THE OXFORD HANDBOOK OF

ENGLISH LITERATURE
AND
THEOLOGY

THE OXFORD HANDBOOK OF

ENGLISH LITERATURE AND THEOLOGY

Edited by

ANDREW HASS,
DAVID JASPER

AND

ELISABETH JAY

OXFORD
UNIVERSITY PRESS

OXFORD

UNIVERSITY PRESS

Great Clarendon Street, Oxford OX2 6DP

Oxford University Press is a department of the University of Oxford.
It furthers the University's objective of excellence in research, scholarship,
and education by publishing worldwide in

Oxford New York

Auckland Cape Town Dar es Salaam Hong Kong Karachi
Kuala Lumpur Madrid Melbourne Mexico City Nairobi
New Delhi Shanghai Taipei Toronto

With offices in

Argentina Austria Brazil Chile Czech Republic France Greece
Guatemala Hungary Italy Japan Poland Portugal Singapore
South Korea Switzerland Thailand Turkey Ukraine Vietnam

Oxford is a registered trade mark of Oxford University Press
in the UK and in certain other countries

Published in the United States
by Oxford University Press Inc., New York

© Oxford University Press 2007

British Library Cataloguing in Publication Data

Data available

Library of Congress Cataloging in Publication Data

The Oxford handbook of English literature and theology
edited by Andrew Hass, David Jasper, and Elisabeth Jay.
Includes index.
ISBN–13: 978–0–19–927197–9 (alk. paper)
ISBN–10: 0–19–927197–6 (alk.paper)
1. Christian literature, English–History and criticism.
2. Christianity and literature–Great Britain.
3. Bible and literature.   4. Bible–In literature.
5. Theology in literature.   I. Hass, Andrew.   II. Jasper, David. III. Jay, Elisabeth.
PR145H37 2007
820.9′38261—dc22   2006038887

Typeset by SPI Publisher Services, Pondicherry, India
Printed in Great Britain
on acid-free paper by
Biddles Ltd., King's Lynn, Norfolk

ISBN 0–19–927197–6   978–0–19–927197–9

1 3 5 7 9 10 8 6 4 2

Contents

PART THREE: LITERARY WAYS OF READING THE BIBLE

PART FOUR: THEOLOGICAL WAYS OF READING LITERATURE

PART SEVEN: AFTERWORD

LIST OF CONTRIBUTORS

George Aichele is Professor of Philosophy and Religion at Adrian College, Michigan.

Pamela Sue Anderson is Reader in Philosophy of Religion in the University of Oxford.

Simon Bainbridge is Professor of Romantic Studies at Lancaster University.

Timothy K. Beal is the Florence Harkness Professor of Religion and the Director of the Baker-Nord Center of the Humanities at Case Western Reserve University.

Kirstie Blair is Lecturer in English Literature at the University of Glasgow.

Daniel Boscaljon is a graduate student at the University of Iowa in English and Religious Studies.

Lori Branch is Assistant Professor of Restoration and Eighteenth-Century British Literature at the University of Iowa.

Christopher Burdon is a priest of the Church of England, Principal of The Northern Ordination Course, and Honorary Lecturer at the University of Leeds.

Robert G. Collmer, is Emeritus Distinguished Professor of English, Baylor University, Texas.

Brian Cummings is Professor of English at the University of Sussex and Director of the Centre for Early Modern Studies.

Valentine Cunningham is a Professor of English Language and Literature in the University of Oxford and Senior Fellow and Tutor in English at Corpus Christi College, Oxford.

J. Cheryl Exum is Professor of Biblical Studies and Director of the Centre for the Study of the Bible in the Modern World at the University of Sheffield.

Luke Ferretter teaches English Literature at Baylor University, Texas.

Paul Fiddes is Professor of Systematic Theology in the University of Oxford, and Principal of Regent's Park College in the University.

Cath Filmer-Davies was a Senior Lecturer in English at the University of Queensland, Australia, and a writer, editor and broadcaster.

Michael Fox is an Assistant Professor in the Department of English and Film Studies at the University of Alberta.

Donald Gray is a Canon Emeritus of Westminster, Chairman of the Alcuin Club, and President of the Society for Liturgical Study.

Kevin Hart is Notre Dame Professor of English and Concurrent Professor of Philosophy at the University of Notre Dame, Indiana.

Andrew W. Hass is Lecturer in the School of Languages, Cultures and Religions at the University of Stirling.

Peter S. Hawkins is Professor of Religion at Boston University, where he is also Director of the Luce Program in Scripture and Literary Arts.

Thomas Healy is Professor of Renaissance Studies at Birkbeck College, University of London.

Alastair Hunter is Senior Lecturer in Hebrew and Old Testament Studies at the University of Glasgow.

Alison Jasper is Lecturer in the School of Languages, Cultures and Religions at the University of Stirling.

David Jasper is Professor of Literature and Theology at the University of Glasgow.

Elisabeth Jay is Director of the Institute of Historical and Cultural Research at Oxford Brookes University where she is also Associate Dean of Arts and Humanities and a Professor of English.

Ian Ker is a member of the theology faculty at the University of Oxford.

David E. Klemm is Professor of Theology, Ethics, and Culture in the Department of Religious Studies at the University of Iowa.

Rhodri Lewis is British Academy Research Fellow at Jesus College, Oxford, a member of the Oxford English Faculty, and affiliated with the Max-Planck-Institut für Wissenschaftsgeschichte, Berlin.

Michael Lieb is Professor of English and Research Professor of Humanities at the University of Illinois.

Tod Linafelt is Associate Professor of Biblical Literature at Georgetown University, Washington, DC.

Lynne Long lectures at the University of Warwick in the Centre for Translation and Comparative Cultural Studies.

Cleo McNelly Kearns is a non-resident fellow at the Center of Theological Inquiry in Princeton, New Jersey.

Scott Masson teaches English at Tyndale University College, Toronto.

Stephen Medcalf was a Lecturer and Reader in English in the School of European Studies at the University of Sussex.

George Newlands is Professor of Divinity at the University of Glasgow and Principal of Trinity College.

Bridget Nichols is Lay Chaplain to the Bishop of Ely.

Kirsten Nielsen is Professor of Biblical Studies at the University of Aarhus.

Tina Pippin is Professor and Chair of the Department of Religious Studies at Agnes Scott College, Georgia.

Adele Reinhartz is the Associate Vice-President for Research at the University of Ottawa, where she also holds the position of Professor in the Department of Classics and Religious Studies.

Scott Robertson serves as a priest of the Episcopal Church in North Ayrshire, Scotland.

Christopher Rowland is Dean Ireland Professor of the Exegesis of Holy Scripture in the University of Oxford.

David Scott is Rector of a parish in Winchester, an honorary Canon of Winchester Cathedral, and an Honorary Fellow of the University of Winchester.

Yvonne Sherwood is Senior Lecturer in Biblical Studies and Jewish Studies at the University of Glasgow.

Norman Vance is Professor of English at the University of Sussex.

Elena Volkova is a Professor in the Department of Comparative Literature and Culture, Faculty of Foreign Languages, of Moscow State University, and Head of the Centre for the Study of Religion, Language, Literature at Moscow Orthodox Academy.

Heather Walton is Senior Lecturer in Practical Theology at Glasgow University and Co-director of the Centre for the Study of Literature, Theology and the Arts.

Nicholas Watson is Professor of English and American Literature and Language at Harvard University.

Helen Wilcox is Professor of English Literature at the University of Wales, Bangor.

Terry R. Wright is Professor of English Literature at the University of Newcastle upon Tyne.

Eric Ziolkowski is the Charles A. Dana Professor of Religious Studies and Head of the Religious Studies Department, Lafayette College, Pennsylvania.

Abbreviations

BCP	Book of Common Prayer
JPS	Jewish Publication Society Bible
KJV	King James Version
LXX	Septuagint
NRSV	New Revised Standard Version
RSV	Revised Standard Version

PREFACE

Planning, co-ordinating and editing a volume containing fifty essays from an international community of scholars was never going to be an easy task, especially since the project has involved negotiating and charting the relationship between two disciplines. The selection and ordering of topics in this book was often hard-fought and the editors must take full responsibility both for those included and omitted.

Although the volume adopts a largely chronological approach, it has not been designed as a history, nor for that matter, a comprehensive work of reference. Rather, the contributors were invited to address key moments and developments in the mutual engagement of theology and literature, and they were given considerable freedom to shape their response to this challenge as they wished. The result is a volume which amply demonstrates the productive diversity of approach called forth when experts in their various fields are invited to engage in interdisciplinary study.

Our thanks go to Hilary O'Shea of Oxford University Press, with whom initial conversations took place. During the course of the book's development, we have been helped and encouraged in every way by the editorial wisdom of Lucy Qureshi and Dorothy McCarthy, together with Jenny Wagstaffe. We are grateful also to the Institute for Historical and Cultural Research at Oxford Brookes University for providing us with funds and resources to work together as editors during the summer of 2005.

Andrew Hass
David Jasper
Elisabeth Jay
November 2006

Acknowledgements

We are grateful to all authors and publishers of copyright material quoted in the essays in this book, and in particular for permission to reprint the following:

The Alternative Service Book: extracts copyright © The Central Board of Finance of the Church of England, 1980; The Archbishops' Council, 1999, reproduced by permission.

W H Auden: 'Between those happenings that prefigure it' and extract from 'Friday's Child' from *Collected Poems* (Faber, 1986), by permission of the publishers, Faber & Faber Ltd and Random House, Inc.

HD (Hilda Doolittle): extract from 'Trilogy: Tribute to the Angels' from *The Collected Poems 1912–1944* (Carcanet/New Directions, 1983), copyright © 1982 by The Estate of Hilda Doolittle, by permission of the publishers, Carcanet Press Ltd and New Directions Publishing Corp.

Geoffrey Hill: 'Of Coming into Being and Passing Away' from *Canaan* (Penguin, 1996), copyright © Geoffrey Hill 1996, by permission of Penguin Books Ltd and from *New and Collected Poems 1952–1992* (Houghton Mifflin, 1994), copyright © Geoffrey Hill 1994, by permission of Houghton Mifflin Company. All rights reserved.

Gordon Jackson: Psalm 2 and Psalm 100 from *The Lincoln Psalter* (Carcanet, 1997), by permission of the publisher, Carcanet Press Ltd.

Peter Levi: Psalm 100 from *The Psalms* translated by Peter Levi, introduction by Nicholas De Lange (Penguin Classics, 1976), copyright © Peter Levi 1976, by permission of Penguin Books Ltd.

C S Lewis: 'Song' from *Spirits in Bondage* (Harcourt Brace, 1984), copyright © 1919 by C S Lewis Pte. Ltd, by permission of the C S Lewis Company and Harcourt, Inc; extract from unnamed poem from *The Pilgrim's Regress* (Fount, 1998), copyright © 1933 by C S Lewis Pte. Ltd, by permission of the C S Lewis Company.

Roddy Lumsden: 'In the Wedding Museum' from *The Book of Love* (Bloodaxe Books, 2000), copyright © Roddy Lumsden, by permission of Bloodaxe Books.

Michele Roberts: extract from 'Restoration Work in Palazzo Te' from *All the Selves I Was* (Virago, 1995), copyright © Michele Roberts 1995, by permission of the publishers, Virago, a division of Little Brown Book Group, and of Gillon Aitken Associates.

David Slavitt: Psalm 100 from *Sixty-One Psalms of David* selected and translated by David Slavitt (Oxford University Press, 1996), copyright © David Slavitt 1996, by permission of the William Morris Agency.

R S Thomas: extracts from 'Ninetieth Birthday', 'The Parish', and 'Priest and Peasant' from *Collected Poems 1945–1990* (J M Dent, 1993), by permission of the publishers, a division of the Orion Publishing Group.

Laurance Wieder: Psalm 100 from *The Poets' Book of Psalms: the complete Psalter as rendered by twenty-five poets from the sixteenth to the twentieth centuries* compiled by Laurance Wieder (Oxford University Press, 1999), by permission of Laurance Wieder.

Rowan Williams: extract from 'Penrhys' from *Remembering Jerusalem* (Perpetua, 2001), by permission of the author and the publisher.

W B Yeats: 'The Travail of Passion', copyright © 1906 by The Macmillan Company, copyright © renewed by William B Yeats, 'The Second Coming', copyright © 1924 by The Macmillan Company, copyright © renewed 1952 by Bertha Georgie Yeats, and extracts from 'Vacillations', copyright © 1933 by The Macmillan Company, copyright © renewed 1961 by Bertha Georgie Yeats, 'The Valley of the Black Pig', copyright © 1906 by The Macmillan Company, copyright © renewed by William B Yeats, and 'The Dawn', copyright © 1906 by The Macmillan Company, copyright © renewed by William B Yeats, all from *The Collected Poems of W B Yeats* edited by Richard J Finneran (Macmillan, 1983), by permission of A P Watt Ltd on behalf of Gráinne Yeats, Executrix of the Estate of Michael Butler Yeats, and also of Scribner, an imprint of Simon & Schuster Adult Publishing Group. All rights reserved.

We have tried to trace and contact all copyright holders before publication. If notified, we will be pleased to rectify any errors or omissions at the earliest opportunity.

PART ONE

INTRODUCTORY ESSAYS

CHAPTER 1

'NOW AND IN ENGLAND' (ELIOT 1968: 50)

ELISABETH JAY

THE aim of this Handbook is to provide a sense of what it might mean to engage in the interdisciplinary study of English literature and theology. The tentative phrasing of this opening sentence is entirely intentional: unlike the serried ranks of biblical commentaries, or magisterial literary histories that thunder forth from the presses, this hybrid venture boasts no unassailable pedigree, or universally acknowledged territory. Yet the *Handbook* begins with a section that lays claim to a tradition embedded in the roots of English literature and producing new shoots and exotic blossoms even in today's multicultural, 'post-secular' society. This introductory chapter will seek to explore the paradox of how it is possible to make the confident assertion that a corpus of material exists which would gain general recognition as constituting the primary sources for study, while also making a virtue of the fact that there is as yet no unified field of interdisciplinary methodology. The task of mapping out the territory has at the very least laid bare some of the terminological pitfalls that await unwary scholars. 'Modernism', for instance, as Cleo McNelly Kearns points out (ch. 10), is nowadays used to identify wholly different periods and politics in the two disciplines, but as her chapter reveals this retrospective critical categorization has in fact helped to obscure the way in which early twentieth-century literature was often inflected by the religious issues of theological modernism.

More fundamentally neither 'Theology' nor 'English Literature' are as transparent or uncontested terms as they might at first appear. Not only has each been used to describe both the primary sources and the academic process of studying these sources, but as boundary classifications they have proved shifting and unstable, subject to the changing political forces at work over time within society at large and within academic institutions in particular. If 'Theology' can be translated as 'discourse about God' this begs a number of questions as to what kind of 'God-talk' is permitted or implied, and who, at any particular time, is entitled to do the talking. Theology, of course, has the longer and more venerable history as an academic discipline—the study of English Literature being a nineteenth-century parvenu in both schools and universities—but that might merely be said to compound the chronological slipperiness of the term. If Theology is thought of as a discipline associated with *ex cathedra* pronouncements emanating from the institutions of church and university, then this radically narrows the field for study, excluding both dissenting and non-dogmatic texts, and most women's voices. And yet if we nowadays feel inclined to admit any writing that invokes the name of God or seeks to divine transcendent meaning and purpose does the field become so inclusive as to be academically unmanageable? English Literature might at first sight seem to offer a more easily agreed body of material but even if we assume that educational institutions are best qualified to mark out the territory it soon becomes clear that there is no longer an immutable canon of material for study and the academic methodologies employed have been subject to revolutionary revision in the last quarter of a century. In short, both terms of the *Handbook*'s title are and have always been strongly politically charged.

Evolutionary models of history customarily identify a relatively simple point of origin or origins from which a linear pathway of developing complexities can then be traced. The origins of Theology and English Literature, however, confound this pattern. Although it is possible to identify formative works written in the vernacular it is still difficult to talk of a 'vernacular tradition' of 'English literature' dealing with theological matters, independently of the Germanic and Celtic cultures which contributed to it, or the Latin and French contexts by which it was influenced, even when seemingly most in revolt against them. It is easy to identify the high points of literary-theological achievement in poems such as *The Dream of the Rood*, but scholars have found it more difficult to know how to deal with the growing body of 'vernacular theology'. Viewed from the standpoint of Latin, the universal language of Christendom, the vernacular mainly presented risks of misinterpretation, error, heresy, and schism as the centre lost linguistic control of and access to its margins. On these same margins, however, theology in the vernacular started to make itself intelligible to new audiences and encouraged the development of literary genres undreamt of by those who saw the vernacular as merely a vehicle for derivative versions of Latin originals.

Whether the mystery plays derived from Latin liturgical pageant or were developed as new vernacular drama remains a matter of debate: what is beyond dispute, however, is that as responsibility for their production moved into the hands of the trade guilds so they began to reflect particular economic and cultural interests. The York Shipwrights, for instance, fashioned the story of Noah to explore its connections with their own craft and way of life, just as twentieth-century feminist readings reworked the biblical tale to represent the experiences of women that had been occluded in the patriarchal focus of the original. In both cases, such engagements, because they originated in a recognition of the immense power these foundational myths exerted, contributed to a struggle which has had consequences both for literature and theology. The secularizing tendencies of these medieval dramas fed into the world of Elizabethan and Jacobean drama and ultimately into the Puritan backlash which sought to regain control of religious representation. (The feminist challenge to patriarchal readings of the Scriptures is still being worked through in many churches today.) The *Handbook*'s opening section does not aim to provide a comprehensive historical survey of the route from the representation of Mr and Mrs Noah in the medieval mystery plays to the recent refashionings of this tale from Genesis by, *inter alia*, Jeannette Winterson (*Boating for Beginners*, 1985) Michèle Roberts (*The Book of Mrs Noah*, 1987), and Julian Barnes (*A History of the World in Ten and a Half Chapters*, 1989). Instead, by focusing upon some of the crucial moments, movements, and turns in the relationship between literature and theology, this section illuminates the high political stakes involved in negotiating or disputing control of the Word.

One of the effects that Julian Barnes achieves by resituating the Noah story in a variety of historical settings is to make us confront complacent habits of reading biblical narrative as fossilized religious discourse, remote from our interpretation of the world around us. Furthermore, by loosing the story from its canonical moorings, he reminds us of art's pivotal role in the wrestle between theological authority and the human imagination for supremacy in detecting or imposing patterns and meaning. Tracing a watery pathway from Noah to the story of Jonah and the whale, Barnes proceeds to consider other perilous voyages in their light. Of the account of James Bartley's 1891 escape from the belly of a sperm whale, he writes:

You may not credit it, but what has happened is that the story has been retold, adjusted, updated; it has shuffled nearer. For Jonah now read Bartley...For the point is this: not that the myth refers us back to some original event which has been fancifully transcribed as it passed through the collective memory; but that it refers us forward to something that will happen, that must happen. Myth will become reality, however sceptical we might be.

(Barnes 1990: 180–1)

As confirmation Barnes offers us the shameful tale of what befell the thousand Jews, who embarked upon the German cruise ship *St Louis*, which sailed in 1939 from Hamburg. In Barnes's hands the account serves as a commentary upon the cruelty the human race has routinely and casually condoned in its primitive lust for tales of providential survival, and so the tales of Noah and Jonah fall into place as analogous narratives, which we have preferred to attribute to the 'fairly repellent morality' of the God of the Old Testament (ibid. 177) than to the human capacity to author and authorize. For the purposes of the *Handbook*, whether we espouse the Jungian collective memory or the proleptic theory of myth proposed here is less relevant than the recognition that theology and literature are discourses which continue to exert political power despite attempts to corral them as 'academic' and thus irrelevant or dead tongues. If nothing else the history of 'the Holy Land' should remind us of the mythic potency exercised by such biblical phrases as 'the Promised Land' and to the risks implicit in regarding 'sacred texts' and officially sanctioned theology as set apart from all other forms of literary endeavour.

It is perhaps no coincidence that the *Journal of Literature and Theology* came into being at very much the same time that novelists working in Britain, such as Barnes, Roberts, Winterson, Sarah Maitland and others, were turning back to the Bible as the imaginative springboard for novels which proceeded as much by narrative cogitation as by easily discernible plot structures. These scholarly revisitings and creative revision-ings of the grand metanarratives came at a time when institutional religious affiliation was markedly in decline and the Christian church, was, as a consequence, losing its power to claim control of a monolithic story of universally applicable truth. British novelists began to turn away from fiction's post Second World War love affair with the analysis of contemporary social mores, and, often fuelled by modish critical theories, to take to speculative wandering among fantasized alternative realities and multiple truth systems. Fiction began to parade a fresh self-consciousness, drawing attention to its own fictiveness, and often employing a fictional narrator whose function was to brood over the impossibility of his/her interpretative role in a world where values could no longer be assumed to be universal. The emergence of the various strands loosely woven into the scholarly activity of 'Literature and Theology' might be traced to some of the same social and intellectual phenomena. Some literary scholars were drawn to it through a sense of perceived loss, wanting to restore to their students the cultural resonance of classical and biblical knowledge which they sensed was fast disappearing. These recruits were often drawn from a generation who had been the last to be handed a canonical map of English literature whose compass points referred to the founding texts of Western civilization and whose more local grid references were formed by the intersection of national institutions and patronage systems with schools and move-ments of writers, usually gendered male. This generation, released from the bondage of the canon by a wave of critical theory, proceeded to lead their successors as students out into a wilderness where texts replaced books, and hermeneutic and linguistic theories were preferred to contextual knowledge. This move coincided with, or was indeed part of a larger cultural change, in which it could no longer be assumed that knowledge of the Christian religion or indeed of Homer and Virgil would form part of the secondary education of the ever-increasing numbers coming into Higher Educa-tion in Britain. Patterns of immigration have certainly contributed to an ethos that no longer finds it appropriate to sow British, or even Western cultural values, in its state schools: it is difficult to exaggerate the extent of the sea-change this represents for a literature embedded in a nationalism embroiled, almost from its inception, in religio-political conflicts.

It is possible to point to R. A. Butler's 1944 Education Act as heralding the moment at which the British ceased to assume that Christianity was hard-wired into the nation's culture. Previous Acts had presumed that religion formed an integral part of education, being concerned only to insist upon a non-denominational provision. This meant that even those authors who had themselves abandoned orthodox Christian belief had to hand a vocabulary and a myth-hoard that they knew they held in common with their readers. John Ruskin's pessimistic prophesy in 1852 that the very fabric of the education of his own childhood was being dismantled: 'If only the Geologists would let me alone, I could do very well, but those dreadful Hammers! I hear the clink of them at the end of every cadence of the Bible verses'(Ruskin 1903–12: xxxvi. 115)—was still unrealized by D. H. Lawrence's day. Lawrence could still perceive himself as being characteristically provocative when he claimed, in his posthumously published essay, 'Why the Novel Matters', that the Bible, along with Homer and Shakespeare, was an exemplar of the novel as the true 'book of life', (Lawrence 1956: 105), and, more importantly, a novel such as *The Rainbow* (1915) is scarcely intelligible without recourse to 'every cadence of the Bible verses'. Not to recognize the reference to Deuteronomy 34: 1–5 in the following passage is to be deprived, not of a piece of vocabulary for which a synonym can easily be found, but of the novel's narrative trajectory which is predicated upon an understanding of civilization as aspiring to new covenants as the journey over the generations is retraced from Genesis to Revelation, from the rhythms of tilling the land to the culture of 'the great city', 'Something she had not, something she did not grasp, could not arrive at. There was something beyond her. But why must she start on the journey? She stood so safely on the Pisgah mountain?' (Lawrence 1970: 195).

For the first time, in 1944, it was thought necessary to make a collective act of worship compulsory in all state-aided schools, suggesting that in post-war Britain neither parents nor teachers could be relied upon to transmit Christian religion as endemic to the nation's values. As the twentieth century wore on church and chapel attendance dwindled to the point when Grace Davie (1999: 49) described the nominal allegiance professed by the many as a condition where the British know which church they are not attending. Although non-attendance at corporate Christian worship does not necessarily signify the death of belief, it does indicate the passing of an intimate—or, increasingly, any—familiarity with Christian liturgy and the Bible. The perception of a divergence between popular culture and a strongly religiously inflected literary heritage is of course, not new. When Marlowe's Dr Faustus reviews the medieval university curriculum that he has mastered and resolves to abandon even 'Divinity', the crowning glory of the academic disciplines, in favour of the 'profit and delight' to be gained through magic and necromancy, the text displays a marked nervousness about its ability to count upon the audience's knowledge of what rests unsaid.

> When all is done Divinity is best.
> Jerome's Bible, Faustus, view it well.
> *Stipendium peccati mors est.* Ha! *Stipendium, etc.,*
> The reward of sin is death. That's hard.
> *Si peccasse negamus, fallimur, et nulla est in nobis veritas.*
> If we say that we have no sin we deceive ourselves, and there's no truth in us. Why, then, belike we must sin, and so consequently die.
> Ay, we must die an everlasting death.
> What doctrine call you this? Che sera, sera:
> What will be, shall be. Divinity, adieu!
> These metaphysics of magicians
> And necromantic books are heavenly.... (*Dr Faustus* (i. i))

Although, as Thomas Healy argues (Ch. 23), the play's overall theological stance is difficult to interpret, it is important that the audience feels upon its pulse the drama of this moment when the threat of the 'wages of sin' is precisely not balanced by the promise of 'eternal life through Jesus Christ our Lord' (Romans 6: 23). Whether this pivotal moment is regarded as the beginning of Faustus's descent into false logic, or the articulation of a challenge to the Christian world order, it is imperative that the entire audience, including those familiar with the Bible only in the vernacular, should be able to experience the frisson occasioned when an anticipated rhythm is unexpectedly jarred and broken.

For scholars of the 1980s the urge to regenerate lost or dying knowledge was complicated by the impossibility of a return to an Edenic world innocent of critical theories. Their mission of recovery seemed questionable to at least two classes of critic: those who doubted the worth of prioritizing the pursuit of lost resonances when the past is, in any meaningful sense, unknowable, and those who, though they valued the effect of a truth felt upon the pulse, privileged personal readings precisely because they offered an escape from the tyranny of the totalizing (white male) discourse in which liberal humanism had so often been couched. This decade, which saw a predictable conservative backlash against the dominance of theory, in the shape of new Historicism, created some strange alliances in literature departments, but in so doing began to weaken the prejudice that distrusted all interest in matters religious or theological as an indication of conservative recidivism or proselytizing fundamentalism. The safest compromise was generally admitted to be the bringing back of the Bible 'as' or 'together with' literature into the seminar room, where it was used, *inter alia*, as an outstanding example of English Renaissance prose, as a complicated example of the cultural politics of production, or simply as a series of source passages. To some of this new cohort of biblical readers, with such honourable exceptions as Robert Alter, it now seemed that adequate theoretical justification existed to validate their annexation of the Bible without the need to learn Hebrew or Greek—always a snag when taking on say Homer or Virgil as taught in rival Classical literature departments: far simpler to venerate the Authorized Version as an aesthetic Ur-text.

Biblical scholars did not remain immune to these winds of change, but were apprehensive of dabbling with theories whose implications might well lead beyond the Judaeo-Christian mind-set. Almost twenty years ago the editors of *The Literary Guide to the Bible*, despite claiming to embrace a 'pluralist' notion of criticism, explicitly ruled out Marxist, psychoanalytic, deconstructionist, and 'some feminist' critics as unlikely to provide help in the task of learning 'how to read the Bible again' (Alter and Kermode 1987: 5–6). Our approach as *Handbook* editors, by contrast, has been simply to seek out the best biblical scholarship available. In this process certain trends have become apparent. Although recent biblical scholarship has been happy to raid literary theory for approaches, such as genre and feminist criticism, which carry obvious affinities for its own concerns, it has often been content to return, with this booty, to its usual occupations, rather than engaging more directly with the subsequent turns of theoretical or 'post-theory' debate. Nevertheless, the growth in readings which regard the individual books of the Bible as contextualized productions of Mediterranean antiquity, and in which St Paul, the chief begetter of Protestant theology and saint for all seasons, becomes Paul a man of his time, is proving divisive for Theology, driving a wedge between systematics and biblical criticism. Not every branch of the discipline has embraced with equal enthusiasm this new cultural space where theology can no longer presume upon even faint echoes of its previous coercive authority. Some theologians have argued, with Graham Ward, that inter-disciplinary dialogue represents a way out of the modernist ghetto where theologians were condemned 'simply to speak to and write for other theologians' (Ward 2000: p. viii). From this perspective the re-engagement with literature appeared potentially revivifying for theology while offering theorists who were reluctant to become trapped in endless linguistic 'play', the possibility of retrieving a framework of ethically based discussion.

Those theologians, on the other hand, who remained apprehensive about popular culture's power to trivialize rather than fertilize might well point for vindication to that recent best-seller, Dan Brown's *The Da Vinci Code* (2003). John Robinson's project, in *Honest to God* (1963), of demythologizing Christianity's 'traditional orthodox supernaturalism' so that it might once again become 'meaningful' for the 'lay' world (Robinson 1963: 8) would appear to have come full circle in Brown's novel which responds to a new popular craving for myth and belief in cultic movements with aspirations to world domination. Brown's novel, which is as devoid of the theological, in the sense of discussion of transcendence, as it is of the pleasures which a good literary style confers, would seem to have gained its reputation from yoking cultural pretentiousness—offering guided tours to the must-sees of European tour-ism—to an interpretation of church history driven by a combination of popular conspiracy theories—the suppression of 'goddess-worship' by the patriarchy, and the presentation of Opus Dei as a sinister religious mafia. The Vatican's decision to authorize an official refutation of the misinformation it believed to be contained in a novel which was selling well even in Roman Catholic bookshops, followed by the decision by Lincoln Cathedral's Anglican dean to permit filming of the book in its precincts, are indicative at the very least of the polarized approaches to cultural engagement now taking place under the umbrella of institutional theology.

It is unsurprising, therefore, that the section 'Literary Ways of Reading the Bible' should be the most marked for the divergent approaches its contributors assumed. Some welcomed the chance to consider the readings which English literature has offered of biblical narratives, while others felt better placed to interpret their brief as applying methodologies derived from literary criticism to biblical texts. In a few cases we have endeavoured to respect the author's original choice of approach, while helping readers to gain a sense of both approaches, by appending to these chapters a brief account of the way in which particular biblical themes, episodes, and symbols have informed English literature.

All the chapters in this section, however, share the premise that literary approaches to the Bible inevitably uncover the hermeneutics at work in the act of translation, as one word or phrase, one mind-set, dogmatic persuasion, or cultural value is privileged over another. The reactions of two reviewers in *The Times* newspaper to *Good as New: A Radical Retelling of the Scriptures* (2004), by John Henson, a retired Baptist minister, offer an interesting guide to the place occupied by the Bible in Britain's contemporary cultural wars. As indicated by the review titles, 'Rocky of Ages' (Whittell 2004), and 'Archibishop blesses a gospel with more sex' (Gledhill 2004), the surface furore raged around the 'inclusivity' of the language employed in the translation, but deeper anxieties about the cultural power afforded by control of the Word were at work than might have been anticipated in a *soi-disant* secular society. The enthusiastic endorsement given by the Archbishop of Canterbury, Rowan Williams, to a translation which he hoped would spread 'in epidemic profusion through religious and irreligious alike' precisely because it does not take the reader into 'a specialised religious frame of reference' was the chief offence. 'Yet isn't that precisely where the Bible is meant to take us? Out of the humdrum, the everyday, to somewhere different, more taxing, better?' argued *The Times* columnist, claiming to speak on behalf of 'England's adult, literate agnostics' in wanting to retain 'the tradition and the calming ritual of unmodernised Church life and language that is most likely to lure us there' (Whittell 2004). At first glance this seems to be simply another version of the medieval rivalry between the establishment's favoured language and the vernacular employed by a missionary church intent upon gaining the broadest transmission for its message. There are, however, interesting differences. This time around 'education' is being aligned with 'scepticism', while an attempt is also being made to neutralize the undoubted attractions of the Bible and formal liturgy by consigning them to the heritage theme park. In this reading, religion's alarming power to disrupt the civilized consensus of 'High Culture' is imaged in the spectacle of an archbishop, the symbolic embodiment of the Establishment's investment in religion as history, preferring the claims of popular culture. Williams's own triple credentials as theologian, priest, and poet to the post of champion of the values of 'High Culture' only accentuate the extent of his 'defection' for those anxious to turn 'the sacred' into a fossilized and aetheticized commodity. The enduring tradition to which Williams himself of course belongs, of the Anglican pastor-poet, is both discussed and exemplified in David Scott's chapter in the concluding section of the *Handbook*.

Failing to recognize the organic connections between language and beliefs can prove curiously disenabling. Both *Times* reviewers chose for especial excoriation the rendering of Mark 1: 9–11, reporting John's baptism of Jesus. The Authorised Version reports the voice from heaven as saying 'Thou art my beloved son, in whom I am well pleased', which is now rendered 'That's my boy! You're doing fine!', but neither review explains precisely what is wrong with this locution. A literary-theological reading might suggest that the generic nature of this praise, applied in modern, usually American, English, to a well-performed act by any younger male, does not seem to offer any specific recognition of a Father–Son relationship between two parts of the Trinity. Instead, the *Times* reviewer has nothing but 'good taste', a curiously fickle, and often culturally localized principle, on which to ground his criticism: the choice of the word 'dipped' in the same narrative episode: 'Then Jesus came from Nazareth to be dipped by John in the Jordan' is simply dismissed as 'cringe-making' (Whittell 2004). A literary-theological commentary might take into consideration that this word had been chosen by an American Baptist, whose sect had, over three centuries ago, acquired the nickname of 'dippers' on account of their practice of baptism by total immersion, before proceeding to question whether the word resonates differently for British readers.

The cultural specificity of the encounter between readers and writers was one reason for preferring to limit ourselves to English literature, rather than 'literatures in English' when broadening the discussion beyond the Bible, and so the *Handbook* largely ignores the textual and credal negotiations that took place when English literature was read beyond British shores. Such an account would have to include the glimpse offered in Olive Schreiner's *The Story of an African Farm* (1998/188), of how it must have felt to the child of a German-born, Lutheran-turned-Wesleyan missionary, and an English, Wesleyan mother who was to finish her days in a South African, Roman Catholic convent, to pore, at the far ends of the Empire, over the pages of literature produced in England, and to what extent the common reading inheritance she shared with her fellow freethinkers in England was to draw her closer to them or to sharpen her profound feeling of alienation. To read the relationship in the opposite direction, George Eliot's work has had an impact on American fiction, as seen most recently in Cynthia Ozick's *The Puttermesser Papers* (1997), but to trace the way in which it has fed into a literary heritage with its own theological traditions, not to mention the knowledge of writings from many non-English-speaking cultures that immigrants brought with them, would require a companion volume.

From today's anti-imperialist perspective, this volume contains at least one blatant anomaly. Why have we annexed, for English Literature, James Joyce, who regarded England as little more than an obstacle between that 'fauborg called St Patrice' and continental Europe? Or, rather, to invert the question, how could we possibly omit an author for whom addressing the theological matters abroad in the Judaeo-Christian tradition of his times was an imperative so great that it not only forced scholars to pay attention even in the two or three decades after the Second World War when theology had almost entirely disappeared from the agenda of literary scholarship, but was also to spark an exploratory reworking of his materials on another continent in Vikram Seth's *A Suitable Boy* (1993). Joyce's *œuvre* lays out the problem inherent in the current enterprise with devastating clarity. Between 1801 and 1921 Ireland was, politically speaking, an integral part of the United Kingdom, but as the reactions of those English-born, Oxford-educated Roman Catholic converts, John Henry Newman and Gerard Manley Hopkins showed, culturally speaking, the lives of their fellow Romanists in this distant part of the kingdom were almost wholly unfamiliar. This perception of an alien encounter between co-subjects and brothers in Christ was not one-sided: in *A Portrait of the Artist as a Young Man* (1916), Stephen Dedalus mulls it over from the perspective of the Dublin student taught by an English convert to the Jesuits:

The language in which we are speaking is his before it is mine. How different are the words *home, Christ, ale, master,* on his lips and on mine! I cannot speak or write these words without unrest of spirit. His language, so familiar and so foreign, will always be for me an acquired speech. I have not made or accepted its words. My voice holds them at bay. My soul frets in the shadow of its language.   (ibid. 189)

If what constitutes the tradition of 'English literature' is contentious, to restrict 'theology' in this volume to the Judaeo-Christian might seem equally perverse at a time when departments of Theology and Religious Studies rightly require their students to familiarize themselves with a variety of global religions. The recent fashion for characterizing opposing tendencies in today's society as examples of either 'tribalism' or 'globalism', serves to obscure the way this has developed from a much older Western tradition of categorizing into 'Old' and 'New' dispensations, 'orthodox' and 'sectarian' movements, 'darkened' and 'enlightened' periods or conceptions. Joyce's upbringing in Catholic Ireland enabled him to interrogate England's entrenched hierarchical assumptions, in such a way as to prepare his readers for embracing the exilic, European Judaism, embodied in Leopold Bloom. From a Jesuit perspective, Stephen Dedalus's speculations remind us, if 'the vain pomps' of Anglicanism had figured in the pilgrimage made by the convert English dean of studies on his way to finding 'the one true Church', the Church of England was scarcely to be differentiated from any other heretical sect.

From what had he set out? Perhaps he had been born and bred among serious dissenters, seeking salvation in Jesus only and abhorring the vain pomps of the establishment. Had he felt the need of an implicit faith amid the welter of sectarianism and the jargon of its turbulent schisms, six principle men, peculiar people, seed and snake baptists, supralapsarian dogmatists?   (ibid. 188)

The *Handbook*'s historical bias has undoubtedly favoured a rather traditional canon, and the editors were particularly aware, in selecting authors for inclusion in the third and fourth sections, that almost every choice involved the rejection of a viable alternative. For instance, we might have chosen James Hogg's portrayal of extreme Calvinism in *The Private Memoirs and Confessions of a Justified Sinner* (1997/ 1824) to represent Romanticism's engagement with Scottish Presbyterianism, rather than Wordsworth, Coleridge, and Blake's differently unorthodox, but more Anglocentric offerings. The Wesley brothers might have ousted Bishop Butler, and Gerard Manley Hopkins might have been preferred to Newman or Keble. Within the Anglican tradition, some will query why the Welsh-centred poetry of R. S. Thomas has not merited a full chapter. Hymnody, as a discrete generic category, is a marked absence from 'Theology as Literature', but this area has been particularly well-served in recent years, notably by J. R. Watson (1997). The theological and literary texts we arrived at are not only heavily weighted in favour of the Anglican as opposed to the Jewish, Roman Catholic, or Dissenting traditions, but also predominantly English and male. But to pretend that things had been otherwise, in a handbook that seeks to convey, at least in skeletal form, a sense of the key moments of English literature's relationship with theology, would be historically misleading.

Until the 1851 Religious Census, which revealed the hitherto concealed extent of godlessness abroad in the nation, it was the official assumption that Britain was a

Christian nation, and this ensured both that theology was inextricably bound up with politics, and that men dictated educational policy and what was published. Although religious toleration became incorporated into the law of the land in 1689, theology not acceptable to the prevailing regime still found it hard to gain a hearing. There has been much valuable work done in the last couple of decades on the ways that women, over the centuries, have articulated their theological speculation in private journals and unpublished poetry, and in publications such as hymns, novels, religious drama, autobiographies, biographies, anonymous reviewing, and works of overtly non-sectarian devotional meditation. A survey work, entitled *Religious Thought in the Nineteenth Century* (1896), probably reflected the public perception well in allocating only 8 of its 396 pages to women's contribution, but the nineteenth century had in fact seen a decisive shift in wresting theological debate from the control of the clerisy. Discussion of the consequences of Higher Criticism, for instance, had moved beyond the control of the church and the academy into the pages of more generally available periodical essays, novels, and poetry. Culture, that is, heralded by Matthew Arnold as the substitute for God, drifted away from the religious authority that had fashioned its delivery through its control of the two universities. The full-blown privatization of religion, legitimating individual 'spirituality', that we are witnessing now, had its origins in the complex circumstances that saw the growth of a mechanized publishing industry and the spread of literacy promoting a wider dissemination of ideas that were often absorbed through the private practice of reading, which, in turn, had an inherent tendency to encourage the notion of the right of the individual conscience to make out its own faith.

The inclusion of two chapters discussing feminist theology and literature speaks to the definitive emergence, in the final thirty years of the last century, of women's voices as both ideological and economic forces, and to the profound difference that feminist critical theories have made to the two major disciplines with which this handbook deals. In a future edition of the *Handbook* I would look forward to seeing comparable space devoted to gender theory and the impact that this is having on literary-theological reflection in academic circles, within faith communities, and in thoughtful and adventurous fiction such as Michael Arditti's *Easter* (2000).

This chapter has described a historical trajectory that could be interpreted as leading to the final crumbling away of institutional religion, the breakdown of shared values, and the disappearance of a distinctively national literature, or as the empowerment of the laity in a wider community no longer hedged about with effectively policed border controls. Full empowerment, however, involves access not only to the data but to knowledge about how that data has been produced and used in the decision-making processes that have led us to where we are now. The *Handbook* therefore is designed not only for those academically committed to the interdisciplinary study of Literature and Theology but for any general reader interested in the cultural state we find ourselves in 'Now and in England'.

WORKS CITED

ALTER, ROBERT, and KERMODE, FRANK (eds.). 1987. *The Literary Guide to the Bible*. London: Collins.

ARDITTI, MICHAEL. 2000. *Easter*. London: Arcadia Books.

BARNES, JULIAN. 1990. *A History of the World in Ten and a Half Chapters*. London: Picador.

BROWN, DAN. 2003. *The Da Vinci Code: A Novel*. London: Bantam.

DAVIE, GRACE. 1999. *Religion in Britain since 1945*. Oxford: Blackwell.

ELIOT, T. S. 1968. 'Little Gidding', *Four Quartets*. London: Faber.

GLEDHILL, RUTH. 2004. 'Archbishop blesses a gospel with more sex'. *The Times*, 23 June, 20.

HENSON, JOHN. 2004. *Good as New: A Radical Retelling of the Scriptures*. New Alresford: O Books/John Hunt.

HOGG, JAMES, 1997. *The Private Memoirs and Confessions of a Justified Sinner*. Ware: Wordsworth Editions. First published 1824.

HUNT, J. 1896. *Religious Thought in the Nineteenth Century*. London: Gibbings.

JOYCE, JAMES. 1963. *A Portrait of the Artist as a Young Man*. Harmondsworth: Penguin.

LAWRENCE, D. H. 1970. *The Rainbow*. Harmondsworth: Penguin.

—— 1956. *Selected Literary Criticism*, ed. Anthony Beal. London: Heinemann.

MARLOWE, CHRISTOPHER. 1971. 'Doctor Faustus', *The Plays of Christopher Marlowe*, ed. Roma Gill. Oxford: Oxford University Press.

OZICK, CYNTHIA. 1997. *The Puttermesser Papers*. New York: Knopf.

ROBERTS, MICHÈLE. 1987. *The Book of Mrs Noah*. London: Methuen.

ROBINSON, JOHN A. T. 1963. *Honest to God*. London: SCM.

RUSKIN, JOHN. 1903–12. *The Works of John Ruskin*, ed. E. T. Cook and A. Wedderburn. 39 vols. London: George Allen.

SCHREINER, OLIVE. 1998. *The Story of an African Farm*. Oxford World's Classics. Oxford: Oxford University Press. First published 1883.

SETH, VIKRAM. 1993. *A Suitable Boy*. London: Phoenix House.

WARD, GRAHAM. 2000. *Theology and Contemporary Critical Theory*. 2nd edn. London: Macmillan.

WATSON, J. R. 1997. *The English Hymn: A Critical and Historical Study*. Oxford: Clarendon.

WHITTELL, GILES. 2004. 'Rocky of Ages', *The Times: Body and Soul*, 26 June, 2.

WINTERSON, JEANNETTE. 1985. *Boating for Beginners*. London: Methuen.

CHAPTER 2

THE STUDY OF LITERATURE AND THEOLOGY

DAVID JASPER

IN recent times the study of 'literature and theology' or 'literature and religion' has been granted, if often somewhat grudgingly, its place in the curriculum of the academy, often uncomfortably suspended between academic departments of literature and theology, or part of a larger enterprise which is concerned with religion and the arts. Within churches and Christian communities there has been a rather bemused acknowledgement of the power and importance of literature, resulting in such phenomena as 'narrative theology', and the rather naive gestures towards the power of 'story', such as were made in the 1981 Report of the Doctrine Commission of the Church of England, *Believing in the Church*, in which story and liturgy were linked in an essay which begins:

Recent theology...has thrown up a new term which we might want to use: 'story'. Story, like myth, is a word with many possible meanings. On the one hand, it is hallowed in Christian usage: 'Tell me the old, old story'; on the other, it can be used in a debunking way, as when people say that Christianity is 'only a story' or 'only a collection of old stories'. (Barton and Halliburton 1981: 79)

Behind such debunking lie passages in the Pastoral Epistles, 1 and 2 Timothy, that urge the reader to pursue the truth and avoid 'godless and silly stories', the Greek word being μυθοι ('myths') which, in its Homeric form simply means story or narrative.

As critical understanding of the relationship between literature and theology became more nuanced and sophisticated in the later twentieth century, students in the field became aware that once this door had been opened, other doors presented themselves and the study expanded to other arts—the visual, cinema, architecture, dance, music. The list begins to seem endless. These will not be our concern in this handbook, important though they are. Perhaps, at best, we can lead the way towards further studies in these wider fields, but much remains to be done in establishing precisely what the relationship between literature and theology is or can achieve.

In his book *Literary Theory: An Introduction*, Terry Eagleton offers as a 'single explanation' for the rise of the study of English literature in the nineteenth century, 'the failure of religion'. From the early twentieth century Eagleton (1996: 20) quotes from the inaugural lecture of a Professor of English Literature at Oxford, George Gordon: 'England is sick, and . . . English literature must save it. The Churches (as I understand) having failed, and social remedies being slow, English literature has now a triple function: still, I suppose, to delight and instruct us, but also, and above all, to save our souls and heal the State.' In the earlier years of the twentieth century, however, most critics who gave any attention to the relationship between literature and theology or religion wrote from within the traditions of Christian practice and belief, seeing literature as ultimately dependent on the truths of Christian theology in succession to such earlier critics as Dr. Samuel Johnson, or even further back the seventeenth-century poet Andrew Marvell, who expressed his fears for John Milton's attempt to 'rewrite' the Bible narrative in Paradise Lost.

> When I beheld the Poet blind, yet bold,
> In slender Book his vast Design unfold,
> *Messiah* Crown'd, *Gods* reconcil'd Decree,
> Rebelling *Angels*, the Forbidden Tree,
> Heav'n, Hell, Earth, Chaos, All; the Argument
> Held me a while misdoubting his Intent,
> That he would ruine (for I saw him strong)
> The sacred Truths to Fable and Old Song . . .   (Marvell 1969: 64)

Marvell's sentiments are forcefully echoed in the following century by Dr Johnson, most eloquently in his *Life of Waller* in the *Lives of the Poets* (1781), and it was a common theme with him: his biographer Boswell writes that the good doctor presented his 'dissertation upon the unfitness of poetry for the aweful subjects of our holy religion . . . with uncommon force and reasoning' (Boswell 1953: 1293).

T. S. Eliot's 1935 essay 'Religion and Literature', a landmark in the critical field, follows essentially the same vein as Johnson. A convert to High Anglicanism, Eliot begins on a lofty note: 'What I have to say is largely in support of the following propositions: Literary criticism should be completed by criticism from a definite ethical and theological standpoint. In so far as in any age there is common agreement on ethical and theological matters, so far can literary criticism be substantive' (Eliot 1951: 388). For Eliot, literature stands under the judgment of 'explicit ethical and theological standards' and, apart from all other literature, the Bible is 'the report of the Word of God'. If it is considered simply as 'literature' then its literary influence will soon be at an end.

Early in this essay, Eliot makes the rather startling claim that 'we have tacitly assumed, for some centuries past, that there is *no* relation between literature and theology'. What he calls the 'common code', that is, the culturally specific context by which moral judgements are made, is frequently detached from questions of faith and theology. For his part, however, like Johnson before him, Eliot, with all the fervour of a convert, carries the light of his Christian profession before all his acts of literary judgement. He writes:

It is our business, as Christians, *as well as* readers of literature, to know what we ought to like.... What I believe to be incumbent upon all Christians is the duty of maintaining consciously certain standards and criteria of criticism over and above those applied by the rest of the world; and that by these criteria and standards everything that we read must be tested.   (ibid. 399)

With Eliot we are indeed a far cry from Professor George Gordon and the sense of the 'failure of religion'. And Eliot's claims for a specific Christian reading of literature have continued to find a large public in the English-speaking world through what might seem an unlikely ally for this elegant, Anglo-Catholic intellectual on the edge of Bloomsbury—it is in the hugely influential work of C. S. Lewis and a more recent body of evangelical Christian scholars in Britain and North America who continue to insist on reading literature with a 'Christian perspective'. Lewis, a much better literary critic than he was a religious thinker, was a popular apologist with a rather donnish aptitude for fiction and fantasy writing after the style of the nineteenth-century Scottish writer George Macdonald. Perhaps, in the end, he will be best remembered in his more personal and autobiographical writings, *Surprised by Joy* (1955), and above all *A Grief Observed* (1961), a narrative which traces his process of mourning after the death of his wife.

The influential evangelical Christian tradition of literary criticism and, later, theory which has flourished since Lewis was writing in the middle years of the twentieth century may be characterized by a remark of Ruth Etchells (1983: 7) that 'it is timely, not least in view of the Christian roots of Western civilization, to further the discussion of what might be the characteristics and insights of a specifically Christian criticism. Such criticism must have a theological grounding'. An important volume of essays in this tradition by both British and American scholars, *The Discerning Reader* (1995), edited by David Barratt, Roger Pooley, and Leland Ryken, follows T. S. Eliot in seeking to stabilize what it perceives as the anxiety in English studies and literary theory over both content and values, offering a 'Christian response' to key texts from *Paradise Lost* to the novels of Margaret Atwood and Thomas Pynchon, as well as major theoretical issues. Christian English literary studies in the United States have been more anxious to relate trends and movements in literary theory to well-defined Christian beliefs and assumptions, as in the volume edited by Clarence Walhout and Leland Ryken entitled *Contemporary Literary Theory: An Appraisal* (1991). More recently, and more subtly, the British scholar Luke

Ferretter has contributed his book *Towards a Christian Literary Theory* (2003) to this field.

A generally more sophisticated debate about the relationship between literature and theology has its roots in the work of an Oxford New Testament scholar and theologian, Austin Farrer. Farrer's Bampton lectures for 1948, published as *The Glass of Vision*, set out to explore the relationship between three things, 'the sense of metaphysical philosophy, the sense of scriptural revelation, and the sense of poetry' (p. ix). The book attracted the critical wrath of one of the leading literary critics of the day, Helen Gardner, specifically in her book *The Limits of Literary Criticism: Reflections on the Interpretation of Poetry and Scripture* (1956). Ironically, she accuses Farrer of reading the Bible, and specifically the New Testament, as if it were *literature* rather than a record of historical facts. While she respects Farrer's 'profoundly poetic and Christian imagination' (ibid. 36), she criticizes his neglect of the irrefutable facts of Christianity, setting up a clear distinction between the business of literature and 'fiction' and the more solid historical concerns of theology. At almost the same time, however, a literary scholar from Cambridge, T. R. Henn, was working on a study of the Bible as literature, which was to bear fruit as an essay in the influential new version of *Peake's Commentary on the Bible* (1962), and later a full-length book *The Bible as Literature* (1970). Henn's interest in the literary aspects of the biblical texts stems from his assertion that 'the Bible is burned into the timber of English; and this is not wholly because of its character as a sacred text' (1962: 8). It has provided literature with proverbs and parables, and themes, sacred and profane, for epic, satire, tragedy, farce. Henn suggests that 'one might say, at a guess, that one-third of the poems in our language bear traces of its imagery or thought'. From this interest in the Bible *and* literature, Henn devotes his energies to the Bible *as* literature. It was precisely this project that Eliot and then Helen Gardner viewed with such suspicion, as a denial of the historical specificity of the sacred text. Yet Austin Farrer's work on the literary genius of the gospels was to be taken up much later by another literary critic whose interest was in the nature of narrative and how we interpret it. In his influential book *The Genesis of Secrecy* (1979), Frank Kermode, a Cambridge professor of English, studies the Gospel of Mark alongside James Joyce's *Ulysses*, the novels of Henry James and other modern fiction. 'As to Farrer,' Kermode (1979: 63–4) remarks, 'His work was rejected by the establishment, and eventually by himself, largely because it was so literary. The institution knew intuitively that such literary elaboration, such emphasis on elements that must be called fictive, was unacceptable because damaging to what remained of the idea that the gospel narratives were still, in some measure, transparent upon history.' In the end, both Gardner and Kermode, for different reasons, seem to accept the wedge driven between the Bible and 'literature', while acknowledging its profound influence on English literature. Kermode developed his interest by editing, with the Hebrew scholar Robert Alter, *The Literary Guide to the Bible* (1987), a volume which celebrates Scripture not so much as a 'religious monument' as a 'literary experience', literary critics deliberately invading the territory of 'academic biblical scholarship' (Alter and Kermode 1987: 1–8) in literary readings of the Bible.

At the same time, the work of the Canadian critic Northrop Frye and later Gabriel Josipovici, both professors of English literature, identified the literary power and authority of the Bible as intrinsic to its authority as a sacred text, and thus, they argued, its permeation of European literature is both a literary and a religious phenomenon. 'A sacred book', Frye (1982: 3) wrote, 'is normally written with at least the concentration of poetry.' His study of the Bible begins with his work on William Blake, from whom the title of his book, *The Great Code*, is drawn, and his belief that the Bible is the single most important influence in the imaginative tradition of Western literature. The argument implicit in Frye—that the authority of the Bible is inextricably both literary and sacred—is made explicitly by Jospovici, joining together that which both Gardner and Kermode seemed to put asunder:

[Did] the Bible derive its authority in spite of its narratives? That its mode of narration was quite unrelated to its status? Why did scholars and theologians not at least consider the possibility that, on the contrary, the two were interrelated, and that the Bible had kept its place in our culture because of rather than in spite of them?   (Josipovici 1988: p. xi).

Indeed, this cultural pre-eminence remains powerful into the age of postmodernity with the publication of *The Postmodern Bible* (1995), and in the work of such critics as Stephen Moore, who relates the New Testament closely to a living literary tradition whose greatest modern exponent is James Joyce in a form of biblical commentary that is a 'postmodern analogue of the premodern text that it purports to read'. Mark's Gospel, Moore (1992: pp. xvii, 71) suggests, is 'a nocturnal writing . . . a Gospel of the dark, close kin to the oneiric writing that finds its most daring model in Joyce's *Finnegans Wake*.'

But let us now turn to more general critical considerations of the relationship between literature and theology in the twentieth century and beyond. The influence of the theologian Paul Tillich and a few others in the 1950s in North America initiated an interest in what Stanley Romaine Hopper described in 1951 as the 'spiritual significance' of poetry from an existentialist perspective (Hopper 1992: 19–37). But it was in the 1960s that three very different voices were heard, making serious claims for the study of literature and *religion*. The American Jesuit scholar William F. Lynch, in a series of books, makes great claims for the significance of the 'literary imagin-ation' and the Western literary tradition stretching back to Greek tragedy in the 'Christian' adventure of the 'completely definite'. On the whole, Lynch (1960) rejects the fragmented tendencies of the modern world, which he illustrates in, among others, the works of Graham Greene and T. S. Eliot. Perhaps even more significant is the work of Nathan A. Scott Jr., first at the University of Chicago and later the University of Virginia. Although he began publishing as early as 1952, Scott began to be known in the next decade for his work on modern poetry (especially Eliot and Auden), Samuel Beckett and Ernest Hemingway. Deeply influenced by Heidegger and existentialist thinking, Scott's repeated theme is the central importance of the 'theological horizon' in the literary landscape of the twentieth century, a time indeed characterized by fragmentation and isolation. For Scott, the enduring stability of the literary imagination and the poetic was fundamental in the construction of religious belief, and he looks back to English literature of the nineteenth century, in his last major book *The Poetics of Belief* (1985) specifically to S. T. Coleridge, Matthew Arnold, and Walter Pater, in order to build a philosophy of religion based on the faculty of the imagination.

The third voice from the United States of the 1960s is that of the highly original theologian Thomas Altizer, whose radical 'death of God' theology is still being worked through. His work begins with a book on the poet William Blake, *The New Apocalypse: The Radical Christian Vision of William Blake* (1967), and for four decades he has developed his theological thinking through close readings of Blake, James Joyce, and other 'mythic' writers. Altizer stands apart from other American scholars in the field of literature and religion inasmuch as he is specifically concerned with the business of theology itself. The more common American tendency towards cultural studies has been sharply defined by Giles Gunn, whose important book *The Interpretation of Otherness* (1979) sets out to 'reconstitute the discussion' of the relations between literature and religion 'on the plane of the hermeneutical rather than the apologetic, the anthropological rather than the theological, the broadly humanistic rather than the narrowly doctrinal' (ibid. 5).

One of the exceptions to this tendency in the United States has been a professor of comparative literature, Robert Detweiler, whose work takes the field into the postmodern world, and whose book *Breaking the Fall* (1989) explores the issue not so much of religious *texts*, as of religious *reading*, and the nature of a religiously reading community as a kind of 'church' of readers. Detweiler shares with Scott and others a sense of a world in a condition of societal and religious fragmentation, preserved only by the coherent vision of poets and imaginative writers.

The critical study of literature and religion has been an enterprise shared between many cultures in Europe and North America, not to speak of more recent voices in Australia, South Africa, and elsewhere. But in a handbook whose primary focus is on English literature and theology, although the critical work of North American scholars is immensely important, more space must now be given to the work done in Great Britain itself, where such 'interdisciplinary' scholarship is often less regarded, and important figures accordingly not given the credit that should be their due. Mention has already been made of Helen Gardner, whose work as a professor of English literature followed closely the conservative approach of T. S. Eliot, and whose Memorial Lectures she delivered in 1968, initiating a discussion on religion and tragedy that would be continued by others such as Ulrich Simon in later years. Only a few years later the American literary scholar Roy Battenhouse produced a massive volume entitled *Shakespearean Tragedy: Its Art and Christian Premises* (1971). In 1966, Gardner delivered the Ewing Lectures with the title 'Religious Poetry', with particular emphasis on the seventeenth-century English poets George Herbert and John Donne, linking their particular style and 'wit' to the literature of the New Testament itself: 'The paradoxes, twistings of Scripture, borrowings from the liturgy, allegorical interpretations, the use of typology, all these things reach back through the centuries of Scriptural commentary and liturgical use to the early Fathers, and indeed to the New Testament itself' (Gardner 1971: 174). But particular attention should be given to a group of British theologians of the second half of the twentieth century whose contribution to *theology* and English literature was immense, who generally received little credit for their work from either the theological or the literary establishments of their day, and whose legacy is now in danger of being forgotten. Of particular significance are Martin Jarrett-Kerr, F. W. Dillistone, John Coulson, John Tinsley, Ulrich Simon, and Peter Walker. In his Introduction to the proceedings of the First National Conference on Literature and Religion held in Durham University in 1982, Dillistone wrote:

Over a considerable period, certainly since the ending of the Second World War, there has been a growing interest in America in the relationship between literature and religion ... since returning to England in 1952 I have realized that there has been hesitation, even suspicion in academic circles in this country [Great Britain] when attempts have been made to suggest that theology and English literature have much to contribute to one another and to learn from one another.   (Jasper 1984: 1)

As a distinguished exception to this suspicion, Dillistone mentions John Coulson, a scholar of nineteenth century theology and literature, whose book *Religion and Imagination* (1981) is addressed to the 'student and teacher of religion' and celebrates the gain to be made from 'cultivating a properly imaginative response to literature in general' (ibid. p. v), appreciating the reinforcement of imaginative forms and religious beliefs. In this book, Coulson looks back directly to J. H. Newman's masterwork, the *Essay in Aid of a Grammar of Assent* (1870), advocating the importance of literature for the study of religious thought and the nature of religious 'assent'. He argues that literature does more than simply 'reflect' the beliefs of a community, for the study of literature reveals the *form* of the questions which, at least in the nineteenth century, *should* have concerned theologians, but with the exception of Newman, did not. Coulson (1981: 5) illustrates his contention in a study of the poetry of T. S. Eliot's *Four Quartets*, suggesting that 'Eliot's poetry exemplifies what Newman's theology explains'. Literature at its best requires and justifies an imaginative assent (what the Romantic poet S. T. Coleridge might have called the 'willing suspension of disbelief') and thus teaches us the nature of such assent.

Coulson is concerned to explore the *craft* of literature as an important means of understanding the nature of religious assent. Such a concern also runs through the work of Dillistone himself, who as a teacher of theology was always anxious to commend to his students the 'unfamiliar territory' of literature. Reading novels, poems, and plays was not simply an optional extra for his students, but rather a necessary step in religious understanding. Dillistone's early work, *The Novelist and the Passion Story* (1960), was a preliminary essay in exploring biblical narrative 'as fiction', offering a literary challenge to the largely historical paradigms of biblical criticism, and showing the novel as a demonstration of a theological theme, that is 'the power of redemptive suffering' (ibid. 22). In a sequence of later theological books, Dillistone invariably begins within a literary context—for example, with Eliot's *The Cocktail Party* in what is perhaps his most important work, *The Christian Understanding of Atonement* (1968). Encountering literature, he argues, shifts the theological mind from proposition and 'statable message' to a respect for the power of symbol and intuition, and he frequently returns to the American poet Wallace Stevens's *The Necessary Angel*, where Stevens writes:

The extension of the mind beyond the range of the mind, the projection of reality beyond reality, the determination to cover the ground, whatever it may be, the determination not to be confined, the recapture of excitement and intensity of interest, the enlargement of the spirit at every time, in every way, these are the unities, the relations, to be summarized as paramount now.   (Stevens 1951)

Very different from Dillistone's measured thought is the work of Ulrich Simon, Professor of Christian Literature at King's College, London. Born into a German Jewish family, his father died in Auschwitz in 1943, and Simon eventually settled in England and became an Anglican priest. His book on atonement theology, *Atonement: From Holocaust to Paradise* (1987), has an urgent, personal tone. His recourse to literature as a source of theological reflection is rooted in literature's capacity to go beyond any conclusions we may claim to have reached, a valuable corrective to the 'systematic' theologian. Simon returns repeatedly to the plays of Shakespeare, and especially the tragedies where 'there are no mechanics to work the balances'.

When I lectured for a whole term on the Atonement to theological students this play (*Measure for Measure*) was the text on which to draw. It gives an extreme case which could make bad law, but does not. It could also sentimentalize mercy to discredit it, but does not. Shakespeare orchestrates a polyphonic discourse which hovers between the extremes of tragedy and comedy. Hence no-one ever gets to the bottom of this play; whenever one returns to read or see it a new element of substance is perceived.   (ibid. 54)

Simon is profoundly aware of the endless dramatic challenge which literature presents to the religious conscience and to the conclusive tendencies of theology, not least in a twentieth century soaked in blood and human cruelty. (Apart from the murder of his father, Simon's brother was a victim of Stalin's repressive regime.) In all his work he returns to the great literary tradition of tragedy in the West, and seeks a necessary synthesis between Christian existence and tragic involvement. The literature of tragedy, and perhaps Shakespeare above all, presents a massive challenge to the Christian conscience and to a theology of the cross that has too often denied the tragic reality of the human condition, and yet is not without hope. For Simon, tragedy and Christianity exist in a creative dialectic: 'Christianity is tragic because of the Cross, and tragedy becomes Christian through the Resurrection' (Simon 1989: 145).

In this group of twentieth-century English 'literary' theologians, another very different voice is that of Martin Jarrett-Kerr. A monk of the Community of the Resurrection, Mirfield, and one of those involved in the early battle against apartheid in South Africa, Jarrett-Kerr seemed to have read everything, and was always ready to defend the freedom of literature to speak and challenge: he was deeply involved also in the 'Lady Chatterley' trial—speaking in defence of D. H. Lawrence—and wrote a still-valuable study of Lawrence's work. At the centre of Jarrett-Kerr's approach to the study of literature and theology is the question of 'commitment', writing at a time when for many the value of literature seemed almost to be its freedom from commitment; the poet, the novelist, as was being claimed, should not be tied down, and one of the most vocal in this claim for freedom was Lawrence himself. Lawrence wrote in a brief essay entitled 'Why the Novel Matters' (see Elisabeth Jay, Ch. 1 above):

The Bible—but *all* the Bible—and Homer and Shakespeare: these are the supreme old novels. These are all things to all men. Which means that in their wholeness they affect the whole man alive, which is the man himself, beyond any part of him. They set the whole tree trembling with an excess of life, and they do not just stimulate growth in one direction. (Lawrence 1956: 105)

For Jarrett-Kerr himself, literature's very freedom is indicative of a far more powerful commitment than simply *to* a creed or system of belief. In a late essay entitled 'Literature and Commitment: "Choosing Sides"', Jarrett-Kerr wrote:

There is a type of commitment which has not yet been mentioned, although it relates to Addison, Pascal and Milton and a whole mountain-range behind them. So far we have considered only man's commitment to...(beliefs, principles, systems, forms, styles, aspirations...). But what of a commitment believed to have been made (or continually being made) not *by* man, but *to* man? Commitment by whom or what? Let us call it by some 'outside' power or powers. (Jasper 1984: 116)

Theology remains at the heart of Jarrett-Kerr's concerns, and for him the beauty and mystery of literature is indicative of divine commitment to *us*—it is, in other words, revelatory. Reading literature as literature (and not a simply a vehicle for theology or dogma) is a way to perceive more clearly the workings of the divine in creation.

The final member of this group of British theologians to be considered, and the list is by no means exhaustive, is an Anglican bishop, Peter Walker, a poetic spirit whose writings on the poet W. H. Auden are both deeply spiritual and penetrating. Walker, too, is committed to literature because what he calls the truth of poetry reveals that which is, in Auden's own words, 'beyond our comprehension but not beyond our attention' (Jasper 1984: 63). Walker's own labyrinthine prose demonstrates the dilemma of the student of literature and theology: always called to be 'both/and', both a critic and a theologian, a poet and a critic, never simply *using* literature for theological purposes of finding theological themes in narratives, but sensitive to the demands of both forms of discourse and their disciplines. The point is clearly made by the former Bishop of Durham David Jenkins in a comment made in 1964, published under the editorship of John Coulson (1964: 219):

The dreadful thing about so much theology is that, in relation to the reality of the human situation, it is so superficial. Theological categories (really mere theological formulae) are 'aimed' without sufficient depth of understanding at life insensitively misunderstood. Theologians need therefore to stand *under* the judgments of the insights of literature before they can speak with true theological force of, and to, the world this literature reflects and illuminates.

This illumination, however, as John Tinsley once reminded us, is not direct but 'slant'. In a brief but influential article entitled 'Tell it Slant', Tinsley (1983: 163–70) uses the poetry of the American Emily Dickinson (and also the thought of Kierkegaard) to warn theologians against their tendency to 'unequivocal assertions' and be content with 'ambiguity and paradox'.

During the past twenty years there has been a steady stream of work from British scholars in the field of literature and theology from both the literary and the theological side, not least in the pages of the journal *Literature and Theology*, published from Oxford since the early 1980s. A few comments may be worthy of note. Much of the most creative writing has been from a group of scholars of the literature of the nineteenth century, a period characterized by the dilemma of the 'critical spirit and the will to believe'. The work of T. R. Wright, Elisabeth Jay, and Valentine Cunningham in particular has focused on theological readings of texts and the importance of the novel above all in the nineteenth century as a subtle barometer of religious opinion and belief. Wright furthermore wrote a volume entitled *Theology and Literature* (1988) which explores the 'creative tension' between theology and literature, their differences being of ethos and discipline: 'Much theology... tends towards unity and coherence, a systematic exploration of the content of faith which attempts to impose limits on the meaning of words, while literature, as Ezra Pound insisted, is often dangerous, subversive and chaotic, an anarchic celebration of the creative possibilities of language' (ibid. 1). Yet, for all their differences, according to Wright, theology and literature share a common enemy, that is, a pervasive literalism which blocks many people from understanding the nature of Christian belief. What Wright is really aiming for, along with a number of other literary critics such as Michael Edwards, is a poetics of faith, which is an understanding of the nature of theology *through* literature, or even theology itself *as* a poetry of faith. In his chapters on the novel, poetry, and drama, Wright seems to suggest that theology, as a basically rather simple activity, needs to learn from the complexity of literature and its forms. Writing of the language of theology in the plays of Samuel Beckett, he suggests that 'in order to be comprehensible... it needs to be seen within its total context as part of a complex and pluriform set of linguistic and literary codes' (ibid. 199).

The opposite position is taken by the 'literary theologian' Paul S. Fiddes, whose book *The Promised End: Eschatology in Theology and Literature* (2000) explores a complex eschatological theology from various perspectives through specific literary texts from *King Lear* to the novels of Martin Amis. Fiddes begins with a peculiarly modern, or even postmodern problem in literature—how to bring a book to an end (he explores the alternative endings of John Fowles's novel *The French Lieutenant's Woman*), and four literary 'models' for exploring the sense of an ending as offered by four critics, Frank Kermode, Northrop Frye, Jacques Derrida, and Paul Ricœur.

We might say, then, that the study of literature and theology is alive and well, though it remains unsystematic and patchy. The texts of English literature and the doctrines of theology continue to enjoy creative conversations, though perhaps not much more than that, and the fundamental terms of the two fields of study remain unchanged. That change, specifically in theology, may now be beginning to happen as we move ever further from the almost entirely Christian culture that has been the context for most English literature until the present day, and at the same time the churches that have been the guardians of Christian theology continue a seemingly irreversible slide into institutional decay. So far we have looked almost exclusively at the work of theologians and literary critics. But we should also recognize the work of cultural critics in both America and Great Britain, and situate the study of literature and religion within the field of cultural studies. A classic example of such work is J. Hillis Miller's book *The Disappearance of God* (1965), in which Miller examines five Victorian writers—Thomas de Quincey, Robert Browning, Emily Brontë, Matthew Arnold, and Gerard Manley Hopkins—in all of whose work is found in different ways, Miller argues, a consciousness of the disappearance of God, perhaps the fundamental shift in the transition to modernity in English literature and culture. This is to be clearly distinguished from the more dramatic 'event' of the 'death of God' in Hegel and Nietzsche. It is the subtle sense, caught in the delicate folds of literary narrative and poetry, of the gradual withdrawal of the deity from human affairs and experience. In Miller's (1965: p. x) words:

Though literature is a form of consciousness, consciousness is always consciousness *of* something. A work of literature is the act whereby a mind takes possession of space, time, nature, or other minds. Each of these is a dimension of literature. Literature may also express a relation of the self to God. I have chosen to approach five writers from a theological perspective because in [them] theological experience is most important and determines everything else.

The point, perhaps, is that these writers are all very different in their religious views, but they all participate in a general cultural shift which involves a theological sea-change that is perceived in literature long before it is even acknowledged or articulated by the theologians themselves. Now if, turning back to another cultural literary critic Terry Eagleton, a Professor of Cultural Theory, Victorian English studies did indeed emerge out of the 'failure of religion', it ought to be noted that one of his more recent works, *After Theory* (2003), is saturated with *theological* language, though it is not the theology of the Church and Christian tradition as such. Indeed, it is a theology that arises from the corpse of organized religion, though its vocabulary is familiar, and it begins with the work of poets and playwrights. In one chapter Eagleton (2003: 174) begins with the 'poetry' of the Hebrew prophets:

Take, for example, a revolutionary document like the Book of Isaiah. The poet who wrote this book opens with a typically anti-religious bout of irascibility on the part of Yahweh, the Jewish God. Yahweh tells his people that he is fed up with their solemn assemblies and sacrificial offerings . . . and counsels them instead to 'seek justice, correct oppression, defend the fatherless, plead for the widow'.

He continues with a discussion of 'a materialist morality' as illustrated by *King Lear*, concluding on a significantly theological note: 'Only when this paranoid monarch accepts that he stinks of mortality will he be *en route* to redemption.' (ibid. 182).
Protestantism and its theology, it seems, is far from dead.

A more elitist cultural critical approach to the relationship between theology and literal is found in the work of George Steiner, described by one of his admirers, Robert Carroll (1994: 262), as 'a metaphysician of art, literature, and culture, and some may regard him therefore as a theologian *manqué*'. The presence of deity, though carefully veiled, is everywhere present in Steiner's writings on literature, and in one of his best-known books, *Real Presences* (1989), Steiner

> proposes that any coherent understanding of what language is and how language performs, that any coherent account of the capacity of human speech to communicate meaning and feeling is, in the final analysis, underwritten by the assumption of God's presence. I will put forward the argument that the experience of aesthetic meaning in particular, that of literature, of the arts, of musical form, infers the necessary possibility of this 'real presence'. (ibid. 3)

The difficulty with reading Steiner, so deeply learned within the tradition of European literature, is his location only in the very highest echelons of literary and artistic culture and his intolerance of anything less. One of the great virtues of studying the relationship between religion and literature is that it recognizes no intellectual class barriers, rediscovering the roots of theological thinking and practice in the deepest, common roots of human experience—an experience more than the purely intellectual. Steiner, together with that other mandarin of literary culture, the American Harold Bloom, is ultimately too intellectual to follow the broader community of religious readers. Thus Bloom loftily begins his book, *The Western Canon* (1995) with the words: 'I feel quite alone these days in defending the autonomy of the aesthetic . . . Aesthetic criticism returns us to the autonomy of imaginative literature and the sovereignty of the solitary soul, the reader not as a person in society but as the deep self, our ultimate inwardness' (ibid. 10).

Very different from such cultural isolation is the turn of literature and religion studies in recent years to various forms of liberation theology and theory. For example, the claims of women to read and write, to see and to be heard, have produced radical rereadings of biblical texts and also a revision of the literary canon which has often been defined and limited in many subtle ways by the patriarchal hegemony that can be traced back ultimately to the church and its controlling theology. New texts and new readings of texts spring out of what Elisabeth Jay (1995: 118) has called 'feminism's originating vision of oppression, marginality and difference [which] can seem very easily to translate into the Christian desire to work ceaselessly for "heaven on earth" if (and this "if" is still the stumbling block for many feminists) we are prepared also to embrace the notion of "goodwill toward men"'. Of even more recent date is the interest of religion and literature in post-colonial cultures, a matter not at all alien to the concerns of English literature. For the spirit of British colonial and imperial adventurism was driven by, among other more material forces, a missionary zeal to convert the 'heathen in their blindness', territorial acquisition seen as fulfilling the prediction of Genesis 28: 14: 'you shall spread abroad to the west and to the east and to the north and to the south, and all the families of the earth shall be blessed in you and in your offspring'. The consequence of this after the decline of British and European imperialism has been the growth of literatures, outside the scope of this volume, in Africa, India, the Caribbean, Canada, and Australasia that seek cultural independence, yet remain rooted in the literary and religious culture of a Britain perceived as oppressive rather than liberating.

Developments in the field of literary theory in the later part of the twentieth century have had a profound effect upon the study of literature and theology, though in fact the link is an ancient one through the art of hermeneutics or the theory of interpretation within both Jewish and Christian traditions in the West. Though a standard study by Terence Hawkes, *Structuralism and Semiotics* (1977), focuses almost exclusively on the twentieth century, in fact students of St Augustine of Hippo's work *On Christian Doctrine*, dating from the fourth century CE, will quickly become aware of his very sophisticated theory of semiotics in his reading of Scripture. Yet if structuralism in literary studies was not only a way of reading and understanding but also a way of perceiving and thinking about the world, it was with the rise of post-structuralism and deconstruction that theological questions became acutely and even overtly a part of literary theory. Within structuralist thought in literary schools, learning from the linguistic theory of Ferdinand de Saussure, the structures of texts are perceived as self-regulating, without appeals beyond themselves to order and generate patterns of meaning. Within deconstruction this could be perceived as a threat to the very notion of theology itself. The point is made rather wordily by the French theorist and critic Jacques Derrida in a chapter of his book *Of Grammatology* (1967, trans. 1974) entitled 'The End of the Book and the Beginning of Writing': 'language itself is menaced in its very life, helpless, adrift in the threat of limitlessness, brought back to its own finitude at the very moment when its limits seem to disappear, when it ceases to be self-assured, contained, and *guaranteed* by the infinite signified which seemed to exceed it' (1974: 6). For 'infinite signified' we may, of course, read the traditional notion of 'God' or the Divine. But if literary theory has seemed to take us away from the business of theology, it may be that its task of exploring the theoretical implications of literary practice, is, in fact, closely allied to theology's business with religion and religious experience. A significant volume of essays of the 1980s, to which Derrida also contributed, Sanford Budick and Wolfgang Iser's *Languages of the Unsayable* (1989), addressed in literature and philosophy an age-old problem of theology. The cover advertisement for the book expresses it very clearly: 'The articulation of the unsayable, of negativity—that which has been excluded by what is sayable—is one of the most important and fascinating areas of contemporary humanistic study,' while Derrida (ibid. 3–5) begins his own essay in the book by referring to the traditions of 'negative theology' and his literary distinc-tion from them. Poetry, like theology, it might be said, has long understood its task as the articulation of that which is essentially 'unsayable' but yet known and acknow-ledged, and literary theorists are now simply exploring that which the poet has often expressed with telling simplicity. George Herbert, for example, in the early seven-teenth century, explored the nature of prayer as that which is beyond explanation, in a series of metaphors and images ending with the utterly simple yet mysterious phrase: 'something understood' (Herbert 1967: 27).

From the side of theology and religious studies, a few critics have adopted the language and methods of 'secular literary criticism' to explore the literature of the Bible and sacred texts, but far more significant has been the recognition by many literary critics of the close relationship between their theoretical concerns and the concerns of theology, and of the emergence of ancient forms of textual interpretation in modern literary studies. In particular ancient Jewish midrashic approaches to texts have been rediscovered in postmodern literary criticism. In the volume *Midrash and Literature* (1986), edited by Geoffrey H. Hartman and Sanford Budick, essays on Milton, Defoe, and Romantic poetry look back to the Bible and its midrashic interpretation. For example, in Harold Fisch's essay on *Robinson Crusoe*, he writes: 'The story of Robinson's many trials on the island may be read as a kind of midrash on Jonah.... Defoe's book... is not only about a man who undergoes a moral testing on a desert island: it is about the process of interpretation itself, its pitfalls and menaces' (ibid. 218, 221). English literature itself here becomes part of biblical interpretation and an element in the long history of interpreting the sacred texts.

Apart from this recent revival in literary theory of ancient Jewish methods of interpretation, almost all the study of literature and theology in Britain and North America, as we have been following it, has been from within the dominating Christian tradition. Things, however, are changing, and one of the most public debates over literature and theology in the 1980s in England took place within the context of Islamic culture: the furore caused by the publication of Salman Rushdie's novel *The Satanic Verses* (1988). It is clear that within post-colonial literatures, other religious voices are beginning to be heard, and yet the greater part of the present volume must be concerned with literature and Christianity. Perhaps the growing awareness of the multicultural demands upon its critical attention has somewhat halted the flow of 'literature and theology' since its flowering in the 1960s and beyond. Perhaps also there has been a recognition that *inter*disciplinarity inevitably leads to *multi*disciplinarity, and attention to literature has expanded to other arts as well—the visual arts and, to a lesser extent, music. Or perhaps the hesitation apparent in such academic studies has another and less definable root.

As long ago as 1967, George Steiner published a volume of essays entitled *Language and Silence*. Steiner and many others after the Holocaust, such as Theodore Adorno, have struggled with the question as to whether it is possible to say anything after such an event in human history. Arguably, however, where theology has stumbled and fallen silent, the voices of the poets and writers have continued to speak and be heard—Celan, Wiesel, Levi, and others. Literature continues to speak, even in the midst of silence, and possibly because it has always been sensitive, in a way that theology paradoxically has often not been, to the inaudibility of the word, to the silence and darkness of God. What Eliot in *Four Quartets* described as the 'music heard so deeply | That it is not heard at all' is a poetic recognition of that 'eloquent silence' that is acknowledged in the traditions of mystical theology, and a recognition by the poet of Valentine Cunningham's perception that 'theology has never, ever, not dealt in the aporetic, the desert experience, the *via negativa*. Aporia infects the very ecstasy of the believer' (Cunningham 1994). Most recently, the growing interest in mysticism and negative theology has opened up new channels also in literature and theology. If deconstruction in literary theory and studies has worked against structures and systems, not least the systems of theology, then it has allowed the return to certain alternative traditions of radical dissent: mystics, at least within the Christian tradition, have often had the characteristics of being at once saintly *and* persecuted. At the same time many of them have been major writers and poets. In a major and unfinished work, entitled in English *The Mystic Fable* (1982), Michel de Certeau asserts that, at least since the seventeenth century, mysticism has been primarily a literary phenomenon. It is hardly surprising then, as theological interest in and studies of mysticism proliferate, that the study of literature and theology has begun importantly to suggest that our own time is experiencing not so much a dilution of belief as a shift away from traditional theological and ecclesial forms of belief and that literature is (and perhaps always has been) a major expression of religious beliefs and experiences that have often been suppressed by the very guardians of theology. The radical implications of this for literature (and perhaps why literary critics like Jonathan Culler have often, and sometimes rightly, been so suspicious of theology and 'religion') were suggested long ago in the 1960s by the radical theologian Thomas Altizer in his essay on the poet William Blake, stating that 'faith has never been able to speak in the established categories of Western thought and theology... because it has so seldom been given a visionary expression' (Altizer 1968: 182). The claim is extreme and provocative, but it is precisely such provocation which has inspired poets, since the prophets of the Hebrew Bible itself, to the ruin of sacred truths in seeking to express that which is ultimately beyond human expression, and it is why the study of the relationship between theology and literature remains so important, often so irritating, and so fascinating. It is why such devout, Christian poets as Gerard Manley Hopkins or R. S. Thomas have found their most profound voice at the very moment when their theological world seems to falter, while others more sceptical have thrown shards of light in dark places in spite of, or perhaps because of, their unbelief.

WORKS CITED

ALTER, ROBERT, and KERMODE, FRANK (eds.). 1987. *The Literary Guide to the Bible*. London: Collins.

ALTIZER, THOMAS, J. J. 1967. *The New Apooalypse. The Radical christian vision of william Blake*. 2000 Awora, colorado: Davies.

—— 1968. 'William Blake and the Role of Myth', in Thomas J. J. Altizer and William Hamilton, *Radical Theology and the Death of God*. London: Penguin.

BARRATT, DAVID, POOLEY, ROGER, and RYKEN, LEYLAND (eds.) 1995. *The Discerning Reader: Christian Perspectives on Literature and Theory*. Grand Rapids: Baker Books.

BARTON, JOHN, and HALLIBURTON, JOHN. 1981. 'Story and Liturgy', in *Believing in the Church: The Corporate Nature of Faith*. A Report by the Doctrine Commission of the Church of England. London: SPCK.

BATTENHOUSE, ROY W. 1971. *Shakespearean Tragedy: Its Art and Christian Premises*. Bloomington: Indiana University Press.

BIBLE AND LITERATURE COLLECTIVE, THE. 1995. *The Postmodern Bible*. New Haven: Yale University Press.

BLOOM, HAROLD. 1995. *The Western Canon: The Books and School of the Ages*. London: Macmillan.

BOSWELL, JAMES. 1953. *Life of Johnson*. 3rd edn, 1799. Oxford: Oxford University Press.

CARROLL, ROBERT P. 1994. 'Toward a Grammar of Creation: On Steiner the Theologian', in Nathan A. Scott, Jr. and Ronald A. Sharp (eds.), *Reading George Steiner*. Baltimore: Johns Hopkins University Press.

COULSON, JOHN (ed.). 1964. *Theology and the University: An Ecumenical Investigation*. London: Darton, Longman, & Todd.

—— 1981. *Religion and Imagination: 'In aid of a grammar of assent'*. Oxford: Clarendon.

CUNNINGHAM, VALENTINE. 1994 *In the Reading Gaol: Postmodernity, Texts and History*. Oxford: Blackwell.

DERRIDA, JACQUES. 1974. *Of Grammatology*. Trans. Gayatri Chakravorty Spivak. Baltimore: Johns Hopkins University Press.

—— 1989. 'How to Avoid Speaking: Denials', in Sanford Budick and Wolfgang Iser (eds.), *Languages of the Unsayable: The Play of Negativity in Literature and Literary Theory*. New York: Columbia University Press.

DETWEILER, ROBERT. 1989. *Breaking the Fall: Religious Readings of Contemporary Fiction*. San Francisco: Harper & Row.

DILLISTONE, F. W. 1960. *The Novelist and the Passion Story*. London: Collins.

—— 1986. *The Christian Understanding of Atonement*. London: James Nisbet.

EAGLETON, TERRY. 1996. *Literary Theory: An Introduction*. 2nd edn. Oxford: Blackwell.

ELIOT, T. S. 1951. *Selected Essays*. 3rd edn. London: Faber & Faber.

ETCHELLS, D. R. 1983. *A Model of Making: Literary Criticism and its Theology*. Basingstoke: Marshall Morgan & Scott.

FARRER, AUSTIN. 1948. *The Glass of Vision*. Westminster: Dacre.

FERRETTER, LUKE. 2003. *Towards a Christian Literary Theory*. London: Palgrave Macmillan.

FIDDES, PAUL S. 2000. *The Promised End: Eschatology in Theology and Literature*. Oxford: Blackwell.

FRYE, NORTHROP. 1982. *The Great Code: The Bible and Literature*. London: Routledge & Kegan Paul.

GARDNER, HELEN. 1956. *The Limits of Literary Criticism: Reflections on the Interpretation of Poetry and Scripture*. Oxford: Oxford University Press.

—— 1971. *Religion and Literature*. London: Faber & Faber.

GUNN, GILES. 1979. *The Interpretation of Otherness: Literature, Religion and the American Imagination*. New York: Oxford University Press.

HARTMAN, GEOFFREY H., and BUDICK, SANFORD (eds.) 1986. *Midrash and Literature*. New Haven: Yale University Press.

HENN, T. R. 1962, 'The Bible as Literature', in Matthew Black and H. H. Rowley (eds.), *Peake's Commentary on the Bible*. Rev. edn. London: Thomas Nelson.

—— 1970. *The Bible as Literature*. London: Lutterworth.

HERBERT, GEORGE. 1967. *A Choice of George Herbert's Verse*, ed. R. S. Thomas. London: Faber & Faber.

HOPPER, STANLEY ROMAINE. 1992. *Stanley Romaine Hopper: The Way of Transfiguration. Religious Imagination as Theopoiesis*, ed. R. Melvin Keiser and Tony Stoneburner. Louisville, Ky.: Westminster/John Knox.

JASPER, DAVID. 1984. *Images of Belief in Literature*. Basingstoke: Macmillan.

JAY, ELISABETH. 1995. 'The Woman's Place', in David Barratt, Roger Pooley and Leyland Ryken (eds.), *The Discerning Reader: Christian Perspectives on Literature and Theory*. London: Apollos.

JOSIPOVICI, GABRIEL. 1988. *The Book of God: A Response to the Bible*. New Haven: Yale University Press.

KERMODE, FRANK. 1979. *The Genesis of Secrecy: On the Interpretation of Narrative*. Cambridge, Mass.: Harvard University Press.

LAWRENCE, D. H. 1956. *Selected Literary Criticism*, ed. Anthony Beal. London: Heinemann.

LEWIS, C. S. 1955. *Surprised by Joy*. London: Geoffrey Bles.

—— *A Grief Observed*. London: Faber & Faber.

LYNCH, WILLIAM F. 1960. *Christ and Apollo: The Dimensions of the Literary Imagination*. Notre Dame: University of Notre Dame Press.

MARVELL, ANDREW. 1969. *The Poems of Andrew Marvell*, ed. Hugh Macdonald. London: Routledge & Kegan Paul.

MILLER, J. HILLIS. 1965. *The Disappearance of God: Five Nineteenth-Century Writers*. New York: Schocken.

MOORE, STEPHEN D. 1992. *Mark and Luke in Poststructuralist Perspectives: Jesus Begins to Write*. New Haven: Yale University Press.

NEWMAN, JOHN HENRY. 1870. *An Essay in Aid of a Grammar of Assent*. 1979. Notre Dame: University of Notre Dame Press.

RUSHDIE, SALMAN, 1988. *The Satanic Verses*. London: Viking.

SCOTT, NATHAN A., JR. 1985. *The Poetics of Beliefs: Studies in Coleridge, Arnold, Pater, Santayana, Stevens and Heidegger*. Chapel Hill, NC: University of North Carolina Press.

SIMON, ULRICH. 1987. *Atonement: From Holocaust to Paradise*. Cambridge: James Clark.

—— 1989. *Pity and Terror: Christianity and Tragedy*. London: Macmillan.

STEINER, GEORGE. 1967. *Language and Silence: Essays on Language, Literature and the Lahuman*. New York: Athenaeum.

—— 1989. *Real Presences: Is There Anything in What we Say?* London: Faber & Faber.

STEVENS, WALLACE. 1951. *The Necessary Angel: Essays in Reality and Imagination*. London: Faber & Faber.

TINSLEY, JOHN. 1983. 'Tell it Slant', *Theology* 83.

WALHOUT, CLARENCE, and RYKEN, LEYLAND (eds.) 1991. *Contemporary Literary Theory: A Christian Appraisal*. Grand Rapids: Wm. B. Eerdmans.

WRIGHT, T. R. 1988. *Theology and Literature*. Oxford: Blackwell.

FURTHER READING

BLOND, PHILIP (ed.). 1998. *Post-Secular Philosophy: Between Philosophy and Theology*. London: Routledge.

BLOOM, HAROLD. 1989. *Ruin the Sacred Truths: Poetry and Belief from the Bible to the Present*. Cambridge, Mass.: Harvard University Press.

CUNNINGHAM, VALENTINE. 1975. *Everywhere Spoken Against: Dissent in the Victorian Novel*. Oxford: Oxford University Press.

—— 2002. *Reading After Theory*. Oxford: Blackwell.

DAVIE, DONALD. 1978. *A Gathered Church: The Literature of the English Dissenting Interest, 1700–1930*. London: Routledge & Kegan Paul.

DETWEILER, ROBERT, and JASPER, DAVID (eds.) 2000. *Religion and Literature: A Reader*. Louisville, Ky.: Westminster/John Knox.

EDWARDS, DAVID L. 2005. *Poets and God: Chaucer, Shakespeare, Herbert, Milton, Wordsworth, Coleridge, Blake*. London: Darton Longman & Todd.

HENN, T. R. 1970. *The Bible as Literature*. London: Lutterworth. (An expanded version of his earlier essay in *Peake's Commentary*.)

JASPER, D. 1992. *The Study of Literature and Religion: An Introduction*. 2nd edn. London: Macmillan.

—— and PRICKETT, STEPHEN (eds.) 1999. *The Bible and Literature: A Reader*. Oxford: Blackwell.

—— and WRIGHT. T. R. (eds.) 1989. *The Critical Spirit and the Will to Believe: Essays in Nineteenth Century Literature and Religion*. London: Macmillan.

JAY, ELISABETH. 1979. *The Religion of the Heart: Anglican Evangelicalism and the Nineteenth Century Novel*. Oxford: Oxford University Press.

RYKEN, LEYLAND. 1979. *Triumphs of the Imagination: Literature in Christian Perspective*. Downers Grove, Ill.: InterVarsity Press.

SAID, EDWARD. 1983. *The World, the Text, and the Critic*. Cambridge, Mass.: Harvard University Press.

SHERRY, PATRICK. 2003. *Images of Redemption: Art, Literature and Salvation*. London: T & T Clark.

VANCE, NORMAN. 1985. *The Sinews of the Spirit: The Ideal of Christian Manliness in Victorian Literature and Religious Thought*. Cambridge: Cambridge University Press.

WARD, GRAHAM. 2003. *True Religion*. Oxford: Blackwell.

PART TWO

THE FORMATION OF
THE TRADITION

CHAPTER 3

ORIGINS IN THE ENGLISH TRADITION

MICHAEL FOX

Towards the conclusion of the book of Job, Heliu (NRSV: Elihu) observes of God: 'Si uoluerit extendere nubes quasi tentorium suum, et fulgurare lumine suo desuper, cardines quoque maris operiet' ('If he will stretch out clouds as his tent, and lighten from above with his light, he shall also cover over the ends of the sea'; Job 36: 29–30). Pope Gregory the Great (c.540–604), interpreting these verses in his monumental commentary, the *Moralia in Iob*, likens the stretching out of the clouds to the opening of the way of preaching to his ministers, who spread over the compass of the world. Because words are not sufficient as a means of persuasion, God also brightens from above with his light: these 'fulgura' ('lightnings' or 'brightnesses') are to be understood as 'miracula' ('miracles'). The 'clouds', then, rain down words, and make miracles known by the power of their glittering light, thus turning even the furthest reaches of the world to divine love and faith. How, says Gregory, do we know this to be true? Well, we have seen that God has penetrated the hearts of nearly all peoples and has joined in one faith the differences of the east and west, and we have also the specific example of Britannia: 'Ecce lingua Brittanniae, quae nihil aliud nouerat, quam barbarum frendere, iam dudum in diuinis laudibus Hebraeum coepit Alleluia resonare' (*Moralia* 27. 11. 21, ed. Adriaen (1979); 'Behold the tongue of Britain, which knew nothing other than a barbarous gnashing, already a little while ago began to resound in divine praises the Hebrew Alleluia').

If the conversion of the English to Christianity is the most recent example of the power of God's words and miracles which Gregory, writing near the end of the sixth century, can provide—and it may be, in fact, that this reference was added somewhat after the composition of the bulk of the commentary—then, by the time Bede (c.673–735) was composing his *Historia ecclesiastica gentis Anglorum* (*The Ecclesiastical History of the English People*), which was completed in 731, the status of Gregory as the 'Apostle of the English' was firmly established. Bede not only incorporates the whole of the passage from Gregory's *Moralia* in his own history, commenting that the combination of words and miracles is specifically appropriate to the conversion of the English, but, to a brief biography of Gregory, also appends the traditional explanation for Augustine's mission of conversion (*HE* 2. 1). One day, before he becomes pope, Gregory happens to see some boys for sale in the marketplace. On account of their appearance, it seems, Gregory enquires about their origins and their faith. Upon learning that they are pagans, Gregory expresses sorrow that their appearance should so contradict their spiritual condition and asks the name of their race, their country of origin, and the name of their king. The people, he learns, are called *Angli*, their country is *Deiri*, and their king *Ælle*. Although as yet unknown to the slaves and their people, the appropriateness of their salvation is immediately clear to Gregory, who sees in the name of the race a reference to angels (*angeli*), their future companions in heaven, in the name of the country a reference to their deliverance *de ira [Dei]* ('from the wrath [of God]'), and, in the name of their king, the first two syllables of the *Alleluia* which shall resound throughout their land (*HE* 2. 1).

The manner in which Gregory, by playing with language (the Latin verb is *adludere*) is able to demonstrate the innate suitability of the race for Christianity is particularly appropriate for understanding the complex relationship between Christian and pagan, or Germanic, and Latin and vernacular in the early English tradition (Liuzza 2001). For example, perhaps the best-known 'miracle' in Bede's *Historia ecclesiastica* is the story of the (probably) illiterate cowherd, Cædmon, who, with the gift of singing having been given to him by God, converts Latin Scripture (which he learned *per interpretes*, in English) into Old English poetry (*HE* 4. 24). In other words, Cædmon takes the Latin of Christianity and, using what had been both the language and the verse-form of Germanic paganism, turns it into vernacular verse. Further, in sharp relief to written Latin traditions, it would seem that Cædmon's versification is based largely upon oral principles, as writing is nowhere mentioned in Bede's account of the miracle.

Bede relates that the miracle took place in the monastery at Streanæshalch (Whitby), under the rule of the abbess Hild, and thus between 657 and 680. Cædmon, already well advanced in life, had learned nothing of songs, and so, when it sometimes happened at the feast that the harp would pass from hand to hand for the entertainment of the company, he would depart as his turn came near. On this particular occasion, Cædmon has a dream in which a figure appears to him and commands him to sing something ('Canta mihi aliquid'; 'Sing something for me'). When pressed, Cædmon finally sings a short song on a suggested topic, the beginning of all creation ('principium creaturarum'), here presented in an early Northumbrian version:

Nu scylun hergan   *hefaenricaes uard,*
metudæs maecti   end his modgidanc,
uerc *uuldurfadur,*   sue he uundra gihuaes,
eci dryctin,   or astelidæ;
he aerist scop   aelda barnum
heben til hrofe,   *haleg scepen,*
tha middungeard   *moncynnæs uard;*
eci dryctin,   æfter tiadæ
firum foldu,   *frea allmectig.*   (Smith 1968: 38–40)

(Now [we] shall praise   the guardian of the heavenly kingdom,
the might of the creator   and his design
the work of the father of glory,   as he, of every wonder,
eternal lord,   established the beginning.
He first shaped   for the children of men
heaven as a roof,   holy creator;
then earth   the guardian of the race of men,
eternal lord,   afterward prepared
the land for people,   lord almighty.)

Though the poem is relatively short, it is not an unsophisticated piece. David Howlett argues for the orthodox and Trinitarian nature of the poem, suggesting, among other more complicated arguments, that this is reflected in the length of the poem (nine lines), the number of times God is named (also nine), and the number of independent clauses in the poem (three, or an introduction with three, depending on how one treats 'sue' in line 3). Although there is some disagreement on the distribution of terms, the different persons of the Trinity are generally agreed to be present in the poem (Howlett considers the Father the 'hefaenricaes uard', the Son the 'metudæs maecti' and the Holy Ghost 'his modgidanc' (Howlett 1974; 1997: 262–74); but Huppé finds the Trinity in the 'metudæs maecti' (the Father), 'his modgidanc' (the Son) and the 'uerc uuldurfadur' (the Holy Spirit) (Huppé 1959: 111)). Even if Howlett's term for the Holy Ghost is not counted, critics have often noted that *Cædmon's Hymn* contains many different epithets for God (seven unique, or eight epithets altogether, in italics above). If we read the poem this way, one might also observe that the poem contains forty-two words, and fourteen of these, or precisely one-third, are terms for God. Further, in the repetition of 'uard' ('guardian') first with 'hefaenricaes' and then with 'moncynnæs' the poet shows the two facets of God's creation, first heavenly, then earthly (from 'In principio creauit Deus caelum et terram'; 'In the beginning God created heaven and earth' (Gen. 1: 1)). In the latter instance, the (relatively rare) assonance between 'middungeard' and 'uard' (which is more obvious in the West Saxon forms 'middangeard' and 'weard') has the further effect of emphasizing the relationship of God to the earth. Examples of the poetic craft of the hymn might be multiplied, but it should be obvious that the structure and language of the poem are highly suggestive and complex.

Bede's presentation of *Cædmon's Hymn* also reflects how he himself understood its significance. First of all, this gift of song is a result of the grace of God, and thus to be classed among the 'miracula'. Miracles are generally understood to effect salvation, but it has also been noted that Bede incorporates miraculous content in his *Historia ecclesiastica* in order to 'confirm the place of the English as a chosen people' (Rowley 2003: 229). Thus, Bede's account emphasizes that proper credit for Cædmon's skill lies with God—'diuina gratia' ('divine grace') is mentioned four times in the chapter—and that the wise men of the monastery and the abbess Hild herself all recognize that fact. For Bede, this was 'the miracle that solemnized the birth of Christian poetry in English' (Huppé 1959: 101). Cædmon's poetry is not, however, an end in itself: not only did his teachers become his audience, but he guided the souls of many to disdain earthly things, and to desire heavenly life, and this turning from sin and the world was always the aim of his singing.

One of the most interesting features of Bede's story is that Bede himself includes only a Latin paraphrase of the poem in the text, and warns his readers that the translation of poetry is a particularly difficult thing: 'Hic est sensus, non autem ordo ipse uerborum' ('This is the sense, but not, however, the order of the words'). While scribes have dutifully added the Old English text in the margin or at the conclusion of the *Historia ecclesiastica* (there are twenty-one manuscripts containing the Old English version of *Cædmon's Hymn*), Bede himself did not, and this has on occasion raised the issue of back-translation (O'Donnell 2004: 421–2). Bede's Latin has only recently been the subject of scrutiny as translation and as verse in its own right, but, where the Old English invites general comparison with Scripture, the liturgy, or Latin verse such as the Genesis poem of Hilary of Arles (Huppé 1959: 108–9), Bede's Latin contains words and phrases which would scan as part of a Latin hexameter, especially in the final lines, and parallels in one phrase ('culmine tecti') with such poets as Vergil (*Aeneid*), Juvencus (*Euangelorium libri IV*), Paulinus of Nola (several *Carmina*) and Sedulius (*Carmen paschale*), as well perhaps, as Aldhelm (*De laudibus uirginum*); another phrase ('humani generis') is very common in Latin hexameters and prose (Orchard 1996: 413; O'Donnell 2004). What is important to note, therefore, is that Bede clearly saw fit to place Cædmon in a poetic tradition which had been a Latin poetic tradition, both pagan and Christian. Cædmon's particular achievement, at least as Bede would have it—and we must realize that Bede's emphasis on God's grace is effectively divine sanction of such activity—is to advance the vernacular language and the vernacular tradition of alliterative verse to the status of Latin as a vehicle for communicating Christian doctrine and theology, a fact perhaps particularly made clear by the way Bede's Latin paraphrases the Old English (O'Donnell 2004) and the way Bede borrows from Scripture throughout the chapter (Orchard 1996: 403–4). In more recent times, the lasting influence of *Cædmon's Hymn* and its innovations can be seen in W. H. Auden's 'Anthem' (Szarmach 1998).

The story of Cædmon, then, though the poetry of his which is certainly preserved is limited to this nine-line 'hymn', has much to tell us about the status of Latin and vernacular literature in the late seventh century. Men were accustomed to sing at the feast, and it seems this singing must have been in Old English, in a style much like Cædmon's; in other words, no particular surprise or significance is expressed or attached to the mechanics of Cædmon's verse (O'Donnell 2004: 430–1). Vernacular poetic traditions must have been well established already. Bede informs us that

Cædmon's poetic career, which consists of instruction in the course of Christian history, rumination, and transformation of that instruction into verse, spanned a wide range of subjects:

Canebat autem de creatione mundi et origine humani generis et tota Genesis historia, de egressu Israel ex Aegypto et ingressu in terram repromissionis, de aliis plurimis sacrae scripturae historiis, de incarnatione dominica, passione, resurrectione et ascensione in caelum, de Spiritus Sancti aduentu et apostolorum doctrina; item de terrore futuri iudicii et horrore poenae gehennalis ac dulcedine regni caelestis multa carmina faciebat.   (Colgrave and Mynors 1969: 418)

(He sang about the creation of the world, the origin of the human race and the complete history of Genesis; about the departure of Israel from Egypt and the arrival in the promised land; about many other stories of sacred scripture; about the incarnation, passion, resurrection and ascension into heaven of the Lord; about the coming of the Holy Spirit and the teachings of the apostles; he also made many songs about the terror of future judgement, the horror of the torments of hell and the sweetness of the heavenly realm.)

This body of verse, however, has long been noted to resemble the collection preserved in Oxford, Bodleian Library, Junius 11, a manuscript which is perhaps to be dated to between 960 and 990 (Lockett 2002), and which contains the poems known to the modern era as *Genesis A, Genesis B, Exodus, Daniel,* and *Christ and Satan.* Franciscus Junius, who first published the contents of the manuscript in 1655, was convinced that these were the collected works of Cædmon. Though we now know that this is not the case, Bede's estimate of the range of topics upon which Cædmon sang may be of surprising importance in the development of English literary traditions, as this way of considering Christian history develops in an interesting, and, it seems to me, particularly English way throughout the medieval period. In any case, as Jeff Opland (1980: 120) has summarized the situation: 'Almost all of the extant Old English poetry is Christian or biblical; it may be that the very existence of this poetry is directly attributable to the singular success achieved by Cædmon in exploiting the secular native poetic tradition for pious ends.'

Cædmon, in Bede's estimation, had no peer as a composer of religious poetry in Old English. Bede himself, however, was reported in Cuthbert's *Epistola de obitu Bedae* (*Letter on the Death of Bede*) to be 'doctus in nostris carminibus' ('learned in our [vernacular] songs'), and the most significant Anglo-Latin poet of the late seventh and early eighth centuries, Aldhelm of Malmesbury, was also said to be an accomplished Old English poet. Of Bede's works we have only Cuthbert's description of what is known as *Bede's Death Song*, a five-line admonition for the moment of death; of Aldhelm's Old English compositions not one has survived with his name attached. However, the twelfth-century historian William of Malmesbury in his *Gesta pontificum Anglorum* preserves the tradition that Aldhelm was an accomplished vernacular poet—'Poesim Anglicam posse facere, cantum componere, eadem apposite uel canere uel dicere' ('He was able to make English poetry, to compose song, and likewise to sing or recite appropriately')—whose abilities were esteemed even by King Alfred. In fact, William relates an anecdote about how Aldhelm used to recite from a bridge after the semi-barbarous people had hurried off after mass, combining matter of 'high sentence' with frivolous things, and finally leading the people back to a sound state of mind (Hamilton 1870: 336; Opland 1980: 120–1; Orchard 1994: 5). This intermingling of Christian and native material (the words of Scripture among things 'ludicrous') is perhaps related to contact between Latin and vernacular traditions, for it would seem that even Aldhelm's Latin verse shows evidence of Old English influence, and Aldhelm was the first medieval poet to compose a substantial body of Latin verse as a non-native speaker of Latin (Lapidge 1979; Orchard 1994). Recently, it has been suggested that there is evidence that Aldhelm's reputation as a composer of vernacular verse was current as early as the time of Alfred (in the late ninth century), and that Aldhelm may have been the author, or closely associated with, the Old English *Exodus* (Remley 2005).

Besides *Caedmon's Hymn, Bede's Death Song*, and the so-called *Leiden Riddle*, all of which survive in early Northumbrian versions (Smith 1968), the only other extant vernacular poem with a certain claim to some kind of early existence in Anglo-Saxon England is *The Dream of the Rood*. The complete poem survives only in a late tenth-century manuscript, Vercelli, Biblioteca Capitolare, CXVII (known as the Vercelli Book), but fragments of the poem are preserved on the Ruthwell Cross, a massive stone cross which has been dated as early as 670, though most believe it to be a product of the early to mid-eighth century. Though it is generally accepted that the verses on the Ruthwell Cross are extracts from a more substantial text, the precise relationship between the cross and the poem is impossible to determine (Pope and Fulk 2001: 65), and the runic text may even be a later addition to the cross. *The Dream of the Rood* begins with a traditional Old English poetic opening (lines 1–3), which at once aligns the poem with such works as *Beowulf* and *Andreas* and establishes it as probably the earliest medieval vernacular example of the dream vision which is later to figure so prominently in the works of Langland and Chaucer. The poem consists of four main sections, the vision of the cross and those regarding it (lines 4–23), the introduction to the speech of the cross (lines 24–7), the speech itself (28–121), and the conclusion, in which the dreamer recounts his prayers and longing for the cross, including mention of the redemptive nature of the crucifixion and a vision of the masses being led back into heaven by Christ triumphant (lines 122–56).

What is remarkable about the poem from a doctrinal point of view is the balance between the poet's view of the crucifixion as Christ's triumph (as Son of God) and Christ's suffering (as man): 'Their paradoxical fusion in the crucifixion is suggested first by the alternation between the jewelled radiant cross and the plain and blood-covered cross in the prelude, and secondly and much more subtly and powerfully by the two figures of the heroic victorious warrior and the passive enduring cross' (Woolf 1958: 137–8). However, this is not a dualism of the poet's invention, as Rosemary Woolf has pointed out, but rather 'reflect[s] exactly the doctrinal pattern of thought of [the poet's] time', before a 'comprehensive and consistent soteriological theory' evolved with Anselm in the eleventh century (ibid. 138 and 142). The influence of pagan Germanic culture is clear in the emphasis on Christ as a warrior, but it has also been argued that the death of Baldr in Old Norse mythology lies behind the observation that 'weop eall gesceaft' ('all creation wept', 55) at the death of

Christ (of course, Baldr's death may in turn have been influenced at an earlier stage by the biblical account of Christ's crucifixion). The importance of the cross, and the cult of the cross, is clear from other works such as Cynewulf's *Elene*, the homiletic Old English 'Finding of the True Cross' (Bodden 1987), and evidence from the *Anglo-Saxon Chronicle* which suggests that Alfred may have received a fragment of the true cross from Pope Marinus in 883 [882]. Among thematic parallels with other Old English texts such as *The Wanderer*, we might also note that the poet, through the repetition of such phrases as 'elne mycle' (34a, 60a, 123a) and 'mæte werede' (69b, 124a) to describe Christ, the cross, and the dreamer, in the first instance, and Christ and the dreamer in the second, affirms the fundamental similarity of nature and will between Christ and man. Though the influence of earlier Christian Latin poetry (most notably the hymns of Venantius Fortunatus), the liturgy, and the Nicene Creed have all been suggested (Patch 1919; Ó Carragáin 1982; Grasso 1991; Holderness 1997), *The Dream of the Rood* remains the most compelling and unusual witness to the union of vernacular verse and Christian theology, perhaps in the history of English literature.

While *Cædmon's Hymn* and *The Dream of the Rood* are sophisticated poems which stand at important junctures in the English tradition, there is relatively little disagreement about the nature of Christian influence in each. The same, however, cannot be said for *Beowulf*. Though it is an accepted fact that *Beowulf* draws in imaginative ways 'on biblical stories of creation, of Cain and the giants to form part of its mythic structure' (Godden 1991: 207), there is really no scholarly agreement on how to read and/or understand the (largely critically constructed dichotomy of) Christian and pagan elements in the poem (Irving 1997; see also Klaeber 1911–12; Hill 1994). What readers of *Beowulf* have sometimes ignored is the poem's manuscript context.[1] We must first of all keep in mind that *Beowulf* appears in the composite manuscript Oxford, Bodleian Library, Cotton Vitellius A. xv, specifically, the latter codex, known as the Nowell Codex, which contains *The Passion of St Christopher*, the *Wonders of the East*, the *Letter of Alexander to Aristotle*, *Beowulf*, and *Judith*, in that order. It has often been suggested that the common link between these texts is an interest in 'monsters' (most recently and thoroughly by Orchard 1995), but it might also be observed that the two other poetic texts in the manuscript contain explicitly religious material, a life of the dog-headed saint, Christopher, and a verse paraphrase of the Old Testament story of Judith and Holofernes. The *Wonders of the East* and the *Letter of Alexander to Aristotle* both derive from Latin traditions of writing about the east, and seem also to be related to the Latin *Liber monstrorum* (*Book of Monsters*), which, incidentally, has also been linked to the Wessex of Aldhelm and the beginning of the eighth century (Lapidge 1982). As Andy Orchard has made clear, the *Liber monstrorum* contains a sophisticated mixture of three kinds of material: Christian prose sources (such as Augustine and Isidore), pagan prose sources (mainly the

---

[1] On the importance of manuscript context and organization to understanding (Christian) Old English poetry, see Raw (1991: 228) and Caie (2004).

Alexander material) and Vergil (Orchard 2003: 133–7), and one might therefore profitably consider *Beowulf* in just such a light.

In assessing the religion of *Beowulf*, Paul Cavill has quite rightly pointed to the two salient facts: 'the poem deals with characters who were historically heathen' and 'the poem as it is recorded in the manuscript is the product of a Christian poet' (Cavill 2004: 16). Therefore, it might first of all be helpful to isolate the passages in the poem which refer explicitly and clearly to Old or New Testament events. Though no certain reference to the New Testament has been identified, there are three separate passages which clearly refer to Old Testament history. The first appears near the beginning of the poem, in the passage which introduces the ravager of Heorot, the monster Grendel:

> Wæs se grimma gæst   Grendel haten,
> mære mearcstapa,   se þe moras heold,
> fen ond fæsten;   fifelcynnes eard
> wonsæli wer   weardode hwile,
> siþðan him scyppend   forscrifen hæfde
> in Caines cynne—   þone cwealm gewræc
> ece drihten,   þæs þe he Abel slog;
> ne gefeah he þære fæhðe,   ac he hine feor forwræc,
> metod for þy mane   mancynne fram.   (102–10)[2]

(The grim spirit was called Grendel, notorious border-stepper, he who held the moors, fen and fastness; the wretched man occupied the land of monsters for a time, after the creator had cursed him among the kin of Cain—the eternal lord avenged that killing, that he [Cain] slew Abel; he [Cain] did not rejoice in that feud, but he, the lord, banished him far from the race of men on account of that crime.)

The second is in many ways a reiteration of the first, part of the introduction of Grendel's mother after Beowulf's slaying of Grendel (1255b–1265a), and briefly introduces the biblical flood of Genesis 6 (1260–1b), which will become the topic of the third passage, the much-discussed depiction of the struggle of the giants with God and of the flood on the hilt of the sword which Beowulf brings up from the mere:

> Hylt sceawode,
> ealde lafe,   on ðæm wæs or writen
> fyrngewinnes,   syðþan flod ofsloh,
> gifen geotende   giganta cyn,
> frecne geferdon;   þæt wæs fremde þeod
> ecean dryhtne;   him þæs endelean
> þurh wæteres wylm   waldend sealde.   (1687b–1693)

(He [Hrothgar] examined the hilt, the old remnant, on which was written the beginning of the ancient struggle, after which the flood, the rushing sea, slew the race of giants—they achieved a terrible end; that was a nation strange to the eternal lord; to them on account of this the ruler gave a final reward through the surge of waters.)

---

[2] Quotations from *Beowulf* are taken from Klaeber (1950).

Though these passages are relatively brief, their significance to the poem is difficult to overstate. First of all, the poet locates the origin of Grendel and his mother—and (I would argue), through several strategies, mainly of repetition and variation, the dragon—in Cain's killing of Abel. The 'monsters' of *Beowulf* owe their existence ultimately to Cain, from whom sprang a surprising list of monsters, including 'eotenas ond ylfe ond orcneas', all the 'untydras' (111–12). God banished Cain on account of the killing of Abel, and the poet cleverly aligns that curse (Gen. 6: 11–12) with God's later decision to eradicate evil on the earth (then populated also by giants, the product of a curious union between either rebel angels and human women, or the righteous (male) ancestors of Seth and the corrupt (female) ancestors of Cain) by means of the flood (Gen. 6: 5–7). Though the characters in the poem are not aware of it, therefore, they occupy a world defined by Christian cosmology, and in fact may participate in a reflex of the struggle between Cain and Abel, and between God and the giants (in discussion of the development of the Cain and Abel allusion, much has been made of the link to Augustine's notion of the conflict between the city of man and the city of God; see Osborne 1978). This scriptural framework has the effect of aligning Beowulf and, to a lesser extent, other characters in the poem with those who oppose Cain and the giants, that is, ultimately, with God and, through typology, with the righteous Christian (though see Kaske 1967 on the term 'eoten' and difficulties in its interpretation in the poem).

While these three passages represent the sum of the certain scriptural references in the poem, there are many other points of possible influence. The first, and one of the most important, is the 'creation' song, sung by the scop in Heorot, which so angers Grendel:

> Sægde se þe cuþe
> frumsceaft fira   feorran reccan,
> cwæð þæt se ælmihtiga   eorðan worhte,
> wlitebeorhtne wang,   swa wæter bebugeð,
> gesette sigehreþig   sunnan ond monan
> leoman to leohte   landbuendum,
> ond gefrætwade   foldan sceatas
> leomum ond leafum,   lif eac gesceop
> cynna gehwylcum   þara ðe cwice hwyrfaþ.   (90b–98)

(He who knew how to tell about the beginning of mankind, so long ago, said that the almighty created the earth, the bright beautiful land, compassed by water; the triumphant one established the sun and the moon, lamps as light for earth-dwellers, and adorned the corners of the earth with limbs and leaves; he also shaped life for each of the races, of those which move about, alive.)

The court poet's song of creation obviously resembles the Genesis account of creation, and Caedmon's rendering of that account (quoted above). As it stands, it need not necessarily be biblical: for example, the Carthaginian minstrel Iopas sings a song not so different in Vergil's *Aeneid* (1. 740–6). However, the *Beowulf*-poet makes it clear that it is the noise of the hall, and perhaps this particular 'song', which makes Grendel suffer. Given the association of Grendel with Cain, we (the audience) immediately associate the *scop*'s song with praise of the Christian creator, and thus we have here an instance of what has been called a persistent 'ironic divide' between different levels (or frames) of narration in the poem, the 'pagan perspective...circumscribed by the broader Christian worldview possessed by the poet and his audience' (Sharma 2005: 247), and, in this case, by Grendel himself. Hrothgar's 'reading' of the hilt (quoted above) is another excellent example of these different narrative perspectives in the poem, as is the assertion of the poet that the Danes, not knowing any better, have entrusted their souls to the 'gastbona' ('soul-slayer') (175–88; see also Robinson 1985: 31–4, who calls this the 'double perspective' of the poem).

Of the many Old English texts in which parallels to *Beowulf* have been found, two of the more intriguing in this context are *Genesis A* and *Genesis B*.[3] Friedrich Klaeber first noted possible borrowings in *Beowulf* from *Genesis A*, but these are somewhat difficult to evaluate (Klaeber 1910, summary in Orchard 2003: 167). Most interesting is the suggested parallel between Beowulf and Nimrod, both the mightiest men of their respective days. Two particular parallels between *Beowulf* and *Genesis B*, assuming the direction of influence to be from *Genesis B* to *Beowulf*, have important thematic ramifications. First of all, Hrothgar promises Beowulf ample reward before and after the contest with Grendel: 'Ne bið þe wilna gad, | gif þu þæt ellenweorc aldre gedigest' (660b–661); 'Ne bið þe nænigre gad | worolde wilna, þe ic geweald hæbbe' (949b–950) ('There will not be a lack of good things for you, if you come through that courageous deed with your life'; 'There will not be any lack of good things for you in the world, of those over which I have power'). In case the reader misses it the first time, the poet twice uses the formula 'wilna gad' in Hrothgar's promises to Beowulf, and it is surely striking that this is precisely how God phrases his promise in *Genesis B*'s rather free rendering of the injunction in Genesis 2: 16–17:

'Ac niotað inc þæs oðres ealles,   forlætað þone ænne beam,
wariað inc wið þone wæstm,   ne wyrð inc wilna gæd.'   (235–6)

('Enjoy everything else, but leave that one tree alone; guard yourselves against that fruit, and there will not be a lack of good things for you [two].')

In this instance, Hrothgar (who in fact tends to speak in a more 'Christian' way than any other character in the poem) uses the words of God in a way which should convince us that the narrative has significance beyond the literal events there presented. Certainly, again, Hrothgar uses language which neither he nor the characters within the artistic narrative frame might be expected to understand. Later in the poem, in the context of his 'sermon', Hrothgar muses on the inscrutability of earthly rewards in a way which implicitly contrasts his own power with God's (compare 950b with 1727b):

[3] *Genesis A* and *Genesis B* are the modern titles of the continuous paraphrase of Genesis material in the Junius manuscript. What distinguishes one from the other is the unusual origin of *Genesis B*, a transliteration of an Old Saxon Genesis from the mid-ninth century, perhaps pressed into service when the Old English Genesis was found to be missing material on the fall of man. On *Genesis B* and the Old Saxon Genesis, see Doane (1991), from which all *Genesis B* quotations are taken.

> 'Wundor is to secganne,
> hu mihtig god   manna cynne
> þurh sidne sefan   snyttru bryttað,
> eard and eorlscipe;   he ah ealra geweald.'   (1724b–1727)

('It is a wonder to say how mighty God, to the race of men, through his broad spirit, dispenses wisdom, land, and nobility; he has power over all things.')

Hrothgar's expression of wonder at the order of the world seems to echo the questioning tone of *Genesis B* as the poet attempts to make sense of the fact that God, fully aware of the outcome of the temptation of Adam and Eve, would ever allow such a thing to take place:

> Þæt is micel wundor
> þæt hit ece god   æfre wolde,
> þeoden, þolian   þæt wurde þegn swa monig
> forlædd be þam lygenum   þe for þam larum com.   (595b–598)

(That is a great wonder, that eternal God, the lord, would ever allow it, that so many might be led astray by the lies which came from that teaching [i.e. the words of the serpent].)

If the connection between these two expressions of wonder is a valid one, then we may see here a shared concern for understanding the nature of the created world, one from the mouth of a (partially enlightened) pagan king, and one from a Christian poet considering the defining event in Christian (earthly) history. The former, without revelation, cannot see the divine order; the latter, with it, remains unable clearly to justify the ways of God to man.[4]

Despite the fact that there is no critical agreement on New Testament references in *Beowulf*, several possibilities have been suggested. The most significant of these resides in a single word, 'non' (1600a; 'nine', the ninth hour of daylight), the time of day (three o'clock in the afternoon) at which the Scyldings and Hrothgar give Beowulf up for dead after his plunge into the mere, for it is precisely at the ninth hour of the day ('circa horam nonam') that Jesus cries out to God and dies (Matt. 27: 45–50). Possible links between Beowulf and Christ do not end there. Hrothgar, as he praises Beowulf after the defeat of Grendel, also praises Beowulf's unnamed mother (942b–946a) in a manner which has been seen as an echo of Luke 11: 27. Further, the very fact that Beowulf rides to his final encounter with the dragon (a creature which must at least in part have been evocative to the poem's audience of the dragon of the Apocalypse in, among other references, Rev. 12: 7–9) in the company of twelve

---

[4] Indeed, while the *Genesis B* poet is generally agreed to deal less harshly with Adam, and especially with Eve, than is standard in early medieval examinations of the fall, the question of theodicy in man's fall was of no small significance in Anglo-Saxon England. Ælfric, for example, in his translation and adaptation of Alcuin's *Quaestiones in Genesim* (*Questions on Genesis*) breaks the question down into a matter of creation 'non posse peccare' ('not to be able to sin') and 'posse non peccare' ('to be able not to sin'), and suggests that the devil's daily temptations are opportunity for meritorious struggle (*Interrogationes Sigewulfi*, Interrogatio 36). One might compare these considerations with the admonitions of Dame Studie in Langland's *Piers Plowman*: 'Wilneth nevere to wite why that God wolde | Suffre Sathan his seed to bigile' (10. 119–20).

companions, one of whom is a thief, is certainly suggestive of Christ, as might be the return of the treasure ultimately to the earth, just as Judas's silver is buried, unwanted, in Potter's Field. Though few are convinced that Beowulf was meant to be seen as a type of Christ, there are other Old Testament figures with whom he bears comparison, namely Moses, Samson, and David in his battle with Goliath (Horowitz 1978; Orchard 2003: 142–5), and compelling links have also been made to hagiography, and the battles of saints with dragons (Rauer 2000).

The fact that New Testament references are few or non-existent, however, does not render specifically New Testament theology irrelevant to the poem (Cavill 2004). Several of the scriptural references generally assumed to be from the Old Testament, in fact, are also in the New. For example, though the story of Cain and Abel is related in Genesis 4, Cain is also mentioned in Hebrews 11: 4 and Jude 11, and, in fact, even connected to the devil in 1 John 3: 12, as he is not anywhere in the Old Testament. More importantly, the very cosmology of the poem, with a heaven and a hell of eternal punishment, is necessarily New Testament and Christian, and Cavill precisely summarizes this aspect of the theology of the poem:

The poet makes reference to Old Testament biblical history (Cain and Abel, the Flood, and so on), but at various points the poem and the characters express a New Testament understanding of God, the devil, judgement, heaven and hell; and indeed the Old Testament. The poet makes a perfectly reasonable distinction (for an Anglo-Saxon Christian, at least), between history and revelation: the creation, flood and giants of Genesis were to him history, the shared history of the world... heaven, hell and the devil were revealed truth about spiritual reality. (Cavill 2004: 38)

Still, terms and passages remain which are problematic. For example, how are we meant to understand 'ealde riht' (2330a; 'Old Law'?) or 'soðfæstra dom' (2820b; 'judgement of the righteous'?); Cavill's discussion of the latter and its interpretative possibilities is illustrative of the difficulties which yet inhere in our understanding of the 'theology' of Beowulf (Cavill 2004: 20–4; see also Irving 1997: 189–91).

A large portion of the corpus of writing in Old English which survives is homiletic in nature, and it might then come as no surprise that there are also points of contact between Beowulf and the vernacular homiletic tradition (Orchard 2003: 151–62). Three significant points of influence have been widely discussed in Beowulf scholarship: the narrator's comment on the idol-worshipping Danes (175–88), the description of the mere (especially 1357b–1364 and 1408–17a), and Hrothgar's 'sermon' (1700–84, but especially 1758–68). Curiously, while the first has long been suggested as a possible interpolation, both for the sentiment expressed, and the 'wa...wel' ('woe...weal') structure which appears often both in poetry and prose (including the much-discussed conclusion of The Wanderer), and may derive from the Beatitudes (Orchard 2003: 153), and the third has, on the basis mainly of theme and polysyndeton, recently been suggested to be a tenth-century interpolation (Lapidge 2000: 38–9), the only passage for which a clearly related source survives has, so far as I know, never been suggested as an interpolation. The description of the home of Grendel's mother has long been recognized to share dramatic verbal similarities with the description of hell in Blickling Homily xvi, a description which must have its ultimate source in the apocryphal *Visio Pauli*, though the precise relationship between the three works is still not without uncertainty. In any case, the use of Paul's vision of hell in the description of Grendel's mere is a master stroke: again using language which would not be familiar to the characters within the poem, the poet associates the monsters of Beowulf's career (including the dragon, through the repetition of such landmarks as the 'har stan') with the beasts that issue from the mouth of hell. In fact, many redactions of the *Visio Pauli* also include a 'draco igneus', a beast from whose mouth issue all sorts of lesser amphibious monsters, and this beast may well have influenced the poet's conception of Grendel, his mother, and the 'nicras' of the mere.

Early students of *Beowulf* were inclined to invent a character known as the 'Christian interpolator' to explain Christian elements in the poem. However, as the preceding discussion will have shown, Christianity is inextricably woven into the very fabric of the poem, its mythology, its setting, and its themes, and this is generally true of most Old English literature. Though the theology of the poem is not particularly complex, it may be that the poem in this respect is more representative of mainstream Anglo-Saxon theology than one might think. Even such named Old English authors as we have, and one primarily thinks of Ælfric and Wulfstan in this context, were hardly devoted to issues of theological complexity. Ælfric, for example, perhaps in a conscious echo of King Alfred's plan to translate into Old English 'the books most necessary for all men to know', set out, by summarizing Carolingian and English learning, 'to provide the means of religious education in the vernacular' (Clemoes 1959: 30)—even, almost 400 years before Wyclif, participating in a plan to translate substantial portions of the Bible; Wulfstan in turn continues the tradition, both rewriting Ælfrician texts and producing new works which reflect his own interests and shifting emphases (Godden 2004: 373–4). However, both Ælfric and Wulfstan are quite rightly celebrated for their various achievements, and their impact was probably felt long after the Norman Conquest of 1066 (below; Wormald 2004: 19–23).

One of the primary theological concerns of Anglo-Saxon authors seems to have been to recount and explicate the extra-scriptural fall of the angels. The angelic fall was a problem which had much exercised Augustine, but which had been simplified to a great extent, particularly by Gregory, before being virtually ignored by writers such as Bede and Alcuin. Old English writers, however, found in the fall of the angels a subject which seems to have been particularly dear to them, for we find substantial treatments of angelic history in Old English poetry (including, most significantly, *Genesis A*, *Genesis B*, *Christ and Satan*, and *Solomon and Saturn*), and in certain homiletic works. The primary concern in these works, apparently, has been to place the angelic fall in the context of the human fall, and then to examine, to differing degrees, certain theological issues regarding free will, sin, grace, and salvation in that light. Indeed, grace and free will become two of the most significant areas of theological speculation among Anglo-Saxon writers, though this speculation takes place mainly in homiletic works, and other specifically 'religious' texts (Grundy 1991;

Kleist 2000). In the poetry of the Junius manuscript, and in the homilies of Ælfric and Wulfstan, and perhaps the Rogationtide homilies, Vercelli XIX–XXI, the inclusion of angelic history has been linked to Augustine's conception of the catechetical 'narratio', a kind of basic 'sermon' for those new to the faith which relates the basics of Christian history, and the Christian faith, in a particular kind of way (Day 1974). Such a sermon also had Latin models, known to the Anglo-Saxons, such as Martin of Braga's *De correctione rusticorum* and Pirmin's *Scarapsus*, but the insistence on a precise sequence of events, from creation and angelic history to Last Judgement, seems to have become a particularly English way of looking at Christian history, and to have achieved its highest art in the works of John Milton.[5]

In the centuries after the Conquest, therefore, we find such works as the (probably) Anglo-Norman *Mystère d'Adam* (also known as the *Ordo repraesentationis Adae*) a work which, as it delves into the psychology of Adam and Eve, could be read as a twelfth-century *Genesis B*, and which may have been intended to present the complete cycle of Christian history (Woolf 1963). While the precise origin of medieval English drama is obscure, the possibility of development from the tenth-century 'Quem quaeritis?' ('Whom do you seek?') tropes, preserved in Winchester Troper and in the *Regularis concordia*, for example, would make for another interesting bridge between Anglo-Saxon England and the later period (Bedingfield 2002). The (later) Middle English mystery cycles, indeed, are an interesting case, for it would seem that their particular interest in presenting the complete course of Christian history, from angelic creation and fall to Last Judgement, develops naturally from the various incarnations of Augustine's scheme for the *narratio*: they share a basic didactic function, and share a desire to show the relationship between events, how, for example, Adam's sin and Christ's passion are related. Further, the situation as the mystery cycles begin to develop early in the fourteenth century must have been quite similar to the situation in the late tenth and early eleventh centuries in England: most of the laity had no access to, and could not understand, the Latin Bible.

Thus, what has been called 'the tradition of biblical paraphrase' continues after the Conquest, and again furnishes the material for much of the writing which survives from the twelfth and thirteenth centuries. The Fourth Lateran Council of 1215, with its emphasis on clerical reform and the instruction of the laity, would only have reinforced the need for these basic summarizing texts (Morey 2000: 2). However, there are other, less obvious links between the Anglo-Saxon period and the later Middle Ages. For example, one might compare Anglo-Saxon treatments of the creation and fall with Langland's, particularly the fascinating socio-political critique in which angels become Christ's knights, acting first, and only, to protect truth (*Piers Plowman*, Passus 1. 105–35), or the overall summary of Christian history (with the dramatic participation of Lucifer himself) in Passus 18–19. Even the notion of the

---

[5] Though the connection is not generally accepted, it has been suggested that Milton had access to the Junius manuscript in some form, and that either its texts or its illustrations (perhaps described to him by a third party) were an influence on *Paradise Lost* (Gajšek 1911; Lever 1947; Bolton 1974; Leasure 2002). In any case, the tradition of (English) writing about Genesis is a particularly rich one (Evans 1968).

righteous heathen, the subject of much discussion among students of *Beowulf* (see, in particular, Donahue 1965), makes an appearance in Langland (Chambers 1924; Russell 1966). One of Langland's primary aims must have been to communicate what might be termed a fundamental vernacular theology, precisely the aim, for example, of Ælfric. In fact, it may be that Langland's alliterative verse is another legacy ultimately of Ælfric, for it has been argued that Ælfric's 'rhythmical prose', which has recently been argued to be better described as verse (Bredehoft 2004), was a model for Layamon's *Brut*, and, in turn, for the alliterative revival of the fourteenth century (Cable 1991: 42–52; Brehe 1994). In other words, at least in the case of Langland and the *Gawain*-poet, not only the foundation of vernacular theological subject matter, but also the style of communication might be traced to the products of the tenth-century Benedictine reform movement, particularly Ælfric and Wulfstan.

It has repeatedly been remarked that early medieval theology is conservative, derivative and primarily oriented toward practical application (Wrenn 1969; Gatch 1977: 4). Nevertheless, at the significant points of intersection between theology and the earliest English literature, such as in *Cædmon's Hymn*, *The Dream of the Rood*, *Beowulf*, and the Genesis poems, one sees a highly sophisticated 'blending of traditions' (Orchard 1996: 402). Mainly, these traditions are Christian and pagan and Latin and vernacular, but there is also evidence of an innovative blending of styles or genres, particularly between poetry and homiletic prose, in ways which anticipate and influence the literature and thinking of post-Conquest England. Just as for Gregory the race of the Angles can in their appearance signify angels and salvation to come, so can what must originally have been a completely pagan notion of fate, or *wyrd*, become subordinated to a Christian God, and yet leave the modern reader with the vague sense that the poet intended either something more, or something less. And so, in the words of the poet of *Maxims II*: 'Þrymmas syndan Cristes myccle,| Wyrd byð swiðost' (4b–5a; 'The powers of Christ are great; fate is [or "will be"] strongest').[6]

WORKS CITED

ADRIAEN, MARCUS (ed.) 1979. *S. Gregorii Magni Moralia in Iob*. CCSL 143, 143A, and 143B. Turnhout: Brepols.

BEDINGFIELD, M. BRADFORD. 2002. *The Dramatic Liturgy of Anglo-Saxon England*. Woodbridge: Boydell.

BJORK, ROBERT E., and NILES, JOHN D. (eds.) 1997. *A Beowulf Handbook*. Lincoln: University of Nebraska Press.

---

[6] Exactly how to punctuate this part of the poem (here Dobbie 1942) is the subject of some debate (i.e. should there be a full stop after line 4?). One might compare the opening of *The Wanderer*, which speaks of the Lord's mercy, but culminates with the famous gnomic statement that 'wyrd bið ful aræd' (5b; 'fate is completely determined'?).

BODDEN, MARY-CATHERINE. 1987. *The Old English Finding of the True Cross*. Cambridge: D. S. Brewer.

BOLTON, W. F. 1974. 'A Further Echo of the Old English *Genesis* in Milton's *Paradise Lost*'. *Review of English Studies* 25: 58–61.

BREDEHOFT, THOMAS E. 2004. 'Ælfric and Late Old English Verse'. *Anglo-Saxon England* 33: 77–107.

BREHE, STEVEN. 1994. 'Rhythmical Alliteration: Ælfric's Prose and the Origins of Layamon's Metre', in Françoise Le Saux (ed.), *The Text and Traditions of Layamon's Brut*. Cambridge: D. S. Brewer, 65–87.

CABLE, THOMAS. 1991. *The English Alliterative Tradition*. Philadelphia: University of Pennsylvania Press.

CAIE, GRAHAM D. 2004. 'Codicological Clues: Old English Christian Poetry in its Manuscript Context', in Paul Cavill (ed.), *The Christian Tradition in Anglo-Saxon England: Approaches to Current Scholarship and Teaching*. Cambridge: D. S. Brewer, 3–14.

CAVILL, PAUL. 2004. 'Christianity and Theology in *Beowulf*', in Paul Cavill (ed.), *The Christian Tradition in Anglo-Saxon England: Approaches to Current Scholarship and Teaching*. Cambridge: D. S. Brewer, 15–39.

CHAMBERS, R. W. 1924. 'Long Will, Dante, and the Righteous Heathen'. *Essays and Studies by Members of the English Association* 9: 50–69.

CLEMOES, PETER. 1959. 'The Chronology of Ælfric's Works', in id. (ed.), *The Anglo-Saxons: Studies in Some Aspects of their History and Culture presented to Bruce Dickins*. London: Bowes & Bowes, 212–47; repr. in (and cited from) Paul E. Szarmach (ed.) 2000. *Old English Prose: Basic Readings*. New York: Garland, 29–72.

COLGRAVE, BERTRAM, and MYNORS, R. A. B. 1969. *Bede's Ecclesiastical History of the English People*. Oxford: Clarendon.

DAY, VIRGINIA. 1974. 'The Influence of the Catechetical *narratio* on Old English and Some Other Medieval Literature'. *Anglo-Saxon England* 3: 51–61.

DOANE, ALGER N. 1991. *The Saxon Genesis*. Madison: University of Wisconsin Press.

DOBBIE, ELLIOTT VAN KIRK. 1942. *The Anglo-Saxon Minor Poems*. ASPR 6. New York: Columbia University Press.

DONAHUE, CHARLES. 1965. '*Beowulf* and the Christian Tradition: A Reconsideration from a Celtic Stance'. *Traditio* 21: 55–116.

EVANS, J. M. 1968. *Paradise Lost and the Genesis Tradition*. Oxford: Clarendon.

GAJŠEK, STEPHANIE VON. 1911. *Milton und Cædmon*. Vienna: W. Braumüller.

GARDE, JUDITH N. 1995. *Old English Poetry in a Medieval Christian Perspective: A Doctrinal Approach*. Cambridge: D. S. Brewer.

GATCH, MILTON MCC. 1977. *Preaching and Theology in Anglo-Saxon England: Ælfric and Wulfstan*. Toronto: University of Toronto Press.

GODDEN, MALCOLM. 1991. 'Biblical Literature: The Old Testament', in Malcolm Godden and Michael Lapidge (eds.), *The Cambridge Companion to Old English Literature*. Cambridge: Cambridge University Press, 206–26.

—— 2004. 'The Relations of Ælfric and Wulfstan: A Reassessment' Townend 2004: 353–74.

GRASSO, ANTHONY R. 1991. 'Theology and Structure in *The Dream of the Rood*'. *Religion and Literature* 23: 23–38.

GRUNDY, LYNNE. 1991. *Books and Grace: Ælfric's Theology*. Medieval Studies 6. London: King's College.

HAMILTON, NICHOLAS E. S. A. (ed.) 1870. *Willelmi Malmesbiriensis Monachi De Gestis Pontificum Anglorum*. London: Longman.

HILL, THOMAS D. 1994. 'The Christian Language and Theme of *Beowulf*', in Henk Aertsen and Rolf Bremmer, Jr. (eds.), *A Companion to Old English Poetry*. Amsterdam: VU University Press, 63–77.

HOLDERNESS, GRAHAM. 1997. 'The Sign of the Cross: Culture and Belief in *The Dream of the Rood*'. *Literature and Theology* 11: 347–75.

HOROWITZ, SYLVIA. 1978. 'Beowulf, David, Samson and Christ'. *Studies in Medieval Culture* 12: 17–23.

HOWLETT, DAVID R. 1974. 'The Theology of *Cædmon's Hymn*'. *Leeds Studies in English* 7: 1–12.

—— 1997. *British Books in Biblical Style*. Dublin: Four Courts.

HUPPÉ, BERNARD F. 1959. *Doctrine and Poetry: Augustine's Influence on Old English Poetry*. Albany: State University of New York.

IRVING, EDWARD B. 1997. 'Christian and Pagan Elements'. Bjork and Niles (eds.) 175–92.

KASKE, ROBERT E. 1967. 'The *eotenas* in *Beowulf*', in Robert P. Creed (ed.), *Old English Poetry: Fifteen Essays*. Providence, RI: Brown University Press, 285–310.

KLAEBER, FRIEDRICH. 1910. 'Die Ältere Genesis und der Beowulf'. *Englische Studien* 42: 321–38.

—— 1911–12. 'Die christlichen Elemente im *Beowulf*'. *Anglia* 35: 111–36, 249–70, 453–82; 36: 169–99; now trans. Paul Battles. 1996. *The Christian Elements in Beowulf*. Old English Newsletter Subsidia 24. Kalamazoo: Medieval Institute, Western Michigan University.

—— (ed.) 1950. *Beowulf and the Fight at Finnsburg*. 3rd edn. Boston: Heath.

KLEIST, AARON. 2000. 'Striving with Grace: The Sources of Ælfric's Doctrine of Free Will'. Unpubl. Ph.D. dissertation, Cambridge University.

LAPIDGE, MICHAEL. 1979. 'Aldhelm's Latin Poetry and Old English Verse'. *Comparative Literature* 31: 209–31.

—— '*Beowulf*, Aldhelm, the *Liber monstrorum* and Wessex'. *Studi Medievali*, 3rd ser., 23: 151–92.

—— 'The Archetype of *Beowulf*'. *Anglo-Saxon England* 29: 5–41.

LEASURE, T. ROSS. 2002. 'The Genesis of *Paradise Lost*: What Milton May Have Seen in the Junius Manuscript'. *Cithara: Essays in the Judaeo-Christian Tradition* 41: 3–17.

LEVER, J. W. 1947. '*Paradise Lost* and the Anglo-Saxon Tradition'. *Review of English Studies* 23: 97–106.

LIUZZA, ROY. 2001. 'Religious Prose'. *A Companion to Anglo-Saxon Literature*, ed. Phillip Pulsiano and Elaine Treharne. Oxford: Blackwell, 233–50.

LOCKETT, LESLIE. 2002. 'An Integrated Re-examination of the Dating of Oxford, Bodleian Library, Junius 11'. *Anglo-Saxon England* 31: 141–73.

MOREY, JAMES H. 2000. *Book and Verse: A Guide to Middle English Biblical Literature*. Urbana: University of Illinois Press.

Ó CARRAGÁIN, EAMON. 1982. 'Crucifixion as Annunciation: The Relation of *The Dream of the Rood* to the Liturgy Reconsidered'. *English Studies* 63: 487–505.

O'DONNELL, DANIEL P. 2004. 'Bede's Strategy in Paraphrasing *Cædmon's Hymn*'. *Journal of English and Germanic Philology* 103: 417–32.

OPLAND, JEFF. 1980. *Anglo-Saxon Oral Poetry: A Study of the Traditions*. New Haven: Yale University Press.

ORCHARD, ANDY. 1994. *The Poetic Art of Aldhelm*. Cambridge: Cambridge University Press.

—— 1995. *Pride and Prodigies: Studies in the Monsters of the Beowulf-Manuscript*. Cambridge: Brewer.

—— 1996. 'Poetic Inspiration and Prosaic Translation: The Making of *Cædmon's Hymn*', in M. Jane Toswell and Elizabeth M. Tyler (eds.), *Doubt Wisely: Studies in English Language and Literature in Honour of E. G. Stanley*. London: Routledge, 402–22.

—— 2003. *A Critical Companion to Beowulf*. Cambridge: D. S. Brewer.

OSBORNE, MARIJANE. 1978. 'The Great Feud: Scriptural History and Strife in *Beowulf*'. *Publications of the Modern Language Association* 93: 973–81; repr. in Peter S. Baker (ed.) 1995. *Beowulf: Basic Readings*. New York: Garland, 111–25.

PATCH, HOWARD R. 1919. 'Liturgical Influence in *The Dream of the Rood*'. *Publications of the Modern Language Association* 34: 233–57.

POPE, JOHN C., and FULK, R. D. 2001. *Eight Old English Poems*. 3rd edn. New York: W. W. Norton.

RAUER, CHRISTINE. 2000. *Beowulf and the Dragon: Parallels and Analogues*. Cambridge: D. S. Brewer.

RAW, BARBARA C. 1991. 'Biblical Literature: The New Testament', in Malcolm Godden and Michael Lapidge (eds.), *The Cambridge Companion to Old English Literature*. Cambridge: Cambridge University Press, 227–42.

REMLEY, PAUL. 2005. 'Aldhelm as Old English Poet: *Exodus*, Asser and the *Dicta Ælfredi*', in Katherine O'Brien O'Keeffe and Andy Orchard (eds.), *Latin Learning and English Lore: Studies in Anglo-Saxon Literature for Michael Lapidge*. 2 vols. Toronto: University of Toronto Press, i. 90–108.

ROBINSON, FRED C. 1985. *Beowulf and the Appositive Style*. Knoxville: University of Tennessee Press.

ROWLEY, SHARON M. 2003. 'Reassessing Exegetical Interpretations of Bede's *Historia ecclesiastica gentis Anglorum*'. *Literature and Theology* 17: 227–43.

RUSSELL, GEORGE H. 1966. 'The Salvation of the Heathen: The Exploration of a Theme in *Piers Plowman*'. *Journal of the Warburg and Courtauld Institute* 29: 101–16.

SHARMA, MANISH. 2005. 'Metalepsis and Monstrosity: The Boundaries of Narrative Structure in *Beowulf*'. *Studies in Philology* 102: 247–79.

SMITH, ALBERT H. (ed.) 1968. *Three Northumbrian Poems*. London: Methuen.

SZARMACH, PAUL E. 1998. '*Anthem*: Auden's *Cædmon's Hymn*', in Richard J. Utz and Thomas A. Shippey (eds.), *Medievalism in the Modern World: Essays in Honor of Leslie J. Workman*. Turnhout: Brepols, 329–40.

TOWNEND, MATTHEW (ed.) 2004. *Wulfstan, Archbishop of York: The Proceedings of the Second Alcuin Conference*. Studies in the Early Middle Ages 10. Turnhout: Brepols.

WOOLF, ROSEMARY. 1958. 'Doctrinal Influences on *The Dream of the Rood*'. *Medium Ævum* 27: 137–53.

—— 'The Fall of Man in *Genesis B* and the *Mystère d'Adam*', in Stanley B. Greenfield (ed.), *Studies in Old English Literature in Honor of Arthur G. Brodeur*. Eugene: University of Oregon Books, 187–99.

WORMALD, PATRICK. 2004. 'Archbishop Wulfstan: Eleventh-Century State Builder'. Townend 2004: 9–27.

WRENN, CHARLES L. 1969. 'Some Aspects of Anglo-Saxon Theology', in E. Bagby Atwood and Archibald A. Hill (eds.), *Studies in Language, Literature and Culture of the Middle Ages and Later in Honor of Rudolph Willard*. Austin: University of Texas, 182–9.

FURTHER READING

BJORK, ROBERT E., and NILES, JOHN D. (eds.) 1997. *A Beowulf Handbook*. Lincoln: University of Nebraska Press.

COLGRAVE, BERTRAM, and R. A. B. MYNORS. 1969. *Bede's Ecclesiastical History of the English People*. Oxford: Clarendon.

GARDE, JUDITH N. 1995. *Old English Poetry in a Medieval Christian Perspective: A Doctrinal Approach*. Cambridge: D. S. Brewer.

GATCH, MILTON MCC. 1977. *Preaching and Theology in Anglo-Saxon England: Ælfric and Wulfstan*. Toronto: University of Toronto Press.

GODDEN, MALCOLM, and LAPIDGE, MICHAEL (eds.) 1991. *The Cambridge Companion to Old English Literature*. Cambridge: Cambridge University Press.

GRUNDY, LYNNE. 1991. *Books and Grace: Ælfric's Theology*. Medieval Studies 6. London: King's College.

HUPPÉ, BERNARD F. 1959. *Doctrine and Poetry: Augustine's Influence on Old English Poetry*. Albany: State University of New York.

MOREY, JAMES H. 2000. *Book and Verse: A Guide to Middle English Biblical Literature*. Urbana: University of Illinois Press.

ORCHARD, ANDY. 2003. *A Critical Companion to Beowulf*. Cambridge: D. S. Brewer.

PULSIANO, PHILLIP, and TREHARNE, ELAINE (eds.) 2001. *A Companion to Anglo-Saxon Literature*. Oxford: Blackwell.

ROLLINSON, PHILIP B. 1973. 'The Influence of Christian Doctrine and Exegesis on Old English Poetry: An Estimate of the Current State of Scholarship'. *Anglo-Saxon England* 2: 271–84.

WILSON, JAMES H. 1974. *Christian Theology and Old English Poetry*. The Hague: Mouton.

WOOLF, ROSEMARY. 1986. *Art and Doctrine: Essays on Medieval Literature*, ed. Heather O'Donoghue. London: Hambledon.

CHAPTER 4

VERNACULAR BIBLES AND PRAYER BOOKS

LYNNE LONG

INTRODUCTION

IN Europe, from the advent of Christianity until towards the end of the twentieth century, the Bible remained unchallenged as the central text within the cultural polysystem, functioning as an agent for language enrichment and as a source text for literary inspiration, commentary, and reference. The Bible was the one text that could be quoted or referred to in the knowledge that listeners and readers would recognize the allusions. Even more importantly, as Coulson (1984: 8) puts it 'In almost all the classics of English or European literature written before the nineteenth century their authors assume the truth of the Christian faith.'

In England, theology and literature have always enjoyed a close relationship, first through the medium of the oral tradition and later through the influence of translated English Bibles and prayer books. As the English language stabilized and developed, translations of the Bible and the Liturgy reflected those changes and provided examples of the vocabulary, syntax, and style of the times. The establishment in the seventeenth century of a single translation allowed unprecedented stability that brought the King James Version to be regarded as 'the touchstone, the national book, the formative mental structure for all English speaking people' (Nicolson 2003: 236). The 1611 KJV Bible was the culmination of a series of translations during the Reformation and founded a deep-rooted tradition. As the Bible provided subject matter, a source of reference and analogy, and a model for narrative and poetic language, its influence on literature was naturally strong. Exactly how did the vernacular Bibles and prayer books through the ages influence English writers and help to shape the canon of English Literature?

The Early Influence of the Bible on Vernacular Literature

For almost the first thousand years the influence and tradition of Christian theology in Britain was mainly through oral channels. Christianity had arrived through the Roman Empire, but its impact had waned until Augustine of Canterbury's mission from Pope Gregory brought a more ordered conversion at the end of the sixth and the beginning of the seventh century (Daniell 2003: 31). Few people, apart from the missionary monks who brought Jerome's official Latin Vulgate Bible to Britain, possessed the education to read the manuscript, and even if they had, there were not enough copies to go round. The Christian message was first transmitted through preaching, the singing of Psalms, prayers, the performance of poems and stories, and even into the later Middle Ages, oral material in the form of plays, hymns, and carols supported the written text. Lack of literacy, however, did not particularly signal a lack of intelligence. Life simply worked in a different way (see Clanchy 1993: 233). The collective memory was where the important features of the contemporary culture resided: history, literature, and Bible stories. The effect on formal language of the oral transmission of the Bible, particularly through prayers and preaching, must have been considerable, but by its nature such influence is difficult to detect except in a very general way. It shows up best in proverbs and sayings in current use taken directly from the Bible, in the language of sermons, letters, journals, and wills, or in the many direct and oblique references to the Bible in literature through the centuries.

Most cultures, English included, have an oral vernacular literary tradition that precedes written literature and runs concurrently with an elite classical written literature. Anglo-Saxon poetry was performed orally long before it was written down and had its own specific conventions separate from the classical Latin and Greek literary models. Rhythm and repetition in oral vernacular poetry aided memory, as did alliterative half lines (Ong 1982: 34). All kinds of narrative were used as subject matter, battles, heroic exploits, journeys, Bible stories, and Christian liturgy joined the Anglo-Saxon poetic tradition through the poetry of Cædmon (d. 670–80) and others such as the eighth-century Cynwulf (Bede 1990: 248; see further Fox, Ch. 3 above). Cædmon's work is recorded a century later, through translation, in Bede; the anonymous Christian poets that followed survive in written fragments in the Exeter Book (Exeter Cathedral Library) and the MS Junius II manuscript in the Bodleian Library (Kennedy 1963: 8). It seems that, as in unlettered communities today, there was considerable literary activity before the actual writing process dominated English culture. Evidence of the same kind of pre-textual orality is to be found in the Bible itself and Walter Ong (1982: 37) points out how the oral features of the creation narratives as translated from Genesis into seventeenth-century English have changed into print-based features by the twentieth century as the literary culture in English gradually moved from oral to written.

As well as in works by Cædmon, Cynwulf, and other anonymous Anglo-Saxon poets, Christian literature flourished in the form of partial translations from the Bible and also as sermons that began life as oral performances and were later written down. King Alfred's translation project of the ninth century is said to have included his own version of the Psalms (Shepherd 1969: 370). Ælfric's extracts from the Old Testament, Wulfstan's sermons, the Blickling collection of homilies, the Old English glossing of the Lindisfarne and Rushworth Latin Gospels, and finally the Anglo-Saxon Gospels of the tenth century all combined to form a body of vernacular literature based on or translated directly from the Bible. After the Norman Conquest there were also many translations of religious literature from French, at first enriching the English canon, later necessary as the use of spoken French waned and people required texts in one of the many dialects of English (Blake 1996: 136–7). Lives of the Saints, rules for communities of women, apocryphal stories of Jesus' life, and the Christian history of the world in the metrical form of *Cursor Mundi* are some examples of the kind of translated literature generated by biblical and other Christian sources for an increasingly literate readership. Eventually, in the latter part of the fourteenth century came the first complete translation of the Bible into English.

THE MEDIEVAL POLITICS OF THE VERNACULAR

In the late thirteenth and early fourteenth centuries there was a movement in Europe away from Latin towards the vernacular by writers who felt that they had perhaps exhausted the possibilities of Latin. Dante Alighieri (1265–1321) used his mother tongue to write his masterpiece *La Commedia*, combining classical and religious sources. Petrarch (1304–74) and Boccaccio (1313–75) experimented with writing poetry and narrative in Italian rather than Latin. The twelfth century chivalric romances of Chrétien de Troyes and the many German writers who were so influenced by him had laid the foundation for a vernacular literature, but one which was not intrinsically religious. An important development came when Jean de Meun (*c.*1240–*c.*1305) completed Guillaume de Lorris's vernacular *Roman de la*

Rose in the early fourteenth century, providing one of the most influential classical literary texts of the age. English romances of the time included *Havelock the Dane* and *King Horn*. Throughout Europe vernaculars were becoming recognized vehicles for high-status national literatures.

The rise of the vernacular literatures coupled with the political situation made the Wycliffite English Bible of the 1380s a translation waiting to happen. England was a very different place from the land that the missionary Augustine had known and was experiencing an unsettled period of linguistic and political development, shaking off the final traces of Norman French domination. The church had developed into a powerful political institution, some of whose practices were badly in need of reform. The institutional language of communication and scholarship and the language of the Bible, remained in high-status Latin. English still functioned as the less sophisticated, low-status language of the common people, as the contemporary arguments against translation by Thomas Palmer and William Butler suggest (Deanesly 1966: 428 no. 4). Making an English translation of the Bible from the official Latin Vulgate of Jerome was an act that challenged the authority of the church and initiated linguistic separation from the wider Latin-speaking church in Europe. Translating into English also opened up the text directly to a growing newly literate lay audience and introduced the possibility of error or change through the translation process (ibid. 401) or in the process of unmediated interpretation.

Politically, the use of English reflected the more general move of the time in Europe towards nationhood and national identity. Socially, a vernacular translation narrowed the gap between the Latin literate elite and the ordinary English reader (ibid. 226). On a religious level, an English Bible provided an authority other (and arguably higher, as the Word of God) than the Church itself. On a literary level, the Wycliffite version was a reflection of the vernacular movements in Europe as well as part of a growing literature of religious writing in English. The English vernacular movement, associated with but not exclusive to the Lollards, began in the early part of the fourteenth century to accommodate a rising number of people who were literate in English only.

MEDIEVAL LITERATURE IN ENGLISH

Richard Rolle (*c.*1300–49) wrote lyrical prose in English as well as sermons in Latin. He translated parts of the Scriptures, of which the Psalms and two commentaries remain, and some of his Latin works were immediately translated into English. Rolle was instrumental in creating a lyrical vocabulary in English for the translation of some of the more challenging parts of the Hebrew Bible, such as the Song of Songs. Julian of Norwich (*c.*1342–1416) and later Margery Kempe

(1373–1438) continued the tradition of writing religious experiences in English (Goldie 2003: 110).

Around the time of the Wycliffite translation, there was other literary activity connected with the vernacular and the challenge it presented to the established order. *The Vision of Piers Plowman*, an alliterative poem in English reworked twice by its author William Langland (*c.*1330–87), questions the current state of medieval society against a background of Christian principles preached by the clergy but often neglected in practice. It was one of the most popular poems of the time with over sixty manuscripts surviving, some of them well annotated (Langland 1995: p. xix). Direct and indirect references to the Bible abound, but appear to be translations made directly from the Latin Vulgate by the poet himself, like other contemporary writers, as they often make better sense than the contemporary Wycliffite Bible. The author weaves Bible quotations, hymns, liturgy, and doctrines into his text, some-times using Latin to authenticate his source in the style of a sermon. For example in Passus 6, lines 75–7, he begins the quotation from Psalm 69: 28 in Latin and finishes it in English:

> *Deleantur de libro viventium*: I sholde noght dele with hem,
> For Holy Chirche is hote, of them no tithe to aske
> *For let them not be written with the righteous*

> (Langland 1995: 98)

Langland's work epitomizes the situation of the time in many ways. It questions the hierarchical structure of medieval society and its hypocrisy by a comparison with the Gospel teachings: it encourages the examination of a personal path to salvation. At the same time it illustrates the possibilities of easy transfer from Latin to English in the writing of Scripture-based literature. The Wycliffite translation did exactly the same, but by means of a direct challenge to the established hierarchy. But for Langland the Wycliffite translation of the Bible was not so much an influence on literature as an encouragement to the laity to seek direct access to the Scriptures to explore the meaning of Christianity; it was also an encouragement to writers to use English. He was exploring very similar paths to those taken by the Wycliffite group.

A more technically complex literary piece of the same time, outstanding for the intricacy of its form, survives in the *Pearl* poem. Extant in the single manuscript that is shared by the two companion poems, *Cleanness* and *Patience*, and the story of *Sir Gawain and the Green Knight*, *Pearl* is based firmly on the literature of the New Testament, particularly the Gospel of Matthew and the Book of Revelation, with further considerable references to the Psalms and various parts of the Old Testament. Like Langland, the dreamer/jeweller of *Pearl* has religious issues to be explored. Grieving at the loss of his small daughter, his pearl, he has a dream in which his theological questions are answered by the daughter herself, speaking directly to him from heaven, using scriptural references to support her arguments as in a sermon. Lines 500–72, for example, are a complete translation, within the poetic conventions the author has set himself, of Matthew 20: 1–16, the 'sothfol gospel of God almygt' (Andrew and Waldron 1996: 77). The translation appears to be the author's own, as it is not taken from the Wycliffite or Anglo-Saxon versions. Interestingly, lines 709–12 encourage anyone who can read to look at the book and be made aware of how Jesus walked among the people and how they brought their children to him:

> Rygtwysly quo con rede,
> He loke on bok and be awayed
> How Jesus Hym welke in areþede,
> And burnez her barnex vnto Hym brayed.   (ibid. 87)

This implies that the author was aware that an English version of the Gospels was available and was happy to advocate its use.

Langland's work and the Pearl poem were a continuation of 'a native tradition of alliterative writing which goes back to Old English' (Anderson 1996: p. ix), and as written literature represent the last echoes of Anglo-Saxon oral tradition. However, they engage with a knowledgeable and questioning audience and look forward to a vernacular literary discourse that was emerging from several sources, including translations, interpretations, or representations of the Bible.

The work of Geoffrey Chaucer (1343–1400), product of the French influence of fabliaux and romance (Blake 1996: 133), received much contemporary acclaim in the courtly environment where it was published (by performance) and *The Canterbury Tales* was one of the first texts later printed by William Caxton. Writing during the same era as the work of the Wycliffite translators and aiming at a similar literate but non-Latin reading audience, Chaucer combined classical and religious sources, borrowed stories and structure from Italian vernacular literature, and drew his philosophy from Boethius and Augustine. His satire of the church and his exploration of medieval society are well known from *The Canterbury Tales*; his use of and reference to Christianity and the Bible is often perplexing.

Chaucer's treatment of his subject matter illustrates the traditional tension between the classical and the Christian, and between the subversive and the orthodox. His retelling of the classical tale of *Troilus and Criseyde* reveals a few Christian anachronisms in the dialogue, Criseyde's 'by that God that bought us bothe two' in Book III line 1165, for example (Benson 1987: 529), but the main surprise in Chaucer's version is Troilus's rise to Christian heaven after death and the writer's final fervent prayer mentioning Christ, the Trinity, and Mary. Similarly, 'The Clerk's Tale' of the patient Griselda, a classical story sourced from Petrarch, though not religious in origin is connected by the poet directly to St James's Epistle 1: 12–14:

> As seith Seint Jame, if ye his pistle rede;
> He preeveth folk al day, it is no drede
>
> (ibid. 152. 1154–5)

In line 1118, Griselda physically receives the 'crown of life' promised in James 1: 12 to those who come through the test. Chaucer seems anxious to make strong connections between his classical source and the Christian context of the day. He may have feared that by writing in English, using classical sources, and satirizing the clergy, he was not endearing himself to the establishment. Certainly the passage at the end of 'The Parson's Tale', 'Here taketh the makere of this book his leve', reads as a confession and retraction of all the non-religious material he has produced (ibid. 328). Here Chaucer quotes Romans 15: 4, 'Al that is written is written for oure doctrine [learning]', and asks for prayers 'that Crist have mercy on me and foryive me my giltes'. The biblical references are not from the Wycliffite translation: in fact with his use of 'giltes' for 'sins' he echoes the Anglo-Saxon Gospels (Bosworth 1888: 24, Matt. 6: 12). Chaucer's retraction seems to indicate the tension he felt between classical and Christian sources and the danger felt both in his criticism of the Church and in using English as his literary medium.

PROBLEMS FACED BY THE WYCLIFFITE TRANSLATORS

The Wycliffite Bible stands at a period of change in both language and literature. The English language was undergoing huge and rapid development as the Anglo-Saxon and Norman French influences settled down together and gradually transformed into what we now call Middle English. The fact that the Wycliffite translation, the work of several hands, was revised almost immediately, this time by a single translator, is a reflection of how difficult the process of translation was and how rapidly the target language was shifting. A standard English was yet to be established: well into the fifteenth century the printer William Caxton laments the diversity of English dialects in the Prologue to *Eneydos* (Pollard 1903: 240). Apart from the shifting target language, the single Latin source text available presented its own problems. The reviser and writer of the second version of the Wycliffite Bible gives in his Preface an account of the strategies of translation and in particular the difficulties of translating words with more than one meaning. 'But in the translating of words equivocal, that is, that hath many significations under one letter, may lightly be peril' he says; '. . . Therefore a translator hath great need to study well the sentence [sense] both before and after, and look that such equivocal words accord with the sentence' (ibid. 198). Translating the Bible into English was never going to be a simple matter.

Social and political changes were equally swift and dramatic in the fourteenth century and the whole enterprise of Bible translating so sensitive that the translators were under continual pressure. State and church worked together closely in the medieval and early modern period so that distinguishing between the two was difficult: John Wyclif (*c.*1330–84), priest and reformer, had attacked the power of the papacy and questioned the civil authority of the church (Daniell 2003: 71). As Scripture formed the basis of his challenge, a Bible in English would support his ideas and allow a wider audience to understand the evidence. The church hierarchy generally resisted the movement towards a vernacular Scripture as undesirable, unnecessary, and, in Wyclif's case, bound to be heretical. Common people were considered to be incapable of reading the Scriptures without mediation, officially because they lacked the necessary learning, but also because the church was keen to resist any dilution of its control over interpretation of the Bible.

There was considerable support for the use of the vernacular among Oxford academics, but in 1407 the seventh constitution of the Oxford Council prohibited both the translation of Scripture into English and the reading of Scripture in English unless specifically approved by church authorities (Craigie 1940: 143). In this way the Wycliffite version became proscribed, although complete and partial manuscripts continued to circulate (Wright 2001: 204).

The Wycliffite group translated from the Latin Vulgate using the commentaries of the ancient doctors, particularly Nicholas of Lyra, as sources of reference (Pollard 1903: 194). Their translation was fairly literal and faithful to the Latin even to the point of unintelligibility. The resources available to William Tyndale, translating one hundred and forty or so years later, were much better, as was the method of reproduction and distribution of texts. What remained the same were the strict hierarchical divisions in society and the reluctance of the church authorities, including Henry VIII, to allow translations in the vernacular that might cause heresy and lead to dissent.

THE MYSTERY PLAYS

The fifteenth century, the time between the Wycliffite translation and Tyndale's English Bible, has traditionally been regarded as one of the low points in English literature, falling as it does between the achievements of Chaucer and Shakespeare. Certainly the dislocation caused by the Wars of the Roses, war with France, and several outbreaks of plague prevented the settled patronage necessary for the kind of literary success that later took its place in the canon of English literature. Interestingly, during this period, Bible translation was represented by the cycles of Mystery Plays initiated in the fourteenth century to celebrate the new feast of Corpus Christi (Happé 1975: 19). Acted and produced by the town guilds, the plays developed gradually to suit local needs and were at their most popular in the fifteenth century. The cycles covered the story of the whole Bible, from Genesis to the Gospels, and reinforced church doctrine at the same time as providing entertainment for the townspeople. Characters from the Bible stories, while keeping to the scriptural narrative, nevertheless have the concerns of the medieval population, questioning tithes and moaning about the cold, their wives/husbands, and their employers. The plays were a way of examining the issues likely to be causing unrest and dissent among the audience and reinforcing compliance with church practices by demonstrating the results of disobedience to God's law. In *The Killing of Abel* in the Townley cycle, the foul-mouthed Cain objects to sacrificing some of his crop to God because he has so little (a reference to the payment of tithes by the poor). The audience may laugh at his rude language and sympathize with his poverty but to support him is also to condone the murder of his brother. Others, such as the *Shearmen and Taylor's Play* of the Coventry cycle, explain and reinforce the doctrine of the Holy Trinity or the virginity of Mary (ibid. 346). The interpretation of the Bible as a support for church doctrine and practice became a Reformation issue bound up with direct access to the text and connected with the way the text was translated/interpreted. The next century saw the beginning of a startling activity in the realm of Bible translation.

WILLIAM TYNDALE (*c.*1494–1536)

It was always William Tyndale's intention to translate the Bible into English. He tells his reader as much in the Preface to the Pentateuch of 1530 and relates how he unsuccessfully sought the patronage of Bishop Tunstall in order to do it (Bray 1994: 34–5). Like the Wycliffite group, he worked at a time of political and religious turmoil and, also like the Wycliffite group, his translation was a response to the need for reform of religious practices. A vernacular Bible would remove the mediatory role of the clergy and lessen the power of the church. 'I had perceived by experience', says Tyndale, 'how that it was impossible to establish in the lay-people any truth, except the Scripture were laid plainly before their eyes in their mother tongue' (ibid. 33). The scriptural experience of laypeople so far had been mediated through sermons or through the popular play cycles which provided domesticated and indoctrinated versions of the Scriptures rather than the plain text that Tyndale wanted.

In order to complete his translation, Tyndale moved to Germany in 1524, where Martin Luther had published a German translation of the New Testament two years earlier. Luther's attacks on the teaching of the church were by this time well known throughout Europe and had been condemned as heresy. Those humanists such as Desiderus Erasmus (1466–1536) who had at first supported both Luther and intellectual reform in the church were obliged to endorse orthodoxy or be associated with a heretic (see Bejczy 2001: 118–19). Henry VIII himself received the title *fidei defensor* from the Pope for a tract written in his name against Luther. Luther's translation of the Bible was part of his programme of reform and, like Wyclif and the Lollards, linked the concept of vernacular Scriptures with heresy and dissent.

William Tyndale was undeterred by the political climate and pressed ahead with his own project. Erasmus' Greek New Testament of 1516 and the emended Latin Vulgate combined with some contemporary vernacular versions to provide better source texts than had been available to the Wycliffite group. Tyndale's extensive knowledge of languages and his gift for translation gave him the insight to realize that English could be a better vehicle for the Hebrew original than Jerome's Latin. He recognized too, in his 1525 New Testament, that the polished Latin of the Vulgate reflected neither the koine Greek of the gospel writers nor the Aramaic oral source. He was not the first to comment on the disparity between early sources and Vulgate, as both Erasmus and Lorenzo Valla (1405–57) before him had made similar observations (Long 2001: 122), but he was the first to respond accordingly in terms of translation style (see Lawton 1990: 67).

Unfortunately Henry VIII's obsession with heresy was such that the quality of Tyndale's translation was acknowledged only subliminally by the use of it as the basis of future English translations. Tyndale's inclusion of a substantial proportion of the glosses from Luther's New Testament together with the perceived mistranslation of the Latin for 'priest' into 'elder', 'church' into 'congregation', and 'charity' into 'love' confirmed the heretical connection. Accordingly many copies of the New Testament were confiscated and burned when they arrived in England. Tyndale himself was burnt at the stake in 1536, after two years in prison on the Continent and before he was able to complete the Old Testament.

Tyndale considered his translation as a work in progress that would be improved in future editions. The Epilogue to the second (1526) New Testament asks the reader not to be offended at 'the rudeness of the work now at the first time'. 'In time to come', he says, 'we will give it its full shape' (Pollard 1903: 116). In the extraordinary translation activity that followed Tyndale, the complete Bible was finally given its full English shape.

AFTER TYNDALE: ENGLISH BIBLES IN THE REIGN OF HENRY VIII

Although Henry VIII was afraid of heresy, and more importantly dissent and subversion through heresy, he also recognized the advantage and prestige of having the Bible in English. In the proclamation of 1530 it was announced that his advisers considered it unnecessary for the common people to have the Scriptures in English. Nevertheless, if the people 'do utterly abandon and forsake all perverse, erroneous and seditious opinions' found in the contemporary English books, the King would provide a translation 'by great, learned and Catholic persons' if he thought the time appropriate (Hughes and Larkin 1964: 196). Encouraged by the possibility of a change in attitude and by Henry's break with Rome in 1534, Miles Coverdale (1488–1568) produced a complete translation of the Bible in 1535. Under the protection of Thomas Cromwell, the King's pro-reform chancellor, he took over 'the ministration of other that began it before' (Robinson 1940: 169). The political climate had softened somewhat since the adverse reaction to Tyndale's New Testament, but nevertheless Coverdale wrote in his still officially unauthorized first edition an elaborate dedication to the King just to be on the safe side (printed in Pearson 1845). His sources were substantially Tyndale for the New Testament with some minor adjustments and 'sundry translations, not only in Latin but also of the Dutch [German] interpreters' (ibid. 12). His aim was above all for clarity of expression even if that meant departing a little from the original.

Meanwhile Archbishop Thomas Cranmer was anxious to promote an official authorized version that could be used in churches all over England. In 1537 he wrote excitedly to Cromwell, sending him a copy of one Thomas Matthew's translation of the Bible which had been published in the same year. He asked Cromwell to try to get the King to licence this translation because it was the best he had read so far, 'until such time that we, the bishops, shall set forth a better translation, which I think will not be till a day after doomsday' (Pollard 1903: 215).

Thomas Matthew was a pseudonym for John Rogers, a Lutheran and follower of Tyndale. The fact that he felt a pseudonym was necessary confirms the unsettled and dangerous nature of the practice of Bible translation. He used as much of Tyndale's translation as was available, including some previously unpublished parts of the Old Testament, but added some notes of his own which could have been considered provocative. The origin and association of Matthew's Bible may not have been satisfactory, but it was closer to the Hebrew and Greek originals than Coverdale's. Thomas Cromwell therefore determined to combine the best of the two versions and asked the more moderately disposed Coverdale to revise Matthew's contentious translation. Coverdale obliged and produced in 1539 the first of many revisions that come under the title of The Great Bible. Archbishop Cranmer oversaw two further revisions in 1540 after Thomas Cromwell's fall and execution (Isaacs 1940: 175).

The making of an English Bible to be used in parish churches shows how far reform had progressed in just a few years. Cromwell's injunction of 1538 required each parish priest to provide 'one book of the whole Bible of the largest volume, in English, and the same set up in some convenient place within the said church that you have cure of, whereas your parishioners may most commodiously resort to the same and read it' (Bray 1994: 179). The use of an English Bible in the churches, and later the use of the English Prayer Book for services, was not only a breakthrough in Reformation terms but also the beginning of a cultural and linguistic phenomenon that continues to influence English literature.

ENGLISH REFORMATION LITERATURE

The production of literature in English related to the Bible in the first half of the sixteenth century reflected the early turmoil of the Reformation. It was limited mainly to tracts presenting or restraining polemic views or to accounts of persecution. William Tyndale contributed *The Obedience of a Christian Man* in 1528, pleasing the King as it advocated obedience to authority. Thomas More's *Dialogue Concerning Heresies* of 1529, a defence of the burning of Tyndale's New Testament and an analysis of the contentious words in the translation, provoked a reply from Tyndale: *An Answer unto Sir Thomas More's Dialogue* (1531). More replied with *A Confutation of Tyndale's Answer* (1532). It is interesting to reflect that More's *Utopia* of 1516 had described a society where there was religious freedom.

There was considerable translation activity during this time stimulated perhaps by the Reformation interest in the text of the Scriptures and in the Protestant and humanist writings from Europe. Translation also provided a way of being creative without involving responsibility for the source text. In 1550, John Cheke, the young Prince Edward's tutor, privately translated the Gospel of Matthew into English and made it an exercise in using Anglo-Saxon rather than Latin- or Greek-based vocabulary (Isaacs 1940: 181). John Foxe's first edition of *Acts and Monuments*, published in Strasburg in 1554, was in Latin. Court literature in the form of sonnets from Thomas Wyatt (1503–42) and Henry Howard Earl of Surrey (1517–47) included many translations from or imitations of Petrarch's sonnets. Although written in the 1530s, the poems by Wyatt and Surrey circulated privately and were not published until 1557 as the popular *Tottel's Miscellany* (see Hamrick 2002; Rollins 1965). Wyatt translated the Penitential Psalms into verse in 1540; Philip Sydney (1554–86), poet and soldier for the Protestant cause, left his translated Psalms incomplete at his death to be finished by his sister, Lady Mary (Sydney) Herbert.

THE BOOK OF COMMON PRAYER

It was during this phase of English literary history that the influence of the English Bible and its accompanying liturgy became most marked. When Henry VIII died in 1547, the process of reform accelerated under the young King Edward VI and his protectors and with it the use of English for religious purposes. The order for an English Bible in every church was renewed; in addition each parson was required to have a New Testament in English and Latin for his own use and to read to the congregation from the Scriptures, as well as saying the Gospel of the Mass in English rather than Latin (Bray 1994: 250–3). The year of Edward's accession also saw the publication of the first of two books of homilies, to which Thomas Cranmer was a major contributor. The homilies presented the Reformation idea of the centrality of Scripture in terms of authority and reference and were designed to restrict the spread of unauthorized beliefs (Greenblatt and Logan 2000: 556). They were read in churches on a cyclical basis and must have become very familiar to congregation and clergy. They continued a long Christian tradition of homiletic writing and oral preaching. Publishing the sermons in English made it clear that they were intended for the edification of the general population as well as for clergy who might use them for preaching. Together with the liturgy they provided a persuasive model of English expression and religious discourse.

The Act of Uniformity of 1549 provided for the first Book of Common Prayer, produced by Cranmer 'and certain of the most learned and discreet bishops, and other learned men of this realm' (Bray 1994: 267) to be used throughout England and Wales. The book is in effect a translation into English of the Latin old rites with adjustments towards the new theology of the Reformation. The idea was to simplify the process of finding the prescribed reading and have all the necessary material in one book to be used by everyone (Cranmer 1549, online document, also in Booty 1976: 15). Coverdale's prose translation of the Psalms, perhaps his best-known achievement, went into the Prayer Book (Daniell 2003: 189). One of the most important sections was the penultimate section, the Articles of Religion, which defined the basis of the Protestant belief and confirmed the Holy Scriptures as containing 'all things necessary for salvation'.

The effect of the Book of Common Prayer was to introduce to every person who attended church a common means of expressing Christian praise and ritual in English. The style and language of the prayer book could not help but reflect the language and style of the vernacular translations of the corresponding years (Brook 1965: 15). There was some controversy about aspects of the translation, in particular about Cranmer's rendering of the words of Communion, which, for some, did not move far enough away from the doctrine of the real presence. As a result, the alterations in the 1552 revision were extensive and among other changes left the wording of the Communion service ambiguous. There was also controversy about the Prayer Book's imposition on congregations that had been accustomed to using their own forms of worship. Despite an assurance in the Preface that private prayers could be said in any language, there were some violent protests in Cornwall and Wales where English was not in common use. The compulsory use of the new Prayer Book was resented as well as its use of English (Haig 1993: 174).

THE GENEVA BIBLE

The progress of the English Reformation was halted temporarily when Edward died, aged 15, shortly after the introduction of the revised Prayer Book. As soon as she had confirmed her position as queen, Henry's elder daughter Mary set out to return the country to Catholicism, and while some welcomed this reverse, others were reluctant to give up the freedoms that had been won with such difficulty, particularly the vernacular services. While there is no mention in the new government's 1554 injunction of the wholesale removal of English Bibles, there is emphasis on a return to the use of the Latin rite and on restoring the authority of the Pope and the practice of celibacy among the clergy (Bray 1994: 317). From Mary's perspective it seemed perfectly possible to restore Catholicism by force and injunction (Cameron 1991: 288). The Protestant reform programme came to an abrupt halt and began to grind slowly into reverse.

Before Edward's death, Cranmer, one of the opposers of Mary's accession and consequently one of the early victims of her regime, had welcomed Protestant scholars from the troubled areas of Europe and made connections, particularly with the German and Swiss communities (ibid. 284). More extreme European Protestant groups, including those headed by John Calvin, John Knox, and Christopher Goodman, had already set up communities in exile abroad at Basle, Zurich, and the independent Protestant state of Geneva. Others unwilling or unable to live in Mary's Catholic England now joined them. These communities were already producing contemporary vernacular translations of the Bible in the main European languages as well as critical editions of the Latin Vulgate, and had gathered considerable scholarly learning and experience in doing so (Daniell 2003: 292). As vernacular Bible activity in England had come to a stop, the Protestant exiles determined to continue abroad and in 1557, William Whittingham, probably helped by other Genevan scholars, published an English translation of the New Testament. Two years later a translation of the Old Testament, the work of several scholars, completed the Geneva Bible. By this time Mary was dead and Henry VIII's second daughter Elizabeth had come to the throne in 1558.

The Geneva Bible became the most popular Bible of the Elizabethan age. It was in manageable quarto size, printed in clear roman type rather than Gothic, and the chapters and verses were numbered for ease of reference. Elizabeth was wary of the text because of its uncompromising commentaries and Calvinist provenance rather than because of the translation itself. The Preface dedicates the translation to the Queen in the usual way, but then takes on a less conciliatory tone. The writer exhorts her to ask God for the 'great wisdom' necessary for the advancement of the true religion and says that she 'must show [her]self strong and bold in God's matters' (Bray 1994: 359–60). It is unlikely that Elizabeth had forgotten John Knox's 1558 treatise, *First Blast of the Trumpet against the Monstrous Regiment of Women,* aimed at her sister Mary in particular but scathing about women in general and women rulers in particular. Nor would Christopher Goodman's pamphlet of the same year, *How Superior Powers Ought to be Obeyed by their Subjects: And Wherein They May be Lawfully by God's Word be Disobeyed and Resisted,* with its preface by William Whittingham, have given the Queen much reason to favour the Genevan Protestant cause. James I, many years later, retained similar misgivings. The ordinary people of England, however, who wanted a clear, reliable, and accessible translation of the Bible, had no such difficulties; the Geneva Bible ran to many editions and was the Bible used by Shakespeare, the writer of the Preface to the King James Bible, John

Milton, and John Bunyan (Greaves 1980: 233). The 1599 version travelled to the New World with the Pilgrims in 1620.

The Revised Book of Common Prayer and the Elizabethan Literary Revival

On Elizabeth I's accession the 1552 edition of the Book of Common Prayer was reinstated and published in 1559 with some small but important changes. Vestments, dispensed with in the previous Protestant liturgy, were reintroduced, and the two forms of words in the Communion service of the previous books were combined, so allowing flexibility of interpretation. Compulsory attendance at church on Sunday and holy days was required by the 1552 and the 1559 Acts of Uniformity. Consequently the entire churchgoing population, except during the five years of Mary's reign, heard, read, and repeated after the priest the English language of the Prayer Book, including substantial readings from the Bible, at least once a week (Arnoult 1998: 28). We might draw the conclusion that the literary flowering in the Elizabethan age had something to do with the widespread use of high-status English as the language of religion.

Translators such as Thomas Hoby (1530–66) and Arthur Golding (1536–1605), poets such as Edmund Spenser (1552–99) and Philip Sidney (1554–86), dramatists and poets such as Christopher Marlowe (1564–93) and William Shakespeare (1564–1616), and sermon writers such as Launcelot Andrewes (1555–1626), all contributed to a rich literary culture. Renaissance writing involved the reworking of multiple sources, but nevertheless much of the literary output demonstrated the specific influence of the English Bibles and Prayer Books of the time in both language and subject matter. Edmund Spenser's *Faerie Queene,* for example, combines England's chivalric heritage with classical and Italian sources to produce a patriotic defence of Protestantism at a time when the Queen's position was threatened by the Pope. Biblical allusions and references are frequent, as are doctrinally significant names and actions, as when the Redcrosse knight gives Prince Arthur a New Testament in Book I, canto IX, stanza 19 (Spenser 1993: 113). Spenser makes reference to the Articles of Religion in the Book of Common Prayer when an appalled Una berates Redcrosse for his surrender to despair:

> Why shouldst thou then despair that chosen art?
> Where justice growes, there growes eke greater grace,
> The which doth quench the brand of hellish smart.   (ibid. 122)

Christopher Marlowe examines a similar vision of redemption and damnation in *Faustus,* though the outcome is different. Marlowe's play also has its own blend of classical and religious elements, but the dramatic intensity comes from the struggle of Faustus who has sold his soul to the devil in return for knowledge. The parallel with Adam and Eve is highlighted in the final scene when he declares, 'The serpent that tempted Eve may be saved, but not Faustus' (scene 13, line 16).

THE BISHOPS' BIBLE OF 1568

Elizabeth's accession and the period of stability that followed brought the Marian exiles back to England. They were keen to push for further Calvinist reform but Elizabeth had determined for her own safety to steer a middle course between severe reform and extreme orthodoxy. She tolerated the Geneva Bible as a piece of scholarship and allowed it to be printed in England but never gave it authorized status. The moderate Archbishop Matthew Parker initiated a project to revise the Great Bible. In 1566 he wrote to William Cecil, the Queen's chancellor, telling him that he had 'distributed the Bible in parts to diverse men' (Pollard 1911: 287) in order that they should revise the translation. In a later letter presenting the completed translation to Elizabeth in 1559, he alludes to the Geneva Bible, mentioning that 'in certain places be publicly used some translations which have not been laboured in your realm having inspersed diverse prejudicial notes which might have been also well spared' (ibid. 295). The Geneva Bible was never printed in England during Parker's lifetime (Daiches 1968: 55 n.). His idea was to correct and restore the Great Bible rather than to produce a new translation, but according to some critics the result did not always bear comparison with the Geneva Bible (Daniell 2003: 345). The resulting translation was to be employed some years later as the starting point for the King James Bible translators.

THE RHEIMS/DOUAI TRANSLATION 1582

During Elizabeth's reign, practising Catholics as well as Protestant extremists found themselves in exile. Catholicism, though tolerated at first, was outlawed after the forced arrival in England of Elizabeth's Catholic cousin, Mary Queen of Scots, deposed from the Scottish throne in favour of her baby son and fleeing from the scandal of her husband's and her secretary's murders. Elizabeth dare not remove this dangerous focus of dissent, but when the Pope made a difficult situation worse by excommunicating Elizabeth and declaring her to be no longer rightful queen of

England, Catholicism became too dangerous to tolerate. The Catholic community was forced to choose between their religion and their country (Long 2001: 176). The Catholic College of Douai, temporarily housed at Rheims, felt that the lack of priests in England together with the propaganda of the Protestant Geneva Bible was severely hampering the promotion of the Catholic cause. Accordingly in 1578, William Allen, later made cardinal by Pope Sixtus V, obtained permission to initiate a 'faithful and catholic translation' (Pollard 1911: 300). Gregory Martin was the first translator, using Jerome's Vulgate as the main source text but comparing it with the Greek original. William Allen and Richard Bristow revised each portion. The resulting translation is often criticized for its latinate style and the refusal of the translators to turn technical vocabulary into words more meaningful to the reader (Isaacs 1940: 191). The Preface is a defensive document, regretting the need to translate and defending the use of the Vulgate. The translation was undertaken only 'upon special consideration of the present time, state and condition of our country, unto which divers things are either necessary, or profitable and medecinable [sic] now, that otherwise in the peace of the Church were neither much requisite, nor perchance wholly tolerable' (Pollard 1903: 302). Although the Vulgate is used as the basis, the Greek influence is evident in the alternative renderings given and also in the treatment of the definite article. At times the latinate wording makes the text almost unintelligible, but in other places Martin has a better turn of phrase and makes use of other versions, even those whose theology he disliked.

The Old Testament did not appear until 1609 in Douai, too late to be consulted by the King James translators who did in fact make use of the New Testament. In the intervening years the Rheims New Testament had been the subject of great controversy. William Fulke produced a dual text of the Bishops' Bible and the Rheims in parallel, with his own rebuttal of the Catholic version in 1589. Gregory Martin, William Whittaker, George Wither, and Thomas Cartwright contributed to the debate as to which translation was 'sincere and true' (Fulke 1583). Thomas Cartwright's anti-Rheims contribution was published as late as 1618, after the King James Bible, showing how great the divisions between conservatives and reformers still were (Greenslade 1963: 163).

THE KING JAMES BIBLE, 1611

The Elizabethan settlement and the Thirty-Nine Articles that set out the precepts of English Protestantism were too broad and open to interpretation to satisfy everyone. On the accession of James I in 1603, the Puritans in particular were anxious to define Protestantism exclusively in relation to Scripture and presented their case at the Hampton Court Conference (Opfel 1982: 4). James, astute, well read, and something of a Bible scholar, was as fully aware of the danger to himself as monarch from a

Puritan reading of scriptural authority as his predecessor had been. Without the support of the bishops, the King knew that his position was vulnerable; the Puritans wanted to dismantle what they saw as an unnecessarily powerful hierarchy in the decision-making machinery of the church. Their spokesman John Rainolds (or Reynolds), drew little support from James for most of his requests except for the proposal that a new translation of the Bible be made. Here was a means to secure religious unity and provide an alternative to the popular Geneva Bible with its anti-monarchist provenance.

James, himself a translator of the Psalms, was enthusiastic about the project and wrote to his archbishop Bancroft asking him to make sure that 'our said intended translation may have the help and furtherance of all our principal learned men within this our kingdom' (Isaacs 1940: 198). Translation was to be by committees, two each at Westminster, Oxford, and Cambridge, composed of scholars and linguists of all the various shades of religious persuasion between high church and Puritan with the notable exception of the outspoken Hugh Broughton (Daiches 1968: 67). Bancroft set out fifteen rules to be followed: number six forbade the use of marginal notes except for explaining the Hebrew or Greek words, number eleven gave authority to ask 'any learned man in the land' for his judgement in places of obscurity (Opfel 1982: 139). The Bishops' Bible of 1559, already appointed to be read in churches, was to be used as a basis for the translation, thus ensuring continuity, but rule fourteen allowed for 'these translations to be used when they agree better with the Text than the Bishops' Bible: Tindoll, Matthew's, Coverdale's, Whitchurch's, Geneva' (Opfel 1982: 140). Politically this approach was sound, as the previous translations were not invalidated but became part of a greater process. As McGrath argues, the King James Bible was conceived as 'a corporate effort in which the achievements of earlier generations could be valued and used by their successors' (McGrath 2001: 177). Even more than that, the policy extended to including the best from contemporary translations and even from versions produced by Calvinists and Catholics.

The Translators' Preface carefully defends the translation process and sets out the strategies used. The writer Miles Smith demonstrates an awareness of the difficulties of the task, 'for whosoever attempteth anything for the public (specially if it appertain to religion, and to the opening and clearing of the word of God), the same setteth himself upon a stage to be glouted upon by every evil eye' (Rhodes and Lupas 1997: 29). Certainly the translation drew criticism, as expected, and took some decades to begin to replace the popular Geneva version in the private prayer life of the ordinary people (see Isaacs 1940: 223; Norton 2000: 90). However, the careful planning of the enterprise, and the use of the best scholars and best available resources at a time of political confidence and literary accomplishment could not help but produce a work of substantial quality. Olga Opfel (1982: 131) considers it 'a miracle and a mystery' that a work of art could be produced under such conditions of committee labour. Isaacs (1940: 204) calls the Authorised Version 'a miracle and a landmark'; Daniell (2003: 427) observes that 'the sheer longevity of this version is a phenomenon without parallel'. The 1611 version was not initially the exclusive source of reference, but in its later forms its cadences and expressions are now deeply embedded in the English culture and psyche, thanks in part perhaps to the Victorian promotion of religion as social morality and empire as evangelical mission. Stability and certainty is what most people require in religion, and the King James Bible in its various editions and revisions has helped to provide that.

The King James Bible dominated the latter part of the seventeenth century and most of the eighteenth. Since unity in worship was what was required, every person who attended church, and that was most of the population, read or heard the English words of the King James Bible, deeply affecting their own speech and writing. It was revised in the second half of the nineteenth century after much debate and continues to flourish today, particularly in some areas of the United States, its archaic language giving status and authenticity to its content.

The Influence of Reformation Bibles and Prayer Books on Seventeenth-Century Literature

William Shakespeare (1564–1616) was active as playwright and poet from the 1590s. All the main English Reformation Bibles and Prayer Books were either already available to him or were introduced during his lifetime. Although he followed the usual Renaissance model of reworking a combination of sources and never used Biblical stories per se for the subject matter of his plays, quotations from and references to the Bible abound in his work. Extensive studies of allusions in his plays to the Bible, the Book of Homilies, and the Prayer Book reveal a writer steeped in the scriptural culture of his time and one who frequently, but not exclusively, uses the Geneva Bible (Noble 1935; Shaheen 1999).

Both John Donne (1572–1631) and George Herbert (1593–1633) drew on their experiences as clergymen, their Articles of Faith, the Bible, and the richness of religious discourse to write their best poetry. Donne circulated his work privately where he could challenge his readers with the overlapping languages of spiritual and secular love. The structure of Herbert's *The Temple* has been described as 'attending to Herbert's wish to situate his devotional lyrics amid the discourses of social practice and historical pattern' (Schoenfeldt 1994: 86). Certainly these two poets situate their lyrics within the social and cultural setting of the time and demonstrate the effect on literature of the religious cultural context. The Sidney/Herbert Psalms greatly influenced both poets (Abrams and Greenblatt 2000: 958).

Aemilia Lanyer (1569–1645) was the first among a growing group of educated women who found in the Protestant affirmation of the supremacy of individual conscience a justification for breaking 'the traditional expectation of womanly silence' (Woods 1993: p. xxxi). Writing or translating religious matter had become an acceptable occupation for a woman. The title of her 1611 poem about the passion of Christ, *Salve Deus Rex Judaeorum*, came to Lanyer in a dream long before she wrote it, so that she felt 'appointed to performe this Worke' (ibid. 139). The poem is most interesting for its reasoned argument against Eve's guilt:

> That undiscerning Ignorance perceav'd
> No guile, or craft that was by him intended
> For had she known of what we were bereav'd
> To his request she had not condescended.   (ibid. 84)

It is a point taken up later in 1667 by Milton in *Paradise Lost* when Eve says to Adam:

> thou couldst not have discerned
> Fraud in the Serpent, speaking as he spake;
> No ground of enmity between us known,
> Why he should mean me ill, or seek to harm.   (IX. 1149–52)

THE ENGLISH BIBLE AFTER THE
KING JAMES VERSION

Even after the King James Bible had established its dominance, biblical translation continued to flourish. In particular there was development with respect to source text editions, proposed revisions of the 1611 version and an increase in the number of translations made by individuals. The Puritans remained unhappy with what they considered to be a distance from the source texts (Isaacs 1940: 225). The 1637 Prayer Book, for example, published in the reign of Charles I, was still considered by some 'too popish'. In 1639 the Puritan Hebrew scholar Henry Ainsworth produced a more literal version of the Old Testament, keeping close to the Hebrew idiom. The unsettled period of the Puritan interregnum, 1649–60, and the re-establishment of the monarchy under different terms involved many in a re-evaluation of political and religious ideology. Religious polarity continued to be a source of contention and bloodshed. In one of the more reflective passages of his diary, Samuel Pepys remarks, 'Thus it was my chance to see the King beheaded at White-hall and to see the first blood shed in revenge for the blood of the King at Charing-cross' (Pepys 1660, online, entry for 13 October).

John Milton (1608–74) may also have been present at that execution. He is perhaps the most politico-religious seventeenth-century writer, producing classical poetry alongside religious pamphlets and basing his epic poem on the story of the Fall in Genesis. For Milton, as for everyone who experienced the Civil War, politics and religion were inseparable and the Bible the repository of 'all things necessary for salvation', including justification for military action.

Work on biblical scholarship continued in spite of political unrest. In 1627 Charles I had received the gift of a complete fifth-century Greek codex, the Alexandrinus, sent to his father James from Cyril Lucar (Parker 2001: 118). This had initiated some debate about the comparative authenticity of source texts. Between 1654 and 1657 Brian Walton took advantage of politically enforced retirement to produce a polyglot Bible that included Ethiopic and Persian versions for comparison (Robinson 1940: 22). John Mill's 1707 critical edition of the Greek New Testament highlighted many variations between sources, while Edward Wells produced a translation that challenged the *textus receptus* by prioritizing earlier readings (Daniell 2003: 510). Variable reading in source texts, a focus on different kinds of translation from writers such as John Dryden and Alexander Pope, and the movement towards clarity of language encouraged individuals to attempt Bible translating. New scientific understanding about the natural world as demonstrated by Robert Boyle and the debate on reason and revelation outlined by John Locke gave the late seventeenth- and early eighteenth-century commentators much on which to reflect (see Clements 2001: 219; Neil 1963: 240). The fashion for paraphrases at the time perhaps reflects the popular reliance on commentary that had been present in the Geneva Bible but lacking in the King James (Sykes 1963: 188).

The development of the novel from Daniel Defoe in 1719 and Jonathan Swift in 1726 encouraged new perspectives on narrative. Daniel Mace's revised critical Greek text of the New Testament published in 1729 had, as well as some new underrated renderings, a completely new kind of English translation written in the lively prose of the day (Byatt 1984, online). The following year saw a revision of the Rheims New Testament; hymn writer Philip Doddridge produced 'a paraphrase and version' of the New Testament between 1739 and 1756, followed in 1764 by 'a new and literal translation' of the complete Bible by the Quaker Anthony Purver. Every new translation or paraphrase quickly found its critics. Perhaps the most controversial was Edward Harwood's liberal translation of the New Testament done in the style 'with which other translations from the Greek classics have lately been executed' (Isaacs 1940: 231). The idea of this free adaptation of the content of the New Testament was to attract young people to read it for its modern style. Isaacs calls it 'a mirror of the later century' and it certainly has the linguistic characteristics of eighteenth-century popular prose rather than the more sonorous language of the Geneva or King James versions.

While individuals were making translations and paraphrases of the New Testament, Richard Challoner was busy revising the Rheims/Douai Bible. He spent over twenty years between 1750 and 1772 bringing out various revisions of both Old and New Testament, changing them substantially from the original sixteenth- and seventeenth-century versions and arguably modelling them more on the language of the Authorized Version.

Proposals and demands for the revision of the King James Version preoccupied the beginning of the nineteenth century. While its function within the liturgy remained dominant, developments in biblical scholarship together with the errors inherent in successive printings made revision a necessity. Eventually an official revision began in

1870 and the New Testament was published in 1881 to a predictable storm of criticism, lamenting the change in familiar wording. The Old Testament followed in 1885.

CONCLUSIONS

The history of English translations of the Bible and their influence on language and literature is a complex one that makes sense only within the separate historical and literary contexts of the various translations. The story is further complicated by religious polemic that even today governs the use of certain translations or vocabulary. What is clear is the centrality of the English Bible, both as a literary text and as a source of theology, to English culture and literature. Even today, when the Bible is less of a shared text, its language is easily recognizable as the distinctive language of religion. We can trace the history of English language through comparing translations of the Bible (Blake 1996: 9) and in order to understand English literature before about 1950, knowledge and understanding of the Bible are essential. It is difficult to look objectively at one's own culture and to see how deeply Christianity has embedded itself there, but with globalization and the integration of English literatures from English-speaking countries outside Britain comparisons begin to arise. Confrontation with religions other than Christianity is more common in the modern multicultural society and the cultural impact of texts central to other religions may bring biblical issues to future prominence.

WORKS CITED

ABRAMS, M. H., and GREENBLATT, STEPHEN (eds.) 2000. *The Norton Anthology of English Literature*, 7th edn. London: W. W. Norton, i.

ANDERSON, J. J. 1996. *Sir Gawain and the Green Knight*. London: J. M. Dent.

ANDREW, MALCOLM, and WALDRON, RONALD. 1996. *The Poems of the Pearl Manuscript*. Exeter: University of Exeter Press.

ARNOULT, SHARON, L. 1998. 'Spiritual and Sacred Publique Actions', in Eric J. Carlson (ed.), *Religion and the English People 1500–1640*. Kirksville, Mo.: Thomas Jefferson University Press, 25–47.

BEDE. 1990. *The Ecclesiastical History of the British People*, ed. D. H. Farmer, trans. Leo Sherley-Price and R. E. Latham. London: Penguin.

BEJCZY, ISTVÁN. 2001. *Erasmus and the Middle Ages*. Leiden: Brill.

BENSON, LARRY. (ed.) 1987. *The Riverside Chaucer*. Oxford: Oxford University Press.

BLAKE, N. F. 1996. *A History of the English Language*. London: Macmillan.

BOOTY, JOHN E. 1976. *The Book of Common Prayer 1559*. Charlottesville: University Press of Virginia.

BOSWORTH, JOSEPH. 1888. *The Gothic and Anglo-Saxon Gospels*. London: Reeves & Turner.

BRAY, GERALD. 1994. *Documents of the English Reformation*. Cambridge: James Clark.

BROOK, STELLA. 1965. *The Language of the Book of Common Prayer*. London: André Deutsch.

BYATT, ANTHONY. 1984. Daniel Mace's New Testament, online at <*http://www.biblecollectors. org/daniel_mace.htm*>. Accessed 21.03.05.

CAMERON, EUAN. 1991. *The European Reformation*. Oxford: Clarendon.

CLANCHY, MICHAEL T. 1993. *From Memory to Written Record*. Oxford: Blackwell.

CLEMENTS, RONALD. 2001. '1700 to the Present', in John Rogerson (ed.), *The Oxford Illustrated History of the Bible*. Oxford: Oxford University Press, 218–41.

COULSON, JOHN. 1984. 'Religion and Imagination', in David Jasper (ed.), *Images of Belief in Literature*. London: Macmillan, 7–24.

CRAIGIE, WILLIAM. 1940. 'The English Versions to Wyclif', in H. Wheeler Robinson (ed.), *The Bible in its Ancient and English Versions*. Oxford: Clarendon, 128–45.

CRANMER, THOMAS. 1549. 'Preface to the Book of Common Prayer', online document at <*http://justus.anglican.org/resources/bcp/1549/front_matter_1549.htm#Preface*>, accessed 23 Feb. 2005.

DAICHES, DAVID. 1968. *The King James Version of the Bible*. Chicago: Archon.

DANIELL, DAVID. 2003. *The Bible in English*. New Haven: Yale University Press.

DEANESLY, MARGARET. 1966. *The Lollard Bible*. Cambridge: Cambridge University Press.

FULKE, WILLIAM. 1583. *A Defence of the Sincere and True Translations of the Holy Scriptures in the English Tongue*, ed. H. C. Hartshorne. Parker Society, 1843.

GOLDIE, MATTHEW BOYD. 2003. *Middle English Literature*. Oxford: Blackwell.

GOODMAN, CHRISTOPHER. 1558. *How Superior Powers Ought to be Obeyed*, ed. Patrick S. Pole. Online document at <*http://www.constitution.org/cmt/goodman/obeyed.htm*>, accessed 3 Mar. 2005.

GREAVES, RICHARD, L. 1980. 'The Nature and Intellectual Milieu of the Political Principles in the Geneva Bible Marginalia'. *Journal of Church and State* 22: 223–49.

GREENBLATT, STEPHEN, and LOGAN, GEORGE M. (eds.) 2000. 'The Sixteenth Century'. *The Norton Anthology of English Literature*. 7th edn. New York: W. W. Norton, i.

GREENSLADE, S. L. 1963. 'English Versions of the Bible 1525–1611', in S. L. Greenslade (ed.), *The Cambridge History of the Bible: The West from the Reformation to the Present Day*. Cambridge: Cambridge University Press, 141–76.

HAIG, CHRISTOPHER. 1993. *English Reformations*. Oxford: Clarendon Press.

HAMRICK, STEPHEN. 2002. 'Tottel's Miscellany and the English Reformation', *Criticism* 44/4: 329–44.

HAPPÉ, PETER. 1975. *English Mystery Plays*. London: Penguin.

HUGHES, PAUL. L., and LARKIN, JAMES. F. (eds.) 1964. *Tudor Royal Proclamations*, i. *1485–1553*. New Haven: Yale University Press.

ISAACS, J. 1940. 'The Sixteenth Century English Versions'. in H. Wheeler Robinson (ed.), *The Bible in its Ancient and English Versions*. Oxford: Clarendon, 146–95.

KENNEDY, CHARLES. W. 1963. *Early English Christian Poetry*. New York: Oxford University Press.

KNOX, JOHN. 1558. *First Blast of the Trumpet Against the Monstrous Regiment of Women*, in Kevin Reed (ed.) 1995. *Selected Writings of John Knox: Public Epistles, Treatises and Expositions to the Year 1559*. Dallas: Presbyterian Heritage.

LANGLAND, WILLIAM. 1995. *The Vision of Piers Plowman*, ed. A. V. C. Schmidt. Everyman. London: Charles Dent.

LAWTON, DAVID. 1990. *Faith Text and History—The Bible in English*. Hemel Hempstead: Harvester Wheatsheaf.

LONG, LYNNE. 2001. *Translating the Bible*. Aldershot: Ashgate.

MCGRATH, ALISTER. 2001. *In the Beginning: The Story of the King James Bible*. London: Hodder & Stoughton.

NEIL, W. 1963. 'The Criticism and Theological Use of the Bible, 1700–1950', in S. L. Greenslade (ed.), *The Cambridge History of the Bible: The West from the Reformation to the Present Day*. Cambridge: Cambridge University Press, 238–93.

NICOLSON, ADAM. 2003. *Power and Glory*. London: HarperCollins.

NOBLE, R. S. H. 1935. *Shakespeare's Biblical Knowledge and Use of the Book of Common Prayer*. London: Society for the Promotion of Christian Knowledge; New York: Macmillan.

NORTON, DAVID. 2000. *A History of the English Bible as Literature*. Cambridge: Cambridge University Press.

ONG, WALTER. 1982. *Orality and Literacy*. London: Routledge.

OPFEL, OLGA S. 1982. *The King James Bible Translators*. Jefferson, NC: McFarland.

PARKER, DAVID. 2001. 'The New Testament', in John Rogerson (ed.), *The Oxford Illustrated History of the Bible*. Oxford: Oxford University Press, 110–33.

PEARSON, GEORGE (ed.) 1845. *Remains of Myles Coverdale*. The Parker Society. Cambridge: Cambridge University Press.

PEPYS, SAMUEL. 1660. Entry for 13 October, online at <*http://www.pepysdiary.com/archive/1660/10/index.php*>, accessed 21.03.05.

POLLARD, ALFRED. 1903. *Fifteenth Century Prose and Verse*. Westminster: Constable.

RHODES, EROLL F., and LUPAS, DIANA (eds.) 1997. *The Translators to the Reader*. New York: American Bible Society.

ROBINSON, H. WHEELER. 1940. 'The Hebrew Bible', in H. Wheeler Robinson (ed.), *The Bible in its Ancient and English Versions*. Oxford: Clarendon, 1–38.

ROLLINS, HYDER EDWARD. 1965. *Tottel's Miscellany*. Cambridge, Mass.: Harvard University Press.

SCHOENFELDT, MICHAEL C. (1994). 'The Poetry of Supplication: Towards a Cultural Poetics of the Religious Lyric', in John R. Roberts (ed.), *New Perspectives on the Seventeenth Century English Religious Lyric*. Columbia: University of Missouri Press, 75–114.

SHAHEEN, NASEEB. 1999. *Biblical References in Shakespeare's Plays*. Newark: University of Delaware Press.

SHEPHERD, GEOFFREY. 1969. 'English Versions of the Scripture before Wyclif', in G. W. H. Lampe (ed.), *The Cambridge History of the Bible*. Cambridge: University of Cambridge Press, ii. 362–86.

SPENSER, EDMUND. 1993. *The Faerie Queen*. London: J. M. Dent.

SYKES, NORMAN. 1963. 'The Religion of Protestants', in S. L. Greenslade (ed.), *The Cambridge History of the Bible, The West from the Reformation to the Present Day*. Cambridge: Cambridge University Press, 175–98.

WOODS, SUSANNE. 1993. *The Poems of Aemilia Lanyer*. Oxford: Oxford University Press.

WRIGHT, DAVID. 2001. 'The Reformation to 1700', in John Rogerson (ed.), *The Oxford Illustrated History of the Bible*. Oxford: Oxford University Press.

FURTHER READING

HUDSON, ANNE. 1988. *The Premature Reformation*. Oxford: Clarendon.

KING, JOHN. N. 1982. *English Reformation Literature: The Tudor Origins of the Protestant Tradition*. Princeton: Princeton University Press.

LANCASHIRE, IAN (ed.) 1994. *A Fruitful Exhortation to the Reading of Holy Scripture.* Online document at <*http://www.anglicanlibrary.org/homilies/bk1hom01.htm*>, accessed 27 Feb. 2005.

LEWALSKI, BARBARA KIEFER. 1979. *Protestant Poetics and the Seventeenth Century Religious Lyric.* Princeton: Princeton University Press.

MARSHALL, PETER, and RYRIE, ALEC (eds.) 2002. *The Beginnings of English Protestantism.* Cambridge: Cambridge University Press.

REX, RICHARD. 2002. *The Lollards.* Basingstoke: Palgrave.

RYRIE, ALEC. 2003. *The Gospels and Henry VIII.* Cambridge: Cambridge University Press.

SHUGER, DEBORA. 1990. *Habits of Thought in the English Renaissance: Religion, Politics and the Dominant Culture.* Berkeley: University of California Press.

CHAPTER 5

THE PROTESTANT AND CATHOLIC REFORMATIONS

BRIAN CUMMINGS

A history of theology in western Europe which failed to place the sixteenth-century religious Reformations at a prominent place in its narrative would make strange reading. Doctrinally, this is a period of astonishing creativity and at the same time agonizing controversy. On the one side it sees the emergence of wholly new ways of imagining Christian thought, dominated by two figures of unquestionable intellectual genius (Martin Luther and John Calvin). These versions of doctrine were not only intellectually fashionable but involved the redrawing of the political map of Europe and the creation of autonomous religious institutions which have survived to the present day. On the other side, in large parts—indeed the larger part—of Europe these new versions of doctrine were decisively rejected, and Catholic orthodoxy reasserted. Yet in the reassertion of Catholic doctrine, while much appears to stay the same, much else is transformed. The new settlement of the Council of Trent is as decisive a watershed in the history of theology as the declaration of the Protestant confessions. Formally and conceptually, Catholic theology was practised in revolutionary ways. Not only did new masters emerge, but a new religious order—the Jesuits—was formed to practise it, alongside yet also in direct competition with older institutions and practices.

A history of literature in the sixteenth century which placed a similar emphasis on the religious Reformations would, until very recently, have looked decidedly eccentric. On the one hand, a few authors might readily have been acknowledged as interested in issues of doctrine, but if so, this would have been seen as a matter of individual affiliation. Devotional literature, in the traditional structure, was confined to the periphery of literary history as a significant but minor genre. The larger concerns of sixteenth- and seventeenth-century literature were assumed to be secular.

In the last ten years such assumptions have been put into disarray. These assumptions have been shown to reflect less the historical conditions of the sixteenth and seventeenth centuries than the prejudices of English as a modern academic discipline. Increasingly it is becoming as hard to separate literary production from the processes of religious change as it is the visual and musical arts, where the Reformation has long been a key object of enquiry. Not only evidently devotional works, but literature across the genres is increasingly seen in this light: the shadow of the Reformation has been observed even across the face of Shakespeare studies, previously regarded as sacred ground for the secular spirit. Moreover, secularization itself can be seen as an important dimension of the reaction to religious division. At the same time, in the converse direction it is becoming clearer that the religious Reformations themselves encompassed from the beginning profoundly literary and textual processes. Early modern religion is caught up in developments in literary media, in the shift from manuscript to print or the politics of the vernacular. In that sense literary and theological history are meeting halfway. If the study of early modern literature is now ready to admit a religious dimension, early modern theology turns out to be equally receptive towards literary methods of analysis.

THE RELIGIOUS REFORMATIONS OF THE SIXTEENTH CENTURY

First of all, it is necessary to clarify what is meant by 'the Protestant and Catholic Reformations'. At one time the word 'Reformation' implied a Protestant version of history, a strong narrative of change in which a decaying and corrupted medieval church gave way with historic inevitability to a movement for reform. On the one hand lay the 'abuses' of the past—a decadent or semi-detached clergy, a venal system of financial inducements, allied to a shopworn intellectual legacy from scholastic theology, now reduced to cliché and jargon. On the other hand lay the 'protests' (hence the term 'Protestants') of a new class, predominantly urban, humanist-educated, morally purified, dedicated to 'new learning' and modernity. This narrative did not have to be narrowly confessional; many of the most urgent voices for 'reform' after all remained Catholic (Erasmus, the Thomist Cardinal Cajetan, or in England Reginald Pole or Thomas More). But this argument was insistently anti-medieval; it made 'Reformation' synonymous with 'Renaissance'; and almost ruthlessly teleological, seeing the sixteenth century through the eyes of the twentieth as part of a historic progress via the Enlightenment and liberal hermeneutics towards science and modernism.

Perhaps in some quarters of the print and broadcast media this view still prevails. It is at present a journalistic cliché to say that Islam is awaiting its 'Reformation', as if such a thing is a known quantity and unequivocally a good thing. Yet such a view of the historical Reformation of early modern Europe is now out of date. Among English historians, a different consensus has emerged (known as the 'revisionist' case): a Protestant Reformation was by no means inevitable, but occurred contingently in different places for different reasons.[1] In England, especially, there was no single process of reform but a series of crises and imposed solutions, by which religious polity went backwards and forwards at least five times in the space of thirty years. As a result, many historians now prefer to use the plural form 'Reformations' to describe the period.[2] Such 'reformations' were political in character, motivated by the needs of Tudor monarchs. Henry VIII first incited evangelicals to aid his break with Rome in the early 1530s, then reined back on them later in the decade as he perceived their demands to pose new threats to social order. Under Edward VI a second, more radical Reformation was instituted, using iconoclasm to break the will of older residual religious practices and enforcing a new austere vernacular religion through Thomas Cranmer's Book of Common Prayer of 1549.[3] After Edward's premature death in 1553, Mary first attempted to restore Catholic ritual and doctrine by default and then, especially in urban, eastern parts of the country, used persecution in her own radical reformation against pertinacious heresy. Elizabeth, inheriting these violent oppositions in 1559, might herself have gone in different directions but chose a path of patient compromise and anxious balance, interrupted by frequent, vicious campaigns against both Catholic recusants and Puritan radicals.

The revisionist case, especially in the work of Eamon Duffy, has emphasized the richness, diversity, and creativity of late-medieval religion (Duffy 1992). Far from falling into decay, fifteenth- and early sixteenth-century parishes were a vibrant scene of new cults and new forms of devotion. Rather than a backward-looking refusal to brace up to modernity, this Catholic culture welcomed innovations such as the printed book or vernacular humanism to enrich its traditions. The destruction of this culture was not inevitable but the result of violent will. As a result, a complex network of communal beliefs and ideas concerning the human body, external nature, the physical universe, time and death was overturned and (in Duffy's view) replaced by a more didactic, verbal, semantic view of religion.[4] Yet popular belief was more stubbornly resistant than the Protestants assumed it would be. In many parts of the country, Catholic sentiment died hard and disappeared only slowly. Elizabeth's famous 'settlement' of 1559, far from finding a natural English middle way between radical (for which, read foreign) extremes (Spain and Geneva), was a ruthlessly expedient political negotiation, balancing one faction against another, coercing conformity from above.

---

[1] See the essays collected in Haigh (ed.) (1987), as a riposte to the classic work (first published in 1964) Dickens (1967).

[2] Following Haigh (1993).

[3] On the 'second' English Reformation see MacCulloch (1999).

[4] For a further exploration of these ideas at a local level, see Duffy (2001).

It should be said that the revisionist case has not been afraid to impose its own stereotypes in turn. In particular, it has been reluctant to find as nuanced a language for describing Protestant forms of religion as it has for late-medieval piety. It has also struggled to find an explanation for the sheer variety—and contrariety—of religious views in the early modern period. Above all, it has failed to account for the violence that characterizes reactions on either side to the apprehension of religious change and unexpected pluralism. To do this, we perhaps need to think less in terms of understanding any of the different traditions in line with their internal merits or persuasiveness, and more in terms of why religious diversity in the sixteenth century is so pervasive and so extreme.

REFORMERS AND MOVEMENTS FOR REFORM

The revisionist account of the English Reformation has also suffered from a certain Anglocentrism. This has partly been a deliberate effort to escape the narrative history offered in the classic account of A. G. Dickens in 1964, which saw English Protestantism as a blood relative of the German Reformation initiated by Martin Luther (Dickens 1974). Dickens emphasized Luther's theological influence and, on a wider historical front, the association between Protestantism in both Germany and England with vernacular national identity. In reaction to Dickens, it has been pointed out that Luther was not much read in England after the reign of Henry VIII, and that even during his reign Henry himself was consistently anti-Lutheran. The revisionists argue that the English Reformation has little in common with Luther's in Germany. While this may be true in terms of a direct legacy, the importance of Luther lies not just in theological originality (more will be said on this below). Luther is also a symptomatic figure for religious change in its widest experience. He began his career as a monk in a religious order already split over issues of reform (the Augustinians). It was on a mission to advance the observant cause that he visited Rome in 1510 (several years before his intellectual crisis) staying in the convent by S. Maria del Popolo. At this stage he was also a conventional scholastic theologian, trained in Lombard's Sentences and in the Ockhamist nominalism of the German *via moderna*. Late in 1517 he came into public view by intervening in the promulgation of Indulgences in Saxony. At first sight, the Ninety-Five Theses of 31 October can also be seen in the light of late-medieval disputes. The form of the theses follows a scholastic disputation. To Archbishop Albrecht of Brandenburg the quarrel seemed at first a typical monastic affair involving Augustinians on one side and Dominicans promoting the Indulgences on the other (Oberman 1989: 187–97; Brecht 1985: 205–6).

Luther, it turned out, was no ordinary monk. His attacks on Indulgences proceeded not from idle contrariness but a passionate and imaginative personal theology arising from his university lectures. Also, to an extent that has been missed in traditional studies of the Reformation, he was a brilliant literary innovator, commanding an extraordinary range of styles. A small central kernel of theological ideas (not all of them in themselves original)—on penitence, humility, faith, justification, grace—are expressed, as the occasion demands, with terse metaphoric gravity, or edgy irony and parody, or oratorical high flourish, or caustic folkloric (often scatalogical) satire. Something of this range can be seen in his three masterpiece treatises of 1520 (the *Babylonian Captivity*, *To the German Nobility*, and *The Freedom of a Christian*), one in exuberantly controversial scholastic Latin, the second a furiously political vernacular philippic, the last a lyrical personal testament produced in both languages.

Historians still struggle to make historical sense of Luther, and thus also of the movement that came with him. Was he a Hercules Germanicus (as in Hans Holbein the Younger's woodcut of 1523; Scribner 1994: 32–4) or (in Diarmaid MacCulloch's recent phrase) 'an accidental revolutionary' (MacCulloch 2004: 123)? Was he a late, wayward, scholastic or a scion of Erasmian humanism, a heretic who (unlike John Wyclif or Jan Hus) got away with it, or a premonition of modern identity? Perhaps the answer to these questions is sought too internally; however original Luther was, the context in which he worked was different in a number of ways from a century before for Hus. One difference was the complexity of imperial politics: Luther received protection from the local elector Frederick the Wise which meant that the ecclesiastical proceedings against him were aborted. Another was the dissemination of his writing in printed books. This is not a matter of number of copies simply (early printed books had low print runs) but more of intellectual autonomy. Luther's ideas had an independent aura of authority.

This is what lends support to the argument that this is not a mere recurrence of medieval forms of heresy on a larger scale. The appearance in Wittenberg of a religious group professing radical ideas with political protection and doctrinal self-sufficiency enabled a sense that this was not a sect but a different way of practising Christianity. This emboldened priests in other cities and smaller imperial states attracted to Luther's theology to preach new doctrines from the pulpit with something like impunity. Nuremberg in 1521 allowed posts in three churches to be occupied by Lutheran sympathizers. Cities in the Low Countries, such as Antwerp and Ghent, were also vulnerable to the spread of dissident ideas, inciting the agents of the new emperor Charles V to take draconian measures to regain control. Outside the jurisdiction of the emperor in Switzerland, in 1522 Huldrych Zwingli openly promoted alternative doctrines in the Grossmünster in Zurich. His parishioners ate sausages in Lent and Zwingli himself married. In Basle, Oecolampadius made similar moves; by 1523, there were reformed preachers in Schaffhausen and even St Gallen, site of a famous and ancient abbey (Gordon 2002: 86–118). Within the Empire, in free cities such as Strasburg—despite formally accepting the decree of Worms against Luther—reforming preachers were also tolerated. Martin Bucer, a former Dominican, arrived in 1523, full of quotations and ideas from Luther. Oecolampadius preached in Augsburg as well as Basle. Perhaps most emblematic of all these converting or cohabiting cities was Konstanz, which a hundred years earlier had been the seat of the condemnation of both Wyclif and Hus (Cameron 1991: 168–85).[5]

Almost all these radical preachers, like Luther himself, were also prolific writers. No wonder that Luther said that he himself did nothing, the word did it all. Luther was a colossus of the printed book. As a direct result of the Lutheran controversy, printing was established in around thirty new cities in Germany. Production of books in the German language increased tenfold in the six years following the Ninety-Five Theses (Flood 1998: 29, 43). Along with controversial works his catechisms and sermons were bestsellers. From 1522 they were followed by his enormously influential editions of the Bible. The coincidence of scriptural methodology and written dissemination is anything but accidental. Luther instinctively realized, and quickly others like Zwingli and Bucer understood it too, that his religion was profoundly verbal. It was a religion of verbal meaning, above all biblical meaning, understood in the mind of the believer and transferred from one believer to another by word of mouth or by reading from the page. Zwingli was perhaps quickest to see that with this came an ambivalence or even antipathy to a religion of visible things or bodily practices, whether in the cult of the saints or the real presence of the sacraments.

In the years that followed, preaching, doctrine, and writing became more pressingly intertwined with questions of church polity. Some states and magistrates formally professed a new confession, and in Augsburg in 1530 a first attempt was made to model a new confessional formula as an authoritative summary of reformed dogma. A still more striking renovation of church order was attempted in the episcopal city of Geneva beginning in 1536 (MacCulloch 2004: 196–7, 236–41). In Geneva, more than anywhere else, a blueprint was drawn up which combined a radical vision of theocratic social organization with the zealous promotion of a divine literature. Geneva, a prototype of the modern metropolis, lay at the crossroads between France, Italy, the Empire, the federated cantons of Switzerland, and the free cities of Germany. It was a location for ideas in action without visible boundaries, the city as printed book. For this role it found its ideal intellectual magistrate in Calvin, one of the most prolific and versatile writers of the age.[6] Perhaps no figure from the sixteenth century is more difficult to apply sympathetic imagination to in our own time. Yet like modern gurus such as Freud, Heidegger, or Derrida he inspired both intense following and intense loathing, a sense either that nothing could make sense without him or that he made nonsense of everything sacred or true. In this context it should be realized that controversy is part of the attraction and vilification part of the mystique.

Calvin (who was a lawyer from Picardy) earlier toyed with launching a stronger pace of reform in France, but found cities (Basle, Lausanne, and Strasburg as well as Geneva) more appropriate to his methods. He arrived in Geneva by accident but naturally attributed to this a divine providence which sought to take advantage of the peculiar situation of that city. Only recently independent of the Duchy of Savoy, the

---

[5] On earlier heresies see Cameron (1991: 70–8).
[6] For a complete bibliography see Peter and Gilmont (1991–2000).

fledgling city-state craved a new political order which could make sense of religious radicalism. Calvin was born for the part. An exile himself, he happily cooperated with other exiles and immigrants in a rapidly expanding population. He was an instinctive political propagandist and modernizer, a brilliant exponent of verbal media. From the pulpit he created for himself a cult of personality, as a prolific and incandescent preacher. His flair as a publicist found another outlet in printed proclamations, digests, and articles of faith, displayed in public places to inspire, inflame, and regiment the plebs. As well as a demagogue he was an intuitive public pedagogue, promoting clarity and uniformity of ideas through catechism and doctrinal formularies, inculcated in churches and schools, and through books. He understood the importance of youth and education, transforming the public school system and instituting a rigorous humanist Collège of higher learning. Above all, he recognized the power and reach of the technology of information. Just as Wittenberg metamorphosed through Luther from an eastern rural backwater into one of the most prolific centres of German printing, so Calvin's Geneva became a model for innovation and productivity in the knowledge industry. Master exponents of the trade escaping from religious suppression in Paris and Lyons were encouraged to settle and revive their work in French-speaking Geneva. Here they could restore their networks of distribution in a liberal economic framework and a sympathetic religious culture (Calvinist protestantism always found a natural home in urban, educated merchant classes). The doyen of exile printers was the Estienne family, Paris masters who now produced for Calvin some of the most technically perfect books on the European scene.

For the printers, this enabled them to return to, and compete for, business in their old markets without physically returning from exile. For Calvin, it aroused the dream of a religion without physical boundaries, a congregation without limits. From his sermons on the text of Scripture he constructed commentaries on the whole Bible, ready to interpret God for anybody willing or able to read. Principal of all his books was the *Institutio Christianae religionis*, concerning (as it declared in the opening sentence) the entirety of 'the knowledge of God and of ourselves' (Calvin 1960: i. 35). This summary of Christian doctrine was first published in 1536 and was revised and expanded throughout Calvin's life, at first in Latin and then from 1541 also in the purest and coolest French.

It was Calvin's ambition to recreate a universal church of the book. In this sense Geneva was not so much the location of his evangelical mission as its colophon. As a first step he addressed a Preface to 'son prince et souverain seigneur' King François I of France pleading for an end to religious persecution and a reformation of the church in line with Christ's truth (Calvin 1957–63: i. 27). This is not (he declares like revolutionaries before and after) a new church, but the old rediscovered in its proper guise. When he first wrote these words in August 1535 (before he arrived in Geneva) he may have had some realistic hope of converting the French nation; with every passing edition the reprinting of the same words must have sounded more piously optimistic. Although reformed Collèges were formed in Bordeaux and elsewhere, and reformist views penetrated urban classes in some cities, and parts of the gentry (including the King's sister Marguerite de Navarre in their ambit), Calvin's

France remained obstinately orthodox. Indeed, Marguerite regarded her views as evangelically Catholic rather than in any way heterodox. It was largely the same story in Italy, where the views of the so-called *illuminati* remained within the bounds of the church—indeed in some cases the leading members of such groups (such as Gasparo Contarini) were also members of the Papal Curia.

The English Reformations and the Crisis in Europe

For political reasons religion in England was exposed to different forces. At first, Henry VIII encouraged his bishops in an active campaign to extirpate any signs of the Lutheran heresy, and even signed his name to a refutation of Luther's ideas on the sacraments. In due course, the great matter of the king's divorce from Catherine of Aragon encouraged a different approach to theology, as proofs were sought to justify the sovereignty of the English monarch over religious affairs. Thomas Cranmer, who was one of Henry's researchers, suddenly found himself archbishop of Canterbury as he eased through the theological niceties that allowed both the king's new marriage to Anne Boleyn and the Act of Supremacy in 1534.[7] While Anne used her influence to encourage the appointment of her evangelical clients to vacant bishoprics, Cranmer dabbled with learned enthusiasm in Continental Reformed doctrine. His long correspondence with Bucer in Strasburg began in 1531. Meanwhile writings previously regarded as dangerously seditious began to be tolerated, sometimes by peculiar routes. William Tyndale, who had first sought (and was refused) permission from Cuthbert Tunstall, the humanist bishop of London, to translate Scripture in 1523, worked in secret (pursued by Henry's agents) in Germany and the Low Countries for the rest of his life (Daniell 1994: 83–7). But Queen Anne owned a copy of his revised New Testament of 1534 and when Cranmer with Thomas Cromwell, the vicegerent of spiritual matters, decided to promote an official English Bible (the Great Bible of 1539), large portions of Tyndale's work were silently included. Protestant writers faced continual threats of persecution throughout the 1530s (Tyndale himself was caught and executed abroad in 1536) but their books were beginning to have influence. Other writers in the circle of Anne and of Cromwell, such as the humanist courtier and poet, Sir Thomas Wyatt, bear the traces of this new theology.

   Yet it was by no means clear that England was poised to embrace the Protestant line wholeheartedly. At an earlier stage in his reign Henry had endorsed Sir Thomas More's campaign as chancellor against heresy. More combined a zealous programme of persecution with a wary attachment to the humanist ideals of his youth. His

---

[7] Cranmer became archbishop late in 1532 and Anne became queen in 1533. See MacCulloch (1996: 75–6, 79–97).

collaborator from the halcyon days of *Utopia* (1516), Erasmus, now occupied an ambiguous position in contemporary religious debate. Erasmus's satires of a corrupt clergy and papacy, and his championing of new methods of theology against the scholastic rule were considered by conservatives to be precursors of Lutheranism. Yet the Lutherans equally suspected him of lukewarm time-serving in the cause of the gospel. More (at least in the quiet of his own mind) tried to keep the two principles— reform in method but unswerving obedience to the authority of the Church in doctrine—in balance, but cracks were appearing throughout Catholic Europe. Reginald Pole, another of the king's faithful servants, left for exile over the regal divorce. Once in Italy, Pole became associated with Contarini (both were noblemen) and through him with a Spanish refugee, Juan de Valdés. Valdés developed a theology of a personal encounter with grace through faith. His followers, who were known as the *spirituali*, numbered prominent members of the Roman aristocracy such as Vittoria Colonna; Colonna was an intimate friend of Michelangelo, now at work on the Last Judgement in the Sistine Chapel.

Valdés's ideas led in different directions. Two of his acolytes, Bernardino Ochino and Pietro Martire Vermigli, became leading lights in their religious orders (the Capuchins and the Augustinians) before breaking off into Protestant sects, leading them into northern Europe and for a time to England. Valdés himself was suspected by the Inquisition—perhaps correctly—of enjoying Luther's writing a little more than was good for him, although his own version of spiritual progress was not radically predestinarian as Luther's and Vermigli's became. Pole warned Colonna of the importance of maintaining the doctrine of the church, but he, too, was attracted by the modern slant of the *spirituali*, and the heady mix of humanist erudition and personal salvation they enjoined. Paul III made cardinals of Pole, Contarini, and Giovanni Pietro Carafa in 1535 (along with Bishop John Fisher, whom Henry VIII promptly made a martyr). In 1537 Pole, Contarini, and Carafa jointly formed a commission which published a report *De emendanda ecclesia* and looked forward to a General Council of the church to resolve the issues of the new theology and to reshape Christianity for a modern world (MacCulloch 2004: 213–18).

What lay in common between reforming ideals in both Catholic and Protestant camps was a commitment to personal piety, an attraction to humanist learning and bookish devotion, and a suspicion or distaste for a religion exclusive to an insular and sometimes corrupt clergy. If in northern Europe this sometimes led to outright rebellion against the church, in the south it could just as easily result in the revival or creation of reformed religious orders. These had something in common with late-medieval trends; after all, Erasmus was brought up in the traditions of the *Devotio Moderna*, and Luther belonged to the reformist wing of the German Augustinians. The Italian equivalents were the Oratories. The most spectacular of these developments was the Society of Jesus, under the peculiar aegis of Ignatius Loyola, a Spanish nobleman and former soldier. The movement was formally founded in 1540 with the help of Contarini, who had followed a course of Loyola's *Spiritual Exercises*.

England continued to be caught between these different axes of the European crisis in religion for generations, and experienced a greater volatility of religious polity than almost any other nation. As a result, religion in England claimed a particularly ambiguous role in the construction of identity, since every group at some point found itself branded as heretical and therefore also potentially as treasonable. Just as easily it could find itself back on top. At each of these movements of policy there was an intellectual migration, as persecuted minorities moved across the channel and encountered the latest ideas. Bucer from Strasburg and Ochino and Vermigli from Italy became the mentors of Edwardian evangelicalism at Cambridge and Oxford, then their books were burned under Mary. Pole returned from Rome to be archbishop of Canterbury, but no sooner was his counter-reformation spirituality in fashion than it was out again. The Protestant exiles of the 1550s came back with a vengeance, bringing Geneva home with them. Now it was the Catholics who went underground or abroad to Italy, northern France, or the Spanish Netherlands; they re-emerged as Jesuits.

A spectacularly charismatic movement with a mission to live out in the world a highly individualized and literate theology, the Jesuits had more in common than might be thought with their Protestant opposite numbers. For a while, there were even attempts at a rapprochement across the religious divide. At Regensburg in 1541 Contarini on the one side, and Bucer on the other—with even England seeking representation in the form of Stephen Gardiner, a leading conservative in Henry's national church—were among those commissioned to seek a basis for reconciliation. At first good will seemed to be prevailing, and some agreement was found on justification, Luther's sticking point. But on the subject of the mass and of the sacrament of confession the participants got nowhere. To some relief both in Rome and Wittenberg, peace did not break out. Instead a clearer sense of difference emerged. Ochino shuffled off in disappointment to Zurich, Vermigli to Strasburg. Carafa, soon to become Pope Paul IV, declared his complete vindication at this defection of the *spirituali*. He himself had always said they were just Protestants in disguise. Meanwhile, the Jesuits, also Carafa's bugbears, attached themselves more forthrightly to the interests of orthodoxy; as the 1540s drew to a close, they discovered their *métier*: the confutation of heresy and the promulgation among the laity of confession and the mass. It was the Jesuits who later came to set the agenda for a proposed Catholic revival in England in defiance of all heresy. When the Council of Trent finally convened for the first of its sessions in 1545, a few months before the death of the first and greatest Protestant of them all, Luther, its mission was set in stone: to restate more vigorously than ever obedience to a single truth of doctrine.

THEOLOGY AND LITERARY HISTORY

To the extent that the Reformation has registered in histories of literature and literary method, influence has been measured in terms of a history of ideas. English literature is seen as the beneficiary, or otherwise, of religious change in a number of isolated authors. Sometimes the effect is seen to be for the worse (Fox 1989: 209–31). Henrician evangelicals such as Tyndale, Miles Coverdale, John Frith, and Robert Barnes hardly figure in older studies, and when they do are seen as instinctively suspicious of literary effects, anti-humanist and literal-minded to a fault. This simply repeats the polemical satire of More that his Protestant enemies were stupid as well as malicious. Yet More hardly fares better in such accounts: whereas the younger More is regarded as a figure of humanist irony and sensitivity, the post-Reformation More, embroiled in controversy and persecution, is seen as a fugitive from imaginative fiction. The religion of other court humanists such as Wyatt and the Earl of Surrey has also received short shrift. Wyatt, whose Lutheran language in the penitential psalms has already been noted, is usually contrasted with Surrey, who was from a conspicuously Catholic family. Yet in both cases this is felt to be irrelevant to their literary careers, which are safely secular, humanist, and Petrarchan in character.

Such a bias tells us more about twentieth-century literary studies than it does about those of the sixteenth century. The first correction to make here is that while humanism may (eventually) lead in the direction of cultural secularization, it does not result from it. Erasmus, to take only the most famous example, began his study of Greek authors precisely to gain access to the original words of scripture (Cummings 2002: 102–11). His most celebrated work was an edition of the New Testament in Greek (1516) with a whole volume attached of theological as well as philological interpretation. From one of the prefaces to this work he constructed a new statement of hermeneutic method, the *Ratio verae theologiae*, as important a manifesto in the history of literary theory as it is in the history of theology. His educational, grammatical, and rhetorical works, such as *De recta pronuntiatione* and *De copia*, while they excoriate the principles of scholastic method, do so not in the interests of removing literary study from the arena of religion but rather making it all the more central. His most widely read book, the *Moriae encomium*, is a polemical justification of the benefits of literature in transforming European piety and religious learning.

Erasmus was read with forensic intensity on all wings of the religious debates of the 1520s. There were reasons for each opposed camp to claim him as an ally (whether as a forerunner of Protestant ideas or as ultimately a champion of orthodoxy against Luther in *De libero arbitrio*) but it was more common for both sides to consign him to the enemy. Erasmus's theological writing is crucial to an understanding of the century, but not only because of its content. Indeed, it is as true for the Reformation in general as it is for Erasmus individually that developments in literary process influence religious debates as much as the other way around.

Many futile attempts have been made to align Erasmus with a particular confessional identity. Yet such attempts may miss completely his relevance to the relationship of theology and literature in the sixteenth century, and to the history of literature in general. Erasmus has been kidnapped by traditional literary history to impose a secular model on the development of vernacular literatures. In England, an Erasmian literary method has been conflated with a Petrarchan literary practice as a way of establishing a line from Wyatt and Surrey through the Elizabethans, beginning with Sir Philip Sidney and Edmund Spenser, towards the courtly and classicized poetry of the early Stuarts surrounding Ben Jonson, and on to Andrew Marvell and John Dryden before and after the Restoration. The literature of the public theatre, including most of all the master of them all, Shakespeare, is tacked onto this narrative as belonging to a similar humanist tradition. The concerns of this literature are assumed to be overwhelmingly secular, and only accidentally religious. A separate tradition has been understood to exist of devotional literature, written (it seems) for separate people, and requiring (in modern literary histories) separate chapters to expound them. This is the case even when an author, such as John Donne, writes in both spheres: an extraordinary typological division has been imposed, splitting his life in two. Only an acknowledged genius, in the case of John Milton, has escaped; yet even then, the interpretative history of *Paradise Lost* has become isolated as a result.

To a remarkable degree, this narrative held sway in very different schools of literary interpretation on both sides of the Atlantic in the twentieth century. Since 1980, and the publication of Stephen Greenblatt's *Renaissance Self-Fashioning*, a new set of literary theories (feminist, psychoanalytic, anthropological, post-structuralist, deconstructionist) has held sway in the name of a new form of historicism applied to early modern literature (Greenblatt 1980). Yet the model of *literary* (as opposed to political) history has largely, and uncritically, followed the familiar one of humanist revival and secular triumph, displayed in a canon of authors (above all, Shakespeare) that has remained astonishingly static and conservative. Religion has been the ugly duckling of the New Historicism as much as it was of the New Criticism. Greenblatt's book anticipated this by endorsing the canon of Wyatt, Marlowe, Spenser, and Shakespeare. Yet it also contained the intimation of a different approach in its initial chapters devoted to two central figures of the early Reformation, More and Tyndale. These chapters took as their point of departure the history of the printed book and the vernacularization of Scripture. Although the rest of the book failed to take up this challenge, Greenblatt opened up the possibility of a quite different account of the history of early modern literature in which religion plays a central part.[8]

In such a context it takes a religious historian, Patrick Collinson, in *The Cambridge History of Early Modern English Literature*, to point out that around two-thirds of all the items in the *Short Title Catalogue* of English books between 1475 and 1700 are religious (Collinson 2003: 374–98). What are the consequences of this for a history of literature? Are we really to infer (as we might from a glance at the syllabuses of modern English departments) that religious books were produced for a different community of readers, living as if in a different culture? Studies of publishing, bookselling, and book ownership have shown that this is, of course, not the case. Wills and inventories, among the gentry and the university educated, but also among the middling sort in cities and towns, show eclectic tastes. This is a reading public absorbing what we would class as both secular and sacred reading, controversial or pietistic prose mixed with literary fiction or drama. Many of the most popular books of the age were religious, beginning of course with the Bible. The Geneva Bible of

---

[8] Greenblatt (2001), takes up interests left to one side in 1980.

1560, which included contentious and highly theological annotations, became from the 1580s onwards (with revised notes by the Oxford Puritan Laurence Tomson in the case of the New Testament) one of the most widely owned and read books in English literary history. Shakespeare must have owned one at least from the 1590s, and read some of the notes as well as the text (Shaheen 1987: 28). Although works of theology were much less widely read than moral, devotional, or catechistical material, theological issues were part of everyday life (Green 2000). Far more than the theatre (so often lauded by misty-eyed modern critics as the voice of popular London) the open air arena of Paul's Cross was the literary and ideological forum of Tudor and Stuart life, with crowds of several thousands attending sermons throughout the year. Many of these sermons were on highly explosive and recondite matters, such as predestination, election, or the Christian mass.

While different genres of writing have their own distinctive history and identity, the lines of division in the literary world of post-Reformation England do not form in the ways we might expect. Traditional literary history has sometimes missed this point because of the lacuna that has built up between the reigns of Henry VIII and of Elizabeth. New work on the Edwardian and Marian Reformations has shown that Tudor religion was much more literary than previously thought, and that Tudor literature was intricately caught up in religious controversy (Betteridge 2004: 87–173). Religious polemic was commonly presented in the form of verse or dialogue or drama. Robert Crowley, for example, is known to literary history as the first printer of *Piers Plowman* in 1550. He also wrote a large body of poetry himself, including epigrams, satires, and political poems. In 1551 he was ordained, and after the reign of Mary he reappeared later in Elizabethan England as an old-fashioned supporter of the new vanguard of Puritanism. William Baldwin, who like Crowley worked in printing (he assisted Edward Whitchurch, the publisher of the first Book of Common Prayer in 1549) was the author of a complex and ambiguous fiction entitled *Beware the Cat*. Written in 1553 but not published until 1570, Baldwin provides a link between Erasmus and the Elizabethans that has otherwise proved so elusive.

Marian writing has received even less attention than Edwardian, and has suffered from the inevitable stereotype of reactionary conservatism. However, it now appears that Marian literature was part of a serious programme of political and religious reform, which has been obscured by the historical accident of Mary's early death. Miles Hogarde, a prolific writer in prose and verse, attempted to apply the principles of Pole's reforming humanism (Pole was now of course archbishop of Canterbury and the papal representative at the English court) to roll back the evils of the Protestant heresy. He did this both by means of polemic—as in the prose work *The Displaying of the Protestants*—and in revising and reforming some of the techniques of late-medieval devotion, as in his poem *The Path waye to the towre of perfection*, which combines dream vision, allegory, and the confessional style of Thomas More's late works (Betteridge 2004: 150–64).

Restoring the energy of the religious Reformations to a history of English writing is an important means of enabling both a more continuous interpretation of the passage from fifteenth- to sixteenth-century literature and an analysis of the differences. Richard Tottel's anthology of *Songs and Sonettes* has long been seen as an epochal moment in English literature, as a representative moment of Renaissance renewal and an inauguration of the secular triumph that leads to the Elizabethan sonneteers and especially to Shakespeare himself. In this story the date of the work has appeared almost coincidental. Yet 1557 was the apogee of Marian reform, and also (not coincidentally) the height of the Marian persecution. Tottel's miscellany, it can now be appreciated, is a conscious attempt to appropriate the poetic masters of Henry's reign—principally Wyatt and Surrey—in the interests of a new historical order. The book is therefore both deliberately nostalgic for the literary genres of the pre-Reformation past, yet at the same time polemically voguish in its theme of literary renewal and revival. By one of the ironies of history, within a year Mary was dead and her sister inherited the throne in order to reinstitute a Protestant hegemony. Tottel's book was therefore reappropriated for the new literary regime and, instead of being the model for a counter-reformation aesthetic, fed into the literary self-projection of Protestants and Puritans, beginning with those most political of Protestant writers, Sidney and Spenser.

THEOLOGY AND LITERATURE

Religion was the maker and breaker of political order throughout the sixteenth and early seventeenth centuries in Britain. Theology in turn was the language in which political ideas were tested and the main source of political controversy, the scene both of brittle enforcement and seditious fantasy. Rather than seeing literature as a free space beyond the personal and public agonies of religious change, it is more realistic to see the enormously rich literary production of the end of the sixteenth and beginning of the seventeenth centuries as part of a world in which words mattered intensely for exactly these reasons. Tottel's first printing project after the accession was a literary celebration of Elizabeth's entry into London. It contained an image of the Marian martyrs redeeming the sins of England's Babylonian captivity and an allegorical pageant glorifying the new Protestant order. Yet it soon became apparent that the Elizabethan order required a more complex cultural ideology if it was to survive. The sixteenth century produced a legacy of anxieties and disorders concerning religious practice which left their mark on all aspects of social and cultural everyday life. So far I have suggested ways in which the linear history of English literature might be reinterpreted via the Reformations. In this last section I will briefly suggest some of the theological topics which consumed and transformed the literary imagination.

Luther's early theology was embroiled with the issue of justification. While the revolutionary nature of Luther's inwardness has been exaggerated—subjectivity is crucial to late-medieval piety as well as to late-medieval literature—it is easy enough to see how Luther's doctrinal imagination provided a crucial vocabulary for the articulation of subjectivity later in the century. Luther's intensely verbal methods for investigating individual faith provided a model both for literary interpretation (in his concentration on the semantics of the biblical texts) and for self-analysis and self-presentation. Wyatt's Psalms are an early example of the effect of this way of thinking in English, and at the same time of how a medieval mode of devotion could be assimilated to new pressures. Yet it is a mistake to see this in narrowly confessionalized terms, or to apply too dogmatic an interpretation to the theology involved. In responding to the demands of Protestants for a sophisticated language of the self, Catholic theology proved equally adept at turning inward. The spirituality of the Jesuits, beginning with Ignatius's *Spiritual Exercises* (itself one of the most influential books of the century) reinterpreted the modes of penitence and the confessional to create a language of subjectivity of extraordinary improvisatory power. The implications of both these modes of thinking (Lutheran or Ignatian) for literature are only beginning to be realized.

In the first decades after Henry's break with Rome, as policy on religion raged back and forth, the fiercest points at issue turned out to be rather different. On the one hand, evangelicals stressed the importance of the vernacular in relation to Scripture and liturgy. Conservative opponents—perhaps encouraged in their inhibition by the weight of English experience of the Lollard heresy—viewed the vernacular with often violent suspicion (Cummings 1999: 821–51). The suppression of the vernacular, in the form of Arundel's Constitutions of 1409, had a long history. To a degree not found in Germany, the capacity of the vernacular to embody religious value remained a conflict for years. Censorship laws went back and forth on questions such as marginalia, annotation, and interpretation.

What this conflict reveals is a deeper uncertainty about sacred meanings. If traditional Catholics showed their solidarity with orthodoxy by doubting the ability of English words to do the work of prayer or blessing or the institution of the mass, Protestants showed their scepticism with orthodoxy by doubting the interaction of words and things altogether. Such complex issues as the real presence can only briefly be handled in a short survey. Many Protestants—such as Luther—remained relatively conservative on the issue of the mass. Yet when Luther wrote *hoc est corpus meum* in chalk on a table at Marburg in 1529 and proceeded to argue about the nature of metaphor with Zwingli, he showed his usual genius for finding the point on which agreement could not easily be made. Protestants argued about the sacrament of the eucharist as much with other Protestants as with Catholics. Under Henry as well as Mary, this was the issue most likely to lead to trial for heresy.

We are inclined now as literary historians to attempt to resolve these questions in doctrinal terms, and much effort has been spent in identifying the positions of different factions. Such factions matter to the personal biography of many Tudor individuals, including writers. Yet underlying both dispute and violent punishment is an anxiety which is much more immediately relevant to the history of literature. The mass involved problems of signification and linguistic meaning which were beyond the capacity of any single commentator or theologian to resolve.

It is in this light that we need to approach one final theological controversy of the sixteenth century, concerning the ultimate destiny of the believer. Predestination is not the easiest idea to explain to a modern reader, perhaps especially to a modern English student. The idea of eternal damnation prescribed as the inevitable destiny of souls who have not yet lived or even been conceived is, shall we say, hard to sell in a commercial, materialist, and permissive society. Yet here again we have lost sight of the ways that Calvin's thought touched a contemporary nerve. Predestination involved a total explanation for the world, and appeared to give the believer access to an ineluctable logic. It exposed, even as it attempted to alleviate, the sense of loss experienced through the decline (in Protestant England) of the doctrine of purgatory and the cult of the dead. It explained the faults in other people or other societies with grim exactitude; and to the self it offered rigorous questioning and testing. Those who adhered to the doctrine also felt the benefits of solidarity with co-believers combined with an equally satisfying alienation from those beyond the group.

From a literary point of view, predestination is again more than a doctrine, it is a way of looking at the world. It offers both a key to interpreting the texts of Scripture, and just as crucially, a way of generating narratives in relation to the self and history (Cummings 2002: 283–7, 396–417). Just as concepts of fate and destiny, differently constructed, created the fabric from which Greek mythology and tragedy could be elaborated, so theories of providence and predestination offered the Tudor and Stuart imagination complex ways of understanding time and causation. In the intervening centuries the idea of predestination has been parodied to the point of crudity, but to see the gravity and immediacy of the idea we need look no further than three masterpieces of English sixteenth- and seventeenth-century literature: *Doctor Faustus, Hamlet,* and *Paradise Lost.* The version of determinism in each work is different, but in each work the individual spectator or reader is confronted with a vision of mortality and uncertainty that is profoundly disturbing. It would not be possible for any of these works to be constructed in the way they are without the intervening medium of the post-Reformation language of theology.

WORKS CITED

BETTERIDGE, TOM. 2004. *Literature and Politics in the English Reformation.* Manchester: Manchester University Press.

BRECHT, MARTIN. 1985. *Martin Luther: His Road to Reformation 1483–1521.* Philadelphia: Fortress.

CALVIN, JEAN. 1957–63. *Institution de la religion chrétienne,* ed. Jean-Daniel Benoît. 5 vols. Paris: Vrin.

—— 1960. *Institutes of the Christian Religion,* ed. J. T. McNeil, trans. F. L. Battles. 2 vols. Philadelphia: Westminster.

CAMERON, EUAN. 1991. *The European Reformation.* Oxford: Oxford University Press.

COLLINSON, PATRICK. 2003. 'Literature and the Church', in David Loewenstein and Janel Mueller (eds.), *The Cambridge History of Early Modern English Literature.* Cambridge: Cambridge University Press.

CUMMINGS, BRIAN. 1999. 'Reformed Literature and Literature Reformed', in David Wallace (ed.), *The Cambridge History of Medieval English Literature.* Cambridge: Cambridge University Press, 821–51.

—— 2002. *The Literary Culture of the Reformation: Grammar and Grace.* Oxford: Oxford University Press.

DANIELL, DAVID. 1994. *William Tyndale: A Biography.* New Haven: Yale University Press.

DICKENS, A. G. 1967. *The English Reformation.* Rev. edn. London: Collins.

—— 1974. *The German Nation and Martin Luther.* London: Arnold.

DUFFY, EAMON. 1992. *The Stripping of the Altars: Traditional Religion in England, 1400–1580.* New Haven: Yale University Press.

—— 2001. *The Voices of Morebath: Reformation and Rebellion in an English Village.* New Haven: Yale University Press.

FLOOD, JOHN L. 1998. 'The Book in Reformation Germany', Jean-François Gilmont (ed.), *The Reformation and the Book.* Aldershot: Ashgate.

FOX, ALISTAIR. 1989. *Politics and Literature in the Reigns of Henry VII and Henry VIII.* Oxford: Blackwell.

GORDON, BRUCE. 2002. *The Swiss Reformation.* Manchester: Manchester University Press.

GREEN, IAN. 2000. *Print and Protestantism in Early Modern England.* Oxford: Oxford University Press.

GREENBLATT, STEPHEN. 1980. *Renaissance Self-Fashioning: From More to Shakespeare.* Chicago: Chicago University Press.

—— 2001. *Hamlet in Purgatory.* Princeton: Princeton University Press.

HAIGH, CHRISTOPHER (ed.) 1987. *The English Reformation Revised.* Cambridge: Cambridge University Press.

—— 1993. *English Reformations: Religion, Politics and Society under the Tudors.* Oxford: Clarendon.

MacCULLOCH, DIARMAID. 1996. *Thomas Cranmer: A Life.* New Haven: Yale University Press.

—— 1999. *Tudor Church Militant: Edward VI and the Protestant Reformation.* Harmondsworth: Penguin.

—— 2004. *Reformation: Europe's House Divided 1490–1700.* Harmondsworth: Penguin.

OBERMAN, H. A. 1989. *Luther: Man between God and the Devil.* New Haven: Yale University Press.

PETER, RODOLPHE, and GILMONT, JEAN-FRANÇOIS. 1991–2000. *Bibliotheca Calviniana: Les Œuvres de Jean Calvin publiées au XVIe siècle.* 3 vols. Geneva: Droz.

SCRIBNER, R. W. 1994. *For the Sake of Simple Folk: Popular Propaganda for the German Reformation.* Rev. edn. Oxford: Clarendon.

SHAHEEN, NASEEB. 1987. *Biblical References in Shakespeare's Tragedies.* Newark: University of Delaware Press.

FURTHER READING

ASTON, MARGARET. 1988. *England's Iconoclasts, i. Laws against Images.* Oxford: Clarendon.

COLLINSON, PATRICK. 1988. *The Birthpangs of Protestant England: Religious and Cultural Change in the Sixteenth and Seventeenth Centuries.* London: Macmillan.

KING, JOHN N. 1982. *English Reformation Literature: The Tudor Origins of the Protestant Tradition*. Princeton: Princeton University Press.

LEWALSKI, BARBARA. 1979. *Protestant Poetics and the Seventeenth Century Lyric*. Princeton: Princeton University Press.

MCEACHERN, CLAIRE, and SHUGER, DEBORAH. 1997. *Religion and Culture in Renaissance England*. Cambridge: Cambridge University Press.

MCGRATH, ALISTER E. 1999. *Reformation Thought*. 3rd edn. Oxford: Blackwell.

MARSHALL, PETER. 2002. *Beliefs and the Dead in Reformation England*. Oxford: Oxford University Press.

NEILL, MICHAEL. 1999. *Issues of Death: Mortality and Identity in English Renaissance Tragedy*. Oxford: Oxford University Press.

SCHOENFELDT, MICHAEL C. 1999. *Bodies and Selves in Early Modern England: Physiology and Inwardness in Spenser, Shakespeare, Herbert, and Milton*. Cambridge: Cambridge University Press.

SHELL, ALISON. 1999. *Catholicism, Controversy and the English Literary Imagination: 1558–1660*. Cambridge: Cambridge University Press.

SIMPSON, JAMES. 2002. *1350–1547: Reform and Cultural Revolution*. The Oxford English Literary History 2. Oxford: Oxford University Press.

WALKER, GREG. 2005. *Writing Under Tyranny: English Literature and the Henrician Reformation*. Oxford: Oxford University Press.

WALSHAM, ALEXANDRA. 1999. *Providence in Early Modern England*. Oxford: Oxford University Press.

CHAPTER 6

THE ENLIGHTENMENT

RHODRI LEWIS

1

IF one pauses to think about the Enlightenment, it is usually in terms of the 'age of reason'—the triumph of the modern, secular, and scientific over the variously antiquated, irrational, and superstitious practices which held sway in European society and thought until the eighteenth century. Despite the fact that the very term 'Enlightenment' comes from the German *Aufklärung*, it is a movement that is usually considered to have had French as its mother tongue. Its chief protagonists are taken to be Voltaire, Diderot, d'Alembert, and the cohort of *philosophes* who gathered together in Paris to pour the cold water of scepticism on commonly received ideas about religion, philosophy, and politics. Reason was their credo, and as discussions of divinity were by definition supra-rational, they had little time for theology. Their chief organ was the *Encyclopédie* (published between 1751 and 1772), a work whose very title gives an idea of the universal applicability that the *philosophes* took reason to have, but fails to hint at the herds of sacred cows slaughtered within its thousands of pages. On this account, the aim of the Enlightenment was to wake reason from its centuries of slumber. In so doing, it would usher in an age in which humankind could recognize its proper position in the world and cosmos for the first time, then reform its beliefs and habits accordingly. Indeed, the opposition of Enlightenment thought to the *ancien régime*, or old order of political, philosophical, social, and religious ideas, is often cited as a cause of the French Revolution—just as, to a lesser extent, it is seen to underpin the American Revolution that preceded the events of 1789. In its turn, the French Revolution is taken to be a sort of accelerated image of the Enlightenment, banishing the dead hand of the church and monarchy, and marking the authentic beginning of a secular and egalitarian modernity.

The Enlightenment, then, does not seem to have been the friend of either religion or theology. Britain did not have a revolution and did not have self-styled *philosophes*; it also opposed, with its armies, the march of progress in both France and the fledgling United States. Bearing both these points in mind, it is legitimate to ask: what possible use is there in considering the impact of Enlightenment theology on English literature? Leaving on one side the thought that 'Enlightenment theology' looks suspiciously like an oxymoron, the very question seems divided against itself. To be sure, it is easy to comprehend a Scottish Enlightenment (think of David Hume and Adam Smith), and England certainly came to have its philosophical and political radicals (consider Thomas Paine's *Rights of Man*, or the young Wordsworth celebrating the new 'dawn' marked by the French Revolution), but the Enlightenment itself would appear to have been a European something from which most of the British Isles was insulated by the sea, roast beef, and a distrust of big ideas.

As is so often the case, the simpler the question, the more difficult it can be satisfactorily to answer it. It will not be surprising to learn that things were, in fact, more complicated and far more interesting than this. In the course of this essay, I hope to explain why. This will involve investigating: (1) the meaning and usefulness of the term 'Enlightenment'; (2) the origins and evolution of British Enlightened thought, which emerged a number of decades *before* that of France or Scotland; (3) the animating role of theological debate, controversy, and speculation within this. It will become clear that there was such a thing as a British, and specifically English, Enlightenment, and that far from being religiously iconoclastic, it was characterized by deep theological commitment. Crucially, it considered itself no less Enlightened for this. I make no claims to treat of the entirety of either British or European Enlightened thought, but only to consider aspects of the British Enlightenment that are touched by theological concerns. Finally, I will sketch some aspects of the relationship between British Enlightened thought and literature. This was in no sense the product of one-way traffic, with works of literature simply responding to and reflecting the theological and philosophical preoccupations of the age. Rather, at a time in which books (be they textbooks, novels, plays, poems, or sermons), periodicals (such as Addison and Steele's *Spectator*) and other printed materials were more widely available and read than ever before, literary texts came both to shape and to animate the whole gamut of Enlightened thinking. (For useful overviews of the British Enlightenment, see Porter 2000; Himmelfarb 2004.)

2

'In the beginning was the Word'. The famous phrase with which John's gospel opens is of particular resonance here because the 'Word' in question translates the Greek term *logos*, which also denotes 'reason'. And reason, as the text of Proverbs 24: 27 (a favourite text of many Enlightenment and proto-Enlightenment philosophers and theologians) has it, is 'the candle of the Lord'. The rational faculties are innate to all humankind, and through their proper exercise it is possible to shed valuable light on the natural world, human nature, morality, and the providence of God. The things revealed in this light would, it was held, complement the truths revealed in sacred Scripture, and came to be known as 'natural religion'. This is best understood as the ability to know something of God, and of properly ethical behaviour, without the benefit of revelation, or of the divine *logos* on which the Christian religion was founded. The metaphor of human reason as a tool with which to illuminate the universe was a powerful one, and it is precisely this that lies at the heart of the notion of an 'Enlightenment'.

This notwithstanding, the term 'Enlightenment' as understood in the context of this chapter has rather a messy genealogy. Echoing a usage current in eighteenth-century France, d'Alembert, writing in the preface to the *Encyclopédie* (1751), remarked on the 'century of enlightenment' (*siècle de lumières*) in which he wrote. Outside France, however, the term gained currency only very much later. In 1784, the Berlin Academy invited debate on the question, 'What is Enlightenment [*Aufklär-ung*]?', and one of those to answer the challenge was the philosopher Immanuel Kant. It was only when his essay was translated into English in 1798 that the term entered the English language. Even then, it was not commonly used in its current sense until the early twentieth century. (See Schmidt 1996; 2003.) In England, rather, the term was adjectival. English writers discussed, with the polymathic Dissenter and theorist of light, Joseph Priestley, the virtues of an 'enlightened age' (Priestley 1782: ii. 467), while Edmund Burke was even able to use the term ironically in lamenting the 'patriotic crimes of an enlightened age' in his 1790 *Reflections on the Revolution in France* (Burke 1986: 166). As will become clear below, the implications of this go beyond lexicographical curiosity, and are suggestive of a tradition of English thought that was interested in the pursuit of a form of reason far closer to that of Proverbs than to that embraced by the French *philosophes*. That said, the term 'Enlightenment' *does* remain a convenient shorthand with which to denote the activities of those writers, philosophers, scientists, and theologians who inhabited the 'age of reason'. If we are careful not to use the term narrowly to describe the activities and aspirations of the Parisian *philosophes*, then little harm can come of it. Nevertheless, while stylistically ungainly, it is closer to the truth to think of several discrete 'Enlighten-ments', occupying distinct but overlapping intellectual spheres.

3

The Parisian Enlightenment, far from speaking to eternity of the neglected but universal truths of rationality, justice, and human freedom, was a response to the peculiar tensions of French political and religious history. Ideas never emerge from a historical vacuum, and to demonstrate what I mean, a brief historical digression is necessary. Despite decades of religious conflict, most notoriously represented by the 1572 St Bartholomew's Day massacre, Henri IV had granted French Protestants toleration, and protection, with the 1598 Edict of Nantes. But such liberal policies were anathema to the most powerful of Henri's successors, Louis XIV. This most absolutist of monarchs took the expression of his will to be the only legitimate basis of government, and modestly liked to be referred to as the 'Sun King' (not so much Enlightened, as The Light). Louis could not admit any form of free discussion or dissent, and disliked the idea that anyone might answer to a God who did not have his royal seal of approval. In 1685, he revoked the Edict of Nantes, driving French Protestants (largely Huguenots) into exile in England, the Netherlands, and Switzerland. Likewise, throughout his reign he persecuted the Jansenist order—whose prominent members included Blaise Pascal and the Port-Royal philosophers—as a threat to the rigorously hierarchical Gallican church he wished to impose. By 1710, he had disassembled their monasteries, and with Papal connivance the Jansenists were banished in 1713. The point to make here is that, in its oppressive determination to stifle free debate and any form of theological enquiry, the policies of Louis XIV's Gallican church account almost entirely for the anticlerical and anti-theological animus of the *philosophes* who are traditionally thought of as the standard-bearers of the Enlightenment. Since the pious dogma of the church was instrumental to the repressive intellectual and political climate in which the *philosophes* found themselves, they were naturally in opposition to both it and its teachings. Britain, however, had a very different experience of institutionalized religion, and it is here that the origins of the British Enlightenment lie.

It need hardly be said that one of the reasons England was different was the very fact of its Reformation, and the existence of the Anglican Church. Although a strain of Calvinism—most obvious in the growth of Puritanism, but given wider licence by the 1618 Synod of Dort—became the dominant doctrinal position within the Church of England, this began to be questioned in the last decade of the seventeenth century. Richard Hooker's *Of the Laws of Ecclesiastical Polity* (the first five volumes of which were published during 1593–7, the last three in 1648 and 1661) is the classic expression of these views. At once identifying himself with the tolerationism of Erasmus and founding a new tradition of liberal Anglican thought, Hooker sought to emphasize the role of the individual in bringing about his own salvation through the use of reason to contemplate Scripture, God, and the world. In so doing, he was seeking to counterbalance the bleak orthodoxies of Calvinist anthropology, in which thinking reasonably was viewed as a 'carnal' sin leading inexorably to human pride. Hooker also argued strongly against any form of theocratic government (of the sort found in Calvinist Geneva), proposing that the church be integrated within the civil law of the commonwealth. Hooker's views exerted a great deal of influence in the seventeenth century, principally through William Chillingworth, the so-called 'Great Tew circle' of thinkers, and Edward, Lord Herbert of Cherbury. It would, however, be a mistake to view this proto-Enlightened pattern of thought as an exclusively English tendency, as Protestant writers from continental Europe—principally from Huguenot France and the Netherlands—also played a key role in its development. The most important of these include Philippe Duplessis-Mornay, Jacobus Arminius, and Hugo Grotius. Indeed, by the beginning of the eighteenth century, British Enlightened thinkers were part of a pan-European Protestant Enlightenment; one specifically opposed, after the dispersal of the Protestants from France in 1685, to the implications of Gallican religious, intellectual, and political tyranny.[1] The crucial point to take from this is that while the Parisian Enlightenment was driven to secularism by its anti-Catholicism, the Reformation had opened up discursive channels which enabled the Protestant Enlightenment to take place *within* the bounds of traditional theological debate. (See Trevor-Roper 1967; Tyacke 1987.)

4

The religious conflicts of the mid-seventeenth century—on the European canvas, the Thirty Years War; on the English, the Civil Wars—offered short shrift to such doctrinally liberal thought, and it was not until after the Restoration of the monarchy and Church of England in 1660 that it began fully to come of age in England. Motivated in large part by opposition to the heat and intemperance of much theological discourse in the 1640s and 1650s, the emergence of a 'Latitudinarian' party of theologically and ecclesiologically broad-minded clergymen was crucial to this development. Influential early Latitudinarians included John Wilkins, Benjamin Whichcote, Edward Stillingfleet, and the future archbishop of Canterbury, John Tillotson. However, while their brand of rational religion was advanced in theologically sophisticated terms from the early 1660s onwards, they did not find themselves on the right side of church politics until after the 1688 Glorious Revolution, and the accession of William and Mary to the throne. (See McAdoo 1965; Rivers 1991–2000.) John Locke was much influenced by their thought, and his *The Reasonableness of Christianity as Delivered in the Scriptures* (1695), while sparking a good deal of controversy, came to be amongst the most influential expressions of rational religion. If religion is the practice of reverence towards God, then theology is the enquiry into the doctrines and rules on which this practice is based. For Locke, the relationship between the two is intrinsically related: the practice of using reason for the purpose of theological enquiry is essential to the proper worship of God. As he had expressed it towards the end of his *An Essay Concerning Human Understanding* (1690):

---

[1] Consider, e.g., the way in which the intellectual world-views of John Locke and Edward Gibbon were informed by the long periods that they spent in contact with Protestant scholars and thinkers. In Locke's case, this was the result of his political exile in Amsterdam for most of the 1680s; in Gibbon's, through his immersion in the scholarly culture of Swiss-Calvinist dissent in Lausanne. (See Pocock 1999.)

Reason is *natural Revelation*, whereby the eternal Father of light, and Fountain of all Knowledge, communicates to Mankind that portion of Truth which he has laid within the reach of their natural Faculties: *Revelation* is natural *Reason* enlarged by a new set of Discoveries communicated by GOD immediately, which *Reason* vouches the Truth of, by the Testimony and Proofs it gives, that they come from GOD.   (Locke 1975: 698)

Theology, furthermore, is the master-discipline which Locke and his followers used both to structure and to give meaning to their entire philosophical endeavour. By 1759, William Warburton could remark uncontroversially that 'Locke is universal'. This Enlightened success was largely owing to the efforts of popularizers such as the Dissenting educationalist Isaac Watts. His *Logick: or the Right Use of Reason in the Enquiry after Truth* (1725) distilled Locke's writings in textbook form for ease of consumption by a broader audience, and went through more than twenty editions by the end of the eighteenth century. (Rivers 1991–2000; Locke 2002.)

The rational theologians sought to downplay the fundamentally fallen nature of humankind central to Calvinist doctrine (with its concomitant belief that redemption was only possible through grace), and emphasized the freedom of human beings in determining their own salvation. Central to this freedom was the proper exercise of human reason. This was understood in two different but complementary ways: (1) in the sense immediately familiar to us, as to do with the ratiocinative faculties, the fullest possible exercise of which was deemed to be crucial to understanding the universe in which we live; (2) as 'right reason', the innate moral sense of right and wrong (something like conscience), the exercise of which was essential to living a virtuous life. These two concepts of reason, with all that they entail, came to dominate the English, and British, Enlightenment. They demand to be unpacked in a little more detail.

In the first case, reason has a twofold significance: first, in that it could only be common to all human beings through the agency of their Creator, then it is *ipso facto* proof that God exists; second, in that it allows for the proper comprehension of the universe, then it provides humankind with the opportunity to honour God through becoming learned readers of the book of nature. In other words, the proper exercise of reason allowed for what is known as the 'argument from design': the rational study of nature reveals the laws and inherent order underpinning it; without a divine author, these could not exist; therefore, God exists. This pattern of argument was central to many justifications of science in the long eighteenth century (*c.*1690–1830), as to learn more about nature was to learn more about God's power and—as this power is subject to the laws he has created to govern nature—virtue. The arguments of natural philosophers such as Robert Boyle and John Ray assumed a greater importance in the English intellectual milieu after the foundation of the Royal Society in 1660. Many of its members were Anglican clergymen as well as scientists, and—just as Locke did—saw their differing pursuits as aiming at a common end: truth and the greater glory of God. As Thomas Sprat, later bishop of Rochester, had put it in his polemical *History of the Royal Society* (1667), given that the 'universal Disposition of the *Age* is bent upon a *rational Religion*' (Sprat 1667: 374), then natural philosophy should be seen as the ally of any theologian seeking to combat Puritan enthusiasts, Roman Catholics, and/or atheists.

The only problem with this was that despite the advances in learning that had been made since the Renaissance—advances that had made increasingly apparent the obsolescence of received systems of natural philosophy—scientists were not confident in proposing a theory of how it was that nature worked. As expressed in the agreeable hyperbole of Alexander Pope's (1978: 651) couplet, however, a solution soon presented itself:

> Nature and Nature's Laws lay hid in Night.
> GOD said, *Let Newton be*! and All was Light.

Isaac Newton published his *Philosophiae naturalis principia mathematica* (*The Mathematical Principles of Natural Philosophy*) in 1687, and his *Opticks* in 1704. Both revolutionized the way in which it was possible to think about nature. Although Newton made no claim to knowledge of final causes (he was, he said, an experimental rather than hypothetical philosopher), he offered a compelling account of the forces holding the universe together. Most importantly, he had deduced the law of universal gravitation, in which every particle of the universe was attracted to every other particle with a force varying directly as the product of their masses, and inversely as the square of their distances. Gravity could only be a power emanating from God, and was evidence of his goodness in regulating the operations of the universe. Newton's theory was thus able to accommodate theology, experimental science, and mathematics in a simple but powerful conceptual framework. The implications of this were not lost on theologians or natural philosophers, and when Robert Boyle endowed a series of Royal Society lectures, Newton's admirers Richard Bentley, Samuel Clarke, and William Whiston—along with works such as William Derham's *Physico-Theology* (1713)—all gave powerful accounts of natural religion indebted to the Newtonian theologico-philosophical synthesis. While it generally conquered all before it, the Newtonian view of the universe did not go unchallenged: leaving aside the question of Newton's well-hidden but heretical religious views (including a thoroughgoing disbelief in the Trinity), it was attacked by the German philosopher Gottfried Wilhelm Leibniz for proposing a 'clockwork' world in which God's only function was to wind up the mechanism when appropriate. These criticisms echoed those of the more conservative and mystical members of the Church of England. Nevertheless, Leibniz was effectively answered by Samuel Clarke, and by the 1730s, the Newtonian world-view had become one of the hallmarks of Enlightened (and enlightened) thought. (See Manuel 1974; Jacob 1976; Westfall 1980; Dobbs and Jacob 1995; Feingold 2004.)

If the use of reason was key to understanding the book of nature, however, it was also to be deployed in reading the book of scripture, the Bible. Building on the work of Renaissance biblical scholars (themselves employing critical methods and standards stretching back to the Church Fathers Origen and Augustine), Enlightened students of Scripture began to propose that traditional interpretations of Scripture were based either on corrupt textual readings or on the deliberate imposition of church doctrines on the sense of the biblical text. It was held that the interpretation of the Bible should concentrate on the philosophical and rational nature of Scripture, with doctrine elaborated from this, not vice versa. The history of the world as given in the Bible was brought into disrepute both in terms of its detail and chronology (the question of the origin of language was particularly vexed), while biblical miracles and prophecy were increasingly understood as something which could not have been literally true. Thomas Hobbes, Isaac La Peyrère, and Baruch (or Benedict) de Spinoza were the immediate parents of this rationalist tradition, and it was furthered by the works of the French scriptural scholars Jean Le Clerc and Richard Simon—which were quickly translated into popular English editions. The influence of these writers was pervasive (not least on Locke and Newton), but it was in the writings of John Toland, Anthony Collins, and Thomas Woolston that the new method of biblical study was given its most penetrating English voice. Collins's *Discourse of the Grounds and Reasons of the Christian Religion* (1724) goes as far as suggesting that traditional interpretations of the Bible depended on wilful wrong-headedness. The stakes were high: in 1696, a 20-year-old student called Thomas Aikenhead was hanged in Edinburgh. His crime? The blasphemy of doubting that Moses wrote the first five books of the Old Testament.

Jonathan Swift was no friend to Enlightened—or 'freethinking'—scholarship. However, one of his attempts to skewer what he took to be the dangerous absurdity of such views (in *Mr Collins's Discourse of Free-Thinking* (1713)) gives a particularly clear account of the issues in question:

The Priests tell me I am to believe the *Bible*, but *Free-thinking* tells me otherwise in many Particulars: The *Bible* says, the *Jews* were a Nation favoured by God; but I who am a *Free-thinker* say, that cannot be, because the *Jews* lived in a *Corner* of the Earth, and *Free-thinking* makes it clear, that those who lived in *Corners* cannot be Favourites of God. The *New Testament* all along asserts the Truth of Christianity, but *Free-thinking* denies it; because Christianity was communicated but to a few; and whatever is communicated but to a few, cannot be true; for that is like *Whispering*, and the Proverb says, that there is no Whispering without Lying. (Swift 1939–69: iv. 30)

Those who would desacralize biblical study would come in for many more attacks, not all of them as witty as Swift's. Nevertheless, by the end of the century, the Oxford Professor Robert Lowth would be delivering his *Lectures on the Sacred Poetry of the Hebrews* (1787). Far from being the ultimate source of spiritual truth, the Bible had become an object of literary investigation. (See Frei 1974; Rossi 1984; Force and Popkin 1994.)

The notion of 'right reason' might seem harder to get a handle on than that of reason in its most obvious sense. This needn't be the case. John Milton, writing in his unpublished manuscript treatise, 'On Christian Doctrine', expresses its meaning and importance clearly: 'Further evidence for the existence of God is provided by the phenomenon of conscience, or right reason ... if there were no God, there would be no dividing line between right and wrong' (Milton 1953–82: vi. 132). While subtly reinforcing the argument from design then, the doctrine of right reason (which was also referred to as that of 'common notions', 'truths of natural inscription', or 'first principles') was taken as the basis of Latitudinarian ethical thought. Humankind had an instinctive moral faculty, and virtuous behaviour resulted from the proper exercise of it, rather than from obeying the dictates of impassioned clergymen—a key biblical text in this respect was inscribed by Paul, in Romans 2: 14–15. The most powerful Enlightened expression of this view comes in the work of Anthony Ashley Cooper, third earl of Shaftesbury, by which time right reason had come to be known as either 'moral sense' or 'common sense'. There are three chief aspects to Shaftesbury's moral theory as expressed in his *Characteristicks of Men, Manners, Opinions, Times* (1711). First, as we have seen, are the innate notions of right and wrong, the natural tendency of human beings to sympathy and to moral sentiment, expressed as politeness. (This can, at times, look like an ethics of good breeding.) Second, the emphasis on education—this natural faculty does not always operate of its own accord, and needs to be encouraged through discipline and reflection, particularly in those who are less well-bred. Third, the aesthetic—the moral sense is a bit like aesthetic good taste, the faculty through which we decide what is beautiful, and what is ugly. (See Cooper 1999: 167–92; Rivers 1991–2000: i. 62–6, ii. 114–52; Klein 1994.) Moreover, as the emphasis on politeness and sympathy implies, for Shaftesbury virtue is social and, when expressed as benevolence or charity, is the key to a cohesive society: 'Virtue is the good, and Vice the ill of everyone' (Cooper 1999: 170). Shaftesbury's views were extremely influential. After his death in 1713, they were prominently propagated by Frances Hutcheson, Joseph Butler, Richard Price, and—in their most nuanced terms—in Adam Smith's *Theory of Moral Sentiments* (1759). They bequeathed to the eighteenth century its characteristic language of sentiment, sympathy, and sociability. (See Mullan 1988; Rivers 1991–2000: ii. 153–237.)

These two senses of reason were not seen by all Enlightened thinkers as equally valid. Locke, for instance, fully repudiated the suggestion that there might be innate moral truths impressed on human consciousness (Locke 1975: 65–84), and believed that morality could be realized only through the properly rational study of nature, human nature, and—for those with the benefit of Christian revelation—Scripture. The moral faculty, like the cognitive faculty, was naturally a *tabula rasa*, only inscribed through experience, proper guidance, and wisdom. As phrased in his *Reasonableness of Christianity*: 'The same spark of the Divine Nature and Knowledge in Man, which making him a Man, shewed him the Law he was under as a Man; Shewed him also the way of Attoning the merciful, kind, compassionate Author and Father of him and his Being, when he had transgressed that Law' (Locke 2002: 190). Newton went even further than this, and claimed that morality itself could be better understood through a fuller grasp of the natural world. Towards the end of his *Opticks*, he proposed that: 'If natural Philosophy in all its Parts, by pursuing of this Method [i.e. Newton's], shall at length be perfected, the Bounds of Moral Philosophy will also be enlarged' (Newton 1952: 405). Understanding the ways of nature is a part of our duty to (and further reveals our duty *towards*) God, but also makes plain our moral duties to ourselves and to one another. In their different ways, for Locke, Newton, and many others in their wake, the moral law is to be discovered by looking outside ourselves (up at the heavens, perhaps) rather than by looking directly within. Even when human beings and their beliefs are the subject of study, they are to be looked at as philosophical objects, rather than as innately virtuous subjects.

Not every Enlightened thinker, however, shared such views. Pope's *Essay on Man* (1733)—a philosophical poem in heavy intellectual debt to the thought of Pope's hero, Henry St John, Viscount Bolingbroke—is typically pithy. Imagining a number of angels beholding the goings on of humankind down on earth, Pope (1978: 251) describes how:

> Superior beings, when of late they saw
> A mortal Man unfold all Nature's law,
> Admir'd such wisdom in an earthly shape,
> And shew'd a NEWTON as we show an Ape.
>   Could he, whose rules the rapid Comet bind,
> Describe or fix one movement of his Mind?
> Who saw its fires here rise, and there descend,
> Explain his own beginning, or his end?
> Alas what wonder! Man's superior part[2]
> Uncheck'd may rise, and climb from art to art:
> But when his own great work is but begun,
> What Reason weaves, by Passion is undone.

Pope portrays a version of Enlightened thought which emphasizes the potential of human knowledge, but which is circumscribed by a proper sense of what this can reasonably be expected to achieve. Rather than contemplating the cosmos with a view to determining the lineaments of either God or morality, Pope suggests that 'The proper study of Mankind is Man' (Pope 1978: 250). In so doing, Pope not only echoes Bolingbroke, but foreshadows much criticism of Newtonian natural religion from within the Church of England. Mid-eighteenth-century Cambridge had a flourishing community of Lockeans, prominent amongst whom were Edmund Law, Joseph Clarke, and Daniel Waterland. They held that humankind should turn away from the attempt to rationalize God, as to do so would be both theologically and methodologically unsound. (See Gascoigne 1989; Young 1998.) Yet for all their differences, these various ideas of reason did coalesce in the attempt to provide a rational basis for the Christian religion. The argument is not that reason is not important in disputing theology—which, after Locke, is the intellectual master-subject, determining man's place in both the cosmos and society—any more than it is about relegating theology to the realm of the sub-rational. Rather, the arguments are about how *best* to deploy reason within theological dispute and reflection.

However, in the movement away from a Reformed religious belief that was underwritten by faith alone, there was no guarantee that reasonable thought would remain religious in any orthodox sense. To the consternation of many clerics and mainstream theologians, this turned out to be the case. Once reason had been admitted as the chief criterion for the interpretation of Scripture, a number of heretical views—long proscribed by the authority of the church—began to flourish. Socinianism and Arianism were chief amongst these, and sought to deny the divinity

---

[2] 'superior part' = rational faculties.

of Christ (and thus the coherence of the Trinity) at the same time as proposing the underlying truth of the Christian religion.

A closely related, but more extreme, version of such doctrines is usually considered under the heading of 'deism': the belief that the Christian religion as revealed in the Bible is misleading and redundant—that the only true theology could be *natural* theology. In discussing biblical scholarship above, we have already encountered Toland (who published his *Christianity not Mysterious* in 1696) and Collins; in concert with Matthew Tindal, they made names for themselves in taking the religious ideas of Locke and the Latitudinarians to what seemed their logical conclusions. Moreover, some of their ideas overlap very closely with those of Shaftesbury. As Tindal's *Christianity as Old as the Creation, or the Gospel a Republication of the Religion of Nature* (1730)—whose title gives more than a gentle nod towards what is comprised within its covers—has it: 'God, at all times, has given mankind sufficient means of knowing whatever he requires of them' (Tindal 1730: 7). Just as God had allowed human beings to determine for themselves what hurts and pleasures their bodies, so he had allocated them rational faculties for determining the good of their souls in reading the book of nature. Suggesting that the salvation of people's souls was in some sense dependent on a corrupt biblical text interpreted by corrupt and greedy churchmen was, Tindal held, nothing short of monstrous. This did not endear Tindal or his theological fellow-travellers to the Anglican hierarchy, and they drew fire from a wide range of critics, including Joseph Butler and the Newtonian apologist Samuel Clarke. But foremost amongst these was George Berkeley, philosopher and bishop of Cloyne. He referred to them as 'minute philosophers' (on account of their diminution of virtue and religiosity), and compiled a philosophical dialogue, *Alciphron* (1732), in which he sought comprehensively to rebut deist arguments. (See Rivers 1991–2000; Champion 1992.) Other Christian denominations opposed deism, despite which they went far beyond the attachment to natural religion evidenced in Anglican thought. In so doing, these rational Dissenters were exploiting the political freedom provided by the move away from the Calvinist theocratic model. If the Socinian heresy can be seen to have parented Unitarianism, then the entire Methodist movement, founded by John Wesley, can be seen in this rational light—as should both the theological and scientific works of Joseph Priestley. (See Haakonssen 1996; Schofield 1997.)

Collins, anticipating the responses the publication of his beliefs would provoke, pre-emptively regretted the shotgun blasts with which the orthodox tended to attack freethinkers: '*If any good Christian happens to reason better than ordinary, they presently charge him with Atheism, Deism, or Socinianism: as if good Sense and Orthodoxy could not subsist together*' (Collins 1713: 84). Collins protests the injustice of this, but such attacks were to some degree pertinent. Deism, Socinianism, and other heresies are considered above; more worrying for the theologian, however, is the threat of atheism.

As the orthodox suspected, by making religious belief subject to rational knowledge rather than to faith and adherence to Scripture, the door was opened to the falsifiability of religion. In other words, if belief in God depended on some version of the argument from design, then if one could prove the invalidity of the argument or the absence of a design, then there would be no reason to believe in God. Although Newton's theories seemed to have seen off the threat of overt atheism, natural religion was about to be attacked by an adversary from whose arguments it has not thus far recovered. This was the Scottish philosopher David Hume. Hume's first manoeuvre was to redefine reason as an instrumental, rather than innately virtuous, human attribute. As he famously phrases it in his *Treatise of Human Nature* (1739–40), 'Reason is, and ought only to be, the slave of the passions' (Hume 1978: 415). It is a subordinate intellectual tool, able to distinguish between conditions of truth and falsity, but not between right and wrong; it cannot thus be a source of morals. Hume then took his sceptical razor to the argument from design in the posthumously published *Dialogues Concerning Natural Religion* (1779): to seek the first cause of the world (i.e. God) was uncertain and useless, on account of the fact that the whole subject was 'beyond the reach of human experience', and therefore entirely conjectural. Better to suspend judgement, and move on to things that can usefully be comprehended and discussed; the Christian religion was a metaphysical hypothesis like any other. (See Hurlbutt 1965; Norton 1982; Rivers 1991–2000; Hunter and Wootton 1992.) In making religion dependent on the proper use of reason and/or right reason, the Enlightenment made it almost impossible to present a form of religious belief dependent on faith as anything other than the elevation of authority or convenience over intellectual truth. Without rational support, religious belief thus became indefensible. Of course, attempts to counterbalance the variously redefined claims of reason are not hard to find—any number of Evangelical revivals aside, certain aspects of Romanticism were an attempt to reassert the value of a religion of nature (secularized, and apprehended through the imagination rather than reason)—but the influence of religious scepticism is one of the most obvious legacies of Enlightened thought.

Viewed in this light, the British Enlightenment can, in retrospect, be seen to have been more the friend of philosophy than theology. But in positioning Hume towards the *end* of my discussion of British Enlightened thought, I am being deliberately provocative. Misleading, even, in that British clergymen and theologians dismissed Hume's ideas as irreligious (and therefore wrong), and would continue propounding 'common-sense' theories of natural religion well into the nineteenth century. However, what I do hope to have demonstrated is the fact that Hume belonged to very much the same generation as the Parisian *philosophes*, thereby pointing up two little-grasped facets of eighteenth-century thought. First, that the British Enlightenment occurred well before that in Paris. Second, and somewhat counter-intuitively, that it was the pious efforts of these English-speaking thinkers which opened up the intellectual space that made the rational iconoclasm of the *Encyclopédie* possible at all. (See Israel 2003.) Whether this was a good thing is a question that must be left to individual judgement. What it does clearly address is the absolute centrality of keeping an open and active historical mind when thinking about what the Enlightenment, or Enlightenments, actually were.

5

The interpenetrative nature of the relationship between Enlightened thought and literature in Britain is already clear from many of the examples used in the pages above. Although it is thus impossible to talk about the Enlightenment as if it were something impacting upon literary works from the outside, it remains to offer some suggestions as to how the Enlightenment, properly understood, influenced the development of English literature. Perhaps a little paradoxically, the most obvious literary legacy of the Enlightenment and its theology was not an idea at all: rather, it was the totemic figure of Isaac Newton, exegete of light. We have already seen his importance in Pope's work, and his name rapidly became a leitmotif combining a sense of the Enlightened comprehension of nature with that of the individual human struggle to master the world. The two parts of his historical character did not always sit easily together (witness e.g. William Blake's troubled relationship with Newton and his thought), but they would exert a literary magnetism that remained potent enough to draw in both Wordsworth and Coleridge. (See Wylie 1989; Feingold 2004.)

For the remainder of this chapter, however, I would like to return to ideas. In no sense is what follows a survey of English Enlightened literature; rather, I should like to provide several topics that might prove food for thinking further about the relationship between Enlightened theology and English literary writing.

It is tempting to view the increasing availability of printed works (be they of literature or anything else) across the long eighteenth century as a purely quantitative phenomenon—that cheaper production methods and economies of scale made hitherto exclusive works available to a broader social audience. As far as it goes, this is true. But it ignores the qualitative impact of print, which finally enforced the idea that literature was something read rather than heard. Consider, for instance, the mock-scholarly footnotes to Pope's *Dunciad* (1728, 1729, 1743); however euphonious the couplet it annotates, a footnote cannot be read aloud. Crucially, print culture also provided for the emergence of a new, and subsequently enduring, literary genre: namely, the novel. Its name is not misleading, for it was exactly this: a novel literary development, responsive to and reflecting the concerns of an Enlightened age. If neither morality nor the knowledge of God, the world, or ourselves was innate—if the self, after Locke, was a *tabula rasa*—then the novel was a literary form which represented the emergence of an at times anxious self-consciousness. Likewise, it was something in and through which an identity could be inscribed. In so doing, it owed much to seventeenth-century spiritual autobiography. From Daniel Defoe's *Robinson Crusoe* (1719) to Samuel Richardson's eponymous epistolary heroines *Pamela* (1740–1) and *Clarissa* (1748) to the abortive attempt at autobiography comprised in Laurence Sterne's *Tristram Shandy* (1759–67), the uncertainties of life and of selfhood were something to be worked out within the covers of this new literary medium. (See Watt 1957; McKeon 1987.)

The so-called 'sentimental' novel—hugely popular throughout the second half of the eighteenth century—was the most emphatic embodiment of these tendencies. In these works, feeling—seen as coterminous with sentiment, sympathy, spontaneity, and sincerity—was the guiding light of protagonists struggling within a heartless world. Whether or not these protagonists prevail within the action of novels they inhabit (and very often, they do not), their integrity and moral status as exemplary human beings is manifest. Throughout, their language and patterns of thought bear the clear stamp of Shaftesbury. Richardson's *Pamela*, *Clarissa*, and *Sir Charles Grand-ison* (1754) set the tone for the sentimental novelists, and were followed by innumer-able other works. In additions to Sterne's writings, two of the most prominent of these were Oliver Goldsmith's *Vicar of Wakefield* (1764) and Henry Mackenzie's *The Man of Feeling* (1771). As Richardson put it, the authenticity of his characters' experiences is vouchsafed by their writing 'to the moment', or as soon as their feelings became apparent to them. The sentimental vogue was given further impetus by journals such as the *Lady's Magazine* (which ran from 1770 to 1832), which in turn points to a key aspect of much early novelistic culture: its feminization. Not only did these novels prioritize a distinctly feminine form of virtue, but they were read most significantly by women and, most significantly, marked the first time that female authors—including Charlotte Lennox, Sarah Fielding, Charlotte Smith, Maria Edge-worth, and Mary Hays—were able effectually to shape moral debates and practices. (Perhaps even more revealingly, many male authors took a female *nom de plume* in publishing their works.)

The role of fiction in inculcating public virtue is in fact central to the emergence of the novel. If morality lay within, in discovering and making use of one's innate sense of right and wrong, then the novel sought to teach the existence of these universal truths through literary examples. This position was theorized in manuals such as the *Lectures on Rhetoric and Belles Lettres* (1783) of Hume's friend Hugh Blair, a hugely popular work which would go through a great many editions by the mid-nineteenth century. It is thus no accident that those hostile to the increasing ambitions of the novel saw it as undermining the role played by the printed sermon and as a corrupting influence on the young, particularly upon young ladies. It would be hard to describe Henry Fielding as a sentimentalist—for instance, his *Shamela* (1741) remorselessly parodies Richardson's lachrymose virtue—but in the publica-tion of *Tom Jones* (1749) he too showed himself committed to the propagation of new and socially improving notions of human behaviour. Fielding was also a magistrate actively involved with a series of social reforms taking the idea of charity as their cornerstone, and his literary endeavours can be seen as of a piece with these in terms of their motivation. (On the previous two paragraphs, see Todd 1986; Dwyer 1987; Mullan 1988; Barker-Benfield 1992.)

But literary novelty did not have it all its own way any more than the novel did. A case in point is the heated debate on the relative merits of ancient and modern authors that began in the mid-1690s and rumbled along for another forty years. Dubbed the 'Battle of the Books' by Swift (in the preface to his *A Tale of a Tub* (1704)), its combatants argued about whether or not the modern age could see further than antiquity, in so doing advancing the competing critical claims of reason and author-ity, learning and taste. The essence of the quarrel lies in the opposition between the Newtonian natural theologian and classical scholar Richard Bentley on the one hand, and literary wits such as Swift and Pope on the other. Bentley believed that classical texts could be improved by modern philological scholarship, which appar-atus—just as would happen when they were applied to sacred Scripture—often undermined received critical opinion. Those entering the lists on behalf of the ancients took a directly opposite view, holding that ancient texts were to be both venerated and imitated in the attempt to develop a suitably polite and civilized standard of literary discourse. Rather than annotating and altering the sense of classical literary texts, then, it was needful to make them more accessible to the taste of the contemporary reading public. It was in this spirit that Pope completed his translations of Homer's *Iliad* (1715–20) and *Odyssey* (1725–6) in easily digestible rhyming couplets. As Bentley would remark, these made for a 'pretty' poem, but had little to do with Homer. Their popularity, however, was enormous. The diver-gence between these two approaches was writ yet larger when it came to editing English classics, including Shakespeare and Milton. Lewis Theobald, an admirer of Bentley's critical methods, deployed the whole range of philological scholarship in producing a superb edition of Shakespeare's works, only for Pope to produce a popular edition of his own (of negligible scholarly value). Adding insult to injury, Pope then pilloried him as the pitiably dull 'Tibbald' of the *Dunciad*. (See Levine 1991.) Here then, we see the beginnings of a duality in literary studies that remains with us today: literary texts, like literary criticism, should be both acute and access-ible, but when forced to compromise between these two qualities, where should the editor or critic trim?

More importantly for a better understanding of the Enlightenment, this also marks the decoupling of the two kinds of reason that characterize English Enligh-tened thought. The ratiocinative faculties cherished by Bentley were of little use to a milieu in which right reason—transformed into the language of aesthetic taste, style, and civility—was the *sine qua non* of literary achievement. Shaftesbury had tri-umphed over Locke and Newton. Burke's *Philosophical Enquiry into the Origin of our Ideas of the Sublime and the Beautiful* (1757) both usefully amplifies this point and provides a convenient terminus for this essay. In it, Burke asserts the primacy of the imagination, passions, and senses in both aesthetic appreciation and creation, adding that this is simply the exercise of a 'sentiment common to all mankind' (Burke 1999: 63). In so doing, Burke identifies himself with a recognizable facet of Enlightened thinking, but also heralds the end of this variously rational tradition, at least within the literary sphere. Literature, like theology, showed itself to be something that could not bear too much rationality. Thus, at the same time as he attempted to stake a claim as a good Enlightenment man, Burke allows us retrospectively to discern that the seeds of Romanticism had already been sown. The literary mind would no longer profess to be a (divinely lit) rational mirror of the world or of the self, but would begin to conceive of itself as something that had to generate its own light—a light that would be generated not by reason, but by the imagination.

WORKS CITED

BARKER-BENFIELD, G. J. 1992. *The Culture of Sensibility: Sex and Society in Eighteenth-Century Britain*. Chicago: University of Chicago Press.

BURKE, EDMUND. 1986. *Reflections on the Revolution in France*, ed. Conor Cruise O'Brien. Harmondsworth: Penguin.

—— 1999. *A Philosophical Enquiry into the Sublime and Beautiful, and Other Pre-Revolutionary Writings*, ed. David Womersley. Harmondsworth: Penguin.

CHAMPION, JUSTIN. 1992. *The Pillars of Priestcraft Shaken: The Church of England and its Enemies, 1660–1730*. Cambridge: Cambridge University Press.

COLLINS, ANTHONY. 1713. *A Discourse of Free-Thinking*. London: [no printer].

COOPER, ANTHONY ASHLEY (Third Earl of Shaftesbury). 1999. *Characteristics of Men, Manners, Opinions, Times*, ed. Lawrence E. Klein. Cambridge: Cambridge University Press.

DOBBS, BETTY JO TEETER, and JACOB, MARGARET. 1995. *Newton and the Culture of Newtonianism*. Atlantic Highlands, NJ: Humanities Press.

DWYER, JOHN. 1987. *Virtuous Discourse: Sensibility and Community in Late Eighteenth-Century Scotland*. Edinburgh: John Donald.

FEINGOLD, MORDECHAI. 2004. *The Newtonian Moment: Isaac Newton and the Making of Modern Culture*. New York: Oxford University Press.

FORCE, JAMES A., and POPKIN, RICHARD H. (eds.) 1994. *The Books of Nature and Scripture: Recent Essays on Natural Philosophy, Theology and Biblical Criticism in the Netherlands of Spinoza's Time and the British Isles of Newton's Time*. Dordrecht: Kluwer.

FREI, HANS W. 1974. *The Eclipse of Biblical Narrative: A Study in Eighteenth- and Nineteenth-Century Biblical Hermeneutics*. New Haven: Yale University Press.

GASCOIGNE, JOHN. 1989. *Cambridge in the Age of the Enlightenment: Science, Religion and Politics from the Restoration to the French Revolution*. Cambridge: Cambridge University Press.

HAAKONSSEN, KNUD (ed.) 1996. *Enlightenment and Religion: Rational Dissent in Eighteenth-Century Britain*. Cambridge: Cambridge University Press.

HIMMELFARB, GERTRUDE. 2004. *The Roads to Modernity: The British, French and American Enlightenments*. New York: Alfred A. Knopf.

HUME, DAVID. 1978. *A Treatise of Human Nature*, (ed.) L. A. Selby-Bigge and P. H. Nidditch. Oxford: Clarendon.

HUNTER, MICHAEL, and WOOTTON, DAVID (eds.) 1992. *Atheism from the Reformation to the Enlightenment*. Oxford: Clarendon.

HURLBUTT, ROBERT H., III. 1965. *Hume, Newton, and the Argument from Design*. Lincoln: University of Nebraska Press.

ISRAEL, JONATHAN I. 2003. *Radical Enlightenment: Philosophy and the Making of Modernity 1650–1750*. Oxford: Oxford University Press.

JACOB, MARGARET C. 1976. *The Newtonians and the English Revolution, 1689–1720*. Hassocks: Harvester.

KLEIN, LAWRENCE E. 1994. *Shaftesbury and the Culture of Politeness: Moral Discourse and Cultural Politics in Early Eighteenth-Century England*. Cambridge: Cambridge University Press.

LEVINE, JOSEPH M. 1991. *The Battle of the Books: History and Literature in the Augustan Age*. Ithaca: Cornell University Press.

LOCKE, JOHN. 1975. *An Essay Concerning Human Understanding*, ed. Peter H. Nidditch. Oxford: Oxford University Press.

—— 2002. *Writings on Religion*, ed. Victor Nuovo. Oxford: Clarendon.

McAdoo, Henry R. 1965. *The Spirit of Anglicanism: A Survey of Anglican Theological Method in the Seventeenth Century*. New York: Charles Scribner & Sons.

McKeon, Michael. 1987. *The Origins of the English Novel*. Baltimore: Johns Hopkins University Press.

Manuel, Frank E. 1974. *The Religion of Isaac Newton*. Oxford: Clarendon.

Milton, John. 1953–82. *The Complete Prose Works of John Milton*, ed. Don M. Wolfe et al. 8 vols. New Haven: Yale University Press.

Mullan, John. 1988. *Sentiment and Sociability: The Language of Feeling in the Eighteenth Century*. Oxford: Clarendon.

Newton, Isaac. 1952. *Opticks; Or, A Treatise of the Reflections, Refractions, Inflections and Colours of Light*, ed. I. Bernard Cohen et al. New York: Dover.

Norton, David F. 1982. *David Hume: Common-Sense Moralist, Sceptical Metaphysician*. Princeton: Princeton University Press.

Pocock, J. G. A. 1999. *Barbarism and Religion*, i. *The Enlightenments of Edward Gibbon, 1737–1764*. Cambridge: Cambridge University Press.

Pope, Alexander. 1978. *Complete Poetical Works*, ed. Herbert Davies. Oxford: Oxford University Press.

Porter, Roy. 2000. *Enlightenment: Britain and the Creation of the Modern World*. London: Penguin.

Priestley, Joseph. 1782. *A History of the Corruptions of Christianity*. 2 vols. Birmingham: J. Johnson.

Rivers, Isabel. 1991–2000. *Reason, Grace and Sentiment: A Study of the Language of Religion and Ethics in England, 1660–1780*. 2 vols. Cambridge: Cambridge University Press.

Rossi, Paolo. 1984. *The Dark Abyss of Time: The History of the Earth and the History of Nations from Hooke to Vico*. Chicago: University of Chicago Press.

Schmidt, James (ed.) 1996. *What is Enlightenment? Eighteenth-Century Answers and Twentieth-Century Questions*. Berkeley: University of California Press.

—— 2003. 'Inventing "the Enlightenment": Anti-Jacobins, British Hegelians and the *Oxford English Dictionary*'. *Journal of the History of Ideas* 64: 421–43.

Schofield, Robert E. 1997. *The Enlightenment of Joseph Priestley: A Study of his Life and Work from 1733 to 1773*. Philadelphia: Pennsylvania State University Press.

Sprat, Thomas. 1667. *The History of the Royal Society of London*. London: John Martyn.

Swift, Jonathan. 1939–69. *The Prose Works of Jonathan Swift*, ed. Herbert Davis et al. 16 vols. Oxford: Blackwell.

Tindal, Matthew. 1730. *Christianity as Old as the Creation; Or, the Gospel a Republication of the Religion of Nature*. London: Wilford.

Todd, Janet. 1986. *Sensibility: An Introduction*. London: Methuen.

Trevor-Roper, Hugh R. 1967. 'The Religious Origins of the Enlightenment', in id., *Religion, the Reformation and Social Change*. London: Macmillan.

Tyacke, Nicholas. 1987. *Anti-Calvinists: The Rise of English Arminianism, 1590–1640*. Oxford: Clarendon.

Watt, Ian. 1957. *The Rise of the Novel: Studies in Defoe, Richardson and Fielding*. London: Chatto & Windus.

Westfall, Richard. 1980. *Never at Rest: A Biography of Isaac Newton*. Cambridge: Cambridge University Press.

Wylie, Ian. 1989. *Young Coleridge and the Philosophers of Nature*. Oxford: Clarendon.

Young, Brian W. 1998. *Religion and Enlightenment in Eighteenth-Century England: Theological Debate from Locke to Burke*. Oxford: Clarendon.

FURTHER READING

FEINGOLD, MORDECHAI. 2004. *The Newtonian Moment: Isaac Newton and the Making of Modern Culture.* New York: Oxford University Press.

FREI, HANS W. 1974. *The Eclipse of Biblical Narrative: A Study in Eighteenth- and Nineteenth-Century Biblical Hermeneutics.* New Haven: Yale University Press.

ISRAEL, JONATHAN I. 2003. *Radical Enlightenment: Philosophy and the Making of Modernity 1650–1750.* Oxford: Oxford University Press.

LEVINE, JOSEPH M. 1991. *The Battle of the Books: History and Literature in the Augustan Age.* Ithaca: Cornell University Press.

LOCKE, JOHN. 2002. *Writings on Religion,* ed. Victor Nuovo. Oxford: Clarendon.

MCKEON, MICHAEL. 1987. *The Origins of the English Novel.* Baltimore: Johns Hopkins University Press.

MANUEL, FRANK E. 1974. *The Religion of Isaac Newton.* Oxford: Clarendon.

MULLAN, JOHN. 1988. *Sentiment and Sociability: The Language of Feeling in the Eighteenth Century.* Oxford: Clarendon.

PORTER, ROY. 2000. *Enlightenment: Britain and the Creation of the Modern World.* London: Penguin.

RIVERS, ISABEL. 1991–2000. *Reason, Grace and Sentiment: A Study of the Language of Religion and Ethics in England, 1660–1780.* Cambridge: Cambridge University Press.

TREVOR-ROPER, HUGH R. 1967. 'The Religious Origins of the Enlightenment', in id., *Religion, the Reformation and Social Change.* London: Macmillan.

YOUNG, BRIAN W. 1998. *Religion and Enlightenment in Eighteenth-Century England: Theological Debate from Locke to Burke.* Oxford: Clarendon.

CHAPTER 7

ROMANTICISM

SCOTT MASSON

'Romanticism' is notoriously difficult to define, but not so much because of the ongoing scholarly debates about its period or its politics. It is because a resistance to definition to a certain extent defines it. This resistance is inherent in the ephemeral trajectory that Romanticism casts as its path. Romantic writing characteristically strives to transcend all bounds, all definition. As the German poet Novalis explained to his readers: 'By investing the commonplace with a lofty significance, the ordinary with a mysterious aspect, the familiar with the prestige of the unfamiliar, the finite with the semblance of infinity, I thereby romanticise it' (Furst 1980: 3). One of his contemporaries and perhaps the principal Romantic theorist, Friedrich Schlegel, succinctly defined it as 'a progressive universal poetry' (ibid. 4). He explained it by contrast with foregoing types: 'Other types of poetry are complete and can now be wholly analysed. Romantic poetry is still in the process of becoming; this indeed is its very essence, that it is eternally evolving, never completed . . . It alone is infinite, just as it alone is free, recognizing as its prime law that the poet's caprice brooks no law' (ibid. 5) Shelley employed similar terms, though like Wordsworth he saw no break between the poetry of his own age and that of the past. For Shelley, all poetry tended to progressive universality: 'All high poetry is infinite; it is the first acorn, which contains all oaks potentially' (1965: vii. 131).

Another of its most important features appears in the midst of the contrast Friedrich's brother A. W. Schlegel made between the 'fixed' classical forms and themes of writing and the romantic. He connected the new class of poetry to an anthropological development, as if a new race of spiritual human being had evolved for whom the Romantic poet assumed a prophetic voice: 'The whole play of vital motion hinges on harmony and contrast. Why should this phenomenon not also recur on a grander scale in the history of mankind? Perhaps in this notion the true key could be found to the ancient and modern history of poetry and the fine arts.

Those who accepted this have invented for the particular spirit of modern art, in contrast to ancient or classical, the name "romantic"' (Furst 1980: 33). In this contrast Schlegel expressed the standard opinion of his contemporaries that the ancients, particularly the Greeks, had articulated a grand but essentially static vision of human nature. While the Romantics much admired the vision, they considered it impossible to revert back from their own sentimental age to its *naïveté* (the descriptions 'naive' and 'sentimental' were those of the influential poet, dramatist, and historian Friedrich Schiller). Nor was there reason for considering the Greeks' static views superior. On the contrary:

Among the Greeks human nature was self-sufficient; it was conscious of no defects, and strove for no other perfection than that which it could actually attain through its own powers. A higher wisdom teaches us that mankind, through a great transgression, forfeited the place to which it was originally destined, and that the whole aim of its earthly existence is to strive to regain its lost possession, which it can never achieve on its own...So the poetry of the ancients was the poetry of possession, ours is that of longing.   (Furst 1980: 33–4)

This narrative of loss has Christian overtones. Yet with its high claim to creativity, Romanticism's 'longing' to overcome discord and fragmentation suggests that human redemption and eschatological fulfilment on earth lay within the power of the artist. The Romantic narrative is not simply one of Messianic fulfilment though, for its belief in the 'natural' benefit of organic creative *processes* to society indefinitely forestalls any such conclusion. In fact, in its basic tendency to reject order and harmony as a sign of unenlightened, 'naive' thinking, Romanticism also opposed the authoritative and the orthodox, in form and content, in literature and theology. The reason lay in its alternative explanation for what Schlegel called humanity's 'great transgression'. As T. E. Hulme (1924: 117) explains, rather than adhering to the Christian doctrine of original sin, the Romantics were schooled by Rousseau that

man was by nature good, that it was only bad laws and customs that had suppressed him. Remove all these and the infinite possibilities of man would have a chance. This is what made them think that something positive could come out of disorder, this is what created all religious enthusiasm. Here is the root of romanticism: that man, the individual, is an infinite reservoir of possibilities; and if you can so rearrange society by the destruction of the oppressive order then these possibilities will have a chance and you will get Progress.

It will be necessary to explore these characteristics of Romanticism in greater detail to get a fuller picture.

ROMANTICISM AND THE ENLIGHTENMENT

The Romantic Movement emerged at different times in different countries during a period spanning roughly from the mid-eighteenth to the mid-nineteenth century. Although the exact period is debatable no one disputes the existence of the phenomenon. The marks of Romanticism can be found wherever the Enlightenment was embraced, and often most strongly where it was. The Enlightenment tends to be associated with eighteenth-century France, but we can see some of its characteristics in seventeenth-century England, and it certainly dominated the thinking of the American revolutionaries. In common, they viewed absolute monarchy as dangerous and evil and rejected orthodox Christianity. (See, on the Enlightenment, Ch. 6, by Rhodri Lewis, above.)

In terms of religious belief, Enlightenment thinkers tended towards a heresy called deism. They maintained a functional idea of God as a first principle, a giver of 'laws' by which the universe was ordered and could thereby be understood. In pursuing the idea of natural revelation, they also rejected the church's claim that God had revealed himself to humanity in the Bible, seeing that traditional claim as a 'naive' if not vulgar expression of what could be more clearly ascertained through the use of reason. What was new about this was the postulate of autonomy attached to reason, or 'pure reason' as Immanuel Kant called it. In the concept of autonomy, literally the 'law of the self', reason made a radical departure from any and all 'external' forms of authority. It made its turn inward and to the infinite, as Hulme suggested, in the name of progress.

As was readily apparent in the appeal it made to the infinite, Romanticism represented a sort of continuation of Enlightenment ideology. Yet it often under-stood itself in more or less explicit opposition to it for one important reason. A thinker of the Enlightenment characteristically espoused a belief in progress through the use of science and reason, eschewing all traditional teaching, particularly that of the church, as 'unexamined prejudices'. The Romantics, for whom Rousseau is probably the first representative, deplored such principled detachment. After all, some of the chief ills of social prejudice were isolation, exclusion, and alienation. While they hardly supported the church, they emphasized the importance of an 'organic' connection to the world, and thus tended to assert the continuing validity of what was old and, more importantly still, original, and that included the trappings of Christendom.

In this emphasis, it is important to note that the Romantics retained the Enlight-enment's prejudice against prejudice; they simply regarded its practice of reason as the clearest manifestation of prejudiced thinking. It is for this reason that William Wordsworth in his Romantic manifesto *Preface to Lyrical Ballads* (1800) was unwill-ing to engage in the 'selfish and foolish hope of reasoning the reader into an approbation' (Wordsworth and Coleridge 1963: 236) of his poems. He preferred to 'use a language arising out of repeated experience and regular feelings [which] is a more permanent and far more philosophical language than that which is frequently substituted for it by Poets, who think they are conferring honour upon themselves and their art in proportion as they separate themselves from the sympathies of men' (ibid 239–40). By connecting humanity with something 'prior to critical judgment' he intensified the Enlightenment's attack on prejudice, turning it against reason as well. This had a somewhat ironic consequence. By making out what he called the primal sympathies of our 'nature', i.e. the provenance of the heart, to be a higher court than reason, the provenance of the mind, he put them beyond rational criticism (or dispute), while also making feelings the judge of all things. They thereby became absolutely authoritative in a way that no monarch could ever have hoped to be. And since they brooked no external opposition, the priesthood of the believer replaced the priesthood of all believers.

ROMANTICISM'S SECULAR THEODICY

It was through feeling that the Romantics made the otherwise incongruous alliance between the infinite, their simulacrum of God, and the natural. This alliance functions in what the critic M. H. Abrams has aptly described as Romanticism's 'secular theodicy'. The term theodicy was coined by the German philosopher G. W. Leibniz in 1710 for his argument justifying the goodness of God in the face of the reality of the suffering and evil in the world which appears to repudiate it. In Romantic writing, it appears in the play of natural origins within its common narrative of a fall from innocence, only to be recovered through the redemptive power of poetry.

While Romanticism thus largely departs from Leibniz's attempt to do this on behalf of the Christian faith—the great poet and critic Samuel Taylor Coleridge being the notable exception, particularly in his later works—there is no doubt that the demonstration of a goodness to be recovered, or created, is a seminal 'spiritual' aspect of Romantic writing. It probably constitutes the main interest for anyone studying Romanticism and religion. This consonance makes Romanticism appear to be an ally to the Christian faith, and some have seized upon it as such, including most notably the liberal wing of the Anglican Church in the nineteenth century. For them, Wordsworth's insistence on humanity's innate 'spiritual sense' presented a bulwark against the increasingly prevalent mechanistic and deterministic views of human nature. In practice, however, Romantics followed their Enlightenment predecessors in denying the validity of the revelation of God in the Bible or the validity of the church's witness to him. The change lies in the fact that the Romantic identifies the active power behind both in the person of the poet.

The manner in which it does so will receive fuller exposition when we look at Romantic poetics, but the result is clear. Romanticism tends to posit an alternative 'theological framework' in place of the Christian narrative of creation, fall, exile, and redemption. 'Origins' play a crucial role throughout this narrative framework. The Romantic narrative suggests a quasi-Pelagian state of humanity's *original* goodness at the 'dawn of consciousness'; it attributes the fall to the advent of society and, more specifically, to its use of reason sequestered from 'life', i.e. its departure from its naive *origins* (against which it casts the contemporary age's 'sentimental' condition as one of exile or alienation, which the poet most keenly feels); and it sees redemption (and progress) as coming in the form of *originality*, specifically through the reconciling power of the poetic *imagination*.

None of these narrative states are entirely coherent or consistent with logical explanation, because in its appeal to origins Romanticism steadfastly avoids the notions of causality or any agency that would allow it. The main reason for this aversion probably lies in one of the key theological beliefs that Romanticism inherits from deist thinkers, that the supernatural realm does not exist, or if it does, that it is in some way subordinated to the natural, or subsumed within it. We can see this, for example, with respect to the transition between the original state, essential goodness or harmony, and the second, a state of fallenness or discord. Such a metaphysical transition begs the question of how it transpired. If humanity really was originally good, which the Christian faith also affirms, how did it ever come to fall? The answer provided in Christian doctrine is through the act of a supernatural adversary, Satan. Since, however, the supernatural realm and the beings therein are held not to exist, the Romantics, like the deists before them, tend to reject this out of hand. Romanticism emends the deist account, however, by attributing supernatural power to the processes of the human imagination rather than to its notion of God as erstwhile original principle, now an 'absentee landlord'.

The absence of God remains significant, though, as the divine space in which the imagination can work. We can also see this absence 'inhabited' in the Romantic narrative in the transition from the contemporary state of exile—expressed variously as a loss of innocence, an increasing sense of alienation or even, to use Blake's neutral term, 'experience'—to what follows, redemption. Yet this too begs the question. If we come into the world of contemporary society as 'fallen' beings, how can we restore ourselves to original goodness? It would seem impossible, unless what we call 'good' is not wholly good and 'evil' not wholly evil. In other words, the Romantic account of the fall presupposes that good and evil have no radical or supernatural sense; indeed, that they are relative terms. What the Bible calls sin is reformulated as a defective or false form of knowledge. The result of this is what Thomas Carlyle termed Romanticism's 'natural supernaturalism'. God becomes naturalized, and nature divinized.

Romanticism has been effectively embraced by much of the Western world as its spiritual mentor. Books on finding God through walks in the woods abound. It is not for this chapter to provide an extensive historical account of how this transpired, but merely to note that it has and to describe how it functions. Before commencing an exposition of the poetics of Romanticism, it would be useful to recount the manner in which it functions around a theodicy of origins.

VARIATIONS ON THE THEODICY OF ORIGIN

One of the salient features of Romanticism, certainly in comparison to foregoing conceptions of literature, is that it uses the predicate of originality as a term of highest praise, as it does for the one who is capable of attaining it, that is, the poetic genius. It is pre-eminently in the Romantic period that we note the return to the ancient pagan notion that the poet is divinely inspired, although it differs markedly in so far as the modern claim bears the salvific and eschatological weight of centuries of Christian thought. Milton, of course, made what appeared to be a similar claim for divine inspiration in *Paradise Lost*, and he was a model for the Romantic poets in this and other respects, but it should be noted that there is little of what we would now call originality in that poem. On the contrary, it may be the most conspicuously learned and allusive poem in the English language. Nor would Milton have wished for it to have been otherwise. Originality, traditionally speaking, was not something for which an artist strove. On the contrary, in any culture in which the notion of truth has narrative content, the idea of good art is contingent on its adherence to established conventions, whether in the form of allusion, form, style, setting, or whatever else conforms to it. Far from banishing the artist's creative powers, they form the backdrop of the familiar that allows us to recognize what is distinctive.

Romanticism in this sense is wholly different. As we have seen, it departs from the conventional and the orthodox indiscriminately, regarding the orthodox as merely another spurious convention, in this case of a religious variety. In and of itself, the result of Romanticism's departure from convention and orthodoxy is obscurity. Yet the potency of its eccentric and exotic references lies in what is implied by departing from these same conventions and norms: a renewal of the spirit that lies beyond them.

We can detect this in the form of theodicies of origin everywhere in Romantic writing: we find it in its setting, often in the Middle Ages or among primitive or native peoples, at any event before the onset of civilization; we find it in the arcane practices and mysterious characters it depicts, untainted by conventional or civilized behaviour; we find it in the allegedly more primitive mythological terms in which it chooses to express itself (rather than in the conventional poetic terms of critical orthodoxy), though it similarly elevates poetry above prose as a more spontaneous and sincere mode of expression; we find it in the way in which it elevates the court of private feeling, untutored by social constraints, above that of public debate or approbation; we see it in its heroes, who tend to be ostracized or misunderstood 'original geniuses' rather than exemplary models for others to follow; we see it in its poetic form, which tends to emphasize 'organic' process rather than 'mechanical' completion; and finally we see it in the way it sets the 'natural', for which is to be understood the good, in utter opposition to the artificial, civilized, or conventional.

It is in adherence to a theodicy of origins that we should understand the poet William Wordsworth's affinity for the simplicity of peasant life and the closeness to nature. Nor are such sentiments connecting the heart with nature isolated. His praise for the 'primal sympathies' of the heart finds its correlate in Keats's conviction of the 'holiness of the heart's affections' and in Percy Shelley's self-referential definition of love as 'that powerful attraction... beyond ourselves, when we find within ourselves the chasm of an insufficient void, and seek to awaken in all things that are, a community with what we experience within ourselves' (1965: vi. 201) It is first in the Romantic movement too that we detect a valorization of the previously undiscovered realm of intimacy, the 'spiritual origin' of outward social conventions; and it is there that we find a sanctification of human love that will actually even present itself in defiance of the community, not as an act of participation in it, let alone in its Christian sense as a human analogy of God's love for his Bride, the church.

ROMANTICISM AND SOCIETY

Romanticism's fascination with origins, in other words, is nothing like a sign that it sees the need to uphold the wisdom or legitimacy of tradition. On the contrary, it signifies the desire to escape to a place or a state assumed to be prior to *any* defined order, not a return to one of the past. Yet the diversity of these references to origins gives little clue to what provokes the shared rebellion against order. To understand what does, we must look to the thing against which the Romantics appeared united in their contempt: the evil presented by mass society. This is perhaps difficult to understand in a time in which it is commonplace to use 'society' as a generic description of all people within a given nation, who are assumed to be united by a common will. More confusingly still, it is also commonly used in the social sciences as a description for all peoples throughout the course of human history. We must rid ourselves of this generalization to understand the change here.

Prior to the eighteenth century, there really was no such thing as 'society' as a political entity. Historically one could speak of tribes and kingdoms and empires, of the *polis* and the *res publica*, but there was no term to describe a collective phenomenon to which a single will could be posited, as is now understood to be the case with our word 'society'. When the word 'society' was used, it was to describe a group of individuals banded together for a common and usually nefarious purpose, as still used in 'criminal society'. The lack of a term for a collective with political power and a united will owes itself in part to the fact that in terms of sharing political power the majority of mankind were irrelevant. The American and French Revolutions, of which more will be said in a moment, brought a great shift in this respect. Yet the Romantics were all at one point or another strongly supportive of the Revolution. In what sense then could they be said to be antisocial?

It is in the sense that they opposed the way in which mass society regarded its members to be impersonal or, more precisely, stripped them of the integrity of personhood, which was a legacy of Classical individualism and the Church Fathers' teaching on the concept of the person (as a result of their reflection on the Trinity). Although the degradation of this was arguably the substance of their objection, with the exception of the later work of Coleridge, it was certainly not its tenor. Their objection lay in the sense that the integrity of personhood was being crushed in the process of assuming, or forcing, the assent of the individual to the one will of society without any recourse. And it invariably transpired without any recourse, for no *one* could be said to represent society in a way that he could claim responsibility for its actions and be held thus accountable. The Christian faith became particularly odious in the light of this development because its allegiance to an unworldly king made it appear similarly unaccountable, and added the promise of eternal reward or punishment thereto. Perhaps this congruence may explain the sense that theological liberals had that it was necessary to play down the supernatural idea of heaven and hell to make the faith acceptable.

Considerable responsibility for the attack on personal integrity though must be attributed to the Enlightenment's concept of human autonomy. In his short treatise *What is Enlightenment?* (1784) Immanuel Kant (1959) famously defined the Enlightenment as 'man's release from his self-incurred tutelage', i.e. his emancipation from his historical reliance on authorities other than himself. No generation should be bound to the creeds or customs of a bygone era, he argued, for it was an offence against human nature whose true destiny lay in progress. The formula Kant prescribed for progress was indeed that of self-reliance. The love of self would invariably translate into the love of all, and vice versa: 'Self-love thus pushed to social, to divine | Gives thee to make thy neighbour's blessings thine', chimed Alexander Pope (1964: 162) in agreement.

What needs to be noted about this agenda, however, is that the progress implicit in this idea of autonomy, literally this 'law of the self', makes no appeal to others for its conduct. It is self-interpreting and self-regulating. This means that autonomy is not only radically opposed to the integrity of tradition, it means that unlike individuality, with which it is commonly confused, it has no inherent regard for the existence of others. In that sense, the progress it proposes invariably comes at the cost of radical isolation for the individual and the oblivious denigration of others. This became most apparent when a late form of Romanticism, social Darwinism, was embraced by the twentieth-century totalitarian state. In it, society's embrace of the life-processes of labour 'thus pushed to social, to divine' seemed to justify the sacrifice of the individual in the name of the progress of the 'life' of a 'healthy' society.

Kant's check on this was in his 'ethical' command: to treat others as if they were ends, not means to ends. Yet the command no longer had any bearing on what he had already declared integral: the autonomy of the self. Individuality, on the other hand, whether we see it in the creation account in Genesis, whereby human integrity is a function of human nature, male and female, being *in imago Dei*, or in its Classical conception at the heart of the politics of Greece and Rome, depends on the presence of others. Human plurality is the condition of human individuality, since being an individual is to have one's personal distinctiveness acknowledged by others. Although Romanticism tended to share the Enlightenment postulate of autonomy, we should understand the frequent Romantic portrait of a poet in lonely social isolation or even exile, as well as its characteristic rebellion against authority, as a reaction against the rapid and progressive degradation of personal integrity.

Thus for all the propaganda surrounding human equality around the time of the Revolution, what mass society really brought was uniformity. Yet it only did that by imposing its demand for conformity. Only after this had transpired, and it did so over the course of the nineteenth century, would it make any sense to study humanity in the way proposed by an emergent branch of learning, the behavioural sciences, i.e. as if humanity were merely a species of animal like any other. Wordsworth certainly sensed the indignity that was being done, complaining in his 1802 *Preface to Lyrical Ballads* that the sensibility in England was being corrupted by 'the great national events which are daily taking place, and the increasing accumulation of men in cities, where the uniformity of their occupations produces a craving for extraordinary incident, which the rapid communication of intelligence hourly gratifies'. These are acting, he laments, 'to blunt the discriminating powers of the mind' and 'reduce it to a state of almost savage torpor' (Wordsworth and Coleridge 1963: 243). Coleridge would only add to his friend's sentiments with his lifelong crusade against pantheism and the precursors to evolutionary materialism.

With society's demand for conformity of behaviour among its members and with its antagonism towards the traditional institutions of human order, from familial to ecclesiastical to political, which had legitimized and protected the individual person, it is easy to understand both Romanticism's sense of alienation and its need to defend personal integrity against the current 'orthodoxy', which Blake's poem 'London' described as contemporary society's 'mind-forged manacles'. Romanticism's appeal for the need to 'return to origins' stems from a sense of being alienated from the world, and of being beset and invaded by the social order of the present age without defence against its 'authority'.

ROMANTICISM AND HISTORY

The relationship of Romanticism to the French Revolution is a somewhat complex one. On the one hand, virtually every Romantic was sympathetic with the Revolution in France at one stage or another, and most regarded continued political allegiance to it to be essential to the cause. Shelley (1965: i. 206) spoke for many of his contemporaries in condemning Wordsworth for having once 'like to a rock-built refuge stood | Above the blind and battling multitude' only later to desert 'truth and liberty'. Yet since the Revolution did not eradicate the problems wrought for human liberty and human integrity by social conformity, and in fact in many respects seemed to exacerbate them, it was perhaps not cowardice or the apathy of age that prompted Coleridge and Wordsworth to rethink the project in more radical 'theological' terms at a distance from Jacobin politics. Romantic politics, if the apposition of the two words does not already imply an inherent contradiction, is by nature utopian and non-partisan.

For Romanticism provided no practical response to enlightened society's radical attack on the human person; it offered an imaginative one, rooted in what Words-worth termed 'feeling'. The intent in this emphasis was not to trivialize poetry or reject politics, although some greeted it in such terms at first; on the contrary, it marked nothing other than an unprecedented power being attributed to poetry as a political | theological act. To understand the power attributed to 'feeling', we will need to look to the quasi-theological tenor of Romantic poetics. What will become clear is that since Romanticism merely opposed the Age of Reason's prescription for the progressive emancipation of humanity from the vulgarity and immaturity of the past through the use of 'reason' with its contrary programme of insoluble connection to its roots through the use of 'feeling', it implicitly assumed the validity of its idea of progress without question. It simply adapted it to include and celebrate the mystery of these roots or origins at its very heart.

In this sense, Romanticism did not genuinely oppose the Enlightenment; it reformulated it into a secular theology of historical progress. This has often been observed from without, but it is presented as a manifesto of sorts at the time (in a document published only in 1917) known as *The Oldest Systematic Programme of German Idealism* (1796), ascribed variously to Hegel, Hölderlin, or Schelling. The programme asserts as a self-evident truth that 'as the whole of metaphysics will in future come under *morality*—of which Kant only gave an *example* with his two practical postulates and *exhausted* nothing, this ethics will be nothing but a complete system of all ideas... The first Idea is naturally the notion *of my self* as an absolutely free being.' This assertion is given its theological freight in what follows: 'With the free self-conscious being, a whole *world* emerges at the same time—out of the nothing—the only true and thinkable *creation from nothing*' (Bowie 1990: 265).

To effect this, however, the author asserts the necessity of the craft of the poet. Poetry must return to its original service: 'at the end again (it) becomes what it was at the beginning—*teacher of (History) Mankind*; for there is no philosophy, no history anymore, poetry alone will survive all the remaining arts and sciences'. To that end, he calls for 'a new mythology', one adapted to the age of reason: it 'must be in the service of the Ideas, it must become a mythology of *reason*' or, as he clarifies, a 'monotheism of reason of the heart', a 'polytheism of imagination and of art'. The path to the marriage of reason and imagination will be long and hard, but if the common man can only be made reasonable and the philosopher 'mythological', the result will be little less than apocalyptic: 'enlightened and unenlightened must finally shake hands, mythology must become philosophical and the people reasonable, and philosophy must become mythological in order to make the philosophers sensuous. Then eternal unity will reign among us' (ibid. 266–7).

This programme reveals the underlying subtext of Romanticism. Implicitly or explicitly, it is a means for completing the Enlightenment. For with its emphasis upon the interconnectedness of all things, it no longer upheld the idea of progress as an ideal, as the Enlightenment had, but as a historical narrative of continuous advance from society's murky origins, its fabled 'dawn of consciousness', towards the present. It is thus no accident that modern liberal historiography began in this era; nor is it that the modern nation-state's identity was established on ethnic lines in the Victorian period that followed. Nationalism along ethnic lines and the 'right of self-determination' signifies if nothing else the fact that Romanticism's mythology of origins had rapidly attained the mark of official legitimacy. The evolutionary theory that Charles Darwin presented in his *The Origin of the Species*, for all the scandal it provoked when it appeared in 1859, had a similar sense of inevitability about it in the light of Romanticism's belief both in the indivisible unity of all things and the idea of imperceptible progress *through creation*, seen most clearly in the poet's own imaginary activity. Darwin's evolutionary theory, as he himself acknowledged, was clearly anticipated not only by his grandfather Erasmus Darwin but by a host of cultural studies dating at least as far back as Maupertuis, Diderot, Lessing, and Herder.

In the narrative the human sciences provide about society as a *body* with one will, emerging from a primordial soup at the 'dawn of consciousness' and progressing over time from an age of myth to an age of reason, perhaps we can see a strange fulfilment of the prophecy Wordsworth made in his 1802 *Preface to Lyrical Ballads*: 'if the time should ever come when what is now called Science, thus familiarized to men, shall be ready to put on, as it were, a form of flesh and blood, the Poet will lend his divine spirit to aid the transfiguration, and will welcome the Being thus produced, as a dear and genuine inmate of the household of man' (Wordsworth and Coleridge 1963: 254). The myth of society and its progress is a result of this transfiguration, and it became the opium of the masses.

ROMANTIC POETICS: ORGANICISM

In terms of literature, we can see the mysterious power of origins wielding its influence perhaps most clearly in the term most strongly identified with Romanticism, namely in imaginative originality. The imagination has pride of place among all major Romantic writers. Its emphasis among them may in fact lie behind the notorious slipperiness of the term 'Romanticism'. With the exception of Byron, who somewhat refreshingly satirized its self-congratulatory pretence—while nonetheless using its idea of rebellion against convention for his own sublime heroes—it is a poetic power capable of reconciling contraries, overcoming discord, and restoring a state of unity and goodness that had existed in the universe before it somehow lapsed into evil, alienation, and suffering. Once again, mystery surrounds the details of these, in large part because it receives mythopoetic terms appropriate to the feeling of the loss rather than discursive terms that would record a reason for it. In fact, the very idea of a definite account of origins or ends runs contrary to the spirit and methodology of Romanticism.

As already suggested, one reason for this was to avoid the 'rational' notions of agency or causality. But it also had a positive reason. In the place of the concept of personal agency, we find a new anthropological concept emerging in the Romantic period: that of the organism. Along with proposing a new understanding of human nature, it also accommodated Romanticism's revolutionary 'theological' notion of creativity: its supernatural naturalism. For inherent in the model of the organism are the attendant ideas of ceaseless process, growth, and connection to the world. Furthermore, the organic model suggests an imperceptible and mysterious origin at every point in which there is 'living' progress. Just as we observed this function within its historical narrative of original goodness, fall, and imaginative reconciliation, we can see allusions to mysterious origins at work in the *form* of Romantic poetry. The fragment as poetic form, the trope of Romantic irony, the elliptical narrative pattern, the characteristic appeal to silence and absence, even the use of the long dash—all these are symptoms of Romanticism's underlying organic poetics.

This model of artistry marks a significant departure from the traditional view of the artist as a maker, *homo faber*, acting *in imago Dei*, which gained repeated expression in the neoclassical age with its common description of the artist as a *secondus Deus*. The poet most strongly associated with organicism, is of course, Coleridge. Yet far too much has been made of this. As Thomas McFarland has convincingly demonstrated, Coleridge fought pantheism in all its forms throughout his life, and a thoroughgoing organicism is simply what he labelled pantheism, or 'hylozoic atheism'. He insisted, on the contrary, that 'even the philosophy of nature can remain philosophy only by rising above nature, and by abstracting from nature' (Coleridge 2002: 218), 'and thus nature itself, as soon as we apply Reason to its contemplation, forces us back to a something higher than nature as that on which it depends' (ibid. 140) For Coleridge it was the God of the Christian faith: 'No Trinity, no God—is a matter of natural Religion as well as of Christianity, of profound Philosophy no less than of Faith' (Coleridge 1959: 283–4).

This insistence probably lay at the heart of the criticism Keats expressed towards Coleridge in a famous letter discussing what had made Shakespeare the great poet he was: his 'negative capability'. Coleridge could never join Shakespeare in the ranks of the great poets, Keats mused, because unlike him he was 'incapable of remaining content with half knowledge'. Yet with a great poet, he explained, 'the sense of Beauty overcomes every other consideration, or rather obliterates all consideration' (To George and Tom Keats, 21–7 Dec. 1817). Or, as he put it elsewhere: 'The Genius of Poetry must work out its own salvation in a man: It cannot be matured by law & precept, but by sensation and watchfulness—That which is creative must create itself' (To J. A. Hessey, 8 Oct. 1818). Therein lay the key to Wordsworth's present greatness: he wrote after 'the Chamber of Maiden thought' had 'gradually darkened' and society had advanced to the present age, to the point where 'we see not the ballance [*sic*] of good and evil', yet he was able to make us 'feel the "burden of the mystery"', a fact which Keats attributed to the 'general and gregarious march of intellect' (To J. H. Reynolds, 3 May 1818).

ROMANTIC POETICS: THE SUBLIME

Behind these sentiments lay another influence. There was a genuine spiritual urgency related to perhaps the most important aesthetic category of the period, that of the sublime. Some explanation here is necessary. In the Enlightenment, the concept of the sublime underwent a process of redefinition. It was initially associated with powers that produced overwhelming sensations, from those of the original poetic genius—Milton and Shakespeare were the most commonly cited examples—to that in nature. The *locus classicus* for the sublime in nature was a mountain of sufficient grandeur to evoke the awful sense of a Divine maker. Sites such as the Alpine Mont Blanc, to which numerous Romantic poems were devoted, became places of pilgrimage for the many who were persuaded by deist 'arguments from design' to read nature as a book revealing divine intention.

Edmund Burke's *Philosophical Enquiry into the Origins of Our Ideas of the Sublime and Beautiful* (1757) made a crucial step in discussions on the subject when he reformulated the idea of the sublime as a sensation related to an object into one of subjective affect. For Burke, the sublime was intimately connected with the relationship between individual and society. While he presented the beautiful as a function of something like an instinct towards sociability, which thus encouraged the procreation of the species, he connected the sublime with the instinct of self-preservation, evident in the face of the threat of annihilation. The feeling of the sublime was a fearful response to something of grandeur or power; once again, it had a social use: promoting the survival of the species. Tellingly, Burke even associated the two aesthetic categories with particular affective responses: beauty with a relaxation of the bodily functions, even to the point of indolence, and the painful sublime with a requirement of 'exercise or labour' to overcome it. This is not far off the psychologizing of the faith that soon followed, and we can even see the seeds for the sociologist Max Weber's famous thesis that the origins of capitalism lay in the Protestant work ethic. William Blake too might have had such theological-somatic arguments in mind when he asserted in one of his 'Proverbs of Hell' (1790) that 'Damn braces. Bless relaxes.'

The advance Immanuel Kant made on the concept in his third critique, *Critique of Judgement* (1790), may be the most significant. It came by dissociating the sublime from human artifice as well as distancing it from Burke's suggestion that aesthetic perceptions were related to human social instincts. Indeed, Kant's discussion of the sublime is the key point in his argument for the 'purposiveness without purpose' in aesthetic objects. Unlike foregoing discussions, he associated the sublime with objects of nature alone, which made it easier for him to avoid the question that a poem would beg, namely in what relationship it stood to its Maker's intentions. For Kant, the feeling of sublimity in nature derives from the very fact that it is not the vehicle of any message. The ironic result of this rather dubious severance of object from intention, however, was not to limit the significance of the artist, it was to absolutize him in a way that has since proved irresolvably troublesome.

While it does mark his opposition to deist arguments, Kant's main purpose in relating the sublime to nature is to show how the sublime objectifies the otherwise hidden role of the judgement as a form-giving faculty. The fact that the sublime, by definition beyond our perception, fails to appear as an object of beauty demonstrates that we enjoy it not primarily because it suggests infinity, but because it lacks *any form*. In other words, through its own lack of appearance the sublime provides the best evidence of the creative power of imagination. Thus Shelley concludes his 1817 poem 'Mont Blanc' with the question: 'And what were thou, and earth, and stars, and sea | If to the human mind's imaginings | Silence and solitude were vacancy?' (Shelley 1965: i. 233).

ROMANTIC POETICS: THE IMAGINATION

Here and elsewhere, Shelley assumes divine powers for the imagination, making it not only the true origin of human religion and culture but its only recourse for future renewal and redemption. Thus he adopts a 'Satanic' stance against 'rationalist' thought in his *A Defence of Poetry* (1822), reformulating Luther's definition of sin as a state of being 'curved in upon ourselves' to suggest that the external world is curved in upon us, a bond of necessity which only the freedom of poetry can break. 'All things exist as they are perceived; at least in relation to the percipient. "The mind is its own place, and of itself can make a Heaven of Hell, a Hell of Heaven." But poetry defeats the curse which binds us to be subjected to the accident of surrounding impressions... It creates anew the universe' (Shelley 1965: vii. 137).

William Blake, though influenced by Jacob Boehme's mysticism, Freemasonry, and millenarian thought rather than by Kantian philosophy, speaks in unison with the other Romantics when he too attributes this original sense to the imagination at the conclusion of the first series of his anti-deist tract 'There is No Natural Religion' (1788). As so often in the period, its 'redemptive' creative power is a means of overcoming the 'death' offered by a more 'reasonable' religion: 'If it were not for the Poetic or Prophetic character, the Philosophic & Experimental would soon be at the ratio of all things. & stand still, unable to do other than repeat the same dull round over again' (Blake 1965: 1) He expands upon this in the 'Application' of the second series, where he writes, 'He who sees the Infinite in all things, sees God. He who sees the Ratio only, sees himself only. Therefore God becomes as we are, that we may be as he is' (ibid. 2). Blake's God is the creative force behind all religions, as his prophetic 'voice crying out in the wilderness' exclaims in his 'All Religions are One' (1788): 'As all men are alike (tho' infinitely various), So all Religions &, as all similars, have one source. The true Man is the source, he being the Poetic Genius' (ibid. 3). Similarly, in his annotations to the Idealist philosopher George Berkeley's *Siris*, he writes: 'Man is all Imagination God is Man & exists in us & we in him' (ibid. 654).

The quintessential definition of the Romantic imagination, however, has long been held to belong to Samuel Taylor Coleridge. In chapter 13 of his *Biographia Literaria* (1817) he writes:

The IMAGINATION... I consider either primary, or secondary. The primary IMAGINATION I hold to be the living Power and prime Agent of all human Perception, and as a repetition in the finite mind of the eternal act of creation in the infinite I AM. The secondary Imagination I consider as an echo of the former, co-existing with the conscious will, yet still identical with the primary in the *kind* of its agency, and differing only in *degree*, and in the *mode* of its operation. It dissolves, diffuses, dissipates, in order to recreate; or where this process is rendered impossible, yet still at all events it struggles to idealise and to unify. It is essentially *vital*, even as all objects (*as* objects) are essentially fixed and dead.   (1983: 304)

The similarities this definition bears to the organicism of his contemporaries is evident.

Later in life, Coleridge was to regard his 'metaphysical disquisition at the end of the first volume of the *Biographia* as 'unformed and Immature' with at best 'fragments of the truth' (1990*b*: 293). He objected to it because it too closely approximated Schelling, whom he had come to regard as 'the reviver of pantheist Atheism with Romish Pseudo-Catholicism for its mythological Drapery' (1990*a*: 5262). As already stated, it was an error he sought to correct in his later work. Yet the references to human agency in it, and of imaginary activity as a *repetition* in the finite mind of that of its Divine Maker is at odds with this organicism. It is also clear that he regarded God as a supernatural being in accordance with church teaching. But the clearest evidence is in the aim long expressed for his *magnum opus*: 'The purpose of the whole', he wrote, is 'a philosophical Defence of the Articles of the Church' (1959: 534).

WORKS CITED

BLAKE, WILLIAM. 1965. *The Poetry and Prose of William Blake*, i, ed. David V. Erdman. Garden City, NY: Doubleday.

BOWIE, ANDREW. 1990. *Aesthetics and Subjectivity: From Kant to Nietzsche*. Manchester: Manchester University Press.

COLERIDGE, SAMUEL TAYLOR. 1959. *Collected Letters of Samuel Taylor Coleridge*. iii. *1807–1814*, ed. Earl Leslie Griggs. Oxford: Clarendon.

—— 1983. *Biographia Literaria: or Biographical Sketches of My Literary Life and Opinions*, ed. James Engell and W. Jackson Bate. Princeton: Princeton University Press.

—— 1990*a*. *Notebooks*, iv. *1819–1826*, ed. Kathleen Coburn and Merton Christensen. Princeton: Princeton University Press.

—— 1990*b*. *Table Talk*, ed. Carl Woodring. Princeton: Princeton University Press.

—— 2002. *Opus Maximum*, ed. Thomas McFarland. Princeton: Princeton University Press.

FURST, LILIAN R. (ed.) 1980. *European Romanticism: Self-Definition: An Anthology*. London: Routledge & Kegan Paul.

HULME, T. E. 1924. *Speculations: Essays on Humanism and the Philosophy of Art*. London: Routledge & Kegan Paul.

KANT, IMMANUEL. 1959. *Foundations of the Metaphysics of Morals and What is Enlightenment?* New York: Liberal Arts.

POPE, ALEXANDER. 1964. *An Essay on Man*, ed. Maynard Mack. London: Methuen, 1964.

SHELLEY, PERCY BYSSHE. 1965. *The Complete Works of Percy Bysshe Shelley*, ed. Roger Ingpen and Walter E. Peck. 10 vols. New York: Gordian; London: Ernest Benn.

WORDSWORTH, WILLIAM, and COLERIDGE, S. T. 1963. *Lyrical Ballads: Wordsworth and Coleridge*, ed. R. L. Brett and A. R. Jones. London: Methuen.

Further Reading

ABRAMS, M. H. 1971. *Natural Supernaturalism: Tradition and Revolution in Romantic Literature.* New York: W. W. Norton.

CLARK, TIMOTHY. 1989. *Embodying Revolution: The Figure of the Poet in Shelley's Poetry.* Oxford: Oxford University Press.

ENGELL, JAMES. 1981. *The Creative Imagination: Enlightenment to Romanticism.* Cambridge, Mass.: Harvard University Press.

FRANK, MANFRED. 1989. *Einführung in die frühromantische Aesthetik.* Frankfurt am Main: Suhrkamp.

FURST, LILIAN R. (ed.) 1980. *European Romanticism: Self-Definition: An Anthology.* London: Routledge & Kegan Paul.

LACOUE-LABARTHE, PHILIPPE, and NANCY, JEAN-LUC. 1988. *The Literary Absolute: The Theory of Literature in German Romanticism.* New York: SUNY.

MASSON, SCOTT. 2004. *Romanticism, Hermeneutics and the Crisis of the Human Sciences.* Aldershot: Ashgate.

MCFARLAND, THOMAS. 1969. *Coleridge and the Pantheist Tradition.* Oxford: Clarendon.

PORTER, ROY. 2004. *Flesh in the Age of Reason: How the Enlightenment Transformed the Way We See Our Bodies and Souls.* London: Penguin.

PRICKETT, STEPHEN. 1996. *The Origins of Narrative: The Romantic Appropriation of the Bible.* Cambridge: Cambridge University Press.

—— 1976. *Romanticism and Religion: The Tradition of Coleridge and Wordsworth in the Victorian Church.* Cambridge: Cambridge University Press.

SIMPSON, DAVID. 1979. *Irony and Authority in Romantic Poetry.* Totowa, NJ: Rowman & Littlefield.

WEISKEL, THOMAS. 1976. *The Romantic Sublime: Studies in the Structure and Psychology of Transcendence.* Baltimore: Johns Hopkins University Press.

CHAPTER 8

THE INFLUENCE OF GERMAN CRITICISM

DAVID E. KLEMM

'Critique' (or, alternatively, 'criticism', for the German term *Kritik*) is a universal power of human enquiry, an ingredient in some measure within every historical tradition. Over an extended moment in Western culture, however, one bridging the Enlightenment and Romanticism, critique arose with an extraordinary force that disrupted, transformed, and redirected the preceding traditions, including those of English literature. Critique, in this world-transforming appearance, had its genesis in German Protestantism for contingent historical reasons, but its eschatological consequences were universal. All subsequent thinking, including that of English literature, was gradually taken into the all-pervasive influence of the new critical world-view. *The Oxford Handbook of English Literature and Theology* rightly seeks to take account of the nature of critique, as well as major responses to it, in order to comprehend the formation of the tradition properly. I begin this chapter by describing the chief forms of critique before briefly outlining some major points of impact on English literature.

WHAT IS CRITICISM (*KRITIK*)?

The context for the appearance of critique was the slow revolution that led to the formation of the modern world. This process was 'the passage from a world whose structure and laws were preexisting and immutable givens for every member of society, to a world that could discover its own nature and define its norms itself' (Todorov 2002: 9). Most decisively with the German philosopher Immanuel Kant (1724–1804), critique provided the justification for the newfound freedom to make individual choices concerning all the common values and expectations inherited from the past. For Kant, 'Our age is the genuine age of criticism, to which everything must submit' (Kant 1997: 100–1). Enlightenment is the movement that embraces and applies criticism as 'humanity's emergence from its self-incurred immaturity' in a passage to autonomous adulthood (Kant 1970: 54). Over the course of the nineteenth and twentieth centuries, critique assumed new forms, mostly in Germany. Its ramifications spread in global directions to set the agenda for serious reflection today. Not without struggles and resistance, the historic appearance of critique has gradually pushed all prior conceptions of thinking into the past as typical of previous centuries but no longer directly applicable. What precisely *is* criticism in this sense of the term?

Critique is the real power in the human soul to dislodge the being of whatever was previously accepted as self-evident or known. Humans have always exercised this capacity, but in the late eighteenth and early nineteenth centuries, critique called into question the received view of the nature of thinking. Previously, in the Western tradition, dominated by Aristotle, thinking was conceived as abstraction: the intellect possesses a natural power of receiving the universal, essential form of objects given to experience, and of taking that form into itself (abstracting it from the particular object), while maintaining itself as an immaterial object, that is, without becoming the known object itself (Rorty 1979: 40). For example, the mind receives the universal form of 'treeness' from a particular tree and takes the form into itself; thinking, 'This is a tree,' without itself becoming a tree. The particular tree is thereby represented as a concrete instance in time and space of a universal essence ('treeness') that is neither temporal nor spatial. Within this picture, the abstracted essence is viewed as the being or substance of the particular object. In this way, the mind was held to have direct access to the metaphysical world of being through its capacity to receive and abstract essences.

This model of thinking as abstraction had immense prestige and for centuries was largely accepted as self-evidently true (although the record of dissent is also impressive). The critical revolution fully manifested itself when Kant dislodged this model of thinking as abstraction by showing that there is no natural continuity between perceived particulars (Kant called them 'intuitions') and abstracted essences (Kant's 'concepts'), as the abstraction model presupposes. Most decisively, however, Kant also presented a superior model showing how knowledge is possible as a synthesis of a sensuous element (the concretely given 'intuition', or perceived particular within time and space) with an intellectual element (the abstractly conceived thought or 'concept', which is itself neither temporal nor spatial). Kant no longer confused the being or essence of a thing with the naturally abstracted universal thought-element. Rather, following Kant, the being or essence of the thing is conceived as the connection, along with the connecting activity, between a particular intuition, received by the faculty of sensibility, and a universal concept, conceived by the faculty of understanding. According to Kant's model, knowledge is a justified synthesis between two independently derived elements—the sensible intuition and the intellectual concept—which are different in kind and have a different origin (Kant 1997: B377, B76). Knowledge is the demonstrated correspondence between these two elements.

In other words, Kant demonstrated that what had been taken as the self-evident givenness of something to thought (e.g. the tree in its treeness) in fact conceals some unreflected prior connection between a fallible human concept (e.g. the concept 'tree') and experience of some kind (e.g. the intuition of this thing). This connection comes to language precisely in the copula (e.g. 'is') within the form of a judgement (e.g. 'This *is* a tree'). To dislodge self-evidence means to disconnect the immediacy of the connection between thought and experience, to scrutinize both the applied concept and the perceived intuition, and to question the truth-status of the judgement by seeking justification (or sufficient reason) for positing the identity-in-difference between concept and intuition. Because the 'being' of a thing is the connection between concept and intuition, critical consciousness therefore questions the truth of being in its self-evident appearance.

Kant's critical philosophy could not be successful without showing how knowledge as justifiable synthesis of concepts and intuitions is possible. The problem arises because concepts and intuitions are for Kant different in kind. Concepts are universal, predicable of many different intuitions; intuitions are particular, they fall under concepts as their sensible exemplification. Moreover, the problem was exacerbated, because Kant's analysis of concepts shows that they have both empirical and pure or transcendental elements to them. For example, the concept of a tree includes both empirical features, such as 'a long-stemmed woody perennial plant with one main trunk', and also pure elements, transcendental concepts, which are the conditions of the possibility of applying empirical concepts. These transcendental elements include the pure a priori categories of understanding, for example substance and causality. Because the mind in the nature of the case deploys transcendental concepts, when we think, 'This is a tree,' we necessarily think that this long-stemmed plant is a substance and that it stands in causal relationship with other things in the world around it.

A problem arises for critical philosophy, however, at just this point. How can one justify the use of transcendental (non-empirical) concepts? As Kant says, 'pure concepts of understanding being quite heterogeneous from empirical intuitions, and indeed from all sensible intuitions, can never be met with in any intuition. For no one can say that a category, such as that of causality, can be intuited through senses and is itself contained in appearance.' So, if knowledge is the justifiable subsumption of intuitions under concepts, and concepts include transcendental categories as the condition of their possibility, 'How, then,' Kant asks, 'is the subsumption of intuitions under pure concepts, the application of a transcendental category to appearances, possible?' (ibid. B177). Kant answers this problem with his doctrine of schematism, which I shall now review in order to draw out some results that were profoundly influential on English literature.

Minimally, Kant tells us that to combine concepts with intuitions, 'there must be some third thing, which is homogeneous on the one hand with the category, and on the other hand with the appearance, and which thus makes the application of the former to the latter possible' (ibid. B177). At the empirical level, the third thing is an *image*—such as the image of a dog in general, which enables synthesis between the universal concept of a dog and a particular intuition of a furry, four-legged animal. This empirical image is a product of *reproductive imagination*, a function of the empirical subject. Such images can be connected with a concept, however, only by means of a transcendental schema of a pure concept. A transcendental schema is a product of pure a priori *productive imagination*, a product of the *transcendental 'I'*, through which, and in accordance with which, images themselves first become possible (ibid. B181). Now, the transcendental 'I' is strictly speaking unknowable, because it is neither concept nor intuition, yet it is a necessary condition of any knowing. What about the transcendental image? Here is one truly brilliant part of Kant's doctrine.

According to Kant, the pure image is a 'transcendental time determination' (ibid. B185); it is the form of the transcendental ego's timing of being. In the *Transcendental Aesthetic* portion of the *Critique of Pure Reason*, Kant had determined that space and time are 'pure intuitions' and not concepts. Consequently, a pure image as transcendental time determination is a necessary characteristic of pure intuition. If so, with this seemingly insignificant technical move, Kant solves the problem of justifying knowledge. He does so by arguing that pure intuitions of time fall under pure concepts, making synthesis of concepts and intuitions possible through the production of pure images. Schemata, i.e. determinations of pure intuitions of time, satisfy the homogeneity requirement in that they are at once both intellectual (homogeneous with a pure concept) and sensuous (homogeneous with an intuition). And schemata thereby also assure the applicability of concepts to experience. Previously time and space were viewed as the ultimate objective properties of the universe; with Kant, they become pure intuitions through which the transcendental 'I' temporalizes and spatializes being.

Now, what are the decisive issues that emerge in this form of rational critique? I want to focus on two issues. First, critique determines the realm of objectivity at two levels: that of (1) empirical experience, and that of (2) the transcendental conditions for thinking empirical reality. The transcendent domain of supernatural reality, including God and the eternal world of spiritual realities, no longer has any objective status. Prior to critique, supernatural reality was purportedly understood (abstracted) by metaphysical thinking, which is now shown not to constitute knowledge as justifiable synthesis. More specifically, Kant shows that the faculty of reason is limited to ordering the concepts of understanding into a unity, by means of the ideas of the world, the freedom of the self, and God. The ideas of pure reason, however, cannot in principle refer to any possible intuitions, empirical or transcendental (ibid. B359). Consequently, although they are necessary for the systematic unity of thinking, they have a strictly regulative function and cannot constitute knowledge. In this way, the power of critical questioning desacralizes the world, driving out supernatural beings, such as angels and demons, God and the devil. The other side of the destructive power of critique is the new, creative picture of a world constituted in its being largely by the powers of transcendental imagination. This picture will be massively influential for literary thinkers. The problem it poses is: How can we humans, who long for the sacred, live in a world emptied of transcendent divinity? One answer that will eventually emerge is: we live in an empirical world in which we yet receive signs of a transcendental depth of meaning, living symbols of the unknowable divine.

Second, critique distinguishes in principle between the objectivity of the world and the subjectivity of the 'I' who synthesizes it. The subject is precisely *not* a possible object; the 'I' systematically eludes any thinking that aspires to become knowledge. 'I' am not anything that can objectively appear, for 'I' am always necessarily the one to whom things (thoughts, perceptions) do appear. Whatever appears as objective cannot be a subject, and the subject cannot appear as any sort of object. Moreover, in reflecting on the conditions of the possibility of knowledge, Kant's critical philosophy brings out the reflexive structure of finite human thinking: the thinking 'I' operates within strict limits that determine its finitude, yet the 'I' infinitely recognizes those limits and recognizes its own recognizing of those limits. The question here is: What is the meaning of the fact that the transcendental 'I' infinitely recognizes its being both as creative power synthesizing the world and as a finite power, operating within definable limits? One answer that will come forth is: 'I' am a self-conscious living contradiction, infinitely projecting meaning on the basis of and into a finite set of relations among myself, others, and the world, and infinitely taking responsibility for the meanings I project.

Historical Criticism

If rational critique destroys the traditional forms of metaphysical theology and religious belief, can biblical revelation provide a solid basis for theology and religion? Historical criticism, as it builds from Semler to Strauss, answers 'no'. Just as Kant gives us a critique of pure reason, Johann Semler (1725–91), presents in principle a critique of any possible revelation based on the historical investigation of scriptural texts. Johann Semler was a contemporary of Kant, who probed deeply into the historical character of all human thinking, as well as into the character of the historical process itself. Whereas Kant's rational critique focuses on the identical formal structures of the human mind, Semler's historical critique highlights the differences in thinking that can be traced back to the ways that individual human lives are shaped by, and themselves shape, history. Historical criticism is thus the reverse side of rational criticism. In this context as well, critique is the power to dislodge what appears as self-evident. Prior to historical criticism, it was broadly assumed that the Bible is the Word of God in that its real content, given in the literal sense of the text, both presents an accurate picture of what happened in history and is authoritatively true, because the Bible in its entirety and unity was authored by God through inspired human witnesses. Semler's historical criticism denies the verbal inspiration theory by disconnecting the unreflected connection between the literal sense of a document and both its historical meaning and its theological truth (Hornig 1961: 65–73). By contrast, Semler systematically distinguished between sacred Scripture and the Word of God (Semler 1967: 60). What does this mean in practice?

According to Semler's principles, even if the historical critic can establish the literal sense of Paul's claim to the Romans that human beings are justified by faith and not by works, the critic does not yet know the meaning of Paul's letter in its historical context, for meaning is dependent on the specific interests, intentions, and points of view of Paul in relation to those of the Roman community. The historical critic asks: What are Paul's interests in saying so? Whom is he trying to persuade, and for what reasons? Additionally, according to Semler, the historical critic in principle cannot say on the basis of studying Paul's text whether or not God would agree with Paul that human beings are justified by faith and not by works. How do we know that Paul's word is also the Word of God? Thus criticism cuts itself off from the mainstream of orthodox biblical theology. Semler, in the true style of critique, dislodges the idea that revelation can be received on the basis of biblical (or any other scriptural) authority and makes revelation dependent on the free judgement of the human mind. How does he do so?

In his major work, *Abhandlung von freier Untersuchung des Canons* (*Treatise on the Free Investigation of the Canon*) (1771), Semler read the Bible as a collection of documents in the history of religions, not as straightforward divine revelation. As Hornig (1961: 223–36) reports, in this regard Semler drew an important distinction between the ideas of a bygone age and the linguistic vehicles, or modes of presentation, of those ideas. For example, Semler understood the image of demonic possession in the New Testament as a vehicle for conveying the idea of psychological disturbance or psychiatric illness. This insight led to his accommodation theory: Jesus knew what the idiom of demonic possession signified, but he employed it just the same to accommodate his teaching to the common level of understanding (Frei 1974: 60–1). Consequently, the critical reader of the Bible cannot, for example, take the stories of miraculous exorcism of demons as evidence that Jesus is Son of God because he saves people from the devil and evil demons. These stories have another intention, which is to show that salvation is in fact freedom from sin (Hornig 1961: 226). Nor can the historical critic accept at face value, for example, the New Testament claims to be the fulfilment of the Old Testament. It was in the interest of the New Testament communities so to present themselves, given that they were really establishing a new religion distinct from Judaism. How, then, can the historical critic make individual judgements about the theological truth of claims made in these documents?

Semler held that the human mind possesses what could be called an original, universal revelation, which consists in the ability to determine whether something purporting to be the Word of God is in fact what it claims to be. The criteria are (1) whether the material content of the purported revelation corresponds to the rational, moral idea of God, and (2) whether the language of revelation has the capacity to transform ethically the one who receives it (Semler 1967: 26; Hornig 1961: 106–11). True revelation elevates its hearer to a higher level of ethical existence than he or she would otherwise have achieved; it does not present information about God or the world. In this way, Semler both respects historical differences among presentations of possible revelation and provides a critical norm for the free judgement thereof.

David Friedrich Strauss (1808–74) brought historical criticism to a razor-sharp edge. According to Strauss, historical criticism destroys the illusions of dogmatism by distinguishing the historical from the mythical in the Gospel accounts concerning Jesus. In the words of Hans Frei, by 'myth' Strauss referred not to 'deliberate inventions', but rather to 'unconscious folk poeticizing, the manifestations of a culture's rather than an individual consciousness' (Frei 1985: 235). Applied to the Gospels, the term 'evangelical mythus' denotes 'a narrative relating directly or indirectly to Jesus, which may be considered not as the expression of a fact, but as the product of an idea of his earliest followers' (Strauss 1994: 86). In his highly controversial *Life of Jesus* (1835), Strauss developed a thoroughgoing analysis and interpretation of myth in the New Testament, arguing dialectically against both the supernaturalist accounts of the dogmatists, who simply accepted stories of immediate divine intervention in historical events as true, and the rationalist explanations of these stories as errors or even as deliberate fabrications on the part of the original witnesses. Strauss's mythical interpretation claimed to resolve the difficulties attending both supernaturalist and rationalist views by explaining the text on the basis of its arising out of a common cultural consciousness at the time.

Strauss used two sets of criteria for drawing the distinction between myth and history, and he unflinchingly applied them to the New Testament documents. The first, negative criterion has two parts: (1) The New Testament accounts are not historical (i.e. they could not have taken place in the manner described), but are rather mythical, 'when the narration is irreconcilable with the known and universal laws which govern the course of events' (Strauss 1994: 88). Strauss had in mind not only physical laws of causality, but known laws of succession and psychology. (2) Narrated events cannot be considered historical if they are internally inconsistent or in contradiction with other accounts (ibid. 88). The second, positive criterion is that New Testament accounts may be considered as myth (or even legend) when the form or substance of the narrative is poetical.

Strauss gave a coherent mythical explanation for what had been considered the mysteries of Christian faith (the birth accounts and infancy narratives of Jesus, stories of his baptism, temptation, and transfiguration, his miracles and healing ministry, and above all, his resurrection from the dead). But in so doing, Strauss's historical criticism dislodged the connection—so crucial for traditional Christian faith—

between the (mythical) idea of the Christ as divine Son of God and the particular, historical person of Jesus. With the publication of *Life of Jesus*, Strauss became infamous overnight: 'The all but universal revulsion against it cost him his academic career and turned him into a homeless wanderer among his peers' (Frei 1985: 222).

RESPONSES TO CRITICISM

The responses to criticism in both its rational and historical forms were deep and diverse. The major movements of thought in the nineteenth and twentieth centuries all flow out of the shock of encounter with critique and the apparent destruction of both metaphysical and biblical theology. The questions driving each of these currents of thought were: What happens to religion, literature, and theology in an age of criticism? Does criticism lead thinking into an abyss from which there is no return, or does the path of criticism lead thinking towards clarity concerning truth, beauty, and goodness? Consider these patterns of response:

1. *Transcendental or absolute idealism* was a powerful effort to reconstitute philosophical theology beyond the purely destructive aspects of critique. Its fundamental strategy was to move the unknowable, yet necessary, self-conscious transcendental subject of the Kantian schematism doctrine from its position as unexplainable surd into the first principle and self-evident starting point of philosophy—either as absolute ego (Fichte in the *Science of Knowledge* of 1794), self-intuition (Schelling in the *System of Transcendental Idealism* of 1800), or Absolute Spirit (Hegel in the *Phenomenology of Spirit* of 1807). Consider, for example, Fichte's programme in the *Science of Knowledge*. For Fichte, the ground of all empirical experience is not itself empirical, but is 'the self-positing I' ('*das sich setzende Ich*'). This technical term refers not at all to the empirical consciousness of an individual person, but to a transcendental structure that makes empirical consciousness possible. The self-positing 'I' is a transcendental consciousness that is conscious of itself as consciousness and, as such, is both subject of thinking and object thought—not at all in the nature of a thing but, wholly in the nature of pure activity. In this sense, the 'I' posits its own being absolutely (Fichte 1970: 99): its thinking is its being, and its being is to think. From this starting point, Fichte deduces the forms and laws of all conscious activity. In spite of its greatness of purpose and execution, ultimately German idealism was unable to ward off the threat of solipsism, and lurking behind it was the abyss of nihilism (something Fichte himself was able to see by the year 1800).

2. *Ethical voluntarism* (e.g. Fichte in *Vocation of Man* of 1800), or the will to believe, recognized that the idealist dream of absolute knowing comes to nothing. As Fichte (1987: 63–4) wrote, if '[a]ll I know is my consciousness itself', then

Nowhere is there anything which endures, neither outside of me nor in me, but only ceaseless change. Nowhere do I know of any being, not even of my own. There is no being. I myself do not know at all and don't exist. There are images: they are all that exist . . . images which do not represent anything, without meaning and purpose. I myself am one of these images.

This passage records a genuine encounter with nihilism, to which Fichte responds with a decision to accept some unknowable beliefs, such as that the human vocation is not merely to know but to *act* on behalf of 'the conception of a moral world', even though that conception is not strictly speaking knowable. Only by believing what is unknowable can life assume dignity and purpose, ceasing 'to be an empty game without truth and meaning' (ibid. 75). *Fideism* (e.g. Jacobi's philosophy, 'which has its essence in not-knowing' (Jacobi 1987: 122), that is, in immediate self-consciousness as feeling) is a variation of this response, in that it decides for faith as an answer to cognitive nihilism. The feeling of unity with oneself is nothing to know, but is the site where 'the human being finds God' (ibid. 138). Schleiermacher is sometimes interpreted as a kind of fideist, as is Kierkegaard.

3. A new tradition of *German aesthetics* (e.g. Schiller, Friedrich Schlegel, Hölderlin, Novalis, Schelling) arose on the basis of creative appropriations of Kant's philosophy, especially the *Critique of Judgement*, as Bowie (2003) and Hammermeister (2002) have made clear. The major authors united behind the conviction that the Absolute as the ultimate unity of opposites transcends knowledge; nonetheless, the work of art can present the Absolute in and for feeling and aesthetic intuition. In this way, aesthetics supersedes theology, the artistic image transcends the speculative concept, and the Bible rises from the ashes of criticism to be read as art.

4. *Radical criticism* arose on the conviction that because religious and theological thinking cannot be about supernatural things, since such things exceed human knowing, religion and theology must be forms of coded language that is really about something else. Ludwig Feuerbach (1804–72) is a key figure here. He propounded a rigorous projection theory to explain religion as 'the dream of the human mind'. Religious consciousness of the infinite is not what it appears to be; religious consciousness is self-consciousness alienated from itself and projected in objective form onto the infinite background of human reason, will, and affection. Feuerbach (1957: p. xxxvii) argued that 'the true sense of Theology is Anthropology, that there is no distinction between the *predicates* of the divine and human nature, and, consequently, no distinction between the divine and human *subject*'. Thus what religion views as objectively divine is in truth the divinity of human nature. His successors in radical criticism include Marx, Nietzsche, and Freud. Given this review of critique and the basic responses to it, I turn now to a brief account of how English literature was influenced by critique in the late eighteenth and early to mid-nineteenth centuries.

SOME POINTS OF CONTACT BETWEEN GERMAN KRITIK AND ENGLISH LITERATURE

Samuel Taylor Coleridge (1772–1834) is the major figure when we consider the direct influence of German critical thought on English literature of the nineteenth century (Ashton 1999: 496). As a young man Coleridge engaged in serious study of German critical thought, beginning with his reading of Schiller in 1794, which inspired him not only to learn the language well but also to live in Germany (1797–9) so as to imbibe the new critical atmosphere at first hand (ibid. 29). Coleridge's own vocation oscillated between poet and philosopher, and he not only read and mastered German literature and aesthetics, but was in a class of his own among Englishmen in truly absorbing the arguments of Kant, Schelling, and other critical philosophers (such as Lessing and Herder) (ibid. 48). Although Coleridge sometimes recapitulated the ideas or even the words of Kant, or others, without citation (ibid. 28), he appropriated in a truly critical way Kant and post-Kantian thought. He was never a mere passive receiver of ideas, but rather creatively and constructively thought through the critical questions for himself, arriving at his own unique synthesis of ideas and symbols (ibid. 46).

The cultural and social climate in England was uncongenial for Coleridge's serious engagement with German critical thought, however, and Coleridge paid a price in isolation and misunderstanding for his commitment to mastering the new critical medium. 'Kantism' was ridiculed at the time for its obscurantism, moral turpitude, and latent atheism, although only a caricature of Kant's thought was known in England. The new German critical thought was identified with 'Jacobinism' in the public mind, and in Coleridge's lifetime there was little public interest in things German (ibid. 30). Coleridge was undaunted; he deliberately chose to dislodge the unreflected negative opinion of German thought by his own critical spirit and to raise it to a higher synthesis.

Higher synthesis was always Coleridge's aim. Inheriting the critical split between subjectivity and objectivity from Kant, he was intent on reconciling the 'I am' and the 'it is', spirit and nature, in a living unity-in-polarity (Jasper 1999: 28). To do so, he self-consciously deployed the means of language as both objective thing and subjective thought ('Language is the sacred Fire in the Temple of Humanity') (quoted ibid. 26). Words, like human beings, are living agents—unities of subjectivity and objectivity (Coleridge 2004: 572). Claude Welch examines how, in true Kantian style, Coleridge approached his task by analysing the conditions of the possibility of synthetic thinking at four successive levels.

First, Coleridge distinguishes between reason and understanding in a way that changes the Kantian formula. Understanding is the power of knowing phenomena—objects of sensory experience; reason is the power of forming universal and necessary ideas or spiritual truths in the subjective–objective medium of language—as symbols that are ideas and ideas that are symbols (ibid. 555–60). Consider, for example, a poetic expression of Coleridge's idea in 'Effusion XXXV' (1795), whose title was later changed to 'The Eolian Harp'. Coleridge (ibid. 18–19) writes:

> And what if all of animated nature
> Be but organic Harps diversly fram'd
> That tremble into thought, as o'er them sweeps,
> Plastic and vast, one intellectual Breeze,
> At once the Soul of each, and God of all?

Second, Coleridge examines and exalts the power of imagination as the function of reason enabling it to transcend understanding; imagination is distinct from fancy, which remains tied to sense experience (ibid. 488–9). Third, Coleridge unifies theoretical and practical reason, by arguing that a moral sense of goodness, guided by conscience, is an ingredient in rational enquiry (Welch 1985: 11). Fourth, Coleridge unifies reason and will in faith; willing reason is faithful to the spiritual truths which grasp and are grasped by willing reason (Coleridge 2004: 571–2; Welch 1985: 13). Progressing through these four levels of self-critical reflection leads the mind to a place that is simultaneously light and dark, where reason paradoxically both transcends itself and fails to transcend itself by remaining true to its own limits. The site of this failing success or successful failure is the linguistic symbol—the site of spiritual realities truly but partially enshrined in language, through the imagination, as 'a repetition in the finite mind of the eternal act of Creation in the infinite I AM' (Coleridge 2004: 488, quoted in Jasper 1999: 26).

William Wordsworth shared a profound (though troubled) friendship and collaboration with Coleridge; the two men mutually influenced each other, as Abrams (1953: 180–2) points out. With respect to studying German language, literature, and philosophy, however, Wordsworth was nowhere close to Coleridge, who consumed the works of new German criticism with boundless energy. Nonetheless, the uncanny proximity of some of Wordsworth's distinctive poetic ideas to their counterparts in contemporary German criticism commands any reader's careful attention.

One such idea in Wordsworth is that of the 'spot of time', in which the poet forms an unbreakable relationship to a self-defining moment, event, and place. The spot of time is thus the emergence of a transcendental depth of meaning within everyday experience. In Geoffrey Hartman's (1987: 169) words concerning the episode describing the death of Wordsworth's father in the 1850 *Prelude* (Wordsworth 1979: XII. 292–333), 'Wordsworth called the episode a "spot of time," to indicate that it stood out, spotlike, in his consciousness of time, that it merged sensation of place and sensation of time (so that time was *placed*), even that it allowed him to physically perceive or "spot" time.' In this incident, Wordsworth is a 13-year-old schoolboy who anxiously anticipates his return home for Christmas by climbing a crag overlooking the crossing point of two highways from which he could see the expected horses coming and where he impatiently wished that time would pass. Ten days later, his father died,

> And I and my three brothers, orphans then,
> Followed his body to the grave. The event,
> With all the sorrow that it brought, appeared
> A chastisement.

With some vague feeling of retribution, the poet continues,

> Yet in deepest passion, I bowed low
> To God, Who thus corrected my desires...

As is clear from the above example, Wordsworth's 'spot in time' was no mere romantic fancy, but a word-event arising out of a traumatic conjunction of events, fused together as a loss partially healed in time by poetic language.

The significant background of Wordsworth's various spots of time is the generalized cultural experience of the interiorizing of religion in the poetic recognition of time transcending itself into eternity experienced as intensity of the moment (Marshall 2000: 63–4). Wordsworth refers neither to scriptural citation nor to dogmatic allusion to mark his recollection of a religious experience. Rather, his poetry engages the individual language of an individual intuition and feeling of the universe. Take, as an example, these lines from Wordsworth's *Tintern Abbey*:

> ...I have felt
> A presence that disturbs me with the joy
> Of elevated thoughts; a sense sublime
> Of something far more deeply interfused,
> Whose dwelling is the light of setting suns,
> And the round ocean and the living air,
> And the blue sky, and in the mind of man;
> A motion and a spirit, that impels
> All thinking things, all objects of all thought,
> And rolls through all things. Therefore am I still
> A lover of the meadows and the woods,
> And mountains; and of all that we behold
> From this green earth;
>
> (Wordsworth 2004: 64)

The connection with Friedrich Schleiermacher, one of the great minds of German criticism, is clear. In his famous *On Religion: Speeches to Its Cultured Despisers* (1799), Schleiermacher (1996: 22) defines religion not as metaphysics, nor morality, but as 'intuition and feeling. It [i.e. religion] wishes to intuit the universe, wishes devoutly to overhear the universe's own manifestations and actions, longs to be grasped and filled by the universe's immediate influences in childlike passivity.' Religion for Schleiermacher is individual, and Wordsworth's poem captures the feeling and intuition that marks the individuality of Christianity—Schleiermacher's term is 'holy sadness' for the mood that reflects the unresolvable tensions between finitude and infinity (ibid. 115, 119); Wordsworth (2004: 64), in *Tintern Abbey*, speaks of 'The still, sad music of humanity'.

Thomas Carlyle (1795–1881) was an important defender of German criticism across the nineteenth century in Britain. In his famous article of 1827 in the *Edinburgh Review* on 'The State of German Literature', Carlyle set out to contradict the prevailing British opinion of German literature as absurd, immoral, and, in general, in bad taste. Carlyle wrote, 'Far from being behind other nations in the practice or science of Criticism, it is a fact...that they [the Germans] are distinctly and even considerably in advance. Criticism has assumed a new form in Germany...[where it is] ultimately a question on the essence and peculiar life of poetry itself' (Ashton 1980: 75). By all accounts, Carlyle, though far from being absolutely successful, did have a profound effect on warming the otherwise cold British attitude towards German critical thought.

Like Coleridge, Carlyle turned to German thought seeking an idealism in philosophy and literature that could save him from the aridity of British empiricism and utilitarianism; and he found it. In 1820, he began seriously learning the German language, and in 1825 he translated into English Goethe's *Wilhelm Meisters Lehrjahre*, for which Carlyle was less than fully enthusiastic. He began a quite lengthy relationship with the great man, Goethe, by correspondence. Goethe very much fancied the image of Carlyle working away in the Scottish Highlands on German literature, and Goethe promoted Carlyle's reputation in German circles. Goethe had particular words of praise for Carlyle's *Life of Schiller* (1825), in which Carlyle paid homage to Schiller's moral and political idealism, as well as to the moral basis of his aesthetics (ibid. 91). Rosemary Ashton (ibid. 92) calls the work 'a landmark in Anglo-German relations, being the first English biography of a great German writer'. The biography praises Kant and accounts for Kant's influence on Schiller, but it also reveals Carlyle's limitations when it came to understanding Kant's critical philosophy. Carlyle had no fondness for Coleridge (indeed, the latter disappointed him when they met in 1824), yet Carlyle took his (mis)reading of Kant (e.g. the distinction between understanding and reason) straight from Coleridge's *Aids to Reflection*.

Carlyle's fascination with German thought culminated in his highly idiosyncratic *Sartor Resartus* (1833–4), a peculiar mixture of reflections on the state of society and universe, along with characterizations of Goethe, Jean Paul, Novalis, Fichte, Kant, and others. In this mercurial work, Carlyle speaks through the fictional mouthpiece of Teufelsdröckh, who is himself ironically called into question by a doubting editor, making it very difficult to grasp Teufelsdröckh's actual philosophy—much less the thought of Carlyle. Admittedly, Carlyle was not a systematic thinker; he was most comfortable with Germany's poets. Yet he was the creative conduit of much of the influence of German criticism on British literature.

Another great mediator of German critical thought into the English literary context was Mary Ann Evans (1819–80), who wrote under the pseudonym of George Eliot. Her life and literary career, it is frequently noted, brilliantly epitomize the process that many people underwent as critical thinking was more thoroughly appropriated and even transformed on British soil. She made a life-changing transition, as a result of exposure to critique, from being a rather simplistic religious soul into being a serious enquirer concerning the meaning of human existence in relation to the sacred dimension of life. Every thinker who truly journeyed down the path of criticism had to make decisions about what, if anything, survives the negativity of critical thought in theology, religion, and ethics. George Eliot pursued this path with extraordinary courage, reinterpreting the heart of the Christian message in broadly humanistic, yet religiously sensitive terms of love, sympathy, goodness, and duty as universal goals of a self-critical and responsible humanity. She accomplished her goals through a strenuous programme of study and translation of German and

French sources in critical thought, reflecting on critical questions in essays, and writing major works of fiction.

George Eliot grew up with a strong evangelical Christian piety as a schoolgirl in Warwickshire. The break with her naive faith came through reading Charles Hennell's *Inquiry Concerning the Origin of Christianity* (1838), which incorporated many of the insights of biblical criticism found in more systematic form in Semler and Strauss. For Eliot, higher criticism destroyed any possible supernatural or miraculous basis for dogmatic Christianity. She stopped taking communion, which precipitated a break in relations with her father that was resolved after three weeks with no loss of integrity on her part. Higher criticism was an ambiguous power for Eliot; it destroyed her church identity, but it also set her the lifelong task of poetically expressing the core insights of the Christian story.

Her acquaintance with a group of unorthodox thinkers in Coventry, which at various times included the Brays, Brabants, and Henells, led to Eliot being invited to translate David Friedrich Strauss's *Life of Jesus* into English during the years 1844–6. She also translated Spinoza's *Ethics* in 1849 and possibly the *Tractatus Theologico-Politicus*, neither of which she published (Ashton 1980: 156). In 1854, she translated Ludwig Feuerbach's work of radical criticism, *The Essence of Christianity* (1841), which she enjoyed much more than Strauss's dry analyses. Eliot claimed that 'With the ideas of Feuerbach I everywhere agree,' not only in their negative, destructive aspect, but also in so far as they raise to supreme importance sympathy for others, human love as divine, the spontaneity of goodness, and the sublimity of duty. In short, she embraced Feuerbach's 'religion of humanity'.

George Eliot's impressive series of novels embody in poetic form the critical insights of Strauss and Feuerbach. In *Scenes of a Clerical Life* (1858), *Adam Bede* (1859), *The Mill on the Floss* (1860), *Silas Marner* (1861), *Romola* (1863), *Middlemarch* (1872), and other works, George Eliot gives testimony in fiction to her belief that 'the idea of God, so far as it has been a high spiritual influence, is the ideal of a goodness entirely human (i.e., an exaltation of the human)' (Ashton 1980: 160; and see Keuss 2002).

Finally, I want to point to a more ubiquitous influence of German critical thought on English literature with reference to Emily Brontë (1818–48) and her novel *Wuthering Heights* (2004). No explicit references exist to show that Emily Brontë was directly influenced by German critical thought. To our knowledge, she did not learn the German language or study Kant. But by the time that Emily Brontë wrote *Wuthering Heights* in 1847, the central ideas of German critical thought were so thoroughly appropriated into British culture that they began to appear frequently in literary expression.

Wuthering Heights is an extraordinary novel, full of ambiguity and indeterminacy. Indeed, it is impossible to say precisely what kind of novel it is. Written well after the end of the Romantic era, *Wuthering Heights* reveals many influences from the central Romantic poets—Wordsworth, Coleridge, Blake, Byron, Shelley, and Keats—along with influences from novelists Jane Austen and Sir Walter Scott. Indeed, several motifs of the novel simply drip Romanticism (ibid. Intro. p. xiii): the theme of eternal, tragic love between Catherine and Heathcliff, with its features of madness, extravagance, and torment; the rootedness of this love in the wild moors which inspired it; the closeness to primitive nature of the Earnshaw family in general, and of Catherine and Heathcliff in particular; the struggle between passion and reflection, symbolized by the two houses—Wuthering Heights and the Earnshaw family versus Thrushcross Grange and the Linton family; and the apparent triumph of passion over reflection as 'The relative peace of Thrushcross Grange is ultimately over-powered by the influence of *Wuthering Heights*' (ibid. notes 430).

However, I want to focus quite specifically on one formal feature of *Wuthering Heights*, which as such presents the substantial content and meaning of the novel. I have in mind the narrative structure of *Wuthering Heights*, which manifests very clearly and precisely the idea, stemming from Kant's critical philosophy, of a self-critical subjectivity, as spelled out above in this chapter. *Wuthering Heights* is, of course, written in the first-person narrative voice, which displays the systematically elusive nature of the narrating 'I' and the reflexive structure of human thinking. The inscrutable 'I' of narration is always different from the one (himself or herself) who is also a character in the events and about whom he or she narrates. Moreover, the finitude of the narrating 'I' is clear: the narrator is not omniscient but learns about events as the plot progresses and makes mistakes in understanding events as he/she goes along; yet the narrating 'I' ties it all together into a unified whole, showing the infinite power of imagination to synthesize disparate episodes into narrative unity. We have embedded in the structure of narration the form of selfhood as a living contradiction between an infinite power of imagination and entanglement in finite, limited sets of relationships.

Moreover, the shift in narrative voice from Lockwood to Nelly Dean intensifies the theme of a living contradiction, a doubling of identity. The shift elevates the doubling from one within the self (as a doubling between infinite and finite aspects of the self) to the level of an 'I–Thou' encounter between selves. Recall that the 'I–Thou' relationship, later made famous by Martin Buber, first appears in the context of critical thought in Fichte's *Vocation of Man* (1800), when Fichte's narrating 'I' attempts to forestall solipsism, and hence nihilism, by granting independent free existence to the Other (Fichte 1987: 76–7). Here, in *Wuthering Heights*, the narrating 'I' doubles between two very different concrete narrators who are also situated in the plot. Lockwood is a stranger to the moors, having just arrived from London, and is generally mystified by the people he meets and events he observes. Nelly is the stable nurse and housekeeper, figure of continuity and steadfastness, who intimately knows and is known by Catherine and Cathy. Neither narrator is impartial or passive to the action. Somehow the elusive true point of view on the complex story is hidden in the gap between the narrators. The doubling of narrators formally mirrors the doubling in identity going on in the plot between Catherine and Heathcliff, who are mysteri-ously identical in their difference, so close that Catherine says, 'Whatever our souls are made of, his and mine are the same' (ibid. 98).

But most importantly, the first-person, doubled, narrative voice tells its story in long-term retrospective. The narrative of three generations of Earnshaws and Lintons begins in 1801, with Lockwood's surprise visit to Heathcliff, as narrated by Lockwood; it shifts into the voice of Nelly Dean when the disturbed Lockwood returns to Thrushcross Grange and listens to Nelly, who returns the story to the past, beginning in 1771, in order to bring events full circle back to the present moment in 1801. The form of first-person, long-term retrospective enables the author to suggest the view that past time is not past but continues to intrude on present time; just as present time is not merely present, but is the outcome of the past—the decisions and actions which have determined what it means to be in the present. *Wuthering Heights* is a tale of events that are literally unforgettable and hence numinous, even if in a tortured way. This theme of memory is backed up by appearances of ghosts—Catherine's spirit appears to Lockwood in ch. 3 and Heathcliff's ghost purportedly appears to the villagers in ch. 34. Are these ghosts 'transcendent' (supernatural) beings, or are they symbols of the eternal presence and influence of events past, refigured in memory yet potent in affect, hence 'transcendental' conditions of present experience?

My concluding point is that by the time of *Wuthering Heights*, the ideas we associate with German critical thought have deeply penetrated English literature— for better or for worse. From heroic beginnings, championed by Coleridge and Carlyle, to wider dissemination by Wordsworth and Eliot, the revolution crystallized by German critique gradually permeates the field of English literature, as we see in the case of Emily Brontë's *Wuthering Heights*.

Works Cited

ABRAMS, M. H. 1953. *The Mirror and the Lamp: Romantic Theory and the Critical Tradition.* Oxford: Oxford University Press.

ASHTON, ROSEMARY. 1999. 'England and Germany', in Duncan Wu (ed.), *A Companion to Romanticism.* Oxford: Blackwell, 495–504.

—— 1980. *The German Idea: Four English Writers and the Reception of German Thought 1800–1860.* Cambridge: Cambridge University Press.

BOWIE, ANDREW. 2003. *Aesthetics and Subjectivity: From Kant to Nietzsche.* 2nd edn. Manchester: Manchester University Press.

BRONTË, EMILY. 2004. *Wuthering Heights.* Intro. and notes (423–32) Rebecca Johnson. New York: Pocket Books. First published 1847.

COLERIDGE, SAMUEL TAYLOR. 2004. *Coleridge's Poetry and Prose*, selected and ed. Nicholas Halmi et al. New York: Norton.

FEUERBACH, LUDWIG. 1957. *Essence of Christianity*, trans. George Eliot. New York: Harper & Row.

FICHTE, JOHANN GOTTLIEB. 1970. *Science of Knowledge with the First and Second Introductions*, ed. and trans. Peter Heath and John Lachs. New York: Meredith.

—— 1987. *Vocation of Man*, trans. Peter Pruess. Indianapolis: Hackett. First published 1800.

FREI, HANS. 1985. 'David Friedrich Strauss', in Ninian Smart et al. (eds.), *Nineteenth Century Religious Thought in the West.* Cambridge: Cambridge University Press, i. 215–60.

—— 1974. *Eclipse of Biblical Narrative: A Study in Eighteenth and Nineteenth Century Hermeneutics.* New Haven: Yale University Press.

HAMMERMEISTER, KAI. 2002. *German Aesthetic Tradition.* Cambridge: Cambridge University Press.

HARTMAN, GEOFFREY H. 1987. *Unremarkable Wordsworth*. Foreword Donald G. Marshall. Minneapolis: University of Minnesota Press.

HORNIG, GOTTFRIED. 1961. *Anfänge der historisch-kritischen Theologie*. Göttingen: Vandenhoeck & Ruprecht.

JACOBI, FRIEDRICH HEINRICH. 1987. 'Open Letter to Fichte', in Ernst Behler (ed.), *Philosophy of German Idealism: Fichte, Jacobi, and Schelling*. New York: Continuum.

JASPER, DAVID. 1999. *Sacred and Secular Canon in Romanticism*. New York: St Martin's.

KANT, IMMANUEL. 1997. *Critique of Pure Reason*, trans. and ed. Paul Guyer and Allen W. Wood. Cambridge: Cambridge University Press.

—— 1970. *Kant's Political Writings*. 'What Is Enlightenment?', ed. with intro. and notes Hans Reiss, trans. H. B. Nisbet. Cambridge: Cambridge University Press, 54–60.

KEUSS, JEFFREY F. 2002. *A Poetics of Jesus: The Search for Christ Through Writing in the Nineteenth Century*. Aldershot: Ashgate.

MARSHALL, DONALD G. 2000. 'Schleiermacher and Wordsworth'. *Christianity and Literature* 50: 53–68.

RORTY, RICHARD. 1979. *Philosophy and the Mirror of Nature*. Princeton: Princeton University Press.

SEMLER, JOHANN S. 1967. *Abhandlung von freier Untersuchung des Canons* (1771). Texte zur Kirchen- und Theologiegeschichte 5. Gütersloh: Mohn.

STRAUSS, DAVID FRIEDRICH. 1994. *Life of Jesus Critically Examined*, ed. with intro. Peter C. Hodgson, trans. George Eliot. Ramsey, NJ: Sigler. First published 1835.

SCHLEIERMACHER, FRIEDRICH. 1996. *On Religion: Speeches to Its Cultured Despisers*, translated and ed. Richard Crouter. 2nd edn. Cambridge: Cambridge University Press. First published 1799.

TODOROV, TZVETAN. 2002. *The Imperfect Garden: The Legacy of Humanism*, trans. Carol Cosman. Princeton: Princeton University Press.

WELCH, CLAUDE. 1985. 'Samuel Taylor Coleridge', *Religious Thought in the Nineteenth Century*. Cambridge: Cambridge University Press, iii. 1–28.

WILLIAM WORDSWORTH. 1979. *Prelude, 1799, 1805, 1850*, ed. Jonathan Wordsworth et al. New York: Norton.

—— 2004. *Selected Poems*, ed. with intro. and notes Stephen Gill. London: Penguin.

FURTHER READING

BOWIE, ANDREW. 1997. *From Romanticism to Critical Theory: The Philosophy of German Literary Theory*. London: Routledge.

BRONTË. EMILY. 1998. *Wuthering Heights*, ed. Patsy Stoneman. New York: Columbia University Press.

HODGSON, PETER C. 2000. *The Mystery Beneath the Real: Theology in the Fiction of George Eliot*. Minneapolis: Augsburg Fortress.

NEWLYN, LUCY (ed.) 2002. *The Cambridge Companion to Coleridge*. Cambridge: Cambridge University Press.

VIDA, ELIZABETH M. 1993. *Romantic Affinities: German Authors and Carlyle: A Study in the History of Ideas*. Toronto: University of Toronto Press.

WELLEK, RENÉ. 1965. *Confrontations: Studies in the Intellectual and Literary Relations Between Germany, England, and the United States During the Nineteenth Century*. Princeton: Princeton University Press.

CHAPTER 9

....

THE VICTORIANS

....

T. R. WRIGHT

INTRODUCTION: THE CHALLENGE OF LITERATURE TO THEOLOGY

....

THERE can, of course, be 'no one definitive picture of Victorian England', as Philip Davis (2002: 9) admits at the beginning of his excellent study of *The Victorians*. If there could be, most critics admit, then Walter Houghton's magisterial study of *The Victorian Frame of Mind* would probably be it. Houghton certainly provides a framework for beginning to understand the emotional and intellectual tensions within the period, the conflict between what he calls 'the critical spirit' and 'the will to believe' characteristic of so many thinkers during the long and changing reign of Queen Victoria. Other surveys of the period talk with greater new historical self-consciousness of *Inventing the Victorians* (Sweet 2001), of 'the construction of Victorianism' within the limits of our own interpretative assumptions (Thomas 1994: 1). All recognize the differences between the early and late decades of the period, the impossibility of generalizing intelligently about a reign which began with the revolutionary fervour and anxiety of the 1830s only to develop a more confident belief in technological progress evident in the Jubilee years (1887 and 1897).

All historians of the period also agree that religion was the dominant issue of the period. Boyd Hilton (1988: 3) labels the years up to 1865 *The Age of Atonement*, finding even the language of social and economic thought imbued with 'evangelical eschatology', a discourse hinging on the core Christian doctrine of the atonement. The early Victorians inherited from the evangelical movement of the turn of the century the belief, in the words of one of its leaders, William Wilberforce, that the world was 'in a state of alienation from God ... lost in depravity and sin'. It 'ought to be the object of every moral writer', Wilberforce argued, 'to produce in us that true and just sense of the intensity of the indignity of sin' so that we should seek and receive the redemption offered by Christ (ibid. 4). This strong sense of the fall into original sin, David Newsome (1997: 207) suggests, helps to explain why Darwin came as such a shock to the Victorians. For if the account in Genesis could not be trusted,

If there was no Adam and Eve, there was no Garden of Eden. If no Eden, there was no Temptation, and no Fall of Man. If no Fall of Man, what became of original sin and the requirement of redemption? So, a thirteen-year-old schoolboy named George Macaulay Trevelyan reasoned, from learning that Darwin had proved the Bible to be untrue, 'the fabric of Christian doctrine instantaneously fell away in ruin'.

Some well-known lines from Tennyson's *In Memoriam* also capture the way in which the emerging theories of evolution and the discoveries of geology of the early Victorian period seemed to undermine the argument from design, the belief encapsulated in Paley's *Natural Theology*, still standard reading for ordinands at the beginning of Victoria's reign, that a benevolent and providential purpose was discernible from the order of creation. Nature for Tennyson (1969: 912) seemed no longer 'careful of the type' while Man's trust that 'God was love indeed | And love Creation's final law' was undermined by the fact that 'Nature, red in tooth and claw | With ravine, shrieked against his creed'.

Just as Tennyson turned for answers to an inner voice, partly that of his dead friend Arthur Hallam, partly Christ, and partly conscience, so, Hilton (1988: 5) argues, his contemporaries began around 1870 to shift the 'centre of gravity' of their theology from the atonement to the incarnation, from transcendence to immanence. The influential collection of essays edited by Charles Gore in 1889, *Lux Mundi,* took as its subtitle, *A Series of Studies in the Incarnation.* The Oxford theologians responsible for these essays, like their Cambridge counterpart B. F. Westcott, found in Browning, who was much quoted in their pages, a more optimistic belief that 'this world's no blot for us | Nor blank; it means intensely, and means good' (Newsome 1997: 228). It is significant in itself that these theologians should turn to poetry for an expression of their newly rediscovered faith in the ultimate goodness of creation. But the interdisciplinary field of literature and theology does not simply involve the citing of literary texts as illustrative of characteristic attitudes and beliefs of a particular period. It is more important to understand how forms that we tend to label 'literary', devices such as metaphor, symbol, and narrative, themselves generate theological meaning. Faith too is not simply a matter of giving assent to a number of doctrinal propositions but of entering with the whole personality into a different imaginative world.

This is an insight which a range of Victorian writers of all theological persuasions can be shown to have understood. Stephen Prickett sees a Romantic tradition going back to Wordsworth and Coleridge running through the Victorian period, particularly evident in the Tractarians, in Keble and Newman, but also in liberal theologians such as Maurice and Arnold, who attempt to get behind the metaphors of 'the kingdom of heaven' and to uncover the symbolic and sacramental nature of Christianity (Prickett 1976). John Coulson points to a similar common tradition behind the distinction Newman makes between notional and real assent, the former a matter of mere conception, the latter of the whole imagination (Coulson 1981: 82). Philip Davis (2002: 115) quotes Isaac Williams in Tract 87 explaining the Tractarian idea of 'reserve', that the faith is not best conveyed by explicit doctrinal propositions, 'any more than our Lord does in His own teaching', but by 'the tone of a person's whole thoughts'. The word 'tone' here, Davis explains, 'is the literary-religious word that marks the whole subtle, inner working of the *spirit* of a real person, hidden deep within both his language and his silence'. It may no longer be a term in current literary-critical use, redolent as it is of I. A. Richards and *Practical Criticism*, but it has a venerable literary and religious history.

A more liberal theological tradition which developed from the Romantics included such Victorian sages as Thomas Carlyle, John Ruskin, and Matthew Arnold. For Carlyle (1908: 385), writing *On Heroes and Hero-Worship* in 1841, the poet had become the true priest and prophet of his age: 'Men of Letters are a perpetual priesthood, from age to age, teaching all men that a God is still present in their lives ... he is the light of the world.' Similarly, for Carlyle, it is 'Literature, so far as it is Literature', which is the true 'apocalypse of nature', revealing the 'open secret' of the universe' (ibid. 391).

John Ruskin made a similar spiritual journey, partly under the influence of Carlyle, from a narrow evangelical upbringing to the worship of art. His autobiography, *Praeterita*, published between 1885 and 1889, begins by lamenting that his mother had it 'deeply in her heart to make an evangelical clergyman of me', forcing him to 'learn long chapters of the Bible by heart' and to read it through from cover to cover 'about once a year' (Ruskin 1994: 5). These habits remained with him as an Oxford undergraduate: 'It had never entered into my head to doubt a word of the Bible,' he reports, 'but the more I believed it, the less it did me any good', merely reinforcing in him a sense of his own worthlessness (ibid. 151). Eventually he rebelled, abandoning his evangelical beliefs along with its habits and transferring his sense of awe to art and nature. The biblical quotation, 'He hath made everything beautiful in His time', he recounts, 'became for me henceforward the interpretation of the bond between the human mind and all visible things' (ibid. 242). As Linda Peterson (1986: 72) suggests in her illuminating study of *Victorian Autobiography*, Ruskin reversed the standard evangelical formula, interpreting the biblical text by experience rather than experience by the biblical text.

Perhaps the most outspoken challenge from literature to theology of the Victorian period came in Matthew Arnold's *Literature and Dogma* of 1873. For Arnold too the 'received theology of the churches and sects' had become 'a hindrance ... rather than a help' to the understanding of the Bible (1968: 151), which was couched in 'literary not scientific language' (ibid. 189). Arnold accepted some of the findings of higher critics such as Strauss (discussed by David Klemm in the previous chapter) but insisted that to read the New Testament properly required 'a larger, richer, deeper, more imaginative mind than his' (ibid. 158). Some of Arnold's attempts to gloss traditional theological terms have understandably attracted ridicule, but his critique of what he calls 'the pseudo-science of dogmatic theology' (ibid. 382), his attempt to separate Christianity from some of the metaphysical assumptions enshrined in its historic creeds (discussed in more detail by Luke Ferretter later in this volume) struck a chord with many of his contemporaries.

In looking at the Victorians in the context of the development of 'literary' modes of understanding theology, it would be possible, of course, to follow the development of certain theological concepts in works of literature. It is a method which works well enough in Michael Wheeler's study of *Death and the Future Life in Victorian Literature and Theology,* which traces the four last things (Death, Judgement, Heaven, and Hell) through a wide range of literary texts. My own preference, however, is for a generic organization which highlights the way in which literary form shapes theological meaning (Wheeler himself, incidentally, returns in the final section of his book to a reading of four literary texts in the light of his earlier theological framework). I will proceed in the next section of this chapter therefore to explore the novel, which became the dominant literary form during this period. It is there, I suggest, that we can find some of the most powerful accounts of the theological understanding characteristic of the Victorians.

Victorian poets also provide a 'literary' account of the age's engagement with Christianity. For the third section of this chapter, on the verse of the period, I have chosen to focus primarily on the dramatic monologue, perhaps the single most important literary invention of an age when the theatre itself is widely regarded as undergoing a relatively barren time. The point of the dramatic monologue, I will argue, is that it explores the particular significance of a particular individual's experience of religion in a particular place and time. This, I suggest, is both genuinely incarnational, theological meaning being embodied in history, and also a direct challenge to any form of systematic theology which confines itself to abstractions. In poems such as 'Easter-Day', not technically a dramatic monologue but exemplifying many features of that form, Browning not only attempts an answer to Clough's poem of the same title but explores what it means to hold the different theological positions exemplified in the course of the poem. Many of Browning's dramatic monologues grapple with the issues of higher criticism and scientific discovery which were undermining Victorian faith in similar highly specific, historical terms. These poems also illustrate the way in which the Victorians came increasingly to recognize that no individual mind could claim to grasp the totality of religious truth. The most they could achieve was an understanding of certain aspects of it. This, I would argue, is one of the most profound insights Victorian literature can claim to have contributed to theology.

THE VICTORIAN NOVEL: FROM THE TENDENTIOUS TO THE GENUINELY IMAGINATIVE

As early as the 1840s, as Kathleen Tillotson (1954: 13) observes in her study of the fiction of that decade, the novel was 'in process of becoming the dominant literary form'. 'Such is the universal charm of narrative,' as Sir Walter Scott had argued in a review of *Emma* employed by Robert Lee Wolff (1977) as an epigraph to his monumental survey of the religious novels of this period, 'that the worst novel ever written will find some gentle reader content to yawn over it, rather than to open the pages of historian, moralist, or poet.' The title of Margaret Maison's survey of Victorian religious novels, *Search Your Soul, Eustace,* gives some idea of the tendentious and exhortatory nature of many of these novels at a time when 'fiction became the pulpit, the confessional and the battlefield' of theology (Maison 1961: 5). Whether urging readers to *Rest in the Church* (the title of an 1847 novel by Elizabeth Harris whose main claim to fame is having prompted Newman to reply with *Loss and Gain*), warning against the danger of wicked Jesuits (as in Mrs Trollope's *Father Eustace* also of 1847), or simply advocating the virtues of a particular brand of Anglicanism or Dissent, many of the novels catalogued by Wolff and Maison, both of whom organize their material mainly along denominational lines, have little literary or even theological merit; they are of interest primarily to the historian as representative and illustrative of their age. At least some of these novels, however, have genuine theological value.

The major novelists of the period were often caustic about the crudely tendentious co-option of the genre. Thackeray had his fictive correspondent write in *Punch* in 1851, 'My dear Snooks...the scene, in the 200th number, between the Duke, his Grandmother, and the Jesuit Butler, is one of the most harrowing and exciting I ever read...Unless he writes with a purpose, you know, a novelist in our days is good for nothing' (Tillotson 1954: 116). George Eliot in 1856 was even more severe on what she called 'Silly Novels by Lady Novelists' in which the conventions of romantic fiction were simply modified so that 'tender glances are seized from the pulpit stairs instead of the opera box' while the conversation of the lovers is 'seasoned with quotations from Scripture, instead of quotations from the poets' (Eliot 1963: 318). Robin Gilmour (1993: 89) has written scathingly about such 'cassock-rippers'. Trollope has one of the characters of his novel *Three Clerks* outline the plot of his planned religious novel: 'Sir Anthony reforms, leaves off drinking, and takes to going to church every day. He becomes a Puseyite, puts up a memorial window to the Baron, and reads the Tracts. At last he goes over to the Pope, and gives over his estate to Cardinal Wiseman' (Tillotson 1954: 116). Even the major novelists could be partisan, as Dickens with his portrait of dissenters (Cunningham 1975: 198), Charlotte Brontë with her prejudice against Catholics and Puseyites, or Trollope himself with his satire on evangelicals such as the infamous Mr Slope of *Barchester Towers*.

Perhaps the most interesting Victorian religious novels are those categorized by Maison as of 'Lost Faith' or 'Towards Unorthodox Faith'. These novels may have been written out of need, the desire to express and communicate the spiritual torments suffered by their authors, but not quite so obviously to persuade or convert. I want to focus on four examples of this genre, two from the 1840s, Geraldine Jewsbury's *Zoe* and James Anthony Froude's *The Nemesis of Faith*, both of which achieved notoriety in their own time but now illustrate the problems as well as the potential power of the genre, and two of the 1880s, Olive Schreiner's *The Story of an African Farm* and Mrs Humphry Ward's *Robert Elsmere*, which can, in my view, lay claim to genuine literary and theological merit. In these later novels the literary form is in some respects crucial to the theological insight achieved, which is one of the key justifications of this interdisciplinary field.

Few modern readers, I suspect, would concur with Jane Carlyle's response on reading the manuscript of *Zoe*: 'It is a wonderful book!—Decidedly the *cleverest* Englishwoman's book I ever remember to have read' (Jewsbury 1989: 5). It has decidedly 'silly' propensities (in George Eliot's sense), telling as it does of the unconsummated but passionate romance of its deuteragonists, the Catholic priest Everhard Burrows and the eponymous Zoe. The novel's subtitle, *The History of Two Lives*, reflects the structure of the book, since the two lives are clearly destined to come together but not until they have taken dramatically separate directions which make a conventional romantic conclusion impossible. Everhard is educated for the priesthood. At the English College in Rome, however, as privileged access to extracts from his journal reveal, he buys 'theology at the price of religion'. His faith, he laments, after four years of study, 'from being a sacred and mysterious object of belief' becomes merely 'a collection of doctrines to be disputed' (ibid. 122).

The two plots come together when Everhard, already suffering from nagging doubts about the faith he is so voluminously defending, is sent by the Rector to the college established by Zoe's husband, Francis Gifford, for the education of the sons of English Catholics. Lengthy theological conversations with Zoe further erode his faith while increasing his romantic attraction to her, which reaches an absurdly melodramatic conclusion when he rescues her from a fire and takes her (for safety) into the chapel, where his long-sublimated passion for her bursts forth in full cassock-ripping vein. He subsequently abandons the priesthood and attempts for a while to teach a secular religion of 'brotherhood' before penning on his deathbed a letter of undying love to Zoe.

Zoe probably deserves the label 'silly novel' in Eliot's sense of playing theological variations on a romantic theme. Jewsbury, it could be argued, fails fully to develop what insights she has into the dryness of the scholastic theology then dominant in Rome and its questionable demand of compulsory celibacy in the clergy. Everhard keeps his vow of celibacy on the grounds that it had been made to the God in whom he continues to believe rather than to the church. This is supposed to benefit Zoe, leaving her with 'no unsatisfied yearning ... to become more to him than she already was' (ibid. 315). She is left to cradle his final letter into eternity, allowing readers to weep cathartically satisfying tears. To the extent that they may also be provoked into asking questions about Catholic teaching, however, the novel can be said to provide a significant contribution to contemporary theological discussion.

The same recognition, with similar reservations, can be accorded to Froude's (1849) novel *The Nemesis of Faith*, which quickly achieved the same scandalous notoriety as *Zoe*. A copy of the novel was publicly burnt by the sub-rector of Exeter College, from which Froude immediately resigned his fellowship. The reviews called it 'a Blasphemous Book', 'a *manual of infidelity*', 'one long series of attacks on Christianity' (Ashton 1989: 76). In some ways this last description is accurate, since the first part of the novel consists of a series of letters by the 'hero' of the novel,

Markham Sutherland, explaining his doubts about a range of Christian doctrines. To begin with he objects to the God of the Old Testament, whom he sees as 'jealous, passionate, capricious, revengeful' and cruel (Froude 1904: 11). Then there is the doctrine of hell, especially if considered in store for 'our daily companions— the people we meet at dinner or see in the streets' (ibid. 15). The doctrine of the atonement, in which God requires Christ's innocent sacrifice in payment for human sin, causes him further agonies (ibid. 70). As a young man about to take holy orders, it is clearly significant that Sutherland has difficulties with these doctrines. Believing, like Newman, that 'Life is change', he follows another hero of his, Carlyle, in denying 'the eternity of any creed or form at all' (ibid. 33–4). He nevertheless goes ahead with his ordination, only to resign under pressure from his rector and bishop.

The Nemesis of Faith is formally fragmented, borrowing from German literature (perhaps through Carlyle) a number of characteristic Romantic devices: letters, comments from an editor (Arthur, the addressee of the letters) and a section entitled *Confessions of a Sceptic,* recording how Newman 'magnetised' us, drawing us (apparently against our better judgement) into what could only be a temporary belief in full-blooded dogmatic Catholicism. The real twist in the story, and perhaps the 'silliest' part of the novel, is that the resultant scepticism into which Sutherland falls exposes him to temptation in the form of a married woman. His doctrinal doubts, it seems, lead him to abandon morality altogether. He is on the verge of suicide on the banks of Lake Como when a former Oxford acquaintance, now, like Newman, a Catholic priest, convinces him once more of 'the intensity of sin' (ibid. 220). Sutherland is persuaded to confess, convert, and enter a monastery, only for this solution to his problems also to prove illusory: 'his new faith fabric had been reared upon the clouds of sudden violent feeling, and no air castle was ever of more unabiding growth' (ibid. 226).

This is the nemesis of faith of the title; Froude would later comment that excessive 'credulity' brings about 'the wreck of the character of weak but not ill-minded individuals who had been taught to lean upon a crutch, and found the crutch itself breaking in their hands' (Ashton 1989: 77). In an autobiographical memoir from the 1890s, when he had become the respected Regius Professor of Modern History at Oxford, Froude claimed that the novel 'exhibited in an imaginative form the common doctrine of the established authorities, that infidelity led to immorality' (ibid.). That, of course, would have made it the nemesis of doubt. Froude, I suppose, was attempting to establish a middle ground between the path exemplified by Newman, who turned to ecclesiastical authority as a buttress *against* doubt, and the other extreme of abandoning all faith, including all morality. But the fragmentary form of the novel, its patchwork of letters, editorial comments, and confessions does to some extent capture the *Sturm und Drang* of the period, the sense of the poor protagonist adrift on the competing waves of extreme authoritarian faith and complete religious scepticism.

To move from these two novels of the 1840s to the opening chapter of Olive Schreiner's *The Story of an African Farm* of 1883 is to enter a totally different literary world in which the intellectual difficulties which trouble the characters of Jewsbury and Froude become fully dramatized, part of a convincing, in some ways terrifying, psychological world. 'The full African moon' of the opening sentence pours down onto a farmhouse in which young Waldo has just wakened from sleep to find his thoughts chiming in synchrony with the loud ticking of his father's hunting watch. The young boy, whose imagination is dominated by his father's daily reading of the family Bible, is not just concerned, as Sutherland was, with the question of hell, but obsessed by it, by the sheer numbers of people who must go there (if it exists). As the watch continues its remorseless ticking, the boy dwells on the fact that 'every time it ticked *a man died!*' Schreiner presents the boy's terrified mental state:

> 'Dying, dying, dying!' said the watch; 'dying, dying, dying!'
> He thought of the words his father had read that evening—'*For wide is the gate, and broad is the way, that leadeth to destruction, and many there be which go in thereat.*'
> 'Many, many, many!' said the watch.

Waldo screams out, 'Stop them!, Stop them!' and calls on God to 'save them', weeping in sympathy for the lost souls of his imagination (Schreiner 1998: 3–4). It is all, as in *Zoe*, highly dramatic but more psychologically convincing here as part of the imaginative world of an uneducated boy fed with this violent biblical material while having no theological, historical, or interpretative framework within which to place it.

The early chapters of *The Story of an African Farm* can be comic as well as terrifying, along the lines of the similarly poignant childish literalism of Edmund Gosse in *Father and Son*. Just as the young Gosse experiments with prayer and idolatry, beseeching the Lord for a humming top and bowing down before a chair, to be disappointed at his lack of response on both occasions, so the young Waldo experiments with sacrifice along the lines of the Old Testament. He builds a small altar, lays his mutton chop upon it, and calls upon God to consume it with fire, concluding when nothing happens that he must be as hateful to God as Cain, whose own sacrifice was equally unpleasing: 'He will not hear my prayer. God hates me' (ibid. 7). He resolves accordingly to hate God while continuing to love Jesus. What makes this convincing as literature, I would argue, as well as theology (of a particularly complex sort), is the way Schreiner presents a fully realized psychological profile of a boy deeply imbued with the Bible but lacking the intellectual resources to understand it.

As Waldo grows up, the novel turns into a more characteristic Victorian 'novel of doubt'. Chapter 5 finds him worrying Strauss-like over the discrepancies between the different gospel accounts of the resurrection. Like Markham Sutherland too he objects to the violence to be found in the Old Testament, in particular Jael being celebrated for hammering a nail through Sisera's skull in the Book of Judges (ibid. 33). He makes one final attempt to attract God's attention, clasping his hands and praying 'very loud' but, gaining no answer, he concludes, like the narrator on the night of Tess Durbeyfield's rape, that 'Baal was gone a-hunting' (ibid. 93). The second part of the novel falls apart structurally, dividing its attention between a range of characters, not only Waldo but Lyndall struggling with similar doubts and fears while the narrator pontificates at length about the sadness of losing faith. But the power of the first part of the novel brings something new to the genre, demonstrating a depth of realism in the treatment of religious experience.

The final 'novel of doubt' I want to consider is perhaps the most famous, Mrs Humphry Ward's *Robert Elsmere* of 1888, which became a publishing sensation after the reigning prime minister, Gladstone, published a 10,000 word review on the 'Battle of Belief' it represented. This sparked off a wide-ranging debate in the highbrow journals first in Britain and then in America on the future of Christianity (Sutherland 1990: 128). Ward herself claimed that it was the 'shock of indignation' she felt on listening to the Bampton Lecture of 1881, by John Wordsworth, which linked 'unsettlement in religion' with immorality in conduct, which drove her to defend 'the patient scholars and thinkers of the Liberal host', men such as Stanley, Jowett, and her uncle Mathew Arnold, against such slurs:

> How could one show England what was really going on in her midst? Surely the only way was through imagination; through a picture of actual life and conduct... Who and what were the persons of whom the preacher gave this grotesque account? What was their history? How had their thoughts and doubts come to be? What was the effect of them on conduct?   (Ward 1918: 168)

Robert Elsmere answers these questions in three bulky volumes, tracing the development of her eponymous cleric from his courtship of the deeply religious Catherine Leyburn, through the unsettling of his faith in the supernatural side of Christianity under the influence of a local squire, to the final phase of Elsmere's life, when he brings 'The New Brotherhood of Christ' to the slums of London.

The power of this novel, as with Schreiner's, I would argue, lies in its exploration of the psychology of its central figure, as the falseness of his position gradually dawns upon him. Ward records Elsmere's reading of Wendover's anti-Christian polemics:

> Robert had lit on those pages in the Essay on the Gospels where the squire fell to analysing the evidence for the Resurrection, following up his analysis by an attempt at reconstructing the conditions out of which the belief in the 'legend' arose. Robert began to read vaguely at first, then to hurry on through page after page, still standing, seized at once by the bizarre power of the style, the audacity and range of the treatment.   (Ward 1952: 274)

Ward captures the sheer intellectual excitement of reading biblical criticism (no mean feat), as well as the psychological effect on Elsmere, who feels 'as though a cruel torturing hand were laid upon his inmost being'. He sinks back upon his chair, head in hands, aware of the possible consequences for himself, his career, and his family of doubting such a central element of orthodox Christianity.

The lengthy theological conversations Elsmere undergoes with Wendover, with his tutor Grey (clearly modelled on the Liberal Anglican Idealist T. H. Green), and with his wife are probably less important, and less interesting to a reader than Elsmere's inner conflict as he moves slowly from a supernatural to a fully 'natural' or 'human' Christianity. Grey, for example, assures him rather predictably that the pain of 'parting with the Christian mythology' is all part of 'the education of God'. God, Grey insists, 'is in criticism, in science, in doubt, so long as the doubt is a pure and honest doubt'.

He should 'learn to seek God, not in any single event of past history, *but in your own soul*' (ibid. 345). Elsmere finally plucks up the courage to confide his doubts about the incarnation and the resurrection to his wife, who has little time for 'all these critical and literary considerations' (ibid. 352–3). But the point is that these *are* genuinely 'critical and literary' considerations; they arise from the kind of 'critical and literary' reading Matthew Arnold and others had given to the Bible and they find expression here in literary form, through the novel's exploration of Elsmere's inner conflicts.

Much of the final part of the novel, describing Elsmere's work in the slums of London, is filtered through the eyes of a friend, Hugh Flaxman, who records for the benefit of his sympathetic aunt the founding of 'The New Brotherhood of Christ', in which he sees the same spirit as in the early Church, 'the spirit of devotion, through a man, to an idea'. He describes their first service, in which Elsmere reads 'a passage from the life of Christ' and then 'expounds it ... as a lecturer might expound a passage of Tacitus, historically and critically'. After that, however, 'when the critic has done, the poet and the believer begin', bringing out 'the pure human pity of the story' (ibid. 553–4). Again, the point is that it takes 'a poet' to appreciate the full pathos of the story, which appeals first and foremost to the imagination.

All of these novels, it could be argued, have their flaws; none of them totally escape the tendentiousness characteristic of nearly all Victorian fiction. But all four of the novels I have considered seem to me to contribute something not only to literature but to theology, providing portraits of religious experience (albeit negative experience, doubt more than faith) which help readers to understand more fully what such experience involves. It is, of course, a very traditional defence of literature, that it helps us to understand different ways of thinking and feeling. But it is nevertheless important to recognize what literature can contribute to theology in this respect, deepening and expanding the understanding of faith characteristic of more straightforward theological discourse.

VICTORIAN POETRY: DRAMATIC MONOLOGUES AND HISTORICAL PERSPECTIVES

As with the novel, 'Victorian religious poetry', in Cynthia Scheinberg's words, became 'an important site for presenting divergent religious perspectives', representing the variety of religious communities that had found legitimacy within the period, from the dissenting and Catholic traditions given full status as citizens in 1828 and 1829 to the Jewish poets beginning to appear at its close (Scheinberg 2000: 160). In what remains probably the most influential volume on the religious poetry of the period, *The Disappearance of God* (1963), J. Hillis Miller argued the case for 'the homogeneity of the culture' of the age. While admitting that 'we can neither explain why people stop feeling and believing in an old way, nor why a new way of feeling and believing appears simultaneously in widely separate individuals', like 'a great wave breaking on the shore', Miller (2000: 3–4) believed (in 1963 at least) that such a phenomenon was most observable in its literature. By 2000, in the preface to a revised edition of *The Disappearance of God*, Miller confessed to being less confident about the existence of such a 'universal spooky Zeitgeist' (ibid. p. xi). It remained the case, however, in his view, that the five writers studied in his volume shared a similar concern with the loss of connection to the traditional Christian God and struggled to 'bring him back to earth as a benign power inherent in the self, in nature, and in the human community' (ibid. 15). But they did so, Miller insists, in different, historically specific ways.

The dramatic monologue, according to Miller, should be acknowledged not only as the characteristic poetic form of the period but as 'the literary genre of historicism... aware of the relativity, the arbitrariness of any single life or way of looking at the world' (ibid. 107–8). Browning, for example, 'assumes that there is no way to create an absolute system of thought which will allow man to put himself in the place of God and see things *sub specie aeternitatis*... Reality for man lies in the acceptance of a finite perspective on the world' (ibid. 107). The best way to avoid overconfidence in the absolute truth of one's own position is therefore, as in *The Ring and the Book*, to be aware of the existence of multiple different perspectives: 'There is no "Truth", only a large number of little subjective truths' (ibid. 145). Miller reads *The Ring and the Book*, Browning's monumental retelling of the 'events' surrounding a historic murder trial as seen by a number of the participants, as a heroic attempt to achieve 'God's own infinite perspective' simply by multiplying the points of view (ibid. 149), reaching towards a mathematical infinity.

The point about the dramatic monologue, however, is that it advertises what in other poetry is sometimes concealed, that the perspective offered is a particular one, limited to one person at a particular time and place. Even lyric poems such as 'Dover Beach', Matthew Arnold's melancholy lament over the 'long withdrawing roar' of the Sea of Faith, presents the imaginary views of a particular lover addressing his beloved in a particular setting. Swinburne too puts his lament, 'Thou hast conquered, O pale Galilean', into the mouth of a pagan Roman of the fourth century, drawing attention to the particular context in which those words were uttered by the apostate Emperor Julian (Brett 1965: 159–61). Hardy is less obviously historical or dramatic in 'God's Funeral' but that makes it no less problematic for A. N. Wilson to read this poem as straightforward evidence not just for Hardy's feeling 'that God had died' but for the collective experience of religious bereavement of 'Western Humanity' (Wilson 2000: 10).

Hardy's poem, of course, should not be read literally even as a statement of what *he* believed, let alone 'Western Humanity'. Hardy (1985: 441) used often to complain that 'people *will* treat my mood-dictated writing as a single scientific theory'. 'God's Funeral', it should be noted, dramatizes several divergent points of view. The persona, for example, observes two separate groups of mourners at this funeral: one group see the concept of God along Feuerbachian lines as a 'man-projected Figure' reflecting human emotions such as jealousy and ferocity while another claims that he remains a living person. The persona himself sympathizes with both groups but remains 'speechless', observing towards the end of the poem yet a third group, 'a certain few' who claim to see a gleam of light on the horizon. The poem ends with the persona 'dazed and puzzled' twixt the gleam and gloom', suspended in agnostic indecision (Hardy 1930: 307–9). It is, as Wilson suggests, characteristic of the period, not because it represents some homogenous Victorian experience of 'collective nervous breakdown' (Wilson 2000: p. xii) but because it registers specific alternative positions with none of which it can be content.

Another influential book on Victorian religious poetry, David Shaw's *The Lucid Veil*, takes its title from Tennyson's metaphor for the paradoxical representation character-istic of poetry, which is 'neither a mirror, that clearly reflects the world, nor a mask that hides it' but a veil which 'filters both God and nature through a screen of analogy'. Metaphors, symbols, and similar poetic strategies re-present reality through a kaleido-scope of linguistic devices which shed new light on what might otherwise be taken for familiar 'objects' (Shaw 1987: 3). Shaw analyses, for example, the way 'all confident definitions of God have a way of dissolving' in a poem such as Clough's 'Hymnos Ahymnos', which begins by invoking an ambiguously located divinity,

> O thou whose image in the shrine
> Of human spirits dwells divine.

The suggestion here that he only exists in the human heart is reinforced by the refusal at the end of the poem even to demand the predicate of existence of him: 'I will not ask to feel thou art'. Clough, in Shaw's words, denies himself 'the comfort of . . . pre-maturely stable ideas about God' (ibid. 138–40), opening up the unorthodox possi-bility of an immanent but not transcendent deity.

There are poems in which Clough seems definite enough. The persona of 'Easter Day', subtitled 'Naples 1849', for instance, allows himself the clear denial, 'Christ is not risen!' Each stanza repeats this refrain with slight variations, as the poem explores the consequence of this conviction for someone who had once been convinced of the truth of the resurrection:

> We are most hopeless who had once most hope
> We are most wretched that had most believed.
>   Christ is not risen.

> (Brett 1965: 36–41)

Unable, however, to let the matter rest as a literal statement of a fixed truth, Clough added a second poem 'Easter Day II', in which the persona hears

> Another voice that spake, another graver word,
> Weep not, it bade, whatever hath been said,
> Though He be dead, He is not dead.
>   In the true Creed
>   He is yet risen indeed,
>   Christ is yet risen.

> (ibid. 42)

A less delicate consciousness than Clough's might be tempted to suggest, pragmatically at least, that he ought to make up his mind on the subject, but the remainder of the poem tries to establish what this 'true Creed' is, in what sense it remains true that Christ is 'yet risen' (ibid. 43). It would be possible to 'translate' these poems, to paraphrase their 'meaning' in terms of the abandonment of literal belief in a physical resurrection but this would be to miss the experience of reading them, the emotional impact of this conviction on a particular character in a particular place in 1849.

Similarly, in order to 'reply' to Clough, Browning chose to write a complex pair of poems, 'Christmas-Eve' and 'Easter-Day', published together as a slim volume the following year. The first, as Mary Pollock explains, is a cross between a dream vision and a Menippean satire while the latter, with its opening lament, 'How very hard it is to be | A Christian', is a dialogue between two conflicting views about the nature and demands of faith. The former is the more readable, though it too embodies self-contradiction, the whole point of the Menippea being 'the narrator's tendency to undermine and satirize his own position in the text' (Pollock 2003: 113). Far from Clough's exotic Neapolitan location, 'Christmas-Eve' begins with its persona taking refuge from a sudden downpour in an undistinguished nonconformist chapel. He is soon so bored by the sermon, however, that he falls asleep and is magically trans-ported (in a dream) to two alternative religious locations. The first is St Peter's, Rome, where he cannot but be impressed by the liturgy, the incense, bells, and garments, seeing 'the error; but above | The scope of error', the 'love of those first Christian days' (Browning 1994: 402). He then gets transported to a German univer-sity lecture room, where he captures some of the intellectual excitement, the 'buzzing and emotion' as the 'hawk-nosed high-cheek-boned Professor' makes his way to his lectern. The content of the lecture, however, reducing the 'Myth of Christ' to a 'popular story' expressive of an eternal idea (ibid. 404–5), leaves him dissatisfied, so he is only too pleased to wake up back in the dingy nonconformist chapel in time for 'the tenth and lastly'. 'I choose here,' announces Browning's persona (ibid. 408), but not before he has made it clear that there are also elements of truth to be found in the alternative locations he has explored.

A number of Browning's dramatic monologues approach the 'Christ-event' from different vantage points. Two fictional first-century characters, for example, find themselves unable to accept the message preached by the early church. Cleon, a poet, cannot accept that a 'mere barbarian Jew' such as St Paul could have access to secrets shut from him, dismissing the message preached by 'certain slaves | Who touched on this same isle' as unbelievable: 'Their doctrine could be held by no sane man' (ibid. 452). Karshish, the Arab physician comes a little closer to the event, finding himself fascinated by Lazarus's claim to have been resurrected by the incarnate God. Though Karshish too finds this 'strange', he ends the poem dwelling on the possibility that the 'very God', the 'All-Great, were the All-Loving too' (ibid. 426). These characters remain suspended on the brink of belief, unable to accept what they nevertheless find strangely attractive.

Perhaps Browning's most profound and powerful poem, however, approaching even closer to the heart of the mystery surrounding the incarnation, is 'A Death in the

Desert' (1864). The death in question is that of St John, narrated by one Pamphylax, whose story, dictated to Phoebus, comprises the subject of a parchment manuscript introduced at the beginning of the poem by its owner and read (at the end) by the heretical Cerinthus, who remains unconvinced by Christ's divinity. This complex enfolding of different layers of perception embodies in its form what Eleanor Shaffer (1975: 210) sees as the point of the poem: 'The inaccessibility, the uncertainty of what really happened, the unreliability of personal witness and of document, the saturation in folk tale and dogmatic expectation characterize all historical events, not simply because they happened long ago, but because we cannot perceive in any other way.' Browning, who had read both Strauss's and Renan's *Life of Jesus* (the latter published in 1863), marvelled at their complacency in believing that they had come closer to 'stating a fact' than St John himself (De Vane 1955: 261–2). What actually constitutes a 'fact' is precisely what this poem explores.

Pamphylax's account of St John's death, after establishing in vivid detail the dramatic surroundings of this 'event', presents the apostle realizing the enormity of his predicament, that he, the last person to have had direct contact with Christ, is about to die. He imagines future generations questioning the historicity of the events recorded in his Gospel. John recognizes that people will have very different notions of God, of history, and of the miraculous, that 'man was made to grow', to 'apprehend Him newly at each stage'. His own Gospel will be read differently, with less emphasis on the miraculous elements, 'wrought | When, save for it, no faith was possible', and more on its overall theological significance: 'This book's fruit is plain, | Nor miracles need prove it any more' (Browning 1994: 488–9). Browning's apostle's meditation on the nature of Christian faith and the extent to which it is related to history, I would claim, remains one of the most significant pieces of writing on this subject of any period, all the more powerful because the complex layers of narrative dramatize as well as explain the nature of the evidence.

Browning is equally incisive on the shortcomings of natural theology, whether in 'Caliban upon Setebos', in which Shakespeare's character indulges in a comic variety of Calvinism, full of anthropomorphic arguments from his own temperament to that of God, in 'Bishop Blougram's Apology', in which a worldly and pragmatic Catholic bishop attempts to persuade a sceptical journalist of the validity of Pascal's wager (that he might as well place his money on full-blooded faith since the consequences of being wrong are less awful), or in 'Mr Sludge the Medium', a satire on spiritualism in which the urgent need for some kind of faith becomes increasingly apparent. The point of all these monologues, however, as of all the poems considered in this section, is that they embody a *dramatic* representation of a particular point of view, embedded in a particular context, shaped by the assumptions and interpretative framework of the time. Any reading of any piece of Victorian writing, of course, requires these considerations to be taken into account. What is so impressive about Browning in particular and the Victorian dramatic monologue in general is that these 'new historicist' considerations are already embodied in the poems themselves. These literary texts, in other words, contain a highly self-conscious reflection on the nature of Victorian faith. They represent, I would claim, a more interesting, intelligent, and persuasive form of theology than the many volumes of straightforward essays and sermons published in the period.

WORKS CITED

ARNOLD, MATTHEW. 1968. *Literature and Dogma*. Ann Arbor: University of Michigan Press.

ASHTON, ROSEMARY. 1989. 'Doubting Clerics: From James Anthony Froude to *Robert Elsmere* via George Eliot', in David Jasper and T. R. Wright (eds.), *The Critical Spirit and the Will to Believe: Essays in Nineteenth-Century Literature and Religion*. London: Macmillan, 69–87.

BRETT, R. L. (ed.) 1965. *Poems of Faith and Doubt: The Victorian Age*. London: Edward Arnold.

BROWNING, ROBERT. 1994. *The Works of Robert Browning*. Ware: Wordsworth Editions.

CARLYLE, THOMAS. 1908. *Sartor Resartus and On Heroes and Hero-Worship*. London: J. M. Dent.

COULSON, JOHN. 1981. *Religion and Imagination*. Oxford: Clarendon.

CUNNINGHAM, VALENTINE. 1975. *Everywhere Spoken Against: Dissent in the Victorian Novel*. Oxford: Clarendon.

DAVIS, PHILIP. 2002. *The Victorians*. Oxford: Oxford University Press.

DE VANE, WILLIAM CLYDE. 1955. *A Browning Handbook*. 2nd edn. New York: Appleton-Century-Crofts.

ELIOT, GEORGE. 1963. *Essays of George Eliot*, ed. Thomas Pinney. London: Routledge & Kegan Paul.

FROUDE, J. A. 1904. *The Nemesis of Faith*. London: William Hutchinson.

GILMOUR, ROBIN. 1993. *The Victorian Period: The Intellectual and Cultural Context, 1830–1890*. London: Longman.

HARDY, THOMAS. 1930. *The Collected Poems of Thomas Hardy*. London: Macmillan.

—— 1985. *The Life and Work of Thomas Hardy*, ed. Michael Millgate. Athens: University of Georgia Press.

HILTON, BOYD. 1988. *The Age of Atonement: The Influence of Evangelicalism on Social and Economic Thought, 1785–1865*. Oxford: Clarendon.

JEWSBURY, GERALDINE. 1989. *Zoe: The History of Two Lives*. London: Virago.

MAISON, MARGARET. 1961. *Search Your Soul, Eustace: Victorian Religious Novels*. London: Sheed & Ward.

MILLER, J. HILLIS. 2000. *The Disappearance of God: Five Nineteenth-Century Writers*. Urbana: University of Illinois Press.

NEWSOME, DAVID. 1997. *The Victorian World Picture*. London: John Murray.

PETERSON, LINDA H. 1986. *Victorian Autobiography: The Tradition of Self-Interpretation*. New Haven: Yale University Press.

POLLOCK, MARY. 2003. *Elizabeth Barrett and Robert Browning: A Creative Partnership*. Aldershot: Ashgate.

PRICKETT, STEPHEN. 1976. *Romanticism and Religion: The Tradition of Coleridge and Wordsworth in the Victorian Church*. Cambridge: Cambridge University Press.

RUSKIN, JOHN. 1994. *Praeterita*, ed. A. O. J. Cockshut. Keele: Ryburn.

SCHEINBURG, CYNTHIA. 2000. 'Victorian Poetry and Religious Diversity', in Joseph Bristow (ed.), *The Cambridge Companion to Victorian Poetry*. Cambridge: Cambridge University Press, 159–79.

SCHREINER, OLIVE. 1998. *The Story of an African Farm,* ed. Joseph Bristow. Oxford: Oxford University Press.

SHAFFER, E. S. 1975. *'Kubla Khan' and 'The Fall of Jerusalem'.* Cambridge: Cambridge University Press.

SHAW, W. DAVID. 1987. *The Lucid Veil: Poetic Truth in the Victorian Age.* London: Athlone.

SUTHERLAND, JOHN. 1990. *Mrs Humphry Ward: Eminent Victorian, Pre-eminent Edwardian.* Oxford: Clarendon.

SWEET, MATTHEW. 2001. *Inventing the Victorians.* London: Faber & Faber.

TENNYSON, ALFRED LORD. 1969. *The Poems of Tennyson,* ed. Christopher Ricks. London: Longmans.

THOMAS, JANE. 1994. *Victorian Literature from 1830 to 1890.* London: Bloomsbury.

TILLOTSON, KATHLEEN. 1954. *Novels of the 1840s.* Oxford: Clarendon.

WARD, MRS HUMPHRY. 1918. *A Writer's Recollections.* London: Collins.

—— 1952, *Robert Elsmere.* London: Thomas Nelson.

WHEELER, MICHAEL. 1990. *Death and the Future Life in Victorian Literature and Theology.* Cambridge: Cambridge University Press.

WILSON, A. N. 2000. *God's Funeral: A Biography of Faith and Doubt in Western Civilization.* New York: Ballantine.

WOLFF, ROBERT LEE. 1977. *Gains and Losses: Novels of Faith and Doubt in Victorian England.* London: John Murray.

FURTHER READING

BUDD, SUSAN. 1977. *Varieties of Unbelief: Atheists and Agnostics in English Society, 1850–1960.* London: Heinemann.

CHADWICK, OWEN. 1970. *The Victorian Church.* 2 vols. London: Adam Black.

—— 1975. *The Secularization of the European Mind in the Nineteenth Century.* Cambridge: Cambridge University Press.

COCKSHUT, A. O. J. (ed.) 1966. *Religious Controversies of the Nineteenth Century.* London: Methuen.

CUPITT, DON. 1984. *The Sea of Faith: Christianity in Change.* London: BBC.

HANSON, ELLIS. 1997. *Decadence and Catholicism.* Cambridge, Mass.: Harvard University Press.

HOUGHTON, WALTER E. 1957. *The Victorian Frame of Mind.* New Haven: Yale University Press.

JAY, ELISABETH (ed.) 1983. *The Evangelical and Oxford Movements.* Cambridge: Cambridge University Press.

—— 1979. *The Religion of the Heart: Anglican Evangelicalism and the Nineteenth-Century Novel.* Oxford: Oxford University Press.

REARDON, B. M. G. 1966. *Religious Thought in the Nineteenth Century.* Cambridge: Cambridge University Press.

—— 1971. *Religious Thought in the Victorian Age.* London: Longmans.

ROWELL, GEOFFREY. 1974. *Hell and the Victorians.* Oxford: Clarendon.

Victorian Religion. 2003. Special issue of *Victorian Literature and Culture* 31 / 1 (March).

CHAPTER 10

MODERNISM

CLEO MCNELLY KEARNS

To introduce the term 'modernism' into a discussion of the intersections between literature and theology is to risk complicating rather than clarifying the issues at stake. In the first place, modern literature and modern theology are two relatively distinct discourses with different orientations and contexts—and each term is within its own domain highly contested and perhaps even, many would argue, counter-productive. Modernism in theology has its roots in the Enlightenment and in nineteenth-century philosophy and biblical criticism, and in Romantic and Victorian liberal and progressive thought. It draws upon Kant, Hegel, and the higher criticism, and it enters into dialogue with, among other things, Darwinian science and the general high bourgeois culture of its time. However, though the influence of its orientations and engagements persists to this day, many of the towering figures of twentieth-century theology, from Karl Barth to Hans Urs von Balthasar, were *not* modernists strictly speaking, and were often highly critical of liberal suppositions and methods even where they sometimes drew on or deployed them. Modernism in literature and the arts, by contrast, is an almost purely twentieth-century phenomenon and is to some extent a matter of style and form rather than content and ideas, though it has more ties to theology and more concern with theological issues than literary and cultural critics have often appreciated.

Theological modernism effectively began in nineteenth-century Germany, where theologians such as Schleiermacher and Troeltsch began to perceive that one way out of scholastic and Calvinist aporias and the subsequent dismissal of religion during the Enlightenment lay in Kant's philosophy of religion. This philosophy delineated a clear separation between reason and faith, and it thus opened a space in which the latter could be articulated on a new basis, a basis of immanence, feeling, and contemporary cultural and personal experience. Modernism of this kind went hand in hand with a Hegelian historicizing of the unfolding of spirit and a sense of the providential evolution of divine manifestation towards universal salvation. These affirmations translated, perhaps too readily, into romantic vapours, cheap progressivism, and perennial philosophy, but they helped theology to recover from what many had thought were the devastating blows of eighteenth-century British Enlightenment critique. Furthermore, they also led to a willingness to embrace the surrounding culture and were patient of engagement with the rising cultural prestige of science. This general theological outlook also inspired and informed the higher criticism and new initiatives in textual approaches to Scripture and tradition, the sphere in which modernism in theology bore its most lasting fruit.

From Germany, and building on a strong internal discourse of enlightenment, modernist ideas quickly reached the British intelligentsia, their original source. Among the most prominent expositors of the new and modern point of view was the English Jesuit George Tyrell. Writing to his friend and like-minded colleague Baron von Hugel, Tyrell summarized his position, a useful statement, in brief, of the modern religious point of view:

Hence I am driven to a revolutionary view of dogma. As you know, I distinguish sharply between the Christian revelation and the theology that rationalizes and explains it. The former was the work of the inspired era of origins. It is prophetic in form and sense; it involves an idealized reading of history past and to come. It is, so to say, an inspired construction of things in the interests of religion; a work of inspired imagination, not of reflection and reasoning. It does not develop or change like theology; but is the subject-matter of theology...The whole has a spiritual value as a construction of Time in relation to Eternity. It gives us the world of our religious life. But I do not feel bound to find an independent meaning in each element; or to determine prematurely what elements are of liberal, and what of purely symbolic value— which is the core of historic fact and which of idealization. My faith is in the truth, shadowed by the whole creed; and in the direction it gives to spiritual life—in the Way, the Life and the Truth.   (Petre 1920: 57–8)

The extent to which these views sound conventional or uncontroversial today is the extent to which a generalized modernism was rapidly diffused in British and American culture in the twentieth century and became well established, at least among the intelligentsia, both within and without the Catholic Church.

This diffusion did not occur without resistance. There followed on this nineteenth- and early twentieth-century expansion something of an immediate countermovement towards repression. It was foreshadowed in Leo XIII's encyclical *Aeterni Patris* (1879). Pope Leo, believing that a return to a repristinated and reified understanding of scholasticism was the only possible position for a church under political and cultural siege, exhorted the magisterium to 'restore the golden wisdom of St. Thomas'. Some thirty years later, Tyrell was suspended from his ministry and expelled from the Society of Jesus for modernist tendencies, and Pius X in the papal document *Pascendi* (1907) formally condemned modernism and attempted to make a return to scholasticism the official theology of the Church. (This stance would probably have horrified Thomas himself, who was in many ways the modernist of his day.) This attempt by the papacy to close the door on a widespread and intellectually compelling movement had the ironic effect not only of destroying several great careers and setting Catholic biblical scholarship back by generations but of putting the term 'modernism' itself on the general cultural map. The major figures condemned in this document include Alfred Loisy (1857–1940) as well as Tyrell (1861–1909) and von Hugel (1852–1925). As Marianne Thormahlen notes in her introduction to an important recent anthology of essays on the modernist movement in literature, none of these figures made use of the word 'modernism' itself in public until after the papal condemnation (Thormahlen 2003: 124). That condemnation had, however, the unintended consequence of making the term part of the general intellectual commerce of the period.

Eventually, however, modernism's best offspring—the movement its conservative opposition dubbed *nouvelle théologie*—succeeded just before, during, and after the Second World War in reorienting Catholic intellectual life to a new direction, modern in a somewhat different sense. This theology, developed by such deeply reflective and learned figures as Jean Danielou, Henri de Lubac, Yves Congar, and M-D Chenu, arose from a discreet but persistent exploration of Christian texts and traditions with an eye both to their historical context and to their contemporary relevance (Daley 2004). As Danielou describes its challenges, a theology of this kind

must treat God as God—not as an object, but as the Subject par excellence, who reveals himself when and as he will; as a result, it must be penetrated, first of all, with a religious spirit. Second, it must respond to the experiences of the modern mind, and take cognizance of the new dimensions which science and history have given to mind and society. Finally, it must become a concrete attitude before existence—one unified response that engages the whole person, the inner light of a course of action in which the whole of life is engaged.   (Cited ibid. 5)

The *nouvelle théologie* contributed to what was perhaps modernization's most stunning public success: the reform movement culminating in Vatican II. This reform not only 'purged' the liturgy and many of the thought forms of the Church of centuries of scholastic elaboration, but opened the path for Catholic theology and biblical criticism to draw on contemporary methods and experience and on philosophical movements from existentialism and hermeneutics to phenomenology and deconstruction.

This was not the whole story, however, for Catholic resistance to these new currents remained important, both within the magisterium and in the pew, and Catholic conservatism in doctrine and morals had from the first a deep cultural impact, not only on the faithful, but on the wider culture as well, creating a conservative profile for the Roman Church still operative today. At the same time, the Catholic understanding of and reaction to this phenomenon influenced a number of the writers of the twentieth century, not always in the direction of dissent. For as we shall see there was something in religious and philosophical modernism— as opposed to modernism in the arts—that seemed to many twentieth-century writers inadequate to the experience of two world wars and a holocaust, and antithetical to the complex, sometimes apocalyptic, sometimes classical, symbolic, imaginative, and restorative energies they sought to reclaim.

Protestant modernism in Britain and America had roughly the same nineteenth-century seedbed as did Roman Catholic modernism: the higher criticism, political liberalism, the rise of science, anticlericalism, and a desire to break down dogmatic reification and moral absolutism and bring Christian belief into better contact with contemporary realities. These assumptions quickly flowed not only into a flourishing biblical scholarship but into the Broad Church and Anglican modernist movements in Britain and into Unitarianism in America. The major figures in Britain—such divines as B. F. Streeter and Dr. Sanday—are now no longer household names, but the positions they held and defended are widely accepted in Christian circles and often the more powerful for being tacitly assumed. Paul Badham (1998: 78), in his useful study of Anglican modernism then and now, defines the still important issues these positions raise in terms of the following axioms:

1. Belief that the objective existence of God can be shown to be compatible with modern philosophy and science.

2. Belief that religious experience is foundational for faith and that such experience is part of the common heritage of the world's faiths.

3. Belief in the reality of life after death understood in terms of the immortality of the soul.

4. Belief that the divinity of Christ must be expressed in such a way that it is compatible with the equally important doctrine of his humanity and oneness with us and that it genuinely reflects what historical study of the Gospels tells us about Jesus' life and thought.

In the USA, a German-influenced, broad Unitarianism and the philosophies of religion—Emersonian, idealist, and eventually pragmatic—to which it gives rise were immensely influential in the nineteenth century, though from the first they had their critics. Emily Dickinson, for instance, was able to be acid as well as acute about this tendency.

> He preached upon 'Breadth' till it argued him narrow—
> The Broad are too broad to define
> And of 'Truth' until it proclaimed him a Liar—
> The Truth never flaunted a Sign—
>
> Simplicity fled from his counterfeit presence
> As Gold the Pyrites would shun—
> What confusion would cover the innocent Jesus
> To meet so enabled a Man!

This poem captures well the complexities at issue in the reception of modern theological ideas, for while it pokes fun at a so very up-to-date, so very *enabled* clergyman, it does so in the name of what is also a highly modernist construct: a humane and innocent Jesus upon whom tradition has thrown a false and elaborate overlay, and whose very name serves as a kind of touchstone for simple faith and historical truth.

Within a few years of the papal condemnation of modernism in 1907, the modernist movement in both Catholic and Reformed circles also began to gather steam among the general educated public, accruing a wide range of connotations and implications, both intellectual and cultural. These connotations included what S. M. Hutchens (1999: 1) describes succinctly as 'a posited end to the assertion of religious dogma as prescriptive public truth'. Great interest at this time followed and continues to follow initiatives in biblical criticism toward stripping away secondary and mythological elements from the faith in favour of a new understanding of its historical manifestations and of a rational though not dismissive reappropriation. The desideratum, as many see it, is to disestablish Christianity and cleanse it not only of the weight of gothic and scholastic mediations and constraining social conventions but of the more fanciful, symbolic, allegorical, and apocalyptic and apocalyptic-messianic interpretations of its truths, even those of Scripture itself. As Hutchens (ibid. 2) also notes, modernism in this sense posits 'as an epistemological entrance requirement' that all prior canons of knowledge and method and their condensed symbols be subject to critical reconstruction, though it cannot tell us by what canon this is to be done once these prior canons enter the door.

This positive invocation of a general, across-the-board examination and critique of religion, based on criteria outside the realm of faith, targeted as antiquated and mystified any position smacking of apocalyptic and/or participating in what previous ages had elaborated as a full messianic understanding of the figure of Jesus. Robert Jenson (2004: 12) puts it pungently, if somewhat tendentiously: 'modernity's great theological project was to suppress apocalyptic, and to make messianism into [mere] guru-worship'. A new understanding of Christianity, it was thought, might arise from this suppression, an understanding based on a progressive sense of history and a submission to scientific criteria. This basis would not leave the church without faith and tradition, but it would value these without the sacrifice of intellectual rigour, scientific advancement, rigorous textual criticism, and radical cultural and political engagement. The figure of Rudolf Bultmann comes to mind here, the New Testament scholar who inaugurated a project of 'demythologizing' the Gospels that, as it seems in retrospect, only a dyed-in-the-wool modernist could imagine as possible or desirable.

Bultmann is instructive here, however, in another way, for his religious vision was not confined by exegetical method. He was a profound man of faith, and he was open to and inspired by the extremely rigorous anti-modern theological perspective offered by the work of his younger colleague Karl Barth. Barth, perhaps the most outstanding theologian of the twentieth century, challenged in many ways the liberal political and revisionist predispositions of his time and sought to restore an apocalyptic, engaged, and deeply messianic vision to Christian understanding. To Barth we shall return in a moment. First, however, we must note among the moderns a number of somewhat younger and later figures, including Richard and Reinhold Niebuhr, whose base of operations was the USA and whose engagement with the liberal politics and art of the 1930s to the 1960s was, like that of Troeltsch and others before them, founded in a historically critical understanding of Christianity and a strong desire to subject the faith to reasonable revision.

To some extent, two other great twentieth-century theologians were in a qualified way moderns as well: Paul Tillich and Dietrich Bonhoeffer, at least in the sense that they were deeply engaged with contemporary culture and politics, somewhat distanced from ecclesiastical structures and orthodoxies, and completely opposed to the idolatrous power of institutions, both state and church. Tillich, who sought a kind of revision of the doctrine of God in terms of the ground of being, saw theology less as a matter of reflection on revelation than as a search for answers to 'ultimate questions', while Bonhoeffer's life of sacrificial political engagement drew upon the prophetic capacity of modern liberalism to witness to a gospel sense of discipleship and to a historical Jesus seen as a model for spiritual leadership in the face of evil.

The attenuations of a nineteenth-century religious outlook, however updated, did nonetheless, here as in Catholicism, breed a certain resistance, a resistance with many opposing, profound, and still-ramifying manifestations, including the rise of neo-orthodoxy on the one hand and fundamentalism on the other. Granted, Protestant modernism was neither resisted with such institutional force as Roman Catholic modernism (though many refined theologians vigorously rejected it), nor did it win the day in quite so definitive a fashion. From the first, however, it had its dissenters, both from above, so to speak, in the flourishing movement of neo-reformed-orthodoxy around the great, left-leaning, and philosophically sophisticated figure of Karl Barth, and from below in the hotly and passionately held fundamentalism and evangelical fervour of many clergy as well as laity.

The key moment in this shifting current was perhaps the period just before and during the First World War, a period that inaugurated major shifts in the culture of Europe and America in almost every domain. Among other things, very early, in 1914, as Europe began to fall apart, the modern theologian Troeltsch, like many of his colleagues, compromised himself in the eyes of some Christians by supporting the Kaiser's war policies and by moving from the chair of Systematic Theology at Heidelberg to a chair in the History and Philosophy of Civilization in Berlin. Highly critical of Troeltsch's move, the young Barth began to look to Kierkegaard rather than to Kant and Hegel for philosophical inspiration and to adumbrate a radical apocalyptic vision of Christianity as the encounter with what today, in a different language and context, might be called the *tout autre*. In 1919 he published his controversial and widely read commentary on Romans. Its attack on liberal theology for failing to provide a sharp enough critique of culture and politics to mount a serious resistance to imperialism seemed prophetic when the so-called 'Faith Movement of German Christians' showed itself ready to embrace Nazism, and the official church leadership in Germany seemed to lack either ethical or theological resources to combat this collusion.

The youthful Barth, rusticated for a time in his early years to the leadership of a parish made up largely of the industrial poor, was struck by the impotence of liberal theology in addressing the lives of his parishioners, and had to conclude that the bourgeois religious perspective in which he had been trained offered them very little, and that his pastoral responsibility must carry him beyond its terms and horizons (Jenson 2004: 5). Giving up definitively on natural theology and on the possibility of a happy collaboration between Christian understanding and contemporary social and political culture, Barth then began the articulation of a theology based strictly on 'vertical' revelation from above and not on the surrounding dominant culture, whether enlightened or not.

The first initiative here was the commentary on Romans, a publication which instantly made him a celebrity. He then gathered about him a movement of sorts, drawing the older Bultmann in its train and including Emil Brunner. The group published a journal, *Zwischen den Zeiten*, defining their moment in history as one of crisis, a moment, as the journal's title indicates, seen as a kind of suspension, 'between the times'. Robert Jenson (ibid. 6) captures the theological and indeed the aesthetic energies of this movement well:

For what is there *zwischen den Zeiten*, between the times? Theologically, there is that dimensionless perch between time and eternity, between death and resurrection. Culturally, there is the breathless moment between deconstruction of the established grasp of reality and the gift of a new one—the moment of Cézanne's *Bathers*. Politically, there is revolution. And in Germany all of these were there at once.

Barth's own work emerged from this moment, and although it later modulated into a somewhat less apocalyptic exposition as he attempted to give narrative and Christological content to the encounter between time and eternity, it was a modulation with an edge. It gave him a critical purchase on both liberal religion and contemporary politics, helping to sustain his profound resistance to National Socialism.

Barth's critique of nineteenth-century assumptions about religion and theology is still widely influential today, though less so perhaps in the pew than in the study. Even those whose perspective remained in some sense more hospitable to the surrounding culture and more engaged with natural theology than his have had to reckon with his cogent analyses. Tillich and Bonhoeffer, for instance, emerging from the same experiences of the trauma of war and holocaust that Barth saw coming, while both loosely speaking 'modern' in their move away from ecclesiastical structures and into direct engagement with the world (though both were also profoundly pessimistic and existential, rather than progressivist and scientific in orientation), nevertheless developed their thought very much in conversation with Barth and they shared his personal and principled opposition to the reigning paradigms in society and politics, whether liberal or conservative.

Tillich, for instance, though often contrasted to Barth, saw his theology as in part constructed to 'answer' the Barthian call. As late as 1963, in a set of lectures for the general public, he wrote a moving statement that weaves together a new theological vision with a deep suspicion of progressivism and social planning:

Today we have to resist the meaningless 'forwardism' determining our inner and outer experience. Most of us can offer this resistance only as victims of the structures of our times. But the scars received in our lives may be the basis for sensitive speaking... But even then we will have to keep on resisting—against control by others, against 'management' of persons, against all abuse of men and women. This certainly includes the abuse of forcing them into their own salvation.   (Tillich 1996: 61)

Thus although modernist hopes and perspectives informed and inspired these theologians, they were in various ways as critical of a hyper-rationalized modern identification with the powers that be as was Barth himself. What Barth, Bultmann, Tillich, Bonhoeffer, and the leading figures of Vatican II shared, however—and shared in distinction from many of their postmodern heirs—was a sense that it is possible to cleanse Christian tradition of secondary formations and to return to a kernel, a bedrock, a bottom line to be discerned in Scripture and history upon which theological vision may be built anew.

It is interesting to note that none of the figures mentioned so far tackled directly or commented in an extended way on the two major and growing challenges to religious faith in this period: the social theory of Karl Marx and the psychologies of Sigmund Freud and Carl Jung. The Marxist view of religion as the 'opium of the people' and the Freudian view of it as a form of mystification and unconscious projection gained instant attention and growing currency among the intelligentsia throughout the period, and so as time went on did Jung's association of the sense of divinity with a transpersonal collective unconscious. These opinions influenced—though they did not entirely captivate—many artists and writers. Indeed it might be argued that the most important theological or rather atheological statements of the modern period were Marx's *Critique of the German Ideology* (1846), Freud's *Civilization and its Discontents* (1930), and Jung's *Answer to Job* (1952). Each of these offers a sharp critique of religion, and each is scornful of theological mystification, but each also arises from within a Jewish and Christian discourse and can hardly be conceived without the valorization of social justice and personal self-examination found in these faith traditions. Each was also eventually to spawn intense engagements from theologians and religious writers in the postmodern period.

Whatever its limitations, the impact of the modernist movement in theology on the literary and artistic modernism of the twentieth century was more profound than many later critics have supposed. It was not, however, monolithic nor was a modern religious outlook always the general theological orientation of choice for modern writers and artists. In the first, place, as we have seen, by the time at which the literary figures we call moderns were making their contributions, not only had the Roman Catholic Church formally condemned the modernist movement, but such major theologians of the period as Barth were already to some extent reacting against or moving beyond modern theology *strictu dictu*. And although their own innovations were placing them firmly in the camp of the avant-garde, the literary moderns were reacting *against* some modernizing tendencies in religion and culture, even when they regarded these as inevitable and in some respects liberating. Among other things, as I have said, modernism in the arts is primarily a matter of form, rather than content, of style rather than of thought per se, though form carries, for moderns in particular, its own freight of meaning: philosophical, political and theological.

At a deeper level, however, it must be admitted that the modernist ethos in religion was in many respects counter to the interests of art and artists. Demythologizing? The reduction of complex symbols into linear propositions? The cleansing and rectifying of tradition? A sense of the datedness of the past and its lack of pertinence

to the present? Optimism about the forward march of progress? Rejection of apocalyptic sensibility? Philosophical idealism? Pure science? None of these gestures or
positions or projects entirely suited the book of a modern writer, certainly not a
Joyce, a Pound, a Yeats, or an Eliot, especially not after the traumas and dislocations
of the First and then the Second World Wars. For in driving a wedge between the
rational and the mythological, the appeal of the new and the beauty of the old,
meaning and symbol, personal feeling and scientific consensus, modern theology left
little space for either art or genuine engagement with the darkness of human suffering
and mass-manufactured death and destruction.

Under the pressure of their need for both aesthetic pertinence and political
engagement, many artists and writers resisted not only the absolutisms, moral and
political, of various forms of clerical and cultural *ancien régime*, but the equally
barren vistas of the up-to-date liberal response. This response seemed to offer only a
denatured and pre-programmed agenda that threatened to ignore or elide political
and personal breakdown, to cut itself off from classical and pagan sources of
inspiration and renewal, and to flatten out all difference into an unending and sterile
same. At the same time, much in a generalized and widely diffused kind of 'modern
thinking' continued to have its appeal to men and women of letters, due among other
things to the critical historicism of its approach to biblical texts, its scholarly
approach to other cultures, its potential universalism and hospitality to Bohemian
and oppositional lifestyles, and above all to a deep and relatively unconstrained
exploration of the experience and meaning of sex. Thus, the relationship of most
modern artists to modern theology and religion was and remained ambivalent and
hard to determine.

Contributing to the complexity of the issues at stake was a further problem. For
though the term 'modern' occasionally occurs in nineteenth-century literature and
more often in twentieth-century novels, where it is a kind of canting jargon—often
used tongue in cheek—for all that is trendy and outré in art and morals, modernism
in literary studies is largely the sober retrospective construct of critics of the second
half of the twentieth century. Its profile is drawn by those readers for the most part
tuned and sympathetic to the new twentieth-century aesthetic and trying to measure
a major change in sensibility (cf. Thormahlen 2003: 124). This change was immediately and intuitively apparent to its first audience, but it was defined more precisely
by later critics, for whom modernism was a largely formal innovation entailing a
family of features, among them the writing of self-consciously difficult and demanding texts, the representation of sex and violence as constituent elements of human
life, a deployment of high learning in a vernacular idiom, linguistic experimentation
and the breaking of a certain conventional decorum in social, literary, and religious
domains.

Most of these later critics, from F. R. Leavis to Malcolm Bradbury, approached
modernism with discernment and respect, but they were often tone deaf to its
religious roots, seeing its provocative and impious discourse as arising from nothing
more than a kind of enlightened secularism. As we shall see, this was often not the
case, and the range of religious reference and dimension of spirituality inherent in

modern art seems to have often eluded these otherwise very acute readers. Children of a later, highly secularized cultural moment, they were subject to the notion that religion can be neatly hived off from philosophy and art—indeed that these perhaps supersede it—a view not unrelated to nineteenth-century aestheticism. Literary modernism as usually defined in the critical literature is thus not only different from theological modernism but is often defined in ways divorced from religious issues altogether.

We can now see, *pace* these critics, that modern artists—like the 'terribly modern' young things who liked, bought, and indeed flaunted their work—were probably more aware of the serious theological and religious issues underlying this new art and aesthetic, and more engaged with these matters, than the literary and cultural critics who followed them. Certainly this is true of the major figures of the period. T. S. Eliot is the most obvious example here, at once a major poet, an innovative critic, and, in his mature years, a practising Christian of great theological and philosophical subtlety and sophistication. Not only did Eliot deal with Christian themes in his work, but he made a direct contribution to Christian thought both through his participation in the Anglican Lambeth Conference and through his work on the committee for a revised translation of the New Testament.

Equally engaged, though from a dissenting point of view, were such writers as Yeats, Pound, and Joyce. The latter, for instance, was explicit about the difficulty and yet necessity he found in escaping the constraints of ethnicity, traditional faith, and identification with a single cultural heritage and social location. 'When the soul of man is born in this country,' says his young Irish hero in *Portrait of the Artist as a Young Man,* 'there are nets flung at it to hold it back from flight. You talk to me of nationality, language, religion. I shall try to fly by those nets' (Joyce 1991: 206). At the same time, it must be said that Joyce's disengagement from Catholicism and Irish politics and his movement toward a kind of gnosticism and pan-European cosmo-politanism emerged not from some merely rationalist and secular set of assumptions and presuppositions, but from a highly charged and consciously developed counter-vailing spiritual vision, one still informed and illuminated by the past. Among other things, his profound appreciation of the tension between Hebraism and Hellenism—to borrow the phrase of the great nineteenth-century critic Matthew Arnold—emerged from and depended on this spiritually informed vision.

(It might be noted here that a great many manifestations of modern sensibility, though not all, are closely tied to a persistent strain of gnosticism in Western culture, where gnosticism is defined as general orientation toward a dualistic theology according to which orthodox institutional religion is no more than a mask for a profoundly dark human situation, caught between an ideal notion of divinity and an equally strong sense of moral and ethical chaos. This gnosticism is explicit in the work of Lawrence Durrell, who is well aware of its historical roots, its theological implications, and its possible intersections with the new psychologies of Freud and Jung; and it marks the sensibility of, among others, D. H. Lawrence and Norman Mailer as well, most extravagantly in the latter's neglected magnum opus, *Ancient Evenings.*)

Yeats is yet another modern poet who departed from Christianity, but not in order to move towards a modern, rational liberalism in religion, but rather to embrace (though perhaps never quite literally) an esotericism the extent of which continues to astound the more secular of his critics and readers. His poem 'Vacillations', among his most important, ends with an apostrophe to Baron von Hugel, the Christian modernist noted above. It concludes:

> Must we part, Von Hugel, though much alike, for we
> Accept the miracles of the saints and honour sanctity?
> The body of Saint Teresa lies undecayed in tomb,
> Bathed in miraculous oil, sweet odours from it come,
> Healing from its lettered slab. Those self-same hands perchance
> Eternalised the body of a modern saint that once
> Had scooped out pharaoh's mummy. I—though heart might find relief
> Did I become a Christian man and choose for my belief
> What seems most welcome in the tomb—play a pre-destined part.
> Homer is my example and his unchristened heart.
> The lion and the honeycomb, what has Scripture said?
> So get you gone, Von Hugel, though with blessings on your head.

As his inclusion of pharaoh's mummy in this list of miracles might signal, Yeats was more interested in the belief in a world of spirits hidden from and more 'real' than obvious earthly phenomena, spirits that may be invoked to intervene actively in human life, than he was in orthodox Christianity, though he was insistent that these forms of spirituality were by no means as far apart as many thought. His interest in the occult, like that of many of his contemporaries, was in part a provocative gesture, in part a way of courting the muse, and in part a genuine spiritual commitment. The fine line between and among these motives is traced with great finesse and theological sophistication by several recent scholars (Helmling 1988; Longenbach 1988). In general, however, the increasingly high level of scholarship in matters cultural, some small but growing measure of direct contact with other traditions once thought to be entirely mystified and inscrutable, and a deeper philosophical and historical sophistication prevented many modern writers from falling into the sillier forms of spiritualism.

Ezra Pound, another dissenter from the modern Christian consensus, was also deeply engaged with religious and spiritual issues, though he did not think theologically in quite the way that Joyce or Eliot did. He shared with Yeats an interest in the occult and in gnosticism (Longenbach 1988; Miyaki 1991), but his apprehension of these was tempered by a finer sense of cultural mediation and a more honed aesthetic sensibility than many others could deploy. (The greatest of his contemporaries recognized in Pound this superior sensibility, and were the more mortified by the curious intellectual and ethical failures of his later political and social vision.) Indeed, Pound stands as *primus inter pares* among modernism's several great heretics, figures whose opposition to orthodox Christianity arose neither from liberal revisionism nor from secular materialism, but from a deep and impassioned concern with matters spiritual and an engaged critique of the attenuated forms Christian life and belief had come in their time to take.

Not every modern artist departed from Christianity or from traditional forms of representation in such extreme directions, either in terms of beliefs or aesthetics. Wyndham Lewis, for instance, after many experiments in both painting and writing involving both form and content, returned not only to traditional religious constructs but to portraiture and to the conventional structure of the novel. Eliot, having written the echt-modern poem *The Waste Land*, perhaps the greatest single achievement of modern poetry, took up dramatic lyric, the popular theatre, and something resembling more the meditative devotional poetry of the past than the innovative forms of the modernist sense of the future. Joyce, Pound, and Woolf, to mention only a few other representative figures, continued to be committed to a break with conventional form as well as content, but their later work moved, in the judgement of many, very close to the edge of unintelligibility and seemed to approach a cul-de-sac, aesthetically, personally, and to some extent ethically as well. So, at least, in the case of Woolf, who ended her life, and Pound, whose tragic investment in Italian fascism brought not only his reputation but in many respects his poetry to grief.

Thus many major figures in the modern arts, while avant-garde in orientation, were far more antagonistic to modernist revisionism in religion than might be supposed— or at least to modernist revisionism in its more reductive and unimaginative forms. Indeed, a surprising number of these figures remained or became close to traditional pre-modern forms of religious belief and practice. The Catholics, Anglo-Catholics, and/or converts Eliot, Stevens (late in life), David Jones, Allen Tate, W. H. Auden, Evelyn Waugh, G. K. Chesterton, Hilaire Belloc, and Paul Claudel all come to mind here, a list to which we must add the names of J. R. R. Tolkien, C. S. Lewis, the eccentric but interesting Charles Williams, and the great American modern literary critic Cleanth Brooks. A certain *nostalgie du cloître* may be observed even in figures who did not formally embrace high Anglicanism or Catholicism, such as Hilda Doolittle, Gertrude Stein, Wyndham Lewis, and Henry James. In the reformed tradition there was among others Marianne Moore, whose letters reveal not only a regular churchgoer but in many respects a deeply Protestant sensibility.

An important context for both the orthodox and the unorthodox theologies of modern artists remains to be discussed: the phenomenon the French historian of letters and cultural critic Raymond Schwab (1984) long ago identified as 'the oriental renaissance', an influx of Eastern philosophy and religion into European and American culture beginning in the nineteenth century and growing exponentially in importance today. For during the modern period, and with a depth of effect that we are only beginning to measure, the discovery of the huge, relatively unknown and unmapped 'old worlds' of Indic and Chinese culture and religion (to which we might add the 'primitive' world of African rhythms and forms) not only challenged European hegemony over religious truth but profoundly relativized the context in which that truth was understood and pursued. While arrogance and colonial myopia often dominated the reception of this infusion of new visions and perspectives, the effect of this intercultural contact was profoundly transforming, both in religion and in the arts.

Even in the very early modern period, many theologians and divines in Britain already wrote in the light of this oriental renaissance. The eminent Rowland Williams began his career with a major study on Christianity and Hinduism, while such equally prominent figures as B. H. Streeter and A. C. Bouquet took up the relatively new term 'comparative religion' and advocated its pursuit. These initiatives were largely based on a model of progressive revelation that makes Christ the fulfilment of all prior forms of religious understanding. Though this model now seems inadequate, the very gesture of placing, say, early Buddhism and the early church on the same plane, if only for purposes of comparison, was radical in both its immediate and long-term implications. This gesture was informed by the work of, among others, the great scholar of oriental texts and languages Max Muller and the early mythographer Sir James G. Frazer. Muller's remarks on these new perspectives capture both their potential and their limitations:

If we have once learned to see in the exclusive religion of the Jews a preparation of what was to be the all-embracing religion of humanity, we shall feel much less difficulty in recognizing, in the mazes of other religions, a hidden purpose; a wandering in the desert, it may be, but a preparation also for the land of promise. (Muller 1872: 23; cited in C. Kearns 1987: 132–3)

The effect of this oriental renaissance appears even more extensive in literature, though here again the new vistas opened out by comparative culture and religion are explored as much from a need to escape from modernist reductions as to harvest the scholarly, philosophical, and theological fruits of openings to the East. Yeats was intrigued by Eastern traditions and collaborated on a translation of Patanjali's yoga sutras, which was to become an influential text among the American intelligentsia in the next century. T. S. Eliot was long engaged with Buddhism and Hinduism, among other things for its refinement of meditative technique and its validation, though with great critical and philosophical sophistication, of mystical experience (ibid.). Ezra Pound not only rendered a number of classics of Chinese religion and literature into English, but was deeply steadied and guided by his understanding of Confucianism (G. Kearns 1980).

Eliot himself best understood the cultural possibilities and tensions arising from liberal, enlightened modernism in religion. Though the conservative positions on these issues he came to embrace displeased the politically correct both then and now—'how unpleasant to meet Mr. Eliot | with his garb of clerical cut', to quote his own spoof—his analysis of the issues at stake was without peer. His key critical terms, 'dissociation of sensibility', 'the objective correlative', and 'tradition and the individual talent' all arise form modernist concerns. The first of these points to an inability to feel thought on the pulse and is for Eliot the result of a modern divorce between sense and sensibility. The second represents a modernist attempt to bridge the subjective world of philosophical idealism, private experience, and esoteric knowledge, with what he calls 'open wisdom' and the new realism of science. The third, and the rich discourse of tradition in Eliot's work to which it leads, is perhaps the most productive of his critical concepts, arising from his study of American philosophers William James and Josiah Royce. Royce in particular, though Eliot could critique his philosophical arguments with a rapier mind honed on the finer work of F. H. Bradley, helped move him towards an understanding of cultural hermeneutics as spiritual practice.

Eliot saw in the initial *moment* or insight of artistic inspiration a necessarily heterodox impulse, an impulse in the best work then classically chastened and disciplined into an orthodoxy of both form and content that re-envisions the tradition even as it carries that tradition forward. (This is an understanding remarkably similar to that of Wallace Stevens, whose great poem 'An Ordinary Evening in New Haven' is in part a meditation, less resolved than acutely stated, on the problem of revelation and interpretation.) He fully took on board the Kantian and later the proto-phenomenological and deconstructive critique of Thomism in philosophy, the importance of the higher criticism in biblical studies and the appeal of cultural relativism when faced with, among other things, the profound influx of Eastern philosophy and religion into the Western cultural matrix. Alert to the modern heresies of esotericism, gnosticism, and paganism in his own work as well as that of his contemporaries, Eliot also understood that to meet with an adequate poetics and ethics the deep questions and traumas of contemporary life, not to mention the dislocations of a debased sexuality, required stronger medicine than a simple nineteenth-century Hegelian and idealist revisionism.

In 1927, after a long period of interest in Buddhism and Hinduism, Eliot joined the Anglican Church. He did so to some extent for practical or more precisely for pragmatic reasons in the philosophical sense. To 'become' a Buddhist, he thought, was to require of himself a change in mental orientation that would take him too far from his own language and culture to bear fruit (Kearns 1987: 131–59). In reflecting on this decision, Eliot articulated well the journey he himself had traced through both the appeal and the critique of modern thought to an understanding of the need for some traditional religious framework in which to carry on spiritual practice. 'The difficult discipline', he writes, 'is the discipline and training of emotion; this the modern world has great need of; so great that it hardly understands what the word means; and this I have found is only attainable through dogmatic religion' (Eliot 1930: 156).

This return to orthodoxy, though orthodoxy far more relativized, nuanced, and deconstructive in philosophical location than might appear, must, however, be counterbalanced by a recognition of its roots in Eliot's profoundly modernist project, both in literature and theology. In his early years, he put this project in terms that almost any modern theologian or writer could endorse: 'The life of a soul does not consist in the contemplation of one consistent world but in the painful task of unifying (to a greater or lesser extent) jarring and incompatible ones, and passing, when possible, from one or more discordant viewpoints to a higher which shall somehow include and transmute them' (cited in Kearns 1987: 85).

Thus while a literary and critical modernism seems on the surface independent of and at times oblivious to theological modernism, the modernist stances taken by major twentieth-century artists and writers raise theological issues and concerns with which they are very much engaged. These issues are incarnated in their stylistic and formal innovations as well as in their range of interests, both often sensitive as well as challenging to conservative and orthodox understandings of Christianity and prescient with respect to problems to come. These include problems of comparative religion, esotericism, spiritualism, and pagan and natural theology as well as questions of politics, ethics, and revolutionary change. Engagement with these matters did not, moreover, prevent many moderns from finding their way towards religion, Christian and otherwise, on terms both new and old.

WORKS CITED

BADHAM, PAUL. 1998. *The Contemporary Challenge of Modernist Theology.* Cardiff: University of Wales.

DALEY, BRIAN. 2005. '*La Nouvelle Théologie* and the Patristic Revival: Sources, Symbols and the Science of Theology'. Unpublished paper. Center of Theological Inquiry. Princeton, NJ. Cited by permission.

ELIOT, T. S. 1930. 'Religion without Humanism', in Norman Foerster (ed.), *Humanism and America.* New York: Farrar & Rinehart.

HELMLING, STEVEN. 1988. *The Esoteric Comedies of Carlyle, Newman and Yeats.* New York: Cambridge University Press.

HUTCHENS, S. M. 1999. 'Modernism and Theology: Book Review of *The First Moderns: Profiles in the Origins of Twentieth-Century Thought by William R. Everdell*', in *Touchstone: A Journal of Mere Christianity.* July/August: 1–2. Available online at <http://www.touchstonemag.com/archives/article.php?id=12-04-101-b>.

JENSON, R. W. 2004. 'Apocalyptic in Twentieth Century German Theology'. Unpublished paper. Center of Theological Inquiry. Princeton, NJ. Cited by permission.

JOYCE, JAMES. 1991. *Portrait of the Artist as a Young Man.* New York: New American Library.

KEARNS, CLEO. 1987. *T. S. Eliot and Indic Traditions: A Study in Poetry and Belief.* Cambridge: Cambridge University Press.

KEARNS, GEORGE. 1980. *Guide to Ezra Pound's Selected Cantos.* New Brunswick. Rutgers University Press.

LONGENBACH, JAMES. 1988. *Stone Cottage: Pound, Yeats and Modernism.* Oxford: Oxford University Press.

MIYAKE, AKIKO. 1991. *Ezra Pound and the Mysteries of Love: A Plan for the Cantos.* Durham, NC: Duke University Press.

MULLER, MAX. 1872. *Lectures on the Science of Religions.* Cited in Kearns.

PETRE, M. D. (ed.) 1920. *George Tyrell's Letters.* London: Fisher Unwin.

SCHWAB, RAYMOND. 1984. *The Oriental Renaissance: Europe's Rediscovery of India and the East 1680–1880,* trans. G. Patternon-Black and V. Reinking. New York: Columbia University Press.

THORMAHLEN, MARIANNE (ed.) 2003. *Rethinking Modernism.* Basingstoke: Palgrave Macmillan.

TILLICH, PAUL. 1996. *The Irrelevance and Return of the Christian Message.* Cleveland: Pilgrim.

Further Reading

Bradbury, Malcolm, and McFarlane, James (eds.) 1978. *Modernism 1890–1930*. Atlantic Highlands, NJ: Humanities Press.

Bratten, Carl. E., and Jenson, Robert. 1995. *Map of Twentieth Century Theology: Readings from Karl Barth to Radical Pluralism*. Minneapolis: Fortress.

Danielou, Jean. 1946. 'Les Orientations presentes de la pensée religieuse'. *Études* 79/5.

Jenson, Robert W. 1995. *Essays in Theology of Culture* (Grand Rapids: W. B. Eerdman).

Martz, Louis. 1998. *Many Gods, Many Voices*. Columbia: University of Missouri Press.

Ward, Graham. 1998. *Barth, Derrida and the Language of Theology*. New York: Cambridge University Press.

CHAPTER 11

·····

POSTMODERNISM

·····

KEVIN HART

ANY general consideration of postmodernism must begin with more than a ritual bow to Jean-François Lyotard whose *The Postmodern Condition: A Report on Know-ledge* (1984) extended and accelerated the circulation of the word inside and outside the academy. Right at the start of his book, Lyotard notes that in the United States the word is already used by sociologists and critics and that 'it designates the state of our culture following the transformations which, since the end of the nineteenth century, have altered the game rules for science, literature, and the arts' (p. xxiii). If one looks hard enough, one can find 'postmodern' as far back as the 1870s, and only if one plugs one's ears can one avoid hearing it today. As the word is used in more and more contexts, its meanings multiply, migrate, adapt to new environments, and cross-fertilize one another. Confusion can be kept to a minimum, at least to begin with, by clarifying what the word means in *The Postmodern Condition* before encountering its more exotic senses. Lyotard uses 'postmodern' to denote the impact of twentieth-century cultural transformations 'in the context of the crisis of narratives [*récits*]' (ibid. p. xiii), and thereby brings literature—both narrative practice and reflection on that practice—onto centre stage in discussion of the postmodern.

'Narrative' includes a good deal more than fiction, however, as is made plain no later than the second paragraph of Lyotard's introduction. What interests him is science—knowledge in general rather than the hard sciences in particular—and its disdain for narrative, which it tends to discount as fable. Science has needed to legitimate itself, Lyotard says, and has done so by producing a metadiscourse called philosophy. Modern sciences are those that attempt to justify themselves and that seek universality for their claims by appealing 'to some grand narrative, such as the dialectics of Spirit, the hermeneutics of meaning, the emancipation of the rational or working subject, or the creation of wealth' (ibid. p. xxiii). The postmodern, by contrast, is signalled by 'incredulity toward metanarratives' (ibid. p. xxiv), a stance that has arisen partly because the sciences have had so much success they no longer seek legitimation outside themselves and partly because people no longer look for or even expect to find reliable metaphysical grounds for anything. Nowadays we find ourselves in a world constituted by many regional language games—descriptive, denotative, and prescriptive, as well as narrative—in which we participate and which do not add up to being a 'world' in quite the unified and solid sense that was assumed as recently as the Victorian age.

Several positions and problems that have become characteristic of debate about the postmodern are apparent in Lyotard's opening remarks on the topic. First, the modern is associated with science, and consequently with clarity and rigour as necessary conditions of discourse, whereas the postmodern is a suspicious attitude towards the ways in which science has legitimated itself. If postmodernists produce arguments to support their views, these are subsidiary to the sceptical stance towards origins and ends that sets them apart from the moderns. The postmodernist will be a pragmatist, although not always of the card-carrying kind. One difficulty generated by the contrast between science and pragmatism is that some writers, widely regarded as central to postmodernism, reach their positions by closely following a train of reason. If the Jacques Derrida of *Glas* (1974; trans. 1986) does not fit the bill, the author of *Speech and Phenomena* (1973) does. Second, although 'modernity' is often used to name a historical period, Lyotard commends it as a mode of thought and sensibility. St Augustine is modern, as are Descartes and Proust, while Montaigne is postmodern, as are Sterne and the later Wittgenstein. A dualism inhabits much talk of the postmodern, then, regardless of whether that talk is polemical or philosophical; and the structure is called into question when people invoke the pre-modern or make finer discriminations (as in talk of late modernity and para-modernities, for example). To Lyotard's credit, there is no question at least of cleanly dividing the modern from the postmodern or of rigidly determining the modern in history. The postmodern is not what succeeds the modern but is the modern 'in the nascent state' which Lyotard (1984: 79) insists is a constant situation. At the start of the modern, the postmodern will already have been at work.

Such is the strange logic of the future anterior. Lyotard's fleshing out of this logic in the vocabulary of modern transcendental philosophy has been highly influential. 'The postmodern would be that which, in the modern, puts forward the unpresentable in presentation itself; that which denies itself the solace of good forms, the consensus of a taste which would make it possible to share collectively the nostalgia for the unattainable; that which searches for new presentations, not in order to enjoy them but in order to impart a stronger sense of the unpresentable' (ibid. 81). The postmodern is therefore to be approached by way of the sublime as formulated by Kant yet disengaged from the specific moment of the *Critique of Judgement* (1790) and distributed across the centuries. To be sure, Aristotle, Longinus, and Burke explored the sublime before Kant put pen to paper yet, for Lyotard, Kant best identifies and diagnoses its contradictory flavour and justifies avant-garde activity. Subtle and interesting as the point is, people regularly recur to the commonsense meaning of 'postmodern' as coming after the modern, the sense that was already in use by the American sociologists and critics whom Lyotard acknowledges at the start of his book. If nothing else, the practice is evidence of the power that the modern still holds over us, for temporal succession—including cause and effect, growth and decline—is one of the habits of perception we call 'modern'.

Kant is not one philosopher among others for Lyotard. His aesthetic of the sublime is the very place where 'modern art (including literature) finds its impetus and the logic of avant-gardes finds its axioms' (ibid. 77). Other French philosophers of the same generation had said much the same thing about the same time. Yet Lyotard relies on Kant more heavily, and adapts him more thoroughly, than they do. Several things need to be brought to light in the Frenchman's use of the critical philosophy. The first is that no incredulity is expressed towards the Kantian metanarratives: that Enlightenment properly comes only when we learn to live within the limitations of thought and focus on ethical action, and that genius proceeds without reference to concepts. We might wonder if *The Postmodern Condition* urges a metanarrative of the rise of the avant-garde, a privileged history of artistic practice and theory passing from the third *Critique* to Jena Romanticism to the New York School (Lyotard 1991: 98). The second point is related to this concern, for a relationship seems to be assumed between postmodernism and the avant-garde. Third, and more obscurely, there is a correlation implied between the Romantic sublime and the death of God that had already been hinted in the definition of the postmodern in the words 'nostalgia for the unattainable' (ibid. 81) and in the choice of the word 'paganism' to evoke the postmodern condition (Lyotard and Thébaud 1985: 16).

For many critics, the idea of the avant-garde is tied to the modern, and with the exhaustion of modernism and the expression of doubts about the linear literary history on which it relied, there comes the diminution of the avant-garde, its last flourishing being the New York School and its last literary figure of stature being John Ashbery. Rejecting this consensus, Lyotard maintains that the avant-garde remains alive and well, and its vitality is to be found in its relentless investigation of the presuppositions of the modern. In its own ways, he says, this inspection of what makes and unmakes modernism is a form of what Freud called *Durcharbeiten* (Lyotard 1992: 93). Just as the patient works through the meanings of his or her neurosis in order not to repeat it, so the avant-garde labours in rethinking the assumptions, trajectories, and destinations of the modernist project. It will quickly be seen that the analogy works only within a narrow range of contemporary writing and does so best in the projects that are usually styled 'experimental': language poetry, sound poetry, and so on. Not all the literature that invites being called postmodern is also avant-garde. There is no coercive reason to think that a critical inspection of modernism's assumptions will always result in a direct path to avant-garde writing. The lessons that Roy Fisher has learned from Wallace Stevens and T. S. Eliot are not the same as those that Peter Riley has taken to heart in reading his masters from the same period, and the same could be said of the different modernist heritages prized by prose writers such as Zadie Smith and D. M. Thomas. It must also be said that, especially in Britain, much recent writing that identifies itself as avant-garde shows little or no sign of the analytic labour that Lyotard values. The poetry of

Jeremy Prynne, for example, is more than likely to strike the reader schooled in modernism as mandarin and fatigued rather than energized and exciting.

At any rate, to understand the postmodern as Lyotard promotes it we must first grasp the Kantian doctrine of the sublime. And to do that, we need to distinguish the sublime from the beautiful. Neither word denotes properties in nature or art; each refers to a judgement about one or the other. Rather than yielding theoretical knowledge about anything, which would enable us to prove the aesthetic value of a natural scene or a poem, aesthetic judgements point to the subjectivity of the judge although not always to the uniqueness of his or her taste. As is well known, for Kant we get to know the world about us by bringing our intuitions of it into line with the categories of the understanding. Analogously, when judging a particular object to be beautiful, the imagination apprehends the form of what is intuited and refers it to the understanding. There is a free accord between the two faculties. Since only form is apprehended, no determinate concept is at issue and consequently no cognition takes place: there is solely a pleasure that enhances life. This delight can be communicated, and it is reasonable to expect that others will come to agree that something is beautiful. With each judgement of beauty there is a community to come.

No such balance or presumptive agreement is found in judgements of the sublime, however. For here the relevant faculties are judgement, imagination, and reason, the last faculty being incommensurate with the first two. Ideas of reason—God, freedom, and immortality—have no counterpart in experience, Kant tells us, and he adds that a feeling of the sublime occurs when such an idea is presented to the imagination. The totality of something unlimited cannot be thought by the imagination and that faculty is consequently overwhelmed by what has presented itself. With beautiful objects, which are always bounded, the imagination could freely enter into play with another faculty. Now it finds itself forced to obey an alien law: the unpresentable idea brings forth the utmost seriousness in the one to whom it is presented. Lacerated by the presentation of the idea, the imagination recoils in self-sacrifice, and is rewarded with what Kant calls 'negative pleasure', an expansion of the soul that comes when the imagination realizes that it can only represent the unpresentability of a presentation. This feeling of contradiction, pain and pleasure together, is, as Kant learned from Burke, the signpost of the sublime.

There is no sublime experience without the feeling of self-sacrifice, Kant argues. 'The *astonishment* amounting almost to terror, the awe and thrill of devout feeling, that takes hold of one when gazing upon the prospect of mountains ascending to heaven, deep ravines and torrents raging there, deep-shadowed solitudes that invite to brooding melancholy, and the like—all this, when we are assured of our own safety, is not actual fear. Rather, it is an attempt to gain access to it through imagination' (Kant 1952: 120–1). On Lyotard's reading, there is no sublime experience without an awareness of death. Where Kant envisages a recovery of selfhood to follow the act of self-sacrifice in sublime experiences, Lyotard sees only the loss of the subject. More broadly, he takes the 'retreat of regulation and rules' to imply 'the death of God' (Lyotard 1986: 11). He might have quoted Barnett Newman, the American abstract expressionist whose art he admires. In his essay, 'The Sublime is Now',

Newman (1948: 53) states, 'We are freeing ourselves of the impediments of memory, association, nostalgia, legend, myth or what have you, that have been the devices of Western European painting. Instead of making cathedrals out of Christ, man or "life," we are making them out of ourselves, out of our own feelings.' Now if Lyotard is correct, the reader of postmodern literature might think that he or she will not only experience a feeling of contradiction but will also be exposed to a withdrawal of the law which would lead to his or her becoming an atheist. Clearly, there would be very high stakes in deciding whether to read Virginia Woolf or Graham Swift. But are things quite so straightforward or so dire?

The moralist at least need have no fear of people reading postmodern literature as conceived by Lyotard. Seriousness is produced by an encounter with the sublime, as we have seen, and Kant tells us that there is an essential relation between the sublime and *Sittlichkeit*, morality. Yet the religious person who reads Kant will recall that the adoption of the moral law removes God from the theatre of human action, so that morality is *de facto* although not *de jure* co-ordinate with the death of God. We are to act as if God were not there to help us. Believers might also be concerned that attention to the sublime serves to replace the practice of religion. The accent is removed from worship and placed firmly on sublime feelings and ethics. Kant himself would be chary of suggestions that the former can have religious significance. Not all those influenced by him would agree, however. The nineteenth and twentieth centuries provide us with 'religion within the limits of art' as well as 'religion within the limits of reason' (Lacoue-Labarthe and Nancy 1988: 77). Only those postmodernists wedded to 'religion without religion', in which the way to God goes solely by way of ethics, remain faithful to Kant's suspicion that, considered by itself, worship is at best empty and at worst a distraction from what religion actually asks of us. Others take the sublime, and indeed the category of feeling, to be the peculiarly modern way in which we are religious.

One index of the sway that the sublime holds on postmodern men and women would be a tendency to iconoclasm. Here it might reveal itself in a prizing of social justice over and above religious ritual, or in a desire to think of a God beyond metaphysics. Another index would be a taste for the fragmentary. The postmodern sublime would point us to literary and spiritual works that elaborate themselves by denying us the satisfaction of form. Pascal's *Pensées* would supply us with a powerful example from the past, while Simone Weil's notebooks and Edmund Jabès's *Le Livre des questions* (1963–73) would speak to us in related ways in the present. In terms of the visual arts we recall that, iconoclastic as they are, Barnett Newman's most demanding works probe spiritual impulses from positions unfamiliar to most overtly committed Christian artists. 'Genesis', 'Abraham', 'Covenant', 'Joshua', and, above all, 'Stations of the Cross', are cases in point.

Orthodox Christians will object to Lyotard that a retreat of rules and regulations does not imply the death of God, although it might indicate the closure of a certain metaphysical notion of the deity. They will also say that God cannot adequately be discussed in terms of the sublime, and that two quite different senses of 'transcendence' are in play when talking of God and the sublime. The objection invites us to consider whether there is, as Lyotard seems to assume, just the *one* postmodernism, an attitude of derision that extends to the dominion of God as well as philosophical metanarratives. A unitary understanding of postmodernism would be an odd thing. For there is no 'concept' of the postmodern as Lyotard conceives it. Modern science, largely based on experiment, generates philosophy to legitimate it, thereby calling forth the scepticism of postmodern men and women. Similarly, one might say, the avant-garde, with its total reliance on the experimental, gives rise to a theory of culture ('modernism') at the risk of being subject to a postmodern winking at the desire for legitimation. When literary historians tell us that the greatest poetry is always avant-garde we should look at them with suspicion and charge them with holding a naive linear view of literary history, one that, in any case, has reached its limit in postmodern times when the marginal is routinely incorporated into the dominant culture. Or one might say, more technically, that postmodernists do not secure their theory at the level of second-order discourse reflecting on first-order texts. For them, distinctions between first- and second-order discourses, or, if you wish, between theory and practice, can be shown to be divided and equivocal.

There are British novels that grapple with the religious and that can be plausibly called postmodern. Salman Rushdie's *The Satanic Verses* (1989) begins with angels and the death of God, and belongs in the world of Islam, although how close to the margins of that world is open to dispute (ibid. 16, 30). Graham Swift's novel *Waterland* (1983) works off the Christian story by brooding throughout on Mary Metcalf's 'liaison ... with God' (ibid. 100–3); Jim Crace's *Quarantine* (1998: 193) focuses on a mad Jesus who, dying, becomes 'all surface, no inside ... a dry, discarded page of scripture now'; and Julian Barnes's *A History of the World in 10 $\frac{1}{2}$ Chapters* (1989) develops a cheeky rereading of the legends of Noah's Ark and Jonah in the whale, and offers a new, disenchanted interpretation of heaven. Yet affirmations of a vigorous Christianity can be found in postmodern writing in Britain. Radical orthodox theologians John Milbank, Graham Ward, and Catherine Pickstock are postmodern both by virtue of criticizing modernity (in its elevation of space over time, in its nihilism, and in its culture of death) and by addressing many of the themes, from the city to cyberspace, that preoccupy secular postmodernists. Could it be that the only site in which the postmodern and theology vigorously engage one another in Britain is in the work of theologians? I will return to the question.

Nothing would be gained by simply tagging the British novelists named above as 'postmodern' and then moving on. In fact, most of what makes them interesting would be lost, and we would be in danger of misrepresenting them and rendering postmodernism as a homogenous movement. If Swift, Rushdie, Crace, and Barnes use any of the standard equipment of postmodern writing—a subversion of representation, a prizing of surfaces over depths, a disposition towards lightness rather than seriousness, a love of the intertextual, a taste for the non-functional—they do so in a cautious and reserved manner. To compare these writers with their older French contemporaries, people such as Philippe Sollers and Louis-René des Forêts, would result in more perplexity than clarity about defining the postmodern. The ways in which history and politics figure in postmodern British narrative writing help to separate it from its French counterpart. Speaking very generally, one might say that the French postmodernists are drawn to question *le politique* (the political) when they write, and that they therefore involve themselves in philosophical questions, and, further, that they do so even when they are addressing *la politique* (politics). The British, by contrast, are more likely to respond to the lessons of geography, society, and history as directly experienced. One of Barnes's narrators might say, 'We all know objective truth is not obtainable, that when some event occurs we shall have a multiplicity of subjective truths which we assess and then fabulate into history, into some God-eyed version of what "really" happened' (1989: 243), but the reader never feels that the rug is being pulled completely from under his or her feet. Look outside the door: the butcher's shop is still across the road, the postman is turning round the corner, and the newspaper is on the step. Yet when Michel Foucault (1967, 189) tells us that 'there is nothing to interpret...for fundamentally everything is already interpretation', we know that for him there is no rug, and no floorboards either, despite the glittering array of facts offered in his histories.

Even if we restrict ourselves to Lyotard's understanding of the postmodern, we would want to say that the British novelists I have named participate in the postmodern without ever quite belonging to it. Nor do the French or the Americans, of course, but a Michel Deguy or a Charles Bernstein participates more fully than his British counterparts, the one participating also in the echoes of surrealism and the other in the aftershocks of the Black Mountain School. I take the distinction from Derrida's essay 'The Law of Genre' (1992: 230) where he is concerned to show that every text participates in one or more genres but never belongs to any one genre in the sense of having a continuous and uninterrupted border around it. Only the most naive epigones could be accused of treating the postmodern as a *genre*—of art, philosophy, or anything. Yet we might say that Barnes, for example, participates in postmodernism in that he treats Judaeo-Christianity as an archive of stories that can be put together in new ways, without worrying about the whole, yet does not belong to it in any thoroughgoing way, if only because his conception of religion as myth places him in the company of exemplary moderns such as Feuerbach, Strauss, Frazer, and Bultmann. Even here, though, there is a need for nuance and shading. Barnes is perfectly capable of twisting 'myth' around to make it more postmodern, as in his reflections on Jonah. 'For the point is this,' he says, 'not that myth refers us back to some original event which has been fancifully transcribed as it passed through the collective memory; but that it refers us to something that will happen, that must happen. Myth will become reality, however sceptical we might be' (1989: 181). To that bold claim, only a hardened and shameless postmodernist could demur by distinguishing between *l'avenir* and *à venir*, a future present and what is to come, and insisting that thinking in terms of any present is characteristic of the modern mindset.

To reflect on the contemporary British theologians I have named, along with others such as Oliver Davies, Laurence Hemming, Joseph O'Leary, and even Denys Turner, would be to doubt whether Lyotard's sense of the postmodern is sufficiently large to accommodate what they do and how they do it. They are less concerned with finding a 'stronger sense of the unpresentable' than with doing other things that a taxonomist might consider postmodern. John Milbank (1998: 131–56) refigures the postmodern as the post-secular, and argues that it involves a half-turn towards the pre-modern: hence his fascination with St Augustine. Oliver Davies dreams of a theological language that no longer relies on *ousia*; Laurence Hemming, who actively seeks a philosophy of being, is concerned to examine the ways in which the sublime and the divine have been braided together; Joseph O'Leary thinks of faith as a deconstructive principle that can be used to overcome Western metaphysics, especially as found in St Augustine; while Denys Turner gingerly appropriates the language of deconstruction in his consideration of mysticism. Certainly the word 'postmodernism' itself can be traced to another source than the one that Lyotard supplies. When Bernard Iddings Bell published his *Postmodernism and Other Essays* in 1926, he was not placing himself in a Kantian heritage or under the sign of modern atheism but subscribing to something far older, that, when fully re-emerged from the obscurity to which it had been banished by Schleiermacher and Feuerbach, would be opposed to both: an orthodox theological stance that had found religious liberalism or modernism intellectually reductive and spiritually unsatisfying. Few theologians today have heard of Bell. Even so, in the work of contemporary theologians with a traditionalist bent—Denys Turner and John Webster, for example—the word 'postmodernism' can refer to something that troubles theological as well as cultural modernism.

So we must be very careful talking of postmodernism when religion is in the air. Strange cross-fertilizations might have occurred that are not immediately apparent to the eye or the ear. On the one hand, the word might denote a theological position in accord with at least some attitudes, desires, or conclusions associated with postmodernism as usually understood. Such would be the case with work that commends approaching God by way of serving the other person, or talking of 'God without being', or considering the various strategies of apophaticism, or reflecting on the constitutive inadequacy of our response to the divine call, or imagining doing theology in cyberspace. On the other hand, to talk of postmodernism in the context of religion could mean a post-liberalism in either its narrow sense (as proposed by George Lindbeck) or the broader sense of Chalcedonian orthodoxy that Bell had in mind and that is affirmed from different positions by Milbank and others.

In treating English literature and theology from the perspective of postmodernism we can do more than reflect on (*a*) fiction influenced by cultural postmodernism that also touches on religious matters, and (*b*) theology marked by postmodernism in one or another sense. We need to take account of attempts in Britain to make 'literature and theology' into a discipline in its own right and to assess the ways in which that has been shaped by postmodern concerns. Positive interest in the field becomes apparent in the Victorian age, in Matthew Arnold's *Literature and Dogma* (1873) and Stopford Augustus Brooke's *Theology in the English Poets* (1880). Negative interest is heavily underlined in William Empson's *Milton's God* (1961). Only with Helen Gardner's *Religion and Literature* (1971) are questions posed and considered in an intelligent modern way by a critic of standing. Postmodern concerns might be seen to begin with Frank Kermode's *The Sense of an Ending*. Here Kermode (1967: 28) proposes that apocalyptic writing provides a source from which we derive both literary fictions and our sense of historical crisis: 'changed by our special pressures, subdued by our scepticism, the paradigms of apocalypse continue to lie under our ways of making sense of the world'. If Kermode drew on religion to help him understand narrative in all the complexities that postmodernism saw there, he was to become more interested in biblical criticism. *The Literary Guide to the Bible* (1987), edited by Kermode and Robert Alter, bypasses the postmodern. Indeed, when the Bible and Culture Collective produced their volume, *The Postmodern Bible* (1995) they excoriated Alter and Kermode for excluding 'feminist, ideological, psychoanalytic, deconstructive, or Marxist approaches', dominant concerns of poststructural and postmodern criticism. 'We are convinced', the Collective added, 'that the critical practices explicitly excluded from Alter and Kermode's account will be increasingly vital to a biblical scholarship responsive to a postmodern culture' (Bible and Culture Collective 1995: 7). Certainly those practices were felt strongly, first in the United States and then in Britain, in the final years of the twentieth century and the first years of the twenty-first century.

Postmodern interests in literature and religion are evident in the journal *Literature and Theology*, published by Oxford University Press, from its inception in 1987 to the present day. The journal's founding editor, David Jasper, has been intrigued by the postmodern for many years. His most decisive involvement with it, however, is *The Sacred Desert* (2004) in which he declares that he sees ' "religion" as a defining characteristic of post-modernity' and that it is only on a journey through the desert—inner as well as outer—that 'theology and its language can find new life' (ibid. 4). Like the radical orthodox theologians, Jasper is sharply critical of modernity; it has 'failed to understand anything about the desert except as a place to be wearily traversed by one or two brave souls in the service of Empire' (ibid. 57). Unlike them, he looks for inspiration to Thomas J. J. Altizer and Don Cupitt, two Godless theologians whose work Milbank and company would regard as anaemic liberalism of the very worst kind. Desert Fathers such as Paphnutius and Sarapion would find little to celebrate in Jasper's desert spirituality. Then again, the Desert Fathers were not interested, as Jasper certainly is, in the literature of the desert. A closer companion on the journey is Edmond Jabès, although the tutelary spirit is the American postmodern theologian Mark C. Taylor.

Another worthy in the British world of theology and literature is George Steiner whose *Real Presences* (1989), inflated and imprecise though it sometimes is, made a significant contribution to debate. For Steiner, the questions 'What is poetry, music, art? How can they not be? How do they act upon us and how do we interpret their action?' are 'ultimately theological questions' (ibid. 227). In itself the claim is far from new. St Bonaventure elaborated it, in a quite different context and style, in his *De reductione artium ad theologiam*: all debates in the humanities can be traced back to theological issues. Yet the claim *is* worth making again, and a Christian could explore it while keeping in mind Erich Pzywara's (1929: ii. 667) notion of *reductio in mysterium*, the leading back from the particulars of our lives to the divine mystery that supports life itself. Steiner's constant target is deconstruction, one of the two or three crucial movements in the higher intellectual reaches of postmodernity. Like Derrida, however, Steiner (1989: 3) proposes a transcendental argument, 'that any coherent understanding of what language is and how language performs, that any coherent account of the capacity of human speech to communicate meaning and feeling is, in the final analysis, underwritten by the assumption of God's presence'. In fact, Steiner deviates from this argument the more deeply he gets into his subject. First, he allows the felt absence of God to be just as effective as the divine presence in supporting 'certain dimensions of thought and creativity' (ibid. 229). And second, he passes from assuming that God is present to pretending that he is. 'We must read *as if* ' (ibid.), he says, meaning, I take it, that we must wager that there is a God—or regret there is no God—if we are to read at the highest level.

On hearing Steiner's injunction, we are likely to recall Wallace Stevens (1954: 486) talking of 'the intricate evasions of as' and be less than willing to follow the directive to read *as if*. Also, we might remember a French writer whom Stevens loved, Maurice Blanchot, who argues in *L'Espace littéraire* (1955) that literature is linked to a sense of the sacred (H. Stevens 1972: 879). Blanchot (1982: 243), however, acknowledges, with a backwards glance to Hölderlin and Heidegger, that the gods have departed, and that the last vestige of the sacred that remains to us is the approach of what he calls *le Dehors*, the Outside, 'a suffocating condensation where being ceaselessly perpetuates itself as nothingness'. One may well doubt whether we need the hypothesis of the Outside in order to read Mallarmé, Rilke, and Kafka, the authors who most intrigue Blanchot in this book. Yet we may be pleased that Blanchot does not ask us to pretend to believe in or to care about a deity he and many of his readers find incredible. To have faith in God is a wholly good thing, but to pretend to believe in God in order to read or write better is bad, and to ask people to do so is even worse.

Like several other critics of stature, including Harold Bloom and Christopher Ricks, Steiner points to Geoffrey Hill as the finest of contemporary British poets. His 'dramatization of the Christian condition' is, as Steiner puts it in an endorsement for *Canaan*, a part of his poetic strength. That Hill is postmodern would not be a judgement likely to be offered by Steiner, perhaps for very good reasons. After all, it is often unclear when critics declare '*X* is postmodern' whether the predication is descriptive or evaluative or both. Are we illuminated about the work when told that Browning is Victorian or that Petronius is modern? Scarcely; and 'postmodern' is, as we have seen, far less clear than either judgement. So when Vincent Sherry (1987: 243) tells us that 'Hill is postmodernist in his openness to the processes of his art, his situating the traces of the language as they crisscross his poems' we are likely to be nonplussed. To begin with, to say that Hill is postmodern*ist* rather than postmodern misses the mark, for there is nothing in his poetry or his criticism that leads us to think he subscribes to views associated with Lyotard or with any other theoretician of the postmodern. Nor does the formulation distinguish avant-garde from postmodern practice: one might well be postmodern yet write very differently from aficianados of the avant-garde such as Emmanuel Hocquard or Lyn Hejinian. And what does it mean for someone to be open 'to the processes of his art' or to situate 'the traces of the language'? Neither formulation is at all clear.

The Geoffrey Hill of *Tenebræ* (1978) is not Christian but is intently concerned with diagnosing the religion's ascetic practices and his own reluctance to make an act of faith despite an almost overwhelming desire to do so. 'That Hill takes Christianity seriously', Sherry (1987: 156–7) says, 'may in itself be offensive to contemporary critics'. It is hard to know what to do with such a sentence. Could anyone have written 'That Jabès takes Judaism seriously...may in itself be offensive to contemporary critics' or 'That Rushdie takes Islam seriously...may in itself be offensive to contemporary critics'? Not even a critical study hostile to *Le Livre des questions* or *The Satanic Verses* would call forth such a sentence. And if it did, the study's assumptions would be put to the question. Yet the sentence prompts the question whether a poet can address Christianity, as a believer or not, and still be postmodern. The sonnets of 'Lachrimæ', for instance, show no interest in affirming surfaces instead of depths, they seek to understand rather than debunk, and there is no attempt to make form overflow content. At first blush, then, there is nothing postmodern about them. Their very form, the sonnet, implies content, it might be said: the way in which they organize a world of feeling and intellect is at odds with postmodernity. A postmodern sonnet, if there is such a thing, would look more like something in Ted Berrigan's *The Sonnets* (1964) than anything as polished as 'Lachrimæ'.

Yet these are not the only or even the most suitable criteria to bring into play. Some people sympathetic to Milbank's understanding of the postmodern might read 'Lachrimæ' and observe that the sequence is post-secular, that its half-twist towards the pre-modern indicates a deep discontent with the modern, that it contests transparency of language, and that it perpetually exceeds the project of modernism in learning, with equal attention, from the Mallarmé of 'Plusieurs Sonnets' and the Lope de Vega of the religious lyrics. A second reading will give appropriate shading to 'post-secular', for the sequence addresses the relations of poetry and religion, registering the ways in which art and incarnation double each other, and how religious devotion becomes at once drawn out and perverted by representation. For example, the court of James I, as evoked in 'The Masque of Blackness', the second of the 'Lachrimæ' cycle, might well resemble 'Midas' feast' but so too does the church, at least when it comes to icons and liturgical vessels. That there is an admiration and a questioning of modernism in Hill is beyond doubt, yet because the working through of the modernist heritage does not lead to poems that square with the poetics of Tom Raworth or Denise Riley should not make us conclude that the work is therefore not postmodern. *Durcharbeiten* tends towards psychic health; it has no necessary end in avant-garde poetics. Hill questions modernism, to be sure, but also he puts pressure on art and the artist in general, not to mention their honourable and dishonourable relations with art as religion and religion as art. No postmodernist has presented a more savage attack on representation than the one that readers will find in Hill.

Tenebræ testifies that in Britain theology and the postmodern engage one another in poetry as well as in theology. 'Lachrimæ' is not centred in a faith seeking understanding but in a sensibility that seeks to understand oneself and others in order perhaps to have faith. If at times self-reflection frays into self-admiration for maintaining a delicate balance between belief and disbelief, and moving questioning decays into arid intellectualism, at other times the poetry has a powerful simplicity. That is never more so than in the final poem of the sequence, 'Lachrimæ Amantis', a translation of a sonnet by Lope de Vega ('¿Qué tengo yo qui mi amistad procuras?'). It is telling that in the original Spanish, written of course by a Catholic—and one who finally entered holy orders but without finding serenity—the poet suggests that he will never actually wake to welcome Jesus who knocks on his window each night. He will do so tomorrow, he says, only to say the same thing the next day and every other day. With Hill it is different. His speaker drowses 'half-faithful for a time | bathed in pure tones of promise and remorse: | 'tomorrow I shall wake to welcome him'. Maybe he will not, maybe he will.

By the time of *Canaan* (1996), Hill is in communion with the Episcopal Church, and is writing lyrics that are less anguished about the act of faith and are more formally iconoclastic than those in *Tenebræ*. Consider 'Of Coming into Being and Passing Away':

> Rosa sericea: its red
> spurs
>   blooded with amber
> each lit and holy grain
> the sun
>   makes much of
> as of all our shadows—
>
> prodigal ever returning
> darkness that in such circuits
> reflects diuturnity
>   to itself
> and to our selves
>   yields nothing
> finally—
>   but by occasion
> visions of truth or dreams
> as they arise—
>   to terms of grace
> where grace has surprised us—
> the unsustaining
>   wonderously sustained
>
>   (Hill 1996: 4)

A reader devoted to Lyotard's understanding of the postmodern would celebrate the 'stronger sense of the unpresentable' that is evident here compared with 'Lachrimæ', and would point to the breaking of form, the bristling ambiguities, the raiding of literary history in gestures if not in content (the lyric places itself in the heritages of Emily Dickinson and Paul Celan). Here, the reader might say, is the postmodern sublime, with the retreat of rules and regulations, the exposure to death ('yields nothing | finally—'), from which the poet pulls back at the last moment in his acceptance of being surprised by grace (rather than by sin, as in Stanley Fish's *Paradise Lost*).

Yet the poem seeks to give us not so much an idea of reason as the 'terms of grace', conditions and limits that must be accepted: life in a familiar world of shadows, and roses near the end of the season. One can be reconciled to Christianity, the poem implies, not because it embodies nostalgia for the unattainable but because it speaks of a God who sustains the world in being. To decide to affirm that God is, as one theologian puts it, 'a miraculous experience, one not deducible from experiences already had' (Jüngel 1983: 33). In the wake of that decision visions and dreams of truth can be translated into the peculiar language of theology (the 'terms of grace'). That they are visions *or* dreams lets doubt intrude and longing emerge. Hill might hope that the poem clasps faith and style in its one movement. Elsewhere, he tells us that he prizes those moments when 'grammar and desire are miraculously at one' (Hill 2003: 118). Cant postmodernism, as he would see it, goes in the opposite direction, seeking a divergence between the two and eschewing any possibility of the miraculous. Even if we set aside Hill's reflections as a critic, to call a lyric such as 'Of Coming into Being and Passing Away' postmodern pure and simple would be to yield to the demands of the insistent and tedious taxonomist. The poem does not evince a sceptical attitude towards metanarratives; it is uninterested in them. Nor does it develop a play of surfaces or delight in devices that exceed the poem's economy. If it invites being called 'postmodern', it does so in another sense of the word, one that neither leads ineluctably to the avant-garde nor discounts an articulation of literature and theology.

Works Cited

BARNES, JULIAN. 1989. *A History of the World in 10 $\frac{1}{2}$ Chapters*. New York: Alfred A. Knopf.

Bible and Culture Collective (ed.). 1995. *The Postmodern Bible*. New Haven: Yale University Press.

BLANCHOT, MAURICE. 1982. *The Space of Literature*, trans. Ann Smock. Lincoln: University of Nebraska Press.

CRACE, JIM. 1998. *Quarantine*. Harmondsworth: Penguin.

DERRIDA, JACQUES. 1973. *Speech and Phenomena: And Other Essays on Husserl's Theory of Signs*, trans. and intro. David B. Allison, pref. Newton Garver. Evanston: Northwestern University Press. First published 1967.

—— 1986. *Glas*, trans. John P. Leavey Jr. and Richard Rand. Lincoln: University of Nebraska Press.

—— 1992. 'The Law of Genre', in *Acts of Literature*, ed. Derek Attridge. New York: Routledge.

FOUCAULT, MICHEL. 1967. 'Nietzsche, Freud, Marx.' Colloque de Royaumont, *Nietzsche*. Paris: Minuit.

HILL, GEOFFREY. 1996. *Canaan*. London: Penguin.

—— 2003. *Style and Faith*. New York: Counterpoint.

JASPER, DAVID. 2004. *The Sacred Desert: Religion, Literature, Art, and Culture*. Oxford: Blackwell.

Jüngel, Eberhard. 1983. *God as the Mystery of the World: On the Foundation of the Theology of the Crucified One in the Dispute between Theism and Atheism*, trans. Darrell L. Guder. Grand Rapids: Eerdmans.

Kant, Immanuel. 1952. *The Critique of Judgement*, trans. James Creed Meredith. Oxford: Clarendon.

Kermode, Frank. 1967. *The Sense of an Ending*. Oxford: Oxford University Press.

Lacoue-Labarthe, Philippe, and Nancy, Jean-Luc. 1988. *The Literary Absolute: The Theory of Literature in German Romanticism*, trans. Philip Barnard and Cheryl Lester. Albany: State University of New York Press.

Lyotard, Jean-François. 1984. *The Postmodern Condition: A Report on Knowledge*, trans. Geoff Bennington and Brian Massumi. Minneapolis: University of Minnesota Press. First published 1979.

—— 1986. 'Complexity and the Sublime', *ICA Documents 4: Postmodernism*, ed. Lisa Appignanesi. London: Free Association.

—— 1991. 'The Sublime and the Avant-Garde', in *The Inhuman: Reflections on Time*, trans. Geoffrey Bennington and Rachel Bowlby. Stanford: Stanford University Press.

—— 1992. *The Postmodern Explained to Children: Correspondence 1982–1985*, trans. Julian Pefanis and Morgan Thomas. Sydney: Power Publications.

—— and Thébaud, Jean-Loup. 1985. *Just Gaming*, trans. Wlad Godzich, afterword by Samuel Weber. Minneapolis: University of Minnesota Press.

Milbank, John. 1998. 'The Sublime in Kierkegaard', in Phillip Blond (ed.), *Post-Secular Philosophy: Between Philosophy and Theology*. London: Routledge.

Newman, Barnett. 1948. 'The Sublime is Now'. *The Tiger's Eye* 6.

Pzywara, Erich. 1929. 'Katholizismus', in *Ringen der Gegenwart*. 2 vols. Augsburg: Filser.

Rushdie, Salman. 1989. *The Satanic Verses*. New York: Viking.

Sherry, Vincent. 1987. *The Uncommon Tongue: The Poetry and Criticism of Geoffrey Hill*. Ann Arbor: The University of Michigan Press.

Steiner, George. 1989. *Real Presences: Is There Anything in What We Say?*. London: Faber & Faber.

Stevens, Holly (ed.). 1972. *Letters of Wallace Stevens*. New York: Alfred A. Knopf.

Stevens, Wallace. 1954. *Collected Poems*. New York: Alfred A. Knopf.

Swift, Graham. 1983. *Waterland*. New York: Poseidon.

Further Reading

Davies, Oliver. 2001. *A Theology of Compassion: Metaphysics of Difference in the Renewal of Tradition*. London: SCM.

Hart, Kevin. 2004. *Postmodernism: A Beginner's Guide*. Oxford: Oneworld.

Hemming, Laurence. 2002. *Heidegger's Atheism: The Refusal of a Theological Voice*. Notre Dame: Notre Dame University Press.

—— and Lacoue-Labarthe, Philippe. 1997. *Retreating the Political*, ed. Simon Sparks. London: Routledge.

Lyotard, Jean-François. 1986. 'Defining the Postmodern', *ICA Documents 4: Postmodernism*, ed. Lisa Appignanesi. London: Free Association.

Nancy, Jean-Luc. 1976. 'Tout le reste est literature', in *Le Discours de la syncope*, i. *Logodaedalus*. Paris: Aubier-Flammarion.

O'Leary, Joseph S. 1985. *Questioning Back: The Overcoming of Metaphysics in Christian Tradition*. Chicago: Winston.

Turner, Denys. 1995. *The Darkness of God: Negativity in Christian Mysticism*. Cambridge: Cambridge University Press.

PART THREE

LITERARY WAYS OF
READING THE BIBLE

CHAPTER 12

THE BIBLE AS LITERATURE AND SACRED TEXT

PETER S. HAWKINS

OVERVIEW

ANY consideration of the 'Bible as Literature and Sacred Text' must begin by recognizing the problematic nature of that deceptively simple conjunction, 'and'. Although it may imply an easy equivalency—the Bible is both a work of literature *and* the Word of God—these two identities have never rested easily with one another. For centuries, appreciation for Scripture's artistry sprang from the devout conviction that its divine Author would offer nothing less than perfection. The Bible was also pervasive: a universal subtext, a web of story and metaphor that was always *already* in mind. It was God's Book and as such 'required reading' even for those who could not actually read. Now, by contrast, biblical writing is typically considered a human endeavour that warrants our critical consideration for historical and aesthetic reasons. Given the Bible's importance to Western literature (not to mention to our culture as a whole), we study it to 'get the references', to gain some notion of the biblical literacy that until recently almost any writer both possessed and expected to find in a reader. The frequency of university courses on 'The Bible as Literature', or the priority given to the term 'Literature' in the title of this entry, suggests how commonplace it has become to treat the Scriptures as any other compendium of narrative or poetry—except, that is, for its extraordinary influence.

Yet, if many people today read the Bible for its prose, or are as likely to encounter it in English departments as in church or synagogue, discussion of the 'Bible as

Literature' shows that there is still a need to claim Scripture's literary status because it retains some notion of sanctity or authority—of being a 'Holy Bible'. By contrast, no one would think of offering 'Homer as Literature' because neither the *Iliad* nor the *Odyssey* is regarded any longer as sacred text. However canonical these epics may be as literary works, they have utterly lost the scriptural status they enjoyed in the ancient world. Some would say that this is now also true for the Bible, and see it only as an important (if problematic) human document that has provided us with stories to retell—in film as well as writing. Yet the furore that attended Martin Scorsese's *The Last Temptation of Christ* or Mel Gibson's *The Passion of the Christ*, especially when compared to the bland reception given to *Troy* (a recent adaptation of Homeric and Virgilian material), indicates that the Scriptures have not yet become 'mere' literature.

Scriptural Writers

One might well ask whether there is any indication in the Bible itself that its authors thought of it as 'literature', that is, as 'writing which has claim to consideration on the ground of beauty of form or emotional effect' (*OED* iii). Does it even make sense to speak of the Bible as a 'book' when the Scripture itself is not a single work but rather *ta biblia*, an anthology of 'the books' written over centuries and brought together, after a contentious winnowing process by communities of Jews and Christians who believed these writings to be sacred? Surveying this extraordinarily various material, what is there that invites a reader to approach the text as literary art? Many of the Psalms, of course, are beautiful lyric poems and Jesus' parables in Luke are masterful short stories. One cannot deny the presence elsewhere in Scripture of narrative technique or rhetorical flourish, sometimes of a high order. Very occasionally a biblical author will confide an effort to 'find pleasing words, and [write] words of truth plainly' (Eccles. 12: 10, NRSV) or, like Luke at the opening of his Gospel, express his intent to render an 'orderly account' of events so that the reader 'may know the truth about which you have been instructed' (1: 3–4). In both these cases of authorial aside, however, what matters is truth-telling, not style. The Word of the Lord is meant to be heard and obeyed. Thus St Paul writes in 2 Tim. 3: 16, 'All Scripture is inspired by God and is useful for teaching, for reproof, for correction, and for training in righteousness, so that everyone who belongs to God may be proficient, equipped for every good work.'

From what we can tell from the biblical writers themselves, therefore, they expect us to listen and learn, to be changed by the text, not entertained. Or as the Book of Common Prayer would have it, the words of Scripture are given by God so that we may 'hear them, read, mark, learn, and inwardly digest them'. Beauty may be their attribute; it is not their *raison d'être*.

EARLY CENTURIES OF THE COMMON ERA

Rabbinic Judaism avoided aesthetic evaluations or judgements. A Hellenized Jew such as Philo could apply Greek notions of poetry to Hebrew texts, saying that men of old—presumably Moses in the Song of the Sea and David in the Psalms—composed 'hymns and songs to God in all sorts of meters and melodies' (Philo 1960: 29–30), but the rabbis stayed clear of analysing the Bible's 'poetry'. This is not to say they did not attend to the language of Scripture. They were passionately committed to mining the riches of individual Hebrew words and phrases, each of which connected any given text in Torah to every other; each intended by the divine Author to reveal a fine point of law or lore. Although they understood that the Torah spoke in the 'language of men', the rabbis did not focus on human composition or artistry.

The Church Fathers, also writing in the early centuries of the Common Era, were of a mixed mind. Some opposed Athens to Jerusalem, to recall Tertullian's famous contrast, and maintained that the evangelists and apostles 'had no need of rhetorical art' (Justin Martyr), showed 'no power of speaking or of giving an ordered narrative by the standards of Greek dialectical or rhetorical arts' (Origen), and produced 'no sounding sentences nor magnificent diction nor excessive or useless order of arrangement of words and sentences' (John Chrysostom) (Norton 1993: i. 17, 21, 22). Christ called fishermen to follow him and spread the nets of the divine Word far and wide: the very artlessness of their recorded speech was proof that the disciples bore witness not to the wisdom of men, to the 'wisdom of this world', but rather to the power of God. Their teaching was treasure contained in 'earthen vessels' (2 Cor. 4: 7).

Yet the same Fathers who praised the simplicity of God's Word in contrast to the artfulness of the dominant pagan culture did so in quite competent rhetoric, as befitted their fundamentally rhetorical education. They were also able, as in the case of 'golden tongued' John Chrysostom, to compose gorgeous sermons and hymns that showed how well Jerusalem could manage when it wanted to rival Athens for sheer verbal glory.

Exactly contemporary with those who argued that the Bible had nothing to do with Greek literature or its literary standards were those who celebrated a peculiar biblical eloquence. It was said to be older than the ancient music of Greece, free from the fabrications of fable and myth, and of an order of beauty superior to every pagan model. Thus the early third-century *Didascalion Apostolorum* urges its audience to avoid the books of the heathen altogether: if Christians wanted historical narrative, they should go to Kings; if philosophy, the Prophets; if songs, the Psalms. Jerome asks, 'What has Horace to do with the Psalter? Vergil with the Gospels? Cicero with the Apostles?' (Jerome 1988: vi. 35). In part he is suggesting that we must choose between the one and the other, in part claiming that because of Scripture, there is no longer any need for pagan masters. The cultured despisers of Christianity mocked the Old Latin biblical text that Jerome had set out to transform and improve in his own Vulgate translation. At least in their original tongues, he argued, the Scriptures were without equal—not only true, but also eloquent and accomplished *as writing*: 'What is more musical than the Psalter? What is fairer than the hymns of Deuteronomy or Isaiah? What is more solemn than Solomon, what more polished than Job?' (ibid. 484).

At first, Augustine famously did *not* find the biblical text to be beautiful at all. There was nothing in the Old Latin language to admire for anyone who had been taught to evaluate strictly on the basis of style: 'When I first read the Scriptures . . . they seemed quite unworthy of comparisons with the stately prose of Cicero' (Augustine 1978: 3. 5). In retrospect, he understood this youthful blindness to have been the result of pride; he could not see that the Bible's 'gait was humble, but the heights it reached were sublime'. Yet as *Confessions* go on to show, the sacred texts steadily increased in stature once Augustine entered the church's fold: 'It is surely true that as the child grows these books grow with him.' Ambrose taught him to read the Prophets allegorically, and thereby made sense of their obscurity. At the climactic moment of his conversion, it is the Epistle to the Romans that he takes up and reads, finding his salvation through a single verse and, in Scripture itself, his future calling as a Christian preacher and exegete. Finally, it is the powerful communal singing of the Psalms that makes his baptism so memorable.

By the time Augustine produces the fourth book of *On Christian Doctrine*, he is no longer concerned with the deficiencies of the Old Latin or the alleged lowliness of the Scriptures, but instead assures the neophyte preacher that everything necessary in the way of rhetoric is to be found in the Bible. So magnanimous is the sacred text, moreover, that it can be all things to all people. The rhetorician will find in Amos or Paul (as well as in Cicero) the tools for powerful preaching to the high and mighty; at the same time, the common person will not be put off by grandiloquence. The words of Scripture 'are not composed by human industry, but poured forth by the Divine mind both wisely and eloquently, with a wisdom that is not bent on eloquence, but an eloquence that does not depart from wisdom' (Augustine 1958: 4. 7. 21).

THE MIDDLE AGES

In his understanding of the Bible's 'holy literature', as in so much else, Augustine's word became authoritative in the West. Cassiodorus (1969), in his *Introduction to Divine and Human Readings*, claimed that the art of rhetoric had its beginning in the Scripture, which was replete with all the tropes and figures one could want; yet the ornaments of rhetoric did not exist to beautify Scripture but rather are glorified by having Scripture's own dignity conferred on them. The Venerable Bede, in his *Art of Metrics*, goes so far as to treat the 'classics' and the Scripture together, classifying biblical books according to poetic structures shared with Homer and Virgil. Proverbs, Ecclesiastes, and the Psalms can be compared to the first three of Virgil's

Georgics, and Job to the *Iliad* and the *Aeneid*. It is not, of course, that Scripture is the same as literature; rather, it is 'literature plus', a text that could stand up to literary scrutiny but that was, as a divine inspiration, essentially incomparable.

An aspect of the Bible's 'plus' is the multiplicity of its meanings. Although the number of 'senses' that Scripture was thought to have might vary, it was the fourfold exegesis formulated by John Cassian that became normative. In *Conferences* 14. 8 Cassian (1985: 160) took the allegorical reading of Hagar and Sarah offered by St Paul in Gal. 4: 21–31 as a way of describing the various 'senses' in which a single biblical text could be true. Thus, when the Scriptures speak of Jerusalem they mean not only the historical city, but also 'in allegory as the church of Christ, in anagoge as the heavenly city of God "which is mother to us all," in the tropological sense as the human soul which, under this name, is frequently criticized or blamed by the Lord'. Whereas pagan fables might be given allegorical readings, they had no literal or historical veracity: their 'facts' were only fictions. In the Bible, on the other hand, every fact revealed a compound mystery. Christian exegetes also saw a typological relationship between the Testaments: the New was believed to unlock the Old, to contain Christian meanings that remained hidden until the gospel provided the key.

It is an indication of the daring of Dante Alighieri that he deployed biblical typology as fully as he did for his known purposes, and even went so far as to claim a uniquely biblical, fourfold polyvalence for his *Commedia*, thus alleging at least a quasi-scriptural identity for himself and the 'sacred poem | to which heaven and earth have both set a hand' (*Par.* 25. 1-2). Dante's bold claims for his vernacular text came at the same time that translations of the Bible were being brought into the language of the people. In England, the trend began with the medieval mystery plays that took the church's Vulgate and turned it into a dramatic vernacular aimed at an entire city, and then with Richard Rolle, who translated the Latin Psalter in the mid-fourteenth century. A few decades later, John Wyclif and his colleagues produced what has come to be called the Wyclif Bible. In the fifteenth century, on the Continent, Erasmus translated the New Testament's Greek into Latin and Luther the entire Bible into German. Their efforts in turn influenced the work of William Tyndale, who translated the first five books of the Jewish Bible (the Pentateuch), Jonah, and the New Testament. Tyndale was joined in his efforts by Myles Coverdale (remembered now primarily for his Psalter), who, along with others, produced the first complete English Bible of the Reformation in 1553. Other translations followed, most notably the Calvinist-inflected Geneva Bible (1560), the Bishops' Bible (1568), and the Roman Catholic Douai-Rheims completed in 1610. One year later, the Authorized Version (better known as the King James Bible) appeared.

Contrary to myths that have grown up around it, as David Norton has demonstrated, the King James Bible only gradually and fitfully became synonymous with 'Bible' in the English-speaking world; by the nineteenth century, however, it was hailed as a literary achievement rivalled only by Shakespeare. This celebration came at the expense of its consideration as a sacred text by a Divine Author. But before this apparent triumph of literature over religion transpired, there were writers who very much revered the Bible as 'holy', and still esteemed it as a Word more to obey than to admire, but who nonetheless spoke passionately about its literary power.

Whereas the biblical translator did this work in prose, poets dealt with the sacred text not only by taking it out of Hebrew, Greek, or Latin and bringing it into English, but also by refashioning it within the modes and conventions of vernacular versification. Here one thinks of the spate of poetry that issued from the English Reformation from the sixteenth century and into the early eighteenth. Poets who translated the whole Psalter into English verse include Philip Sidney and his sister Mary Sidney Herbert, George Wither, George Sandys, and Christopher Smart. Many others, however, tried their hand at parts of the whole. George Herbert's rendition of Psalm 23 is among the best examples of this genre. The King James Bible's 'green pastures' become in Herbert's rendering 'the tender grass', and God's 'goodness and mercy', 'thy sweet and wondrous love'. The effect of the paraphrase is to naturalize the Scripture into an English pastoral landscape, to convert the Psalm into quatrains and alternating rhymes—a transformation of Hebrew poetry into an Anglican hymn. Thus, David comes to sing a new song in the idiom of Herbert's time, place, and language, while Herbert himself in some sense becomes a biblical poet, co-author with the Psalmist.

THE SEVENTEENTH CENTURY

In the English seventeenth century the Bible was revered not only as eloquent, but as a sacred work that contained and therefore validated various styles of writing. Someone like Donne, for whom the Almighty was a 'Metaphorical God' delighting in subtlety and enigma, praised the Bible for the complex verbal delights that corresponded not only to God's nature but to Donne's own intricate poetry and prose: 'the Holy Ghost in penning the Scriptures delights himself not only with a propriety but with a delicacy and harmony and melody of language, with height of metaphors and other figures' (Donne 1953–62: vi. 55). George Herbert viewed the Scriptures otherwise. Perhaps because he was a country parson, Herbert believed while the 'book of books' contained 'moving and ravishing texts', the preacher was not 'to be witty or learned or eloquent, but [rather] holy' (Herbert 1981: 63). Herbert the poet, of course, exhibits all four of these characteristics in abundance: he assimilates scriptural text and teaching into 'utmost art'. Nonetheless, his poetry emulates the 'simplicity' of the biblical word, managing to be at once intimate and complex.

Perhaps no one in the history of English literature quarried the Scriptures as extensively as did John Milton, not only in his doctrinal and polemical prose but in the great poems for which he is remembered: *Paradise Lost*, with its extraordinary gloss on the opening of Genesis; *Samson Agonistes*, with its reworking of the Book of

Judges; and *Paradise Regained*, a retelling of Satan's temptation of Christ as found in Matthew and Luke. Milton's choice of biblical over classical models expresses his preference for Mount Zion, his exaltation of its 'majestic unaffected style' above the Parnassian oratory of Greece and Rome (*Paradise Regained* 4. 359; Milton 1972); yet his embrace of the biblical text was not an emulation of its 'unaffected style' or of the typically Puritan approach to language. Milton the poet chose 'no middle flight' (*Paradise Lost* 1. 14; ibid.), but consistently soared, in full majesty, demonstrating a mastery of classical rhetoric and literary form. In the poet's autobiographical interventions throughout *Paradise Lost*, he suggests that, like the holy men of Scripture who took the Spirit's dictation, he too was an inspired writer on the order of Prophets and Evangelists. If so, then Milton gives us a Baroque Bible that demonstrates the happy concord of Athens with Jerusalem—a quasi-sacred text that was also (unmistakably, unapologetically) a true work of literature.

Milton's contemporary and fellow Dissenter, John Bunyan, also mined the Scriptures in his immensely popular *Pilgrim's Progress* (1678). But rather than find a narrative base in Genesis or Judges, or pull out all the rhetorical stops, Bunyan writes a Christian allegory permeated with biblical thought and language. He aimed to reflect God's 'solidity', to set off the beauty of divine truth, not by poetic dazzle but by straightforwardness.

THE EIGHTEENTH CENTURY

Although there were still those who argued a great gulf fixed between mere poesy and the truth of God's Word—Samuel Johnson famously asserted it was 'too simple for eloquence, too sacred for fiction, and too majestick for ornament' (Johnson 1967: 847)—the eighteenth century marks the development of a notion of a distinctive biblical poetry: ancient, sublime, and (in the English of the King James Bible translators), a masterpiece of style. Some (like Jonathan Swift) would emphasize its 'simplicity'; for others it was its 'sublimity' that was most striking. Andrew Lowth, in his influential *Lectures on the Sacred Poetry of the Hebrews* (Latin, 1753; English, 1787) presented the Hebrew of Scripture as a language of passion: its free spirit appears all in a rush, laying bare the 'affections and emotions' of the biblical writer (Lowth 1829: 114–15). Lowth is best remembered for his discussion of parallelism as the defining feature of biblical poetry. Perhaps even more important, however, was his extension of the category of 'poetry' (via parallelism) to include the Prophets: one who spoke under the influence of divine inspiration could be variously named 'a prophet, a poet, or a musician'. With regard to the individual styles of the prophets, Lowth judged Isaiah more perfect than Jeremiah while Ezekiel was 'deep, vehement, tragical': the three taken together 'may be said to hold the same rank among the Hebrews, as Homer, Simonides, and Aeschylus among the Greeks' (ibid. 183).

Lowth's own free verse translation of Isaiah attempted to demonstrate this claim in English; it also underscored his conviction that to tell the 'truth' about the sacred text, one had to attend to its particular *literary* quality—in the case of the Old Testament prose, its brevity and succinctness, and in poetry, versification that reveals the essential parallelism of the original.

At roughly the same time that Lowth was writing about the poetry of the Bible, and the King James Bible was on its way to apotheosis, Scripture was also (at least among the intelligentsia) something of a neglected masterpiece. In a 1763 journal entry James Boswell mentions reading the Genesis story of Joseph and his brothers, 'which melted my heart and drew tears from my eye'. He notes, however, that although the sacred writings are 'simply and beautifully told', people of distinction were woefully ignorant of them (Boswell 1950: 196–7). If, however, they were to read the story of Joseph without being aware that it was taken from the holy book which they otherwise affected to despise, they would be touched by its beauty and literary merit.

Not that everyone acknowledged the latter. Horrified by the content of the Bible— 'the obscene stories, the voluptuous debaucheries, the cruel and torturous executions, the unrelenting vindictiveness'—Thomas Paine was able in *The Age of Reason* to find almost nothing 'simply and beautifully told'. According to him, the Book of Joshua was 'only fit to amuse children', Ruth 'an idle bungling story... about a strolling country girl creeping slyly to bed to her cousin Boaz', and Ecclesiastes 'the solitary reflections of a worn-out debauchee'. Of the Gospels, he says, 'it is impossible to find in any story so many glaring absurdities, contradictions, and falsehoods'; the New Testament as a whole 'is like a farce in one act' (Norton 1993: ii. 130–1). Only Job and a few of the Psalms escape this critical devastation.

THE NINETEENTH CENTURY

By 1800, however, Paine was very much a minority voice among writers, who were busy exchanging classical themes for biblical ones, even though many were hardly orthodox or even barely Christian. William Blake was steeped in the King James Bible and caught its diction and its prophetic and apocalyptic tones as he worked to build a poetic Jerusalem in 'England's green and pleasant land'. His notion of the Bible was highly idiosyncratic and heterodox; it stood replete with 'imagination and visions from end to end'. Jesus and his disciples were all artists, and both Testaments of Scripture together formed 'the great code of art' (Blake 1978: i. 665). Although William Wordsworth was not as ostensibly 'biblical' as Blake, he celebrated the 'poetic diction' of the Bible (that is, the King James Version) in his preface to the revolutionary *Lyrical Ballads* (1800). Thanks in part to the dissemination of Lowth's ideas about Hebrew as a 'simple and unadorned' language marked by an 'almost ineffable sublimity', Wordsworth found a model for a common man's vernacular that he was himself striving to compose. His colleague Samuel Taylor Coleridge praised the Old Testament as 'the true model of simplicity of style' (Norton 1993: ii. 153 n. 22); he also proclaimed that 'Sublimity is Hebrew by birth!' (ibid. 158). Once again, the Bible could be all things to all people. Twentieth-century publication of Coleridge's extensive biblical criticism latterly reveals him to have been a serious thinker about the Scripture's aesthetic unity as inseparable from its religious content; he also felt its power personally: 'In the Bible there is more that finds me than I have experienced in all other books put together' (Jasper and Prickett 1999: 61). More typical of Romantic criticism was William Hazlitt's impressionistic effusions over the King James Bible, which ranged from the 'Orphic hymns' of David and the 'gorgeous visions of Ezekiel' to those less spectacular passages in which one found 'a depth and tenderness of feeling, and a touching sympathy in the mode of narration' (Norton 1993: ii. 171).

Because the Bible had come in the nineteenth century to be appreciated as a work of art quite apart from a sacred context or identity, it could be redeemed in the eyes of those who found themselves at odds with religion. Lord Byron, a notorious infidel, was interested enough in the Old Testament to author *Hebrew Melodies* and *Cain*; his atheist friend Percy Bysshe Shelley was, in Byron's words, 'a great admirer of Scripture as a composition' (ibid. 164). Indeed, in his 'Defence of Poetry', Shelley esteems the book of Job a 'sublime dramatic poem' and the Song of Songs a model 'of poetical sublimity and pathos', and claims that Jesus and his disciples were imbued with 'the astonishing poetry of Moses, Job, David, Solomon, and Isaiah' (Shelley 1926–30: vii. 196). He finds it impossible to imagine what the moral condition of humankind would have been had Dante, Petrarch, Chaucer, Shakespeare, and Milton never existed, if Greek literature had not been revived, or if 'Hebrew poetry had never been translated' (ibid. 132–3). It is as if the Bible, no longer uniquely God's book, had entered the ranks of a purely *literary* canon, properly placed on the same shelf as Sophocles, the *Canzoniere*, and *The Canterbury Tales*. What was once believed to be uniquely inspired could almost be listed casually as one 'inspiring' work among others.

'Almost', because at least for the nineteenth century—in spite of the ardent aesthetic celebration of the King James Bible, in Saintsbury's (1912: 157–8) words, as 'the prowess and the powers of the English tongue'—Scripture occupied a place not even Shakespeare could rival, even if the tide of faith had ebbed for the elite and the Bible lost its once unequalled authority. In Thomas Macaulay's memorable 1828 claim, 'if everything else in our language should perish, [the King James Bible] would alone suffice to show the whole extent of its beauty and power' (Norton 1993: ii. 179). A few decades later, Matthew Arnold spoke of the Bible as the cornerstone of 'letters' ('poetry, philosophy, eloquence'). Quite apart from whatever it might have to say about religion, it offered 'the one great literature for which the people have had a preparation' (ibid. 273), a resource rich in poetry and philosophy which, if read for literary and historical substance and not for doctrine, could be inspiring for all. Furthermore, the Bible could be read for pleasure, and indeed must be. As Arnold later wrote in the preface to his Hebrew translation, *Isaiah of Jerusalem*, it was not enough to translate the books of Scripture accurately, for 'they must be translated so as to be deeply enjoyed, and to exercise the power of beauty and sentiment' (ibid. 276). Does this mean that he took the Prophet's words only as poetry and literature? Arnold poses this question in his preface but does not answer it directly. Instead, he says how very highly he values 'the power of poetry and literature upon men's minds', suggesting that it is precisely 'letters', not religion, that give access to the deepest truth. In any case, Arnold lets delight have the last word: not even from 'our own Shakespeare and Milton' has he 'received so much delight and stimulus as from Homer and Isaiah' (ibid.). Any proper curriculum would have to include both 'poets'.

THE TWENTIETH CENTURY

By the early twentieth century, others took up where Arnold left off: Richard Moulton, whose academic career took him across the Atlantic from Cambridge to the University of Chicago, began a one-man 'Bible as Literature' industry with publications bearing such titles as *The Modern Reader's Bible* (1895) and *The Literary Study of the Bible* (1899). Moulton was fascinated by the Bible's 'morphologies' (literary genres) and assumed that *all* Scripture had a literary quality to it. In 1895, folklorist Sir James G. Frazer edited *Passages of the Bible Chosen for their Literary Beauty and Interest*: his work was for those, like himself, who loved the Bible divested of 'purely theological import'. Frazier was convinced that only portions of the Scripture deserved to be called 'gems' and thus made his anthology accordingly: he culled what was worth reading and forgot the rest. A selective approach was also followed by William Ralph Inge in *Every Man's Bible: An Anthology* (1934): by carefully choosing texts from the treasury of Scripture, he hoped to use literary brilliance as a means to lure readers back to the Word of God. In either case, whether the anthologist is a sceptic or an apologist for Christianity, by the twentieth century one of the Bible's major selling points to the contemporary audience—and perhaps the decisive one—was its quality as writing.

For some, the 'Bible as Literature' movement sounded a death-knell for the future of the text. T. S. Eliot, for instance, argued in 1935 that the Scripture had been formative in Christian culture only because it had *not* been treated as narrative or poetry but rather 'as the report of the Word of God': 'the fact that men of letters now discuss it as "literature" probably indicates the *end* of its "literary" influence' (Eliot 1953: 33). For C. S. Lewis in 1950, who took issue with the literary adulation of the KJB, the Bible was 'so remorselessly and continuously sacred that it does not invite, it excludes or repels, the merely aesthetic approach. You can read it as literature only by a *tour de force*' (Lewis 1962: 48–9).

Objection to the 'Bible as Literature' has by no means been limited to traditionalist Christians from an earlier moment in the twentieth century: James Kugel (1981: 304) ends *The Idea of Biblical Poetry* by speaking in the voice of a Jewish 'we' that includes those, like himself, who shudder to hear the biblical Joseph described as 'one of the most believable characters in Western literature'. For Kugel, Joseph cannot properly be taken as a character or the Bible placed on the same shelf with other pieces of literature:

And as true as this may be for us, how much truer must it have been when his story was first set down? That initial narrative act, 'Come gather round and let me spin a tale,' is not the starting point of biblical history. Its premise—'Let me tell you what happened to Joseph-our-ancestor, let me tell you how things came to be as you know them actually to be now'—is significantly different. Not to speak of 'Let me tell you how God saved us' [or] 'Let me tell you God's teaching.'   (ibid.)

Kugel certainly does not deny that the Bible has literary features worth noting (although he takes issue with the whole notion of 'Hebrew poetry'); he denies that 'we' can understand Scripture aright only as a work of literature rather than as what it presents itself to be—God's Word.

Something like Kugel's contrast between spinning a tale and handing down God's teaching is to be found in Erich Auerbach's essay 'The Scar of Odysseus', placed at the outset of *Mimesis: The Representation of Reality in Western Literature* (1946)—a text commonly taken to mark the beginning of contemporary excursions into 'Bible as Literature'. Auerbach argues that the binding of Isaac in Genesis 22 is no better established in history than the hero's return in *Odyssey* 19: both are legendary. What differentiates the two, however, is that whereas Homer's bard is merely telling a story, the Genesis narrator has composed an 'effective version' of what he believes to be true: 'What he produced, then, was not primarily oriented toward "realism" (if he succeeded in being realistic, it was merely a means, not an end); it was oriented toward the truth' (Auerbach 1957: 14). Truth-telling in the Bible, moreover, always involves a veil of darkness, an untold story, a background that recedes into mystery.

These characteristics do not represent merely a stylistic tic of the Hebrew writer: style develops out of a theological understanding of a God who always 'extends into depths', whose mind is fathomless, ultimately unknowable (unlike the Homeric gods, who are 'comprehensible'). The perceived unity of the Bible is also ultimately a theological construct, for although pieced together from myriad sources, Scripture nonetheless coheres by virtue of a continuous 'vertical connection' between its many characters and episodes and a mysterious divine plan. 'The greater the separateness and horizontal disconnection of the stories and groups of stories in relation to one another...the stronger is their vertical connection, which holds them all together and which is entirely missing in Homer' (ibid. 17). A universal history runs through-out the Law and the Prophets, a Master Story that not only knits up the whole but distinguishes biblical writing from all other ancient literature.

Auerbach (ibid. 11) offers more than a contrast between 'two equally ancient and equally epic texts', between two 'styles' of literature. In this reckoning, one compels belief; the other invites a suspension of disbelief; one presents itself as truth (the Bible 'is tyrannical—it excludes all other claims', ibid. 14) and the other does not (Homer's world 'exists for itself, contains nothing but itself', ibid. 13). Yet, if this comparison is the formal agenda of the essay, the rhetorical force of Auerbach's passionate analysis takes us beyond any neutral discussion of diverse literary strategies. Rather, the essay reads like a defence and illustration of scriptural truth against the lies of the poets, however compelling those tale-spinners may be. There is no 'we' in Auerbach, as there is in Kugel, to suggest that he belongs to a community of readers who would shudder to consider Abraham, like Odysseus, 'one of the most believable characters in Western literature'. There is only a critic operating apart from any discernible religious position who, however unintentionally, recalls the stacked deck of the Athens–Jerusalem debate. Homer is 'literature', the Bible 'sacred text'.

Auerbach's treatment of the Bible in *Mimesis* marked a turning point in how Scripture would be read critically in the twentieth century. First, Auerbach was a Romance literature specialist by training, not a biblical scholar. As a result, he felt no obligations to the historical-critical method that tended to divide the received text into smaller and smaller units, shaped by different redactors (e.g. J, E, D, and P in the Hebrew Bible or, in the New Testament, the three Synoptic Gospels, John, and the supposed antecedent of all four, Q). By contrast, he read the Bible as he read Homer (or, later in *Mimesis*, Dante, Cervantes, and Virginia Woolf)—as a unified text, and as a literature that could hold its own against the classics. He was not the first to bring the scriptural canon into dialogue with secular works; but for twentieth-century academics working in English or Comparative Literature, *Mimesis* seemed in the 1970s to open a door to biblical study that would enable, in the words of the editors of the 1987 *Literary Guide to the Bible*, 'all manner of new possibilities, a revision of past readings, a modern Bible' (Alter and Kermode 1987: 4).

Second, Auerbach did this as a Jew, albeit one who wrote more about Christian texts than Jewish ones, and who devoted much of his study to traditional figural readings of the Bible that tended to discard the Old Testament 'foreshadow' in favour of New Testament and ecclesiastical 'fulfilment'. His professional Bible, so to speak, was Christian, as indeed it has been almost entirely throughout our discussion thus far. This bias continues to be the case, for obvious reasons, among those who regard the Bible as foundational to an overwhelmingly Gentile English literature and 'Western cultural tradition', pre-eminently Northrop Frye in *The Great Code* (1982) and its sequel, *Words with Power* (1990). Nonetheless, Auerbach's Jewishness, however indirectly, may have fostered a general discussion of the Bible as Jews have always viewed it, not as an *Old* Testament but rather as an integral whole, written in Hebrew, and perhaps best considered within such Jewish modes of interpretation as one finds in the eleventh-century commentator Rashi or among the rabbinic Midrashim. The Jewish spectrum of such work is broad, ranging from Harold Bloom's energetic iconoclasm in *The Book of J* to Geoffrey Hartman's Continentally–influenced criticism, to the *explication de texte* readings of literary critics such as Robert Alter or Meir Sternberg, to the work of those trained in biblical study, such as Shimon Bar-Efrat, Adele Berlin, David Damrosch, and James Kugel.

It should not be concluded that this surge of interest in the Hebrew Bible means that little new work has been done on the Christian text. Northrop Frye has already been mentioned. Among the first New Testament scholars bringing a literary critical approach to post-Second World War biblical studies was Amos Wilder in several books including *The Bible and the Literary Critic* (1991). Hans Frei's *The Eclipse of Biblical Narrative* (1974) calls for a turning away from history and towards story, with the meaning of the Scripture understood to depend not on historical accuracy but rather on 'history-like' narrative. In the United Kingdom, Gabriel Josipovici's *The Book of God* (1988) argues for the 'magnificent conception' of the Christian Bible as a unity from Beginning to End, as well as for the Scripture's peculiar representation of reality through stylistic disjunctions or 'stutters'. The Bible calls into question 'our ability to make sense of the past, and of stories to explain ourselves or describe the world' (ibid. 306); often against the wishes of its interpreters, Scripture works to stay 'open'. David Jasper and Stephen Prickett separately have produced many works on the Christian Bible prior to their collaboration in *The Bible and Literature: A Reader* (1999). Useful to understanding the evolving impact of the Scripture in both the United Kingdom and America is David Norton's two-volume *A History of the Bible as Literature* (1993). Just prior to the 400th anniversary of the King James Bible, moreover, there also seems to be no dearth of interest in how that revered 'English classic' came to be.

One way to gauge the late-twentieth century scene is to look at *The Literary Guide to the Bible* (1987) co-edited by Robert Alter and Frank Kermode, two literary critics turned biblical scholars, one American and one British. This oft-cited collection of essays promises (according to the book jacket) to 'rediscover the incomparable literary richness of a book that all us of live with and many of us live by'. Here is a Bible 'incomparable' in its richness as literature and a force to contend with for any literate person; on the other hand, we also have a book that 'many of us live by'. These believers in a sacred text may be only a minority compared to 'all of us', but they are nonetheless to be accounted for.

The volume is multi-authored and, as the editors say, 'pluralist' and 'eclectic'. Because very little is offered to someone coming to the Bible as a sacred text, (Evangelical scholars Leyland Ryken and Tremper Longman III moved to fill that gap in 1993 with their *Complete Literary Guide to the Bible*.) Diversity of approach, which now characterizes the 'Bible as Literature' field, is intentionally limited. Alter and Kermode exclude many post-structuralists because allegedly they do not approach the Bible as 'literature of high importance and power' (1993: 4) but are motivated primarily by ideology or social structures. Among those omitted are 'Deconstruction-ists and some feminist critics who demonstrate that the text is necessarily divided against the self' (ibid. 6). To find such alternative readings one must turn to Mieke Bal, to the essays in Regina Schwartz's *The Book and the Text: The Bible and Literary Theory* (1990) or to the Bible and Culture Collective's *Postmodern Bible* (1995).

Alter and Kermode represent two quite different approaches to the Bible, despite all they have in common: training in the interpretation of secular literature and an ease in moving from biblical narrative to nineteenth- and twentieth-century fiction. In several works of his own, Alter deals exclusively with the Hebrew Bible, which he celebrates through many sensitive close readings of a literature characterized by its

wild heterogeneity (e.g. its inclusion of genealogies, etiologies, laws, lists, and enu-
merations along with the more readily recognized genres of poetry and narrative).
Biblical style—which provides a strong sense of unity for this multi-authored,
heavily redacted work—is extraordinarily allusive and self-referential. It revels in
puns and wordplay; its penchant for repetition brings about shades of meaning
rather than simple reiteration, and its 'composite artistry', its 'collage' of sources,
allows for multiple interpretations of characters and events that foreclose easy
judgement.

Is the Bible then 'literature'? Alter (1992, 20) asserts that 'we are in fact better
readers of biblical narrative because we are lucky enough to come after Flaubert and
Joyce, Dante and Shakespeare'. This does not mean, however, that biblical writers
were aiming in the first instance to be interesting, enjoyable, or admirable. Rather,
their 'original emphases' were 'theological, legislative, historiographic, and moral'.
Nonetheless, study of the Hebrew shows 'a delight in the manifold exercise of literary
craftsmanship' that is absolutely inseparable from the meaning and purpose of the
sacred text (Alter and Kermode 1987: 14–15). In this regard, as well as in his preference
for close reading, Alter is the descendent of Auerbach in *Mimesis*: the Bible's singular
style *is* its representation of reality.

But what is 'real' in biblical literature? Alter, like Auerbach, writes about the Hebrew
Bible as if (to recall Gertrude Stein) there is a 'there' there—if not actual history, then
the conviction of the historical. The text, for all its careful shaping of tradition, points
to something beyond itself: 'The biblical outlook is informed, I think, by a sense of
stubborn contradiction, of a profound and ineradicable untidiness in the nature of
things, and it is toward the expression of such a sense of moral and historical reality
that the composite artistry of the Bible is directed' (Alter 1981: 154). For Frank
Kermode, on the other hand, there is finally nothing beyond the biblical text, nothing
off the page. The Gospel of Mark, for instance, is opaque, not 'transparent' to anything
but its own textual antecedents in the Hebrew Bible, or to the demands of story itself:
Judas has a role in the Gospel because a betrayal needs a betrayer; Pilate exists because a
trial needs a judge. Whereas both Auerbach and Alter accept the premise of biblical
historicity, and talk in their different ways about a mysterious divine 'background'
towards which the text points, Kermode (1979: 123) rejects 'the old comfortable fictions
of transparency, the single sense, the truth'. At most there is only 'an uninterpretable
radiance', a sudden flare of obscurity. The text exists for itself, to recall Auerbach on
Homer, and 'contains nothing but itself'.

Kermode's conviction of the Bible's 'opacity' does not seem to be shared by the
many novelists and poets who, in the last decades, have reflected on what the Bible
has meant to them personally—as a sacred text to embrace, an authority to rail
against, or a powerful Word no writer of any stripe can gainsay. Expressions of
religious identity and practice (even if more a part of childhood than of adult life)
abound in such American anthologies as *Congregation: Contemporary Writers Read
the Jewish Bible* (1987), *Incarnation: Writers on the New Testament* (1990), *Joyful Noise:
The New Testament Revisited* (1997), and *Killing the Buddha: A Heretic's Bible* (2003).
Josipovici (1988: 300) suggests that the appeal of the Bible to contemporary writers is

precisely what it was for Dante and Proust, Kafka and Celan—the lure of 'something which is other than literature, something essentially truer and more necessary than literature could ever be'. It may well take the existence of a sacred text to inspire the human literature we need to read.

PRESENT TRENDS

In both the United Kingdom and North America, it is commonplace to speak of the precipitous decline in biblical literacy. At the same time, stores overflow with new translations, study-guides, videos, DVDs, and computer software. The population targeted by this merchandise probably consists of Jews and Christians already reading a 'Holy Bible'. It is this authoritative text, moreover, that is increasingly invoked in the political arena, at least in the United States: what the Bible 'says' is what counts, not how it says it. By contrast, interest in the Bible as Literature—even as *sacred* literature—is largely confined to the secular academy, where form is studied more closely than content.

At the same time that the Bible draws these specialized readerships, a general fascination with literature *about* the Bible has exploded on the American scene. One thinks of runaway best-sellers, *The Bible Code* (1997) and *The DaVinci Code* (2003), which are, each in its way, biblical mystery stories. In addition, those books that did not make it into the New Testament canon—the Gospels of Thomas and Mary Magdalen, for instance—are now capturing the public's imagination, raising questions about what was sacrificed in the making of orthodoxy. And, as has indeed been the case since Henry Fielding gave us *Joseph Andrews* (1742), the first novel in English, the Bible remains a source of literary inspiration in popular fiction. Tim LaHaye's apocalyptic 'Left Behind' series takes up where the Book of Revelation leaves off. Although wordless in Genesis, Dinah narrates her (vastly expanded) experiences in *The Red Tent* (2001); while celibate in the Gospels, Jesus' sex life is 'decoded' in *The DaVinci Code*. Whether or not these Bible-infused works manage to lure their readers back to the original source text, the traditional best-seller is making many best-sellers.

We began by noting the problematic 'and' yoking the possibly antithetic terms, 'literature' and 'sacred text'. Yet what we find in the end is less a dichotomy than a complicated interplay between the two. At present, academics explore the literary quality of the Bible, religious leaders and politicians proclaim its principles, novelists use it to launch their own stories, filmmakers make it into box-office hits, and pop singers mine it for their lyrics. In an era of so-called biblical illiteracy, when paradoxically the Bible has never been more available, it remains to be seen what its future will be—either as a human classic or a divine revelation.

WORKS CITED

ALTER, ROBERT. 1981. *Art of Biblical Narrative*. New York: Basic Books.

—— 1992. *The World of Biblical Literature*. New York: Basic Books.

—— and Frank Kermode (eds.). 1987. *Literary Guide to the Bible*. Cambridge, Mass.: Harvard University Press.

AUERBACH, ERICH. 1957. *Mimesis: The Representation of Reality in Western Literature*. Garden City, NY: Doubleday.

AUGUSTINE. 1958. *On Christian Doctrine*, trans. D. W. Robertson. The Library of Liberal Arts 80. New York: Liberal Arts.

—— 1978. *Confessions*, trans. R. S. Pine-Coffin. New York: Penguin.

Bible and Culture Collective (ed.). 1995. *The Postmodern Bible*. New Haven: Yale University Press.

BLAKE, WILLIAM. 1978. *William Blake's Writings*, ed. G. E. Bentley. 2 vols. Oxford: Clarendon.

BOSWELL, JAMES. 1950. *Boswell's London Journals, 1762–1763*, ed. Frederick A. Pottle. London: Heinemann.

CASSIAN, JOHN. 1985. *Conferences*, trans. Colm Luibheid. Mahwah, NJ: Paulist Press.

CASSIODORUS. 1969. *An Introduction to Divine and Human Readings*, trans. Leslie Webber Jones. New York: Norton.

DONNE, JOHN. 1953–62. *The Sermons of John Donne*, ed. George R. Potter and Evelyn M. Simpson. 10 vols. Berkeley and Los Angeles: University of California Press.

ELIOT, T. S. 1953. *Selected Prose*, ed. John Hayward. Harmondsworth: Penguin.

HERBERT, GEORGE. 1981. *The Country Parson: The Poems*, ed. John N. Wall. New York: Paulist Press.

JASPER, DAVID, and PRICKETT, STEPHEN (eds.). 1999. *The Bible as Literature: A Reader*. Oxford: Blackwell.

JEROME. 1988. *The Principle Works of St. Jerome*, trans. W. H. Fremantle. A Select Library of Nicene and Post-Nicene Father. 2nd ser. 14 vols. Grand Rapids: Eerdmans.

JOHNSON, SAMUEL. 1967. *Johnson, Poetry & Prose*, ed. Mona Wilson. Cambridge, Mass.: Harvard University Press.

JOSIPOVICI, GABRIEL. 1988. *The Book of God: A Response to the Bible*. New Haven: Yale University Press.

KERMODE, FRANK. 1979. *The Genesis of Secrecy: On the Interpretation of Narrative*. Cambridge, Mass.: Harvard University Press.

KUGEL, JAMES L. 1981. *The Idea of Biblical Poetry: Parallelism and Its History*. New Haven: Yale University Press.

LEWIS, C. S. 1962. *They Asked for a Paper*. London: Bles.

LOWTH, ROBERT. 1829. *Lectures on the Sacred Poetry of the Hebrews*. Andover, Mass.: Codman.

MILTON, JOHN. 1972. *The Poems of John Milton*, ed. John Carey and Alistair Fowler. New York: W. W. Norton.

NORTON, DAVID. 1993. *A History of the Bible as Literature*, i. *From Antiquity to the Present*; ii. *From 1700 to the Present Day*. Cambridge: Cambridge University Press.

PHILO. 1960. *The Contemplative Life*, trans. F. H. Colson. Cambridge: Cambridge University Press.

RYKEN, LELAND, and LONGMAN, TREMPER, III (eds.). 1993. *A Complete Literary Guide to the Bible*. Grand Rapids: Zondervan.

SAINTSBURY, GEORGE. 1912. *A History of English Prose Rhythm*. London: Macmillan.

SCHWARTZ, REGINA (ed.). 1990. *The Book and the Text: The Bible and Literary Theory*. Oxford: Blackwell.

SHELLEY, PERCY BYSSHE. 1926–30. *The Complete Works of Percy Bysshe Shelley*, ed. Roger Ingpen and Walter E. Peck. 10 vols. New York: C. Scribner's Sons.

FURTHER READING

BAR-EFRAT, SHIMEON. 1989. *Narrative Art in the Bible*. Sheffield: Almond.

BERLIN, ADELE. 1983. *Poetics and Interpretation of Biblical Narrative*. Sheffield: Almond.

DAMROSCH, DAVID. 1987. *The Narrative Covenant: Transformations of Genre in the Growth of Biblical Narrative*. San Francisco: Harper & Row.

FREI, HANS. 1974. *The Eclipse of Biblical Narrative: A Study in Eighteenth and Nineteenth-Century Hermeneutics*. New Haven: Yale University Press.

FRYE, NORTHROP. 1982. *The Great Code: The Bible and Literature*. New York: Harcourt Brace Jovanovich.

—— 1990. *Words with Power: Being a Second Study of 'The Bible as Literature'*, San Diego: Harcourt Brace Jovanovich.

JASPER, DAVID, and PRICKETT, STEPHEN (eds.). 1999. *The Bible as Literature: A Reader*. Oxford: Blackwell.

JOSIPOVICI, GABRIEL. 1988. *The Book of God: A Response to the Bible*. New Haven: Yale University Press.

NORTON, DAVID. 1993. *A History of the Bible as Literature*. i. *From Antiquity to the Present*; ii. *From 1700 to the Present Day*. Cambridge: Cambridge University Press.

STERNBERG, MEIR. 1985. *Poetics of Biblical Narrative: Ideological Literature and the Drama of Reading*. Bloomington: Indiana University Press.

WILDER, AMOS N. 1991. *The Bible and the Literary Critic*. Minneapolis: Fortress.

CHAPTER 13

THE PENTATEUCH

TOD LINAFELT

To consider the Pentateuch in a 'literary' way, we might ask about its own literary features, or we might ask how those literary features have been absorbed by subsequent writers within the Western tradition that owes so much, and in so many ways, to the Pentateuch or Torah—that is, the first five books of the Bible. This chapter will largely focus on the first question, with the hope that by doing so, the second, addressed briefly at the end, might be given a greater literary context in which to be understood. Ultimately, we want to address a more embracing question: in what ways does the Pentateuch contain subtle and artful material that might prove compelling not only to later generations of English poets, novelists, dramatists, and Christian thinkers, but also to a modern reader whose interest may well go beyond the strictly historical or theological?

It is hard to deny that in many respects the Pentateuch is among the most 'unliterary' works of literature that we have. This judgement is not entirely attributable to the mass of legal material one encounters, to 'getting bogged down in Leviticus' as the phrase so often goes. For even those portions of the Torah made up of what we might think of as classical Hebrew narrative (most of Genesis, the first half of Exodus, parts of Numbers) exhibit a style that often seems simple, even primitive, in comparison with great works of world literature from the *Iliad* and the *Odyssey* to the *Tale of Genji*. For example, biblical narrative works with a very limited vocabulary, and it often repeats a word several times rather than resorting to synonyms. Its syntax too seems rudimentary to modern ears, linking clause after clause with a simple 'and' that reveals little about their syntactical relation (a system linguists call 'parataxis'), instead of using complex sentences with subordinate clauses ('hypotaxis'). Notice, for example, the dogged repetition of 'face' and the run-on syntax in the following very literal translation of Gen. 32: 21 (where Jacob is sending ahead of him a very large gift to his estranged brother Esau, in the hope that Esau will be placated over Jacob's earlier stealing of his blessing): 'For he said, "Let me cover his face with the gift that goes before my face and after I look upon his face perhaps he will lift up my face."' And if translations tend to obscure these features, even when one is not reading the Hebrew one is bound to notice the paucity of metaphorical description, the brevity of dialogue, the lack of reference to the interior lives of characters, the limited use of figural perspective, and not least the jarring concreteness with which God is imagined to be involved in human history.

Many of these features are elements of biblical literature's 'drastic economy of style', to borrow a phrase from Robert Alter. We may compare, for example, Homer's use of sometimes startling metaphors in describing a scene with the (essentially anonymous) biblical authors, who by and large avoid such elaborate figurative language. Contrast this description in the *Iliad* of the death of a single, obscure Trojan charioteer—'Patroclus rising beside him stabbed his right jawbone, | ramming the spearhead square between his teeth so hard | he hooked him by that spearhead over the chariot-rail, | hoisted, dragged the Trojan out as an angler perched | on a jutting rock ledge drags some fish from the sea, | some noble catch, with line and glittering bronze hook' (16. 480–5, Fagles 1990 trans.)—with the blunt recounting in Gen. 34 of the massacre of an entire city by two of Jacob's sons: 'Simeon and Levi, Dinah's brothers, took each his sword, and came upon the city unopposed, and they killed every male. And Hamor and Shechem his son they killed by the edge of the sword' (citations here and below are from Alter 2004). Indeed, biblical narrative tends to avoid description of any sort, metaphorical or otherwise. The principle applies, with some exceptions of course, not only to physical description— so that we are rarely told what either objects or people look like—but also, and more importantly, to the inner lives, thoughts, and motivations of characters in the narratives. It would be a mistake, however, to take this economy of style as an indicator of the Bible's simplicity or primitiveness as a work of literature. In fact, as I will endeavour to show, it is primarily this terseness that lends biblical narrative, and thus the Pentateuch, its distinctive complexity as literature.

Before considering in more detail the workings of narrative in the Pentateuch it is necessary to say a few words about, first, the cultic and legal material that comprises such a significant portion of these five books and, secondly, the poems and poetic fragments that comprise a much smaller group of passages. On the one hand, I am reluctant to give short shrift to the cultic and legal texts—dealing with the construction of the tabernacle, sacrificial rituals, dietary laws, etc.—that one finds in the second half of Exodus and throughout most of Leviticus and Deuteronomy and much of Numbers. This material has already suffered from a less-than-benign neglect both in the history of Christian religious interpretation, which has been inclined to view it as irrelevant in the wake of the gospel, and in Western literary history, which has gravitated to the surrounding stories and poems as sources of inspiration. On the other hand, for all its interesting complexity, its real depth of religious sensibility, and in Deuteronomy at least its high rhetorical flair, the cultic and legal material in the Pentateuch is in the end not quite what we think of as literature. There may indeed be structuring principles both large and small at work in this material that indicates more intentionality in its shaping than is immediately apparent (for one of the most recent and interesting theories along these lines, see Douglas 1999; 2004), and certainly the legal texts both demand and reward the sort of close reading that we tend to associate with poetic and narrative texts (such a reading would bring out, for example, the complex and competing social codes that lie behind the list of sexual prohibitions in Leviticus 18), but these texts are finally more discursive than literary.

The poetry that one finds in the Pentateuch may take the form of relatively long, formal set-pieces (Gen. 49: 1–27; Exod. 15: 1–18; Deut. 32: 1–43) that would seem to have existed independently before being inserted by an author or an editor into their present narrative contexts, and which often serve as markers of transition in the larger structure of a book or in the Torah as a whole, or it may take the form of shorter poems (sometimes just a line or two) that were in all likelihood composed by the author of the surrounding narrative. In either case the most salient characteristic of ancient Hebrew poetry, what allows us in fact to call it poetry, is present, namely parallelism. That is, a line of Hebrew biblical poetry is composed of usually two, but sometimes three, short segments or cola placed in parallel relationship to each other. In the most obvious form of this parallelism the second colon will correspond both semantically and syntactically to the previous. Thus, in the line from Moses' victory song in Exod. 15, 'Your right hand, O Lord, is mighty in power. | Your right hand, O Lord, smashes the enemy', every element from the first half of the line is matched in the second half of the line. But clearly the ancient poets felt a good deal of freedom in articulating the parallelism of the line, as work in recent decades by Robert Alter, Adele Berlin, and James Kugel have made clear, and it is only rarely that one encounters the sort of strict phrase-by-phrase parallelism that we see above.

Puns, wordplays, alliteration, and the like, as well as the Hebrew syntax, are mostly lost in translations (although those by Alter and Fox do an admirable job of carrying these over into English), but there is still a great deal to be seen in the semantic parallelism, or parallelism of meaning, between one colon and the next even in English translation. Frequently the relationship between the cola is one in which the second will heighten or intensify the emotional register of the first, as we see in Jacob's response to being shown Joseph's tunic, recently dipped in the blood of a slaughtered kid by his scheming brothers: 'A vicious beast has devoured him, | Joseph torn to shreds!' (Gen. 37: 33). The image of Joseph being devoured by a wild animal is bad enough, but the grief-stricken father goes on to imagine his son as torn to shreds. Or the second cola might take an image from the first and make it more concrete or specific, as in Exod. 15: 14 where in the line, 'Peoples heard and they quaked, | trembling seized Philistia's dwellers', the generic reference to peoples is specific by reference to the Philistines. Or the second colon might offer a temporal or narrative-like progression from the first, as in Exod. 15: 10: 'You blew with your breath—the sea covered them over. | They sank like lead in the mighty waters.' Often there will be more than one way of articulating the parallelism of the line, and much of the pleasure of reading biblical poetry is to be found in trying to work out just how the second or third colon relates to the first.

The longer, more imposing poems often serve as markers of an overarching design—usually of endings or transitions—in one of the individual books or in the Pentateuch as a whole. So the ending of the book of Genesis is marked by the long poetic blessing that the elderly Jacob extends to his twelve sons (representing the twelve tribes of Israel) in Ch. 49. The poem draws together themes from the previous family-oriented stories in Genesis—especially the promise of fertility and the rivalry among brothers—and it points forward to the coming tribal and national history of Israel (e.g. 'The sceptre shall not pass from Judah' (49: 10)), while also lending a formal closure to the long and storied life of the ancestor Jacob: 'And Jacob finished charging his sons, and he gathered his feet up into the bed, and he breathed his last, and was gathered to his kinfolk' (49: 30). Likewise, the justly famous poem in Exod. 15, traditionally known as the 'Song at the Sea', marks a particularly significant moment in the larger narrative of Exodus: the story moves geographically from Egypt to the wilderness and thematically from liberation to covenant, even as the people of Israel move from slavery to freedom. The end of the Torah as a whole is doubly marked, first by the 'Song of Moses' in Deut. 32, which praises God's saving actions on behalf of Israel, and second by the blessing that Moses extends, as Jacob did earlier, to the twelve tribes in Deut. 33. There is a good deal of linguistic evidence to indicate that these poems or songs (Hebrew *shirah*), along with the 'Song of Deborah' in Judg. 5, are among the oldest portions of the Bible. Thus they are sometimes read as a source of clues in reconstructing tribal history or social structure, but they are also compelling as acts of literature in their own right, exhibiting not only the various types of parallelism but also heightened diction, the sort of vivid and arresting metaphors that are generally lacking in Hebrew narrative, and, especially in the case of Exod. 15, a strophic structure.

The shorter poetic utterances serve either to impart a formal tone or ceremonial gravitas to a situation or to heighten the intensity or the emotional register of a character's speech. For the latter, we saw above the verse form of Jacob's brief lament over Joseph, and among other examples we might add the following: God's outburst over the violence of Sodom and Gomorrah, 'The outcry of Sodom and Gomorrah, how great! | Their offense is very grave' (Gen. 18: 20); Sarah's exclamation at the birth of Isaac, 'Laughter has God made me, | whoever hears will laugh at me' (Gen. 21: 6); and the reaction of Moses, who has just received the tablets of the commandments from God, to the sound of the people celebrating around the golden calf, 'Not the sound of crying out in triumph, | and not the sound of crying out in defeat. | A sound of crying out I hear' (Exod. 32: 18). The effect of lending a formality of tone to an utterance may be seen particularly in short speeches of God, for example God's articulation of the consequences of the eating of the fruit in Gen. 3: 14–19, the exhortation to Cain in Gen. 4: 6–7, and endorsement of Moses over Aaron and Miriam in Num. 12: 6–8; but the use of verse also serves a sort of ceremonial function on the lips of human characters, as in Isaac's blessings of Jacob and Esau in Gen. 27, Jacob's response to God's promised blessing in Gen. 28 ('How fearsome is this place! | This can be but the house of God, | and this is the gate of the heavens' (v. 17)) and his grievance against Laban in Gen. 31: 36–40, and Balaam's several blessings of

Israel in Num. 23 and 24. Many of these shorter examples of verse are not set off as poems in the major translations, but the attentive reader will be able to catch them by the use of parallelism and a more formalized diction and may then ask why the author has set off this particular speech or piece of dialogue in verse form.

The legal, cultic, and poetic sections notwithstanding, to speak of the literary art of the Pentateuch is to speak primarily of its narrative art. It is still the case that in beginning to think about the narrative art of the Bible one could do no better than to read Erich Auerbach's 'Odysseus' Scar', the opening chapter of his book *Mimesis: The Representation of Reality in Western Literature* (1953), in which he compares biblical narrative style with Homeric epic style. Auerbach offers the first and best modern articulation of how the drastic terseness of biblical narrative is not just the absence of style but is in fact a distinctive and profound literary mode in its own right. Auerbach famously describes Homeric style as being 'of the foreground', whereas biblical narratives are by contrast 'fraught with background'. In other words, in the *Iliad* and the *Odyssey* both objects and persons tend to be fully described and illuminated, with all essential attributes and aspects—from physical descriptions to the thoughts and motivations of characters—there in the foreground for the reader to see. But with biblical narrative such details are, for the most part, kept in the background and are not directly available to the reader. So, as I noted at the outset, we are very rarely given physical descriptions of either objects or people in the biblical narrative. (This contrasts with cultic texts where, for example, we are given quite detailed descriptions of the tabernacle and its furnishings; see Exod. 25–7.) What do Adam and Eve look like? We do not know. Abraham? Sarah? Moses? We do not know. As Auerbach puts it in his comments on Gen. 22, where God commands Abraham to sacrifice his son Isaac, it is unthinkable that the servants, the landscape, the implements of sacrifice should be described or praised, as one might expect in Homer: 'they are serving-men, ass, wood, and knife, and nothing else, without an epithet' (9). Occasionally a certain quality is ascribed to some person or object: we are told that Eve perceives that the tree of knowledge is 'lovely to look at' (Gen. 3: 6), and likewise we are told that Joseph is 'comely in features and comely to look at' (Gen. 29: 6). But as a rule such minimal notations are given only when necessary to introduce some element that is important to the development of the plot. In the present cases the attractiveness of the tree of knowledge leads, of course, to the eating of its fruit (but what kind of fruit?—we are not told, the long tradition of the apple notwithstanding), and Joseph's attractiveness leads, in the next verse, to the sexual aggression of Potiphar's wife and thus indirectly to Joseph's imprisonment. And even here one notices that one is not told what it is that makes the fruit lovely to look at or what exactly makes Joseph so beautiful.

Beyond a lack of physical description in the biblical stories, one notices too that descriptions of personal qualities are largely absent. That is, characterization is rarely explicit, but rather must be teased out of the narrative based on what characters do and say. The presentation of Esau and Jacob in Gen. 25 illustrates this nicely. It is true that we are told that Esau is 'a man skilled in hunting, a man of the field' (v. 27), but the essential characterization of Esau as impulsive and unreflective, indeed almost animal-like, is conveyed by action and dialogue. Thus, coming in from the field to discover that his brother Jacob has prepared a stew, Esau inarticulately blurts out, 'Let me gulp down some of this red red stuff, for I am famished' (v. 30). Alter (2004: 131) notes that Esau 'cannot even come up with the ordinary Hebrew word for stew (*nazid*) and instead points to the bubbling pot impatiently as (literally) "this red red"'. And then, after agreeing to trade his birthright to Jacob in exchange for some of the stew, Esau's impetuous, action-oriented character is suggested by the 'rapid-fire chain of verbs' (ibid. 132): 'and he ate and he drank and he rose and he went off' (v. 34). The character of Esau is starkly contrasted in the story with the character of Jacob. If Esau is all instinct and action, Jacob is all calculation and deliberation. The stew is prepared and waiting for the return of Esau from the field, and one cannot fail to notice the mercantile manner in which Jacob first suggests, and then demands formal confirmation of, the trading of the birthright: 'And Jacob said, "Sell now your birthright to me." And Esau said, "Look, I am at the point of death, so why do I need a birthright?" And Jacob said, "Swear to me now"' (vv. 31–3). These initial thumbnail characterizations of Esau and Jacob will be fleshed out further two chapters later, in Gen. 27, where the blind Isaac is deceived into bestowing his blessing on Jacob rather than the intended son Esau. The elaborate ruse carried out by Jacob, with to be sure the invaluable help of his mother Rebekah, in which he impersonates Esau, confirms his calculating ambition even as it adds outright deceit to his résumé of character traits. Jacob will become a consummate trickster as the story proceeds—though he will also, as an elderly man, be tricked by his own sons—but he is never actually described by the narrator as tricky or deceptive, in the way that Odysseus is described repeatedly in terms of his resourcefulness or Achilles in terms of his rage, for example, but instead has his character revealed by what he says and what he does. Esau, for his part, will play a lesser role in the narrative that follows, although his reappearance in Ch. 33 is striking and in some ways unexpected, but both his inarticulateness and his utter lack of calculation are revealed by his response upon hearing that Jacob has stolen his blessing: 'he cried out with a great and very bitter outcry and he said to his father, "Bless me, too, Father"' (v. 34); and again, a few verses later, '"Do you have but one blessing my father? Bless me, too, Father." And Esau raised his voice and wept' (v. 38). By not directly revealing the qualities of character of the actors in the narrative, the narrator puts the onus of interpretation on the readers, who must work out on their own—albeit with hints given—what they think of these characters. To repeat, this is not the *absence* of characterization, but is a *certain mode* of characterization, and in fact a fairly complex mode at that.

We may best see the complexity of this mode of characterization, and indeed of the Bible's economy of style more generally, when it comes to the inner lives of the characters. Readers of Western literature, and especially modern literature, are used to having access in one form or another to the thoughts, feelings, and motivations of the characters about whom they read. But in the in biblical narrative we often get only the briefest of descriptions, as with Abraham's grief upon the death of Sarah: 'And Sarah died in Kiriath-Arba, which is Hebron, in the land of Canaan, and Abraham came to mourn Sarah and to keen for her' (Gen. 23: 2). Or on the death of Moses: 'And the Israelites keened for Moses in the steppes of Moab thirty days, and the days of keening in mourning for Moses came to an end' (Deut. 34: 8). One might object that since both Sarah and Moses had lived long and fruitful lives their deaths lack the tragedy of noble Greek heroes such as Hector, who was cut down in his prime over the affairs of his less-noble brother Paris (whose abduction of Helen from Sparta causes the Trojan war), and thus inspire less intense expressions of mourning. But even with more obviously tragic deaths we see in biblical narrative the restraint of the narrator, who acknowledges the grief of the survivors but refrains from allowing them full expression of it. We noted above, for example, Jacob's response to what he takes to be evidence of his young, beloved son Joseph's death: 'A vicious beast has devoured him, | Joseph torn to shreds!' (Gen. 37: 33). In a scene that seems intended to characterize Jacob as an extravagant mourner, the narrator goes on to describe Jacob as rending his clothes and donning sackcloth and refusing to be comforted by his other children: ' "Rather I will go down to my son in Sheol in mourning," and his father keened for him' (37: 35). Yet even here the few scant lines in Hebrew do not come close to matching the sixty lines of direct lament over the death of Hector in the *Iliad*.

Consider also the notoriously ambiguous story in Lev. 10 of the burning of Nadab and Abihu, the sons of Aaron. (On the ambiguities of the story see esp. Greenstein 1989; Beal and Linafelt 1995.) The reader is told that the two young priests brought 'strange fire' or 'alien fire' before the Lord, 'and fire came out from before the LORD and consumed them, and they died before the LORD' (10: 2). Moses very quickly offers a sort of cryptic theodicy, cast as a line of verse, in the face of the shocking event: 'This is what the LORD spoke, saying, "Through those close to Me shall I be hallowed | and in all the people's presence shall I be honoured" ' (10: 3). No more laconic response could be imagined, both to the death of the young men and to Moses' extemporaneous theologizing, than that attributed to Aaron: 'And Aaron was silent.' Surely we are to imagine Aaron's grief as real and deep—indeed, a few verses later Moses forbids Aaron and his other sons to go through the public rituals of mourning while they are consecrated for service in the temple (10: 6–7)—and yet all we are given is his silence. Unless one imagines this silence to indicate a complacent assent to what has just been witnessed, the narrator gives us, to borrow from Auerbach again, 'a glimpse of unplumbed depths'. It is, in short, a silence that is 'fraught with background', a silence that demands interpretation on the part of the reader. Is Aaron feeling pure shock? Overwhelming sadness? Anger at God? Confusion or despair? Is his silence a rejection of Moses' statement of God's intent? And if so, on what basis? The fact is that we are given no access whatsoever to the inner life of Aaron, and because we do not know what he is thinking we also do not know what motivates his silence.

It is with regard to this latter issue, the question of character *motivation*, that we may see the importance of recognizing the distinctively terse mode of biblical narration. As we have seen in the story of Jacob and Esau, the narrator reveals very little about the inner lives of characters, instead reporting mainly action and dialogue, or what the characters *do* and what they *say*. If we are given little or no access to the thoughts and feelings of the characters about whom we read, then it follows that the motivation behind what they do and say is also largely obscure. The importance of this obscurity of motivation can scarcely be overstated for any literary reading of the Pentateuch or for biblical narrative in general, since it more than anything else is what gives the literature its profound complexity as it forces the reader to negotiate the many possible ways of imagining the characters' inner lives. And it is worth noting that much of the Bible's extraordinary influence on Western literature takes the form of later authors imaginatively filling in these unstated motivations (on which see the final section of this chapter).

Let me try to justify, briefly, my claim about the obscurity of character motivation with reference to the literature itself. First, we may take Gen. 22 as the *locus classicus* of the ambiguity of character motivation in the Pentateuch. In a story that has never failed to engage the imagination of interpreters ancient or modern, God commands Abraham to take his son Isaac and sacrifice him as a burnt offering. Although a few chapters earlier we have seen Abraham challenge the justness of God's decision to destroy Sodom and Gomorrah, here Abraham says nothing in response. Instead, there is the narrator's terse report: 'And Abraham rose early in the morning and saddled his donkey and took his two lads with him, and Isaac his son, and split wood for the offering, and rose and went to the place that God had said to him. On the third day Abraham raised his eyes and saw the place from afar' (vv. 3–4). Abraham's silent obedience here is often taken to be motivated by an untroubled and unquestioning faith in God, which, depending on one's perspective may be seen positively as an expression of ultimate piety or negatively as an expression of unfeeling religious fanaticism. But both interpretations fail to recognize the fundamental literary convention of the refusal of access to the inner lives of characters. The fact that we are not *told* of Abraham's inner, emotional response to the demand that he slaughter his son does not mean that he *has no* inner, emotional response. I think that we are to assume that he does, but rather than describing it for us or allowing Abraham to give voice to it the narrator leaves us guessing as to what that response might be and thus also as to his motivation for his actions. Now, it is possible to fill that gap left by the narrator with an inner calm that reflects absolute faith, but it is equally possible to imagine that Abraham is feeling anger, disbelief, and even disgust (with God for demanding the slaughter? with himself for not protesting?). And however one fills the gap of Abraham's inner life initially, surely it is complicated by Isaac's calling out to him in v. 7, 'Father!', and by the plaintive question that follows, 'Here is the fire and the wood but where is the sheep for the offering?' It is precisely because we do not know what Abraham is thinking or feeling that his brief response to Isaac's question takes on a deeply ironic double meaning. On the one hand, it may be read as a ruse, if not an outright lie, to deflect any suspicions that may be dawning on the son; on the other hand, it may be read as a straightforward statement of faith that a sheep will indeed be provided. It may even be the case here that the author makes use of the ambiguities of Hebrew's seemingly rudimentary syntax in order to signal the potential irony to the attentive reader. For there is no punctuation in the Hebrew text and one may also construe the syntax to read: 'God will see to the sheep for the offering: *namely*, my son.'

To go back to Abraham's initial response to Isaac, we may see how what at first instance looks like wooden repetition may in fact be a subtly modulated use of a key word or theme. When God first calls out to Abraham to begin the episode, Abraham's response is 'Here I am'; when Isaac calls in the middle of the episode, on the way to the place of sacrifice, Abraham's response is, once again, 'Here I am, my son'; and when, at the climactic moment when the knife is raised over the boy, the angel of Lord calls out 'Abraham, Abraham!' (22: 11) his response is again 'Here I am.' In each case the single Hebrew word *hinneni*, 'here I am' or 'behold me', is repeated by Abraham. To substitute a synonym for the sake of variety, as for example the JPS Tanakh does in translating the second occurrence as 'Yes, my son,' is to lose a concrete expression of what is certainly a central theme for the story, namely the anguished tension between the demands of God and the ethical demands of another human being (Abraham's own child no less!). Every ethical fibre in Abraham's being must be demanding that he should not kill his son, and yet this is what God demands that he do. He responds 'Here I am' to both God and Isaac, and yet he cannot be fully 'there', fully present, to both equally. It is only with the third, very late, repetition of 'Here I am' that the tension is resolved and Abraham is no longer caught between these opposing demands on his loyalty. One might say that Abraham's threefold response provides the underlying armature for the story, marking the beginning, the middle, and the end. Although the single word *hinneni* is literally repeated each time, it acquires a new depth of meaning—and certainly a new tone—with each repetition. And to the end of the story it remains the case that we are never quite sure what Abraham is thinking as he first travels in silence, then responds to his son, then binds and raises the knife, and finally sacrifices the ram instead.

If we do not know what motivates Abraham in Gen. 22, it is also the case that we do not know what motivates Isaac to make his enquiry as to the whereabouts of the sheep or what he is thinking as his father binds him and lays him on the makeshift altar. But by this point we are not surprised by this fact, since we have begun to see that the biblical authors make use of this convention in order to allow for depth of character and depth of meaning. It is perhaps somewhat more surprising to note that this convention applies to God too, who is after all a character in these narratives as well, and so the *literary* art of biblical narrative has distinct *theological* implications. What motivates God to demand the sacrifice of Isaac? The narrator refused to tell us, though for any reader, religious or not, this must certainly be a compelling question. We are told that 'God tested Abraham' (22: 1); but this does not give us an answer to our question. The sense of the word 'test' (Hebrew *nissah*) is something like 'trial' or 'ordeal', and so God decides to put Abraham through an ordeal, presumably to test his mettle. (A comparison with the opening chapters of Job is apt.) But why, and to what end? Is it to find out how strong Abraham is under pressure? To see whether he values his son more than he values God? Does God genuinely learn something new about Abraham, about humanity, or about God's self through this test? ('Now I know...' (22: 12).) Without knowing what motivates God or what God is thinking as the knife is raised, we cannot finally even know whether Abraham has passed or failed the test. Most readers assume that he has passed, but a few have dared to suggest that God wanted not blind obedience from Abraham but resistance—after all, such resistance was honoured when Abraham argued on behalf of Sodom and Gomorrah—and that in failing to argue with God, Abraham failed to show the strength of character that God hoped to see (see e.g. Wiesel 1976: 93–4; Fewell and Gunn 1993: 52–4). If such a reading seems strained, especially in the light of 22: 16, the fact that it is nonetheless possible—if only just—witnesses to the profound but productive ambiguity of Hebrew literary style, which exploits to great effect its distinctive economy of style.

There is very much more that could be said about the literary art of the Pentateuch, especially about the patterns or structures that biblical authors and editors have used to construct both individual stories and larger blocks of material (on these elements, see Fishbane 1979; Fokkelman, 1987a, b; Rosenberg 1984; Trible 1978; and Walsh 2001). I mentioned at the beginning of this chapter the jarring concreteness with which God is imagined in the Pentateuch as active in the world: God walks in the garden of Eden and enjoys the evening breeze; God shows up at the tent of Sarah and Abraham to promise them offspring; God destroys Pharaoh's army at the Red Sea; God inscribes with God's own hand the tablets of the covenant at Sinai; and in the final, poignant scene of the Torah at the end of Deuteronomy, God buries Moses after allowing him a vision of the Promised Land that he is not finally to enter. But if the Hebrew literary imagination is relentlessly concrete in its workings, including its imaginings of God, it does not follow that it is without subtlety. In fact, divine agency and human agency are almost always imagined in these narratives as being inextricably bound together in such a way that neither is autonomous or effective in and of itself. And so, God announces to Rebekah in Gen. 25 that the elder of her twins (Esau) will serve the younger (Jacob), but two chapters later when the time has come to deliver the blessing to the proper son God has apparently left the matter to Rebekah to work out, which she does with great effectiveness. Joseph may declare in Gen. 50 to the brothers who, thirteen chapters and many years earlier had sold him into slavery, that 'While you meant evil toward me, God meant it for good,' but the story also makes clear that it is largely his own wits and talent, rather than any supernatural intervention, that allows him to survive and prosper in Egypt.

Even in the Exodus story, where God's saving action seems more tangible than anywhere in the Bible, the divine plan requires human agents for implementation. And so after the flurry of first-person active verbs in which God resolves to liberate Israel from slavery ('I have seen . . . I have heard . . . I have come down to rescue . . . I will bring them up . . . [3: 7–8]), God shifts unexpectedly to the second person, saying to Moses, 'And now, go that I may send you to Pharaoh, and bring my people the Israelites out of Egypt' (3: 10). Moses quite naturally responds, 'Who am I that I should go to Pharaoh and that I should bring out the Israelites from Egypt?' God's answer is telling with regard to the interdependence of divine and human agency: 'For I will be with you' (v. 12). Who is it that liberates Israel—God or Moses? It is both. But even that answer is too simple, since the liberation of Israel requires not only the cooperation of God and Moses but of *Israel* as well. Thus, Moses dutifully announces to the enslaved Israelites God's plan to liberate them, which God has again stated in a flurry of first-person verbs: 'I will take you out...I will rescue you from bondage...I will take you...I will be your God...I will bring you to the land I promised' (Exod. 6: 6–8). The response? 'They did not heed Moses because their spirits had been crushed by cruel slavery' (author's trans.). The point would seem to be a sociological one: that the people cannot be liberated before they are ready, and after generations of bondage and hard labour it will take more than promises to get them ready; only after seeing the very real power of Pharaoh broken by repeated plagues are the Israelites able to summon the energy to come out of Egypt.

Pharaoh himself is no less a site of this fundamental tension, in this case paradox, of divine sovereignty and human agency. On the one hand, *God* claims responsibility for 'hardening' Pharaoh's heart so that he refuses to allow Israel to leave (Exod. 7: 3; 14: 4); but on the other hand, Pharaoh is said by the narrator to have hardened *his own* heart (8: 11, 28). And still other times a passive voice is used, so that Pharaoh's heart 'was hardened' or 'became hard' (7: 14; 8: 15; 9: 4), thereby leaving the agency behind the hardening unclear. This shifting of agency allows the narrative to retain a sense of God's sovereign activity in history, while at the same time affirming the moral culpability of Pharaoh, whose repeated promise of freedom is never fulfilled and thus represents rather realistically the psychology of tyranny (Walzer 1985). Logically, we as readers may want to know, which was it? Did God harden Pharaoh's heart, or did Pharaoh harden his own heart? But the story refuses to come down on one answer or another, giving us a 'both/and' that reflects a pronounced trend in biblical narrative, on display nowhere more than in the Pentateuch: to render not only the inner lives of both humans and God, but creation and history itself, as unfathomably complex and finally irresolvable. This pervasive tension between the human and the divine, between the cosmos and individual action, is undoubtedly what gives this material such rich possibility for further literary consideration and expression.

We see this possibility manifested in the literary adoption and reworking of what the Pentateuch has so impressively handed down to Western literature: many of its most foundational tales, including the creation and fall, the flood, the story of Cain and Abel, Abraham's sacrificing of Isaac, the story of Jacob, Joseph's saga, the Exodus narrative, and the evolution of the Judaic law. The mythic status of the pre-historical books, told in economic, yet often concrete, detail, and the absoluteness of the *Lex talionis* and the Decalogue pitted against human frailty and relativism have ensured that they reappear throughout English literature. But certain figures and themes have resonated more strongly in some periods than others. Changes in the nature of divine governance, for instance, were of particular interest to those who lived through England's Civil War period. Cain's exclusion from salvation struck particular theological and psychological chords with the Romantics, while their pantheistic interests led them to frequent reimaginings of the creation. The flood appealed as an example of divine intervention, as did Babel Tower, and Sodom and Gomorrah, to all those who felt they lived in periods of either peculiar wickedness or of imminent millennial change. The Exodus story and the wandering in the wilderness have carried more obvious analogies for the American experience, although the Promised Land has continued to provide Utopian promise for all writers with reformist agendas.

The following references cannot be more than indicative, although they do attempt to include one or two less well-known examples together with works from the traditional canon. For many English readers Milton's *Paradise Lost* has unconsciously supplanted the Bible's account of the creation and fall, and is certainly better known than Dryden's *The State of Innocence and the Fall of Man*, Pope's *Essay on Man*, or Blake's revisioning in *The Four Zoas*. Among modernist texts Conrad's *Heart of Darkness*, Joyce's *Finnegans Wake*, and D. H. Lawrence's *The Rainbow* continue to explore versions of pre- and post-lapsarian existence, while in the twentieth century William Golding's fiction repeatedly returned to these myths.

Tales of the flood preoccupied novelists of the 1980s (see Ch. 1, above), though earlier examples might include George Eliot's *The Mill on the Floss* and C. Day Lewis's *Noah and the Waters*. The *Akedah*, Abraham's sacrificing of Isaac, appears in works as diverse as Thomas Browne's *Religio Medici*, Thomas Hardy's *Tess*, Wilfred Owen's 'The Parable and of the Old Man and the Young', and Lawrence's 'England, my England'. The Jacob/Esau narrative incurs brief treatment in poems such as Donne's *Holy Sonnets* No. 11, and Keble's *The Christian Year*, and is treated at greater length in Salman Rushdie's *Midnight Children*, while 'wrestling Jacob', in addition to providing subject matter for Charles Wesley's 'Wrestling Jacob' and Christina Rossetti's 'Weeping We Hold Him Fast Tonight', achieved renewed popularity as a consequence of post-Freudian theoretical readings. The story of Joseph seems to have enjoyed a particular affinity for the stage from Renaissance drama to Rice and Webber's *Joseph and The Amazing Technicolor Dreamcoat*, or, less surprisingly, for the picaresque form, as in Fielding's *Joseph Andrews*.

The most famous brooding upon *Lex talionis* is to be found in Shakespeare's *Merchant of Venice*. The first of the Ten Commandments' injunction against representation has doubtless militated against their artistic rendition, but the nineteenth century in particular was remarkable for sardonic reflections on a so-called Christian nation's observance of the Decalogue. Clough's 'The Latest Decalogue' and Hardy's *Far from the Madding Crowd* and *Jude the Obscure* here provide notable examples.

WORKS CITED

ALTER, ROBERT. 2004. *The Five Books of Moses: A Translation with Commentary.* New York: W. W. Norton.

AUERBACH, ERICH. 1953 [1946]. *Mimesis: The Representation of Reality in Western Literature.* Princeton: Princeton University Press.

BEAL, TIMOTHY K., and LINAFELT, TOD. 1995. 'Sifting for Cinders: Strange Fires in Leviticus 10: 1–5'. *Semeia* 69/70: 19–32.

DOUGLAS, MARY. 1999. *Leviticus as Literature.* Oxford: Oxford University Press.

—— 2004. *Jacob's Tears*. Oxford: Oxford University Press.

FAGLES, ROBERT. 1990. *Homer's Iliad*. New York: Viking.

FEWELL, DANNA, and GUNN, DAVID M. 1993. *Gender, Power, and Promise: The Subject of the Bible's First Story*. Nashville: Abingdon.

FISHBANE, MICHAEL. 1979. *Text and Texture: Close Readings of Selected Biblical Texts*. New York: Schocken.

FOKKELMAN, J. P. 1987a. 'Genesis', in Robert Alter and Frank Kermode (eds.), *The Literary Guide to the Bible*. Cambridge, Mass.: Harvard University Press.

—— 1987b. 'Exodus', in Robert Alter and Frank Kermode (eds.), *The Literary Guide to the Bible*. Cambridge, Mass.: Harvard University Press.

FOX, EVERETT. 1995. *The Five Books of Moses*. The Schocken Bible. New York: Schocken.

GREENSTEIN, EDWARD. 1989. 'Deconstruction and Biblical Narrative.' *Prooftexts* 9: 43–71.

KUGEL, JAMES L. 1981. *The Idea of Biblical Poetry*. New Haven: Yale University Press.

ROSENBERG, JOEL. 1984. 'Biblical Narrative', in Barry W. Holtz (ed.), *Back to the Sources: Reading the Classic Jewish Texts*. New York: Summit.

TRIBLE, PHYLLIS. 1978. *God and the Rhetoric of Sexuality*. Overtures to Biblical Theology. Philadelphia: Fortress.

WALSH, JEROME T. 2001. *Style and Structure in Biblical Hebrew Narrative*. Collegeville, Minn.: Michael Glazier.

WALZER, MICHAEL. 1985. *Exodus and Revolution*. New York: Basic Books.

WIESEL, ELIE. 1976. *Messengers of God: Biblical Portraits and Legends*. New York: Summit.

FURTHER READING

ALTER, ROBERT. 1981. *The Art of Biblical Narrative*. New York: Basic Books.

—— 1985. *The Art of Biblical Poetry*. New York: Basic Books.

BARTHES, ROLAND. 1977. 'The Struggle with the Angel', in *Image, Music, Text*. New York: Hill & Wang.

BERLIN, ADELE. 1983. *Poetics and Interpretation of Biblical Narrative*. Sheffield: Almond.

—— 1985. *The Dynamics of Biblical Parallelism*. Bloomington: Indiana University Press.

BIBLE AND CULTURE COLLECTIVE. 1995. *The Postmodern Bible*. New Haven: Yale University Press.

BRUEGGEMANN, WALTER. 1982. *Genesis*. Interpretation. Atlanta: John Knox.

DAMROSCH, DAVID. 1987. *The Narrative Covenant*. New York: Harper & Row.

DOUGLAS, MARY. 1993. *In the Wilderness: The Doctrine of Defilement in the Book of Numbers*. Sheffield: JSOT.

FRIEDMAN, RICHARD ELLIOTT. 1997. *Who Wrote the Bible?*, 2nd edn. San Francisco: HarperCollins.

GUNN, DAVID M., and NOLAN FEWELL, DANNA. 1993. *Narrative in the Hebrew Bible*. Oxford: Oxford University Press.

LEVINSON, BERNARD. 1997. *Deuteronomy and the Hermeneutics of Legal Innovation*. Oxford: Oxford University Press.

POLZIN, ROBERT. 1980. *Moses and the Deuteronomist*. New York: Seabury.

STERNBERG, MEIR. 1985. *The Poetics of Biblical Narrative*. Bloomington: Indiana University Press.

ZORNBERG, AVIVAH GOTTLIEB. 1995. *Genesis: The Beginning of Desire*. Philadelphia: Jewish Publication Society.

—— 2001. *The Particulars of Rapture: Reflections on Exodus*. New York: Doubleday.

CHAPTER 14

JUDGES

TIMOTHY K. BEAL

LIKE the literature that precedes and follows in the Hebrew Bible (Joshua and 1–2 Samuel), the book of Judges is clearly the product of a complicated literary history involving the interweaving, revising, and editing of multiple literary and oral traditions concerning the early formation and deformation of Israel in the land of Canaan. But recognizing this complexity must not distract us from the remarkable literary qualities of the book in its final form. Indeed, many of these qualities are the result of its complex literary history, which has resulted in a narrative whose surface structure is often undermined by the seething of political and theological chaos brought on by tensions between the various perspectives and voices it has incorporated. It is a book whose coherence is in many ways found in its dissymmetry. In recent decades, such tensions between surface structure and deep chaos, predictable repetition and disturbing interruption, have made the book of Judges a significant focus of study for new literary approaches in biblical studies and a rich resource for writers of English literature.

OUTLINE AND STRUCTURE

The book of Judges may be divided into three main parts: 1: 1–3: 6, accounts of tribal conquest and failure in Canaan; 3: 7–16: 31, the cycles of thirteen judges who delivered Israelites from oppression by other peoples; and 17: 1–21: 25, narratives of atrocity, civil war, and collapse among the tribes of Israel. Each section is briefly described below.

1. Accounts of Conquest and Failure (Judges 1: 1–3:6)

Judges opens with a series of short narratives recounting successful and failed conquests in the land of Canaan after the death of Joshua (Josh. 24: 29). This material may be divided into two subsections, 1: 1–2: 5 and 2: 6–3: 6, each of which emphasizes Israel's unfaithfulness and includes a divine speech (2: 1–5, 20–3) in which God determines to abandon them in the mess they have made for themselves.

The first subsection (1: 1–2: 5) recounts specific stories of Israelite tribal settlement in Canaan. While it begins by listing success stories, it finishes with failures. Judah 'could not drive out the inhabitants of the plain' (1: 19), the Benjaminites 'did not drive out the Jebusites who lived in Jerusalem' (1: 21), Menasseh 'did not drive out the inhabitants of Beth-shean and its villages, or Taanach and its villages, or the inhabitants of Dor and its villages . . .' (1: 27), and so on (1: 28–35). By the end of Ch. 1, it is clear that the conquest has been far from total, and that the Israelites are settling in a land largely populated by other peoples and their gods. The section closes (2: 1–5) with a theological explanation of their failure, delivered by an angel of Yhwh in language strongly reminiscent of Deuteronomy: because the Israelites have not kept their covenant with God, God will not drive out the inhabitants of the land. They will be relentless adversaries and their gods will be ever-present snares.

The second subsection (2: 6–3: 6) serves as a bridge between the opening series of conquest narratives and the cycles of judges that follow in the main body of the book (3: 7–16: 31). On the one hand, as a conclusion to the opening series, it retells the death of Joshua (2: 6–10) and reiterates the Deuteronomic message that the failure of the tribes to remove the other inhabitants was divine punishment for their failure to keep God's law (2: 20–3). On the other hand, as an introduction to what follows, the text sandwiched between Joshua's death and God's reiteration of Israel's punishment for its unfaithfulness provides an outline of the cycle of crisis and deliverance that will run through most of the book:

Then the Israelites did what was evil in the sight of Yhwh and worshipped the Baals; and they abandoned Yhwh, the God of their ancestors, who had brought them out of the land of Egypt; they followed other gods, from among the gods of the peoples who were all around them, and bowed down to them; and they provoked Yhwh to anger. They abandoned Yhwh, and worshipped Baal and the Astartes. So the anger of Yhwh was kindled against Israel, and he gave them over to plunderers who plundered them, and he sold them into the power of their enemies all around, so that they could no longer withstand their enemies. Whenever they marched out, the hand of Yhwh was against them to bring misfortune, as Yhwh had warned them and sworn to them; and they were in great distress.

Then Yhwh raised up judges, who delivered them out of the power of those who plundered them. Yet they did not listen even to their judges; for they lusted after other gods and bowed down to them. They soon turned aside from the way in which their ancestors had walked, who had obeyed the commandments of Yhwh; they did not follow their example. Whenever Yhwh raised up judges for them, Yhwh was with the judge, and he delivered them from the hand of their enemies all the days of the judge; for Yhwh would be moved to pity by their groaning because of those who persecuted and oppressed them. But whenever the judge died, they would relapse and behave worse than their ancestors, following other gods, worshipping them and bowing down to them. They would not drop any of their practices or their stubborn ways.   (Judg. 2: 11–19)

So the cycle goes: the people abandon YHWH; indignantly, YHWH responds by abandoning the people; they become oppressed by other peoples in the land; they cry out for deliverance; compassionately, YHWH responds by raising a judge who delivers them; the judge eventually dies, and the cycle begins again. Significantly, this summary of the cycle ends not with the deliverance and restoration of the people, but with their relapse into apostasy and YHWH's return to anger. Thus the cycle's ending anticipates where the Israelites will find themselves at the end of the book.

2. The Judges (3: 7–16: 31)

The main body of the book is comprised of the stories of thirteen judges, set within the repeating cycle summarized in 2:11–19, above. The judges are: Othniel (3: 7–11); Ehud (3: 12–20); Shamgar (3: 31); Deborah (4: 1–5: 31); Gideon (6: 1–8: 35); Abimelech (9: 1–57); Tola (10: 1–2); Jair (10: 3–5); Jephthah (10: 6–12: 7); Ibzan (12: 8–10); Elon (12: 11–12); Abdon (12: 13–15); and Samson (13: 1–16: 31). Six of the accounts are very brief, providing only a few details about the judge and his accomplishments (Shamgar, Tola, Jair, Ibzan, Elon, and Abdon).

The relatively short account of Othniel, the first judge, neatly encapsulates the cycle: the people turn away from YHWH whereupon he brings foreign oppressors against them. They cry for help. He then raises a deliverer who defeats the oppressors and the people enjoy 'rest'. In each of the subsequent stories of major judges (Ehud, Deborah, Abimelech, Jephthah, and Samson), however, this cycle is but the framework within which a much richer and more complex narrative is placed, so that the particular ambiguities and tensions within each story are far more compelling than the general simplicity and predictability of the overall pattern of repeating cycles. Indeed, as Lillian R. Klein suggests, in Yeatsean terms, the narrative of Judges is not so much a series of repeating cycles, coming around to the same place again and again, as it is a 'widening gyre' whose 'centre cannot hold' (Klein 1988; see also Exum 1990).

The story of Samson, the last judge in the book, is perhaps the most exceptional within this framework. Although presented as the last reiteration of the cycle, his story diverges significantly from those of preceding judges, in that he breaks vows, marries a non-Israelite, and does not ally with other Israelite tribes in his battles against the Philistines. Thus his story functions as a bridge between the reiterative judges' cycles in the main body of the book and the final section, which emphasizes atrocity, corruption, civil war, and collapse among the tribes of Israel.

3. Atrocity, Civil War, and Collapse (Judges 17: 1–21: 25)

The last five chapters of the book depict the failure of the Israelite tribes to create and maintain coherence. The overall movement of the narrative is toward increased apostasy—the shrine of Micah and the idolatry of the Danites (17: 1–18: 31)—and, most strikingly, the escalation of violence, especially violence against women—the rape of the unnamed woman (or 'Levite's concubine', 19: 1–21), which leads to the massacre of the Benjaminites (20: 1–48) and the subsequent repopulation of the tribe by means of murder, rape, and kidnap (21: 1–25).

Towards the beginning of this final section, and then again as the very last word at the end of the book, the narrator provides this summation of the state of tribal Israel: 'In those days there was no king in Israel; all the people did what was right in their own eyes' (17: 6; 21: 25; the first part of this statement, that there was no king, is also repeated in 18: 1 and 19: 1). As a frame around these last stories in Judges, this statement both highlights the unravelling of the tribal system and indicates the solution, namely a united monarchy.

In a nutshell, then, we may say that the overall shape of the book of Judges is this: a series of temporary comings together of Israelite tribes under judges in response to particular crises, framed by narratives emphasizing the ultimate failure of the tribes to unify and thrive in the land of Canaan. Despite the central stories of deliverance, the first and last words of the book are words of incompletion, disintegration, and collapse.

HISTORY OF INTERPRETATION

1. Christian Tradition

In the earliest (ante-Nicene) history of Christian biblical interpretation, there are few substantive treatments of the book of Judges. During the Nicene and post-Nicene periods, however, with the rise of allegorical modes of interpretation, interest in its stories grows demonstrably. Many interpreters, for example, find the miracle stories in the Gideon cycle to be revealing of various aspects of God's grace before and after Christ. Most noteworthy in this regard, if also most unfortunate, are allegorical interpretations of the story of Gideon's fleece (6: 36–40). According to this interpretation, the fleece represents Israel and the dew represents grace. The fleece on the first morning, wet with dew while the ground around it remained dry, represents the grace of God before Christ, residing with Israel alone. The fleece on the second morning, completely dry while the ground around was soaked, represents God's abandoning of Israel in order to shower his grace on the rest of the world. Concerning the second morning, Augustine, for example, writes in *On Original Sin* (Ch. 29): 'Like the rain in the fleece it [i.e. grace] was latently present, but is now patently visible amongst all nations as its "floor," the fleece being dry,—in other words, the Jewish people having become reprobate' (similarly Sermon 81. 9; Ambrose, *Of the Holy Spirit*, 1; Jerome, Letter 58; Cyril of Jerusalem, *Catechetical Lectures*, 15).

As Christianity increasingly claimed to have superseded Judaism as the rightful heir of God's promise to Abraham, examples of this supersessionist allegorical reading of Gideon's fleece become more popular. Indeed they are found throughout the history of Christian interpretation to this day. Even the Protestant reformer Martin Luther, despite his general dismissal of allegorical interpretation in favour of more literal treatment of biblical texts, was inclined to this allegorical reading. In his lecture on Psalm 104, he describes the Jews of the law as skinned and reprobate, with the grace of God now flowing freely over the rest of the world's floor: 'If you hear and see any figure of the Law, it will appear altogether flesh and thick, but when you will have separated it from the spirit, you will behold the skin in which the flesh was, but the flesh has been emptied . . . Yet the flesh was in that skin. And Gideon's fleece received the dew, that is, with the letter stripped off, the law is spiritual. . . . Therefore the former is judgment, the latter righteousness . . . the former hardness, the latter sweetness' (*First Lectures on the Psalms*, Ps. 104: 2 (319)).

During the Christian Middle Ages, the most prevalent and popular interpretations of Judges were typological, finding the meaning of the Old Testament in the Christology of the New Testament and subsequent Church doctrine. Consider, for example, the illuminated *Speculum humanae salvationis* (fourteenth and fifteenth centuries), in which the following figures from Judges anticipate Gospel themes: Jephthah's virgin daughter, willingly sacrificed for her father's zealous vow, prefigures the dedication of Mary's virginity; Samson's slaughter of many with a jawbone prefigures Jesus prostrating his enemies with a word (John 18: 6); Samson's carrying off the gates of Gaza prefigures Jesus breaking out of the tomb; and Jael's piercing of Sisera with a tent peg and Samson's slaying of the lion prefigure Mary's and Jesus' conquering of the devil. By such typological interpretations, made popular to the European masses through visual artistic representations such as the *Speculum*, the Mother Church was asserting its monopoly on Christ who was presented as having a monopoly on Scripture. This subordination of the Old to the New obviously served the Church's larger political purpose of creating and distinguishing a religiously homogenous Christian Europe in opposition to the perceived threat of Islam and Judaism, which affirmed the independent authority of the Old.

Throughout the history of Christian interpretation, in addition to allegorical and typological trends, there has been a more literal strain of interpretative discourse focused on drawing moral lessons from the characters and stories of Judges. Perhaps these go back to the early summons in the apocryphal Sirach and in the New Testament book of Hebrews to remember the judges as heroes of faith, praising these 'famous men . . . whose hearts did not fall into idolatry and who did not turn away from the Lord' (Sir. 44: 1; 46: 11), 'who through faith conquered kingdoms, enforced justice, received promises' (Heb. 11).

The fact that Hebrews mentions Barak but not Deborah (the judge in Judges 4–5, who questioned Barak's courage and resolve) and Jephthah but not his daughter, moreover, may be an early symptom of the patriarchal anxiety that runs through most of this moralistic interpretative tradition. Consider, for example, Calvin's concern, in his commentary on 1 Tim. 2: 12 ('I permit no woman to teach or have authority over a man'), that God's call on Deborah to be judge not be taken as justification of women leaders in the church: 'If anyone bring forward, by way of objection, Deborah and others of the same class . . . the answer is easy: Extraordinary acts done by God do not overturn the ordinary rules of government, by which he intended that we should be bound' (Calvin 1948).

2. Jewish Tradition

Rabbinic interpretations of Judges in the Talmud, Midrash, Targums, and various other commentaries reflect a tradition-dependent accrual of interpretative dialogue. Within this dialogue, there is, on the one hand, a certain deference to the readings of earlier rabbinic authorities, and, on the other hand, a certain openness to new and innovative readings that challenge earlier ones. Indeed, when reading rabbinic interpretative history on Judges, one has the sense that a new and surprising insight drawn from a previously unnoted detail in the text might break into the dialogue at any point. In contrast against Christian interpretative tradition, moreover, the import of these new insights need not be theological or doctrinal.

Some of the most creative rabbinic interpretative traditions begin with a play on words in the Hebrew text. Consider the story of the future judge Othniel's capture of a city named Kiriath-Sepher (1: 13). Noting that this name literally means 'the city of the book' or 'city of writing', *Talmud Murah* 16a celebrated him less as a warrior and more as a great scholar who, by dialectical reasoning alone, recovered the seventeen hundred laws that had been lost during Israel's mourning over the death of Moses. Indeed, Othniel is remembered in certain rabbinic traditions as a great scholar who set up an academy for the study of Torah and was allowed to enter into Paradise alive (see citations in Ginzberg 1968: 185 n. 23).

Other rabbinic readings are concerned to sort out potential contradictions between stories in Judges and other biblical texts. How, for example, can the Moabites be Israel's enemies in the Ehud cycle when Ruth, David's grandmother, was a Moabite? Facing the problem head on, Midrash Ruth *Rabbah* (2: 9) asserts that King Eglon was none other than Ruth's (and her sister Orpah's) father, discerning the seeds of Ruth's righteousness in Eglon's openness to divine revelation as evidenced in the fact that he got up from his throne when Ehud told him that he had a message from God for him (Judg. 3: 20; see also *Talmud Sanhedrin* 60a). As a poetically appropriate reward for this sign of reverence, God determined to raise a descendent of Eglon to sit on the throne of Israel (David).

Whereas Christian tradition was suspicious of tricksters such as Ehud and especially Jael, rabbinic tradition has been generally positive. Sisera, for example, was believed to deserve his grotesque death at the hand of Jael, on accounting of his own egregious acts of oppression and abuse as king (Midrash Numbers *Rabbah* 10: 2). Picking up on Deborah's praise of her as 'most blessed of women in tents', and reading 'women in tents' as a reference to the women of Israel, she is considered to be as praiseworthy as Sarah, Rebecca, Rachel, and Leah (for a much fuller discussion, including speculations about whether or not she and Sisera had sex before she killed him, see the extensive discussion of rabbinic literature on this story in Gunn 2005).

3. Modern Biblical Criticism and the Deuteronomistic History

With the rise of modern higher criticism of the Bible in Europe during the eighteenth, nineteenth, and early twentieth centuries, scholars increasingly focused on the literary history of the book of Judges, attempting to identify its various textual sources and produce an archaeology of the book's final form. Soon biblical criticism of the text of Judges had become a highly specialized discipline aimed at disentangling multiple literary strands and cataloguing them according to a chronology of literary development. In the wake of Wellhausen's seminal formulation of the Documentary Hypothesis in his *Prolegomena to the History of Ancient Israel* (1878), scholars raced to find the same literary history in Judges. They discovered three of the four strands—the Jahwist (J), the Elohist (E), and the Deuteronomist (D)—along with independent literary sources identified with later editors. Within this disciplinary approach to Judges, there was almost no interest in the stories, let alone the book as a whole, as literature.

Although arguments for the presence of J and E in the book gradually lost ground, the strong presence of D continues to be recognized by most biblical critics to this day, especially in those 'framework' passages, discussed above, that reiterate the cycle of apostasy, oppression, repentance, and deliverance. Most scholars continue to follow Martin Noth (1943) in locating the book within the biblical narrative of the Deuteronomistic History (abbreviated DtrH), which runs from Deuteronomy through 2 Kings. Shaped by the theology of Moses' teachings in Deuteronomy, this narrative gives account of the Israelite conquest of the land, the Davidic monarchy, the divided kingdoms of northern Israel and Judah, Assyria's defeat of the northern kingdom, and Babylon's defeat and exile of the southern kingdom. In the light of Deuteronomy, defeat and exile are interpreted as the result of the failure to maintain pure religious devotion to YHWH, allowing Torah to be compromised by relations with non-Israelite peoples and their gods. At the same time, Deuteronomy also asserts that repentance will lead to deliverance.

4. Literary Approaches

Although Noth himself was not particularly interested in the Bible as literature per se, it could be argued that his focus on the stories of Judges as part of a larger narrative, the DtrH, which displayed clear editorial intentionality and thematic unity, opened the way to literary approaches to the book. Robert G. Boling's 1975 Anchor Bible Commentary on Judges is an early example. He criticized earlier treatments of the story of the Levite and the unnamed woman (aka 'the Levite's concubine') in Judges

19–21 for their unwillingness to allow the narrator 'anything resembling a Mosaic consciousness' characteristic of the Deuteronomist (ibid. 278). By contrast, he identified a certain 'tragicomic' sense of irony within the story, a 'grim humour' to its treatment of characters, institutions, and events. Indeed, the question of how to understand Judges in relation to literary terms such as irony, tragedy, and comedy continues to be central in literary criticism of Judges to this day (on which see esp. Exum 1980; 1981; 1989; Gunn 1985; 1987; 1992; and Klein 1988). Boling also identified a thematic relationship between this story and that of Lot in Sodom (Gen. 19), arguing that the Judges narrative was not merely imitating the Genesis text, as other more dismissive interpreters had alleged, but was using this biblical motif of hospitality intentionally, as part of its narrative craft. Here, too, Boling anticipates a major literary approach to Judges, namely intertextual analysis (e.g. Gunn 1992; Beal and Gunn 1992).

Within the disciplinary tradition of scholarship on the DtrH, Robert Polzin's multi-volume formalist literary-critical study of Deuteronomy through 2 Kings as a narrative whole was particularly important in breaking new ground for literary approaches. In his first volume, *Moses and the Deuteronomist: Deuteronomy, Joshua, and Judges* (1980), he presented Judges in terms of an ideological struggle between, on the one hand, 'authoritarian dogmatism' which held strictly to an original authoritative law and, on the other hand, 'critical traditionalism' which sought to sustain a law tradition by reinterpreting it in the light of new circumstances. Similarly, David Jobling's structural analysis (1986) presents Judges in terms of irresolvable tensions between pro- and anti-monarchic strains, opening ways for its exilic audience to develop new 'political theologies' (see also Webb 1987 and Klein 1988).

A major literary innovation within biblical studies came with James Muilenberg's call, in his 1968 presidential address to the Society of Biblical Literature, to move beyond the analysis of biblical sources and forms into what he called 'rhetorical criticism'. By this he meant to call for greater focus on the rhetorical intentionality of biblical texts in their final literary form. Modelling the approach on biblical poetry, he demonstrated how closer critical attention to rhetorical markers (e.g. repetitions, shifts in speaker) yields important clues to the intentionality of the text itself. Like the literary movements called formalism and New Criticism in literature studies, then, Muilenberg's rhetorical criticism presumed that the rules for understanding a text's meaning and intentionality are to be found through close literary analysis of the text itself rather than through research into its social, historical, and literary backgrounds.

The influence of Muilenberg's rhetorical criticism on literary approaches to the Bible is not so much due to the reception of his publications, which were relatively few, as it is due to his students. A teacher of legendary (even prophetic) proportions, his scholarly disciples include Walter Brueggemann, Edwin Good, and Phyllis Trible, among many others. Each of these has taken Muilenberg's rhetorical criticism in new directions and has in turn been highly influential on a new generation of graduate students and biblical scholars.

In the book of Judges, Phyllis Trible's rhetorical-critical analysis of the stories of Jephthah's daughter (Chs. 10–11) and the Levite and the unnamed woman (Chs. 19–21) in her *Texts of Terror: Literary-Feminist Readings of Biblical Narratives* (1984) have been particularly influential, helping to ignite a revolution in biblical studies centred on feminist literary-critical analysis.

In the hands of Trible, rhetorical criticism went beyond any identification of a straightforward, univocal intentionality within these stories. Within the larger narrative structures formed through repetitions and other literary elements, she attended exegetically to the minutest details of the text, even and especially those details that could undermine the narrator's larger, overarching patriarchal intentions. Thus, for example, through close analysis of the patterns of verbal subjects, she shows how the 'unnamed woman', as she is first to call her (aka 'the Levite's concubine'), is converted from an agent who might threaten male subject-ivity into an objective means of mediation between men—first between master (Levite) and father, then between master and host, and finally between master and the tribes of Israel. And this last mediation, as the master cuts her raped body into pieces and distributes them to the tribes, will lead to further violence against women and children. Likewise, she shows how the story of the tragic death of Jephthah's daughter is used in service of the larger cause of Israelite deliverance (cf. 1 Sam. 12: 11).

Texts of Terror was based on a series of lectures on preaching (the Lyman Beecher Lectures) at Yale Divinity School. This context is important to keep in mind. Addressing an audience of preachers, and embracing feminism as a 'prophetic movement' (1984: 3), Trible called for a kind of biblical storytelling that might, through attention to particular rhetorical details in the text, expose the patriarchal interests of those texts *as well as* the patriarchal anxieties that drive them. For such anxieties are also openings for destabilization and deconstruction, which in turn open the possibility of something new. In her hands, then, as in the hands of Good and Brueggemann in other biblical texts, rhetorical criticism identified ways in which the narrative might undermine, even deconstruct, itself. Indeed, although *Texts of Terror* shows no explicit interest in engaging the literary-theoretical discourses of deconstruction and post-structuralism, its analyses of how patriarchal biblical nar-ratives subvert their own conscious intentions demonstrate how deconstruction happens within a text.

Trible's influence on literary approaches to Judges, let alone her influence on literary biblical criticism and theology more generally, can hardly be overstated. In fact, literary approaches to Judges have been dominated by feminist analysis, and almost always have been in dialogue with her work, even and especially when they diverge from it or move beyond it (see e.g. the many essays by Exum, Gunn, Fewell, and esp. Fewell and Gunn 1990; and the outstanding collections edited by Brenner and Yee).

Of comparable influence in literary approaches to Judges is the opus of three books (1987; 1988*a*; 1988*b*) and other essays by critical theorist and cultural analyst Mieke Bal. Whereas Trible's most influential contributions were her literary-critical analyses of particular stories within Judges, especially those stories about sexual politics and violence, Bal's have concerned the analysis of larger narrative structures, patterns, and dissymmetrical relations within the book.

As discussed earlier, the various stories in Judges resist neat interrelationships with one another. They resist coherence. Bal argues that interpretation history (esp. modern criticism) has produced a coherent reading of Judges based primarily on an 'eagerness to narrow history down to a narrative of war and political leadership' and driven by an androcentric point of view which serves 'to subordinate the stories about women to the major historiographical project, which is nationalistic and religious, and in relation to which the murder stories are just the unpleasant but unavoidable fulfilment of the divine plan' (1988a: 13). By foregrounding the political-religious emergence of Israel, interpreters have backgrounded, if not ignored altogether, issues of gender-based violence and domestic conflict. This coherency muffles the voices of the female victims under the clamour of men's battles and the political collaborations as the tribes move towards nationhood.

Yet, Bal shows, the book of Judges is riddled with intertextual tensions that undermine such attempts to establish narrative coherence (ibid. 34; cf. 281 n. 4). No coherence can comprehend entirely and absolutely all the voices of such a polyvocal book. Bal's feminist counter-coherent analysis attends to the various texts within the book of Judges as they appear in tension with each other. Focusing on three stories of women killing men and three stories of men killing women, she reveals a fundamental dissymmetry within the larger narrative: a 'dissymmetry of power: power over the body, over life, over language' (ibid. 32), organized around stories of gender-based violence. In Bal's intertextual counter-coherence, then, the book is denied a univocal coherence, and the suppressed voices of victimized women are amplified. Moreover, the female murderers are no longer comprehended merely as war heroines; rather, they introduce maternal anger into the book (ibid. 197–8). They kill for the murdered daughters.

5. Cultural-Historical Approaches

In recent years, a new direction in Judges studies has begun to emerge. We might call it the cultural history of Judges. Rather than focusing exclusively on the biblical text in itself, as a literary object, new approaches are exploring the afterlives of this book in literature, music, visual culture, political discourse, and religious communities. Examples to indicate the range of possibilities opening here would include the critical analysis of cultural representations of Delilah by J. Cheryl Exum (1996) and 'How the West Was Not One', by Jennifer Koosed and Tod Linafelt, which reads Judges in relation to the film *Unforgiven* and Luce Irigaray's essay, 'This Sex Which Is Not One' (1996). The most important resource in this new field is certainly David M. Gunn's monumental, nearly comprehensive commentary on the social and cultural history of Judges in the Blackwell Bible Commentary series (2005).

JUDGES IN ENGLISH LITERATURE

Judges has proven to be a rich repository for writers within the English tradition, largely because of the many levels on which the original stories operate, from the personal love story of Samson's entanglement with Delilah to the struggle of a nascent Israel to establish and define itself in relation to and over against the other nations. Within the history of English literature, we may identify two major trajectories of literary production in which stories and characters from Judges figure prominently: Christian typology and edifying history (Gunn 2005). Within these two trajectories, the narrative poetics of the book and its stories has had very little influence. Paying scant attention to the book's own narrative strategies of coherence and incoherence, symmetry and dissymmetry, characters are extracted from their literary context and exploited in various ways for their theological and moral potentials. After discussing these two trajectories, we will consider a third trajectory that undermines the first two, that is, literature that draws from Judges as a means of addressing the theological problem of tragedy. Although less dominant in the history of English, this trajectory is more closely allied with the narrative poetics of the book itself.

First, Judges has been used by writers as a resource for Christian typology. Among many possible examples, consider the seventh stanza of the Metaphysical poet George Herbert's softly intense 'Sunday' in *The Temple* collection (1633), which he completed while on his deathbed. In this poem, Samson's removal of the doors prefigures Christ's victory in death, 'unhinging' of the Lord's Day, giving access to the heavens for all humankind:

> The rest of our Creation
> Our great Redeemer did remove
> With the same shake, which at his passion
> Did th' earth and all things with it move.
> As Sampson bore the doores away,
> Christs hands, though nail'd, wrought our salvation,
>   And did unhinge that day.

Such poetic prefigurings, of course, continue the theological tradition that goes back to the early church fathers of reading the characters and events of Judges in terms of a Christian grand narrative of redemptive history. At the same time, it highlights the fact that literature and theology is often a literary craft, and that literature often *is* theology.

Second, Judges has figured prominently in what Gunn aptly describes as 'edifying histories', that is, literary discourses of national identity that glorify the trinity of God, country, and patriarchy—in short, the fatherland.

The political and polemical elements of Judges are often seized upon in situations of national strife. We see, for example, the figure of Gideon appropriated by Andrew Marvell in praise of Cromwell and by Tennyson, in his poem 'Napoleon', which celebrated England's triumph over Napoleon at Trafalgar.

The Philistines, who figure prominently as Israel's and especially Samson's antagonists in Judges, frequently come to represent the enemies of English high culture as well. Probably this literary use of the Philistines of Judges begins with John Milton's 'brief epic', *Samson Agonistes* (1671), in which Samson is represented as a tragic hero who struggles to tame or defeat this Philistine nature. Centuries later, in *Culture and Anarchy* (1882), Matthew Arnold drew inspiration from Samson's heroic struggle in his own plea on behalf of the culture of English in its struggle against those he called 'British Philistines'. In fact, the idea of a 'Philistine' as someone who is crass and uncultured was drawn primarily from Judges via Arnold.

Within this edifying history of English culture and fatherland, Jephthah's daughter is frequently exalted as a national heroine on account of her self-sacrifice in honour of her father's vow. In 'Jephtha's Daughter' (1815), for example, George Gordon Lord Byron has Jephthah declare boldly to her father,

> I have won the great battle for thee,
> And my Father and Country are free!
> When this blood of thy giving hath gushed,
> When the voice that thou lovest is hushed,
> Let my memory still be thy pride,
> And forget not I smiled as I died.

Likewise Tennyson, in 'A Dream of Fair Women' (1832), has her exclaim, posthumously, 'How beautiful a thing it was to die | For God and for my sire!'

Not surprisingly, we see this same orientation towards moral and spiritual edification in popular Christian devotional literature, which draws models for godly living from the biblical characters. Here, as with Byron, Tennyson, and others, gender-based concerns about the praiseworthiness of the women of Judges have been central. The beginnings of this literary tradition within Christianity are found in the popular 'character Bibles' of the nineteenth and twentieth centuries. Of Jael, for example, Cunningham Geikie writes in *Characters of the Old Testament*, 'The end was noble enough; the means brave to a marvel; but the heart that could have planned and carried them out was anything rather than that of a woman' (1884: 140). On the other hand, Robert F. Horton, in his very popular *Women of the Old Testament: Studies in Womanhood*, writes that to say that Jael's action was not praiseworthy is to 'lower our whole estimate of Deborah herself', since Deborah calls her 'blessed' (1898: 126). Whereas Jael's nobility seems questionable, most writers are quick to praise Jephthah's daughter for submitting to Jephthah's vow, even if they condemn the vow itself as rash and foolish. The most effusive of these is Alexander Whyte, in *Biblical Characters*, who celebrates her for her influence on future generations: the young women who journeyed to the mountains each year to lament her death (Judg. 11: 40) 'came back to be far better daughters than they went out. They came back softened, and purified, and sobered at heart. They came back ready to die for their fathers, and for their brothers, and for their husbands, and for their God' (1905: 31).

Despite such glorifications of Jephthah's sacrifice for her father and fatherland, her horrifically tragic story remains as something of a trauma in English theological and literary tradition. It and other tragic stories like it in Judges (Samson and the unnamed woman, for example) resist the desire for edification that we see expressed in Byron, Tennyson, and Whyte. Indeed, contradicting their songs of praise for her sacrifice is a body of literature that laments, protests, and questions her tragic fate, often placing her alongside her literary soul mate from Greek tragedy, Agamemnon's daughter Iphigenia in Euripides' play, *Iphigeneia in Aulis*.

In Shakespeare's tragedy *Hamlet* (II. ii. 404–421), for example, Hamlet speaks to Polonius of Jephthah's daughter, whom Jephthah 'loved passing well'. He calls Polonius Jephthah, intimating that he, too, has foolishly sacrificed his own virgin daughter by keeping her from marriage (recall that, before her death, Jephthah's daughter spends two months in the mountains with her companions, bewailing her eternal virginity). Several lines later (II. ii. 457–64), Hamlet refers to Pyrrhus' spilling of the 'blood of fathers, mothers, daughters, sons, | Bak'd and impasted with the parching streets ... | Roasted in wrath and fire, | And thus o'ersized with coagulate gore,' thus indirectly providing a particularly vivid description of Jephthah's daughter's whole-burnt sacrificial body.

More profound in its resistance to the tragedy of Jephthah is Georg Friedrich Händel's last oratorio, *Jephtha* (1752), with words by Thomas Morell (who explicitly connected Jephthah's daughter to Euripides' *Iphigenia* by giving her the name Iphis). Here is a powerful expression of unquiet submission that, over the centuries, has left audiences uncertain and questioning of the necessity of her sacrifice and the clarity of God's will. Recent performances of the oratorio, moreover, have carried echoes of more recent dread tragedies of war that are the spawn of foolish vows and that culminate in unnecessary child sacrifices. In the 2005 English National Opera production, for example, Katie Mitchell's staging of the oratorio in a bombed-out 1940s hotel clearly placed the story in the context of the Israeli-Arab War (note, by the way, Israel's Operation Jephtha, 13 April 1948, the aim of which was to clear eastern Galilee of Arabs).

In these works, as in Trible's essay—a work of narrative literature in its own right—the story of Jephthah's daughter and others like it in Judges are treated as terrible tragedy. As such these works contribute to a literary-theological tradition that undermines the moralizing tendencies in biblical interpretation and resists the economy of sacrifice that so pervades patriarchies and patriotisms, past and present. And here we find the deep volatility and inherent dissymmetries of Judges returning in ways that continue to open new spaces to raise theological questions that are as urgent today as ever.

WORKS CITED

BAL, MIEKE. 1987. *Lethal Love: Feminist Literary Readings of Biblical Love Stories*. Bloomington: Indiana University Press.

—— 1988a. *Death and Dissymmetry: The Politics of Coherence in the Book of Judges*. Chicago: University of Chicago Press.

—— 1988b. *Murder and Difference: Gender, Genre, and Scholarship on Sisera's Death*. Bloomington: Indiana University Press.

BEAL, TIMOTHY K., and GUNN, DAVID M. 1992. 'Ideology and Intertextuality: Surplus of Meaning and Controlling the Means of Production', in Danna Nolan Fewell (ed.), *Reading Between Texts: Intertextuality and the Hebrew Bible*. Louisville: Westminster/John Knox.

BOLING, ROBERT G. 1975. *Judges*. Anchor Bible. Garden City: Doubleday.

CALVIN, JOHN. 1948. *Commentaries on the Epistles to Timothy, Titus, and Philemon*, trans. William Pringle. Grand Rapids: Eerdman.

EXUM, J. CHERYL. 1980. 'Promise and Fulfilment: Narrative Art in Judges 13'. *Journal of Biblical Literature* 99: 43–59.

—— 1981. 'Aspects of Symmetry and Balance in the Samson Saga'. *Journal for the Study of the Old Testament* 19: 2–29.

—— 1989. 'The Tragic Vision and Biblical Narrative: The Case of Jephthah', in J. Cheryl Exum (ed.), *Signs and Wonders: Biblical Texts in Literary Focus*. Atlanta: Society of Biblical Literature.

—— 1990. 'The Centre Cannot Hold: Thematic and Textual Instabilities in Judges'. *Catholic Biblical Quarterly* 52: 410–31.

—— 1996. *Plotted, Shot, and Painted: Cultural Representations of Biblical Women*. Sheffield: Sheffield Academic Press.

FEWELL, DANNA NOLAN, and GUNN, DAVID M. 1990. 'Controlling Perspectives: Women, Men, and the Authority of Violence in Judges 4 and 5'. *Journal of the American Academy of Religion* 56: 389–411.

GEIKIE, CUNNINGHAM. 1884. *Old Testament Characters*. New York: James Potts.

GINZBERG, LOUIS. 1968. *The Legends of the Jews* trans. Henrietta Szold. Philadelphia: The Jewish Publication Society, iv.

GUNN, DAVID M. 1985. 'The Anatomy of a Divine Comedy: On Reading the Bible as Comedy and Tragedy', in J. Cheryl Exum (ed.), *Tragedy and Comedy in the Bible*. Decatur: Scholars Press.

—— 1987. 'Joshua and Judges', in Robert Alter and Frank Kermode (eds.), *The Literary Guide to the Bible*. Cambridge, Mass.: Harvard University Press.

—— 1992. 'Samson of Sorrows: An Isaianic Gloss on Judges 13–16', in Danna Nolan Fewell (ed.), *Reading Between Texts: Intertextuality and the Hebrew Bible*. Louisville, Ky.: Westminster/John Knox.

—— 2005. *Judges*. Blackwell Bible Commentaries. Blackwell.

HORTON, ROBERT F. 1898. *Women of the Old Testament: Studies in Womanhood*. London: Service & Paton.

JOBLING, DAVID. 1986. 'Deuteronomic Political Theory in Judges and 1 Samuel 1–12', in *The Sense of Biblical Narrative*. Sheffield: Sheffield Academic Press, ii.

KLEIN, LILLIAN R. 1988. *The Triumph of Irony in the Book of Judges*. Sheffield: Almond Press.

KOOSED, JENNIFER and LINAFELT, TOD. 1996. 'How the West Was Not One', in Alice H. Bach, ed., *Biblical Glamour and Hollywood Glitz*. Atlanta: Scholars Press.

LUTHER, MARTIN. 1513–15. *First Lectures on the Psalms*.

NOTH, MARTIN. 1943 (tr. 1981). *The Deuteronomistic History*. Sheffield: Sheffield Academic Press.

POLZIN, ROBERT. 1980. *Moses and the Deuteronomist: Deuteronomy, Joshua, and Judges*. New York: Seabury.

TRIBLE, PHYLLIS. 1984. *Texts of Terror: Literary-Feminist Readings of Biblical Narratives*. Minneapolis: Fortress.

WEBB, BARRY G. 1987. *The Book of the Judges: An Integrated Reading*. Sheffield: Sheffield Academic Press.

WELLHAUSEN, JULIUS. 1878 (trans. 1885). *Prolegomena to the History of Ancient Israel*, trans. J. S. Black and A. Menzies. Edinburgh: A & C Black.

WHYTE, ALEXANDER. 1905. *Biblical Characters: Gideon to Absalom*. London: Oliphants.

FURTHER READING

ALTER, ROBERT. 1981. *The Art of Biblical Narrative*. New York: Basic Books.

—— 1990. 'Samson without Folklore', in Susan Niditch (ed.), *Text and Tradition: The Hebrew Bible and Folklore*. Atlanta: Society of Biblical Literature.

BACH, ALICE. 1998. 'Rereading the Body Politic: Women and Violence in Judges 21'. *Biblical Interpretation* 6:1–19.

BAL, MIEKE. 1990. 'Dealing/With/Women: Daughters in the Book of Judges', in Regina M. Schwartz (ed.), *The Book and the Text: The Bible and Literary Theory*. Cambridge: Blackwell.

BEAL, TIMOTHY K., and GUNN, DAVID M. 1999. 'The Book of Judges', in John H. Hayes (ed.), *The Dictionary of Biblical Interpretation* (Nashville: Abingdon).

BOS, JOHANNA W. H. 1988. 'Out of the Shadows: Genesis 38; Judges 4: 17–22; Ruth 3'. *Semeia* 42: 37–67.

BRENNER, ATHALYA. 1990. 'A Triangle and a Rhombus in Narrative Structure: A Proposed Integrative Reading of Judges iv and v'. *Vetus Testamentum* 40: 129–38.

—— (ed.) 1993. *A Feminist Companion to Judges*. Sheffield: Sheffield Academic Press.

CAMP, CLAUDIA V. 2000. *Wise, Strange and Holy: The Strange Woman and the Making of the Bible*. Sheffield: Sheffield Academic Press.

CRENSHAW, JAMES L. 1978. *Samson: A Secret Betrayed, a Vow Ignored*. Atlanta: John Knox.

DAY, PEGGY L. 1989. 'From the Child Is Born the Woman: The Story of Jephthah's Daughter', in Peggy L. Day (ed.), *Gender and Difference in Ancient Israel*. Minneapolis: Fortress.

FEWELL, DANNA NOLAN. 1992. 'Judges', in Carol A. Newsom and Sharon H. Ringe (eds.), *The Women's Bible Commentary*. Louisville, Ky.: Westminster/John Knox.

—— 1995. 'Deconstructive Criticism: Achsah and the (E)razed City of Writing', in Gail Yee (ed.), *Judges and Method: New Approaches in Biblical Studies*. Minneapolis: Fortress.

FEWELL, DANNA NOLAN, and GUNN, DAVID M. 1993. *Gender, Power, and Promise: The Subject of the Bible's First Story*. Nashville: Abingdon.

FUCHS, ESTHER. 1989. 'Marginalization, Ambiguity, and Silencing: The Story of Jephthah's Daughter'. *Journal of Feminist Studies in Religion* 5: 35–45.

GREENSTEIN, EDWARD L. 1981. 'The Riddle of Samson'. *Prooftexts* 1: 237–60.

HAMLIN, E. JOHN. 1990. *Judges: At Risk in the Promised Land*. Grand Rapids: Eerdmans.

LASINE, STUART. 1984. 'Guest and Host in Judges 19: Lot's Hospitality in an Inverted World'. *Journal for the Study of the Old Testament* 30: 37–59.

MATTHEWS, VICTOR H. 1992. 'Hospitality and Hostility in Genesis 19 and Judges 19'. *Biblical Theology Bulletin* 22: 3–11.

NIDITCH, SUSAN. 1989. 'Eroticism and Death in the Tale of Jael', in Peggy L. Day (ed.), *Gender and Difference in Ancient Israel*. Minneapolis: Fortress.

—— 1990. 'Samson As Culture Hero, Trickster, and Bandit: The Empowerment of the Weak'. *Catholic Biblical Quarterly* 52: 608–24.

REINHARTZ, ADELE. 1992. 'Samson's Mother: An Unnamed Protagonist'. *Journal for the Study of the Old Testament* 55: 25–37.

SCHNEIDER, TAMMI. 2000. *Judges*. Berit Olam. Collegeville: Liturgical Press.

STERNBERG, MEIR. 1990. *The Poetics of Biblical Narrative: Ideological Literature and the Drama of Reading*. Bloomington: Indiana University Press.

STONE, KEN. 1995. 'Gender and Homosexuality in Judges 19: Subject-Honour, Object-Shame?' *JSOT* 67: 87–107.

—— 2000. 'Concubine (Secondary Wife of a Levite)', in Carol Meyers, Toni Craven, and Ross Kraemer (eds.), *Women in Scripture*. New York: Houghton Mifflin.

YEE, GALE A. 1993. 'By the Hand of a Woman: The Metaphor of the Woman Warrior in Judges 4'. *Semeia* 61: 99–132.

—— (ed.) 1995. *Judges and Method: New Approaches in Biblical Studies*. Minneapolis: Fortress.

CHAPTER 15

PSALMS

ALASTAIR HUNTER

INTRODUCTION

As compared with the narrative sections of Scripture, the psalms pose a more daunting challenge to literary readings in current times. For while narrative lends itself to visual and cinematic interpretations, and provides storylines and ironic play in abundance, the poetic themes and tropes of the psalter and the linguistic devices it deploys are far harder to render accessible to a modern ear, even for those still familiar with it through its presence in Christian worship and the liturgy of the synagogue. And, as is the case with all poetic forms, the question of translation intrudes much more forcefully than for literature with a more directly semantic intention. Thus, though the prophetic and wisdom books are also composed broadly speaking using the *conventions* of poetry, the translator/interpreter has more to pin his or her hopes to than the poem itself. For I take it to be axiomatic that it is the very sounds and patterns, structures and phonetic interplay, which carry the soul of poetry, and without which the meaning is a decidedly poor second cousin. Of course, in a volume such as the present one, the given language is English and the understanding is that the readers both of this book and of the texts with which it concerns itself will read primarily in English. But that does not entirely dispose of the problem. The choice of which biblical translation—or translations—to read from remains, and can make a significant difference. Thus it is important to say something about how this particular aspect of the literariness of the psalms has been handled in recent decades.

TRANSLATING THE PSALMS

I shall confine my remarks to questions relating specifically to the rendering of the Psalms in 'suitable' English—a subset of problems relating to translation in general and the translation of poetry in particular. In my own recent study of the Psalms I devote two chapters to, respectively, theory of translation and the choice of a 'best fit' English version from those generally available (Hunter 1999: 3–32). While it is clearly an option for each interpreter to produce his or her own 'Englishing' of whichever psalms they might wish to discuss, the problem here is that the general reader is doubly excluded from the original; first, in not having direct access to Hebrew, and secondly, in being confronted with an opinion which may well be idiosyncratic, and about which no consensus (in the form of commentary and/or public liturgical use) has developed. Obviously this particular rubric—the requirement for a publicly acknowledged set of translations—carries far less weight where the psalms, either as a whole or any subset of them—constitute literary pieces in English in their own right, quite regardless of their faithfulness to the originals.

In this regard, a literary collection like that of Donald Davie (1996) has striking virtues. It assumes (without reprinting them) the familiar King James versions, but provides a wide range of poems produced over some four centuries, from Coverdale to modern translators such as David Frost and Gordon Jackson, which fall some-where between my demand for public accountability and the freedom of the indi-vidual to interpret entirely creatively. Davie makes the interesting point that up to the end of the eighteenth century it was common to find major poets trying their hand at rendering the Psalms, but that after Robert Burns 'the task is delegated to worthy persons who make few or no pretensions to being poets in (as we oddly say) their own right' (Davie 1996: p. xxii). He attributes this to the principles of self-expression, individualism, and originality espoused by the Romantic Movement. Thus even that most overtly religious of poets, Gerard Manley Hopkins, offers nothing in the line of psalms translation. He has one interesting piece, 'Thee, God, I come from, to thee go, | All day long I like fountain flow' (Mackenzie 1990: poem 161), which has clear echoes of those psalms in which the poet, conscious of his/her sinfulness, seeks to hide from God, only to be discovered by God's mercy. It begins with the thought, frequently expressed in the Old Testament, that we come from and return to God. Davie (1996: 290) understands 'Thou art indeed just, Lord' (Mackenzie 1990: poem 177) as based on Ps. 119: 137–60; the superscription, however, refers rather to Jer. 12: 1. It is more than a little interesting, therefore, to note the number of volumes which have appeared in recent years, beginning with Peter Levi's translation for Penguin Classics in 1976, comprising either new translations of part or all of the Psalter, or compendia of translations—such as Davie (1996), which, curiously, uses none of Levi's translations and makes no reference to that edition.

It is not possible in the short space of this chapter to pursue the detail of the arguments which rage in the battleground of translation theory; the reader is directed both to my own work (Hunter 1999: 3–32) and especially to Davie (1996: pp. xxviii–lviii) where much that is sensible and insightful is offered. Davie is, admittedly, neither an Old Testament nor a Hebrew scholar, and some of what he has to say is coloured by somewhat outdated academic information. But he was a poet, and as such could offer insights which leave the more prosaic world of the scholar some distance behind. He is also, it must be said, opinionated—no bad thing when so much of what is offered as interpretation in the biblical field is anodyne. The essence of the argument—leaving aside the sheer difficulty of translating poetry—focuses on the unresolved tension between, on the one hand, the desire to match the linguistic peculiarities of the original as closely as possible, and on the other, the feeling that we should be free to represent the *sense* of the original even if that necessitates very paraphrastic translations. If the poetry of the source text is somehow to be conveyed, it seems obvious that some kind of faithfulness to the sounds and forms of the Hebrew is in order; but there are very narrow limits to what is possible. At the other extreme, we find compositions in English which could be said to be inspired by (or instigated, or prompted by) a Hebrew psalm, but which should be judged strictly in their own terms. In modest disagreement with Davie, I would include the Countess of Pembroke's magnificent version of Ps. 139 (ibid. 77) in this category, as also his own adaptation of Ps. 39 (ibid. 329).

The most useful modern editions are, first, five single-authored collections or part collections: Levi (1976), Frost, Emerton, and MacIntosh (1977), Jackson (1997), Slavitt (1996) and Wieder (2003); and secondly, two eclectic editions: Davie (1996) and Wieder (1995). The last two overlap, not surprisingly, in their selections from older poets, but have almost nothing in common with poets of the twentieth century, and are surprisingly distinctive in their coverage of the earlier centuries (only fifteen poets are found in both anthologies, and only nineteen individual psalms are shared). The reader who wants to gain an overview of the psalms in English since the beginning of the sixteenth century will find much to ponder in Davies and Wieder.

POETIC FEATURES OF THE PSALMS

It is questionable, in spite of the almost ubiquitous presence of psalms in many traditions of worship, whether compositions designed for strictly liturgical use should be admitted as poetry. The near-parodic admiration for the Anglican Book of Common Prayer in self-styled literary circles (and the associated opprobrium attached to the *Alternative Service Book*) suggest that the element of distance may lend enchantment here, as in so many areas. The problem lies in the apparent discovery that *what* is said does not merit the poetic intensity of *how* it is said: for unless modern versions are hopelessly incompetent—and this is not my own experience of the matter—the difference lies in the removal of what may be a spurious element of mystery. It is manifestly not true that current English is incapable of expressing the numinous, the transcendent, or the inspirational; but it may be that traditional religious sources of these phenomena no longer carry such weight for most modern readers. It is, of course, a moot point whether the psalms—either individually or as a whole—were composed for cultic or liturgical situations. Some surely were, some may have been adapted to such use, and others may have begun life as personal *cris de cœur* and may therefore best be understood in those terms. There is a world of difference between the emotion of Ps. 23 and that of Ps. 119: the former can still, it seems, be captured by modern readers, the latter is remote from our secular perceptions. On the other hand, a rabbinic consciousness, for which Halacha is a primary desideratum, might warm to its elaborate and highly structured celebration of the Torah of Moses.

So far so good; but emotional response is only one small aspect of how we read poetry. A second very important dimension is that of metaphor and metonym: the standard devices by means of which language in general, and poetry in particular, attempt to create effect and enhance meaning by tempting the reader into strictly non-logical responses. This is not the place for an elementary lesson in linguistic tropes; but without some awareness of them we are likely to find ourselves adrift from the modus operandi of the psalms. This is a real danger in certain religious circles, where images and phrases in the psalms are often interpreted as literal prophecies of events in (most commonly) the life of Jesus. This misprision[1] begins in the New Testament, where Ps. 2: 7 'You are my son; today I have begotten you' is cited in Matt. 3: 17 to prove that Jesus is the Son of God. There are numerous other examples which have successfully pre-empted the use of the psalms for many Christians, and have led some forms of scholarly approach into a vain quest for historical contexts or social life-settings based on fragmentary evidence within the texts.

Literary tropes, even when we recognize their presence, can still present snares for the unwary. Some we do not have the linguistic ability to recognize because our knowledge of Hebrew is lacking: a good example is to be found in Ps. 29: 2 which the King James Version renders 'Worship the Lord in *the beauty of holiness*' (my italics). Later versions try 'holy splendour' (NRSV), 'the splendour of his holiness' (NIV) and 'in holy attire' (REB). What any of these phrases actually signifies is, sadly, a continuing mystery. Others suffer from the fact that accurate translation misrepresents the metaphor. In Hebrew the word for heart (*leb*) is regularly applied to matters of the will, the mind, and the intellect; its literal translation produces a completely different English metaphor, to do with the emotions or the affections. Thus a passage such as Prov. 3: 5, 'Trust in the Lord with all your heart', while perfectly comprehensible in English, constitutes a religious imperative which, however valid, seems not to belong to the Hebrew original. Thirdly, certain kinds of literary device which maintain their semantic fields through translation may nevertheless lose some of

---

[1] I use this somewhat recondite term in homage to one of the leading readers of the Old Testament of recent years, the late Robert P. Carroll, for whom it was a favourite term.

their effect through the transformation of the terms between the two cultures. 'The Lord is my shepherd' undoubtedly depends upon a profession which belongs to both ancient Israel and modern society; but that may be all they have in common. I do not imagine that the psalmist ever conceived of him/herself as being coralled by a couple of sheepdogs, for example. Another pervasive example, the frequent use made of kingship and autocratic hereditary rule to describe God and God's relationships with humankind poses problems of a different kind for peoples familiar with democracy and constitutional monarchy or elected presidential office. The only models we have currently for autocracy are negative in the extreme. These examples, and many others, present problems for translation on the one hand, and for our reception of the psalms' poetic aspects on the other. Brown (2002) addresses the question of metaphor directly, though mostly in the interests of explaining how they function theologically and in their contextual terms. Some of Gordon Jackson's compositions address the contemporary problems head-on in attempting to provide meaningful renderings. Here is one example which might serve as a taster for others in his collection:

> Psalm 2
> Why are the nations up in arms, and men drawn into insane dreams?
> The world's rulers are in accord—against God and the Lord's Anointed:
> 'Old God's authority is at an end—long live the Revolution!'
> The Lord in heaven is laughing; to him their threats are a joke.
> But one day his top will blow, and his fury flow like lava.
> *Here on my holy mountain, behold the man, the Anointed*
> I say what I hear the Lord speak—
>   *You are my Son; this day I have begotten you:*
> *The nations are yours for the asking, the ends of the earth your estate:*
> *With a sceptre of iron judge them; smash them to smithereens.*
> Learn wisdom smartly, O Captains and Rulers, remember your place:
> Bow to the Lord in fear, and rejoice in him with trembling:
> Kiss the Son, stay his displeasure, and beware his infolded fire;
> Once it erupts it will engulf all but the blessed he shelters.

There is a neat juxtaposition of current usage with eschatological threat in this translation which almost succeeds in injecting new force into the somewhat tired imagery of empires at war which inhabits the original, while the italicized passages have the effect of removing the troublesome Christological reading from direct to reported speech ('I say what I hear the Lord speak'), which restores its metaphoric character and strips out its spurious theological authority.

The psalms are also replete with structural devices which present varying degrees of difficulty. The phenomenon of parallelism, first identified by Bishop Lowth in the eighteenth century, can, to some extent, survive translation—though where it depends crucially on the order of words in the original Hebrew it is often masked. Here translators may have the choice, which poetic convention offers, of an unusual word order in English, but surprisingly few take it up. There is a pleasing instance in Ps. 121: 3–5, where the Hebrew order is:

> 3. He will not let your foot slip,
>   He will not slumber,
>   *He who protects you.*
> 4. For sure, he will not slumber,
>   He will not fall asleep,
>   *He who protects Israel.*
> 5. *Yahweh is your protector*

Notice the skill with which the psalm delays the subject, at the same time as it enhances the identity of the subject in three stages, from the simple 'he who protects you', through the more all-embracing 'he who protects Israel', to the final revelation that it is none other than Yahweh who is the protector. The eight versions I myself have consulted (Hunter 1999: 15–32) lose this effect by reordering verses 3 and 4; yet it poses no serious problems of translation, as my own basic translation (above) shows. This failure to follow what is a rather central aspect of the structure of the psalms is interesting, for it suggests that the primary motivation for most scholarly translation was to reach a quite conventional kind of received English. Many of the secondary versions to be found in Davie and Wieder will have based themselves on earlier English renditions, though Levi's translation of Ps. 121 directly from the Hebrew is no better. Berlin (1985) is still the best study of parallelism in the psalms; Hunter (1999: 46–61) examines structure more generally. It is, of course, difficult to go more than a certain distance into structural features on the basis of translations alone; and this is even more true of aspects such as paronomasia, assonance, consonance, and dissonance, alliteration, and the repetition of keywords and roots. But such difficulties are true of all poetry in translation, and need not delay us especially here.

I began this section by querying whether it is proper to treat the psalms as poetry; I suggest that the evidence we have reviewed is sufficient to provide a qualified affirmative, but only if a serious effort is made to represent these works in translation with their own recognizable structural features while at the same time endeavouring to revivify the metaphoric and metonymic basis from which they operate. This is in many ways the exact reverse of what has commonly happened; but the work of Jackson and others offers some hope that surprising and refreshingly new poems can still be found in this ancient collection.

LITERARY PSALMS: THE SIXTEENTH TO THE NINETEENTH CENTURIES

The great period of biblical translation which culminated in the Authorized (King James) Version of 1611 stimulated a parallel literary interest in the psalms which influenced poets such as Donne, Herbert, Milton, and the Sidneys. From the review of Davie and Wieder in the section 'Translating the Psalms', above, we have already seen that they represent only a fraction of what was a very considerable activity. Between them, these two collections represent seventy-eight different poets, of whom only about a dozen were active in the twentieth century. Given the huge influence of the Bible in literature of the pre-Romantic periods this is hardly surprising; what is more interesting is the significant interest in extensive translation since 1976 (Levi, Frost, Jackson, Slavitt and Wieder), which seems to suggest that the modern decline in influence of the King James Version has spurred efforts to recapture a body of verse which was in danger of fast disappearing from view.

Some psalms, of course, have never lost their fascination: the *De Profundis* ('Out of the depths', Ps. 130); the exiles' vengeful lament (Ps. 137) 'by the waters of Babylon'—not least for its incarnation at the hands of Boney M; the great celebration of the ineluctable presence of God which is Ps. 139 ('If I take the wings of the morning, and dwell in the uttermost parts of the sea, even there shall thy hand lead me', vv. 9–10, KJV); and of course Ps. 23 whose words have accompanied countless of the dead on their final journey, and which Holladay (1996: 359–69) characterizes as 'an American secular icon'. Others are heard by secular audiences in a variety of choral guises: 'Why do the heathen rage' (Ps. 2: 1) in the *Messiah*; 'Bringing in the sheaves' (Ps. 126: 6) in the well-known spiritual; Stravinsky's *Symphony of Psalms* (38: 13–14; 39: 2–4, 150); Bernstein's *Chichester Psalms* (108: 2; 100; 23; 2: 1–4; 131; 133: 1); and the antiphonal performance of psalms in the Anglican choral evensong—for many today perhaps as much an aesthetic as a religious experience. Through their use in the Book of Common Prayer many individual phrases from the psalms have entered the common stock of English; the considerable number included in the *Oxford Dictionary of Quotations* is eloquent testimony to this enduring aspect of the literary role of the Psalms.

Historically speaking, the stimulus to serious literary work on the Psalms came from the Reformation emphasis on vernacular worship and the particular need for English psalms, given their key role in the Anglican liturgy. Most of those who have direct experience of them in this respect will know them either from the uninspired and generally uninspiring metrical versions—which are occasionally redeemed by magnificent music—or from the prose translations of Miles Coverdale in the Book of Common Prayer. The challenge to create truly *poetic* translations was first, and arguably most impressively met by Sir Philip Sidney (Pss. 1–43) and his sister Mary, Countess of Pembroke (Pss. 44–150, and revisions of her brother's work). Both, of course, worked from English prose translations; but their real strength lay in the application to this work of secular poetic conventions and a willingness to be adventurous in structure, rhyme, metre, and metaphor. Pritchard (1992: 8) offers this assessment:

The 'Sidneian Psalms', as Donne called them in his celebratory poem, begun by Sir Philip Sidney in the 1580s and completed after his death by his sister Mary, constituted, in their fusion of technical sophistication and religious commitment, a major cultural intervention. This poetry, so little known nowadays, which did so much to transform the quality of seventeenth-century religious lyric—it is hard to imagine the poetry of George Herbert being the same without it—was a considered response to the writers' complex political, religious, literary and personal situation.

The truth of this assessment may be easily demonstrated by setting out for comparison Mary Sidney's rendering of the first four verses of Ps. 130, that of Sternhold and Hopkins (1562), and the Scottish Metrical Psalter of 1560–64; this latter is notably more succinct than either of the other two:

Mary Sidney

> From depth of grief
>   Where drowned I lie,
> Lord for relief
>   To thee I cry:
> My earnest, vehement, crying, praying,
> Grant quick, attentive hearing, weighing.
>
>   O Lord, if thou
>   Offences mark,
>   Who shall not bow
>   To bear the cark?
> But with thy justice mercy dwelleth,
> Whereby thy worship more excelleth.

Sternhold and Hopkins

> Lord, unto thee I make my moan,
>   when dangers me oppress;
> I call, I sigh, complain, and groan,
>   trusting to find release.
> Hearken, O Lord, to my request,
>   unto my suit incline,
> And let thine ears, O Lord, be pressed
>   to hear this prayer of mine.
> O Lord our God, if thou survey
>   our sins, and them peruse,
> Who shall escape? Or who dare say,
>   I can myself excuse?
> But thou art merciful and free,
>   and boundless in thy grace,
> That we might always careful be
>   to fear before thy face.

Scottish Metrical Psalter

> Lord, from the depths to thee I cried.
>   My voice, Lord, do thou hear:
> Unto my supplications' voice
>   Give an attentive ear.
> Lord, who shall stand, if thou, O Lord,
>   Shouldst mark iniquity?
> But yet with thee forgiveness is,
>   That feared thou mayest be.

It would be unkind to berate the metrical version for not being what it was never intended to be, or to forget the exigencies of strict metre necessitated by the simple tunes required for popular worship. While it is sad that for a great many people the only knowledge of the psalms as poetry consists of a body of what is, at best, mundane verse and at worst doggerel, nevertheless this body of work too is part of the literary heritage of the psalms, and one which has shown remarkable powers both of survival and of influence. Nevertheless, without making unreasonable claims for the Sidneys, their influence is undoubted, certainly meriting Donne's accolade, 'They tell us *why*, they teach us *how* to sing' (Davie 1996: 98).

While critics are agreed that George Herbert was influenced by the Sidneys' psalms, it is perhaps curious that he produced little himself by way of psalms translation. Only one is known, a metrical version of Ps. 23 (ibid. 117) which is remarkably unlike his other verse. Davie notes the conjecture that 'he contrived a special rusticity so as to appeal to an unlettered congregation used to the old version of Sternhold and Hopkins'. However, Freer (1972: 12) suggests that, from a religious point of view, Herbert may have seen virtue in those very lame and ill-formed verses which would have been used by his congregation, and quotes a verse from 'The Elixir' in support:

> All may of thee partake:
> Nothing can be so mean,
> Which with this tincture (for thy sake)
> Will not grow bright and clean.

This poem itself has something of the structure and rhythm of the metrical psalms, though its use of these is far more subtle. It is not suprising that it has become itself a well-known hymn, together with 'Let all the world in every corner sing' and 'King of Glory, King of Peace' (which has some links with Ps. 116). The reminiscences of the style of the Sidneys are clear in all three, and suggest that the liturgical tradition missed an opportunity when it failed to develop these as choral items. Herbert himself, arguably, writes *as if* he were a psalmist, and a number of his poems can be read in that way. Consider, for instance, 'Affliction (IV)': here is precisely the mood and pattern of so many psalms of lamentation, though in Herbert's individual voice. I quote here the first and last two stanzas, and suggest a comparison with Pss. 57 and 70 from a fairly long list of possible exemplars:

> Broken in pieces all asunder,
>> Lord hunt me not,
>> A thing forgot,
> Once a poore creature, now a wonder,
>> A wonder tortur'd in the space
>> Betwixt this world and that of grace.
>
> Oh help, my God! let not their plot,
>> Kill them and me,
>> And also thee,
> Who art my life: dissolve the knot,
>> As the sun scatters by his light
>> All the rebellions of the night.

> Then shall those powers, which work for grief,
>   Enter thy pay,
>   And day by day
> Labour thy praise, and my relief;
>   With care and courage building me,
>   'Till I reach heav'n, and much more thee.

These, and similar examples, testify to the truth of Patrides' claim (1974: 10) that 'so profoundly was Herbert engaged with the Psalter that its echoes reverberate across his poetry, to an extent unmatched by any other poet in English Literature'.

Herbert succeeds in conveying a religious sensibility which, however foreign to the modern consciousness, is given eloquent voice by poetry which combines elegance of structure with a genuine passion. His older contemporary, Donne, while notable for his celebratory poem on the Sidney psalms, affords surprisingly little else of direct relevance to our subject. His specifically religious poetry ('On The Progress of the Soul', 1612, and a variety of groups including the 'Holy Sonnets', the 'Divine Meditations', and a 'Litany', written probably at various points through his career) is too precisely focused on Christian themes to offer any direct echo of the psalms—this is especially true of the 'Holy Sonnets'. The 'Divine Meditations', a sequence of nineteen sonnets, is infused in its earlier stanzas with something of the psalmists' sense of being both creaturely and unhappy—made by God, but despairing in the face of death and the enemies of the soul. But Donne's theology is in the end too Calvinist to be truly in harmony with the thought of the psalmists, who never—even in their bleakest moments—abandoned the hope that the individual might experience God's mercy. Compare, for example, the concluding lines of the 'Meditations' (Smith 1976) with the sentiments of the psalm whose superscription attributes it to David after Nathan takes him to task for the Bathsheba affair:

> I durst not view heaven yesterday; and today
> In prayers and flattering speeches I court God:
> Tomorrow I quake with true fear of his rod.
> So my devout fits come and go away
> Like a fantastic ague: save that here
> Those are my best days, when I shake with fear.

Psalm 51: 7–13

> Purge me with hyssop, and I shall be clean;
>   wash me, and I shall be whiter than snow.
> Let me hear joy and gladness;
>   let the bones that you have crushed rejoice.
> Hide your face from my sins,
>   and blot out all my iniquities.
> Create in me a clean heart, O God,
>   and put a new and right spirit within me.
> Do not cast me away from your presence,
>   and do not take your holy spirit from me.
> Restore to me the joy of your salvation,
>   and sustain in me a willing spirit.

> Then will I teach transgressors your ways,
> and sinners will return to you.

The psychological difference is instructive. Donne, who never committed any crime as heinous as murder in the interest of adultery, finds it hard to conceive of mercy, while the psalmist's verse is imbued with optimism, however sombre his crimes.

Donne has one significant work of biblical translation—a version of Lamentations ('The Lamentations of Jeremy') in a rigorous ten-syllable metre with a strict *aabb* rhyming pattern over virtually all of its 390 lines. The character of the biblical book of Lamentations is that of an extended psalm of lament, but of a national rather than individual kind. This might therefore be seen as Donne's contribution to the genre of psalms translation; as such, it perhaps suits a certain melancholic note in his own character, and is in keeping with—though superior to—the techniques of the metrical psalms. Thus, summing up this aspect of Donne and Herbert, we find in the former a clear respect for the psalms of Philip and Mary Sidney, with little sign of emulation; and in the latter an undoubted stylistic influence through his religious poetry in general, but ironically only one psalm rendered, and that in the standard metrical mode. While this may reflect simple preference on the part of these poets, it is tempting to speculate that something in the liturgical use of the psalms themselves precluded a genuinely literary approach; the Sidneys constitute a potential that was never truly developed—until, dare we suggest, the twentieth century.

Milton produced versions of Pss. 1–8 (composed in 1653) and 81–8 (composed in 1648), together with a versification of Ps. 136 which is familiar as the hymn 'Let us with a gladsome mind', supposedly composed when he was 15, and a paraphrase of Ps. 114 from the same period. The difference between the two groups is striking: the earlier group is in strict common metre (8/6/8/6) rhymed *abab*, as if they were deliberately modelled upon the metrical collections. Despite their qualities, they did not become part of that liturgical tradition, leaving Milton's main contribution to worship the somewhat awkward piece from his teenage years. The second group to be composed is poetically more interesting in its deployment of a variety of metre, rhythm, and rhyme pattern. Psalm 3 in particular uses one of the forms found in the Sidney psalms, and the sheer diversity that is compressed into this short collection is reminiscent of the same phenomenon in the former. A brief quotation from Ps. 3 must suffice to illustrate this point:

> Lord how many are my foes
> How many are those
> That in arms against me rise;
> Many are they
> That of my life distrustfully thus say,
> No help for him in God there lies.
> But thou Lord art my shield, my glory,
> Thee through my story
> Th' exalter of my head I count;
> Aloud I cry'd
> Unto Jehovah, he full soon reply'd
> And heard me from his holy mount.

Milton, interestingly, does seem to have worked directly from the Hebrew. Mary Ann Radzinowicz (1989: 94), in her monograph *Milton's Epics and the Book of Psalms*, suggests that the poet took this metrical freedom directly from the character of the Hebrew psalms: 'Milton's willingness to translate eight Psalms in a wide variety of metres without imposing a traditional English one suggests that he thought Hebrew verse observed its own kind of ancient freedom, overruling the preference for any single English metrical practice. Like the verse of Pindar, that of David privileged rhythm over meter.' This does not account for the strict metre and rhyme in Ps. 81–8: did Milton work from English exemplars in this instance, or are we to read them as a virtuoso performance in a strict form which, having been accomplished, left him free to experiment in Ps. 1–8? Whatever the answer to these questions, we find in Milton's versions a virtual synopsis of the English psalms tradition of the sixteenth and seventeenth centuries.

Three other names merit mention: Isaac Watts and Christopher Smart in the eighteenth century, and James Montgomery in the nineteenth. Watts might best be described as a jobbing versifier, while Montgomery is more broadly a hymnographer, whose work has contributed hugely (as indeed has Watts's) to hymnaries in most anglophone Christian traditions. Smart is more interesting—an erratic poet most famous for his long unfinished poem 'Jubilate Agno' in which (amongst many other things) he celebrates his cat Jeoffry. The poem was written during a period of incarceration for supposed insanity—though one might imagine that a man who could find reason to praise God through his pet cat was saner than most of us. Both Davie and Wieder include generous examples of Smart's psalm versions; Wieder provides seventeen: only Mary Sidney has a greater number in Wieder's *The Poets' Book of Psalms*. A flavour of his work is to be found in Ps. 134, which conforms to a kind of faintly jolly metrical rhythm, but succeeds nonetheless in conveying a certain strangeness not out of keeping with the poet and his source:

> Attend to the musick divine
>   Ye people of God with the priest,
> At once your Hosanna combine
>   As meekly ye bow to the east.
>
> Ye servants that look to the lights
>   Which blaze in the house of the Lord,
> And keep up the watch of the nights
>   To bless each apartment and ward,
>
> The holy of holies review,
>   And lift up your hands with your voice,
> And there sing your anthem anew,
>   In praise to Jehova rejoice.
>
> The Lord that made heav'n and earth
>   Which rules o'er the night and the day,
> His blessing bestow on your mirth,
>   And hear you whenever ye pray.

LITERARY APPROACHES TO THE PSALMS: THE TWENTIETH CENTURY

A path which I have not chosen to go down in this chapter is to review the many biblical translations which have appeared in English since the nineteenth century. In my own work, *Psalms* (Hunter 1999: 15–32), I gave some consideration to the choice of an English version amongst eight possible twentieth-century versions; that, however, leaves at least as many again unconsidered. It would be futile here either to list or to attempt to evaluate what is a burgeoning literary, religious, and (it must be said) commercial enterprise. Thus I will confine my comments in this final section to translations which have either a clear poetic purpose or a liturgical direction independently of biblical translation per se. This means that I will *not* here consider Harry Mowvley's *The Psalms: Introduced and Newly Translated for Today's Readers* (1989), but *will* note the so-called 'Gelineau Psalms' because of their explicit liturgical purpose. The principal collections, then, are the Gelineau Psalms (1963), Levi (1976), Frost (1976), Slavitt (1996), Jackson (1997), and Wieder (2003). Of these, two are expressly liturgical in purpose (Gelineau and Frost); the others seek explicitly to make English poetry out of the psalms. I have reproduced for purposes of comparison the translations of Ps. 100 made by these four, since these may be assumed to have an explicitly literary purpose. I have arranged them in two pairs, the first two being by English poets (Levi and Jackson), the second pair North American (Wieder and Slavitt). They illustrate rather effectively the different options open to those bold enough to undertake such an enterprise, and do so along what appear to be cultural lines (though admittedly the sample is far too small to permit of any sweeping conclusions). Thus Levi, certainly, and Jackson to a degree preserve a kind of sobriety of tone, a more literal faithfulness to the original which mutes their own poetic voice. The other two quite strikingly depart from the Hebrew to create new poems which have their own very clear authorial sound, without losing a recognizable connection with the Hebrew. The reader is invited to make his or her own appraisal of the results.

Peter Levi

> Shout to God all the earth,
> serve God with rejoicing,
> come to him with shouting and gladness.
> Know that God is God,
> he made us, we are his,
> his people and the sheep of his flock.
> Enter his gates with thanksgiving
> and his courts with praise.
> Give thanks to him and bless his name.
> God is good and his mercy is everlasting,
> and his faithfulness is for every generation.

Gordon Jackson

> Give glory to God, all men of the earth,
>> be glad that you serve him,
>>> let his presence fill your hearts to bursting
>>>> and his goodness fill your praises;
> You know that the Lord is God,
>> that he it was made us,
>>> that we are his,
>>>> his very own flock that he loves and provides for;
> So enter with confidence through his gates,
>> fill his courts with your praises,
>>> give him such thanks as you have to give him,
>>>> and bless his holy name;
> For the Lord is good and his love will never run out,
>> and his truth will stand the test of all generations.

Laurance Wieder

> It helps to make a lot of noise
> When on earth. We did not,
> Were modest, too, until God made us
> Enter squally bawling thank-yous
> In our lifetime, children's children.

David Slavitt

> Let every nation chorale to the Lord
> a Dio, con brio
>> in love and joy before Him.
>> Sing to him and adore Him
>>> with a resonant tonic chord,
>>> acknowledging God as the Lord.
> He made us and all else there is.
> We are his sheep; our meadow is His.
>> In joy we intone our thanks and praise.
>> let us in elegant harmony raise
>>> our voices to sing;
>>> He is good, and He is one,
>>> from mother to daughter, from father to son.

I turn finally to a brief comment on the theory of literary approaches to the psalms. There is, of course, considerable overlap with theory in general, for which there is ample resource in other places. My own *Psalms* (Hunter 1999: 62–99) provides an overview which those who wish to test the postmodern waters may find helpful; however, it must be said that there is not a wealth of material on this subject, though there are many studies of individual psalms and groups of psalms. More often than not they deal with historical-critical and linguistic points which belong to a different field of specialism. Robert Alter (1985) is a notable exception: well worth reading both for its wealth of information and for its elegant style.

Detailed discussion of a whole range of literary aspects of biblical poetry is provided, taking in wisdom and prophetic texts as well as the psalms, and concluding with a brief chapter, 'The Life of the Tradition' which addresses some of the topics we have considered at more length in this chapter. Alter concludes his study (ibid. 211–13) with a brief discussion of a modern Israeli poem (by Tuvia Rüvner) which opens with a double citation from the psalms. Virtually all the language in the poem is recognizably biblical, yet also recognizably modern Hebrew in its original form. It is certainly the case that there is considerable intertextuality in the biblical psalms; thus the contemporary poet's use of biblical material to create modern poetry (which is highly developed in Israeli verse) has close analogies with the psalms themselves. For even though modern poems rarely serve a *directly* religious purpose, the very denseness of biblical allusion creates an expectation and a response in the reader which is not that distant from what one might experience reading a biblical psalm and recognizing its intertext: a good example is the way that Ps. 8 toys with the creation account in Gen. 1 and 2. The recognition of this link allows the reader space to read between, and indeed outside, the lines and thereby to build a response in a far wider interpretative field than he or she might at first have expected. While modern Israeli poetry is technically outside the remit of this chapter, it is perhaps worth noting that the poem by Tuvia is by no means an isolated example; the traditions of the Psalter (and of the Old Testament as a whole) are to be found alive and well in Israel today. Perhaps the most stimulating study in English of this phenomenon is David Jacobson's *Does David Still Play Before You?*; for a complete review of Hebrew verse through three millennia, Carmi (1981) is indispensible.

I shall conclude with a brief account of an important essay by Harold Fisch (1988), 'Psalms: The Limits of Subjectivity'. In it he asks whether, unlike other biblical poetry, which often has a strong dialogic character, the psalms can be read as meditations, in the Romantic sense of 'a self-consciousness which expresses itself essentially in monologue' (ibid. 108). He goes on to argue that rather than monologues the psalms are a kind of 'whispered inner dialogue', but one in which, because of the communal dimension, the 'I/thou' regularly segues into a 'we/thou' (ibid. 108–14). But a further reversal takes place, as

the trials and struggles of the community often take on the character of a lonely, individual ordeal in which the suffering soul cries out to God and is answered. What one would want to say is that, paradoxically, the ongoing covenant drama involving God and the people is constantly interiorized to become the drama of a lonely soul, crying in anguish, trusting and despairing. The people in short take on the marks of a lyrical subjectivity, giving us idiolect and sociolect all together.   (ibid. 105)

The psalms are also characterized by a level of formulaic language—words conscious of themselves and of their contexts. 'Every phrase in the Psalms is a kind of quotation . . . To put it very simply, we could say that we have here a kind of poetry reflexively conscious of the importance of poetry' (ibid. 119). A fitting observation with which to conclude.

WORKS CITED

ALTER, ROBERT. 1985. *The Art of Biblical Poetry*. Edinburgh: T & T Clark.

BERLIN, ADELE. 1985. *The Dynamics of Biblical Parallelism*. Bloomington: Indiana University Press.

BROWN. WILLIAM P. 2002. *Seeing the Psalms. A Theology of Metaphor*. Louisville, Ky.: Westminster/John Knox.

CARMI, T. 1981. *The Penguin Book of Hebrew Verse*. Harmondsworth: Penguin.

DAVIE, DONALD (ed.) 1996. *The Psalms in English*. London: Penguin.

FISCH, HAROLD. 1988. *Poetry with a Purpose. Biblical Poetics and Interpretation*. Bloomington: Indianapolis University Press.

FREER, COBURN. 1972. *Music for a King. George Herbert's Style and the Metrical Psalms*. Baltimore: Johns Hopkins University Press.

FROST, DAVID L., EMERTON, J. A., and MacINTOSH, A. A. 1977. *The Psalms: A New Translation for Worship*. London: Collins.

GELINEAU, JOSEPH. 1963. *The Psalms: A New Translation. Translated from the Hebrew and Arranged for Singing to the Psalmody of Joseph Gelineau*. London: Collins.

HUNTER, ALASTAIR. 1999. *Psalms*. London: Routledge.

JACKSON, GORDON. 1997. *The Lincoln Psalter*. Manchester: Carcanet.

LEVI, PETER. 1976. *The Psalms*. Harmondsworth: Penguin.

MacKENZIE, NORMAN H. (ed.) 1990. *The Poetical Works of Gerard Manley Hopkins*. Oxford: Clarendon.

PATRIDES, C. A. (ed.) 1974. *The English Poems of George Herbert*. London: J. M. Dent & Sons.

PRITCHARD, R. E. (ed.) 1992. *The Sidney Psalms*. Manchester: Carcanet.

RADZINOWICZ, MARY ANN. 1989. *Milton's Epics and the Book of Psalms*. Princeton: Princeton University Press.

SLAVITT, DAVID R. 1996. *Sixty-One Psalms of David*. New York: Oxford University Press.

SMITH, A. J. 1976. *John Donne. The Complete English Poems*. Harmondsworth, Middlesex: Penguin Books.

WIEDER, LAURANCE (ed.) 1995. *The Poets' Book of Psalms*. New York: Oxford University Press.

—— 2003. *Words to God's Music. A New Book of Psalms*. Grand Rapids: Eerdmans.

FURTHER READING

I have tried, in the brief compass of this essay, to touch on a range of matters which could be said to relate to the general subject, 'Literary ways of reading the Psalms'. It will by now be clear that there is much more that could be said, and much more written, in respect of all of the individual topics addressed. The bibliography will lead those in search of more information into relevant resources; for those who would like more, but not *too* much more, the following three books already listed are a good starting point: Alter (1985); Davie (1996); Hunter (1999). To these I would add:

HOLLADAY, WILLIAM L. 1996. *The Psalms Through Three Thousand Years*. Minneapolis: Fortress.

CHAPTER 16

SONG OF SONGS

J. CHERYL EXUM

THE Song of Songs, the Bible's only love poem, is arguably the most lyrical poetry in the Bible. Nowhere else do we find such rich, sonorous, and sensuous vocabulary, such densely metaphorical language, such vibrant and striking imagery, such imaginative flights of fancy, and such freedom from formal poetic conventions, except perhaps in Deutero-Isaiah and Job. Whereas in a typical couplet of Hebrew poetry the second line normally repeats, emphasizes, extends, or modifies the first—a phenomenon frequently referred to as parallelism—in the Song couplets and triplets display little of the regularity or balance that is the hallmark of ancient Hebrew poetry.[1] Rather they seem to rush forward, spilling over each other, as though impelled by the desire they communicate. Unlike the lyricism of Deutero-Isaiah and Job, where the poetry has a purpose in addition to providing pleasure—to console in the one case, to convince in the other—the Song's erotic lyricism seems to exist purely for the pleasure of the reader.

Lyric poetry is essentially a discontinuous form. In typical lyric fashion, the Song surges forward and repeats itself, returning to themes and images and playing variations upon them that establish echoes across the time and space of the poem. The Song meanders. It does not proceed in a linear fashion; there is no plot (though there is some narrative development within the speeches of the female protagonist). Nor is there any development in the relationship between the Song's lovers. Instead there are only speeches—for it is through the voices of lovers that the poet shows what being in love is like—and a relationship that is always and everywhere already in progress. Symmetry and balance are created by structuring devices such as chiasmus

---

[1] Couplets and triplets are usually represented in translation by indentation. Terminology for describing lines or couplets or units of poetry differs widely, and the nature of couplet composition, or parallelism, in Hebrew poetry has been much discussed; for a general discussion, see Alter 1985: 3–26.

(an *abb'a* or *abcb'a* pattern), inclusio (where a unit begins and ends in the same way), and by repetition within and among sections of the Song. Other features such as assonance, alliteration, sound play (paronomasia), parataxis, enjambement, and ellipsis contribute substantially to the overall poetic effect. Many of these features, however, do not come across well in translation. Fortunately this is not the case with the features that matter most, the poetic strategies by means of which the poet seeks to immortalize a vision of love as mutual desire, sensual pleasure, and sensory delight, a vision in which love is experienced as astonishing, overwhelming, confident, undeterred, deep, and strong as death.

> Place me as the seal upon your heart,
>   as the seal upon your arm,
>   for love is strong as death . . .   (8: 6)

In this poem celebrating love, life, the pleasures of the flesh, and the beauty of the world, the mention of death, near the end, comes somewhat unexpectedly. Though death is spoken of only once, the affirmation that love is strong as death and its corollary, that death is strong as love, hold the key to the poem's *raison d'être*: to immortalize a particular vision of love in the face of death. This poem about desire— in which lovers engage in a continual game of seeking and finding in anticipation, enjoyment, and assurance of sensual gratification—bears witness to the poet's desire to make present, through language, what cannot be captured on the page, the lovers whose multiple identities enable them to stand for all lovers, and ultimately for love itself.

The poet employs a range of interconnected strategies to show us, rather than simply tell us, that love is as strong as death. The most striking is the illusion of immediacy, the impression that, far from being simply reported, the action is taking place in the present, unfolding before the reader. The key to this unfolding is the dialogue format. The Song is a dialogue between a man and a woman (and occasionally the women of Jerusalem). That it represents itself as offering both a woman's and a man's point of view is part of its supreme artifice and artistry, for a moment's reflection tells us the Song is not a transcription of a lovers' tryst. Voices that seem to reach us unmediated are the voices of lovers created for us by the poet (Fox 1985: 253–6). By presenting the lovers in the act of addressing each other, the poem gives us the impression that we are overhearing them.

The lovers are always taking their pleasure or just about to do so. The erotic imperative—the call to love by means of grammatical forms that suggest present time—lends urgency to the moment: 'draw me after you', 'let us run' (1: 4), 'tell me' (1: 7), 'rise up', 'come away' (2: 10, 13), 'turn' (2: 17), 'open to me' (5: 2), 'let me see' (2: 14), 'let me hear' (2: 14; 8: 13). Coupled with imperatives, vocatives strengthen the impression of the lovers' presence at the moment of utterance: 'you whom I love', 'my sister, bride', 'O fairest of women'. The present moment is also vividly captured by participles: in 2: 8–9, for example, the man is approaching, bounding over hills, standing, knocking—his activity arrested in time and space. The question, 'What is this coming up from the wilderness?' (3: 6), gives rise to the illusion that we are watching, along with the speaker, our eyes riveted upon something just entering our field of vision, poised between the wilderness and the unspecified location of the speaker.

A related technique for immortalizing love is conjuring. Throughout the Song, speech embodies desire by calling bodies into being and playing with their disappearance in an infinite deferral of presence. Conjuring seeks to make immanent through language what is absent, the body, to construct the body and endow it with meaning. The man conjures his lover up repeatedly by describing her bit by bit, in densely metaphorical language, until she materializes, clothed in metaphor (4: 1–5, 12–15; 6: 4–10; 7: 2–10).[2] The woman calls her lover forth through her poetic powers of representation only to let him disappear so that she can conjure him up again (2: 8–17; 3: 1–5; 3: 6–11; 5: 2–6: 3).

For the poet's vision of love to live on, the poem must be read. It needs readers to actualize it in the present, in the acts of reading and of appreciation. Having an audience is so important that the poet provides one within the poem. In addition to the voices of the lovers, there is a third speaking voice, that of the women of Jerusalem, who function as an audience and whose presence facilitates the reader's entry into the lovers' seemingly private world of erotic intimacy. For readers, a certain element of voyeurism may be involved in overhearing the intimate exchanges of lovers. Presenting the lovers as aware of and in conversation with an audience is a poetic strategy that makes the relationship between the lovers less private, less closed (and the Song less voyeuristic). The Jerusalem women are sometimes addressed directly (1: 5; 2: 7; 3: 5, 10–11; 5: 8, 16; 8: 4) and they sometimes speak (5: 1, 9; 6: 1; 8: 5; and perhaps 1: 8; 7: 1). At other times their presence, which the lovers do not regard as either intrusive or embarrassing, is simply assumed. The women's presence is a reminder that what seems to be a closed dialogue between two perpetually desiring lovers is addressed to us, the Song's readers, for our pleasure and possibly our enlightenment.[3]

The Song also seeks to involve its readers by encouraging them to relate the lovers' experience to their own experience of love, real or fantasized. The Song is not about specific lovers of the past (except for the vaguest connections to Solomon and Jerusalem). Its lovers are any lovers, types of lovers, and their love is timeless. In the course of the poem, they take on various guises or personalities and assume different roles, as shepherds, for instance (1: 7–8), or vineyard keepers (1: 5–6; 8: 11–12), or royal figures (1: 4, 12; 3: 6–11; 6: 8–9). If the Song gives the impression that the lovers are young because they often appear to be courting, this does not mean the Song is about young love only. The lovers are not to be confused with the poet, who presents them to us both as explorers discovering the delights of intimacy and as

---

[2] Song 7: 1–9 in some English translations, where the versification differs from the Hebrew text (6: 13 = 7: 1 Hebrew, 7: 1 = 7: 2 Hebrew, etc. throughout ch. 7). I follow the Hebrew versification.

[3] Obviously nothing compels readers to accept the poem's invitation to enter the lovers' intimate erotic world or to accept it on the poet's terms. To judge from the admiration, and even adoration, it has elicited over the centuries, the Song is very effective in seducing most readers with its poetic vision of desire.

knowing all there is to know about love. By providing access to only the voices of the lovers, to what they say not who they are, the poet is able to identify them with all lovers.

In the Song, desire is always on the brink of fulfilment, it has an urgency about it (come!, tell me!, make haste!). Fulfilment is simultaneously assured, deferred, and, on a figurative level, enjoyed. The slippage in the Song from one mode to another, the blurring of distinctions between wishing and desiring and consummation is also a blurring between past, present, and future, and is central to the Song's poetic artistry and erotic persuasiveness.[4] It is one of the ways the poem immortalizes love by representing it as always in progress.

Significantly, there is no closure to this poem about desire. It ends with the woman seemingly sending her lover away and calling him to her in the same breath, he as a gazelle and she as mountains of spices where he will cavort: 'Take flight, my love, and be like a gazelle or young deer upon the mountains of spices.' Resistance to closure is perhaps the Song's most important strategy for immortalizing love. Closure would mean the end of desiring, the silence of the text, the death of love.[5] Not only does the Song end without closure, it begins *in medias res*, 'let him kiss me'—a design that makes it, in effect, a poem without beginning or end. Like the love it celebrates, the Song of Songs strives to be never-ending (cf. Munro 1995: 89). The woman's words in the poem's final verse, because they signal both the lovers' separation and their union, suspend their love in time and bring the poem round full circle to desire's first articulation, 'let him kiss me'.

> Let him kiss me with the kisses of his mouth
> for your caresses are better then wine ...   (1: 2)

With its first words (apart from the title) the poem draws the reader into a romantic relationship already in progress. The woman longs for kisses because she knows their intoxicating effect. The erotic imperative in 1: 2–4 ('let him kiss me!', 'draw me after you!', 'let us run!'), together with the direct address to another person ('you'), communicates a sense of urgency and creates the impression that we are overhearing and observing a love affair as it unfolds. The woman begins by speaking of 'him' and 'his mouth' as if her lover is not there with her. In the next breath she addresses him directly, 'your caresses'. We might think of 'let him kiss me with the kisses of his mouth' as an incantation, and the shift from 'let *him* kiss me' to '*your* caresses' an act of conjuring. As if in response to articulated desire, the lover materializes, brought into being by seductively beautiful poetry.

The woman's praise of her partner's lovemaking is followed in 1: 5–2: 7 by a series of short, loosely connected speeches in which alternating voices highlight various

---

[4] On temporal and spatial shifts and their poetic effects, cf. Munro 1995: 117–42.

[5] Brooks (1993: 20) discusses 'the way in which narrative desire simultaneously seeks and puts off the erotic dénouement that signifies both its fulfilment and its end: the death of desiring, the silence of the text'. See also Landy 1983: 113: 'The tension in the Song between the desire of the lovers to unite and the inevitability of their parting is that also between their voice and the silence into which it vanishes, and between love and death—the ultimate parting, the unbroken silence.'

aspects of love. Love emboldens and makes one vulnerable: the woman invites the gaze of the women of Jerusalem, but also feels the need to explain her appearance (1: 5–6). Love is playful. The exchange in 1: 7–8 is teasing and erotically suggestive. The question, 'Tell me, my soul's beloved, where do you graze?', alludes to the man's favourite pastime, feeding or grazing on the lilies (2: 16; 6: 2). There is no direct object, no flock of sheep, as supplied by most translations, for this is one of the many instances of double entendre in the poem. Love is mutual adoration. The man's 'Look at you! You are beautiful, my friend!' is echoed by the woman's 'Look at you! You are beautiful, my love!', and his praise of her, 'Like a lily among thistles, so is my friend among women', is capped by her 'Like an apple tree among the trees of the forest, so is my lover among men'. Love is stimulating and intoxicating (erotic feasting in the wine house, 2: 3–4). It is overwhelming ('I am faint with love', 2: 5). Even when gratified, it cannot get enough. These verses are filled with wonderfully concrete images. The tents of Qedar, the curtains of Solomon, the chariots of Pharaoh, the vineyards of Engedi are not just any tents, curtains, chariots and vineyards, but special ones associated with the richest and most illustrious of rulers both near and far, an exotically remote desert tribe and a renowned luxurious oasis.

Love awakens the senses to nature's beauty and bounty. Vineyards, especially metaphoric ones, need tending (1: 6). The woman speaks of fragrant spices and aromatic woods: nard, myrrh, henna, cedar, cypress. She discourses on flowers and trees, singling out ones beautiful to look at and pleasing to smell ('rose of Sharon', lily, apple tree) and, stimulated by the last of these, the apple tree as metaphor for her lover, she fancies indulging in delicacies to eat (raisins, apples) to accompany the wine and fruit of love that is sweet to her taste. Animals traverse the landscape. Sheep and goats, which need tending, represent domesticity and responsibility, while gazelles and does of the open field are untamed and fleet of foot, a symbol of freedom and spontaneity. Love is spontaneous, free and responsible. Love, says the poet, is intimate and private (the lovers' couch is verdant and their house, a bower sweet, 1: 16–17), but it cannot be kept to itself. It spills over, bursting to announce itself to others: 'Sustain me, refresh me', the woman calls to the women of Jerusalem, reminding us of their presence (2: 5–7). The invitation to the women of Jerusalem to participate in the lovers' pleasure is also an invitation to the reader.

My lover answered and said to me … (2: 10)

In 2: 8–3: 5, for the first time, the Song of Songs acknowledges the presence of a narrator. This narrator is also a character, as distinguished from the poet, whose presence as narrator throughout the Song is deftly effaced. The woman tells a story, or, rather, juxtaposes two stories, each with a narrative movement and a sense of closure, a tension and a resolution. In the first (2: 8–17), she describes her lover's visit to her house and his invitation to her to join him outdoors, where spring's arrival is heralded by flowers coming into bloom, birdsong, budding vines, and fragrance in the air. In the second (3: 1–5), she describes her nocturnal search for her lover and its resolution when she finds him, concluding with an address to the women of Jerusalem, in which she places them under oath not to rouse love before it wishes (cf. 2: 7; 8: 4).

The poet puts words into the woman's mouth, creating her speech (2: 8–3: 5) in which she puts words into her lover's mouth, creating his speech (2: 10–14). Even when using a narrator whose presence is evident (to the point of such an obvious sign of narration as 'my lover answered and said to me'), the poet maintains the illusion of immediacy so central to the Song's poetic effectiveness. The impression that the action is taking place in the present, unfolding before the reader's very eyes, is achieved in the woman's speech through a combination of poetic techniques: (1) the use of the word 'look!' (Hebrew *hinneh*, often translated as 'behold') as a focalizer of present action, (2) the reliance on the erotic imperative to give the impression of the lovers' presence at the moment of utterance ('Rise up, my friend, my fair one, and come away', 'let me see', 'let me hear', 'turn, my love, be like a gazelle') and (3) the prominence given to participles to capture action in process (the man is leaping, bounding, standing, and gazing). When the woman quotes her lover, it is as if we are overhearing him, so unobtrusive is the double narratorial voice, the poet telling us what the woman is telling us that the man is saying.

First heard, then seen at a distance, he materializes through her poetic powers of representation.

> Listen! My lover!
>   Look! He's coming,
> leaping over the mountains,
>   bounding over the hills.
> My lover is like a gazelle
>   or young deer.
> Look! He's standing outside our wall,
>   peering in through the windows,
>   peeking through the lattice.   (2: 8–9)[6]

She brings him to her house from afar, only to send him away in what is not really a sending away, if 'cleft mountains' is a double entendre for the woman herself: 'When the day breathes and the shadows flee, turn, my love, be like a gazelle or young deer upon the cleft mountains' (2: 17). In 3: 1–5 the conjuring begins anew. The lover is not there, and she seeks him, cannot find him, seeks and finally finds him. The lovers materialize and dematerialize in a continual play of seeking and finding, of desiring and experiencing satisfaction, that mirrors the rhythms of love.

At key points in her story, the woman's narrative presence is as adeptly effaced as the poet's own. Her voice not only distinguishes itself as that of a narrator and a character in her own narration, it also merges with the poet's (as its creator) and her lover's (when she quotes him). The distinction between past and present is blurred; for example, the man *spoke*, yet we hear him speaking (2: 10–14); the watchmen *found* the woman, and we hear her questioning them (3: 3). The beginning of the woman's speech is vividly situated in the present: the lover is approaching. The narrated story that follows (what the man *said*) is transformed, through the illusion of immediacy, into the present, as we overhear him *saying*, 'Rise up, my love, and come away'. By the

---

[6] Translations from the Hebrew are mine; for discussion, see Exum 2005.

time he says to her 'let me hear your voice' (v. 14) and she replies in vv. 15–17, the indicators of narration have faded away. And by v. 17 she has conjured her lover up so vividly that she now speaks to him directly: 'Turn, my love, be like a gazelle'.

Again the woman conjures up her lover (3: 6–11). This time he appears as a kingly lover, a Solomon, approaching from afar in a magnificent royal palanquin that we, the readers, see, as though through her eyes, in greater and greater detail as it moves closer and closer. By means of a question, 'What is this coming up from the wilderness?', the woman calls attention to what looks like columns of smoke on the horizon. Next comes an appeal to the sense of smell as the air grows denser, perfumed from unseen censers, as though incense were being burned. Could this be a caravan laden with aromatic powders? One might expect a caravan, since the question, 'What is this coming up from the wilderness?', anticipates as an answer something that is feminine in gender, and the Hebrew word for caravan (ʾorehah) is feminine. But, no, this is not a caravan. Suddenly the woman recognizes the litter—'Look! It is Solomon's litter!'—and we see it too. Although we now see what is responsible for the columns of smoke and the heavy scent in the air, we cannot yet see who it is—apart, that is, from the impressive escort that accompanies the litter. Soon these warriors are close enough for us to distinguish the swords at their sides.

An imaginative transformation takes place as the litter draws closer. It becomes a magnificent palanquin, whose trappings progressively come into view. It is made of wood and has silver posts. As it comes even nearer, we catch a glimpse of its upholstery, with the gold thread woven into it perhaps catching the light, and its cushioned seat covered in expensive purple cloth. Finally we look into its very interior (3: 10), and view the inlaid work that decorates it. And who is inside? Why Solomon, of course, as we might have expected! The palanquin has brought the man in his Solomonic guise before us, and we (as the audience of whom the poem is ever mindful), along with the women of Jerusalem, are invited to gaze upon him, wearing his crown, on what we now discover to be his wedding day—a wedding day that symbolically anticipates that of the lovers.

> Look at you! You are beautiful, my friend!
> Look at you! You are beautiful. (4: 1)

The Song began with short, alternating speeches expressing the lovers' desire, delight in, and praise of each other (1: 2–2: 7). Then the woman had a long, uninterrupted speech from 2: 8 to 3: 11. Now it is the man's turn to offer a long speech. The dialogue format enables the poet to explore the nature of love and longing from both their points of view. Their voices are in harmony and their desire is mutual, but they do not talk about love in the same way. Whereas the woman's characteristic mode of speaking about love is to tell stories in which she and her lover are characters, the man relies on figurative language to describe how he experiences love. He looks at her, tells her what he sees, and how it affects him. The majority of the unusual, memorable metaphoric descriptions of the body in the Song are his, including the erotically charged extended metaphor of the woman as a pleasure garden in 4: 10–5: 1. Through metaphoric descriptions of the body the poet invites the reader into the private world of the lovers, offering the reader the pleasure of looking at, and thus knowing, the body. The inventory of body parts is intimate, the images are sometimes erotic, the overall picture is sexually suggestive. At the same time, metaphor functions as a way of keeping the reader out and preserving the lovers' privacy: the lovers seem to have their own private code, and the metaphors conceal more than they display.

The man begins by inviting his lover to see herself through his eyes ('Look at you, you are beautiful...'), and he describes, by means of striking metaphors, her eyes, hair, teeth, lips, mouth, cheeks, neck, and breasts (4: 1–5). Clearly the description is not meant to inform the reader what the woman looks like, for it does a very poor job of that. It is, moreover, addressed to the woman herself; that is, within the context of the poem the man is telling his lover how he perceives her (though of course everything in the poem is ultimately addressed to the reader). Typically an image receives more attention than its referent. Her hair is not like a flock of goats, but like a flock of goats moving down a mountainside, and not just any mountainside, but Mount Gilead. Her neck is not like a tower, but like the tower of David, a tower built in courses, and on those courses shields are hung, a thousand of them, all kinds of shields that a warrior might wield. Sometimes, as in the case of the tower, it seems almost as if the poet has forgotten the referent in the interest of developing the image. The images seem to be striving for completion, as if to compensate for the dividing up of the body into parts by creating a total picture. Here we find the kind of specificity and attention to detail, the interest in particulars, that makes the poetry so elegant. The comparisons are rendered more dynamic through parataxis (the juxtaposition of referent and image without connecting verbs): 'your hair, like a flock of goats winding down Mount Gilead', 'like a slice of pomegranate, your cheek', and so on.

The man's speech becomes more erotically explicit as it progresses. Similes focusing on the woman's facial features and comparing them to the sorts of things one might see in the world of nature or architecture yield to one long, elaborate metaphor for the woman that is more sexually suggestive but less specific with regard to the body part or parts in question (no doubt due to the intimate nature of the description). The similes in 4: 1–5 tend to distance the object of desire; the body is looked at but not approached. In 4: 6, the distance is eliminated, as the man puts himself in the picture: 'I will make my way to the mountain of myrrh and the hill of frankincense.' In 4: 1–5 the woman is a landscape upon which goats and sheep gambol, gazelles feed, and a decorated tower stands. In v. 6 she becomes the landscape her lover will frolic upon and feed on. He continues to describe her body metaphorically, but, in the rest of his speech, he approaches it as source of comestibles and unguents that he will savour with delight (and, by the end, relish with abandon).

He who gazed upon her and very deliberately catalogued her charms is devastated when she looks at him: 'You have captured my heart with one glance of your eyes' (4: 9). In 4: 10–11 he responds to her praise of his lovemaking in her fervent declaration of desire with which the Song began (1: 2–4) by praising her lovemaking in similar terms. He develops her imagery further by adding spices to the perfumes of which she spoke, and milk and honey to the wine. He goes on to describe her as sweet-tasting and sweetly scented, a garden of choice fruits and spices, and a spring of fresh, flowing water. This description is different from the one vividly picturing selected parts of her body, one by one, in startling metaphors, with which he began. Not only is it more intimate and sensuous but also he is less interested now in an inventory of her features than in what she represents for him: voluptuous bounty and life. Her lips, for example, are not compared to something sweet, but are themselves the source of nectar. And in place of an inventory in which only one simile or metaphor represents each body part, the man now relies on a cluster of metaphors to create an overall picture of the woman as a fragrant and fecund garden, where a bountiful meal of erotic delights awaits him.

Suddenly, the woman speaks (4: 16), and with her words, the speech, which had been wholly the man's, becomes antiphonal. It is as if, her lover's speech having reached an erotic crescendo, she cannot keep quiet any longer. She interrupts, taking up his image of her as a fragrant garden of choice fruits, and invites him to come to his garden and there to taste all love's pleasures. The seamlessness of the imagery communicates the lovers' complete concord. He ardently accepts the invitation and underscores both his claim to all the pleasures of the garden and his savouring of them by repeating the possessive pronoun 'my': 'I come to *my* garden, *my* sister bride, I pluck *my* myrrh with *my* spice, I eat *my* honeycomb with *my* honey, I drink *my* wine with *my* milk.' The final word belongs to the women of Jerusalem, who encourage the lovers in their mutual intoxication: 'Eat, friends, drink yourselves drunk on caresses!' Enter this poetic garden of eroticism, says the poem to its readers.

> My lover has gone down to his garden,
>   to the beds of spices,
>   to graze in the gardens
>   and to gather lilies.
> I am my lover's and my lover is mine,
>   he who grazes among the lilies.   (6: 1–3)

Although they are types, representatives of all lovers rather than identifiable individuals, the lovers seem to take on distinct personalities as we get to know them. They are consistent in the way they each talk about their love and in the way love makes them behave—she telling stories in which he courts her and she seeks him (2: 8–3: 5; 5: 2–6: 3), he praising her charms in vivid metaphorical language (4: 1–15; 6: 4–10; 7: 2–10) and laying claim to the pleasures she offers (5: 1; 7: 9–10). This consistency enables us to build a picture of them and encourages us to feel we know them. The woman's second long speech (5: 2–6: 3) is a variation of her first. Here her account of a visit by her lover is seamlessly interwoven with her story about seeking him in the city streets at night, whereas in her first long speech the two episodes were simply juxtaposed. In her earlier 'story', the man came courting in the daytime, inviting her to join him outside; now he comes courting at night, and asks her to let him inside. The first time she sought him in the city streets at night, she found him immediately after encountering the city watchmen. This time she encounters a setback: the watchmen strike her and take her wrap from her.[7] Curiously, she seems unaffected by what is clearly a disturbing incident in the poem.[8] As it transpires, however, it seems that her lover was never really 'lost'. When questioned, she reveals that she knows where he is: in his garden (6: 2). The garden in the Song is both the place where the lovers enjoy the fruits of love and a double entendre for the woman herself and, specifically, her sexuality. The lovers are thus together.

The revelation at the end of the speech that the woman did not need to look for her lover at all has bearing on the interpretation of her 'story' in which first he is there, seeking entry to her chamber, and then he is gone and she chases him in the streets. It cautions us against an overly literalistic reading of these verses as if they needed to be explained as an event in the life of the lovers or as a dream. While it begins by exploiting the lyric potential of a dream ('I was sleeping but my heart was awake'), the woman's speech is first and foremost an instance of the Song's blurring of the distinctions between longing and gratification, desire and its satisfaction. It begins with an elaborate double entendre for erotic play and ends with a dramatic feat of conjury.

The woman's 'story' unfolds on two levels, and offers the most sophisticated, well-developed example of double entendre in the poem. On one level, it appears that the man is outside her chamber at night, seeking admittance. He departs before she can get up to let him in, and she goes out in the city streets in search of him. On the erotic level, Song 5: 2–7 is an account of coition veiled by the indirection of language (Cook 1968: 123–4), not a stage-by-stage description to be deciphered by matching body parts and fluids to oblique references, but an overall suggestiveness of sexual intimacy created by the pace, the imagery, and the choice of terminology. The repeated use of 'open', for instance, without a direct object, such as 'door', draws attention to its sexual sense: 'Open to me, my sister, my friend' (5: 2); 'I rose to open to my lover' (5: 5); 'I opened to my lover' (5: 6). Though translations differ, it is hard to miss the sexual innuendo in 'My lover reached his hand into the opening, and my insides were stirred because of him' (5: 4), especially since 'hand' is sometimes used in Hebrew as a euphemism for 'penis'. On the erotic level, the search for the lover that follows his withdrawal may express the woman's desire for further gratification—the literary equivalent of 'I can't get enough of you!'

At the point when her search for her lover seems to end disastrously, with her beating at the hands of the watchmen, the woman's narrative becomes a dialogue with the women of Jerusalem that enables her story to reach the desired outcome, the

---

[7] The text is ambiguous regarding the severity of the attack; her words could be interpreted to mean that they struck her, perhaps only once, which resulted in bruising, or that they beat her, seriously wounding her.

[8] Love's willingness to undergo suffering is a topos of love poetry. Nevertheless, even if the woman seems unaffected by this setback, it is not so easy for modern readers to dismiss the fact that it is a woman whom the poet represents as abused by men in a role of authority. Her lover does not undergo suffering for her sake, and, even if the poet had portrayed him as doing so, it is hard to imagine a man experiencing this kind of treatment. The situation seems to reflect the social mores and expectations of the poet's society, in which men enjoyed a social freedom that women did not share.

union with her lover. Instead of finding her lover at the end of a search through the city streets (cf. 3: 4), she 'finds' him through describing him. She conjures him up by depicting him from head to foot in simile and metaphor, until he is there, in his garden, with her, in an image of sexual intimacy. The presence of the women of Jerusalem as interlocutors (5: 9; 6: 1) who enable the 'seeking' of the lover to end successfully in 'finding–by-praise' (Cook. 134) is the most vivid instance of audience participation in the poem. As elsewhere, the women's participation functions to draw the reader into the world of the poem (cf. 2: 7; 3: 5; 3: 10–11; 5: 1; 8: 4–5). They and we are the audience of the woman's narrative in 5: 2–7, and we are the audience of their dialogue with the woman, which seems to be taking place before us, in 5: 8–6: 3.

On this one occasion, the woman adopts her lover's typical mode of speaking about love. Three times he describes her, from her head downwards in 4: 1–5 and 6: 4–7, and from her feet to her head in 7: 2–6. Though she describes his body only once (5: 10–16), the fact that she, too, owns the gaze plays an important role in the poet's vision of love as shared delight and pleasure. Like desire, looking in the Song is constructed as mutual. Each lover delights in the other's body. Each describes the loved one part by part, organizing the body in an effort to know it, and investing each part with meaning through a simile or metaphor whose import cannot be reduced to prose paraphrase. An important difference is that, unlike his descriptions of her, her description of him is textually motivated. She describes him in answer to a question raised by the women of Jerusalem, who ask, 'What distinguishes your lover from any other lover?' His descriptions, in contrast, are represented by the poet as spontaneous outbursts inspired by the sight of her. He deals with her body in parts to cope with the overpowering feelings she arouses in him, processing her body part by part and clothing it in images (cf. Landy 1983: 176). She treats his by parts to cope with his seeming absence and to conjure him up through the evocative power of language. Although the poet gives the lovers a different status with respect to the gaze, readers see the man in the same way that we see the woman, through an inventory of body parts described metaphorically.

> You are beautiful, my friend, like Tirzah,
>> lovely as Jerusalem,
>> as awesome in splendour as they.
> Turn your eyes away from me,
>> for they overwhelm me.   (6: 4–5)

In response to the woman's speech, which ends with her 'finding' him by praising his physical charms, one by one, until she has successfully conjured him up, the man now launches into a long speech in which he conjures her up by praising her physical charms in detail, not once but twice. As in his first long speech (4: 1–5: 1), he is concerned primarily with looking at her, describing what he sees, and telling the world how it affects him. Here in his second long speech (6: 4–7: 10), his two descriptions of the woman's charms (6: 4–10 and 7: 2–10) frame a short and rather cryptic first-person narrative about a visit to the nut garden (6: 11–12). Unfortunately the text of these two verses is so corrupt that it is impossible to tell who goes to the nut garden or what happens there. If the woman is the subject of these verses, then she interrupts the man's speech here, to tell of her visit to the nut garden (an incipient story). The man then calls her back into the poetic present so that the description of her charms can resume: 'Come back, come back, O Shulammite! Come back, come back, that we may gaze upon you.'[9] He includes others in his desire to gaze—the audience within the poem, the women of Jerusalem, and the audience of the poem, its readers.

The man begins and ends his speech with descriptive praise. Each time he describes his lover's body metaphorically, part by part, and then moves on to extol her perfection in other, more varied ways. He finds her captivatingly beautiful, desirable, and awe-inspiring. He has said all this before, in his first long speech, but lovers never tire of saying, or of hearing, familiar words of affection and adoration. The inventories of body parts are presented for the visual pleasure they offer to the onlookers, who include the poem's readers. The degree to which they objectify the loved one is counterbalanced by the extent to which the lover is affected. The man does not just look. He loses himself in the vision of beauty he sees before him when he surveys the body of the woman he loves. He is overwhelmed by her eyes (6: 5) and held captive in her tresses (7: 6)—overcome by the very features he contemplates. The first description (6: 4–10) is an inclusio that foregrounds these feelings; it opens and closes with the depiction of the woman as 'as awesome in splendour as they' (the royal cities of Tirzah and Jerusalem in v. 4, the moon and sun in v. 10), expressing his sense of awe at her aspect. 'Who is this that looks down like the dawn, beautiful as the moon, splendid as the sun, as awesome in splendour as they?' (6: 10) is either the man's rhetorical question or a question he puts in the mouths of the queens, concubines, and other women he conjures up to praise his beloved in vv. 8–9. Either way, it expresses his point of view. The second description (7: 2–10) begins with his lover's feet and moves up to her head, completing, as it were, the picture with which he began, in which he described only her head and face.

The final metaphoric description of his lover's body gives way to a metaphor for the man's desire when he puts himself into the picture. Putting himself in the picture he constructs of her is not unlike her telling stories in which both he and she are characters. Neither lover constructs the other without being affected themselves—without becoming part of the story or entering the picture. He ended his first long speech with a metaphor of the woman as a garden of erotic delicacies on which he proceeded to glut himself; he ends this one with a metaphor of her as a palm tree that he will possess by climbing and laying hold of its clusters. In response, the woman once again interrupts her lover's speech at the point where it reaches an erotic crescendo. Just as she invited him to come to his garden and eat its choice fruits

---

[9] Song 7: 1 is one of the few places in the Song where the identity of the speaker is not apparent. I understand the first couplet of 7: 1 as the man's speech, because the gaze gives rise to a description of the woman seen through his eyes; the speaker could, however, be the women of Jerusalem. The second couplet probably belongs to the woman. Shulammite is not a proper name. It alludes, through wordplay, to Solomon, and is probably a derivative of the same root, *šlm* (from which the word *shalom* is also derived), meaning 'the perfect one' (Fox 1985: 157–8).

at the end of his first long speech, here, at the end of his second long speech, she invites him to spend the night in the countryside and to visit the vineyards: 'There I will give you my love' (7: 13).

> You who dwell in the gardens,
>   companions are listening for your voice.
> Let me hear it!   (8: 13)

As it nears its conclusion, the Song returns to the mode in which it began, with a series of shorter speeches, where the voices of the woman, the man, and the women of Jerusalem intermingle, and the transitions from one topic to another are more abrupt. Like the opening of the poem, these verses are a kind of montage, with alternating voices expressing various aspects of love. Among the things said here about love, none is more important than the climactic affirmation of love's power:

> Place me as the seal upon your heart,
>   as the seal upon your arm,
> for love is strong as death,
>   jealousy as adamant as Sheol.
> Its flames are flames of fire,
>   an almighty flame.
> Floods cannot quench love,
>   nor can rivers sweep it away.
> Should a man offer all his wealth for love,
>   it would be utterly scorned.   (8: 6–7)

Although the poem's readers are its ultimate audience, within the world of the poem this succinct credo on the subject of love is spoken by the woman to her lover. For the first and only time, she does not speak specifically about her love or their love, but about love itself. There is never any sense of insecurity about love in the Song. The mention of jealousy is thus somewhat surprising, since jealousy, in Hebrew as in English, is a violent emotion, aroused when a rival is felt to threaten an exclusive relationship. What rival does the poet have in mind? The woman shows no jealousy of other women; indeed, she finds it only natural that women should adore her lover (1: 3–4). Here, just as she speaks about love in general, she speaks about jealousy in general and not about any jealousy of her own. For the Song of Songs, love's ultimate rival is mortality. In the face of the ineluctable claim of death and Sheol, the abode of the dead, on the loved one, the woman audaciously declares, on behalf of the poet, that love—and specifically love in its violently possessive form, jealousy—is just as unyielding, just as adamant in its refusal to let go of the object of its desire, as its rival, death.

The climactic affirmation of love probably does not come at the end of the poem because there it would be too much like closure. Rather than bringing the poem to closure, the poet chooses to end it with the man's request to hear his lover's voice (8: 13). Her reply, in which she sends him away and allusively calls him to her at the same time (8: 14), takes us back to the beginning, for only when the woman seems to send her lover away can the poem begin again with longing and the quest to gratify desire—with a voice that implores, 'Let him kiss me with the kisses of his mouth!' Like the companions who listen for the woman's voice, the Song's readers listen too—for the voice of the poet, who speaks about love through the voices of lovers.

The Song of Songs is present everywhere in English literature, referred to frequently by Chaucer in *The Canterbury Tales*, and translated into English numerous times in the English Protestant tradition. William Baldwin's *The Canticles or Balades of Salomon* (1549) was published with the intention that the translation would drive 'out of office the bawdy tales of lecherous love', and it is clearly dependent on the Great Bible of 1538, which entitles the book the 'Ballet of Balettes of Salomon'. Edmund Spenser translated the Song into English, and although his work is lost, its influence on his other poetry, particularly in his portrayals of women, is very evident. By the seventeenth century the Song and commentaries upon it provided a bridge between secular love poetry and sacred lyrics for such poets as George Herbert, Andrew Marvell, and Henry Vaughan. In *The Reason of Church Government* (1642), Milton describes the poem as a 'divine pastoral drama', and in the seventeenth and eighteenth centuries dramatic readings of the poem became popular. Robert Lowth in his lectures as Professor of Poetry at Oxford (1741–51) argues against excessive allegorizing of the poem, and anticipated readings of the poem in the Romantic period such as that contained in Lord Byron's *Hebrew Melodies* (1815) ('She walks in beauty, like the night'). The Romantic celebration of the poem's eroticism as against the tradition of reading it as an allegory in which the lover is interpreted as God or Christ, and the beloved as the Church or even the Virgin Mary, finds its culmination in Thomas Hardy's *Jude the Obscure* (1895), where Sue Bridehead decries 'such humbug as could attempt to plaster over with ecclesiastical abstractions such ecsctatic, natural, human love as lies in that great and passionate song'. The Song has been granted less attention in the literature of the twentieth century.

WORKS CITED

ALTER, ROBERT. 1985. *The Art of Biblical Poetry.* New York: Basic Books.

BROOKS, PETER. 1993. *Body Work: Objects of Desire in Modern Narrative.* Cambridge, Mass.: Harvard University Press.

COOK, ALBERT. 1968. *The Root of the Thing: A Study of Job and the Song of Songs.* Bloomington: Indiana University Press.

EXUM, J. CHERYL. 2005. *Song of Songs, A Commentary.* Old Testament Library. Louisville, Ky.: Westminster/John Knox.

FOX, MICHAEL V. 1985. *The Song of Songs and the Ancient Egyptian Love Songs.* Madison: University of Wisconsin Press.

LANDY, FRANCIS. 1983. *Paradoxes of Paradise: Identity and Difference in the Song of Songs.* Sheffield: Almond.

MUNRO, JILL M. 1995. *Spikenard and Saffron: A Study in the Poetic Language of the Song of Songs.* Sheffield: Sheffield Academic Press.

FURTHER READING

BLOCH, ARIEL, and CHANA, BLOCH. 1995. *The Song of Songs: A New Translation with an Introduction and Commentary.* Afterword by Robert Alter. New York: Random House.

ERNST, JUDITH. 2003. *Song of Songs: Erotic Love Poetry,* adapted and illus. Judith Ernst. Grand Rapids: Eerdmans.

FALK, MARCIA. 1990. *The Song of Songs: A New Translation and Interpretation,* illus. Barry Moser. San Francisco: HarperSanFrancisco.

LANDY, FRANCIS. 1987. 'The Song of Songs', in Robert Alter and Frank Kermode (eds.), *The Literary Guide to the Bible.* Cambridge, Mass.: Belknap, 305–19.

CHAPTER 17

PROVERBS, ECCLESIASTES, JOB

KIRSTEN NIELSEN

PROVERBS, Ecclesiastes, and Job form the main part of the wisdom literature of the Old Testament. They share an interest in everyday life and the desire to create order out of human experiences, but they offer no single theology that can be described as 'wisdom' theology—only a common concern for the conditions of human life and for human experience as the basis for theology. Their conceptual origin is of a world created and therefore ordered, but they disagree on whether man is capable of perceiving that order. They agree that the path to wisdom is through experience, but whether an underlying order can be construed from human concrete experiences is debatable.

In Prov. 3: 13 the man who finds wisdom is considered blessed. Moreover, 'By wisdom the Lord laid the earth's foundations, by understanding he set the heavens in place; by his knowledge the deeps were divided, and the clouds let drop the dew' (Prov. 3: 19–20). It is characteristic of Proverbs that humans are seen as capable of insight into the creation and of acting in accordance with it.

This is otherwise in Ecclesiastes, where wisdom fails to lead to blessing. On the contrary: 'Then I applied myself to the understanding of wisdom, and also of madness and folly, but I learned that this, too, is a chasing after the wind. For with much wisdom comes much sorrow; the more knowledge, the more grief' (Eccles. 1: 17–18). Thus the problem in Ecclesiastes is that although God 'has made everything beautiful in its time,' humanity cannot fathom what God does. (Eccles. 3: 10–11) How then should life be lived? The Preacher's answer is clear. We must receive what God gives in the way of good gifts and enjoy them as long as they last: 'It is good and proper for a man to eat and drink, and to find satisfaction in his toilsome labour under the sun during the few days of life God has given him—for this is his lot' (Eccles. 5: 18).

In the book of Job God presents himself in chs. 38–41 as the Creator who has ordered everything according to his will. But human insight into this is dubious. With the words, 'Where were you when I laid the earth's foundation? Tell me, if you understand...' God provokes Job, and Job bows his head (Job 38: 4). However, the question here is whether Job's self-subjection to the mighty God implies that he has actually changed his attitude to his own life. His friends claimed that his misfortunes were God's justified punishment for his sins, whereas Job continued to maintain his innocence. And according to God, Job's friends are not speaking the truth, only Job is. (Job 42: 7). The book of Job gives no immediate solution to Job's problem, which is the disparity between experience and transmitted teaching. In his own experience he has felt how the good do not always thrive and the wicked do not always suffer. God agrees with Job that he is pious and righteous and he therefore ultimately blesses him with more than he had enjoyed before, but it hardly solves Job's problem that he finally receives more riches and a new family of children.

The three wisdom books are concerned with the human condition; they are not accounts of historical persons but tales of everyman. Though they were generated by a particular culture at a particular point in history, they do not refer to historical events or persons and are therefore not linked to the story of the salvation of Israel. The attribution of Ecclesiastes to the wise King Solomon must not be understood as a historical definition but as a claim for the book's depth of insight. Nor should the description of Job as a rich man from the land of Uz be read geographically but rather as what might best be described as literary information.

This wisdom literature of the Old Testament permeates English literature from the earliest texts of Old English. Perhaps the greatest of wisdom writers in the tradition is Geoffrey Chaucer, whose *Canterbury Tales* (*c*.1387), and above all the 'Tale of Melibee', draw heavily upon the biblical literature of wisdom. This tradition of wisdom continues through the poetry of Spenser and Milton, and although it wanes during the classical period of the eighteenth century and in Romanticism (apart from William Blake's fascination with the character of Job), it resurfaces in the nineteenth century, above all in Herman Melville, and then, as we shall see, in the literature of the twentieth century.

READING STRATEGIES: IMAGERY AND INTERTEXTUALITY

The wisdom books are part of Israel's national literature and must be read as such. This idea is not new: reading the Bible as literature has long been a recognized approach (cf. Ch. 12 above, by Peter Hawkins). But a literary reading is not an isolated method. Rather we should speak of various reading strategies that can be selected to analyse and interpret a biblical text. The two specific strategies chosen here focus upon imagery analysis and intertextual reading.

Imagery

Most wisdom literature takes the form of poetry, and therefore one of its most important characteristics is its imagery. With the aid of metaphors, similes, parables, and allegories, readers are invited into an active interpretation of the given propositions in order to see the world in a new way. The abundance of images contain an immense potential of significance and meaning, whereby different parts can be activated in different situations. The openness of the text therefore adds to its relevance in new situations where it is open for reinterpretation.

The word 'imagery' is used specifically of pictorial language, be it metaphor, simile, parable, or allegory. Common to these forms is that they simultaneously denote something valid and something invalid. When a king is compared with a lion, the reference is not to the number of paws or colour of fur but rather to certain skills and behavioural patterns of lions, as in the proverb: 'A king's wrath is like the roar of a lion; he who angers him forfeits his life' (Prov. 20: 2). In brief, while all the potential meanings of a statement are relevant literally (*conjunctive use*) only a few are relevant when the statement is understood metaphorically (*disjunctive use*) (Nielsen 1989: 30–1). A characterization of Old Testament imagery (ibid. 65–6) may be summarized in these four points:

1. Imagery acts in a specific context by an interaction between two different statements.
2. Information can be derived from imagery in the form of new proposals for understanding reality (*informative function*).
3. The object of imagery is to involve the audience in such a way that by entering into the interpretation they take it over as their own perception of reality (*performative function*).
4. Imagery can be reused in another context, with the possibility of new interpretation and new evaluation of the informative and performative function respectively.

It is clear from this that the reader plays an especially active role in the interpretation of the image-laden texts, though it must be pointed out that the various forms of context in which the images appear serve to limit the possibilities for interpretation. Thus not only the literary context in which the image appears but also the conventions of the particular culture play a significant role; in its broadest sense the context might be said to act as linesman to the language play of the imagery.

Intertextuality

An intertextual reading has the further advantage over reading the individual text as an isolated work of art in that potential meanings become available in the wisdom texts that are not clear from the isolated reading. The intertextual dialogue allows for other aspects, whether these are intended by the 'writer' or result from the introduction of new intertexts in the literature of a later age.

The term *intertextuality* is used here in the broad sense of the word to signify that no text comes into existence or can be read as an isolated unit; each text is part of a network. In theory this network is limitless across literature, but in practice a meaningful interpretation can only be undertaken within certain parameters. My own studies suggest a useful distinction between three types of intertextual reading:

1. the intertextuality that the 'author' designates through various markers;
2. whatever intertextual links the editorship can create;
3. what later tradition or the individual includes by way of intertexts.

By 'author' I mean not the historical person who may have written the text in question but the authorial voice that expresses itself in the text and which through various markers points to the relevant intertexts. When, for example, Ruth is repeatedly referred to as 'the Moabite woman', i.e. belonging to the hated Moabites, the marker requests the reader to recall the Moabite traditions in order to understand this particular narrative of a female progenitor which the book of Ruth constitutes. The word 'marker' is used here in the same way as in Tryggve Mettinger's (1993) article on intertextuality in Job. Mettinger underlines that markers have 'a double character', and quoting the literary critic Michael Riffaterre, he provides the following definition of their function: 'They are both the problem, when seen from the text, and the solution to that problem when their other, intertextual, side is revealed' (ibid. 264). Occasionally the intertextual relation can be compared to the phenomenon that Harold Bloom (1973: 5) has drawn attention to in the context of poetry: 'My concern is only with strong poets, major figures with the persistence to wrestle with their strong precursors even to the death.' This is a view that proves fruitful in, for example, an analysis of the book of Job and its 'battle' with the Esau-Jacob traditions.

Proverbs as Literature

The book of Proverbs (see Bullock 1995: 19–33) belongs in the category of wisdom literature, which has often led scholars to study the proverbs solely as the teaching of how life is ordered. According to the book life is marked by a moral righteousness which implies that the good thrive and the evil suffer. This righteousness is not hidden from man but can be learned, and man can thus work towards leading a good life, for God himself is the guarantor that everything is as it should be, and that he will therefore act from within this righteousness.

This brief summary requires further elaboration which can draw on the imagery used about wisdom's attraction as its starting-point. A recurrent term in the first chapters of Proverbs is 'wisdom', ḥokmah, which is feminine gender in Hebrew. In ch. 8 wisdom is portrayed as a woman who invites young men to come to her instead of letting themselves be lured by the woman 'dressed like a prostitute' whom they have been told to shun in ch. 7, for 'her house is a highway to the grave, leading down to the chambers of death' (Prov. 7: 27). Wisdom is at once identified as the prostitute's opposite, even though her audience are the same young men and her invitation to approach her, '... on the heights along the way, where the paths meet ... beside the gates...' (Prov. 8: 2–3) is reminiscent of the prostitute's behaviour.

The image of the inviting woman who calls out to inexperienced men and promises 'to bestow wealth on those who love me' (Prov. 8: 21) speaks volumes— much more than the bald statement simply that wisdom is good. For through the image the readers are revealed as those who are to be lured, and thus do not themselves seek wisdom.

Wisdom herself says that she was the first of God's creations. She has existed 'from eternity', she was there before the oceans and the mountains came into being, before he set the heavens in place, 'when he gave the sea its boundary so the waters would not overstep his command, and when he marked out the foundations of the earth. Then I was the craftsman at his side. I was filled with delight day after day, rejoicing always in his presence, rejoicing in his whole world and delighting in mankind' (Prov. 8: 29–31). The figure of Dame Wisdom (or in Chaucer Dame Prudence), appears regularly in medieval English literature, though in the morality play of *Wisdom* (c.1460) she appears dressed as Christ the King in contest with Lucifer as counsellors of Anima (Soul). In the twentieth century, Leonard Cohen's *Book of Mercy* reintroduces Dame Wisdom as 'Our Lady of the Torah'.

Behind the ancient image of wisdom as a woman lies a possible further factor. In his book on wisdom and Proverbs the German scholar Bernhard Lang (1986) argues that Prov. 1–9 should be ascribed to a society where not only Yahweh was worshipped but also other gods such as Baal, El, Shemesh, and the feminine Astarte. Lang's thesis is that Wisdom is still one of the gods worshipped in ancient Israel. In later Judaism and Christianity she lost her divine status, for there was no room for other gods; the breakthrough of monotheism demanded a new interpretation of wisdom. She became more a poetical figure, a literary personification. Lang thus shows how Wisdom is an example of a divinity being redefined to secure monotheism. At the same time, she enters into the traditions of literature well prepared for her role.

Lang's interest is in the history of religion, while mine is in the imagery that formulates the link between the divine world and wisdom. In choosing his imagery to depict wisdom, the 'author' of Proverbs successfully demarcates the special relation between not only humankind and wisdom but also God and wisdom. Wisdom is not merely the possession of available knowledge, she is a dialogue partner who was there from the beginning and still woos men from every corner of the earth. Lang's emphasis on the ancient goddess behind the image can therefore help more recent literature in the English tradition to take the imagery seriously and interpret Wisdom as an actress in a man's world. At the same time a further advantage of reading the image of wisdom in this way is that the proverbs themselves are not removed from their theological context in the Old Testament, as some scholars prefer. Taken *out* of context most proverbs can be interpreted solely as everyday experiences of how life normally functions. For instance, the proverb, 'A hot-tempered man stirs up dissension, but a patient man calms a quarrel' (Prov. 15: 18), does not in itself give rise to the inclusion of a divine guarantor within its parameters. But in its context it forms part of the portrayal of the elements on which Wisdom built the world from the beginning.

Proverbs is constructed in such a way that chs. 1–9 serve as a theological intro-duction to the rest of the book, which primarily has the character of an anthology of individual proverbs (but see, however, ch. 31, which is a wisdom poem). Here we find proverbs that in isolation express general common sense and everyday experience.

> Go to the ant, you sluggard;
> consider its ways and be wise!
> It has no commander,
> no overseer or ruler,
> yet it stores its provisions in summer
> and gathers its food at harvest.
> How long will you lie there, you sluggard?
> When will you get up from your sleep?
> A little sleep, a little slumber,
> a little folding of the hands to rest—
> and poverty will come on you like a bandit
> and scarcity like an armed man.
>
> (Prov. 6: 6–11)

A proverb of this type builds on experience: sloth does not bring any reward. Similarly: 'Do not love sleep or you will grow poor; stay awake and you will have food to spare' (Prov. 20: 13). If readers of the biblical literature lack the theological context, such a proverb speaks only of what man himself has seen, but if they see it in continuation of the first chapter, they can better understand who has created such a righteousness in life, and who is therefore the guarantor that virtuous effort is rewarded. Whether such a context is always evident in the later literary tradition is another matter.

Seen as mini-narratives the many individual proverbs allow readers to work actively on the interpretation and to become part of the narrative themselves. The proverb about the king's anger and the lion's roar (Prov. 20: 2) draws on a number of scriptural intertexts that employ the image of a lion attacking a herd and dragging its victim away, for example Hosea 5: 14, to develop a narrative on the need for caution when confronting one who is stronger. Read in the light of the subsequent proverb, which considers it honourable to withdraw from conflict since it is only fools who pick quarrels, a further nuance is added: a man of honour knows his limits.

The proverb thus enters into critical dialogue with other texts where honour is otherwise linked to battle and victory. Indeed, our interpretation of the wisdom tradition in the Bible may be profoundly influenced by later literary texts.

Where a form-critical analysis of the individual proverbs often limits their understanding and perhaps categorizes them by form and content only, a reading that includes both imagery and intertextuality opens up their potential meanings and thus ensures their continued relevance. For an intertext is not just a text that deepens the meaning, it can act as a critical challenge. Thus Ecclesiastes contains a number of examples which show that the expected links in life do not in fact materialize, for example between effort and reward:

> All man's efforts are for his mouth,
> yet his appetite is never satisfied.
>
> (Eccles. 6: 7)

Job speaks correspondingly of an experience-based criticism of the wisdom of the ancients and thus against the tradition of proverbs linking guilt to fate. When his friend Eliphaz argues that, 'As I have observed, those who plough evil and those who sow trouble reap it' (Job 4: 8), the argument is taken from the world of proverbs (cf. Prov. 22: 8) and reflects a confidence that there is a precise connection in life between the two. The book of Job can also therefore be incorporated as a critical intertext to the classical wisdom of the book of Proverbs. For Job's experience and God's assessment of him tell a different story. Job has *not* done wrong: 'he is blameless and upright, a man who fears God and shuns evil' (Job 1: 8, see also 42: 7), and yet he loses everything he owns. In his *Illustrations of the Book of Job* (1825), the poet Blake portrays Job as a kind of Romantic hero, stressing the justice of his questioning of God. The Romantic interest in Job's rebellion continues into the nineteenth century, Tennyson even learning Hebrew in order to translate the book—a project he never achieved.

Within the genre of wisdom, literary experience plays a decisive role. But precisely for that reason, in the very approach to wisdom lies a critical potential. For when the experience of the connection between guilt and fate is turned into a dogma that embraces everyone for all time, the dogma will inevitably be challenged by other experiences suggesting that life is not so simple. A good example of this is the Preacher's experiences.

ECCLESIASTES AS LITERATURE

Ecclesiastes is a highly complex text. Scholars have made various attempts over the years to explain the frequent occurrence of conflicting statements, particularly by employing literary criticism to distinguish between various sources or by emphasizing the nature of the work as a collection of maxims.[1] A similar method is adopted by Robert Gordis (1955), whose thesis is that the work contains a long series of quotations which are used either to support the Preacher's own views or as contrasts to these. The problem is, how do we determine whether these are indeed quotations? In the history of research one solution has been to turn the conflicting views into a basic structure for the work, reflecting the tension between traditional wisdom and the Preacher's view. But why do the two views appear side by side, if the Preacher only shares one of them?

A literary reading applying the two strategies outlined above sees the unity in the book as its point of origin, which is also in line with recent scholarship on the subject (Fox 1989). It is therefore judicious to take the opening words of the book as its point of departure: ' "Meaningless! Meaningless!" says the Preacher, "Utterly meaningless! Everything is meaningless" ' (Eccles. 1: 2). This opening has often led scholars immediately (and overhastily) to brand the Preacher a pessimist, who contradicts everything that the optimistic proverbs express. Literature has almost exclusively focused on the pessimism of Ecclesiastes, perhaps the most notable example being ch. 96 of Melville's *Moby Dick* (1851), which reads, 'The truest of all men was the Man of Sorrows, and the truest of all books is Solomon's, and Ecclesiastes is the fine tempered steel of woe. "All is vanity." ALL. This wilful world has not got hold of unchristian Solomon's wisdom yet.' In *Man and Superman* (1903), George Bernard Shaw refers to the 'profound truth of the saying of my friend Koheleth, that there is nothing new under the sun, *Vanitas vanitatum*.'

The Hebrew word *hebel*, which is often rendered as 'meaninglessness' or 'emptiness' appears about seventy times in the Old Testament, roughly half of them being in Ecclesiastes, making it a clear leitmotif in the book. It is difficult to translate *hebel* with a single word. The original meaning is probably 'a gust of wind' (see Isa. 57: 13), but by extension it can be used of what is fleeting, hard to grasp, transient, worthless, absurd, what is vanity or even emptiness. Applying the image of a gust of wind, *hebel* to the whole of Ecclesiastes as a metaphor serves to summarize the main ideas in the book.

In its totality the structure of Ecclesiastes supports this interpretation. In both the first and the last chapters we find the distinctive '*Hebel*...Everything is *hebel*' (Eccles. 1: 2, 12: 8). But what is the subject that can be summarized in the image of the gust of wind? The main thought in the book is that man does not control his own existence, just as he cannot control the wind. Wisdom, which according to Proverbs is a means by which to see through life and manage it, leads, according to Ecclesiastes, only to pain (Eccles. 1: 18). The wealth which should be a consequence of the wise man's conduct has come to the Preacher but has proved to have

---

[1] This treatment of Ecclesiastes builds on an unpublished Danish doctorate by Pastor Leise Christensen, 'Modsigelsens nødvendighed. Kontinuitet via ambiguitet i Ecclesiastes' (The Need for Contradiction. Continuity via Ambiguity in Ecclesiastes) Ph.D. in the Faculty of Theology, Aarhus University, October 2000.

no durability. Both the fool and the wise man must die and give up their riches. And this too is *hebel* (Eccles. 2). The fact that death is the conclusion to every human life forces the Preacher to maintain that man is therefore like the animals (Eccles. 3). Similarly, the repression of society, the prevalence of injustice, and human mutual envy lead the Preacher to think of a gust of wind (Eccles. 4). In chapter after chapter these motifs are varied, but heaviest of all to bear is the pain that man cannot see through life: 'I have seen the burden God has laid on men. He has made everything beautiful in its time. He has also set eternity in the hearts of men; yet they cannot fathom what God has done from beginning to end' (Eccles. 3: 10–11). (See further, Fox 1999: 192).

It is against this background that the conflicting statements about the enjoyment of life and the pleasure it gives make sense, not as negations of a basically pessimistic attitude to life but as a necessary supplement. For the Preacher is an observer who collects his experiences, and for that very reason he must give up the attempt to create a synthesis, since his own experiences prove that just as evil happens, so does good—and both come from God (Eccles. 3: 12–13). He must therefore encourage his readers to enjoy the good things they are given and in the brief time they are allotted. Ecclesiastes must be read as a collection of observations that reflect the reality which is the human lot, and because life is like a gust of wind which comes and goes and which no one can grasp or control, so the Preacher can only advise his readers to be present in the moment.

The Preacher has experienced not only injustice and death but also the following: 'Then I realized [saw] that it is good and proper for a man to eat and drink, and to find satisfaction in his toilsome labour under the sun during the few days of life God has given him—for this is his lot. Moreover, when God gives any man wealth and possessions, and enables him to enjoy them, to accept his lot and be happy in his work—this is a gift of God' (Eccles. 5: 17–18). Here the Preacher is not creating a new system but guiding his readers to a life-wisdom that rests on life-experience, where an active God grants both fortune and misfortune. These are the conditions 'under the sun' where man lives.

Taking our starting-point in the central metaphor enables us to make sense of the apparently contradictory statements in Ecclesiastes. If, moreover, we employ an intertextual approach, we could say that Ecclesiastes is very much in dialogue with the view of wisdom found in Proverbs. If the Preacher did not have positive wisdom as part of his spiritual baggage, the clash between experience and the transmitted tradition would not have been so painful. And without a teaching that urged the link between guilt and fate, the 'gust of wind' would not have been so fitting a metaphor for Ecclesiastes. English literature, however, has on the whole resolutely emphasized the negative aspect of Ecclesiastes. Thackeray's *Vanity Fair* (1848) concludes its play with the question, 'Ah! *Vanitas Vanitatum!* Which of us is happy in this world?' Yet it may be said that G. K. Chesterton expresses something of the more ancient balance, though in a very different context, in his *George Bernard Shaw*: 'That all is vanity, that life is dust and love is ashes, these are frivolities, these are jokes that a Catholic can afford to utter.'

JOB AS LITERATURE

The Book of Job is an account of how through no fault of his own a pious man is struck by misfortune because Satan manages to convince God that it is worth testing Job's godliness. The book consists partly of a framework narrative depicting the test and the concluding compensation, partly of a number of dialogues between Job and his friends in which Job maintains his innocence and accuses God of treating him unjustly. His friends on the other hand attempt to convince Job that God has struck him down justly. In the closing chapters of the dialogue God finally takes the floor, with the result that Job bows down to him and withdraws his charges. English literature has tended to focus upon two specific issues. The first is that of the righteous man unjustly treated by God—the question of theodicy, or even more, the incoherence of the book. Job's 'problem', which is the question of how a benevolent Creator can permit unspeakable sufferings in the world, is the centre of Muriel Spark's brilliant novel *The Only Problem* (1984). As the central character in Muriel Spark's novel, Harvey Gotham, says, 'The *Book of Job* will never come clear. It doesn't matter; it's a poem.' On the whole, literature has tended not to be persuaded by God's final speeches. Following Blake, I. A. Richards's *Job's Comfortings* (1970) rejects the final reconciliation of God and Job.

The second issue in literature is the theme of Job's comforters, who have become a byword for bad advice, from Burton's 'Schismaticks' and 'Hereticks' in *The Anatomy of Melancholy* (1621), to Byron's 'bad pilots when the weather is rough' in *Don Juan* (1819–24), while Spark's Harvey Gotham laments 'the futility of friendship in times of trouble'.

The book is difficult to place under a single formula. One approach has been to distinguish between the pious Job of the narrative framework, who accepts both good and bad from God's hand without a murmur, and the Job of the dialogues who rebels against God. Scholars have therefore often attempted through source-criticism or tradition-criticism to prove that there are two distinctive Job figures and thus two separate sources for the book of Job (see Baker 1978). However, these attempts do not change the fact that if one reads the book as a literary unity, its purpose is precisely the *juxtaposition* of the narrative framework, Job 1–2 plus 42: 7–17 with the dialogues, 3: 1–42: 6, to create a major drama. In the process a question mark is placed on the friends' theology, with its clear perception of the link between guilt and fate as well as on the narrative framework's happy ending. Within one and the same drama we are presented with differing views of how the created world is ordered, and how God intervenes in the world.

In the introduction, chs. 1–2, God and Satan play the determining roles, disagreeing on the sincerity of Job's piety but agreeing to let it be tested. Job's friends, who come to comfort him, also by and large agree with one another. Though they employ various explanatory models, they share the common theme that suffering should be regarded as meaningful, either because there is a reason for it, or because it has a purpose. In this context Elihu, who follows up after Job's concluding speech, can also be seen as part of this group of friends in his emphasis on God's justice in the case of Job. After Elihu, God himself makes a magniloquent speech about the world and the order with which it is created. But on the subject of Job's suffering he is silent. Here readers must enter the drama themselves and decide whether behind God's words on the passage of nature lies a commentary on Job's fate—though this is doubtful once they have read Job 28, a long poem on the secrecy of wisdom. Only God knows the path to wisdom, it says; and man's task is 'The fear of the Lord—that is wisdom, and to shun evil is understanding' (Job 28: 28). How then does the framework narrative with God's rejection of his friends in favour of Job relate to the other voices in the drama? How open is the Book of Job to interpretation? The book's imagery and its intertextual links provide an approach.[2]

'In the land of Uz there lived a man whose name was Job' (Job 1: 1). To understand the significance of these two facts readers need to know the language and culture in which the book was written. Scholars have attempted to locate Uz and point to two possibilities: Aram or Edom. If we employ the historical-critical approach in which texts are located in relation to actual history and geography we must therefore note that Job is not an Israelite but comes from one of the neighbouring countries. On the other hand, if we assume that the Old Testament is primarily literature, then perhaps Uz serves as a marker pointing to the intertextuality within which the book should be read. Of the two, Edom seems the more likely, being the territory of Esau, the progenitor of the Edomites, just as Jacob was the progenitor of the twelve tribes of Israel. This is in line with the fact that the entire introduction to Job is kept in a popular narrative style. A comparison with narratives in any other OT books leads naturally to those of the three patriarchs, Abraham, Isaac, and Jacob, and in particular to Isaac and his two sons, Esau and Jacob.

In the Israelite consciousness the names 'Esau' and 'Jacob' denote jealousy between brothers and a battle for paternal blessing. 'There was a man who had two sons...' is how many stories begin, to which the readers' response is, 'Which one did he love most?' and 'How did the brothers react when they discovered that they were rivals?' Many a family drama has revolved around being the eldest or the preferred youngest; the parable of the Lost Son and the tragedy of King Lear spring immediately to mind. The father-figure in Job is not his earthly but his heavenly father. In other words God is depicted in the image of a patriarch, before whom his sons assemble, including one who bears the name of Satan, meaning 'the adversary'. In the well-known conversation that follows God reminds Satan of Job: 'Have you considered my servant Job? There is no one on earth like him; he is blameless and upright, a man who fears God and shuns evil' (Job 1: 8). Like any other proud father God singles out his favourite child, and like so many other elder brothers who feel sidelined by this endless praise of the favourite son Satan reacts with jealousy and the desire to denigrate Job's motives by accusing him of being a timeserver. He predicts that if God withdraws his blessing, Job will show his true colours and curse God to his face. When God agrees,

---

[2] The following presentation builds on Kirsten Nielsen 1998.

Job is tested by Satan. Job survives the ordeal and is rewarded, but there is no further mention of Satan, at least not under that name!

Scholars have normally interpreted the opening scene in heaven as God summoning his council to court like an earthly king, one of his councillors being Satan whose task is to spy on God's subjects and report back on them in heaven. But this reading fails to explain why God gives way to such a loose suspicion as Satan presents. Nor does it make sense of what Satan imagines he is achieving by speaking ill of the king's favourite. And readers must also wonder why Satan is not punished in the end. If, on the other hand, the scene is understood not as an official gathering of king and council but as a description of the relationship between a father and his two sons, then it is not unreasonable for one of the sons to succumb to jealousy of his brother, who may be absent but who is nevertheless in spiritual terms always present. Why not discredit and then usurp him? Indeed, the close relationship to his father makes this 'elder son' the obvious candidate to be his father's favourite. Moreover, the father's yielding to the jealous Satan is better understood if Satan is regarded as one of his sons and if the suspicion that is sown is that Job is a deceiver, whose loyalty and love are pure calculation. Lastly, it makes more sense for a father to refrain from chastising his jealous son than to withhold punishment from a councillor who has offended the king's faithful servant.

When viewed as a new version of the drama between Esau and Jacob, the book of Job is revealed as a treatment of a blessing and a curse. Similarly both narratives deal with how the blessing is assured through a struggle with God himself: 'I will not let you go unless you bless me,' shouts the patriarch Jacob in his struggle with the Stranger. And when God indeed blesses him, he exclaims, 'I saw God face to face, and yet my life was spared.' Jacob called the place Penuel, which in Hebrew means 'God's face' (Gen. 32: 26–31).

Correspondingly, the entire dialogue section in Job can be read as one long struggle with God, a struggle to get so close that they can actually meet in a legal action. A close reading of Job shows that the word for face, *pānīm*, is a key concept in the dialogue. What Job is demanding is a face-to-face meeting with God; and indeed they do finally meet. God answers Job out of the storm and Job submits with the words: 'My ears had heard of you but now my eyes have seen you. Therefore I despise myself and repent in dust and ashes' (Job 42: 5–6). Job has his wish to see God fulfilled.

God's speeches are often criticized for not addressing Job's problem. But if we bear in mind their dramatic function together with our surprise that Satan goes unpunished, then part of the explanation must be as follows. The two monsters, Behemoth and Leviathan, whom God depicts with such pride, are known in a Near East tradition as beasts of chaos, which must be overcome before the creation can take place. In Job 40–1 they are turned respectively into God's supreme work (Job 40: 19) and a 'king over all that are proud' (Job 41: 34). But as God's creatures they are also limited by God's power, as is Satan when he sets out to test Job (Job 1: 12; 2: 6). The two beasts of chaos thus play the same role in the speeches as Satan does in the introduction. Just as God, in the image of a father, can be tempted by one son to test the other but must set limits on the test, so does God have a similar relationship to the huge beasts of chaos. He has created them and set limits on their destruction, but he will not annihilate them. They are his, and therefore surrounded by his care. This is true of the beasts of chaos as well as the Satan who goes unpunished in Job. In spite of everything he is his father's son.

Further evidence of the father metaphor and the model of a father and his two sons is to be found in the name of 'Job', which is not a coincidence but an apposite marker. In a number of articles the American W. F. Albright, one of the pioneers of Old Testament archaeology, has shown that Job is a common name in the Near East (Albright 1943: 7–17; 1954: 222–33). It appears in the form *a-ya-ab* partly in a list of Egyptian slave names from the eighteenth century BCE, partly in one of the Amarna letters from around 1300 BCE. The Hebrew name Job is a contracted form meaning, 'Where is father?' So also through the choice of name readers are given a clue as to the image that forms the basis of the book of Job: that of a father surrounded by his sons.

In English literature, Job is deeply embedded in intertextual allusions. Milton's *Paradise Regained* (1671) draws heavily upon Job, even to its structure, while the same poet's *Samson Agonistes*, published simultaneously with *Paradise Regained*, closely relates Samson with the Job story. In prison in Gaza, the blind Samson is visited by friends (the Chorus) to comfort him (Lewalski 1966).

WISDOM AND THE IMAGES OF GOD

These examples of metaphorical and intertextual readings of the three Old Testament wisdom books as literature lead to the consequences that this approach has for understanding the conception of God in these texts. Wisdom literature deals with the ordering of existence and the conduct necessary to lead a good life. But as can be seen from Proverbs and Ecclesiastes, the problem is that when experience is the path to knowing God's will and purpose for the world, and since experiences differ so widely, any attempt to create a cohesive system must sooner or later fall apart. The reason why the many proverbs claiming that life is stamped with a particular order have nonetheless been preserved is presumably the simple fact that they are used when the situation applies, and not when experience dictates something else. The book of Proverbs is like a reservoir from which one can draw language for one's experience or for a necessary injunction. In addition, the image of wisdom as a woman who actively offers herself to readers also allows for a relation to her to be personal rather than being to a closed system. Another way to respond is to follow the Preacher in giving up on the search for a system and rejoicing instead over the good days that do come one's way. Alternatively, like Job's friends, one can steadfastly insist that there is a discernible purpose in what happens to Job, whether or not he will admit it. The wisdom poem in Job 28 points out human limitations and therefore recommends piety as the path to the good life. And then there is the 'narrator' in Job, who allows these various voices to state their case with an explanation for Job's fate. These voices never in the end become one, but there is a narrative voice inviting readers to imagine life as a play about an eternal triangle between a father and his two sons.

On the basis of his cultural traditions and theological models the author of Job has created a drama that allows the reader the opportunity to assume different positions along the path to the happy ending. Like all good literature the drama is also an exercise in living in this world. For the author's contemporaries the figure of Job and the acceptance of his rebellion against God were equally important opportunities as Job's subjection and God's re-establishment of his wealth. Over the years many critics have complained about the banality of the book's happy ending and have believed that the real Job is the one who meets God himself and is satisfied with that. But the Book of Job is more than just dialogues. Its strength lies in the fact that it does not settle for describing a man who has to subject himself to God when he meets him, but also depicts a God who in his meeting with a man must also yield—and enable Job to live his life again. This God makes reparation. With such an image of God, who is neither an automaton merely guaranteeing that everything happens according to a fixed order, nor an unpredictable tyrant following his own whims without regard for human life, the author has found a middle way between the two dangers that threaten the idea of wisdom. In the former lies the danger of creating a mechanistic universe, in which both God and man are confined by infrangible legalities; in the latter is the danger that the world becomes a place where only chance rules. The book of Job makes a substantial contribution to avoiding these pitfalls, just as the goddess behind wisdom in Prov. 8 helps to maintain the personal will behind the world's order. And this is presumably the personal will to which the Preacher relates when in Eccles. 7: 14 he raises himself above the pain of man's lack of insight into God's plans and exclaims:

> When times are good, be happy;
> but when times are bad, consider:
> God has made the one
> as well as the other.
> Therefore, a man cannot discover
> anything about his future.

The selectivity as well as the persistence with which later literature has taken the tradition of the Old Testament to itself is indicative of the ultimate difference between literature and theology. Literature, finally, is not concerned to establish the nature of God standing behind the complexities of the world order. It is, however, deeply concerned with the humanistic issues of suffering, of wisdom, and of the tragedy of human experience. Perhaps, in the end, Spark's fictional scholar of the book of Job, Harvey Gotham, himself a modern 'Job' figure, was right when he asserted: 'The *Book of Job* will never come clear. It doesn't matter; it's a poem'. The poet is not a theologian—though in the case of Job itself, perhaps its theological author is one of the world's great poets.

WORKS CITED

ALBRIGHT, W. F. 1943. 'Two Little Understood Amarna Letters from the Middle Jordan Valley'. *Bulletin of the American School of Oriental Research* 89: 7–17.

—— 1954. 'North-West Semitic Names in a List of Egyptian Slaves from the Eighteenth Century BC'. *Journal of the American Oriental Society* 74: 222–33.

BAKER, J. A. 1978. *The Book of Job: Unity and Meaning*. Sheffield: JSOT.

BLOOM, HAROLD. 1973. *The Anxiety of Influence: A Theory of Poetry*. Oxford: Oxford University Press.

BULLOCK, C. HASSELL. 1995. 'The Book of Proverbs', in Roy B. Zuck (ed.), *Learning from the Sages: Selected Studies on the Book of Proverbs*. Grand Rapids: Baker Books.

FOX, MICHAEL, V. 1989. *Qohelet and his Contradictions*. Sheffield: Almond.

—— 1999. *A Time to Tear Down & a Time to Build Up*. Grand Rapids: Eerdmans.

GORDIS, ROBERT. 1955. *Kohelet—the Man and his World*. 2nd edn. New York: Schocken.

LANG, BERNARD. 1986. *Wisdom and the Book of Proverbs: A Hebrew Goddess Redefined*. New York: Pilgrim.

LEWALSKI, BARBARA. 1966. *Milton's Brief Epic: The Genre, Meaning and Art of 'Paradise Regained'*. Providence, RI: Brown University Press.

METTINGER, TRYGGVE, N. D. 1993. 'Intertextuality: Allusion and Vertical Context Systems in Some Job Passages', in Heather A. McKay and David J. A. Clines (eds.), *Of Prophets' Visions and the Wisdom of Sages: Essays in Honour of R. Norman Whybray*. Sheffield: Sheffield Academic Press.

NIELSEN, KIRSTEN. 1989. *There is Hope for a Tree: The Tree as Metaphor in Isaiah*. Sheffield: JSOT.

—— 1998. *Satan—the Prodigal Son? A Family Problem in the Bible*. The Biblical Seminar 50. Sheffield: Sheffield Academic Press.

FURTHER READING

FARMER, KATHLEEN S. 1998. 'The Wisdom Books. Job, Proverbs, Ecclesiastes', in Steven L. Mackenzie and M. Patrick Graham (eds.), *The Hebrew Bible Today: An Introduction to Critical Issues*. Louisville, Ky.: Westminster/John Knox.

GREENBERG, MOSHE. 1987. 'Job', in Robert Alter and Frank Kermode (eds.), *The Literary Guide to the Bible*. London: Collins.

WILLIAMS, JAMES G. 1987. 'Proverbs and Ecclesiastes', in Robert Alter and Frank Kermode (eds.), *The Literary Guide to the Bible*. London: Collins.

CHAPTER 18

PROPHETIC LITERATURE

YVONNE SHERWOOD

THE Prophets, as Luther put it, 'have a queer way of talking'. He means 'queer' in the old-fashioned sense and is not talking about sudden gender shifts in prophetic imagery (see e.g. Micah 4: 6–13 and Isaiah 42: 14–16 and discussions by Runions 2003 and Stone 2001). This 'queer' way of talking has tended to keep prophetic texts on the sidelines of recent interdisciplinary conferences on the Bible as Literature. The Bible has tended to field the narrative books, such as Samuel or Genesis, as its main speakers, because they can be relied on to speak eloquently for the Bible as a consummate work of art. One of the reasons that the Prophets have been confined to the peripheries is because the new literary study in Biblical Studies has usually defined itself in opposition to historical criticism, with its emphasis on the text as an uneven composite of sources. The untidy Prophets have proved difficult to fit into models of literature defined on holistic, New-Critical lines. Herbert Marks (1989: 212) puts the problem well:

The received texts [of the Prophets] are cluttered and chaotic, and the signs of literary shaping have studiously to be recovered from under a welter of vestiges and interpolations. Even where deliberate patterns may be traced, they frequently overlie one another, like the superimposed figures of paleolithic cave art—the successive tradents, authors and editors having valued polyphony and suggestive destiny more than formal decorum. The presence of discordant features that resist assimilation may result in part from the peculiar status of the Israelite literature as evolving Scripture, a repository of collective traditions that could more safely be expanded or rearranged than cancelled. But regardless of its cause, it contributes largely to the aesthetic impact of the collections, which in the self-occlusion of their rough formal structures, as in the sheer abundance of their 'difficult ornaments' are the reflection or perhaps the model of Israel's image of the divine.

Compiled according to a system that seems perverse by Western (conceptual, philo-sophical) standards, oracles are often placed adjacent to one another on the basis of a shared pun or catchword. So, for example, Isa. 58: 13–14 (a thoroughly traditional interpretation of the sabbath) is appended to vv. 1–12 (a radical reinterpretation of fasting) because the two are joined by the keyword s.b.t. ('sabbath' or 'to rest'). By using sound, rather than sense, as a primary linking principle, prophetic literature insists on its distance from Western philosophy and theology—with its emphasis on consistency—and from related ideas of literature as a unifying craft. It also fore-grounds the permeable boundaries between the oral and the written. Continuity of sound leads to lurches of meaning, as the text turns on what Marks calls 'redactional hinges'. This sense of radical rotation is exacerbated by the process whereby subse-quent users update, supplement, and change (without erasing) the pre-existing text. As later Judaean readers add a caveat of Judaean restoration to the book of Amos's oracles of Israelite destruction, the book lurches, as one commentator puts it, from the 'blood and iron' of 1: 1–9: 10 to the 'lavender and roses' appendix of 9: 11–15.

'Inconsistency' is much more than a regrettable accident produced by the editorial process. Editorial hinges seem strangely of a piece with prophetic literature's already lurching world. The compilation of different divine words on the basis of a single catchword seems strangely *fitting* in the context of a prophetic style that revels in the hinged word, the word that carries its opposite around within itself. For example Isa. 5: 1–7, the so-called 'Song of the Vineyard', concludes: 'He expected justice (*mishpat*) but saw bloodshed (*mishpach*), righteousness (*tsedeqah*) but heard a cry (*tse-aqah*).' The poet relishes the ability of the word to slip into its opposite at the slightest nudge. The book of Hosea takes the name of the northern kingdom, 'Ephraim', then splits it into 'healing', 'adulterers', 'wild ass', 'fruit', 'flourishing', and 'bakers', which are all punning permutations of the core letters. It then expands (over-cooks?) the baker metaphor so that it rises to yeasty proportions: the people are hot with lust, hot with anger, they are made to a bad recipe like half-baked, half-done syncretistic cakes (Hos. 7: 4–8). As Harold Fisch (1990: 146) observes, the disintegration and backslid-ing of Ephraim is performed in the 'backsliding' and disintegration of the word/name. Similarly, the book of Amos splinters the name of the Yahwistic shrine 'Gilgal' into the fragmented, anagrammatic phrase *ha-gilgal galoh yigleh*: 'Gilgal shall surely go into exile' (Amos 5: 5–6). The splintering of the name of the shrine into the least expected meaning, 'exile', pushes sense beyond its accepted borders and sends 'true', or better, normative meaning into exile. This convulsion of sense seems strangely fitting in a book that dates itself in relation to the earthquake (Amos 1: 1), and then subjects tradition to distortions that would register on the Richter Scale.

Amos's aniconic vision of the basket of summer fruit (Amos 8: 1–3) performs prophetic literature's dispersal/exile of normative, standard meaning. The sumptu-ous image seen by the prophet—literally a 'basket of summer'—makes the divine gloss that follows counterintuitive to say the least: 'The end has come for my people Israel and I will no longer pass them by. And the singing women of the palace shall howl on that day. So many corpses, strewn everywhere. Hush.' Defying visual/conceptual logic, the 'vision' sets up an absolute disjunction between the image and the verbal non sequitur that follows. Visually, it is as perverse as, say, a still life with fruit with the caption 'Women Wailing and Corpses Lying Everywhere' or an apple overwritten with the words 'The End' in the style of René Magritte (for illustrations see Sherwood 2001). All that holds the 'vision' together is the purely sonic connection between 'end' (*qaits*) and 'summer' (*qayits*). The vision is in fact an 'auracle' held together by the fragile thread of pun. It is an a-visual vision, a non-revelatory revelation, in which an appeal to the eye is a decoy for the real (hidden) target, which is the ear. The punning deception is reminiscent of the scene in the *Epic of Gilgamesh* where Utnapishtim tells the citizens of Shuruppak who are about to be drowned in a flood, that they will be given 'morning cakes' (*kukku*), concealing the real meaning 'darkness' (*kukku*), and 'wheat' (*kibtu*), concealing the real meaning 'heaviness' (*kibittu*). But in an academic culture where metaphor is a sign of high literature and punning the lowest form of wit, biblical commentators have felt very uneasy about this over-reliance on the (mere) sound and shape of words. As if to insist that the Hebrew prophet is emphatically *not* using words as cavalierly as a Jacques Derrida, a Ferdinand de Saussure, or a James Joyce, critics have argued that what Amos saw was really a basket of *rotten* fruit, thus giving the vision meaningful conceptual, metaphorical ground to stand on (see Sherwood 2001). But this ameliorating translation misses the relish of the disjunction between fruit and corpses, feast and devastation, and the *enjoyment* of true (occulted) meaning lurking in the hidden corners of sound. The 'vision' of the basket of summer fruit can be read not as an anomaly but as an icon for the poetics of prophecy. For it creates interpretative panic by snatching away the solid (conceptual) ground beneath our feet and ruptures epistemological security in its blinding, blurring disregard for that most reliable of senses, sight.

The fragmentary nature of the prophetic books is reflected in their religious and cultural afterlives, where they tend to circulate as fragmentary phrases. That most famous of the Prophets, Isaiah, the so-called 'fifth gospel', is in fact known through small phrase-shards such as 'the prince of peace', 'swords into ploughshares', the 'man of sorrows', 'no peace for the wicked', and 'the wolf dwelling with the lamb' (see Sawyer 1996). It is no accident that the 'prophetic' book that has had the richest cultural afterlife is the book of Jonah—the book that has defected from the prophetic genre altogether and become narrative, literary criticism's favoured biblical genre (see Sherwood 2000a). This generic defection has, ironically, made Jonah the cultural darling of the 'Prophets'. Generally, the reception of prophecy and particularly the adoption of 'prophecy' as a literary figure tends to focus on prophecy as a generic category, so transcending awkward textual specifics. Prophecy has been understood as a high aesthetic category meaning variously, and by no means coherently, inspiration, dissidence, individualism, innovation, and supreme craft.

One of the many consequences of the complex cultural negotiations between the Bible and the Enlightenment was the deflection of worship into an aesthetic mode, so that the Bible became the 'best' book, in an aesthetic sense, as Matthew Arnold put it (Arnold 1960 (1861)). In this scheme, the Prophets (in a general, generic sense) took their place among the superlatives, in the heights. The group of artists that included

Paul Gaugin and Pierre Bonnard adopted one of the Hebrew terms for 'prophet' and called themselves the '*nabis*', showing how far the Prophets had become the kind of culture figures that writers and artists wanted to be seen hanging out with. A similar set of superlatives prevails in biblical criticism, where prophetic literature is commonly praised for its 'consummate artistry' and 'polished literary art' (e.g. Westermann 1985 (1969): p. xi).

As a generic literary category 'Prophets' have been understood as 'poets' according to two basic literary templates: Renaissance rhetoricians or Romantic poets. Biblical critics have frequently employed the idea of the prophet as rhetorician or consummate Renaissance gentleman-craftsman. The biblical prophets are regularly seen as experts in the Renaissance art of *prodessare* and *delectare*, seducing 'harde harted evill men' to the love of virtue 'as if they tooke a medicine of cherries' (Sidney 1987 (1595): 121). Writing in 1991, Yehoshua Gitay imagined Isaiah wielding a range of rhetorical instruments extracted from Renaissance works such as Peacham's *The Garden of Eloquence* (1593) and Scaliger's *Poetics libri septuem* (1561), including (among other things) *antanaclasis, attemperatio, perfectum confidentae, pleonasmus, synonymia, provocatio, copulatio*, and *tremenda majestas*. In 1984, Richard Clifford prefaced his study of Deutero-Isaiah with a citation from Shakespeare's Henry VIII:

> He was a scholar, a ripe and good one;
> Exceeding wise, fair-spoken and persuading:
> Lofty and sour to them that lov'd him not
> But to those men that saught him, sweet as summer.   (IV. ii. 50–4)

(Symptomatic of the preferred literary emphasis on the sweet is the title of Clifford's study: *Fair Spoken and Persuading* rather than 'Lofty and Sour'.) This idea of the prophet as graduate from Rhetoric School in fact has a long pedigree in English Literature. In 1656 Abraham Cowley spoke of a 'Prophet's College' moderately endowed with a 'Hall, Schools, Library and Synagogue' and 'Reverend Doctors teaching courses', while in 1713 Antony Collins, a friend of John Locke, described the Prophets as 'bred in Universities call'd Schools of the Prophets' (cited in Heschel 1975: 152–3).

The alternative model for prophetic poets could not be further away from the accomplished graduate of 'Prophet School' clutching his diploma. William Blake saw prophetic literature as the ancient template for the Romantic poem produced entirely '*without Labour or Study*' (Blake 1988 (1803): 71; my italics), so turning Prophets into something approaching the literary equivalent of the sacred icon as *acheiropoiete*, that not made by human hands. (Compare the Rhetorical emphasis on sublime handicraft, superlatively 'made'). But although the emphasis is on inspiration rather than craftsmanship, deviation rather than conformity, Romantic literary models still attempted to *unify* the disparate text through the figure of the inspired character-author at its heart. Working on the principle that, as Schiller put it, 'Like the Deity behind this universe [the poet/prophet] stands behind the work; he is himself the work, the work is himself', or that as Herder suggested, 'the book is the impression [*Ausdruck*] of a living human soul' (cited in Abrams 1971: 236–8), the

Romantic model facilitated the substitution of Jeremiah the book with Jeremiah the man. Prophecy was thus converted into narrative (as biography), or its poetic equivalent, lyric (poetry in the first person). Prophetic literature became potentially as consumable as the narrative 'prophet' Jonah, once it was consolidated around a central 'I'.

The rise of the Prophets in the later eighteenth century as a model of refined primitivism by way of cultural counterpoint to the Augustans is well documented in classic studies by Abrams (1971), Roston (1965), and Prickett (1989). Robert Lowth's *Lectures on the Sacred Poetry of the Hebrews* (1753) and his commentary on Isaiah (1778) were hugely influential in this regard. The latter was used by Coleridge in his 1795 lectures, and influenced Wordsworth's *Prelude* and Blake's *The Marriage of Heaven and Hell.* As European cultures increasingly defined themselves in relation to 'Hebrew' and 'Hellenistic' precursors, Romantic writers became increasingly eager to partake of the 'sublimity' that, as Coleridge maintained, was 'Hebrew by birth' (cited in Roston 1965: 125). Blake styled himself as a 'Voice crying in the Wilderness'; one 'dictated to' even 'against [his] will' by the 'Spirit of Prophecy'; 'Secretary to Authors in Eternity'; and recipient of a 'fourfold vision' (Blake 1988 (1803): 71). In his *Memorable Fancy* he imagined a meal with Isaiah and Ezekiel, during which a rather different Isaiah to the fair-spoken rhetorical craftsman leant over and confided in him: 'I saw no God, nor heard any, in a finite organical perception; but my senses discover'd the infinite in everything, and as I was then perswaded, & remain confirm'd, that the voice of honest indignation is the voice of God, I cared not for the consequences, but wrote.' In *The Prelude*, Wordsworth bound 'Prophets' to 'Poets' precisely around the experience of being bound by covenants made for them against their will (*Prelude* IV. 341–4; cf. e.g. Jer. 1: 47) and saw Prophets and (Romantic) Poets as 'connected in a mighty scheme of truth' (XII. 301–2). In a fusion of the biblical and the classical, Coleridge and Shelley saw the poet-prophet as an Aeolian harp, 'played on by one vast intellectual breeze' or as 'passive slave of some higher and more omnipotent Power' (Coleridge, 'The Eolian Harp'; Shelley, 'Essay on Christianity'). The oxymoronically alienated and inspired figure of the Hebrew prophet became a touchstone for the Romantic tradition of the *poète maudit*, more blessed and cursed than his fellow men—though it should be noted that the Romantics often enjoyed a far greater proportion of social blessing than the Prophets. It is hard to imagine Hosea or Ezekiel achieving the social approbation of a Wordsworth and having their chairs and walking sticks revered as sacred relics by their fans. Though subsiding in intensity, the Romantic pairing of prophecy and poetry lingers well into the nineteenth and twentieth centuries, for example in William Carlos Williams's dubious etymological reflections on the 'nabi' as 'one whose mind bubbles up and pours forth as a fountain, from inner divine spontaneities, revealing God' ('A Backward Glance O'er Travelled Roads', clearly inheriting the Wordsworthian idea of prophecy as the 'spontaneous overflow of powerful feelings' (Wordsworth 1965 (1800): 246)). Replaying a now well-worn cultural axiom, Jeanette Winterson juxtaposes the *prophet* as 'voice crying in the wilderness' to the *priest* with his set words, old words, and 'words of power' (Winterson 1985: 186).

The role of Romanticism as 'inspiration' for biblical scholarship on the Prophets is far less widely conceded than the influence of the Hebrew prophets on Romanticism (though for brief exceptions see Barton 1996 (1988): 156; Conrad 1991: 6–12; Blenkinsopp 1983: 29). However, the reciprocity of the relationship is unselfconsciously laid bare in late nineteenth- and early twentieth-century commentaries as they gush, for example, about how the 'ancient Orient' produced 'powerful personalities...grasped by the storms of the age, trembling with passion, who, touched by the divinity in secret hours attained the sublime courage to proclaim thoughts that they, they completely alone, perceived within themselves' (Gunkel 1987 (1923): 23), or depict Amos as a 'desert shepherd with the nomad's hatred of buildings' and a 'keeper of sheep, who stood in close touch with Nature and drew lessons from her which dwellers in cities seldom ever learn' (Smith 1912: 41; Canney 1919: 547). Reading the text as a cardiac print-out of the prophetic heart, scholars on the Prophets have tended to see the 'flickering unrest' of Hosea and Jeremiah and the 'majestically rolling sentences of Isaiah' as a map of the prophets' 'inner emotions' (Gunkel 1987 (1923): 47), and have claimed that, as a consequence of his disastrous marriage to a prostitute, Hosea the book/man 'breaks itself up into sobs' (Ewald 1875: 218). (At this point Romanticism turns mawkish and merely sentimental.) Unaware of the way in which metaphors of 'baking' come from the decomposition of 'Ephraim', the critical consensus until quite recently has been that Hosea was a baker, so demonstrating the translation of the prophetic text into biography or lyric. And in biblical criticism, as in 'culture' in a more diffuse sense, the influence of Romanticism can still be felt. A 1996 commentary describes Ezekiel as the poet of the 'vine, the shepherd and the cedar tree', rather than, say, bloody babies, dancing bones, and boiling pots (R. E. Clements 1996: 6; cf. Ezek. 16; 37; 24). James Mays informs us that Amos's 'rich and polished speech warn[s] that he is not to be taken for a simple and uncultured person' 'countryman from Tekoa that he was' (Mays 1969: 6). Like all true Romantic poets, Amos is really a sensitive, cultured soul who is really only visiting the country.

In literary and Christian theological terms, which are rarely entirely separate from one another, the Prophets in the general sense have become the strand of the Old Testament with which English-speaking (Christian and post-Christian) cultures have identified most closely. They have been defined by passages such as the showdown between prophet and priest in Amos 7: 10–16 (over-read as prophetic *opposition* to temple and cult) and by images of the new heart of flesh or circumcision of the heart (Jer. 4: 4; Ezek. 36: 26). And not without some justification, they have been credited with the invention of 'ethical monotheism'—which in Christian theological classifications is seen as the virile strand of Old Testament religion that survives the demise of weaker 'Law'. It seems that the rise of the figure of the prophet in English Literature is more than just a cultural accident, traceable back to historical idiosyncrasy and the singular influence of Lowth. Though the figure of the poet as a quasi-prophetic figure has a much earlier pedigree in English Literature (putting in an appearance in Milton's self-definition as God's 'secretary', or George Herbert's 'call' to poetry, for example), there are reasons why the figure of the prophet comes into his own as a cultural symbol at the end of the eighteenth century. For this emergent iconic literary/religious hero represents the Enlightenment individualism that is an outgrowth of a Protestant Reformation, as opposed to Judaism and, more to the point, Catholicism (the realm of ritual and cult). It is no accident that this volume includes a chapter on Prophetic Literature but not on 'Law and Priestly Literature', or that the chapter on the Pentateuch inevitably pays far more attention to the narrative passages, even though Pentateuch/Torah is in a very real sense dominated by 'Law'. The literary privileging of the prophet as exponent of an individual religion of the heart and dissenter against the cult is an outgrowth of a Protestant antithetical categorization of the Law and the Prophets, in which the Prophets come to represent those progressive individuals who peered above the parapet of the Old and glimpsed the New (the New being Christianity, Reformation, and Enlightenment, all rolled into one so that the joins barely show). The irony is that sustaining this idea has depended on transcendentalizing and generalizing the idea of Prophets and not reading the actual texts too closely. For Prophets are as difficult to read, in literary (and theological) terms, as Law.

Although they miss a great deal when used separately, the Romantic and Rhetorical models work curiously well together. It seems far from accidental that attempts to describe prophetic literature have drawn on models from the opposite ends of the literary spectrum, for together they highlight the curiously oxymoronic cohabitation of control *and* deviance, subversion and settled form. The Rhetorical model is helpful in that it acts as a counter-balance to Romanticism, conveying something of the structure and repetition that makes scholars suspect that the Prophets went to the same cultural genre 'school' (whatever that might have meant in practice). Poetic parallelism offers a form of genre constraint not dissimilar to the sonnet: the prophets, as God himself puts it, 'steal . . . words from one another' (Jer. 23: 20); and oracles follow certain basic formulae so closely that the moment of prophetic 'inspiration', so treasured by the Romantics, is in fact modelled on a basic template known as 'The Call'. Conversely, however much as Romanticism might anachronistically amplify prophetic 'individualism', it helpfully highlights the fact that the Prophets do seem less subject to generic controls than, say, the average psalmist. Or to put it another way, it suggests that lack of restraint and the overthrow of tradition is intrinsic to prophetic poetics, in a way that is not the case for the Psalms. In reading ancient Hebrew literature we may anachronistically amplify the idea of the individual 'writer' striving for difference. But nevertheless it seems to be true that there is something about prophecy, as opposed to other biblical literary forms, that comes closest to the idea of literature as what Derek Attridge (1988) calls 'peculiar language'.

Despite their potential, particularly when used together, Romantic and Rhetorical models are currently employed as a kind of *Apologie for Prophesie*. They tend to be used to place the reader in the position of the deflected worshipper, constantly praising, and cover over seeming untidiness in aesthetic apologetics about unity and craft. While more pronounced in the Rhetorical model, even the Romantic model is prone to apostrophize the 'graces of method, order, connexion and arrangement' which act as a restraint on the 'irresistible violence' of the 'prophetic impulse' (so Lowth 1807 (1778): 85–6). Romanticism and Rhetoric both tend to tug prophetic criticism in the direction of a sometimes tedious litany that *praises* rather than *describes*. In post-Enlightenment exchanges in which religious value is both reinforced by, and converted to, literary value, a worshipful 'Holy, Holy, Holy' (cf. Isa. 6) is changed to 'Marvellous!', 'Sublime!' and 'What a fine example of *copulatio!*'. The Prophets, as the pinnacle of biblical writing, reflect that cultural inclination to superlative that has been present ever since the earliest attempts to study the Bible as literary art. Robert Boyle's *Some Considerations Touching the Style of the Holy Scriptures* (1653) addresses itself to a strawman who prefers the Odes of Pindarus to the Psalms of David, and affirms 'the Beauty, the Symmetry and the Magnificence' of the biblical literature and its 'significant and *sinewy*' quality; and Stennet in his 1709 *Version of Solomon's Song* engages in similar panegyric, while adding an uncomfortable wriggling caveat that 'tis more modest and becoming to lay the fault on our own ignorance, if we don't see that Beauty and Elegance which the antient Hebrews did' (cited in Roston 1965: 52–6). (One is reminded of Augustine's confessional comments about the seeming crudeness and unworthiness of the Old Testament, particularly the Prophets and the Law (Augustine 1999: 80, 140).) Uncomfortable intimations of a 'sinewy' quality, or 'seeming' lack of Beauty, or 'violence' suggest that one of the reasons for the lavish application of superlatives to biblical literature is aesthetic apologetic. These superlatives are particularly liberally applied to the Prophets.

In order to come a little closer to the actual prophetic texts, I want first to compare prophecy to other genres within the biblical canon, and then to literary and cultural forms outwith the Bible. For thankfully for the Prophets, and for us, there are more definitions of literature than those supplied by Romanticism, Rhetoric, and the new literary criticism of the Bible with its almost exclusive preference for composite narrative art. I want to start with the inner-biblical comparison and look at prophecy alongside Wisdom (broadly sketched, the books of Proverbs, Ecclesiastes/Qoheleth, and Job (cf. Nielsen, Ch. 17 above)). Much can be gleaned about the difference between these two genres by looking at how they talk about words and what they are trying to *do* with words. Wisdom words are proffered as choice delicacies to be savoured, tried on the palate, and combined in new thought-recipes (Job 12: 11). They are described as 'apples of gold in settings of silver': jewels to be set in a sentence as a precious stone is set in a ring (Prov. 25: 11). The dominant impression is of writers/ speakers carefully putting words in place like old-fashioned typesetters, and striving, through very precise wordsmithery, for something like the Augustan ideal of 'what oft were thought, but ne'er so well expressed'. Good Wisdom words can be recognized by their ability to soothe, kiss, and *nourish*. Wisdom, far more than Prophecy, would merit comparison with Sidney's rhetorical 'medicene of cherries'. Bad Wisdom words can be identified by their tendency to sting like vinegar or run with an ugly gait like a lame man's legs (Prov. 24: 26; 18: 20; Job 16: 5; cf. *The Instruction of Amen-em-opet* 1: 13; Prov. 25: 20; 26: 7). The Wisdom writer describes himself as putting *mots justes* together in order to build a solid verbal siege barrier against his opponent, or lining up words like chess pieces before playing a game (Job 33: 5; 16: 4). In a 'whirlwind' of discourse, he seeks out the words that will act as a fixed point or a 'mooring stake for the tongue' (*The Instruction of Amen-em-opet* 1. 15–16). Though the Wisdom writers employ riddles, those riddles are presented as something like a crossword puzzle—tributes to the capacity of the circle of the Wise to decode them (Prov. 1: 5–6). The riddle functions to support the cohesion of the inner circle and to oil the wheels of social/linguistic exchange.

Prophetic words, in contrast, often present themselves as slashing through the social fabric and the language that sustains it. They are, for example, words that slice the people in two, leaden weights that lie heavy on the land, and *fire* that devours people like wood (Hos. 6: 5; Amos 7: 10; Jer. 5: 14). The (all-)consuming nature of the prophetic word is dramatized in the body of the prophet, who is curiously both its subject (speaker) and its object (victim)—a paradox performed in the figure of ingesting the scroll/word (Ezek. 3: 1–3; Jer. 15: 16). The prophet is frequently overwhelmed by 'his' text, which dramatizes its control of him rather than his control of it by compelling him to participate in what Maimonides called 'crazy [repellent] actions' (Maimonides 1963: 98b). Subject to an imperative not his own, submitting to a social/bodily abjection that would be anathema to the Wisdom writer, he must, for example, go naked and barefoot, marry a prostitute, betray what he 'is' by transgressing priestly prohibitions, or offer up parts of his own body as physical stage for prophetic tropes (Jer. 13; Hos. 1–3; Ezek. 4–5). The object of these divine command performances seems often to be to perform the heaviness of the oracle/word as 'burden' (*masa*). As if in a visceral interpretation of the idealized Wordsworthian metaphor of being bound/covenanted against his will, the prophet must bind himself and submit to a yoke of straps and bars (Ezek. 4 and 5; Jer. 27 and 28; cf. Amos 7: 10). As the supra-social nature of the prophetic word is dramatized in asocial excessive actions, so it 'speaks' its non-eloquent credentials in the prophet's silenced, stammering, stuttering mouth (Ezek. 2: 26; cf. Isa. 6: 5 and the uncircumcised mouth of Moses in Exod. 6: 12). As prophetic visions thwart the eye, so prophetic oracles 'speak' of oracles of silence, deaf ears, closed eyes, and sealed books (Isa. 6: 6–9; 21: 11–12; 29: 11). Instead of proffering flatteringly entangled puzzles as tributes to the intelligence of one's conversation partner, prophetic texts proffer mind-blinding visions (a 'basket of summer' means 'corpses'), and make strangely elliptical pronouncements such as 'Therefore I will do this to you, O Israel; because I will do this to you, prepare to meet your God, O Israel', or 'Write the vision; make it plain upon the tablets'—circling around, without detailing, the 'vision' or the antecedent of 'this' (Hab. 2: 2–4; Amos 4: 12; cf. Marks 1990). A scene in which crowds gather round and praise the poet as one who plays the tongue like a musical instrument would, one imagines, make the Wisdom writer glow with pride, but is anathema to Ezekiel (33: 30–2). In a statement that makes Rhetorical apostrophes to craftsmanship seem rather wide of the mark, Ezekiel classes it as failure to be perceived as a 'maker of metaphors' or an exponent of (mere) craft (cf. 20: 49). Similarly, the prophetic desire for words strong enough to *strike* us, and make the audience cry out for straight/smooth things and 'pretty songs' in *contrast* (Isa. 30: 11; Jer. 6: 14; Ezek. 13: 8–13) questions the automatic tendency to place prophetic poetry in the beautiful, superlative heights of 'art'.

Rather than acting as mooring stakes in the whirlwind, prophetic words typically subject language to the force of the whirlwind and rip up the moorings of tradition. The book of Amos, for example, describes the 'Exodus' of the Ethiopians, Philistines, and Arameans; converts sheol (the place of death) to the place of refuge; turns the divine warrior against his own nation; makes the 'day of the Lord' a day of destruction; and abases the precious idea of remnant in the bedraggled, bloodstained image of a pathetic piece of ear retrieved from the lion's mouth (Amos 9: 7–8; 9: 2; 5: 18–20; 4: 12). Prophetic 'rhetoric' seems to define itself through the denial of the luxury of stretching out in accepted meanings, rather as the rich and secure in Amos are denied the luxury of stretching out in their ivory beds (Amos 6: 4–7). It seems to be seeking out radical defamiliarisation, making our own homes and traditions unfamiliar and strange to us—a process that Amos makes graphic and overt in relentless portrayals of the destruction of the house (Amos 3: 15; 6: 9–11; 5: 19; cf. 6: 1 and 5: 11). Prophetic style seems actively to scavenge for words and phrases that, in Wisdom terms, *fail*, stinging like vinegar or running like a lame man's legs (Prov. 25: 20; 26: 7). If it is true that, as Coleridge sagely put it, no metaphor runs on all four legs at once, prophetic metaphors tend to limp, hop, and stagger like the image of a God bloodied and battle-dazed and staggering like a drunk (Isa. 63: 1–6; cf. the discussion in Sawyer 1993).

If a good metaphor represents, according to Nelson Goodman, a 'happy if bigamous second marriage' for a word (Goodman 1968: 73), prophetic metaphors are like bizarre and dysfunctional marriages on the verge of breakdown. As if to dramatize the fact, the first three chapters of the book of Hosea are based entirely on a dysfunctional marriage between a 'prostitute' and a prophet, in which the metaphor/allegory, like the marriage itself, is, to say the least, strained. Though sanitized by centuries of domestication and homilies to 'love', feminist and womanist critics have recaptured the shock of the graphic, corporeal imagery of Hosea 1–3—language that would have been equally scandalous to its original audiences, though differently so. Comparisons with Wisdom's emphatic separation of the religious man and the adulterous woman expose by contrast the intolerable scandal of telling a male elite, effectively, ' "You are a slut" says the Lord' (cf. Prov. 7). In Ezek. 23, Judah and Samaria have their 'virgin bosoms…handled' and their 'breasts pressed' by Egyptians with penises like those of stallions (Ezek. 23: 3, 8). The description of the 'mincing' and 'tinkling' women who trip up the Judah catwalk in Isa. 3: 16–26 reminds me of Hamlet's virulent denunciation of Ophelia. But it is as if a more vulgar Hamlet were to say 'You jig, you amble and lisp and nickname God's creatures, and make your wantonness your ignorance…therefore the Lord will afflict your heads with scabs and expose your xxxx's' (euphemistically translated 'secret parts' in most translations; cf. *Hamlet* iii. ii. 142–8). Though the shock is exacerbated in cultures whose idea of Bible, religion, and literature have been shaped by the Christian preference for the realm of the spirit/soul as opposed to the body, it is hard to imagine any culture that could have easily assimilated these pornoprophetic and visceral images as the acme of literariness or high culture. And this seems to be precisely the point.

Over the last decade the towering metaphor of nation-as-prostitute has dominated the critical literature (see e.g. O'Brien 2002; Weems 1995). The next important step may be to stop considering this as a special image apart and to start considering this perverse figure as in some sense typical of a prophetic style. The declaration 'I am the husband and you are the whoring wife' is cut from the same peculiar literary cloth as the God of Jeremiah's ragged 'You are the loincloth and I am the loins' (13: 11) (far less well-known than his 'You are the clay and I am the potter' (18: 10)) or Amos's perverse description of famine as the equivalent of dental floss: the gift of cleanness of teeth (Amos 4: 6). We could even go further and say that the scandalous effects of the nation-whore metaphor are relatively mild compared to other prophetic statements that are not just striking, but existentially inconstruable. The message of the book of Amos is impossibly, and so by way of infinite provocation, 'You are dead' (Sherwood and Caputo 2004): far worse (more infinitely inconceivable) to be a dead nation than a living whore. The nation-prostitute image is in some sense iconic for a genre that is frequently rude well beyond the bounds of *provocatio*, in which the prophet is more inclined to see himself as administering poisoned 'wormwood' words rather than 'fair-spoken' cherry-medicine (Jer. 9: 15). And any attempt to deal fairly with prophetic rhetoric would have to engage with the counter-intuitive equation of the true with the 'sour'. In comparison with the rather banal criteria laid out in the book of Deuteronomy—where the true prophetic word is the one that conforms to the commandments or that is fulfilled (and so *becomes* 'true') in the future (cf. Deut. 13: 1–5 and 18: 15–22)—prophetic literature has its own, more interesting, criteria for the true prophetic word. Whereas the good Wisdom word is the word that is palatable and that successfully *does* things, the true prophetic word is often (by definition?) the word that, in its very unpalatableness, demonstrates its unwillingness rhetorically to seduce its audience—indeed that often, indeed typically, alienates and *fails*. It may be no accident that Jonah's short, bizarre oracle in Jonah 3: 4–5 is one of the few superlatively successful oracles in the prophetic corpus, for the prophetic word proper seems to be, by definition, the word that provokes 'stout/strong' opposition against it (Mal. 3: 13). In J. L. Austin's (1975) terms, the prophetic word often defines itself as a failed performative that does *not* do what it wants to do with words, at least in human-social terms.

The image of the verbally and physically abused woman-nation, graphic well beyond the decorous bounds of *copulatio*, is also not out of place in the highly corporeal prophetic corpus. It finds ready companion metaphors in the nation-baby found covered in blood with cord uncut (Ezek. 16), the image of sin as the stain of menstrual blood (Isa. 64: 6) and the spectacle of blood poured out like dust and flesh like dung (Zeph. 1: 17). One of the most fascinating features of prophetic poetry is perhaps the one least written about: the way it makes itself felt through the skin and through the body. But, with its images of writhing on beds too short with covers too short (Isa. 28: 19), of being slopped like liquid from one container to another (Jer. 48: 11), or of lying face down and making your back like a street for the oppressors to pass over (Isa. 51: 23), this is a poetry that feels profoundly the insecurities and vacillations of being human and that makes itself felt physically on the flesh. When read, rather than generalized, the Prophets can seem almost 'Levitical' in their emphasis on the body (so jeopardizing the distinction between Prophets and Law). They transgress against the presumed decorum of Culture and Literature, and go into the body, well beyond the easily poeticized and spiritualized zone of 'heart'. They subject the figure of the national and individual body to verbal and visual decomposition, laying bare the body politic as 'a pile of bruises and sores and bleeding wounds that are not squeezed out, or bound up or softened with oil' in a graphic, typically prophetic gloss on the biblical aphorism that 'All people are like grass' (Isa. 1: 6; cf. 40: 6). One of the key prophetic tropes is the *entropy* of human figures (in the sense of both bodies *and* traditional metaphors and concepts), thus exposing the mortality and fragility of human being and human structures. (Compare the comments on the disintegration of the name and identity of 'Ephraim' above.) This fluid decomposition is mirrored in alchemical mutations and convulsions in landscape, cosmos, and time, in which morning overtakes evening, the harvester precedes the sower, streams turn to pitch, soil to brimstone, and the hills and valleys melt like wax before the fire (Amos 9: 13; Isa. 34: 9; Joel 2: 31; Nah. 1: 5; Mic. 1: 4).

The *difference* of prophetic literature can be clearly seen if we look at the book of Isaiah, beyond the Christmas and Easter out-cuts. Alongside and even within well-known passages such as Isa. 6: 1–9: 7, we stumble across images of, for example: Zion like a shelter in a cucumber field (1: 8); the earth staggering like a drunkard (24: 20); Assyria as a razor shaving the genitals of the body politic (7: 20); the divine command to 'dull their ears' and *prevent* understanding (6: 9–10); and landscapes that, as one student commented, look like the 'post-nuclear holocaust landscapes of *Threads*'. Images of redemption forge on just as determinedly into the outlands of the ludicrous and the counter-intuitive, as if determined to scandalize credulity. Once the veneer of familiarity is removed, what could be more implausible than the wolf cosying up with the lamb (11: 6)? Radical reversal becomes the only principle that can be relied on in eschatological visions where valleys are raised and mountains brought down low (40: 4). The many lesser-used Isaian images of redemption are those that make extreme category mistakes and turn on very squeaky hinges. Liturgies and literary canons make little use of scandalously mixed metaphors such as the worm Jacob who turns into a sharp-toothed threshing sledge, the God warrior who suddenly metamorphosizes into a woman in labour, drying up the earth with her panting, and the image of the nations suckling on the breasts of kings—not just a category, but a gender 'mistake' (41: 14–16; 42: 13–15; 60: 16).

Modern readers could be forgiven for feeling that images of God-in-labour, genital-razors, and nations sucking on kings' breasts fall short of contemporary ideals of *belles lettres*. Comparison with other Ancient Near Eastern literatures suggests that seeming subversion at least *partly* emerges from mistakenly applying a dehistoricized, transcendental 'literary' to a corpus between twenty-eight and twenty-three centuries old. However, the hostile responses of the Prophets' original audiences recorded as part of the texts (as an intrinsic part of their self-understanding), taken together in comparison with other genres in the biblical canon and prophetic texts from neighbouring cultures, suggest that Hebrew prophecy is also, particularly, actively, excessively seeking difference—and this for a particular reason. For, with the exception of Jonah, prophecy is the *extended recording of divine speech*. In Wisdom literature the hidden God does not speak directly, with the exception of his brief 'response' from the whirlwind in the book of Job (Job 38–41) and the speech of Hokhmah/Woman Wisdom in Proverbs. For all that she inverts theological gender stereotypes, Woman Wisdom's speech—essentially 'Come to me and learn prudence and acquire intelligence'—treads a far more conservative line than 'You are the loincloth and I am the loins'. Only in Job 38–41 does Wisdom edge closer to prophetic texts like Amos (the whirlwind is strikingly close to the earthquake) as God overthrows Wisdom's chessboard with a cavalcade of wild words/animals, the effect of which is to do far more than 'argue' 'Did you create the world/language?' and 'Is this not my wor(l)d with which I can do as I please?'

Too little attention has been directed towards prophetic theology and its impact on prophetic literature. Whereas the Psalms tend to protect the image of God beneath a fairly conservative repertoire of images (God as sheltering wing, canopy, booth, shield, cooling shade, and so on), the Prophets, in contrast, risk all kinds of heterogeneous linkages between Godness and bear-ness, Godness and illness, Godness and femaleness, and Godness and rottenness. They describe God as a woman in labour, a she-bear or wild animal mangling its prey; maggots/pus in the body politic and rot in the nation's joists; the one who sexually overpowers the prophet; and, most radically, the Not-I-Am, the inversion of the already cryptic/open name of Exod. 4 (Isa. 42: 14–15; Hos. 13: 8; 5: 12; Jer. 20: 7; Hos. 1: 8). In a particularly tight covenant between 'literature' and 'theology', a prophetic theology of God as radical other, the one who can be who he will be to the point where he overthrows the accepted canon of himself, surely impacts on the whole form of prophetic 'literature', for that whole body of literature is conceived as divine speech. In a tantalizingly under-developed observation, Robert Alter (1985: 141) thinks of prophetic poetry as the act of imagining what God would sound like if he spoke in the Hebrew language. How could God's seeing be described except as a radical distortion of our seeing? How could God be imagined to speak, except as a radical dis-ordering of our speech? If the presence of God causes the 'foundations' and the thresholds to shake (Ezek. 1: 28; Isa. 6: 1–6; Amos 9: 1) or the earth to melt (Amos 9: 5), then will not language shake and melt as God speaks 'our' language? If God's thoughts are not our thoughts (Isa. 55: 8–9) does it not follow that his language is not our language, his metaphors not our metaphors? If God is beyond compare (Isa. 40: 25) might it not follow that his metaphors are those that strain the principle of comparison altogether, even to the point of collapse? If prophecy is writing and speaking itself, as genre, as answer to the imagined question 'How could God's speech and a God's-eye view of the world be made to feel sufficiently other, sufficiently different?', then 'difference' seems too mild a word for the kind of difference the genre is looking to achieve.

It is a commonplace going back at least to Aristotle that literary language must work within common, shared language and yet remake it in such a way that we think that it has produced something else entirely, called literature. To this end it must strive for 'strange words and metaphor and ornamental words that prevent the diction from being ordinary and mean' (*Poetics* 1458a). All literature can only emerge as such through self-conscious negotiation between ordinary and extraordinary language (so Attridge 1988) but must continue to pay its dues to ordinary language if it is not to become solipsistic and meaningless. A careful writer-philosopher such as Aristotle is particularly insistent that a writer must pay his/her dues to the communal, for 'a riddle will result if someone writes exclusively in metaphor', 'barbarism will result if there is an exclusive use of strange words', and 'normal speech' must be used to 'keep the diction clear' (*Poetics* 1458a). Prophecy is an acute case of the literary—a kind of hyperliterary—striving within language for a beyond so excessive that it speaks (as if) from God, to us, and yet speaks to us in words we know or words related to the words we know already. It must speak otherwise to the point where it dispossesses us of the illusion of 'our' language and authorship (our control over language) which is why it makes the Prophets subjects and objects/victims of the word. In prophecy, both sides of the equation are particularly marked: prophecy must speak to us in shared words, and yet radically dispossess us of shared words and traditions. It has most in common with those forms of literature that strive most extremely to make language peculiar to itself, including what Aristotle would call 'barbarism' and 'riddles', sonic sense paired with conceptual nonsense and anagrams and puns.

   This is why, when it is finally and belatedly incorporated into the canon of the Bible as Literature, prophetic literature may well do us the important service of expanding our definitions of 'literature'—particularly the conservative, moderate, refined aesthetic that we tend to associate with the Bible. It may be equally, if not more, appropriate to think of the Prophets alongside modernists such as Joyce and Pound, than to imagine them as avid readers of Peacham's *Garden of Eloquence* or Wordsworth's *Prelude*, or as a kind of state-sanctioned poet laureate. Hints of alternative literary companions can be found in the margins of the critical tradition: for example in Hermann Gunkel's insightful observation, in the midst of his Romanticism-inspired gush, that there is something about prophetic literature that is 'dark', 'stammering', 'secretive', 'colossal', and '*baroque*' (Gunkel 1987 (1923)). In contrast to Wisdom literature's words modelling themselves on the 'apple of gold in a setting of silver', Gunkel at least hints that we might think of prophecy alongside the poetry that we term, in a word that itself derives from the term for an oddly twisted pearl, 'baroque'. Developing Gunkel, I suggest potential analogies between John Donne and the Prophets in the hope that this figure who was belatedly incorporated into the literary canon will help us to read this literature not yet fully incorporated into the biblical literary canon (see Sherwood 2002; compare Helen Wilcox, ch. 24 below). Echoing Prophecy's propensity to turn on creaking 'hinges', editorial or otherwise, Donne's poetry veers round sharp conceptual corners. As if mimicking swerves from worms to threshing sledges or warriors to women, *A Valediction: Of Weeping* makes tears that were, a line ago, like 'coins' mutate into 'wombs'. These and other strained metaphors that 'violently yoke heterogeneous elements together' (as Samuel Johnson complained) give us a template for prophecy's 'metaphysical conceits'. The precocious pairing of starvation and the gift of clean teeth finds fittingly audacious companions in claims that baptism is 'like' a wardrobe (from *Sermons*, in Potter and Simpson 1953–62: ii. 66); a flea is a 'like' a marriage cloister ('The Flea'); God is 'like' a 'holy thirsty dropsy' coursing through the body (*Divine Poems* 15); and the overcoming of the soul by God is 'like' begged-for rape or siege (Holy Sonnet 10: 'Batter my Heart…'). The last two strained/ strange metaphors have precise correlates in the prophetic corpus (Hos. 5: 12 and Jer. 20: 7) though the fact that these are never mentioned in literary commentaries is perhaps symptomatic of an over-sanitized view of biblical literature. By seeking the 'two-faced, three-angled, and self-multiplying ambiguity of meaning' (Davies 1994: 5), Donne, like the Prophets, exposes the intrinsic mutability, fluidity, and plasticity of all things. He undoes language to undermine names and identities: as Hosea undoes Ephraim, Donne undoes 'Donne'. And, as in the Prophets, this mortification of human language, human power and human concept is intimately tied to a God who can 'blast the State with a breath, melt a Church with a looke, moulder a world with a touch' (Potter and Simpson 1953–62: ix. 195). The Prophets and Donne seem to share that 'unpoetic' poetic quality that led C. S. Lewis to disparage Donne as 'shaggy and savage' and Coleridge to term him 'rhyme's sturdy cripple' ('Notes on Donne', in A. L. Clements 1992: 145–7, 357). It may be a nice irony that Donne ultimately offers a better analogy for prophetic literature than Coleridge precisely because he, like Ezekiel, is determined not 'siren-like to tempt', but to utter 'harsh' songs that 'teare' the tender labyrinth of the ear' (Satire II in Milgate 1967 and ibid. 66; cf. Ezek. 13: 8–13; 20: 49; 28; Isa. 30: 11; Jer. 6: 14). In 'The Litanie', Donne describes the prophetic poetics on which he models his own. Perfectly encapsulating some of the paradoxes discussed here, he sees it as characterized by (1) rhythmic discipline, (2) a love of 'secrets', and (3) a particularly unpoetic brand of 'poetiqueness'.

Taking our cue from the Prophets and their metaphysical conceits, we can create new (mis)pairings across epochs and the genres, so pushing our ideas of prophetic literature beyond Romanticism, Rhetoric, and the fairly circumscribed idea of literature that presides over the new biblical literary criticism. Indeed, the process has already begun. Hebert Marks (1990; 1989) has explored 'prophetic stammering' in stuttering conversation with Mallarmé and Dante, and has pushed the implications of Romanticism beyond its often trivializing and saccharine representations in biblical criticism into a more probing exploration of the Prophets and the Sublime. Thomas Jemielity's *Satire and the Hebrew Prophets* (1992) has disrupted a still-prevalent naive representationalist view of prophetic literature by pointing to the extreme caricatures that would rival any by Swift, Brueghel, or Bosch. Insights on the Prophets can also be found in unexpected corners of the literary canon. The breathless provocation of prophetic literature is parodied, but also powerfully imitated, in Donald Barthelme's (1982: 264–5) 'tongue-lashing' in his 'A Manual for Sons'. Emerging from a Christian-influenced aesthetic that has tended to favour the spiritual and the transcendental above and against the flesh, biblical literary critics, like literary critics in general, are increasingly exploring literature in relation to politics, culture and society, and the body. Indeed this questioning of literature as a hermetically sealed category seems to be particularly urged by prophetic literature as it foregrounds its own materiality in deeply visceral imagery and scenes of ingesting and performing the word. Beyond rather trivial analogies with 'street-theatre', critics have begun to ask more searching questions about prophetic performance. Mark Brummitt has looked at Jeremiah's dramas in comparison with the Brechtian *Lehrstücke*; Teresa Hornsby has taken Ezekiel 'off-Broadway'; and I have attempted to explore prophetic 'art' alongside contemporary that deviates from the sanctity of the gallery/museum imagined as the secular equivalent of a church (Brummitt 2005; Hornsby 2005; Sherwood 2000*b*). Such analogies suggest alternative definitions of art, for example as that which, as Francis Bacon says, 'returns us to the vulnerability of the human situation' (cited in Buck 1997: 10). They give us new ways of thinking about prophetic literature beyond ideas of the product of quasi-divine 'inspiration' or consummate craft.

WORKS CITED

ABRAMS, MEYER H. 1971. *The Mirror and the Lamp: Romantic Theory and the Critical Tradition.* Oxford: Oxford University Press.

ALTER, ROBERT. 1985. *The Art of Biblical Poetry.* Edinburgh: T & T Clark.

ARNOLD, MATTHEW. 1960 (1861). 'On Translating Homer', in R. Super (ed.), *On the Classical Tradition.* Ann Arbor: University of Michigan Press, 97–216.

ATTRIDGE, DEREK. 1988. *Peculiar Language: Literature as Difference from the Renaissance to James Joyce.* London: Methuen.

AUGUSTINE. 1999. *The Confessions*, trans. M. Boulding. New York: New City.

AUSTIN, J. L. 1975 (1962). *How to Do Things with Words*, ed. J. O. Urmson and Marina Sbisa. Cambridge, Mass.: Harvard University Press.

BARTHELME, DONALD. 1982. 'A Manual for Sons', in *Sixty Stories.* Harmondsworth: Penguin, 249–71.

BARTON, JOHN. 1996 (1988). *Reading the Old Testament: Method in Biblical Study.* London: Darton, Longman & Todd.

BLAKE, WILLIAM. 1988 (1803). 'From a Letter of 25 April 1803 to Thomas Butts', in Michael Mason (ed.), *William Blake.* Oxford: Oxford University Press, 70–1.

BLENKINSOPP, JOSEPH. 1983. *A History of Prophecy in Israel.* Philadelphia: Westminster.

BRUMMITT, MARK. 'Title', 2006. 'Of Broken Pots and Dirty Laundry: The Jeremiah *Lehrstücke*'. *The Bible and Critical Theory* 2/1: 3.1–3.10.

BUCK, LOUISA. 1997. *Moving Targets: A User's Guide to British Art Now.* London: Tate Gallery.

CANNEY, M. A. 1919. 'Amos', in A. S. Peake (ed.), *A Commentary on the Bible.* London: Thomas Nelson & Sons, 547–54.

CLEMENTS. A. L. (ed.) 1992. *John Donne's Poetry.* London: W. W. Norton.

CLEMENTS, ROLAND E. 1996. *Ezekiel.* Louisville, Ky.: Westminster/John Knox.

CLIFFORD, R. J. 1984. *Fair Spoken and Persuading: An Interpretation of Second Isaiah.* New York: Paulist Press.

COLERIDGE, SAMUEL TAYLOR. 1992. 'Notes on Donne', in Clements (1992: 145–7).

CONRAD, EDGAR J. 1991. *Reading Isaiah.* Minneapolis: Fortress.

DAVIES, STEVIE. 1994. *John Donne*. London: Northcote House.

EWALD, GEORGE W. 1875. *Commentary on the Prophets of the Old Testament*, i. *Joel, Amos, Hosea and Zechariah*, trans. J. F. Smith. London: Williams & Norgate.

FISCH, HAROLD. 1990. *Poetry with a Purpose: Biblical Poetics and Interpretation*. Bloomington: Indiana University Press.

GITAY, YEHOSHUA. 1991. *Isaiah and His Audience: The Structure and Meaning of Isaiah 1–12*. Assen: Van Gorcum.

GOODMAN, NELSON. 1968. *Languages of Art: An Approach to a Theory of Symbols*. Indianapolis: Bobs-Merrill.

GUNKEL, HERMANN. 1987 (1923). 'The Prophets as Writers and Poets', trans. James L. Schaaf, in D. L. Petersen (ed.), *Prophecy in Israel*. Philadelphia: Fortress, 22–73.

HESCHEL, ABRAHAM. 1975. *The Prophets*. New York: Harper & Row, ii.

HORNSBY, TERESA. 2006. 'Ezekiel Off-Broadway'. *The Bible and Critical Theory* 2/1: 2.1–2.8.

The Instruction of Amen-em-opet, in J. B. Pritchard (ed.) 1969. *Ancient Near Eastern Texts Relating to the Old Testament*. Princeton: Princeton University Press, 421–5.

JEMIELITY, THOMAS. 1992. *Satire and the Hebrew Prophets*. Literary Currents in Biblical Interpretation. Louisville, Ky.: Westminster/John Knox.

JOHNSON, SAMUEL. 1992 (1779–81). 'The Metaphysical Poets', from *Lives of the Poets*, in A. L. Clements (1992: 142–5).

LOWTH, ROBERT. 1807 (1778). *Isaiah: A New Translation: With Preliminary Dissertation and Notes Critical, Philological and Explanatory*. 2 vols. London: J. Nichols.

MAIMONIDES, MOSES. 1963. *The Guide of the Perplexed*, trans. S. Pines. Chicago: Chicago University Press.

MARKS, HERBERT. 1989. 'The Twelve Prophets', in R. Alter and F. Kermode (eds.), *The Literary Guide to the Bible*. London: Fontana, 207–33.

—— 1990. 'On Prophetic Stammering', in Regina Schwartz (ed.), *The Book and the Text: The Bible and Literary Theory*. Oxford: Blackwell, 60–80.

MAYS, JAMES L. 1969. *Amos*. Old Testament Library. London: SCM.

MILGATE, W. (ed.) 1967. *John Donne: The Satires, Epigrams and Verse Letters*. Oxford: Oxford University Press.

O'BRIEN, JULIA. 2002. *Nahum*. Readings: A New Biblical Commentary; Sheffield: Sheffield Academic Press.

POTTER, G. R., and SIMPSON, E. M. (eds.) 1953–62. *The Sermons of John Donne*. 10 vols. Berkeley and Los Angeles: University of California Press.

PRICKETT, STEPHEN. 1989. *Words and the Word: Language, Poetics and Biblical Interpretation*. Cambridge: Cambridge University Press.

ROSTON, MURRAY. 1965. *Prophet and Poet: The Bible and the Growth of Romanticism*. London: Faber & Faber.

RUNIONS, ERIN. 2003. 'Zion is Burning: Genderfuck and Hybridity in Micah and Paris is Burning', in *How Hysterical: Identification and Resistance in the Bible and Film*. New York: Palgrave, 93–114.

SAWYER, JOHN. 1993. 'Radical Images of Yahweh in Isaiah 63', in Philip R. Davies and David J. A. Clines (eds.), *Among the Prophets: Language, Image and Structure in the Prophetic Writings*. Sheffield: Sheffield Academic Press, 72–82.

—— 1996. *The Fifth Gospel: Isaiah in the History of Christianity*. Cambridge: Cambridge University Press.

SHERWOOD, YVONNE. 2000a. *A Biblical Text and Its Afterlives: The Survival of Jonah in Western Culture*. Cambridge: Cambridge University Press.

SHERWOOD, YVONNE. 2000*b*. 'Prophetic Scatology: Prophecy and the Art of Sensation', in Stephen D. Moore (ed.), *In Search of the Present: The Bible through Cultural Studies*. Semeia 82; Atlanta: Scholar's Press, 183–224.

—— 2001. 'Of Fruit and Corpses and Wordplay Visions: Picturing Amos 8.1–3'. *Journal for the Study of the Old Testament* 92: 5–27.

—— 2002. '"Darke Texts Needs Notes": Prophetic Poetry, John Donne and the Baroque'. *Journal for the Study of the Old Testament* 27/1: 47–74.

—— and CAPUTO, JOHN D. 2004. 'Otobiographies, or How a Torn and Disembodied Ear Hears a Promise of Death', in Y. Sherwood and K. Hart (eds.), *Derrida and Religion: Other Testaments*. New York: Routledge, 209–39.

SIDNEY, SIR PHILIP. 1987 (1595). 'An Apologie for Poesie', in Richard Dutton (ed.), *Sir Philip Sidney, Selected Writings: Astrophil and Stella, The Defence of Poetry and Miscellaneous Poems*. Manchester: Carcaret, 102–48.

SMITH, GEORGE A. 1912. *The Early Poetry of Israel in its Physical and Social Origins*. London: Henry Frowde.

STONE, KEN. 2001. 'Lovers and Raisin Cakes: Food, Sex and Divine Insecurity in Hosea', in Stone (ed.), *Queer Commentary and the Hebrew Bible*. Sheffield: Sheffield Academic Press.

WEEMS, RENITA J. 1995. *Battered Love: Marriage, Sex and Violence in the Hebrew Prophets*. Minneapolis: Augsburg Fortress.

WESTERMANN, CLAUS. 1985 (1969). *Isaiah 40–66: A Commentary*, trans. David M. G. Stalker. London: SCM.

WINTERSON, JEANETTE. 1985. *Oranges are not the Only Fruit*. London: Pandora.

WORDSWORTH, WILLIAM. 1965 (1800). 'Preface to the Lyrical Ballads', in R. L. Brett and A. R. Jones (eds.), *Lyrical Ballads: The Text of the 1798 Edition with the Additional Poems and Prefaces*. London: Methuen, 241–72.

—— 1971 (1805–6). *The Prelude: A Parallel Text*, ed. J. C. Maxwell. Harmondsworth: Penguin.

FURTHER READING

CONRAD, EDGAR. 1999. *Zechariah*. Readings: A New Biblical Commentary. Sheffield: Sheffield Academic Press.

GEORGE, D. H. 1986. 'Reading Isaiah and Ezekiel Through Blake', *New Orleans Review* 13: 12–21.

KUGEL, JAMES L. (ed.) 1990. *Poetry and Prophecy: The Beginnings of a Literary Tradition*. Ithaca: Cornell University Press.

LANDY, FRANCIS. 1995. *Hosea*. Readings: A New Biblical Commentary. Sheffield: Sheffield Academic Press.

MISCALL, PETER D. 1993. *Isaiah*. Readings: A New Biblical Commentary. Sheffield: Sheffield Academic Press.

CHAPTER 19

THE SYNOPTIC GOSPELS

GEORGE AICHELE

No other texts in the Bible have been so received or transformed in English Literature as the texts of the Gospels. The multiple canonical Jesus narratives have been resurrected again and again in the poems, dramas, and stories of generations of English writers, and these narrative afterlives reflect and transfigure both the content, what Jesus says and does, and the form, how his words and deeds are represented, in the biblical accounts. Both facets confront readers with complicated questions of narrative truth and meaning, structure and ideology. This chapter will consider how the Synoptic Gospels are themselves the subject of literary study, and how they have lent themselves to successive literary creations within the tradition.

TRUTH

Literary study of the Synoptic Gospels cannot dispense with the question of denotation (or 'reference'). Denotation is the power of words to indicate some object, whether actual or imaginary. It is the relationship of language to reality, the ability of words in a sentence to signify something that exists in some way, and thus it establishes the truth value of the sentence, its status as 'true' or 'false'. Identifying the denotation of language in the Gospels is crucial to determining the truthfulness of their respective stories. Are the Gospels histories—that is, stories that describe something that actually happened with some degree of accuracy—or are they fictions, imaginative constructs whose relation to the real world of the reader is indirect or even non-existent? A third option is that the Gospels are a complex mixture of history and fiction that must be sorted out by the reader before she can determine the truth value of the stories.

No written text can guarantee its own truthfulness, and the distinction between history and fiction is itself a product of ideology, which is discussed further below. Nevertheless, the question of denotation is unavoidable in relation to any book of the Bible, and it is especially controversial in relation to the Gospels. Many readers of the Bible believe that the Bible is true in some way, and particularly that Jesus and his followers really said and did at least some of the things that are narrated in the Gospels. For such readers, Coleridge's 'willing suspension of disbelief' or 'poetic faith' (1920: 169) will not do. The texts of Matthew, Mark, and Luke are versions of a single true story, featuring one actual person named Jesus. The Gospels serve as three accounts of a single historical truth, rather like stories of a single event in different newspapers. Thus Matthew's Gospel is often called 'The Gospel *According to* (Saint) Matthew', and so forth.

Between these three denotations of a single historical reality there can be no serious incompatibility, merely differences of theological emphasis or relatively trivial discrepancies of description. These differences are resolved by the narrative harmonizations that began with the second-century Christian, Tatian, and are still popular among readers today, often in the form of reconstructions of 'the historical Jesus'. Tatian's harmony was eventually condemned by the early church, but popular literary treatments of the Gospels, including retellings of the life of Jesus as well as other considerations of 'the Gospel' as though it were a single thing, often piece them together as though they narrated a single story. By harmonizing the diverse birth, resurrection, and other episodes, readers obliterate their differences, creating a super-gospel, not unlike Paul's 'gospel'.

The opposite extreme from this view treats the Gospels as fictions. Fictional language also denotes, but in a different way than non-fictional language does. In fiction, denotation is 'split' (Jakobson 1987: 85) and the poetic function of language dominates over the referential function, in contrast to non-fictional language, where the referential function dominates. Split denotation is quite evident in fictional texts such as Laurence Sterne's *Tristram Shandy* (1967) or Flann O'Brien's *At Swim-Two-Birds* (1966). It is not so evident in the Synoptic Gospels, but it does appear. If Mark 16: 8 is the 'proper' ending of the Gospel of Mark, as most scholars think, then the women at the tomb 'said nothing to any one, for they were afraid' (RSV). However, if the women said nothing to anyone, then the story of the empty tomb and the young man's words to them were never told to any others. Because these matters evidently are being 'told' to others in the text of Mark itself, that Gospel implies that its story is fictitious. As it does on numerous other occasions, Mark points to itself, as well as to the events described. In contrast, the Gospels of Matthew and Luke each narrate (different) encounters between the disciples and Jesus after the resurrection. In each case, this reduces the evident fictionality of the story.

If they are fictions, the three Synoptic Gospels narrate three distinct stories, which are evidently similar to one another but cannot be presumed to be 'the same story'. Differences between the stories appear in large chunks of narrative that are unique to (or absent from) each Gospel, such as birth stories or resurrection appearances, or the Sermon on the Mount. They also appear in major differences of theme or message such as Jesus' relation to God, Israel, the Gentiles, or his followers. Furthermore, they appear in minor but often quite significant variations in language, such as Jesus' reply to Peter at Caesarea Philippi, or his last words. These three stories denote three different Jesuses, each of whom has a mother named Mary and disciples named Peter, James, and John. Each Jesus speaks enigmatically but provocatively and also performs miracles, and each one is crucified by the Romans. Whether any of these accounts denotes historical reality is irrelevant to the reader's understanding of it, just as the historical accuracy (or lack of same) of Shakespeare's play, *The Tragedy of Julius Caesar* (1952), adds nothing to its literary 'truth'.

On close reading, it is clear that the Synoptic Gospels do not tell the same story. Nevertheless, despite significant differences between the Gospels, it is hard to regard the striking similarities between them as mere coincidence. Emphasis on these similarities leads to the third option—that is, that underlying the incompatibilities, there might be some historical relationship between the three Synoptic Gospels, as well as the non-canonical gospels, a trajectory of oral and literary development in terms of which they all could be better understood. This trajectory might even reach all the way back to some actual 'historical Jesus'. Once again, the Gospels are all thought to denote the same person, Jesus, but their deviations from a single true story are now seen to be the product of historical, theological, and literary factors.

The Gospels of Matthew, Mark, and Luke are similar to each other (and all are different from John) in their 'mode of presentation' (Frege 1952: 57) of Jesus. The Gospel of John was probably written after the others, by an author who may or may not have known one or more of them. Large pieces of text are shared, nearly verbatim, between Matthew, Mark, and Luke. Hence these Gospels are called 'synoptic'. During the last few centuries, various accounts have been offered to explain the historical and literary relations between the Synoptic Gospels. The most widely accepted theory states that the Gospel of Mark was written first, after which Matthew and Luke were each written. Each of these latter two Gospels in its own distinctive way draws upon Mark, 'correcting' Mark's theological and literary failings and incorporating material from at least one other common source, as well as material that appears uniquely in each of them.

The narratives in the Synoptic Gospels are usually realistic ones. When supernatural events occur in them, they are marvellous intrusions from another 'world'. Otherwise, the Gospel's characters and settings reflect a world that is not unlike our own. However, like any other narrative world, this world is represented in words, and most words are universals; they can never describe completely any actual object. Ingarden (1973: 142) claimed that actual objects possess an infinite manifold of properties or 'sides', but narrated objects are inevitably composed of a finite selection of 'states of affairs'. Unlike the 'unequivocally determined', unique, actual object, the narrated object is composed of general determinants and thus contains 'spots of indeterminacy' (ibid. 246–9). A 'round', realistic character in any story, whether fictional or not, is quite 'flat' compared to any actual person (cf. Chatman 1978: 131–4). Literary realism is not reality but rather the illusion of reality—that is, of denotative completeness. A realistic narrative simultaneously reveals the denoted object and conceals its incompleteness.

This denotative incompleteness, which is inherent in language and which renders every narrative at least somewhat fictional, arises in the signifier. The material stuff of the signifier interferes with denotation, disrupting narrative completeness and resisting meaning; the signs themselves impede the reader's understanding. Again, this appears most clearly in novels such as *Tristram Shandy* or James Joyce's *Finnegan's Wake* (1967), but it is true of any written text. This incompleteness demands completion in the act of reading, which produces one of many possible illusions of complete denotation. Without the concretization supplied by an actual reading, the literary work could not exist (an unread text has no meaning), but through that concretization, the story is in effect rewritten by the reader. Multiple, incompatible interpretations of the literary work are thus the inevitable result of denotative incompleteness.

Roland Barthes distinguished between 'readerly' and 'writerly' texts as two possible relations between reader and text. The readerly text (such as the traditional novel) is realistic, and the reader is 'plunged into a kind of idleness...[where] instead of gaining access to the magic of the signifier, to the pleasure of writing, he is left with no more than the poor freedom either to accept or reject the text' (Barthes 1974: 4). The meaning is 'obvious' and the story is realistic. In contrast, the writerly text refuses the reader's desire for understanding and thus demands a more active role on the reader's part. The denotation of reality is problematic in this text.

Both texts require the reader to make choices that determine the text's meaning, but the writerly text makes the reader's complicity in the formation of meaning evident, while the readerly text conceals it. The writerly text demands conscious labour, a deliberate rewriting on the part of the reader, that the readerly text does not. Readerliness and writerliness are functions of both the reader's pre-understanding (ideology) and the signifier. Lewis Carroll's poem 'Jabberwocky' is more readerly to Humpty Dumpty than it is to Alice (1982: 95–7, 137), but 'Jabberwocky' is probably more writerly (and less realistic) than Tennyson's 'The Lady of Shalott' (2005) for any actual reader. Similarly, the Gospel of Mark is more writerly than is the Gospel of Luke.

Denotation is also a factor in the construction of literary unity. By establishing the story's truth-value, denotation helps to make the story 'one'—to fix its boundaries and its focus, that is, the identity of its contents. Denotation makes the story 'the same' from one textual embodiment to another, even across differences of language or medium. Different reading strategies seek to sustain or to interrogate narrative unity. 'Narrative' and 'reader-response' criticisms emphasize the structural unity of the narrative and the reader's role in identifying its meaning, respectively. They seek a coherent message attached to the text, to be uncovered through valid exegesis. In contrast, deconstructive, post-colonial, and queer criticisms emphasize discontinuity and denotative breakdown, often exploring the text's meaning possibilities in non-traditional reading contexts. Feminist criticisms vary widely, some seeking to restore unity and others to challenge it.

The literary unity of each Gospel is neither self-evident nor intrinsic to the text. Fragmentation of narrative unity appears in the three endings of the Gospel of Mark. As Aristotle noted, the end of a story defines its unity (1967: 24–30). Both the longer and the shorter added endings of Mark reflect differences in vocabulary from the rest of Mark, and each of them eliminates the self-referentiality of Mark 16: 8 with resurrection appearances and reconciliations between Jesus and his disciples, as do Matthew and Luke. However, this results in three distinct, incompatible endings for Mark—in effect, three Gospels of Mark.

Some scholars have argued that the Gospel of Mark was damaged before it could be disseminated, and that an original and theologically satisfactory ending after Mark 16: 8 was lost. Here historical argument is used to repair literary difficulty. Other scholars claim that the reader has already been given a key to the 'correct' under-standing of Mark's abrupt ending, clues presented elsewhere in that Gospel that fill in the gaps and satisfy the needs of orthodox faith. In other words, Mark is a puzzle that has just one correct solution. These scholarly speculations supplement the text's incomplete denotation. However, if ancient readers knew what Mark's author meant by the ending at 16: 8, and where the clues were, then why was there a desire to repair that ending? Mark's two added endings, and the resurrection appearances in Mat-thew and Luke, suggest that this desire was strong.

Meaning

Signification involves both denotation and connotation. Connotation (or 'sense') is what a word says about the denoted object, the mode of presentation of that object in language. It is the intersection between a specific, concrete utterance (*parole*) and the linguistic repertoire (*langue*) of the language-user—that is, the word's relation to other words or sentences within the general system of the language, as filtered by a set of culturally determined codes. Connotation produces a second level of meaning, with denotation as the primary level. The entire denotative sign (signifier–signified) becomes the signifier of another signified:

> signifier↔signified (Connotation)
> ↗ ↖
> signifier↔signified (Denotation)

However, as Barthes (1974: 128) said, 'denotation is not the truth of discourse: . . . [denotation is] a particular, specialized substance used by the other [connotative] codes to smooth their articulation'. In other words, denotation is a diminished form of connotation. Connotation is meaning running wild, the engine of what Eco (1976: 15), following Pierce, calls 'unlimited semiosis'. Connotation implies that there is no proper or firm connection between meaning and language. Meaning is not located 'in' any individual text, but rather it flows between texts and readers, and between texts and other texts. This free flow of semiosis is most evident in writerly texts.

Although intertextuality and unlimited semiosis are two sides of the same coin, they are perpetually at war. In order for a coherent message to be received, the potential for excessive or multiple connotations must be limited. The need to control connotation plays a major part in the functioning of the reader's intertextual network. The individual reader is among other things an accumulation of all the texts that she has read, an intertextual web that constantly grows and diminishes as she reads new texts and forgets old ones. Each text is read in the light of countless other texts, which themselves were read in the light of yet other texts. The reader does not choose this network, and she usually is not even particularly conscious of it. If she does gain some level of critical awareness of the web of texts, that too happens intertextually.

One form of this control of connotation is identification of genre. Genre describes the structure of the literary unit, and more specifically (in relation to the Gospels) the type of narrative involved. Genre restricts the kind of meaning peculiar to the text in question, both the sort of objects to which a given text points (its denotations) and other texts that have similar structures (its connotations). A history book has a different relation to reality than a work of fiction, and a tragic hero is a different sort of character, and lives in a different sort of world, than does a comic buffoon.

Genre is not an objective structure of the text, but rather a set of denotative and connotative codes that the reader brings to the text, in the form of expectations, assumptions, and prior reading experience. The text's significance appears in the tension between the incompleteness of the text as a collection of signifiers and the reader's desire for completeness and truth. That desire is satisfied in part when the reader establishes the codes through which the text will be understood. Even a deliberate reading against the grain of codes established by some genres presupposes that the true grain of the text's meaning has already been identified. Yet even though it is the reader who identifies the text's genre, the reader is not free to read that text in terms of whatever genre she wishes.

If the genre of the Gospels is misidentified, then understanding of them will be mistaken, or impossible. However, there is a great deal of disagreement about the gospel genre. The Synoptic Gospels all share similar narrative structures, on both the micro level (the 'forms' of form criticism) and the macro level (plot, characters, language). They are formally distinct from the Gospel of John and from many of the non-canonical gospels. Nevertheless, the Synoptics do not all clearly belong to the same genre. The designation 'gospel' may itself be merely a matter of historical coincidence (the appearance of the word *euaggelion* ('gospel') in Mark 1: 1, coupled with Paul's frequent use of that word) or of irrational tradition.

That scholars continue to debate what the appropriate genre might be for the Synoptic Gospels is an index of the lack of consensus about their meaning. Some claim that there is no one gospel genre, and that 'gospel' denotes only the content of the message, not its structure. Just as it may be argued that the Synoptic Gospels tell three distinct stories, so it may be that each of them belongs to a different genre. The genre of ancient biography 'fits' Luke well, but that does not mean that it is appropriate for Matthew, which may be better understood as prophetic history, or for Mark, which appears to be an extended parable.

Other forms of intertextual control of the meaning of the Synoptic Gospels are also employed by readers, including creeds, catechisms, sermons, and rituals of the Christian churches. The Gospels play an important part in the worship and theological reflection of Christians, and all these activities are themselves texts that may figure in the intertextuality of a reading. However, identification of the connotations of the Gospels is most influenced by the canon of the New Testament. The fact that Matthew, Mark, Luke, and John are the only Gospels within the Christian Bible helps to control the meaning of each one of them, and of the whole New Testament. That the books of the Bible are all usually bound together in a single codex encourages people to read them as a single book with a single proper sequence. The placement of the four Gospels at the beginning of the New Testament, and the 'synoptic' similarities between three of them, encourages the reader to think that these books belong together and suggests that they represent four versions of one story. It also suggests that they all mean the same thing, a single truth.

The resulting connotations are what many people mean when they describe Matthew, Mark, and Luke as 'Gospels'. If other texts, such as the gospel of Thomas or the Protevangelium of James, had been included in the New Testament—or if one or more of the Synoptics had been omitted from it—then understanding of the Gospel genre would be different, as would the connotations that emerge for each of the Gospel stories. The Christian canon cannot exclusively determine the identity of the Gospel genre, since there are instances of other literary genres also in the canon, and since other texts identified as gospels are not in the canon. Nevertheless, the biblical canon provides an intertextual mechanism that powerfully influences the connotations of its constituent texts.

The canon offers Barthes's 'poor freedom' of the readerly text to Christian ideology. The Bible limits the semiosis of its constituent texts, producing Gospels that speak clearly and with authority to the believing reader. Both the physical location of Mark between Matthew and Luke, and the understanding that all three Gospels belong to the same genre, encourage the reader to read Mark in the light of the other two Gospels and thereby restrain Mark's unorthodox connotations. The appearance of the word 'gospel' numerous times in other New Testament texts, especially the letters of Paul, also influences understanding of the meaning of that word, and of the Gospel texts.

The canon presents the Bible (and thus the Gospels) as authoritative and meaningful. Many Christians believe that the canonical texts possess some inherent quality that identifies them (and them alone) as the authoritative word of God.

To add books to or take them away from this collection would be blasphemous. The books of the Bible have been imbued with this inherent quality either by God, their spiritual author, who inspired the human writers, or else by the Church, which authorized them by accepting them into the canon, again with the aid of divine inspiration. God has put his self-evident mark upon the Bible, and the text manifests its own divine origin. The apparent diversity of the Gospels serves some divine purpose.

This theological claim is an older version of modern secular belief that a book's author controls the text's meaning through the process of writing it, and that readers are obliged to hunt for and respect the author's intention. The author's intention identifies the story's genre and limits its connotations. Secular humanists who may have little use for God or the Bible insist that an intrinsic quality marks the 'great books' or 'classics' of 'literature', which are also called a 'canon', as the products of godlike human art.

For humanistically inclined biblical scholars, the historical human author's intention serves as a way to secure proper understanding of the biblical text, once the allegorical search for timeless meaning is no longer credible. For these readers, the connotations of phrases such as 'Son of man' or 'kingdom of God' in the Gospel of Luke are limited to what Luke's author wanted them to mean—or perhaps even to what Jesus wanted them to mean, since these phrases are presented as his spoken words. Likewise, the intentions of Mark's author, if we knew them, would greatly clarify the disturbing ending of that Gospel.

Another strategy that leads to similar results (as Mark's ending again indicates) takes the form of identification of the book's original or intended audience as the proper determinant of the story's connotations. What the author could expect the first audience to know already (prior to reading the book) resolves literary or theological problems in the story. For this approach, the Gospel of Mark's ending at 16: 8 is not troublesome because its first readers already understood certain things, and especially that Jesus is the unique Son of man, as well as the Son of God. Similarly, the horrific saying at Matt. 27: 25 may become less anti-Jewish if 'all the people' was understood to mean that Matthew's first readers were themselves included in that 'people' who were responsible for the death of Jesus.

If a text is intrinsically meaningful, then any competent reader should be able to decipher that meaning. However, not all competent readers perceive the alleged mark of God on the biblical texts. Only certain Christian readers are able to recognize this inherent characteristic and to fully appreciate the Bible as God's word, and thus reading competency, according to this view, is not only a matter of literacy, but also of faith. For these readers, the connotations that God (or each Gospel's author) intended become more important than the actual signifiers that make up the texts. Once again, historical or theological supposition rescues literary difficulty. The author's (or God's) meaning-filled intention is spelled out in a story that supplements or even replaces the text of each Gospel. This is yet another form of intertextuality.

STORY

Although speculation about the Gospels' actual authors is inconclusive, each of the Gospels projects its own 'implied author' (Chatman 1978: 148–51). When one talks about 'Mark's messianic secret' or 'Matthew's portrayal of Jesus as the new Moses', the names 'Mark' and 'Matthew' connote distinct perspectives embedded in the stories that are crucial to any understanding of them. Different implied authors tell different stories. This implied author is a simulacrum of narrative unity, integrating disparate elements into a single, meaningful story. It counters writerly factors in the text that tend to tear the story apart. The implied author is not a person but rather a narrative construct, the product of an ongoing intertextual negotiation between reader and text—it is the effect of the connotative and denotative codes that the reader applies to the text.

Like genre, the implied author is 'given' to the reader intertextually. The reader cannot impose on the story whatever perspective she wants, any more than she can choose to make the story signify whatever she wants. Thus although the Gospels' implied authors are subjective phenomena, distinctions between them cannot simply be made up, or wished away. As a function of the reader's understanding, the implied author is both a narrative function and a theological one. Different understandings of the implied author reflect differences of ideology as well as different understandings of the role of ideology in reading.

Although the Synoptic Gospels are usually understood as three versions of a single story, they have distinct implied authors who present the reader with different and arguably incompatible characterizations of Jesus. Matthew's 'second Moses' who emphasizes the law (5: 17–20) but dies abandoned by God (27: 46) is not the same as Luke's 'Lord', who belongs in his 'Father's house' (2: 49) and who is comfortable even on the cross (23: 43, 46). The 'messianic secret' theory offers a way to overcome some of Mark's ambiguities regarding Jesus, but that theory requires that the reader has already read Matthew or Luke (which tend to resolve those ambiguities), or is otherwise familiar with Christian thought, and thus already expects that a Gospel will present Jesus as the Christ. Mark's Jesus is either an inept keeper of secrets, or else there is no secret, but merely profound obscurity (11: 33). If the reader does not already know who Jesus is before she starts to read Mark, she will very likely still not know by the end of Mark.

Christmas stories and genealogies in the Gospels of Matthew and Luke help to identify Jesus theologically. Jesus' conception and birth as God's son is vividly narrated. Mary's pregnancy is supernaturally produced, and both of Jesus' parents acknowledge his divine Father. Nevertheless, there are significant differences between the two Christmas stories. Each story sets the stage for a larger story of Jesus, but in two different ways. In Matthew, Joseph plays a central role, whereas in Luke, Mary is the focal character. Matthew's account is filled with overt references to the Jewish Scriptures, but Luke's few quotations are unmarked, and Luke's story sounds more like a pagan tale of divine–human rape. However, both stories make it clearer than Mark does that Jesus actually is 'the Son of God', clarifying the connotation of that phrase. Mark's lack of a birth story and later reference to Jesus as the 'son of Mary' (6: 3, compare Luke 4: 22) suggests that Jesus' birth was not only quite natural but probably illegitimate.

Many stories in the Synoptic Gospels serve as commentaries on the Jewish Scriptures ('the law and the prophets'). The Gospel's text denotes another biblical text, and the Gospel's story interprets and appropriates the cited text. Miracles attributed to Elijah or Elisha are resurrected in the deeds of Jesus. The reader's familiarity, or lack of familiarity, with Old Testament texts yields differences in the significance of shared words or phrases in the Gospels, even as the gospel texts direct the connotations of precursor texts. In each of the Synoptics, Jesus preaches the 'kingdom of God' ('heaven' in Matthew), often in parables which present the kingdom as a 'secret'. In all three Gospels, Jesus explains his use of parables by quoting LXX Isa. 6: 9–10, but with significant differences. Mark 4: 11–12 and Luke 8: 10 follow Isaiah closely, and according to them Jesus speaks in parables *so that* 'those outside' will not understand. Jesus' parables are not invitations but obstacles. Matthew 13: 13 rewrites Isaiah and eliminates the harshness of the saying, and as a result Jesus tells parables *because* the crowd does not understand.

In all three of the Synoptic Gospels, Jesus speaks often about a 'Son of man', a common phrase in the Jewish Scriptures. Jesus describes this Son of man as both human (for example, '[t]he Son of man must suffer many things, and be rejected by the elders and chief priests and scribes, and be killed', Luke 9: 22) and also divine ('whoever is ashamed of me and of my words, of him will the Son of man be ashamed when he comes in his glory and the glory of the Father and of the holy angels', Luke 9: 26). 'The Son of man' in Jesus' words is usually understood to connote Jesus himself, understood as a unique being with a special relation to God. However, in Mark 3: 28, 'the sons of men' are not only sinners and blasphemers, but also plural. The Markan context suggests that these multiple sons of men are the crowd sitting about Jesus, whom he calls his 'brother and sister and mother' (3: 32–5). These people may include Jesus among their number, but these sons of men are not innocent, unique saviours. They are ordinary human beings, which is what 'son of man' usually connotes in the Jewish Scriptures. Luke omits and Matthew rewrites (12: 31) the saying in Mark 3: 28, in both cases obliterating the plural sons of men and further defining the identity of Jesus as the Son of man.

Comparable differences (and similarities) are played out in relation to other major synoptic themes. Jesus' sojourn in the wilderness and his temptation by Satan is briefly noted in Mark's Gospel but narrated in great detail in both Matthew and Luke. These latter temptation stories are much the same, and they both emphasize Jesus' rejection of Satan's offers. In contrast, Mark never clearly states that Jesus did not succumb to temptation and even hints that he might be 'possessed by Beelzebul' (3: 22). Each of the Gospels associates numerous miracles with Jesus, but sometimes in Mark it is not clear whether a miracle has been performed at all (5: 22–4, 35–43), or who the miracle has been performed by (7: 25–30), or who controls the miraculous powers (5: 25–34). Matthew and Luke often 'correct' such stories by emphasizing Jesus' supernatural powers and his ability to use them.

Likewise, Jesus' relations to his disciples and to his family are stormy throughout Mark. The disciples often do not understand Jesus and are sometimes even hostile (8: 32–3), and his family thinks that he is crazy (3: 21), but others understand him quite well (12: 12, 28–34). As a result, Mark's distinction between outsiders and insiders (4: 11) becomes paradoxical (Kermode 1979). In contrast, the disciples have no difficulty understanding the secret of the kingdom in Matthew and Luke, and both of these Gospels omit any parallel to Mark 3: 21. Matthew and Luke either soften Mark's tensions and paradoxes or eliminate them altogether.

The Gospels all conclude with passion and resurrection stories. In both Mark and Matthew, Jesus in Gethsemane is unwilling to die, and he cries out that he has been abandoned at the moment of his death (Mark 15: 34–7). Not unlike the Gospel of John, Luke presents Jesus as calm and assured, both in the garden (except for 22: 43–4, missing in the oldest manuscripts) and on the cross, where he promises to be with the faithful thief 'today in paradise' (23: 43). Luke also puts different last words in the mouth of Jesus, words that connote Jesus' closeness to God (23: 46). Both Matthew and Luke present post-resurrection stories that fill the gap left by Mark's empty tomb ending, although again their stories are quite different from each other. In contrast to Mark's ending at 16: 8 (but like Mark's added endings), it is clear in these resurrection stories that Jesus has not only risen from the grave, but he has met with the disciples and given them instructions to create a church.

IDEOLOGY

Both denotation and connotation are impossible without some physical signifier, whether sound, script, or pixel. This signifying material interferes with the story's meaning and unity. As Socrates said, nothing can rescue the signifier (Plato 1973: 97). The signifier is frail, and its transmission is always vulnerable. However, ideology rescues the signified meaning of the text, assuring the reader that hers is the proper understanding. Ideology is not in the text itself, like a message in a signifying bottle, put there by an author (or God). Nor is ideology in the reader, at least not in the sense that, like Lewis Carroll's Humpty Dumpty, the reader might choose to make words mean whatever she wants (1982: 136). Ideology lies between reader and text, both connecting them and controlling the connection. It defines a proper intertext, a system of restraints through which unlimited semiosis is brought to a halt and within which acceptable readings can occur. On the highest level, this takes the form of what Foucault (1972) called 'discursive formations', fundamental linguistic structures which are generally invisible but which control the possibility (or impossibility) of saying some particular thing at some particular time. On a lower level, ideology takes the form of actual networks of texts that are read, and especially the canon of the Bible. Because we take them for granted, even these more explicit controls on understanding may seem quite natural.

Every reading expresses one ideology or another, and conflict between readings is often conflict of ideologies. Ideology is not bad—indeed, it is inescapable. However, because ideology is not rational, it may be dangerous, and because it is normally invisible, its power is considerable. All readers read from concrete social and material locations, and no reader has privileged access to some site of valid, objective truth, such as the mind of the text's author, the social context of its production, or 'what really happened'. In so far as such authorities are invoked, it is because some ideology sanctions them. Likewise, the claims of some readers to use objectively neutral ('scientific') methods are ideological manoeuvres that conceal the interests of the readers themselves.

Ideology appears in assumptions that support historical analysis of the Synoptic Gospels. Historical assumptions regarding what the first readers of a text already knew, or what the actual author intended, derive from ideological assumptions about the relevance of those matters to contemporary understanding. Ideology also appears in literary analysis of the Gospels. Decisions to treat the Gospels as fictions or historical accounts, or some mixture of both, and the various intertextual ways through which readers concretize the stories, 'reading out' the meaning (Chatman 1978: 41), inevitably reflect ideological differences.

Ideological influence on reading is more evident in relation to relatively writerly texts such as the Gospel of Mark, where the reader must work harder to make sense of the text—that is, to explore and contain its connotations. Mark's writerliness is more open to non-Christian readings than are either Matthew or Luke. These latter, more readerly Gospels fill many of Mark's narrative gaps and jolts. They consistently rearrange or revise large chunks of material taken from Mark, or they place it in narrative contexts where what was theologically confusing or even troublesome in Mark's Gospel becomes more clearly orthodox in its new setting. Despite significant differences between them, both Matthew's and Luke's stories are theologically more acceptable to Christian readers than is Mark's story. Nevertheless, what may be most evident in relation to Mark is true also, but in more subtle ways, for the other two Synoptic Gospels. As Barthes (1974) demonstrated, even the most readerly text becomes writerly, if read carefully.

Biblical scholars and Christian theologians frequently assume the ideological authority of the canon for the significance of their readings. Acceptance of the canon as the proper intertextual frame for reading the Gospels restricts the possibilities for understanding them. This ideological bias becomes apparent when biblical texts are read in the light of different, non-canonical intertextualities. Postmodern recognition of unlimited semiosis opens the prospect of a wider range of readings of the Synoptic Gospels. The decision to read the Gospels against the grain of the Christian canon and tradition—as is the case in queer, post-colonial, radical feminist, or deconstructive readings—attends to the writerly aspect of the texts and opens up new connotative possibilities. Such readings play in almost midrashic fashion on contradictions, lacunae, and aporias within or implied by the story. They read the text closely, and they are concerned neither with the internal coherence of the story nor with its consistency with Christian dogma.

Reading any of the Synoptic Gospels in intertextual juxtaposition with non-biblical texts instead of (or in addition to) the canonical ones produces understandings that challenge prevailing ideologies. This is quite a different thing from the widespread citation or paraphrasing of Gospel texts (often harmonized) in secular literature, which becomes another form of commentary and is often quite orthodox. In contexts provided by non-biblical texts, 'the hermeneutical flow' is 'reversed' (Kreitzer 2002), and the meaning of the story is no longer directed by the canon. The signifiers are unchanged, but the meaning is transfigured.

Ideology is also a factor in translation of the Scriptures. No modern reader is a native speaker of ancient Greek. Hence translation always figures in the understanding of the Gospels. Different modern English translations present different signifiers than the source texts and therefore tell 'the same story', or represent 'the same Jesus', only if the reader's ideology allows them to do so. The theological bias of some translations is well known, but other important issues are often overlooked. The widely accepted dynamic equivalence theory of translation asserts that adequate translation of biblical texts will always be possible, but it ignores the materiality of the signifier in favour of widely accepted and often unquestioned theological interpretations. For example, the NRSV translation of *tois huiois tōn anthrōpōn* ('the sons of men') in Mark 3: 28 as 'people', while dynamically equivalent, conceals the fact that this same phrase in the singular is always translated as 'Son of man' when it appears in sayings of Jesus, where it is usually thought to denote only himself. The ideological desire that the singular phrase *ho huios tou anthrōpou* in the words of Jesus should uniquely denote Jesus overpowers the contrary signifier. The coincidence of phrase in the material text disappears in favour of inclusive language and theological dogma.

Scholarly acceptance of dynamic equivalence in translation again suggests that theological issues play a large role in critical study of the Bible. Widespread acceptance of the possibility of a 'dynamically equivalent' transfer of meaning maintains both the opposition between reality and appearance (an ideology of representation) and the notion of the canon as a channel of a divine message.

Like historical readings, literary readings of the Gospels are also theological readings. They may not be overtly theological, but they will never entirely avoid the theological dimension. Theology is among other things a defence mechanism, an attempt by ideology to rationalize itself. Even for the non-believer, the Synoptic Gospels' stories are filled with denotations and connotations that are ultimately theological. A careful reading of any Gospel will not be ideology-free, but it will attempt to confess its own bias. It will make explicit the theological codes, and any other codes, through which that reading has been made possible, and it will show how those codes have been applied to the text. An overt ideology is still an ideology, but one that no longer entirely controls the reading.

TRADITION

These literary aspects of the Synoptic Gospels—truth, meaning, story, and ideology—help to inform, and in many respects constitute, a tradition of literature drawing from Matthew, Mark, and Luke. In terms of form, the interrogation of the truth claims of the gospel narratives by the higher critics, and in particular David Friedrich Strauss's plea that they be read as poetic myth, was influential on subsequent approaches to narrative, as has been shown in Ch. 9 above, on the Victorians. The problems of document authentication posed by the Synoptic Gospels have continued to reverberate in works as different as Robert Browning's 'Death in a Desert' and Margaret Atwood's *The Handmaid's Tale*. In regards to content, the details of Jesus' life, beginning with the birth narratives, have been a source of poetic inspiration in such eminent writers as John Donne (Holy Sonnets, 'Nativitie'), John Milton ('On the Morning of Christ's Nativity'), S. T. Coleridge ('A Christmas Carol'), G. M. Hopkins ('The Blessed Virgin Compared to the Air We Breath'), Oscar Wilde ('Ava Maria Gratia Plena'), T. S. Eliot ('Journey of the Magi'), and W. H. Auden ('For the Time Being: A Christmas Oratorio'). As in birth, so in death: the passion and crucifixion of Jesus, which has inspired a rich tradition in painting, has also led to numerous literary works, from the early York Crucifixion Play to Herbert's *The Church* ('Good Friday', 'The Passion', 'The Sepulchre', 'Easter I & II', for example), Wilfred Owen's 'At Calvary Near the Ancre', and Geoffrey Hill's 'Canticle for a Good Friday', to name but a few. Other aspects of Jesus' life and ministry have also been represented from the Gospels, both in poetry and in novel form—for example, the inauguration of his ministry in Milton's *Paradise Regained* and Jim Crace's *Quarantine*, or Jesus and Mary Magdalene in Robert Southwell's 'Mary Magdalene's Complaint at Christ's Death' and Michele Roberts's *Wild Girl*. The parables of Jesus have received particular attention in all literary forms, whether directly in poetry (Christopher Smart's *The Parables of Our Lord and Saviour Jesus Christ*, or Christina Rossetti's 'A Prodigal Son'), or indirectly in Chaucer's *Canterbury Tales*, which incorporate religious parables of many kinds, or in the novel form, such as Bunyan's *Pilgrim's Progress*, or more obliquely in the novels of Thomas Hardy. One might even argue that the Gospel form itself has been rewritten in various literary forms. Here we might think of Blake's 'The Everlasting Gospel' as a clear poetic example, though we could say that the novel form as a whole owes much to the parabolic approach in its vivid narratives drawn from common life that compel us into active thought.

WORKS CITED

ANDERSON, JANICE CAPEL, and MOORE STEPHEN, D. (eds.). 1992. *Mark and Method*. Minneapolis: Fortress.

ARISTOTLE. 1967. *Poetics*, trans. Gerald Else. Ann Arbor: University of Michigan Press.

BARTHES, ROLAND. 1967. *Elements of Semiology*, trans. Annette Lavers and Colin Smith. New York: Hill & Wang.

—— 1974. *S/Z*, trans. Richard Miller. New York: Hill & Wang.

BIBLE AND CULTURE COLLECTIVE. 1995. *The Postmodern Bible*. New Haven: Yale University Press.

CARROLL, LEWIS (Charles Dodgson). 1982. *Through the Looking Glass*, in *The Complete Illustrated Works*. New York: Crown.

CHATMAN, SEYMOUR. 1978. *Story and Discourse*. Ithaca, NY: Cornell University Press.

CHILDS, BREVARD S. 1979. *Introduction to the Old Testament as Scripture*. London: SCM.

COLERIDGE, SAMUEL TAYLOR. 1920. *Biographia Literaria*. Cambridge: Cambridge University Press.

EAGLETON, TERRY. 1991. *Ideology*. London: Verso.

ECO, UMBERTO. 1976. *A Theory of Semiotics*. Bloomington: Indiana University Press.

FOUCAULT, MICHEL. 1972. *The Archaeology of Knowledge and the Discourse on Language*, trans. A. M. Sheridan Smith and Rupert Sawyer. New York: Harper & Row.

FREGE, GOTTLOB. 1952. *Translations From the Writings of Gottlob Frege*, trans. and ed. P. T. Geach and M. Black. Totowa, NJ: Rowman & Littlefield.

INGARDEN, ROMAN. 1973. *The Literary Work of Art*, trans. George G. Grabowicz. Evanston: Northwestern University Press.

JAKOBSON, ROMAN. 1987. *Language and Literature*, ed. Krystyna Pomorska and Stephen Rudy. Cambridge, Mass.: Belknap.

JOYCE, JAMES. 1967. *Finnegan's Wake*. New York: Viking.

KERMODE, FRANK. 1979. *The Genesis of Secrecy*. Cambridge, Mass.: Harvard University Press.

KREITZER, LARRY J. 2002. *Gospel Images in Fiction and Film*. Sheffield: Sheffield Academic Press.

MOORE, STEPHEN D. 1989. *Literary Criticism and the Gospels: The Theoretical Challenge*. New Haven: Yale University Press.

NIDA, EUGENE, and TABER, CHARLES R. 1982. *The Theory and Practice of Translation*. Leiden: E. J. Brill.

O'BRIEN, FLANN (Brian Nolan). 1966. *At Swim-Two-Birds*. New York: Penguin.

PLATO. 1973. *Phaedrus*, trans. Walter Hamilton. Harmondsworth: Penguin.

SANDERS, JAMES A. 1984. *Canon and Community*. Philadelphia: Fortress.

SHAKESPEARE, WILLIAM. 1952. 'The Tragedy of Julius Caesar', in *The Complete Works*. New York: Harcourt, Brace & World, 809–45.

STERNE, LAURENCE. 1967. *The Life and Opinions of Tristram Shandy*. Harmondsworth: Penguin.

TENNYSON, LORD ALFRED. 2005. 'The Lady of Shalott'. The Literature Network www page <http://www.online-literature.com/tennyson/720/>, accessed 25 March 2006.

FURTHER READING

ANDERSON, JANICE CAPEL, and MOORE, STEPHEN, D. (eds.). 1992. *Mark and Method*. Minneapolis: Fortress.

BARTHES, ROLAND. 1967. *Elements of Semiology*, trans. Annette Lavers and Colin Smith. New York: Hill & Wang.

BIBLE AND CULTURE COLLECTIVE. 1995. *The Postmodern Bible*. New Haven: Yale University Press.

CHATMAN, SEYMOUR. 1980. *Story and Discourse*. New York: Cornell University Press.

CHILDS, BREVARD S. 1979. *Introduction to the Old Testament as Scripture*. Minneapolis: Augsburg Fortress.

EAGLETON, TERRY. 1991. *Ideology*. London: Verso.

MILLER, J. HILLIS. 1990. *Tropes, Parables, Performatives: Essays on Twentieth-Century Literature*. London: Harvester Wheatsheaf.

MOORE, STEPHEN D. 1989. *Literary Criticism and the Gospels: The Theoretical Challenge*. New Haven: Yale University Press.

NIDA, EUGENE, and TABER, CHARLES R. 1982. *The Theory and Practice of Translation*. Leiden: E. J. Brill.

QUINE, WILLARD VAN ORMAN. 1960. 'Translation and Meaning', in *Word and Object*. Cambridge, Mass.: MIT, 26–79.

SANDERS, JAMES A. 1984. *Canon and Community*. Philadelphia: Fortress.

CHAPTER 20

THE GOSPEL OF JOHN

ADELE REINHARTZ

Like other books of the New Testament, the Gospel of John can be viewed from a variety of perspectives. For the Christian church, it is sacred Scripture that enshrines eternal truths about God, Jesus, humankind, and the relationships among them. For historians, it is a potential source of information about the historical Jesus, and/or about the hypothetical community of Jewish-Christians at the end of the first century whom many scholars see as the group within which and for which the Gospel was written. But for those who love stories, the Fourth Gospel is a rich narrative that entices and mystifies simultaneously. Even as it unequivocally proclaims the message that Jesus is the Messiah, the Son of God, it also teases the reader with its double and triple entendres, its allusive use of language, and its elliptical statements. Most intriguing, however, is the way that the Gospel reaches out directly to the reader, across the miles and the years that lie between, to invite the reader into the story and into its way of perceiving the world.

One passage that extends this invitation clearly and explicitly is 20: 30–1, generally taken to be the Fourth Gospel's conclusion and statement of purpose: 'Now Jesus did many other signs in the presence of his disciples, which are not written in this book. But these are written so that you may come to believe that Jesus is the Messiah, the Son of God, and that through believing you may have life in his name.' The Gospel thus envisages an active relationship between the reader and the text, one that is not neutral but, on the contrary, demands the reader's commitment to the truths that it proclaims.

In prescribing the ideal reader's response to its contents, the Gospel explicitly acknowledges its own textuality and also beckons us to consider it not only as a spiritual resource or historical source, but precisely as a literary work. It is only relatively recently, however, that literary criticism, sometimes referred to as narrative criticism, has been viewed as a useful, or even a legitimate approach to the Gospel of John. Some scholars believed that it is not appropriate to apply methodologies developed for the study of imaginative literature to ancient texts, especially to sacred Scripture, and even more so to texts that, for some readers at least, are deemed to be historical. Others felt that resorting to literary criticism somehow negated or diminished the 'gains' of historical criticism (Culpepper 1983: 8).

In large measure, it was R. Alan Culpepper's 1983 book, *The Anatomy of the Fourth Gospel*, that opened the way for the inclusion of literary-critical methodologies. In the decades since the publication of this seminal work, many articles and books have utilized literary-critical theory or otherwise focused on the literary aspects of the Gospel. Culpepper explicitly states that he did not intend his book to supplant historical criticism or to challenge the results of previous research (ibid. 5). He does, however, anticipate that a literary-critical approach might lead to insights unattainable through historical methodologies.

Some twenty or more years later, the climate has changed. Today, devoted historical critics employ literary criteria, and literary criticism, or even literary theory, may no longer strike them as starkly antithetical, and threatening, to the historical-critical enterprise. Brown's posthumous *Introduction to the Gospel of John*, edited and prepared for publication by Francis Moloney, is a revision and expansion of his introduction to the two-volume Anchor Bible commentary (Brown and Moloney 2003). While it still gives pride of place to historical criticism, this book acknowledges the importance of dealing with the Gospel in its final form, as a complete narrative. It is thus a measure of the degree to which literary-critical approaches to the Fourth Gospel have become mainstream in the two or more decades since the publication of Culpepper's *Anatomy*.

This essay will provide a brief introduction to the literary-critical study of the Gospel of John. It will consider the following issues: (1) The Fourth Gospel's literary structure and the basic narrative elements such as plot, setting, characterization, and chronology; (2) some of the literary devices that pervade the Gospel; (3) the ways in which literary approaches to the Fourth Gospel resonate in English literature; (4) a number of the major literary-critical approaches that have been applied to the Gospel. Finally, it will address the question of the Gospel of John and historical criticism, to show how literary-critical approaches can actually complement and even illuminate historical concerns, as Culpepper had promised.

At the outset, it is important to clarify my usage of the terms 'Gospel', 'author', and 'evangelist'. By 'Gospel', I refer to the Gospel of John in its present form, that is, as it is found in the critical edition of the New Testament based on textual criticism of the manuscripts. In this essay, however, quotations will be in English, taken from the New Revised Standard Version of the New Testament (1989). As for authorship, New Testament scholars are in agreement that the precise identity of the author is not known, and that the Gospel probably underwent a lengthy and complex process of composition before reaching its present form. For the purposes of this discussion, I use the terms 'author' and 'evangelist' interchangeably, as a shorthand way of referring to that unknown person or group of people who had a hand in the composition of the Gospel. For the most part, these terms do not have in mind historical personages so much as the 'implied author', that is, the persona that emerges from the Gospel, or, rather, is constructed in our own consciousness when we read the Gospel. Similarly, the terms 'implied' or 'original' or 'intended' reader do not refer to specific, historical individuals or groups but rather the image of an ideal reader who would agree with and feel him- or herself addressed by the Gospel in its present form.

NARRATIVE ELEMENTS

Narrative Structure

Even before literary criticism began to be applied explicitly to the Fourth Gospel, scholars had incorporated literary observations in their analyses of the Gospels. One such observation is that the Gospel can easily be divided into two sections, with the break occurring at the end of Ch. 12. C. H. Dodd (1953) referred to Chs. 1–12 as the Book of Signs, and 13–21 as the Book of Glory. This division recognizes the differences in content and focus between these two sections. Dodd also commented in detail on the integral relationship between the Gospel's narrative and its discourse material. For example, the so-called Bread of Life discourse in 6: 22–65 takes place after the narrative of the feeding of the multitudes; it refers back to that event and expounds on the spiritual meaning of that event as well as its implications for the relationship between God and humankind.

The Book of Signs also has a distinct structure built around a series of stories that recount the 'signs' (miracles) that Jesus does in order to manifest his glory to those characters in the Gospel who are able to understand the true meaning of the acts that they are witnessing. The signs include the changing of water into wine at the wedding at Cana (John 2: 1–11), the healing of a nobleman's son (4: 46–54), the healing of a lame man (ch. 5), the multiplication of the loaves and fishes (6: 1–14), Jesus walking on water (2: 16–21), the healing of a blind man (Ch. 9), and the raising of a dead man named Lazarus (Ch. 11). Each of these narratives follows a general pattern that consists of the identification of a problem or dire situation, the expectation that Jesus can alleviate the problem, momentary uncertainty as to whether Jesus will act, the accomplishment of the miracle, and the narrator's note as to its significance. This narrative structure emphasizes that all Jesus' acts revealed and testified to his identity as the Son of God.

The Nature of the Johannine Narrative

The evangelist viewed Jesus' acts as significant beyond the witnesses within the narrative. As 20: 30–1 states, Jesus' signs were potentially revelatory not just for those who saw them at the time, but also for all those who later read about them in the pages of the Fourth Gospel. According to J. Louis Martyn, those later readers constituted a community, usually referred to as 'the Johannine community', whose experiences were written, if obliquely, within and between the lines of the Gospel narrative. These later readers, argues Martyn, would have read the Gospel on two levels, as a story of Jesus and as a record of the community's own painful experiences in conflict with the 'synagogue'—the Jewish community—among whom they lived (Martyn 2003).

Whether we can in fact read the specific experiences of the Johannine community directly out of the Gospels' story of Jesus is doubtful, in my view, yet the evangelist's apparent awareness of the post-Easter reader does imply that at the very least the story of Jesus was told in a way that resonated with, if it did not precisely describe, the lived experience of later believers. That is, it hints at a set of relationships and issues with which that community is struggling, the most important of which is the issue of how the community views itself *vis-à-vis* Judaism. In telling its story of Jesus in a way that sets up a strident dichotomy between Jesus and the Jews, this group may well be giving expression to its own fraught relationship with the Jews around them, and the difficulty of developing a self-identity that claims the legitimacy of Judaism and at the same time distinguishes itself from Judaism in significant ways (Reinhartz 1998; 2001). Thus we might say that the Gospel contains both a historical narrative, set in early first-century Judaea and Galilee, and an ecclesiological narrative, set some years later, probably within a Diaspora group or community that revered the teachings expounded in the Gospel.

There is yet a third level to the Gospel narrative, one we may term the cosmological story. The prologue and many other passages in the Gospel situate the story of Jesus in the larger narrative of God's relationship with the world or even the broader cosmos. The connection between the historical and cosmological levels is made explicit in 1: 14: 'And the Word became flesh and lived among us.' That is, God's divine, pre-existent Word descended into this world to take on human identity. The cosmological level of the Gospel's narrative implies that the story of Jesus has meaning far beyond the story's details, extending to the entire universe and for all time.

Setting and Plot

Each of these three narrative levels places Jesus and his story in a different setting and describes the central conflict in a different way. The geographical setting of the historical tale is first century Galilee, Samaria, and Judaea. The experience of these areas, particularly Judaea, under Roman dominion, is not a major focus of the

Gospel but it is the backdrop against which all of the action takes place, and which makes some of it, such as the chief priests' nervousness concerning the crowds' responses to Jesus, comprehensible (11: 48).

The central conflict on the historical level is that between Jesus and a group called the Jews. The contours of this group vary according to the context. At times the term apparently refers to a subgroup of Jews, namely, the authority figures among them (e.g. 9: 18); at other times it would seem to refer to a larger, amorphous group (12: 9). The conflict escalates through specific incidents that can be viewed as violations of Jewish law, such as the Sabbath laws (5: 16), or Jewish beliefs, such as those pertaining to prophecy (7: 52), and reaches its climax in the passion narrative when Jesus is condemned to death.

The setting of the cosmological tale, by contrast, is universal space and time. Jesus is incarnate as a specific human being in a specific time and place, but he is always existent, both before and after this specific incarnation, and he is present everywhere, to all who believe in him as the Christ and Son of God. On the cosmological level, the plot is propelled by the conflict between God and Satan; it reaches its climax at the crucifixion/resurrection event, in which Jesus, the Son of God, does battle with the Jews, who have the devil as their father (8: 44), and vanquishes 'the ruler of this world'. On the level of the ecclesiological tale, the setting is not specific, but would be extended to anywhere that there is a presence of a group that adhered to the Johannine expression of faith in Jesus as the Messiah and the Son of God. This narrative level entails the conflict between this group and all those who persecute them for their beliefs.

On all three levels, the enemy is represented or symbolized by 'the Jews', as the Jewish authorities and crowds who do not believe in Jesus in the historical tale, the ones who ostracize or, according to Martyn, expel and persecute the Johannine community in the ecclesiological tale (Martyn 2003), and the 'children of Satan' (cf. John 8: 44) in the cosmological tale.

Characterization

The protagonist of the Gospel is of course Jesus, who is the pre-existent Word within the cosmological tale and lives on within the Johannine community through the Gospel account as well as through the activity of the Paraclete or Advocate (14: 26; 15: 26). Despite these varied roles, Jesus, as a literary figure, is flat and two-dimensional. He lacks the complexity, the fallibility and hence the potential for growth, change, and development that would make him interesting as a literary figure. This is hardly surprising. Someone who is the incarnate Son of God cannot at the same time be shown as flawed, imperfect, or lacking in any way; his divine identity leaves no room for change, improvement, or self-discovery.

Not only Jesus but most of the other characters in this Gospel also lack depth. The disciples and other followers such as Mary Magdalene and Mary and Martha of Bethany illustrate varied levels and types of faith in Jesus. The Gospel does not draw them as full-fledged characters in their own right, and it is not interested in them as such but only as representatives of particular responses to Jesus. In dialogue with Jesus, they act as the foil that provides the opportunity for Jesus to proceed with his discourses. The Jews who fail to believe in Jesus are always negative, while the disciples are always good, if somewhat lacklustre, unimaginative, and lacking in insight. A possible exception to the overall flat characterization is Nicodemus, who approaches Jesus in John 3 and may, or may not, move towards faith by the end of the story (cf. 7: 50; 19: 39). To varying degrees, then, the characters model the process of faith and understanding that the implied author wants his reader to experience through reading the book. Yet, as we shall see below, the Gospel often places its readers in an ironic, superior relationship to its literary characters.

Use of Time

One of the characteristic features of narrative literature is its complex use of time and time markers (cf. Genette 1979). Overall, the Gospel of John, as a historical tale, moves forward chronologically, from the appearance of Jesus near the Jordan where John was baptizing, to his crucifixion. The references to three Passover seasons (John 2: 13; 6: 4; 12: 1) imply a time span of just over two years at the very least.

At certain points, the Gospel is very precise in defining the chronological relationships among a series of events. For example, the events in John 1: 19–2: 11 occur over the period of a week, with the intervals indicated by internal temporal markers at the beginning of each small section (e.g. 'the next day', in 1: 29, 1: 35, 1: 43; 'on the third day', in 2: 1). Other events, such as the cleansing of the temple and the multiplication of the loaves and fishes, are connected with external temporal markers such as the Jewish festival of Passover (2: 13; 6: 4).

But the Gospel also provides a number of analepses (flashbacks) and prolepses (anticipations) that momentarily remove the reader from the chronological sequence. For example, the introduction of Mary of Bethany in John 11: 2 refers forward to her anointing of Jesus' feet, which does not occur until John 12: 3. John 4 refers to the imprisonment of John the Baptist as a future event, which, interestingly enough, is not recounted in this Gospel but is familiar to us from the Synoptics. Some of the prolepses serve a theological purpose, namely, to demonstrate that Jesus is the long-awaited messianic prophet (Reinhartz 1989). This purpose can be seen in a narrative pattern in which prophetic statements that Jesus makes in the Gospel are fulfilled within the narrative itself at a subsequent point. For example, prophecies about Jesus' future crucifixion and resurrection (e.g. 3: 14) are fulfilled in John 19–20. In other cases, the narrator points out that one event or another was not understood until after Jesus' death (2: 23). These analepses and prolepses add texture and provide a means through which the Gospel reaches out to its later readers. In doing so, they also provide a bridge from the historical to the ecclesiological levels—the era of the community—and finally to the cosmological level, including that future eschatological time in which all believers will join Jesus in his Father's house (14: 2).

Style

The Gospel of John has a distinctive style that distinguishes its narrative and its protagonist from the Synoptic Gospels and the Synoptic Jesus. The Gospel creates a closed and exclusive world, with its own view of reality and its own terms of reference. Some scholars use this observation as a basis for conjecturing about the social relationships in the 'real world' between the Johannine community and its surroundings; Wayne Meeks (1972), for example, argues that the self-referential quality of the text signals a society that has its boundaries rather tightly drawn around it. From this he concludes that the Johannine community lived in some isolation from other early Christian groups.

Whether or not one believes that it is possible to draw a straight line from the self-referential literary qualities of the text to the 'real' community that may lie behind the Gospel, it is obvious that both the Johannine narrator and the Johannine Jesus use characteristic phrases that draw attention to the key points in the Gospel's portrait of Jesus and its understanding of his significance for humankind.

Examples of Characteristic Vocabulary

Signs. The Gospel narrator, as well as Jesus, use this term to describe Jesus' revelatory miracles (e.g. 2: 11, 4: 54, 20: 30–1). The Gospel is equivocal as to whether and how the signs should be used as the basis for faith. For example, the first sign, the wedding at Cana, is an action that contributes to the faith of the disciples who see it as a revelation of Jesus' glory (2: 11). But later, Jesus, along with the evangelist, is suspicious of the faith of the crowds who saw the signs that he had done (2: 2–25). The same suspicion is evident in Ch. 6, where some among the crowd who had benefited from the 'sign' of the multiplication of loaves and fishes came to make him king (6: 14).

'*Very truly, I tell you*'. Jesus punctuates some of his discourses with this phrase as a way of emphasizing one or another point that is germane to his self-revelation. In 5: 19, for example, Jesus declares: 'Very truly I tell you, the Son can do nothing on his own, but only what he sees the Father doing.' He continues in this vein in 5: 21: 'Very truly I tell you, the hour is coming, and is now here, when the dead will hear the voice of the Son of God, and those who hear will live.'

'*Woman*'. Jesus calls almost all of the major female characters in this Gospel 'woman' (the exceptions are Mary and Martha of Bethany). In the story of the wedding at Cana, Jesus' mother draws his attention to the fact that the wine has run out. He responds: 'Woman, what concern is that to you and to me? My hour has not yet come' (2: 4). In 4: 21, Jesus reveals to the Samaritan woman that a time will soon come when worship will occur neither on Mount Gerizim, the Samaritans' holy mountain, nor on Mount Zion, the Jews' holy site, but all will worship God 'in spirit and in truth' (4: 23). In 20: 15, Jesus asks Mary Magdalene, 'Woman, why are you weeping? Whom are you looking for?' as a prelude to revealing himself to her as the risen Lord. Harsh as this usage may sound to our ears, the narrative contexts suggest that the Johannine Jesus uses the vocative 'woman' not to distance himself from these female figures but to announce a revelation meant for their ears (and ours) alone.

'I AM' (Ego eimi). In seven passages, Jesus uses 'I am' without a predicate. For example, in 4: 25, the Samaritan woman declares: 'I know that Messiah is coming . . .' Jesus responds: 'I am [he], the one who is speaking to you.' In John 8: 57, the Jews mock Jesus: 'You are not yet fifty years old and have you seen Abraham?' Jesus replies: 'Very truly, I tell you, before Abraham was, I am' (8: 58). This absolute usage is an echo of God's self-revelation in Exod. 3: 14 (the 'burning bush' story) in which God identifies himself as 'I am who I am'. In using this expression, Jesus therefore underscores his identity as God's divine son.

These examples demonstrate the strong connection between Jesus' language in this Gospel, and the Gospel's Christology, in which Jesus is first and foremost the Son of God. These revelatory formulae may well have been familiar to the audience from biblical sources and also employ a repetition of refrains in order to underscore the revelatory moments in his speech.

Rhetoric of binary opposition. Throughout the Gospel, the evangelist takes pains to explain the superiority of his vision of salvation through Christ. He does so in large measure through the use of contrasting metaphors. One set of metaphors describes opposing states of being, such as light/darkness, life/death, above/below, from God/not from God. The other set comprises dichotomous activities, such as believing/disbelieving, accepting/rejecting, doing good/doing evil, loving/hating. The positive element of each pair denotes a positive relationship to Jesus and hence to God; the negative element of each pair denotes opposition to Jesus, that is, the rejection of the claim that Jesus is the Christ, the Son of God. Accepting Jesus demonstrates a love for God, for Jesus, and for fellow believers (15: 12–17). Rejecting Jesus is tantamount to hating God.

By means of this rhetoric of binary opposition, the Gospel associates the Jews closely with the negative pole of each of the dichotomous pairs. Jesus accuses the Jews of not having the love of God in them (8: 42), and tells the disciples that his enemies hate both himself and his Father (15: 23–24). Most troubling is the claim that the Jews are children not of God but of the devil (8: 44), which is consistent with this dualistic rhetoric. The statement is perhaps a logical inference from the evangelist's conviction that in rejecting Jesus, the Jews distance themselves from God. But it has had an unfortunate afterlife in the history and culture of the West as a cornerstone of anti-Semitic rhetoric already evidenced in the Book of Revelation, which refers to the 'synagogue of Satan' (Rev. 2: 9) to this very day.

Literary Devices

In addition to characteristic language, the Fourth Gospel employs a number of literary devices.

Irony. At numerous points, the narrator draws the reader into collusion over against the characters in the story. For example, in John 2: 21–2, the narrator informs the reader that Jesus' words about rebuilding the Temple in three days refer to the resurrection of his own body. The readers, with the narrator's help, therefore know something that the disciples do not, for the disciples remembered, that is, understood, this only after Jesus was raised from the dead (2: 22).

Misunderstanding. One particular type of irony in this Gospel involves an exchange in which Jesus' dialogue partner misunderstands Jesus' words by taking them literally. Doing so affords Jesus the opportunity to expound on the spiritual significance of his own statements. A clear example is Jesus' dialogue with Nicodemus. Jesus tells Nicodemus that unless someone is born again, or born from above, he or she cannot enter the kingdom of God. Nicodemus takes Jesus literally, and asks how it is possible for someone to enter the mother's womb a second time and then be born anew (3: 4). Jesus then corrects Nicodemus' mistaken interpretation and explains that he was referring to rebirth from water and the spirit, not a literal re-enactment of the physical birth process through which we all come into the world as human beings (3: 5).

Symbol and metaphor. The language in the Gospel is drawn from everyday life but it also is charged with spiritual meaning in the context of Jesus' words and deeds (cf. Koester 2003). For example, in John 6, the Bread of Life discourse, the image of the bread of life alludes to the Exodus story in which God provided sustenance for the Israelites as they wandered in the desert after their liberation from Egypt. In the Johannine context, however, the image refers to Jesus' body which believers must consume in order to be saved, and secondarily perhaps to Jesus' words and teachings. From the point of view of early Christian practice there may be yet another layer to this symbolism, as an allusion to the eucharist, though it remains a matter of controversy as to whether the Gospel 'intends' a reference to this practice. Another potent image is the Temple, which in the Gospel symbolizes Jesus' body and person, and, beyond the Gospel, may have become a symbol for the Johannine community itself (cf. Coloe 2001).

Parables and figurative vignettes. The Jesus of the Gospels of Matthew and Luke frequently speaks in parables, which are short stories, often in a pastoral setting, that refer beyond themselves to the kingdom of God (Dodd 1967). The Johannine Jesus, on the other hand, uses figurative language but usually not in the context of parables. Some scholars, however, argue that the passage about the vine leaves and vine dresser in John 15: 1–6 and the good shepherd passage in John 10: 1–5 are in fact parables (e.g. Martyn 1978: 117; Painter 1991: 53–74). This question has not been fully resolved, but on literary grounds one would tend to distinguish between these passages, which are essentially extended metaphors, and parables, which tell a short story involving characters, a problem or conflict, and a resolution (Reinhartz 1992: 54–62).

Intertextuality. Another feature or device that adds to the texture of the Gospel is intertextuality, or its allusions to other texts and images with which we may presume familiarity on the part of the original audience. For example, John 1 contains some rather explicit allusions to Genesis. Its well-known opening line, 'In the beginning was the Word, and the Word was with God, and the Word was God,' echoes Genesis 1: 1, 'In the beginning when God created the heaven and the earth', particularly in the light of Hellenistic and other Jewish traditions which posit the divine Word as the agent of creation. The Johannine Prologue also uses the imagery associated with Lady Wisdom to describe Jesus. John 1: 3 describes Jesus as being active in the divine creation of the world, a role that Prov. 8 attributes to Wisdom (cf. especially 8: 30). In its description of the pre-existent Word as becoming flesh and living, 'tabernacling', among Israel, the Prologue sounds much like the Wisdom of Ben Sira 24, in which Wisdom declares that 'the Creator of all things gave me a command, and my Creator chose the place for my tent. He said, "Make your dwelling in Jacob, and in Israel receive your inheritance." Before the ages in the beginning, he created me, and for all the ages I shall not cease to be' (24: 8–9) (Scott 1992). The encounter between Mary Magdalene and the risen Jesus in John 20, for its part, alludes to the exchange between the bride and her beloved in the Song of Songs (Reinhartz 1999).

These literary devices draw readers into the narrative and encourage them to see themselves as being directly addressed by the Gospel. Temporarily, at least, they can also view themselves as superior to some of the characters within the Gospel story itself who, not having the benefit of the narrator's commentary, do not fully comprehend the significance of the words and the works which they themselves have witnessed until the crucifixion/resurrection event.

John and English Literature

One does not have be a professional exegete to recognize that the Fourth Gospel is an artful, highly literary text. The extensive use of the Gospel of John in literature testifies to the fact that at least some readers have been delighted as well as inspired by the allusive language and other features of this text in the writing of their own works. The Gospel of John has resonated throughout Christian literature since the second century, perhaps even in the New Testament itself, given that 1 John, which may or may not have some relationship to the person or groups whose witness and words are preserved in the Fourth Gospel, directly borrows from the Gospel of John.

Within the field of English literature, references or allusions to the Gospel of John appear frequently in both poetry and prose. One of the most popular sections of the Gospel is the Prologue, and, in particular, the association or identification of Jesus as the divine Logos or Word. In some cases, the reference is theological or cosmological. An example is Emily Dickinson's 1955 poem 'A Word Made Flesh is Seldom': 'A Word made Flesh is seldom | And tremblingly partook . . . A Word that breathes distinctly | Has not the power to die' (cf. Jasper Prickett and Hass 1999: 88–9). In this poem, the focus is precisely on the moment or the idea that the Word became flesh and dwelt among humankind.

In other cases, the application is somewhat more profane. In Shakespeare's *Romeo and Juliet*, John 1: 16 provides the language with which Romeo proclaims his love for Juliet to Friar Lawrence: 'I pray thee, chide me not. Her I love now | doth grace for grace and love for love allow' (ii. iii. 85–6; Sims 1966: 47; cf. John 1: 16: 'And of his fullness have all we received, and grace for grace', KJV). In Shelley's play, *The Cenci*, Beatrice is described in the language of John 1: 5, which speaks of Jesus as the 'light shineth in the darkness; and the darkness comprehended it not' (John 1: 5). Beatrice is originally one whose 'bright loveliness | Was kindled to illumine this dark world' (iv. i. 121–2). She is 'the light of life' (iv. iii. 42; v. iv. 134—Shelley 1994: 83). In *Prometheus Unbound*, Asia's character is described in ways that echo the Johannine Logos, suggesting that 'her identity cannot be divorced from that of her masculine counterpart, the central Christ-figure of the poem' (Shelley 1994).

W. B. Yeats, in turn, plays 'in deconstructive fashion' with a number of Johannine texts, especially John 1: 1. This can be seen, for example, in 'The Song of the Happy Shepherd', in which the poet declares that 'Words alone are certain good' and then opines that 'even this good | God is no more substantial than poets' breath:' 'The wandering earth itself may be | Only a sudden flaming word, | In clanging space a moment heard' (Poems 7—Purdy 1994: 47).

The Gospel of John also frequently appears in contexts associated with sexuality. The encounter between Jesus and Mary Magdalene in the garden (Ch. 20) has long fuelled speculation with regard to their personal relationship. In the apocryphal Gospel of Mary, admittedly not a work of English literature, the disciples refer to Mary as having a special, loving relationship with Jesus; they seek her report of the words that he imparted to her when he appeared to her in the garden (King 2003; Meyer and de Boer 2004). In Nikos Kazantzakis' *The Last Temptation* (1960), Jesus holds himself responsible for Mary Magdalene's descent into prostitution. While on the cross, Jesus fantasizes that he marries Mary, and conceives a child by her, only to see her and her unborn child die. In José Saramago's *The Gospel According to Jesus Christ* (1994), Jesus is depicted as living in an intimate relationship with Mary Magdalene from the time he first meets her at age 18 until his death. She is his most loving and constant companion. This theme has surfaced most recently in Dan Brown's runaway bestseller, *The Da Vinci Code* (2003), which claims that Jesus and Mary Magdalene married and had a child, the descendants of whom are still alive today.

Jesus' words to Mary in the garden, 'Do not touch me' (Latin: *Noli me tangere*) resonate in many works of English literature. Mary Magdalene appears, for example, as the speaker in Robert Southwell's 'Mary Magdalen's Complaint at Christ's Death', in which she promises 'Though my life thou drav'st away, | Maugre thee my love shall stay' (Jasper Prickett, and Hass 1999: 295). In Tobias Smollett's *The Expedition of Humphry Clinker* (1771), the narrator recounts a remark of his uncle, referring to his wife, the narrator's aunt, as a '*noli me tangere* in my flesh, which I cannot bear to be touched or tampered with' (ibid. 295). In D. H. Lawrence's *St. Mawr* (1925), a female character sympathizes wearily with Jesus' comment to Mary Magdalene and explains:

I feel like all bruises, like one who has been assassinated. I do so understand why Jesus said: *Noli me tangere* Touch me not, I am not yet ascended unto the Father. Everything had hurt him so much, wearied him so beyond endurance, he felt he could not bear one little human touch on his body. I am like that. I can hardly bear even Elena to hand me a dress. As for a man—and marriage—ah, no! *Noli me tangere, homine*! I am not yet ascended unto the Father. Oh, leave me alone, leave me alone!   (ibid.).

Other Johannine passages, however, also provide fodder for references to or discussions pertaining to sexuality. Chaucer's Wife of Bath discusses the differences between sex and marriage by commenting on the wedding at Cana (John 2: 1–11) and Jesus' conversation with the Samaritan woman (Ch. 4). With regard to the second example, the Wife, like Johannine exegetes before and after her time, is not sure whether Jesus, in declaring to the woman that 'thou hast had five husbands; and he whom thou now hast is not thy husband' (4: 18, KJV) was referring to the Samaritan's currently illegal husband as her fifth or sixth (Besserman 1998: 150–1). Mary of Bethany's act of anointing Jesus' feet and wiping them with her hair appears in Yeats's poem 'The Travail of Passion', alongside images of and allusions to the Gospel accounts of Jesus' Passion:

> When the flaming lute-thronged angelic door is wide;
> When an immortal passion breathes in mortal clay;
> Our hearts endure the scourge, the plaited thorns, the way
> Crowded with bitter faces, the wounds in palm and side,
> the vinegar-heavy sponge, the flowers by Kedron stream;
> We will bend down and loosen our hair over you,
> That is may drop sweet perfume, and be heavy with dew,
> Lilies of death-pale hope, roses of passionate dream.
>
> (Poems 70—Purdy 1994: 49–50).

A less likely text, John 14: 2–3—'In my Father's house are many mansions: if [it were] not [so], I would have told you. I go to prepare a place for you. And if I go and prepare a place for you, I will come again, and receive you unto myself; that where I am, [there] ye may be also'—appears in a sexual context in 'Crazy Jane Talks With the Bishop'. Jane interprets Jesus' place to mean the manger. 'Love is God, the place, the stable. Jane thus insists that God acts through sexuality' (ibid. 104).

Elsewhere, the Gospel of John provides fodder for anti-Jewish representations. The most famous example, perhaps, is Shakespeare's *The Merchant of Venice*, in which Launcelot's speech about his master, the Jew Shylock, draws on the Johannine Jesus' declaration that the non-believing Jews have the devil as their father (John 8: 44). Launcelot proclaims in Act II Scene 2:

Certainly my conscience will serve me to run from this Jew my master. The fiend is at mine elbow, and tempts me, saying to me, 'Gobbo, Launcelot Gobbo, good Launcelot,' or 'good Gobbo,' or 'good Launcelot Gobbo, use your legs, take the start, run away.' My conscience says, 'No; take heed, honest Launcelot; take heed, honest Gobbo;' or, as aforesaid, 'honest Launcelot Gobbo; do not run; scorn running with thy heels.' Well, the most courageous fiend bids me pack: 'Via!' says the fiend; 'away!' says the fiend; 'for the heavens, rouse up a brave mind,' says the fiend, 'and run.' Well, my conscience, hanging about the neck of my heart, says very wisely to me, 'My honest friend Launcelot, being an honest man's son,'—or rather an honest woman's son;—for, indeed, my father did something smack, something grow to, he had a kind of taste;—well, my conscience says, 'Launcelot, budge not.' 'Budge,' says the fiend. 'Budge not,' says my conscience. 'Conscience,' say I, 'you counsel well;' fiend, say I, 'you counsel well:' to be ruled by my conscience, I should stay with the Jew my master, who, God bless the mark! is a kind of devil; and, to run away from the Jew, I should be ruled by the fiend, who, saving your reverence, is the devil himself. Certainly, the Jew is the very devil incarnal; and, in my conscience, my conscience is but a kind of hard conscience, to offer to counsel me to stay with the Jew. The fiend gives the more friendly counsel: I will run, fiend; my heels are at your commandment; I will run.

These examples are by no means exhaustive. Indeed, the Gospel of John, along with Revelation, seems to be have been one of the most popular and influential New Testament texts for English writers and poets, its symbols and stories resonating throughout the entire history of English literature.

Literary-Critical Approaches

The Gospel of John is rich with possibilities for literary-critical analysis. As a literary text, it remains just beyond our grasp; no one theory or approach can properly find a place for all of its elements. Far from being a drawback, this is actually an advantage, for it ensures that the Fourth Gospel will continue to tantalize us, and to yield fruitful insights with each new method.

A brief glance at recent publications shows that the Gospel of John has lent itself rather well to just about all the major trends in literary criticism in recent years, including structuralism (e.g. Stibbe 1994a, b), new historicism (e.g. Conway 2002), post-colonialism (e.g. Dube Shomanah and Staley 2002), and autobiographical criticism (Staley 1995; Kitzberger 1999). One approach that has been extremely fruitful in Johannine studies is feminist criticism. Feminist criticism is not a discrete methodological approach; rather, it employs the full range of literary, social-scientific, and historical critical approaches but through the lens of issues pertaining to women and gender, such as the textual representation of women, the use of female imagery, and the structure of gendered relationships (cf. Levine and Blickerstaff 2003). For example, Mary Magdalene can be discussed as a historical figure, in order to discern whether or not she was one of the group whom the Gospel designates as disciples (D'Angelo 1999; Schneiders 2003), or in order to examine her literary role in John 20 (Reinhartz 1999; Winsor 1999), or her afterlife in the history of interpretation, including popular culture (Schaberg 2002). Another area of interest is the use of wisdom language, and the wavering gender applications of this initially female imagery to a male figure such as Jesus (Conway 2003).

My own approach is drawn primarily from reader-response criticism. This approach posits that meaning resides not specifically in the text or in the intention of the author but in the complex interactions between the reader and the text. Thus one can examine the impact that text may be designed to produce in the reader (faith, leading to eternal life), and the information and attitudes that readers may be bringing to the text in their attempt to create meaning (knowledge of the Hebrew Scriptures; knowledge of certain events in Jesus' lifetime and in the lives of those around him, such as the arrest of John the Baptist). Reader-response criticism encourages us to distinguish between the implied and the real reader, and the implied and real author. These distinctions help to remind us of the distances in time, place, genre, and sensibilities, between the text and the historical events and personages that the text conjures up both within and outside the narrative as such. This approach has allowed some interaction or interface between literary and historical criticism. In particular, it has undergirded a critique of the theory that the Fourth Gospel directly describes the expulsion of Johannine Christians from the synagogue. It does so by drawing attention to the ways in which the earliest readers may well have read this text, based on hints within the text itself (Reinhartz 1998; 2001).

Most recently, my work has used reader-response criticism as a foundation for ethical criticism, an approach that has been articulated most persuasively by the literary critic Wayne Booth, entitled ethical criticism (Booth 1988). Ethical criticism goes beyond both reader-response criticism and historical criticism to encourage a reader to engage in a more fundamental way with a text, much as we engage with the friends in our lives. Using this approach, one can analyse the distinct subject positions—such as compliance, resistance, sympathy, or engagement—that we undertake as readers of text and the ways in which that subject position either facilitates or inhibits one's readiness to interact with the views of texts that are distant from our own traditions and sensibilities (Reinhartz 2001).

John and History

At the outset of this discussion, I referred to the resistance to literary criticism on the part of historical critics. A close look at the corpus of Johannine scholarship, from the Church Fathers to today, shows that most interpretations, whether they acknowledge it or not, utilize the Gospel's literary features in developing and expounding their own historical or theological hypotheses. Origen's famous description of the Gospel of John as the spiritual Gospel (Origen, *Commentary on the Gospel According to John* 1. 40 (1989: 42)) is an assessment of its content, and a declaration that the Gospel should have an impact on the reader that goes beyond informing him or her about events that may have happened to a historical figure. More recently, source critics, who are interested in reconstructing the written sources that the evangelist may have used in composing the Gospel, use literary criteria in order to formulate their hypotheses. Rudolph Bultmann, for example, distinguished among several sources including a signs source, and a revelatory discourse source (Bultmann et al. 1976). Bultmann's theories reflect his assessment that the distinctions in genre between narrative and discourse, and his analysis of similarities and differences between these materials and those of other groups, all reflect the evangelist's use of different prior written sources. On this basis, he concludes that Jesus' discourses are influenced by the Gnostic redeemer myth in which the saviour descends from heaven and ascends again. In addition, his theory posits the existence of a redactor who rearranged the components of the Gospel and thereby disrupted some of the integrity of the original document. This theory reflects a belief in the Fourth evangelist as a consistent writer; hence all elements, whether narrative or theological, that disrupt that consistency were laid at the feet of a figure other than the evangelist.

Later scholars, such as R. T. Fortna, accepted and developed the notion of a written signs source but not the existence of other written sources or the activity of an ecclesiastical redactor (Fortna 1970). Raymond E. Brown (Brown 1966; 1979), while accepting much of Fortna's work, also postulated a number of successive editions of the Gospel in which material was added and revised in accord with the ongoing development of tradition as well as the experiences of the (hypothetical) Johannine community. These hypotheses regarding the Gospel's composition history are historical in the sense that they pertain to the historical circumstances that may have influenced the process by which the Gospel attained its present form, but they involve analyses of and judgements about the Gospel's literary characteristics, and such questions as whether or not it is to be seen as unified work.

Perhaps the most influential historical hypothesis is that of J. Louis Martyn (2003). As I have already mentioned briefly, Martyn argued that the Gospel of John is a two-level narrative, one level telling a story of Jesus who had been crucified as the consequence of a conflict with the Jewish authorities of his time, and the second level telling the story of a Christian community that had been expelled from the synagogue by the Jewish authorities of their time, some six decades after Jesus' death. This theory has become virtually axiomatic in recent Johannine scholarship, but it must be noted that even this fundamentally histor-ical-critical hypothesis is based on literary considerations, namely, that certain incidents that the Gospel recounts are anachronistic to the time of Jesus and thus reflect the late first-century context in which the Gospel was written. Further, it makes a number of basic literary assumptions: that the Gospel is written in a way that encodes and alludes to this context and that it would have been read that way by its original audience.

The turn to the literary initially suggested to some scholars that historical ques-tions should not be put to the Fourth Gospel, and/or that the Fourth Gospel was not amenable to historical research precisely because it is such a literary work, and because it seems to operate in its own world (Kysar 2005). Yet at the same time, there are others who are indeed asking, or returning to, historical questions, yet with a consciousness of the literary elements of the Gospel. Some are now suggesting that the Fourth Gospel may provide some data for historical Jesus research, and that it should not be sidelined from this enterprise. One proponent of this approach is Paula Fredriksen, who argues that in certain respects the Fourth may offer a more accurate, or at least a more plausible set of data than the Synoptics. An awareness of the Gospel as a literary work can also help us to see which elements may indeed reflect ancient tradition or even historical realities (cf. Fortna and Thatcher 2001; Fredriksen 1999).

A second historical issue is the history of the Johannine community. Approaching the Gospel as a literary text does not rule out the possibility that it does in some fashion reflect the realities, or the perceived realities, of an ancient community of followers of the Johannine understanding of Jesus. But the literary-critical approaches do point out and emphasize the artfulness of the Gospel's presentation, and also allow us to consider the distance between ourselves and the original readers of the Gospel, and the assumptions that we make. At the same time, we need to take into account the possibility that the Gospel story is told in a way that would appeal directly to a late first-century audience, and that at the very least it would resonate with their current issues and struggles even if it is not a direct reflection of those struggles or it does not allow us to reconstruct them precisely if at all.

As we noted at the outset, Culpepper's foray into literary criticism of the Fourth Gospel was motivated in part by a desire to show that an approach to the Gospel as a literary rather than a straightforward historical text illuminates aspects of the Gospel that other methodologies fail to address. Not all scholars have been convinced by Culpepper or by the many books that followed suit. John Ashton (1994: 165), for example, explicitly questions the value of narrative criticism, and suggests that in fact it is very limited in its ability to illuminate aspects of the text beyond what other approaches can do. He calls literary critics to task for failing to take full measure of the Gospel's declared historical intentions, and for ignoring or eliding the profound differences between fiction and non-fiction. Implicit in this critique is a fundamental objection to the use of methods first developed in the study of imaginative literature to texts that do not construct themselves as fiction.

Yet in my view Ashton's critique is misplaced. The methods developed in the study of fiction are useful in the study of the Gospels not because they are similar or dissimilar in their stated relationship to external 'reality' but because they are narratives. The elements of plot, setting, character, and the details of style and literary devices are not specific to fiction as such, but to narrative, that is, to any text, imaginative or historical or somewhere in between, that tells a story. Patently this is true of the Gospel of John as it is of many ancient texts within the canon and outside it.

If postmodernism has taught us anything, it is that we must interrogate the facile binary oppositions in which we are accustomed to classify the world. Surely one such binary opposition is that between fiction and non-fiction, and another between literature and history. One may legitimately debate whether or not one or another narrative segment within the Gospel, or symbol, or character, or dialogue is or is not illuminated by literary theory. But it seems to me beyond dispute that all exegetes, whatever their specific methodological commitments, are first and foremost readers of the text. If it does nothing else, literary criticism can foster a sensitivity to the literary elements of the Fourth Gospel, and an awareness of what moves, and what assumptions, one is making when one reads the Gospel as a believer, as a non-believer, as a theologian, as a historian, or as some or none of these.

WORKS CITED

ASHTON, JOHN. 1994. *Studying John: Approaches to the Fourth Gospel*. Oxford: Clarendon.

BESSERMAN, LAWRENCE L. 1998. *Chaucer's Biblical Poetics*. Norman: University of Oklahoma Press.

BOOTH, WAYNE C. 1988. *The Company We Keep: An Ethics of Fiction*. Berkeley: University of California Press.

BROWN, RAYMOND EDWARD. 1966. *The Gospel According to John*. Anchor Bible 29–29 A. Garden City, NY: Doubleday.

—— 1979. *The Community of the Beloved Disciple*. New York: Paulist Press.

—— and MOLONEY, FRANCIS J. 2003. *An Introduction to the Gospel of John*. Anchor Bible. New York: Doubleday.

BULTMANN, RUDOLF KARL, BEASLEY-MURRAY, G. R., HOARE, RUPERT WILLIAM NOEL, and RICHES, JOHN KENNETH. 1976. *The Gospel of John: A Commentary*. Philadelphia: Westminster.

COLOE, MARY L. 2001. *God Dwells with Us: Temple Symbolism in the Fourth Gospel*. Collegeville, Minn.: Liturgical Press.

CONWAY, COLLEEN M. 2002. 'The Production of the Johannine Community: A New Historicist Perspective'. *Journal of Biblical Literature* 121: 479–95.

—— 2003. ' "Behold the Man!" Masculine Christology and the Fourth Gospel', in Stephen D. Moore and Janice Capel Anderson (eds.). *New Testament Masculinities*. Atlanta: Society of Biblical Literature, 163–80.

CULPEPPER, R. ALAN. 1983. *Anatomy of the Fourth Gospel: A Study in Literary Design*. Philadelphia: Fortress.

D'ANGELO, MARY ROSE. 1999. 'Reconstructing "Real" Women in Gospel Literature: The Case of Mary Magdalene', in Ross Shepard Kraemer and Mary Rose D'Angelo (eds.). *Women and Christian Origins*. New York: Oxford University Press, 105–28.

DODD, C. H. 1953. *The Interpretation of the Fourth Gospel*. Cambridge: Cambridge University Press.

—— 1967. *The Parables of the Kingdom*. [London]: Collins.

DUBE SHOMANAH, MUSA W., and STALEY, JEFFREY LLOYD. 2002. *John and Postcolonialism: Travel, Space and Power*. London: Sheffield Academic Press.

FORTNA, ROBERT TOMSON. 1970. *The Gospel of Signs: A Reconstruction of the Narrative Source Underlying the Fourth Gospel*. London: Cambridge University Press.

—— and THATCHER, TOM. 2001. *Jesus in Johannine Tradition*. Louisville, Ky.: Westminster/John Knox.

FREDRIKSEN, PAULA. 1999. *Jesus of Nazareth, King of the Jews: A Jewish Life and the Emergence of Christianity*. New York: Knopf.

GENETTE, GÉRARD. 1979. *Narrative Discourse: An Essay in Method*. Ithaca, NY: Cornell University Press.

JASPER, DAVID, PRICKETT, STEPHEN, and HASS, ANDREW. 1999. *The Bible and Literature: A Reader*. Oxford: Blackwell.

KING, KAREN L. 2003. *The Gospel of Mary of Magdala: Jesus and the First Woman Apostle*. Santa Rosa, Calif.: Polebridge.

KITZBERGER, INGRID R. 1999. *The Personal Voice in Biblical Interpretation*. London: Routledge.

KOESTER, CRAIG R. 2003. *Symbolism in the Fourth Gospel: Meaning, Mystery, Community*. Minneapolis: Fortress.

KYSAR, ROBERT. 2005. *Voyages with John: Charting the Fourth Gospel*. Waco: Baylor University Press.

LEVINE, AMY-JILL, and BLICKENSTAFF, MARIANNE. 2003. *A Feminist Companion to John.* Feminist Companion to the New Testament and Early Christian Writings. London: Sheffield Academic Press, 4–5.

MARTYN, J. LOUIS. 1978 (1968; 1979). *The Gospel of John in Christian History: Essays for Interpreters.* Theological Inquiries. New York: Paulist Press.

—— 2003. *History and Theology in the Fourth Gospel.* New Testament Library. Louisville, Ky.: Westminster/John Knox.

MEEKS, WAYNE A. 1972. 'The Man from Heaven in Johannine Sectarianism'. *Journal of Biblical Literature* 91: 44–72.

MEYER, MARVIN W., and DE BOER, ESTHER. 2004. *The Gospels of Mary: The Secret Tradition of Mary Magdalene, The Companion of Jesus.* San Francisco: HarperSanFrancisco.

ORIGEN and HEINE, RONALD E. (ed.) 1989. *Commentary on the Gospel according to John.* Fathers of the Church. Washington, DC: Catholic University of America Press, v. 80, 89.

PAINTER, JOHN. 1991. 'Tradition, History and Interpretation in John 10', in Johannes Beutler and Robert Tomson (eds.). *The Shepherd Discourse of John 10 and Its Context.* Cambridge: Cambridge University Press, 53–74.

PURDY, DWIGHT H. 1994. *Biblical Echo and Allusion in the Poetry of W. B. Yeats: Poetics and the Art of God.* Lewisburg: Bucknell University Press.

REINHARTZ, ADELE. 1989. 'Jesus as Prophet: Predictive Prolepses in the Fourth Gospel'. *Journal of the Study of the New Testament* 36: 3–16.

—— 1992. *The Word in the World: The Cosmological Tale in the Fourth Gospel.* The Society of Biblical Literature Monograph Series 45. Atlanta, Ga.: Scholars Press.

—— 1998. 'The Johannine Community and its Jewish Neighbors: A Reappraisal', in Fernando F. Segovia (ed.). *'What is John?' Literary and Social Readings of the Fourth Gospel.* Atlanta: Society of Biblical Literature, ii. 111–38.

—— 1999. 'To Love the Lord: An Intertextual Reading of John 20', in Fiona Black, et al. (eds.). *The Labour of Reading: Essays in Honour of Robert C. Culley.* Atlanta: Scholars Press, 56–69.

—— 2001. *Befriending the Beloved Disciple: A Jewish Reading of the Gospel of John.* New York: Continuum.

SCHABERG, JANE. 2002. *The Resurrection of Mary Magdalene: Legends, Apocrypha, and the Christian Testament.* New York: Continuum.

SCHNEIDERS, SANDRA MARIE. 2003. *Written That You May Believe: Encountering Jesus in the Fourth Gospel.* New York: Crossroad.

SCOTT, MARTIN. 1992. *Sophia and the Johannine Jesus.* Sheffield: JSOT.

SHELLEY, BRYAN. 1994. *Shelley and Scripture: The Interpreting Angel.* Oxford English Monographs. Oxford: Clarendon.

SIMS, JAMES H. 1966. *Dramatic Uses of Biblical Allusions in Marlowe and Shakespeare.* Gainesville: University of Florida Press.

STALEY, JEFFREY LLOYD. 1988. *The Print's First Kiss: A Rhetorical Investigation of the Implied Reader in the Fourth Gospel.* Chico, Calif.: Scholars Press.

—— 1995. *Reading with a Passion: Rhetoric, Autobiography, and the American West in the Gospel of John.* New York: Continuum.

STIBBE, MARK W. G. 1994a. *John's Gospel.* New Testament Readings. London: Routledge.

—— 1994b. *John as Storyteller: Narrative Criticism and the Fourth Gospel.* Monograph Series (Society for New Testament Studies); 73. Cambridge: Cambridge University Press.

WINSOR, ANN ROBERTS. 1999. *A King is Bound in the Tresses: Allusions to the Song of Songs in the Fourth Gospel.* Studies in Biblical Literature 6. New York: Peter Lang.

Further Reading

Bennett, Fordyce R. 1997. *A Reference Guide to the Bible in Emily Dickinson's Poetry.* Lanham, Md.: Scarecrow.

Carter, Thomas. 1905. *Shakespeare and the Holy Scripture, with the version he used.* London: Hodder & Stoughton.

Conway, Colleen M. 1999. *Men and Women in the Fourth Gospel: Gender and Johannine Characterization.* Atlanta, Ga.: Society of Biblical Literature.

Culpepper, R. Alan. 1983. *Anatomy of the Fourth Gospel: A Study in Literary Design.* Philadelphia: Fortress.

Jasper, David, Prickett, Stephen, and Hass, Andrew. 1999. *The Bible and Literature: A Reader.* Oxford: Blackwell.

Martyn, J. Louis. 2003. *History and Theology in the Fourth Gospel.* New Testament Library. Louisville, Ky.: Westminster/John Knox.

Meeks, Wayne A. 1972. 'The Man from Heaven in Johannine Sectarianism'. *Journal of Biblical Literature* 91: 44–72.

Reinhartz, Adele. 2001. *Befriending the Beloved Disciple: A Jewish Reading of the Gospel of John.* New York: Continuum.

Wright, T. R. 2000. *D. H. Lawrence and the Bible.* Cambridge: Cambridge University Press.

CHAPTER 21

APOCALYPTIC LITERATURE

CHRISTOPHER ROWLAND

THERE are many different kinds of prophecy in Christendom. One is prophecy which interprets the writings of the prophets...Another kind foretells things to come which are not previously contained in Scripture, and this prophecy is of three types. The first expresses itself simply in words, without images and figures—as Moses, David, and others of the prophets prophesy about Christ, and as Christ and the apostles prophesy about Antichrist, false teachers, etc. The second type does this with images, but alongside them it supplies their interpretation in specific words—as Joseph interprets dreams, and Daniel both dreams and images. The third type does it without either words or interpretations, exclusively with images and figures, like this book of Revelation and like the dreams, visions, and images that many holy people have had from the Holy Spirit...So long as this kind of prophecy remains without explanation and gets no sure interpretation, it is a concealed and mute prophecy and has not yet come to the profit and fruit which it is to give to Christendom.   (Luther, *Prefaces to the New Testament* 1546; Luther 1960: xxxv. 399–400)

Luther's later Preface to the Book of Revelation in 1530, from which this is taken, not only exhibits a clear recognition of the difference in genre among the biblical prophetic and apocalyptic texts, especially Daniel and Revelation, it also echoes earlier attempts to differentiate among visions. The fourfold character of vision is set out by Richard of St Victor (Dronke 1984: 146): physical sight which contains no hidden significance; a mode of sight such as when Moses beheld the burning bush; the seeing through visible things to the invisible, and finally contemplation of the celestial without the mediation of any visible figures.

The term 'apocalypse' denotes a particular literary type found in the literature of ancient Judaism, characterized by claims to offer visions or other disclosures of divine mysteries concerning a variety of subjects, especially those to do with the future ('eschatology'). When we find cataclysmic events described in these texts, they are often labelled 'apocalyptic' because they resemble the world-shattering events described in John's visions in the book of Revelation. There is only one apocalypse in the Hebrew Bible, the book of Daniel, though the discovery of fragments of an Enoch apocalypse among the Dead Sea Scrolls remind us that apocalyptic was a widespread phenomenon in Second Temple Judaism (the religion which came to an end with the destruction of Jerusalem in 70 CE).

Apocalyptic literature has obvious links with the prophetic texts of the Hebrew Bible, and particularly with the future hope of the prophets. The concern with human history and the vindication of Israel's hopes echoes prophetic themes, several of which have contributed to the language of the book of Revelation, particularly Ezekiel, Daniel, and Zechariah. There are also some similarities with the Wisdom books of the Hebrew Bible, with its interest in understanding the cosmos and the ways of the world. The most obvious apocalyptic or revelatory moment in the Wisdom corpus is the opening and dramatic climax of the book of Job. This climax enables Job's entirely reasonable stance to be transcended, and for Job to move from understanding on the basis of hearsay to understanding based on apocalyptic insight (Job 42: 11).

DANIEL

The one Old Testament apocalypse (regarded as a prophetic book in the Christian Bible, placed after the prophecy of Ezekiel but in the Writings in the canon of the Hebrew Bible) contains a mixture of stories concerning the activity of a Jewish elite in Babylon, chief among whom is Daniel, their activities in discerning the mysterious dreams and signs which confront Babylonian kings, and the limits of compromise which lead to persecution. The second half of the book is a series of visions about the future purposes of God, which, though given in the time of the Exile, relates to the political situation in the middle of the second century BCE. Its scope is international and relates the life of the righteous people to the succession of world empires and offers them the promise of eschatological vindication (Dan. 12: 2 contains the first explicit doctrine of resurrection in the Bible). (See Collins: 1993.)

In Daniel a significant part of the book has to do with the royal court in Babylon, and ch. 2 offers an interpretation of Nebuchadnezzar's dream. Here are men who are comfortable, respected Jews who have a good reputation in the land of their exile, though there is nostalgia for Zion (Dan. 6: 10) and limits on what the Jews described in these stories are prepared to compromise. As in Revelation, idolatry is the problem (Dan. 3). The fiery furnace and the lions' den are the terrible consequence for those who refuse to conform. Yet there is evidence of admiration on the part of the king and a reluctance to see these significant courtiers die. Nebuchadnezzar is depicted with a degree of sympathy (unlike Belteshazzar in Dan. 4). Those who resist the imperial system are prepared to face suffering but have miraculous escapes.

Daniel presents individuals who are immersed in the life of the pagan court. Very differently, Revelation countenances no such accommodation. There is a more distanced and antagonistic attitude to empire. Although Rev. 18 reflects, briefly, on Babylon's fall from the perspective of the kings, the mighty, and the merchants, the position is one of vigorous rejection of the power and effects of empire and of satisfaction at the ultimate triumph of God's righteousness (14: 11; 19: 3). The only strategies are resistance and withdrawal (18: 4). Accommodation may be a sign of apostasy (Rev. 2: 20 ff.). In Revelation persecution is expected to include suffering and death (2: 11; 6: 9; 7: 14; 11: 7; 13: 10; 12: 11).

Luther was right to note the difference between Daniel and Revelation. However enigmatic the meaning of the texts, the genres of the two books are quite different and leave the reader with different approaches to the original visions. Whereas Daniel is almost always offered some kind of interpretation (e.g. in chs. 2, 10–11), in which an angel explains the obscure images, such an explanation is almost completely lacking in Revelation which allows the interpreter greater latitude in the way in which the original vision is interpreted.

In one important sense the kind of effect that both have had on subsequent literature and art has taken little account of these differences. The book of Revelation itself is an indication of the fact that Daniel, from a very early time, was an influential text for later visionaries (along with Ezekiel). Indeed, the particular interpretations are ignored in favour of a reuse of the visionary images in the new visionary situation, two hundred years later. Thus, for example, the interpretation of Daniel's vision of the beasts arising out of the sea becomes a vehicle of a powerful political critique of the contemporary polity in Rev. 13. Nevertheless, the Danielic vision is interpreted synchronically rather than diachronically. Thus, it is not a succession of empires but a fourfold imperial oppression. The frequent allusions to Daniel in both Revelation and 2 Esdras show that whatever the precision of the interpretations offered Daniel, this prophetic text allowed the possibility of later appropriation and renewed actualization. Alongside Revelation (and indeed in the extant literature attested earlier), the Book of Daniel formed a foundation of Christian eschatological expectation.

Interest in the book of Daniel in the New Testament revolves around two issues: Christology and eschatology. With regard to the first, the presence, distinctively, in the New Testament of the phrase 'the Son of man' on the lips of Jesus, as well as allusions to Dan. 7: 13, indicates the importance attached to this chapter in defining the role of Jesus as the mediator of divine authority. The political character of this kind of reading is implied as the ultimate triumph of the Son of man over the reign of the beasts, suggesting an end of the dominion of the empires of this age (cf. 1 Cor. 15: 25). In the book of Revelation (as also in the roughly contemporary 2 Esdras 13), Dan. 7 has become the source of the political critique which is found in Rev. 13, where there is an implicit link of the beasts of Daniel with the rule of the contemporary beast, the Roman Empire. To this extent Daniel provided a crucial catalyst for early Christian writers as they sought to expound the significance of Jesus in the light of their eschatological convictions about him.

The earliest commentary (and indeed one of the earliest biblical commentaries) now extant on either book is Hippolytus' commentary at the beginning of the third century (Daley 1991). This differs from later interpretations which are more the detailed explication of the eschatological scenario and in this respect show greater affinity with the detailed explanations which are to be found in the angelic interpretations in Daniel itself. Hippolytus, who wrote in Rome around the beginning of the third century CE, explains the vision of Nebuchadnezzar with regard to the world empires of antiquity, by interpreting ch. 2 in the light of ch. 7 where the terrible fourth beast of Dan. 7 is identified with Rome. Like many Christian interpreters after him, Hippolytus sees the coming of Christ taking place in the fifth period of an age of the world lasting seven thousand years. The commentary concerns an account of human history in the light of Daniel. Indeed, Hippolytus notices what subsequent scholarship has noticed, namely, that the prophecies of Dan. 9–10 concern the time of Antiochus Epiphanes in the middle of the second century CE. He interprets Dan. 9: 25 as the first coming of Christ, and Daniel's sealed book is that which the Lamb opens in Rev. 5: 6. A new dimension of the prophecy starts with 9: 26 and the following verses refer to the fulfilment of the eschatological promises. The vision in Dan. 10 is a vision of the pre-existent Christ (as also is Dan. 12: 6), and Hippolytus interprets the different parts of his appearance of the gifts which he brought. Chapter 11 continues to adopt a mixture of history and eschatology, in part about the time of Antiochus, which anticipated the time of Antichrist, and that of Antichrist. Apart from the way in which Hippolytus apportions some parts of the book to past history (from Hippolytus' perspective) and others to the future, we find him making links with the other canonical apocalypse, so Dan. 11: 36 is linked with Rev. 11. Thus, in the earliest Christian commentary we find the connections already made which would be systematized and expanded in subsequent eschatological expositions, where Revelation and Daniel are woven together.

With the emergence of the self-conscious eschatological timetabling which was the legacy of the Joachite revolution in the twelfth century, the book of Daniel's futurism was mapped onto Revelation, an interpretative move that had been made as far back as the commentary of Hippolytus, to yield a major resource for the description of the divine plan for human history. The influential commentator on Revelation, Joseph Mede (1586–1638), whose detailed exegesis of that book offered a way of unlocking both its hermeneutic and its message, allowed others, such as Isaac Newton, to expound the wisdom of the providential ordering of history evident in the prophetic texts. The legacy of this kind of approach to apocalyptic literature is evident in the often complex and detailed descriptions of the meaning of the prophetic texts and the way they relate to one another in the exposition of the future. This has its culmination in the synthetic eschatology in the modern period, which has become a cornerstone of modern eschatological scenarios. The Scofield Reference Bible (1909) popularized a view which has a long pedigree, and which owed not a little to the eschatological interpreter John Nelson Darby (1800–82). Darby's link of the rapture of 1 Thess. 4 to the material in Daniel and Revelation (and other biblical prophetic books) in particular, has led to an enormously influential set of beliefs on the future of the world and the relationship of the elect to it.

The Geneva Bible's marginal notes on the Book of Daniel are a salutary reminder that we are dealing with a text which was exegetical dynamite in its ability to support and inform struggles for change. Calvin continues the line taken by Hippolytus with a strictly historical reading of the statue of Dan. 2, though he reads the stone which shatters the statue Christologically. It is Christ who destroys all worldly empires: 'outside of Christ whatever is splendid and powerful in the world, and wealthy and strong, is fleeting and passing and of little worth' (Calvin (1993: 106) on Dan. 2: 45; Parker 1993).

A more immediate, existential, and potentially revolutionary kind of reading of the book is also found. Thomas Muentzer (c.1483–1525) is a case in point. His reputation is as the dangerous fanatic whose resort to violence drew upon himself and his companions a horrible retribution in the midst of the German Peasants' Revolt in 1525. In what must be one of the most remarkable sermons preached in the early Reformation period, the so-called Sermon before the Princes, Muentzer depends on Dan. 2 for a final, critical challenge to local rulers to throw in their lot with the common people and themselves be the agents of the imminent eschatological harvest. According to Muentzer, Nebuchadnezzar shamed the people of God by his actions, by accepting what God had to say to him and proving himself to be a worthy recipient of the divine mysteries. The soothsayers of his own court resembled the ecclesiastical intellectuals of Muentzer's own day in presuming to interpret the divine mysteries without really understanding either them or the Almighty. Muentzer, like Daniel and all the true prophets before him, was equipped to do what every pious person could do as the result of the indwelling Spirit. Muenzter's interpretation of the statue fits into a long history of eschatological doctrine in which the 'fifth kingdom' is the decisive one. At the height of the English Revolution in the seventeenth century the doctrine of the 'Fifth Monarchy' (namely, that the succession of world empires predicted in Dan. 2 and 7 had come to its end and that the reign of King Jesus was about to be established) was extremely influential among revolutionary groups. In the establishment of this 'fifth monarchy', the saints were given an active role, being Christ's instruments in the establishment of the kingdom of God on earth (Capp 1972).

A century later than Thomas Muentzer, in England, there arose another prophetic figure with views on the interpretation of prophetic texts linked to practical action, but with more of that sense of passive resistance within the constraints of history that we find in the book of Daniel. Gerrard Winstanley's writing career spans the years 1648 to 1652, the period from the second Civil War to the last years of the Commonwealth. As far as we know, no further theological and political writings are now extant (Sabine 1941). From April 1649 to March 1650 Winstanley's life and writing was intimately bound up with the practice of communism in rural Surrey.

According to Winstanley, private property is the curse of the fall, and those who possess it have gained it by oppression or murder. Its prevalence is typified by the rule of the Beast through a professional ministry; the kingly power; the judiciary; and 'the buying and selling of the earth, which correspond to the four beasts in the book of Daniel. In this passage, the process of 'updating' Daniel, already evident in Revelation and 4 Ezra, is at work but now applied to the particular manifestation of tyranny evident in the English monarchical state.

What is striking about these readings of Daniel is the ready way in which writers relate the images to their own time. They differ from many readings of Daniel, ancient and modern, in that they do not depend on their meaning in the ancient world.

OTHER APOCALYPTIC TEXTS:
1 ENOCH AND 4 EZRA

1 Enoch opens with an alternative account of the corruption of the earth parallel to the opening chapters of Genesis (See Nickelsburg 2001; Stone 1990.) Enoch's position in heaven means that he can intercede on behalf of the fallen angels. Enoch eventually reaches Paradise. In the next section of the book, the Parables, probably much later than the opening chapters and with many features which distinguish it from the rest, we have a heterogeneous collection of material which mixes an account of Enoch's activities with God. In this, Enoch describes a figure 'like a son of man' (this section of 1 Enoch has many connections with the 'Son of man' sayings in the gospels). In ch. 72 we have a section dealing with astronomical material, which Enoch reads in the heavenly tablets. Enoch passes on other awesome visions concerning the future of the earth, one of which is long and symbolic. The book closes with a collection of advice and warning from Enoch to his children with woes for the rich and powerful and vindication for the humble and meek.

The book of 2 Esdras is an important witness to Second Temple eschatological belief (Sanders 1977: 409–18) and its influence persisted into the early modern period (Hamilton 1999). In 4 Ezra (the Jewish apocalypse found in 2 Esdr. 3–14) there is another concern: the apparent inscrutability and mercilessness of God. At times it appears that Ezra's concerns are more merciful than the divine reply. Such sentiments, however, are dealt with by urging the righteous to concentrate on the glory which awaits those who are obedient to God. From angelic revelation Ezra learns that the righteous need to view all things in the light of the eschatological consummation rather than concentrate exclusively on the apparent injustices of the present. The righteous are urged to attend to their destiny and concentrate on obedience to the law of God. There is a questioning of the way the world is. There emerges, possibly for the first time in such an explicit form, evidence for a hope for a new age which is transcendent, though it appears alongside the conventional hope for a this-worldly reign of God (7: 28–9; cf. 5: 45; Rev. 20–1).

The apocalypse of 4 Ezra purges the mind of any presumption of ability to fathom the wisdom of God, by showing it an erroneous assumption engendered by a corrupted mind. Those who, like Ezra, continue in obedience, a way of life which seems so pointless, receive reassurance that faithful endurance will pay off ultimately. That is the only kind of answer on offer in this tantalizing apocalypse. The persistent concern throughout the earlier part of the dialogue between Ezra and the angel is the exploration of the conditions for understanding the ways of God.

REVELATION

The Apocalypse is a different sort of text to those discussed above. Daniel is pseudonymous and was probably written in the second century BCE at the height of the crisis which threatened Jerusalem and its temple under the Seleucid king Antiochus IV. John's apocalypse does not claim some kind of authority via an apostle (although John shares the same name as the son of Zebedee and the book was linked with John from a very early stage in the early church). John's authority depends on his prophetic call (1: 9–11). Revelation (or 'unveiling'—the meaning of the word 'apocalypse') was the catalyst in succeeding centuries for a variety of eschatologically inclined movements and readings of history. (See Kovacs and Rowland 2004.) It is representative of that spirit of early Christianity which allied expectation of historical change with visionary intuition, endowing its message with authenticity.

Traditionally the date of the book has been towards the end of the reign of the emperor Domitian (the mid-90s), who took action against some members of the imperial household for their atheism (though the charge of atheism could equally have been levelled at sympathizers of Judaism as Christianity). Evidence from Rev. 17 itself suggests that an earlier date is equally likely, perhaps after Nero's death in 68, when there were four claimants to the office in a year (Galba, Otho, Vitellius, and Vespasian who finally became emperor). Evidence for persecution in Asia Minor at the time of Domitian is sparse apart from Revelation, though there appears to have been harassment of Jews at the end of Domitian's reign. Domitian claimed for himself the title *dominus ac deus noster*. The external evidence is strong for a Domitianic date, but the internal evidence of this chapter points in the general direction of a date for the Apocalypse three decades earlier.

Revelation is part of a tradition and is a continuation of much of what has gone before. Ezekiel and Daniel have influenced the form and content of the book of Revelation. From the Christophany at its opening, via the visions of heaven, the dirge over Babylon, the war against Gog and Magog, and finally the vision of the new Jerusalem, it bears the marks of influence of the written forms of the ancient prophetic imagination on the newer prophetic imagination of John of Patmos. Daniel is an ingredient of John's vision from almost the first verse to the last: the vision of the human figure in ch. 1; the vision of the beast in ch. 13, and the designation of the character of the book as 'what must take place after this' are all indebted to Daniel. Daniel's beasts from the sea become in John's vision a terrible epitome of all that is most oppressive and yet eerily akin to the way of perfection symbolized by the Lamb that was slain, as the similarity to the character of the Lamb of the description of the head of the beast in Rev. 13: 3 and 17: 8 suggests. So this unique example in the early Christian literature of the apocalyptic genre is profoundly indebted to Jewish apocalyptic ideas.

The vision of Christ marks the start of John's revelation. After the instruction to write the letters to the seven churches, John is called to heaven in the spirit and is granted a vision of the divine throne with one seated upon it. There is at the start of this new dimension of John's vision, a vision of the throne which owes some of its details to Ezek. 1 and Isa. 6. The seer is offered a glimpse of a reality which is cut off from normal human gaze and opened up only to the privileged. Revelation 4, however, is subverted in ch. 5. John sees the scroll with seven seals, which contains the divine will for the inauguration of the eschatological process. The means of the initiation of that process turns out to be the coming of the Messiah, the Lion of Judah. The paradox is that this messianic Lion turns out to be a Lamb with the marks of death. It is the Lamb's marks of slaughter that qualified it to have this supreme eschatological role and to share the divine throne (Rev. 7: 17).

The sequence of seals, trumpets, and bowls is initiated by the Lamb taking the heavenly book (chs. 5, 6, 8–9, and 16). It is the predetermined evolution of the divine purposes in history as the structures of the world give way to the messianic age (the millennium). The opening of the seals had unleashed the Four Horsemen with their destructive potential. This is suddenly interrupted in ch. 7: the sealing of the servants of God with the seal of the living God. There is a contrast here similar to that found in chs. 13 and 14.

In chs. 10–11 the seer is involved in the unfolding eschatological drama of the apocalypse when he is instructed to eat the scroll and commanded to prophesy. The prophetic commission is followed in ch. 11 by a vision in which the church is offered a paradigm of the true prophetic witness as it sets out to fulfil its vocation to prophesy before the world. Juxtaposed with the vision of the two witnesses, their death and vindication, is another vision about persecution. The message is quite a simple one: a pregnant woman is threatened by a dragon and gives birth to a male child who is precious to God as the Messiah. That is followed immediately by the account of another struggle in which there is war in heaven between Michael and the dragon who had persecuted the woman. Michael and his forces prevail, meaning there is no longer a place in heaven for the dragon. The vision seems to suggest that the picture of a heavenly struggle is closely linked with the earthly struggle of those who seek to be disciples of Jesus to maintain their testimony.

A hostile attitude to the Roman Empire emerges in the Book of Revelation. The position is one of vigorous rejection of the power and effects of empire, and of satisfaction at the ultimate triumph of God's righteousness (14: 11; 19: 3). The book concludes with visions of the victory of the Son of Man over the enemies of God and the messianic reign on earth which precede the Last Judgement and the coming of the New Jerusalem.

Only in chs. 20–2 is the resolution of the contrary states of heaven and earth, good and evil, which is seen at its starkest in the contrast between the praise of the heavenly host in ch. 4 and the injustice and rebelliousness of humanity, achieved in the new Jerusalem, where God dwells on earth with men and women. The location of the throne of God runs like a thread binding the different visions of the Apocalypse together. It is the destiny of the elect and a sign of authority in the universe, contrasting with that other locus of power in the cosmos which deludes the world's inhabitants (2: 13; 13: 2). In Rev. 21 the tabernacling of God with humankind is fulfilled in the new creation. There is a contrast between the vision of the new Jerusalem in ch. 21 with the initial vision of the heavenly court in ch. 4. In Rev. 4 the seer is granted a glimpse into the environs of God. This contrast between heaven and earth disappears in the new creation where the tabernacle of God is with humanity. God's dwelling is not to be found above the cherubim in heaven; for his throne is set right in the midst of the New Jerusalem where the living waters stream from the throne of God and his servants, marked with the mark of God, will see him face to face.

Apocalypse in History

The book of Revelation points the way to the main contours of apocalyptic interpretation which were already set within the earliest period of Christianity. These were the visionary appropriation of Scripture, the search for meaning in mysteries, and the 'actualizing' of visions. When Scripture is appropriated in a visionary way, the words offer the opportunity to 'see again' what had appeared to prophets and seers in the past, becoming a means of prompting new visions whereby higher spiritual realities may be discerned. Though there are only occasional prompts to quest for the meaning of the mysteries (e.g. 17: 9 cf. 1: 20, 4: 3), Revelation has prompted scores of ingenious attempts to unlock its mysteries. Finally, in 'actualizing' Revelation, particular visions are picked out and identified with, or believed to be embodied in contemporary events. (See Rowland 1998; Kovacs and Rowland 2004; Patrides and Wittreich 1984.)

Early Christian appropriation of the Apocalypse offered evidence that a doctrine of the resurrection and this-worldly eschatology played their part in the writings of both Justin (*Trypho* 80) and Irenaeus (*Adv. Haer.* 26. 1–36. 3). The popularity of apocalyptic ideas among such movements as Montanism led to a growing suspicion of the book. Although in several key respects he had been anticipated by Origen, Tyconius' reading of the book of Revelation (*c.*400), which had a profound influence on the mature Augustine and thence on later Christendom, stressed the contemporary rather than eschatological import of the visions. The book is used to interpret contemporary ecclesial life. The text becomes a tool facilitating the discernment of the moral and spiritual rather than searching out the eschatological in the text. The mature Augustine continued in this tradition. He accepted an approach to Scripture which enables Revelation to be a source of insight both eschatologically and for the contemporary church. Augustine's approach to empire in *The City of God* is in certain key respects at one with the dualistic and suspicious attitude evident in earlier Christian apocalyptic interpretation.

The later Middle Ages saw the emergence of the influential reading by Joachim of Fiore, which used Revelation as a hermeneutical key to understand both Scripture and the whole of history. Joachim broke decisively from the Augustinian tradition in being willing to find significance in history. The sixth period is the crucial time and a beginning of the time of renewal and eschatological conflict. What is distinctive about this kind of interpretation is the way in which the present was infused with eschatological vitality, and the renewal movements, especially the Franciscan movement, imbued with eschatological significance.

Revelation did not dominate the interpretative horizons of Reformers such as Calvin, even if the whole period was pervaded with a sense of destiny and the struggles within church and state were seen as evidence of the Last Days. Luther initially outlined his reasons for relegating the book to a subordinate place within the canon of the New Testament, in words which echo much earlier (and later) assessments in the Christian tradition. He believed that it was neither 'apostolic or prophetic' because 'Christ is not taught or known in it' and 'to teach Christ is the thing which an apostle above all else is bound to do' (*Preface to the New Testament*), though he subtly modified his view of Revelation in the later editions of his New Testament from 1530 onwards. Luther came to the view that the pope was Antichrist, a view held also by Calvin. A fascinating witness to the interpretation of Revelation in the early Calvinist tradition is provided by the Geneva Bible, which offers a typical example of the historicizing interpretation of the day (Hill 1993). It enables us to see how Revelation was used as part of the ecclesiastical struggle of the time. Its reformed protestant leanings are everywhere apparent. As may be expected, there is identification between Rome and Antichrist (the papacy is the inheritor of the power of the Roman Empire, in the interpretation of the two beasts of Rev. 13).

The evidence of an extensive use of Revelation is apparent, however, in the writings of Melchior Hoffman (d. *c.*1534), who was a significant influence on radical Anabaptism at Münster. The Melchiorite interpretation of Revelation is an unusual example of the use of the book in the practice of a millenarian politics which, like the revolutionary actions of Thomas Müntzer a decade earlier (and more recent examples such as the Branch Davidian community at Waco), did not remain at the level of utopian idealism but resulted in violent attempts to establish an eschatological theocracy. Despite the sense of an expectation of imminent fulfilment, what one finds in the post-Münster Anabaptism is the sense of being in the penultimate period, rather than in the eschatological commonwealth on earth.

The link between Revelation and radical politics is particularly evident in the English Civil War writing of the seventeenth century. The rule of the Beast is not merely eschatological but is seen in the political arrangements of the day and the professional ministry. Only the high point of medieval interpretation of the Apocalypse in the fourteenth century, in the wake of Joachim of Fiore's groundbreaking interpretation, can rank with the seventeenth century as a golden age of the interpretation of the Apocalypse. This was a particularly turbulent period of history when England had its one period of republican rule. The learned and ingenious explanations of Joseph Mede, who saw biblical prophecy as a sign of divine providence, stand in marked contrast with other readers of the Apocalypse in a time of political upheaval. The seventeenth century saw a surge of radicalism, along with a flowering of women's religious activity in England, which coincided with a crisis in religious and political life (Mack 1992). A key doctrine which was to become extremely influential among revolutionary groups held that the succession of world empires predicted in Dan. 2 and 7 had come to its end and that the reign of King Jesus was about to be established. The influence of the Apocalypse was to permeate English religion through the individualized reading of the apocalyptic narrative in Bunyan's *Pilgrim's Progress*, itself a product of a period when the revolutionary politics of the mid-seventeenth century were on the wane.

Alongside the place of Revelation in radical religion in the seventeenth century, there was a rich tradition of interpretation, in which the careful exposition of the book was carried out in more measured and less heated atmosphere, encouraging a long tradition of apocalyptic speculation. Chief among these was Joseph Mede (1586–1638) whose work had enormous influence on subsequent generations. His synchronic approach to the visions has been typical of many commentators on Revelation down to the present day, and his work was frequently quoted in subsequent centuries. The approach to Revelation which saw in it an account of universal history in which contemporary events could be found had a new lease of life at the time of the French Revolution.

The use of the Apocalypse as a repository of prophecies concerning the future has been there from the start and reached an influential climax in the work of Joseph Mede. Yet in the last two hundred years it has become very much part of a growing trend of eschatological interpretation. In this kind of interpretation, influentially supported by the Scofield Reference Bible, the book of Revelation convinces the elect of their secure place in the divine purposes. From the early modern period, interpreters such as Hugo Grotius (1583–1645) argued the book of Revelation's meaning was almost entirely related to the circumstances of John's own day. This view was echoed in Catholic scholarship from the same period, when there was an attempt to play down the contemporary link with the Roman Catholic Church by relating Revelation's images to the eschaton. This position now dominates modern historical scholarship, where attention is paid entirely to the book in its ancient context. From the earliest references to the book in the second century CE, John's vision has been linked to the social and political realities of late first-century Asia Minor, with its imperial cult.

DIFFERING WAYS OF READING REVELATION

Approaches to the Apocalypse may be categorized in the light of whether they refer to past, present, or future. In the Apocalypse itself, past, present, and future are interrelated: eschatological visions (Rev. 6–22) grow out of the past (Rev. 5), and have an import for life in the present (Rev. 2–3). In classifying interpretations of the Apocalypse there seem to be two basic types of hermeneutical approach to the text. The first could be described as 'Decoding'. This involves presenting the meaning of the text in another, less allusive, form, showing what the text *really* means, usually with great attention to the details of the text and their meaning. The interpreter renders the images of the Apocalypse in another form, usually relating to historical events or persons. The Apocalypse only occasionally prompts the reader to 'decode' the meaning of the apocalyptic mysteries (17: 9; cf. 1: 20 and 4: 3). In this respect it is different from its biblical counterpart, the book of Daniel, which is replete with detailed elucidation of its visions. Nonetheless, some have sought precise equivalence between every image in the book and figures and events in history, resulting in a long tradition of decoding interpretation. An image is seen to have one particular meaning, and the interpreter assumes that if the code is understood in its entirety the whole Apocalypse can be rendered in another form and its inner meaning laid bare. There is also a peculiar form of decoding in which individuals 'act out' details of the text, in effect decoding the text once and for all in that person.

A different form of interpretation is one that refuses to translate the images but instead uses them metaphorically, so that the image is applied to another situation or person, not by way of equating the two but by a process of juxtaposition, to cast light on that to which the image has been applied. In this way, the imagery of the Apocalypse is juxtaposed with the interpreter's own circumstances, whether personal or social, so as to allow the images to inform understanding of contemporary persons and events, and to serve as a guide for action. This interpretation has deep roots in the Christian tradition, going back at least to the time of Tyconius. In contrast with decoding, it preserves the integrity of the textual pole and does not allow the image or passage from the Apocalypse to be identified solely with one particular historical personage or circumstance. The text is not prevented from being actualized in different ways over and over again. This is crucial. The book becomes a resource not just for the generation of the Last Days but a resource for the religious life in every generation. An example of this is understanding the book's images as an allegory of the struggles of the individual soul, in which the Apocalypse serves as a model of the progression from despair and darkness to the brilliance of the celestial city. This pattern lies behind two of the great literary texts that describe a spiritual journey: Dante's *Divine Comedy* and Bunyan's *Pilgrim's Progress* which are both deeply indebted to the Apocalypse, for their narrative form as well as for particular images (Herzman in Emmerson and McGinn 1992: 398–411).

A further form of interpretation is the appropriation by visionaries of passages where the words of the Apocalypse either offer the opportunity to 'see again' things similar to what had appeared to John, or prompt new visions related to it. So in the visions of Hildegard of Bingen, for example, many details of John's text reappear. Others, such as William Blake, exhibit a less direct relationship to the letter of the text. In his works the images and symbols of Apocalypse appear in different guise, woven into the tapestry of Blake's own visionary world and incorporated into his idiosyncratic *mythopoiesis*.

EXAMPLES OF THE TREATMENT OF THE BIBLICAL TRADITION OF APOCALYPTIC LITERATURE WITHIN ENGLISH LITERATURE

Medieval texts such as *Piers Plowman*, which envisions an age in which the world is free from greed and pride, have a clear apocalyptic dimension in both form and content (Bloomfield 1962; Kerby-Fulton 1990). The poem known as *The Pearl*, written in England in the fourteenth century, depicts The New Jerusalem in detail; the main textual source is the book of Revelation. In John Gower's (*c.*1330–1408) *Vox Clamantis* (*Voice of One Crying Out*), the writer identifies himself with the voice of John the Baptist, crying in the wilderness, as well as that of John of Patmos in the book of Revelation. The poem is written in the form of a dream vision, a popular poetic genre in the fourteenth century.

Several of Shakespeare's plays contain lines or phrases echoing those from the book of Revelation, and *King Lear* (1608) is notable among them (Fisch 1999). The plot of *Lear*, in the king's personal journey into madness and his recovery, gives it an apocalyptic theme, in addition to and beyond the lyrical references to end-times or Revelation language (such as Gloucester's speech in i. ii, or Lear's psychologizing interpretation of Armageddon's storms in iii. iv).

John Milton's indebtedness to the book of Revelation in *Paradise Lost* (1667) comprises many elements. There is the invocation of the Apocalypse at the beginning of Book IV, the entire account of the war in Heaven and the woes and visions of the end in the last two books. It is the emphasis of the Apocalypse on the historical process that is most akin to *Paradise Lost*; the unilinear course of time on earth, with Christ at its centre, linked with battles and events in Heaven taking place in relation to this, link Revelation and *Paradise Lost*'s narratives together.

There is an apocalyptic dimension to a series of George Eliot's novels, especially her *Romola*, set in late fifteenth-century Savonarolan Florence, whose inspiration comes from the book of Revelation. The Florentine setting of *Romola* involves a city overwrought with prophesies and end-timed hysteria (though, curiously, the book of Revelation does not appear to have been a significant influence on the historical Savonarola, even if it did inspire such artists as Botticelli, in his 'Mystic Nativity'). Similarly, in *Daniel Deronda* we find a young Jew who discovers 'his prophetic vocation and mission to gentile society', while in Middlemarch, 'apocalyptic imagery provides a kind of metaphorical drama'. An important strand in the characterization of the minister Rufus Lyon in *Felix Holt* is his detailed interpretations of the book of Daniel.

Elsewhere, in Dickens's *A Christmas Carol* (1843), the vision shown to Ebenezer Scrooge, of his 'Christmas Past, Christmas Present, and Christmas As Yet To Come' and guiding through his past to his bleak future by the spirits that visit him, has been termed his personal 'apocalyptic journey'. Its visionary nature, and relation with the future may link it with Revelation, but it also has concepts of individual autonomy and of choice to change behaviour, which are perhaps more from other influences. In Joseph Conrad's *Heart of Darkness* (1899–1902) most of the biblical allusions of the book owe more to the Old Testament. Yet the journey undertaken by the protagonist Marlow, up the Congo River in search of the missing agent Kurtz, may be read nonetheless as an individual apocalyptic journey, in the same vein as Bunyan's *Pilgrim's Progress*, searching the darkness of the individual and of humanity.

During their formative period in the early 1790s, the first generation of Romantic poets incorporated in their poems a vision of the French Revolution as the early stage of the abrupt culmination of history, in which there will emerge a new humanity on a new earth that is equivalent to a restored paradise (Burdon 1997; Paley 1999).

In 1793, while still a student at Oxford, Robert Southey wrote *Joan of Arc: An Epic Poem*. In it Joan is granted a vision of a 'blest age' in the future when, in a violent spasm not quite named the French Revolution, humanity shall 'burst his fetters', and 'Earth shall once again | Be Paradise'. In 1793, Wordsworth concluded his *Descriptive Sketches* with the enthusiastic prophecy (which precisely matches the prophecy he attributed to the Solitary in his later poem *The Excursion*) that events following the French Revolution would fulfil the millennial prophecy of the book of Revelation. In those happy early years of the revolution, Coleridge shared this expectation, in a historical sequence that he succinctly summarizes in his prose argument of the plot of *Religious Musings* (1794) as 'The French Revolution. Millennium. Universal Redemption. Conclusion.' Two decades later, the young Percy Shelley recapitulated the millenarian expectations of his older contemporaries. His early principles, Shelley said, 'had their origin' in those views that 'occasioned the revolutions of America and France'. Shelley's *Queen Mab*, which he began writing at 19, presents a vision of the woeful human past and the dreadful present, as preceding a blissful future 'surpassing fabled Eden', of which most features are imparted from biblical millennialism.

Living at this time was, arguably, the person who has understood most about Revelation without ever explicitly commenting upon it, William Blake (1757–1827; Burdon 1997; Paley 1999). Blake inhabited and was suffused with the world of the Bible in a way without parallel. In Blake's own prophecy the images of Revelation are woven into the fabric of his own visionary mythology. Blake recognized the prophets of the Bible as kindred spirits and he wrote in their style and used their images, but for his own time and in his own way. Throughout the 1790s, Blake's writing and designs return to the themes of prophetic struggle and the need to be aware of the dangers of the prophetic spirit degenerating into 'the apostasy of state religion'. He was inspired by Revelation, which seemed to offer a different perspective on the world, to challenge a system which oppressed the poor and turned the religion of Jesus into a series of commandments. In his words and pictures Blake offered an 'apocalypse' or an unveiling of, and opportunity to open eyes to, other dimensions of life, and an awareness of the epistemological shift which was required of dulled human intellects.

As we have seen, among the English Romantic poets at the beginning of the nineteenth century, apocalypticism had an important place. Thus, William Wordsworth can describe the act of imagination as an 'apocalyptic' experience every bit as overwhelming, and in some sense even more vivid and real as experience of the real world. In Book VI of 'The Prelude' he describes the way in which he has been steadily making his way across Europe towards Italy, and has been full of anticipation of the moment when he and his companions will cross the Alps. He discovers that he has actually missed this eagerly anticipated event, however, and in place of the actuality of the experience Wordsworth's imagination takes over and creates the vision in his mind's eye. This exercise of creative imagination enables him to have an experience of the physical sight he had missed. It was every bit as over-whelming as the actual experience itself and indeed of proportions akin to that experienced by John in his apocalyptic vision: 'The unfettered clouds', he writes, 'and region of the Heavens, | Tumult and peace, the darkness and the light | Were all like workings of one mind, the features | Of the same face, blossoms upon one tree; | Characters of the great Apocalypse, The types and symbols of Eternity, | Of first, and last, and midst, and without end.' In this act of imagination the last book of the Bible offers the poet the framework of his visualization and is the most appropriate way in which the poet can grasp and explain the enormous significance of what has happened to him. Nature itself expanded the horizons of the interpreter as the poet sought to express the meaning of 'the great Apocalypse' (Abrams 1971: 105–7; further Paley 1999).

The greatest poetry of the age was written not in the mood of revolutionary exaltation, but in the mood of revolutionary disenchantment and despair, after the succession of disasters that began with the Reign of Terror in 1793–4. A number of the major Romantic poems, however, did not break with the formative past, but set out to salvage grounds for hope in a new and better world. That is, Romantic thought and imagination remained apocalyptic in form, but with a radical shift from faith in a violent outer transformation to faith in an inner moral and imaginative transform-ation—a shift from political revolution to a revolution in consciousness—to bring into being a new heaven and new earth.

William Butler Yeats lost his Christian faith as a boy, but remained a man of profoundly religious temperament. A passionate celebrant of life on earth, he nevertheless maintained a lifelong search for a world beyond. This led him to various kinds of mysticism, to folklore, theosophy, spiritualism, and neo-Platonism—not in any strict chronological order, for he kept returning to and reworking earlier aspects of his thought. An immersion in the poetry of William Blake, whose *Works* (1893) he edited with Edwin Ellis, encouraged his interest in apocalyptic literature, and, in the 1890s, he himself wrote poems on apocalyptic themes.

Yeats writes of the poet's visionary-aware sight in the poem *The Valley of the Black Pig* (1896):

> The dews drop slowly and dreams gather: unknown spears
> Suddenly hurtle before my dream-awakened eyes,
> And then the clash of fallen horsemen and the cries
> Of unknown perishing armies beat about my ears.
> We who still labour by the cromlech on the shore,
> The grey cairn on the hill, when day sinks drowned in dew,
> Master of the still stars and of the flaming door.

Similarly, in *The Second Coming* (1921) Yeats echoes apocalyptic themes:

> Turning and turning in the widening gyre
> The falcon cannot hear the falconer;
> Things fall apart; the centre cannot hold;
> Mere anarchy is loosed upon the world,
> The blood-dimmed tide is loosed, and everywhere
> The ceremony of innocence is drowned;
> The best lack all conviction, while the worst
> Are full of passionate intensity.
>
> Surely some revelation is at hand;
> Surely the Second Coming is at hand.
> The Second Coming! Hardly are those words out
> When a vast image out of Spiritus Mundi
> Troubles my sight: somewhere in sands of the desert
> A shape with lion body and the head of a man,
> A gaze blank and pitiless as the sun,
> Is moving its slow thighs, while all about it
> Reel shadows of the indignant desert birds.
> The darkness drops again; but now I know
> That twenty centuries of stony sleep
> Were vexed to nightmare by a rocking cradle,
> And what rough beast, its hour come round at last,
> Slouches towards Bethlehem to be born?

T. S. Eliot's *The Wasteland* (1922) is a work of crisis literature that reveals truths about the past, present, and/or future in highly symbolic terms, and was intended to provide hope and encouragement for people in the midst of severe trials and tribulations. Many refer to *The Wasteland* as an 'apocalyptic poem', with all its imagery of a dried-up, arid present and expected future, contrasted with allusions to a richer, more fertile and vivid past. *The Wasteland* of the desert, the modern city, modern life, is rife with wars physical and sexual, spiritually broken, culturally decaying, dry and dusty. The topic of memory, particularly when it involves remembering the dead, is of critical importance as memory creates a confrontation of the past with the present, a juxtaposition that points out just how badly things have decayed. The 'dystopia' of the modern present is seemingly made all the more harrowing in parts of the poem by the absence of God now or in the future: there is no hope for the apocalyptic resurrection, no truth to be revealed at the close of life, rather, in our world the dead are dead, and the living are merely waiting to die. The poem's apocalypticism may therefore be a form of anti- or counter-Book of Revelation. Yet another T. S. Eliot poem *The Journey of the Magi* (1927) offers a reflection on the First Coming and expectation/desire of the Second.

In a similar vein to Eliot's poetry, works such as Aldous Huxley's *Brave New World* (1932), George Orwell's *Nineteen Eighty-Four* (1948), Ray Bradbury's *Fahrenheit 451* (1953), and Margaret Attwood's *Oryx and Crake* (2003), are often termed apocalyptic. Where they take their cue from the book of Revelation, it has been argued, is in their 'dystopian' nature'—being not a prediction of a terrible future, but a nightmare of the present. Taking such a view requires a reading of John of Patmos's apocalypse as a nightmarish prediction and future dream of revenge and deliverance from the persecution being suffered in the period of the book's conception.

Each of these novels reveal the discomforts, concerns, and perceived threats of the times and cultures in which they were written. By taking particular aspects within their present, they project into the future a nightmare scenario, often with the intention of awaking their present readership to a potential worse future. The respective aspects of their present are: industrial mass-production applied to humanity; the totalitarian state on a world scale; a meaningless society living only for trivial entertainment; and, most recently and, therefore, perhaps reflecting closest our current fears in the West, genetic engineering and climate change, which could wipe out the human race.

At the beginning of the twenty-first century, the book of Revelation is on the one hand the centrepiece of the theological map of a major swathe of Christianity while being largely ignored or reviled by the rest. It is hard to see much connection between this and its powerful inspiration of art and literature down the centuries, or for that matter to see that it could be something different from the map of the end of the world which has made it such a happy hunting ground of eschatological prognosticators of the last two centuries. In a pragmatic world its imaginative and evocative images seem only disturbing or disordered. What fired the imagination of Blake, or even Augustine in *The City of God*, is largely lost on a world where safety and predictability are at a higher premium. Such suspicion and marginalization cannot detract from the extraordinary power and influence its images have had down the centuries, and to which art and liturgy, piety as well as literature, have borne witness.

WORKS CITED

ABRAMS, M. H. 1971. *Natural Supernaturalism: Tradition and Revolution in Romantic Literature*. New York: Norton.

BLOOMFIELD, M. W. 1962. *Piers Plowman as a Fourteenth Century Apocalypse*. New Brunswick: Rutgers University Press.

BURDON, C. 1997. *The Apocalypse in England: Revelation Unravelling 1700–1834*. London: Macmillan.

CALVIN, J. 1993. 'Daniel I, Chapters 1–6', *John Calvin's Lectures on the Book of the Prophecies of Daniel*, trans. T. H. L. Parker. Grand Rapids: Eerdmans.

CAPP, B. S. 1972. *The Fifth Monarchy. A Study in Seventeenth Century Millenarianism*. Oxford: Oxford University Press.

COLLINS, J. J. 1993. *Daniel*. Hermeneia. Minneapolis: Fortress.

DRONKE, P. 1984. *Women Writers of the Middle Ages: A Critical Study of Texts from Perpetua to Marguerite*. Cambridge: Cambridge University Press.

ELLIOTT, E. B. 1851. *Horae Apocalypticae; or A Commentary on the Apocalypse, Critical and Historical*. 4 vols. London: Seeley.

EMMERSON, R. and McGINN, B. 1992. *The Apocalypse in the Middle Ages*. Ithaca: Cornell University Press.

FISCH, H. 1999. *The Biblical Presence in Shakespeare, Milton and Blake*. Oxford: Clarendon.

HAMILTON, A. 1999. *The Apocryphal Apocalypse: The Reception of the Second Book of Esdras (4 Ezra) from the Renaissance to the Enlightenment*. Oxford: Oxford University Press.

HILL, C. 1993. *The English Bible and the Seventeenth Century Revolution*. London: Penguin.

KERBY-FULTON, K. 1990. *Reformist Apocalypticism and Piers Plowman*. Cambridge: Cambridge University Press.

KOVACS, J. and ROWLAND, C. 2004. *Revelation: The Apocalypse of Jesus Christ*. Oxford: Blackwell.

LUTHER, M. 1960. *Luther's Works*, xxxv. *Word and Sacrament*, ed. E. T. Bachman and H. T. Lehmann. Philadelphia: Fortress.

MACK, P. 1992. *Visionary Women: Ecstatic Prophecy in Seventeenth Century England*. Berkeley: University of California.

NICKELSBURG, G. W. E. 2001. *1 Enoch 1: A Commentary on the Book of 1 Enoch Chapters 1–36, 81–108*, ed. Klaus Baltzer. Minneapolis: Fortress Press.

PALEY, M. 1999. *Apocalypse and Millennium in English Romantic Poetry*. Oxford: Clarendon.

PARKER, T. H. L. (ed.) 1993. *Calvin's Old Testament Commentaries Daniel I Chapters 1–6*, Grand Rapids: Eerdmans.

PATRIDES, C. A., and WITTREICH, J. A. (eds.) 1984. *The Apocalypse in English Renaissance Thought and Literature: Patterns, Antecedents and Repercussions*. Ithaca: Cornell University Press.

QUALLS, B. 2001. 'George Eliot and Religion', in George Levine (ed.), *The Cambridge Companion to George Eliot*. Cambridge: Cambridge University Press, 119–37.

ROWLAND, C. 1998. 'Revelation', *New Interpreter's Bible*. Nashville: Abingdon, xii.

SABINE, G. 1941. *The Works of Gerrard Winstanley with an Appendix of Documents relating to the Digger Movement*. Ithaca: Cornell University Press.

SANDERS, E. P. 1977. *Paul and Palestinian Judaism*. London. SCM.

STONE, M. E. 1990. *Fourth Ezra*. Hermeneia. Philadelphia: Fortress.

Further Reading

Aune, D. E. 1997–8. *Revelation.* World Biblical Commentary 52a. Dallas: Word.

Carey, F. 1999. *The Apocalypse and the Shape of Things to Come.* London: British Museum Press.

Charlesworth, J. H. 1983. *The Old Testament Pseudepigrapha.* New York: Doubleday, i.

Cohn, N. 1957. *The Pursuit of the Millennium.* London: Paladin.

Collins, J. J., McGinn, B., and Stein, S. (eds.) 2000. *The Encyclopedia of Apocalypticism.* 3 vols. New York: Continuum.

Daley, B. 1991. *The Hope of the Early Church.* Cambridge: Cambridge University Press.

Forey, M. 1994. *Apocalypse in Spencer and Milton.* D.Phil., Oxford University.

Froom, L. 1946–54. *The Prophetic Faith of Our Fathers.* 4 vols. Washington, DC: Review & Herald.

Reeves, M., and Hirsch-Reich, B. 1972. *The Figurae of Joachim of Fiore.* Oxford: Oxford University Press.

Rowland, C. 1982. *The Open Heaven.* London: SPCK.

Van der Meer, F. 1978. *Apocalypse: Visions from the Book of Revelation in Western Art.* London: Thames & Hudson.

Wainwright, A. W. 1993. *Mysterious Apocalypse.* Nashville: Abingdon.

PART FOUR

THEOLOGICAL WAYS OF READING LITERATURE

CHAPTER 22

LANGLAND AND CHAUCER

NICHOLAS WATSON

MEDIEVAL THEOLOGY AND THE CHURCH

WHEN Langland and Chaucer were writing in the last decades of the fourteenth century, Christian theology had much the intellectual and cultural authority that science does now. This had been so for many centuries and was to be so for several more. Like modern science, late medieval theology—especially the scholastic theology developed in the universities from the twelfth century on—was a specialized, sophisticated, and constantly developing body of thought and experiment, the full state of whose hypotheses at any given moment was grasped in detail only by a few professionals, but which was still vital to many different discourses, institutions, and careers. As with modern science, medieval theology's claim was that its account of the cosmos was the truest possible. Yet, as also with modern science, real power lay less in this claim itself than in the status its workings-out conferred on theology as an applied discipline, as near kin to the medieval mechanical sciences (navigation, engineering, and the like) as to its only intellectual competitor, philosophy. Indeed, medieval theology's claim to importance was even more closely tied to the fact that it got things done than is true of modern science. Science distinguishes between the discovery of knowledge and its commercial application: the phrase 'good science' refers, not to useful or lucrative science, but to intellectually sound science. By contrast, it was (and is) axiomatic that even the most abstruse theology should have positive practical implications. Good theology was not only rationally sound but beneficial. Theology that could be shown to be useless or damaging, on the other hand, however well reasoned—and whether its deficiencies were taken as a sign of heresy, moral blindness, arrogance, or careerism on the part of the theologian—was, by definition, 'bad': a perversion of the discipline from its true ends and of truth itself (see e.g. Aquinas, *Summa contra Gentiles*, Book 1).

The product of an amalgam between the Hebrew and Christian Scriptures and Graeco-Roman metaphysics, medieval Christian cosmology was neither more nor less anthropocentric than its post-Copernican counterparts, but it was theocentric. It understood the cosmos as the creation of a being whose attributes could be seen as surely in his handiwork as in his communications, through revelation, with human-kind. Humankind mattered only as the summit of creation, made on the sixth day after both the angels and the earth and its other creatures as an uniquely intricate commingling of spiritual and physical substances. According to Edmund of Canter-bury's *Mirror of Holy Church* (*c.*1225), only humans 'hath beoinge [*existence*] with stones, livinge with herbes [*plants*], felinge [*sensation*] with beestes, resoun with angeles' (Horstmann 1895–6: i. 243–4). Despite its fall from perfection into evil—an event grounded in the fall of the angel Satan which momentarily seemed to threaten the viability of the entire cosmos as an instrument of praise—humankind retained a blurred image of its creator: its trinity of mental faculties (memory, reason, will) a created microcosm of the uncreated Trinity of Father, Son, and Holy Spirit. Indeed, this image—according to Walter Hilton's *Scale of Perfection* (*c.*1390), once 'wonderli faire and bright' but now 'disfigured and forschapen [*deformed*]' (Bestul 2000: 2. 1)—could be partially restored in this life, in preparation for its full restoration in the next, as a result of the central event in history: the incarnation of God in the person of Christ. In medieval Christian thought, this event was momentous both in practice and in theory: in practice, because it transformed the effects of the fall on human-kind; in theory, because it revealed something definitive about the being of God—his love, as creator and redeeemer, for his creatures. Hence the unsustainability, in vernacular and official theology, of any distinction between practice and theory, the useful and the true. Because God had lived and died in human form, the attributes, needs, and responsibilities of people must be central to the discipline's purpose as a mode of thought.

Medieval theology was thus notionally responsive to social, political, and ethical issues with an immediacy modern science cannot match. Yet the persistent attempts by nineteenth- and twentieth-century intellectuals to understand this responsiveness idealistically, as the basis of a now lost sense of cultural coherence and community (Robertson 1962; Duffy 1992), founder on the history of a single institution, an institution that was at once created by theology and provided it with its home and the source of its power: the church. The church was imagined in a number of ways: as a Noah's ark, protecting the people of God from evil (especially through the liturgy, the daily round of religious services performed in churches and monasteries); as the vehicle of God's continuing revelation to his people (especially through the teaching of his word by the clergy to the laity); as the body of Christ, sustained in being by the sacraments (especially baptism, confession, and the mass). Yet while these images convey real information about how the church made theology communally and individually meaningful, the church was also a bureaucracy, the purity of whose ideals was always at risk from the warring uses to which it put them or was itself put—especially uses involving money and power. As the most powerful, ancient, and complex institution in Europe, the church was inevitably (perhaps by definition) more corruptible than other bureaucracies, both because of its status and because it had largely invented the ethical structures that defined corruption. Medieval accounts of hell often populate its reaches with the corrupt clergy, while it was taken for granted that the Antichrist—Satan's last attempt to bring Christianity down, whose coming heralded the final days before the Judgement—could arise only within the church, as a seductively complete perversion of its ideals, a sedimentation of all the smaller perversions it had perpetrated through time (McGinn 2000). Even in theory, only the 'invisible' church—the *idea* of the church sustained by and in its virtuous members—was pure. The institutional church (the 'visible' church) was anything but that.

As expressed in the history of the church, the utilitarian nature of medieval theology thus took many forms, not all contributing to coherence or community. Theological debates within the church, such as that over the Franciscan ideal of poverty (Burr 1989), inevitably played out in tandem with struggles for institutional power. As a result, official theology—from the doctrines justifying the sale of indulgences to the debates about the 'powers' of God, which coincided with a struggle between the papacy and the Holy Roman Emperor for primacy (Coleman 1981)—tended to become ever more concerned with power as such. The models of community theology did produce in this environment were often organized around exclusion, not inclusion. A key example is the position promulgated at the Fourth Lateran Council in 1215, as part of Pope Innocent IV's programme to create a Christendom united in knowledge of one creed, from which heretics and non-Christians would be expelled: 'Una vero est fidelium universalis Ecclesia, extra quam nullus omnino salvatur [*there is one universal church of the faithful outside which absolutely no-one is saved*]' (Tanner 1990). It is true that reactions against church corruption also found expression through theology: the prophetic theology of visionaries such as Bridget of Sweden (d. 1373) or Catherine of Siena (d. 1378), critics of the papacy who were fervent supporters, and the learned theology of scholars such as John Wyclif (d. 1384), a critic who was emphatically not, are equally cases in point. (Wyclif's claim that the church's jurisdiction was spiritual, not temporal, agitated contemporaries, including Chaucer and Langland.) But the definitions of community accompanying calls to reform could be narrower than those they sought to replace. Wyclif's followers held that the laxity of the visible church proved the Antichrist had come. For them 'extra quam nullus omnino salvatur' referred only to the invisible church, 'alle that schulle be saved' as *Book to a Mother* has it: a select company whose membership was known to God alone (McCarthy 1981: 2).

One standard account of the late-medieval scene, derived from competing definitions of church and community such as these, describes a centralized but vulnerable institution pitted against a variety of reformist forces whose power grew—especially after the election of rival popes in the Great Schism of 1378—until in the sixteenth century their theologies became cohesive enough, and their support from secular states strong enough, to bring about the permanent schism known as the Reformation (Tierney 1964). The state did play an increasingly important spiritual role throughout Europe. Yet the church was itself a reformist body, whose insistence on educating its members, especially once the Fourth Lateran Council made confession a duty for all, knowingly risked the reactions against its corruption that energized the reformers. The secularization of the late-medieval church—as it increasingly organized its pastoral responsibilities around the salvation of the laity, and as the laity responded by taking increasing charge of this process (Vauchez 1993)—was so various as to make any simple account of conflict between church and reformers reductive. It is true that reaction against church corruption included reaction against the more abstruse reaches of its theology, which some saw as so abstract as to have betrayed its reason for being. Vernacular theological writings often contrast the rational sterility of *scientia* (formal learning) with the affective utility of *sapientia* (inner knowing), arguing that the uneducated understand divine truth better than religious professionals (Gillespie 2007), and by Langland and Chaucer's time secular theologies that regard the laity as central to the church are commonplace. Yet such writings can be as uneasy about reform as they are antagonized by church corruption. Caught between competing views of the role of the church, the responsibilities of the individual Christian, and the possibility of salvation for all but the most pure, Langland and Chaucer are among those who refuse to take sides, focusing their writerly energies on analysing both the problems and their possible, often mutually incompatible, solutions.

Langland, Chaucer, and Theology

Both Langland's *Piers Plowman*, written and rewritten at least three times between the 1360s and the 1380s, and Chaucer's *Canterbury Tales*, left unfinished at the poet's death in 1400, are much engaged with Christian theology, its incarnation in the church, and the religious role played by secular society. This is a truism in the case of *Piers Plowman*, whose convoluted narrative is all about attempts to reform the church, Christian society, and the sinning individual, or about the implications of these attempts' invariable, if never total, failure. It has been much less a truism in that of *The Canterbury Tales*, which, despite its framing around pilgrimage and focus on religious themes, is still often understood as the wellspring of a specifically secular tradition of English literature, whose concerns are more likely to be expressed through engagement with classical philosophy or late-medieval political theory than through any serious confrontation with theology.

Part of the reason the poems are read so differently has to do with differences in their literary reference-points and critical histories. Although formally connected with the dream vision, *Piers Plowman* mainly works with genres of writing developed within the late-medieval institutional church (monastic, scholastic, pastoral, or satirical), whereas *The Canterbury Tales* also makes use of the neoclassical and courtly genres favoured by the French and Italian poets on whom Chaucer modelled much of his earlier career. Late-antique philosophical thought, Graeco-Roman history and mythology, and contemporary literary theory all mattered to Chaucer as they did not to Langland—much as they mattered to the poets (from Lydgate to Wyatt to Spenser) who established Chaucer's reputation after his death—and have defined our understanding of Chaucer's interests for so long that their subordination to an overarching religious framework in *The Canterbury Tales* is hard to take seriously. Langland's religious interests do not suffer such misinterpretation, but contributed to a decline in his reputation after the sixteenth century (Spenser is the last major poet to read him carefully), as theological thought (more volatile than philosophy well into the modern era) grew away from him, its concerns increasingly translated into different idioms and dogmatic structures.

The more significant differences between the two poets for our purposes, however, are those between the narratorial stances adopted within their poems and the trajectories of the poems themselves. Langland initially represents his poetic 'I' (who crystallizes into the character Will), first as a critical observer of, then as a sinful participant in, the world of his poem, maintaining an extraordinarily flexible relationship between poet, poem, and world in which the intellectual quest of the poet, the spiritual journey of the narrator, and the historical development and decline of Christian society are presented in ever-changing balance. As *Piers Plowman* goes on, however, the narrator's dreams increasingly come to be constructed prophetically, as Will progresses from dreamer to visionary, and the poem from expositions of 'treuthe' by a personified heavenly Holy Church to a series of a visions of the life, death, and resurrection of Christ, and thence to a final, apocalyptic vision of the invasion of the contemporary church by the forces of corruption:

And there by conseil of Kynde [*nature/the Creator*] I comsed to rome [*began to roam*]
Thorugh [*through*] Contricion and Confession til I cam to Unitee [*unity, i.e. the Church*].
And there was Conscience conestable [*constable*] Cristene [*Christendom*] to save,
And bisegede, soothly, with seven grete geaunts [*giants, i.e. the seven deadly sins*]
That with Antecrist helden [*fought*] harde ayein Conscience.   (XX. 212–16)[1]

Langland never wholly succumbs to the prophetic voice—both because the figures of authority in his poem can never quite agree about the meaning of the events unfolding within it and because it is not always clear who actually constitutes a figure of authority—but *Piers Plowman* nonetheless ends in a pronouncedly public mode, as the narrator's personal needs and desires are swallowed up in the near-complete moral collapse of the visible church with which the poem ends.

---

[1] Quotations from *Piers Plowman* are taken from Schmidt 1997, an edition of the B text; in citations, capital roman numerals refer to passus numbers, arabic numbers to lineation within the passus. Many of Langland's revisions between A, B, and C are relevant to this essay, but the textual complexities are such that it has seemed best to work with a single version of the poem.

By contrast, when not telling his own tales, Chaucer's 'I' represents himself as a mere transcriber of a seemingly casual assemblage of stories with no personal relation to himself: a pilgrim associated with no trade whose nature can thus not be opened to the reader by the satirical *General Prologue*. When this distance breaks down with the concluding 'Parson's Tale'—a pastoral treatise on contrition, confession, and satisfaction which rejects the aesthetic principles on which the poem is based ('Thou getest fable noon ytoold for me [*you don't get me telling any fables*]' (X(I). 31))—the solemn mood that ensues leads to the narrator's penitential rejection of much of his own œuvre:

Wherfore I biseke you mekely, for the mercy of God, that ye preye for me that Crist have mercy on me and foryeve me my giltes; and namely of my translacions and enditynges of worldly vanitees, the whiche I revoke in my retracciouns; as is the Book of Troilus; [...] the Book of the XXV Ladies [*i.e. The Legend of Good Women*]; [...] the tales of Caunterbury, thilke that sownen into [*tend towards*] synne; [...] and many another book, if they were in my remembrance, and many a song and many a leccherous lay, that Crist for his grete mercy foryeve me the synne.   (X(I). 1084–6)[2]

Where Langland's Will moves quickly 'thorugh Contricion and Confession' back to his vision of a society in collapse, Chaucer's narrator—heeding the call to penitence in a very different style from Will—abandons the world represented by the poem, no more making any public pronouncement upon it than has the Parson, whose *Tale* insistently treats the moral flaws it describes as material for private confession rather than social satire. All humour and flexibility gone, the narrator evaluates his writings only in so far as they affect his own hope of salvation. If the ending of *Piers Plowman*, with its modern-seeming account of a dystopian world in which 'the best lack all conviction while the worst | Are full of passionate intensity' (W. B. Yeats, 'The Second Coming'), is written in a public mode inflected by the apocalyptic language of prophecy, the ending of *The Canterbury Tales*, whose sobriety so disappoints modern readers that it is often ignored or read ironically, is written in a private penitential mode inflected by the Parson's language of pastoral theology.

The contrast between the narratorial stances of the two poems, and between their endings, reflect important differences both between the two authors' self-presentation, and between their views of the theological role of poetry and the meaning of Christian history. Langland is driven by his belief in impending apocalypse to push beyond his uncertain sense of his prophetic voice and speak publically to Christian society as a whole about its predicament. His need to imagine a 'good theology', a version of truth that performs what it promises, overrides all else. Averse to Langland's vatic view of poetry and perhaps to his apocalypticism, Chaucer rests firmly within his role as a layperson with no authority to pronounce on public matters, unwilling to make

---

[2] Quotations from *The Canterbury Tales* are taken from Benson 1987, and follow the reference conventions used in that volume: citations are by fragment number (using both of the two main systems for distinguishing fragments, one with upper-case roman numerals, the other letters) and line number within fragment. Many of Chaucer's other poems are, of course, relevant to this essay, but it has seemed best to focus on his best-known and most overtly theological work.

judgements even on private morality when he has no formal responsibility to do so (Cooper 1999). As a result, although *Piers Plowman* and *The Canterbury Tales* both depict contemporary Christian society and draw on the same satirical traditions for their raw material, the two poets represent this society in different ways. Langland's characters, most of whom are personifications, quickly become exemplary of the cosmic spiritual forces of good and evil; even Langland's narrator, Will, is not only a poet and sinful individual but an aspect of the human psyche (the energy of purpose, desire, affect, stubborness). Chaucer's characters, by contrast, live in a world which, for all its comic confusion, anticipates the moral theology imposed on it by 'The Parson's Tale' in the sense that it contains individualized agents whose virtues, sins, and destinies—like the tales they tell—are personal before they are exemplary (Patterson 1978). Langland's Friar Flatterer almost single-handedly brings about the collapse of Unity, worming his way into the church, then offering absolution on easy terms to lay people: a perversion of the penitential system which allows Sloth and Pride their long-desired point of entry (XX. 305–80). When Chaucer's Friar quarrels with the Summoner, on the other hand, their hatred may point to a wider problem with ecclesiastical funding but hardly threatens the end of the world, while the association between friars and corrupt confessional practice in 'The Summoner's Tale' itself resolves into a brilliant, blasphemous joke about farts and spiritual *afflatus* whose specifically moral significance is left unclear (III(D). 2222–94). If Langland's characters play distinct parts in a single apocalyptic history, Chaucer's are protagonists in an indefinite series of experimental fictions.

None of this is to say that *The Canterbury Tales* is uninterested in social issues or fails to bring large theological ideas to bear on those issues. Despite the poem's dissimilarities from *Piers Plowman*, its thinking about society, ethics, and human understanding is far more theological than is usually admitted and also more Langlandian, clearly marked by Chaucer's reading of his older contemporary. But where *Piers Plowman* is nothing less than a critique of formal theology and of the late-medieval church that taught, sustained, and profited by it, *The Canterbury Tales* takes theology and the church, in all its corruption, as objects of study rather than critique, refusing the responsibility for their reform that Langland fervently acknowledges. In so doing, Chaucer for the most part also refuses—until the rounding up that is 'The Parson's Tale'—the responsibility to write 'good theology', offering instead an intellectualized series of meditations on themes, religious and secular, whose common element is their attention to the philosophical limit case: the extreme, as distinct from the exemplary, instantiation of an issue (Miller 2005). Not Langland's generic sinner Haukyn, weeping in his spotty 'cote of Cristendom' (XIII. 272–3), but the oft-married Wife of Bath, with her aggressive sermon on the spiritual validity of the second best and refusal of Christ's counsel of perfection (Blamires 1989); not Langland's ignorant penitents, wandering like animals in their search for Truth until instructed by Piers (V. 513–642), but the 'litel clergeon', whose illiteracy is understood by the Prioress and the Virgin alike as synonymous with saintliness; not Langland's theological doctor, made spiritually useless by careerism yet respected by Clergy, Scripture, and Conscience (XIII. 1–201), but the Pardoner, whose powerful understanding of penitential theology is in service to a mode of deliberate evil which depends on bringing others to repentance: floating free of moral commentary as these portraits do, any of them might 'sownen into synne'. Inside Chaucer's modest refusal to adjudicate the intricate cases constructed by *The Canterbury Tales* a real potential for destabilizing the faith rather than building it—a real possibility of 'bad theology'—lies coiled. The last-minute act of penitence that is the *Retractions* may be less a remorseful response to a consciously worldly poem than it is a layman's acknowledgement of the relentless pressures his poem has placed on the ethical and theological models that have come under its eye.

PIERS PLOWMAN: THE CRITIQUE OF FORMAL THEOLOGY

As vernacular, fictive, and poetic projects by writers outside the institutions in which formal theology was produced—university, monastery, pulpit—both *Piers Plowman* and *The Canterbury Tales* are by definition something other than official contributions to religious thinking. *Piers Plowman* makes this clear from the outset, representing itself as the dreams of a man who has gone out 'wide in this world', dressed 'in habite as an heremite unholy of werkes', in search, not of the truths he finds, but merely of 'wondres [*marvels*]' (Prol. 3–4). A member of an old and informal religious profession—one which maintained an ambiguous position somewhere between clerical and lay—a hermit might write theology of a prophetic or a satirical kind. Langland was probably aware of Richard Rolle (d. 1349), England's last major eremitic writer, whose elaborately rhetorical Latin and English works are trumpeted from the spiritual 'desert' of a cell already irradiated by the perfection of heaven and almost separate from the church they address (Godden 1984; Watson 1991). But Langland's narrator is an 'unholy' hermit: one of the unstable hermits satirized as *girovagi* as early as the sixth-century *Benedictine Rule* and characterized only a few lines into *Piers Plowman* as 'grete lobies and longe [*big tall lubbers*] that lothe were to swynke [*work*]' (Prol. 55). Despite the freedom with which he criticizes all he sees, his prophetic credentials are, and stay, extraordinarily weak. Having failed to leave the world behind as a hermit should, indeed suffused with curiosity about the world, and lacking both institutional and spiritual authority and any clear social status, the narrator's self-depiction is as wavering as Rolle's is clear. Unable to decide even if he is a hermit, a cleric in minor orders, or married with children (XVIII. 427–8; XX. 193–8), when he is asked to justify his poetic 'makynge' the best reply he can make is that he writes merely for comfort and fun (XII. 16–24). Such flexibility or evasiveness is essential to the unconstrained way in which *Piers Plowman* ranges over matters ecclesiastical, social, political, and moral without ever committing itself to a single viewpoint. But it hardly makes for easy judgements on the reader's part about the judgements constantly handed down by the narrator and many of the characters he encounters.

All this narrator can at first do well is to dream everything—church, state, and society—with dispassionate attention to the gap that opens up at all social levels between ideal and practice as soon as any of these entities is set in narrative motion. However confident Holy Church's opening exposition of a world divided into True and False—a life loyally lived in a manner proper to one's station and a life of rebellion and greed—the poem's action constantly shows well thought-out reformist initiatives beset by the law of unintended consequences, as they run headlong into forces more obdurate than the theological theory behind them has planned. Summoned by Conscience and the king to reform secular society, Reason attempts to impose strict justice, the disciplined practice of everyday life, and communal contrition for sin, telling the king to 'rende out my guttes' if he does not succeed (IV. 186). Yet a trickle of resistance to his program—the wink Waryn Wisdom gives Lady Mede after her defeat in the lawsuit between Peace and Wrong (IV. 154); the rapid defections from the pilgrimage to Saint Truth by a pardoner and a prostitute (V. 639–42)—soon grows into a flood. As a mildly penitent society loses its way, straying like 'beestes over baches and hilles', the conservative forces of ignorance and inertia quickly reassert themselves (V. 514). Piers Plowman's attempt to continue Reason's initiative by having society reform itself by *doing*—ministering to its physical needs as a means of furthering its spiritual ones—is equally short-lived. Mere exhortation achieves nothing, and Hunger, summoned to compel the idle back to work, is too blunt an instrument for moral purposes (VI). Throughout the poem, theories, models, collective initiatives, all crumble in this way under the dead weight of the narrative 'and then'. Even in the penultimate passus, with its account of history from biblical times to the present, a single conjunction separates the creation of a Christian society under Piers and the inevitable rise of the forces of corruption against him: 'Now is Piers to the plow—*and* Pride it aspide, | And gathered hym a gret oost [*host*]' (XIX. 338–9).

Of moral idealism itself, the narrator nonetheless has a traditionalist's appreciation, longing for the simplicity of the 'estates' model that divided society into those who fight, those who work, and those who pray, and movingly recreating the language in which the liturgy evokes Christ's incarnation and the forgiveness of sins (e.g. I. 148–74; V. 479–506). But his dreams cannot begin to imagine these ideals having any sustained application until he learns that reform must begin with the individual, embarking on a quest for Dowel [*Do well*] that first exposes, then redeems, the self-righteousness that lies behind his own desire to master and criticize the world, rather than engage with his own soul (VIII–XV). This process leaves uncertain much that other didactic poems would consider it good to be clear about: formal theological questions about the role of education in the spiritual life; the place of community in a world where only individuals 'do well'; the question of whether even those who 'do well' are thereby saved. But the process does have the effect of urging the poem ever further from theories into the realm of impulsive evangelical action. Theological theory fares badly in this part of the poem, where idle laymen and ambitious academics are satirized in the table talk of the 'heighe men' who find the fall irrational, or of the doctor who patronizingly defines Dowel as 'do as clerkes techeth' (X. 103; XIII. 116). The narrator's own speculations about the fate of the learned at first seem no better, as he plunges through badly digested Bible verses and snippets of Augustine to the ironic conclusion that even a little learning is a dangerous thing: 'Ye, men knowe clerkes that han corsed the tyme | That ever thei kouthe or knewe moore than *Credo in Deum patrem* [*I believe in God the Father*]' (X. 466–7). Yet his anti-intellectualism is supported elsewhere in a poem which seems dissatified with any merely theoretical knowledge when 'kynde knowynge [*intuitive knowledge*]' of the truth is possible (I. 138). The dreamer is shrewd in his own definition of Dowel, not as knowledge, but as painful experience—' "To se muche and suffre moore, certes," quod I, "is Dowel" ' (XI. 410)—and is right to assume that 'good' theology must be closely responsive to the human predicament, however wrong he sometimes is about that predicament itself.

The place of formal theology in *Piers Plowman* is represented, on the one hand, by a series of personifications—including Holy Church, Reason, Wit, Study, Clergy, and Scripture—and, on the other, by the poem's use of Latin quotations from biblical, patristic, and scholastic sources. These offer a collective representation of learned authority around and about which the poem thinks in the most diverse ways. Despite the moral authority of a second set of allegorical personages, with whom the poem is closely identified, including especially Conscience and Piers—who grasps truth not intellectually but intuitively, 'as kyndely as clerc doth his bokes' (V. 538)—it sometimes seems that these sources of formal authority provide avenues to 'treuthe' with which the narrator's vernacular ruminations and even the poem's consistent elevation of Piers as a religious ideal cannot compete. As we saw, in the second vision a single narrative links the reformist efforts of a figure of formal authority, Reason, and the poem's complex figuration of intuitive authority, Piers. Piers's attempts to bring society to God culminate in his publication of a pardon, sent by Truth, guaranteeing forgiveness of sins to all the estates of society if they fulfil their professional and personal duties responsibly and with charity (VII). But the unity between Reason and Piers, formal and intuitive authority, is permanently broken when a priest gives a formal theological reading of this pardon and shows that Piers's optimistic claim to have found a means of forgiveness for all can be reduced to two harsh lines of the Athanasian Creed: 'Et qui bona egerunt ibunt in vitam eternam. Qui vero mala, in ignem eternum [*And they that have done good shall go into life everlasting and they that have done evil into everlasting fire*]' (VII. 110). Piers's response—to tear the pardon apart, give up his plough, and devote himself to 'preieres and . . . penaunce'—is read differently by different scholars (Lawler 2000), not least because the priest, while formally correct, speaks so contemptuously that we cannot be sure his intervention is 'good' theology: what he says may be true but is it useful? Nonetheless, the poem seems to imply here that Piers's ignorant optimism—his desire to find a version of Christian truth applicable to all estates of society—has urged him into theological error. Here we might choose to see the learned, perhaps priestly, author of *Piers Plowman* reining in the complacencies of his dreamer by formally correcting his great visionary creation, Piers.

Yet it is not clear that the formal theology represented by the Athanasian Creed has much permanent influence on the poem. Despite the cautions offered by the learned personifications in the third vision (VIII–XII), the narrator's attacks on learning, and his frenetically optimistic salvation theology—which at one point manoeuvres in a matter of lines from the terrifying formal theological statements 'Many are called but few are chosen' (Matt. 22: 14) to the desperate intuitive claim that it is impossible for baptized Christians, feudally bound to their lord, 'rightfully to reneye [*renege*]' their saving faith (XI. 112–14, 126)—dominate the thinking of the last visions of *Piers Plowman*. Despite the occasional moderating voice (the most coherent of which is Ymaginatif's in Passus XII), the poem's view of learning and respect for theological caution never recovers from Conscience's decision to abandon Clergy and go off on pilgrimage with the vagabond Patience (XIII. 180–215)—he who reduces theology to three words by claiming as a 'liflode [*means of sustenance*]' adequate for all Christians 'a pece of the Paternoster [*Lord's Prayer*]—fiat voluntas tua [*thy will be done*]' (XIV. 48–9). At the climax of the poem, Christ's harrowing of hell (XVIII), Langland in his turn suspends the precepts of formal theology, holding out—despite the pronouncements of the Fourth Lateran Council—a hope of universal salvation that even the poem's closing vision of universal corruption cannot negate, endorsed as it is by Christ's own words: 'For I were an unkynde kyng but I my kyn holpe [*unless I helped my kinsfolk*]—| And nameliche [*especially*] at swich a nede ther nedes helpe bihoveth [*where there is a great need for help*]' (XVIII. 399–400). All earlier promises in this vein, such as Piers's pardon, are contractual, using the poem's penitential dictum 'redde quod debes [*repay what you owe*]' to suggest that salvation is due to all who do right. It is this that renders them vulnerable. By contrast—like his appearance as the Good Samaritan, interrupting his journey to Jerusalem to tend the man fallen among thieves (XVII. 48–83)—Christ's words and deeds here are impulsive, putting his promise beyond the criticism of official theologians like the cavilling priest. Conceding little credence to formal authority as such, *Piers Plowman* here rests its vulnerable claim to 'treuthe' on nothing more than its own ability to imagine, passionately but coherently, a Christ to whom anything less than the full pardon of sinful humanity is unthinkable (Watson 1997).

For all this, the extent to which *Piers Plowman* actively rejects formal theology must not be exaggerated. Not only does Langland presuppose the truth of the Scriptures and the writings of the fathers, he firmly endorses more recent theological doctrines, such as the doctrine of purgatory and those underlying the sacrament of confession. His poem's attacks on academic intellectualism (*scientia*) and affirmation of the value of inner knowledge (*sapientia*) have a centuries-long history in monastic thought, uneasy from the first about the scholasticism associated with the university (Simpson 1990). Characters such as Conscience and Patience, who stand opposed to the narrator's more assertive attempts to fashion truth in the image of his desires as well as to academic learning, also derive from this tradition. Learning is never attacked, except by the narrator at his most shrill. Even though he is left behind,

Clergy retains the poem's respect, as a figure who, says Conscience, if he could ever be brought into harmony with Patience, could help to do great things in the world:

If Pacience be oure partyng felawe [*partner*] and pryvé [*intimate*] with us bothe,
There nys [*is*] no wo in this world that we ne sholde amende,
And conformen [*dispose*] kynges to pees, and alle kynnes londes [*the lands of all peoples*]—
Sarsens [*Moslems*] and Surre [*Syrians*], and so forth alle the Jewes—
Turne into the trewe feith and intil oon bileve [*one faith*].   (XIII. 207–11)

This glimpse of a revived role for Latin theological learning as an instrument for the conversion of the world suggests that Conscience and Patience are weakened by the failure of learned theology to support their enterprise. Ideally, Clergy, Conscience, and Patience *would* work together.

Still, the failure of Clergy is real. As the poem ends and Conscience leaves a desperately corrupted visible church to go a second time on pilgrimage, he goes in search, not of Clergy, but of Piers: the only figure able to destroy Pride (XX. 383). Whatever Piers represents—be it Christ, be it the invisible church, be it the principle of integrity (Aers and Staley 1996)—his centrality to the poem's spiritual quest is hardly a ringing endorsement of the achievements of formal theology.

THE CANTERBURY TALES: THEOLOGY AND WORLDLINESS

Even more than *Piers Plowman*, *The Canterbury Tales* immediately divests itself of any claim to theological authority, presenting itself as the product of a specifically secular view of Christian society. As in the older poem, religious beliefs and mores jostle for recognition within the all-absorbing affairs of the world. But where *Piers Plowman* sees the 'fair feeld ful of folk' which provides its setting in the eschatological light of the narrator's first glimpse of the place, positioned 'bitwene' tower and dungeon, heaven and hell (Prol. 17), Chaucer's pilgrims make their way to Canterbury illumined by no such spiritual radiance. Indeed, the syntax of the famous sentence with which the poem opens turns even the miracles performed by St Thomas, whose shrine is the goal of the pilgrimage, into natural effects of the seasonal rebirth that is spring: '*Whan*' (inspired by the 'breeth' of the west wind) the 'croppes' grow and 'foweles maken melodye', '*Thanne*' (inspired by how Thomas has helped them 'whan that they were seeke') 'longen folk to goon on pilgrimages' (I(A). 1–18). Although the pilgrims assemble at the Tabard 'in a compaignye'—a loosely non-hierarchic organization (Wallace 1997) but described in an order that firmly places 'those who pray' (Prioress, Monk, and Friar) behind 'those who fight' (Knight, Squire, and Yeoman)—their 'felaweshipe' is initially a matter of 'aventure', and is sealed, not by prayers and mutual pledges of charity, but by 'soper', 'strong...wine', and the ministrations of the Host (I(A). 24–6, 750).

Perhaps there are echoes in this supper of a late-medieval understanding of Christian society as the body of Christ on earth (see 1 Cor. 12–14): an understanding which found its ritual expression in the communal supper of the mass and its public celebration in the late-medieval feast of Corpus Christi (Rubin 1991). The title 'Hooste [*innkeeper*]' used for Harry Bailey, who is the master of ceremonies for the *Tales*, seems to pun on the word 'host', the wafer which becomes Christ's body when consecrated by the priest. To follow the implications of this pun to one logical conclusion, the 'felaweshipe' of pilgrims is perhaps, then, an image of Christian community as a whole, so that the pilgrimage offers a partial analogue to Langland's inclusive theology of salvation. If so, the dictum 'nobody is saved outside the church' ('extra quam nullus...salvatur') would here imply its opposite: 'nobody inside the church is damned' (as Will argues in *Piers Plowman* XI. 123–36). But is this right? The best evidence for the Host/host pun is, ironically, the Host's blasphemous invocations of Christ's body—by 'Goddes bones', 'nayles and blood', 'Goddes digne passioun', etc. (II(B¹). 1166; VI(C). 288; II(B¹). 1175). Repetitition of these blasphemies at key moments between tales helps hold the poem together but also rouses the Parson to a stern reproof—'What eyleth the man, so synfully to swere?' (II(B¹).1171; see also X(I). 586–604)—and later finds sinister echoes in the 'othes...dampnable' which punctuate the conversation of the three desperate young rioters at the opening of 'The Pardoner's Tale' (VI(C). 472). If the Host is truly representative of the body of Christ on earth, membership of that body must bestow salvation on easy terms indeed, unless we take the Parson's reproof (and the sombre tale he tells) seriously, as suggesting the opposite: not the ease, but the *difficulty* with which the worldly are redeemed. This is not the kind of issue Chaucer tends to resolve. At best an ambiguous image of the divine presence latent within the 'felaweshipe', the Host seems to be a figure of the strange ways in which the sinful and the sacred combine in *The Canterbury Tales*, both in his own character and in the secular society he represents.

Unlike *Piers Plowman*, whose enquiry into the best form a just society might take imagines a series of incommensurable possibilities—some moderately reformist, others revolutionary—*The Canterbury Tales* starts from the premises that society is de facto governed by the secular and that secular society is de facto neither just nor primarily interested in religious concerns, however far religion bounds its temporal existence and the eternal destinies of its members. *Piers Plowman* first introduces us to Holy Church as a beautiful woman who descends from Truth's tower to provide an authoritative interpretation of the 'feld ful of folk' (I. 2). Whether we associate it with the Host, the Monk ('a manly man' (I(A).167)), or the Parson beating the bounds of his parish (I(A). 491–5), the church in *The Canterbury Tales* exists entirely in the world, and in all but the last case has become indistinguishable, even in principle, from the world's concerns; the Monk regards the rule confining him to his cloister as 'old and somdel streit [*narrow*]'—for, if it is followed, 'how shal the world be served?' (I(A). 174, 187). Here, religious ideas and ideals are always first seen in relation to worldly usefulness: 'Me were levere than a barel ale | My wyf at hoom had herd this legende ones!' is all the Host can say to the tale of the virtuous Griselda (IV(E). 1212c–d). Indeed, until the Parson invites the pilgrims to consider their lives penitentially, most such ideas to all appearance have no morally persuasive force at all. In *Piers Plowman*, formal theology seems insufficiently adapted to the needs of secular society; Holy Church can expound the world but she cannot make it virtuous. Here, both the church and religion as a whole are adapted all too well, serving the interests of those who adhere to them so directly that their spiritual function can seem irredeemably compromised.

If 'good' theology is defined as a combination of the useful and the true, *The Canterbury Tales* generally understands the true as beyond its mandate but keeps a fierce focus on the category of the useful, repeatedly asking 'useful for what and to whom?' This is so even before the poem turns away from the classical setting of *The Knight's Tale*—the arena of much of Chaucer's other poetry—to focus, Langland-style, on Christian, often contemporary Christian, society. On one level, Theseus's defence of divine justice at the end of 'The Knight's Tale' is one of the most impressive theological expositions in Chaucer's poetry, glimpsing, from a pagan land centuries before Christ's Incarnation, a providential purpose (described in Boethian Christian terms) behind the flux of sublunary life (I(A). 2987–3074) (Minnis 1982). As theology, this speech is a clear improvement on the state polytheism Theseus also patronizes, with its worship of vicious and fickle planetary energies. Yet the setting of the speech makes its political expediency clear, for by identifying Theseus with a benificent providence (rather than, for example, with the chaotic power of Saturn) the speech sacralizes his rule, strengthening his hold over Thebes, Amazonia, and Athens (as the earthly representative of the 'Firste Moevere' (I(A). 2987)) in much the same way as does Palamon's marriage to Emily. Whether he is viewed as an ideal ruler or as a tyrant conqueror, Theseus uses theology to his advantage as clearly here as Nicholas uses it in the Miller's riposte to 'The Knight's Tale', when Nicholas convinces John the carpenter to identify himself with Noah, chosen by God to survive a new flood, and Alison to identify herself with Mary: 'And *angelus ad virginem* [the angel came to the Virgin] he song' (I(A). 3216). John's simple devotion, seemingly fed on a diet of local miracle plays, proves his undoing, as his student lodger casts him in the role of another elderly carpenter: not Noah but Mary's husband Joseph, blasphemously represented (in the fabliau version of events stage-managed by Nicholas) as cuckolded by the Holy Spirit (Watson 2000). Like the Wife of Bath asking commonsense questions that subvert a millennium-old tradition of celebrating virginity over matrimony—'And certes, if ther were no seed ysowe, | Virginitee, thanne whereof sholde it growe?' (III(D). 71–2)—all these characters have their theologies just where they want them.

Given the explicit connections the tales make between the theological views of their tellers or protagonists and their worldly positions and interests, it is not surprising that one of the two prose tales—whose very form seems to indicate the temporary suspension of the ironic—should bring theology and worldly interest together on a conceptual, as well as a personal or political level. In the narrator's own

'Tale of Melibee', worldly self-interest is represented, not as ethically suspect nor as a cause for ironic commentary but as both virtuous and difficult. It takes Prudence, the injured Melibee's wife, many thousands of words to bring her husband to an understanding that his desire for passionate revenge is folly and that his true interests lie in reconciliation with his enemies. Only once he has already accepted her interpretation of these interests (as lying with honour, not wealth, communal peace, not violence, and so on) can Melibee also understand that worldly self-interest, rightly understood, is the same as spiritual self-interest. Deflecting his final throw at revenge at the end of the tale, Prudence at last makes explicit the equation between Melibee's behaviour towards others and God's towards him: 'Wherfore I pray yow, lat mercy been in youre herte, | to th'effect and entente that God Almighty have mercy on yow in his laste juggement. | For Seint Jame seith in his Epistle: "Juggement withouten mercy shal be doon to hym that hath no mercy of another wight"' (VII(B2). 1866–8/*3056–8). As Melibee offers forgiveness to his enemies and commends himself and them to the forgiveness of a God 'so free and so merciable' (VII(B2). 1885/*3074), worldly self-interest turns out to lead, by many twists and turns, all the way to the imitation of Christ.

Replacing the ludicrous 'Sir Thopas' as the narrator's own contribution to the tale-telling, 'The Tale of Melibee' can plausibly be read as Chaucer's defence of the potential value of a religious system in which the spiritual and the worldly fully interpenetrate: a system ordered by the cardinal virtue of prudence, represented in traditional iconography with three eyes, one for the past, one for the present, one for the future. While there are other serious religious tales—we can certainly count 'The Man of Law's Tale', 'The Second Nun's Tale', and 'The Parson's Tale'—none of these is integrated with the world of the pilgrim 'felaweshipe' in the same way as 'The Tale of Melibee'. In these tales, virtuous Christian behaviour is either linked to the heroic past in which Constant sails the storm-tossed seas in her open boat and Cecilia preaches the word from her boiling bath, or occasions an end to tale-telling, as the Parson's analytic rejection of sin replaces the Host's inclusive but self-interested acceptance. The fact that the Host responds to 'The Tale of Melibee' by blaming his wife for failing to check his own passionate outbursts—'For she nys no thyng of swich pacience | As was this Melibeus wyf Prudence' (VII(B2). 1895–6/*3086–7)—suggests that the tale is as relevant to him as it is to its protagonist, and when the linked themes of marital counsel and domestic hen-pecking next emerge in the barnyard comedy of 'The Nun's Priest's Tale' the breadth of the tale's applicability is confirmed. Chaucer seems not to have decided what should follow 'The Man of Law's Tale' (a tale told perhaps by the Shipman, perhaps by the Squire, perhaps by the Wife of Bath) and links 'The Second Nun's Tale' with the world of the pilgrims in a deliberately strained way, as Cecilia's bath gestures forwards to the alchemical imagery of the 'Canon's Yeoman's Tale'; nothing follows 'The Parson's Tale' except the 'Retractions', as the narrator leaves the world and its interests to prepare for death. Positioned between the ideals represented by the Host and the Parson, 'The Tale of Melibee' may provide *The Canterbury Tales* with the nearest thing to a theological centre: a place from which the poem's desire to recognize the demands of the world and its acknowledgement of the final primacy of spiritual values can be recognized and reconciled; a consciously 'good' theological system based not (like the Parson's) on penitence but on prudence, and one which, as a direct result, can operate within the world while also protecting the eternal interests of its adherents.

Yet if 'The Tale of Melibee' shows religion and worldliness coexisting without succumbing to the hypocrisy of the Pardoner or the subversiveness of the Wife of Bath, one equally serious tale serves as its antonym: 'The Clerk's Tale', a study not of prudence but of obedience that constitutes one of the most extreme examples of Chaucer's fondness for the limit case. 'The Clerk's Tale' brings into tense union two related discourses of obedience: one social, concerning the obedience of subjects to rulers and wives to husbands; the other theological, concerning the soul's obedience to God (Georgianna 1995; Newman 1995: ch. 3). Urged to marry, Walter confirms his absolute authority over his subjects by choosing the lowest-born of them as bride, effectively creating his queen from nothing, as God created the world; urged to obey him, his bride Griselda swears 'that nevere willyngly, | In werk ne thoght, I nyl yow disobeye, | For to be deed', consecrating herself to Walter as though he were indeed God (IV(E). 362–4). When Walter subjects Griselda to a series of cruel tests, his association with divinity is apparently compromised, as the Clerk and Walter's subjects bewail his cruelty; only in the tale's conclusion is the association partly readmitted: 'For greet skile is he [*God*] preeve [*test*] that he wroghte [*created*]. | But he ne tempteth no man that he boghte [*redeemed*]' (IV(E). 1152–3). No such qualifications apply to Griselda, all concurring that her obedience is Christlike, even though her example is said to be 'inportable [*intolerable*]', unless it applies only to humanity's need to be 'constant in adversitee' before God (IV(E). 1144, 1146). 'Inportable' here admits the practical limits to the parallel between the kinds of obedience Griselda signifies: a parallel which, taken beyond a certain point, becomes too painful, perhaps too socially disruptive, to be useful. According to the tale, however, no such limit exists in theory; even if Walter's cruelty were real, Griselda, in her acceptance of all, would still be an ideal wife and subject.

The explicit gap between practice and theory, usefulness and truth, opened up at the end of 'The Clerk's Tale' makes overt the sense in which the tale is itself 'inportable', both to the Clerk and to readers. The only workable defence of Griselda's virtue is to acknowledge that cruel husbands and rulers like Walter really are the image of God. Understood didactically, 'The Clerk's Tale' thus describes humankind's relation to God as abject on one side, capricious on the other, endorsing the rights of husbands and rulers to be Godlike in a style similar to Walter. To reject the truth of this is to dismiss Griselda, and the quality of obedience, either as lacking in virtue or as irrelevant to real life, a position to which the Clerk comes close in his envoy: 'Grisilde is deed, and eek hire pacience, | And bothe atones buryed in Ytaille' (IV(E). 1177–8). Like so many of *The Canterbury Tales*, 'The Clerk's Tale' secularizes religion, applying theological structures to a human situation in which (as in both 'The Knight's Tale' and 'The Tale of Melibee') the secular power has become fully identified with spiritual authority, so that the divine inhabits the world mainly by analogy. But where the union of worldly and spiritual prudence in 'The Tale of

Melibee' is fruitful, that of worldly and spiritual obedience in 'The Clerk's Tale' is barren, 'inportable', its truth claims at odds with utility: Walter, in his curiosity and perversity, cannot be the analogue of a loving God any more than Griselda, in her fulsome obedience, can be that of the exemplary wife; yet neither can these analogies be properly resisted. Here, more than anywhere else in *The Canterbury Tales*, Chaucer the humble layman might have feared the capacity of Chaucer the speculative thinker to write in ways that 'sownen into synne', to explore religious truth in ways that might be considered to constitute 'bad theology'.

WORKS CITED

AERS, DAVID, and STALEY, LYNN. 1996. *The Powers of the Holy: Religion, Politics, and Gender in Late Medieval English Culture*. University Park: Pennsylvania State University Press.

AQUINAS, THOMAS. 1975. *Summa contra Gentiles*, trans. Anton C. Pegis. 5 vols. London: University of Notre Dame Press.

BENSON, LARRY (ed.) 1987. *The Riverside Chaucer*. 3rd edn. Boston: Houghton Mifflin.

BESTUL, THOMAS H. (ed.) 2000. *Walter Hilton: The Scale of Perfection*. Middle English Texts Series. Kalamazoo: TEAMS.

BLAMIRES, ALCUIN. 1989. 'The Wife of Bath and Lollardy'. *Medium Aevum* 58: 224–42.

BURR, DAVID. 1989. *Olivi and Franciscan Poverty*. Philadelphia: University of Pennsylvania Press.

COLEMAN, JANET. 1981. *Piers Plowman and the Moderni*. Rome: Edizioni di Storia e Letteratura.

COOPER, HELEN. 1999. 'The Four Last Things in Dante and Chaucer: Ugolino in the House of Rumour'. *New Medieval Literatures* 3. Oxford: Clarendon, 39–66.

DUFFY, EAMON. 1992. *The Stripping of the Altars: Traditional Religion in England 1400–1580*. Yale: Yale University Press.

GEORGIANNA, LINDA. 1995. '"The Clerks' Tale" and the Grammar of Assent'. *Speculum* 70: 793–821.

GILLESPIE, VINCENT. 2007. *Looking in Holy Books: Essays on Late-Medieval Religious Writing in England*. Aberystwyth: University of Wales Press.

GODDEN, MALCOLM. 1984. 'Plowmen and Hermits in Langland's *Piers Plowman*'. *Review of English Studies* 35: 129–63.

HORSTMANN, CARL (ed.) 1895–6. *Yorkshire Writers: Richard Rolle of Hampole, an English Father of the Church*. 2 vols. London: Swan Sonnenschein.

LAWLER, TRAUGOTT. 2000. 'The Pardon Formula in *Piers Plowman*'. *Yearbook of Langland Studies* 14: 117–52.

McCARTHY, ADRIAN JAMES (ed.) 1981. *Book to a Mother: An Edition with Commentary*. Salzburg Studies in English Literature. Salzburg: Institut für Anglistik und Amerikanistik.

McGINN, BERNARD. 2000. *Antichrist: Two Thousand Years of the Human Preoccupation With Evil*. New York: Columbia University Press.

MILLER, MARK. 2005. *Philosophical Chaucer: Love, Sex, and Agency in the Canterbury Tales*. Cambridge Studies in Medieval Literature 55. Cambridge: Cambridge University Press.

MINNIS, A. J. 1982. *Chaucer and Pagan Antiquity*. Cambridge: D. S. Brewer.

NEWMAN, BARBARA. 1995. *From Virile Woman to Woman Christ: Studies in Medieval Religion and Literature*. Philadelphia: University of Pennsylvania Press.

PATTERSON, LEE. 1978. 'The "Parson's Tale" and the Quitting of the "Canterbury Tales"'. *Traditio* 34: 331–80.

ROBERTSON, D. W., JR. 1962. *A Preface to Chaucer: Studies in Medieval Perspective*. Princeton: Princeton University Press.

RUBIN, MIRI. 1991. *Corpus Christi: The Eucharist in Late Medieval Culture*. Cambridge: Cambridge University Press.

SCHMIDT, A. V. C. (ed.) 1995. *William Langland: The Vision of Piers Plowman: A Critical Edition of the B-Text Based on Trinity College Cambridge ms B.15.17*. 2nd edn. London: Dent.

SIMPSON, JAMES. 1990. *Piers Plowman: An Introduction to the B-Text*. Longman Medieval and Renaissance Library 1. Harlow: Longman.

TANNER, NORMAN. 1990. *Decrees of the Ecumenical Councils*. 2 vols. Washington: Georgetown University Press.

TIERNEY, BRIAN. 1964. *The Crisis of Church and State, 1050–1300*. Hoboken, NJ: John Wiley.

VAUCHEZ, ANDRÉ. 1993. *The Laity in the Middle Ages: Religious Beliefs and Devotional Practices*. South Bend, Ind.: University of Notre Dame Press.

WALLACE, DAVID. 1997. *Chaucerian Polity: Absolutist Lineages and Associational Forms in England and Italy*. Paolo Alto: Stanford University Press.

WATSON, NICHOLAS. 1991. *Richard Rolle and the Invention of Authority*. Cambridge Studies in Medieval Literature 13. Cambridge: Cambridge University Press.

—— 1997. 'Visions of Inclusion: Universal Salvation and Vernacular Theology in PreReformation England'. *Journal of Medieval and Early Modern Studies* 27: 145–87.

—— 2000. 'Christian Ideologies', in Peter Brown (ed.), *A Companion to Chaucer*. Oxford: Basil Blackwell, 75–89.

YEATS. W. B. 1967. *Collected Poems*. New York: Macmillan.

FURTHER READING

General

AERS, DAVID, and LYNN STALEY. 1996. *The Powers of the Holy: Religion, Politics, and Gender in Late Medieval English Culture*. University Park: Pennsylvania State University Press. Study of religious thought and writing in fourteenth-century England, with chapters on Langland and Chaucer.

BROWN, PETER (ed.) 2000. *A Companion to Chaucer*. Oxford: Basil Blackwell. Essays on aspects of Chaucer's thought and writing with special emphasis on *The Canterbury Tales*.

GILLESPIE, VINCENT. 2005. *Looking in Holy Books: Essays on Late-Medieval Religious Writing in England*. Aberystwyth: University of Wales Press. Collection of essays on aspects of late-medieval English spirituality.

HUDSON, ANNE. 1988. *The Premature Reformation: Wycliffite Texts and Lollard History*. Oxford: Clarendon. Study of the most important English religious movement of the late Middle Ages.

KUNG, HANS. 2001. *The Catholic Church: A Short History*. London: Orion. Consciously polemical study of the growth of the Catholic Church around the papacy.

SIMPSON, JAMES. 2004. *The Oxford English Literary History: Reform and Cultural Revolution, 1350–1547*. The Oxford History of English Literature, ii. Oxford: Clarendon. Controversial account of Langland and Chaucer's literary and religious milieu.

SWANSON, R. N. 1993. *Church and Society in Late Medieval England.* Oxford: Basil Blackwell. Study of the role of the church in late-medieval English society.

WALLACE, DAVID (ed.) 1999. *The Cambridge History of Medieval English Literature.* Cambridge: Cambridge University Press. Collection of essays on Langland, Chaucer, and contemporaries.

Piers Plowman

BENSON, DAVID. 2004. *Public Piers Plowman: Modern Scholarship and Medieval English Culture.* University Park: Pennsylvania State University Press. Second part of the book focuses fruitfully on Langland's debt to the common religious culture of his time.

CARRUTHERS, MARY. 1973. *The Search for Saint Truth.* Evanston, Ill.: Northwestern University Press. Study of *Piers Plowman* as a search for knowledge.

MANN, JILL. 1979. 'Eating and Drinking in *Piers Plowman*'. *Essays and Studies,* NS 32: 26–43. Account of one of Langland's principal allegorical images with special reference to the eucharist.

SIMPSON, JAMES. 1990. *Piers Plowman: An Introduction to the B-Text.* Harlow: Longman. Introduction to *Piers Plowman,* with special focus on the role of affective knowledge.

Yearbook of Langland Studies. 1987– . Annual journal dedicated to Langland studies, with comprehensive annotated bibliography.

The Canterbury Tales

Chaucer Review. 1966– . Journal dedicated to Chaucer and his contemporaries.

BESSERMANN, LAWRENCE. 1998. *Chaucer's Biblical Poetics.* Norman: University of Oklahoma Press. Recent study of Chaucer along lines generally influenced by Robertson 1962.

COOPER, HELEN. 1999. 'The Four Last Things in Dante and Chaucer: Ugolino in the House of Rumour'. *New Medieval Literatures* 3. Oxford: Clarendon, 39–66. Important reading of Chaucer's religiosity in relation to Dante's.

FOSTER, EDWARD E., and CAREY, DAVID H. 2002. *Chaucer's Church: A Dictionary of Religious Terms in Chaucer.* Aldershot: Ashgate. Useful reference volume.

ROBERTSON, D. W., JR. 1962. *A Preface to Chaucer: Studies in Medieval Perspective.* Princeton: Princeton University Press. Controversial and influential attempt to claim a version of Augustinian Christianity as key to a proper, didactic understanding of all Chaucer's works.

Studies in the Age of Chaucer. 1979– . Journal dedicated to Chaucer and his contemporaries. Contains annual annotated bibliography of Chaucer scholarship.

WATSON, NICHOLAS. 2005. 'Chaucer's Public Christianity'. *Religion and Literature* 37: 1–18. Study of *The Canterbury Tales* as a public statement of a distinctively lay version of Christianity.

CHAPTER 23

SHAKESPEARE AND MARLOWE

THOMAS HEALY

> There's a divinity that shapes our ends
> Rough-hew them how we will.
>
> > (*Hamlet* v. ii. 10–11; Shakespeare 1988)
>
> I count religion but a childish toy,
> And hold there is no sin but ignorance.
>
> > (*The Jew of Malta*, Prologue, 14–15; Marlowe 1969)

Theology infuses the plays and poems of Shakespeare and Marlowe, as it does virtually all Elizabethan and Jacobean culture. The questions are, what theology, and is there any consistency in its employment? There is critical controversy concerning the nature of Herbert, Donne, or T. S. Eliot's catholicism, there is debate about the orthodoxy of Milton's perception of the Trinity, and about Langland's inclination to Lollardy; but their Christianity is not called into question. As the quotation from *The Jew of Malta* above illustrates, though, the parameters of what Marlowe's and Shakespeare's theology may consist appear wider—in Marlowe's case to the extent of asking whether theology is present in his work only to be defamed.

With both dramatists, some contemporaries or near contemporaries showed unease over what were perceived as their plays' unorthodox religious positions. Thomas Beard's *The theatre of Gods iudgements* (1597) used Marlowe's violent death at the age of 29 to claim that God had acted against a non-believer, one who had affirmed: 'our Sauiour to be but a deceiuer, and Moses to be but a coniurer and seducer of the people, and the Holy Bible to be but vaine and idle stories, and all religion but a deuice of pollicie' (ibid. 148). While Shakespeare's life never prompted such outbursts against his possible irreligion, Hamlet's assertion of godly providence above was not felt to be present in all Shakespeare's plays. Late seventeenth-century audiences found *King Lear*'s conclusion too pessimistic and Nahum Tate rewrote it in 1680, allowing Cordelia and Lear to live. The sense of utter and inconsolable loss that Lear suffers was experienced as too bleak, contrary to a providentially governed universe that seeks humanity's well-being. Tate's version subsequently kept Shakespeare's from the stage for the following one hundred and fifty years.

The weight of modern critical evaluations about both playwrights' work, however, has been to discover moral and religious outlooks at the heart of their drama. With Marlowe, the most influential mid-twentieth-century view was that his major characters (Tamburlaine, Faustus, The Jew of Malta) were 'overreachers': they exceed the limits of a divinely governed universe and so tragically decline (Levin 1954). Reading Marlowe's plays within this framework, it is possible to assert his Christian orthodoxy, his drama is witnessed as illustrative warnings against transgressing God's order. To understand the plays in this manner, however, seems difficult to reconcile with many of their elements—e.g. proposing that we must appreciate *Doctor Faustus*'s concluding chorus as being without glibness and irony when it exhorts us:

> Only to wonder at unlawful things,
> Whose deepness doth entice such forward wits
> To practise more than heavenly power permits.
>
> (Epilogue, 6–8)

Shakespeare's celebration as one of the British 'worthies' from the eighteenth century meant that his drama became increasingly envisaged as articulating a national spirit that almost inevitably portrayed it supporting the institutions of church and state. Cranmer's prophetic salute of Elizabeth's future glory in *Henry VIII*, which amidst the foretelling of secular peace and material plenty for the nation, also ordained that under Elizabeth 'God shall be truly known' (v. iv. 36) appeared to indicate that Shakespeare unambiguously supported Anglican Protestantism. By the mid-twentieth century, the British predominately viewed Shakespeare as articulating the spirit of a golden Elizabethan world that combined a secular and sacred *via media*. The questioning of Shakespeare's political orthodoxy in the 1980s, however, increasingly brought his theology under new scrutiny, with renewed claims made both for a more radical Protestantism or, more recently, Roman Catholicism, underpinning his dramatic vision (Hamilton 1992; Wilson 2004). Further, since the early nineteenth century, Shakespeare's drama has played differing but distinctive roles in the emerging national cultures of Europe and the United States as well as former British colonies. His plays, particularly in translation, have been reconstructed into a myriad of protean forms that often allows their religious sentiments readily to accord with diverse theological orthodoxies.

Atheism, paganism, classical stoicism, liberal Anglicanism, severe Calvinism, persecuted Roman Catholicism: the gamut of arguments about Marlowe and Shakespeare's theology are seemingly as varied and ingeniously derived as the claims about the authors' possible identities: Francis Bacon, Lords Rutland or Oxford, each another! Rather than proposing that these various theological outlooks that critics have found in their work are resolvable, this chapter will attempt to outline some of the reasons why such often contradictory positions have been argued: why Marlowe's and Shakespeare's religion seems so hard to clarify. For reasons largely of space, I shall focus on their plays. Their poetry does not spell out their theological inclinations any more clearly, and although Shakespeare's sonnets or Marlowe's *Hero and Leander* are widely read, these writers' reputations especially rest with their drama.

Leaving aside the matter of adoption by different cultures outside Britain, three issues notably complicate attempts to explore religion with Shakespeare and Marlowe. First, our understanding of the complexities surrounding the nature of both Protestantism and Roman Catholicism in England at the end of the sixteenth century is still far from secure and this is only enhanced when we add the question of contemporary religious culture's relations with the new commercial theatres in London, which both dramatists principally wrote for. In addition, our knowledge of these authors' biographies is sketchy to the point of non-existent regarding their personal views. Extrapolation from reputation, hearsay, and reported opinions, or general circumstantial supposed evidence is frequently used to assert authorial viewpoints that there is no genuine proof to support. We possess no letters, journals, or private papers for either man. Drama is not an exercise in biography and attempts by some to select certain characters or dramatic episodes as notably revealing about their author's genuine beliefs are largely the products of over-stimulated critical fantasies. Peter Holland's entry on Shakespeare and Charles Nicolls's on Marlowe in the *New Dictionary of National Biography* supply the most accurate account of these authors' lives and religion.

Second, English drama as a literary genre in the late sixteenth century departed from being part of its society's wider religious observances as it had been in the Middle Ages. The secular dramas that Marlowe and Shakespeare excel at create characters and dramatic incidents that are not built on familiar moral types or straightforward plots designed to assert shared social, moral, and religious values. Although both Shakespeare and Marlowe have been examined as part of serious literary culture for a few centuries, they initially participated in a popular theatre where issues of literary value, such as integrity or consistency of vision, needed to accommodate the demands of commercial entertainment. Literary criticism has sometimes tried to separate Renaissance drama's supposed serious elements from those seen as directed to the demands of low-life audiences in the pit. Such attempts, though, tend to ignore the ways these plays employ ribaldry, the grotesque, and social topsy-turveyness to challenge orthodox norms by which élite characters attempt to control their environments, including religious perspectives. Though for slightly different reasons, much current literary criticism finds the simultaneous presence of farce and tragedy in Shakespeare's and Marlowe's drama no less awkward to deal with than previous generations. For instance, many critics, if not audiences, are uncomfortable with presenting *The Tempest*'s Caliban as 'some monster of the isle' as

Stefano describes him (ii. ii. 65). At present, he is far more likely to be portrayed as an unfortunate victim rather than as a clownish villain.

Third, and in some respects most significant, Renaissance drama is designed as performed language. This makes these playwrights something of an anomaly in this section called 'theological ways of *reading* literature'. Both Shakespeare and Marlowe were part of a theatre world where plays were principally acted rather than read in textual form—in Shakespeare's case he operated as a director and as an actor as well as a playwright. Their plays were envisaged as being completed in their staging and, as Elizabethan dramatists usually offer few clues about how they imagined an ideal staging of their work, the play-texts are incomplete in ways that poetry and novels are not. Performance always differs, if only slightly, from previous stagings, even within the same production. Arguing that a play or a character reflects specific theological values is difficult to do with any precision because such interpretations necessarily fix how they imagine the language is performed and its relation to the spectacle of the staging. This is further compounded with both Marlowe's and Shakespeare's work by the fact that the editions of texts we possess are not fully authorial but the products— to lesser or greater extents depending on how many versions of a play exists and its paths of transmissions—of later editorial processes. In the case of Marlowe's *Doctor Faustus*, for example, we have two very different versions of it, neither of which is fully authorial, while the only early text we possess of *The Jew of Malta*, one of the period's most popular plays, dates from 1633, forty-two years after it was first performed and forty after the author's death. Similarly, numerous Shakespeare plays have scenes or speeches that exist in different versions and early sources of a number of the plays are exclusively dependent on the 1623 First Folio of his works, which appeared eight years after his death.

'A great offence from the church of God'? Theatre and Religion in Elizabethan London

At the start of the Reformation in England, the new Protestants celebrated players along with printers and preachers as crucial conduits through which the reform movement could spread its ideas. Drama for early English Protestantism remained important for religion, as it had been in the Middle Ages. Indeed, for some decades of the mid-sixteenth century when both Marlowe and Shakespeare were young it was possible to witness both new Protestant plays and older Roman Catholic ones. Shakespeare could have seen Lord Leicester's Men (a peer with pronounced Protestant sympathies) performing in Stratford in 1572 and 1576, while the nearby Coventry mystery cycle originating in the Middle Ages continued to be performed annually until 1578. However, the relation between religion and drama began to fracture in Elizabeth's reign. There were government orders in both 1559 and 1589 against playing 'matters in divinity', largely stemming from fears of stirring divisions within Protestantism rather than associating plays with Roman Catholic practices. While these orders seem not to have been vigorously enforced, by the 1580s some of the more strident elements within the now dominant Protestant Church of England orchestrated a series of pamphlet attacks on the London theatres as sinful places that directly conflicted with the efforts of the godly to win souls to religion. The Court, however, would have none of it; the theatres remained open. Nor did such attacks appear to affect the conduct of thousands of Londoners who regularly flocked to Southwark on the Thames's south bank to witness performances in the new commercially run theatres being built there. Indeed, by helping to make theatrical distractions seem a questionable activity, such attacks may have helped to heighten the playhouses' attractions (Mullaney 1988).

For a Calvinist element within the English Church, the new commercial theatres of the 1580s had chosen entertainment over edification; they had become places disorderly and unstable. Ideologically, they now exemplified Calvin's fears about 'theatres of the world' where humanity might be stunned, dazzled, and blinded by the world's allurements that falsely promised grace and sweetness (Diehl 1992). Further, in their eyes, the city's ostensible moral health might be directly equated with its physical and commercial health. The Corporation of London argued: 'to play in plague time is to increase the plague by infection; to play out of plague time is to draw the plague by offendings of God, upon occasion of such plays' (Chambers and Greg 1908: 173). Refusing to regulate activities that were imagined as contrary to God's desired reformation of England might have immediate and deadly results for all.

Yet, even among those with strongly held Protestant beliefs there was no consensus about the moral value of watching plays. Defending drama in the early seventeenth century, Thomas Heywood explicitly counters the charge that theatrical spectacle is inappropriate by citing various examples of when it allegedly had been effective in helping to restore moral order (Heywood 1973). He claims instances when those witnessing performances in which murders are enacted found themselves drawn to confess similar crimes. The spectacle that is filled with the incidents of dramatic excitement (blood, lust, revenge) is not morally corrupting the audience, Heywood argued, rather it is helping to cleanse the community of a moral pollution that infects it: 'What can sooner print modesty in the soules of the wanton ... then by discouvering to them the monstrousnesse of their own sin' (sig. G2v). Dramatic display could be witnessed as an effective vehicle to root out sin and help preserve the godly English. Despite vocal criticism in some quarters, English Protestantism never abandons its interest in drama as an instrument for reform, even among those of Calvinist inclinations within the English Church.

There was, therefore, no consensus about drama's role in relation to religion in Elizabethan London; but with the Government anxious about the staging of religious issues, theatre companies were not in a position to perform works that engaged in specific theological controversies. There was also no clear relation between theological perspectives and views towards drama. A man of a Calvinist disposition such as the Earl of Leicester could promote his own drama troupe while those with similar theological outlooks in the Corporation of London might decry playing altogether. Literary criticism in particular tends to categorize England's religious positions during this period by rather fixed and well-delineated categories: Calvinist or Puritan, episcopalian Anglican, Roman Catholic, and so forth, with the assumption that each of these categories has a well-defined set of principles. The reality was very different, with positions shading into one another. Religious perspectives, too, might be focused around allegiances in complex patronage networks or through a developing sense of national consciousness and these outlooks frequently have only a tenuous link to doctrine. The Protestantism of a substantial number of England's population can be more easily found reflected in their fears about foreign threats (real, of course, in the case of Spain during the 1580s), or about more surreptitious and even supernaturally sinister invasions by the forces of Antichrist, than it can be observed around distinctions about Christ's real as opposed to transubstantiated presence in the communion celebration. Further, since the English Church claimed to be the true catholic church and many of its clergy favoured rich trappings in church ceremonies, as the monarchy did in its civil and religious conduct, outside precise liturgical observances it is frequently hard to distinguish how a Roman Catholic recusant devotional aesthetic differs from devotional expression promoted with Anglican episcopalianism. It is often easier to distinguish this episcopal faction's perspectives from those maintaining more reformed Puritan observances, even though both groups belong within the same church.

Within the vast literature that emerges from the English Church arguing over doctrinal complexities, there are a variety of rhetorically strenuous polemics proclaiming the righteousness of one stance against the myriad sinfulness of others. In such writing, Roman Catholicism may be rhetorically proclaimed as the antithesis of the English Church. In contrast, even in many plays by authors of recorded Protestant sympathies, it is surprisingly rare for jingoistic reductivist views to be articulated. For example, *Sir Thomas More*, which contains some work by Shakespeare, is the product of a group of playwrights, largely of known Protestant dispositions. It seems to have been written for Lord Strange's Men, a company that also tended to perform plays with notable Protestant sympathies. Yet, rather than attacking More, the play celebrates his integrity, his administrative ability, his friendlessness to players, and his concern for the poor. While the play is vague about his doctrinal opposition to Protestantism, his death is presented sympathetically. In its final words from the Earl of Surrey, More is: 'a very learned worthy gentleman' who 'seals error with his blood' (Munday 1990: v. iv. 119–20). *Sir Thomas More* participates in the Humanist convention of the rise and fall of the man of virtue and shares much in common with a similar play *Thomas Lord Cromwell*, which commemorates Henry VIII's first Protestant chancellor. Thus, central historical characters of the English Reformation who were doctrinally and politically opposed to one another could appear on the stage some sixty years after their deaths in portrayals which minimize their religious hostility and which celebrate common virtues.

Interestingly, one of the period's surviving plays that is decidedly antagonistic to Roman Catholicism is Marlowe's *Massacre at Paris*, also probably first performed by Lord Strange's company in 1593. The existing text is short and unquestionably corrupt but there is nothing to suggest that it does not reflect Marlowe's intent. It presents the religious turmoil between Protestantism and Catholicism in France, centrally the 1572 St Bartholomew's Day Massacre that, especially in Paris, saw large numbers of Protestants butchered by the Guise faction. The Duke of Guise's cry of 'Religion: *O Diabole*' is part of a presentation that neatly makes the equation between political ambitiousness and spiritual corruption (I. ii. 66). The play concludes with the 1589 assassination of Henri III by a friar and the coming to power of the Protestant Henri of Navarre, with the possibility of England and France joining in an anti-papal alliance. Characteristically, Marlowe shows no particular interest in doctrinal difference, religion is presented as part of a potentially supernaturally inspired 'great game' about gaining secular power.

Shakespeare, too, particularly in his earlier work, can adopt anti-papal portrayals. His *Life and Death of King John* (*c*.1595) is more moderate in tone than the anonymous aggressively anti-Roman play *The Troublesome Reign of King John* that it is based on, but Shakespeare, too, celebrates John as attempting to throw off papal authority. John's condemnation of Europe's other kings for remaining subservient to the pope heightens a sense of English religious virtue that would have pleased John Foxe, one of the greatest advocates of England's Reformation, from whose *Acts and Monuments* much of Shakespeare's historical information is drawn. John links papal corruption to one of the issues the Protestant reformers particularly disliked, the sale of indulgences:

> Though you and all the kings of Christendom
> Are led so grossly by this meddling priest,
> Dreading the curse that money may buy out,
> And by the merit of vile gold, dross dust,
> Purchase corrupted pardon of a man,
> Who in that sale sell pardon from himself ;
> Though you and all the rest so grossly led
> This juggling witchcraft with revenue cherish;
> Yet I alone, alone do me oppose
> Against the Pope, and count his friends my foes.   (III. i. 88–97).

Though such examples suggest that both Marlowe and Shakespeare tended to support popular appeals to emerging English nationalism that grew out of the conflicts generated by the Reformation, various aspects of their reputations have been offered to suggest that they were actually challenging such positions. The charge of atheism levelled against Marlowe at the time of his death and which has contributed much to his subsequent critical reputation for writing unorthodox drama emerges from slanders that probably had their origins in the English Church's attempts to curb unorthodox viewpoints. Marlowe's death was rapidly turned into a *cause célèbre* about his impiety by those such as Thomas Beard, quoted above, who opposed the theatre. This, though, seems only to have enhanced Marlowe's theatrical standing among playgoers. *The Jew of Malta* and *Doctor Faustus* in particular were two of the most frequently revived plays from the early 1590s until the theatres closed in the 1640s. Contemporary arguments around the moral integrity or depravity of the theatre helped to create a reputation around Marlowe for impiety that often came to seem actual biography for later generations. But there is no firm evidence that Marlowe championed religious heterodoxy in his life, though nothing to suggest he had a particularly devotional cast of mind. While he held a Parker scholarship at Cambridge that was intended for boys going to enter the church, this never seems to have been a serious possibility for him.

Similarly, suggestions of Shakespeare's recusancy built on the possibility (and it is no more than that) of his father John's continued, quiet, adherence to the old religion need to be tempered by remembering that his father was of a generation that had been born into Roman Catholicism, witnessed Henry VIII's modest Reformation and the more evangelical one under Edward VI, and Mary's restoration of Catholicism and Elizabeth's of Protestantism; whereas his son lived his entire life under Elizabeth's and James's Anglican settlement. It is worth comparing Shakespeare's position with his patron, Henry Wriothesley, 3rd Earl of Southampton, a man known for his adherence to militant Protestant causes but whose father frequently spent time in the Tower on account of his fervent Roman Catholicism. Though Shakespeare cultivated social position in Stratford, what we know of his life does not exhibit any pronounced inclination towards formal religion. When Shakespeare does address the relatively recent history of his own era in plays such as *Henry VIII*, he is generally sympathetic to the Tudor Reformation (figures such as Wolsey and Gardiner are presented as self-interested, while Cranmer is a character of integrity and piety—though so is Katherine of Aragon).

'COME, I THINK HELL'S A FABLE': THE RISE OF SECULAR THEATRE

The mystery plays that Marlowe or Shakespeare may have witnessed at Canterbury or Coventry in their youth were dramatizations of biblical stories. Performed by guilds or other groups within their communities they explicitly interpreted Christian theology for their audiences. With the advent of the Reformation, Protestants such as John Bale emended medieval drama to promote what were seen as less idolatrous spectacles, though still pursuing moralized themes that commonly employed highly stylized characterizations of virtues and vices. For instance, *Nice Wanton,* dating from the late 1550s, advocates the need to educate children to fear God and obey their parents. The indulged child Dalila ends up dying of syphilis in a whorehouse and, at the play's conclusion, her mother warns the audience about the dangers of young people being given too much liberty without parental good governance.

Such dramatized representations of clearly defined virtues and vices are challenged in the late 1580s by Marlowe's *Tamburlaine*:

> Nature, that fram'd us of four elements
> Warring within our breasts for regiment,
> Doth teach us all to have aspiring minds.
> Our souls, whose faculties can comprehend
> The wondrous architecture of the world
> And measure every wandering planet's course,
> Still climbing after knowledge infinite
> And always moving as the restless spheres,
> Wills us to wear ourselves and never rest
> Until we reach the ripest fruit of all,
> That perfect bliss and sole felicity,
> The sweet fruition of an earthly crown.
>
> (1 *Tamburlaine* II. vii. 18–29)

The celebration of human potential is a Renaissance commonplace but Tamburlaine's conclusion here is not typical. The 'perfect bliss and sole felicity' human endeavour is expected to pursue is a heavenly not earthly crown. Tamburlaine's statement on its own might appear to signal his moral corruption: conventionally if he articulates sentiments like this he would be a figure of vice. What Marlowe and Shakespeare's drama does instead is to propose that such clear distinctions according to established religious codes are debatable. Tamburlaine confounds the era's views about characterization. He is a shepherd of humble origin (not an aristocrat accidentally lost in the wood) yet he conquers half the world. He is cruel and relentlessly ambitious but, as the speech above shows, immensely articulate, intelligent, and possessed of a fine sensibility. Yet above all, he is successful. Especially in the first play (there are two parts to *Tamburlaine,* but the first part appears to have been conceived as an independent play with the second following from its success), Tamburlaine pursues an unchecked acquisition of opulence and material abundance without a *nemesis.*

> I hold the Fates bound fast in iron chains
> And with my hand turn Fortune's wheel about;
> And sooner shall the sun fall from his sphere
> Than Tamburlaine be slain or overcome.
>
> (1 *Tamburlaine* I. ii. 174–7)

The first play ends with Tamburlaine's egoistic self-presentation confirmed by events. Even in the second play, where he increasingly appears despotic and cruel, Tamburlaine finishes his reign with a quiet death surrounded by family and friends: he is not tormented either physically or mentally. Throughout both plays, Tamburlaine presents himself as the 'scourge of God'. While it can just possibly be argued that this implies he actually operates on behalf of a providential Christian God who uses him to prevent the Turkish and other Eastern empires from invading Europe and threatening the Christian West, his usual dramatic impact is far more decisively as a challenger of Christian moral norms, a precursor of the Nietzschean superman. The English dramatic tradition that Marlowe and Shakespeare inherited was clear about the dire consequences of sin and its punishment in either this life or in an afterlife. Marlowe's *Tamburlaine* offered a new secular theatre a self-fashioning figure uninterested in an afterlife, a character who inhabits a dramatic world wholly defined by immediate material concerns. For the space of a few hours an audience might witness a spectacle of excess and inflated possibilities that rewarded rather than punished those prepared to abandon existing social and moral norms. Witnessing *Tamburlaine*, it would require an extremely sober disposition to notice that the spectators were more likely to be among Tamburlaine's victims than his beneficiaries and that his conquests are so dependent on his own extraordinary energy that they require his unique individual drive to sustain them. As with his followers in the play, his vigour and magnificence attract audiences. Yet Marlowe's play is not principally designed to challenge existing moral and theological beliefs directly. It differs, too, from earlier dramatic conventions in not being overtly didactic. Tamburlaine's inhabiting the exotic east with its inflated scale of proportion creates an exaggerated world that is notably dissimilar to that outside the theatre. Medieval moral geography had argued that the further you travelled from the centres of religion and civilization (traditionally Jerusalem and Rome) the more monstrous the world literally became and the less you could expect the standards of godly conduct to apply. It is plausible that early audiences enjoyed Tamburlaine's abandoning convention on the same principle that English buccaneers used to defend their conduct in plundering the Pacific a century and more after: 'there is no God this side of Cape Horn'. The play seems more interested in having audiences suspend their moral and religious orders rather than having them subverted or challenged.

Shakespeare, too, similarly eschews a drama that allows religious or moral values to be unambiguously approved. One of the features of both medieval drama and early Protestant plays is that a divine government is not in question. While there may be differing interpretations of how it manifests itself and its laws, the underlying acceptance of a supernatural moral order is not at issue. Shakespeare seems far more interested in varieties of possibilities, part of his drama's success is the way he combines various perspectives into cohesive pieces of theatre.

In *The Tempest*, one of the last plays he wrote, Prospero attempts to stage a moral reformation of those characters who have sinned against him and robbed him of his dukedom:

> Though with their high wrongs I am struck to th'quick,
> Yet with my nobler reason 'gainst my fury
> Do I take part. The rarer action is

> In virtue than in vengeance. They being penitent,
> The sole drift of my purpose doth extend
> Not a frown further.   (v. i. 25–30)

The trouble for Prospero is that the principal offenders, his brother Antonio and Sebastian the brother of the King of Naples, do not show penitence. To stage his circle of forgiveness at the play's conclusion, Prospero is forced to attain their compliance through threats of exposure. The finale of his design is to reveal the King of Naples's son Ferdinand and his daughter Miranda. This is a play-within-a-play, a tableau which Prospero envisages betokens the union of Naples and Milan through the couple's union. But what greets the spectators does not really meet his purpose. The couple are displayed playing at chess:

MIRANDA Sweet lord, you play me false.
FERDINAND No, my dearest love,
  I would not for the world.
MIRANDA Yes, for a score of kingdoms you should wrangle,
  An I would call it fair play.   (v. i. 174–8)

Within Prospero's carefully managed revelation, what we discover is not ideal concord but dissimulation. Chess is the game of kings based around the capture of a kingdom. That Ferdinand attempts this by illegal moves and then denies it does not argue greatly for the harmonious union of the kingdoms that Miranda and Ferdinand's marriage is supposed to ensure. It is hardly a moment of solace for Prospero to discover that his daughter is ready to allow such actions and indeed is prepared to sanction them as 'fair play'.

In the play, the significance of this exchange is somewhat ignored in the joy of father and son being reunited, but Miranda compounds her willing delusion by naively greeting her treacherous uncle and the complicit Neapolitans as 'goodly creatures': 'How beauteous mankind is! O brave new world | That hath such people in it' (v. i. 185–7). Rather than a successful comic end that sees reconciliation arising from a godlike Prospero showing mercy to the penitent, *The Tempest* suggests that little has changed. Shakespeare's play neatly exposes the morally prescribed theatre Prospero wishes to stage as a contrivance. The rest of the play's characters refuse to play their roles according to the norms that Prospero wishes.

Of course, it might be argued that Shakespeare is exposing human limitations in organizing our world, even when characters possess powerful magic, thus pointing to mankind's essentially fallen condition. In the play's epilogue, Prospero pleads with the audience for release from his island:

> And my ending is despair
> Unless I be relieved by prayer,
> Which pierces so, that it assaults
> Mercy itself, and frees all faults.
> As you from crimes would pardoned be,
> Let your indulgence set me free.
>
> (Epilogue 15–20)

The prayers and indulgences he seeks are the audience's applause. The idea that earthly petition could necessarily influence the divine was a fraught area between Roman Catholicism and Protestantism, with Protestants seeing the Roman Church's sale of indulgences as particularly corrupt, as we have seen, an issue that Shakespeare attacked in *King John*. Shakespeare is being playful here, but *The Tempest*'s epilogue reinforces the play's general concern with issues of illusion and reality. Prospero addressing the audience as participants in this drama formally includes it within the working of *The Tempest*. Shakespeare bridges the world created on the stage with the real one external to it, suggesting that, if 'all the world's a stage' it may be marked out by pursuit of artifice and contentment with illusion rather than a determination to grasp at higher things.

'VERY LIKE A WHALE': THEOLOGY AND PERFORMANCE

Attempts to determine either Shakespeare's or Marlowe's theological framework in their drama inevitably confronts the fact that their plays were designed for performance. Interpretation of dramatic language cannot be decided simply by reading a text without imagining its enactment: what dialogue or a speech means is determined by its dramatic context. Since the nineteenth century, dramatists have attempted to control this through writing elaborate descriptions about how scenes should be staged and by providing indications about how the text is to be delivered. Examining a play-text by Harold Pinter, for instance, it is striking that the author's meticulous directions for stage arrangement and speaking are often more extensive than the actual words to be delivered. Marlowe and Shakespeare rarely provide more than a hint about staging: most directions in current editions are the products of later editors and admirers. Shakespeare in particular played a full part in the running of the theatre, probably directing some of his own plays but certainly being available to discuss their staging with his company. Regrettably, no records of such interactions exist. The length of a dramatic performance, too, could vary considerably: plays might be performed in longer or shorter versions to meet the requirements of a production's circumstances (this is customary today, too: it is rare to see an uncut text of the longer Shakespeare plays). Given the ubiquity of this practice, it is possible that both writers conceived their plays as adaptable dramatic vehicles. Rather than working from the premise of finished texts, they may have imagined their plays as comprising scenic units that could be arranged according to theatrical requirements.

Some of the implications of these issues may be illustrated by considering Hamlet's speech 'To be, or not to be'. Frequently presented as a soliloquy that reflects his mental state, this speech is often seen as encapsulating a virtual philosophy about the meaning of existence. What prevents Hamlet from pursuing self-annihilation is the possibility of an afterlife:

> To sleep, perchance to dream. Ay, there's the rub,
> For in that sleep of death what dream may come
> When we have shuffled off this mortal coil
> Must give us pause.   (III. i. 67–70)

Hamlet considers the misfortunes that attend human life, reasoning that 'the pale cast of thought' prevents decisive action, deciding that only:

> . . . the dread of something after death
> The undiscovered country from whose bourn
> No traveller returns, puzzles the will
> And makes us rather bear those ills we have
> Than fly to others that we know not of?
> Thus conscience does make cowards of us all.   (III. i. 80–5)

The speech is extraordinary for its eloquence but also for the apparent absence of theology in it. Although Hamlet acknowledges the possibility of an afterlife, and of one less agreeable than the present, it is 'the undiscovered country', it does not resemble heaven or hell, purgatory or limbo, or the similar destinations of organized religion. Also striking is Hamlet's refusal to acknowledge any religious or moral law to remain alive. It is cowardliness, the fear of the unknown, which prevents action rather than obedience to godly dictum. Perhaps most conspicuous in the speech is its refusal even to debate that life might be inherently good, preferable in itself to death. Hamlet's appears a largely godless universe, or one that is certainly devoid of providential government.

These are remarkable thoughts even for current Western cultures in which the concept of suicide is usually viewed as unfortunate but not criminal. But it seems even more astonishing for Shakespeare's era when suicide was a crime against both God and the state, commonly labelled 'self-killing' or 'self-murder'. As the monarch's subject, legally his property, individuals did not have the right to kill themselves as this was stealing the monarch's possession. Suicide was, of course, utterly prohibited by church law. As the priest argues with Laertes about Ophelia's suicide later in the play, she has only been granted burial in consecrated ground because of royal pressure. A suicide should literally be an outcast of the church.

Hamlet's speech gains further interest when we compare it to an earlier version printed in the 1603 First Quarto of the play (virtually all modern editions follow the account printed in the 1623 Folio). Here, it is much less eloquent but noticeably more orthodox in its theology. Hamlet makes a similar point about dreaming after death, though now the afterlife is a certainty:

> For in that dream of death, when we awake,
> And bourn before an everlasting Judge,
> From whence no passenger ever retur'nd,

> The undiscovered country, at whose sight
> The happy smile, and the accursed damn'd.

(Quarto 1 ll. 1720–4)

He concludes that life must be endured: 'for a hope of something after death'. The Folio version, therefore, relates a much darker, theologically pessimistic conceptualization. Despite being couched in the formal eloquence of the period, it is a meditation that can seem strikingly modern. But a substantial question looms: 'what type of speech is this?' It is not necessarily a soliloquy at all.

In the scene, Claudius and Polonius have placed Ophelia as bait in a gallery where Hamlet normally walks; they hope any conversation between the two will reveal the cause of Hamlet's supposed lunacy. Polonius has been arguing that this is the result of a passion for Ophelia, but Claudius is sceptical. Throughout the play Hamlet is under constant observation, he does not know who, if anyone, he can trust. Immediately before his entry to the gallery and the reciting of the 'To be' speech, Claudius and Polonius have concealed themselves to spy on him. It is perfectly conceivable to stage this so that Hamlet is aware of their presence, that he knows that he is being overheard. This is the issue raised by the speech's performance. Rather than a genuine private rumination, it may be witnessed as a public performance in which Hamlet attempts to convince these spies that he is melancholic, possibly deranged, but not a danger. Hence he offers a declamation that proposes action stifled by contemplation. Hamlet is representing himself as a harmless introvert. What appears to later generations a potentially profound consideration about existence may actually be a feigned reflection. Recasting the speech in the later Folio version to remove its theological dimension, Shakespeare may have sought to strengthen Hamlet's appearance of madness because, for all its eloquence and sophistication, the prince's discourse utterly overlooks the God-directed nature of the universe, and thus has no basis in sense according to the period's understanding. It is a type of empty profundity that a depressed undergraduate who has been reading too much in classical literature might come out with.

This is no more than a plausible possibility, of course. It might be argued that even if designed to dupe Polonius and Claudius (who instantly sees through Hamlet's ostensible madness) the speech still stands as an astonishing statement for its era. Yet, it illustrates how circumstances of performance may have a profound effect on what is being said. If this is the case with one speech in one scene, these varying potentials for grasping a play's concerns are constantly present throughout the whole. To take another example, Isabella's reaction to the Duke's proposal of marriage at the end of *Measure for Measure*—a wordless response about which there is no indication about how it is to be performed expect through interpretation of what has taken place—effectively has the potential to transform the play from comedy to tragedy or vice versa.

We may further witness the difficulties for determining theology in plays that are unstable vehicles for stating ideas by considering Marlowe's *Doctor Faustus*. In many respects this play appears theologically orthodox. Faustus sells his soul to Lucifer for twenty-four years, during which period he gains a reputation as a conjuror. At the conclusion, Faustus desires to turn to Christ for forgiveness but finds he cannot. He realizes that his brief interlude of notoriety will be paid for with eternal damnation and curses his fate before he is captured by devils. In one version of the play, there is a scene in which scholars subsequently discover his limbs 'all torn asunder' (v. 3). In many respects Marlowe's work formally conforms to the earlier morality tradition, showing that human learning (Faustus is a famous academic) is a danger to spiritual salvation when accompanied by worldly ambition.

As has long been recognized, however, Marlowe's Faustus is not a simple two-dimensional morality figure and his fate has puzzled later commentators who have considered him both villain and hero. Some of this difficulty arises because there are two distinct versions of the play, one (the A text) published in 1604 and another (the B text) published in 1616. A number of modern editions print both versions, so substantial are their differences. Much recent criticism has favoured the A text because its presentation of Faustus's fate is potentially more uncertain: there is no scene of him dismembered, for example, leaving the nature of his 'damnation' more open to question. There is frequently a modern desire to imagine that Faustus 'confounds hell in Elysium' (I. iii. 60) as he boasts to the devil Mephistopheles—he denies a conventional Christian construction to the afterlife. Yet, in its strange blending of practical high jinks, pseudo-philosophical debate, eloquent poetry, and farcical bantering it often seems that Marlowe is attempting both moral edification and unconstrained spectacle with *Doctor Faustus*. This creates glorious theatre but can be intellectually confusing. Rather than successfully marrying the apparent polarities of education and entertainment, Marlowe's language compromises the demands of both, providing no secure understanding of what this dramatic piece is attempting to achieve. In either version *Doctor Faustus* is a play that seems constantly to defer clarifying its philosophical or metaphysical speculations while it pursues its various self-generated performances. Yet, such problems about interpreting what exactly is 'The form of Faustus' fortunes good or bad' (Prologue, 8) which the opening chorus claims it will present for an audience's applause are compounded by the play existing in two versions that only enhance the parameters of what those forms may be.

An awareness of its own theatricality is a feature shared by both Marlowe and Shakespeare's drama. Staging plays-within-plays, for instance draws attention to drama as artifice. Such actions constantly question what may be real, what can be believed. It is frequently difficult to decide who is deliberately putting on various roles and who appears genuine. Hamlet proposes no answer to this dilemma: 'We defy augury. There's a special providence in the fall of a sparrow. If it be now, 'tis not to come. If it be not to come, it will be now. If it be not now, yet it will come. The readiness is all' (v. ii. 164–8). Seeking to establish theology in these plays is to engage with dramatic spectacles that present mirrors to the world. But what type of reflections they offer: accurate or distorted, eloquent or confused, clear or shadowy, comic or tragic, perhaps all of these simultaneously, is never settled as they change each time they are enacted. Although both these dramatists have much to teach us, they are not didactic in that their art does not offer a fixed view that insists we witness the world of God or of man in a precise way.

WORKS CITED

BEARD, THOMAS. 1597. *The Theatre of Gods Judgements*. London: Printed by Adam Islip.

CHAMBERS, E. K., and GREG, W. W. (eds.) 1908. *Dramatic Records from the Lansdowne Manuscripts*. London: Malone Society.

DIEHL, HOUSTON. 1992. 'Dazzling Theatre: Renaissance Drama in the Age of Reform', *Journal of Medieval and Renaissance Studies* 22: 211–36.

HAMILTON, DONNA. 1992. *Shakespeare and the Politics of Protestant England*. Lexington: University of Kentucky Press.

HEYWOOD, THOMAS. 1973. *An Apology for Actors*. New York: Garland, facsimile reprint.

LEVIN, HARRY. 1954. *The Overreacher*. London: Faber & Faber.

MARLOWE, CHRISTOPHER. 1969. *The Complete Plays*, ed. J. B. Steane. Harmondsworth: Penguin. All citations to Marlowe's work to this edition.

MULLANEY, STEPHEN. 1988. *The Place of the Stage: License, Play and Power in Renaissance England*. Chicago: University of Chicago Press.

MUNDAY, ANTHONY, et al. 1990. *Sir Thomas More*, ed. Vittorio Gabrieli and Giorgio Melchiori. The Revels Plays. Manchester: Manchester University Press.

New Dictionary of National Biography. 2004. Oxford: Oxford University Press.

SHAKESPEARE, WILLIAM. 1988. *The Complete Works*, ed. Stanley Wells, Gary Taylor, et. al. Oxford: Clarendon. All citations to Shakespeare's work to this edition except where noted.

WILSON, RICHARD. 2004. *Secret Shakespeare: Studies in Theatre, Religion and Resistance*. Manchester: Manchester University Press.

FURTHER READING

CHANEY, PATRICK (ed.) 2004. *The Cambridge Companion to Christopher Marlowe*. Cambridge: Cambridge University Press.

DOBSON, MICHAEL, and WELLS, STANLEY (ed.) 2001. *The Oxford Companion to Shakespeare*. Oxford: Oxford University Press.

GRAZIA, MARGRETA DE (ed.) 2001. *The Cambridge Companion to Shakespeare*. Cambridge: Cambridge University Press.

HEALY, THOMAS. 1994. *Christopher Marlowe*. Writers and their Work. Plymouth, Northcote House.

KASTAN, DAVID SCOTT (ed.) 1999. *A Companion to Shakespeare*. Oxford: Blackwell.

LAKE, PETER, and QUESTIER, MICHAEL. 2002. *The Antichrist's Lewd Hat: Protestants, Papists and Players in Post-Reformation England*. New Haven: Yale University Press.

WHITE, PAUL WHITFIELD. 1993. *Theatre and Reformation: Protestantism, Patronage and Playing in Tudor England*. Cambridge: Cambridge University Press.

CHAPTER 24

HERBERT AND DONNE

HELEN WILCOX

'*INTERPRETATIONS of religious meaning* have always been *central* to the criticism of certain sixteenth- and seventeenth-century English writers who engaged closely with the religious cultures and controversies of their day' (Andersen and Sauer 2001: 3; my italics). This statement is undoubtedly true of a large number of early modern English authors—including those discussed in the chapters preceding and following this—but I would suggest that it is more applicable to George Herbert and John Donne than to any of their contemporaries. The aim of this chapter is to demonstrate that the critical fortunes of these two poets over the centuries have been dependent not only on changes in literary taste but also on shifts in theological readings and devotional interests—and that the process of reading their work today can be greatly enriched by this awareness. The chapter falls into three parts, each defined by a chronological focus: the first locates Donne and Herbert in their seventeenth-century devotional cultures; the second examines the theological nature of later critical responses to their writings, and the third highlights the religious issues inherent in any interpretation of their poetry. For, as Herbert noted in 'Jordan (II)', the religious poet seeks out 'quaint words' in order to speak of 'heav'nly joyes' (Herbert 1941: 102), and it is precisely such 'words', as Donne claimed in a 1629 sermon, that have always 'busied the whole Church' (Donne 1953–62: ix. 70). Thus, in their mutual dependence upon contested and often sacred words, devotional poetry and the business of theology are necessarily intertwined.

I

John Donne (1572–1631) and George Herbert (1593–1633) belonged to the first generations of English authors who grew up after the Reformation had firmly taken hold under the church settlement of Elizabeth I. Nevertheless, the two poets' religious experience, much like the history of the English Church in the late sixteenth and early seventeenth centuries, was by no means free of dilemma or controversy. Donne was born into a Catholic family, descended on his mother's side from the prominent English martyr, Sir Thomas More. Donne's uncle Jasper Heywood was head of the Jesuit mission attempting to reconvert England in the 1580s, and the poet's own brother Henry died in Newgate while imprisoned for harbouring a Catholic priest (Bald 1970; Flynn 1995). Donne himself, however, converted to the Church of England and was ordained a priest in 1615 in St Paul's Cathedral, London, of which he became dean from 1621 until his death ten years later. These bare facts disguise a lifetime of doctrinal fascination and uncertainty, as reflected in the opening lines of his *Holy Sonnet* 18:

> Show me deare Christ, thy Spouse, so bright and clear.
> What! is it she, which on the other shore
> Goes richly painted? or which rob'd and tore
> Laments and mournes in Germany and here?
>
> (Donne 1985: 446)

The 'richly painted' Catholic church, or the plain and sorrowful Protestant tradition—which was the true church, the bride of Christ? This question is never far from the surface of Donne's writing, secular and sacred alike.

George Herbert, by contrast, was brought up in the context of the Church of England under the powerful influence of his devout mother, Magdalen Herbert (herself a friend of Donne), and appears to have had little doubt about the answer to Donne's fundamental enquiry. In his poem 'The British Church', Herbert praises the Anglican Church for its middle way between the 'painted' Catholic Church and the 'undrest' Calvinist tradition:

> I joy, deare Mother, when I view
> Thy perfect lineaments and hue
>   Both sweet and bright.
> Beautie in thee takes up her place,
> And dates her letters from thy face,
>   When she doth write.
>
> A fine aspect in fit array,
> Neither too mean, nor yet too gay,
>   Shows who is best.
>
> (Herbert 1941: 109)

Although Herbert seems to have been more confident than Donne about where to find Christ's true 'Spouse', it took him a long time to commit himself to be ordained in her service (Charles 1977), and his lyrics such as 'Affliction (I)', addressed to God, suggest a life of inner struggle as well as physical affliction:

> At first thou gav'st me milk and sweetnesses,
>   I had my wish and way:
> My dayes were straw'd with flow'rs and happinesse;
>   There was no moneth but May.
> But with my yeares sorrow did twist and grow,
> And made a partie unawares for wo.
>
> (Herbert 1941: 47)

When Herbert did eventually learn to live with the 'wo' as well as the 'sweetnesses' of his relationship with God, he left his academic and courtly circles to become rector of the modest country parish of Bemerton, near Salisbury, where he ministered for only three years before his early death in 1633 (Charles 1977).

An immediate insight into the theological reception of the two poets' writing may be gained from the early publication history of their works. Herbert's collection of devotional lyrics, *The Temple*, was published posthumously under the guidance of Nicholas Ferrar and the Little Gidding community, thus locating the author in the devout Arminian tradition favoured by Charles I and Archbishop Laud (although, since Ferrar's name is not mentioned in the early editions, this identification has been of greater significance to modern admirers than to Herbert's seventeenth-century readers). Interestingly, the original publication of *The Temple* by the Cambridge university printer was almost prevented on theological grounds: the vice-chancellor objected to the lines in 'The Church Militant' that radically suggested the Christian religion in England was 'on tip-toe', ready to 'passe to the *American* strand' (Herbert 1941: 196). Herbert's words were being scanned for their potential to cause religious and political controversy, and their publication was only permitted once the vice-chancellor had agreed that, although Herbert 'had many heavenly Speculations, and was a Divine Poet', yet his readers were not likely to 'take him to be an inspired Prophet' (Walton 1670: iv. 75). Ironically, only two years later a preacher from Ipswich, Samuel Ward, made the same claim that 'the Gospel stood on tiptoes' ready to desert England—and was imprisoned by Archbishop Laud for so doing (Prynne 1646: 361). Herbert's poems, which were said by the poet to be an image of 'the many spiritual Conflicts that have past betwixt God and my Soul' (Walton 1670: 74), in fact trod very close to more public—and politically dangerous—conflicts. Devotional poetry, not polemical in itself, could unwittingly provide fuel for fiery theological controversy, occasionally even for both sides of the same argument.

Although Donne is best known by modern readers as a witty and outspoken love poet, he was famed in his own day principally as the author of controversial treatises and an inspired preacher. His secular poems circulated extensively in manuscript—a clear indication of an already wide readership—but his first printed publication was *Pseudo-Martyr* (1610), a book-length prose argument in support of the king's religious policies, asserting that Catholics could take the oath of allegiance to the Crown.

Thus Donne was no stranger to theological conflicts; indeed, it seems that he relished the challenge of intense doctrinal debate, despite (or perhaps precisely because of) his family's close experience of its dangers. When he published his autobiographical prose meditations, *Devotions upon Emergent Occasions* (1624), Donne demonstrated that his self-conception was not only spiritual but also thoroughly denominational. In the dedication, he identifies his ordination to the priesthood of the Church of England as his 'second' or 'Supernatural' birth, giving identity to him in his adult life (Donne 1975: 3; Strier 1996: 102). An extant copy of the third edition of the *Devotions* (1627) contains an anonymous handwritten inscription, claiming: 'Here Wit and Piety together shine; | That, shows the Poet; This, the sound Divine' (Smith 1975: 78). This contemporary evidence confirms that Donne's early reputation was as a divine, learned in doctrine and theological insight, as well as a dazzling poet. During his lifetime Donne had published a small number of occasional sermons, and in 1651 the London publisher Humphrey Moseley highlighted the link between the poet and priest, writing that Donne, 'the highest Poet our Language can boast of', was also 'an excellent Preacher' (Cartwright 1651: preface n.p.). It is therefore fair to assume that, like Herbert, Donne was considered by his contemporaries and early readers in unavoidably religious terms, and that, like Herbert's, his work was viewed through the scrutinizing lens of theological appreciation.

What does it mean to read a poem theologically? It can, of course, imply that the major impact of the text lies in its insights concerning God and his creation, which may be analysed in theological terms alongside the Bible and the Church Fathers. This was the principle upon which with George Ryley operated in his painstaking 1715 commentary, *Mr Herbert's Temple . . . Explained and Improved*, in which he extrapolates the doctrinal and moral significance of Herbert's poems (Ryley 1987). Theological reading can also mean that poetic evidence is used polemically, as in the controversies surrounding the publication and early uses of *The Temple*. But perhaps more common than both of these types of theological reading are the situations in which the texts are given a more practical religious function, as inspiration for private prayer and meditation, or as material for liturgy and worship. After the posthumous publication of the poems of Donne and Herbert, coincidentally in the same year (1633), their poetic works were quickly put to didactic, musical, and liturgical use. Large numbers of their devotional lyrics are to be found in spiritual commonplace books, meditations, pamphlets, and sermons, while Herbert's were also thought useful for younger readers. Extracts from his poems reappeared in a later seventeenth-century versified ABC entitled 'Youth's Alphabet: or, Herbert's Morals' (Wilcox 1984), and Stanley Fish has convincingly demonstrated the parallels between *The Temple* and early modern children's catechisms (Fish 1978). Meanwhile, Donne's 'Hymn to God the Father' was set to music by seventeenth-century composers such as Hilton and Humphrey: Izaak Walton refers to the 'most grave and solemn Tune' to which it was 'often sung to the *Organ* by the *Choristers* of St. *Pauls* Church' towards the end of Donne's own lifetime (Walton 1670: i. 55). As Ramie Targoff has rightly argued, it is misleading to construct 'impermeable boundaries between personal and liturgical poetry' when reading seventeenth-century poems

(Targoff 2001: 87). Several of Herbert's lyrics were the inspiration for solo devotional songs, composed by musicians such as Lawes, Blow, and Purcell, but in 1697 thirty-two of his poems were adapted for communal singing in the nonconformist tradition, published as *Select Hymns taken from Mr. Herbert's Temple* (Wilcox 1987). In these practical ways, the works of Donne and Herbert remained prominent in the religious cultures of seventeenth-century England and were absorbed into the traditions of those who read and appropriated them.

The allegiances of the admirers of Donne and Herbert were surprisingly varied. The contrasting locations of the poems' musical use—from St Paul's Cathedral to nonconformist chapels—suggests the accessibility of their work to otherwise antagonistic theological traditions. In 1637 Donne was described by the puritan minister Nathaniel Whiting as 'a Poet, and a grave Divine', while three years later he was honoured by the Cavalier poet George Daniel of Beswick as 'the reverent Donne, whose quill God purely fil'd' (Smith 1975: 119, 123). Achsah Guibbory writes of Herbert that 'the work of few poets has been so sharply contested, as readers have sought to identify his poetry with particular religious positions' (Guibbory 1998: 44). Just after the publication of *The Temple*, Herbert's poems were praised in an outspoken poem by John Polwhele, commending their anti-puritan 'Catholique Conformitie' (Wilcox 1979: 153), and from 1647 onwards Herbert's *Temple* was published together with Christopher Harvey's *Synagogue*, the latter being a set of distinctly pro-ceremonialist poems in imitation of Herbert's collection. By contrast, Richard Baxter, one of the leading nonconformist theologians of the later seventeenth century whose writings were seen as 'a Treasure of Controversial, Casuistical, Positive and Practical Divinity' (Bates 1692: 90), proclaimed the Anglican Herbert's lyrics as the finest example of '*Heart-work* and *Heaven-work*' he knew (Baxter 1681: A7ᵛ). These responses from opposite ends of the ecclesiastical spectrum importantly remind us that early theological ways of reading the texts of Donne and Herbert could be surprisingly flexible, even in such a polemical age.

However, the work of Donne and Herbert was appropriated by many in the Restoration period as particularly emblematic of royalist Anglican spirituality from the era before the Civil War. This nostalgic image of pre-Commonwealth orthodoxy was promoted by the biographer Izaak Walton, whose *Lives of Dr. John Donne, Sir Henry Wotton, Mr. Richard Hooker and Mr. George Herbert* explicitly recalled and reconstructed those lost 'happy daies of the Nations and the Churches peace' (Walton 1670: A7ʳ). Donne emerges from Walton's pages as a kind of Anglican Church Father, identified with Augustine and Ambrose for 'learning and holiness' (ibid. i. 37). Herbert is portrayed as an exceptionally holy figure who, when asked in what words he would pray, answered, 'O Sir, the Prayers of my Mother, the Church of *England*, no other Prayers are equal to them' (ibid. iv. 67). Walton knew that he was writing these *Lives* for 'succeeding Generations' (ibid. 80), but even he might have been surprised at how pervasive his interpretations were. His biographies enshrined a kind of Anglican piety that, however surreptitiously, still influences readings of the poets' works to this day.

II

By the end of the seventeenth century, the poetry of Herbert and Donne was waning in popularity. Dryden consigned Herbert's verse to a mythical 'Acrostick Land' in 1682 (Dryden 1963: 64), and the German poet Christian Wernicke wrote in 1697 that 'no Englishman ever reads' the work of Donne or Quarles (Smith 1975: 163). If their decline in this period and their almost total neglect in the eighteenth century were largely due to changes in poetic taste and the rise of neo-classicism, their subsequent revival may be said to be as much based on theology as on aesthetics. An early hint of renewed interest came in the mid-eighteenth century when John Wesley, founder of the Methodists, transcribed and adapted large numbers of Herbert's lyrics as hymns; he was so fond of *The Temple* that it was later suggested, 'Had there not been a Herbert, it is probable that there might never have been a Wesley' (Patrides 1983: 16). This claim, though extravagant, gives some indication of the part played by theological responses to the seventeenth-century writers in the later history of Christianity in England. In the early nineteenth century, Coleridge responded to Donne primarily as a prose writer, finding 'Armouries for the Christian Soldier' in the work of 'this admirable Divine': 'such a depth of intellect, such a nervousness of style, such a variety of illustration, such a power of argument' (Coleridge 1955: 205). Reading Donne's sermons, Coleridge often found truth in those powerful arguments—such as Donne's claim that the church's authority is as important as that of the Bible—but Coleridge was aware that to agree with this one 'must bear to be thought a Semi-papist, an Ultra High-Churchman' (Coleridge 1955: 179). Coleridge's reaction to Herbert, whom he regarded as 'a true poet', was not concerned with specific kinds of Anglicanism (as it was in the case of Donne), yet his commentary on *The Temple* was still couched in ecclesiastical, terms:

To appreciate this volume, it is not enough that the reader possess a cultivated judgment, classical taste, or even poetic sensibility, unless he be likewise a *Christian*, and both a zealous and an orthodox, both a devout and a *devotional* Christian. But even this will not quite suffice. He must be an affectionate and dutiful child of the Church, and ... find her forms and ordinances aids of religion, not sources of formality; for religion is the element in which he lives, and the region in which he moves.   (ibid. 534)

Coleridge's comments—though often challenged by later readers—demonstrate the importance of religion as the 'element' in which both poet and reader live: the theological dimension is the necessary context of both text and interpretation.

As the nineteenth century progressed, the works of Donne and Herbert began to enjoy a revival in popularity through the reopening of some of the theological controversies from two hundred years earlier. The seventeenth-century clash between puritan and ceremonialist ideologies was mirrored in the nineteenth-century debates between the evangelicals and the followers of the Oxford movement—and the poets, particularly Herbert, supplied excellent material for strengthening arguments and inspiring visions. John Keble, for instance, a prominent figure in the Anglo-Catholic

Oxford movement, was often paralleled with Herbert both as a poet (his collection *The Christian Year* seeming to resemble *The Temple*) and as a churchman: 'there is the same zeal and energy in pastoral duties, the same love of paradox in language, the same reverence for antiquity and for the ceremonies of the church', wrote an anonymous author in 1838 (Patrides 1983: 23). On the other hand, an unsigned review in the *Christian Remembrancer* of 1862 commended Herbert's life and works not to those who favoured ceremony and tradition but to those who practised so-called 'muscular Christianity', stressing that Herbert, like Charles Kingsley and others in that movement, believed that 'the work and excellence of man lies *in* the world and not *out* of it' (ibid. 241). In the midst of these conflicting interpretations, the writer and art historian John Ruskin was also a great admirer of Herbert, largely for the poet's personal spirituality. In 1845 Ruskin wrote to his parents: 'I really *am* getting more pious than I was, owing primarily to George Herbert, who is the only religious person I ever could understand or agree with' (Ruskin 1972: 108). As in the seventeenth century, therefore, the range of responses to and interpretations of Herbert's work among the Victorians is striking, yet the later readers are once again united in using the poems for theological purposes, whether personal or public.

Donne continued to have an uncertain reception in the nineteenth century, being the more baroque and extravagant poet and therefore less amenable to Victorian piety. As the Presbyterian minister George Gilfillan wrote in 1860, Donne's poems may have had 'lofty spirituality' and were the product of a 'great' mind, but that mind was also 'trammelled and tasteless', mixing beauty and originality with lines that were 'either bad, or unintelligible, or twisted into unnatural distortion' (Smith 1975: 423). One way for nineteenth-century readers to cope with Donne's uneasy intensity was to liken him, as Walton had done, to St Augustine. Richard Trench, Archbishop of Dublin, made this specific parallel in 1868, asserting that Donne's writings demonstrated 'the same passionate and personal grasp of the central truths of Christianity, linking itself as this did with all that he had suffered, and all that he had sinned, and all through which by God's grace he had victoriously struggled' (ibid. 455). The theological force of Donne's Augustinian struggle was only fully appreciated in the early twentieth century, when T. S. Eliot, in particular, combined a modernist fascination for Donne's energetic aesthetics with a theological appreciation of the traditions for which Donne stood. This was the heyday of the reception of early seventeenth-century devotional writers: Eliot's essays and poems are repeatedly respectful of, and deeply indebted to, the achievement of Donne and Herbert (as well as Lancelot Andrewes, Richard Crashaw, and a host of their more secular contemporaries). While Eliot's admiration of Donne focuses on the unprecedented unity of thought and feeling in his writing—'a thought to Donne was an experience' (Eliot 1951: 287)—it is the specific combination of theological ideas with emotions that he appreciates in Herbert's poetry: 'his mind is working continually both on the mysteries of faith and the motives of the heart' (Eliot 1932: 361). In both cases, it becomes impossible to separate the theological reading from an emotional engagement with the seventeenth-century text.

The critical fortunes of Donne and Herbert since the watershed of T. S. Eliot's intervention have been unmistakeably bound up with the theological emphases, and critical loyalties, of those who have interpreted their poetry. A representative debate was the encounter of William Empson and Rosemund Tuve over Herbert's 'The Sacrifice'. While Empson took a 'New Critical' approach to the poem, carefully analysing the ambiguity and originality of Herbert's language (Empson 1930: 284–93), Tuve pressed the case that Herbert's inspiration derived from the medieval liturgical tradition and should be understood—and admired—in that context (Tuve 1952). As the critical readings of Donne and Herbert multiplied in the second half of the twentieth century, the focus was not so much on *whether* the poets' works should be interpreted in the light of theological or ecclesiastical sources, as *which* traditions were most influential. In 1954 Louis Martz published *The Poetry of Meditation*, in which he demonstrated the structural and intellectual influence of the Roman Catholic meditative tradition on the work of Donne, Herbert, and their contemporaries. Among Martz's most important claims was that Donne's Holy Sonnets 'are, in the most specific sense of the term, meditations, Ignatian meditations: providing strong evidence for the profound impact of early Jesuit training upon the later career of John Donne' (Martz 1962: 53). The theological balance of the poets' sources was tipped back in 1979 by Barbara Lewalski's *Protestant Poetics and the Seventeenth-Century Religious Lyric*, in which she argued that reformed biblical aesthetics were more significant for the early modern English devotional poets than the Continental counter-reformation practices outlined by Martz. Lewalski asserted that the most important source for Herbert's lyrics, for example, was not the meditations of St François de Sales (as suggested by Martz) but the Bible, and that 'Herbert undertakes nothing less than the task of becoming a Christian psalmist' (Lewalski 1979: 316). The fascinating opposition of these two perspectives on the seventeenth-century devotional lyric—each of which is thoroughly theological in approach—set the terms for subsequent critical readings of both Herbert and Donne.

Recent interpretations of the work of the two poets continue to be acutely conscious of the controversies concerning key doctrines and church practices by which these priest-poets were surrounded. Meg Lota Brown, for example, has helpfully pointed out how the 'principles of case divinity', in dealing with issues of conscience, inform Donne's writings (Brown 1995: 14), while Achsah Guibbory has shown that seventeenth-century disagreements over religious ceremonial can serve as a key to interpreting the work of Herbert and his contemporaries (Guibbory 1998). The continuing critical debates about the poets' spiritual allegiances may be seen particularly clearly in biographical readings of Donne's work: was the whole of his intensely argumentative output written in the shadow of his apostasy (Carey 1981), or did he remain true to his Catholic inheritance (Flynn 1995)? In Herbert's case, the critical focus tends to be on the theological assumptions inherent in his lyrics of praise and pain: does *The Temple* depict a Calvinist sense of human dependence on God (Strier 1983), an Anglican *via media* (Hodgkins 1993), or continuity with the tradition of St Thomas Aquinas (Young 2000)? However these questions are answered, it is evident that theology, history, and literary texts in the early modern period are inseparable—and will go on being so. Donne's art, for instance, has recently been examined in the context of the mixed reception of his Catholic contemporaries (Shell 1999), while the individual vocation expressed in Herbert's lyrics has been placed at the intersection of Protestantism and social change (Malcolmson 1999). The critical approach of New Historicism has inspired a significant sense of two-way traffic between texts and their cultural contexts, which has in turn emphasized the function of poetry as evidence of cultural and ecclesiastical history. Detailed knowledge of early modern theological issues can indeed enrich our understanding of the poetry of Herbert and Donne, but it is equally true that a study of their works can 'expose the fault lines and tensions in the early Stuart church' (Shami 2001: 88).

III

In the first two sections of this chapter, we have seen the importance of theological controversies in the early reception of Herbert and Donne, and the continuing critical fascination with the poets' devotional influences and allegiances. But let us turn finally to the experience of the modern reader who wishes to engage personally with the poems but is not a church historian or literary critic. Is it possible to read the *Holy Sonnets* and *The Temple* in a way which is not theological?

To answer this question, it is necessary to reconsider the definition of theology. I have already suggested that what we might call theological readings of literary texts are not always scholarly, doctrinal, or polemical; they can also involve practical and devotional responses, such as treating the lyrics as hymns, prayers, or handbooks of morality. It is certainly possible to read Herbert and Donne without joining in the hunt for signs of latent Catholicism or extreme Calvinism yet still taking a theological approach, as a recent book-length devotional study of Herbert's 'Prayer (I)' has demonstrated (Lennon 2002). However, I would contend that even an apparently non-religious interpretation of these works will also inevitably involve an encounter with some of the central concerns of theology: the nature of God, the power of grace, the experience of sin and despair, and the language of spirituality. The poems challenge us theologically in their expression of affliction and fear, wit and wonder. As Walter de la Mare wrote of Donne's first *Holy Sonnet*, 'Reading him, we do not throw off the world; we are not, as by a miracle, made innocent and happy.' The materials of his verse are 'extremes of exultation and despair, passion and disillusionment, love, death, the grave, corruption...' (Smith and Phillips 1996: 364–5), which combine in witty language to form a passionate theology of experience. Herbert's poetic art is by nature 'prayerful', as the title of Terry Sherwood's critical study reminds us (Sherwood 1989), and to write (and read) this devotional poetry is to analyse the state of the soul, discover the nature of redemption, and come into contact with the divine—that is, to engage in the business and the consequences of theology. As the speaker of 'The Quidditie' tells God, 'a verse' is 'that which while I use | I am with thee' (Herbert 1941: 69–70).

Readers of Donne and Herbert cannot avoid being struck by the dynamism and range of the ways in which being 'with' God finds expression in the poems. At the centre of theological enquiry lies the issue of who or what God is, and the opening lines of Herbert and Donne's devotional lyrics afford direct and dramatic impressions of the speakers' sense of God. Donne, a lawyer by training and disputatious by nature, engages with a God who also (it seems) works by logical principles and enjoys an argument. Donne's first *Holy Sonnet* begins with a direct challenge to this resilient God: 'Thou hast made me, And shall thy worke decay?' (Donne 1985: 434). The encounter between speaker and God in Donne's religious writings is energetic and, at times, bruising. As Donne famously demonstrated in *Holy Sonnet* 14, his rhetoric invokes an active Trinity willing to intervene and knock him into shape spiritually: 'Batter my heart, three-person'd God; for, you | As yet but knocke, breathe, shine, and seeke to mend' (ibid. 443). The verse is as powerful and uncompromising as the God whom Donne's anguished persona constructs and desires. By contrast, Herbert (1941: 62) writes (in 'Mattens') with a tone of wonder, amazed by the God who can be interested in frail humanity: 'My God, what is a heart, | That thou shouldst it so eye, and wooe, | Powring upon it all thy art [?].' His poems depict a loving and loyal God who renews the life of his creation, as in the opening of 'The Flower': 'How fresh, O Lord, how sweet and clean | Are thy returns! ev'n as the flowers in spring' (ibid. 165). It would be wrong, however, to suggest that the speaker's relationship with God in Herbert's lyrics is always harmonious. There are many moments in *The Temple* when God is defined by his apparent absence—when, as in 'Deniall', prayer seems unable to 'pierce' his 'silent eares' (ibid. 79)—and the speaker's tone of adoration is displaced by frustration and anger. The beginning of 'The Collar' typifies this mood: 'I struck the board, and cry'd, No more. | I will abroad' (ibid. 153). Nevertheless, by the time we reach the conclusion of this and almost all Herbert's poems, the chief divine characteristic is consoling love, a quality which restores the speaker to intimacy with God: 'Me thoughts I heard one calling, *Child!* | And I reply'd, *My Lord*' (ibid. 154). Donne, on the other hand, achieves closeness with God at the ends of his poems through fear rather than an inclusive divine presence: in *Holy Sonnet* 9 he hopes that God will show his mercy by being willing to 'forget' rather than remember him and his sins (Donne 1985: 440), and *Holy Sonnet* 19 closes with the admission that his 'best dayes' are 'when I shake with fear' (ibid. 447).

What is at the heart of the covenant between the human soul and God—terrifying or reassuring—as explored in the work of Donne and Herbert? The centre of Donne's theology is the crucifixion and, as he observes in *Holy Sonnet* 13, 'the picture of Christ crucified' is never far from his mind's eye. In *Holy Sonnet* 11 he applauds the 'strange love' which caused Christ to clothe himself in 'vile mans flesh, that so | Hee might be weake enough to suffer woe' (ibid. 441). Donne's finest occasional poetic meditation, 'Goodfriday, 1613. Riding Westward', concentrates on the vision of Christ's 'flesh . . . rag'd and torn' on the cross which is paradoxically so 'present yet unto my memory' that the speaker is afraid to turn towards the east and see God die (ibid. 455–6). In a typical combination of audacity and humility, Donne argues that he will only turn his face towards God once he can be sure that God will recognize the divine 'Image' in this chastened human being. Though equally corrected and humbled, Herbert's persona is generally not so bombastically terrified as Donne's, but rather is overwhelmed by God's love and the gift of grace. Herbert's Christ is typically already risen and, as the poem 'Easter' celebrates, will take the believer 'by the hand, that thou likewise | With him mayst rise' (Herbert 1941: 41). The love of God and his creation is a reciprocal relationship in Herbert's experience: as 'Clasping of Hands' repeatedly asserts, almost in the manner of a secular love lyric, 'Lord, thou art mine, and I am thine' (ibid. 157). The last lyric poem of *The Temple*, 'Love (III)', sums up this theology of redeeming love in terms of a host welcoming his guest. The speaker, 'guiltie of dust and sinne', senses his unworthiness to accept this divine hospitality— the offered gift of spiritual sustenance, of the eucharist, of the promised heavenly banquet—but at every turn he is reassured by 'Love', who is Christ himself. Finally, the speaker must concede and accept: 'You must sit down, sayes Love, and taste my meat: | So I did sit and eat' (ibid. 189).

As 'Love (III)' makes clear, the greatest difficulty for the speaker in Herbert's *Temple* is to acknowledge that grace is an all-encompassing gift that requires, in its most extreme manifestations, merely a mute and passive acceptance on the part of the believer. Herbert's sonnet 'The Holdfast' confronts this theological problem: how can one who has nothing actually make any admission of that human condition? For 'to have nought is ours, not to confesse | That we have nought' (ibid. 143). While Herbert's speakers struggle to let go of their role in the process of redemption, Donne's are incessantly active and busily confessing their fallenness. His short 'Hymn to God the Father' claims at least five different kinds of error and weakness, from his birth into original sin to the deep 'sinne of feare' with which he approaches death; the poem drives the point home by using the word 'sinne' itself eight times in the process. The most important lesson for Donne's persona, as in *Holy Sonnet 7*, is 'how to repent' of all those sins, an action which he boldly asserts will be 'as good | As if thou hadst seal'd my pardon, with thy blood' (Donne 1985: 439). Thus, even as we read the work of Donne and Herbert on its apparently personal and 'lowly ground' (ibid.), we are once again confronted with one of the crucial debates of theological tradition: is the redemption, as expressed in the power of Christ's sacrifice and in the sacraments, the only source of salvation, or can individual human actions be just 'as good' in contributing to the saving of souls?

Although the poems of Herbert and Donne are profoundly serious in their confrontation with some of these central issues of theology—the characteristics of God, the place of human spiritual endeavour, and the achievement of salvation— they are also marked by exquisite and ironic wit. Donne's 'Hymn to God the Father' has a famously punning refrain, drawing in the names of the poet and his wife Anne More in the repeated confession: 'When thou hast done, thou hast not done, | For, I have more' (ibid. 490). Herbert's poems assert a sense of immanent wit both in the creation—as he claims in 'The Church-porch', 'All things are bigge with jest'

(16)—and in language itself. In his sonnet 'The Sunne', Herbert (1941: 168) delights in the fact that the words 'sun' and 'son', which may both properly be used as titles for Christ, sound identical: 'How neatly doe we give one onely name | To parents issue and the sunnes bright starre!'. Language itself, the medium of poetry, has a theological significance for Donne and Herbert; both poets assert that the source of linguistic subtlety and beauty is divine. In Expostulation 19 of his prose *Devotions Upon Emergent Occasions*, Donne praises God's words as, paradoxically, the only means of expressing the 'inexpressible *texture*, and *composition* of thy *word*' (Donne 1975: 99). The work of both writers is saturated with explicit and implicit biblical echoes (Stanwood and Asals 1986; Bloch 1985), declaring that, as Herbert (1941: 166) puts it with deceptive simplicity in 'The Flower', 'Thy word is all, if we could spell'. The second half of the line highlights the problem faced by all devotional poets but intensely felt by Herbert and Donne: how can earthly writers learn to 'spell', literally and metaphorically, the heavenly and incarnate word? Donne's poem in praise of the Sidneys' Psalm translation admits that those who try to find words for God 'doe the Circle square, | And thrust into strait corners of poore wit | Thee, who art cornerlesse and infinite' (Donne 1985: 467). In 'Jordan (II)' Herbert (1941: 102–3) demonstrates the dangers of trying too hard to find 'quaint words, and trim invention' to write of 'heav'nly joyes'. Not only is language itself inadequate, but poets may in the very attempt 'weave' their own selves—their desires, skills, and pride—'into the sense'. The poem's conclusion, that 'There is in love a sweetnesse readie penn'd: | Copie out onely that, and save expense' (ibid. 103), is at best a partial solution. The fundamental theological problem of *how* to 'copie' the example of divine love, both in language and in life, remains.

Before concluding this account of the work of Herbert and Donne set in a theological light, it is important to note that neither poet was wholly at ease with the impact of strict theologians or ecclesiastical leaders. Herbert refers disparagingly in his lyric 'Divinitie' to fussy and pedantic experts whose 'curious questions and divisions' are destructive of faith (ibid. 134), while Donne's 'Litany' (1985: 465) prays for deliverance from the sort of preacher whose 'infirmitie…diminishes the Word'. But when theology is more broadly defined and positively interpreted, it is clear that their own work has given rise to three major kinds of response which we can properly call theological. First, in the early decades after the publication of their writings, Donne and Herbert inspired readings of a practical, devotional, and sometimes polemical nature. Second, in the nineteenth and twentieth centuries their work gave rise to critical debates centring on the poets' place in early modern doctrine and spirituality. Third, the poems themselves embody and explore fundamental theological questions as experienced in the aesthetics of devotional verse, and do so to such an extent that it is virtually impossible to respond to the poems without dealing with issues such as sin, redemption, and the language of spirituality.

It is fascinating to observe that all three kinds of theological 'use' of the poets' work continue to this day. First, the poems make regular appearances in devotional and liturgical contexts as readings, hymns, and anthems, not only in quiet daily worship but on such public occasions as the enthronement of an Archbishop of Canterbury.[1] Second, the critical arguments concerning the doctrinal traditions and allegiances of the poets are as yet unresolved and, as we have seen, continue to inspire new readings both of the poems and of early modern English religious culture. And finally, the process of reading the poems remains a source of rich encounters between what Carl Phillips has called 'the demands of art and of piety' (Post 2002: 148). The spiritual and the aesthetic are intertwined as the imaginations of writer and reader are fired by the challenge of matching earth and heaven in human language. When the task is— occasionally, fleetingly—fulfilled, then faith and poetry combine, as when the spiritually recovered speaker of Herbert's 'The Flower' declares:

> And now in age I bud again,
> After so many deaths I live and write;
> I once more smell the dew and rain,
> And relish versing... (Herbert 1941: 166)

Works Cited

Andersen, Jennifer L., and Sauer, Elizabeth. 2001. 'Introduction', *Renaissance and Reformation*, Special Issue, 'Literature and Religion in Early Modern England: Case Studies', 25/4: 3–8.

Bald, R. C. 1970. *John Donne: A Life*, ed. W. Milgate. Oxford: Clarendon.

Bates, William. 1692. *A Funeral-Sermon for the Reverend, Holy, and Excellent DIVINE, Mr. Richard Baxter*. London: Brab. Aylmer.

Baxter, Richard. 1681. *Poetical Fragments*. London: T. Snowden for B. Simmons.

Bloch, Chana. 1985. *Spelling the Word: George Herbert and the Bible*. Berkeley: University of California Press.

Brown, Meg Lota. 1995. *Donne and the Politics of Conscience in Early Modern England*. Leiden: Brill.

Carey, John. 1981. *John Donne: Life, Mind and Art*. London: Faber & Faber.

Cartwright, William. 1651. *Comedies, Tragi-Comedies, with other Poems*. London: Humphrey Moseley.

Charles, Amy M. 1977. *A Life of George Herbert*. Ithaca: Cornell University Press.

Coleridge, Samuel Taylor. 1955. *Coleridge on the Seventeenth Century*, ed. Roberta F. Brinkley. Durham, NC: Duke University Press.

Donne, John. 1953–62. *The Sermons of John Donne*, ed. George R. Potter and Evelyn M. Simpson. 10 vols. Berkeley: University of California Press.

---

[1] During the enthronement of Archbishop Rowan Williams on 27 February 2003 (Herbert's feast-day in the Anglican calendar), Herbert's words featured in a hymn, two anthems, and the sermon. The most recent musical setting (at the time of writing this essay) of Donne's 'Hymn to God the Father', in this case by Francis Jackson, had its première at Buckfast Abbey in July 2005. The continuing liturgical interest in the poets is also ecumenical in flavour: a recent critical biography of the Catholic Donne (Edwards 2001) was written by the former provost of the Anglican Southwark Cathedral, while Herbert was quoted in a sermon by the Roman Catholic Bishop of Brentwood broadcast on BBC Radio 4 in October 2004.

—— 1975. *Devotions Upon Emergent Occasions*, ed. Anthony Raspa. Montreal: McGill-Queen's University Press.

—— 1985. *The Complete English Poems of John Donne*, ed. C. A. Patrides. London: Dent.

DRYDEN, JOHN. 1963. *Selected Poems*, ed. James Kinsley. Oxford: Oxford University Press.

EDWARDS, DAVID L. 2001. *John Donne: Man of Flesh and Spirit*. London: Continuum.

ELIOT, T. S. 1932. 'George Herbert', in *The Spectator* 148: 360–1.

—— 1951. *Selected Essays*. London: Faber & Faber.

EMPSON, WILLIAM. 1930. *Seven Types of Ambiguity*. London: Chatto & Windus.

FISH, STANLEY. 1978. *The Living Temple: George Herbert and Catechizing*. Berkeley: University of California Press.

FLYNN, DENNIS. 1995. *John Donne and the Ancient Catholic Nobility*. Bloomington: Indiana University Press.

GUIBBORY, ACHSAH. 1998. *Ceremony and Community from Herbert to Milton: Literature, Religion and Cultural Conflict in Seventeenth-Century England*. Cambridge: Cambridge University Press.

HERBERT, GEORGE. 1941. *The Works of George Herbert*, ed. F. E. Hutchinson. Oxford: Clarendon.

HODGKINS, CHRISTOPHER. 1993. *Authority, Church, and Society in George Herbert: Return to the Middle Way*. Columbia: University of Missouri Press.

LENNON, DENNIS. 2002. *Turning the Diamond: Exploring George Herbert's Images of Prayer*. London: SPCK.

LEWALSKI, BARBARA KEIFER. 1979. *Protestant Poetics and the Seventeenth-Century Religious Lyric*. Princeton: Princeton University Press.

MALCOLMSON, CRISTINA. 1999. *Heart-Work: George Herbert and the Protestant Ethic*. Stanford: Stanford University Press.

MARTZ, LOUIS L. 1962. *The Poetry of Meditation: A Study in English Religious Literature of the Seventeenth Century*. Rev. edn. New Haven: Yale University Press. First published 1954.

PATRIDES, C. A. (ed.) 1983. *George Herbert: The Critical Heritage*. London: Routledge & Kegan Paul.

POST, JONATHAN F. S. (ed.) 2002. *Green Thoughts, Green Shades: Essays by Contemporary Poets on the Early Modern Lyric*. Berkeley: University of California Press.

PRYNNE, WILLIAM. 1646. *Canterburies Doome*. London John Macock for Michael Spark Senior.

RUSKIN, JOHN. 1972. *Ruskin in Italy: Letters to his Parents 1845*, ed. Harold I. Shapiro. Oxford: Oxford University Press.

RYLEY, GEORGE. 1987. *Mr. Herbert's Temple and Church Militant Explained and Improved.*, ed. Maureen Boyd and Cedric C. Brown. New York: Garland.

SHAMI, JEANNE. 2001. '"Trying to Walk on Logs in Water": John Donne, Religion, and the Critical Tradition'. *Renaissance and Reformation*, Special Issue, 'Literature and Religion in Early Modern England: Case Studies', 25/4: 81–99.

SHELL, ALISON. 1999. *Catholicism, Controversy and the English Literary Imagination, 1558–1660*. Cambridge: Cambridge University Press.

SHERWOOD, TERRY G. 1989. *Herbert's Prayerful Art*. Toronto: University of Toronto Press.

SMITH, A. J. (ed.) 1975. *John Donne: The Critical Heritage*. London: Routledge & Kegan Paul.

—— and PHILLIPS, CATHERINE (eds.) 1996. *John Donne: The Critical Heritage*. London: Routledge, ii.

STANWOOD, P. G., and ASALS, HEATHER ROSS (eds.) 1986. *John Donne and the Theology of Language*. Columbia: University of Missouri Press.

STRIER, RICHARD. 1983. *Love Known: Theology and Experience in George Herbert's Poetry*. Chicago: University of Chicago Press.

STRIER, RICHARD. 1996. 'Donne and the Politics of Devotion', in Donna B. Hamilton and Richard Strier (eds.), *Religion, Literature and Politics in Post-Reformation England*. Cambridge: Cambridge University Press.

TARGOFF, RAMIE. 2001. *Common Prayer: The Language of Public Devotion in Early Modern England*. Chicago: University of Chicago Press.

TUVE, ROSEMUND. 1952. *A Reading of George Herbert*. Chicago: University of Chicago Press.

WALTON, IZAAK. 1670. *The Lives of Dr. John Donne, Sir Henry Wotton, Mr. Richard Hooker and Mr. George Herbert*. London: Richard Marriott.

WILCOX, HELEN. 1979. 'Puritans, George Herbert and "Nose-twange"'. *Note and Queries* 26/2: 152–3.

—— 1984. '"Heaven's Lidger Here": Herbert's *Temple* and Seventeenth-century Devotion'. David Jasper (ed.), *Images of Belief in Literature*. London: Macmillan, 153–68.

—— 1987. '"The Sweet Singer of the Temple": The Musicians' Response to Herbert'. *George Herbert Journal*. 10: 47–60.

YOUNG, R. V. 2000. *Doctrine and Devotion in Seventeenth-Century Poetry*. Woodbridge: Boydell & Brewer.

FURTHER READING

BLOCH, CHANA. 1985. *Spelling the Word: George Herbert and the Bible*. Berkeley: University of California Press.

CHARLES, AMY M. 1977. *A Life of George Herbert*. Ithaca: Cornell University Press.

ELIOT, T. S. 1994. *George Herbert*. Reissue of 'Writers and their Works' series. Plymouth: Northcote House.

FRONTAIN, RAYMOND-JEAN, and MALPEZZI, FRANCES M. (eds.) 1995. *John Donne's Religious Imagination. Essays in Honor of John T. Shawcross*. Conway: University of Central Arkansas Press.

GUIBBORY, ACHSAH. 1998. *Ceremony and Community from Herbert to Milton: Literature, Religion and Cultural Conflict in Seventeenth-Century England*. Cambridge: Cambridge University Press.

LEWALSKI, BARBARA KEIFER. 1979. *Protestant Poetics and the Seventeenth-Century Religious Lyric*. Princeton: Princeton University Press.

MARTZ, LOUIS L. 1962. *The Poetry of Meditation: A Study in English Religious Literature of the Seventeenth Century*. Rev. edn. New Haven: Yale University Press. First published 1954.

PATRIDES, C. A. (ed.) 1983. *George Herbert: The Critical Heritage*. London: Routledge & Kegan Paul.

ROBERTS, JOHN R. 1973. *John Donne: An Annotated Bibliography of Modern Criticism, 1912–1967*. Columbia: University of Missouri Press.

—— 1988. *George Herbert: An Annotated Bibliography of Modern Criticism, 1905–1984*. Rev. edn. Columbia: University of Missouri Press.

SMITH, A. J. (ed.) 1975. *John Donne: The Critical Heritage*. London: Routledge & Kegan Paul, i.

—— and PHILLIPS, CATHERINE (eds.) 1996. *John Donne: The Critical Heritage*. London: Routledge, ii.

SUMMERS, JOSEPH H. 1981. *George Herbert: His Religion and Art*. Repr. Binghamton, NY: Medieval and Renaissance Texts and Studies. First published 1954.

CHAPTER 25

JOHN MILTON

MICHAEL LIEB

BACKGROUND

THE scholarship on Milton's theology is immense, in part because Milton is essentially a theological poet. In fact, he has always been looked upon as a theological poet. From the eighteenth century onwards, such groups as the Arians, the Socinians, and the Unitarians claimed him as their own. *Paradise Lost*, in particular, enjoyed a reading audience as large as that of the Bible. Even today's new historicist, gender-related, post-colonial, and postmodern criticism must address theological issues underlying Milton's works. There is no lack of scholarship on the subject of Milton's theology. Titled '*Bright Essence*' (1971), the volume of seminal essays compiled by William B. Hunter et al. alone attests to this fact. Almost every book and article published on Milton, however, addresses some aspect of his theological views, including the nature of Milton's God (Empson 1961; Danielson 1982), the developing concepts of Christian doctrine from the beginnings of the church up through the Reformation (Evans 1968; Patrides 1966), the concept of hypostasis in his rendering of Jesus (MacCallum 1986), and a host of related issues.

Despite the plethora of books and articles devoted to various aspects of Milton's doctrinal beliefs, the question of *how* to read his works theologically has not received the attention it deserves (see Fish 1967/1998; 2001). Knowing Milton's views and reading his works are two different enterprises. In order to address the second issue, one must determine precisely what a 'theological reading' of Milton's works entails. What are the assumptions of such a reading? How do they operate? And how does one know if those assumptions are borne out by what happens in the poetry? In the case of the Miltonic œuvre, the answers to those questions have long involved recourse to the *De Doctrina Christiana*. With the posthumous publication of the *De Doctrina* in 1825, the world of Milton scholarship felt confident that it had all the answers to the various conundrums that had plagued it before the discovery of the manuscript. Although readers were either delighted with or horrified by the various heterodoxies evinced by the treatise (among them, mortalism, materialism, monism, polygamy, and Arianism), at least they felt that they had a 'handle' on Milton's putative theological beliefs as manifested in the poetry. No longer were they obliged to surmise that Milton was a member of this school or that—it was all there in the prose. All one had to do was look it up.

Glossing the Text

Assumptions of this nature became the basis of the 'classic' work on the subject: Maurice Kelley's *This Great Argument: A Study of Milton's 'De Doctrina Christiana' as a Gloss upon 'Paradise Lost'* (1941). From the time of its publication to the present, this book has been canonized by its adherents as the key to how Milton's epic is to be read as a 'theological document'. Although it is arguable that its detractors have become more persuasive than its adherents, the book must be given its due as a monument to how one might finally understand the theological intricacies and doctrinal premises of Milton's epic. The foreword to the book amounts to a credo that reflects the author's determination to defend his approach to a poem that is professedly theological, that is, a poem with its own codes, its own cues, and its own protocols in its unfolding of the story of all things. Eschewing what he claims is the prevailing school of 'critical mysticism' concerning *Paradise Lost*, Kelley dismisses any attempt to discover hidden meanings through distinctions such as conscious and unconscious modes of production. For these purveyors of the psychological approach, it is the world of the unconscious that matters, rather than what Kelley terms 'professed' and 'conscious' meanings. In place of this critical mysticism or 'intuitive criticism', Kelley offers an approach 'more logical and more productive of defensible conclusions' in the study of the theological bearing of Milton's epic. Kelley's book is grounded in the belief that 'the poet himself has something definite to say, and that he is more interested in conveying this message than in stimulating his readers to an irresponsible and uninhibited exercise of their associative powers'. The problem, Kelley observes, is that in attempting to communicate his message by means of poetic discourse, the poet 'may not be completely successful'. The reason for this lack of success stems from the annoying connotative associations that words possess. The language of theological poetry runs the risk of being undone by the ambiguities it masks. As a result, this mode of discourse tends to be less precise than the discourse of prose. For that reason, Kelley turns to 'Milton's own writings for a less ambiguous statement of the dogma, aims, and argument of his epic'. Kelley has found that statement, that *clavis*, in Milton's systematic theology, the *De Doctrina Christiana* (Kelley 1941: pp. viii–ix).

Confident that he has the key to unlock the mysteries of the text, Kelley declares in the subtitle of his book that what he has produced is a study of Milton's *De Doctrina Christiana* as a 'gloss' upon *Paradise Lost*. 'Gloss': what precisely does Kelley have in mind? Etymologically grounded in the Latin *glossa* (which in turn derives from the Greek γλωσσα: tongue, language), the term gloss was traditionally applied to certain kinds of interpretative practices extending back to the Middle Ages and earlier. In fact, the medieval period witnessed the production of glosses, *scolia*, or lexicons of various sorts for the purpose of explicating difficult words or texts by means of which the glossarist would unlock otherwise occluded meanings. His discourse might assume any number of shapes, including marginal glosses, interlinear glosses, or both. The text most often subjected to this form of interpretation was the Bible. Here, one encounters undertakings such as the *Glossa Ordinaria*, the very title of which suggests the nature of its utility for those who required immediate recourse to the meanings of a word, a passage, or an even larger unit of discourse. Bearing the imprint of multiple glossarists, the *Glossa Ordinaria* became a standard of all such glossarial endeavours. Biblical glosses found their correspondence in the area of the legal proceedings of the church. The product of ecclesiastical regulation, canon law attracted its own mode of interpretative discourse consistent with the proper glossing of texts.

In England, the term 'gloss' emerged during the early modern period when it too assumed the form of 'a word inserted between the lines or in the margins of a text' as a way of disclosing as clearly as possible the true meanings of a foreign or otherwise difficult word in the text. Like all such interpretative endeavours, the act of glossing a text was not without its detractors. Especially in its association with legal and ecclesiastical matters, 'glossing' was often viewed as a 'sophistical or disingenuous' form of interpretation (*OED*, s.v.). Although not all glosses were so conceived, those disinclined to embrace any attempt to contain the text within the narrow room of a particular glossarist's predilections greeted the idea of the gloss with suspicion, if not with disdain. For such detractors, the act of glossing a text carried with it the potential for being guilty of misleading and even duplicitous practices. Reflecting such an outlook, Milton himself was no friend of the glossarists. In the *Defensio Prima*, for example, he does not hesitate to castigate his enemies by declaring that they 'have spent more time and pains turning over glossaries and pompously publishing laborious trifles than in the careful and diligent reading of sound authors' (Milton 1931–8: vii. 187). For the Milton of *Paradise Lost*, the greatest practitioner of the gloss proved to be none other than that most suspect of interpreters—Satan himself. Thus, Satan is early accused by God of preparing to tempt Adam and Eve with 'his glozing lies' (*PL* 3. 93). 'Glozing' carries as much the meaning of deception as it does the idea of commenting upon or interpreting (*OED*, s.v.). In short, the world of Miltonic discourse is one in which the act of glossing is liable to assume a bearing at once suspicious and duplicitous.

Even at its most benign, the glossarial methodology prevalent in his own time is one that Milton himself initially adopted, only to reject it, as the guiding compositional principle of the *De Doctrina Christiana*. The story of his desire to approach the Bible in the vein of the glossarists is told in the epistle to the reader that prefaces the theological treatise. There, Milton recounts the arduous task he undertook to produce a work that, by its very nature, would be *sui generis*. 'I entered', he says, 'upon an assiduous course of study in my youth, beginning with the books of the Old and New Testament in their original languages, and going diligently through a few of the shorter systems of divines, in imitation of whom I was in the habit of classing under certain heads whatever passages of Scripture occurred for extraction, to be made use of hereafter as occasion might require.' Moving from the shorter systems to 'some of the more copious theological treatises', he found in both 'any instances adverse reasonings either evaded by wretched shifts, or attempted to be refuted, rather speciously than with solidity, by an affected display of formal sophisms, or by a constant recourse to the quibbles of the grammarians' (Milton 1931–8: xiv. 6–7). Both with respect to the 'shorter systems of divines' and to the 'copious theological treatises', Milton has in mind the theological works that prevailed during his time. Essentially grounded in the exegetical manoeuvres of the biblical gloss or the so-called *locos communes*, Milton is at pains to dissociate himself from the common practices of the glossarists (whether of the shorter systems or of the copious treatises) that he knew only too well. By means of this dissociation, Milton devises a systematic theology that eschews the easy glosses of both the earlier and the later glossarists. The *De Doctrina Christiana* reflects this desire to be at once *sui generis* and infused with what is commonly referred to as the 'hermeneutics of suspicion'.

I contend that Maurice Kelley's way of reading *Paradise Lost* theologically should be greeted with a corresponding hermeneutics of suspicion, first because of its assumptions about the relationship between theological and poetic discourse; second, because of its determination to make correspondences between poem and treatise a one-to-one operation. This approach assumes that what the poem fails to yield about complex doctrinal matters will be set straight by the theological treatise. Implicit in the approach is the conviction that poems can get messy, especially Miltonic poems such as *Paradise Lost*, with its metaphors, poetic diction, periodic constructions, multiple points of view, and its use of the verse paragraphs to drive home its message. For Kelley, such potentially subversive exercises in the dissemination of the true *kerygma* are best understood by the straightforward, unembellished, systematic laying out of doctrine advanced in the theological treatise. Despite the strides that Milton studies have achieved since the publication of Kelley's book, the prevailing belief in the kind of theological reading of Milton's poetry that Kelley endorses continues to obtain among many who approach *Paradise Lost* as a theological poem.

READING THEOLOGICALLY

Even before proceeding to discuss Milton's poetry from a theological perspective, we must be aware of a major issue that confronts anyone who seeks to understand

Milton's doctrinal beliefs, especially as they are reflected in the *De Doctrina Christiana*. This issue concerns the authorship of the theological treatise and, by implication, how such a treatise is to be used once the issue is addressed, if not resolved. Except for the challenge to authorship launched by Thomas Burgess (1829), the nineteenth-century divine, shortly after the publication of the treatise, the provenance of the *De Doctrina Christiana* went unchallenged until William B. Hunter entered the fray. Having ventured forth with some preliminary articles that called Milton's authorship into question, Hunter then produced his monograph '*Visitation Unimplor'd*': *Milton and the Authorship of 'De Doctrina Christiana*' (1998), to argue that we cannot assume categorically Miltonic authorship in whole or in part simply because the academy says so. Although Hunter's arguments have generally gone unheeded or have been cast aside with remarkably little fuss, few have elected to counter Hunter point-by-point. The particulars of the arguments are complex indeed and need not engage us here. Suffice it to say that Miltonists will continue to do battle over the question of authorship for many generations to come. Accordingly, anyone who deems it appropriate to invoke the *De Doctrina Christiana* to serve as a testing ground for clarifying the finer points of theology in Milton's poetry would be well advised to take into account the very real uncertainties that surround the theological treatise, especially in the vexed area of authorship. This is not to say that the theological treatise is no longer germane to Milton's outlook. Rather, it is to alert us to the multiple pitfalls that await any who would approach the treatise with the same glossarial *insouciance* that Kelley undertook to approach the subject in *This Great Argument*. When it comes to *Paradise Lost* (or to any of the other poems that Milton authored) the *De Doctrina Christiana* is no *Glossa Ordinaria*.

So how then is one to read *Paradise Lost* theologically? We begin with the Milton of the antiprelatical tracts, in particular, *The Reason of Church-Government* (1642), which provides invaluable insight into his self-reflections concerning his poetic ambitions. In the introduction to the second book of this tract, Milton distinguishes himself from what he calls those 'libidinous and ignorant Poetasters' who 'lap up vitious principles in sweet pils to be swallow'd down, and make the tast of vertuous documents harsh and sowr', rather than imparting sweetness and light in the Horatian mode (Milton 1931–8: iii. 239). Corresponding to the poetasters are the 'vulgar Amorist' and the 'riming parasite', both of whom receive their inspiration not from the Muse of divine, inspired poetry but from the pagan world of 'Dame Memory and her Siren daughters' (ibid.). Unlike these profane poets, Milton embodies the impulse of true religious devotion, which derives its inspiration from 'devout prayer to that eternall Spirit who can enrich with all utterance and knowledge, and sends out his Seraphim with the hallow'd fire of his Altar to touch and purify the lips of whom he pleases' (ibid. 241). The allusion, of course, is to Isa. 6: 1–7, in which the prophet receives his calling. Beholding 'the Lord sitting upon a throne, high and lifted up' so that 'his train filled the temple', Isaiah is transformed by a vision of the seraphim that cry unto one another 'Holy, holy, holy, is the Lord of hosts: the whole earth is full of his glory.' At the prospect of receiving his calling, the prophet laments, 'Woe is me! for I am undone; because I am a man of unclean lips, and I dwell in the midst of a people of unclean lips: for mine eyes have seen the King, the Lord of hosts.' In response to that lamentation, Isaiah is then purified, when one of the seraphim, having a live coal from the altar in its hand, flies to the prophet, lays the burning coal on his mouth, and declares, 'Lo, this hath touched thy lips; and thy iniquity is taken away, and thy sin purged.' As one whose lips have been purified and whose sins have been cleansed, Milton envisions himself as such a prophet, whose vocation, he declares, is to 'inbreed and cherish in a great people the seeds of virtu, and publick civility, to allay the perturbations of the mind, and set the affections in right tune, to celebrate in glorious and lofty Hymns the throne and equipage of Gods Almightinesse, and what he works, and what he suffers to be wrought with high providence in his Church' (ibid. 238).

POETICS OF THE INEFFABLE

One might argue—with some justification—that Milton's account of his vocation as prophet in the mould of Isaiah is not theology per se, but to adopt such a position would be to accede to a rather narrow view of theology. The point is that in the case of John Milton as poet, as well as polemicist, any attempt to divorce religious experience from theological experience is immediately suspect: for Milton, the two go hand in hand. This is true especially when it comes to a reading of *Paradise Lost*. The proem to the third book tells the tale. It opens with an address to light that delights in what has been called negative theology, a theology of not knowing, of divine ignorance, characteristic of the theology of Dionysius the Areopagite (AD 500?) and Nicholas of Cusa (1401–64). It may be read in fact as Milton's own statement of the *deus absconditus* or hiddenness of God:

> Hail holy Light, ofspring of Heav'n first-born,
> Or of th' Eternal Coeternal beam
> May I express thee unblam'd? since God is light,
> And never but in unapproached light
> Dwelt from Eternitie, dwelt then in thee,
> Bright effluence of bright essence increate.
> Or hear'st thou rather pure Ethereal stream,
> Whose Fountain who shall tell?   (3. 1–8)

Among Milton scholars, a great deal of discussion has centred on the theological implications of this invocation. Scholars argue about the extent to which Milton is either orthodox or heterodox, whether he espouses Athanasian or Arian views, whether he is Trinitarian or anti-Trinitarian, whether his putative emanationism is consistent with patristic readings of the godhead, whether his discourse on the Son of God in the *De Doctrina Christiana* serves as an adequate gloss on his hymn to light in the epic. This is what might be called the 'theological Milton', that is, the construction of Milton as a poet whose poetry re-enacts his theological habits of mind. It is a construction determined to transform the ineffable into theological doctrine. Given the doctrinal basis of Milton's epic and his own theological proclivities, such an approach is understandable, if not inevitable. On the other hand, a careful reading of the text suggests that the inclination to 'theologize' meets with the resistance in the attempt to draw theological conclusions from poetic discourse, especially the kind of discourse that the poet presents at the outset of the third book of his epic. In fact, it is precisely the determination to transform poetic discourse into theological doctrine that the poet of the invocation to light is at pains to counter. Paradoxically, he does so in the very act of invoking the theology of godhead in his paean. That is, at just the point that the poet entertains various ways of construing light as Athanasian or Arian, Trinitarian or anti-Trinitarian, and the like, he suggests his awareness of the ultimate impossibility of comprehending the ineffable through language at all. That is why he offers the alternatives of either/or: Godhead as *either* 'ofspring of Heav'n first-born' *or* as an emanation 'of th' Eternal Coeternal beam' *or* as 'Bright effluence of bright essence increate' *or* as 'pure Ethereal stream'. To offer options about the name and nature of godhead is at once to suggest both the hubris of engaging in such an act ('May I express thee unblam'd?') and the impossibility of naming the un-nameable ('since God is light, | And never but in unapproached light . . .'). The only thing we know is that we cannot know. Poetry becomes the means by which this not knowing is most profoundly expressed.

Where does Maurice Kelley as a glossarist stand in all this? Interestingly, he adopts *neither* the Trinitarian nor the anti-Trinitarian position. Instead, Kelley reduces the possible meanings implicit in 'holy Light' to the realm of the literal. As far as Kelley is concerned, the proem to Book 3 opens with nothing more than 'an invocation to light *in the physical sense*' (italics mine). In place of theology, Kelley (1941: 92–3) substitutes 'physics'. To advance such a view runs the risk of denuding 'holy Light' of its sacrality. As much as Kelley might wish to conceive light in this way, no justifica-tion for such a conception is to be found in the *De Doctrina Christiana* itself. In fact, the theological treatise endorses the sacral dimensions of 'holy Light' throughout. Speaking of the *habitaculum Dei* or 'abode of God' in the treatise, Milton (1931–8: xiv. 29–31) observes that there is a 'habitation of God, where he diffuses in an eminent manner the glory and brightness of his majesty'. Out of the *habitaculum Dei* emanates 'holy Light' in its most glorious form. Disregarding such readings, Kelley leads us (by way of a footnote) to several biblical texts that he would have support his literalist interpretation. These texts include Ps. 104: 2 ('Who coverest *thyself* with a light as *with* a garment') and 1 Tim. 6: 16 ('Who only hath immortality, dwelling in the light which no man can approach unto, whom no man hath seen, nor can see'). As much as Kelley wants these texts to yield a reading of 'holy Light' as entirely physical, they suggest an interpretation that is precisely the opposite. In the process, they reinforce once again the sacrality that underlies the idea of light as 'holy'. Thus, in Ps. 104, the act of covering oneself with light as with a garment involves a deliberate 'metaphorizing' of emanation. The passage represents the light of God as a kind of *pleroma* or 'fullness' that occludes as much as it reveals. Implicit in 1 Tim. 6, the notion of dwelling in light, in turn, suggests in a New Testament context the *shekhinah* or dwelling presence of God, whose emanation once overwhelms the very process of beholding. There is nothing physical as such about 'holy Light': its radiance is simply of the most profound and spiritual sort. The Miltonic form of theology conceived as the 'phenomenology of the ineffable' is pervasive throughout the poetry and, in particular, throughout *Paradise Lost*.

What then is the ineffable? It is the *ineffabilis*, the unutterable, the inexpressible, the unspeakable. As that which utters the unutterable, expresses the inexpressible, and speaks the unspeakable, Milton's epic becomes the vehicle of the divine, the holy (Lieb 1981). By means of his epic, one gains access to the world of the ineffable, the world of the holy, a phenomenon quite set apart from the world of the profane, the commonplace, the diurnal. As that which lies outside the holy, that is, the *fanum* or consecrated area, the world of the profane represents the condition that Milton as poet seeks to transcend in his quest to realize the world of the holy. What is the holy, and how do we recognize it when we see it? The holy is a phenomenon most immediately associated with the work of Rudolf Otto, whose treatment of the subject is seminal. As Otto (1958) defines it, the holy (*das Heilige*) is a manifestation of the overwhelming encounter with the numinous, that power (*numen*) which resides in godhead. An encounter that defies conceptualization, the holy gives rise to a 'creature-feeling' that expresses itself as 'self-abasement' before 'an overpowering, absolute might'. As a revelation of divine 'otherness' (what Otto calls the 'wholly other' or *ganz andere*), the holy embodies a sense of 'awefulness' that is essentially primordial and archaic. Arising from what Otto terms the *mysterium tremendum* or the mystery of mysteries, the experience of the holy assumes many forms: 'It may at times come sweeping like a gentle tide, pervading the mind with a tranquil mood of deepest worship' until it fades away into the ' "profane", non-religious mood of everyday experience'. Or 'it may burst in sudden eruption up from the depths of the soul with spasms and convulsions, or lead to the strangest excitements, to intoxicated frenzy, to transport, and to ecstasy'. In the presence of this 'mystery inexpressible and above all creatures', one is finally bound inextricably to that which one is at a loss to understand, to know, to articulate (ibid. 12–24).

From the perspective of the ineffable, Milton's invocation to 'holy Light' is striking in the extent to which it is aware of the numinous quality of the phenomenon it invokes. The poet knows that this is the *mysterium tremendum* that he calls upon, that, in fact, he 'hails' as one would acknowledge the divine presence of that which is to be hallowed in recognition of its holiness. This is Milton's *ave* to the source of all that is holy. His salutation is therefore a hallowing of that which is hallowed, a call that embodies the poet's own desire (*ave* as *avere*) to be made whole, to be imbued with that luminescence through which the poet himself will partake of the very numen he invokes. Otto speaks wisely of what he calls 'numinous hymns' that are themselves replete with 'numinous sounds' in the creation of poetry that gives voice to the unutterable. Milton's 'Hail' is one of those numinous sounds in its announcement of the numinous hymn to follow. Once again like the prophet Isaiah who appears before the Enthroned Deity in the Holy of Holies, Milton proclaims his

'Holy, holy, holy,' as he awaits the purification of his lips, so that he may speak, utter the unutterable, give expression through the word of his poetry to that which defies articulation (Isa. 6: 1–7). For Milton, the holy emerges not only as a phenomenon of the most archaic sort but as a manifestation of the religious impulse in its most advanced stages of development. As a phenomenon of the most archaic sort, it is conceptualized as a divine beam of light or as a pure ethereal stream, the source of which is both unknown and finally unapproachable and the lineage of which antedates the very creation of the universe. Emerging from the *tehom*, that which Milton in *Paradise Lost* (3. 11) calls the 'rising world of waters dark and deep', it occludes at precisely the point that it reveals, as it 'invests' the waters with its numinous mantle. Its presence overwhelms, and its manifestation resonates with all those qualities of the numinous that enshroud the *mysterium tremendum*. As that which existed before the sun and the heavens were created, however, the presence of God embodied in the ineffable is correspondingly conceived as the means of knowing, as the way in which one comes into knowledge of the 'wholly other' as it unfolds itself within the realm of humankind. As such, it assumes the form of wisdom and understanding 'possessed' by God 'in the beginning of his way, before his works of old'. It is this wisdom, this understanding, who (in personified form) declares: 'I was set up from everlasting, from the beginning, or ever the earth was. When there *were* no depths, I was brought forth: when there *were* no fountains abounding with water. Before the mountains were settled, before the hills was I brought forth.' Thus, wisdom proclaims that when God 'prepared the heavens I *was* there'; wisdom attended God, '*as* one brought up *with him*' and '*was* daily his delight, rejoicing always before him' (Prov. 8: 22–5, 27, 30). Thus, in its later stages of development, the holy reveals itself in that higher wisdom of knowing, of understanding, that is an essential part of God's own self-manifestation from the very foundations of the universe. It is precisely this wisdom that the poet seeks in his quest to express and to celebrate the essential nature of the ineffable in his poetry, in his articulation of the word as a paean to the holy in its bright essence.

Such an experience transcends the immediate concerns of the poet's allegiance to a particular church, denomination, or doctrinal persuasion. Whether one is an Anabaptist or a High Church Anglican is incidental to the kind of associations that engage us here. In Milton studies as well as in studies of other poets deemed to be 'religious', the thrust of prevailing scholarship is to 'locate' the poet within a particular religious milieu. Among other poets of his time, Milton is characteristically seen to reflect a particular poetic disposition that has its immediate source in seventeenth-century debates concerning the place of belief and dogma as an outgrowth of the Reformation. This approach is very much in keeping with what might be called Milton's doctrinal outlook. A theologian in his own right, Milton certainly invites the kind of analysis that views his poetry in the context of his lengthy discourses concerning vexed issues of Christian doctrine. But what I have in mind in addressing the relationship between poetry and the ineffable is an experience rooted in something much more 'primitive' than the immediate milieu in which Milton's poetry (or any religious poetry of a particular time or place) is grounded.

It is this phenomenological perspective that one sees in such scholars as Gerardus van der Leeuw, whose own masterwork *Religion in Essence and Manifestation* (1968) approaches the holy from precisely this point of view. As a phenomenologist, van der Leeuw, like Otto, desires to get beyond the immediate forms of religion in order to gain insight into the essential power that inspired them. Those forms are the denominational or doctrinal postulates of belief through which the numinous is conceptualized. It is the province of the poet to deconceptualize, in effect, to deconstruct, such postulates or, at the very least, call them into question, in the portrayal of the ineffable as that which no creed, no denomination can fully comprehend.

Reading *Paradise Lost*

As one might conclude, the best way to read *Paradise Lost* and *Paradise Regained* theologically is to hold as suspect any interpretation determined to demonstrate that the epic is the 'versified' product of one or more schools of doctrinal thought. One might even go so far as to say that the best way to read Milton's epics theologically is to read *against* the inclination to 'theologize' the poem, or, at least, to be complacent in assuming that all the mystery will be resolved by resorting to a theological treatise the very provenance of which (in whole or in part) has come under fire as indisputably the product of John Milton's authorship. In this context, one might do well to remind himself that the first 'theologians' in the narrative encompassed by *Paradise Lost* are the fallen angels. Those inclined to discuss matters beyond their reach are described as follows:

> [They] ... apart sat on a Hill retir'd,
> In thoughts more elevate, and reason'd high
> Of Providence, Foreknowledge, Will and Fate,
> Fixt Fate, free will, foreknowledge absolute,
> And found no end, in wandring mazes lost.   (2. 557–61)

To see the fallen angels in this posture is to realize the irony implicit in Milton's own agenda of asserting 'Eternal Providence' in order to 'justifie the wayes of God to men' (1. 25–6). In such moments of self-parody, Milton makes a point of dramatizing the precarious position in which one always finds oneself in presuming to venture beyond one's proper station as a creature of God. This is something the fallen angels never learn: their blatant defiance of their limits accordingly results in their fall. With the fallen angels in mind, the poet knows that in his attempt to surpass the boundaries set for him he too runs the risk of those fallen theologians. Thus, he prays that he will not have to endure the fate of such over-reachers as Bellerophon. In his ascent 'above the flight of *Pegasean* wing', the poet fears that he too might be thrown from his 'flying steed', to wander aimlessly as a crazed, blind fool on the '*Aleian* Field' below (7. 4, 17–20). Such, one might suggest, is the fate of those who dabble in forbidden things, as much the stuff of poetry as the stuff of theology. For that reason, *Paradise Lost* counsels us to be 'lowlie wise' (8. 173) in the face of all those temptations to cultivate a knowledge of things that lie beyond our grasp. At the same time, this is an epic of transcendence. It is an epic that invites us to behold God on his throne, to witness the war in heaven and the overthrow of the rebel angels by the Son in his divine chariot. It delights in recounting the creation of the world and the nature of prelapsarian existence. In short, this is an epic that takes immense risks in its portrayal of that which can only be accommodated to the limited capacities of human sense through the mediatorial function of poetic discourse. Any attempt to read that discourse theologically must take into account the insurmountable chasm between divine and human modes of perception.

THE CELESTIAL DIALOGUE

It is with this sensitivity to poetic nuance that such events as the dialogue between the Father and the Son in Book 3 of *Paradise Lost* must be read. This dialogue is at the heart of theological readings, for in it Milton portrays Father and Son speaking to each other in a manner customarily associated with performance on the stage. Recalling that Milton originally intended to write his great work in the form of drama, we should be alert to the dialogic implications of the celestial council scene. That scene in effect enacts what Milton in the *De Doctrina Christiana* calls 'the drama of the personalities in the godhead' (1931–8: xiv. 197). It is this drama (at its heart, 'theological') that has been the source of more entanglements than almost any other events in Milton's poetic œuvre. In response to the drama, readers have asked two fundamental questions: (1) How can a poet presume to portray the unportrayable as 'characters' in a drama; and, (2) assuming that such a portrayal is possible, what can be said about the nature of the relationship between the characters in this drama? To read *Paradise Lost* theologically is to attempt to answer these questions. At the very least, the answers lie not in subjecting the poetry of Milton's epic to the 'glossarial' dimensions represented by the theological treatise. Determining whether Milton was an Arian, a Subordinationist, a Trinitarian, or a Socinian based upon our reading of the *De Doctrina Christiana* does not get us very far into the nature of what I would call Milton's 'poetic theology'. This is a theology of metaphor, paradox, and multiple modes of perception. It is the theology of the poet, not of the theologian. Poetic theology delights in subverting expectations, challenging doctrinal formulation, and confounding the glossarist's determination to render it all clear as day.

One or two examples should suffice. The council scene in Book 3 opens through the delineation of what amounts to the stage setting for high theatre such as one might witness in *Hamlet* or *King Lear*. First, the enthroned Father is described: 'Now had th'Almighty Father from above, | From the pure Empyrean where he sits | High Thron'd above all highth, bent down his eye.' Surrounding him, 'all the Sanctities of Heav'n | Stood thick as Starrs.' On his right side 'the radiant image of his Glory sat, | His onely Son' (3. 56–64). So situated, the Son fulfils his role as one who is 'dextrous' (from the Latin '*dexter*') to perform his Father's work (cf. 5. 741). In this respect, the Son finds his counterpart in the figure of Sin, whose purpose is *sinister*, that is, implicitly situated on the left-hand side and hailed as 'a Sign | Portentous' (2. 760; cf. 10. 322). The significance of the setting of the celestial dialogue for a theological reading is one in which position is everything in life, because *position* implies *condition*. The semiological bearing of the Father–Son relationship reinforces the theological implications of how that relationship is to be interpreted. Milton himself implies as much in his act of situating Father and Son in the playing out of the dialogue. The stakes are high, for if Father and Son are situated or enthroned at the same level, then the parity of their enthronements would imply a parity of their respective natures. The problem is that the dialogue itself subverts, rather than supports, interpretations based upon settings or signs (portentous or otherwise). In fact, the discourse provides cues that actually appear to be contradictory. Thus, judging by what the Father himself declares, we might first assume that the Son is enthroned in a position equal to that of the Father. So the Father celebrates the Son in the following manner: 'Thou hast, though Thron'd in highest bliss | *Equal to God*, and equally enjoying | God-like fruition, quitted all to save | A World from utter loss' (3. 305–8; italics mine). Such a declaration would appear to support an orthodox reading of the dialogue consistent with the kind of description one finds in the proem to Milton's 'On the Morning of *Christs* Nativity' which portrays the Son as one 'wont at Heav'ns high Council-Table | To sit the midst of Trinal Unity' (10–11). The setting is perfectly clear in the early celebration of Christ's nativity.

But matters become problematical in *Paradise Lost*. In the setting for the celestial council scene that Milton's epic portrays, there is no 'Trinal', for there is no direct reference to the Trinity. What then does the phrase 'Equal to God' really mean? The precise *theology* of the phrase is indeterminate, and such a condition is rendered even more perplexing by virtue of the praise later bestowed upon Father and Son by the angelic hosts. Their hymn celebrates the Son in relation to the Father in a manner that questions the very notion of parity. Thus, they conceive the Son as one who, 'regardless of the Bliss wherein hee sat | *Second* to thee [God], offerd himself to die | For mans offence' (3. 408–10; italics mine). So we might be inclined to ask whether the Son is equal to God or second to God? That is, are we to understand the Son as one enthroned at the same level as the Father, a position that implies parity, or, in keeping with Milton's hierarchical universe, is the Son enthroned (either literally or metaphorically) at a lower level, a positioning that implies imparity? Our response to those questions will determine our interpretation of both the dramatic and the theological implications of the dialogue. In either respect the so-called drama of the personalities in the godhead assumes different meanings. With complete parity, we are invited to think of the dialogue as essentially monologue in which one character is portrayed as two, each an aspect of the other. With imparity, we are invited to think of the dialogue as one in which there are two different characters, each with his own personality, his own powers, his own history. From this perspective, the unfolding of the dialogue is such that the Father is able to 'test' the Son, educate him in the ways of what will become his destiny as Messiah, a destiny that the Son willingly and knowingly embraces to establish himself 'by Merit more then birthright Son of God' (3. 309). It really does matter where the Son sits and at what level he is enthroned. What is the answer? It is one in which the poetry complicates itself even further in its conception of who is where and of who exists when. For in God's dialogue with Adam in Book 8, we receive an entirely different rendering of God's 'situation' (a Miltonic word). Responding to Adam's request for a mate, God asks: 'What thinkst thou then of mee, and this my State, | Seem I to thee sufficiently possest | Of happiness, or not? *who am alone | From all Eternitie, for none I know | Second to me or like, equal much less*' (8. 403–7; italics mine). Forget the discourse of Book 3: God is God. There is no other who is equal to him or even second to him.

CUES TO READING

What, then, of our theological reading? I contend that contradictory (perhaps, paradoxical, perhaps oxymoronic) cues of this sort—the very stuff of poetry—are such that we are finally obliged to 'deconstrue' the theological (and semiological) significations we have always taken for granted. In theology (particularly of the systematic sort), such cues are not of immediate concern. In fact, they do not appear to be at issue at all. The use of the *De Doctrina Christiana* to clarify these issues causes more problems than it solves. In its treatment of the Son of God ('De Filio Dei') in the fifth chapter of the first book, the treatise makes clear that its concerns lie elsewhere. Invoking the distinction between 'essentia' and 'substantia', the treatise concerns itself not with 'cues' or 'signs' of any sort but rather with such metaphysical distinctions that are the very stuff of systematic theology. Specifically, the treatise is at pains to demonstrate that the Father and the Son are neither coeternal nor coessential but are rather consubstantial. (The terms 'essence' and 'substance' share a complex and vexed history that extends back to the earliest Church councils.) What this means for the treatise is that the Son is *subordinate* to the Father in all ways, including designations such as 'omnipotence', 'omniscience', and 'omnipresence'. All this is no doubt useful up to a point in the discussion of the Father–Son relationship in *Paradise Lost*, but finally one must come to terms with the actual cues embedded in the poem itself in order to read the poem theologically. This means coming to terms with the essentially ludic nature of the poem as poem. Here is where we must sensitize ourselves to competing discourses that may be reconciled only through careful interpretive manoeuvres that take into account the possibility that these discourses may never be reconciled at all. Given Milton's fundamental adherence to the notion of the *deus absconditus* or 'hidden God', it is only just and fitting that his God be portrayed in this way. For this is a God described as 'invisible'. Indeed, 'Thron'd inaccessible', He is a God whose very skirts are 'dark with excessive bright'. His skirts 'dazzle Heav'n' so profoundly that even the 'brightest Seraphim' dare not approach Him but instead veil their eyes with their wings (3. 380–8). We recall Isa. 6: 2: 'Above it [the throne] stood the seraphim: each one had six wings: with twain he covered his face, and with twain he covered his feet, and with twain he did fly.' This vision lies at the heart of the entire enterprise. For Milton, the vision serves to warn his readers that they must be aware of the dangers that attend upon an interpretation of his poetry, especially *Paradise Lost*. In the fashion of Isaiah, one must be in a position to have his own lips touched by the luminous coals from the altar before he presumes to hold forth on the theology of *Paradise Lost*. Perhaps, this is what Milton calls for when he invokes his 'fit audience'. Although he expected that audience to be 'few' (7. 31), Milton would have marvelled at the extent to which the theological basis of his *opera* (particularly *Paradise Lost*) has given rise to whole schools of thought among Miltonists. If we are to understand that *opera*, we must come to terms with the interpretative dynamics that distinguish this body of works. This will mean defining and redefining one's expectations at every point. If one can maintain not just a calm of mind but a flexibility of mind, the act of reading Milton's poetry 'theologically' will be that much more enhanced.

MILTON'S 'BRIEF EPIC'

The foregoing reading of *Paradise Lost* finds its counterpart in *Paradise Regained*. Once again, Milton's treatise *The Reason of Church-Government* is suggestive. There, Milton (1931–8: iii. 237) distinguishes between two kinds of epic that engage him: the 'diffuse epic' and the 'brief epic'. The first he associates with the epics of Homer, Virgil, and Tasso; the second with the book of Job. If the first looks forward to *Paradise Lost*, the second looks forward to *Paradise Regained*. The model suggested by the book of Job, of course, resides as much in *Samson Agonistes*, Milton's drama drawn from the book of Judges 13–16, as it does in *Paradise Regained*, the epic drawn from the Gospel of Luke 4 (compare Matt. 4). The publication of both poems (epic and drama) in the same volume in 1671 attests to the extent to which Job represents a 'subtext', as it were, to an understanding of the epic, on the one hand, and the drama, on the other. Theologically, *Paradise Regained* reaches back to *Paradise Lost* as well. It is a correspondence for which Milton's Quaker friend Thomas Ellwood might assume some responsibility. Having secured a 'pretty Box' for Milton at

Chalfont St. Giles to escape the plague in 1665, Ellwood relates in his autobiography that, upon a visit to the poet, he was presented by Milton with the manuscript of *Paradise Lost*. After reading and reflecting upon the poem, Ellwood in a return visit responded with the now-famous question: 'Thou hast said here much of *Paradise lost*, but what hast thou to say of *Paradise found?*' Some time after Milton had returned to London, he presented Ellwood with a copy of *Paradise Regained*. '*This*', Milton said in a pleasant tone, 'is owing to you: for you put it into my Head, by the Question you put to me at *Chalfont*; which before I had not thought of' (Ellwood 1906: 199–200). Whether the story is apocryphal is difficult to determine. What is not difficult to determine is the extent to which the diffuse epic sets the stage for the brief one. Thus, in the last two books of *Paradise Lost*, Adam on the Hill of Speculation is made aware of the form redemption will assume in human history. It is a form in which the mystery of the *protevangelium* proclaimed in Gen. 3: 14–15 ('And the Lord God said unto the serpent . . . I will put enmity between thee and the woman, and between thy seed and her seed; he shall bruise thy head, and thou shall bruise his heel') is finally disclosed. In response to his realization of exactly what the phrase 'seed of Woman' implies, Adam declares that 'Needs must the Serpent now his capital bruise | Expect with mortal pain,' but entirely misunderstands the nature of the warfare involved. Mistakenly assuming, however, that that warfare will be physical, Adam asks of his guide, the archangel Michael, to reveal 'where and when | Thir fight, what stroke shall bruise the Victors heel' (12. 383–5). Michael responds in the spirit of Saint Paul (Eph. 6: 10–24): 'Dream not of thir fight, | As of a Duel, or the local wounds | Of head or heel: Not therefore joyns the Son | Manhood to God-head' (12. 386–9). Rather, their warfare will be of the spiritual sort, one that destroys Satan's works in humankind and its offspring through renewed obedience to the 'Law of God' (12. 394–7). Internalized and spiritualized, the soteriology of renewed obedience is what underlies the action of the brief epic, one in which Satan becomes the Son's 'Spiritual Foe', against whom the Son proves his mettle (1. 10). The theology of *Paradise Regained* is one in which the battle in the 'wast Wilderness' is waged within the individual soul of the 'glorious Eremite', who in his sojourn into the Desert is described as having 'into himself descended' (1. 7–8; 2. 111). In the various attempts to understand the theology of *Paradise Regained*, there has been much discussion about the nature of the hypostatical union (Lewalski 1966), a topic addressed in detail in *De Doctrina Christiana* (1. 5). At issue is the way in which Milton conceived the union of God and human in the person of the Son as saviour. But an understanding of the theology of *Paradise Regained* makes it clear that such concepts, although of interest in the attempt to determine the nature of hypostasis, are not of immediate moment to the make-up of the incarnate Son of the brief epic. It is enough to know that in him God has joined manhood to godhead and that the three temptations (often referred to as those of the flesh (*concupiscentia carnis*), the world (*concupiscentia oculorum*), and the devil (*superbia vitae*)) that the Son resists are all-encompassing. (Designating these temptations as 'the triple equation', theologians have traditionally viewed them in the context of the temptations that Eve proved incapable of resisting in Eden.)

SAMSON AGONISTES

If *Paradise Regained* is the narrative that elaborates the soteriological dimensions manifested in *Paradise Lost*, the brief epic likewise finds its counterpart in the dramatic poem *Samson Agonistes*. As suggested, both may be said to draw their inspiration from the book of Job as subtext, a tie reinforced by the fact that both brief epic and dramatic poem appeared in the same volume in 1671. Just as the so-called triple equation in the brief epic is anticipated by the pattern of temptations embodied in the diffuse epic, so the triple equation may be said to extend to a corresponding pattern in the dramatic poem, one in which *concupiscentia carnis* is reflected in the figure of Manoa, *concupiscentia oculorum* is reflected in the figure of Dalila, and *superbia vitae* is reflected in the figure of Harapha of Gath. In addressing these correspondences, one must be careful not to succumb to the temptation of being overly formulaic. If one can speak of a 'theology' that underlies *Samson Agonistes*, it is one in which all formulas are defied and in which the figure of God is entirely hidden. In this context, God once again becomes the *deus absconditus*, a hidden God. If he has any sort of name through which he is identified, that name is 'our living Dread' (l. 1673), a phenomenon that returns us to Rudolf Otto, whose consideration of the holy (*das Heilige*) most aptly describes the experience of 'otherness' (*ganz andere*) that infuses the dramatic poem. In her splendid study *Towards 'Samson Agonistes'*, Mary Ann Radzinowicz sees Milton's dramatic poem as the culmination of his mature literary and theological outlook. If such is the case, then this 'maturity' is one in which the primal forces that underlie *Paradise Lost* are as present in the dramatic poem as they are in the diffuse epic. What is true of the diffuse epic is true of the dramatic poem: the best way to read Milton's poems theologically is to read *against* the inclination to theologize them, or to approach them as the poetic manifestations of a systematic theology.

WORKS CITED

BURGESS, THOMAS. 1829. *Milton Not the Author of the Lately Discovered Arian Work 'De Doctrina Christiana'. Three Discourses, Delivered at the Anniversary Meetings of the Royal Society of Literature In the Years 1826, 1827, and 1828. To Which is Added, Milton Contrasted With Milton, and With the Scriptures*. London: Thomas Brettell.

DANIELSON, DENNIS. 1982. *Milton's Good God: A Study in Literary Theodicy*. Cambridge: Cambridge University Press.

ELLWOOD, THOMAS. 1906. *The History of the Life of Thomas Ellwood*, ed. S. Graveson. London: Headley Brothers.

EMPSON, WILLIAM. 1961. *Milton's God*. London: Chatto & Windus.

EVANS, J. M. 1968. *'Paradise Lost' and the Genesis Tradition*. Oxford: Clarendon.

FISH, STANLEY. 1967. *Surprised by Sin: The Reader in 'Paradise Lost'*. London: Macmillan.

—— 2001. *How Milton Works*. Cambridge, Mass.: Belknap.

HUNTER, WILLIAM B. 1998 *'Visitation Unimplor'd': Milton and the Authorship of 'De Doctrina Christiana'*. Pittsburgh: Duquesne University Press.

—— Patrides, C. A., and Adamson, J. H. 1971. *Bright Essence: Studies in Milton's Theology*. Salt Lake City: University of Utah Press.

KELLEY, MAURICE. 1941. *This Great Argument: A Study of Milton's 'De Doctrina Christiana' as a Gloss upon 'Paradise Lost'*. Princeton: Princeton University Press.

LEEUW, GERARDUS VAN DER. 1968. *Religion in Essence and Manifestation*, trans. J. E. Turner. Princeton: Princeton University Press.

LEWALSKI, BARBARA K. 1966. *Milton's Brief Epic: The Genre, Meaning, and Art of 'Paradise Regained'*. Providence, RI: Brown University Press.

LIEB, MICHAEL. 1981. *Poetics of the Holy: A Reading of 'Paradise Lost'*. Chapel Hill: University of North Carolina Press.

MACCALLUM, HUGH. 1986. *Milton and the Sons of God: The Divine Image in Milton's Epic Poetry*. Toronto: University of Toronto Press.

MILTON, JOHN. 1931–8. *The Works of John Milton*, ed. Frank Allen Patterson et al. 18 vols. in 21. New York: Columbia University Press.

—— 1971. *Complete Poetry of John Milton*. ed. John T. Shawcross. New York: Doubleday.

OTTO, RUDOLF. 1958. *The Idea of the Holy: An Inquiry into the Non-Rational Factor in the Idea of the Divine and Its Relation to the Rational*, trans. John W. Harvey. New York: Oxford University Press.

PATRIDES, C. A. 1966. *Milton and the Christian Tradition*. Oxford: Clarendon.

RADZINOWICZ, MARY ANN. 1978. *Toward 'Samson Agonistes': The Growth of Milton's Mind*. Princeton: Princeton University Press.

FURTHER READING

BRYSON, MICHAEL. 2004. *The Tyranny of Heaven: Milton's Rejection of God as King*. Newark: University of Delaware Press.

CAMPBELL, GORDON, CORNS, THOMAS N., HALE, JOHN K., HOLMES, DAVID I., and TWEEDIE, FIONA J. 1997. 'The Provenance of *De Doctrina Christiana*'. *Milton Quarterly* 31: 67–117.

CONKLIN, GEORGE N. 1949. *Biblical Criticism and Heresy in Milton*. New York: King's Crown.

DOBRANSKI, STEPHEN, and RUMRICH, JOHN (eds.). 1998. *Milton and Heresy*. Cambridge: Cambridge University Press.

FRYE, ROLAND MUSHAT. 1960. *God, Man, and Satan: Patterns of Christian Thought and Life in 'Paradise Lost,' 'Pilgrim's Progress,' and the Great Theologian*. Princeton: Princeton University Press.

GILBERT, ALLAN H. 1942. 'The Theological Basis of Satan's Rebellion and the Function of Abdiel in *Paradise Lost*'. *Modern Philology* 40: 19–42.

HAMILTON, GARY D. 1972. 'Milton's Defensive God: A Reappraisal'. *Studies in Philology* 69: 87–100.

HASKIN, DAYTON. 1994. *Milton's Burden of Interpretation*. Philadelphia: University of Pennsylvania Press.

HONEYGOSKY, STEPHEN RAYMOND. 1993. *Milton's House of God: The Invisible and Visible Church*. Columbia: University of Missouri Press.

IDE, RICHARD S. 1984. 'On the Begetting of the Son in *Paradise Lost*'. *Studies in English Literature* 24: 141–55.

LABRIOLA, ALBERT C. 1981. ' "Thy Humiliation Shall Exalt": The Christology of *Paradise Lost*'.
    Milton Studies 15: 29–42.

LEWIS, C. S. 1942. *A Preface to Paradise Lost*. London: Oxford University Press.

LIEB, MICHAEL. 2002. '*De Doctrina Christiana* and the Question of Authorship'. *Milton Studies*
    41: 172–230.

—— *Theological Milton*. 2006. Pittsburgh: Duquesne University Press.

O'KEEFFE, TIMOTHY J. 1982. *Milton and the Pauline Tradition: A Study of Theme and
    Symbolism*. Washington, DC: University Press of America.

PARK, YOUNGWON. 2000. *Milton and Isaiah: A Journey through the Drama of Salvation in
    'Paradise Lost'*. New York: Peter Lang.

PATRIDES, C. A. 1971. '*Paradise Lost* and Language of Theology', in W. B. Hunter, C. A.
    Patrides, and J. H. Adamson (eds.). *Bright Essence: Studies in Milton's Theology*. Salt Lake
    City: University of Utah Press, 165–78.

REVARD, STELLA P. 1980. *The War in Heaven: 'Paradise Lost' and the Tradition of Satan's
    Rebellion*. Ithaca, NY: Cornell University Press.

ROBINS, HARRY F. 1963. *If This Be Heresy: A Study of Milton and Origen*. Urbana: University of
    Illinois Press.

ROSS, MALCOM M. 1954. *Poetry and Dogma: The Transfiguration of Eucharistic Symbols in
    Seventeenth-Century English Poetry*. New Brunswick, NJ: Rutgers University Press.

SEWELL, ARTHUR. 1939. *A Study in Milton's 'Christian Doctrine'*. London: Oxford University
    Press and Milford.

SHAWCROSS, JOHN T. 1993. *John Milton: The Self and the World*. Lexington: University Press of
    Kentucky.

SHOULSON, JEFFREY S. 2001. *Milton and the Rabbis: Hebraism, Hellenism, and Christianity*.
    New York: Columbia University Press.

SILVER, VICTORIA. 2001. *Imperfect Sense: The Predicament of Milton's Irony*. Princeton:
    Princeton University Press.

SIMS, JAMES H. 1962. *The Bible in Milton's Epics*. Gainesville: University of Florida Press.

—— and LELAND RYKEN (eds.). 1984. *Milton and Scriptural Tradition: The Bible into Poetry*.
    Columbia: University of Missouri Press.

WITTREICH, JOSEPH ANTHONY, Jr. 1986. *Interpreting 'Samson Agonistes'*. Princeton: Princeton
    University Press.

—— 2002. *Shifting Contexts: Reinterpreting 'Samson Agonistes'*. Pittsburgh: Duquesne
    University Press.

YU, ANTHONY C. 1980. 'Life in the Garden: Freedom and the Image of God in *Paradise Lost*'.
    Journal of Religion 60: 247–71.

CHAPTER 26

THE EIGHTEENTH-CENTURY NOVEL

SCOTT ROBERTSON

IT would be an oversimplification to state that the novel was 'born' in the eighteenth century. Nonetheless it is clear that this period provided the socio-economic, cultural, and philosophical conditions wherein this 'new species of writing' could flourish. The restive theological climate of the time with its threatening extremes of enthusiasm and deism (if not the more rare atheism) also coloured the outlook of the pioneer novelists of the time. Reliance upon the providence of God in a world increasingly perceived as unstable served as a major thematic backcloth. In his essay, 'The Depreciated Legacy of Cervantes', the novelist and critic Milan Kundera, makes the following trenchant comment:

As God slowly departed from the seat whence he had directed the universe and its order of values, distinguished good from evil, and endowed each thing with meaning, Don Quixote set forth from his house into a world he could no longer recognise. In the absence of the Supreme Judge, the world suddenly appeared in its fearsome ambiguity; the single divine Truth decomposed into myriad relative truths parcelled out by men. Thus was born the world of the modern era, and with it the novel, the image and model of that world.   (Kundera 1990: 6)

Kundera's contention is that the novel heralded the advent of a new world. But it was no sympathetic herald. The classified world of Leibniz and Newton, the world of determination and rationalization appeared as fearsome as the old order of religion and superstition which it sought to supersede. The novel, as the artistically ambivalent and ambiguous herald to the grand project of progress and enlightenment, endeavoured to temper the optimism of the period. The novel's recognition of the frailness of the human condition and its awareness of the importance of the old stories which had moulded so much of human history were (and are) vital constituents in a form which showed the world its true face. In so doing it offered some sense of security in an environment of increasing diversity and change. The novel, then, holds a dual faceted function. It points to the past, in that it tells stories and it points to the openness of the world by creating worlds of its own. Telling stories honours and continues the tradition of the human propensity to remember. Stories, at their most rudimentary are reflections on existence. They hold within them the seeds of the human spirit. They are our memories writ large. The novel form progresses this tradition in a new and potentially threatening context. This threat is found within the created worlds of the novel. In these worlds readers find themselves. And yet the world remains new and strange.[1] There is indeed a rediscovery of humanity, and yet there is always a horizon that is open to be explored or run away from.

Kundera's assessment of the rise of the novel has merit in that it recognizes both the cultural context within which the novel form arose and the psychological roots from which the novel as an art form draws its energy and power. The common denominator in Kundera's thesis is the denominator par excellence—God, the one in whom all existence has its source. And yet Kundera is distrustful of this heritage. He sees any ideology as a threat to the freedom (for better or worse) which the novel seeks to offer. The novel, he suggests, is not there to argue for a position. That is the role of religion and ideology. As he puts it, 'Man desires a world where good and evil can be clearly distinguished, for he has an innate and irrepressible desire to judge before he understands' (Kundera 1990: 7). The novel, rooted in what Kundera describes as the 'absence of the Supreme Judge', has a different kind of wisdom, namely the wisdom of uncertainty. However, Kundera has exposed a point of tension when he argues that a desire for certainty is innate in the human psyche. I would contend that it is this very tension between the desire for certainty placed alongside the reality of human frailty which is reflected in the rise of the novel, and which, in various ways, is exhibited in the works that will be examined in this chapter.

However, I also believe Kundera has overstated the case at least as far as eighteenth-century England is concerned. Despite the increasingly obvious secularizing agenda it is clear that, as the novel form was in its nascent stages, religion remained a major force. A cursory glance at the publishing history of the eighteenth century would suggest that God appears to be very much present, albeit as yet another player in an increasingly competitive literary market. Brian Young has indicated that the distinction we take for granted between theology and other forms of literature was less pronounced in the time of Defoe or Fielding. He argues that, '[a]lthough long interpreted as an inherently secularizing genre, the eighteenth-century novel was also frequently a form of theological literature' (Rivers 2003: 84). The attitude of the churches and clerics toward romances and other forms of literature obviously varied. The mystic, William Law (1686–1761) would never have countenanced the reading of 'corrupt' texts such as plays, but the substantial figure of William Warburton (1698–1779) lending his weight in favour of the practice, more than compensated. The

---

[1] In a famous essay, 'The Strange New World Within the Bible,' Karl Barth (1928: 28–50) described the Bible in the same way.

ambivalent attitude of the church merely reflected the impossibility of attempting to confine the development of forms of artistic expression that, though grounded in the religious ferment of the late seventeenth and early eighteenth centuries, sought to honour and indeed emulate the erudition of the likes of Virgil, Horace, and Aristophanes.

On a broader scale, the desire to move beyond the destructive internecine conflicts that bedevilled the post-Reformation political sphere promoted a theological atmosphere that, while not devoid of heated rhetoric, leaned more towards dispassionate inquiry and the pursuit of an increasingly rational (and thereby tolerant) basis for faith. The outstanding figure, whose influence in this regard towers over the entire period, was, of course, John Locke (1632–1704). Locke's importance lay primarily in his displacement of the problem of knowledge from the realm of authority to the individual. His *An Essay Concerning Human Understanding* (1690) rejected the long-held notion of 'innate ideas' which impinge upon the mind in favour of experience itself which presents to us the ideas and sensations upon the blank canvas of our minds. This epistemological framework held major implications for theological understanding. If there were no essences where does that leave the notion of revelation, of truth that lies beyond the immediate sense perspective? Locke's new paradigm opened the way to a more reasoned approach to faith. It led, too, to the subsequent theological spats between so-called freethinkers and conservatives.

Locke's fundamentally anthropocentric system provides, then, the philosophical backdrop for the artistic development we now understand as the novel 'whose primary criterion was truth to individual experience—individual experience which is always unique and therefore new' (Watt 2000: 13). As such, the novel becomes an expression of philosophical, theological, and economical individuality in an environment struggling to determine the nature and extent of Providence. In this study we will confine ourselves to four significant authors of the period who, in different ways, exemplify the influence of some or all of these forms of expression and who articulate in fiction their particular attitude towards God's place in the world—a place marked not by 'absence' but by an increasing 'hiddeness'.

Daniel Defoe (1660–1731) was a one-off. His curriculum vitae could itself form the plot of a novel. The wide range of his political, journalistic, and, apparently, clandestine activity served Defoe well when he wished to describe the vagaries of the human traveller, be that the isolated Robinson Crusoe or the worldly wise Moll Flanders. It is, of course, due to the former character that Defoe has made his place in the literary firmament. Ironically, however, this first novel provides us with our greatest interpretative challenge. The fact that Defoe was producing something aesthetically new (or at least was reaching towards that goal) has led to *The Life and Strange Surprizing Adventures of Robinson Crusoe* (1719) becoming something of a critical enigma. In the face of the many competing interpretations of *Robinson Crusoe*, Max Novak is forced to write: 'The variety of structures—spiritual autobiography, traveller's narrative, do-it-yourself utopia, political and economic allegory—fuse into a unity under the realistic surface of the narrative but provide a text that opens itself to a myriad of possible readings' (Richetti 1998: 49). Novak's pessimism aside, there is no mistaking that the development of individual self-consciousness in *Robinson Crusoe* is closely allied to a religious independence which no doubt stemmed from Defoe's own upbringing as a Protestant Dissenter. As Backscheider puts it, '[Defoe's teachers] taught him the revolutionary Protestant idea that God's love gave his people status that no person, no law, could take away' (Backscheider 1989: 16).

One must, however, be careful in conceding purely selfless motives to the religious pronouncements which pepper *Robinson Crusoe*. It is arguable that Defoe's journalistic style is indicative of an acute awareness of the Puritan distaste for fiction. *Robinson Crusoe* sold astonishingly well. The public appetite for spiritual autobiography clearly had a great deal to do with this success. As Rogers (1979: 58) states, 'In 1719 no living Englishman (or woman) could have escaped the power of the religious word; it was the stuff of his culture'. Defoe, political animal that he was, would recognize the importance of maintaining public confidence and it is just possible that in presenting us with such a character, Defoe was simply filling a market need.

I would suggest, however, that *Robinson Crusoe* is more than simply a sop to the market. In a society where possibly a fifth of all children died in their first year and one in three before the age of 5 (Porter 1991: 13) issues such as providence and individual human destiny were almost universally held in sombre focus. In *Robinson Crusoe* we find a conscious, though obviously imperfect, attempt to express such enduring questions of existence. From the Preface, the author makes this abundantly clear stating that he desired to 'justify and honour the Wisdom of Providence'. Defoe had, in fact, already written about disaster some years before *Robinson Crusoe* was published. His work, *The Storm* (1704) describes the events surrounding a natural disaster that struck Britain on 26–7 November 1703 in which around 8,000 people lost their lives. In this work Defoe challenges those who refuse to accept the providence of God in the whole sorry episode.

> I trembl'd as the winds grew high,
> And so did many a braver man than I;
> For he whose valour scorns his sense,
> Has chang'd his courage to impudence.
> Man may to man his valour show,
> And 'tis his virtue to do so;
> But if he's of his Maker not afraid,
> He's not courageous then, but mad.

(The Storm, 414)

Defoe may have had the storm in mind when he writes of that which occurred off the Yarmouth coast in *Robinson Crusoe* (1998: 10–11). Crusoe's response to disaster in all its forms becomes from this point a significant theme in the book and, as a consequence, ought to impact upon our attempts to interpret the work.

Once shipwrecked, Crusoe's 'dismal island' forms an isolated Eden where, ultimately, he not only dominates the land but also learns to discipline his soul, which by this time has become, as Halewood (1964: 346) puts it, 'his antagonist'. Two examples may be offered to support this—first, Robinson's complex repentance, and second, the strange incident when Crusoe's parrot, Poll, speaks to him.

Hunter (1966: 148–9) recognizes that the isolation of Crusoe is a necessary preparatory state for true self-examination. Such isolation, however, also reflects the Puritan emphasis upon the exile of man from the state of blessedness he once enjoyed. The image of Crusoe travelling eastwards from the Brasils to be shipwrecked is suggestive of the exile of Adam to the east of Eden (Gen. 3: 24). Thus Robinson's precarious and lonely position is set before us.

However, the spiritual starkness of Crusoe's situation is not made immediately apparent. Defoe deliberately presents Robinson as a naive, and worldly individual. So, from the ship, 'the instrument of his sin' (ibid. 142), Defoe has Robinson first salvage what he can, but later, as he slowly comes to terms with his situation and begins to establish himself materially, illness overtakes him. Defoe grants Crusoe all the benefits of an abundance of material possessions but then threatens to take away the one material possession of greatest price, his own body. This is the turning point in Crusoe's assessment of his situation. He blindly cries out to God: 'Lord be my Help, for I am in great Distress' (1998: 91). As his health slowly returns to him he begins to muse on the nature of existence and comes to the conclusion that creation presupposes a Creator. Crusoe's next step is to question the purposes of such a Creator in bringing him to such a desolate place. He asks two questions: 'Why has God done this to me? What have I done to be thus us'd?' (ibid. 92) The second question is the one which focuses Crusoe's mind. He recalls his 'dreadful mis-spent Life'. Later, he describes his disobedience toward his father as his 'ORIGINAL SIN', (ibid. 194) an obvious echo of Genesis and of the story of the Prodigal Son.[2] This leads us briefly to assess the odd insertion regarding Poll, the Parrot. Having just returned from his wayward trip on the boat, and lying down in the shade of his 'Country House' (reminiscent of Eden in the cool of the evening), Crusoe hears, as if in a dream, a voice asking the question: 'Where are you?' There is an echo, here, of God's question to Adam in the Garden of Eden following his wayward action in taking the fruit. Like Adam, Crusoe is terrified by the question. The voice not only magnifies Crusoe's sense of isolation (though it may be a device which prefigures the advent of human contact) but also brings into relief Crusoe's precarious hold upon his own spiritual security.

Essentially, Crusoe links his experience of suffering with his spiritual waywardness. His conversion, though in some senses overly stylized, can also be regarded as a significant staging post on his journey to reconcile the perennial conundrum of providence in the face of evil. Robinson sums up his experience thus: 'In a word, as my Life was a Life of Sorrow, one way, so it was a Life of Mercy, another; and I wanted nothing to make it a Life of Comfort, but to be able to make my Sense of God's Goodness to me, and care over me in this Condition' (ibid. 132).

---

[2] Watt and others have emphasized 'the dynamic tendency of capitalism' as the 'real' original sin (Rogers 1979: 61–2). Watt argues that Crusoe actually benefits materially from his enforced isolation. This, of course, ignores the fact that on Crusoe's return to civilization, he has no family to go back to. He is wealthy but remains isolated.

If the epithet 'self-made man' could be applied to Defoe, it would be equally appropriate for Samuel Richardson (1689–1761). Trained as a printer and schooled as a devout Anglican with distinct Puritan leanings, Richardson exemplified the Protestant work ethic and vigorously applied his religion to his work. As a result, we find ourselves increasingly exposed to the deep existential possibilities that the novel form provides. Whereas in *Robinson Crusoe* the nature of existence in the face of suffering is the major but somewhat static subtext, in Richardson's *Pamela* (1740–1) we are confronted with more immediate and dynamic ethical dilemmas. One of the major criticisms of Defoe's novel has been his blatant disregard for Crusoe's nature as a sexual being. Richardson, on the other hand, has sexuality, or more properly, the defence of virtue in a fallen world, at the heart of this, his first novel.

The book was a phenomenal success but the subject matter inevitably led to some criticism. Isaac Watts, for example, whilst thanking Richardson for sending the volumes of *Pamela*, said that the ladies cannot read them without blushing. It was becoming clear that Pamela herself was seen either as an example to all ladies to follow, or as a 'sly minx far less innocent than she appears' (Carroll 1969: 20). The character of Pamela is critical to our assessment of how successful Richardson is in presenting any kind of moral or religious case in the work. There is, however, one significant obstacle in our reaching toward a satisfactory conclusion, namely the novel's epistolary nature.

The dramatic effect that Richardson creates with this technique clearly heightens our sense of intimacy with the characters presented, but what we gain in immediacy we lose in breadth of vision. Indeed, such a constrained position leads to a sense of artlessness concerning, for example, Richardson's portrayal of Mr B.'s reformation (ibid. 25). Ironically, due to this one-sided perspective, one develops a temptation to look down on the virtuous Pamela as a hypocrite. So Littleton (1998: 290) states: 'While Pamela always ascribes her manoeuvres to God's inspiration, the insights with which she counters Mr B's claims tend to create the impression that she succeeds, not by standing on the right ground, but rather by making the ground she stands on the right one.' Similarly, Kearney has argued that Richardson fails to reinforce the power of his own technique by often intruding into the latter part of the work and using Pamela not as a 'sensory sounding-board' but as a moral arbiter (Carroll 1969: 38). Our interpretative strategy then in Richardson, as in Defoe, is preconditioned upon our approach to authorial and aesthetic integrity—a considerable, though not wholly unexpected irony when we attempt to discern the influence of religion upon such works.

Recognizing these difficulties, it is, however, possible to discern certain religious motifs which influence *Pamela*. Chief amongst these is the notion of the Fortunate Fall, the general principle of a tragic descent that ultimately leads to a successful outcome. Thus, emulating the calamity of Joseph in the book of Genesis, Pamela loses her servant position with her mistress and the security such a function entailed. Mr B. subsequently pursues Pamela to the extent of imprisoning her. This confinement lasts forty days, a period of time no doubt reflecting the temptation of Christ in the wilderness. And it is in this period of confinement that Pamela's true feelings about herself and Mr B. are revealed.

Critical to this revelation is Pamela's aborted attempt at suicide in the pond. Pamela, as well as self-indulgently ruminating upon her own funeral, weighs up her present anguish against the possibility that salvation may be near at hand: 'If, despairing of deliverance, I destroy myself, do I not in effect, question the power of the Almighty to deliver me?' (Richardson 1985a: 213) However, through Pamela's resolve to stay the course Providence has mapped out for her, Richardson wishes us to know that, for all Mr B.'s trickery, there is one 'deceitful heart' more treacherous: '[T]hough I should have praised God for my deliverance, had I been freed from my wicked keepers, and my designing master; yet I have more abundant reason to praise him, that I have been delivered from a worse enemy—*Myself*!' (ibid. 214). The heart's fickle nature is a recurring theme in *Pamela* (ibid. 157, 257, 280, 284, 287). It serves a double function in the work. Not only does it entail the straightforward moral assessment of the human condition based on Jer. 17: 9: 'The heart is deceitful above all things, and desperately wicked: who can know it?', but it reveals to us Pamela's own inconsistent feelings toward Mr B. In her confused passion she exclaims: 'O credulous, fluttering, throbbing mischief.' Richardson thereby sanctifies Pamela's moral ambivalence, placing it within the broader scheme of scripturally sanctioned human frailty.

In a letter to Aaron Hill dated 26 January 1746, Richardson bashfully accepts the praise of those 'Friends that complimented my Scribbling as being a New Species of Writing' (Carroll 1964: 78). The 'Scribbling' in question was, of course, to become *Clarissa or The History of a Young Lady* (1747–8), and the friends' assessment was not misplaced. The striking immediacy of the novel, engendered by the same successful epistolary technique as in *Pamela*, lies in the deep psychological portrayal of the main protagonists, the virtuous Clarissa Harlowe and her sexual predator, Robert Lovelace. The immense scope of the work, rich in incidental (some would say pedantic) detail has, paradoxically, a single, largely unreported incident as its heart—the rape of Clarissa. It is this incident, and the individuals affected by it, that has held the attention of contemporary and modern readers alike. The dramatic representation of this act is similar in rhetorical strength to the verse division in John's Gospel where are offered the two words, 'Jesus wept.' Fourteen words from around one million form the critical hub of the novel: 'And now, Belford, I can go no farther. The affair is over. Clarissa lives' (1985b: 883). The brevity of communication serves to accentuate the overwhelming emotional impact of the event. Such, no doubt, was Richardson's intent, and yet he would be less than happy that the presentation of sexuality in the work has, over the years, become the focus of much critical attention. For Richardson primarily saw *Clarissa* not as feminist text but as a 'Religious Novel'. He viewed the state of religion in the country as 'at so low an ebb' and sought to use the novel form as a means to 'do good' (Carroll 1964: 92). The event of the rape, for Richardson, was merely a catalyst to a greater objective, namely the maintenance of Virtue and the promotion of the devout life and holy death. 'Clarissa lives' but only to die.

The common critical thread that has run through subsequent readings of *Clarissa* can be broadly defined as a response to the issues of sex, suffering, and redemption. Through Clarissa's opposition to the clear wishes of her avaricious family, and her subsequent fall into the clutches of the voracious Lovelace, leading to her slow, triumphant journey to the grave, Richardson is pointing his audience to the perils and rewards on offer to those who aim to preserve honour and virtue in the face of an increasingly ungodly society.[3] In the words of Bechler, *Clarissa* sought 'to express in fiction a profound fundamentalist reaction against the rational and pragmatic tendencies of the age' (Myer 1986: 94).

Clarissa's determination to retain her virginity, however, goes beyond being merely indicative of eighteenth-century social mores. Her virginity defines who she is. It is the loss of this which precipitates both Clarissa's increasing religious awareness (or, as some would argue, mania) and her psychological and physical decline. Richardson thus provides us with a curious Protestant 'Virgin' martyr. Clarissa's sexuality is linked with spiritual purity. The purging of defilement, a Catholic notion, is reproduced by the Protestant Richardson in the body of Clarissa as a means to rekindle the spiritual passions.

The suffering that Clarissa endures is therefore not simply confined to the rape itself. The *History* is a total encapsulation of a life increasingly tormented from all quarters. Those, like Lady Bradshaigh, who wished for a more tender, physical resolution missed Richardson's aim, which is to point to suffering as a means to redemption. In his response to such criticism, Richardson outlines his own extensive experience of suffering (he had already buried his first wife and no less than six sons and two daughters) and poignantly concludes: 'From these affecting Dispensations, will you not allow me, Madam, to remind an unthinking World, immersed in Pleasures, what a Life this is of which they are so fond? And to endeavour to arm them against the most affecting Changes and Chances of it?' (Carroll 1964: 110). Richardson defends his own 'trial' of Clarissa on the grounds that she, subsequent to her deflowering, increasingly embodies those moral and religious sensibilities grounded in and proved by suffering. She has been refined in the fire and achieves the only reward possible—beatification.

This spiritual resolution in a holy death evokes the devotional writings of John Tillotson, Roberts South, and John Sharp—all found in Clarissa's library. (Richardson, himself, was close to William Law.) Clarissa spends one-third of the novel moving towards death, perhaps imitative of a similar mathematical division in St John's Gospel regarding the last week of Christ's life which, of course, culminates in the cross. In what Peggy Thompson describes as 'theological alchemy' the sufferings of Clarissa's life are transformed into a state of heavenly bliss. Following in the sacrificial footsteps of Christ becomes, then, the overarching metaphor for Clarissa's life and as such it is not a life wasted. So we hear the words of Lovelaces's erstwhile friend, Belford:

---

[3] In his postscript to *Clarissa*, Richardson (1985*b*: 1495) makes it clear what his religious motivation has been when he says his is 'a work which is to inculcate upon the human mind, under the guise of an amusement, the great lessons of Christianity'.

What a fine subject for tragedy would the injuries of this lady, and her behaviour under them, both with regard to her implacable friends and to her persecutor, make! With a grand objection as to the moral, nevertheless; for here virtue is punished! Except indeed we look forward to the rewards of HERAFTER, which, morally, *she* must be sure of, or who can?

(Richardson 1985*b*: 1205)

Henry Fielding (1707–54) hated *Pamela* and satirized both its content and style with his own *Shamela* (1741)—but he much admired *Clarissa*. These contrasting reactions betray to us a little of the dual-faceted nature of Fielding's own religious sensibilities and his approach to the novel, which he, as God of his own literary universe, described as his 'great Creation' (Fielding 1995: 10. 1. 337). Fielding abhorred hypocrisy, particularly when connected with religion. Yet, at the same time, he had a moral astuteness which recognized (and indeed, in his early novels, celebrated) rather than dismissed human frailty. He had little time for the outward trappings of religion. This is exemplified most clearly in the clerical dress of Parson Adams, the true hero of *Joseph Andrews* (1742). Adams, in this work is repeatedly presented to us as 'dishevelled' (Fielding 1999: 1. 16. 107). But his careless dress-sense has a moral purpose because it exposes the cleric's innocence and goodness of heart. Fielding describes him thus: 'He was a Man of good Sense, good Parts, and good Nature, but was at the same time as entirely ignorant of the Ways of this World, as an infant just entered into it could possibly be' (ibid. 1. 3. 65).[4]

Adams thus comes to us as a holy fool, but only in the sense that he exhibits none of the censoriousness which Fielding found distasteful amongst many of the clergy. Adams, because of his own weaknesses, his shy vanity, and his blindness to the true wiles of saint and sinner alike, shines as a Christlike figure. Covered in pig's blood, and following a fight with a surly innkeeper, Adams proclaims: 'Sir, I am far from accusing you' (ibid. 2. 5. 146). The ridiculous nature of the event hides the vital assessment of Adams' engagement with the world—one who is ready to fight and equally ready to forgive.[5] Such earthy spirituality contrasts markedly with the hypocritical Parson Barnabas who, when questioned by the apparently dying Joseph as to the nature of forgiveness, mumbles: 'That is . . . to forgive them as—as—it is to forgive them as—in short, it is to forgive them as a Christian' (ibid. 1. 13. 96).

There is, then, an abiding sense in Fielding's work that religious profession and professional religion are most definitely held in an instructive dynamic tension. Though clearly a conservative, Fielding understood the temptation faced by the establishment to avoid its moral responsibilities and simply rely on the superficial aspects of their position. In *Tom Jones* (1749) the classic and dramatic example in this regard is the conversation held between Squire Western, Parson Thwackum, and Mr Square the tutor. This discussion follows the incident of the bird in Book 4 which itself serves as the novel's parabolic heart (Fielding 1995: 4. 3, 4. 4). Tom's gift of the

---

[4] Paulson (1996: 112) also sees the crab-stick which Adams carries as 'the physical manifestation of the religion that is required to substantiate good nature'.

[5] In this regard, Weinstein argues that Adams functions 'as a catalyst who brings out into the open the wide spectrum of affectation and hypocrisy which Fielding aims to expose' (Weinstein 1981: 115).

bird, emblematic of a fledgling love, is received by Sophia with greater joy than that with which it is offered. The subsequent betrayal of trust by Blifil and reckless pursuit of 'Tommy' by Tom sets in relief the contrast between blatant self-regard, even narcissism, and the honest, good-natured search for one's true place in the world. Tom literally goes out on a limb that he might reach the prize. It is this recklessness which Fielding wishes to extol. Thwackum and Square in their subsequent puerile discussion regarding revelation and the laws of nature completely miss the point that Squire Western sees only too clearly.[6] Regarding the actions of Blifil, he exclaims: 'Drink about, (says *Western*) Pox of your Laws of Nature. I don't know what you mean either of you, by Right or Wrong. To take away my Girl's Bird was wrong in my Opinion, and my Neighbour *Allworthy* may do as he pleases, but to encourage Boys in such practices is to breed them up to the Gallows' (4. 4. 106). And of Tom, Western has this to say: 'It may be learning and sense for aught I know; but you shall never persuade me to it. Pox! you have neither of you mentioned a word of that poor lad who deserves to be commended. To venture breaking his neck to oblige my girl was a generous-spirited action; I have learning enough to see that' (ibid. 4. 4. 108). The dual defence of the ill-mannered Blifil by Thwackum and Square, and their attack upon the innocent Tom, both serve to illustrate the vacuity of their respective positions. They may have the respective status of divine and philosopher, but, according to Fielding, neither share any of the moral authority one would assume ought to reside in such offices. Thwackum, the representative of redundant, merciless religion is clearly a figure set up to be attacked. Fielding sums him up thus: 'Thwackum was for doing Justice, and leaving Mercy to Heaven' (ibid. 3. 10. 97). He becomes emblematic of Fielding's famous definition of religion as a 'word of no meaning; but which serves as a bugbear to frighten children with' (Goldgar 1988: 38). In a further double assault, he declares: 'Had not Thwackum too much neglected virtue, and Square, religion, in the composition of their systems; and had not both utterly disregarded all natural goodness of heart, they had never been represented as the objects of derision in this history' (ibid. 3. 4. 85). Towards the end of the work, we discover that Square, on his deathbed, converts to Christianity (ibid. 18. 4. 602). However, there is no such meekness in the heart of Thwackum, and this only serves to highlight what, for Fielding (1972: 4), was the worst of crimes, namely hypocrisy—the 'Bane of all Virtue, Morality, and Goodness'. The rational Square is redeemed but the religious Thwackum is not.

Battestin (1959: 70) concludes that, for Fielding, 'Good nature is thus instinctive and independent of the dictates of philosophy and religion, though it is ultimately incomplete without the latter'. In this regard, it is important to take seriously Fielding's (1999: 49) own description of what he was trying to do in *Tom Jones*; he viewed his work as a 'comic epic-poem in prose'. This was not merely a technical description distinguishing his new form of writing from so-called serious Romance (Richardson and Fielding wished to distance themselves from the 'novel' as it was

---

[6] Rosengarten (2000: 67) comments: 'In Thwackum and Square, *Tom Jones* dramatizes in miniature the deism controversy. Divine and desist claim to argue from revelation and reason, respectively.'

understood, preferring the more substantial term, 'history'); it encapsulated Fielding's Latitudinarian outlook. Prior to *Tom Jones*, Fielding had already entered his philosophy into print with *An Essay on the Knowledge of the Characters of Men* (1743), where we find: 'Good nature is that benevolent and amiable temper of mind, which disposes us to feel the misfortunes, and enjoy the happiness of others; and, consequently, pushes us on to promote the latter, and prevent the former; and that without any abstract contemplation on the beauty of virtue, and without the allurements or terrors of religion' (Irwin 1967: 12). In *Tom Jones*, human nature, Fielding (1995: 1. 1. 25) assures us, is the sole focus of our attention. Good nature is that positive aspect of the human character which Fielding wishes to promote literally in the character of Tom Jones. Tom is the vehicle through which Fielding can present his philosophy to a public falling between the two extremes of atheism and enthusiasm.[7] Fielding's middle way attempts to acknowledge the limitations on the human spirit which the atheist and the enthusiast for differing reasons choose to ignore. His is the messy world of well-meaning people getting it wrong. As Damrosch (1985: 270) puts it, 'In Richardson's world you are either defiled or pure. In Fielding's world there are a few great sinners, not many saints, and a wide range of mortals in between'. The true genius of Fielding is that, in criticizing those who are driven by adherence to a particular system that reduces the status of the individual, he does not thereby wish to substitute yet another system. His Latitudinarian leanings encouraged him to recognize and rejoice in the glaringly obvious fallibility of life. The purpose behind all this is that Fielding, as Allen (1991: 63) succinctly puts it, 'is showing the age its face'. Thus Paulson (1996: 102) concludes that, for Fielding, 'The validity of religion is based less on whether it is true or false than on whether it fulfils a social function.'

We have already noted that the outwardly saintly Blifil is, in reality, the darkest of characters in the work. By exposing Blifil, 'the most perfectly political individual in the novel' (Richetti 1999a: 139),[8] for the shallow cad he truly is, Fielding is exposing the threat to society posed by those who, regardless of social position, have no time for benevolence and share no sympathy with their fellows.[9] It is therefore not systems per se, but those individuals within such systems that give cause for concern. Irwin (1967: 21) has noted that, for Fielding, 'any malaise in society can be no more than the sum total of its symptoms'. Fielding's earlier dismissal from the theatre courtesy of Walpole's Licensing Act of 1737, confirmed to him the destructive potential 'at all levels of society, of unconditioned and therefore tyrannical power' (Allen 1991: 54).

The purpose of existence in such a fallible and potentially threatening world is essentially to do the best one can. The greatest expression of this well-meaning

---

[7] See Allworthy's speech, 'Nothing less than a persuasion of universal depravity can lock up the charity of a good man; and this persuasion must lead him, I think into atheism, or enthusiasm' (Fielding 1995: 2. 5. 64).

[8] Mutter sees the name Blifil as an anagram of 'ill fib' (Fielding 1995: Introduction, p. xix). Paulson (1996: 118), somewhat strangely, notices that 'Blifil' rhymes with 'Devil'.

[9] Richetti (1999b: 39) argues that 'the entire plot of the novel rests not just on the personal histories of these characters but on their exploitation and negotiation within the ideology surrounding the country house and the patron–client system'.

behaviour is the pursuit of wisdom, or prudence.[10] The individual blessed with good nature will, however falteringly, actively seek this Holy Grail. So we find ourselves with the basic plot of *Tom Jones*, namely the innocent and equally fallible Tom in pursuit of experience, of prudence, of Wisdom, of Sophia (Battestin 1968: 209).[11] Fielding, therefore, presents to us in the comic/tragic method he practised only too well in the theatre, the fragility of human relationships. Such fragile treasures are worth extolling, and in Tom's pursuit of Sophia we are shown the true cost of such glories. Tom must leave Paradise in order to find it again. So Tom, the 'bastard', leaves Allworthy, the flawed sage and Tom's only true object of affection, in order that he might secure his Sophia and return the prudent heir. Miller (1975: 269) reaches to the heart of the matter when he states:

> Despite, or perhaps because of, Fielding's full sceptical recognition that fallen man—take him all in all—is an ambiguous being, not very strongly deserving of the love of his equally dubious fellows... the persistent emphasis of *Tom Jones* is upon love, the need for love, the necessity of love, both as a freely offered gift and as a jewel worth striving for.

So we witness in *Tom Jones* an emphasis upon practical morality rather than religious determinism. As one scholar has it, for Fielding, '[p]rovidence is not banished, but displaced from this world to the next' (Rosengarten 2000: 92). Fielding remained a good Anglican, but like all good Anglicans he didn't wish to shout about it.

Scampering in the magisterial footsteps of both Richardson and Fielding (writers who had in their contrasting ways effectively set the literary standard for serious works of fiction), there appeared a novel which, at one stroke, set aside that very same standard and redefined how the genre could be produced and apprehended. The cosy world of a closed, providential system as a result became increasingly exposed to the elements. Laurence Sterne's *The Life and Opinions of Tristram Shandy* (1759) from the outset defied the critics who attempted to define it. The question: 'What is *Tristram Shandy*?' has been variously answered by those who view it as merely morally deficient,[12] as a 'genuinely moral work' (Sterne 1998: p. x), as a comment on the indolence of the upper classes (Richetti 1999a: 272) or as an extraordinary precursor to the 'stream of consciousness' fiction of the early twentieth century (Stedmond 1959: 48). Critical agreement is apparently only to be found in the recognition that *Tristram Shandy* is truly one of a kind, and as 'one of the most boldly experimental novels ever conceived' (Dyson 1962: 309).

It has also been duly noted that Locke plays an influential role in *Tristram Shandy*. Locke's *Essay* is explicitly referred to in the novel, and one of its major premises—the

---

[10] 'Prudence and circumspection are necessary even to the best of men' (Fielding 1995: 3. 8. 121). Rosengarten (2000: 76) sees prudence as a neutral quality in Fielding's work, pointing out that Blifil is the most prudent character in *Tom Jones*.

[11] 'Ultimately, her [Sophia's] true identity is ideal, an abstraction' (Battestin 1968: 209). Rosengarten (2000: 77), due to his belief in the neutrality of prudence, disagrees.

[12] Samuel Richardson himself described *Tristram Shandy* as 'disgustful nonsense', in a letter to Mark Hildesley reprinted in *Tristram Shandy*, ed. Howard Anderson (New York: W. W. Norton, 1980), 483, and Leavis (1972: 10) saw it as 'nasty'.

apprehension of reality being based upon sensation—reverberates throughout. Sterne, however, uses the empiricist for his own ends. Locke's theory is placed alongside many of Walter Shandy's odd notions, and Sterne allows us to see how it fares in the Shandean world. In so doing Sterne immediately questions the apparent orderly perception of reality which Locke wishes to present. The account of Tristram's conception, for example, is amusing because it relates timeless psychical experience to the temporal world. The building up of association upon association around this event marks out Tristram. He is the Cain of *Tristram Shandy*, whose mark indicates nothing less than the chaos of human experience, and who is condemned to wander virtually anonymously throughout the work. Sterne is acutely aware of the lie he is telling in presenting the history of Tristram. Sterne introduces a sermon on the Prodigal Son thus:

I know not whether the remark is to our honour or otherwise, that lessons of wisdom have never such power over us, as when they are wrought in the heart, through the groundwork of a story which engages the passions: Is it that we are like iron, and must first be heated before we can be wrought upon? or, Is the heart so in love with deceit, that where a true report will not reach it, we must cheat it with a fable, in order to come at truth?   (Sterne 1973: 94)

Sterne, the preacher, recognizes the power of the fable to communicate the truth. This communication is constituted not so much upon the veracity of facts, but upon a sensibility that is inculcated in the heart of the reader or listener. What he understands so well is that reception of reality is not necessarily an orderly process.

A number of early (and influential) readers did not altogether appreciate the significance of what Sterne was wishing to achieve, namely the presentation of immediate and affecting (as well as amusing) sensation. Johnson dismissed the work as 'odd', George Whitefield allegedly thought Sterne 'scabby', and Horace Walpole found it hard to fathom how a clergyman such as Sterne could produce the commendable sermon on conscience and yet surround it with such bawdiness.

However, it was just such a linkage that brought many others into contact with a subject not normally close to their hearts—religion. This is not to suggest that Sterne has a purely didactic or evangelical motive for *Tristram Shandy*. His prime motivation (other than wishing to be famous) centres around his belief 'that every time a man smiles,—but much more so when he laughs, it adds something to this fragment of life'. These words, from his bold dedication of *Tristram Shandy* (to William Pitt of all people) testify to two key elements in Sterne's writing. He is well aware of the fragility and bittiness of life, yet he is conscious, too, of the human need to bring, however fleetingly, order from chaos. This order is brought about by the unlikely means of the hobby horse. It is through these passionate escape routes from the present that he paradoxically clarifies the world. But of course, as one would expect in *Tristram Shandy*, these passions collide.

Thus we discover the genial and innocent Uncle Toby (with the aid of the faithful Trim) recreating his military experiences in an attempt to recapture his own past and bring purpose to his disorientating present. In a similar vein Walter, Tristram's father, has his own means of facing the world—he looks at it through the lens of antiquated textbooks. Put simply, Uncle Toby is all heart whilst Walter is all head. Tristram, himself, becomes no more than one of Sterne's ciphers of the tenuousness of human existence—his is an existence surrounded by abstraction, distraction, and confusion. He continually fails to get himself born when, in fact, he is the supposed eponymous author. He is a comma. And the moment where we find true corporality in Tristram is either when he is having his nose threatened or when, with the help of a window, he virtually emasculates himself.

What brings about order amongst such chaos is Sterne's belief in experience and his experience of belief. It is experience, however ludicrous and petty, that he offers us in *Tristram Shandy*. But it is offered in the belief that we will laugh because we have faith in the experience Sterne presents, and in the God who 'is the great author and bestower of wit and judgement' (Sterne 1998: 3. 20. 153). In *Tristram Shandy* we are justified by faith in wit and we smile at the judgements of life.

By all accounts Sterne was a gifted and popular preacher. This in itself leads us to recognize a further aspect of Sterne's authorial style. He is a seducer. In a similar vein to Fielding, Sterne intrudes from time to time upon his reader. However, his purpose is less to exhibit erudition and knowledge of the classics as to inculcate a sensibility, an awareness of both the ridiculous and the sublime aspects of human existence. His method of seduction involves recognition of the need for trust. As an author he is, in *Tristram Shandy*, coming alongside us a companion, a fellow traveller. This reassuring presence is required because frequently throughout the work Sterne deliberately leaves us in the dark about what exactly is going on in his world. Unlike Fielding's orderly 'Creation', Sterne's scatological digressions and interruptions, as well as promoting amusement, also engender a sense of anxiety. This tension between the comic and the concerning reflects the sensibility of normal lived experience. Life is profound and petty, sensuous and silly, Pollyanna-ish and pointless. It is all these things and more. And the fact that it is such a contrary, confused and, at times, calamitous experience testifies to just how well observed *Tristram Shandy* is.

The importance of this understanding of sensibility is exhibited most clearly in the sermon on good conscience. It is delivered not by a clergyman but by Corporal Trim, a factor which points to Sterne's desire to further destabilize the traditional sphere of religious and moral instruction and as a result enhance the theoretical possibility of a more positive response. Trim, like the man of the people, Jesus of Nazareth, pro-claims his Sermon on the Mount to an expectant crowd—the Shandy brothers and Dr. Slop. What happens? In a word, chaos—and ultimately in the case of the Roman Catholic Dr. Slop, catatonia. The sermon is exploded by each listener according to the particular hobby horse they happen to be riding. The resulting epistemological anarchy reinforces the truth that all association is, by definition, *free* association. Such liberation is, however, double edged. The joyous comedic chaos of *Tristram Shandy* reveals that there can be no fixed apprehensions. Even that form of commu-nication which we think ought to provide stability and guidance, i.e. the sermon, falls at the same interpretative hurdle. As a result, notions such as Providence become victims in Sterne's time-exploded world of immediate sensation.

The emergence of the novel as a recognizable art form took place in a theological climate which had moved beyond the traditional and, some would say, arid meta-physical speculations of previous generations. The desire for rational debate rather than heretic bloodletting did not however, completely disguise, the tensions which exercised the eighteenth-century mindset. God was indeed in his heaven, but on terra firma the wheels, not only of industry, but also of enlightenment, were gradually turning.[13] The place of the individual in this world was increasingly a focus of legitimate exploration. Thus we have Pope (1905: 25) intone:

> Know, then, thyself, presume not God to scan;
> The proper study of mankind is man.

Consequently, we have been able to trace in our study a slow but steady movement in the presentation of the place of the divine. From the somewhat artless representation of providence in the work of Defoe, through Richardson's world as a proving ground of suffering and redemption, we have journeyed towards an altogether less secure location. Fielding attempts to reassure us with his Shaftesburian morality that all is well. However, notwithstanding his instinctive conservatism, he suspects that the theological assumptions of the past cannot now be taken completely for granted. Providence in his hands is presented as little more than ethical and sociological determination. Fielding intervention replaces divine intervention. Sterne goes even further by demolishing time itself, leaving us floundering for sense, be it human or divine. It is, however, in the floundering that he wishes us to see where life is truly lived. This is exemplified most clearly in his description of how *Tristram Shandy*, itself, comes to be written: 'That of all the several ways of beginning a book which are now in practice throughout the known world, I am confident my own way of doing it is the best—I'm sure it is the most religious—for I begin with writing the first sentence—and trusting to Almighty God for the second' (Sterne 1998: 435–6). The eighteenth-century novel, in the hands of these four great writers, illustrates for us, then, the increasing hiddenness of God and becomes, as a result, the precursor of greater secularization on the literary horizon.

WORKS CITED

ALLEN, WALTER. 1991. *The English Novel*. London: Penguin.

BACKSCHEIDER, PAULA. 1989. *Daniel Defoe: His Life*. Baltimore: Johns Hopkins University Press.

BARTH, KARL. 1928. 'The Strange New World Within the Bible', in *The Word of God and the Word of Man*. London: Hodder & Stoughton.

---

[13] The vexed question as to what actually constituted 'enlightenment' need not concern us here; suffice it to say that it appears reasonable to offer, as Porter (2000: p. xxi) does, a less confining understanding of the term. It was a sensibility rather than a movement.

BATTESTIN, MARTIN C. 1959. *The Moral Basis of Fielding's Art*. Middleton, Conn.: Wesleyan University Press.

—— 1968. 'Fielding's Definition of Wisdom: Some Functions of Ambiguity and Emblem in *Tom Jones*', *English Literary History* 35. Baltimore: Johns Hopkins University Press.

CARROLL JOHN (ed.) 1964. *Selected Letters of Samuel Richardson*. Oxford: Clarendon.

—— (ed.) 1969. *Samuel Richardson*. Englewood Cliffs, NJ: Prentice-Hall.

DAMROSCH LEOPOLD Jr. 1985. *God's Plot and Man's Stories*. Chicago: University of Chicago Press.

DEFOE, DANIEL. 1855. *The Storm: An Essay in The Novels and Miscellaneous Works of Daniel Defoe*. London: Henry G. Bohn.

—— 1998. *Robinson Crusoe*, ed. J. Donald Crowley. Oxford: Oxford University Press.

DYSON, A. E. 1962. 'Sterne: The Novel as Jester', *Critical Quarterly* IV, 309–20.

FIELDING, HENRY. 1972. *Miscellanies*, i, ed. Henry Knight Miller. Oxford: Oxford University Press.

—— 1995. *Tom Jones*, ed. Sheridan Baker. New York: W. W. Norton.

—— 1999. *Joseph Andrews*, ed. Judith Hawley. London: Penguin.

GOLDGAR, BERTRAND. 1988. *The Covent Garden Journal and A Plan of the Universal Register Office*. Oxford: Oxford University Press.

HALEWOOD, WILLIAM H. 1964. 'Religion and Invention in *Robinson Crusoe*'. *Essays in Criticism* 14.

HUNTER, PAUL J. 1966. *The Reluctant Pilgrim*. Baltimore: Johns Hopkins University Press.

IRWIN, MICHAEL. 1967. *Fielding: The Tentative Realist*. Oxford: Clarendon.

KUNDERA, MILAN. 1990. *The Art of the Novel*. London: Faber & Faber.

LEAVIS, F. R. 1972. *The Great Tradition*. Harmondsworth: Pelican.

LITTLETON, JACOB. 1998. 'My Treacherous Heart'. *Eighteenth Century Fiction* 10.

MILLER, HENRY KNIGHT. 1975. 'The 'Digressive' Tales in Fielding's *Tom Jones* and the Perspective of Romance', *Philological Quarterly* 54.

MYER, VALERIE GROSVENOR (ed.) 1996. *Samuel Richardson: Passion and Prudence*. London: Vision.

PAULSON, RONALD. 1996. *The Beautiful, Novel, and Strange*. Baltimore: Johns Hopkins University Press.

POPE, ALEXANDER. 1905. *Essay on Man Epistle II*. London: Cassell.

PORTER, ROY. 1991. *English Society in the Eighteenth Century*. London: Penguin.

—— 2000. *Enlightenment*. London: Penguin.

RICHARDSON, SAMUEL. 1985a. *Pamela*, ed. Margaret A. Doody. London: Penguin.

—— 1985b. *Clarissa*, ed. Angus Ross. London: Penguin.

RICHETTI, JOHN (ed.) 1998. *The Cambridge Companion to the Eighteenth Century Novel*. Cambridge: Cambridge University Press.

—— 1999a. *The English Novel in History*. London: Routledge.

—— 1999b. 'Fielding's *Tom Jones*', *Ideology and Form in Henry Eighteenth Century Literature* Lubbock: Texas Technical University Press.

RIVERS, ISABEL (ed.) 2003. *Books and Their Readers in Eighteenth-Century England: New Essays*. London: Continuum.

ROGERS, PAT. 1979. *Robinson Crusoe*. London: George Allen & Unwin.

ROSENGARTEN, RICHARD A. 2000. *Henry Fielding and the Narration of Providence*. New York: Palgrave.

STEDMOND, JOHN M. 1959. 'Genre and *Tristram Shandy*'. *Philological Quarterly* 38.

STERNE, LAURENCE. 1973. *The Sermons of Mr. Yorick*, ed. Marjorie David. Cheadle: Carcanet.

—— 1998. *Tristram Shandy*, ed. Ian Campbell Ross. Oxford: Oxford University Press.

WATT, IAN. 2000. *The Rise of the Novel.* London: Pimlico.

WEINSTEIN, ARNOLD. 1981. *Fictions of the Self: 1550–1800.* Princeton: Princeton University Press.

FURTHER READING

BOOTH, WAYNE C. 1983. *The Rhetoric of Fiction.* London: Penguin.

DAVIS, LENNARD J. 1987. *Resisting Novels: Ideology and Fiction.* New York: Methuen.

EAGLETON, TERRY. 2005. *The English Novel: An Introduction.* Oxford: Blackwell.

HUNTER, J. PAUL. 1990. *Before Novels: The Cultural Contexts of Eighteenth Century English Fiction.* New York: Norton.

MCKEON, MICHAEL. 1987. *The Origins of the English Novel 1600–1740.* Baltimore: Johns Hopkins University Press.

MCKILLOP, ALAN DUGALD. 1956. *The Early Masters of English Fiction.* Lawrence: University of Kansas Press.

SAMBROOK, JAMES. 1993. *The Eighteenth Century: The Intellectual and Cultural Context of English Literature 1700–1789.* London: Longman.

SKINNER, JOHN. 2001. *An Introduction to Eighteenth-Century Fiction: Raising the Novel.* London: Palgrave.

CHAPTER 27

....

WILLIAM BLAKE

....

CHRISTOPHER BURDON

The labour of that celebrant of Energy and the Prolific, William Blake (1757–1827), has itself generated an energetic and prolific diversity of interpretation. Though little known to his contemporaries and largely forgotten after his death, Blake's huge output of art and poetry inspired a range of twentieth-century readers who drew from him or read into him principles democratic and aristocratic, libertarian and nationalist, activist and quietist, Christian, Gnostic, and atheist. Blake can be held accountable for this confusion. A consistent rebel against the political, religious, and cultural regime under which he lived, he resisted it sometimes by direct and prophetic aphorisms, sometimes by verse of disarming simplicity or 'innocence', but at other times by engravings of extreme obscurity and complexity—emulating Erin's lament in his triumphant poem *Jerusalem* that 'deep dissimulation is the only defence an honest man has left' (*J* 49: 23).[1]

Divergent estimations of how, when, and why Blake dissimulates, of what are the origins and the aims of his obscurity, are the cause of the wildly conflicting range of ideologies he is said to propound and of causes for which he is purloined. Blake's alter ego, the prophetic builder Los, notoriously proclaims,

> I must Create a System, or be enslav'd by another Mans
> I will not Reason & Compare: my business is to create.
>
> (*J* 10. 20–1)

---

[1] All quotations from Blake are from Erdman's edition. References to the engraved books are to the plate and line; those to *The Four Zoas* to page and line, following Erdman's numeration in both cases; those to other works to the page number in Erdman (= E). Individual works are abbreviated thus: *A* = *America*; *BU* = *The Book of Urizen*; *EG* = 'The Everlasting Gospel'; *FZ* = *Vala, or The Four Zoas*; *J* = *Jerusalem*; *M* = *Milton*; *MHH* = *The Marriage of Heaven and Hell*; *SIE* = *Songs of Innocence and Experience*; *VDA* = *Visions of the Daughters of Albion*; *VLJ* = 'A Vision of the Last Judgment'.

Through his 'Poetic Genius' and laborious mode of production Blake the antinomian visionary indeed constructed an increasingly systematic mythopoeia, one which resists elucidation. Yet it purports to be a redemptive system, progressing towards 'The End of The Dream' in his confused and uncompleted epic *The Four Zoas*, when

> The war of swords departed now
> The dark Religions are departed & sweet Science reigns
>
> (*FZ* 139. 9–10)

or towards the climax of his *Jerusalem*, both organized and liberative, when

> The Four Living Creatures Chariots of Humanity Divine Incomprehensible
> In beautiful Paradises expand These are the Four Rivers of Paradise
> And the Four Faces of Humanity fronting the Four Cardinal Points
> Of Heaven going forward forward irresistible from Eternity to Eternity
>
> (*J* 98. 24–7)

Can such a 'System' ever serve or become systematic *theology*? J. G. Davies's *The Theology of William Blake*—a concept and title which would have incurred vigorous protest from the poet—was an informed, valiant, but ultimately unsuccessful attempt to read Blake according to the traditional categories of Christian theology. Davies analysed Blake's 'doctrine of God', his 'doctrine of Christ and redemption', his 'doctrine of man', and his 'ethics', presenting the poet as a sincere but anticlerical Christian (Davies 1948). Certainly Blake is *not* dissimulating when he calls himself a Christian: 'I still & shall to Eternity Embrace Christianity and Adore him who is the Express image of God', he writes in 1802 to Thomas Butts (E 720). Indeed, apart from some revivalist hymns, his is perhaps the most Christocentric poetry ever written in English, and the prominence in his later work of Jesus and of that Saviour's effect in human history cast doubt on the attempts by other scholars—such as Kathleen Raine and Harold Bloom—to read him gnostically or psychoanalytically. But undoubtedly he was, in terms of Christian tradition, not just eccentric but heretical. More convincing than Raine's esoteric Gnostic or Davies's mildly unorthodox Christian is Thomas Altizer's prophet of the death of God, who 'created a whole new form of vision embodying a modern radical and spiritual expression of Christianity' demanding 'a new form of theological understanding' (Altizer 1967: p. xi). Perhaps mediating between such positions is the more historical argument of Robert Ryan that Blake (and other 'Romantic' poets) proclaimed a new religious reformation restoring the spirit of Jesus to a disenchanted world (Ryan 1997: 43–79).

Rather than 'create a system' into which to insert Blake's 'theology', my aim will first be to reflect on *how* this difficult poet-artisan-prophet-artist can be read theologically. I will then examine particular motifs, symbols, and beliefs in Blake and consider how these might inform or subvert Christian and other theologies today.

SEEING, HEARING, AND THINKING BLAKE

Blake's work causes offence to the theological thinker most obviously by its visionary and even authoritarian bent. However transcendent their ultimate subject, theologians are generally trained to think critically and rationally. But for Blake, the *krisis* or judgement is not detached reflection but the actual experience of living, reading, creating, and desiring; the *ratio* or Reason is not the supreme method of thought but an oppressive or death-dealing denial of God, epitomized in the unholy trinity of Bacon, Newton, and Locke. Blake does indeed raise the intellectual or spiritual world above that perceived by the senses, 'the things of Vegetative and Generative Nature' (*VLJ*; E 555), and can be called an insistently dialectical thinker. But his dialectic is 'Mental Fight', and its outcome not demonstrated Truth but the apocalyptic praxis of 'Brotherhood', even 'an improvement of sensual enjoyment' (*M* 1; *MHH* 14). Moreover, the dominant theological strands in the Abrahamic religions have been sceptical of vision and prophecy, especially when these are put forward by a lay artisan: authority rests in Scripture interpreted by institutional tradition. But Blake is insistent on his own vision, which is both personal and cosmic, which uses Christian Scripture as its fulcrum but radically rewrites that Scripture. He does not expound law, gospel, and prophecy. Instead, in his 'Bible of Hell' he 'stamps the stony law to dust', re-presents the gospel of Jesus as antinomian liberty, and dines with Isaiah and Ezekiel on equal terms (*MHH* 25; 23; 12). He is his own prophet, not the exegete of others' wisdom, and he writes his own scripture.

Milton is the work which most insistently explores the poet's own vocation and authority, and near its beginning—significantly seven times over, like the trumpets of the Apocalypse—the poet arrogates the rhetoric of prophet, Bible, and church to proclaim in his own voice, 'Mark well my words! they are of your eternal salvation' (*M* 2–11). 'The Bard', whose song occupies a large part of *Milton* Book 1 and who is both Milton and Blake, asserts uncompromisingly the divine authority of the poet-prophet's words, in a manner bound to engender scepticism in the critical theological mind:

> I am Inspired! I know it is Truth! For I Sing
> According to the inspiration of the Poetic Genius
> Who is the eternal all-protecting Divine Humanity
> To whom be Glory & Power & Dominion Evermore Amen
>
> (*M* 13. 51–14: 3)

On plate 15 of the poem, Milton falls on and enters Blake's left foot, the younger poet taking on his mantle and inspiration to redeem and perfect his mentor's work. Later, on plate 22, the eternal prophetic 'zoa' Los encounters and inhabits the London engraver even more intimately and authoritatively:

> . . . trembling I stood
> Exceedingly with fear & terror, standing in the Vale
> Of Lambeth: but he kissed me and wishd me health.

And I became One Man with him arising in my strength:
Twas too late now to recede. Los had enterd into my soul:
His terrors now posses'd me whole! I arose in fury and strength

(*M* 22 [24]. 9–14)

There follow from Los's lips a proclamation of prophetic authority and from his hands the ceaseless labour of artistic creation—in a Lambeth workshop, in Eternity.

How can the enlightened mind tolerate such assertions of vision and authority? Although in the preface to *Milton* Blake engraves the prayer of the otherwise despised Moses, 'Would to God that all the Lords people were Prophets', it is generally his own prophecy that is foregrounded; and that prophecy is in contention with the spirit of the age, as Los is in contention with another 'zoa' Urizen ('Your Reason'—that is, the Christian and Deist God, the force of nature, law, and religion). Just as the hearing of Scripture is traditionally held to convert the reader and convict him of sin (as in Augustine's *Confessions*, Book 8), so Blake expects the hearing of his own words to be a force of *judgement* on the reader. Over the address 'To the Public' at the beginning of *Jerusalem* he engraves at the top of one side of the plate SHEEP and at the top of the other GOATS, as a sign that the reading of what follows is to be an apocalyptic experience. Nor is this judgement intended to be merely proleptic or symbolic; it is 'the last judgment' now. Into his detailed description of his own outwardly trad-itional picture of the Last Judgment, Blake interjects assertions of the present judging power of his own work and of its eternal origin:

<When> Imaginative Art & Science & all Intellectual Gifts all the Gifts of the Holy Ghost are [*despisd*] lookd upon as of no use & only Contention remains to Man then the Last Judgment begins & its Vision is seen by the [*Imaginative Eye*] of Every one according to the situation he holds ... The Last Judgment is one of these Stupendous Visions[.] I have represented it as I saw it ... The Nature of my Work is Visionary or Imaginative it is an Endeavour to Restore <what the Ancients calld> the Golden Age ... whenever any Individual Rejects Error & Embraces Truth a Last Judgment passes upon that Individual[.]   (E 554–62)

'Vision or Imagination', with which Blake identifies the words of the Bible as well as his own work, 'is a Representation of what Eternally Exists' and so is 'calld Jerusalem'. This is contrasted with 'Fable or Allegory ... Formd by the Daughters of Memory'. It is of course on 'memory' that most religion and theology, most biblical exegesis and literary criticism, are built—on tradition and reason and catechesis and history and on the classical patterns that Blake despised. The theologian, a Daughter of Memory, is challenged by the independence and authority of Blake's work to decide whether she accepts the possibility and the veracity of what the poet has *seen*.

That vision is not with 'my Corporeal or Vegetative Eye' (*VLJ*; E 566); it does not belong to the world of Newton's mathematics or of Venetian painting (two of Blake's pet hates). At the same time it is not a purely solipsistic or Gnostic vision. Blake's understanding, developed from his early *Marriage of Heaven and Hell* through the early prophecies (especially *The Book of Urizen*) and into *Milton* and *Jerusalem*, is that humanity's five senses have contracted, so that the eyes in particular become restricted to 'single vision'. 'Man has closed himself up, till he sees all things thro' narrow chinks of his cavern' (*MHH* 14; cf. *BU* 11. 10–15). True or 'fourfold vision' for

Blake is an apocalyptic *expansion* or transformation of these same senses—not the acquisition of some extraneous or spiritual sense. While the visionary or poet may be the agent of such transformation, this is not a matter of private vision but of the redemption of all humanity, of the 'One Man' or Albion. So the climax of *The Four Zoas* is a moment of vision:

> The Sun has left his blackness & has found a fresher morning
> And the mild moon rejoices in the clear & cloudless night
> And Man walks forth from midst of the fires the evil is all consumd
> His eyes behold the Angelic spheres arising night & day
> The stars consumd like a lamp blown out & in their stead behold
> The Expanding Eyes of Man behold the depths of wondrous worlds
>
> (*FZ* 138. 20–5)

This is a mythical fulfilment of the didactic pronouncements made at the beginning of Blake's career in the engravings *There is No Natural Religion*. On the one hand, 'The desires & perceptions of man untaught by any thing but organs of sense, must be limited to objects of sense'; on the other, 'Mans perceptions are not bounded by organs of perception . . . The desire of Man being Infinite the possession is Infinite & himself Infinite' (E 2–3). And in the vibrant early engraved work *The Marriage of Heaven and Hell*, which is a combination of prophetic oracle, political manifesto, and *ars poetica*, comes the similar pronouncement: 'If the doors of perception were cleansed every thing would appear to man as it is: infinite' (*MHH* 14).

Blake's prophetic work, then, is one of cleansing the doors of perception, which in his later poetry receives an explicitly Christian dedication as well as a claim to visionary authority:

> I rest not from my great task!
> To open the Eternal Worlds, to open the Immortal Eyes
> Of Man inwards into the Worlds of Thought: into Eternity
> Ever expanding into the Bosom of God. the Human Imagination
> O Saviour pour upon me thy Spirit of meekness & love . . .
>
> (*J* 5. 17–21)

Blake thus requires from the theologian, from any critical reader, a suspension of disbelief. Yet this does not mean an uncritical submission to his vision or words, precisely because his creation is a dialectical one. Reading Blake's words and pictures is not just having the doors of your perception cleansed by some direct vision. In a riposte to Dr Trusler, who had said that Blake needed 'somebody to Elucidate my Ideas', he wrote: 'That which can be made Explicit to the Idiot is not worth my care. The wisest of the Ancients considerd what is not too Explicit as the fittest for Instruction because it rouzes the faculties to act' (E 702). Los's labours at his forge and Blake's in his workshop are to be joined by the labours in the reader's mind and senses. Hence the troubling dialectic between text and design in the engraved books, even in the 'Songs of Innocence'. The design frequently does not 'illustrate' the text's content but sits in juxtaposition or in opposition to it: their relationship 'seeks to stimulate the imaginative energy of the reader, who is brought in to play as an active intelligence that must strive to make sense of the difference' (Mee 1992: 17; cf. Burdon 1997: 191–3). Hence also what S. L. Carr calls the 'radical variability' in Blake's engravings (Carr 1986: 182–3). There is no *Urtext* or canonical version of any of these books; rather, each surviving copy divulges to the reader and requires from her a different mental task. The books are particular and highly detailed, literally produced with more labour than any other poet's, yet they are also provisional and indeterminate. And given that Blake's symbolic world draws so heavily on the Bible, such indeterminacy must affect also the reading of Scripture, for Blake's whole ethic and method of production 'challenges the notion of a hegemonic text' (Rowland 2003: 175).

Stephen Behrendt's introduction to *Reading William Blake* explores this dialectical process of writing, drawing, and reading in some detail, remarking that

[w]e cannot approach Blake's illuminated poetry carelessly, without our wits about us. Blake's art challenges us at every turn to confront again the archetypal temptation to our own individual moral, spiritual, intellectual, and aesthetic self-sufficiency, replaying in endless variations the temptation . . . to doubt ourselves and to defer to another. Hence reading Blake's words is an exercise in continual judging and choosing, from which process emerges a sense not just of the 'meaning(s)' of Blake's texts but also, more important, of ourselves as informed readers and as empowered human entities.   (Behrendt 1992: 26)

If this is so, then Blake, the antinomian enemy of 'Religion', is paradoxically the facilitator of a profoundly ethical and religious reading. His very eccentricity, profusion of detail, delight in aphorisms and 'contraries', offensive and authoritarian pose, his madness perhaps, are there to rouse the faculties to act and so initiate a revolutionary praxis of Christian and artistic living (those two adjectives have for Blake the same meaning, as he insists in the address 'To the Christians' prefacing the last book of *Jerusalem).* 'Blake was not the first (see the Book of Revelation) nor the last (see van Gogh's late paintings) to plunge us into a kind of madness to lift us outside the normal so that we can see normality as only one among many imaginable ways of reading, seeing, feeling, thinking, living' (Essick and Viscomi 1993: 10).

It is with this energetic, imaginative, and ultimately practical reading stance that I proceed to outline some of Blake's principal motifs and symbols—his 'beliefs', perhaps—which can inform or infuriate theological thinking. These are: the place of energy and imagination; the notions of 'Divine Humanity' and 'One Man' or Albion; and the depictions of law, sin, liberty, and forgiveness.

'I will not cease from Mental Fight'

Like Jesus, like the biblical prophets, Blake repeatedly summons his readers to 'Awake!'[2] This could be seen as an ascetical call, and certainly Blake's own prolific

---

[2] 'Awake!' in the imperative occurs 41 times in Blake's three major prophecies (× 14 in *FZ;* × 8 in *M;* × 19 in *J).*

labours are a kind of *askēsis*. Yet it is one far removed in spirit—if not necessarily in ultimate goal—from traditional Christian asceticism. Blake opens the main section of his early apocalyptic tract *The Marriage of Heaven and Hell* with erotic designs of embracing and exulting nudes, between which is announced 'Without Contraries is no progression . . . Good is the passive that obeys Reason. Evil is the active springing from Energy' (*MHH* 3). The next three plates develop concisely and polemically these 'contraries', undermining religious and moral dualism, attacking 'those who restrain desire' and proclaiming 'Energy is Eternal Delight', while the 'Proverbs of Hell' that follow (pls. 7–10) celebrate that energy in a witty and deliberate subversion of respectable morality and religion. For Blake in 1790, 'energy' is not moral or mystical but sexual and political. It is embodied in many of the early prophecies in the fiery Orc. In the designs of *America,* Orc is depicted as an amalgam of Prometheus and the risen Christ, in opposition to the Jehovah-like Newtonian god Urizen who attempts to control his universe by physical and moral law. As the myth develops in *The Four Zoas,* the sexual element of Orcian energy diminishes and its political element becomes more coded, yet energy remains 'Eternal Delight'. Jealous Urizen, clutching his books, addresses the chained and tortured Orc in fear of the latter's terrible combination of rage and delight:

> Pity for thee movd me to break my long & dark repose
> And to reveal myself before thee in a form of wisdom
> Yet thou dost laugh at all these tortures & this horrible place
> Yet throw thy limbs these fires abroad that back return upon thee
> While thou reposest throwing rage on rage feeding thyself
> With visions of sweet bliss far other than this burning clime
> Sure thou art bathd in rivers of delight on verdant fields
> Walking in joy in bright Expanses sleeping on bright clouds
> With visions of delight so lovely that they urge thy rage
> Tenfold with fierce desire . . .
>
> (*FZ* 78. 30–9)

To this Orc retorts, 'Curse thy hoary brows . . . my fierce fires are better than thy snows'. The conflict of the two immortals is an ethical and political one, but it is also profoundly theological, allegorizing the biblical antinomy of Moses and Jesus and the Lutheran antinomy of law and gospel. Energy, not order, is the evangelical spirit, embodied as Orc fades from Blake's myth in the redemptive figure of Los and ultimately, in *Jerusalem,* in Jesus the Lamb of God and 'bright Preacher of Life' (*J* 77; cf. *J* 7. 65–70; Altizer 1967: 106–7). And the later, more explicitly Christian Blake does not renounce, though he does refine, his early revelation that 'Energy is the only life and is from the Body' (*MHH* 4).

We might call this a 'dialectical theology': Altizer in particular has aligned Blake with his contemporary Hegel, while Ryan compares him with Karl Barth (Altizer 1967: 28–32; Ryan 1997: 73–5). Yet the conflict of the 'zoas' in Blake's myth moves not towards a logical synthesis, even a provisional one, but towards a humane redemption that *remains* energetic and bodily. The 'contraries' go deeper than dialectical antitheses, to produce what Dan Miller calls 'a counter-dialectic'. 'Blake's "progression"', writes

Miller of *The Marriage of Heaven and Hell,* 'is not necessarily dialectical advance…
The truth of contrariety is just the truth that cannot be told, except in and through
contrary representation' (Miller 1985: 504–5). The 'mental fight' of the zoas, of Blake,
and of his readers is therefore a spiritual one too, which does not flinch from using
military metaphors, such as those from the Letter to the Ephesians that Blake writes as
the epigraph to *The Four Zoas,* or those used to epitomize Los's labours:

> I took the sighs & tears, & bitter groans:
> I lifted them into my Furnaces; to form the spiritual sword.
> That lays open the hidden heart: I drew forth the pang
> Of sorrow red hot: I workd it on my resolute anvil…
> Loud roar my Furnaces and loud my hammer is heard:
> I labour day & night, I behold the soft affections
> Condense beneath my hammer into forms of cruelty
> But still I labour in hope, tho' still my tears flow down.…
> That Enthusiasm and Life may not cease…
>
> (*J* 9. 17–31)

The activity of Los—in *The Four Zoas, Milton,* and *Jerusalem*—is a story of rage
and of labour, but the 'mental fight' issues above all in *building.* There is much
building going on in Blake's prophecies, and not all of it is benign. Urizen frenetically
and solipsistically constructs a 'wide world of solid obstruction', founded on '[t]he
secrets of dark contemplation' and celebrating 'One King, one God, one Law' (*BU* 4).
This is the natural world. By contrast, Los's Golgonooza, the city of art and production, is constructed with human collaboration and intricacy. Golgonooza forms the
architectural foundation of Jerusalem, and it is crucial that in all three poems the city
of eternal redemption does not simply descend from heaven but is the fruit of human
labour and imagination. To engage in its construction is the prophetic calling of
humanity and *a fortiori* of the Christian, that is, the artist: 'Let every Christian as
much as in him lies engage himself openly & publicly before all the World in some
Mental pursuit for the Building up of Jerusalem' (*J* 77; cf. Ferber 1985: 145–51). All is
built by art, not received from divine gift or authority. And—no doubt calling on the
particularity as well as the clear draughtsmanship of his own engraving practice—
Blake insists on the artist's devotion to '*Minute Particulars*'. Abhorring the broad
brushwork and lush colours of Venetian painting, and practising in his own designs a
unique attention to line and detail, he erects this aesthetic principle into an epistemological one as well: 'General Knowledge is Remote Knowledge it is in Particulars that Wisdom consists & Happiness too. Both in Art & in Life General Masses are
as Much Art as a Pasteboard Man is Human' (*VLJ* (E 560); cf. Ferber 1985: 44–5). Los's
triumphant prophetic speech in *Jerusalem,* pl. 91, insists that 'he who wishes to see a
Vision; a perfect Whole | Must see it in its Minute Particulars', while earlier in
the poem 'the living creatures' are Blake's mouthpiece for making it an ethical
principle too:

> He who would do good to another, must do it in Minute Particulars
> General Good is the plea of the scoundrel hypocrite & flatterer:

> For Art & Science cannot exist but in minutely organized Particulars
> And not in generalizing Demonstrations of the Rational Power.
>
> (*J* 55. 60–3)

To read Blake theologically, then, or to undertake theology in a Blakean spirit of energy and imagination requires a practical attention to the particular building blocks of human experience, art, and redemption and a corresponding avoidance of the general or philosophic principle from which proposition and law are derived. And because the particular must be 'organized', Los 'must Create a System, or be enslav'd by another Mans'—though he adds in the next line 'I will not Reason & Compare: my business is to Create', and is described on the following plate as 'Striving with Systems to deliver Individuals from those Systems' (*J* 10. 20–1; 11. 5). Los/Blake is fully aware, even in the midst of the highly stylized and allegorized ordering of Golgonooza in *Jerusalem*, pls. 12–16, that System risks the political and aesthetic surrender of energy to order, of prophecy to Natural or State Religion. As Essick and Viscomi observe of *Milton*,

While his work often celebrates diversity, the energetic expression of individual consciousness, there is an equal and opposite dynamic toward totalizing systems as a way of expressing and giving shape to Blake's sense that everything is connected with everything else.... A poem that seems so digressive, self-interruptive, and wildly heterogeneous is in part the product of a desire for unity and a fear of leaving anything out.   (Essick and Viscomi 1993: 17)

The intricate mythopeia of his longer poems—like the binding together of the *Songs of Innocence and Experience*—enacts Blake's early decree that 'Without Contraries is no progression'. And the building of systems no less than the deliverance from systems is the work of energy and imagination; that is, the dynamic and conflictual 'inspiration of the Poetic Genius | Who is the eternal all-protecting Divine Humanity | To whom be Glory & Power & Dominion Evermore Amen' (*M* 14 [15]. 1–3).

While it is unlikely that Blake was aware of the eastern Christian doctrine of the divine *energeia*, a theological extrapolation of his erotic and artistic sense leads to something not dissimilar.[3] In the early *All Religions Are One* comes the insistence that 'the Poetic Genius is the true Man ... The Religions of all Nations are derived from each Nations different reception of the Poetic Genius which is every where call'd the Spirit of Prophecy' (*E* 1), and in *The Marriage of Heaven and Hell* Ezekiel reveals that 'we of Israel taught that the Poetic Genius ... was the first principle and all the others merely derivative' (*MHH* 12). But this universal poetic imagination later receives a specifically Christian definition as 'the Human Imagination | Which is the Divine Body of the Lord Jesus. blessed for ever' (*M* 3. 3–4; cf. *J* 5. 58–9). The identification of art, imagination, God, and Jesus is clearest in the aphorisms Blake engraved around his copy of the Laocoön, reinterpreted as 'YAH and his two Sons Satan and Adam'. Here we read that 'The Eternal Body of Man is The IMAGINATION. | that is God himself | The Divine Body | Yeshua JESUS we are his Members ... ART is the Tree of

---

[3] The 'energies' of the Trinity are the outgoing powers that create and sustain the world and draw humanity towards Godlikeness.

LIFE | GOD is JESUS.' The words of Jesus about discipleship and gospel are applied to the practice of art, and a man or woman who is not in some sense an artist or who is an 'unproductive Man' 'is not a Christian' (E 273–4). So in Blake's gospel, art replaces conventional religion: 'Prayer is the Study of Art | Praise is the Practise of Art | Fasting etc. all relate to Art.'

The Laocoön aphorisms show a sharp opposition to money and to the commodification of art. Yet this is not, as some interpreters would have it, a mere Romantic aestheticism, for Blake is consistent in identifying the divine work of art and imagination as the building of a free and fraternal 'Jerusalem' and is thus the progenitor more of artisan socialist art than of 'art for art's sake' (Ferber 1985: 54–5). What is extraordinary—what must challenge the theologian to take art and poetry as seriously as philosophy—is the directness of the identifications Blake makes and the confidence with which he derives them from the Bible. 'The Old & New Testaments are the Great Code of Art' (E 274); and though, like Homer, Virgil, and Milton, the Bible is flawed, all of them 'are addressed to the Imagination which is Spiritual Sensation & but mediately to the Understanding or Reason' (E 702–3). It is quite wrong to read this as Romantic anti-intellectualism: an engagement with poetry or art that does not engender 'mental fight' is for Blake sterile, as Milton's stern and apocalyptic rebuke to Ololon insists (*M* 40. 27–41. 28). But the intellect cannot remain bound by Urizenic Reason and Memory (Blake's 'Bacon, Locke & Newton'). Fired by divine imagination, it must take flight, like the birds that inhabit so many of Blake's margins and interlinear spaces or the one 'that cuts the airy way... an immense world of delight' (*MHH* 7). For Blake, energy and imagination, art and labour, simply *are* participation in God or in the Body of Jesus. To pierce the veil of conventional art and religion and apprehend this, and to increase the apprehension by mental fight, this is the ground of evangelical and sensual liberty.

'THE GREAT HUMANITY DIVINE'

Around the head and shoulders of his Laocoön/YAH Blake inscribed: 'All that we see is VISION | from Generated Organs gone as soon as come | Permanent in the Imagination; Considered | as Nothing by the NATURAL MAN' (E 273). His denigrations of 'Nature', 'Natural Man', and 'Natural Religion', of the world of 'Generation', of the 'Vegetative Universe' and 'Corporeal or Vegetative Eye', have led many readers to dub Blake a dualist or even a Gnostic. Undoubtedly his presentation of the material world's creation as a constriction and of Urizen its demiurge as oppressive draws on Platonist, Gnostic, and esoteric traditions (this is especially evident in *The Book of Urizen*). But a Gnostic, even a Christian-Gnostic Blake is ultimately unconvincing for two reasons. First, his myth of redemption is in no sense one of escape from or victory over the sensual world. His dualisms—or, to use his own language, his 'contraries'—are not permanent but dialectical, not metaphysical but ethical. As one of the 'Proverbs of Hell' has it, 'Eternity is in love with the productions of time' (*MHH* 7): the world of time and of the body are the field of redemption. Secondly, the polarity is not between a transcendent and a material world. There is only one world, and what others would call 'the transcendent' is simply for Blake the one world truly seen—hence the repeated emphasis on 'vision'.

The first point can be illustrated from the first two plates of *Europe*. The frontispiece is the famous picture of Urizen/Jehovah known as 'The Ancient of Days'. The solitary Newtonian demiurge crouches within the fearful symmetry of the sun, leaning down to the nether world which he measures with his compasses. Here is the creator Wisdom, whose mastery appears absolute—except that, mysteriously, his white hair is blown to the left by a strong external wind. Its source is found on the opposite right-hand plate, the title page, where, facing away from Urizen, is another ancient symbol of Wisdom: the serpent with its fiery tongue is coiled, not above but among the earth's hills. The wind or spirit, like Shelley's west wind, is that of 'PROPHECY' (this word of the book's title being prominently engraved between the snake's coils and directly opposite Urizen's windswept head). The earthly and heavenly Wisdoms are literally juxtaposed—the free though earthy serpent and the god who circumscribes yet is circumscribed—and their juxtaposition opens up a dialectical reading of the words and designs in the ensuing book. That 'prophecy' ends (on pl. 15) 'in the vineyards of red France' where Los 'Call'd all his sons to the strife of blood', with the picture below of the heroic male nude saviour. On the plates between these the text encodes the European political struggle for liberty, with powerful designs of free spirits—flying birds, more serpents, leaping human nudes—contrasting with realistic depiction of plagues and human suffering and symbolic ones of the source of that oppression in 'Religion hid in War' (*J* 89. 53). Blake's sharp contraries are verbally and visually intertwined and challenge the reader to this-worldly, political judgements, just as for St Paul both 'the Spirit' and the 'principalities and powers' are embodied in this world without their meaning being exhausted by 'the flesh'. The intended outcome of the reading of *Europe*, like that of that other tract of liberty addressed to the Galatians, is not *gnōsis* but *praxis*.

For all his mythical constructions, for all his fluidity of time and space, Blake is therefore an enemy of metaphysical dualism and of a separate realm of the Transcendent. Such a realm is associated in Blake's demonology with Bacon, Newton, Locke, with Jehovah, Moses, and the druids: the world of solipsistic Urizen, in contrast to but in collusion with the merely natural world of Vala. Anticipating Feuerbach, religious dualism is unveiled in both *The Four Zoas* and *Jerusalem* as a human theological and pathological construct. So 'the Slumberous Man', in the power of Urizen and Vala, falls prostrate before the beautiful but 'watry shadow' which has risen 'from his wearied intellect', purloining biblical verses to pronounce himself 'nothing' (*FZ* p. 40), while in the conflicts of Albion in *Jerusalem* ch. 2, Los responds to the prayer for divine deliverance by 'raging',

> Why stand we here trembling around
> Calling on God for help; and not ourselves in whom God dwells
> Stretching a hand to save the falling Man…
>
> (*J* 38 [43]. 12–14)

The worship of the Wholly Other (whether in Jewish, Christian, pagan, or Deist form) is mocked as adherence to 'Nobodaddy' or as man's speech 'idolatrous to his own Shadow' (*FZ* 40. 12), and the positive symbols of transcendence from the book of Revelation and other biblical texts are systematically subverted (Burdon 1999: 16–24). Blake's apocalypse, in Altizer's words, 'ushers in a new Eden that abolishes all those spaces separating an external nature, an autonomous selfhood, and a transcendent God' (Altizer 1967: 196).

If the remote God is an object of derision, there are, however, scattered in Blake's works celebrations of an intimate and joyful *divine presence*. 'Infant joy' is an unmitigated good, even if 'experience' must inevitably unsettle it, and

> Where Mercy, Love & Pity dwell,
> There God is dwelling too.
>
> (*SIE* 18; cf. *SIE* 25, 27)

At the end of both *The Marriage of Heaven and Hell* and *Visions of the Daughters of Albion* the poet proclaims, 'Every thing that lives is holy' (*MHH* 27; *VDA* 8. 10). This is not a vague pantheism but is formulated in conjunction with the brilliantly concise history of religion on pl. 11 of the *Marriage*, where the development of an objectifying 'system' of deities and of priesthood and forms of worship leads men to 'forget that All deities reside in the human breast'. It is in conjunction too with the polemic of pl. 16 where 'I answer, God only Acts & Is, in existing beings or Men'. If we wish to categorize Blake's thought, which here emerges in direct and prophetic form, we cannot call this pantheistic any more than it is dualistic or monistic. It is however both theological and profoundly humanistic, even anthropocentric. And as the myth develops, the thought becomes explicitly Christocentric. For now 'God is Jesus' and addresses the poet at the beginning of *Jerusalem*, 'I am not a God afar off, I am a brother and friend' (*J* 4. 18).

In the book of Revelation, John sees 'the holy city, the new Jerusalem, coming down out of heaven from God, prepared as a bride adorned for her husband' (Rev. 21:2). Yet his vision does not develop Jerusalem as a feminine or human figure, and the subsequent description is in architectural and mathematical terms. Blake's *Jerusalem* radically humanizes the figure of redemption. She is 'the Emanation of the Giant Albion' (that is, Man), depicted in the design of pl. 92 as lamenting beside fallen Man among the ruins of earth and its religions, and celebrated through the lips of Los as 'lovely mild Jerusalem', whose 'gates' and 'walls' are minor features of 'the soft reflected Image of the Sleeping Man' with her 'Head & Heart & Reins' (*J* 85. 21–86. 32). Salvation comes not by submission to or ascent to transcendent divinity but by the renunciation of such pretensions and by the celebration of humanity. So in *America* liberation comes from the earth in the figure of Orc, most notably in the text and designs of pls. 1 and 6. Unmitigated divinity is a painful delusion, as Tharmas laments in his anguish:

> Is this to be A God far rather would I be a Man
> To know sweet Science & to do with simple companions
> Sitting beneath a tent & viewing sheepfolds & soft pastures.
>
> (*FZ* 51. 29–31)

Above all, in Blake's mature myth of the zoas (that is, of fallen and redeemed humanity), the generating force of redemption and of Jerusalem's descent is Urizen's renunciation of his arrogated selfish godhead.

The erotic embrace at the climax of *Jerusalem* (pl. 99) thus celebrates a redemption of God just as much as of man, perhaps a myth of the death of God—at least in the sense that the God of the church and of natural religion vanishes to be replaced by the human Jesus. For some, including Altizer (1967: 63–75), this pattern of death and redemption is read through the doctrinal and biblical categories of incarnation and *kenōsis*.[4] It is true that at the end of the early 'There is No Natural Religion' Blake adapts a familiar patristic motif to engrave 'Therefore God becomes as we are, that we may be as he is' (E 3). But in orthodox Christianity, incarnation is the enfleshment of the spiritual Son or Logos, while in some twentieth-century theology *kenōsis* is the divesting of divinity or of divine attributes. Both terms presuppose a dualist and/or trinitarian metaphysic, whereas for the heterodox Blake the distinction between God and humanity is a consequence of the fall of the 'One Man', of the recalcitrant constricted Albion to whom, in the midst of the mental fight of *Jerusalem* ch. 2, Jesus calls,

> We live as One Man; for contracting our infinite senses
> We behold multitude; or expanding: we behold as one,
> As One Man all the Universal Family; and that One Man
> We call Jesus the Christ: and he in us, and we in him,
> Live in perfect harmony in Eden the land of life,
> Giving, receiving, and forgiving each others trespasses.
>
> (*J* 34 [38]. 17–22)

The mutual redemption is complete after the death of the Urizenic god, the union of the four zoas, and the regeneration of Albion at pl. 96, when

> Urizen & Luvah & Tharmas & Urthona arose into
> Albions Bosom: Then Albion stood before Jesus in the Clouds
> Of Heaven Fourfold among the Visions of God in Eternity
>
> (*J* 96. 41–3)

In other words, Blake discards the Christian machinery of atonement for a practical religion of forgiveness and discards the trinitarian God for 'Divine Humanity | To whom be Glory & Power & Dominion Evermore Amen' (*M* 14 [15]. 2–3).

---

[4] The doctrine of *kenōsis* ('emptying') is built on Paul's hymn to the Christ who 'emptied himself' (Phil. 2: 7).

The term 'Divine Humanity' is taken from the mystical scientist Swedenborg (1688–1772), to whose teaching the young Blake was briefly affiliated (Davies 1948: 31–53; Thompson 1993: 129–61). Despite his satirical rejection of the 'angelic' seer's politics and morality in *The Marriage of Heaven and Hell*, Swedenborg's heretical terminology remained useful to Blake. For while the person and story and death of Jesus are crucial to his narrative of redemption—above the whole poem *Jerusalem* is engraved in Greek 'Jesus only'—his Jesus is not the incarnation of a divine being intervening in human history but the fullness of divine and human history. 'All Things are comprehended in their Eternal Forms in the Divine body of the Saviour the True Vine of Eternity' (*VLJ* (E 555); cf. Altizer 1967: 112–16). Here is a highly imaginative but also practical rewriting not just of Swedenborg but of incarnational theology, of Paul's teaching on the Body, and of evangelical devotion to Jesus. Here is Blake's gospel.

LAW, LIBERTY, AND BROTHERHOOD

Redemption, for Blake as for Paul, is from the power of *law*. But with Blake there is none of Paul's agonizing over the place of Torah. Deliverance is from the 'stony law' of Moses (*MHH* 27; *A* 8. 5)—from the Ten Commandments which Jesus broke (*MHH* 23; *EG* [E 518–24], *passim*), from the oppressive philosophy of 'Moral Virtue the cruel Virgin Babylon' (*M* 5. 27), of black-clad priests and sexual repression (*SIE* 44). The one Law, underwritten by 'One King, one God', is inscribed by iron pen in Urizen's 'Book | Of eternal brass' (*BU* 4. 24–40) and turns 'the Wheel of Religion' (*J* 77; Burdon 1997: 200–8). Blake the radical Protestant is persistently antinomian. Building on Paul, Calvin, and Milton, yet rejecting their theologies of atonement, he presents the Saviour as the Transgressor (*M* 13 [14]. 31) and the system of law and punishment as the outcome not of disobedience or original sin but of humanity's perverse projection of Urizen, who is both God and Satan (*M* 9. 19–29; 38 [43]. 50–39 [44]. 2). The manacles are 'mind-forg'd', and the dismal tree of Mystery grows 'in the Human Brain' (*SIE* 46; 47).

Defeating this deathly law is the *liberty* enacted in Blake's myth by Orc, by Los, by Jesus, and by the repentant Urizen and regenerate Albion. 'Jerusalem Is Named Liberty Among The Sons Of Albion', he engraved on pl. 26 of *Jerusalem*. This is a liberty which must be achieved dialectically, artistically, and theologically, through the negation and death of false gods. And it is a liberty that cannot be spiritualized, for it is comprehensive and bodily, represented in the political cry 'Empire is no more!' (*MHH* 27) and in the celebration of free love (*A* 8. 9–17; 15. 19–26), as well as in the simple joy of unpossessive living:

> He who binds to himself a joy
> Does the winged life destroy

> But he who kisses the joy as it flies
> Lives in Eternitys sun rise.

(E 474)

Above all, liberty is *forgiveness*. In the prefaces to the first and last chapters of *Jerusalem*, Blake insists that this is the teaching and praxis of Jesus 'the bright Preacher of Life', whose spirit 'is continual forgiveness of Sin' (*J* 77; *J* 3). In the address 'To the Deists' that prefaces the third chapter he berates them as the upholders of 'Natural Morality or Self-Righteousness', whereas 'The Glory of Christianity is, To Conquer by Forgiveness' (*J* 52). So '[l]iberty and forgiveness of sins are identical states and values' (Ferber 1985: 126), and for Albion or his sons to seek vengeance is to be 'for ever lost' (*J* 45 [31]. 28–38; cf. *J* 25. 3–11).

The liberty, salvation, and resurrection which Jesus reveals to Albion on *Jerusalem*, pl. 96, are defined simply as *Brotherhood*, without which 'Man is Not' (*J* 96. 16). 'Brotherhood' for Blake is neither natural kinship nor easy friendship; being forged in forgiveness, it is necessarily the brotherhood of enemies (Ferber 1985: 75). More painfully and more evangelically still, resurrection life is defined at the climax of *Jerusalem* as 'Forgiveness of Sins which is Self Annihilation. it is the covenant of Jehovah' (*J* 98. 23). The poet's own prayer to the Saviour at the beginning of the poem is 'Annihilate the Selfhood in me, be thou all my life!' (*J* 5. 22), and before the final chapter of the book is the full-page picture of Albion before the crucified Jesus, mirroring the Saviour's pose and anticipating their conversation about death and self-annihilation (*J* 76; 96. 3–28). Similarly, in so far as there is a human story to *Milton*, it is that of the seventeenth-century poet's redemption through self-annihilation, challenging his Spectre Satan (or God):

> know thou: I come to Self Annihilation
> Such are the Laws of Eternity that each shall mutually
> Annihilate himself for others good, as I for thee.
> (*M* 38 [43]. 34–6; cf. *M* 14 [15]. 30–2; 32 [35]. 10–43)

With remarkable affinity to the words of Jesus as well as to Mahayana Buddhism, Milton/Blake/Los proclaims the possibility of a peaceable kingdom where Selfhood is abolished (cf. Mark 8. 35; Altizer 1967: 179–207). More radically still, Blake builds this possibility on the gospel of the annihilation of God's Selfhood in the death of Christ. This is indeed the ultimate *kenōsis*. Yet the 'emptying' takes place not in or from a transcendent realm but in the human body, in mutual forgiveness, and its goal is not salvation in 'heaven' but fraternal, social, and peaceful existence in history. For Eternity is in love with the productions of time, above all its artistic productions. So, commenting on the revelatory character of Blake's extraordinary illustrations to the book of Job, David Pollard (1992: 34) writes: 'God as sacrifice (as cruciform), as self-annihilating incarnation, is identical with Job as self-annihilating saint, and with Blake as self-annihilating artist. "Christianity is art".' For all Blake's complexity, here in his mature work is a coherent, practical, and radically ascetic vision.

Given this vision, it is small wonder that Blake continued to see his vocation as that of a prophet and evangelist, however few his readers; given this gospel, small wonder too that he continued to see himself at odds with the political and religious structures of his age. He is at odds just as much with those of the twenty-first century. And his artistic theology—for that ultimately is what it is—can now as much as then 'rouse the faculties to act'.

WORKS CITED

ALTIZER, THOMAS J. J. 1967. *The New Apocalypse: The Radical Christian Vision of William Blake.* Ann Arbor: Michigan State University Press.

BEHRENDT, STEPHEN C. 1992. *Reading William Blake.* Basingstoke: Macmillan.

BURDON, CHRISTOPHER. 1997. *The Apocalypse in England: Revelation Unravelling 1700–1834.* Basingstoke: Macmillan.

—— 1999. 'The Pathology of Worship: John's Heavenly Court and *The Four Zoas*', in S. Brent Plate (ed.), *The Apocalyptic Imagination.* Glasgow: Trinity St Mungo.

CARR, S. L. 1986. 'Illuminated Printing: Toward a Logic of Difference', in N. Hilton and T. A. Vogler (eds.), *Unnam'd Forms: Blake and Textuality.* Berkeley: University of California Press.

DAVIES, J. G. 1948. *The Theology of William Blake.* Oxford: Clarendon.

ERDMAN, DAVID V. (ed.) 1988. *The Complete Poetry and Prose of William Blake.* Rev. edn. New York: Doubleday.

ESSICK, ROBERT N., and VISCOMI, JOSEPH (eds.) 1993. *Milton: A Poem.* London: William Blake Trust / Tate Gallery.

FERBER, MICHAEL. 1985. *The Social Vision of William Blake.* Princeton: Princeton University Press.

MEE, JON. 1992. *Dangerous Enthusiasm: William Blake and the Culture of Radicalism in the 1790s.* Oxford: Clarendon.

MILLER, DAN. 1985. 'Contrary Revelation: *The Marriage of Heaven and Hell*', *Studies in Romanticism* 24: 491–509.

POLLARD, DAVID. 1992. 'William Blake and the Book of Job', *There Was a Man in the Land of Uz: William Blake's Illustrations to the Book of Job.* Jerusalem: The Israel Museum.

ROWLAND, CHRISTOPHER. 2003. 'Blake and the Bible: Biblical Exegesis in the Work of William Blake', in John Court (ed.), *Biblical Interpretation: The Meanings of Scripture—Past and Present.* London: T & T Clark.

RYAN, R. M. 1997. *The Romantic Reformation: Religious Politics in English Literature 1789–1824.* Cambridge: Cambridge University Press.

THOMPSON, E. P. 1993. *Witness Against the Beast: William Blake and the Moral Law.* Cambridge: Cambridge University Press.

FURTHER READING

ACKROYD, PETER. 1999. *Blake.* London: Vintage.

BINDMAN, DAVID. (gen. ed.) 1991–5. *William Blake's Illuminated Books.* 6 vols. London: Tate Gallery.

BLAKE, WILLIAM. On-line concordance to Erdman's edition of Blake at <http://www. english.uga.edu/Blake_Concordance>.

DI SALVO, JACKIE. 1983. *War of Titans: Blake's Critique of Milton and the Politics of Religion.* Pittsburgh: Pittsburgh University Press.

ERDMAN, DAVID. 1977. *Blake: Prophet Against Empire*, 3rd edn. Princeton: Princeton University Press.

—— 1974. *The Illuminated Blake.* New York: Dover.

FRYE, NORTHROP. 1947. *Fearful Symmetry.* Princeton: Princeton University Press.

PALEY, MORTON D. 2002. 'YAH & his two Sons Satan & Adam', *Studies in Romanticism* 41: 201–35.

TANNENBAUM, LESLIE. 1982. *Biblical Tradition in Blake's Early Prophecies* (Princeton: Princeton University Press.

VINE, STEVE. 2002. 'Blake's Material Sublime'. *Studies in Romanticism* 41: 237–57.

CHAPTER 28

WORDSWORTH AND COLERIDGE

SIMON BAINBRIDGE

In 1844, John Keble, a leading figure in the Oxford Movement and sometime Oxford Professor of Poetry, dedicated his *Lectures on Poetry, 1832–1841*

TO WILLIAM WORDSWORTH, true philosopher and inspired poet, who by the special gift and calling of Almighty God, whether he sang of man or of nature, failed not to lift up men's hearts to holy things, nor ever ceased to champion the cause of the poor and simple, and so in perilous times was raised up to be a chief minister not only of sweetest poetry but also of high and sacred truth.   (Keble 1912: n.p.)

Two years later, the theological commentator Archdeacon Julius Hare dedicated his book, *The Mission of the Comforter,*

To the honoured memory of SAMUEL TAYLOR COLERIDGE, the Christian philosopher, who through dark and winding paths of speculation was led to the light, in order that others by his guidance might reach the light.   (Hare 1850: n.p.)

These two dedications illustrate the vital role given to Wordsworth and Coleridge in the religious thinking of the Victorian period; both Keble and Hare present their dedicatee as inspired and inspiring, directed by a higher power towards nothing less than the enlightenment of their readers. But these dedications also exemplify the contrasting ways in which the two writers have been read theologically, for if Coleridge is celebrated as a 'Christian philosopher' whose value lies in having found a route through the labyrinth of metaphysical speculation, Wordsworth— while a 'true philosopher'—is hymned primarily as an 'inspired poet' whose 'high and sacred truth' is conveyed in sweetest song.

This contrast between the two writers' roles and the subsequent nature of their influence structures many of the theological readings of their work, as John Tulloch perceptively argued in his important essay 'Coleridge as a Spiritual Thinker' of 1885. Tulloch, a prominent member of the Church of Scotland and author of numerous theological studies, had devoted much of his *Movements of Religious Thought in Britain during the Nineteenth Century* to showing how 'Coleridge exercised a definite influence on Religious Thought', and in his essay he questioned whether H. D. Traill's recent biography of the poet-philosopher had 'recognised that there is a spiritual side to all his thought, without which neither his poetry nor his criticism can be fully understood, cleverly as they may be judged' (Tulloch 1885: p.v; 1991: 157). Despite contesting 'the division between Coleridge the poet and Coleridge the theologian' that Stephen Prickett (1976: 2) has argued had 'hardened into a critical orthodoxy' by the time of Traill's biography, as Tulloch (1991: 158) continues he develops a 'striking contrast between the career of Coleridge and that of his friend Wordsworth' in terms of the relationship between their poetic development and their religious and theological roles. Though Coleridge continued to write poems throughout his life, Tulloch presents his career as structured by a series of phases during which he fulfilled discrete roles, abandoning poetry at just the moment that Wordsworth was consecrating his life to it:

The poet Coleridge passed into the lecturer and the poetical and literary critic, and then, during the final period of his life, from 1816 to 1834, into the philosopher and theologian. It is to this latter period of his life in the main that his higher prose writings belong, and especially the well-known *Aids to Reflection*, which . . . may be said to contain, as his disciples have always held to contain, all the finer substance of his spiritual thought.   (Ibid. 159–60)

For Tulloch, it is in the writings of this later stage that Coleridge's theological importance is to be found, and particularly in *Aids to Reflection* which, despite being 'defective as a literary composition', has been prized greatly by 'all thinkers' on 'divine things': 'To many such it has given a new force of religious insight; for its time, beyond all doubt, it created a real epoch in Christian thought. It had life in it; and the living seed, scattered and desultory as it was, brought forth fruit in many minds' (ibid. 160). Wordsworth, Coleridge's 'counterpart', is no less important or influential, though 'he did not enter the domain of theological speculation or attempt to give any new direction to it' (ibid. 159). Lacking any 'distinctive dogma' and the ability to make 'any fresh insights into religious problems or capacity of co-ordinating them in a new manner', Wordsworth is nonetheless presented by Tulloch as a 'poet of a deeply religious spirit' who 'continued a religious thinker as well as poet all his life' (ibid.). His role is that of 'a preacher and not only a singer', like the Wanderer in *The Excursion*, and his importance lies in his effect on the religious sensibility of his reader:

Wordsworth did for the religious thought of his time something more and better perhaps than giving it any definite impulse. While leaving it in the old channels, he gave it a richer and deeper volume. He showed with what vital affinity religion cleaves to humanity, in all its true and simple phases, when uncontaminated by conceit or frivolity. Nature and man alike were to him essentially religious, or only conceivable as the outcome of a Spirit of life, 'the Soul of all the worlds.   (Ibid.)

Tulloch's portrayal of Wordsworth and Coleridge as 'counterparts' anticipates and is substantiated by the more recent invaluable scholarship of Stephen Prickett and Stephen Gill on the ways in which the two writers were read religiously and theologically in the nineteenth century. As Stephen Prickett (1976: 148) has argued, the 'Coleridge who was important to nineteenth-century thought was Coleridge the metaphysician and theologian, not Coleridge the poet'. Though there were a number of theological readings of Coleridge's poetry, it was primarily the prose—*The Statesman's Manual* (1816), *Lay Sermons* (1817), *Aids to Reflection* (1825), and *On the Constitution of Church and State* (1829)—that proved so important for the admirers of the Sage of Highgate studied by Prickett, figures including J. S. Mill, Julius and Augustus Hare, F. J. A. Hort, F. D. Maurice, F. C. Robertson, George Macdonald, John Keble, and John Henry Newman. Similarly, in the twentieth century, many studies of Coleridge and religion have either examined his theology in relation to nineteenth-century developments in the field (such as Sanders, *Coleridge and the Broad Church Movement* (1942), and Bernard M. G. Reardon, *Religious Thought in the Victorian Age: A Survey from Coleridge to Gore* (1971, repr. 1995)) or offered accounts or syntheses of his religious thinking as contained within his prose (perhaps the three most important such studies being James D. Boulger, *Coleridge as Religious Thinker* (1961); J. Robert Barth, *Coleridge and Christian Doctrine* (1969); Owen Barfield, *What Coleridge Thought* (1971)). David Jasper's titling of his study of 1985 *Coleridge as Poet and Religious Thinker* illustrates a desire to widen the focus of the established forms of these studies to cover the poetry as well as the prose.

By contrast, as Tulloch argued, Wordsworth's importance for religious thought in the nineteenth century derived almost entirely from his poetry (sometimes reinforced by ideas about his life), though we might reverse the emphasis here to claim, as Gill and Robert M. Ryan have, that for many nineteenth-century readers the importance of Wordsworth's poetry (and his life) lay in its spiritual dimensions. Gill (1998: 4) cites the example of Henry Hudson who in 1884 claimed Wordsworth as 'the most spiritual and the most spiritualizing of all the English poets, not Shakespeare, no, nor even Milton, excepted: indeed, so far as I know or believe, the world has no poetry outside the Bible that can stand a comparison with his in this respect'. Two of the best-known examples of nineteenth-century readers who responded to the spiritual power of Wordsworth's poetry were Charles Kingsley and William Hale White ('Mark Rutherford'). In 1844, Kingsley, a reader of Wordsworth since boyhood, described to his wife his response to the text that was the most important of the poet's works for nineteenth-century readers:

I have been reading Wordsworth's 'Excursion,' with many tears and prayers too. To me he is not only poet, but preacher and prophet of God's new and divine philosophy—a man raised up as a light in a dark time, and rewarded by an honoured age, for the simple faith in man and God with which he delivered his message.   (Kingsley 1877: i. 120).

Kingsley's sense of Wordsworth's poetry as spiritually sustaining and enlightening during 'a dark time' was one that echoed throughout the nineteenth century: in 1829, the *Leeds Monthly Magazine* could praise Wordsworth's poetry the more highly because it spoke to an irreligious age (Anon. 1829: 4–13); in 1848, Edward Collins (1848: 13–14, 17) would present the Priest of Nature as 'victor oe'r a recreant age' with his holy musings; in 1864, John Campbell Shairp praised the 'peculiar wisdom' of the poetry that was needed 'by this excitement-craving, unmeditative age' (S. Gill 1998: 67); while in 1880, the Revd H. R. Haweis saw Wordsworth's spirituality as particularly attractive in an age of materialism (Haweis 1880: 241–60). In the 1870s, Kingsley (1888: ii. 286) himself would present the value of the 'great poet, great philosopher, great divine' as preserving him from 'shallow cynical and materialist views of the universe' and protecting him from neglecting 'the spiritual and the eternal', telling the members of the Chester Society of Natural Science that on geological expeditions they should not 'forget to take with you at times a volume of good poetry—say "Wordsworth's Excursion," above all modern poetry. For so you will have a spiritual tonic, a spiritual corrective, which will keep your heart healthy and childlike, to listen to that other and nobler voice of God which speaks through the aesthetical aspects of nature' (ibid.).

The example of William Hale White illustrates how Wordsworth's poetry could give 'religious thought...a richer and deeper volume', to quote Tulloch, without being doctrinal or theological. As he recalled in *The Autobiography of Mark Rutherford* (1881), Hale White's reading of *Lyrical Ballads* while a student of theology prompted a conversion comparable to that of St Paul on the road to Damascus which 'conveyed to me no new doctrine, and yet the change it wrought in me could only be compared with that which is said to have been wrought on Paul himself by the Divine apparition' (White 1881: 23). The effect on Hale White of reading Wordsworth's poetry was, to use Hudson's term, 'spiritualizing':

Instead of an object of worship which was altogether artificial, remote, never coming into genuine contact with me, I had now one which I thought to be real, one in which literally I could live and move and have my being, an actual fact present before my eyes. God was brought from that heaven of the books, and resided on the downs visible in the far-away distances seen from the top of a hill and in every cloud-shadow which wandered across the valley. Wordsworth unconsciously did for me what every religious reformer has done,—he recreated my Supreme Divinity, substituting a new and living spirit for the old deity, once alive but gradually hardened into an idol.   (ibid. 24)

While Coleridge was often conceived in the nineteenth century primarily as a theologian, a number of writers did examine his poetry theologically, and despite the fact that his output seemed limited, theologically it seemed more explicit than Wordsworth's, particularly in terms of the issue of revelation. As George Macdonald (1868: 307) commented in *England's Antiphon*, 'There is little of a directly religious kind in his poetry; yet we find in him what we miss in Wordsworth, an inclined plane from the revelation in nature to the culminating revelation in the Son of Man.' Similarly, in his 1893 lecture on 'The Development of Theology as illustrated in

English Poetry, From 1780 to 1830', Stopford Brooke (1893: 27–8) was able to find a politically inflected theological message in the poetry of the early part of Coleridge's life such as 'Ode to the Departing Year' and 'Ode to France':

The influence of Coleridge as a philosophic prose writer on the growth of liberal theology may justly be said to be great. His influence on it as a poet is inappreciable. In his early days, sympathising with the new ideas about man, he saw in their proclamation a revelation of God, and founded the universal brotherhood of man on God's universal Fatherhood.

But with the revolution's failure, Coleridge's poetic instinct died, forestalling his potential impact on theology:

The miserable close of the Revolution in the attempt of France to enslave Europe drove him out of poetry and out of the ideas he first loved, and the one contribution which he made as a poet to a wider theology—with the exception of his conviction that all nature was the reflection of the universal spirit of God in his own mind—was the closing verse of the *Ancient Mariner.*   (Ibid.)

The understanding of Coleridge's poetic career as short-lived that underpins both Macdonald's and Brooke's assessment of his theological importance can also be seen to inform two other recurrent formulations of the relationship between theology and literature in studies of Coleridge. In the first of these, Coleridge is credited with the initial inspiration or understanding of the workings of God, the divine, or transcendent power which is then passed on to, and fully developed by, Wordsworth (or in some accounts 'Romanticism' more generally). As the *Atlantic Monthly* argued in 1895:

to Coleridge belongs the credit and the immortal honor of having suggested the doctrine which was the motive of Wordsworth's poetry and his own. It was he who became the founder of the Lake School of Poetry, as it is called, whose principle was in such sharp contrast with that which underlay the classical poetry of the last century,—the Neoplatonic doctrine that outward nature is a radiation from a divine life, that supernatural communion is mediated by unearthly powers, that human thought corresponds to some eternal reality.   (Jackson 1991: 211)

This 'doctrine' then gains its fullest expression in Wordsworth, who devotes 'his powers of description, in which he far surpassed Coleridge, to a delineation of the feelings which nature, and nature always as it is revealed in its surpassing loveliness in the Lake Country, inspires in an unworldly soul' (ibid. 211–12).

Related to this sense of Coleridge as the originator of a religious romanticism is the argument that he is its great theorist while Wordsworth is its great practitioner. This reading of Coleridge can be illustrated through the work of J. Robert Barth, the author of several studies of Coleridge in relation to theology. In his book *The Symbolic Imagination: Coleridge and the Romantic Tradition* of 1977, Barth drew on Coleridge's prose writing, and especially his famous statement in *Biographia Literaria* that the imagination is 'a repetition in the finite mind of the eternal act of creation in the infinite I AM' to argue that imagination is an intrinsically religious act, founded upon faith in the human mind's ability to attain something approaching truth, and ultimately upon faith in the divine as an empowering source. It is through the faculty of the imagination that an individual can give meaning to the world, echoing God's initial act of creation. In seeking to develop this argument through a fuller examination of poetry in his more recent *Romanticism and Transcendence: Wordsworth, Coleridge, and Romantic Imagination*, the majority of which focuses on *The Prelude*, Barth (2003: 1–2) argues that 'if Coleridge was the great theorist of the imagination, Wordsworth was, among their contemporaries, its supreme practitioner. Thus if we look to Coleridge for the theoretical grounding of the view of religious imagination proposed in this book, it is in Wordsworth above all that we see this imagination at work.' As Barth argues, the relationship between the two writers is symbiotic, but they remain in their separate roles: 'Wordsworth working within the paradigm— perhaps even the "field of force"—of Coleridge's thought; Coleridge drawing on Wordsworth's poetry as the working material for his theory' (ibid. 2).

While Barth's argument illustrates the frequent division made between Wordsworth and Coleridge as theological and religious writers, it is important to recognize how valuable his work has been in producing sophisticated and nuanced readings of literary works alongside theological texts, a quality that it shares with the scholarship of such critics as Stephen Prickett and David Jasper who have sought to break down the split between Coleridge as poet and theologian. In his *Coleridge as Poet and Religious Thinker*, for example, Jasper (1985: 19) draws on a wide range of Continental and British theology of the Romantic period to provide the foundation for his argument that 'Coleridge's vocations as poet and theologian are... inseparable', an argument he supports through detailed and careful readings of the major poems. For Prickett (1976: 6, 27), Coleridge's later theological speculation arises from the poetry, and cannot be understood without reference to it; indeed, 'Coleridge was, perhaps, unique in being *both* a major artist and a major religious thinker, and this was for him the shaping tension of his whole career.' As an example of the value of considering Coleridge's poetry alongside his theology, Prickett offers a reading of the dualistic nature of *The Ancient Mariner*—with its conflicting requirements of both a religious explanation as an 'ambiguous and mysterious drama of Fall and Redemption through Grace' and a psychological explanation as an 'affirmation of unity and community'—alongside an analysis of Coleridge's theory of the symbol in *The Statesman's Manual*, finding in Coleridge's conception of the Imagination a divinely originating symbolizing activity that can bring 'into a single focus two separate levels of experience, [...] seeing them as a coherent whole' (ibid. 17, 19). As a poem of 'metaphorical or symbolic tension between incompatible yet interdependent worlds', the *Ancient Mariner* can be understood in similar terms as revealing Coleridge's 'growing sense of the transcendent "otherness" of a God of mystery, immanent in the world of nature and human psychology, but simultaneously standing over against that world in judgement' (ibid. 27). The work of writers such as Barth, Prickett, and Jasper develops that of an earlier generation of scholars, such as Basil Willey, who have tended to approach Coleridge's religion and theology in terms of the chronological study of his development (or growth), tracing his shift from 'the Unitarianism of his Cambridge and Somerset days to the Christian orthodoxy of his mature years', as Willey (1971: 222) puts it. Willey himself produced an intellectual biography of Coleridge in 1972 that examined the writer's theological and religious development and the tradition continues in Ronald C. Wendling's *Coleridge's Progress to Christianity: Experience and Authority in Religious Faith* (1995). Over the past few decades, interest in the theological and religious thinking of the later Coleridge (seen for example in David Newsome's (1974, 100–10) account in *Two Classes of Men* of the 'noetic' or 'dynamic' pentad as a figure that could be used to address problems in both literary criticism and theology) has been further stimulated by the publication of the *Notebooks, Marginalia* and *Shorter Works and Fragments* in the Bollingen Series, leading to important work on areas such as Coleridge's biblical criticism, his concept of Logos, and the relationship of his thinking to developments on the Continent (see M. A. Perkins 1994).

It is significant that despite the different political and philosophical emphases of Brooke's and Prickett's theological readings of Coleridge described above, they both cite the *Ancient Mariner*, for this ballad has been central to religious accounts of Coleridge (whose revisions of the poem and additions of the marginal gloss could be seen to invite such readings). As early as 1834, in an (unsigned) review of the *Poetical Works* for the *North American Review*, the Unitarian R. C. Waterston declared Coleridge 'strictly a religious writer' and found in religion a 'key' to the poem which had generally been thought either simply unintelligible or an exercise in the irrational and supernatural (Jackson 1991: 4). Waterston read the poem as follows:

Love is the central, sun-like principle of the moral universe. God is love. Every work in the wide creation is a symbol of that love. This is the great harmony of the whole. The mind of man is a portion of God's universe. It is the living link between it, and Him;—and as it parts with this heavenly principle, it wrenches itself away, by its own unworthiness, from the great whole. It becomes in discord with the spiritual world, as well as the natural; and thus dissevers itself from both. It crushes its best affections, and tears out the very nerve of its inner life. It sins against itself, and the divine law; and must be purified by its own fire. This is the key to the Ancient Mariner. This it is, which gives the whole tale its sublime grandeur. It lays bare the subterraneous springs of the human soul.   (ibid.)

J. R. de J. Jackson (ibid. 3) sees this religious reading of the poem as a 'considerable and prescient departure ... from the criticism written when Coleridge was alive', but during the nineteenth century Christian approaches came to dominate the reading of the *Ancient Mariner*, as David Perkins has argued. Perkins (1996: 426–7) sees this domination as lasting 'for a hundred years, roughly from 1860 to 1960' during which period the readings remained 'vague and general', the shooting of the albatross being interpreted as a violation (rather than a manifestation of original sin) and the blessing of the water snakes as a restoration (but not specifically as supernatural grace). As an example of the longevity of such a generalized Christian approach to the poem, Perkins (ibid. 426–7) cites M. H. Abrams's account in *Natural Supernaturalism* from 1971: 'The persistent religious and moral allusions ... both in the text and in the glosses ... invite us to take the Mariner's experience as an instance of the Christian plot of moral error, the discipline of suffering, and a consequent change of heart. The Mariner's literal journey, then, is also a spiritual journey.' Yet while many readings of the poem remained general in their Christian interpretations, Robert Penn Warren's essay of 1946, 'A Poem of Pure Imagination', signalled the start of a series of more theologically precise readings of the text, many of which, like Warren, made extensive use of Coleridge's essays and letters. Warren presents that narrative of the poem as a sacramental one in which the mariner's shooting of the albatross re-enacts the fall and symbolizes original sin while redemption is gained through his blessing of the water snakes. Warren links this symbolic reading of the poem to an argument which sees the imagination and the creative process as themselves redemptive, so that the poem parallels its own narrative. Warren's interpretation of the poem has been both highly influentially and forcefully criticized, perhaps most notably by William Empson (1973) who emphasized the Unitarian elements of Coleridge's thought at the time he wrote the poem (his refusal to administer Anglican sacraments and his rejection of the doctrine of atonement). The theological elements of Warren's and Empson's arguments are themselves part of Perkins's excellent essay on readings of the *Ancient Mariner* over the past two centuries in which he concludes that the interpretations offered by 'these eminent critics were suggested to them not by their study of Coleridge especially but by wider intellectual preoccupations and deeper emotional experiences, and they constructed a Coleridge to support their interpretations' (ibid. 448).

If, as Perkins argues, theological readings of Coleridge (like any other kind of reading) are as much a product of the critics' 'wider intellectual preoccupations and deeper emotional experiences' as they are the result of an encounter with the text, this might seem to be even more the case with the nineteenth-century contest over the theological content of Wordsworth's poetry; as Stephen Gill (1998: 40) has commented in his excellent study of the celebration of the 'priest of Nature as a source of spiritual power': 'Spiritual power is an almost infinitely elastic term and what people found in, or constructed from Wordsworth, differed greatly. Quakers thought him a Quaker. Anglo-Catholics hailed him as one of themselves. For others it was precisely because it resisted all sectarian labelling that Wordsworth's poetry was so nutritious.' As we have seen in the comments of Keble, Hudson, Kingsley, and Hale White, major claims were made for the spiritualizing and life-changing power of Wordsworth's poetry, but while the Revd F. T. Dibdin (1825: 747) could recommend Wordsworth on the grounds of his 'just and powerful views of religion' in *The Library Companion*, to many the religion of the poetry seemed 'somewhat vague and indeterminate', to quote Alex Patterson (1862: 36).

Wordsworth himself influentially presented his output in ecclesiastical terms, most famously in the 'Preface' to *The Excursion* in which he described the unpublished *Prelude* as having the same relation to *The Recluse* 'as the ante-chapel has to the body of a gothic church' and likened his 'minor Pieces' to 'the little cells, oratories, and sepulchral recesses, ordinarily included in those edifices' (Wordsworth 1949: 2). Writers in their characterizations of the poems often drew on similar ecclesiastical imagery, as when William Spalding (1876: 377) compared *The Excursion* to the 'soul-felt harmony of a divine hymn, pealed forth from a cathedral-organ'. But despite such grand claims for the power of the poetry, the exact nature of the sermon being preached by the Prophet of Nature was often hard to determine. In 1840 Wordsworth (1988: 23) defended himself against this perceived lack of clarity, commenting: 'I have been adverse to frequent mention of the mysteries of Christian faith; not from a want of a due sense of their momentous nature, but the contrary. I felt it far too deeply to venture on handling the subject as familiarly as many scruple not to do'. But Wordsworth's friend Henry Crabbe Robinson offered strikingly different explanations of the issue, noting in 1815 that 'perhaps [Wordsworth] is himself not perfectly clear on the subjects on which his mode of thinking and feeling is anxiously inquired after by his religious admirers' and in 1836 that 'Wordsworth's own religion...would not satisfy a religionist or a sceptic' (Robinson, 1938: i. 158; ii. 481).

A number of the important themes and methodological issues involved in the theological reading of Wordsworth's poetry can be seen in the near lifelong engagement with the poetry of John Wilson, the contributor to *Blackwood's Edinburgh Magazine* who was one of the first to make claims for the poet's genius. As a 17-year-old, Wilson had written to Wordsworth describing *Lyrical Ballads* as 'the book which I value next to my Bible' and in various pieces for *Blackwood's Edinburgh Magazine* in 1818 and 1819 he described Wordsworth as a poet who tuned his mind to nature with a feeling of religious obligation and whose 'seeming self-abstraction from the turmoil of life gives to his poetry a still and religious character that is truly sublime' (Jones and Tydeman 1972: 61; Wilson 1819: 470). Indeed, Wilson would later use an elevated language for the poet himself, remembering a time 'when the Poetry of WILLIAM WORDSWORTH was known but to a few worshippers, to whom it was a religion' and commenting that his poetry would create 'sectarians even in this Natural Religion till the end of time' (Wilson 1835b: 699; 1831: 477). But in a number of pieces of writing, Wilson came increasingly to worry about the lack of reference to doctrine or the role of the church in Wordsworth's religion, describing it in 1827 as 'that of a wanderer in the woods, rather than a frequenter of places of divine worship where Christians meet' and remarking that in the story of Margaret in *The Excursion* the poet seemed to be 'utterly insensible to, or rather utterly forgetful of, religion' (Wilson 1827: 673). Developing these ideas in an extended essay entitled 'Sacred Poetry' in *Blackwood's* in 1828 (later republished in *The Recreations of Christopher North*), Wilson (1828: 925) identified what he thought the 'great and lamentable defect' in Wordsworth's poetry as the lack of any meaningful allusion to 'Revealed Religion'; as a result Wordsworth 'certainly cannot be called a Christian poet'. Focusing on Wordsworth's '"Religion of the Woods"' in *The Excursion*, Wilson argues that the Priest, Pedlar, Poet, and Solitary 'may all, for anything that appears to the contrary, be—deists' and that the 'utter absence of Revealed Religion' in the tale of Margaret 'flings...an air of absurdity over the orthodox Church-of-Englandism...which every now and then breaks out' (ibid. 925–7). But while these essays deny Wordsworth the status of a Christian poet, reassessing the poet's work in 1835 by the light of the setting sun (as he rather prematurely described his old age), Wilson (1835a: 684) was able to reclaim Wordsworth by plotting his poetic career as one of a development towards a mature Christianity, writing that 'In Wordsworth's poetry we see now something far better than the beautiful religion of the Woods. His Ecclesiastical Sonnets are the finest illustrations of Christianity.' Wilson had reviewed *Ecclesiastical Sketches* positively in 1822, praising particularly its treatment of 'Christianity, and great Establishments for the preservation of its doctrines pure and unsullied', and by placing his emphasis on these sketches of the history of the Church of England (rather than on *The Excursion*), Wilson was able to claim Wordsworth not only as 'a Christian Poet' but as the bard of the 'established Church' whose poetry breathes 'so divinely of Christian charity to all whose trust is in the Cross!' (Wilson, 1822: 185; 1835*b*: 710, 708).

Wordsworth's qualification for the title of 'Christian poet' has occupied critics over the past two centuries. Charles Lamb's question on reading *The Excursion* in 1814 'are you a Xtian?' was answered with an emphatic yes as recently as 2001 when William A. Ulmer published his study *The Christian Wordsworth, 1798–1805* (Lamb 1978: iii. 112). But as the example of Wilson illustrates, the answer given often depends on which poems are considered and how his career is constructed. As early as 1815, in a review of *The Excursion* for the *Eclectic Review*, James Montgomery (1815: 19–20) drew attention to the lack of connection between the *natural religion* expressed by the 'Author' and the Wanderer and the more Christian hopes articulated by the pastor, while Wordsworth's friend Henry Crabbe Robinson frequently records in his diary having to defend the poet against attacks such as that from one acquaintance who commented to him: 'I doubt whether Wordsworth is a Christian, if I am to judge of him from *The Excursion*. I think that no better than atheism. At all events, that is not Christianity.' (Crabbe Robinson (1938: i. 65) adds the comment that 'This he afterwards defined to consist in a faith in redemption by Christ and the means of redemption…'.) H. N. Fairchild echoed these sentiments in the middle of the twentieth century, arguing that Wordsworth's failure to incorporate the crucifixion and the resurrection meant he could not be classed as a Christian poet. But, like Wilson, many of those looking for a Christian Wordsworth found reassurance in the later poetry, particularly the *Ecclesiastical Sketches* of 1822 (of which one reviewer commented that the poet had abandoned the divinity of nature for that of 'painted wood, gilt crosses, and priestcraft' (Anon. 1822: 184–5) and *Yarrow Revisited* of 1835. For example, reviewing the latter for the *Christian Remembrancer* (Anon. 1835), the anonymous reviewer saw it as recommending not only religion and morality but church institutions. As the century progressed, it became possible to read the more explicit statements of the later works back into the whole of the poet's output; as Aubrey de Vere (1887: i. 263) commented in his essay 'The Wisdom and Truth of Wordsworth's Poetry', the 'Authentic Theism' of the fourth book of *The Excursion* 'by necessity finds its complement in Christianity—that Christianity so zealously asserted in Wordsworth's maturer poetry, and so obviously implied in the whole of it'.

This nineteenth-century validation of the later Wordsworth for theological reasons has been almost diametrically opposed by the majority of critical assessments of his work in the twentieth which have tended to equate what is presented as a growing Anglicanism with a loss of creative power, an argument summarized in the title of Carson C. Hamilton's 1963 study, *Wordsworth's Decline in Poetic Power: Prophet into High Priest*. For example, in 1919 H. W. Garrod argued that from '1807 on,

Wordsworth sinks deeper and deeper into ordinariness—like a man relapsing into some sensual indulgence; he drugs himself with the humdrum of political and social and religious orthodoxy' (Garrod 1927: 138–40), while David Perkins (1969: 175) has commented that 'with growth of [Wordsworth's] later faith his genius as a poet declined, and there is probably a causal connection'. These changes in the evaluation of Wordsworth, and particularly the move away from seeing his importance in religious terms, can in part be traced back to nineteenth-century developments and particularly Matthew Arnold's favouring of the shorter poems at the expense of *The Excursion* in his edition of the poet, first published in 1879. Countering the approach of 'Wordsworthians' such as Leslie Stephen, whose sense of the importance of the poetry lay in its 'teaching' or philosophy, Arnold criticized those who cited as proof of the poet's excellence passages of 'religious and philosophical doctrine' 'such as we hear in church', arguing that such verse had 'none of the characters of *poetic truth*, the kind of truth which we require from a poet, and in which Wordsworth is really strong' (Arnold 1879: pp. xiv–xx). Arnold's forceful advocacy of this anti-doctrinal, anti-establishment approach to Wordsworth was highly influential, and it is striking how recent accounts of the poet that seek to recover the importance of religion in his work (such as Ryan's *The Romantic Reformation*) frequently do so through a reclamation of *The Excursion*.

In the closing decade of Wordsworth's life, the growing sense of him as a Christian poet and spokesman for the established church gained increasing support from the developing image of him as one who lived an ideal Christian life. This image was consolidated by Christopher Wordsworth's *Memoirs of William Wordsworth* of 1851 which, as Stephen Gill (1998: 35) has shown, presented the poet 'as a die-hard upholder of the National Church'; as William Ewart Gladstone (1851: 151–2) argued in a review of the *Memoirs* for the *Scottish Ecclesiastical Journal*, Wordsworth's letters showed him to be a true Christian, living an unblemished life. As we now know, of course, Wordsworth's life was not as unblemished as either he or Christopher presented it, but this conflation of the poetry and the life has remained influential in Christian readings of the poet, seen, for example in the reasons Lionel Trilling presented in 1951 for considering him an essentially Christian poet. Trilling (1972: 46) provides a lengthy list of the features which he considers Christian:

I have in mind his concern for the life of humbleness and quiet, his search for peace, his sense of the burdens of this life, those which are inherent in the flesh and the spirit of man. Then there is his belief that the bonds of society ought to be inner and habitual, not merely external and formal, and the strengthening of these bonds by the acts and attitudes of charity is a great and charming duty. Christian too seems his responsiveness to the idea that there is virtue in the discharge of duties which are of the great world and therefore dangerous to simple peace... There is his impulse to submit to the conditions of life under a guidance that is at once certain and mysterious; his sense of the possibility and actuality of enlightenment, it need scarcely be said, is one the characteristic things about him. It was not he who said that the world was a vale of soul-making, but the poet who did make the striking paraphrase of the Christian sentiment could not have uttered it had not Wordsworth made it possible for him to do so. And then, above all, there is his consciousness of the *neighbor*, his impulse to bring into the circle of significant life those of the neighbors who are simple and outside the circle of social pride, and those who in the judgement of the world are queer and strange and useless.

While Trilling's account of Wordsworth presents him as a Christian in essence, like a number of the nineteenth-century commentators cited above, it does so in very general terms and does not seek to imply 'completeness or orthodoxy, or even explicitness of doctrine' in the poetry (ibid.). Other readings of the poet, however, have often sought to recruit him to a particular branch of Christianity or to read his poems as expressions of particular doctrinal positions (sometimes even against what is seen as Wordsworth's own conscious beliefs). As Stephen Gill has shown, Wordsworth was recruited by writers on either side of the debate over the Oxford Movement, perhaps most strikingly in the 1842 pamphlet *Contributions of William Wordsworth to the Revival of Catholic Truths*, compiled by Samuel Wilkinson, which claimed that the poet's influence on the Catholic movement had been great (despite failing to find many specific, quotable examples) (S. Gill 1998: 63–7). The opposing reading of Wordsworth in relation to this debate were seen in the pages of the *Westmorland Gazette*, which in December 1854 reported a lecture by George Henry Davis which claimed that Wordsworth's 'writings were one of the principal causes of the late great revival of ceremonial and priestly religion' (Anon. 1854: 5). In an item of correspondence later the same month entitled 'Was Wordsworth a Protestant?', William Pearson (1854: 5; writing as 'An Admirer of Wordsworth and his Poetry') argued that while Wordsworth was charitable towards certain elements of Catholicism, he was nonetheless unmistakably a Protestant.

The argument over Wordsworth's relationship to Catholicism was argued with particular fervour in the 1840s and 1850s (and Gill's account of it is highly recommended), but one persistent element in the Christian readings of the poet over the past two centuries has been the locating of his work within the tradition of dissent, be it Methodism, Quakerism, or even Calvinism. In their review of *The Excursion* for the *Quarterly Review*, Charles Lamb and William Gifford (1814: 104–5) observed that Wordsworth's creed resembled 'an expanded and generous Quakerism' and praised the poem's 'Natural Methodism', while Francis Jeffrey (1814: 4), in his review of the same poem, used the same analogy disparagingly, describing the poem as a 'tissue of moral and devotional ravings... [expressed in the] mystical verbiage of the methodist pulpit'. William Howitt in *Homes and Haunts of the Most Eminent British Poets* of 1847 offered one of the fullest and most developed readings of Wordsworth's poetry in terms of dissent. Asking himself the question what 'is the fundamental philosophy of Wordsworth', Howitt (1847: ii. 273) concludes:

It is, what he, perhaps, would himself start to hear, simply a poetic Quakerism. The Quaker's religious faith is in immediate inspiration. He believes that if he 'centres down,' as he calls it, into his own mind, and puts to rest all his natural faculties and thoughts, he will receive the impulses and intimations of the Divine Spirit. He is not to seek, to strive, to inquire, but to be passive, and receive. This is precisely the great doctrine of Wordsworth, as it regards poetry.

Howitt's subsequent careful reading of the poetry in terms of the traditions and beliefs of Quakerism has been followed in this century by a number of studies which have sought to examine the works in the context of dissent, including important works such as Frederick C. Gill's *The Romantic Movement and Methodism* (1937), Leslie F. Chard's *Dissenting Republicanism: Wordsworth's Early Life and Thought in their Political Context* (1972), Richard E. Brantley's *Wordsworth's 'Natural Methodism'* (1975) and *Locke, Wesley, and the Method of English Romanticism* (1984), James D. Boulger's *The Calvinist Temper in English Poetry* (1980), and Ryan's *The Romantic Reformation* (1997).

A powerful critique of the tendency of some commentators to produce a Wordsworth whose theological position mirrored their own was offered by Walter Bagehot in 1852:

It has been attempted in recent years to establish that the object of his life was to teach Anglicanism. A whole life of him has been written by an official gentleman, with the apparent view of establishing that the great poet was a believer in rood-lofts, an idolater of piscinæ. But this is not capable of rational demonstration.   (Bagehot 1895: i. 31)

For Bagehot, Wordsworth was a 'heretic': 'His real reason for going to live in the mountains was certainly in part sacred, but it was not in the least Tractarian...His whole soul was absorbed in the one idea, the one feeling, the one thought, of the sacredness of the hills' (ibid.). Samuel Taylor Coleridge was similarly unable to detect a theologically satisfactory position in Wordsworth's poetry, commenting that: 'the vague misty, rather than mystic, Confusion of God with the World & the accompanying Nature-worship...is the Trait in Wordsworth's poetic Works that I most dislike, as unhealthful, & denounce as contagious' (Coleridge 1971: 95). Nor was he reassured by the 'the odd occasional introduction of the popular, almost the vulgar, Religion in his later publications', claiming that 'it conjures up to *my* fancy a sort of *Janus*-head of Spinoza and Dr Watts, or "I and my Brother, the Dean"' (ibid. 95). As Bagehot and Coleridge's comments reveal, Wordsworth's 'Nature-Worship', while the most compelling feature of his poetry, was also potentially the most problematic theologically; as Coleridge's reference to Spinoza suggests, it was possible to read Wordsworth's poetry as pantheistic, a philosophy that, in equating God and nature, implied a denial of the personality and transcendence of God. Throughout the nineteenth century, several defences of Wordsworth against the charge of pantheism were offered by writers including Adam Sedgwick (Wordsworth remained 'a man of firm religious convictions' (Gill 1998: 279–80)), Richard Percival Graves ('at no time did [he] identify God and Nature' (ibid. 68)), Stopford Brooke (1910: 85; the 'infinite pleasure of the whole of Nature was felt to be by Wordsworth, not only symbolic of, but actually, the joy of God in His own life'), and Aubrey de Vere (1887: i. 105; 'His imagination was of too spiritual an order to shape itself to material divinities, and his conscience bore witness to a Personal God, the Creator of all things, and Judge of man'). In the more secular twentieth century, critics have been much more willing to accept a pantheistic reading of Wordsworth's early poetry, and the relationship between the roles of religion and philosophy in Wordsworth's response to Nature have been the subject of a number of studies, including Newton P. Stallknecht's *Strange Seas of Thought* (1945), H. N. Fairchild's *Religious Trends in English Poetry*

(1949), H. W. Piper's *The Active Universe* (1962), Jonathan Wordsworth's *The Music of Humanity* (1969), and John A. Hodgson's *Wordsworth's Philosophical Poetry, 1797–1814* (1980). These studies often stress the importance in Wordsworth's developing thought and belief of Coleridge, who has himself been the subject of a number of related studies, including Thomas McFarland's *Coleridge and the Pantheist Tradition* (1969) and Ian Wylie's *Young Coleridge and the Philosophers of Nature* (1989).

While the relationship between God and Nature has been central to theological readings of Wordsworth over the past two hundred years, in the last two or three decades critics have been increasingly concerned with the political and historical dimensions of his religious beliefs. Of course, this approach is not new; in 1868 George Macdonald argued in *England's Antiphon* that it is to the 'terrible disappoint-ment' of the French Revolution that 'we are indebted for the training of Wordsworth to the priesthood of nature's temple' and that when the 'power of God came upon Wordsworth' it brought 'an added insight which made him recognise in the fresh gift all that he had known and felt of such in the past' (Macdonald 1868: 303–4). In the following decade, Stopford Brooke offered the first extended critical reading of *The Prelude* (available only since 1850) in *Theology in the English Poets* to argue that while Wordsworth 'was chiefly saved by his Christianity' from despair following the failure of the revolution, he was only 'partly saved' for 'in rejecting the primary thoughts of the Revolution he rejected half the ideas of Christianity' (Brooke 1910: 153). Whereas these accounts see faith as offering compensation for the failure of political hopes (a model repeated in numerous twentieth-century accounts), M. H. Abrams in his influential book *Natural Supernaturalism* argued that the hopes invested in the Revolution were themselves part of the Romantic 'secularization of inherited theological ideas and ways of thinking' and that with its failure these hopes themselves became internalized: 'faith in an apocalypse by revelation had been replaced by faith in an apocalypse by revolution, and this now gave way to faith in an apocalypse by imagination or cognition' (Abrams 1971: 12, 334). While Abrams's model was one that ultimately saw Wordsworth as moving beyond God and politics to find his true subject in the 'Mind of man', much of the recent theological and religious criticism of the poet has sought to recover more fully what Robert M. Ryan (1997: 1) has described as 'the religious milieu wherein English Romanticism acquired its distinctive character'. Ryan's own study, *The Romantic Reformation*, provides an excellent example of this contextualizing approach presenting Wordsworth, like the other canonical poets of the period, as fully engaged in the religious culture of the time and *The Excursion* as 'an energetic contribution to public religious and political discourse' (ibid. 81). Similarly, much recent work on Coleridge by critics such as Carl Woodring, Leonard W. Deen, Morton D. Paley, Nicholas Roe, Tim Fulford, and Peter J. Kitson has sought to locate his literary output within the context of reformist and dissenting politics (see Fulford 2002). However, in the last few years this historicizing approach to the religious dimensions of Wordsworth's and Coleridge's writing has begun to be challenged by work that draws on the so-called 'theological turn' in Continental philosophy, signalling a revitalized and often highly theorized interest in issues that many of the poets' early readers had responded to, such as the nature of

God and the idea of transcendence. As these developments suggest, the issue of the relationship between literature and religion is regaining a central place in the study of the writing and culture of the Romantic period and the ongoing debate about how best to read Coleridge and Wordsworth theologically is a crucial part of this process.

Works Cited

Abrams, M. H. 1971. *Natural Supernaturalism: Tradition and Revolution in Romantic Literature*. New York: W. W. Norton.

Anon. 1822. 'Review of *Ecclesiastical Sketches*'. *General Weekly Register*. 5 May: 184–5.

—— 1829. 'The Present State of Poetry'. *Leeds Monthly Magazine*. 1 March: 4–13.

—— 1835. 'Review of *Yarrow Revisited*'. *Christian Remembrancer*. 17 (July): 413.

—— 1854. 'Protestant Alliance: Lecture on the Reformation'. *Westmorland Gazette* 37 (2 December): 5.

Arnold, Matthew (ed.) 1879. *The Poems of Wordsworth*. London: Macmillan.

Bagehot, Walter. 1895. *Literary Studies*, ed. Richard Holt Hutton. 3 vols. London: Longmans, Green.

Barfield, Owen. 1971. *What Coleridge Thought*. Middletown, Conn.: Wesleyan University Press.

Barth, J. Robert. 1969. *Coleridge and Christian Doctrine*. Cambridge, Mass.: Harvard University Press.

—— 2003. *Romanticism and Transcendence: Wordsworth, Coleridge, and the Religious Imagination*. Columbia: University of Missouri Press.

Boulger, James D. 1961. *Coleridge as Religious Thinker*. New Haven: Yale University Press.

—— 1980. *The Calvinist Temper in English Poetry*. The Hague: Mouton.

Brantley, Richard E. 1975. *Wordsworth's 'Natural Methodism'*. New Haven: Yale University Press.

—— 1984. *Locke, Wesley, and the Method of English Romanticism*. Gainesville: University Presses of Florida.

Brooke, Stopford A. 1893. *The Development of Theology as Illustrated in English Poetry from 1780–1830. The Essex Hall Lecture, 1893*. London: Philip Green.

—— 1910. *Theology in the English Poets: Cowper, Coleridge, Wordsworth and Burns*. London: J. M. Dent.

Chard, Leslie F. 1972. *Dissenting Republicanism: Wordsworth's Early Life and Thought in their Political Context*. The Hague: Mouton.

Coleridge, Samuel Taylor. 1971. *Collected Letters of Samuel Taylor Coleridge*, v. *1820–1825*, ed. Earl Leslie Griggs. Oxford: Clarendon.

Collins, Edward J. M. 1848. *Windermere; A Poem: and Sonnets*. Kendal: Atkinson & Hamilton.

Dibdin, Revd T. F. 1825. *The Library Companion; or, The Young Man's Guide, and the Old Man's Comfort, in the Choice of a Library*. London: Harding, Triphook, & Lepard.

Empson, William. 1973. Introduction. *Coleridge's Verse: A Selection*, ed. David Pirie. New York: Schocken.

Fairchild, Hoxie Neale. 1949. *Religious Trends in English Poetry*, iii. *1780–1830. Romantic Faith*. New York: Columbia University Press.

Fulford, Tim (ed.) 2002. *Romanticism and Millenarianism*. Houndmills: Palgrave.

GARROD, H. W. 1927. *Wordsworth: Lectures and Essays*. Oxford: Clarendon.

GILL, FREDERICK C. 1937. *The Romantic Movement and Methodism: A Study of English Romanticism and the Evangelical Revival*. London: Epworth.

GILL, STEPHEN. 1998. *Wordsworth and the Victorians*. Oxford: Clarendon.

GLADSTONE, WILLIAM EWART. 1851. 'Review of Christopher Wordsworth's *Memoirs of William Wordsworth*'. *Scottish Ecclesiastical Journal* 7 (17 July): 151–2.

HAMILTON, CARSON C. 1963. *Wordsworth's Decline in Poetic Power: Prophet into High Priest*. New York. Exposition.

HARE, JULIUS CHARLES. 1850. *The Mission of the Comforter*. Cambridge: Macmillan.

HAWEIS, REVD H. R. 1880. *Poets in the Pulpit*. London: Low, Marston, Searle, and Rivington.

HODGSON, JOHN A. 1980. *Wordsworth's Philosophical Poetry, 1797–1814*. Lincoln: University of Nebraska Press.

HOWITT, WILLIAM. 1847. *Homes and Haunts of the Most Eminent British Poets*. London: Richard Bentley.

JACKSON, J. R. DE J. (ed.) 1991. *Coleridge: The Critical Heritage*, ii. *1834–1900*. London. Routledge.

JASPER, DAVID. 1985. *Coleridge as Poet and Religious Thinker: Inspiration and Revelation*. London: Macmillan.

JEFFREY, FRANCIS. 1814. 'Art. 1. *The Excursion*'. *The Edinburgh Review* 24 (Nov.): 1–30.

JONES, ALUN R., and TYDEMAN WILLIAM, (eds.) 1972. *Wordsworth. Lyrical Ballads: A Casebook*. London: Macmillan.

KEBLE, JOHN. 1912. *Lectures on Poetry, 1832–1841*, trans. Edward Kershaw Francis. 2 vols. Oxford. Clarendon.

KINGSLEY, CHARLES. 1877. *His Letters and Memories of his Life*, ed. His Wife. 2 vols. London: H. S. King.

—— 1888. *His Letters and Memories of his Life*, ed. His Wife. 16th abridged edn. 2 vols. London: Kegan Paul, Trench & Co.

LAMB, CHARLES, and GIFFORD, WILLIAM. 1814. 'The Excursion. A Poem'. *Quarterly Review* 12 (Oct.): 100–11.

—— and LAMB, MARY. 1978. *The Letters of Charles and Mary Lamb*. 3 vols. Ithaca: Cornell University Press.

MACDONALD, GEORGE. [1868]. *England's Antiphon*. [n.p.]: Macmillan.

MCFARLAND, THOMAS. 1969. *Coleridge and the Pantheist Tradition*. Oxford: Clarendon.

MONTGOMERY, JAMES. 1815. 'The Excursion'. *Eclectic Review*, 13–38.

NEWSOME, DAVID. 1974. *Two Classes of Men: Platonism and English Romantic Thought*. London: John Murray.

PATTERSON, ALEXANDER. 1862. *Poets and Preachers of the Nineteenth-Century*. Glasgow.

PEARSON, WILLIAM. 1854. 'Was Wordsworth a Protestant?' *Westmorland Gazette* 37 (23 Dec.): 5.

PERKINS, DAVID. 1969. *English Romantic Writers*. Cambridge, Mass.: Harvard University Press.

—— 1996. 'The "Ancient Mariner" and Its Interpreters: Some Versions of Coleridge'. *Modern Language Quarterly* 573: 425–48.

PERKINS, MARY ANNE. 1994. *Coleridge's Philosophy: The Logos as Unifying Principle*. Oxford: Clarendon.

—— 2002. 'Religious Thinker', in Lucy Newlyn (ed.) *Coleridge*. Cambridge. Cambridge University Press, 187–99.

PIPER, H. W. 1962. *The Active Universe: Pantheism and the Concept of the Imagination in the English Romantic Poets*. London: Athlone.

PRICKETT, STEPHEN. 1976. *Romanticism and Religion. The Tradition of Coleridge and Wordsworth in the Victorian Church*. Cambridge: Cambridge University Press.

REARDON, BERNARD M. G. 1995. *Religious Thought in the Victorian Age: A Survey from Coleridge to Gore*. London: Longman.

ROBINSON, HENRY CRABBE. 1938. *Henry Crabbe Robinson on Books and their Writers*, ed. Edith J. Morley. 3 vols. London: J. M. Dent.

RYAN, ROBERT M. 1997. *The Romantic Reformation: Religious Politics in English Literature, 1789–1824*. Cambridge: Cambridge University Press.

SANDERS, CHARLES RICHARD. 1942. *Coleridge and the Broad Church Movement: Studies in S. T. Coleridge, Dr. Arnold of Rugby, J. C. Hare, Thomas Carlyle and F. D. Maurice*. Durham, NC: Duke University Press.

SPALDING, WILLIAM. 1876. *The History of English Literature; with an Outline of the Origin and Growth of the English Language; Illustrated by Extracts; For the Use of Schools and of Private Students. Continued to 1870*. Edinburgh: Oliver & Boyd.

STALLKNECHT, NEWTON P. 1945. *Strange Seas of Thought. Studies in William Wordsworth's Philosophy of Man and Nature*. Durham, NC: Duke University Press.

TRILLING, LIONEL. 1972. 'Wordsworth and the Iron Time', in M. H. Abrams (ed.), *Wordsworth: A Collection of Critical Essays*. Englewood Cliffs: Prentice Hall, 44–66.

TULLOCH, JOHN. 1885. *Movements of Religious Thought in Britain during the Nineteenth Century: Being the Fifth Series of St. Giles' Lectures*. London: Longmans, Green.

—— 1991. 'Coleridge as a Spiritual Thinker'. *Coleridge: The Critical Heritage*, ii. *1834–1900*. London: Routledge, 156–86.

ULMER, WILLIAM A. 2001. *The Christian Wordsworth, 1798–1805*. Albany: State University of New York Press.

VERE, AUBREY DE. 1887. *Essays Chiefly on Poetry*. 2 vols. London: Macmillan.

WARREN, ROBERT PENN. 1989. 'A Poem of Pure Imagination: An Experiment in Reading.' *New and Selected Essays*. New York: Random House, 335–423.

WENDLING, RONALD C. 1995. *Coleridge's Progress to Christianity: Experience and Authority in Religious Faith*. Lewisburg, Pa.: Bucknell University Press.

WHITE, WILLIAM HALE. 1881. *The Autobiography of Mark Rutherford, Dissenting Minister. Ed. by his Friend, Reuben Shapcott*. London: Trübner.

WILLEY, BASIL. 1971. 'Coleridge and Religion'. R. L. Brett (ed.), *S. T. Coleridge*. London: G. Bell & Sons.

—— 1972. *Samuel Taylor Coleridge*. London: Chatto & Windus.

WILSON, JOHN. 1819. 'Crabbe's Tales of the Hall'. *Blackwood's Edinburgh Magazine* 5 (July): 469–71.

—— 1822. 'Wordsworth's Sonnets and Memorials'. *Blackwood's Edinburgh Magazine* 12 (Aug.): 175–91.

—— 1827. 'Aird's Religious Characteristics'. *Blackwood's Edinburgh Magazine* 21 (June): 677–94.

—— 1828. 'Sacred Poetry'. *Blackwood's Edinburgh Magazine* 24 (Dec.): 917–38.

—— 1831. 'An Hour's Talk about Poetry'. *Blackwood's Edinburgh Magazine* 30 (Sept.): 475–90.

—— 1835a. 'Mant's British Months'. *Blackwood's Edinburgh Magazine* 37 (Apr.): 684–98.

—— 1835b. 'Wordsworth's New Volume'. *Blackwood's Edinburgh Magazine* 37 (May): 699–722.

WORDSWORTH, JONATHAN. 1969. *The Music of Humanity. A Critical Study of Wordsworth's Ruined Cottage, Incorporating Texts from a Manuscript of 1799–1800*. London. Nelson.

WORDSWORTH, WILLIAM. 1879. *The Poems of Wordsworth*, ed. Matthew Arnold. London: Macmillan.

—— 1949. *The Poetic Works of William Wordsworth*, v. *The Excursion*, ed. E. Selincourt and Helen Darbishire. Oxford: Clarendon.

WORDSWORTH, WILLIAM. 1988. *The Letters of William and Dorothy Wordsworth; The Later Years, Part 4: 1840–1885*, ed. Alan G. Hill. Oxford: Clarendon.

WYLIE, IAN. 1989. *Young Coleridge and the Philosophers of Nature*. Oxford. Clarendon.

FURTHER READING

ABRAMS, M. H. 1971. *Natural Supernaturalism: Tradition and Revolution in Romantic Literature*. New York: W. W. Norton.

BARTH, J. ROBERT. 2003. *Romanticism and Transcendence: Wordsworth, Coleridge, and the Religious Imagination*. Columbia: University of Missouri Press.

FAIRCHILD, HOXIE NEALE. 1949. *Religious Trends in English Poetry*, iii. *1780–1830. Romantic Faith*. New York: Columbia University Press.

GILL, STEPHEN. 1998. *Wordsworth and the Victorians*. Oxford: Clarendon.

JACKSON, J. R. DE J. (ed.) 1991. *Coleridge: The Critical Heritage*, ii. *1834–1900*. London. Routledge.

JASPER, DAVID. 1985. *Coleridge as Poet and Religious Thinker: Inspiration and Revelation*. London: Macmillan.

PERKINS, MARY ANNE. 1994. *Coleridge's Philosophy: The Logos as Unifying Principle*. Oxford: Clarendon.

PRICKETT, STEPHEN. 1976. *Romanticism and Religion. The Tradition of Coleridge and Wordsworth in the Victorian Church*. Cambridge: Cambridge University Press.

RYAN, ROBERT M. 1997. *The Romantic Reformation: Religious Politics in English Literature, 1789–1824*. Cambridge: Cambridge University Press.

SANDERS, CHARLES RICHARD. 1942. *Coleridge and the Broad Church Movement: Studies in S. T. Coleridge, Dr. Arnold of Rugby, J. C. Hare, Thomas Carlyle and F. D. Maurice*. Durham, NC: Duke University Press.

WILLEY, BASIL. 1971. 'Coleridge and Religion', in R. L. Brett (ed.), *S.T. Coleridge*. London: G. Bell & Sons.

CHAPTER 29

GEORGE ELIOT AND HARDY

NORMAN VANCE

GEORGE Eliot was the first English translator of the iconoclastically post-Christian commentators David Strauss (*The Life of Christ*, 1846) and Ludwig Feuerbach (*The Essence of Christianity*, 1854). But as a novelist she continued to explore connections between divinity (or 'the Unseen') and human goodness in an informal, residually numinous 'Religion of Humanity' which was influenced but not dominated by the secular positivism first developed by Auguste Comte. Her poem 'O may I join the choir invisible' in praise of 'the growing life of man' was often used liturgically at services conducted by English positivists, and was set to music as an almost-sacred cantata in 1883 (Wright 1986: 173–201, 84, 95). She has constantly received the more or less respectful attentions not just of literary critics and fellow-agnostics such as Leslie Stephen (1902) but of theologians (Selby 1896; Hodgson 2001).

Thomas Hardy, much more overtly negative about traditional Christianity in his novels, has been less congenial to theologians, though Pamela Dalziel (2006) has recently demonstrated his sustained religious seriousness. T. G. Selby (1896: 92, 129) condemned his 'terrible and inflammatory impeachments' of moral and religious principle and the 'hopeless note' in much of his writing. Selby's more conservative contemporary Samuel Law Wilson, MA, DD, complained (1897: 382, 396) of 'dabbling in beastliness and putrefaction' in Hardy's later novels and the 'wail of moral helplessness' of his high-handed sinners. In the light of Hardy's occasional statements through his narrators or narrative commentators that Christianity is a transient and outworn faith it is difficult to dislodge G. K. Chesterton's patronizing verdict (1966: 62): 'a sort of village atheist brooding and blaspheming over the village idiot'. Even so, Hardy and Eliot, both selectively attracted to Comte and the Comtean 'Religion of

Humanity' (Wright 1986: 202–17), have much in common as religiously significant writers. Hardy owned, and read at least some of, Eliot's translation of Strauss's *Life of Jesus* (Björk 1985: i. 381). The first number of the originally anonymous serial version of Hardy's *Far from the Madding Crowd* (1874) prompted R. H. Hutton to observe in *The Spectator* (3 January 1874) 'If [it] is not written by George Eliot, then there is a new light among novelists,' and the young Henry James observed rather loftily in *The Nation* (24 December 1874) that 'the author has evidently read to good purpose the low-life chapters in George Eliot's novels'. The common sympathetic concern in Hardy and Eliot with 'low life', the moral and spiritual dignity and difficulty of humble, ordinary people, often presented in rural settings, was a shared legacy from the Wordsworth of 'Michael' or 'The Old Cumberland Beggar', but detailed scholarly work on Hardy and Eliot (Jędrzewski 1996; Jay 1979) has helped to demonstrate that they also shared aspects of a more specifically religious heritage. Hardy as well as Eliot had grown up with the Evangelical habit of Bible reading and serious reflection which never left him and which led to complex but by no means wholly negative critical engagements with traditional theology and institutional Christianity. Even the hostile Samuel Law Wilson (1897: 407), considering Hardy's earlier fiction and the poetry, was forced to admit that 'though exiled from the great Father's house, he has not ceased to cast some longing, lingering looks behind'.

Thinking more of politics and society than of religion, Dr Johnson had urged his friend Boswell to clear the mind of cant. The least that can be said of religious critique in the work of Eliot and Hardy is that it acts on this robust advice, restated after their time by Paul Ricœur who presents atheism as it has developed in the work of Nietzsche and Freud as both a destructive and a religiously liberating force, engaging with what he sees as the 'rotten points' of religion and clearing the ground for 'a faith beyond accusation and consolation' (MacIntyre and Ricœur 1969: 60). Both novelists would have endorsed the implied critique of pitiless 'accusation' or narrowly sanctimonious morality too often associated with conventional religion, and both felt uneasy about glibly metaphysical 'consolation' as opposed to human sympathy. But George Eliot would have rejected the label 'atheist', and despite his anti-religious grumblings it does not sit entirely comfortably on Hardy either. Unwilling to appear as a propagandist rather than an artist, he refused to join the Rationalist Press Association (Wright 1986: 202), and late in life he refused to be included in the secularist Joseph McCabe's *Dictionary of Modern Rationalists* (1920) (Hardy 1978–88: vii. 162). If he was not a conventional believer he was not a conventional unbeliever either, and he could be at least as sceptical of scientific rationalism and the positivist 'Religion of Humanity' as he was of institutional Christianity (Hands 1989: 118).

It needs to be stressed that more or less sceptical novelists, however interested in philosophy and religion, are not philosophers or theologians. Hardy's and Eliot's religious insights disclosed in their creative work over the years are provisional and variable. As Hardy observed in the 1892 Preface to *Tess of the d'Urbervilles*, his novel was 'charged with impressions' rather than formal convictions. *Jude* was similarly defended in the Preface to the first edition (1895) as 'a series of seemings, or personal impressions.' Both writers read widely in controversial literature, but their responses were critical and selective: neither wholeheartedly or enduringly subscribed to the teaching of any of the various post-Christian thinkers they had studied, and it is unnecessarily reductive to try to read their novels as positivist parables or Feuerbachian fables. Neither made any claim to be a systematic religious (or anti-religious) thinker and both addressed religious matters over a long period through dramatized situations, or (occasionally) more or less ironic or poetic self-dramatization, rather than formal disquisition. The tentative pluralism of Eliot's phrase 'experiments in life' applied to her fiction (1954–78: vi. 216–17) resonates with Hardy's 'impressions' or 'seemings'. Rather than attempting to construct an artificially homogeneous theology for either it might be more helpful to consider religion in their work as an evolving series of perceptions mainly arising from and articulated through fictional narratives and lyrical moments of insight or poignant awareness.

The format of Eliot's first published religious reflections, while she was still contemplating turning to fiction, was the book review, in which ideas developed not in a vacuum but in dialogue with the book under review. In the early 1840s, partly under the influence of progressive friends in Coventry, she had vigorously renounced her belief in the dogmatic Christianity of her upbringing. The family tensions and the rebellious anger and antagonism associated with that difficult period gradually receded and she found she could accommodate what was noblest in Christianity. In 1856 the Evangelical austerity that might once have condemned emotional vagueness and frivolous worldliness in manners and material culture in order to emphasize more serious concerns was only slightly displaced into argumentative endorsement of the doctrine of 'realism' in Ruskin's moral aesthetics in a review of the third volume of *Modern Painters*:

The truth of infinite value that he teaches is realism—the doctrine that all truth and beauty are to be attained by a humble and faithful study of nature, and not by substituting vague forms, bred by imagination on the mists of feeling, in place of definite, substantial reality. The thorough acceptance of this doctrine would remould our life.   (Eliot 1992: 248)

Unfortunately, as she noted in another review in the same year, this doctrine had not reached many of the lady novelists of the day who attempted to write on religious themes:

as a general rule, the ability of a lady novelist to describe actual life and her fellow-men, is in inverse proportion to her confident eloquence about God and the other world, and the means by which she usually chooses to conduct you to true ideas of the invisible is a totally false picture of the visible.   (Ibid. 306)

Her stern review of 'Evangelical teaching: Dr Cumming' criticized a fashionable Evangelical preacher who was conspicuously lacking in genuine charity. His rhetorical excesses and his intellectually shoddy religious populism were mercilessly dissected and deplored, not so much because they defended an unbelievable religion as because they wilfully ignored the most vital and enduring part of Christianity, which she was still content to describe in conventional religious language:

of really spiritual joys and sorrows, of the life and death of Christ as a manifestation of love that constrains the soul, of sympathy with that yearning over the lost and erring which made Jesus weep over Jerusalem, and prompted the sublime prayer, 'Father, forgive them', of the gentler fruits of the Spirit and the peace of God which passeth understanding—of this, we find little trace in Dr Cumming's discourses.   (Ibid. 141–2)

Scenes of Clerical Life (1858), her first venture in fiction, can be seen as both a more extended response to Dr Cumming and a series of experiments sifting and testing what Eliot had come to see as the mixed quality of her partly discarded Evangelical heritage. Moral and religious sympathy proves more durable than doctrine. Revd Amos Barton's vanity, thoughtless insensitivity, and intellectual limitations as an Evangelical preacher bring no particular credit to his faith but he is brought close to the heart of Eliot's residual religion of sympathy and suffering when his overworked wife dies and his alienated parishioners respond to his human distress as they never had to his preaching. In 'Mr Gilfil's Love-Story' Maynard Gilfil's spirituality comes out not in his yellowing sermons, short and shallow, but in the depth of his love for the bruised and suffering Tina. The title of 'Janet's Repentance' implies a conventionally Evangelical conversion narrative of the kind that the new Evangelical clergyman Mr Tryan might have been expected to relish, but the topic is cleared of cant by a narrative tracing deliverance from the evil of self-absorbed despair in a degrading and brutal marriage and an awakening to a new life of devotion to others.

The Hebrew word 'Adam' can mean a man, or mankind generally, as well as the first man, the biblical individual called Adam who in the New Testament is linked with spiritual renewal through Christ the redeemer, the second Adam (1 Cor. 15: 22, 45). Eliot's first novel *Adam Bede* (1859) takes advantage of this range of meaning to explore moral and religious issues and the possibilities of renewal in the life of man while apparently concerning itself only with the (fictional) individual Adam Bede. The novel accepts that Methodism, discreetly doing duty for institutional religion more generally, may have lost some of its early fire and fervour. It explores the early days of Methodism in the 1790s and uses that epoch as a metaphor for the fervent beginnings of Christianity itself. Early in the novel Dinah Morris's emotionally effective open-air preaching recalls not merely Wesley and his followers but the out-of-doors preaching and loving ministry of Jesus himself, described by Dinah as 'doing good to poor people' and performing 'miracles to feed the hungry' (Eliot 1996a: 26). Eliot redescribes miracle and mystery as human compassion. Much later, when Bartle Massey seeks to feed the righteous—but betrayed and embittered—Adam, the bread and the wine function as a kind of informal sacrament, symbolizing a kind of renewal as Adam in his distress learns the lesson of mercy which brings him back into the community of love and sympathy and makes him part of it. The sin and sorrow of the world, and the suffering at the heart of the novel, are linked by Dinah not just with the suffering of the crucified Christ but with God himself, 'that Divine Love which is one with his sorrow' (ibid. 328). The pregnant Hetty's distress prompts the narrator to thoughts of the cross (ibid. 364) and the reflection that 'No wonder man's religion has much sorrow in it: no wonder he needs a Suffering God.' This recalls the fifth chapter of Feuerbach's *The Essence of Christianity*, entitled (in Eliot's translation) 'The Mystery of the Suffering God', which addresses itself very specifi-cally to links between human and divine suffering not just in an incarnate Christ but in God himself. But Eliot was not obliged to be an uncritical Feuerbachian and Feuerbach's remorseless insistence that everything in Christianity is pure construc-tion, a merely human projection of subjective feeling, is more extreme than anything in Eliot. It has been suggested (Hodgson 2001: 57) that suffering in *Adam Bede* has links with Luther's emphasis on the cross and human suffering and anticipates post-Holocaust and feminist theologies which present God as no longer impassive and immutable but subject to process and change through direct involvement with suffering and historical development.

The Mill on the Floss (1860) also explores pain and suffering, in the life of Maggie Tulliver, but it moves beyond them. It ends with a sense of reconciliation in death, of recovery of a lost Eden of childhood affection and trust between Maggie and her brother Tom. This love restored in the midst of a catastrophic flood suggests both the view of the *Song of Songs* (8: 7) that 'Many waters cannot quench love' and that as in the biblical lament of David for Saul and Jonathan (2 Sam. 1: 23), which provides an epigraph for the novel as a whole, death need not bring division: 'in their death they were not divided'. The biblical frame of reference is reinforced by allusion to spiritual classics which contributed to the formation of both Maggie Tulliver and the young George Eliot. The landscape of the novel is linked for Maggie with the journey of Christiana in Bunyan's *Pilgrim's Progress* (Eliot 1996b: 41) and indeed Bunyan's pilgrimage narrative, including the passage through 'The Valley of Humiliation', which Eliot uses as her title for Book Fourth of the novel, provides a metaphor for Maggie's constantly frustrated secular progress. Thomas à Kempis's *Imitation of Christ*, which George Eliot had encountered in Richard Challoner's much-reprinted translation (1737), describes the need to accept the crucifixion of self-sacrifice, confirming Maggie's act of renunciation in the last movement of the novel (ibid. 515): 'I have received the Cross, I have received it from thy hand; I will bear it, and bear it till death, as Thou hast laid it upon me.' The Conclusion gestures towards peace and renewal (ibid. 521–2) but stops short of the glibly accepting piety and blandly proffered consolation that would have neutralized Maggie Tulliver's rebelli-ous passion and suffering: 'Nature repairs her ravages—but not all. . . . To the eyes that have dwelt on the past, there is no thorough repair.'

More efficient repair of human damage is offered in *Silas Marner* (1861). The narrative has the simplicity of a fairy tale. The solitary and embittered Silas Marner, robbed of his hoarded wealth, finds the abandoned Eppie by his hearth and with her discovers a new purpose in life. In a sense the miser's gold is replaced by the golden-haired child. The narrative functions as a kind of extended parable of salvation which provides humanitarian fulfilment of the messianic prophecy of Isaiah that 'a little child shall lead them' (Isa. 11: 6). The Bible also describes angels leading the faithful to safety from Sodom, the city of destruction from which Bunyan's Pilgrim set out for the celestial city. Eliot suggests that men still need to taken by the hand and led from threatening destruction, a moral, religious, and a humanitarian imperative, and Eppie shows (Eliot 1996c: 130) how 'the hand may be a little child's'.

Eliot's later novels engage with individual moral agents in relation to a wider social and public, sometimes political, life and the processes by which that shared life evolves. *Romola* (1863) is an erudite historical novel set in fifteenth-century Florence at a time of political and historical crisis when Lorenzo di Medici has died, French influence threatens Florentine autonomy, and the radical preacher Savonarola is a major influence on public life. The public situation brings religion and politics, prophecy and history, and individual lives into sometimes abrasive contact, and while Savonarola is quite sympathetically presented there is a sense both of puritanical excess in his 'bonfire of the vanities' and of an insidious corruption of the prophetic office. The moral ambivalence of prophecy as Savonarola proclaims it is evident from the fact that it inspires both the saintly Romola and the passionately vengeful Baldassare. Romola realizes that the 'wicked folly' of the mad Camilla is excited if not expressly sanctioned by Savonarola (Eliot 1994: 419), and that he is powerless to restrain her religious mania. For the historical narrative to have some moral currency with nineteenth-century readers there had to be some sense of connections and parallels. Savonarola's fervour anticipates the more extreme forms of Evangelical preaching George Eliot had encountered in youth. The pagan exuberance of Politian's celebration of classical deities in the novel has its unspoken romantic counterpart in Schiller's immensely popular lyric 'The gods of Greece'. This is perhaps why Tito's Mediterranean paganism, which makes him a kind of sun-god, an antitype to Savonarola, is so seductively attractive. Tito's evil, which develops only gradually, is not Satanic: it is rather moral cowardice, a self-centred absence of moral courage under duress. As the narrator observes of him (Eliot 1994: 212–13), 'The repentance which cuts off all moorings to evil, demands something more than selfish fear,' even though 'he would still have been glad not to give pain to any mortal'. However, he is brilliantly duplicitous in public life and equally perfidious as a husband. His wronged wife Romola, like Adam Bede before her, develops through suffering and the cross, through renunciation and 'yearning passivity' (ibid. 346), and her individual emotional pilgrimage under Savonarola's spiritual direction is a kind of microcosm or anticipation of larger historical processes which Savonarola tries but fails to direct. The characteristically agonizing progress towards a better world, 'The great world-struggle of developing thought', for her as for Eliot, 'is continually foreshadowed in the struggle of the affections, seeking a justification for love and hope' (ibid. 420).

Felix Holt, the Radical (1866), set at the time of the first great Reform Bill of 1832, is in effect a response to the movement towards further parliamentary reform in the 1860s. As the present writer has argued elsewhere (Vance 1980), the anti-establishment religious radicalism of that 'rusty old puritan' Rufus Lyon, a dissenting minister, is linked by the intricate inheritance plot with both the radical campaign for parliamentary reform and the religiously derived notion of fundamental Law which underpins a more profoundly radical critique of a moribund, morally compromised, and dysfunctional aristocratic society. As always in Eliot personal integrity and moral courage are crucial, the essential moral basis for any enduring social order. The future of the nation seems to lie not so much with politicians and public figures as with thoroughly decent private individuals such as Esther Lyon who marries the political activist Felix Holt. Their wedding is described in the Epilogue (Eliot 1988: 397) as a vindication of 'everything that's good'.

The same era of reform and the same sense of rapid, unnerving social change provide the context for *Middlemarch* (1871–2), her most ambitious and successful novel. Archbishop Trench of Dublin managed to fit a copy inside his hat so he could surreptitiously read it on his knee while apparently listening to speeches on a public occasion (Eliot 1954–78: v. 291). What the Archbishop saw in his hat was in a sense a soberly realist modernized version of exemplary saints' lives. Dorothea Brooke is named after one saint and her progress in life is explicitly compared with that of another, Teresa of Avila. Like the crusading Middlemarch doctor Tertius Lydgate, she has brought a lofty idealism to her adult life which is bruised but in her case channelled rather than defeated by contact with practical realities and constrained circumstances. Unlike St Teresa she does not found a new religious order, but she does at least contribute to 'the growing good of the world', the phrase Eliot uses in the last paragraph of the novel to generalize from her significance and achievement. The impulse to various kinds of reform which pervades the novel is accompanied by aspirations to uncover underlying principle, whether Dorothea's clergyman husband's doomed search for a key to all mythologies or Lydgate's search for basic tissue. Even if neither quest is successful the different narrative strands of the novel combine to disclose another principle, a secular gospel of social benevolence and human interconnectedness, and in ch. 80 the point at which Dorothea awakens to it after personal crisis and the death of private joy is presented as a secular conversion to a new life modelled on religious conversion in Bunyan (Newey 1984). This new life, linking self-sacrifice with social improvement, undogmatically religious in its sense of dedication, is the destiny or aspiration of most of George Eliot's passionate, idealistic heroines from Maggie Tulliver to Romola, eventually seen as a Madonna figure, and it is the life the self-absorbed Gwendolen Harleth needs to find for herself in *Daniel Deronda* (1876).

The Jewish and Zionist theme of this novel, famously deplored by F. R. Leavis who wished it excised from the novel, provides a natural point of connection between politics and the religiously derived if potentially unbalanced or unbalancing sense of rigorous moral imperatives in public and private life which Matthew Arnold had recently labelled 'Hebraism'. The sympathetic account of the Jewish sense of tradition and of the vision of a homeland for the Jews is important in its own right, but it also does duty for a range of recent or contemporary instances of the problem of the righteous nation, notably the race issue in the American Civil War and in the controversial prosecution of Governor Eyre in Jamaica and the Italian struggle to achieve a free and united Italy. It has been observed (Carpenter 1986) that Christian as well as Jewish visions of history are at work in the narrative. The traditional attributes of Christ as prophet, priest, and king are in a sense distributed between the novel's two moral exemplars, Mordecai with his visionary Old Testament rhetoric which recalls Scott's covenanters in *Old Mortality* and Rufus Lyon in *Felix Holt*, and Deronda, Mordecai's Messiah figure who is equipped by education, wealth, and social standing for the public world of national and international affairs and who also functions as an almost oppressively righteous secular priest and confessor, particularly to Gwendolen. Grandcourt's barbed question in ch. 48, 'I suppose you take Deronda for a saint,' provokes Gwendolen to unflattering comparison. Grandcourt's moral ruthlessness, contrasting with Deronda's righteousness, makes him the anti-type of the virtuous public man, supportive of racist oppression and oppressive and tyrannical as a husband.

George Eliot's residually Christian morality attracted the scorn of the more radically post-Christian Friedrich Nietzsche who snorted at 'little moralistic females à la Eliot' and attributed to her a characteristically English inconsistency in not rejecting the morality as well as the metaphysics of traditional Christianity (Nietzsche 1971: 515). Thomas Hardy's much more outspoken condemnation of institutional Christianity and his overt and controversial sympathy for unconventional sexual morality in his later novels, notably *Tess of the d'Urbervilles* and *Jude the Obscure*, might seem closer to the revolutionary spirit of Nietzsche. It might even seem to invite comparison with the extreme view attributed to Dostoevsky's Ivan Karamazov by his enemy, that if God was dead, if belief in God and human immortality had ceased, then everything, even cannibalism, was permitted.

But Hardy stops well short of this. His poem 'God's Funeral' (1908–10) is not a celebration but a sombrely nostalgic fantasy, the speaker 'dazed and puzzled'. He wrote that Nietzsche's ruthless moral teaching could bring 'disaster to humanity' (Hardy 1902; Williamson 1978). His enduring sense of human compassion, which Nietzsche would have dismissed as mere weakness, a feature of 'slave morality', was ultimately formalized as the 'Spirit of the Pities' in his enormous epic drama *The Dynasts* (1903–8). Throughout his writing career Hardy registered a sustained protest against tolerating cruelty or uncharity. In so far as charity is at the heart of Christian morality, Hardy's attacks on the church and churchmen are not so much an indictment of Christianity as of failures in charity, failures, in a sense, to be Christian enough. If one substitutes scribes and pharisees for Hardy's haughty or ineffectual churchmen his work begins to look more Christian in essentials than one might have expected. On the other hand the humane indictment of cruelty raises the problem of theodicy, of how to justify what seems to be divinely tolerated evil: how can a benign, all-powerful God be so cruel as to permit the suffering, natural and man-made, which disfigures the world he created? The problem was not new. As Hardy was well aware, the appalling Lisbon earthquake of 1755 had been more than enough to unsettle any simple confidence in divine providence in Voltaire and others. Hardy's notebooks, which include many extracts from his friend John Morley's *Voltaire* (1872, repr. 1886), also record (Björk 1985: i. 14), from the 1855 edition of G. H. Lewes's *Life of Goethe*, that 'Goethe's religion was all taken out of him by the Lisbon earthquake.'

The sense that neither God nor the amoral natural order as it had been redescribed for Hardy's generation by Darwin and Darwin's popularizer T. H. Huxley can be relied on to ensure human happiness and fulfilment, that nature is at best indifferent, runs through most of Hardy's novels with varying degrees of intensity. Perceptions of natural blight, of natural process doomed to go nowhere, are most apparent in the descriptions of ill-grown trees in *The Woodlanders* (1887), metaphors for the blighted lives of Giles Winterbourne and Marty South.

The popular taste which magazine serials aimed to please would not tolerate too much misery, however, and in his anxiety to be considered a good hand at a serial Hardy was usually prepared to compromise with market forces. Diggory Venn is allowed to marry the widowed Thomasin at the end of *The Return of the Native* (1878), though in a footnote Hardy insists austerely that he would have preferred to leave her a widow. Where possible, in place of formulaic happy endings and implicitly providential plots derived from conventional religious assurance and the artificial conventions of stage comedy, Hardy tends to favour tragic plots with elements of melodrama and farce which grimly mock in their excesses the very idea of a benevolently emplotted universe (Beer 1983: 236–58).

The most farcical of all his novels is perhaps *Two on a Tower* (1882) in which the rather severe Bishop of Melchester makes a conventionally good match by becoming the (third) husband of Viviette, Lady Constantine. Her child born after the marriage is not his: he does not know that she has agreed to this union in a moment of despair after she finds she has become pregnant by the young astronomer Swithin, the man she had thought she had legally married when, unknown to them both, her brutal absentee first husband was still alive. Stargazers become star-crossed lovers. The majestic backdrop of the starry heavens, a source of wonder and awe to Immanuel Kant and the basis of Joseph Addison's great hymn to the Creator 'The spacious firmament on high', signals a blindly terrifying rather than a benignly ordered universe during the hours of darkness when 'there is nothing to moderate the blow with which the infinitely great, the stellar universe, strikes down upon the infinitely little, the mind of the beholder' (Hardy 1993*a*: 64). The bishop conveniently dies and Swithin comes back to Viviette. She dies melodramatically of an overstrained heart touched by sudden joy after despair in the last chapter of the novel, like Gloucester at the end of Shakespeare's *King Lear*, but Swithin, her true lover, gives her full credit for generosity and unselfishness, the biblical charity which 'seeketh not her own' (1 Cor. 13: 5).

Though the bishop ends up looking a little foolish, specifically anti-religious comment tends to be fairly muted in this as in most of the earlier novels. Institutional religion and Bible-reading are accepted as part of the social scene. An inherited fascination with hymns and church choirs provides background for the comedy of *Under the Greenwood Tree* (1872). The mangled Prayer Book allusions and biblical quotations of Joseph Poorgrass in *Far from the Madding Crowd* (1874) are a source of humour more than sardonic irony, and the humorously named Parson Thirdly does no harm even if he does little real good either. Church architecture, religious Dissent, and debate about infant baptism which had once exercised the young Hardy contribute to the rather melodramatic plot of *A Laodicean* (1881), and the title alludes to the church of the Laodiceans described in the New Testament as 'neither cold nor hot' (Rev. 3: 16), but it is not really a religious (or anti-religious) novel: the Laodicean heroine is undecided and capricious in love rather than spiritually lukewarm. The close but difficult relationship between King Saul and the young David in the Old estament provides a model for the relationship between old Henchard and young Farfrae, tradition and modernity, instinct and calculation, in *The Mayor of Caster-bridge* (1886) (Moynahan 1956), but this helps to confer archetypal dignity on Hardy's narrative rather than discredit biblical narrative.

But it becomes increasingly clear that neither church nor churchmen nor perhaps God himself engage very closely with or have much real bearing on the casual harshness of nature and human events as Hardy plots them. In *Far from the Madding Crowd* an overenthusiastic young sheepdog chases Gabriel Oak's sheep over the edge of a chalk-pit and so ruins him as an independent farmer (Hardy 1993b: 41). This more or less natural disaster is rather clumsily linked with man-made disaster on a European scale by linking the scene with Benjamin Haydon's painting of 'Napoleon Buonaparte on the Island of St Helena'. Egdon Heath in *The Return of the Native* (1878) can communicate none of the moral or religious meanings Wordsworth could read into landscape and in a Preface to the 1895 edition it is explicitly linked with the bleak and storm-lashed heath which is the setting for Shakespeare's tragedy *King Lear*.

The harshness of nature, cruel even in its abundance, is made even more explicit in *Tess of the d'Urbervilles* in which Wordworth's phrase 'nature's holy plan' is ridiculed (Hardy 1988: 28). Nature, unrestrained, has given Tess's mother a larger family than can be economically supported. Tess's sexuality, through which her life is blighted and destroyed despite episodes of happiness, is represented as wholly natural: she is defiantly described as 'a pure woman' in the subtitle of the novel, one who has broken none of nature's laws. Yet the novel in a sense anticipates the argument of T. H. Huxley's Romanes Lecture on *Evolution and Ethics* (1893) which warned that natural processes, the amoral Darwinian struggle for survival, provided no satisfactory model for social ethics. If nature is not a reliable guide, the church and social convention are no better, and Hardy condemns the pious censoriousness of Angel Clare's clerical family. Nature and convention between them are represented as having unconsciously connived in wanton cruelty, ultimately driving Tess to her death by execution for murder. This is summed up in a famously controversial and deliberately non-Christian last-minute addition to the text of the last paragraph of the novel (Hardy 1988: 384): ' "Justice" was done, and the President of the Immortals, in Aeschylean phrase, had ended his sport with Tess.'

Hardy's sense in the 1890s of his increasing distance from conventional, institutional Christianity and its rigidly inflexible sexual morality can be linked with the gradual breakdown of his first marriage and his wife's religious conservatism. It is indicated in his later novels by sardonic negotiations of religious themes and ironically truncated biblical quotation. The villainous seducer Alec d'Urberville in *Tess* and the seductress Arabella in *Jude* both undergo short-lived religious conversions which bring no credit either to them or to religion. *Jude* incorporates a kind of inverted *Pilgrim's Progress*, a moral and spiritual regress and a failed apocalyptic vision (Vance 2000). An early perception of Christminster (Oxford) as a 'heavenly Jerusalem' (Hardy 1985: 16), a radiant and enchanting centre of religion and learning, brings Jude to the place only to find in it darkness and despair and a lonely death. The traditional if fragile synthesis of classical and Christian learning in Oxford and in English higher education breaks down completely. Hardy's harshly negative biblical epigraph for the novel, 'The letter killeth', wilfully suppresses the rest of the verse, 'but the spirit giveth life' (2 Cor. 3: 6), letting the quotation stand in condemnation of the letter of the law, particularly the marriage laws, and the narrow legalism of ecclesi-astically sponsored sexual morality, undiluted by the more life-enhancing and hopeful promise of the New Testament dispensation. Just after their children have been killed Jude and Sue overhear sublimely irrelevant clerical argument about the eastward position for celebrating communion. In a savage addition in the 1912 edition Jude exclaims in biblical phrase 'Good God—the eastward position, and all creation groaning!' (Hardy 1985: 356), alluding to Romans 8: 22 without mentioning the redemption or hope specified in the immediately following verses or indeed any possible good that might result. As he is dying he quotes the bitter sayings of the suffering Job, cursing the day he was born (ibid. 426–7), but he is denied Job's final good fortune which vindicates the ultimate mercy of God.

But in *Jude* the suppression and frustration of hope is at least partly man-made rather than metaphysical. Jude's own physical and sexual nature does nothing to help him in his ambitions to become a scholar, or even to continue his occupation as a stone-mason. Exclusive Christminster rather than Christianity blights his life. As often in Hardy, the church and its inadequate, uncharitable teachers and ministers stand condemned not for practising Christianity but for failing to practise or reflect it enough, for failing in charity and compassion. In a sense, it could be argued, Hardy belongs not in an atheistic but in a radically Christian tradition of religious critique and anticlericalism which can be traced back to *Piers Plowman* and its condemnation of cold-hearted clerics practising chastity without charity.

In one of his bleaker short stories, 'The Grave by the Handpost' (in *A Changed Man*, 1913), a father, an old soldier bitterly disappointed in his soldier son, has committed suicide and is buried at a crossroads rather than in consecrated ground. The guilt-smitten son arranges for the biblical words 'I am not worthy to be called thy son', the confession of the penitent Prodigal Son (Luke 15: 18, 19), to be inscribed on his father's tombstone. But the tombstone is never erected, and years later the hope of reunion and reconciliation, implied in the forgiveness of the Prodigal Son in the biblical story, is not realized, even in death, because the son's express wishes are accidentally overlooked and he is not buried beside his father. In the same story the death of both father and son is associated with the singing (to a 'dull air') of a carol by Philip Doddridge which includes the lines, 'He comes the prisoners to release | In Satan's bondage held'. Hardy would have known, and probably expected his readers to know, that the first line of the carol sung in such doleful circumstances was the spectacularly inappropriate 'Hark, the glad sound! the saviour comes', and the events of the story suggest that, nineteen centuries later, the biblical promise of liberation and joy still awaits fulfilment.

But even here Hardy's bitter ironies depend not only on knowledge of Scripture (and the hymnbook) but on continuing respect for the underlying sense of Scripture. Human heedlessness and lack of charity as well as sheer accident contribute to frustrate any kind of reconciliation of the latter-day prodigal son, but that does not of itself invalidate the possibility or the importance of divine as well as human forgiveness and generosity which the parable teaches. The ultimate irony is the discrepancy between the teaching and example of Christ and the work of the church on earth. The harsh ecclesiastical custom of not burying a suicide in consecrated ground, which leads to the humiliating burial at the crossroads, could be seen as the human act which in this instance helps to frustrate, but not to discredit, the essentially Christian process of penitence, spiritual healing, and reconciliation with God and man.

The later Hardy withdrew a little from the despair of *Tess* and *Jude*. He continued to read his Greek Testament and to brood unconventionally on God and man, nature and history. In his poem 'Lausanne: In Gibbon's Old Garden' (1897) in *Poems of the Past and Present* (1901) he saluted the iconoclastic historian of the Roman Empire with fellow-feeling as a maligned truth-teller, but made no attempt to renew Gibbon's ironies and insinuations against the early church. 'A Cathedral Façade at Midnight' in *Human Shows* (1925) accepts Reason's eclipse of 'The coded creeds of old-time godliness', but not without regret. Whatever reason might suggest, scriptural narrative and its cultural consequences retained their hold on Hardy's imagination. In 'In The British Museum' (*Satires of Circumstance*, 1919) he uses the persona of a working man to convey a sense of simple wonder that a 'time-touched stone' from the Areopagus in Athens 'once echoed | The voice of Paul.' The poem alludes to the occasion (Acts 17: 23) when St Paul, visiting Athens, had opportunistically used an altar inscribed 'to the unknown God' to preach the Christian God. With comparable opportunism T. H. Huxley had in 1869 coined the term 'agnostic' from the original New Testament Greek of this phrase (αγνωστω θεω, *agnosto theo*), itself the title of another poem by Hardy. The nature of God might still be unknown and mysterious but it could not be altogether discounted. Folk tradition remembered from Hardy's childhood had fancifully extended the narrative of the nativity to suggest that on midnight on Christmas Eve oxen, who had been represented in the original Bethlehem stable, would kneel in memory of the infant Jesus. Instead of responding with the elegant metropolitan scepticism of a Gibbon or a Voltaire, Hardy's poem 'The Oxen' (1915, in *Moments of Vision*, 1917), which recounts the tradition, ends with actually 'Hoping it might be so'. 'The Darkling Thrush', dated 31 December 1900 (*Poems of the Past and the Present*, 1901), proposed as a kind of epitaph for the nineteenth century, allows the bleak, dead landscape of winter to be transformed by the unexpected song of a thrush, perhaps signalling 'some blessed Hope whereof he knew | And I was unaware'. The word 'blessed' and the capitalized Hope suggest a totally unexpected gleam of what might be Christian hope, one of the three theological virtues, biblically grouped with faith and charity (1 Cor. 13: 13). The moving poems of 1912–13 commemorating his first wife vividly recreate moments of happiness before things went wrong: one of them, 'The Voice', seems to rely on the New Testament metaphor of spirit as wind to bring back his wife as a spiritual presence (Weatherby 1983).

There is less religious bitterness and hostility in the later published work, but it cannot always be sharply distinguished from the earlier because it was often long-meditated, developed from ideas first entertained many years previously. This in itself suggests one should be wary of attributing undiluted atheism to Hardy at any point in his writing career. The poem portentously entitled 'In Time of "The Breaking of Nations"' (1915) in *Moments of Vision* (1915) seems to promise the Old Testament severity of God's judgement against Babylon, breaking in pieces the nations and destroying kingdoms as described in Jeremiah (51: 20), and the original idea came to Hardy during the Franco-Prussian war of 1870. But the theme of undramatic continuity ironically counterpointing public rupture and discord was quietly matured over more than forty years and eventually published during the First World War. The reflection that 'this will go onward the same | Though Dynasties pass' serves as a kind of secular realization of divinely sustained continuity, the promise in the same chapter (Jer. 51: 5) that 'Israel hath not been forsaken.'

It also reminds us that, whether in ancient Babylon or in modern Europe, Dynasties, and what Hardy called 'Dynasts', could come and go. His great epic drama of the Napoleonic Wars, presided over by the Immanent Will, was called *The Dynasts* for ultimately religious rather than political or literary reasons. Hardy had occasionally invoked the Greek tragedians Aeschylus and Sophocles in his novels, as if to suggest that pre-Christian tragic necessity rather than Christian providence governed the life and death of Tess of the d'Urbervilles or the luckless characters of *Jude the Obscure*. But when a scholarly reader asked if the 'Dynasts' of his title came from Aeschylus, from the Greek term δυνάστας (*dynastas*) used to describe the apparent power of the wheeling stars bringing in the seasons at the beginning of the *Agamemnon*, Hardy (1978–88: iii. 197) replied that it came not from Aeschylus but from the Greek of the Magnificat, the song of Mary which has been the hope and the consolation of radical Christians throughout the ages. The revolutionary biblical idea of putting down the mighty, the Dynasts (Greek *dynastas*), from their seats, or thrones (Greek *ek thronon*) (Luke 1: 52) is transferred unironically into the drama.

The intercalated lyric musings of the Spirit of the Pities in *The Dynasts*, presented alongside the speeches of the inexorable Spirit of the Years, dramatize a perpetual tension between Pity and the pitiless sequence of events as they unfold year by year. In theological terms this confrontation could be redescribed as the work of Mercy and Grace in tension with the iron logic of Judgement. In literary terms it represents a vast expansion of the dialectic of opposed strophe and antistrophe in the structure of the choruses commenting on the unfolding action in Greek tragedy. But where in Greek choruses a concluding epode could resolve formal difference, Hardy seems determined to avoid the spurious consolation of glib and easy resolutions. Yet the trajectory of *The Dynasts* suggests the ultimate resolution in human history may come when, by evolutionary processes of amelioration, the blind unconscious Immanent Will eventually acquires full consciousness and the harshness and cruelty of nature and recorded history gradually pass over into a more benign and sympathetic dispensation. While this is hardly orthodox theology it still has what might be described as a theological shape, a progressive teleology which invites comparison with the linkage of physical and psychic nature and historical movement towards a unifying 'Omega' point of assembled consciousness in the controversial religious teaching of the Jesuit scientist Teilhard de Chardin, particularly in *The Phenomenon of Man* (1955). Imaginative fusion of Darwinian and Spencerian evolution with the traditional biblical scheme of 'salvation history' lies behind both writers. In some ways Teilhard's work develops from Henri Bergson's *Creative Evolution*, itself a response to Darwin and Spencer, and at least one early commentator on *The Dynasts* noticed parallels with Bergson, though Hardy had not actually read Bergson at the time (Hardy 1978–88: v. 69–70). As Hardy himself noted in 1907 (Björk 1985: ii. 353–7), his fantasy of an evolving consciousness in the Immanent Will resembled the evolutionary 'New Theology' proposed by the liberal dissenter R. J. Campbell, minister of the City Temple. Like Hardy, Campbell was trying to develop what he called 'the religious articulation of the scientific method' and, again like Hardy, he was looking for a modern solution to the traditional problem of theodicy, a way of not being 'appalled by the long story of cosmic suffering'.

For Hardy, as for many others, the First World War made it much harder to defend any kind of optimism about human affairs. The ultimately progressive dynamic of *The Dynasts* seemed unwarranted. But Hardy's response was not that of the disappointed secular humanist so much as that of the puzzled and caring man of Christian nurture that he had always been: on Christmas Day 1914 he wrote (1978–88: v. 72) that 'the present times are an absolute negation of Christianity'. For him, as for George Eliot, Christianity might have become metaphysically problematic, but it still provided a language and a reference point for moral and social concern, a way of approaching the pain and the possibility of good in the world.

WORKS CITED

BEER, GILLIAN. 1983. *Darwin's Plots*. London: Routledge.

BJÖRK, L. A. (ed.) 1985. *The Literary Notebooks of Thomas Hardy*. 2 vols. London: Macmillan.

CARPENTER, MARY WILSON. 1986. *George Eliot and the Landscape of Time: Narrative Form and Protestant Apocalyptic History*. Chapel Hill: University of North Carolina Press.

CHESTERTON, G. K. 1966. *The Victorian Age in Literature*. London: Oxford University Press.

DALZIEL, PAMELA. 2006. 'The Gospel According to Hardy', in Keith Wilson (ed.), *Thomas Hardy Reappraised: Essays in Honour of Michael Millgate*. Toronto: University of Toronto Press.

ELIOT, GEORGE. 1954–78. *The George Eliot Letters*, ed. G. S. Haight. 9 vols. Oxford: Clarendon.

—— 1988. *Felix Holt, the Radical*, ed. Fred. C. Thomson. The World's Classics. Oxford: Oxford University Press.

—— 1992. *Selected Critical Writings*, ed. Rosemary Ashton. The World's Classics. Oxford: Oxford University Press.

—— 1994. *Romola*, ed. Andrew Brown. The World's Classics. Oxford: Oxford University Press.

—— 1996a. *Adam Bede*, ed. Valentine Cunningham. The World's Classics. Oxford: Oxford University Press.

—— 1996b. *The Mill on the Floss*, ed. Gordon S. Haight. The World's Classics. Oxford: Oxford University Press.

—— 1996c. *Silas Marner, the Weaver of Raveloe*, ed. Terence Cave. The World's Classics. Oxford: Oxford University Press.

HANDS, TIMOTHY. 1989. *Thomas Hardy: Distracted Preacher?* Basingstoke: Macmillan.

HARDY, THOMAS. 1978–88. *The Collected Letters of Thomas Hardy*, ed. R. L. Purdy and M. Millgate. 7 vols. Oxford: Clarendon.

—— 1902. 'M. Maeterlinck's Apology for Nature'. *Academy and Literature* (17 May): 451.

—— 1988. *Tess of the d'Urbervilles*, ed. Juliet Grindle and Simon Gatrell. The World's Classics. Oxford: Oxford University Press.

—— 1985. *Jude the Obscure*, ed. Patricia Ingham. The World's Classics. Oxford: Oxford University Press.

—— 1993a. *Two on a Tower*, ed. Suleiman M. Ahmad. The World's Classics. Oxford: Oxford University Press.

—— 1993b. *Far from the Madding Crowd*, ed. Suzanne B. Falck-Yi. The World's Classics. Oxford: Oxford University Press.

HODGSON, PETER C. 2001. *Theology in the Fiction of George Eliot*. London: SCM.

JAY, ELISABETH. 1979. *The Religion of the Heart: Anglican Evangelicalism and the Nineteenth-Century Novel*. Oxford: Clarendon.

JĘDRZEWSKI, JAN. 1996. *Thomas Hardy and the Church*. Basingstoke: Macmillan.

MACINTYRE, ALISTAIR, and RICŒUR, PAUL. 1969. *The Religious Significance of Atheism*. New York: Columbia University Press.

MOYNAHAN, JULIAN. 1956. '*The Mayor of Casterbridge* and the Old Testament First Book of Samuel', *PMLA* 71: 118–30.

NEWEY, VINCENT. 1984. 'Dorothea's Awakening: The Recall of Bunyan in *Middlemarch*', *Notes and Queries* 31: 497–9.

NIETZSCHE, FRIEDRICH. 1971. *Twilight of the Idols* (1889), in Walter Kaufmann (ed. and trans.), *The Portable Nietzsche*. London: Chatto & Windus.

SELBY, T. G. 1896. *The Theology of Modern Fiction*. London: Charles H. Kelly.

STEPHEN, LESLIE. 1902. *George Eliot*. London: Macmillan.

VANCE, NORMAN. 1980. 'Law, Religion and the Unity of *Felix Holt*', in Anne Smith (ed.), *George Eliot: Centenary Essays*. London: Vision.

—— 2000. 'Secular Apocalyptic and Thomas Hardy', *History of European Ideas* 26: 201–10.

WEATHERBY, H. L. 1983 'Of Water and the Spirit: Hardy's "The Voice"', *Southern Review* 19: 302–8.

WILSON, S. L. 1897. *The Theology of Modern Literature*. London: R. D. Dickinson.

WILLIAMSON, EUGENE. 1978. 'Thomas Hardy and Friedrich Nietzsche: The Reasons', *Comparative Literature Studies* 15: 403–13.

WRIGHT, T. R. 1986. *The Religion of Humanity: The Impact of Comtean Positivism in Victorian Britain*. Cambridge: Cambridge University Press.

FURTHER READING

BEER, GILLIAN. 1983. *Darwin's Plots*. London: Routledge.

DALZIEL, PAMELA. 2006. 'The Gospel According to Hardy', in Keith Wilson (ed.), *Thomas Hardy Reappraised: Essays in Honour of Michael Millgate*. Toronto: University of Toronto Press.

HANDS, TIMOTHY. 1989. *Thomas Hardy: Distracted Preacher?* Basingstoke: Macmillan.

HODGSON, PETER C. 2001. *Theology in the Fiction of George Eliot*. London: SCM.

JAY, ELISABETH. 1979. *The Religion of the Heart: Anglican Evangelicalism and the Nineteenth-Century Novel.* Oxford: Clarendon.

JĘDRZEWSKI, JAN. 1996. *Thomas Hardy and the Church.* Basingstoke: Macmillan.

SELBY, T. G. 1896. *The Theology of Modern Fiction.* London: Charles H. Kelly.

SMITH, ANNE. (ed.) 1980. *George Eliot: Centenary Essays.* London: Vision.

WILSON, S. L. 1897. *The Theology of Modern Literature.* London: R. D. Dickinson.

WRIGHT, T. R. 1986. *The Religion of Humanity: The Impact of Comtean Positivism in Victorian Britain.* Cambridge: Cambridge University Press.

CHAPTER 30

JAMES JOYCE

VALENTINE CUNNINGHAM

> It is a curious thing, do you know, how your mind is supersaturated with
> the religion in which you say you disbelieve.
>
> (Cranly to Stephen, *A Portrait of the Artist as a Young Man*)

Supersaturation: the excessive adding of an element to a liquid, going further than is
strictly necessary, a severely overdone baptism. Joyce's texts come soaked in religion,
supersaturated indeed in the specifically Christian, the Roman Catholic, the Irish
Roman Catholic—an awesomeness of detailing, all the more obsessive as these
writings' bulk expanded in an almost overwhelming exuberance of Catholicized
baroque.

It's an Irish story. As Joyce's ephebic persona Stephen Dedalus notoriously puts it
at the end of *A Portrait of the Artist as a Young Man*, he heads for exile to be able to
'forge in the smithy of my soul the uncreated consciousness of my race' (Joyce 1960:
253).[1] To *forge*, to hammer out, to *make*, like an ancient Greek artificer poet, the
Dedalus whose name he bears, or like the Judaeo-Christian creator God, but also to
invent, to *make up* (that hint of faking in *forge*) for the first time the so far uncreated
conscience of the Irish. Conscience: inward consciousness. His writing will make
Ireland and the Irish know themselves as never before, in particular as Roman
Catholics—as a people steeped in Roman Catholic beliefs, rituals, devotions, litur-

---

[1] I refer to the following versions of Joyce's novels: *Stephen Hero* [*SH*], ed. John J. Slocum and Herbert
Cahoon (London: Jonathan Cape, 1969) (based on the 1st edn., ed. Theodore Spencer, July 1944);
Dubliners [*D*] ([1914], Harmondsworth: Penguin Books, 1965); *A Portrait of the Artist as a Young Man*
[*P*] ([1916] Harmondsworth: Penguin Books, 1960); *Ulysses* [*U*] ([1922], Harmondsworth: Penguin
Modern Classics, 1969); *Finnegans Wake* [*FW*] (London: Faber & Faber, 1939). There has only ever
been one printed version of the full text of *FW* in English, so that page and line references are the same in
every edition.

gies, the daily round of Catholic mindfulness, prayers, rosary, thoughts of the Blessed Virgin Mary, church services, above all the mass. These are the meat and drink of the realism, the quotidian round, of *Dubliners* and *Stephen Hero*, *A Portrait* and much of *Ulysses*, and of the hypertextuality of *Finnegans Wake*.

Dedalus's 'very Catholic home' (Stephen's phrase in *Stephen Hero* (p. 139)) dominates the early pages of *A Portrait*. A domesticity dominated by the religious subject. Exemplarily, the Christmas dinner in *A Portrait* is rifted by the contemporary Irish quarrel over Parnell, a clash about church power and politics and moral theology and what the 'Holy Ghost' meant in Scripture by invoking 'woe' on 'scandal' mongers. The menfolk blame the fat Princes of the Church for meddling in politics and a lack of moral sympathy with the sinner; pious 'aunty' Dante—who won't let Stephen play with Protestants who make fun of the BVM—sticks up for 'God and religion and priest' as the necessary shibboleths of the Irish Catholic home (*P* 34). Stephen's oppressively devout mother, urging his Easter duty on her son, presses in pervasively on *Stephen Hero*. *Ulysses* is racked by the son's guilty refusal to kneel and pray at his dying mother's bedside with which that novel begins. In this family atmosphere there's no being, no selfhood, no self-naming—that move into self-knowledge with which the *Bildungsroman* classically begins—which is not constrained by the name and nature of the divine. '*Stephen Dedalus is my name* ... That was he ... God was God's name just as his name was Stephen'. His schoolfriend Fleming has written 'Stephen Dedalus is my name, | Ireland is my nation. | Clongowes is my dwelling-place | And heaven my expectation' on the flyleaf of his geography book 'for a cod' (*P* 16), but these religious identifyings and placings are no joking matter.

Little Stephen is at Clongowes Wood school, as Joyce was. Like Joyce he moves on to Belvedere College. What happens at Belvedere is the main preoccupation of *Stephen Hero* and hugely dominant in *A Portrait*. At these Jesuit schools heavenly expectations are the perdurable constraint of the Ignatian educational scheme.[2] This is schooling dominated by priests. It's steeped in the pervading odours of sanctity: the incense-laden smell of Catholic ritual—Stephen acts as incense 'boat-bearer'—which is the ground of all the olfactory enticements and incitements of this intensely nose-sensitive hero. At Belvedere Stephen navigates with high emotional intensity between the Scylla and Charybdis of guilty pleasure in masturbation and carnal knowledge with a prostitute, and the duties of confession and repentance enforced by fears of hell (the pages and pages of the Belvedere Retreat sermons on sin and hell in *A Portrait* chill cradle Catholic readers to this day). Penitent after his sexual lapse Stephen tries to live loyally by the manual of the Sodality of the Blessed Virgin Mary—Joyce's Vade Mecum, according to Kevin Sullivan (1958: 116).

Every part of his day, divided by what he regarded now as the duties of his station in life, circled about his own centre of spiritual energy.... On each of the seven days of the week he further prayed that one of the seven gifts of the Holy Ghost might descend upon his soul and drive out of it day by day the seven deadly sins which had defiled it in the past. (*P* 147–8)

---

2 Sullivan (1958) gives the best account of Joyce's Jesuit schooling.

And so on. Joyce's own 'station in life' at this period was a 'prefect' of the Sodality, which involved leading and advising the others, and exemplary practice of virtue and confession and attendance at the sacrament of the eucharist. It carried expectations of a call to the priesthood. Stephen hears that call. A keen self-namer, he imagines being titled 'The Reverence Stephen Dedalus, S.J.' (*P* 161).

It's all a formative domestic and educational religiosity at the core of a totally Catholicized city and country. 'I', says Stephen to Leopold Bloom, surrogate father, twice-baptized Jew (first as Protestant, then as Catholic) in the 'Eumaeus' section of *Ulysses*, 'I belong to the *faubourg St. Patrice* called Ireland for short' (*U* 565). Ireland is Rome's devoutest suburb. According to the mocking legend elaborated in 'The Oxen of the Sun' (*U* 397), the Irish Bull—and Joyce's texts contain a whole herd of them— fattened up on the 'green grass of Erin', is a Papal Bull. Mocking Buck Mulligan wonders in Latin why Irish women should ever prefer lascivious locals to *testibus ponderosis atque excelsis erectonibus centurionum Romanorum*—the ponderous test- icles and heavenly huge erections of the Roman centurions (*U* 400). Latin, the language of Rome and the Fathers of the Church, is of course spoken here. The Papal Bull in question was the one sent by 'farmer Nicholas', i.e. the twelfth-century Pope Adrian IV, otherwise the Englishman Nicholas Breakspear, who gifted Ireland to England's Henry II as a papal fief, thus paving the way for the 'Lord Harry', Henry VIII, and his daughter Elizabeth, to impose their heavy will on the Irish. This is how the double colonizing of Ireland began. 'I am the servant of two masters, Stephen said, an English and an Italian': 'The imperial British state . . . and the holy Roman catholic church' (*U* 26). Irish theology and theological language come from else- where. Stephen's Italian tutor at University College, Father Ghezzi, abuses Bruno the heretic in Italian and pidgin English, sharp reminder for Stephen that 'his country- men and not mine had invented what Cranly the other night called our religion' (*P* 249). The Irish Jesus is made in Italy, to be spoken of in the tones of Belvedere's English Dean of Studies—a convert from English Dissent (and so doubly an alien) who is *astundished* (as *FW* 187. 3 has it) by the strange local word *tundish* (for funnel). 'My soul frets in the shadow of his language', thinks Stephen. 'The language in which we are speaking is his before it is mine. How different are the words *home*, *Christ*, *ale*, *master*, on his lips and on mine!' (*P* 189). The Irishman can't even speak of *Christ* in his own tongue, let alone speak of *home*—the Romanized homeland, colonized by the priests of Rome.

Priests are everywhere. From street after street come the sounds of the mass-bell, as the eucharist is celebrated simultaneously all over the city in chapel after chapel (*chapel*: the Irish word for a Roman Catholic church). 'Abbas father, furious dean . . . see him clambering down . . . clutching a monstrance . . . . And at the same instant perhaps a priest round the corner is elevating it. Dringdring! And two streets off another locking it into a pyx. Dringadring! And in a ladychapel another taking housel all to his own cheek. Dringdring! Down, up, forward, back' (*U* 45). Stephen knows the theology of how Christ's body can be in several places at once—'Dan Occam' thought of *hypostasis* one misty English morning. Jesuit poet G. M. Hopkins, who suffered agonies of body and soul in Dublin's city and its University College, celebrated this phenomenon in his poem 'Spelt From Sybil's Leaves' as Christ playing 'in a thousand places'. He might have had Catholic Dublin in mind. The priest-thronged city.

The central episode of *Ulysses*, 'The Wandering Rocks', is framed by two sets of authoritative possessors of the Dublin street: at the beginning, the Revd John Conmee moving on foot among his familiar urban flock, at the end His Excellency the Vice-Roy Lord Dudley in a majestic cavalcade. Dublin belongs to its twinned masters; the clerical overlordship doubling the imperial. And the street-owning cavalcade of the secular imperium is manifestly outdone for aweing numbers and force in 'Cyclops' when the great host of acolytes, deacons, sub-deacons, abbots, priests, friars, 'saints and martyrs, virgins and confessors' wends its mock-heroic way 'by Nelson's Pillar, Henry Street, Mary Street, Capel Street', chanting the Epiphany Epistle and Gradual (mislabelled the 'Introit'), performing 'divers wonders' en route to blessing Bernie Kiernan's pub in Little Britain Street (*U* 337–8). Admiral Lord Nelson, Henry, Mary, Capel—presumably named for Lord Arthur Capel, Viceroy of Ireland (1672–7)—Little Britain: Dublin's streets are a signifying map of the Anglo-Roman imperial mix. The resources of the mock-heroic—these parodic epic processions—bring smartly home the plenipotential ubiquity of a most powerful church whose claim to the benedictory—'Deus . . . benedictionem tuam effunde super creaturas istas', pray the great Catholic host at Kiernan's pub—is vitiated by its mirroring the imperial force it's hand in glove with. The benediction is 'secundum legem', according to the law of the Latinate deity, a law complicit, it's suggested, with the law of the English master. Rebellious Stephen declares in Nighttown that he 'must kill the priest and the king, at least in his head' (*U* 521).

The Christmas Day quarrel in *A Portrait* is about this galling complicity of the priests of a 'priest-ridden race' in the ruin of Parnell and Home Rule. Stephen is with his father in this family and national division. In *Stephen Hero* he rages against the passive believers of the Dublin slums:

And whenever he encountered a burly-vested priest taking a stroll of pleasant inspection through these warrens full of swarming and cringing believers he cursed the farce of Irish Catholicism: an island [whereof] the inhabitants of which entrust their wills and minds to others that they may ensure for themselves a life of spiritual paralysis, an island . . . in which Caesar [professes] confesses Christ and Christ confesses Caesar that together they may wax fat upon a starving rabblement which is bidden ironically to take to itself this consolation in hardship 'The Kingdom of God is within you'.   (*SH* 150–1)

National *paralysis* from priestedness: it's the keynote of *Dubliners*—the word uttered by the young narrator in the first paragraph of the opening story 'The Sisters' as his priestly mentor Father Flynn lies dying, demented over some unspecified transgression. The boy finds the word strange in his mouth—like *simony* in the Catechism (getting church preferment by paying money: was the old, now paralytic priest a simoniac?). *Paralysis* 'sounded like the name of some maleficent and sinful being'; it fills the boy with fear, 'and yet I longed to be nearer to it and to look upon its deadly work'. This gaze of appalled proximity is what in effect motors *Dubliners*, and indeed

Joyce's whole œuvre. 'I call the series *Dubliners* to betray the soul of that hemiplegia or paralysis which many consider a city.'[3]

This paralysed city is 'dear' but 'dirty Dublin, as Ignatius Gallagher puts it in the *Dubliners* story 'A Little Cloud' ('DEAR DIRTY DUBLIN': it's one of the newspaper headlines in 'Aeolus' (*U* 145)). A city trapped in a Catholicism generating moral shallowness, formalism, violence, guilt, melancholy, ghostedness, repression, and frequently uncritical obedience. In 'Grace', friends of religiously woolly and heavy-drinking Tom Kernan, who falls down the lavatory stairs of a pub, getting all smeared with 'filth' and 'ooze', take him to a Retreat sermon at the Jesuit Church in Gardiner Street by way of moral reform. The sermon is about manliness and rectifying your accounts with the businessman's mammonite God, a kind of Protestantized simony. This ethical-religious flatness follows hard on the group's tragi-comic rhapsodics about papal infallibilty and the Irish submission to it. Mr Cunningham, Catholic loyalist ('our religion is *the* religion') and admirer of Pope Leo XIII ('great scholar and poet': he wrote a Latin poem on 'the invention of the photograph') extols the Irish Cardinal McHale (John of Tuam). At the Vatican Council of 1870 he argued vehemently against the proposed new dogma of papal infallibility, until the Pope declared it a dogma *ex cathedra*, at which point McHale 'stood up and shouted with the voice of a lion: Credo!'

Giving in thus to whatever the church authorizes is for Joyce the essence of Ireland's general paralysis of the insanely faithful. His texts fret continually at the unjust arbitrariness of the Roman dogmas, doxas, rules, pietisms, and their enforcers. A lot of *Stephen Hero*'s anger is provoked by Belvedere's hostility towards Stephen's enthusiastic essay on Ibsen. Ibsen is deemed 'foreign filth'. The Irish, 'happy' in their faith, don't want Ibsen's 'modern pessimism', says the College President, who is open about never having read a line of this offensive material. For Stephen this is cultural disease as Catholic plague. He rants against 'mortifying' 'Jesuit authority', the spreader of this hemiplegic sickness.

The deadly chill of the atmosphere of the college paralysed Stephen's heart. In a stupor of powerlessness he reviewed the plague of Catholicism. He seemed to see the vermin begotten in the catacombs in an age of sickness and cruelty issuing forth upon the plains and mountains of Europe. Like the plague of locusts described in Callista[4] they seemed to choke the rivers and fill the valleys up. They obscured the sun. Contempt of [the body] human nature, weakness, nervous tremblings, fear of day and joy, distrust of man and life, hemiplegia of the will, beset the body burdened and disaffected in its members by its black tyrannous lice. Exultation of the mind before joyous beauty, exultation of the body in free confederate labours, every natural impulse towards health and wisdom and hapinesss had been corroded by the pest of these vermin.   (*SH* 198–9)

Stephen's anger was Joyce's own. 'I spit upon the image of the Tenth Pius', he wrote in 1904.[5] In 1907 Pius X—'our present man' in 'Grace', excused of all failings by the satirized faithful—issued the anti-'modernist' encyclical *Pascendi gregis*. In 1903, as

---

[3] Joyce to Constantine P. Curran (Joyce 1957: i. 59).

[4] John Newman's historical novel *Callista: A Tale of the Third Century* (1855), about early African Christianity.

[5] To Mrs William Murray, New Year's Eve 1904 (Joyce 1957: i. 57).

part of his anti-modernizing project, he had excluded women from church choirs—only males being liturgically sound, he believed. Part of the extended musical business of *Dubliners*'s final story 'The Dead' is Aunt Kate's tirade against this choral edict of Pius X. She's organist at St Mary's Roman Catholic Church in Haddington Road. The edict is 'not just' and 'not right', she says, and this despite her own public respect for the 'Pope's being right' and for the Church's rules (monks sleep in their coffins, she informs Protestant Mr Browne, because that's 'the rule of the order...the rule, that was all').

So Joyce's fictions keenly celebrate law-breakers, resisters of authority and the rules. 'There is no law before impulse', declares Robert in Joyce's play *Exiles*: 'Laws are for slaves' (Joyce 1936: II. 116). Virginia Moseley (1967: 45 ff.) has rightly called *Exiles* a rerun of the Gospels' parable of the Prodigal Son. *Stephen Hero* and *A Portrait of the Artist* are the story of Stephen unslaving himself. He will not submit to the church, he keeps saying in *Stephen Hero*. 'I was sold to Rome before my birth. Now I have broken my slavery', he tells Cranly (*SH* 144). He will not 'go crawling and cringing and praying and begging' to Jesuit 'tomfoolery' about adoring Jesus and Mary and Joseph, and the infallibility of the pope, and 'all his obscene stinking hells' (*SH* 238). 'I will not take service under them. I will not submit to them, either outwardly or inwardly' (*SH* 239). 'I will not serve,' he keeps telling Cranly in *A Portrait*. And he knows this is satanic. Satan, leader of the rebellious angels, was hurled into hell, declares the Retreat preacher, for the sin of pride, 'the sinful thought conceived in an instant: *non serviam: I will not serve*. That instant was his ruin' (*SH* 117). The way forward for the young poet is to adopt Satan's insurgent voice, a fallen discourse. Tellingly, Stephen's treasured phrase, 'A day of dappled seaborne clouds', which incites one of *A Portrait*'s main reflections on the value of words for him—the appeal of 'the poise and balance of the period itself', and how 'a lucid supple periodic prose' might mirror 'an inner world of individual emotions' rather than reflect 'the glowing sensible world through the prism of a language many-coloured and richly storied' (*P* 166–7)—comes from a passage in Hugh Miller's book *The Testimony of the Rocks; or, Geology in Its Bearings on the Two Theologies, Natural and Revealed* (1857) where Miller is imagining Satan's thoughts as he contemplates God's creation. Stephen's cherishing repetition of this aesthetically exemplary phrase from inside Satan's head follows hard on two cases of the old orthodox aesthetico-linguistic order Joyce's proud Satanist is spurning: one, 'a proud cadence' from Cardinal Newman's *The Idea of a University* (1852) about the age-old 'success' of the church ('Whose feet are as the feet of harts and underneath are the everlasting arms') which marks Stephen's refusing of invitations to seek service as a Jesuit priest; the other, Stephen's sneering despisal of a squad of Christian Brothers for their ugly names and get-up—'whose piety would be like their names, like their faces, like their clothes' (*SH* 165–7). Satan has a better style than the low-breed Christian Brothers, better even than Newman himself.[6]

---

[6] The quotations from Newman and Hugh Miller are supplied by the invaluable Joyce annotator Don Gifford (1982: 218–19).

Not kneeling at his dying mother's bedside is the acme of Stephen's non-servitude—not bowing before the mothering authority of Mother Church, the mothering of Mary, the Roman maternal principle embodied in his own most pious mother.[7] It's a local refusal that's consequent on Stephen's larger resistance to the grand, belittling authority of fathers, his own father of course, but much more to the big patriarchal regime of God the Father embodied in the power of the Church Fathers (Aquinas and Co.) and Ireland's priests, all the ordained schoolmasters and pastors who would turn young men back into little boys—the 'dear little brothers in Christ Jesus' the Belvedere Retreat preacher keeps invoking. Temporarily repentant of his whoring, Stephen kneels in the confessional box, regressing for the moment into a little child: 'my child', the confessor keeps saying, and Stephen keeps replying 'father'.

What's at stake in the rebellion is sin, especially the sins of the flesh which have made a man, a church-disobedient grown-up, of Stephen. Stephen is unbowing, Satanically erect—an erectness metonymized in erections: phallic pride, the pride of the masturbator. 'Give it up, my child, for God's sake. It is dishonourable and unmanly.... Pray to our mother Mary to keep you. She will help you my child' (*P* 145). Masturbation is the sin of Onan, biblical archetype of self-pleasurers (he broke the law of levirate marriage by 'spilling his seed on the ground' instead of impregnating his sister-in-law Tamar in Genesis 38), the sin of voyeuristic Leopold Bloom on the beach in the 'Nausicaa' section of *Ulysses*, frigging off at the sight of Irish virgin Gertie MacDowell's enticingly exposed underwear to the sounds of the Litany of Our Lady of Loretto in the nearby church of Mary Star of the Sea, his self-abusive erection parodying the simultaneous elevation of the Host, 'the Blessed Sacrament' in the hands of Father O'Hanlon (*U* 356–62).[8]

There's a good deal of masturbation in 'Circe', the Nighttown episode of *Ulysses*, where men are delighted to turn into polymorphously perverse sexual animals at the House of Bella Cohen, the Jewish brothel-keeper. It's in a daytime version of Night-town, in Dublin's brothel quarter, 'the quarter of the Jews', that Stephen loses his virginity to a prostitute in one of *A Portrait*'s most extraordinary climactic episodes at the end of ch. 2. Dimensions are all. The whore is tiny, doll-like. Propriety induced by the censors Joyce suffered so much from forbids that the girl be described with her legs apart, but her huge doll can be so presented. Stephen is bigger than both. This is where he ceases to be the little child the infantilizing church demands. Here his body learns itself as sinful flesh. His lips perform new words, new work, a new tongue, new

---

[7] Susan Stanford Friedman (1993: 42, 53) is most wrong to argue that 'the dramatic confrontation between mother and son suggests that it is at base his mother, not religion, that he must deny', and that this is 'a flight from the maternal' merely. This involves a misreading of Stephen's dismissive 'O, the Church' in *SH* in his argument with McCann about feminism. (Friedman is better on Stephen's repeated mother-escape attempts—likening him not unhelpfully to Freud's famous fort/da boy, perpetually miming the absence of his mother.)

[8] Parallelisms which haven't escaped the most vigilant, frequently admirable, and sometimes excessive parallel-seeking gaze of Frederick K. Lang (1993: 129). There may even be something in the link between Molly's menstruation (and all the other menstruating females in *Ulysses*) and the wine/blood of the eucharist, which so excites Lang (ibid. 276–8), as it has a long chain of readers going back at least to Harry Blamires (1966).

tongue-work. The whore's kiss replaces the formative kiss of the mother and the body relations of little boy to pious mother ('You put your face up like that to say good night and then his mother put her face down. That was to kiss. His mother put her lips on his cheek; her lips were soft and they wetted his cheek; and they made a tiny little noise: kiss' (*P* 15)). Big now, Stephen won't at first bend his lips to kiss the girl, but 'with a sudden movement she bowed his head and joined her lips to his and he read the meaning of her movements in her frank uplifted eyes'. This is the bowing he will refuse God (the bowed head of prayer), the bedside submission he will deny his mother: a new lip-service, new use of lips and mouth, a new way of utterance, of discourse, for the good Catholic boy who has only kissed his mother and uttered devotions until now. In effect, new worship, new word, new logos, new reading and new reading-matter, new textuality. Stephen is 'conscious of nothing in the world but the dark pressure of her softly parting lips'—lips of both sorts, the ones speakable in publications of Joyce's time and the ones not speakable among polite hearers. 'They pressed upon his brain as upon his lips as though they were the vehicle of a vague speech; and between them he felt an unknown and timid pressure darker than the swoon of sin, softer than sound or odour' (*P* 101). Synaesthesia theologized: the synaesthetic delights of disobedience to the laws of the church.

These are the 'sweets of sin': what Bloom likes about a woman and in a book, warming to the throbbing soft-porn pages of the bookstalls along the Dublin Quays. He'll take *Sweets of Sin*. 'That's a good one', the shopman said, 'tapping on it' (*U* 236). The tome is in Bloom's pocket in Nighttown (*U* 430). Guilty conscience, the (much repeated) *Agenbyte of Inwit*, will crush Stephen back down into 'dear little brother in Christ' size, have him return to confessional kneeling and devotion to the Virgin, but not for long. Once tasted, the masculations of the sinful sweets are for ever; grown-up, he'll soon be flying away, erect, uplifted, the satanic artist alone.

Specially attractive is the smell of prostitutes. They're all *perfumed*. Stephen's has a *perfumed* head. Here's nose appeal for the boy whose sensitive nostrils feature in all of Joyce's fictions about him; a sensitivity apt for a Catholic boy, for Roman religion is odoriferous in the extreme. The incense smell of Roman churches, the potent odours of their kind of sanctity, pervade Joyce's pages. Stephen, Joyce's aesthetic surrogate, craves what the linguistic philospher J. L. Austin called 'performative utterance', words which make things happen. But both of them especially relish that branch of the performative we have (with Jacques Derrida 1992: 300) to call the *perfumative* (it's one of his best puns). Bloom shares this nose alertness. He's quite dotty for smells, especially Molly's. 'Perfume of embraces all him assailed.' 'Perfumed bodies, warm, full.' Bloom sniffs them out everywhere (*U* 168). What happens in Stephen's erotic rite of passage is the swapping of religion's nose-pleasures for a woman's kind—a realization of what he craved and never got from the lovely-smelling body of Emma Cleary in *Stephen Hero*.

Sex with the whore is a most transgressive rite, a perfumative of sinners, a ritual of sin with fallen women. 'He wanted to sin with another of his kind, to force another being to sin with him and to exult with her in sin' (*P* 100). The fallen women gather in the brothel district's 'lighted halls', 'arrayed as if for some rite'; the street gas-lights burn 'as if before an altar'. Having sex outside of marriage is, as Stephen knows, a mortal sin; having it with a prostitute compounds the failure of virtue; having it with what is implied is a Jewish prostitute, one of Christ's crucifiers according to Roman theology of the day, makes it even worse. What stirs Joyce's extended body celebrations most is good Catholics going to the sexual bad in acts of bodily transgression which he puts as necessary to the freeing of the self and art from oppressive theological and ecclesiastical bondage. And the more transgressive, in fact the filthier, the better. Stephen wallows in the filth of his fall. Sexual emancipation comes in the darkest quarters of the city. He's given up following the city's 'kindly lights' (*P* 99: no more of Newman's 'Lead, kindly light' for him). 'He wandered up and down the dark slimy streets peering into the gloom of lanes and doorways, listening eagerly for any sound. He moaned to himself like some baffled prowling beast.' He's turned into the Minotaur, a lecherous beast of the filthy Dublin labyrinth, 'the maze of narrow and dirty streets' and 'foul laneways' where the drunken rioters and 'wranglers' and whores are. The cry he'd repressed for so long, the repressed desire and word, 'broke from him like a wail of furious despair from a hell of sufferers and died in a wail of furious entreaty, a cry for an iniquitous abandonment, a cry which was but the echo of an obscene scrawl which he had read on the oozing wall of a urinal' (*P* 100).

Obscene scrawling is what *Ulysses* would practise on a grand scale—at least according to the legal judgments which banned that novel for obscenity. The Nighttown episode in particular celebrates sexuality with a Rabelaisian abandonment of the orthodoxly couth. Here's the polymorphous perverse in rampant action. Bloom is arraigned by pious ladies on well-founded charges of voyeurism. He's posted them his pornographic photos of Molly 'practising illicit congress' with large blackguards, urging them 'to do likewise, to misbehave, to sin with officers of the garrison'. He appealed to them for masochistic satisfactions, and he appears to get some now, happily 'turning the other cheek' to the hostile hands of adorable females. The black Jewish (Hebrew Bible quoting) whore Zoe touches him up ('How's the nuts?' (*U* 454): Ulysses had his moly, Bloom's got a shrivelled potato in his pocket and testicles there for the asking). Zoe should give up smoking, he advises, and take a chew on him (*U* 454). Mulligan appears as a doctor diagnosing Bloom's 'symptoms of chronic exhibitionism', premature baldness 'from selfabuse', and bisexual abnormality (*U* 464). In nightmare night-time Dublin transsexuality is a norm. Bella turns into butch Bello. Bloom becomes a woman, a piggish one, truffling for oral satisfactions of all kinds. He's a bottom fetishist with a receptive bottom of his own. There's a lot of buggery about. There's even a suggestion that Bloom wants to sodomize Stephen. (Buggery seems to be one of the main transactions comprising the Fall in the Phoenix Park in *Finnegans Wake*.) THE SINS OF THE PAST arise to accuse Bloom of assorted nauseous fetishisms. Bloom is, as Joyce was, a coprophiliac, a 'Dungdevourer' (*U* 488). He doesn't just like sitting on the lavatory thoughtfully excreting (as in that most memorable of bodily exercises at the end of the 'Calypso' section of *Ulysses*) but likes nosing Molly's soiled underclothes and sniffing toilet-paper used by prostitutes (*U* 492). In fact Nighttown repeats and gleefully enacts the contents of Joyce's notorious 1909 love-letters urging Nora Barnacle to perform and write about stimulating excretory acts.[9] *Ulysses* is a fleshy carnivalesque to the most orthodoxy-offending degree Joyce can manage. This is *poiesis*, aesthetic making, as *uropoiesis*—piss-art. Stephen, accused of accosting Cissy Caffrey 'from behind', says, 'pointing to himself and the others': 'Poetic. Uropoetic' (*U* 520).[10] That is, an art which will deliberately pronounce the bodily and sexually unspeakable refused by the right-eously prude. Arraigned by the City Watch, Bloom can only 'murmur vaguely' the unpronounceable password *shibboleth* demanded of the Bible's border-crossing Ephraimites in Judges 12: it comes out as *Shitbroleeth*. His is the word as shit. Joyce certainly does dirt on sex (D. H. Lawrence's definition of pornography), but he delights more in doing sex as dirt. And writing too. It's only in keeping with his master's methods that Shem the Penman, *Finnegans Wake*'s portrait of the writer as Joycean man, should write in his own excrement, *inkenstink*, on his own body, 'the only foolscap available' (*FW* 185).

'Non serviam!' Stephen declares yet again in Nighttown, very drunk, as THE MOTHER vainly apostrophizes the Sacred Heart of Jesus to 'have mercy on him!' and 'Save him from hell' (*U* 517). When in *A Portrait* Stephen tells Cranly that 'I will not serve' (*P* 239), his orthodox chum replies that 'that remark was made before'. And Stephen replies 'hotly', 'It is made behind now.' It's the word from behind: where Satan is and speaks from: the bemerded place and word of the nay-sayer against the divine logos. Speech from the back, backward speech: which is the way a Black Mass is spoken, backwards, from left to right, in fact, heading towards the seat of Satan, the backward Angel who is also to be found on the left hand, in the sinister position. It's also how Jewish texts are read, from back to front, how Bloom remembers his father reading, how the Bible was read before Greek and Roman Christians turned it round in the 'right' direction, pointing towards the right-hand, where Jesus traditionally sits, 'at the right hand of God'. Satanic Bloom knows all this, watching the printer setting type for the newspaper report of Patrick Dignam's funeral, backwards. 'mangiD. kcirtaP. Poor papa with his hagadah book reading backward with his finger to me. Pessach. Next year in Jerusalem. Dear, O dear! All that long business about that brought us out of the land of Egypt and into the house of bondage alleluia' (*U* 124). *Into* the house of bondage, not out of it: Bloom compounds the ancient Hebraic backwardness by reversing the Israelite exiles' direction: backwardness heaped upon backwardness. As it were the work of a Black Mass twice over, anticipatory of Nighttown's inversions and reversions which culminate in a garish confusion of mock eucharistic voices, a great blasphemous Black Mass. '*Introibo ad altare diaboli*', intones Father Flynn. 'To the devil which hath made glad my young days', prays the Revd Mr Haines Love. The elevated host is mocked as Haines Love elevates his 'bare hairy buttocks between which a carrot is stuck'. THE VOICE OF ALL THE DAMNED has The Lord God Omnipotent reigning, backwards—'Tnetopinmo Dog Drol'. And so forth (*U* 527). And these blasphemous words, voices, discourses do

---

[9] Only in *Selected Letters of James Joyce* (Joyce 1975: 181–91).

[10] Curiously misprinted from the 1922 first edition text on as *Neopoetic*.

have it over their orthodox rivals. Which is the tendency, the way, the practice of all of Joyce's writings. They celebrate, repeat, and eventually model themselves, their whole being, on the theologically and ecclesiastically unorthodox, the mocking, blasphemous, and heretical. A blasphemous dog in the orthodox manger ('Do you hold yourself then for some god in the manger, Shehohem, that you will neither serve, nor let serve, pray nor let pray?' *FW* 188: 18–19.)

Ulysses's famous beginning in a mockery of the Catholic eucharist is utterly characteristic. '*Introibo ad altare Dei*', pronounces Mulligan, 'plump' as a medieval 'prelate', his bowl of shaving lather with his razor lying 'crossed' on it doubling as a ciborium or chalice. Shaving soap as the body or blood of Christ. Christ jokingly rewritten as *Christine*. Mulligan has some gold teeth, so he's dubbed *Chrysostomos*, 'golden-mouth'—the nickname of St John 'Chrysostomos', so-called for his eloquence. This jesting banalization, a renowned Church Father redone as Mulligan Chrysostomos by mere virtue of some prominent dental work, is a parodic metamorphosing, a secularizing bring-down of sacred history and tradition, which is simply Joyce's norm. Nothing among his great bulk of Catholic material and reference, the enormous amount of Roman ecclesiology, rituals, liturgies, practices, popes, saints, Fathers, ministers of Roman religion, the words of the sacred texts, the Christian words, concepts, dogmas, theologies, the Christian church's Trinitarian God, Jesus the Son of God and Saviour of the World, the Holy Ghost, Mary the Mother of Jesus, all of which cram the minds of Stephen and Bloom and the ever-mindful, nothing forgetting mind, as it were, of the Joycean text, nothing is safe from lampoon. Early in *Ulysses* Mulligan chants stanzas from Oliver St John Gogarty's Ballad of Joking Jesus ('I'm the queerest young fellow that ever was heard. | My mother's a jew, my father's a bird', and so on at some blasphemous length). *Ulysses* and *Finnegans Wake* are to be thought of as extended versions of that ballad. *Stephen Hero* and *A Portrait* have Stephen in training as that ballad's balladeer. He is the ventriloquist's dummy of Joking Jesus Joyce—James Joyce's favourite persona.

Nothing in this lampooner's Dublin is, as they say, sacred. Not least the eucharist, central rite and sacrament of the Christian church. Joyce's way with the most holy of Christian meals, the feeding of the believer on the body and blood of Christ for essential spiritual nourishment, is an extended case of his persistent religion-ruination game. The eucharist is never not taken mock-seriously, blasphemed, subverted. The long movement in 'Lotos Eaters' beginning with Bloom's dropping in on a mass at All Hallows church, and having his ironic juices set going by a notice about a missionary sermon (might the priest with blue glasses flash them enticingly at natives?), is a characteristic stream of undone and undoing theological and eccelesiological consciousness. 'The cold smell of sacred stone called him.' Cold perfumative. 'Something going on'. 'Shut your eyes and open your mouth. What? *Corpus.* Body. Corpse.... They don't seem to chew it; only swallow it down. Rum idea: eating bits of a corpse why the cannibals cotton on to it' (*U* 82). Wine is better than beer: 'more aristocratic'. It's good that only the priest gets the wine, otherwise 'one old booser worse than another coming along cadging for a drink'; but still this is a 'pious fraud'—'shew wine'. Bloom wishes there were music: he likes 'that old sacred music' (*U* 83), as Joyce himself did. He watches the priest descend the altar steps, 'holding the thing out from him'; repeats some of the prayers straight (as *A Portrait* and *Ulysses* do endlessly): 'O God, our refuge and strength . . .'; 'Blessed Michael, archangel, defend us in the hour of conflict . . .'; reflects on the 'wonderful organization' of the Roman Church, on confession, and 'skindeep' repentance and how much better this is than the Salvation Army's more earnest version ('Reformed prostitute will address the meeting. How I found the Lord'). The Roman system is so complete—'pat' answers for everything from the priest, 'Liberty and exaltation of our holy mother the church. The doctors of the church: they mapped out the whole theology of it' (*U* 84).

Pointfully, Joyce's urban mapping takes Bloom on to the pharmacist's for a prescription. Here's an alternative shrine or church, offering a rival perfumative, alternative corpus work, other kinds of redemption for the body. In the 'reek of drugs, the dusty dry smell of sponges and loofahs', Bloom thinks aporetically of the medicines that can kill, poisons that can cure—pharmaceutical versions of Christ's redemption (life coming from death): 'Remedy where you least expect it'. (No wonder Jacques Derrida, who had long been preoccupied with the aporetic attractions of the pharmakon of Plato, the medicine that poisoned Socrates (Derrida 1981: 61–171), was attracted to this passage: Derrida 1992: 300–1.) With Molly's body-smells on his mind Bloom buys oil, orangeflower water, and white wax for her, lemony soap for himself ('Nice smell these soaps have'). These purchases come to 'three and a penny': 3*s*. 1*d*., three shillings and one penny, three and one, the Trinity in old money: a joke Joyce can't resist (nor can Beckett—compare that flurry of 1*s*. 3*d*. and 3*s*. 1*d*. at the ticket office at the end of his *Watt*). Armed with his soap Bloom heads off for the Turkish baths for some body cleaning. 'Dirt gets in your navel'—the navel whose cord we will learn in 'Oxen of the Sun' connects everybody to Adam and Eve in the Garden of Eden—the connective tissue of the fall, the cause of human dirtiness. But uncleanness and redemptive cleansing are ordinary body matters now—and in a Turkish bath, not in the sacramental waters of the Christian tradition. Polluted, Bloom will pollute the waters. 'Also I think I. Yes I. Do it in the bath. Curious longing I. Water to water' (*U* 86–8). Is it urination he's planning? Uropoeisis; making water? A kind of baptism in his own urine? Another case of the perpetual Joycean mixing of the old theological with its low bodily revised version? 'I think you're getting along very nicely', as a voice says in the literary-theological debates of 'Scylla and Charybdis', 'Just mix up a mixture of theolologicophilolological. *Mingo, minxi, mictum, mingere*' (*U* 205). *Mingo*: I piss. Mixing mixtures is exactly what pharmacists do; it's especially what religio-pharmaceutical Joyce does.

Or is it masturbation he has in mind? The Sin of Onan. That's the suggestion of the episode's ending (*U* 88). 'This is my body', he says, a happy urinator or Onan, appropriating the eucharistic words for the mere relief of the flesh. 'I think I', he says. Bloom always thinks *I*, thinks of *I*, but here the self in interior monologue is thinking, as ever, of its mere bodily functions. This is the self as a refocused *cogito*: I micturate and masturbate therefore I am. The self as a sullied, in-carnate thing.

Hamlet wanted his *solid, sullied* flesh to melt away (*Hamlet* I. ii. 129); Bloom celebrates it rather as the only possible continuing essence.

It's an eating and drinking body, of course, and one dining and wining off parodically eucharistic meat and drink. A sordid ingesting, the tone of whose gross burlesquing of the eucharistic meal is set by Bloom's breakfast pork kidney (*U* 61 ff.): taboo meat for Jews, purchased in a welter of thoughts about Zionist settlements in the Holy Land ('Agendath Netaim'—Hebrew for Planter's Company) growing Jewish lemons, 'without a flaw' (like Old Testament animal offerings to Jehovah, 'without a blemish'), and about the enticing 'hams' of a female customer at the butcher's; meat burned in the pan (a mock burnt-offering: Old Testament type of the sacrificed Christ); meat chewed 'with discernment' (as St Paul told the Corinthian church to eat and drink the body and blood of the Lord). (In the New Bloomusalem of Nighttown, the Holy City is shaped like a 'huge pork kidney' (*U* 459).) Bloom's lunchtime tells a like story. Hungry again, in 'Lestrygonians', he thinks of meat and sacrifice, the Old Testament cuisine of sacrifice and its Christian version in the death of Christ the Lamb of God, in whose cleansing blood sinners need to wash, according to the words of Elisha Hoffman's evangelical hymn 'Have you been to Jesus for the cleansing power? | Are you washed in the blood of the Lamb?' (Hoffman 1878): thoughts prompted by a throwaway announcing the advent in Dublin of American evangelist Alexander Dowie, or 'Elijah' (he's named for the herald of the Messiah in Jewish apocalyptic thought): 'Blood of the lamb . . . Are you saved? All are washed in the blood of the lamb, God wants blood victim. Birth, hymen, martyr, war, foundation of a building, sacrifice, kidney burnt-offering, druid's altars. Elijah is coming.'

Meat is the dominant issue in 'Lestrygonians'—comestibles, womens' bodies—in an explosion of flesh and its appetizing aromas. Incited by the cloth in a shop window (blood-red poplin: a Huguenot import) Bloom thinks of lingerie and Molly and their smells—the smell-taste allurements of exotic (and Jewish) women and food. 'Sunwarm silk. Jingling harness' (a verbal jingling harking back to Stephen's meditation in *A Portrait* (*P* 155), about the connection between words and the things they denote— horse's harness, women's stockings, 'the delicate and sinful perfume' of women's clothing, and his daring to think of a woman 'only amid soft-worded phrases or within rose-soft stuffs'—Stephen's early stab at an incarnational linguistics, or practice of perfumative utterance). 'All for a woman', Bloom goes on, 'silk webs . . . rich fruits, spicy from Jaffa. Agendath Netaim'. 'A warm plumpness settled down on his brain. His brain yielded. Perfume of embraces all him assailed. With hungered flesh obscurely, he mutely craved to adore' (*U* 168) (that wonderful pair of sentences picked out for special mention by Frank Budgen in *James Joyce and the Making of Ulysses*).[11] Bloom tries the Burton restaurant ('pungent meatjuice, slop of greens'), an orgy of nauseous food-shovelling—men 'swilling, wolfing gobfuls' (*U* 168). 'Gulp. Grub. Gulp. Gobstuff' (*U* 169). *Gobstuff*, a mere, but crucial, phoneme away from *God-stuff*.

---

[11] Joyce: 'What I am seeking is the perfect order of words in the sentence. There is an order in every way appropriate. I think I have it. . . . You can see for yourself in how many different ways those words might be arranged' (Budgen 1972: 20).

This is the coarse swallowing which comes from the Irish sceptic's not being able to 'swallow it all', i.e. all the doctrines of St Patrick (*U* 169). To believe is to eat, orthodox dogma of the eucharist has it, and so it is for the doxa's perverter. The parody credo of Shaun the Post in *Finnegans Wake* ('In fact, always, have I believe') is *Greedo!* (*FW* 411. 21), in a passage perverting the Lord's Prayer in terms of eating. 'His hungry will be done!'; 'ghee up, ye dog, for your doggily broth'. Shaun doesn't tell his rosary beads, but recites 'my grocery beans'. Greetings in the *Wake*'s wrenched Christian Year are given rather as *greedings* ('youalldied [Yuletide] greedings' (*FW* 308); 'easter greeding' (*FW* 376. 36–337. 1)).

Bloom's own gobfulls get progressively fouler as Bloomsday goes on. He does eschew a Law-breaking ham sandwich for lunch, but that night in Nighttown (*U* 492–3) he's threatened with having to drink urine ('Lap it up like champagne', says Bello, 'Drink me piping hot'). Does he eat excrement? His stammering confession stops suggestively short: 'I rererepugnosed in rerererepugnant....' In 'Ithaca', in a clamantly pseudo-eucharistic moment (*U* 597), Bloom and Stephen drink in 'joco-serious silence' some Epps cocoa—'Epps's massproduct' (food for the masses and also food for masses): the 'creature cocoa' transformed by Bloom's preparation into a 'massdrink', as by the priest's words the 'creatures' of bread and wine are turned into the body and blood of Christ. W. K. Tindall (1959: 222) long ago pointed out that the botanical name for cocoa is *theobroma*, god-food—which is just the kind of thing Joyce knew and was, as ever, jocoserious about.[12] And not least here, one supposes, because *cocoa* is so close to *caco*, Latin *I shit*, *cack* in English. 'Their feed begins' (*FW* 308)—and the marginal note there anounces 'KAKAO-POETIC'. *Kakaopoesis*: evildoing, or the poetry of foulness and wickedness: the double of *uropoiesis*, and pointedly a rhyming partner of the surely implied *cacopoiesis*. And these foul eucharistics lead inevitably to bad excretion. 'Go the whole hog. Puke it out,' Bello orders (*U* 492).

Bloom's mouth, then, is the excrementitious orifice of the blasphemer (and satirist, especially Irish-satirist, the Swiftian mal-speaker) in action: the mouth of the damned in hell, 'full' as the Clongowes Retreat preacher asserts, 'of blasphemies against God' (*P* 122). Chrystomos as polluted and polluter—the golden mouth as 'excrement yellow' (*U* 425), or lemon-yellow, the colour of Joycean foodstuffs from *A Portrait* on. And not just the mouth. The Bloomian body is a repertoire of bad orifices, the 'vile machine' of Swiftian nightmare ('The Lady's Dressing Room', line 95: Swift 1983: 451), processing ingested bad stuff as excreted bad stuff, shit and piss, spit and vomit. No wonder it's been easy for Joyce interpreters to read Bloom's extended spell on the lavatory in 'Calypso', after the mock eucharist of the pork

---

[12] Tindall's cocoa point is richly expanded by Frederick K Lang (Lang 1993: 260). Lang's is perhaps the best extended inspection of Joyce's transformative use of liturgical and theological things, despite its constant failure to notice Joyce's blasphemous intent—indeed its repeated confused assumption that the liturgical and theological contents are present per se rather than as actors in a grand act of blasphemous displacement. This confusion is widespread among commentators on Joyce's investments in such matters—chief sinner among whom is Virginia Moseley (1967), a keen pleromatist who consistently fails to spot the irony and blasphemy and the desire to outdo and displace, and who would have Joyce a true believer after all.

kidney, as a parodic transubstantiation and to take Stephen and Bloom's shared micturating in 'Ithaca'—this pair of proclaimed heretics and lustful deadly sinners at blasphemous play in an extended parody catechism (*U* 623, 624)—as a mock *asperges*, the sprinkling which precedes the mass (F. K. Lang's point: 1993: 270).[13]

The lair of Shem the Penman in the *Wake* is the abode of this disgraced bodliness—a *literatured* mass of Christian waste-matters, an echoing jokey ruin of distorted, torn-up, mangled religious texts, things, dogmas, a jesting wasteland of de-substantiated Christian substance: 'vivlical viasses,... fallen lucifers,... falsehair shirts, Godforsaken scapulars,... magnifying wineglasses,... ex nuns', vice abbess's, pro virgins'... garters,... lees of whine,... convertible collars,... broken wafers, unloosed shoelatchets, crooked strait waistcoats, fresh horrors from hades,... glass eyes for an eye, gloss teeth for a tooth...' (*FW* 183). The leftover wine (*lees*) and chucked-away bits of wafer indicate a bad eater's contempt for the food elements of the Lord's Supper. Shem's foul excretions are the expectable outcome of the vile post-Christian body: 'messes of mottage,... seedy ejaculations,... blasphematory spits, ...undeleted glete,... war moans...' (*FW* 183–4). *Gleet* is gonorrhoeal discharge from the urethra. *War moans* echo the Salvation Army's magazine the *War Cry*—the moans of a whore, one of the unconverted ones, or an orgasmic sinner at war with (and whining about) orthodoxy. *Messes of mottage* remind of Esau's foolishness in selling his birthright for a 'mess', a meal, a mass, of 'pottage'. *Mot* is *prostitute* in English and *word* in French, so *mottage* is something like *whorish words*. And eating messes of mottage would be very bad mouth work, making a meal of whorish flesh, eating and speaking whorish words—followed by depositing excrementitious messes of this mottage on the floor. In Latin, the language of church and priest, the *Wake* describes Shem's preparation of his inkenstink (*FW* 185). He 'craps' in his hand, urinates joyfully and melliflouously (*laete ac melliflue*) into the vessel containing this mess, makes a writing mix by this micturition (*minxit*), the while singing *magna voce* Ps. 45: 1, '*Lingua mea calamus scribae velociter scribentis*' ('My tongue is the pen of a ready writer': a scribe scribing with ease and speed).[14] Shitting, pissing, mouthing: the busy orifices of the blasphemously carnal writer, laying claim to the scriptural scribe's orifice work. *Eructavit cor meum verbum bonum*, Ps. 45: 1 begins: my heart has belched or vomited out a good word. Joyce the blasphemous vomiter well knew what kind of pious text and utterance he was appropriating for parody.

In Nighttown the vomiting Bloom is appointed a carnivalesque pope. *Habemus carneficem*, prounounces the Bishop of Armagh, pouring on some hair-oil (*U* 458). Not *papem*, nor, crucially, *carnificem*, murderer, mutilator, executioner (as most annotators think), but *carneficem*, a Joyce coinage to mean something like mangler of the flesh, or incarnated do-badder. Incarnation as a bad business. Some fleshy words from the Introit of the Requiem Mass, *Omnis caro ad te veniet*, 'All flesh shall come unto thee', are in Bloom's mind early on (*U* 53). In Joyce's revisionist

---

[13] Gian Balsamo (2004), is a rather good guide to such mocking adaptations.

[14] The Jesuit Joycean Robert Boyle has visited this cloacal passage-at-arms with some force, twice: Boyle, 1966 and 1972.

arrangement, Bloom's body is what all flesh comes to. Those liturgical words get repeated in 'Oxen of the Sun' (*U* 388), where the question of incarnation and transubstantiation arises blasphemously around Mrs Purefoy's pregnancy. 'Incarnation', becoming flesh, is no longer a divine event: it happens in every 'woman's womb'. And this natural flesh-event is glossed as *transubstantiality* (so mere pregnancy is a parody of the Catholic definition of how the bread and wine become the body and blood of Christ in the eucharist), or as *consubstantiality* (a parody of the orthodox credal statement of how God the Father and God the Son are 'one in being', of a shared substance). Revisions could scarcely be more blasphemous. This is the *Greedo*-credo, consuming the ham sandwich of heretical theology, with a vengeance.

Before Bloom eats his stinking gorgonzola sandwich ('with relish of disgust, pungent mustard, the feety savour of green cheese' (*U* 173)), he meditates on the ham on the shelf of Davy Byrne's pub, and on biblical Ham. 'Sandwich? Ham and his descendants mustered and bred [mustard and bread!] there. Potted meats'. Potted thoughts of Ham, these, in a rush of thoughts about religions and eating, both legalized and transgressive: 'Kosher...Yom Kippur fast...Christmas turkeys and geese. Slaughter of innocents. Eat drink and be merry'; missionaries too salty for cannibal taste; a scurrilous limerick about a 'right royal old nigger, who ate or something the somethings of the reverend Mr MacTrigger'. Biblical Ham, the son of Noah, 'saw the nakedness' of his drunken father, for which mysterious (homosexual?) transgression—it keeps being echoed in *Finnegans Wake* as a key part of the Fall in the Phoenix Park—he got his descendants cursed as 'servants of servants', perpetual subalterns. Joyce likes the idea of Ham's sons as the cannibalistic eaters-up of missionaries, a tribe of bad eaters. He's no doubt excited by biblical Ham's fathering of Nimrod, the builder of Babel, and so ancestor of Babelic Dublin in the *Wake*, and of the *Wake* as a Babelic text. And the name of any son of Ham? Why Hamlet, of course: archetype, in Shakespeare's version, and thus for Joyce too, of the troubled, transgressive son at odds with the ghostly father, whose demands ('Remember me!') ruin his life.

Stephen Dedalus is indeed a Hamlet, a descendant of Ham. 'A servant of a servant', he calls himself (*U* 17). Like Shakespeare's Hamlet he's terribly ghosted. Like the Joycean text he has a host of ghostly fathers—all the compelling orthodox prophets, patriarchs, Church Fathers, the commanding authors and compilers of the creeds and liturgies and textbooks on devotion and piety, Aquinas the grand summarizer of Catholic theology, Jerome the translator of the Vulgate Latin version of the Bible, St Ignatius Loyola great adviser on meditation and inspirer of the Jesuits who wrote the educational system Joyce underwent, and Cardinal Newman, founding father of University College Dublin, the alma mater of both Joyce and Stephen. The words of these spokesmen and 'ministers of the Holy Ghost' (*P* 139) haunt Stephen, fill his mind, shape his thoughts and actions.[15] Their words *are* Stephen, as they *were* Joyce. Stephen and Joyce are so familiar with the good words of the good that they seem

---

[15] Maud Ellmann's 1992 article, 'The Ghosts of Ulysses', repr. in Attridge (2004: 83–99), is most pertinent, as well as arrestingly amusing, about Joycean ghostedness.

often to be quoting them from memory. And also misquoting: that sure sign both of the deeply embedded word and worry about it, the so-called 'anxiety of influence' which such distortions always signify in Harold Bloom's influential theory (Bloom 1973; 1975; and *überall*). What happens to the 'proud' cadences of Father Newman (*P* 165), his 'cloistral silver-veined prose' (*P* 175) which so people Stephen's memory, is characteristic of these many misremembered mastering words—they're usually got slightly wrong, and not least in that long 'prayer' from the pervasively influential sermon on 'The Glories of Mary for the Sake of her Son' that Stephen once more recalls before his guilty confession of sin with the prostitute (*P* 139; Don Gifford 1982: 200 gives the correct version).

The shaping word of the Fathers and fathers is the enslaving net that Stephen, and Joyce's text, are struggling with. Stephen starts life as the 'nicens little boy named baby tuckoo' inside his father's story. 'His father told him that story: his father looked at him through a glass: he had a hairy face. He was baby tuckoo.' Who's he? The pronouns are indistinguishable. Baby Stephen and his father are one. His father speaks him and names him. He is the word of his father. This father–son relationship mimes the orthodox relationship of God the Father and God the Son. It stands for all the orthodoxies of the orthodox fathers of Stephen's tradition and education which he struggles to discard: the words of the fathers which he's striving to get out of, to displace and replace by his own story, his own word. *A Portrait* (and *Stephen Hero*) are the story of that wrestling for his own word and name. *Ulysses* marks the struggle's success. Bloom, Jewish, blasphemous, sinful, other, is instated as the desired new father. The struggle is intense, violent with the violence of the Freudian version of this inter-generational fight. The father and the Fathers have to be cut off, castrated, made impotent. The wonderfully complex scene in *A Portrait* (90) in the Cork college's anatomy theatre naturally attracts Freudian and Lacanian analyses (such as Maud Ellmann's 1981: 198–206). Father Simon Dedalus looks for his initials carved on a desk as a student; Stephen sees the embarassing word 'foetus' before he spots the paternal initials; imagines his ghostly father (and the episode is full of student ghosts) cutting the word with a jack-knife; is shocked to find his 'monstrous' sexual thoughts out there, in writing, graphic, *cut in* (as Derrida would say). The father's initials, *SD*, are of course Stephen's own. So it's cut or be cut. No wonder Stephen's nickname is Kinch, *knife*. No wonder, either, that Stephen casts himself as Jacob, the Bible's usurping, trickster hero who wrestles all night with the divine antagonist in Gen. 32 for a blessing and a new name. Dublin, with the Jacob's biscuit factory so prominent (workplace of teasing girls, figures of priested Irish woman-hood (*P* 252); source of the Citizen's missile), is this Jacob's wrestling ring. 'I fear him [the old Irish-speaker] . . . It is with him I must struggle all through the night till day come, till he or I lie dead' (*P* 252).

'He war': the two words Derrida cannily picked out of the multilingual Babelism of the multilinguistic *Wake* (*FW* 258. 12) do indeed encapsulate this Jacobean tragedy of Joyce. He wars, 'he wages war, he declares or makes war', on God and his church; and this struggle for identity, being, a name, the words, is his essence, his very being (he *war*, this is what he *was*, past tense of the verb *to be*, in German) (Derrida 1984:

145–59). To which heterodox end Stephen (and Joyce) call in aid the heretic Fathers, the ones who resisted orthodoxy in the matter of the relationship of God the Father and God the Son, the Trinity, the divinity of Christ. Arius comes to Stephen's mind in 'Proteus' when the sight of some midwives prompts this father-obsessive to yet more thoughts of his parents. The Nicene Creed declares that Jesus was 'begotten not made'; was 'one in being with the Father' (consubstantial, coeternal). Arius split the church by refusing the formula: Jesus was not *homoousias* (of the *same* substance as God, *consubstantial*), but only *homoiousias*, of *like* substance. Stephen knows that he himself was 'made not begotten'. He is of his father's flesh. But perhaps that's what the Creed's *consubstantial* really means: the Father and the Son a merely fleshly pair, 'consubstantial' like him, he with 'my consubstantial father's voice'. It's a patently heretical line of thought he needs Arius to arbitrate. 'Where is poor dear Arius to try conclusions? Warring his life long on the contransmagnificandjewbangtantiality. Ill-starred heresiarch' (*U* 44–5).

Stephen imagines the grand heretics, the old 'Brood of mockers' (*U* 197)—of whom Mulligan is said to be one—Photius, and 'Arius warring his life long upon the consubstantiality of the Son with the Father, and Valentine, spurning Christ's terrine body, and the subtle heresiarch Sabellius who held that the Father was Himself his own son', a 'horde of heresies', all 'fleeing with mitres awry' before 'the church militant'. The *void* awaits them. But this is a void Stephen and *Ulysses* readily plunge into; it's the heresiarchs' theological resistance that Joyce's struggle with the father–son problematic gets modelled on. In the discussion in 'Scylla and Charybdis', where Stephen advances his anxious reflections on the relation of Hamlet to his ghostly father, and Shakespeare's to his son Hamnett, and of Hamlet to Hamnett, Sabellius emerges as the best bet for this fraught son: 'Sabellius, the African, subtlest heresiarch of all the beasts of the field' [i.e. the most Satanic one], who 'held that the Father was Himself His own Son' (*U* 208). Mulligan jeers at the conception, but a Sabellian rewrite of the Apostles' Creed is uttered: 'He Who Himself begot, middler the Holy Ghost, and Himself sent himself, Agenbuyer, between Himself and others . . . sitteth on the right hand of His Own Self' (197–8). (The Jesuit critic Father William Noon is especially revealing about Joyce's Sabellian interests, in Noon (1957), especially in his ch. 6, 'Sabellian Subtleties: The Trinitarian Theme'.) Here's the Son as, in effect, usurper of his Father's fatherhood, overturner and overtaker of the orthodox Father's (and father's) role: a pair whose words and voices are one, seemingly proceeding from the father, but actually from the son, because their identities have been reversed. This is a metamorphosis indeed, even the *metempsychosis* which so haunts *Ulysses*. A metamorphosis indicated with wonderful subtlety in the trangressive metamorphosing of words from Ovid's *Metamorphoses* which follows the Sabellian model's application to Shakespeare and Hamlet (*U* 210). Stephen is thinking again of Dedalus, the 'Old father, old artificer' invoked at the end of *A Portrait*, whose paternal name he bears, and of Dedalus's son Icarus, model of the ephebe he Stephen is. This Icarus's travels are like Joyce's own, back and forth between Dublin and Paris: 'You flew . . . Paris and back . . . Icarus. *Pater, ait.*' It's a momentous intertextual revision, in which son Icarus flies on and father Dedalus falls. In Ovid's *Metamorphoses* 8, the orthodox version, Dedalus keeps asking where the fallen Icarus is: 'Icare, ait . . . Icare, dixit, ubi es?' In Joyce's version, Stephen-Icarus asks in the assumed usurped voice and position of the old father, where father (and every Father) now is: 'Pater, ait'. The flying son has displaced the drowning father; the youth lives and speaks, and in the voice of the old father, the old father who is dead, silent; the father's words, word, logos, sound now only in the tones of the usurping son. (It's an extraordinarily compelling switch that the French writer Hélène Cixous (1998: 100–28) meditates on with great force.)

And all of Joyce's fiction, his fabulation, his textuality, his poetics (revealed in a constant praxis of metatextual reflection) are shaped by this usurping, heretic, father-killing, word-colonizing metamorphosis. The Joycean poetics begin with the 'epiphanic'. Notoriously, Joyce wants us to see his realist, Ibsenite project as a theology-usurping one, as set out in *Stephen Hero*. 'By an epiphany he meant a sudden spiritual manifestation, whether in the vulgarity of speech or in a memorable phase of the mind itself. He believed that it was for the man of letters to record these epiphanies with extreme care' (*SH* 216). Joyce did so (they're published in Joyce 1991: 157–200). Much of his writing can be thought of as such a collection: Joyce as secular *magos* encountering and recording the significant real, the only version of a divinely incarnated realium there now is. In an *epiphany* Stephen finds manifest Aquinas's third requisite of beauty, namely *claritas*, 'radiance' (the other two are *integritas* and *consonantia*, 'integrity' and 'symmetry'). *Claritas* equals *quidditas*, he explains (*SH* 217–18)—glossed as *whatness* in the parallel (revised) passage in *A Portrait* (209). 'His Esthetic was in the main applied Aquinas', we're told (*SH* 81; repeated at *P* 209). It is, rather, Aquinas coopted for secularizing metamorphosis. And so it is across the whole Joycean textual scene. *Dubliners*, Joyce explained, was designed as 'a series of epicleti'[16]—a word derived from *epiclesis*, the old prayer in which the Holy Ghost is invoked to descend upon the elements of the eucharist and/or upon the partakers. Joyce was thus from early on imagining himself as Stephen's 'priest of the eternal imagination, transmuting the daily bread of experience into the radiant body of everliving life' (*P* 221): the writer as priest, by and in whose words the ordinary stuff of the quotidian real is transubstantiated into living-word stuff. Living words: the only living words, at least according to this proud heresiarch ('anarch, egoarch, hiresiarch': *FW* 188. 16). Which is a reversed incarnation: not the Word becoming flesh, but flesh becoming word. Sinful flesh, of course, turned into text. Or *cunt* as *oracle*: as Stephen Hero keeps insisting. He 'called it *oracle* and all within its frontiers oracular' (*SH* 141). Emma tantalizes with her 'inclination for oracle' (*SH* 196). The fleshly oracles of Joyce: they displace the old 'oracles of God'. Here are Joyce's scriptures for those who have ears to hear: his kind of *tympanum* work, whose sexual aspect Joyce greatly enjoys underlining in the 'Sirens' episode, that very musical section of *Ulysses*—in the passage where Simon Dedalus jokes about Ben (Warrior) Dollard's tight trousers that showed off his 'Musical porkers', and about his powerful

---

[16] Joyce (1957: i. 55). Letter dated Early July 1904, in 1975: 22.

bass voice: 'You'd burst the tympanum of [Molly's] ear...with an organ like yours'; 'Not to mention another membrane, Father Cowley added' (*U* 269).[17] These thoughts of musical mouth-ear body-work greatly excite Bloom in that passage: 'Flood of warm jimjam lickitup secretness flowed to flow in music out, in desire, dark to lick flow, invading. Tipping her tepping her tapping her topping her. Tup. Pores to dilate dilating. Tup. The joy the feel the warm the. Tup. To pour oe'r sluices pouring gushes. Flood, gush, flow, joygush, tupthrop. Now! Language of love.' Body language; the language of the body; body-work as word. As in *FW* 584. 3: she 'Tipatonguing him on in her pigeony linguish'. Speaking in tongues as fellatio. As it were the tongue work of Aquinas's Maundy Thursday hymn *Pange lingua gloriosi*, 'Tell my tongue of the victory gained in glorious conflict', the victory of Christ's death on the cross—sung as the Host is carried through the church—perverted to other, merely corporeal tellings. 'I like it', says Stephen in *A Portrait* (209).

And this heretical logocentrism goes very far indeed. It embraces the fantastic blasphemous granting of pseudo-divinity to the neo Father and Son relationship of Bloom and Stephen—or Stoom and Blephen as they appear in Nighttown. Bloom's day is a plot of corrupted Judaeo-Christian rituals and geographies: Bloomsday, 16 June 1904, as (un)holy day or Rabelaisian carnivalesque holiday (*U* 649–50)—'The preparation of breakfast (burnt offering): intestinal congestion and premeditative defecation (holy of holies):... the unsubstantial lunch (rite of Melchizadech):... the bookhunt along Bedford Row, Merchants' Arch, Wellington Quay (Simchath Torah [Rejoice in the Law]): the music in the Ormond Hotel (Shira Shirim [Song of Songs]),' and so on, through the 'holocaust' at Bernie Kiernan's, the 'wilderness' of the Dublin car-drive, the 'rite of Onan' on the beach, the 'heave offering' of Mrs Purefoy's parturition, 'Armageddon' at Bella Cohen's, ending with the 'atonement' at the Cabman's shelter in 'Eumaeus'. Bloom metamorphoses into the *scapegoat* carry-ing the sins of the people into the wilderness ('the land of Ham') (*U* 467). He wears 'a seamless garment marked IHS', intoning, in imitation of Jesus, 'Weep not for me, O daughters of Erin' (*U* 467). He writes his name in the sand in 'Nausicaa', as Jesus did in the presence of the 'woman taken in adultery' in the Gospel: 'I. AM. A', the writing says, a solipsistic version of the tetragrammaton, the unpronounceable name of Jehovah (*U* 379). In Nighttown, 'Women press forward to touch the hem of Bloom's robe' (*U* 460), as a bleeding one did with Jesus. Bloom performs zany miracles (*U* 465). At the end of his cod genealogy we learn that *vocabitur nomen eius Emmanuel*, 'his name shall be called Emmanuel', just like Jesus (*U* 466). He's also a neo St Paul, mocked by the Citizen in 'Cyclops' as 'A new apostle to the Gentiles (*U* 331). In Nighttown he also plays St Peter to Stephen's Jesus ('You were with him', Bella Cohen accuses (*U* 518)). As this neo-Christ, Bloom is the very essence of the heretically fleshly Word. '*Christus* or Bloom his name is', Stephen tells the cabmen in 'Eumaeus', '*secundum carnem*', according to the flesh (*U* 563). Which is to say he's an antichrist—one of Bloom's many manifestations, or hypostases, in Nighttown:

---

[17] A Derridean play on *tympanum* and *hymen* greatly appealing, as it should, to postmodern readers such as Ellen Carol Jones (1993: 257–82), especially the 'Tympanum' section (264–71).

'Reuben J Antichrist, wandering jew' (*U* 472). And a triumphant antichrist, rather than the defeated one of the Bible's apocalyptic book of Revelation. For 'Circe' is an anti-Apocalypse, a triumphant carnival of the blasphemous New Bloomusalem, an apocalypse of the bad body and the sinful word, all egged-on by uncouth American evangelist A. J. Dowie, messianic Elijah come at last. 'A J Christ Dowie' urges the whole debauched crew, 'Florry Christ, Stephen Christ, Zoe Christ, Bloom Christ, Kitty Christ, Lynch Christ', to 'be on the side of the angels' and expect 'the second advent' on Coney Island, to the tune of his 'glory song' from THE GRAMOPHONE, 'The Holy City' of Edward Weatherby and Stephen Adams bastardized: 'Whorusalami-nyourhighhohhhh...' Whorusalem. A new Jerusalem of the whore. The Bible's Scarlet Woman rampant.

We hear THE GRAMOPHONE winding down at that very point. It winds up again, so to say, in *Finnegans Wake*, that extended glossalalic Day of Pentecost, or pun-full fulfilment of the Scriptures: *ut implerentur scripturae* (*U* 424). A pleromatic of Joyce's own scriptures, of course, a text replaying the whole preceding Joycean word-game, but also revamping the church's texts and textuality, a practice of scriptural fulfil-ment as a kind of anagrammatical gibberish, a pentecostal exiling of clear meaning, an extended jubilee of the fallen letter—a textuality delighted in by deconstructionist critics high on postmodernist models of mystagogic textualism (such as Beryl Schlossman, 1985), and encouraged of course by certain of Joyce's closest disciples, especially Eugene Jolas, preacher of the surrealist 'Revolution of the Word' in *Our Exagmination* (Jolas 1929: 77–92). A textual revolution which invests in the kind of linguistic and interpretative bottomlessness that the more recent deconstructive Joyceans want not only to see celebrated by Joyce, especially in *Finnegans Wake*, but want to celebrate Joyce for bringing out as the real linguistic, epistemic, and hermeneutical truth of the Bible and the Christian tradition—discourses with, allegedly, no fixed meanings at all, but existing rather as infinitely rewritable and reinterpretatable sets of meaning potential, as amply exploited by James Joyce. Which is an argument—potently put by Gian Balsamo (2002), and William Franke (2002: pp. v–xiii—that certainly has its force. Except that Joyce's is a neo-logocentrism that does indeed keep touching bottom—and not least with bottom-obsessed Molly Bloom. Not to mention excrement-dotty Leopold Bloom. Dowie-Christ may only return jokily, and the word of his coming may be a mere throwaway covered in gutter-filth. But we never get the olfactory shock of the soiled paper-work of *Ulysses* and *Finnegans Wake* out of our nostrils. And Bloom's dark horse Throwaway did have that funny way of coming in a winner. And of course Molly Bloom's talk goes on and on, and the flow of Anna Livia Plurabelle is an endless circling. Cunt indeed proves oracular. With these grandiloquently eloquent females, at the long climax of *Ulysses* and in the unstoppably cyclical flow of the *Wake*, the voice of the already usurped patriarchal texts is taken over and metamorphosed yet once more into this transformed, unquenchably undone and redone voice of the post-orthodox female: Irish virgin, old pious mother, Blessed Virgin Mary, Mother Church, triumphantly traduced. And, of course, as *Ulysses* suggests, this voice of the transgressive female is, so to say, the voice and text and textuality of Bloom as gifted with an oracular vagina, as in Nighttown, where, as the 'new womanly man', he gives birth miraculously to many sons—including one Chrysostomos—while remaining *virgo intacta*. So that Bloom is both the new father of the new Joycean fatherland and also the Virgin Mary *rediviva*, all in one. Which couldn't be more transgressive, and blasphemous and heretical, and shocking—Bloom all at once the startling Father and Mother of the new logos, the new logocentrism, that Joyce's later texts like to think themselves as comprising.

Works Cited

ATTRIDGE, DEREK (ed.) 2004. *James Joyce's* Ulysses: *A Casebook*. Oxford: Oxford University Press.

BALSAMO, GIAN. 2002. *Scriptural Poetics in Joyce's Finnegans Wake*. Studies in Irish Literature 7. Lewiston, NY: Edwin Mellen.

—— 2004. *Rituals of Literature: Joyce, Dante, Aquinas, and the Tradition of Christian Epics*. Lewisburg, Pa.: Bucknell University Press.

BLAMIRES, HARRY. 1966. *The Bloomsday Book: A Guide through Joyce's 'Ulysses'*. London: Methuen.

BLOOM, HAROLD. 1973. *The Anxiety of Influence: A Theory of Poetry*. New York: Oxford University Press.

—— 1975. *A Map of Misreading*. New York: Oxford University Press.

BOYLE, ROBERT. 1966. '*FW* 185: An Explication', *James Joyce Quarterly* 4 (Fall): 3–16.

—— 1972. 'Miracle in Black Ink: A Glance at Joyce's Use of His Eucharistic Image', *James Joyce Quarterly* 10 (Fall): 47–61.

BUDGEN, FRANK. 1972. *James Joyce and the Making of 'Ulysses', and Other Writings*. London: Oxford University Press.

CIXOUS, HÉLÈNE. 1998. '"Mamãe, disse ele", or Joyce's Second Hand', trans. Eric Prenowitz, in *Stigmata: Escaping Texts*. London: Routledge.

DERRIDA, JACQUES. 1981. 'Plato's Pharmacy'. *Dissemination*, trans. Barbara Johnson. Chicago: University of Chicago Press, 61–171.

—— 1984. 'Two Words for Joyce', trans. Geoff Bennington, in Derek Attridge and Daniel Ferrer (eds.), *Post-structuralist Joyce: Essays from the French*. Cambridge: Cambridge University Press, 145–59.

—— 1992. 'Ulysses Gramophone: Hear Say Yes in Joyce' [1984], *Acts of Literature*, ed. Derek Attridge. New York & London: Routledge, 253–309.

ELLMANN, MAUD. 1981. 'Disremembering Dedalus: A Portrait of the Artist as a Young Man', in Robert Young (ed.), *Untying the Text: A Post-Structuralist Reader*. Boston: Routledge & Kegan Paul, 198–206.

—— 1992. 'The Ghosts of Ulysses', repr. in Attridge (2004: 83–99).

FRANKE, WILLIAM. 2002. 'Literature as Liturgy and the Interpretive Revolution of Literary Criticism', in Gian Balsamo, *Scriptural Poetics in Joyce's Finnegans Wake*. Studies in Irish Literature 7. Lewiston: Edwin Mellen.

FRIEDMAN, SUSAN STANFORD. 1993. '(Self) Censorship and the Making of Joyce's Modernism' in S. S. Friedman (ed.), *Joyce: The Return of the Repressed*. Ithaca: Cornell University Press, 21–59.

GIFFORD, DON. 1982. *Joyce Annotated: Notes for Dubliners and A Portrait of the Artist as a Young Man*. 2nd edn. rev. and enlarged. Berkeley and Los Angeles: University of California Press.

HOFFMAN, ELISHA A. 1878. *Spiritual Songs for Gospel Meetings and the Sunday School*. Cleveland, Ohio: Barker & Smellie.

JOLAS, EUGENE. 1929. 'The Revolution of Language and James Joyce', in Samuel Beckett et al, *Our Exagmination Round his Factification for Incamination of Work in Progess*. Paris: Shakespeare, 77–92.

JONES, ELLEN CAROL. 1993. 'Textual Mater: Writing the Mother in Joyce', in S. S. Friedman (ed.), *Joyce: The Return of the Repressed*. Ithaca: Cornell University Press, 257–82.

JOYCE, JAMES. 1936. *Exiles: A Play in Three Acts* [1918]. London: Jonathan Cape.

—— 1939. *Finnegans Wake*. London: Faber & Faber.

—— 1957. *Letters*, ed. Stuart Gilbert. London: Faber & Faber, i.

—— 1960. *A Portrait of the Artist As a Young Man* [1916]. Harmondsworth: Penguin.

—— 1965. *Dubliners* [1914]. Harmondsworth: Penguin.

—— 1969a. *Ulysses* [1922]. Harmondsworth: Penguin Modern Classics.

—— 1969b. *Stephen Hero* [1944], ed. John J. Slocum and Herbert Cahoon. London: Jonathan Cape.

—— 1975. *Selected Letters*, ed. Richard Ellmann. London: Faber & Faber.

—— 1991. 'Epiphanies', *Poems and Shorter Writings, including Epiphanies, Giacomo Joyce and 'A Portrait of the Artist'*, ed. Richard Ellmann, A. Walton Litz, and John Whittier-Ferguson. London: Faber & Faber.

LANG, FREDERICK K. 1993. *Ulysses and the Irish God*. Cranbury NJ: Associated University Presses.

MOSELEY, VIRGINIA. 1967. *Joyce and the Bible*. De Kalb: Northern Illinois University Press.

NOON, WILLIAM. 1957. *Joyce and Aquinas*. New Haven: Yale University Press.

SCHLOSSMAN, BERYL. 1985. *Joyce's Catholic Comedy of the Word*. Madison: University of Wisconsin Press.

SULLIVAN, KEVIN. 1958. *Joyce Among the Jesuits*. New York: Columbia University Press.

SWIFT, JONATHAN. 1983. *The Complete Poems*, ed. Pat Roberts. Harmondsworth: Penguin.

TINDALL, W. K. 1959. *A Reader's Guide to James Joyce*. London: Thames & Hudson.

FURTHER READING

BALSAMO, GIAN. 2002. *Scriptural Poetics in Joyce's Finnegans Wake*. Studies in Irish Literature 7. Lewiston, NY: Edwin Mellen.

—— 2004. *Rituals of Literature: Joyce, Dante, Aquinas, and the Tradition of Christian Epics*. Lewisburg, Pa.: Bucknell University Press.

CIXOUS, HÉLÈNE. 1998. '"Mamãe, disse ele", or Joyce's Second Hand', trans. Eric Prenowitz in *Stigmata: Escaping Texts*. London: Routledge.

CUNNINGHAM, VALENTINE. 1984. 'Renoving that Bible: The Absolute Text of (Post)modernism', in Frank Gloversmith (ed.), *The Theory of Reading*. Hassocks: Harvester.

DERRIDA, JACQUES. 1984. 'Two Words for Joyce', trans. Geoff Bennington in Derek Attridge and Daniel Ferrer (eds.), *Post-structuralist Joyce: Essays from the French*. Cambridge: Cambridge University Press, 145–59.

DERRIDA, JACQUES. 1992. 'Ulysses Gramophone: Hear Say Yes in Joyce' [1984], *Acts of Literature*, ed. Derek Attridge, New York: Routledge, 253–309.

ELLMANN, RICHARD. 1959. *James Joyce*. London: Oxford University Press.

FRIEDMAN, SUSAN STANFORD (ed.) 1993. *Joyce: The Return of the Repressed*. Ithaca: Cornell University Press.

LANG, FREDERICK K. 1993. *Ulysses and the Irish God*. Cranbury NJ: Associated University Presses.

MOSELEY, VIRGINIA. 1967. *Joyce and the Bible*. De Kalb: Northern Illinois University Press.

NOON, WILLIAM. 1957. *Joyce and Aquinas*. New Haven: Yale University Press.

RABATÉ, JEAN-MICHEL. 1991. *Joyce Upon the Void: The Genesis of Doubt*. Basingstoke: Macmillan.

SCHLOSSMAN, BERYL. 1985. *Joyce's Catholic Comedy of the Word*. Madison: University of Wisconsin Press.

SULLIVAN, KEVIN. 1958. *Joyce Among the Jesuits*. New York: Columbia University Press.

CHAPTER 31

ELIOT, DAVID JONES, AND AUDEN

STEPHEN MEDCALF

THREE of the greatest writers of Christian poetry in English during the twentieth century were converts of varying kinds, whose conversions were fundamentally involved with their special geniuses as poets: David Jones (1895–1973), whose conversion carried him least far, from a not very sacramental Anglicanism to Roman Catholicism, moved because of his understanding of symbolism; W. H. Auden (1907–73) returned, from Anglicanism through unbelief and Marxism, to Anglicanism again, through his awareness of inspiration, of guilt, and of what he learnt from Kierkegaard to call the three stages of the aesthetic, the ethical, and the religious; T. S. Eliot (1888–1965) moved in the widest arc, from Unitarianism which in later life he did not count as Christian, through agnosticism and a close encounter with Buddhism, to Anglicanism at its most sacramental, by an engagement with time and consciousness which took him all his poetic life.

Caliban in Auden's *The Sea and the Mirror*, a libretto (1942–4) in which the characters of Shakespeare's *The Tempest* speak after the action of the play, describes the poet's progress in a way which can be applied to Eliot and Jones as well as to Auden himself. 'Somewhere', he tells the poet, 'you have heard imprisoned Ariel call for help, and now it is a liberator's face that congratulates you from your shaving mirror every morning'; the 'relationship between magician and familiar, whose duty it is to sustain your infinite conceptual appetite with vivid concrete experiences' proliferates and intensifies, until all that you encounter is transformed into 'ever more masterly' poetry. But then 'your strange fever reaches its crisis', Ariel becomes unwelcome to you, you try to dismiss him, but not only does he refuse to go, but when you try to confront him, he turns into Caliban, 'the only subject you have, who is not a dream amenable to magic but the all too solid flesh you must acknowledge as your own' (Auden 1976: 331–3).

In Auden's own life, the description of the moment when Ariel, the genius of poetry as magic, appears as his converse, Caliban, the *id*, seems to correspond to the dreadful occasion in July 1941 when Chester Kallman, who had played the same part in Auden's life as Beatrice in Dante's, and to whom he regarded himself as married, revealed that he had continued his promiscuous ways, and broke off sexual relations between them. (In 1944 Auden wrote to Christopher Isherwood, 'It's O.K. to say that Ariel is Chester, but Chester is also Caliban... Ariel is Caliban seen in the mirror' (Mendelson 1999: 231 n.).) Auden later identified this experience as the final and conclusive stage in his acceptance of Christianity, because it had taken from him the frivolity which he thought is the occupational disease of poets, and obliged him 'to know in person what it is like to feel oneself the prey of demonic powers, in both the Greek and the Christian sense, stripped of self-control and self-respect' (Auden 1956: 1).

Until this providential moment, as he regarded it, the previous progress of his conversion, as indeed of his whole adult thinking life, had from the point of view of his poetry been the feeding of his conceptual appetite with increasingly understood experiences. There remains after Caliban's speech in *The Sea and the Mirror* one song in which Ariel declares his helpless love for Caliban and prophesies their future union until death. And in February 1944, when Auden finished the poem, it seems as if he thought he had achieved a lasting accommodation in himself emotionally, poetically, and religiously.

But it seems likely that the whole account of the poet's progress owes a great deal to Charles Williams's description of the same thing in his *The English Poetic Mind* (1932b): for Auden's conversion and his whole thought at this time was strongly influenced by Williams. Williams bases his description on the development of Shakespeare's plays from their beginnings through the apparently total mastery in appropriating experience which Shakespeare displays in the mature period of his great comedies and history plays, to the crisis most nakedly depicted in *Troilus and Cressida* when Troilus finds that Cressida has played him false: when something is experienced that cannot be happening, only it is. In all Shakespeare's tragedies something of that kind happens: and in Williams's view something similar is potential for every poet. But in English only Shakespeare and Milton confront the crisis at their full poetic power and pass through it to the poetries represented by Milton's *Samson Agonistes*, 'calm of mind, all passion spent', and by Shakespeare's last plays with what Williams calls their 'poetry of pure fact', the poetry of forgiveness, and supremely by *The Tempest* which looks forward in the songs of Ariel to another poetry again, the poetry transcending human emotion of an alien consciousness. All the other English poets have in their various ways evaded or failed to resolve this crisis (Williams 1932b: *passim*).

Whether because Auden was influenced by, or because there is some real validity in, Williams's pattern, it is plain that he fits in among these other poets. He seems to see himself as having resolved the crisis, which yet still exists. That (whatever he thought) he never did in fact transcend it seems to be confirmed by his subsequent life, either in his personal relations, in his poetry in general, or specifically in his sometimes magnificent religious poetry, with which we are here primarily concerned. It must be said that although he explores the riches of Christianity it is not easy to give an integrated account of what he celebrated or to find an assured onward progress after his conversion. His progress up till his conversion is clearer.

His most constant theme, both before and after his conversion seems to be what he said in one of his last verses, in 1975:

> He has never seen God
> But, once or twice, he believes
> He has heard him.

> (Auden 1976: 583)

The verse abbreviates and fulfils what Auden wrote in 1940, when he was still only moving towards Christianity, in the invocation at the end of *New Year Letter*:

> O sudden Wind that blows unbidden
> Parting the quiet reeds, O Voice
> Within the labyrinth of choice
> Only the passive listener hears...

> (ibid. 192)

The conviction that a vision in the one case, and the labyrinth of choice in the other may be self-deception, but yet in both a voice may be self-authenticating, goes back even earlier in Auden's life, as is apparent in Caliban's description of the poet hearing Ariel's call, that is the poetic vocation: Auden never made it clear whether he thought after his conversion that the moment when at the age of 15 at Gresham's School, Holt, he realized he must be a poet was one of the moments when he heard God, but it is probable that he did. What is clear is that opposed to vocation and voice is the poetic gift in so far as it is, as Caliban says, the 'relationship between magician and familiar' which provides 'a dream amenable to magic': in Kierkegaard's scheme, the merely aesthetic.

The notion that art, specifically poetry, may be suspect as magic Auden found explicitly in R. G. Collingwood's *The Principles of Art* (1938), where he also found the doctrine that art should not be 'Magic, a means by which the artist communicates or arouses his feelings in others, but a mirror in which they may become conscious of what their own feelings really are' (Auden 1943, cited in Mendelson 1999: 224). Thus Caliban says that at the end of *The Tempest*, 'when we do at last see ourselves as we are' we also 'hear, not the sounds which, as born actors, we have hitherto condescended to use as an excellent vehicle for displaying our personalities and looks, but the real Word which is our only *raison d'être*' (Auden 1976: 340).

The means are negative and purgative, as we variously see ourselves in the mirror or act on the imagined stage, but the end may be positive: 'we are blessed by that Wholly Other Life from which we are separated by an essential emphatic gulf of which our contrived fissures of mirror and proscenium arch... are really figurative signs' (ibid. 340). More largely Auden once remarked in a broadcast that we should not ask anyone, 'Have you read any good books lately?', but 'Have you been read by any good books lately?' which seems to have been modelled on an aphorism which appears in his and Louis Kronenberger's *Faber Book of Aphorisms*: 'You cannot criticise the New Testament. It criticises you' (Auden and Kronenberger 1962: 82). What Auden sensed positively of the Wholly Other Life was informed by three visions during the 1930s which he would have called mystical or supernatural, although they were not of God but of his fellow human beings.

The first, in June 1933, when he was a teacher at Colwall in the Malvern Hills he called the vision of *agape*: 'a power which, though I consented to it, was irresistible and certainly not mine' (Mendelson 1999: 9), made him aware that he could and temporarily did, love his neighbours as himself. The conviction flows through and dominates his poetry at its most ethical stage in Kierkegaard's scheme, in the 1930s, as a secular ethic sometimes merging with Marxism, expressed in the two voices implied by Caliban, that of the conceptual appetite and that of the vivid concrete experience. At his best they unite, but often enough they fall apart into a sometimes tiresomely arrogant didacticism, and a delighted splendour of language of which the point has somehow gone askew. In all three modes he was apt to say more than he meant: and on this ground he later rejected even some of his best poems of the time, conspicuously the wonderful 'Spain 1937', in his most revolutionary Marxist persona with its undeniably wicked doctrine of 'the conscious acceptance of guilt in the necessary murder' and its ruthless conclusion, also by Auden's later standards wicked, and yet ethical—

> We are left alone with our day and the time is short and
>   History to the defeated
> May say Alas but cannot help or pardon.
>
>   (Auden 1937)

In this poem the very fact of setting down his doctrine so splendidly may have caused, as Caliban implies it should, a revulsion. At any rate, by the end of the 1930s he had abandoned his revolutionary persona for the uncompromising but still secular ethic expressed in 'September 1, 1939', 'We must love one another or die' (Mendelson 1999: 75). In an uncompleted prose teaching of that time, 'The Prolific and the Devourer', he attributed this ethic to Jesus as the greatest of prophets, who had anticipated our ethical needs in the modern rootless life of the cities (ibid. 67). The force with which this possessed him in that year was partly to do with the inexplicably absolute conviction that there exists an ethical centre to demonstrate the evil of Nazism.

Presently he was to reject both poem and essay for a supernatural explanation. This is already latent negatively in 'September 1, 1939' in a conviction of our fallen condition:

> Lost in a haunted wood,
> Children afraid of the night
> Who have never been happy or good
>
>   (Auden 1950: 75)

But a second experience which, although apparently slight, affected Auden as in some sense supernatural, pushed him towards a positive conversion. In July 1936 he met Charles Williams to discuss the *Oxford Book of Light Verse* and

for the first time in my life felt myself in the presence of personal sanctity. I had met many good people before who made me feel ashamed of my own shortcomings, but in the presence of this man—we never discussed anything but literary business—I did not feel ashamed. I felt transformed into a person who was incapable of doing or thinking anything base or unloving.   (Auden 1956: 41)

This experience added an overwhelming substance to itself when in February 1940 Auden read Charles Williams's short history of the Holy Spirit in the church, *The Descent of the Dove* (1939). It was of a kind by which he was more than once deeply affected, an interpretation of history from a surprising personal but persuasive angle: Gerald Heard's *Social Substance of Religion* (1931), which had contributed to his understanding of *agape*, was an earlier example. But it was of these books the one of most lasting value, certainly for Auden, a book which emulates the Old Testament as demonstrating that history is the work of God, and is capable of persuading its readers of its truth. Its influence is pervasive in the latter part of *New Year Letter*, notably in the invocation from which I have quoted, and in others of Auden's poems: one pair of this time, 'Luther' and 'Montaigne', suggests part of its force for him, for Williams displays both figures as directly inspired by the Holy Spirit, in respectively faith and doubt. It reinforced that sense of sanctity which Williams had exemplified for Auden, expressed again in May 1966 in 'Insignificant Elephants', a poem about saints:

> .... all who met them speak
> Of joy which made their own conveniences
> Mournfulness and a bad smell.

> (Auden 1976: 608)

Overwhelmingly *The Descent of the Dove* seems to have introduced Auden to Kierkegaard: although again the first effect of this was negative, in the phrase Williams paraphrased from Kierkegaard, 'Before God man is always in the wrong' (Mendelson 1999: 130). This assertion seemed to give a rationale for Auden's conviction that the Nazis, who denied it, were mistaken and Christians, who affirmed it, right. More positively, again as quoted by Williams, Kierkegaard applied the doctrine to modern times, 'as an effort to be without "the unconditional"'. 'To live in the unconditional, inhaling only the unconditional, is impossible to man; he perishes, like the fish forced to live in the air. But on the other hand, without relating himself to the unconditional, man cannot in the deepest sense be said to "live"'. (Williams 1939: 217). Auden, accepting this, entered on the third, the religious stage of Kierkegaard's scheme.

To discover how the unconditional may be related to man became the central motivating force of Auden's conversion and of his religion. One means, which Williams gave a rationale for in his account of Dante and Beatrice, was the third of Auden's visions of the 1930s, in May 1939, the vision of *eros* when he encountered

Chester Kallman. At Christmas 1941, Auden wrote to Kallman, 'Because it is through you that God has chosen to show me my beatitude. As this morning I think of the Godhead, I think of you' (Mendelson 1999: 183). But the sheerly positive side of this vision had already been twisted askew, as we have seen, by Kallman's self-revelation of July 1941. In the libretto or Nativity Play to which *The Sea and the Mirror* is a companion, *For the Time Being* (October 1941–July 1942), the negative side appears as Joseph's experience of a command, when Mary has told him that she is with child, to continue to believe in her and in God.

For the Time Being is a celebration of the conditions under which the unconditional manifested 'itself under the conditions of existence', in the birth of Christ. These conditions Auden represents as of two kinds: first, the existence of Mary as one 'in a dream of love' who wakes at Gabriel's message to make her choice to bear Christ. For Mary and Joseph Auden seems to have used (of course) the Gospel of Luke, and especially the Magnificat, but also, for the whole play, as one in which time and space are transformed to make the characters of the Nativity story universal, Charles Williams's *Seed of Adam* (Williams 1963).

The second kind of condition is the whole history of humankind's consciousness including the moment of the birth of Christ. For this Auden used (of course) Genesis and Isaiah as traditionally and Messianically interpreted, *Seed of Adam* and Williams's (1938) *He Came Down from Heaven*, but above all C. N. Cochrane's *Christianity and Classical Culture*, which he read in 1941. Cochrane argues persuasively that the establishment of the Roman Empire by Augustus represents the consummation of a particular scheme of human explanation which in ethics, philosophy, and politics alike presents a division of various kinds—form and matter, will and the emotions, controller and controlled—over against which Christianity presented a world explained by the single force of love. Never explicitly but continuously, Cochrane draws a parallel with the twentieth century as nearing an end point in terms of an explanation of the world by the causalities of the scientific enlightenment (Cochrane 1940). With the failure of this, the Unconditional may again reveal itself, as it revealed itself at the consummation and bankruptcy of the classical scheme.

To expound the riches of Auden's sources or the still richer synthesis he made of them is beyond the scope of this chapter. In the first movement, 'Advent', he joins the first century with the Time Being as one in which humankind, separated from its 'immortal and nameless Centre', and abandoned even by the Law which substituted for it, comes to the Abyss for which Auden drew on Paul Tillich as well as Kierkegaard (Auden 1976: 279). In the central passages Mary, the shepherds, the Wise Men, and humankind in general celebrate the knowledge that 'The Father Abyss | Is affectionate | To all its creatures' (ibid. 293). Near the end, Simeon's meditation brilliantly unites Auden's didacticism in describing the conditions and results of the manifestation of the infinite and unconditional in the finite, with his lyric epigrams. One of Simeon's meditations on art presents the abolition both of Tragedy, in the sense of the exceptional hero in the tragic conflict of Virtue and Necessity, in favour of the struggle of 'every tainted will' of each individual, and of Comedy as the ugly and ridiculous, because it now presents all people without merit assisted by the Grace of

God. The Chorus sing 'Safe in His silence, our songs are at play', but in the following section Herod commands the massacre of the Innocents precisely in order to avoid a world in which Justice, Reason, and Idealism may be replaced by God's care for the sinner and the spontaneously, even if only occasionally, good. 'The Rough Diamond, the Consumptive Whore, the bandit who is good to his mother, the epileptic girl who has a way with animals will be the heroes and heroines of the New Tragedy' (ibid. 300). (Auden proclaimed in his T. S. Eliot Lectures in 1967 (Auden 1968: 138–9) his pleasure at Erich Auerbach's similar diagnosis worked out during the war especially in relation to the paradigm of Peter's denial and Christ's trial in the Gospels, published in *Mimesis* (1946).) It is striking however that the whole atonement and the ingression of love in *For the Time Being* is achieved by the incarnation. The passion is only an incident in this, foreseen by Mary in her Lullaby, which beautifully echoes Auden's love lyric 'Lay your sleeping head':

> O shut your bright eyes that mine must endanger
> With their watchfulness...
> How soon will you start on the Sorrowful Way?
> Dream while you may.
>
> (Auden 1976: 293)

However, Auden tried to engage with the passion later in two contrasting ways, first in the sequence *Horae Canonicae*, written between 1949 and 1954, whose setting is essentially Mediterranean—he summered on Ischia during those years—then in *Friday's Child*, which seems to be a deliberate engagement with the Nazi past, written in Austria when he began to summer in Kirchstetten in 1958, in memory of Dietrich Bonhoeffer, and therefore in a Germanic and Northern tradition.

Horae Canonicae was conceived as based on the monastic services of the day which are associated with the events of Christ's passion, and initially Auden intended a grand scheme 'about the relation of history and nature', in which a series of events in general history should be celebrated as well as the passion. But not only did he abandon these schemes, he abandoned all the individual moments of the passion except the crucifixion. In one day, which could be any day except that it ends with a redeemed dawn entirely in contrast with the dawn that begins it, the crucifixion is anticipated and looked back on so far as the narrator is capable. But the narrator's capacity is limited. At Prime, poised between the 'rebellious fronde' of his dreaming mind, and the daytime responsibility of being involved in 'a lying self-made city', he expects a death, but it looks as if it will be his own. At Terce everyone individually sets out on the new day: no one knows but our victim that our choices will involve his death, 'that by sundown we shall have had a good Friday'. At Sext, the three classes which make up every society, the functionaries, the authorities, and the crowd, together crucify him, 'to worship the Prince of this world'. At Nones we begin to forget what we have done: at Vespers we half-remember, when 'I', a nostalgic Arcadian, confront a revolutionary Utopian, unwillingly because he reminds me of the blood, and I remind him of the innocence of our victim, without whose death 'no secular wall will safely stand'. At Compline we cannot and will not until doomsday remember 'what happened | Today between noon and three'. But what our mind rejects our heart, along with the constellations, remembers as 'some hilarity beyond | All liking and happening': and at Lauds we wake to a redeemed nature and a redeemed society in which 'Men of their neighbours become sensible' (ibid. 475–86).

The final sense of time in this sequence Auden summed up in about 1959 in the quatrain:

> Between those happenings that prefigure it
> And those that happen in its anamnesis
> Occurs the event, but that no human wit
> Can recognise until all happening ceases.

(ibid. 539)

But it is evident that the 'anamnesis', a word with which he was familiar in Dom Gregory Dix's *The Shape of the Liturgy* (1945) as signifying the memorial made of Christ in the mass, is not used as Dix would use it of a sacrifice made before God. In so far as sacrificial language is used in *Horae Canonicae* it is used of a sacrifice made, as the Church Fathers tended to think it before Anselm, in payment to the Prince of this world. And the primary effect of the mass and the passion, as described in 'Vespers' and 'Lauds', is on our awareness of one another. In *Horae Canonicae*, it would seem, God's part in the Atonement is to take on himself the dying for ourselves or our fellow members of humankind for which it is our nature to refuse to recognize the need.

And yet, there is a mystery beyond this explanation, else why should the constellations as well as humanity sense the hilarity spoken of in 'Compline'? Auden recognized that the Atonement, like the Incarnation in *For the Time Being* is a mystery only partly apprehensible to finitude and in time. A further pair of apprehensions is offered in *Friday's Child* (who is of course proverbially, as the day of the crucifixion demands, 'loving and giving'). The bulk of the poem proclaims Bonhoeffer's 'religionless Christianity'. As man has now come of age, all the consolations and supports of religion are taken from him and with them the image of an almighty Father, leaving only the powerless Christ of the cross, whom we are free to side with or reject. But to the sense of humanity's unsupported responsibility of choice, Auden adds the even more shocking doctrine of Charles Williams's essay on 'The Cross' (originally published in 1943, reprinted in the collection *The Image of the City* in 1958) that on the cross God accepts his full responsibility for the act of creation on himself, suffering as his creatures do.

> Meanwhile, a silence on the cross
> As dead as we shall ever be
> Speaks of some total gain or loss
> And you and I are free
>
> To guess from the insulted face
> Just what Appearances He saves
> By suffering in a public place
> A death reserved for slaves.

(ibid. 510)

Auden never further integrated these apprehensions of the passion. There is a further doctrine in the antepenultimate line, that of Owen Barfield's *Saving the Appearances* (Barfield 1957), which Auden expressed in such poems as *Ode to Terminus* (Auden 1976: 608–9): that with the incarnation God has given us the responsibility for choosing which scheme of the phenomena of the universe we believe. It is in obedience to this responsibility that in *Precious Five* (1950), Auden accepts that however we may blame 'what is going on', the sky will repeat the command that is, rightly, inscribed on the memorial stone in Christ Church, Oxford, where he used to kneel to receive Communion

> Bless what there is for being.   (ibid. 450)

A complementary doctrine of a presence throughout time forgiving and loving is embodied in *Homage to Clio* (1955), which praises the muse of History but, Auden told J. R. R. Tolkien, is really 'a hymn to our Lady'. The precise opposite of History in 'Spain', she exhibits a 'merciful silence' which

> No explosion can conquer but a lover's Yes
> Has been known to fill . . .
>
> (ibid. 465)

   To Auden's openness, loose ends, and grounding of his faith in personal encounters with voice, sanctity, guilt, and the abyss that demands the Unconditional, the theology of David Jones stands in contrast. In structure it draws on and largely conforms to the liturgy and doctrine of the Roman Catholic Church before the second Vatican council. What transforms it into poetry, having its own contribution to make to theology, is Jones's awareness of what he was doing as visual artist and poet. In *The Anathemata* (1952), which Auden acclaimed in 1970 as the greatest long poem of the twentieth century, he presents humanity as by definition a species that transcends the simple 'utile' by making his artefacts signs. On signification, which we may be aware of in history as soon as we find tools that are deliberately made not only useful but beautiful, rest all human art, ritual, and sacrament. Its consummation is in the incarnation and Christ's 'placing himself in the order of signs' (a phrase Jones took from the French theologian Maurice de la Taille) in the double act of the Last Supper and his passion. The Last Supper asserts that the passion is the sacrifice offered by Christ to his Father of which the mass is the anamnesis and on which the world turns. The poem begins with humankind, 'We already and first of all discern him making this thing other'. 'Other' bears the special meaning of 'significant' and the poem ends with Christ:

> He does what is done in many places
> What he does other
>   He does after the mode
> Of what has always been done
> What did he do other
>   Recumbent at the garnished supper
> What did he do yet other
>   Riding the Axile Tree?
>
> (Jones 1952: 243)

In its most technical form, Jones's theory of signification, which is derived from trends in the Post-Impressionism that was the fashion when he was an art student in about 1920, demands that a work of art must be both a thing in itself and not the impression of anything else, and also that it represents another thing under different forms. He saw in this an analogy with the Catholic and scholastic doctrine that the body of Christ is the eucharistic host, but under different forms. The full doctrine is perhaps both too paradoxical and too personal to work. But it gave him a framework with which to draw into *The Anathemata* an astonishing breadth of history and human culture. In the most magnificent passage of the poem, the second half of 'Rite and Fore-Time', which begins

> From before all time
> the New Light beams for them
>
> (ibid. 73)

and is a sort of comment on the opening of the Epistle to the Hebrews—'God who at sundry times and in divers manners...'—the theory is transposed into a vision of the light which shone in Christ as the motive force of natural as well as human form, giving the one evolving through the geological shaping of the earth into the development of life, and then into the other with the beginnings of art and ritual. It ends, beyond the Passion, as rarely in Jones's work, with a suggestion of the Resurrection:

> How else from the weathered mantle-rock
> And the dark humus spread
> (where is exacted the night-labour
>   where the essential and labouring worm
> saps micro-workings all the dark day long
>   for his creature of air)
> should his barlies grow
>   who said
> I am your Bread?

Nevertheless there is in *The Anathemata* a certain rigidity and limitation which contrasts with Jones's earlier *In Parenthesis* (1937), now widely accepted as the greatest poem to come out of the First World War. There is perhaps no poem which so fully carries out Jones's ambition to represent the fullness of experience, conscious and unconscious, mythic and sensory, under the form of words as does *In Parenthesis*. The growing limitation may be seen in a letter of 1973 asserting 'that in writing *In Paren.* I had no intention whatever in presuming to compare the various maims, death-strokes, miseries, acts of carnage, etc. of the two contending forces, ours or those "against whom we found ourselves by misadventure", with the Passion, self-oblation and subsequent Immolation and death of the cult-hero of our Christian tradition. For that is a unique and profound Mystery of Faith' (Jones 1980: 246).

   On the contrary, one does feel that the armies are sharing in Christ's passion when one contemplates the frontispiece of *In Parenthesis*, a soldier half naked crucified on barbed wire, and its afterpiece, the Lamb pierced again among barbed wire, or when one reads in the last section, as the soldiers wait to go over the top at the Somme:

Or you read it again many times to see if it will come different:
you can't believe the Cup wont pass from
or they wont make a better show
in the Garden.

(Jones 1937: 158)

It may be that it happened to Jones as, in Charles Williams's belief, it happened to Wordsworth with the declaration of war by England against the French Revolution, that the crisis, the thing which cannot be but is happening, came to him when he was hardly a poet at all. His later rigidification will have come from his never entirely freeing himself from the trauma of the Great War.

In contrast to both Auden and Jones, T. S. Eliot encountered not one but three crises during the full flood of his poetic inspiration, which nevertheless seemed on each occasion for a time to be choked. The first phase of his poetry laid out—in 'Portrait of a Lady', 'Prufrock', and 'Rhapsody on a Windy Night'—the field of his struggles: an acute self-consciousness which was both expressed by and issued in, a combat of personas—'to prepare a face to meet the faces that you meet', a hesitation in personal encounter, a sensitivity which made even passing through time painful, and the sense of a gap in the heart of experience. The gaps between lines and images of this time express these things and prepare the way for that use of silences in which Eliot is supreme and which at length made much of the greatness of his religious poetry. It was during this first phase that he laid the foundations of his knowledge of Sanskrit, of Hinduism, and of Buddhism, which added a dimension to his poetry foreign to Jones and Auden. It was also during this time that he experienced what he later identified as the only conversion which affected him through the deliberate agency of another person, to Henri Bergson's philosophy of time and consciousness, which he later abandoned. This phase of his poetry seems to have been ended by a personal crisis at which we can only guess.

During the second phase of his poetry there was a tension between Christianity, Hinduism merging with Buddhism, and despair. The two religious dimensions are represented in 1917 by 'Whispers of Immortality', which has the character of a Buddhist meditation on the hatefulness of flesh, bone, and desire, and 'Mr. Eliot's Sunday Morning Service', which is a merely aesthetic imagination of what it would be like to believe in the incarnation. In this latter poem begins Eliot's concern with the Johannine doctrine 'In the beginning was the Word,' and the employment of silence as what one may compare with the synapses of the nervous system, when 'The Father and the Paraclete' fade away to be replaced by 'The sable presbyters approach | The avenue of penitence.' But these uses are not fully serious, and the poem ends with the ominous presence of a figure who represents all the mean sensuality which Eliot repudiated, but who pervades all his poetry of this time, Sweeney, who is not unlike Auden's Caliban (Eliot 1963: 55–8).

Some of this is taken more seriously in 'Gerontion', a poem of fragmentation and 'fractured atoms' perhaps immediately induced by the death of Eliot's father, but in the context of the immediately post-war world and its anxious attempts to heal itself. Eliot had come across the sermons of Lancelot Andrewes, and a cento of remarks from a sermon of Andrewes on Christ being found a swaddled infant, 'the *Word* without a *word*, the *eternal word* not able to speak a word' as a sign and a wonder, introduces a synapse which enacts what it would be like to receive Christ in Holy Communion:

> Signs are taken for wonders. 'We would see a sign!'
> The word within a word, unable to speak a word,
> Swaddled with darkness. In the juvescence of the year
> Came Christ the tiger
>
> In depraved May, dogwood and chestnut, flowering judas
> To be eaten, to be divided, to be drunk
> Among whispers...

(ibid. 39)

Desperately serious though this is, I do not think it can be taken as any kind of recommendation to believe in Christianity, but rather as the pointing out of an analogy between the difficulty of believing in the incarnation of the Word of God in an infant or in his presence in the communion, and the struggle to use words to say what you mean.

It was perhaps with some such interpretation in mind that Eliot at one stage thought of using 'Gerontion' to introduce *The Waste Land*, though he was easily dissuaded from this by Ezra Pound, who always preferred a poem to stand on its own feet. *The Waste Land* finds its own direction halfway through in 'The Fire Sermon', along with the flow of the Thames from tainted upriver waters to find oblivion in the sea. The title of 'The Fire Sermon', a sermon of the Buddha's, suggests that the whole poem is to be read with a Buddhist slant: and indeed if one were to look for a single word to describe *The Waste Land* it would be *dukkha*, the contingency and impermanence of the world which issues in suffering, and is given its image in the quotation from the Buddha's sermon at the end of this section, 'burning'. But juxtaposed with 'burning' is a phrase from St Augustine's *Confessions* which has a large biblical penumbra: 'O Lord Thou pluckest me out.' It is as if the remedy for the general *dukkha* of the poem might be either the extinction which comes as the river meets the sea to Phlebas the Phoenician, or redemption by God's help. In the last section 'What the Thunder Said', Buddhism is replaced by the moral precepts of Hinduism in the *Brihadaranyaka Upanishad*, 'give', 'sympathize', 'control', though the way they are handled in the poem suggests that the second and third ('each confirms a prison', 'your heart would have responded') are inachievable. But in any case the Hindu scriptures are juxtaposed, as if on an equal level, with an evocation of the Gospels, in which Christ's agony in the Garden is followed by his trial and death, and a phantasmagoric vision of the journey to Emmaus, with Christ perhaps a hallucination. But between the death and the journey there is another journey, which presently Eliot said was the only real poetry in *The Waste Land*, and which ends in a Tantalus-like presentation of his own doctrine of the poetic image as objective correlative: the desire for water creates an image of water:

> Drip drop drip drop drop drop drop
> But there is no water

As in 'Gerontion' the presence of Christ is no more than an image—neither the Hindu ethic nor the gospel brings relief, and the poem ends in a delirious sequence of roughly associated ideas of escape and failure (ibid. 63–86).

Eliot followed *The Waste Land* with two poetries which might be loosely compared to Auden's Ariel and Caliban, and which appeal like David Jones to the origins of art and poetry in ritual, the lyrics of 'The Hollow Men' and the presentation of Sweeney in 'Sweeney Agonistes'. But the ritual in which relief is sought is presented as sheerly a matter of rhythm so far as the modern age is concerned, though the one suggests Guy Fawkes and the other Attic comedy as backgrounds. But Eliot at this time conceived the relief of ritual as simply a discharge from the nervous system, and both works end with the absence of meaning. 'Life is death,' says Sweeney and compares it to the life of a man who has cut himself off by an irrevocable act of murder: 'There wasn't any joint' (ibid. 123–36). 'The Hollow Men' ends equivalently with:

> Between the potency
> And the existence
> Between the essence
> And the descent
> Falls the Shadow

and mirrors this with the breaking off into silence of the Lord's Prayer:

> For Thine is
> Life is
> For Thine is the   (ibid. 89–92).

For Auden, Ariel is revealed as Caliban. For Eliot, Ariel, and Caliban both end with a whimper into silence.

The reasons for Eliot's subsequent transfiguration of both silence and rhythm are too richly abundant to detail here. Much is implicit in his Clark Lectures of 1926 on *The Varieties of Metaphysical Poetry* (Eliot 1993). One thread we may summarize thus: I. A. Richards in 1925 praised *The Waste Land* as a poetry 'severed from all beliefs'; a poetry needed in an age when the scientific approach to the world has extended itself to human psychology, and destroyed that magical view of the world which supposes our desires are justified by their objects. This is a natural interpretation of, for example, the water dripping passage, but when Eliot saw it so presented, he realized that he did not believe it: what Richards saw as a severance from all beliefs, Eliot saw as a belief in itself. To believe in the absence of meaning is itself a belief (Smidt 1961: 63, 69–72). And Richards's argument, extended to the doctrine that (say) falling in love is, like poetry, the creation of an object to satisfy a certain constellation of emotions, Eliot argued, was an unjustified subjectivization of a phenomenon which is as much objective as subjective. Experiences like Auden's of Chester Kallman cannot be merely subjective. In Dante's handling of his love for Beatrice in the *Vita*

Nuova, Eliot found a kind of contemplation which he knew of from his Indian studies in the Yoga Sutras of Patanjali and found an analogy for in the twelfth-century European mystic Richard of St Victor (Eliot 1993). It led him to think differently of the sermons of Lancelot Andrewes. The careful analysis of text which in 'Gerontion' he had simply exploited for its rhythm and for its suitability as a symbol for himself, he now saw as purely contemplative. When he wrote a poem to celebrate his own baptism, 'The Journey of the Magi', he began it with part of Andrewes's exploration of the word *venimus*, 'we are come' to Christ's birth, taken from a text in the Gospel of Matthew, but continued it by way of contrast with images from various sources, including his own experience and the Gospels, which function as symbols of homecoming. And as in the water dripping passage of *The Waste Land*, these end without providing any substance:

> Six hands at an open door dicing for pieces of silver
> And feet kicking the empty wine-skins.
> But there was no information; . . .

But there is now an end to the journey, although only implicit in a semicolon

> ;and so we continued
> And arrived at evening, not a moment too soon
> Finding the place; it was (you may say) satisfactory.
>
>   (Eliot 1963: 109–10)

Had what the Wise Men found been brought into the poem, it would have been treated, as in 'Gerontion', as a correlative of Eliot's search, and as it is in the companion poem to the 'Journey', 'A Song for Simeon'—'the Infant, the still unspeaking and unspoken Word' (ibid. 111–12). How to unite the object of pure contemplation with a poetry of objective correlatives is the task of Eliot's next long poem, *Ash Wednesday*. This emerged first as separate poems, and, when it was published in 1930, Eliot still spoke of it as such. But in fact they form a powerful sequence, governed by an ever-increasing self-consciousness. In the first to be published, the ultimate second part, Eliot brings together more imagery from the Old Testament than perhaps he ever otherwise used, all from the vision of the valley of dry bones of Ezekiel, together with highly personal imagery, in expressing an acceptance of death (ibid. 97–8). The ultimate first part analyses the progress of consciousness that has arrived at this state, first as in psychoanalysis repeating a phrase that will not come out right:

> Because I do not hope to turn again

until language that means what it says is achieved:

> Because I know I shall not know
> The one veritable transitory power—

then attempting to assert the now achieved 'I' until it too breaks down into penitence and a shared plural prayer:

> Consequently I rejoice, having to construct something
> On which to rejoice
> And pray to God to have mercy on us

issuing in a prayer that provides the setting for the second part

> Pray for us now and at the hour of our death.   (ibid. 95–6)

The third part, under the image of a spiral stair, looks back at the first two, seeing them now with horror as a struggle, first with 'The deceitful face of hope and of despair', and then with decay in darkness. When it comes to the third stair, imagery that was used of the lost power of Part One, 'there, where trees flower and springs flow', is picked up with, again as in psychoanalysis, a greater and more honest sense of its attractiveness, imagery of hawthorn blossom and May time, which nevertheless is distraction in the climbing, until broken in on from outside the self altogether, 'strength beyond hope and despair', and issuing in a text from the Gospels which is also the prayer before communion. The prayer issuing from and broken into and ending in silences, asks the Word himself, Christ, to speak

> Lord, I am not worthy
> Lord, I am not worthy
> But speak the word only.   (ibid. 99)

This evocation of grace prepares for the visionary poetry of the fourth part, in which the desert of the second part and of *The Waste Land* blossoms 'In blue of larkspur, blue of Mary's colour'. The fragmentation, the breaking off and the silences of Eliot's earlier poetry become expressions of a contemplation transcending the imagery, and this new fullness in his synapses is expressed in the transformation of the word 'between' from signifying *gap*, as in 'The Hollow Men', to signifying *fullness*:

> One who moves in the time between sleep and waking, wearing
> White light folded, sheathed about her, folded

The image of Beatrice clothed in light in Dante's *Paradiso* is entirely and convincingly remade, but the whole vision ends in silence, once again, 'The token of the word unheard, unspoken', and prayer, 'And after this our exile' a fragment from the *Salve Regina*, a traditional prayer to the Virgin after mass; this, if resorted to, turns out to contain much of the same imagery as *Ash Wednesday* and other of Eliot's poetry in the period leading up to *Ash Wednesday*—the 'vale of tears' and 'eyes of mercy' which occur in 'The Hollow Men', and the child Jesus. But the comparison with the *Salve Regina* again makes clear how much in Eliot's poetry the imagery of prayer is made into something which I. A. Richards, rephrasing the idea of a poetry severed from all beliefs as a matter of 'technical detachment', recognized as even more willing to immerse itself in 'the unknown depths' which exist for the unbeliever and believer alike, than *The Waste Land* (ibid. 100–1).

The involutions of self-consciousness continue in the penultimate and last sections of *Ash Wednesday*. The Word is expressed with what Eliot much later (in 'The

Cultivation of Christmas Trees') described as 'the piety of the convert' (ibid. 117–18) in a parody of mission hymns:

> Where shall the word be found, where will the word
> Resound? Not here, there is not enough silence
> Not on the sea or on the islands, not
> On the mainland, in the desert or the rainland

But the achievement of something from outside any subjectivity is expressed in words taken from the Bible into the liturgy, the verse of the prophet Micah used to represent the implicit voice of Christ from the cross in the Reproaches on Good Friday:

> O my people, what have I done unto thee

Eliot represents this voice as breaking in from 'the centre of the silent Word' on the otherwise egocentric language of the poetry. Curtailed but still reassuring as

> O my people   (ibid. 102–3)

it perhaps provides a centre for the repetition of the first, repeatedly analysed lines of the poem, in yet another form in section VI: 'Although I do not hope to turn again.'

Ash Wednesday was professedly partly modelled on the transformation of personal emotion into contemplation in Dante's *Vita Nuova*: the sixth section makes it possible to begin a new life in a full recognition that what has been dearest is now lost, expressed in Eliot's most personal imagery, drawn from his childhood holidays on the summer coast of New England, the lines beginning, 'From the wide window towards the granite shore'. The section and the poem end by passing into prayer, in Eliot's only direct address (I think) in his poetry to God:

> And let my cry come unto Thee.   (ibid. 104–5)

Ash Wednesday was originally prefaced by the dedication TO MY WIFE, words which probably embody Eliot's last desperate hope that the penitence, grace, and new life expressed in the poem might save their collapsing marriage. He removed them after he had separated from her, a separation coincident with the third blocking of his poetry. The last two poems of this third phase of his poetry, 'Marina' and *Coriolan*, embody broader hopes which also are defeated. In 'Marina', Pericles' astonished recovery of his daughter Marina in Shakespeare's *Pericles*, a scene which Eliot thought 'the dramatic action of beings . . . seen in a light more than that of day', is interwoven with later memories of New England shores, not now expressing loss, but grace reshaping the world. But Eliot superimposed on the tapestry a quotation from Seneca's *Hercules Furens* when Hercules wakes from madness to find that he has killed his children (Eliot 1963: 115; Southam 1994: 246–7). *Coriolan* seems to portray a state at whose centre is a ruler, Coriolanus, whose subjects see him in 'Triumphal March' resting, like the persona of *Ash Wednesday V*, on 'The still point of the turning world'. In the second movement, 'Difficulties of a Statesman', of a poem which was designed to have two further movements, we see him apparently severed from that point and collapsing from within. But how this attempt to create a politics based on the vision of *Ash Wednesday* might have proceeded we cannot tell (ibid. 139–43).

When Eliot's poetry recovered itself, in *Murder in the Cathedral* and 'Burnt Norton', a transformed version of this pattern emerged. Thomas Becket, who has been, and at the beginning of the play still might be, a statesman at the secular heart of society, finds himself obliged to oppose his king in the name of the church. Eliot was commissioned to write the play by Bishop George Bell in the same week that Bell brought the voice of the Confessing Church opposing Nazism in the Barmen Declaration to the House of Lords, and the Barmen Declaration is echoed in reverse in the declarations of the knights at the close of the play on their motives in killing Becket, although the attempt to subject religion to the state implied therein is clearly intended to apply to modern Britain as well as to Germany. Becket has in consequence been transposed from statesman to martyr. But in the personal character of Becket Eliot creates a synthesis of Christianity and Buddhism. Becket is brought by the Four Tempters in a shedding of past and possible lives which parallels that of *Ash Wednesday*, to become both a Christian martyr 'who has lost his will in the will of God and who no longer desires anything for himself' and, in entirely Buddhist language, one who will 'no longer act or suffer' and so will be released from the wheel whose 'pattern is the action | and the suffering'. In both Buddha and martyr the whole chain of causes which constitutes human motive is transcended (Eliot 1969: 245, 259, 261).

'Burnt Norton' begins with thirteen lines that were originally written to illustrate the encounter in *Murder in the Cathedral* with the Second Tempter, who attempts to reconcile Thomas with the King. They introduce, to elucidate choice, the idea of an alternative world which we might have entered if we had decided differently in the past. As they stand by themselves, they seem to exclude this possibility; but they introduce in the poem a vision of an alternative world so powerful, so paradisal, that it changes our idea of eternity, from the point which being always present makes the pattern of the world unalterable, to the point where both worlds, 'What might have been and what has been' are equally present. As in 'Marina', a natural landscape, the garden at Burnt Norton, reveals paradise. In the second movement of the poem another image of eternity, 'the still point of the turning world' returns from 'Triumphal March'. It introduces a vision of eternity, paradoxical and transcending understanding, which is amplified by an image from a novel of Charles Williams, *The Greater Trumps* (Williams 1932a; Gardner 1978: 85), of the whole world as a dance, to show eternity as the reconciling point of the movement of the dance (Eliot 1963: 189–95). When Eliot, in a way appropriately unforeseen when he wrote 'Burnt Norton', added a matching poem, 'East Coker', the dance, now set in a vision of the Middle Ages, follows Erich Auerbach's notion in *Mimesis* of the late medieval view of time, in which a pattern originally constituted by the intuition of eternity survives when that intuition has faded, having only the *creatural*, which is cyclical or fragmented (Auerbach 1953): 'Feet rising and falling. | Eating and drinking. Dung and death.' Into that world Christ enters in a way new to Eliot's poetry, as himself in the passion sharing in and using the fragmentation to heal, 'The wounded surgeon' with 'the healer's art'. The pattern of the world is now seen in each separated moment and with an existentialist sense of time: 'every moment is a new and shocking | Valuation of all we have been.' But the moment at which the poem is specifically set is Good Friday 1940, for which it was written (Eliot 1963: 196–204). In its companion piece, 'The Dry Salvages', the central moment is changed to Lady Day, and a vision of time as patternless, even polytheistic, is cut across by Mary's choice "the hardly, barely prayable prayer of the one Annunciation". This Gospel image of choice is juxtaposed with an image out of the *Bhagavad Gita* in which Krishna tells Arjuna to fulfil his destiny in the present moment: but in the *Gita* this advice is part of the Hindu pattern of cyclical rebirth, which Eliot now conclusively rejects. In the *Gita* the moment of choice as death gives its nature to the entry to another life; in 'The Dry Savages' 'the time of death is every moment' which makes the moment of choice parallel to the existentialist moment of 'East Coker'. But in both quartets, the passion and the annunciation introduce the incarnation: and 'The Dry Salvages' makes the incarnation 'The point of intersection of the timeless with time', the motivation of the saint, who can achieve as in *Murder in the Cathedral* the life of a Buddha: 'right action is freedom | From past and future also' (ibid. 205–13).

In 'The Dry Salvages' this is not an end most of us can hope to achieve. But in the final quartet, 'Little Gidding', the intuition of history as the work of the Holy Spirit appears, once again, as for Auden, from Charles Williams's *The Descent of the Dove*. Eliot of course conceives history more as the later, Christian Auden did in 'Homage to Clio'. But it seems likely that he had in mind the earlier Auden and those notorious closing lines of 'Spain' when he wrote that 'History may be servitude, History may be freedom,' and later that we inherit not only from 'the fortunate' but also from 'the defeated'. History is something within which everyone lives: and perhaps Eliot's most consummate use of the synapse comes between a cento of phrases from Julian of Norwich's *Revelations of Divine Love*, immediately after the lines about the reconciliatory power of History now become personal history:

> And all shall be well and
> All manner of thing shall be well
> By the purification of the motive
> In the ground of our beseeching.

and before an anamnesis of Pentecost:

> The dove descending breaks the air
> With flame of incandescent terror

For 'the ground of our beseeching', that is of our prayer, who for Julian is Christ, is the same God as 'the dove descending'. It is from the silence between the two that the Christian must live (ibid. 214–23).

But Christians need not live so intensely. In his final commemoration of the Christian Year, 'The Cultivation of Christmas Trees', Eliot pictures a possible lifetime in which each Christmas builds on the experiences of childhood:

> So that before the end, the eightieth Christmas
> (By 'eightieth' meaning whichever is the last)
> The accumulated memories of annual emotion
> May be concentrated into a great joy
> Which shall be also a great fear, as on the occasion
> When fear came upon every soul:
> Because the beginning shall remind us of the end
> And the first coming of the second coming.
>
> (ibid. 117–18)

In this professedly minor poem, Eliot uses a web of religious reference, from Christmas to Pentecost, which is textually the occasion 'when fear came upon every soul' (Acts 2: 43), looking back to the first coming and looking forward to the second coming of Christ, to transform his sense in his early poetry of the painfulness of time and the discontinuity of personality, into a sense of time by which it seems almost easy for anyone to become a saint.

This was written before his second marriage, which perhaps was enabled by the capacity to achieve such a vision of experience. But the marriage gave him one more Christian, one might even say Johannine, thing to say, which he puts into the mouth of a lover in 'The Elder Statesman':

> Age and decrepitude can have no terrors for me
> Loss and vicissitude cannot appal me
> Not even death can dismay or amaze me
> Fixed in the certainty of love unchanging.
>
> (Eliot 1969: 583).

The principal issue for Christian theology in the twentieth century was perhaps time, whether one considers the human place in evolutionary history, the scandal of particularity in the incarnation, or the problems about individual choice presented by biological determinism, Marxism, psychoanalysis, and existentialism. We have reviewed Eliot's struggle with time both as lived through and as related to eternity: David Jones offers a religious meaning to time as revealed both in geology and biology and in human history: Auden's principal original contribution to theology was the suggestion that there was an appropriateness to the moment of Christ's birth in human history which is reflected in the present time. Of the three it was Eliot who most consistently and even ruthlessly pursued his problem, raising his poetry in this quest to the edge of what he still wanted to distinguish from it, prayer.

WORKS CITED

AUDEN, W. H. 1937. *Spain*. London: Faber & Faber.

—— 1943. 'Poet of the Encirclement', *The New Republic*, cit. Mendelson (1999: 224).

—— 1950. *Collected Shorter Poems 1930–1944*. London: Faber & Faber.

—— 1956. *Modern Canterbury Pilgrims*, ed. J. A. Pike. New York: Morehouse-Gorham.

AUDEN, W. H. 1968. *Secondary Worlds*. London: Faber & Faber.

—— 1976. *Collected Poems*. London: Faber & Faber.

—— and KRONENBERGER, L. 1962. *The Faber Book of Aphorisms*. London: Faber & Faber.

AUERBACH, E. 1953. *Mimesis*, trans. Willard R. Trask. Princeton: Princeton University Press.

BARFIELD, OWEN. 1957. *Saving the Appearances*. London: Faber & Faber.

COCHRANE, C. N. 1940. *Christianity and Classical Culture*. London: Oxford University Press.

ELIOT, T. S. 1963. *Collected Poems 1909–1962*. London: Faber & Faber.

—— 1969. *Collected Poems and Plays*. London: Faber & Faber.

—— 1993. *The Varieties of Metaphysical Poetry*, ed. R. Schuchard. London: Faber & Faber.

GARDNER, H. 1978. *The Composition of Four Quartets*. London: Faber & Faber.

JONES, DAVID 1937. *In Parenthesis*. London: Faber & Faber.

—— 1952. *The Anathemata*. London: Faber & Faber.

—— 1980. *Dai Greatcoat*, ed. R. Hague. London: Faber & Faber.

MENDELSON, E. 1999. *The Later Auden*. London: Faber & Faber.

SMIDT, K. 1961. *Poetry and Belief in the Work of T. S. Eliot*. London: Routledge & Kegan Paul.

SOUTHAM, B. C. 1994. *A Student's Guide to the Selected Poems of T. S. Eliot*. 6th edn. London: Faber & Faber.

WILLIAMS, C. W. S. 1932a. *The Greater Trumps*. London: Victor Gollanz.

—— 1932b. *The English Poetic Mind*. Oxford: Clarendon.

—— 1938. *He Came Down from Heaven*. London: Heinemann.

—— 1939. *The Descent of the Dove*. London: Longmans & Green.

—— 1958. *The Image of the City*, ed. A. Ridler. London: Oxford University Press.

—— 1963. *Collected Plays*. Oxford: Oxford University Press.

FURTHER READING

On Auden's religious poetry, the most useful books are E. Mendelson (1999), and Arthur Kirsch, *Auden and Christianity*. 2005. New Haven: Yale University Press. But C. N. Cochrane (1940) and C. W. S. Williams (1939) are indispensable.

On David Jones: Jones (1980); R. Hague, *A Commentary on The Anathemata of David Jones*. 1977. Wellingborough: Christopher Skelton; and J. Miles and D. Shiel, *David Jones: The Maker Unmade*. 1995. Bridgend: Seren.

Perhaps the most useful books on Eliot and religion are K. Smidt (1961); H. Gardner (1978); C. McNelly Kearns, *T. S. Eliot and Indic Traditions*. 1987. Cambridge: Cambridge University Press; R. Schuchard's *Introduction to Eliot* (1993); Michael Edwards' chapter 'Eliot/Language', in *Towards a Christian Poetics*, 1984. London: Macmillan; and R. Germer's essay 'T. S. Eliot's Religious Development', in M. Thormählen (ed.), *T. S. Eliot at the Turn of the Century*. 1994. Lund: Lund University Press.

My account of Eliot is an outline of my forthcoming book *An Anatomy of Consciousness: A Study of T. S. Eliot's Poetry as a Single Poem*.

CHAPTER 32

FEMINIST REVISIONING

HEATHER WALTON

> Re-vision—the act of looking back, of seeing with fresh eyes, of entering an
> old text from a new critical direction—is for women more than a chapter
> in cultural history: it is an act of survival.
>
> (Rich 1978: 35)

In her famous essay 'When We Dead Awaken: Writing as Re-vision' (1978), the poet
Adrienne Rich passionately articulates her conviction that women seeking a transformed future must not turn their backs upon the past. She argues that the weight of
history cannot be 'shrugged off' but the burden it imposes upon women might be
transformed into a strange blessing. In particular sacred traditions expressed through
mythology, literature, and art can be revisioned. Although the narratives that sustain
culture are dangerous for women they also carry within them evidence of an unclaimed
inheritance. Through attentive rereadings women may begin to claim their own erased
genealogy. This will entail a painstaking effort of creative interpretation: 'To do this
work takes a capacity for constant active presence, a naturalist's attention to minute
phenomena, for reading between the lines, watching closely for symbolic arrangements,
decoding difficult and complex messages left for us by women of the past' (ibid. 13).

Rich's essay represents a significant moment in the development of contemporary
feminism. Women working in many cultural spheres have sought to critique the
male-centred traditions through which they have been formed and also to engage
with them in order that they might be reclaimed and transformed.[1] The work of the

---

[1] This development within 'second wave feminism' was preceded by the engagement of women
writers throughout the twentieth century with archetypal cultural symbols and ancient myths. See
Humm (1994: 54–73).

pioneering feminist biblical scholar Elizabeth Schussler Fiorenza (1983) can be seen as paradigmatic of this painstaking revisioning labour. She interrogated biblical texts used to subjugate women but also lovingly examined these same Scriptures for traces of the female past. Because the evidence of women's participation in the formation of culture must be assembled from fragments, gaps, and silences, Fiorenza soon came to realize that her work was creative as well as exegetical. The past is not only remembered, it is recreated. This task requires imaginative as well as interpretative resources.

Within the literary sphere feminist revisionists followed similar routes. They critiqued the way male authors employed myths and also sought to rediscover the spiritual wisdom of women which could then be used as a symbolic resource by women writers. This 'women's tradition' had to be both remembered and imagined and the development of revisionist mythology within women's creative writing came to be seen as a political move to address the history of women's cultural exclusion and transform the spiritual archives of Western culture.

My concern in this chapter is to explore this literary revisioning work as it is displayed in the work of two women writers whose attention has been largely focused on the Jewish and Christian traditions. Alicia Ostriker and Michèle Roberts are women whose work arises out of direct political involvement with the women's movement. Both are authors who are deeply immersed in contemporary critical debates and both acknowledge their conversational relationships with other female creative artists. As such it is possible to view their work as representative of a revisionary movement within contemporary women's literature concerned with nothing less than the radical revisioning of religious traditions. However, these women have been chosen not only because of the representative nature of their writing. There are also interesting and significant differences between them which will become apparent in my presentation of their work.

ALICIA OSTRIKER AND EROTIC ENGAGEMENTS WITH TRADITION

From Subversion to Rebellion

The work of Alicia Ostriker provides a helpful introduction to feminist revisioning as she has written a number of critical texts on this subject as well as being a poet who confesses to being 'in love' with her Jewish faith (1997: 7). Ostriker began her writing career as a literary critic and it is in this capacity that she is still best known. Her early published work was on the poetry of William Blake and her criticism of his prophetic writings displays a fascination with the relationship between the poet and religious traditions (Ostriker 1965). Ostriker later interprets Blake's own revisionist myth-making as revealing the vocation of the poet to contest with religious traditions in a passionate, imaginative assault upon authority which is paradoxically based on fidelity to tradition:

Blake's influence on me was crucial... I attempt, like him, to understand where and how the structures of oppressive authority work within culture, and to hear the clanking of the mind-forged manacles. At the same time I attempt to locate in the culture of the past—that very same culture—its liberating imaginative vitality. So part of what I take from Blake is a double stance towards tradition.   (Ostriker 1993: 104)

It is interesting to note that Ostriker was not only concerned with the content of Blake's visionary writings. Her interest was also engaged by his rare and complex verse forms. Ostriker's fascination with poetic form here represents an implicit acknowledgement of the respect that should be shown towards custom and order when attempting radical and disruptive reinterpretations of sacred texts.

Although Blake continues to be beloved by Ostriker (see Ostriker 1990) her growing awareness that his celebration of sexual delight was coupled with a pervasive misogyny caused her to shift her attention away from the male-centred romantic tradition and towards the work of women poets she came to believe were engaged in a fragmented, but identifiable, project to transform the cultural canon. She became convinced that whenever women poets employ 'a figure or a story previously accepted and defined by culture... [they are] using a myth and the potential is always present that the use will be revisionist, that the figure or tale will be appropriated for altered ends, the vessel filled with new wine' (Ostriker 1987: 213).

Ostriker's particular understanding of revisioning owes much to her encounter with 'gynocriticism'[2] and she owes a particular debt to the pioneering work of the feminist writers Elaine Showalter, Sandra Gilbert and Susan Gubar, and Adrienne Rich. Elaine Showalter's early critical texts sought to establish the objective existence of a *women's literary tradition*. Her studies in Victorian women's literature convinced her that women writers, precisely because of their marginal status in culture, have been 'unified by values, convention, experience and behaviours impinging on each individual' and out of this have created a body of writing in which 'female culture is a center... Beyond fantasy, beyond androgyny, beyond assimilation' (Showalter 1977: 319). In this writing women's experience is memorialized and contemporary women readers can return to these texts to uncover significant truths concerning their own identity and inheritance.

Sandra Gilbert and Susan Gubar (1979) contrasted female writers with their male counterparts. Whereas, male artists struggle in oedipal fashion to establish their individual creativity in relation to a powerful inherited tradition, women have been deprived of a matrilineal lineage in which to locate their work. For Gilbert and Gubar the defining hallmark of the female literary tradition is the desire to establish and legitimate female authorship. The women writer defies ancient and

---

[2] The term used to describe women-centred literary criticism as it developed out of feminist awareness in the late 1970s and 1980s.

sacred taboos when she makes her mark on culture and Ostriker (1994: 8) celebrates the audacity that is required by the woman who lays her hands on holy things. 'Touch me not, thou shalt not touch command the texts. Thou shalt not uncover. But I shall. Thou shalt not eat it lest ye die. I shall not surely die . . . What do the stories mean to me and what do I mean to them? I cannot tell until I write.'

Like Adrienne Rich, Ostriker is herself both a poet and a critic. In Rich's work she found confirmation that both women's critical and creative work should be seen as part of a wider political challenge to male authority. Rich also emphasized that the creation of a just society would entail a painstaking forensic examination of traditions which have excluded women in the past. Beneath the surface of culture lies the obscured evidence of women's lives and the significant contributions they have made. In *Diving into the Wreck* Rich (1973: 23) images the perilous voyage of rediscovery that women revisionists must make to places where the dead lie unburied with their treasures half submerged beside them:

> I came to explore the wreck
> The words are purposes
> The words are maps
> I came to see the damage that was done
> And the treasures that prevail.

So from this variety of 'gynocritical' perspectives Ostriker constructs her own vision of women with a recoverable historical tradition, a passion to inscribe their own contribution to the cultural store and a spiritual compulsion to return to the dominant tradition in order to 'know it differently . . . to break its hold over us' (Rich 1978: 35). Her own work is decidedly optimistic in respect to all these points. She refuses to concede that women have ever obeyed the commands to silence that are enshrined in the sacred texts. She believes that feminism has the power to recreate cultural forms to the benefit of both women and men. Furthermore, she declines to approach male-centred traditions as a victim and adopts instead the position of female lover determined to 'seduce' the male tradition for her own pleasure and to make it fertile for new interpretations and fresh forms.

The emerging features of Ostriker's distinctive perspective are set out in her most famous work to date, *Stealing the Language: The Emergence of Women's Poetry in America* (1987). In this she argues that a distinctive literary culture exists amongst women. Up until the beginnings of the feminist awakening in the 1960s this was a hidden tradition; women cryptically disguised their protests against male-centred religious narratives. Emily Dickinson, for example, rails against the domestic piety of her age in searing commentaries upon the conventional authoritarianism of everyday religion. This oppositional stance is only possible, however, because her writing is coded and ambiguous, 'ambivalence ascends to an artistic principle which I shall here call duplicity' (Ostriker 1987: 38), and because few of her works were released for publication during her lifetime. Ostriker argues that in the work of Dickinson (the pre-eminent representative of an emerging dissident tradition) we see subversion, 'yet subversion is not rebellion' (ibid.).

Having demonstrated some of the strategies and subterfuges women poets used in the past to disguise their audacious theological imaginings, Ostriker goes on to claim that the beginnings of a feminist awakening can be discerned in the work of poets writing from the 1960s who had gained the confidence actively to critique male traditions and begin to rewrite the cultural canon. Ostriker tests this understanding through a panoramic survey of over three hundred volumes of poetry written since that time. Describing her method as 'radically inductive' she concludes that her investigations provide firm evidence of a new consciousness amongst women writers many of whom are engaged in radical revisionary work.

The women poets Ostriker investigates draw upon their embodied experiences to produce a distinctive style of writing. 'They draw a map of the female body, the female passions, the female mind and spirit' (ibid. 90). The writing frequently displays unapologetic eroticism and these 'fleshly' texts are particularly effective when brought into relation with religious traditions that have feared and despised women's bodies. Ostriker contends that a woman poet using transgressive bodily metaphors in the retelling of authoritative narratives can have a particularly disturbing impact upon received understandings. Myths are presented as a particularly significant site of cultural struggle and Ostriker argues that 'Where women write strongly as women, it is clear that their intention is to subvert and transform the life and the literature they inherit ... revisionist myth making in women's poetry is a means of redefining both woman and culture' (ibid. 211).

Revisioning the Bible

Stealing the Language is a compelling text packed with delicious quotations from the work of hundreds of women poets. As a work of criticism it remains significant today. But, although it clearly articulates Ostriker's convictions concerning the importance of revisioning it does so in a scholarly style and the 'mythology' which is being revisioned is taken to be the general store of Western sacred traditions. In later works Ostriker's writing on revisioning takes on a more personal tone. She turns her attention towards those women poets who have been particularly significant in her own development, faces the challenges of revisioning the narratives of the Bible and draws upon her own creative writing to make manifest her revisioning project.

Feminist Revision and the Bible (1993) is an elegiac memorial to the 'buried' women of the biblical tradition whose presence is necessary for the male-centred covenantal plot to develop but who somehow vanish from view as the narrative unfolds; 'in each story the disappearance of the female co-ordinates or coincides with the establishment (or re-establishment following a rebellion or fall) of the exclusively male covenant' (ibid. 49). Although these women characters are written out Ostriker claims that they are to be identified with a repressed female divine 'shimmering and struggling at the liminal threshold of consciousness' (ibid. 50) who can be obscured but not overcome. In our own time, Ostriker argues, this divine female is being reborn as women poets reread and rewrite the Bible.

It is to the work of these women poets that Ostriker then turns with an appreciation that their engagement with the Bible is not simply an angry reaction to exclusion. The creative woman writer does not fear the canonical text, she rather desires it. An illustration of the erotic processes at work in revisionist myth-making is presented in Ostriker's account of her own poet mentor H.D., a poet whose approach to the tradition Ostriker views as exemplary. The image of the *palimpsest* is used by the poet to describe the medium upon which poetry is inscribed. Because what is written cannot obliterate what it overscores a religious tradition should not be discarded but reconceived. These convictions generate a religious consciousness which is radically syncretistic as this extract from H.D.'s poetic manifesto 'Notes on Thought and Vision'[3] illustrates:

Christ and his father, or as the Eleusinian mystic would have said, his mother, were one. Christ was the grapes that hung against the sunlit walls of that mountain garden, Nazareth. He was the white hyacinth of Sparta and the narcissus of the islands. He was the conch shell and the purple fish left by the lake tides. He was the body of nature, the vine, the Dionysus, as he was the soul of nature.   (1988: 52)

The figure of Christ inhabits H.D.'s later work appearing in many of the symbolic forms that he has assumed in Christian art and mystical literature. However, he rarely appears alone. The male divine figure is accompanied by a female counterpart who may be consort, bride, sister, Madonna, priestess, or holy wisdom taking poetic form. This divine Lady has assumed many shapes throughout history and H.D. celebrates a new epiphany occurring in modern times through a return of the female divine who does not simply complement her male partner but also restores him (and us) to life again:

> she is Psyche, the butterfly
> out of the cocoon...
>
> her book is our book; written
> or unwritten, its pages will reveal
>
> a tale of a Fisherman,
> a tale of a jar or jars
>
> the same—different—the same attributes
> different yet the same as before.
>
>   (H.D. 1983 [1944]: 570–1)

H.D.'s poems are addressed with reverence and desire to the divine in male and female form. She was bisexual in her loves and also in her writing. Although her most significant relations were with women she relates closely to the body/texts of her male colleagues—with many of whom she was also erotically engaged.[4] Ostriker finds this comprehensive bisexuality attractive. It stands as a figure for the pleasure Ostriker

---

[3] This remarkable text anticipates many of the later concerns of feminist scholars to conceive of an embodied understanding of female creativity. It was written in 1919 out of the traumas of the First World War and the poet's near death in pregnancy, but was not published until 1981.

[4] H.D. had significant relationships with many well-known male modernist writers including Ezra Pound, D. H. Lawrence, and Sigmund Freud.

finds in texts. It is a borderline position between male and female traditions and it desires both.

The erotic imagery that Ostriker uses to describe the relationship between writers and texts reflects her deepening fascination with religious narratives. She maintains that our sacred stories are too precious, too desirable, to be discarded. The female revisionist is both seduced by them and seduces them. Ostriker (1993: 118–19) uses the image of interpenetration to describe an encounter between the woman poet and the tradition: 'To love is to enter and be entered both at once ... to penetrate the other and be penetrated by the other'. In claiming the text invites loving engagement rather than submission Ostriker locates her work in the Jewish midrashic tradition— women poets become midrashists offering their own commentaries upon a tradition that they claim as their inheritance. This role is assumed in a series of poems which form the heart of *Feminist Revision and the Bible* in which Lilith initiates Eve into the mysteries of sexual revolt. In a more recent work, *The Nakedness of the Fathers* (1997), the shift from a paradigm of revisioning to midrash becomes even more pronounced as Ostriker turns her full attention to the foundational narratives of Judaism. This work is close to home in every sense as Ostriker seeks to create a text in which criticism, biography, and imaginative reconstructions of biblical texts are interwoven. 'I am trying in *The Nakedness of the Fathers* to produce a work in which these modes go on simultaneously to interact. Layers of biblical textuality come into play with layers of my own identity and family history. I interpret the Bible while it interprets me ... We intermingle and bleed into each other' (1993: 112).

Bringing these sources together defies the prohibitions against women contaminating sacred objects and allows Ostriker to claim texts that have stood over against women as her own. Although born into a tradition which denied her the opportunity to interpret or transmit the messages of scripture—'Not mine the arguments of Talmud, not mine the centuries of ecstatic study, the questions and answers twining minutely like vines around the living word' (1997: 6)—she has defied the inherited prohibitions: 'We have to enter the tents/texts, invade the sanctuary' (ibid. 7). Once the stories are reclaimed they have the potential to become life-sustaining rather than life-denying and Ostriker claims that the power of revisioning, as she has encountered it in the work of women writers and practised it in her own poetry, is capable of radically reforming current religious understandings. 'By the time the spiritual imagination of women has expressed itself as fully and variously as that of men, to be sure whatever humanity means by God, religion, holiness and truth will be completely transformed' (ibid. p. xiii).

Nakedness of the Fathers ends with a vision of the fruitful erotic encounter between the male-centred tradition and the female revisionist poet[5] and many other women writers have adopted similar erotic imagery in their revisionist work. The novelist and poet Michèle Roberts employs this symbolism in her early writing. Later texts, however, move away from images of sensual desire to offer bleaker pictures of the issues facing women who are inextricably bound up with (or in bondage to) religious

---

[5] Literally fruitful: the work ends with a dreamlike sequence in which God is pregnant and gives birth.

traditions which violate their bodies and their intellects and deny their visions of the divine.

MICHÈLE ROBERTS AND THE VOICES
OF THE LOST

Wild Girl

Roberts is the daughter of a French Catholic mother and an English Protestant father. Much of her writing focuses upon living between worlds, speaking different tongues, and being both a stranger and insider to traditions. She was educated into Catholicism but, perhaps due to her mother's practical and earthly spirituality, she came to see her religion as 'integral as the blood in my veins, passed onto me by my mother like milk' (1983: 52). She also intuitively grasped that within it moved many shadows. Catholic feasts overlaid the older pagan celebrations and rituals around birth, sexuality, and death (ibid. 53). Roberts's childhood years were infused with a sense of communion with the God who animated all things but within this also lurked a sense of yearning for deeper connection to the maternal divine, a 'queenly Virgin Mary, the land flowing with milk and honey, and I was the Israelites in exile yearning to be united with her' (ibid. 54).

Encounters with Marxism and feminism led Roberts to embrace political activism and to repudiate her childhood faith. She sought to 'excise memory and the past, my unconscious and the system of images which had formed me' (ibid. 58). This process of excision was too radical and realizing that she was in danger of self-mutilation, Roberts entered psychotherapy. The Jungian archetypes she encountered enabled her to construct positive images of female identity and thus survive depression. She claimed for herself the archetypal image of the sybil,

the creative woman who is in touch with ancient memories, inspiration, who is an artist. This system of imagery helped me to see that sexuality and spirituality can be connected, need not be at war. Also that a woman can be complete in herself, not a companion or a shadow to a man, but a distinct being, different to him, in her own right.   (ibid. 62)

A new confidence in her spiritual identity was expressed in a revisionist novel that affirms the desiring relations between masculine and feminine archetypes and the love relation that can exist between a free creative woman and ancient religious traditions. In *The Wild Girl, The Book of the Testimony of Mary Magdalene* (1991 [1984]) Roberts employs Jungian archetypes but also draws upon historical traditions marginalized within the Christian West which feminist scholars (e.g. Elaine Pagels 1988; Rosemary Ruether 1983, and Asphodel Long 1992) have argued contain the traces of submerged female traditions. Roberts is particularly indebted to her eclectic study of the Nag Hammadi documents and Gnostic Christian texts. Out of these she creates many images of the reconciliation of the new Adam and the new Eve. She employs her Mary to carry a secret message entrusted to her by Jesus.

> The separation of the inner man and the inner woman is a sickness, a great wound. I, Christ came to repair the separation and to reunite the two and restore to life and health those in danger of dying of this sickness of the soul ... What is this rebirth? How is it to be achieved? The image of this rebirth is a marriage.   (Roberts 1991: 110)

The sexual love between Jesus and Mary is the lens through which Roberts views the misogyny and violence of her inherited tradition. By making her characters lovers Roberts touches the place of pain women experience in relation to the eradication of female sexuality from the dominant tradition. Through presenting women's sexual knowledge as a form of spiritual wisdom Roberts challenges the ancient dualisms that have circumscribed women's power. In the process she re-visions divine and human authority and presents male and female existence as potentially harmonious; capable of generating interpenetrating erotic pleasure rather than perpetual enmity. In the dispensation of the new Adam and the new Eve both genders are embodied, spiritual, and sacred. When employing such symbolism Roberts comes very close indeed to Ostriker's vision of an erotic relation between the male tradition and the female poet which is profoundly generative of new forms.

Fire and Ash

The hopefulness which animates *The Wild Girl* does not disappear from Roberts's later writing but in many of the novels and poetry which follow we are presented with much darker pictures of the quest women must undergo in order to discover again their spiritual inheritance. This is evident if we compare *The Wild Girl* with one of Roberts's most powerful later novels *Daughters of the House* (1992). In the first the narrator presents herself as a witness to truth and commends her story confidently to those who will receive it and pass it on to others. In contrast *Daughters of the House* is about the failure to remember and its consequences. It is about the violence at the root of faith and the hatred of maternal power in monotheistic traditions. It is about death and in particular the death of the mother. The opening words of this novel are far removed from the statements of confidence and faith that introduce *The Wild Girl*.

> Antoinette laughed. She was buried in the cellar under a heap of sand. Her mouth was stuffed full of torn-up letters and broken glass but she was tunnelling her way out like a mole. Her mouth bled from the corners. She laughed a guttural laugh, a Nazi laugh ...
>   Antoinette was dead, which was why they had buried her in the cellar. She moved under the heap of sand. She clutched her red handbag which was full of the shreds of dead flesh. She was trying to get out, to hang two red petticoats on the washing-line in the orchard. Sooner or later she would batter down the cellar door and burst up through it on her dead and bleeding feet.   (Roberts 1992: 1)

This novel, set in rural France during and after the Second World War, tells the story of two cousin/sisters, Leonie and Thérèse, whose mother Antoinette lies dead, beyond speech, her mouth stuffed with torn up letters, the corners bleeding. But although buried, this mother reaches out towards her daughters. Antoinette, the mother, is symbolically linked with a powerful female divine presence. The story tells how this archaic female power was worshipped in the past. The village community had venerated an ancient stone image in a sacred grove. Acts of communal devotion to 'the lady' had marked the passage between fertility and death for generations. Respect for a power beyond 'the name of the Father' had given coherence to the community and enabled it to mediate the destructive and regenerative energy of close social relations. When this form is destroyed by the local priest the village falls prey to the fascistic brutality of the times—a violent force that seeks to destroy all that threatens paternal order.

Sensing the significance of the broken fragments of the lady, Antoinette hides the pieces in the cellar of the family home. To conceal and protect this hidden power she is compelled to engage in collaborative intercourse with the German soldiers occupying the village. Her future is sealed by this act and Antoinette never fully recovers from her wartime experience. Her early death blights the childhood of both girls.

Thérèse copes with Antoinette's death by finding herself another mother, 'she'd been sold one ready made by the priests of her church. Perfect, that Mother of God, that pure Virgin, a holy doll who never felt angry or sexy and never went away. The convent was the only place that she could preserve that image intact' (ibid. 165). She joins a religious order and seeks to assuage her grief through piety and ritual. The holy virgin is venerated as a substitute for her lost mother and the female divine. For many years Thérèse clings to this image but the substitute fails to satisfy her and a restless longing drives her to return to her village and her maternal home. She is seeking her real mother and hoping to provoke Leonie to explore the buried memories of the past.

Leonie does not welcome this return. She has become a village matriarch who actively sustains the family home and the institutions of the local community. Her life is dedicated to obliterating the chaos of origins and preventing the horrors of the past from impacting upon domestic routines and social relations. However, not only does the lady of red fire still lie broken in pieces and buried in the cellar, there are other alien and disruptive presences that have been hidden within the house—a shrine Leonie tends with beeswax and fresh linen. Jewish prisoners had been secreted there prior to their clandestine execution by Nazi sympathizers. But the dead are not quiet.

Leonie must, at last, acknowledge the claims they make upon her. She confronts her mother's death, the tangled roots of her own identity, and opens herself to the confused images and sensations she has repressed. In this new state of awareness she also remembers the war crimes committed in her small village. Empowered by her consciousness of loss Leonie is able to confront what she has expelled from memory. She becomes an agent of change, and possible redemption, rather than a keeper of the house. The novel ends as Leonie opens the door to a room she had previously kept closed. It was a room that as children the sisters had been discouraged from entering 'In case they'd heard those voices crying out and were frightened by them...But history was voices that came alive and shouted' (ibid. 171).

In this later work revisioning is offered to us as a process of becoming aware of dead voices that come alive and shout. Gone are the images of tender desire. This is a desperately painful process as it entails contemplating the violence that has orphaned the daughters and which maintains a culture of hostility towards the stranger. The novel, however, has a positive and redemptive conclusion. This is more difficult to discern in a later novel that confronts the Christian past.

Ghost Writing

Although *Impossible Saints* (1998) is a very funny novel, there is a sense of irrecoverable loss running through it that is more disquieting than that found in *Daughters of the House*. The work, partly inspired by the life of St Teresa of Avila, loosely narrates the story of 'Josephine'—interspersed with other stories echoing the lives of Christian women saints. The story begins as Josephine discovers the clandestine pleasures of reading enjoyed by her mother Beatrice and her woman friends.

Books were their drugs, the magic carpets onto which they flung themselves in order to be borne somewhere else, books lifted them up like powerful caressing hands and cradled them like mothers do, as though they were babies to be held and fed...All the books became one book, they streamed into each other, a channel of sparkling water which kept all the garden green, in the midst of the encircling desert, and never ran dry.   (Roberts 1998: 43)

After her mother's death Josephine discovers that the chest of books her mother has always carefully locked contains not only romances but also books on herbs and medicine, anatomy: dangerous knowledge. It also contains mysterious scrolls wrapped in golden cloth. Josephine and her cousin Magdalena eagerly begin to read these forbidden texts but their transgression (and the 'wanton' behaviour it encourages) are discovered by Josephine's father.

Magdalena was bundled away, and Josephine forbidden ever to see her again. Ferdinand burned all of Beatrice's books that he could find, and the chest that had held them. He made Josephine feed the fire, handing the books to her one at a time. They took a long time to burn. Solid blocks of words, blackening, black, transformed into packets of feathery ash that finally fell apart.   (ibid. 51)

Josephine is sent to a convent from which she does not emerge for many years. She finds sweet comfort there in erotic visions of Christ but this is a time of burning when visionaries and heretics are raised on pyres: 'The world was red' (ibid. 136). Josephine must protect herself by writing her life in orthodox and conventional tones for the Inspectors.[6] But the writing is false. It is constructed out of fear and lying. Her confessor (and lover) advises her that she must begin writing herself again. To do so

---

[6] The narrative here reflects feminist conjectures concerning the written legacy of St. Teresa.

entails leaving the convent and entering Magdalena's house. This is a place of earthly delights where her mother's golden scrolls (rescued by Magdalena) are hidden. These scrolls are Gnostic texts and, reading them, Josephine is enraptured. She is drawn into an untranslatable archaic language. 'Josephine [was] now a part of its grammar, earth sentences, the earth was the speech she could hear, that spoke her and spoke to her, that attracted her into its structure and dissolved her into a part of a speech, a part of earth...She and the earth were the same body' (ibid. 190). Her readings convince Josephine that another form of spiritual life is possible for women that does not entail a renunciation of their sexuality or bodily wisdom but allows them periodically to withdraw from the world to nurture their creative spirits. Such a utopian vision is, of course, unachievable in the time of the Inspectors and Josephine dies leaving only a legacy of writing; her secret life. Small fragments in shrunken handwriting, disordered pages, 'a chaotic pattern which made no sense' (ibid. 238). Even these fragile scattered writings, 'discarded all over the house like vegetable peelings in a bin or balls of fluff under a cupboard' (ibid. 235) are lost or stolen by the guardians of religion. There is nothing left. Her niece Isabel, seeking to remember her aunt, is haunted by the echoes of disjointed phrases and in the end, rather than accept the silence, allows her aunt to invade her imagination. In the warm space of recollection she 'invents' her. 'I reassemble her from jigsaw bits and pieces of writing; from scattered parts. I make her up. She rises anew in my words' (ibid. 290).

The story of Josephine is a story of women and writing. She is forbidden to read, her books are burned, her words are lost; really lost. It is also a narrative of revisioning; of the impossibility of restoring the past and the limits of remembering. The accounts of other Christian women saints whose stories are told alongside Josephine's emphasize the utter annihilation of women's words and voices. Clever, funny, and creative female saints come to life on the pages only to be obliterated. They die 'in the ice of the cave, frozen solid inside it' (ibid. 95). They perish at 'the bottom of the well...flesh and bones rotted and disintegrated and [become] part of the filthy water (ibid. 174). They are 'shrivelled up like an old root buried under moss and branches' (ibid. 209). Josephine herself is dismembered limb from limb. Her bones lost amongst the mixed bones from 11,000 virgins (ibid. 307). In this later work we are confronted with the bleak awareness that the revisionist writer is calling up shadows and spectres from the past. She is unable to breathe life into dry bones.

Possibly She's Absurd

This chapter has explored the work of Alicia Ostriker and Michèle Roberts as exemplifying feminist literary revisioning of theological traditions. Both women approach the religious past sensitive to the history of violence and exclusion it represents for women. Both also claim that women have created their own spiritual traditions and have actively resisted when these were silenced or forbidden. In differing ways Ostriker and Roberts both place the woman writer in the position of inheritor of this spiritual legacy. In poetry and fiction women continue to contest male authority and create their own symbolic landscape through remembering and imagining.

Just as Ostriker and Roberts are taken as representative of a feminist revisioning both can equally be charged with some of the common criticisms that are made of this form of literary intervention. Significant amongst these is the charge that they are following paths established by male exegetes, male 'romantics', psychoanalysts, and literary critics. There is nothing inherently feminist in revisioning per se and the effect of offering multiple rereadings of a sacred tradition is to strengthen that tradition rather than to challenge it. It has also been argued that the notion that myths are the vehicles through which archetypal symbols form culture and the psyche is itself a deeply conservative notion that reflects the critical environment of the 1950s and 1960s and is unsustainable today (see Humm 1994: 55). It has been pointed out that when women attempt to engage with female figures in mythology they are in danger of reinforcing stereotypes rather than reclaiming archetypes. Both Ostriker and Roberts can be accused of offering readers images of female spirituality that are erotic, fleshly, earth-related, and ecstatic—as opposed to the rational, ethical, and transcendent sacred traditions of men. Through so doing they may perpetuate binary and hierarchical understandings of masculine and feminine spheres rather than radically challenging our understandings of gendered identity. It must be admitted that the sacred traditions of Western culture offer a very limited set of roles for women and some religious feminists have preferred to look to the future rather than the past when constructing imaginative projections of female power (see e.g. Carol Christ, 1979: 230). But perhaps the most challenging critique of all is that feminist revisionist myth-making (and associated activities such as the creation of women-centred rituals) encourages women to seek 'imaginary' solutions to social problems. This draws attention away from the need to engage in processes leading to material change. In her important book *Gender and Agency* (2000) Lois McNay argues that symbolic and cultural intervention should never be pursued in isolation from other forms of political action for 'it is only by considering how the indeterminacies of symbolic formulations are mediated that a more precise sense of political agency may be achieved' (ibid. 58).

These criticisms are worthy of serious attention. Engaging with male-centred religious traditions is precarious work for the women artist and both Ostriker and Roberts are aware of the ambivalence of the task they undertake. Ostriker's work is driven by the compulsion of desire. She refuses to be cast as the outsider to tradition. She is the sister, consort, mother, and bride who is prepared to be vulnerable to the (male) other in love in order to generate new visions of the divine. For Ostriker love is always as strong as death. Alongside erotic imagery Roberts offers darker images of the revisioning process. The feminist revisionist writer opens herself up not only to receive the body of her lover and generate new life. She also allows the dead to inhabit her body. The medium cannot herself raise the dead and in bringing the past to view she risks becoming a vehicle for a return of archaic male power as well as female wisdom. But the sacred past calls to the woman artist and she responds.

Roberts's ironic, self-reflexive poem 'Restoration Work in Palazzo Te' (1995) describes the compulsion to attend to this inheritance but acknowledges that the effort may be misguided. In this work a young female mural restorer becomes Psyche searching out Eros.[7] With her diagrams and photographic images she returns to her 'house of desire' to 'revision it' (ibid. 57). But the forms are breaking up, the original paint flakes from the ceiling and is lost. Nevertheless, she continues her work attending to what has almost vanished. Eros resents this attention and stubbornly resists:

> her questioning hands, her
> fingers pattering at him, white
> braille in white dust.
>
> Possibly she is absurd
> Anyway, it is the work that matters   (ibid. 5)

Works Cited

CHRIST, CAROL. 1979 [1975]. 'Spiritual Quest and Women's Experience', in Carol Christ and Judith Plaskow (eds.), *Womanspirit Rising: A Feminist Reader in Religion*. San Francisco: Harper & Row, 228–45.

FIORENZA, ELISABETH SCHUSSLER. 1983. *In Memory of Her: A Feminist Theological Reconstruction of Christian Origins*. London: SCM.

GILBERT, SANDRA, and GUBAR, SUSAN. 1979. *The Madwoman in the Attic: The Woman Writer and the Nineteenth Century Literary Imagination*. New Haven: Yale University Press.

H.D. 1983 (1944–6). 'Trilogy', in *The Collected Poems, 1912–1944*. New York: New Directions, 505–612.

—— 1988. 'Notes on Thought and Vision', in B. Kime Scott (ed.), *The Gender of Modernism*. Bloomington: Indiana University Press, 93–109.

HUMM, MAGGIE. 1994. *A Reader's Guide to Contemporary Feminist Literary Criticism*. London: Harvester Wheatsheaf.

LONG, ASPHODEL. 1992. *In A Chariot Drawn by Lions*. London: The Women's Press.

MCNAY, LOIS. 2000. *Gender and Agency*. Cambridge: Polity.

OSTRIKER, ALICIA. 1965. *Vision and Verse in William Blake*. Madison: University of Wisconsin Press.

—— 1987. *Stealing the Language: The Emergence of Women's Poetry in America*. London: The Women's Press.

—— 1990. 'The Road of Excess: My William Blake', in Gene W. Ruoff (ed.), *The Romantics and Us: Essays on Romantic and Modern Culture*. New Brunswick: Rutgers University Press, 67–88.

—— 1993. *Feminist Revision and the Bible*. Oxford: Blackwell.

—— 1997. *The Nakedness of the Fathers: Biblical Visions and Revisions*, New Brunswick: Rutgers University Press.

PAGELS, ELAINE. 1988. *Adam, Eve and the Serpent*. London: Weidenfield & Nicolson.

RICH, ADRIENNE. 1973. *Diving into the Wreck: Poems 1971–1972*. New York: W. W. Norton.

—— 1978. 'When We Dead Awaken: Writing as Revision', in Adrienne Rich, *On Lies, Secrets and Silences: Selected Prose 1966–1978*. New York: W. W. Norton.

---

[7] Here Roberts echoes the mythology employed by H.D. in *Trilogy* (see above). There seems to be no escape from this strange couple in feminist revisionary writing.

ROBERTS, MICHÈLE. 1983. 'The Woman Who Wanted to Be a Hero', in J. Garcia and S. Maitland (eds.), *Walking on the Water: Women Talk About Spirituality*. London: Virago, 50–65.

—— 1991 [1984]. *The Wild Girl*. London: Minerva.

—— 1992. *Daughters of the House*. London: Virago.

—— 1995. 'Restoration Work in Palazzo Te' in M. Roberts *All the Selves I Was*. London: Virago, pp. 57–58.

—— 1998. *Impossible Saints*. Virago: London.

RUETHER, ROSEMARY. 1983. *Sexism and God-Talk*. London: SCM.

SHOWALTER, ELAINE (1977) *A Literature of their Own: From Charlotte Bronte to Doris Lessing*, London: The Women's Press.

FURTHER READING

HUMM, MAGGIE. 1994. *A Reader's Guide to Contemporary Feminist Literary Criticism*. London: Harvester Wheatsheaf.

OSTRIKER, ALICIA. 1987. *Stealing the Language: The Emergence of Women's Poetry in America*. London: The Women's Press.

—— 1993. *Feminist Revision and the Bible*. Oxford: Blackwell.

RICH, ADRIENNE. 1978. 'When We Dead Awaken: Writing as Revision', in Adrienne Rich, *On Lies, Secrets and Silences: Selected Prose 1966–1978*. New York: W. W. Norton.

SHOWALTER, ELAINE (ed.) 1986. *The New Feminist Criticism: Essays on Women, Literature and Theory*. London: Virago.

WALTON, HEATHER. 2007. *Literature, Theology and Feminism*. Manchester: Manchester University Press.

—— 2007. *Imagining Theology: Women, Writing, and God*. Edinburgh: T & T Clark.

PART FIVE

THEOLOGY AS LITERATURE

CHAPTER 33

CRANMER AND
THE COLLECTS

DONALD GRAY

In the days before universal literacy, linguistic style was most chiefly influenced by that which was heard being read aloud. The place where everyone was subject to this was in church at worship: hence the undoubted impact made by listening to the Bible read in English from the version made by Tyndale or Coverdale, from the 'Great Bible' or, eventually, the Authorised Version. But parallel with that particular aural influence, English church folk had the benefit of Tudor liturgical language assailing their ears. The first major dose of this wholesome and improving medicine was administered by Archbishop Thomas Cranmer (1489–1556) through the Anglican Book of Common Prayer. 'Cranmer's sombrely magnified prose, read week by week, entered and possessed their minds, and became the fabric of their prayers, the utterance of their most solemn and vulnerable moments' (Duffy 1992: 593).

That there is an inevitable connection between Cranmer and the Book of Common Prayer deceives even some of the most devoted admirers of sixteenth- and seventeenth-century liturgical language. In modern-day jargon we must always remember they are not entirely joined at the hip. Cranmer's liturgical work came to a climax in the 1549 and 1552 Prayer Books, in the reign of Edward VI, whereas the most familiar book of traditional worship to present-day worshippers is the popular and memorable book authorized in 1662; that is six reigns later. Therefore there are many celebrated examples of 'Prayer Book language' which are not from Cranmer's pen. However the collects provide a rich source of the Archbishop's art and 'these jewelled miniatures are one of the chief glories of the Anglican liturgical tradition' (MacCulloch 1996: 417).

Yet, even so, of how much of the two Edwardine Prayer Books is Cranmer the author or sole compiler? A seventeenth-century historian (Thomas Fuller 1608–61) assigned to him twelve colleagues in his liturgical work; six bishops and six learned divines. Few of those named had more than a slight acquaintance with liturgical learning. It has been commented that of those named none could equal, let alone rival, the considerable erudition of the chairman. E. C. Ratcliff (1976: 184) thought it most likely that 'the function of the Committee was the function of many other committees, lay as well as ecclesiastical, that is, to approve and adopt whatever the chairman might set before it'. Notwithstanding any of these facts, in this chapter we will continue to speak of 'Cranmer and his collects' being as near the total truth as any evidence can bring us.

Cranmer seems to have begun to study liturgical questions in Nuremberg in 1532 and built up a considerable library on the subject. The Prayer Book of 1549 can be said to be the first gathering together of his many years of reading and thinking about liturgy and worship. As a collection in just a single volume which the clergy would require and the lay folk would give attention to, the Prayer Book was certainly a novel idea to the vast majority of English people, lay and clerks alike, except to that very small proportion of the population who by travel and study had become conversant with the Lutheran Church Orders on the Continent.

There are still those, admittedly a rapidly decreasing number, who can recall the discipline of having been bidden to learn by heart the collect of the week, that is, the collect appointed for each particular Sunday. For many it was a burden, but others believed they greatly benefited from the exercise. This meant that the Prayer Book collects, perhaps uniquely among set prayers, have retained up to the recent past, an honoured place in literary memory and consequentially a definite stylistic influence on the English language, both written and spoken.

The collect is a short and particular type of prayer which is a feature of the worship of Western Christianity. It stands in marked contrast to what has been described as the 'long poetic rhapsodies' of the Orthodox Church (Stephens-Hodge 1964: 15). The Collect asks for one thing and one thing only, and that in the tersest of language. To be good, it must have colour, rhythm, finality, a certain conciseness as well as vigour of thought; but it must be a united petition or it becomes something else rather than a collect. Percy Dearmer wrote: 'We might indeed say that it must be one complete sentence, an epigram softened by feeling; it must be compact, expressing one thought, and enriching that thought so delicately that a word misplaced may destroy its whole beauty' (Dearmer 1919: 149).

Like an epigram, the collect, is content to say one thing, shortly and sharply, and have done with it. Here it differs from what Walter Howard Frere calls 'the oratorical type of prayer' which he believes is one more congenial to the English mind and English language (Arnold and Wyatt 1940: 189). English does not lend itself very well to an epigrammatic type of prayer and both in the sixteenth and seventeenth centuries the English language can be said to have rejoiced in the more rhetorical style. There are admirable prayers of this sort which were composed in each of these centuries and included in the Prayer Book. But these are not, properly speaking, collects. However, tastes change, and in more recent time these more oratorical prayers have lost favour and we have gone back to a love of the epigrammatic. We admire the more concise collect form and appreciate its brevity. Consequently we appreciate the work of Cranmer in the collects, conscious of the fact that in the English language he was labouring under linguistic difficulties. The terse and concise forms of latinate construction, which he knew well and had been versed in from an early age, were no longer available. It was replaced in English by a temptation to floridity, as that fashion grew among 'those who considered that God enjoys extended addresses from his creatures' (MacCulloch 1996: 417).

In its simplest, purest form it seems possible to trace its origin to the early Roman Church. Prayers constructed along the same lines can be found not only in Hebrew religion but also in classical literature, both Latin and Greek. It is therefore probably another case of the church using a form of prayer which had already been found acceptable in other, earlier religions. The writings of Pope Leo (died 461) show that such prayers were familiar in the middle of the fifth century, but it is a matter of some considerable doubt as to whether Leo, as has been suggested, was the author of any of the prayers he cited. The collects are fully developed in the earliest Latin sacramentaries, the earliest surviving books of mass prayers according to the Roman rite, dating from the seventh century (Willis 1968: 103–8).

The first short variable prayer of the eucharist is the collect said by the priest at the end of the entry rite and is related to the specific day or the occasion. It also has a place in the daily offices, although probably not until as late as the eighth century. In the office the collect comes towards the end of the service and is closely related to the concluding prayers. In Anglican prayer books there are also prayers at other services and ceremonies which take the traditional form of the collect.

The derivation of the word has long been a matter of debate. It is now generally agreed that the term 'collect' is Gallican, in origin *collectio:* Gallican because it derives from the liturgical forms in use in Gaul before the adoption of the Roman rite under Charlemagne. In the Gallican rite it referred to the notion of 'collecting the prayers' and has nothing to do with a Roman term *collecta* which signified the collection of the people together for worship. The idea that the collect is so called because it condenses the teaching of the day (e.g. in the lections or Bible readings) has been said to be 'Merely fanciful and not borne out by the facts of the case. Still less reasonable is the idea that it is the prayer which demands a "collected" mind in those who offer it' (Feltoe n.d. [1912]: 211).

The whole body of the prayers which may be classed as collects in the Book of Common Prayer consists of three groups, representing three stages of development. They are, first of all, those which are ancient or pre-Reformation, that is from the Sarum Missal. Next are those presented in 1549, and, lastly, the group which do not concern us at the moment, and derive from the 1662 revision. Nearly two-thirds of the collects belong to the first group, while the second, consisting of those we can call Cranmerian creations, contains nearly four-fifths of the remainder. It must be remembered that additionally many of the older collects received important additions or modifications in 1549 at the hands of the reformers.

In spite of an infinite variety of detail the collect usually consist of five parts. It is a literary form which is as rigid in its structure as a haiku or a sonnet. In the collect thoughts, instead of words, are made to rhyme in definite strophe-patterns, and it has the underlying principles of prose rhythm. One commentator claimed that a listener accustomed to the collect-form can usually tell, after hearing the opening words, approximately how the prayer will continue; not anticipating the actual words, but sensing the pattern (Suter 1940: 29).

The constituent parts of the collect are these:

1. The Address or Invocation. The general rule is that God the Father is invoked either by simple apostrophe or with the addition of an adjective or adjectives describing his power or mercy. The sole Cranmerian exception to this is the collect for the first Sunday in Lent in which the Son is addressed directly. It may be noted that Trinity Sunday also stands outside this principle, as on that day there is doctrinally no distinction of Persons. The invocation being intended, on that day, to be addressed to the Blessed Trinity in Unity. For an example of the Address—the collect for Ash Wednesday, newly written in 1549 began: 'Almighty and Everlasting God'.

2. The Acknowledgement. The address is often, but not always, enlarged or enriched by mention of one or other of the divine attributes or actions, sometimes with a more or less direct use of Scripture. It takes the form of a relative clause. In a classic statement Dean Goulborn said that the acknowledgement gives 'the foundation of doctrine on which our request is made' (Goulborn 1880: i. 3). Instead of an adjective or noun in apposition, we have a clause introduced by a relative pronoun. The statement inside the relative clause will be found to have special significance in view of the petition which follows. It reflects some quality of God which is associated with the request we shall be making in the Petition. Examples are acknowledgements of his power, his grace, his mercy, his readiness to hear or answer prayer. There are some occasions in which we come to God in prayer acknowledging our sinful wickedness, our weakness, and our unworthiness and that may be reflected in the prayer. The Ash Wednesday collect continues, 'which hatest nothing that Thou hast made, and dost forgive the sins of all them that are penitent'.

3. The Petition. This forms the main body of the collect—this is the actual prayer. Now the collect prays for the basic needs of the petitioners, be it forgiveness, protection, guidance, comfort, or love. In the Ash Wednesday collect we continue 'Create and make in us new and contrite hearts'.

4. The Aspiration. Sometimes we find, appended to the particular boon asked for, a statement of the happy effect which may be expected as a result of obtaining it; the reason why we ask, as it were. In those cases it is introduced by the conjunction 'that'. For example, in the collect for Trinity 21, pardon and peace are requested so that we may be better fitted for God's service. In the Ash Wednesday collect: 'That we, worthily lamenting our sins, and acknowledging

our wretchedness, may obtain of Thee, the God of all mercy, perfect remission and forgiveness'.

5. The Pleading. The commonest, simplest, and probably most ancient form of ending a collect is 'through Jesus Christ our Lord'. Christ is our only mediator and advocate and through him alone we draw near to the Father. Historically the pleading contained a doxological ascription of praise, for example 'who liveth and reigneth with thee and the Holy Ghost, one God, world without end'. A collect is not really complete without this ascription, in which God and his glory become once more the centre of the worshipper's thoughts. The Latin collects of the Sarum Missal ended 'Qui vivis' because it was assumed that the priest knew what the correct ending was. Nearly all the 1549 collects end merely 'through Jesus Christ our Lord'. It has been left to subsequent revisions to restore the Trinitarian doxology.

A detailed inspection of the collects in the 1549 Prayer Book reveals that the relative clause of the Acknowledgement or the appended statement of the Aspiration are sometimes omitted. This reduces the collect to its simplest form consisting of just the Address and the Petition with a conclusion in the Pleading. Examples of these 'bald' collects are given later.

It must never be forgotten that Thomas Cranmer spent nearly all his life worshipping according to the Roman rite, with details modified to some extent by the provisions of the Sarum Missal. But they were services in Latin following the rites and ceremonies of the Western church. The first books containing prayers in English were the reforming Primers, which were intended for private, not public, use. They began to appear during the years 1520 to 1545 (Cuming 1983: 26). In them the traditional Hours of Our Lady were supplemented by material which derived from Lutheran sources. It was a crafty method of surreptitiously introducing Lutheran ideas into England under the guise of traditional Catholic piety. But from the point of view of the Prayer Books, the great importance of the Primers is that they contain numerous attempts at rendering the Hours into English. Manuscript Primers had included English versions many years before, but these were available only to the wealthy. Now the invention of printing made services in the vernacular a considerably more practical possibility. They had, of course, been preceded by the use of the translations of the Bible of William Tyndale in the 1520s and Miles Coverdale in the 1530s. These translations resulted in the licensed version known as the 'Great' Bible which in September 1538 Thomas Cromwell ordered to be set up in every parish church. It was to the second edition of this version in April 1540 that Cranmer, as archbishop, contributed a preface in which he set out the reasons, as he saw them, for the use of the vernacular in worship.

In the meanwhile, between 1530 and 1545, small changes and improvement can be detected in the various editions of the Primers, resulting in a gradual approach to what might tentatively be called the literary standards of the Prayer Book. Cranmer had available some earlier efforts of the collect form in English in the Primers, which he could work on and polish, but in many cases he needed to start from scratch (Cuming 1990: 56).

The scarcity of material which could be carried over from the Primers was due, in no small measure, to the fact that they were based on the Hours of the Blessed Virgin Mary and also contained a good deal of provision for saints' days, much of which was becoming increasingly unpalatable to those with reforming zeal. There was also the fact that many of the translations in the Primers can only be described as clumsy. The difference in quality between Cranmer's work and these earlier Primers is notable.

As an example of this we may consider the collect for the fourth Sunday after Trinity in the English translation provided by Robert Redman in the 1537 edition of his Primer, a book which Redman boasts in his preface, 'seemed to men of authority not inconvenient to pass among the common people' in other words available not just for the wealthy (ibid. 28). It reads:

O God the protector of al that trusts in ye without whome nothynge is of value, nothhynge is holy, multyplye thy mercy on vs, that thorowe thy gouernaunce & guydynge we may so passe in temporall goodes, that we lese not the eternall. By Chryst oure Lorde.

When subjected to Cranmer's editorial hand the collect appears in the 1549 Prayer Book in this form:

O God, the protector of all that trust in thee, without whom nothing is strong, nothing is holy; Increase and multiply upon us thy mercy; that, thou being our ruler and guide, we may so pass through things temporal, that we finally lose not the things eternal: Grant this, O heavenly Father, for Jesus Christ's sake our Lord.

But if his polishing techniques were impressive they were eclipsed by the quality of his original compositions. Cranmer's treatment of the eighty-four collects that he needed to provide in the 1549 Prayer Book took three forms. First of all there were the straightforward translations from the Sarum Missal; next adaptations (such as those from the Primers); and thirdly his new compositions. The majority of the third category, not surprisingly, are to be found among the provision for saints' days for the doctrinal reasons already alluded to. He needed to find material for the feasts of Saints Stephen, Philip and James, James, Luke, Andrew, Thomas, Matthias, Mark, Barnabas, John Baptist, Peter, Matthew, Simon and Jude, and All Saints. Most of these collects are based on the Epistle or Gospel or both, set for the feast day.

Some insight into Cranmer's methods can be derived from a letter written to Henry VIII in October 1544. Cranmer is at work on a projected Processional and finds that the Latin original is 'barren and little fruitful'. His reaction is to 'use more than the liberty of a translator: for in some processions I have altered divers words; in some I have added part; in some taken part away; some I have left out whole, either for by cause the matter appeared to me to be little to purpose, or by cause the days be not with us festival-days; and some processions I have added whole, because I thought I had better matter for the purpose, than was the procession in Latin' (Ratcliff 1976: 185).

The first two collects in the church's year, that is, the first two Sundays in Advent, are new compositions by Cranmer, and are recognized as being among his very best work, yet he is content to either translate or adapt from the Sarum Missal all the collects for the long period of the Sundays after Trinity. Geoffrey Cuming (1983: 56) speculated as to whether it was time or perhaps enthusiasm for new composition which ran out.

From the first, further doctrinal bias can be detected in Cranmer's work. For instance he is keen to insert a specific mention of grace or God's goodness into the prayers. Examples of this are in the collect for the first Sunday after Epiphany.

O Lord, we beseech thee mercifully to receive the prayers of thy people which call upon thee; and grant that they may both perceive and know what things they ought to do, and also may have grace and power faithfully to fulfil the same; through Jesus Christ our Lord.

In this collect we note we are to pray that we may 'also have grace and power'; 'grace' does not exist in the Sarum Latin. Nor does the phrase 'by thy goodness' come after the petition praying that we might be mercifully delivered, in the ancient version. Cranmer also carefully omits *meroer* (deserve) from the collects for the next Sunday before Easter and the fourteenth Sunday after Trinity. In order to emphasize the memorial character of the eucharist the Latin *annua expectatione* of the first Mass of Christmas becomes 'the yearly remembrance' and the word *hodie* (today) is pointedly omitted on the Feast of the Epiphany. Cranmer is determined that the hearts and minds of the faithful are turned away from earthly things and are focused heavenward by subtle insertions: on Trinity 4 'that we *finally* lose not the things eternal', and on Trinity 13 'that we may fail not finally to attain thy *heavenly* promises'. *Pietas* provides another example of a questionable translation. Really it means 'fatherly affection', but it is rendered by Cranmer as 'true religion' in Epiphany 5:

O Lord, we beseech thee to keep thy Church and household continually in thy true religion; that they who do lean only upon the hope of thy heavenly grace may evermore be defended by thy mighty power; through Jesus Christ our Lord.

In other collects (e.g. Trinity 20 and 23) he renders *pietas* as 'Godliness' and in yet other collects it is omitted altogether. Evidently, according to Cuming (ibid. 58), Cranmer felt ill at ease with the word.

But it was not wholesale change, far from it. Two-thirds of the *Temporale* (Sundays of the year) and a quarter of the *Sanctorale* (Saints and Holy Days) are fairly straightforward translations, although only three collects (Trinity 11, Trinity 17, and the Annunciation) can be described as being absolutely exact renderings of the Sarum originals. Again, a number of Cranmer's translations are free enough to be described as being more precisely adaptations. Such an example would be the collect for the fourth Sunday in Advent. All the words in italics were added by Cranmer to the Latin original.

Lord, raise up, we pray thee, thy power, and come *among us* and with great might succour us, that whereas through our sins *and wickedness* we be *sore let and* hindered, thy *bountiful grace and* mercy, through the satisfaction *of* thy *Son our Lord*, may speedily deliver us.

The original Latin reads:

Excita, quaesumus, Domine, potentiam tuam, et veni, et magna nobis virtute succurre: ut per auxilium gratiae tuae quod nostra peccata praepediunt, indulgentia tuae propitiationis acceleret. Qui vivis...

It will be noted that Cranmer in his version does not translate either *anxilium* nor *indulgentia,* and *propitiationis* cannot be said to be satisfactorily translated by the English word 'satisfaction'.

One of Cranmer's particular idiosyncrasies of translation has become, down the ages, his trademark; his habit of doubling words. He frequently translates one Latin word by two English words. He is not alone in this; Martin Bucer was also given to it (Whitaker 1974: *passim*) It was labelled by his contemporaries as 'Ciceronian', being a latinate style of balance and antithesis, somewhat given to prolixity. It was a style largely mocked and discarded by stylists by the close of the sixteenth century (Frost 1974: 156). However Cranmer's doubling has contributed to a style of Anglican writing, and even speaking which, while widely imitated, is not always used to the best advantage, nor does it produce the happiest results in speech or writing.

This doubling technique reaches its apogee in two of Cranmer's collects. First of all his rendering of the Sarum collect for the fourth Sunday in Advent, already considered, in which we should note 'sins and wickedness', 'sore let and hindered' 'bountiful grace and mercy'. Secondly, there is the second collect provided for Good Friday, which is a translation of the third of the Good Friday Solemn Prayers in the Sarum Missal.

Almighty and everlasting God, by whose Spirit the whole body of the Church is governed and sanctified; Receive our supplications and prayers, which we offer before thee for all estates of men in thy holy Church, that every member of the same, in his vocation and ministry, may truly and godly serve thee; through our Lord and Saviour Jesus Christ.

Here we notice, 'governed and sanctified' 'supplications and prayers' and 'vocation and ministry', 'truly and godly'. This is the only example of four doubles. Advent 4 has three, and in the first, fourth, and fifth Sundays after the Epiphany and on Lent 5, Trinity 7, and Michaelmas the use of doubles occurs twice in their respective collects. Further there are seven other examples where it occurs once in a prayer. In addition the collect for Easter 4 contains the memorable phrase 'sundry and manifold' which is not represented in the Latin at all. Finally, we must not forget one of Cranmer's most enduring collects (for Advent 2) which contains a famous triplet.

Blessed Lord, who hast caused all holy Scriptures to be written for our learning; Grant that we may in such wise hear them, read, mark, learn, and inwardly digest them, that by patience, and comfort of thy holy Word, we may embrace, and ever hold fast the blessed hope of everlasting life, which thou hast given us in our Saviour Jesus Christ.

'Read, mark, (and) learn' is a regularly quoted piece of advice in English, perhaps often by those who do not know its Prayer Book source.

However this Cranmerian trait is actually not as evident in the collects as it is in other parts of his writings. In total doublets are found in only sixteen out of the eighty-four collects. He seems to have believed it more expressive in exhortations, serving as a kind of aural underlining, reminiscent of the parallelisms of Hebrew verse, making the point more emphatically than a single verb would have done. Attractive though it may seem, there are possible disadvantages. W. H. Frere thought that 'the fashionable literary habit of the day which loved to express one idea by two parallel and synonymous words, has often played havoc with the terseness of the originals. The assimilation of these venerable epigrams to the prevalent style of the rite has been almost too well done. The literary skill of the rite has the defects of its qualities' (Arnold and Wyatt 1940: 110).

The use of doublets by Cranmer can be regarded as evidence of his general tendency towards both expansion and indeed explanation. It also shows itself in the insertion of adjectives and adverbs which are not derived from the Latin originals. One of the most frequent of these additions is the word 'all' and often the phrase 'in all things'. It is also notable that the word 'mercy' and its cognates appear a good deal more than the Latin warrants.

Collects are for use in the worship of the church. They are to be recited, sung, or chanted and not merely read on the page of a book, and for this they need rhythm. Cranmer seems to have appreciated this and was determined to make the English of his collect rhythmical. One way of achieving this was by using more words than are needed just to give its bare meaning. It is not tautology, it has been maintained, but done in order to secure the rhythmical flow of the sentence (Baylay 1913: 3).

It has been observed that the Latin collects in the Sarum Missal extensively display the use of the *cursus*, a system of qualitative prose rhythms for the close of Latin phrases and sentences. There is little doubt that it was a stylistic point known to Cranmer. However, while some modern scholars (including C. S. Lewis) believed that although there is sufficient evidence of *cursus* to suggest that its use is deliberate in the Book of Common Prayer, 'It does not hold the secret of the Prayer Book's music' (Lewis 1954: 217–20). D. L. Frost (1974: 151), in a more recent examination of Prayer Book rhetoric, agreed with Lewis's point, but argued that the *cursus* appears with insufficient frequency to be more than the result of chance.

One part of the stylistic heritage of the Book of Common Prayer is the mediaeval use of wordplay. Such serious wordplay was an important part of the composition of medieval Latin hymns and occurs in Middle English religious prose as well as verse. It involves exploiting the likeness between different words, or playing with the varying meanings of a single word. By this means it was possible subtly and economically to present a variety of ideas at the same time. The Latin collects were a fruitful field for such use of wordplay. In the 1549 Prayer Book versions of those collects it was not possible to reproduce those examples, but it was possible to include some English equivalents. Stella Brook (1965: 131) suggests some possibilities. For instance, in the collect for the second Sunday in Lent there is the repetition of 'ourselves' to compensate for the loss of the chime between *muniamur* and *mundemur* in the Latin original. Brook believed that while the second use of the word is dictated by the needs of English sentence structure the first 'ourselves' is 'a matter of felicitous choice'.

Almighty God, which dost see that we have no power of ourselves to help ourselves; keep us both outwardly in our bodies and inwardly in our souls; that we may be defended from all adversities which may happen to the body, and from all evil thoughts which may assault and hurt the soul; through Jesus Christ our Lord.

Then the further, repetition of the phrase 'which may' helps to balance the ideas of bodies and souls which occur both in the Petition and the Aspiration sections of the prayer.

Alliteration is a firmly established characteristic of English style. R. T. Davies (1963: 34) has stated that Chaucer 'revived and developed for new ends the English alliterative style', derived, ultimately, from long before the Norman Conquest. It is equally a stylistic feature in Latin. It was not possible exactly to mirror its occurrence in translation and instead the Prayer Book collects provide their own examples. For instance, in the collect for the sixteenth Sunday after Trinity:

O Lord, we beseech thee, let thy continual pity cleanse and defend thy Church; and, because it cannot continue in safety without thy succour, preserve it evermore by thy help and goodness; through Jesus Christ our Lord.

The first tentative steps towards the reform of service books commenced in the early 1540s with the appearance of an amended edition of the Sarum Breviary. This was followed by the Litany ordered to be used in the processions supporting the King's intention to invade France. This latter is a Cranmerian masterpiece. Little by little changes were being made but nothing substantial was possible until Henry VIII's comparatively early death aged 55 in 1547. It is very true that the passing-bell for the old King sounded the death knell of the old services. In a little over two years a complete English prayer book was produced. In such a tight programme it was impossible that everything could be stylistically perfect, particularly such a precise, literary product as a collect. It has been conjectured that the 1549 authors worked in a leisurely and thorough way at first, and then were forced to more speedy methods, perhaps delegating some work to less gifted writers.

So it is not surprising that there would have been a few failures among Cranmer's successes. Cuming (1983: 62) says 'some of his collects are flat, and one or two down-right bad, as he would have been the first to admit'. A good collect cannot be thrown off in one sitting. The collect which Cranmer wrote for the feast of St Mary Magdalene has been nominated (Brightman 1915: i. p. xcvii) as his worst effort:

Merciful Father, give us grace, that we never presume to sin through the example of any creature; but if it shall chance us at any time to offend thy divine majesty; that we may truly repent, and lament the same, after the example of Mary Magdalene, and by lively faith obtain remission of all our sins; through the only merits of the Son our Saviour Jesus Christ.

Others have been described as 'bald' collects and are equally said to show signs of weariness or haste. Some which followed literally the Sarum Missal originals are rather arid and uninspired. Examples would be, first of all, the collect for the third Sunday in Lent:

We beseech thee, Almighty God, look upon the desires of thy humble servants, and stretch forth the right hand of thy Majesty, to be our defence against all our enemies; through Jesus Christ our Lord.

or for Passion Sunday:

We beseech thee, Almighty God, mercifully to look upon thy people; that by thy great goodness they may be governed and preserved evermore, both in body and soul; through Jesus Christ our Lord.

Had Cranmer a sense of humour? Walter Frere thought probably not. In an essay which he entitled 'Collects Good and Bad' (Arnold and Wyatt 1940: 187) Frere stated that he believed that it could only be Cranmer's lack of humour which enabled him to pass for use one of the most often prayed of all collects, that which is the second collect at Evensong. It contains a veritable liturgical 'howler'.

O God, from whom all holy desires, all good counsels, and all just works do proceed: Give unto thy servants that peace which the world cannot give; that both our hearts may be set to obey thy commandments, and also that by thee we being defended from the fear of our enemies may pass our time in rest and quietness; through the merits of Jesus Christ our Saviour.

Surely the phrase 'both our hearts' has caused mirth continuously since its first appearance on the Feast of Pentecost 1549; yet Cranmer showed no signs of even being aware of the problem.

These points of gentle criticism are made because the habit of regarding all Cranmer's 1549 Prayer Book collects as necessarily perfect has the danger of destroying that faculty of discrimination which is very important for us always to maintain in matters of liturgical evaluation.

In the collects contained in Cranmer's second major liturgical venture, the 1552 Prayer Book, there were only occasional slight changes of spelling with just one exception; the collect for St Andrew's Day was completely rewritten. The 1549 collect was

Almighty God, which has given such grace to thy Apostle saint Andrew, that he counted the sharp and painful death of the cross to be a high honour, and a great glory; Grant us to take and esteem all troubles and adversities which shall come to us for thy sake, as things profitable for us toward the obtaining of everlasting life.

This collect was defective in the strict reformers' eyes in that it contained information derived from outside the Scriptures. Consequently it was replaced in 1552 by this entirely new collect which could, of course, have been composed by Cranmer himself.

Almighty God, who did give such grace unto thy holy Apostle Saint Andrew, that he readily obeyed the calling of thy Son Jesus Christ, and followed him without delay; Grant unto us all, that we, being called by thy holy Word, may forthwith give up ourselves obediently to fulfil thy holy commandments, through the same Jesus Christ our Lord.

In contrast to the minor changes made in 1552, 106 years after his martyrdom, in the 1662 Prayer Book, more extensive work was done on Cranmer's collects. The revisers went over the collects with much care, altering or removing some obvious blemishes. They also included three entirely new collects, replacing the 1549 collect for Advent 3 and providing collects for Epiphany 6 and Easter Eve which had been collect-less in the earlier Prayer Book. The first two prayers were probably by John Cosin (1594–1672) whose literary work has been much admired and often confused with that of Cranmer. In the 1662 Prayer Book there are twenty changes or amendments in the Temporale, ranging from expansions or developments to the smallest amendment. In the Sanctorale there are sixteen changes of a greater or lesser degree to Cranmer's work.

In subsequent years Cranmer's collects have had a significant place in Anglican liturgical development and through the liturgy have had their effect on English poetry within the church tradition, from George Herbert to John Keble (see Ch. 43 below by David Scott). There was no opportunity for changes in England before the beginning of the twentieth century. In the event the abortive proposals in 1927 and 1928 contained no new Sunday collects, but included many new collects for lesser feasts and fasts. In contrast to this other provinces of the Anglican Communion had been able to revise their prayer books, but in every case a decision was made to retain a large proportion of Cranmer's collects. The result was that the collects remained a major part of the Anglican heritage until the advent of modern language services.

To serve the needs of these new services, now in contemporary language, it was at first naively thought that the problem could be solved fairly easily simply by the abandonment of 'thees' and 'thous' in prayers. It was quickly realized that 'dost', 'hast', 'shalt', 'wilt' and a whole host of other words must be dispensed with in addition if archaisms were to be avoided. Early revisions, such as *The Alternative Service Book* (1980), contented themselves in many cases with no more than 'invisible mending'. For example, in that book, Cranmer's Ash Wednesday collect was rendered:

> Almighty and everlasting God,
> you hate nothing that you have made
> and forgive the sins of all those who are penitent.
> Create and make in us new and contrite hearts,
> that, lamenting our sins
> and acknowledging our wretchedness,
> we may receive from you, the God of all mercy,
> perfect forgiveness and peace; through Jesus Christ our Lord.

There were other less happy attempts to provide contemporary collects in a style which can only be described as sixteenth/seventeenth-century pastiche. They were generally considered a failure.

Nonetheless the eucharist needs what is now often called an 'opening prayer' and if the rest of the service is in modern language it must be preferred to have that prayer also in the same style of language. Whether the shape of the prayer should be collect-like or not continues to be debated. Examples of prayers which could loosely be described as modern collects have been produced, as well as other forms which serve well as opening prayers, but bear little resemblance to the traditional collect. The latest Church of England collect for Ash Wednesday (*Additional Collects*, 2004, 12) reads:

Holy God,
our lives are laid open before you: rescue us from the chaos of
sin and through the death of your Son bring us healing and
make us whole in Jesus Christ our Lord.

However lovers of Cranmer's collects need not despair. It is a fact in these days of often gloomy and depressing church statistics, that attendance at worship in our cathedrals and collegiate churches is a heartening growth area, in particular, for

Choral Evensong. It is a fact underlined by the popularity of the weekly broadcast of that service on BBC Radio 3. This means that the traditional collects retain their honoured place in Anglican public worship and the name of their principal begetter continues to be revered.

Works Cited

Additional Collects. 2004. *Common Worship Services and Prayers for the Church of England.* London: Church House.

ARNOLD, J. H., and WYATT, E. G. P. 1940. *Walter Howard Frere: A Collection of his Papers on Liturgical and Historical Subjects.* Alcuin Club Collections 35. London, Oxford University Press.

BAYLAY, ATWELL M. Y. 1913. *A Century of Collects, Selected and Translated.* Alcuin Club Prayer Book Revision Pamphlets 3. London: A. R. Mowbray.

BRIGHTMAN, F. E. 1915. *The English Rite.* 2 vols. London: Rivingtons.

BROOK, STELLA. 1965. *The Language of the Book of Common Prayer.* London: André Deutsch.

CUMING, GEOFFREY. 1983. *The Godly Order: Texts and Studies Relating to the Book of Common Prayer.* Alcuin Club Collections 65. London: SPCK.

—— 1990. 'Thomas Cranmer: Translator and Creative Writer', in David Jasper and R. C. D. Jasper (eds.), *Language and the Worship of the Church.* Basingstoke: Macmillan.

DAVIES, R. T. 1963. *Medieval English Lyrics: A Critical Anthology.* London: Faber & Faber.

DEARMER, PERCY. 1919. *The Art of Public Worship.* London: A. R. Mowbray.

DUFFY, EAMON. 1992. *The Stripping of the Altars: Traditional Religion in England 1400–1580.* New Haven: Yale University Press.

FELTO, C. L. n.d. [1912], in George Harford and Morley Stevenson, *The Prayer Book Dictionary.* London: Waverley Book Co., n.d.? 1912.

FROST, DAVID L. 1974. 'Liturgical Language from Cranmer to Series 3', in R. C. D. Jasper (ed.), *The Eucharist Today.* London: SPCK.

GOULBURN, E. M. 1880. *The Collects of the Day: An Exposition, Critical and Devotional of the Collects Appointed at the Communion.* 2 vols. London: Rivingtons.

LEWIS, C. S. 1954. *English Literature in the Sixteenth Century.* London, Oxford University Press.

MACCULLOCH, DIARMAID. 1996. *Thomas Cranmer: A Life.* London: Allen Lane Penguin.

RATCLIFF, E. C. 1976. *Liturgical Studies.* London: SPCK.

STEPHENS-HODGE, L. E. H. 1961. *The Collects: An Introduction and Exposition.* London: Hodder & Stoughton.

SUTER, J. W., Jr. 1940. *The Book of English Collects.* New York: Harper.

WHITAKER, E. C. 1974. *Martin Bucer and the Book of Common Prayer.* Alcuin Club Collections 55. Great Wakering: Mayhew-McCrimmon.

WILLIS, G. G. 1968. *Further Essays on Early Roman Liturgy.* Alcuin Club Collections 50. London: SPCK.

Further Reading

BARBEE, C. FREDERICK, and ZAHL, PAUL F. M. 1999. *The Collects of Thomas Cranmer.* Grand Rapids: Eerdmans.

BROOK, STELLA. 1965. *The Language of the Book of Common Prayer.* London: André Deutsch.

CUMING, GEOFFREY. 1990. 'Thomas Cranmer: Translator and Creative Writer', in David Jasper and R. C. D. Jasper (eds.), *Language and the Worship of the Church.* Basingstoke: Macmillan.

—— 1983. *The Godly Order: Texts and Studies relating to the Book of Common Prayer.* Alcuin Club Collections 65. London: SPCK.

MARTIN R. DUDLEY, 1994. *The Collect in Anglican Liturgy.* Alcuin Club Collections 72. Collegeville, Minn.: Liturgical Press.

MacCULLOCH, DIARMAID. 1996. *Thomas Cranmer: A Life.* New Haven: Yale University Press.

CHAPTER 34

JOHN BUNYAN

ROBERT G. COLLMER

SEVENTEENTH-CENTURY Puritanism offers a remarkable spectrum of political and religious diversity. Specifically, Monica Furlong (1975: 17) asserted that Puritanism produced 'two geniuses in the persons of John Milton and John Bunyan'. The complexity of thought and range of knowledge possessed by John Milton stand in sharp contrast to the apparent simplicity and narrowness of view of John Bunyan. Yet the concern of both these visionaries was Christian theology as applied to their worlds—one primarily political, the other personal. For Milton's thought we have, beyond the great poems—*Paradise Lost, Paradise Regained*, and *Samson Agonistes*— the political writings and the systematic theology, unpublished until after his death, *De Doctrina Christiana*. From Bunyan, who wrote some sixty works (all but twelve published during his life), we have his imaginative books—*The Pilgrim's Progress* (*PPI, PPII*), *The Life and Death of Mr. Badman* (*BM*), and *The Holy War* (*HW*)— plus didactic works, his spiritual autobiography, *Grace Abounding to the Chief of Sinners* (*GA*), his systematic theology, *A Confession of my Faith* and *A Reason of my Practice* (*CR*), and other doctrinal writings. About Milton as a thinker on religious matters there is no doubt concerning his capacity, although the shape of his thoughts has been variously construed. Bunyan as a thinker deserves more attention.

Both writers cast much of their theology in literary forms. For Milton the patterns were set by classical or ancient standards, such as the epic, Greek drama, and Pauline epistolary style. Bunyan presents a different case. His theology is firmly Bible-based: as Christopher Hill (1989: 169) asserts, 'The Bible is Bunyan's sheet-anchor, his defense against despair and atheism. He would have been lost if he had abandoned it.' But it is the Bible refracted through Bunyan's experience, and therefore tracing the content and form of his writings means beginning with Bunyan's life: his theology is his life. His literary creations were not abstractions but sprang from problems and successes in his immediate experience or in the experience of persons with whom he associated.

A survey of Bunyan's early life reveals the cultural impediments he had to overcome. Born in 1628 at Elstow, a village near Bedford in southern England, he came, as he wrote in *GA*, from a father's household 'of that rank that is meanest, and most despised of all the families in the Land' (p. 7). Even discounting the temptation among some persons who have achieved prominence to stress their pitiable origins, one concedes that Bunyan lacked the advantages of a son born into a prosperous family such as that of Milton. As he explains in *GA* (ibid.), encouraged by his parents, his early education in a school sufficed for him to learn to read and write, though 'to my shame I confess, I did soon loose [*sic*] that little I Iearned'.

His first encounter with the world beyond Bedford came when he was conscripted into the army on the Parliamentary side in late 1644; he served until 1646. As a young man in Bedford, he let 'loose the reins to my lusts' and 'was the very ringleader of all the Youth that kept me company, into all manner of vice and ungodliness' (*GA* 9). This way of life prevailed until his marriage (his wife's name is not recorded) in about 1649. Although he and his wife had not 'so much houshold-stuff as a Dish or Spoon betwixt us both' (*GA* 10), she did bring as dowry two popular religious books— Arthur Dent's *The Plain Mans Path-way to Heaven* and Bishop Lewis Bayly's *The Practice of Piety*. From this marriage came three daughters, including blind Mary, and a son. He pursued the trade of a tinker, or brazier, an itinerant repairer of pots and pans, through much of his life, for his (second) wife, Elizabeth, described him in 1660 as a 'Tinker, and a poor man' (*A Relation of My Imprisonment* 132).

As a child he suffered what he called 'terrible dreams', which he claimed came from God because of his 'cursing, swearing, lying and blaspheming the holy Name of God' (*GA* 8). He feared divine judgement and the torment of hell with devils and fiends. At the age of 9 or 10, while he was in his 'many sports and childish vanities', he was 'cast down and afflicted mentally'. Periods of depression entered Bunyan's mind throughout his life.

In the middle of the 1650s Bunyan experienced temporary relief from his anxieties. He recorded the end of his struggles: 'Now did my chains fall off my Legs indeed, I was loosed from my affliction and irons, my temptations also fled away: so that from that time those dreadful Scriptures of God left off to trouble me; now went I also home rejoycing, for the grace and love of God' (*GA* 74). In 1655 he joined the 'visible saints' in the Bedford church, which became known as Bedford Meeting and in the middle of that decade, with no university training and no authorization beyond the local church group, Bunyan began to preach, for in 1656 on the title-page of a lengthy tract he described himself as 'By the grace of God, Preacher of the Gospel of his dear son'.

In 1660 his troubles with the authorities of the restored monarchy and the re-establishment of the Church of England erupted. He was arrested for attending a conventicle and preaching without a licence near Bedford. He remained in prison in Bedford until 1672 with infrequent periods of liberty. In 1676–7 he was reincarcerated for about six months. Richard L. Greaves (2002: 494) estimated that he 'spent more time in prison than almost any other nonconformist'. Had he compromised he would not have undergone what he called 'above eleven years imprisonment . . . this tedious tract of time'.

After his release from prison he continued as pastor of the church in Bedford, but increasingly he honed his skills in writing. It is widely accepted by historians that during his second, six-month imprisonment he wrote *The Pilgrim's Progress*, Part One. This was followed by his other three well-known imaginative books. Didactic treatises and a variety of works, including a book for boys and girls to teach them morality through the use of emblems as well as a guide for spelling, followed. Though continuing his ministry in Bedford and the surrounding villages, he frequently journeyed to London, where he engaged printers for his books and preached in nonconformist halls. Many of his works contain digests of sermons.

Tradition holds that he died as a consequence of having been drenched during a ride by horse to minister to a quarrelling son and father. He died in London and is buried in Bunhill Fields, the cemetery occupied by prominent dissenters. Bunyan's simplicity within greatness is reflected by the entry in the Bedford church book: 'wednesday the 4th of septembr was kept in prayre huemilyation for this heavy stroak upon us [,] the death of Bro. Bunyan'. It was the year 1688; he was 60 years, the same number of years as the number of books he wrote.

Always for Bunyan the Bible was his basic guide for putting experience into word. The title-page for *PPI* quotes Hosea 12: 10: 'I have used Similitudes'. He proclaimed a precedent for his work in the Holy Scripture, but there were other books with which he was familiar. For example, he may have structured the dialogues he employed in *PP* after Dent. Lewis Bayly offered much of the preparation for dying in the medieval *ars moriendi* genre, which controls the ultimate goal of *BM*. Beyond these two books lies one that Bunyan claimed he encountered in an old copy, Martin Luther's commentary on the book of Galatians, where Bunyan said, 'I found my condition in his [Luther's] experience, so largely and profoundly handled, as if his Book had been written out of my heart' (*GA* 43). This dense book in a modern edition of more than five hundred pages reveals a capability for concentration in Bunyan's mind beyond that of an ordinary autodidact. In his first imprisonment he purchased John Foxe's lengthy work usually entitled *Book of Martyrs* (original, 1563). Though he disclaimed 'Duncist Sophistry', he appeared to have read Bible commentaries, for example, on the book of Revelation, and books by Ranters and Fifth Monarchists. He mentioned the beliefs of Islam though he did not claim to have read the Koran. More imaginative reading from before his conversion lingered in his mind, for he confessed (in *A Few Sighs from Hell*; 1980: 333) that he used to enjoy 'a Ballad, a Newsbook, *George* on Horseback, or *Bevis* of *Southhampton* . . . some book that teaches curious arts, that tells of old fables'. The exploits of knights that entertained him in his youth insinuated into his mature imaginative creations.

A caveat arises concerning the Bible and Bunyan's style. A person of one book is often decried as limited in knowledge and vision, but that objection does not always apply to the Bible. First, the Bible is not just one book; it is a library of books, for it contains history, myth, law, drama, poetry, parables, tales, and nature descriptions among other genres. Bunyan quoted from the King James and the Geneva Bibles, both of which included the Apocrypha, which he also mentions with respect. In the case of the Geneva Bible the illustrations accompanying the text expand the imagination. Second, a specific vitality and immediacy distinguished Bunyan's method of Bible reading. Literally it spoke inwardly to him. In *GA* when the Bible became, as he said, 'precious', the encounter spawned active verbs—a scripture 'on me did then fasten with conviction'; 'This Scripture did then trample all my desires'; 'it was so fresh . . . that it was if it talked with me'; 'these words broke upon my mind'; 'This Scripture made me faint and fear, yet it kindled fire in my soul'; 'wo be to him against whom the Scriptures bend themselves'. For Bunyan, words, particularly what he considered the words of God, bound into the Bible, became living beings.

The document from which the above quotations came is, of course, *Grace Abounding to the Chief of Sinners*. This book, published in 1666 during Bunyan's long imprisonment, has provoked a great deal of critical comment, for instance, from William James in *The Varieties of Religious Experience* (1902). James labelled it an autobiography. From *GA* James (1928: 157) deduced that Bunyan 'was a typical case of the psychopathic temperament, sensitive of conscience to a diseased degree, beset by doubts, fears, and insistent ideas, and a victim of verbal automatisms, both motor and sensory'. But the work proceeds not from a desire to write a story of the author's life, nor from the hope to write another Puritan self-examination. It is not a record of searching, in Calvinistic terms, to determine whether he was among the Elect. It is dedicated, Bunyan says in the preface, 'to those whom God hath counted him worthy to beget to Faith, by his Ministry in the Word'. He goes on to remind his church members, 'I stick between the Teeth of the Lyons in the wilderness'—the gaol in Bedford.

The usual reaction of a person imprisoned and, according to his own opinion, unjustly, is to rail against the legal system. Bunyan did not do this, but he wrote a report, *A Relation of the imprisonment of Mr. John Bunyan. . . . written by Himself.* This contains, mostly as dialogue, the record of the charges and responses involving Bunyan. It includes the report of Elizabeth's oral defence of her husband before the judges in the Swan Chamber in Bedford. It was published separately in 1665, one year before *GA*. *Grace Abounding* comes from a purpose Bunyan later (1672) explained in *CR*, which is the closest he came to writing a systematic theology. Most of Bunyan's thinking on theology came in fragments, often products of controversies with other religious thinkers or cases of conscience from immediate questions of faith and/or practice. *A Confession* is no exception because it starts by telling the (non-specific) reader, 'Sir, I Marvail not that both your self, and others do think my long Imprisonment strange (or rather strangely of me for the sake of that) for verily I should also have done it my self, had not the Holy Ghost long since forbidden me' (*CR* 135). He defined the subject as no 'other doctrine or practice, then what I held, professed, and preached when apprehended, and cast in Prison' (ibid.). So to understand *GA* one should study what Bunyan in *CR* claimed he had believed.

He cloaked his doctrinal positions in a narrative, so *GA* is a theological work told in story form, Bunyan's own story. Yet the emphasis is not on Bunyan except as experience reveals 'grace abounding'. Since he wrote for his congregants, he set forth the events of his conversion and union with the Bedford 'visible saints'. It was a common practice in nonconformist fellowships for aspiring members to stand before the congregation and tell of their spiritual journey. In *CR* (165) he asserted that 'by the word of faith and of good works; moral duties Gospellized; we ought to judge of the fitness of members...to fellowship...a confession of this by word and life, makes this inward circumcision visible'.

He wrote it as an apology for his life leading up to his imprisonment in order to draw the reader into taking on the same experience. It is a mistake to assume that it is within the long line of autobiographies with their often self-serving motives. It is then different from, for example, St Augustine's *Confessions*, for it is directed to those he calls his 'Children...for your further edifying and building up in Faith and Holiness, &, yet that you may see my Soul hath fatherly care and desire after your spiritual and everlasting welfare' (ibid. 3). The recounting of events from Bunyan's life is selective, not definitive. Significant details are missing, for example, the name of his first wife.

To sustain the reader's interest, Bunyan fashioned events in his life that would attract a reader. The years between 1640 and 1670 in England contained much military activity, so Bunyan fashioned a bellicose tone to his book. *Grace Abounding*, with its recounting of mental battles to reveal the faith inside Christian-Bunyan and its emphasizing conduct as a precondition for entrance into the communion of saints, characterized his life. Nowhere in *GA* does he describe a baptismal act or the Lord's Supper, both ordinances in the Bedford group. For him 'Water baptism and the supper of the Lord' are 'not the fundamentals of our Christianity; nor grounds or rule to communion with Saints: servants they are, and our mystical Ministers, to teach and instruct us, in the most weighty matters of the kingdom of God' (*CR* 160). *Grace Abounding* is a confession of faith and morals directed towards those members of his congregation who might have joined after he entered the group, or persons with doubts of his beliefs resulting from his years of gaol time. It is also a tract to persuade outsiders to emulate what he later called his pilgrimage. It is a literary re-creation of Bunyan's beliefs and practice. It does not show what Alfred Noyes (1928: 105) called 'a congenital defect of the mind', but a description, as Bunyan recalled or constructed, of what God's grace did through him that led him into the communion of the saints in this world with the anticipation of entrance into the Celestial City. But before Bunyan arrived at the religious position sustaining *GA*, he had encountered other expressions of belief. Two are extensively set forth in *GA*; a third is briefly mentioned.

He explained that early in his pursuit of belief, 'I met with some *Ranters* books, that were put forth by some of our Country men; which Books were also highly in esteem by several old Professors [persons who only claimed to be religious]' (*GA* 18). The Ranters were an obscure, plebeian cluster of persons who emerged in England about 1649 and flourished for three or four years. They were not an organized sect; maybe, as one historian, J. C. Davis (1986), insisted, they did not exist but were a creation of deviant 'yellow-journalist' writers. Marxist critics from 1970 on, such as

A. L. Morton (1970) and Christopher Hill, praised them for their anti-establishment views. Most knowledge of them comes from detractors. Their supposed ideas sprang from a sort of pantheism, which meant that God was in everyone and everything, so sin did not exist independently of persons created by God; hence, all actions are permitted. It was an extreme antinomianism, that is, opposition to all rules, including personal and civil law. Blasphemy, adultery, and the belief that Christ had come to free them from societal controls, prevailed. The Ranter whom Bunyan met denied that 'there was a God, Angel, or Spirit, and would laugh at all exhortations to sobriety' (ibid. 18). Without arguing with him, Bunyan, 'abominating those principles, left his company forth with' (ibid. 19). Ranterism is for him encapsulated in one person.

Another group was the Quakers, whom he encountered after the Ranters and against whom he continued to write polemics from the 1650s through the 1680s. For Bunyan the movement was so pervasive that he did not summarize it within one person as he did for Ranterism. Geoffrey F. Nuttall's *Studies in Christian Enthusiasm: Illustrated from Early Quakerism* (1948), though written fifty years ago, is still a solid introduction. The first of Bunyan's works, *Some Gospel-truths Opened*, opposed the Quakers and from *GA* a reader can deduce Bunyan's concept of Quakerism as follows: The Bible is not the Word of God, but the Spirit of God dwells in every person; Christ's blood and body are within the saints; there will be no resurrection of the bodies of the dead; the Jesus who died on the cross did not ascend into heaven and will not return to earth in a Second Coming.

He dealt hurriedly at one point in his spiritual report with other, non-Christian religions and their followers. In *GA* (33) he claimed the Devil, the Tempter, raised a question: 'How can you tell but that the Turks had as good Scriptures to prove their *Mahomet,* as the Saviour, as we have to prove our *Jesus* is; and could I think that so many ten thousands in so many Countreys and kingdoms, should be without the knowledge of the right way to Heaven...?' He never answered that question: 'Onely by the distaste that they [such questions] gave unto my spirit, I felt there was something in me that refused to embrace them' (ibid. 34). Bunyan attempted no rational argument. Little logic appears in *GA*, for the work was never intended for a group either antagonistic or neutral. It was the explanation of the way God's grace had dealt with him and everything he said came from his position as a sort of father writing to his children.

The second major work, *The Pilgrim's Progress,* the book on which rests his prominence, the most widely translated book in the world written originally in English, appeared in 1678 though it may have been written much earlier. Some critics place its composition during the second imprisonment of 1676–7 though others, such as Hill and Greaves (2002: 638), think it was composed earlier, maybe as early as 1668. Drawing upon the medieval traditions of allegory, its target readership was defined in the author's apologia as persons not on a spiritual journey ('The Book will make a Travailer of thee'), people who seek out oddities ('Art thou for something rare and profitable?'), forgetful ones ('Art thou forgetful?'), bored people ('...may the minds of listless affect'), melancholics ('Would'st thou divert thy self from Melancholy?'), lovers of riddles ('Would'st thou read Riddles?'), and persons who seek to learn about themselves ('Would'st read thy self, and read thou know'st not what | And yet know whether thou art blest or not | By reading the same lines?'). He had earlier in this defence appealed to the precedent in the Bible of 'Types, Shadows and Metaphors'. He cited the style of writing in dialogue ('...men [as high as Trees] will write | Dialogue-wise') alluding possibly to Dent. The final lines of the apology ask the reader to 'Lay my Book, thy Head and Heart together'. The purpose was to entice by mental tricks, if you will, to effect a change in the heart.

He chose a modality as venerable as Homer's *Odyssey* (surely unknown to him), with places as familiar as paths, ditches, sloughs, big houses, and hills of Bedford-shire, in language of proverbs and everyday, colloquial speech, with adventures echoic of knightly adventures from his boyhood reading. Paradoxically, however, he chose 'progress', a word associated with royalty (we remember T. S. Eliot's Prufrock 'could swell a progress'). Before Bunyan's time and not necessarily related to his example, 'progress' did not mean an upward advance. The modern connota-tion emerged in the eighteenth century. He peopled his book with types similar to the moods or states of being (a character Hopeful) and thoughts (Atheist) he had set out for his congregation in *GA*. The underlying theology is clearly Calvinist.

The story of *PP* is well known. A man, Graceless, with a burden on his back, flees from his family, home, and the City of Destruction to begin a journey. A spectrum of characters, many of whom are patently transparent to the reader though not always to Christian (who undergoes a name change after meeting with Evangelist), meet him along the road. They vary from the naïve (Pliable), through the deceptive (Mr Worldly Wiseman), to the monstrous (Apollyon, so unforgettably illustrated by William Blake), including a sexual seductive (Wanton, only described by Faithful), all the inhabitants of Vanity Fair, especially the unjust Lord Hategood and the biased jurors, the grotesque Giant Despair and his wife, Diffidence (who is an addition by Bunyan in the second edition). As the story unfolds, the deceivers and violent begin to recede though Christian's struggles nevertheless persist even to the point of death.

The last person to accompany Christian and his companion Hopeful (who replaces the martyred Faithful at Vanity Fair), and who stays with them until the River of Death, is Ignorance. He is the most interesting character who is wrong. He is sophisticated in religious language, believes in God and Jesus, but, according to Christian, lacks saving faith, and he ends by being bound hand and foot by Shining Ones and cast into hell. Probably many of the readers of *PP*, not terrified into acceptance of Bunyan's message, found themselves like Ignorance, not knowing the truth as Bunyan defined it. This character clearly stands for the Anglican Latitudinarian of the Restoration Period. On the other hand, of the characters with goodness there are, besides Evangelist, the Interpreter, the Porter, the women Discretion, Prudence, Piety, and Charity, Faithful (an example of a fellow from the gathered church), then Hopeful, the shepherds, and the Shining Ones who welcome travellers into the Celestial City.

Bunyan's next foray into a narrative with a moral was *The Life and Death of Mr. Badman* which came in 1680 two years after *PP*. Abandoning the allegorical form of the earlier work, it portrays the obverse of the man who seeks the Celestial City. The editors of this work in the Oxford Edition, James F. Forrest and Roger Sharrock, classify it as a 'Puritan rogue novel' rather than an allegory. The nineteenth-century editor of Bunyan's works, George Offor, apologized for its raciness calling it 'the only work proceeding from the prolific pen and fertile imagination of Bunyan, in which he uses terms that, in this delicate and refined age, may give offence'.

The letter to the Courteous Reader is one of the longest introductions that Bunyan affixed to any of his books, revealing the pains to which he went to make his purpose clear and to abort objections. The work falls into a large field called moral theology, which concerns the application of dogma to the human condition. The thesis is the following: 'If it was a transgression of Old, for a man to wear a Womans Apparel, surely it is a transgression now for a sinner to wear a Christian Profession for a Cloak. Wolves in Sheeps Clothing swarm in England this day. Wolves both as to Doctrine, and as to practice too' (*BM* 10). The doctrine and practice from *CR* of 1672 reappear. In the quotation above he continues, 'Some men make a Profession [of faith], I doubt [i.e. fear], on purpose that they may twist themselves into a Trade, and thence into an Estate; yea, and if need be, into an Estate Knavishly, by the ruin of their Neighbour; let such take heed, for those that do such things have the greater damnation' (*BM* 10). Bunyan intended to attack persons who use religion to gain respectability and attain their position by dealing dishonestly in commerce. He claimed that he had witnessed the conduct he describes: 'all the things I discourse of, I mean as to matter of fact, have been acted upon the stage of this World, even many times before mine eyes' (*BM* 1). He admonishes the immediate reader: 'Christian, a Profession according to the Gospel, is, in these dayes, a rare thing' (*BM* 10).

Like *PP*, the book is written in dialogue—literally, with slight background or description—between two persons, Wiseman (Bunyan's voice) and Attentive (like Bunyan's ideal congregant) as they discuss the life and death of Badman, who has recently died. Wiseman says, 'I will tell you a story. When I was in prison, there came a woman to me that was under a great deal of trouble' (*BM* 48). The men talk from morning until evening. Into the recounting of the events of his life enter other stories to drive a point which serve also to relieve the downward spiral of Badman's conduct. They reflect the manners in Bunyan's congregation and community. Six of these ancillary stories are drawn from Samuel Clarke's *A Mirrour or Looking-Glass for both Saints and Sinners* (second edition, 1654).

Wiseman tells of Badman's life in order to satisfy Attentive's major interest, namely, the manner of his death. Though Badman's parents were godly, he was 'very *bad*', given to lying and stealing from gardens and orchards: 'he swarmed with sins, even as a Begger does with Vermin, and that when he was but a Boy' (*BM* 24). 'He reckoned himself a mans Fellow, when he had learnt to Swear and Curse boldly' (*BM* 27). Wiseman cites examples of cursing—'*God-damme, God perish me*, or the like' (*BM* 30). His father apprenticed him to a 'very devout person; one that frequented the best Soul-means ... Very meek and merciful', who did not 'overdrive young *Badman* in business' (*BM* 38). But the boy fell under the influence of 'three young Villains', who taught him uncleanness (Bunyan's word for sexual looseness, sometimes a term for syphilis), drunkenness, and stealing from his master. Wiseman describes the consequences of going with whores, where 'often follows this foul sin, *the foul Disease*, now called by us the *Pox*' (*BM* 51). After he had completed his apprenticeship ('I think he had a Bastard laid to his charge before he came out of his time' (*BM* 61), Badman secured two hundred pounds from his father and set himself up in business. But he managed his affairs poorly and soon found himself in his shop with nothing with which to pay his creditors.

Badman then decides to look for a rich, devout wife. Wiseman describes how his companions counselled him to appear religious. This section is a parallel of the Theophrastian character of the spuriously pious pretender. (We might recall Milton's attack in *Areopagitica* on the man of business who divorces his religion from his practice.) This is a central point of *BM*. The girl was without father and mother and easily susceptible to Badman's wiles, who claimed he had plenty of money and sought only an 'honest and godly wife' (*BM* 67). After marrying he soon returned to his old haunts and habits, kept his wife from her religious activities, and consumed her money. His conduct 'killed her in time, yea it was all the time a killing of her' (*BM* 71). Usually she gave in to his demand to avoid religious gatherings, but she once took a stand and told him she was going to a meeting. At this point he 'sware ... that if she did go, he would make both her, and all her damnable Brotherhood (for so he was pleased to call them) to repent their coming thither ... he meant, he would turn Informer, and so either weary out those that she loved, from meeting together to Worship God; or make them pay dearly for their so doing; the which if he did, he knew it would vex every vein of her tender heart' (*BM* 79). Wiseman calls the hidden church group, harassed by informers, 'Meeters'.

Wiseman describes Badman's business practices—'the new engine of breaking [going into bankruptcy to avoid paying creditors]', using deceitful weights and measures, double-billing his customers, extorting, 'griping and grinding the face of the poor', domineering by appearance, and being proud. Bunyan, through the voice of Wiseman, belabours certain 'religious' persons, particularly women, 'for going with their Bulls-foretops [hair piled up in front of the head], with their naked shoulders, and Paps hanging out like a Cows bag' (*BM* 125).

Badman has a temporary change of heart. Having drunk most of the day and into the night at an ale-house, he falls off his horse and breaks his leg. In bed he regrets his mode of life, asks for the prayers of the devout neighbours, and takes thought of his wife and child. But after recovery he regresses to his old ways. Wiseman concludes, '[H]ence usually is sick-bed Repentance, and the matter of it: To wit, to be saved from Hell, and from Death, and that God will restore again to health till they mend ... this kind of Repentance is by God compared to the howling of a dog' (*BM* 139–40). His pseudo conversion 'broke her [his wife's] heart, it was a worse disappointment to her than the cheat that he gave her in marriage ... she dyed bravely' (*BM* 140–1).

He soon remarried, but this wife was very different. She had forced him to marry after he had promised to do so while drunk. Their life together was contentious, 'for their railing, and cursing, and swearing ended not in words: They would fight and fly at each other, and that like Cats and Dogs' (*BM* 146).

Indeed, the last years of Badman's life are miserable and poverty stricken. Since Bunyan entitled his book like the old stories, he spends a long time on the process of dying and not just the life, of Badman. One-eighth of the book depicts this process. Badman's physical condition 'was dropsical, he was consumptive, he was surfeited, was gouty, and, as some say, he had a tang of the Pox in his bowels' (*BM* 148). Unlike Christian in *PPI*, he shows no troubled conscience and Wiseman sums up his passing as follows: 'As quietly as a Lamb. There seemed not to be in it, to standers by, so much as a strong struggle of Nature: and for his Mind, it seemed to be wholly at quiet' (*BM* 157). Bunyan opposed the long-established criterion that as a tree falls, so does it lie; that is, the manner of dying reveals the true quality of a person's conduct, hence, his or her eternal destiny: 'The opinion of the common people concerning this kind of dying, is frivolous and vain; for Mr. *Badman* died like a Lamb or as they call it, like a *Chrisom* child' (*BM* 165). (Recall that Falstaff died like a Chrisom child.) Appearances, however, are not necessarily what they seem.

In *BM* more obviously than in any other of his major works, Bunyan drew either directly or indirectly on a literary genre exemplified as far back as Chaucer's 'Pardoner's Tale', that is the exemplum. The difference, however, is that instead of being a single, concentrated story leading to a moral lesson, *BM* is a string of stories from the life of one man. Thus his methods in cheating in business appear in detail, each segment being an independent unit. The problems of his second marriage are set forth as a story that could stand by itself. The reader's interest is held in abeyance by being continually teased into waiting for another episode. In the progression downward many events are presented as small short stories. This book, though little read in modern times, shows Bunyan in a practical posture, concerned for honesty in economic dealings, the relationship between religion and morality, the conduct of husbands towards their wives, and the difficulty of judging people from externals only. It is a lively, earthy, and entertaining work.

The Holy War, published two years later in 1682, is considered by some critics his best imaginative work apart from *The Pilgrim's Progress*. Lord Macaulay asserted that, were it not for that, it would have been the 'best allegory that ever was written'. Some phrases from this book have become familiar in English, for instance, 'The men that turn the World upside down' (*HW* 40, originally biblical), 'amazing grace' (*HW* 45, better known later from John Newton's hymn), 'One word more' (*HW* 112, the title of a Robert Browning poem). Of archetypal patterns, *PPI* is the journey while *HW* is the siege of a city, for, as Christopher Hill (1989: 252) has said, Bunyan wrote his *Odyssey* first: 'his *Iliad* proved much more difficult'. Bunyan here was drawing upon his experience as a soldier over thirty years before.

At least three levels of allegory control *HW*—(1) cosmology, including Christian history; (2) personal history (more uses of 'I was there' than in any other preface); (3) seventeenth-century English history. Elements of the political struggles within Bedford and Bedfordshire are present, and even hints of a future millenarian, or chiliastic, perfect world appear.

The full title gives the digest, a holy war—*made by Shaddai upon Diabolus, For the Regaining of the Metropolis of the World. Or, the Losing and Taking Again of the Town of Mansoul.* It is a war made by God the Father (Shaddai) against Satan (Diabolus) and his army, and is an account of the retaking of the city of the soul (Mansoul, which is feminine) which had been occupied by Satanic forces. It includes the fall of humanity from Edenic bliss through the dealings of God with Devil-controlled mankind until the arrival of the Son of God, Emanuel (God with us in the person of Jesus Christ). It shows that on a cosmological scale grace acts against evil to rescue humanity: on a personal level, it describes Bunyan's conflicts from *GA.*

As mentioned above, multiple levels of allegory exist, but they are imposed from the analysis by the reader, not from Bunyan's own preface, 'To the Reader'. He does, however, admit his work is 'My riddle', but he entices the reader to look at his notes 'In the window', that is, in marginalia. In no other work did Bunyan call attention to his marginalia though most of his books carried these digests, biblical citations, sometimes a hand pointing to a passage in the text. Recent scholarship has stressed the physical appearance of the pages of Bunyan's books. *The Holy War* is a spiritual autobiography with military imagery, a self-centred work that avoids discussion of large theological issues: 'This famous Town of *Mansoul* had five gates, in at which to come, out at which to go, and these were made likewise answerable to the Walls; to wit, *Impregnable,* and such as could never be opened, nor forced but by the will and leave of those within' (*HW* 8–9). The only theological urgency lies in the appeal of 'pastoral Arminianism'.

The first movement of the war occurs when the giant Diabolus and his minions lay siege to Mansoul. Captain Resistance is killed, and Diabolonians occupy the town. The method of control, hence of the soul of Everyman, has parallels with the political practices of 'new modelling' (*HW* 18), a loaded term in seventeenth-century England (recall the New Model Army of the Cromwellians). Some opposition to Diabolus is asserted by Mr Recorder, conscience, but he is old and 'debauched', while a high-born person, Willbewill, is seduced by the power bestowed upon him by Diabolus and thus becomes his spokesman.

The news of the occupation of Mansoul by Diabolus reaches the King of the Universe, Shaddai, and his Son, Emanuel, the latter 'a Sweet and comly person, and one that had always great affection for those that were in affliction, but one that had mortal enmity against *Diabolus,* because he was designed for it, and because he sought his Crown and Dignity' (*HW* 29). The van of the army is assembled, of which the captain is Boanerges (representing the thundering preachers of Bunyan's time), while the bulk of the army is led by Emanuel, with forty-four battering rams and twelve slings (the twelve apostles) to hurl stones. The town is entered and Diabolus is taken prisoner; the people of Mansoul who had followed Diabolus, instead of being executed, are forgiven and treated well, even being invited to a celebration with food, music, and entertainment. The leaders of the Diabolonians are tried in court—reminiscent of the trial in Vanity Fair, but with honest judges and juries, and the leaders are crucified. Diabolus, not put on trial, is humiliated and driven out of the city 'to inherit the parched places in a salt land, seeking rest but finding none' (*HW* 93). Bunyan had to let the antagonist free in order to continue the tale of the fights that would ensue inside Mansoul even during the reign of the Son and thus he revealed his own struggles that irresistible grace against the Adamic man did not obliterate.

Emanuel gives the city a new charter (the New Testament) and sets up a chief officer, Mr Gods Peace. Temporarily there is nothing but 'harmony, quietness, joy and health' (*HW* 150). It lasts one summer. Mr Carnal Security, partially a Diabolonian, 'a busie man', rises in influence. About this time a plague sweeps through Mansoul—a possible allusion to the plague of 1665, maybe an illness in Bunyan's own life. In Mansoul there lurk in dark places Diabolonians who establish contact with Diabolus and his army outside. The leaders in Mansoul decide to make a night sally into Diabolus's army, but the attack fails. Diabolus retaliates with a night attack and retakes the city, reducing it to a 'den of Dragons, an emblem of Hell, and a place of total darkness' (*HW* 204). Many of the inhabitants oppose Diabolus, and for two and a half years Mansoul is a cauldron of strife. A petition is sent to Emanuel to rescue the city; he comes again and initially defeats the army of Diabolus. But Diabolus enlists a new army of twenty-five thousand soldiers (ten thousand Doubters with fifteen thousand 'Bloodmen') to lay siege to Mansoul. The Bloodmen are shown to be 'chicken-hearted' and captives are taken before Emanuel to be judged. Several Doubters are tried before judges and one particular Doubter is condemned to death; he is Election-doubter. Bunyan commented, 'To question Election is to overthrow a great Doctrine of the Gospel . . . by the best of laws he [Election-doubter] must die' (*HW* 240–1). The author's Calvinism shows here at its most harsh.

The allegory of *The Holy War* attracts the devotee of military events and it documents Bunyan's faith and experience in a fast-moving narrative. In a vindication of his 'Pilgrim', a poem appended to *HW*, Bunyan rebuts the rumour that *PPI* was not written by himself—'Some say that *Pilgrims Progress* is not mine.' Indeed, he affirms:

> It came from mine own heart, so to my head,
> And thence into my fingers trickled.   (*HW* 274)

In 1664 he published the second part of *PP* and again referred to pretenders to his work:

> 'Tis true, some have of late, to Counterfeit
> My Pilgrim, to their own, my title set.

The Apology at the beginning of *PPII* contains Bunyan's most extensive presentation of his literary method. He denounces the opposers of *PPI* who faulted him for using excessive humour, for writing too abstractly, for obscuring truth in dark images, for writing a romance (a novel). He relies on the popularity of the first part in various lands and in different social levels, and with both men and women, and he vindicates his status as an author through the wide acceptance of his writing about the pilgrim.

The story of *PPII* features Christian's wife, Christiana, and her four sons. Though the narrative describes many places traversed by Christian, it carries a unique emphasis. Instead of one person who leaves his origins to pursue a goal for himself, this part shows that the gathered church of the redeemed is a community. As Bunyan adapted his theology to his purpose, so he employed echoes of *PPI* in *PPII*.

The action begins in the City of Destruction with Christiana having a dream in which she sees her husband 'in a place of Bliss' (*PPII* 285). A visitor, Secret, tells her of an invitation from God to forgive her sins and to invite her 'to his table' (ibid.). Accompanied by her sons and a hired girl, Mercy, Christiana departs. They have scarcely started on their way when the women are approached by two ruffians who seek to seduce them. The women shriek and 'put themselves under those Laws that are provided for the Protection of Women' (*PPII* 299). They go to the House of the Interpreter and there see what Christian had seen, though one added vision is of a man with a muckrake (which gives us a word common in modern political discourse, 'muckraker'). Other scenes are shown, and emblems that appeal to young readers of *PPII*. At the house they are required to enter a bath of sanctification so that they will be clean for the rest of their journey. Interpreter provides his servant, Great-heart, a fighter, to accompany the band. He represents the godly minister of the congregation who explains the places where Christian walked. At the Porter's Lodge the boys recite the catechism, which Christiana had taught them. Here Mr Brisk, pretending to religion, attempts to persuade Mercy to marry him, but she refuses. Near here one of the sons, Mathew, takes ill from having eaten fruit from someone else's orchard. He is cured by a physician, Mr Skill. The boys learn spiritual lessons from sights in the natural world. Before they leave the Porter's Lodge, one of the occupants, Prudence, who has directed the boys in religious matters, plays upon a 'pair of Excellent Virginals' (*PPII* 331) and sings. Mr Great-heart, who has been temporarily absent in order to go back to the Interpreter's house, rejoins the group bringing a bottle of wine plus 'parched Corn' and a 'couple of Pomegranates' for Christiana and Mercy and figs and raisins for the boys. These may suggest participation in holy communion.

They proceed on their journey, passing through the Valley of Humiliation and the spot where Christian defeated Apollyon, and here Great-heart vanquishes the giant Maull, who used 'to spoyl young Pilgrims with Sophistry' (PPII 340). On their way they receive good food, especially at Gaius' Inn, with an elaborate meal of symbolic elements. Here Mercy and Mathew are married, and Gaius gives a daughter to another son of Christiana. Later the two other sons marry.

The band continues and passes through Vanity, where in some quarters religion is considered honourable because of the examples from Christian and Faithful. Towards the end of the journey they come near Doubting Castle, and a decision is made to attack Giant Despair, to free captives in the castle, and to raze it to the ground. With the four (now) young men and another pilgrim, old Honest, Great-heart kills the giant. Then follows a grotesque scene at which the group dances to the accompaniment of violin and lute. One man 'could not Dance without one Crutch in his Hand, but I promise you, he footed it well; also the Girl was to be commended, for she answered the Musick handsomely' (*PPII* 374). The entire book has much concern for music and dancing and food and drink.

They meet shepherds, who welcome them and provide the 'Feast of things easy of Digestion' (*PPII* 376). The shepherds give them gifts of things which they desired, including a large looking-glass for Mercy: 'About *Christianas* Neck, the Shepherds put a Bracelet, and so they did about the Necks of her four Daughters, also they put Ear-rings in their Ears, and Jewels on their Fore-heads' (*PPII* 379). The group must now cross the Enchanted Ground, where a witch, Madam Bubble, is the mistress. She offers them the vanities of this life, 'laugheth Poor Pilgrims to scorn, but highly commends the Rich' (*PPII* 391). Eventually they come to rest in the Land of Beulah, where pilgrims wait to enter the Golden Gates: 'they *heard* nothing, *saw* nothing, *felt* nothing, *smelt* nothing, *tasted* nothing, that was offensive to their Stomach or Mind' (*PPII* 393). Only the water from the River of Death was slightly bitter, but it turned sweeter when it reached their stomachs.

Near the River of Death they meet Valiant-for-Truth, who is soon summoned to cross to the Celestial City, where the 'trumpets sounded for him on the other side' (*PPII* 398) And Christiana 'came forth and entered the R*iver* with a *Beck'n* of Fare well, to those that followed her to the River side' (*PPII* 395). The narrator does not tarry to see the others enter the Celestial City because they had to stay to bring willing persons to the gathered church.

PPII has created controversy concerning the position of women in Bunyan's thought. For instance, that the women had to be accompanied most of the way by a male warrior suggests that women on their own cannot fight spiritual battles. The softening of encounters by referring to what Christian had experienced as mere reports implies that women learn their religion through a man, particularly the husband. Yet the book also shows that the church as represented by Christiana and her sons and an outsider, Mercy, is a welcoming, nurturing, often joyful fellowship.

When Bunyan died he left a legacy of work, especially the five books described above, that has reached around the world and spoken to many classes of people. By trade a tinker, he was also an artist-thinker on profound theological matters.

WORKS CITED

BUNYAN, JOHN. 1765. *A Relation of the Imprisonment of Mr. John Bunyan*. London: James Buckland. Reprinted in *The Works of John Bunyan*, ed. George Offer. Glasgow: Blackie & Son, 1854, i.

—— 1966. *Grace Abounding to the Chief of Sinners and The Pilgrim's Progress from this World to that which is to come*, ed. Roger Sharrock. London: Oxford University Press. (*GA*, *PPI*, *PPII*)

—— 1980a. *The Holy War*, ed. Roger Sharrock and James F. Forrest. Oxford: Clarendon. (*HW*)

—— 1980b. *Some Gospel-truths Opened and A Vindication of Some Gospel-truths Opened, A Few Sighs from Hell*, ed. T. L. Underwood with assistance of Roger Sharrock, in *Miscellaneous Works*. Oxford: Clarendon, i.

—— 1988. *The Life and Death of Mr. Badman*, ed. James F. Forrest and Roger Sharrock. Oxford: Clarendon. (*BM*)

—— 1989. *A Confession of My Faith and A Reason of My Practice*, ed. T. L. Underwood, in *Miscellaneous Works*. Oxford: Clarendon, iv. (*CR*)

DAVIS, J. C. 1986. *Fear, Myth and History: The Ranters and the Historians*. Cambridge: Cambridge University Press.

FURLONG, MONICA. 1975. *Puritan's Progress*. New York: Coward, McCann & Geoghegan.

GREAVES, RICHARD L. 2002. *Glimpses of Glory: John Bunyan and English Dissent*. Stanford, Calif.: Stanford University Press.

HILL, CHRISTOPHER. 1989. *A Tinker and a Poor Man: John Bunyan and His Church, 1628–1688*. New York: Alfred A. Knopf.

JAMES, WILLIAM. 1928. *The Varieties of Religious Experience: A Study in Human Nature*. London: Longmans, Green.

MORTON, A. L. 1970. *The World of the Ranters: Religious Radicalism in the English Revolution*. London: Lawrence & Wishart.

NOYES, ALFRED. 1928. *The Opalescent Parrot*. London: Sheed & Ward.

NUTTALL, GEOFFREY. 1948. *Studies in Christian Enthusiasm: Illustrated from Early Quakerism*. Wallingford, Pa.: Pendle Hill.

FURTHER READING

As an illustration of the wide dispersion of *The Pilgrim's Progress* beyond the limits of English, Isabel Hofmeyr's *The Portable Bunyan: A Transnational History of The Pilgrim's Progress* (Princeton University Press, 2004) with its emphasis on Africa is valuable. Several books of collected essays show diversity of approaches to Bunyan, his milieu, and his works:

COLLMER, ROBERT G. (ed.) 1989. *Bunyan in Our Time*. Kent, Ohio: Kent State University Press.

KEEBLE, N. H. (ed.) 1988. *John Bunyan: Conventicle and Parnassus: Tercentenary Essays*. Oxford: Clarendon.

LAURENCE, ANNE, OWENS, W. R., and SIM, STUART (eds.) 1990. *John Bunyan and His England, 1628–88*. London: Hambledon.

NEWEY, VINCENT (ed.) 1980. *The Pilgrim's Progress: Critical and Historical Views*. Liverpool: Liverpool University Press.

CHAPTER 35

BISHOP BUTLER

LORI BRANCH

ONE of the great ironies of the history of theological writing in England is that Bishop Joseph Butler (1692–1752) comes to us as, in Horace Walpole's words, 'wafted in a cloud of metaphysics', the author of an intellectually rarefied, stylistically stultified, and unattractive theology. In fact, Butler conscientiously refused to pursue eccentric curiosities or engage in speculative theology. Rather he viewed his intellectual projects—scientific in spirit, clouded only by the careful qualifications of his claims—as eminently practical extensions of his pastoral duties as a clergyman. In surveying Butler's works and their impact across the eighteenth and nineteenth centuries, this essay will suggest that in the rise and fall of Butler's influence we see the way in which religion in modernity has tended to become rationalized and secularized into a morality that has no need of faith. In the apologetic quest for rational arguments in favour of Christianity, Butler came to affirm the element of *uncertainty* in religious belief to an extent so disturbing in the Age of Reason that some Christians complained that, rather than helping matters, he had hurt his cause. Certain sceptics even claimed that he had driven them away from belief. Butler's gradual recognition of the subtle ways in which people shape their propensity to believe or not to believe led him from the analysis of natural events that was part and parcel of his analogy between nature and religion, to an interest in church ritual and self-construction. The trajectory of his career finds a mutually illuminating parallel in that of William Wordsworth (1770–1850), who from *Lyrical Ballads'* 'spontaneous overflow of powerful feeling' found himself increasingly interested in the rituals of daily life that shape spontaneous responses, ultimately writing his most historically ambitious work, *Ecclesiastical Sonnets*, on the Church in England, and even offering cautious support to the Tractarians. The irony of each man's career lies in the way that his potentially radical constructivist notions were downplayed and his works co-opted for nearly a century as 'proof' of the truth of Christian revelation. Reduced to philosophy or aesthetics, the startlingly religious elements of Butler's works, like those of Wordsworth's, have most often been underestimated or ignored. This, beyond Butler's contribution to the history of ideas, is the cultural significance of his appeal for the eighteenth and nineteenth centuries: the larger story of faith in modernity masquerading as certainty, misrecognizing itself as an abstract system of propositional truths, and the secularization of religion and theology that results. What our present cultural, intellectual moment affords in the critical reassessment of Butler is the recovery of his full and particular religiousness; that is, his acknowledgment of the process of believing as neither purely rational nor irrational, neither completely logical nor mystical, and a recognition of the way that his own works set the stage for their interpretation in entirely another way.

BUTLER'S MAJOR WORKS: THE ROLLS CHAPEL SERMONS AND *THE ANALOGY OF RELIGION*

> It is come, I know not how, to be taken for granted, by many Persons, that Christianity is not so much as a Subject of Inquiry; but that it is, now at length, discovered to be fictitious. And accordingly they treat it as if, in the present Age, this were an agreed upon Point, among all People of Discernment; and nothing remained, but to set it up as a principal Subject of Mirth and Ridicule.
>
> (Butler, Advertisement to the *Analogy*)

Butler was born in 1692 at Wantage, in Berkshire, to a devout, middling-sort Presbyterian family which intended him for the ministry. After attending the Dissenting academy at Gloucester (which later moved to Tewkesbury), in a decision about which we have almost no information, he converted to the Church of England and pursued an ecclesiastical career. On his ordination in 1718, Butler was appointed to his first position in the church, Preacher to the Rolls Chapel in Chancery Lane, London. His first publication had been an anonymous 1716 edition of his theological correspondence with Samuel Clarke, but the first work that went to press under his name was a collection of homilies from this post, *Fifteen Sermons Preached at the Rolls Chapel*, which appeared in 1726. Perhaps no other volume of sermons has had such a wide secular readership, in large part because the plan of the volume as a whole was that of a carefully worked-out ethical treatise, one that Samuel Taylor Coleridge and Lord Acton considered among the most important in English and greater even than the *Analogy*.

Like the positions of many moral writers of the eighteenth century, Butler's views were implicitly defined against those of Thomas Hobbes (1599–1679). 'Every man is Enemy to every man,' wrote Hobbes in *Leviathan* (1651), and taking 'this inference, made from the Passions', Hobbes contended that the 'known disposition' of mankind is to war, selfishness, and violence: 'to invade and destroy one another' (Hobbes 1651: 1. 13. 185–6). Distasteful as it was, this view of humanity also begged the question of what sort of God—if there be one at all—would have created such creatures or could hold them responsible for 'vices' that were natural to them. Like other moral writers, and like their enemy Hobbes, Butler was greatly influenced by the scientific method and inductive reasoning of an age that stood in awe of the discoveries of Galileo, Kepler, and Newton, and sought similar grounding for religion and theology. As E. C. Mossner (1936a: pp. xii, xi, 240) put it in his classic *Bishop Butler and the Age of Reason*, Butler's writings 'present a cross-section of the later Age of Reason in England', and the main cultural movement to which they testify is the new role of science: 'what Locke is to philosophy, what Newton is to science, what Burke is to politics, Butler is to theology'. 'No writer of the period,' another of Butler's commentators has written, 'more fully represents the true influence of Newton on later thinkers than does Butler himself' (Baker 1923: 10).

It is in this scientific spirit that the Rolls Chapel sermons, foreshadowing Butler's later work, propose to treat morals inductively and pursue that aim through the carefully wrought organization of the volume as a whole. The first three sermons deal with the nature of man and focus on a notion that many writers asserted in contradistinction to Hobbes, that virtue consists in following nature and vice in deviating from it, not vice versa. For Butler, a human being is a microcosm of the natural world, driven by two great forces—rational self-love and benevolence—managed by the watchful eye of conscience, which Butler also calls the 'principle of reflection'. The other sermons in the collection address this conscientious balance between benevolence and self-love: in the governance of the tongue (Sermon IV), in compassion (V and VI), self-deceit (X, exemplified by the character of Balaam in VII), resentment and forgiveness (VIII and IX), in the love of neighbour (XI and XII), the love of God (XIII and XIV), and the ignorance of man (XV).[1]

In these early sermons, we glimpse the contours of the work upon which Butler's fame and influence were largely to rest: namely, a naturalistic account of the human being along the lines of the natural world portrayed by the science of the day, and yet, crucially, one in which benevolence and conscience played a significant, helpful role. That account Butler put forward in *The Analogy of Religion, Natural and Revealed, to the Constitution and Course of Nature*, published in 1736. After a brief 'Advertisement' and Introduction, the treatise consists of a diptych—'Of Natural Religion' and

---

[1] In arguing for a notion of balance between self-love and benevolence, and therefore against the polarity of interested and disinterested actions which was characteristic of both cynical and sentimental ethical writers, Butler nevertheless sets off down the path that many eighteenth-century British moral philosophers—Shaftesbury, Hutcheson, Smith, down to Bentham—also follow, making benevolence one's 'true interest' and ending in the utilitarian notion of virtue calculable as the 'greatest good for the greatest numbers'.

'Of Revealed Religion'—followed by two shorter dissertations, 'Of Personal Identity' (the most widely anthologized of Butler's writings today) and 'Of the Nature of Virtue'. The Introduction announces Butler's three great themes: the centrality of probability to human life and reasoning, the impossibility of determining a priori the conditions which nature or religion ought to fulfil, and the analogy between nature and religion. It also sets the tenor of the work as a humble account of the reaches of human uncertainty, made palatable by notions of likelihood and of a reasonable similitude between observable nature and religion.

In this spirit of painstaking, humble defence of the reasonableness of Christianity, Butler was responding not only to an increasing faith in science and to the scepticism that seems perennially to spring from empiricism, but to the religious fallout of seventeenth-century Europe and of England in particular. A new discourse of religion had emerged in the seventeenth century, born of disgust with the wars of religion as much as of Renaissance Platonism, and best embodied in Lord Herbert of Cherbury's *De Veritate* (1624). In reaction to the Thirty Years War and the widespread desire to circumnavigate treacherous theological controversies, 'religion' in English Protestant hands was, in Graham Ward's terms, simultaneously 'globalized and privatized'; it became increasingly abstract, universalized, and private, and less and less particular. The early modern mind/body duality which we see in Descartes, and which Locke extended into the political realm, opened up a newly secular imaginative space, and the sort of universalistic, utilitarian logic that is fundamental to capitalism increasingly pervaded other areas of thought and behaviour, contributing to religion's increasing vagueness and privatization. In such contexts, particular doctrines about the nature of God or Christ seem less and less *necessary*; what seems beneficial about religion, rather, are the Christian civic virtues that enable capitalism to flourish (Ward 2003: 52–65). This rationalized, generalized understanding of 'religion' ultimately gave rise to the academic study of philosophy of religion and comparative religion, but in the late seventeenth and early eighteenth centuries it already manifested itself in the rise of Deism, a belief in a benevolent Deity, stripped of Christian particularity, that set the cosmos spinning according to rational, benign principles.

It is this transformation of and challenge to traditional Christianity, in the twin forms of Deism and scientifically and philosophically inflected scepticism, that the *Analogy* seeks to respond to. To Deists, Butler essentially replies that their optimism is prey to the same sceptical responses as Christianity; they are no more immune from belief, he argues, than are Christians. To sceptics, on the other hand, he replies that *probability*, however short it might fall of mathematical certainty, is based in reasonable reflection on experience and is central to all human endeavour, and he locates probability's roots in an admittedly humbler form of argument than strict demonstration, that is analogy. Lack of certain knowledge should not (and, he points out, in practice does not) stop us from all manner of necessary action. For many, this was a compelling line of reasoning. James Boswell recounts that Samuel Johnson once answered a sceptic by asking him to consider the case of a man who is ill: 'I call two physicians; they differ in opinion. I am not to lie down and die between them. I must do something'—or, as Boswell (1993: 180–1) put it, 'in short, he gave him more familiarly the able and fair reasoning of Butler's *Analogy*. Johnson's reply is true to the spirit of Butler's aim, to show that both nature and revealed religion are systems designed by God that can illuminate each other, enough so that persons can make reasonable decisions and take actions in the world. Working out these ideas, Butler argues, for instance, in Part 1 of the *Analogy*, that belief in life in a future state is natural and reasonable based on our human experience. Because it is natural for creatures to live at one time with different capabilities from those they possess at later times, he contends, the analogy of religion makes it credible to think that we may exist after death in a state very different from our present condition. Butler extends this sort of reasoning to argue for the naturalness of notions of rewards and punishments in the next life (based in our foresight of consequences to our actions; Part 1, ch. 2), the perfect morality of this future reward and punishment (1. 3), and the notion of earthly life as a period of trial and discipline for the future state (1. 4–5).[2]

The final chapter of the opening section of the *Analogy*—'Of the Government of God, considered as a Scheme or Constitution, imperfectly comprehended'—is in many senses the heart of the book. It sounds the full exposition of Butler's great theme hinted at in the fifteenth Rolls Chapel sermon, and the one that makes him most potentially radical: that of human reason's incomplete comprehension of reality. God's government of the natural world, explains Butler, is 'a Scheme, quite beyond our Comprehension':

In this great Scheme of the natural World, Individuals have various peculiar Relations to other Individuals of their own Species. And whole Species are, we find, variously related to other Species, upon this Earth. Nor do we know how much farther these Kinds of Relations may extend.... There seems indeed nothing, from whence we can so much as make a Conjecture, whether all Creatures, Actions and Events, throughout the whole of Nature, have Relations to each other.... Nor can we give the whole Account of any one thing whatever: of all its Causes, Ends, and necessary Adjuncts; ... And things seemingly the most insignificant imaginable, are perpetually observed to be necessary Conditions to other things of the greatest Importance: So that any one thing whatever, may, for ought we know to the contrary, be a necessary Condition to any other. The natural World then, and natural Government of it, being such an incomprehensible Scheme; so incomprehensible, that a Man must, really, in the literal Sense, know nothing at all, who is not sensible of his Ignorance in it: this immediately suggests, and strongly shews the Credibility, that the moral World and Government of it may be so too. (Butler 1736: 1. 7. 181–3)

If there are things about the natural world of which we are ignorant, then by analogy there well may be aspects of God's moral government that are likewise incomprehensible to us. Defending the various means which God may use to accomplish divine goodness and justice, Butler stresses not man's total but his *partial* ignorance.

---

[2] There is still no standard modern edition of Butler's complete works. Most commentators use the edition by J. H. Bernhard, *The Works of Bishop Butler* (London: 1900), which retains Butler's original paragraphs and their numeration. I have elected to use editions printed in Butler's lifetime, accessible at most research libraries through Eighteenth-Century Collections Online. For the *Analogy*, citations refer to part, chapter, and page (rather than paragraph) number, as paragraph numbers vary in subsequent editions.

Such a line of reasoning provides an answer to objections to the world's injustices, without abandoning our rational faculties; we simply must keep in mind, Butler suggests, that we may not be able to judge of the whole from the admittedly small portion of events we witness.

After clearing a discursive space for reasonable if not irrefutable religion, Part II of the *Analogy* then turns to the revealed religion of Christianity. Revealed religion confirms and republishes natural religion, he argues, such that anyone appalled by the irreligion and amorality of the world around him should take comfort in this confirmation of his moral sensibility, by prophecies and miracles. To Butler's mind, revealed religion and the institutional church remind people of the reality of natural religion and keep them mindful of it. Christianity entails, however, both moral and positive precepts, moral precepts being those naturally revealed, and positive precepts being those doctrines that we could not deduce from nature, including the Trinity, Christ's divinity and incarnation, his sacrifice for us, his mediation between God and man, and the role of the Holy Spirit in the renewal of human nature.

Crucially for Butler, the positive precepts of Christianity are important as *means* serving religion's ultimately *moral* ends (see e.g. ibid. 2. 1). This prioritization of morality as the heart of religion, however, leaves Butler to explain what could be seen as the superfluous role of the supernatural in Christianity. A great deal of the second half of the *Analogy* is thus devoted to understanding the place of miracles and prophecies *vis-à-vis* natural religion. Butler affirms that nothing about the analogy of nature mitigates against revelation and miracles, but rather that extraordinary events within nature parallel miracles in revealed religion. Chapter 3 of this section recapitulates Butler's theme of the limits of human reason: given the idea of a divine revelation, the analogy of nature would suggest, he argues, that it is credible and even probable that we would be incompetent judges of it and that many things in revelation would appear strange and objectionable. Put another way, nature itself is greatly different from what we might a priori have expected it to be (one argument that surely has grown stronger since Butler's day), and thus in religion, too, we should, as it were, expect the unexpected, or anticipate that religion would reveal surprising and even counterintuitive truths. The pertinent and all-consuming question about Christianity, then, is not whether it is what one might expect but whether it is in fact a real revelation of divinity.

It is in the face of this ultimate question, Butler claims, that we are to make the greatest use of our reason. For 'the Faculty of Reason', despite all its shortcomings, Butler famously reveres as 'the candle of the Lord within us' (Part 2, Conclusion, 428).[3] Since in Butler's eyes nothing is objectionable about Christian morality, Christianity can be rationally discredited as a revelation only if there is no proof of its attesting miracles or prophecies. And so it is to these potential objections to Christianity that he turns the latter part of his analysis. He considers at length

---

[3] Butler's footnote identifies this famous phrase as a quotation from Prov. 20: 27, which in the Authorised Version reads 'The spirit of man is the candle of the LORD, searching all the inward parts of the belly.' Butler's adaptation of 'the spirit of man' to 'the Faculty of Reason' is itself noteworthy.

Christ's mediatorship as Prophet, Priest (and Sacrifice), and King, arguing along the way our inability to judge the necessity of Christ's mediation, the common occurrence of the innocent suffering for the guilty, and the virtuous nature of Christ's voluntary suffering (2. 5). In the seventh chapter he evaluates the miracles, prophecies and other evidences that support Christianity as a genuinely divine revelation. Christianity was accepted on the basis of its miracles, he argues, in the age in which those miracles were to have taken place, and given the great prejudice and penalties against accepting Christianity in those days, this makes its miracles quite credible. In the end, Butler acknowledges that his argument is a particularly circumscribed one, seeking not to demonstrate the irrefutable truth and certainty of Christian teaching, but rather to show that the Christian religion is not altogether unreasonable, impossible, or incompatible with the notions of knowledge and the natural world that had grown up in the late seventeenth and early eighteenth centuries.

BUTLER'S LATER CAREER AND THE 'CHARGE ON EXTERNAL RELIGION'

In the 1720s, Butler's Rolls Chapel sermons had attracted the attention of Queen Caroline, and Bolingbroke recounts that she was even more impressed by the *Analogy* and studied it enough to understand the intricacies of its argument. She drew Butler into her intellectual circles and on her deathbed in 1737 received communion from his hands, recommending him to the King for preferment. In 1738 George II followed her wishes, and two years after the publication of the *Analogy*, Butler was consecrated bishop of Bristol, a poorly paid post which, after 1740, he occupied together with the deanery of St Paul's. A decade later and only two years before his death, Butler was made bishop of Durham. These last fourteen years of his life, occupied not so much with philosophical writing as with the pastoral concerns of priests and parishes, brought Butler's intellectual work to an interesting and little noted turn, and the last two years at the vibrant See of Durham certainly loom large in this transformation. In his thirteenth Rolls Chapel sermon, Butler (1726: 256) had addressed 'the Love of God' in order to prevent readers from concluding that for him religion was 'so very reasonable, as to have nothing to do with the Heart and Affections'. But Butler's religion as it appeared in his writings was indeed quite rationalized, and even utilitarian in its religiously moralistic way; hours spent reading the *Analogy* can make the Christian God seem a lifeless conclusion to an argument, and arguments for religion rarely make people more devout. After spending his early career defending the faith in arguments and propositions, Butler seems eventually to have felt the need for some other method to rouse people to a living piety and a daily recollection of their faith. He made clear in his notorious meeting with John Wesley that enthusiasm and revivalism were not, to his mind, the way to real, lasting spiritual awakening. By the time he was in his late fifties, serving in Durham cathedral, famous for its impressive and well-attended choral services throughout a century when the worship of the Established Church notoriously languished, Butler became convinced that it was the liturgical life of the parish that cultivated the piety and religious consciousness that his age seemed to have lost.

In 1751, the year after his transfer to the bishopric of Durham and the year before his death, Butler delivered to the clergy of his diocese what would become known as his charge on 'External Religion', which scandalized not a few readers when it appeared in print and elicited accusations of popery that would be resurrected eighty years later in the heat of controversy over the Oxford Movement. Butler had perhaps foreshadowed the charge's line of reasoning in the *Analogy*, by emphasizing (in 1. 5) that practical habits of virtue are formed and strengthened by repeated acts of virtue, but in this address he went much further. Butler began this sermon, which he titled 'A Charge Deliver'd to the Clergy at the Primary Visitation of Durham', in much the same way he began the *Analogy*, lamenting the general decay of religion in his day and the age's 'zeal for negation' or scepticism. But rather than combating disbelief with argument as he had done before, Butler turned his attention to the decline of religious faith in itself. Twice in the charge he refers to the influence of religion as 'wearing out' in men's minds and hearts, language that evokes the image of a printed or written text that is rubbed out with use or of clothing that is tattered with wear, and so pointing to the need continually to mend, remember, and reinscribe it, to construct or perform it (Butler 1751: 5, 18). Over and over again Butler stresses that it is the business of the clergy to stir up the devotion of the people, mainly through common conversation rather than sermons or argument. Revered as the great answerer of sceptics, Butler here likens answering sceptical objections in a sermon to encouraging someone to manage their finances prudently by 'stating formally the several Objections which Men of Gaiety or Speculation have made against Prudence, and the Advantages which they pleasantly tell us Folly has over it' (ibid. 13).

The want of religion among the generality of people, Butler says, is due not so much to speculative disbelief or active denial of religion, as to 'Thoughtlessness and the common Temptations of Life'. 'Your chief Business therefore,' he tells his clergy, 'is to endeavour to beget a practical Sense of it upon their Hearts':

And this is to be done, by keeping up as we are able, the Form and Face of Religion with Decency and Reverence, and in such a Degree as to bring the Thoughts of Religion often to their Minds; and then endeavouring to make this Form more and more subservient to promote the Reality and Power of it. The Form of Religion may indeed be where there is little of the Thing itself; but the Thing itself cannot be preserved amongst Mankind without the Form. And this Form frequently occurring in some Instance or other of it, will be a frequent Admonition to bad Men to Repent, and to good Men to grow better; and also be the Means of their doing so.   (Ibid. 1751: 13–14)

Beyond the scandal this sermon ignited, Butler in it effects a remarkable and almost complete reversal, within the span of one lifetime, of Puritan and Dissenting sentiments about worship. Butler's parents and grandparents, like other Dissenters, refused to conform to the Established Church after the Restoration not only because of the episcopacy but because of the Book of Common Prayer, and 'forms' of prayer increasingly bore the brunt of criticism as Nonconformists gravitated either to minimalist forms of worship or to spontaneous 'free prayer'. In a dramatic turnabout, this son of Presbyterian parents and pupil of an intellectually rigorous Dissenting academy came full circle, ninety years after the Act of Uniformity, arguing as bishop for the limitations of argument and the benefits of forms to cultivating a vibrant, living faith. More drastically still, he appealed to Islam and Catholicism to make his case:

That which men have accounted Religion in the several Countries of the World, generally speaking, has had a great and conspicuous Part in all Publick Appearances, and the Face of it been kept up with great Reverence throughout all Ranks, from the highest to the lowest; not only upon occasional Solemnities, but also in the daily Course of Behaviour. In the Heathen World, their Superstition was the chief Subject of Statuary, Sculpture, Painting, and Poetry. It mixt itself with Business, Civil Forms, Diversions, Domestick Entertainments, and every Part of common Life. The Mahometans are obliged to short Devotions five Times between Morning and Evening. In Roman-catholick Countries, People cannot pass a Day without having Religion recalled to their Thoughts, by some or other Memorial of it; by some Ceremony or public religious Form occurring in their Way: Besides their frequent Holidays, the Short Prayers they are daily called to, and the occasional Devotions injoyned by Confessors. By these Means their Superstition sinks deep into the Minds of the People, and their Religion also into the Minds of such among them as are serious and well-disposed.   (Ibid. 14–15)

More striking even than Butler's appreciation of Muslim and Catholic ritual is his implicit awareness of the extent to which British life and its emerging public sphere were both secular and secularizing. In the modern organization of business and productivity, Butler notes, people easily pass entire days without visible, public reminders of their religion. The paucity of attention to the church he explicitly connects to the appetite for the material luxuries of the day. 'In the present turn of the Age, one may observe a wonderful Frugality in every Thing which has respect to Religion,' he laments, 'and Extravagance in every Thing else' (ibid. 17).

In this increasingly secular daily life, Butler admonishes ministers to remind people to pray of their own initiative throughout the day—morning and evening, in family and in secret, at meals and in one's work—and to promote public prayer on great feasts and other occasions and to infuse power and life into their communal services. They must, he says,

Admonish them to take Heed, that they mean what they say in their Prayers, that their Thoughts and Intentions go along with their Words, that they really in their Heart exert and exercise before GOD the Affections they express with their Mouth. Teach them, not that external Religion is nothing, for this is not true in any Sense; it being scarce possible, but that it will lay some sort of Restraint upon a Mans Morals; and 'tis moreover of good Effect with respect to the World about him. But teach them that Regard to one Duty will in no Sort atone for the Neglect of any other. Endeavour to raise in their Hearts such a Sense of GOD as shall be an habitual, ready Principle of Reverence, Love, Gratitude, Hope, Trust, Resignation, and Obedience. Exhort them to make use of every Circumstance, which brings the Subject of Religion at all before them, to turn their Hearts habitually to Him; to recollect seriously the Thought of his Presence *in whom they live and move and have their Being*, and by a short Act of their Mind devote themselves to his Service.—If, for Instance, Persons would accustom themselves to be thus admonished by the very Sight of a CHURCH, could it be called Superstition?   (Ibid. 22–3)

With that rhetorical question Butler answers, it is important to notice, not sceptics or Deists, but Protestants more broadly, whose sensibilities seem at least as responsible as scepticism for the decline in faith that Butler laments. Earlier in the charge he had noted in passing how the Reformers had considered various rituals and observances 'Wrong and Superstitious' and so abolished them, and thus 'reduced the Form of Religion to great Simplicity...nor left any Thing more of what was external in Religion than was, in a Manner, necessary' (ibid. 15). The problem with this necessitarian line of thinking, Butler came to think, was that this bare minimum is so easily neglected by so many, and 'Thus they have no customary Admonition, no public Call to recollect the Thoughts of GOD and RELIGION from one Sunday to another' (ibid.). By the end of 'A Charge', it is hard to say who or what is more to blame for the much-noted decline of religion in eighteenth-century British life: his old enemy, scepticism, or the distraction of worldly luxury, or the Reformers who began the process of removing religion from the forms of daily communal worship and the ritual year.

Also remarkable here is how close Butler came, by the end of his life, to some of the most pressing themes in our contemporary academic conversations about religion. The French sociologist of religion Danièle Hervieu-Léger has argued for a definition of religion that takes into account a decisive transformation of Western religion in modernity. Though she argues that the essential characteristics of religion in modernity are fragmentation, individualization, and lack of mediation by a community or religious institution, she observes, somewhat as Butler did, that pre-modern religion involved performative forms of believing and processes of self-formation that connect the individual to a lineage of belief across history and a living community of believers in time, notably ritual and rite (Hervieu-Léger 2001: 35, 83, 88, 123). Not unlike Butler in his account of reasoned uncertainty, philosophers and literary theorists are increasingly concerned with understanding faith *as faith* and not as knowledge or a system of propositions as it came to be understood in the Reformation and Enlightenment.[4] In a similar vein, the anthropologist Talal Asad (2003: 200–1) has suggested that new scholarship should concern itself with understanding how, when, and by whom the categories of religion and the secular are mutually defined—implying that in this mutual definition religion in the West has undergone a profound rationalization and secularization. In the scope of his career, Butler seems to have developed a certain awareness of these changes, articulating important insights as to the limitations (though not impotence) of reason as well as to the performative nature of faith and knowledge that reason's limitations both make

---

[4] I have in mind here works of Jacques Derrida, John Caputo, and Slavoj Žižek.

possible and necessitate. This awareness was not, however, to be his legacy to the eighteenth and nineteenth centuries.

'IRREFRAGABLE PROOF': BUTLER'S EIGHTEENTH- AND NINETEENTH-CENTURY REPUTATION

> Sacred to the memory of Joseph Butler, D.C.L., twelve years Bishop of this diocese, and afterwards bishop of Durham... Others had established the historical and prophetical grounds of the Christian religion and that sure testimony of its truth, which is found in its perfect adaptation to the heart of man. It was reserved for him to develop its analogy to the Constitution and Course of Nature. And laying his strong foundations in the depth of that great argument, there to construct another and irrefragable proof; thus rendering Philosophy subservient to Faith; and finding in outward and visible things the type and evidence of those Within The Veil.
>
> (Butler's epitaph, written by Robert Southey and erected at Bristol Cathedral in 1834)

William Seward, in his *Anecdotes of Some Distinguished Persons*, marvelled that the 'abstruse work' of the *Analogy* was a favourite book with Queen Caroline, who claimed that she read every day at breakfast 'that book which Dr. Hoadley, Bishop of Winchester, said he never could look into without making his head ache' (Seward 1796: 356). The *Analogy* elicited similarly diverse reactions from its first appearance, a fact which itself speaks to the perceived salience of the challenges to Christianity which it essayed, albeit to some too painstakingly, to address. The erroneous notion that Butler's work went unnoticed in his day and was acclaimed only a century later can perhaps be traced to Leslie Stephen's article on Butler in the *Dictionary of National Biography*. It was remedied in Mossner's *Bishop Butler and the Age of Reason* in 1936, which documented the stir the *Analogy* created almost instantly at court as well as in literary and theological circles and is still the account of Butler's influence which studies of Butler both acknowledge and qualify. In 1737 David Hume was answering Butler's arguments one by one in letters to Henry Home, and in the 1740s Henry Fielding's *Tom Jones* shows familiarity with Butler's *Sermons*, and Edward Young's *The Complaint: or, Night Thoughts* was probably influenced by the *Analogy*'s concerns and approaches. The Rolls Chapel sermons and the *Analogy* each went through four editions in Butler's lifetime and, Mossner (1936*a*: 178–86) points out, by the time of his death in 1752, Butler was already regarded by his contemporaries as something of a champion of the faith against sceptics and Deists who, like Hume and

Henry Dodwell, nonetheless highly respected him. In the 1750s Butler was, in Mossner's words, already 'coming to be esteemed popularly as the perfect Church-man', and in 1755 both the Sermons and the *Analogy* were included in the republished *Advice to a Young Student* as recommended reading at Cambridge (ibid. 186, 187–8). Abroad, the *Analogy* was translated into German in 1756, and at home in the decades that followed, writers from Richard Price, Thomas Reid, Dugald Stewart, and James Beattie were all influenced by his moral thought. Samuel Johnson corresponded with him, and Butler can be seen as the forerunner of the Romantic theological tradition of Coleridge, who extolled his Sermons as 'full of thought and sound views of theology' (Harris 1988: 196; Mossner 1936b: 207).

Pointing to the scores of editions of Butler's work in the United States and Great Britain in the late eighteenth and early nineteenth centuries, Mossner (1936a: 197, 201–3) also observes that 'the general tendencies of the eighteenth century were to become accentuated in the nineteenth, until before mid-century Butler had attained the apparent security of an acknowledged classic', mainly as required reading in moral philosophy at Cambridge and Oxford, beginning in the 1830s and meant to ward off Benthamism. Butler's ascendancy was further secured with the publication of the famous *Bridgewater Treatises* (1833–6), the ultimate exposition of the argument from design which attempted to reconcile theology with science, combining the approach of the *Analogy* with Paley's *Natural Theology* in examining 'the power, wisdom, and goodness of God as manifested in the Creation'. In Mossner's account, the 1830s to 1860s marked the period of Butler's greatest adulation. As one American professor would confess in 1837, 'We do not propose to review the writings of Bishop Butler. We should almost as soon think of reviewing the writings of the Apostle Paul' (ibid. 205).

As much needed as Mossner's corrective was, it nonetheless had its shortcomings. Mossner embedded his account of Butler's influence in a larger meta-narrative of the 'decline of reason'—the decline of abstract, mathematical, inductive reason, and the rise of empirical, scientific experimentalism which, in his account, generated two responses: scepticism, represented by Hume, and enthusiasm, epitomized by John Wesley. Mossner saw Butler as indicative both of a reaction against the prevalent seventeenth-century doctrine of the sufficiency of reason in all aspects of human life, including in religion, and of the new leaning toward empirical science. And in Mossner's story, Butler is in part to blame for the demise of reasonable religion which had in the seventeenth century, he says, given us religious toleration as well as Latitudinarianism and its logical offshoot, Deism (ibid. 125, 177). Mossner (ibid. 124) went so far as to speak of 'Butler's attack on reason', which can be fully understood only in the paired contexts of 'the assaults' of the agnostic David Hume and the enthusiast John Wesley.

Mossner's narrative does not take into account, however, what in the intervening three-quarters of a century have become fairly accepted concepts in eighteenth-century studies: the empirical nature of emotionalism and sentiment itself, and the larger continuities of inductive and deductive thought. In a variety of eighteenth-century contexts and genres, sentiments and emotions were taken as empirical sense data, providing evidence alternatively of spiritual grace, of refined sensibilities, or of the morality of particular actions. In this sense, Wesleyan enthusiasm may be seen not as the refusal of reason but an outgrowth of it, the deliberate pursuit of religious and subjective experiences testifying to the action of divine grace. Likewise there are by now well-rehearsed difficulties with regarding empiricism as superseding rationalism; writers from the Restoration onwards almost never use one of these modes of reasoning to the exclusion of the other, and scholarship has come more often to emphasize what inductive and deductive strategies share, namely belief in the possibility of certain, propositional truth and spiralling, doubt-inducing standards for confirming and proving that knowledge. Again, in this sense, Humean scepticism, like Butler's careful self-qualification, is no repudiation of reason, but its recognition of an impasse within itself. Similarly, Butler's form of reason and increasing cultural faith in empirical forms of truth-validation share with seventeenth-century thought the location of meaning and truth in abstract laws and systems. The larger cultural significance of Butler's work, then, is not its overturning of seventeenth-century reason, but its fulfilment of it, its working out of its aims and logics, and in turn, the cultural work that Butler's writings were perceived to perform. Within Butler's work, we see an honest appraisal from within an increasingly demanding empirical reason that complete certainty is not to be had. But without, we find something fascinating: for all his insistence on uncertainty, Butler's work is taken up and championed by religious readers for over a century precisely as the *proof of* religion, a surprising pattern that Butler's works themselves entrench: for as much as they affirm his awareness of uncertainty, they also continually reference the logical process of analogy as 'Proof' of 'Religious Truth'.

For most of the first two centuries after their appearance, the appeal of Butler's writings lay not in their measured claims to probability, but in their scientific approach, in Butler's battling with sceptics and Deists on their own ground and so giving religion the aura of reasonable, scientific validity that seemed ever more necessary for it to be meaningful at all. Butler's insistence on the imperfection of human comprehension of God's system of governing the world was washed out in the blinding appeal of a probability that was ultimately indistinguishable from what Southey glorified in Butler's epitaph as 'irrefragable proof'. Perhaps the most egregious example of this co-optation of Butler's views is Thomas Comber's 1748 tract *An Attempt to Shew the Evidence of Christianity Equal to a Strict Metaphysical Demonstration*, which in a mere sixteen pages offers eight absolute demonstrations—each punctuated by a resounding '*Q. E. D.*'—that Christianity is and *must* 'CERTAINLY', 'INFALLIBLY', 'NECESSARILY' be true (Comber 1748: 9–13). Comber's lengthy subtitle mentions Butler by name and claims to pay proper regard to Butler's sentiments, casuistically explaining how his own 'strict metaphysical demonstration' is in no way inconsistent with Butler's humbler reliance on analogy and probability!

For less bombastic readers and writers, too, Butler functioned as the '*Q. E. D.*' of the Christian faith, a writer to whom one turned for assurance that sceptical objections had been dealt with once and for all. Examples of the evangelical, didactic, and even devotional use of Butler abound across the eighteenth and nineteenth centuries; Edmund Burke is a case in point. When James Barry, the historical painter whom Burke patronized and had educated in Italy, showed signs of wavering in his faith, 'Burke "put into his hands and strongly recommended him to read" Butler's *Analogy*', and Barry was so impressed with what he read that he placed Butler in the group of divines in his picture of 'Elysium' (Mossner 1936*a*: 189). Hugh Blair, who in his *Lectures on Rhetoric and Belles Lettres* complained of the style of Butler's 'abstract philosophical essays', in his sermons considered that the rational validity of scepticism had been outright demolished by the 'masterly hand of Bishop Butler' (Blair 1785: ii. 329; 1790: iii. 376). In *Strictures on the Modern System of Female Education*, Hannah More (1800: i. 214) recommended that all serious young women should read the *Analogy*, alongside other solid stuff like Watt's or Duncan's *Logic* and Locke's *Essay Concerning Human Understanding*, profitable substitutes for 'enervating and absurd books' and rational remedies for the ills of 'English Sentiment, French Philosophy, Italian Love-Songs, and fantastic German imagery and magic wonders'.

Perhaps the most delightful and surprising tribute to Butler's growing popularity as the one who proves Christianity, and one not generally cited, was the *Analogy*'s having been rendered in verse. In 1793, 'A Poem on the Analogy between Natural and Revealed Religion' occupied thirty-six closely printed quarto pages of the Reverend George Butt's *Poems in Two Volumes*. Butt (1741–95) was a Church of England incumbent, ultimately of Kidderminster, who made his literary name with *Isaiah Versified* (1784) and published prolifically in many genres, mainly works of kindly didacticism like 'Stories on the Church Catechism'. Butt was known for his animated pulpit style and artless charm, and in contrast to the political ambitions of many clergy he cultivated relationships with people both in and outside his flock, such that many of Kidderminster's numerous Dissenters could be seen in his church on festival days (Aston 2004: 2). In the lengthy Preface to his adaptation of Butler, Butt (1793: ii. 200, 11) wrote that this 'defence' of Christianity, an attempt to make Butler's 'golden book' of the *Analogy* 'more forcible and sublime' through 'imagination and warmth of expression', was the 'purposed literary labour (in the poetic form) of my whole life'. It was, he claimed, the first half of a grand scheme which would be completed by a later prose work that would '*display*' Christianity (ibid. 199)—presumably the religious novel *Felicia* which he was penning at the time of his death and which his daughter Mary Martha Sherwood published in 1824 as *The Spanish Daughter*. In the 1790s, rendering Butler's proof of Christianity in poetry that could penetrate the heart seemed for Butt as practical a pastoral duty as writing the *Analogy* had been for Butler.

In the early nineteenth century, Butler's influence grew, providing a much-needed tool against utilitarian thought in the universities and inspiring the key figures of the Oxford Movement. The logical conclusion of Tractarianism in Roman Catholicism contributed to Butler's falling esteem, but as Mossner (1936*a*: 205–28) points out, the larger reason for the decline was the rise of evolutionary science and the *Analogy*'s unsuitability for addressing the challenges it posed to Christian teleology. One important supplement to Mossner's narrative has been Jane Garnett's essay on the pattern of Butler's reputation over the second half of the nineteenth century, 'Bishop

Butler and the *Zeitgeist*. Garnett argues that in the latter part of the nineteenth century a new, nuanced appreciation of Butler arose, particularly of his positive recognition 'of the fragmentary nature of human perception, and his emphasis on the value of reasoning from probability'. Among at least a few thinkers at the century's end, 'Butler's works were seen as significant precisely because they did *not* pretend to constitute an absolute system, and indeed because they argued against excessive confidence in systems' (Garnett 1992: 64, 96, my emphasis).

While it might be tempting to end an account of Butler's reception as Garnett does, highlighting what seems like a more authentic appreciation of his thought, that view must be balanced by tracing that part of Butler's heritage which seems both to brush his writings against the grain and yet to share with them important continuities. The last great nineteenth-century thinker to be substantially influenced by Butler was Matthew Arnold. In *God and the Bible* Arnold would confess that 'my obligations of all kinds to this deep and strenuous spirit are very great', and next to John Henry Newman, Butler is the most quoted theological writer in Arnold's religious works (Harris 1988: 197, 193). In 'Matthew Arnold, Bishop Joseph Butler, and the Foundation of Religious Faith', Terry Harris delineates the precise extent of Butler's influence on Arnold and also where they part ways. While Arnold located himself in the rationalistic tradition of Butler's *Analogy*, he diverged from both Butler and Coleridge on their acceptance of uncertainty and the necessity of faith, seeking a basis for Christianity, in Arnold's words, 'in something which can be verified, instead of in something which has to be assumed' (ibid. 195). The tug from probability towards certainty is the force that finally splits Arnold from Butler: 'Arnold cannot accept Butler's proposal to act on probability because in Butler's system there "can be nothing demonstrable or experimental, and therefore clearly known"' (ibid. 203). 'Two things about the Christian religion must surely be clear to anybody with eyes in his head,' Arnold (1883: p. xi) opined in *God and the Bible*: 'One is, that men cannot do without it; the other, that they cannot do with it as it is'—namely, with its stories and teachings growing less credible by the day in the light of contemporary philosophy, science, and textual criticism. Ultimately this desire to reconstruct or rehabilitate Christianity led Arnold to 'replac[e] Christian theology with a Christian ideal based on morality' (Harris 1988: 204, 200). Where Butler, Coleridge, and Newman allowed for what Harris calls transcendental faith, Arnold did not. But crucially, 'Arnold still discovered in Butler a foundation for his own reconstruction of Christianity'—its 'natural truth', its fundamental morality, and its rational defence through experiential verification (ibid. 208). Famously, Arnold's favourite form of experiential verification would be the poetic, and he inaugurated the secularization of Wordsworth mentioned earlier when he so vehemently rejected those who fail to see Wordsworth's '*poetic* truth' and instead insist on extrapolating from Wordsworth 'an ethical system, as distinctive and capable of systematic exposition as Bishop Butler's' (Arnold, 1898: pp. xx, xviii). Arnold wanted an ethical system as systematic as Butler's, but free of faith and completely verifiable—by the new secular, ethical empiricism of literature.

The deep connection between Butler and the Arnold who ultimately parted ways from him was their shared preference for certainty over belief and the failure to imagine any benefits of faith as opposed to certainty in religion or morality, which subsequently collapse into one. The trajectory of Butler's influence was determined by the desire he shared for rational certainty, and in spite of his humble insistence on *un*certainty—an erasure invited, it might be argued, by his rationalist approach itself. We learn from the pattern of Butler's reception history what is perhaps the greatest risk faith runs in defending itself in an age of reason: in following the apostle's dictum, it must be ready to give an account for its hope, but without that account losing the very character of hope and faith. In Butler's life and works we glimpse the cost of the rationalization of faith and the de-Christianization of Christianity: when the self is conceived of as both an object in the given world and a scientific observer of that world, it becomes impossible to conceive of religion, ritual, and sacrament as constructing or even shaping the self in any positive way, and, incapable of such shaping or transformation, the individual Christian life can no longer be thought of as 'irrefragable proof' of Christianity. Without martyrdom, miracles, or monasticism, the modern religious subject as we see it taking shape in Butler's writings is less and less a believer, and increasingly a subject of and to knowledge.

WORKS CITED

ARNOLD, MATTHEW. 1883 [1875]. *God and the Bible: A Review of Objections to 'Literature and Dogma'*. New York: Macmillan.

—— (ed.) 1892. *The Poems of Wordsworth*. New York: Thomas Y. Crowell.

ASAD, TALAL. 2003. *Formations of the Secular: Christianity, Islam, Modernity*. Stanford: Stanford University Press.

ASTON, NIGEL. 2004. 'Butt, George (1741–1795)'. *Oxford Dictionary of National Biography*. Oxford: Oxford University Press. <http://www.oxforddnb.com/view/article/4221>, accessed 16 March 2005.

BAKER, ALBERT. 1923. *Bishop Butler*. London: SPCK.

BLAIR, HUGH. 1785. *Lectures on Rhetoric and Belles Lettres*. 3 vols. London.

—— 1790. *Sermons, by Hugh Blair*. 3 vols. London.

BOSWELL, JAMES. 1993 [1786]. *The Journal of a Tour to the Hebrides*. With Samuel Johnson, *A Journey to the Western Islands of Scotland*, ed., with intro., and notes, Peter Levi. New York: Penguin.

BUTLER, JOSEPH. 1726. *Fifteen Sermons Preached at the Rolls Chapel*. London: W. Botham.

—— 1736. *The Analogy of Religion, Natural and Revealed, to the Constitution and Course of Nature. To which are added Two brief Dissertations: I. Of Personal Identity. II. Of the Nature of Virtue*. 2nd edn., corrected. London: John & Paul Knapton.

—— 1751. *A Charge Deliver'd to the Clergy, at the Primary Visitation of the Diocese of Durham, In the Year, M DCC LI*. Durham: I. Lane.

BUTT, GEORGE. 1793. *Poems in Two Volumes*. Kidderminster: G. Gower.

COMBER, THOMAS. 1748. *An Attempt to Shew the Evidence of Christianity Equal to a Strict Metaphysical Demonstration, Wherein Proper Regard is paid to the Sentiments of those excellent Writers Mr. Hooker, Mr. Chillingworth, Dr. Rogers, Bishop Butler, Dr. Conybeare, &c. on this important Subject*. 3rd edn. London: John Gilfillan.

GARNETT, JANE. 1992. 'Bishop Butler and the *Zeitgeist*: Butler and the Development of Christian Moral Philosophy in Victorian Britain', in Christopher Cunliffe (ed.), *Joseph Butler's Moral and Religious Thought: Tercentenary Essays*. Oxford: Clarendon.

HARRIS, TERRY G. 1988. 'Matthew Arnold, Bishop Joseph Butler, and the Foundation of Religious Faith'. *Victorian Studies* 31: 189–208.

HERVIEU-LÉGER, DANIÈLE. 2001. *Religion as a Chain of Memory*, trans. Simon Lee. New Brunswick, NJ: Rutgers University Press.

HOBBES, THOMAS. 1651 [1985]. *Leviathan*, ed. and Intro. C. B. Macpherson. New York: Penguin.

MORE, HANNAH. 1800. *Strictures on the Modern System of Female Education*. 8th edn. London: T. Cadell & W. Davies.

MOSSNER, ERNEST CAMPBELL. 1936a. *Bishop Butler and the Age of Reason: A Study in the History of Thought*. New York: Macmillan.

—— 1936b. 'Coleridge and Bishop Butler'. *Philosophical Review* 45: 206–8.

SEWARD, WILLIAM. 1796. *Anecdotes of some distinguished persons, chiefly of the present and two preceding centuries. Adorned with sculptures*. 3rd edn. London.

TENNANT, R. C. 1982. 'The Anglican Response to Locke's Theory of Personal Identity'. *Journal of the History of Ideas* 43: 73–90.

WARD, GRAHAM. 2003. *True Religion*. Oxford: Blackwell.

FURTHER READING

BAKER, ALBERT. 1923. *Bishop Butler*. London: SPCK.

CUNLIFFE, CHRISTOPHER (ed.) 1992. *Joseph Butler's Moral and Religious Thought: Tercentenary Essays*. Oxford: Clarendon.

DARWALL, STEPHEN. 1995. 'Butler: Conscience as Self-Authorizing'. *The British Moralists and the Internal 'Ought': 1640–1740*. Cambridge: Cambridge University Press, 244–87.

MOSSNER, ERNEST CAMPBELL. 1936. *Bishop Butler and the Age of Reason: A Study in the History of Thought*. New York: Macmillan.

CHAPTER 36

....

KEBLE AND *THE CHRISTIAN YEAR*

....

KIRSTIE BLAIR

'EITHER poetry is growing more religious, or religion more poetical', noted the religious poet Josiah Conder in an 1825 review, two years before John Keble published his collection of 'hymns' as *The Christian Year* (Conder 1825: 354). The movements which ensued within the Church of England, in part at least inspired by Keble's book, demonstrated that both these assertions were true. *The Christian Year*, one of the most influential works of poetry of the nineteenth century, is now seldom read or taught, and critical interest in it has generally centred upon its acknowledged effect on other writers of the Victorian period—among them Alfred Tennyson, Matthew Arnold, Gerard Manley Hopkins, and Christina Rossetti. Keble's aesthetic theories, of which *The Christian Year* is the fullest embodiment, have, however, maintained an implicit or explicit presence in critical readings of Victorian poetry and poetics, from M. H. Abrams's account of these theories in terms of Freudian repression and sublimation in the 1950s, to twenty-first century re-examinations of Keble in the light of renewed interest in literary affect and the significance of emotion. But he remains underestimated in comparison to other authors of his status in the nineteenth century, when his name and his work would have been as familiar to the literate reader as the names of the other Victorian writers discussed in this volume. While Keble was never their equal in terms of literary merit, *The Christian Year* must be considered one of the primary works of literature and theology of its time, and a crucial example of reading literature as theology and vice versa.

Throughout the religious turmoil and change of the nineteenth century, *the Christian Year* was an immensely popular and familiar text, not only for Anglican middle-class readers but also, according to contemporary writers, across denominations and classes, read by Dissenters and Roman Catholics as well as High Anglicans, sold on railway stalls as well as in high-class religious bookshops, and referenced by writers from Thackeray to Ouida (Cruse 1935: 47–9; Blair 2004: 8–9). One memorial tribute claimed, with typical extravagance, that 'its circulation the world over almost defies statistics, and is practically well-nigh beyond the bounds of calculation' (Grant, in Keble 1886: p. xxvi). Keble's close friend and biographer, John Taylor Coleridge, comments in one of the many hagiographical tributes to Keble and *The Christian Year* after his death: 'It has not been a book for the library... but a book for every individual, found in every room, companion in travel, comfort in sickness, again and again read, taken into the mind and heart, soothing, sustaining, teaching, purifying, exalting' (Coleridge 1866: 6). Coleridge's account is typical in that it locates the power of *The Christian Year* less in its literary merit than in its affective influence. For many nineteenth-century critics, it seemed wrong to apply aesthetic standards of judgement to Keble's poems, both because it was hard to see past the image of Keble himself as a beloved saint, and because the aims of *The Christian Year* were primarily religious rather than poetic. Keble himself, reviewing Conder and other authors in his early article on 'Sacred Poetry', argued that 'we naturally shrink from treating [sacred poems] merely as literary efforts', and that analysing their aesthetic qualities risked disturbing the reader 'in a devotional exercise' (Keble 1877: 81). John Henry Newman (1994: 36) echoed this in his discussion of *The Christian Year* in *Apologia Pro Vita Sua*: 'It is not necessary, and scarcely becoming, to praise a book which has already become one of the classics of the language... Nor can I pretend to analyse, in my own instance, the effect of religious teaching so deep, so pure, so beautiful.' Newman, perhaps slightly disingenuously, avoids any discussion or praise of *The Christian Year* as literature, and reads it in relation to its religious influence on the individual.

Many contemporaries, like Coleridge, described the experience of reading Keble's poems in curative terms, as calming, consoling, and healing to both mind and body. Newman (1979: 48–9) wrote to Robert Wilberforce in 1828 that his dying sister 'told us that during the acuteness of her previous spasms she had received great comfort from being able to repeat to herself Keble's hymns'. Wilberforce, who believed that 'Nothing that has come out for these last hundred years can bear a moment's comparison' to Keble's poems, similarly recited them at his wife's deathbed (Newsome 1993: 82). These were poems which were fundamentally perceived as *useful*. Aesthetic value was considerably less relevant than the creation of affect, the way in which these poems might work upon their reader. Indeed, Keble was only persuaded to publish them on the grounds that they might serve as 'helps to the memory of plain, good sort of people' (Letter to Hurrell Froude, 26 September 1825, cited Coleridge 1870: 121). What Keble hoped these readers would 'remember' were the words of the Book of Common Prayer, and the concomitant authority of the church and of God himself. *The Christian Year* was not an end in itself, but rested entirely on the forms, ceremonies, and language of the Established Church and of the Bible. To read it purely as literature would, in his eyes, have been effectively sacrilege.

The subtitle of *The Christian Year, Thoughts in Verse for the Sundays and Holydays Throughout the Year*, makes the dependence of the poetry on the liturgical calendar immediately evident. Keble's advertisement to the volume, indeed, states that his object is to bring the reader's thoughts and feelings 'into more entire unison with those recommended and exemplified in the Prayer Book' (Keble 1914: p. i). After the two opening pieces for 'Morning' and 'Evening' prayer, the poems begin with 'Advent Sunday' and progress through the year to 'Sunday Next Before Advent', concluding with a set of special poems for saints' days and particular occasions—confirmation, marriage, baptism, and so forth. Although the poems were not specifically written to correspond with the texts for each day, they were arranged to relate thematically to them. *The Christian Year* is thus a 'concept' volume, designed to be read in conjunction with the Sunday lessons and as a gloss upon them, to highlight the importance of the authorized forms of Anglican worship, and to renew interest in them. This was not an entirely original idea. In 1811 and 1812, Reginald Heber, later Bishop of Calcutta, published hymns in the *Christian Observer* with a prefatory notice describing them as 'part of an intended series, appropriate to the Sundays and principal holy days of the year' (cited in Brice 1894: 110). Heber's collection, *Hymns, Written and Adapted to the Weekly Church Service of the Year*, also came out in 1827, following James Montgomery's *The Christian Psalmist* (1825), which selected appropriate hymns for Anglican worship and included a polemical preface arguing for their importance. John Julian notes in his *Dictionary of Hymnology* that by 1833 up to ten collections of hymns were published each year, as Anglicans increasingly realized the potential of church music in worship (Julian 1892: 334). Keble's poems were not wholly in this tradition, however, because their complex structures and rhythms meant that (with a few notable exceptions) they could not easily be sung. Although Keble generally referred to his poems as 'hymns', in the sense of works designed primarily to praise God, this seems to reflect his unease at claiming poetic talent as well as his desire to emphasize their devotional purpose and use-value; in the letter to Froude cited above, for instance, he repeatedly and self-deprecatingly describes his poems as 'things' (Coleridge 1870: 121).

The fact that the poems, unlike sung hymns, were not part of the actual church service probably helped to create their immense appeal. *The Christian Year* was significant in that it was both a public and private collection: public, in that it referred to an external system of worship and worked in tandem with its ceremonies, but private in its expression of feeling (Froude initially felt that the poems were worryingly 'Methodist' in their overt account of emotion (cited in Williams 1892: 22)) and in the fact that it could be read alone, or in the family circle. The Arnold family, for example, despite the increasing estrangement between Thomas Arnold and Keble—who had been close friends at Oriel—on religious grounds, included Keble's poems in their Sunday devotions, and both Thomas and Mary Arnold referred to them in their journals and letters (Kline 2004: 144–6). It seems that *The Christian Year* was in large part described and marketed as a book for repeated private perusal, as shown by the number of editions designed to be pocket-sized. Contemporary accounts emphasize how many Victorians carried it with them when abroad (perhaps a reflection on its Englishness as much as its powers of consolation) and presented it as a gift to friends and relatives. The attention and care which readers devoted to it can be seen not only in the frequency of allusions in Victorian literature, but in the markings left on individual copies: Christina Rossetti, for instance, illustrated her favourite poems, as well as underlining key phrases or passages (see D'Amico 1987).

The way in which readers responded to *The Christian Year* blurred the line between reading a work as literature or as theology. It was a collection which evidently could not be fully appreciated without some knowledge of the Established Church, and which had specifically Christian designs. G. B. Tennyson (1981: 6) observes in his important account of Tractarian poetics that *The Christian Year* is the best nine-teenth-century example of 'devotional poetry', in that it is 'poetry that grows out of and is tied to acts of religious worship'. In literary terms, it was difficult to argue, even for the most dedicated devotees of the volume, that Keble's somewhat awkward, stilted, self-consciously literary diction and form, and his frequently clichéd imagery, were signs of great poetic merit. Yet the poems, at their best, are simple, confident, masterly in their use of form and rhythm as persuasive tools and, most importantly, memorable. The dependence of the language on the Bible and other sources might also seem less a hindrance than a help, giving each poem a sense of familiarity: 'I could hardly believe the lines were not my own and that Keble had not taken them from me,' as Newman put it (To Jemima Newman, 10 May 1828, Newman 1979: 69). Moreover, the form of the volume, the way in which the poems fitted together to create a unity of purpose, made it seem, in Stephen Prickett's (1976: 104) words, like 'a living, active, organic whole charged with divine meaning'. One of the greatest poems of the nineteenth century, Tennyson's *In Memoriam* (1850), with its seasonal cycles and series of connected yet separate short poems, may owe its form to Tennyson's careful reading of *The Christian Year* (see Scott 1989).

Thomas Mozley (1885: 31) summed up the contrasting views on the volume in an 1828 letter to his sister:

I do not know poetry on which there are such various opinions. Some think it will outlive all other human poetry whatever, others that it will be unheard of fifty years hence: some think it simple, others far-fetched; some think it only requires a little pure feeling for the most unlearned to enter into it, others that it is unconstruable to every one, and probably to the author himself.

Written shortly after first publication, Mozley's suggestion that there were voices of dissent in Oxford would, in a few decades time, be drowned out by the consensus that *The Christian Year* was unrivalled as devotional verse and that Keble himself was the ultimate nineteenth-century role model for the Christian and Anglican life. Literary readers, such as Matthew Arnold, might later reject many of the precepts of *The Christian Year*, or might, like Arthur Hugh Clough, reject the church itself, but they still struggled to escape its pervasive influence in their work. Given the status of *The Christian Year* as the best-selling book of poetry of the period, it was hard for Victorian poets not to engage with it on some level. As I argue below, and as many critics have observed, such engagements were simultaneously literary and theological. The way in which these poems represent the natural world and man's place in it, their perception of order and harmony, their attitude towards feeling and its expression, their conception of the role of the poet and of poetry, and even their political motives, all read through form and rhythm as well as language, were profoundly important for later Victorian writers. *The Christian Year* offered a manual for everyday Christian behaviour, apparently embodied in the person of the poet himself and his idyllic life as a country pastor. But it also offered a guide to the poetic life, repeatedly reflecting on the status of poetry in relation to religion and furthering, in its own afterlife, the notion that poetry should be gauged according to the power it had to create feelings in the reader. Each of the 'theological' ideas discussed below was also a poetic idea, one that could potentially be appropriated by writers who had little sympathy with the religious and social ideals which Keble stood for.

The theological roots of *The Christian Year* are on one level very simple, resting on Keble's passionately conservative view of the church and the individual's role in it, summed up by obedience to authority. On another level, however, *The Christian Year* came to be seen as a reflection of and commentary upon the tenets of the Oxford Movement, or Tractarianism, and thus took on specific and more subtle political and theological resonances. When Keble published the volume in 1827, he did in part see it as an intervention in church affairs, and in several poems he laments the current state of Christianity in Britain and highlights the need for reform. But at the same time he clearly did not set out to produce either a theological treatise, such as Butler's *Analogy*, or a call to arms, such as the *Lyra Apostolica* of 1836. The fact that *The Christian Year* can to some extent be read as both is due to the events of the 1830s and 1840s. Keble was perceived as one of the founders of the Oxford Movement—Newman famously dated the start of the Movement from his Assize Sermon on 14 July 1833—even though his actual involvement was relatively little compared to other participants. While Newman, Pusey et al. fought their battles in Oxford, Keble was contentedly living as a rural priest, primarily occupied with parish business and local affairs. It would be a misrepresentation to underplay his participation in Tractarianism, given his notable contributions to the *Tracts for the Times*, his lectures as Oxford Professor of Poetry between 1832 and 1841, his letters, articles, sermons, and scholarly editions of religious works, but from 1835 onwards he was firmly based in Hursley in Gloucestershire and had given up all interest in preferment or Oxford privilege. Asked about his involvement with Tractarianism in later life, he famously said that he looked upon his time with Newman and Pusey as 'a sort of parenthesis' in his normal life (Williams 1892: 118).

When one of his memorial writers observes that in 1833 'our Poet suddenly transformed into a Theologian' (Grant, in Keble 1886: p. xxxiii), then, he expresses the perception of the time, but leaves out the fact that it was Keble's poetry, rather than any of his explicitly theological contributions to Tractarianism, which shaped notions both of his religious views and of Tractarian theology more generally. To take one well-known instance of how his poetry was read as theology, the poem 'Gunpowder Treason' (Keble 1828), added to the volume after the first edition, caused a dispute over the doctrine of the Real Presence because of the lines:

> O come to our Communion Feast:
>   There present, in the heart
> Not in the hands, th'eternal Priest
>   Will His true self impart.   (ll. 49–52)

When 'Not in the hands' was cited by a bishop in the 1850s as proof that Keble did not believe in Christ's presence in the bread of holy communion, he was forced publicly to clarify his position by arguing that his intended meaning was 'not *only* in the hands' (Yonge 1871: 351–2). He reluctantly altered the phrase, in 1866 and subsequent editions, to 'As in the hands'. Charlotte Yonge (ibid. 352) notes, a little defensively, that Keble 'probably had no idea what a theological authority [these lines] had become'. In fact Keble believed that he had already dealt with the debate over 'Gunpowder Treason' in the Preface to his tract *On Eucharistical Adoration*—failing quite to recognize that it was not his tracts people were reading for his theology, but his poetry (Keble 1859: p. xiv, discussed in Coleridge 1870: 169–72). *The Christian Year*, both to those who were already adherents of the Tractarian cause, and those who did not necessarily support it, came to epitomize the best aspects of the movement.

Those elements of Keble's poetry which were most influential in the direction taken by the Oxford Movement, by religious poetry, and, indeed, by the Church of England itself, can be loosely divided into conservatism, a focus on how the everyday and banal could be integrated into a Christian life, the use of nature and landscape in symbolic and typological ways, a concentration on reserve and on caution in expressing feeling, and an emphasis on form and ritual. These could be summed up as constituting what James Pereiro (2004) has recently analysed as the Tractarian 'ethos', a concept coined by Keble, standing for the dominant moral tone of faith, love, and trust essential to Christian life. As already noted, *The Christian Year* and Keble's other writings also participated in a vital nineteenth-century argument about the conjunction of poetry and religion, their operation and their affective power. Stephen Prickett (1976: 32) has acutely commented that: 'Religious language differs only from so-called "ordinary" language in degree and mode. Openly symbolic, tensional, and stereoscopic, it reveals that this is also the condition of ordinary language. We come to understand poetic language via religious language, not vice versa.' Coleridge and Wordsworth, in Prickett's view, inaugurated this belief in the nineteenth century, but it was the Tractarian poets and critics who formed it into a central theological tenet. In an 1846 essay on Keble, Newman (1872: 442) famously defended the claims of the Roman Catholic Church by highlighting its use of form and ritual to express emotion, 'Her very being is poetry; every psalm, every petition, every collect, every versicle'. Newman implicitly borrows here from Keble's earlier lectures on poetry and from the statements he made in Tract 89, 'On the Mysticism Attributed to the Early Fathers of the Church'. Keble's (Keble 1912: ii. 481) concluding Oxford lecture, given in 1841, for instance, expounded upon the relation between poetry and religion, stating: 'In short, Poetry lends Religion her wealth of symbols and similes: Religion restores these again to Poetry, clothed with so splendid a radiance that they appear to be no longer symbols, but to partake (I might almost

say) of the nature of sacraments.' Religion and poetry are here mutually dependent.
A year or two earlier, in Tract 89, Keble (1840: 144) noted of the symbolic language of
patristic theology that just as man uses poetic language to express his most intense
emotions and beliefs obliquely, so: '[God] condescends in like manner to have a
Poetry of His own, a set of holy and divine associations and meanings, wherewith it is
His will to invest all material things.' All religious exercises are therefore also poetical
(as well as vice versa), because God has chosen poetry as the means to convey
religious teaching and feeling. We read God's presence in the world in the same
way as we read a poem, with attention to imagery and analogy—as Keble wrote in the
opening lines of one of the most discussed poems in *The Christian Year*, 'Septuages-
ima Sunday', 'There is a book, who runs may read | What heavenly truth imparts', the
book of Nature.[1]

The 'Dedication' to *The Christian Year* suggests that the roles of poet and priest are
identical:

> O happiest who before Thine altar wait,
>   With pure hands ever holding up on high
>   The guiding Star of all who seek Thy gate.
> The undying lamp of heavenly Poesy.   (ll. 17–20)

Keble frequently apostrophizes poets as those with the power to convey God's vision
to others. *The Christian Year* is filled with musical imagery, suggesting that the true
poet possesses the ability to create harmony and unity. In 'The Circumcision of
Christ', Keble asks:

> Wouldst thou a poet be?
> And would thy dull heart fain
> Borrow of Israel's minstrelsy
>   One high enraptured strain?
>
> Come here thy soul to tune,
> Here set thy feeble chant,
> Here, if at all beneath the moon,
>   Is holy David's haunt.   (ll. 45–52)

Minstrelsy and ministry are never far apart in Keble's verse. The commanding 'here'
in lines 50–1 is both the imagined geographical and temporal location of Christ's
circumcision (an event Keble reads as foreshadowing his sufferings on the Cross),
and the textual location of the Bible verse referring to it. 'Here' is also potentially the
here and now of Keble's poem itself. Given that this *is* a poem on the circumcision, it
is already situated in the space of 'holy David's haunt', and hence it performs its own
injunction and suggests that the poet might profitably tune himself or herself to the
harmonies of Keble's own verse. The tone, as often in *The Christian Year*, is one of
patronage and command, assertion as well as humility. Keble's exhortations to poets
often imply that he has peculiar insight into their role:

---

[1] 'Septuagesima Sunday', lines 1–2, in Keble 1914. All further references to *The Christian Year* are from
this edition.

> Sovereign masters of all hearts!
> Know ye, who hath set your parts?
>
> ('Palm Sunday', 9–10)

'Set your parts' again uses a musical analogy to imply that the true poet is in tune and in time with God's will, a concept that, as I have argued elsewhere, can be read through the controlling rhythms of the verse itself (Blair 2003). Other poets may not recognize God's command, but Keble knows it, intimately and thoroughly.

If the poet's role is to convey God's will, poetry also helps him or her to become a better Christian by providing a means of measured expression. In his poetic theories, largely borrowed from Wordsworth and Coleridge, Keble argued that poetry serves to contain and channel damaging or embarrassing emotions. It exerts a calming and soothing effect on both writer and reader, and through this leads the mind to God: 'The very practice and cultivation of poetry will be found to possess, in some sort, the power of guiding and composing the mind to worship and prayer' (Keble 1912: ii. 482–3). Reading poetry such as Keble's own, as Coleridge noted, the reader should be left 'loving, grateful and reverential towards his Maker', contented with his or her place, and obedient to God's will (Coleridge 1870: 162). This is poetry which is not simply based upon a religious service, it acts in the same way as one of the forms of the church itself.

One of the main reasons for *The Christian Year*'s attraction was precisely the sense of reassurance and confident security it seemed to offer, in a time when the authority of the church and of the Bible, not to mention of Christianity itself, was being considerably undermined. Keble had no interest in engaging with the doubts and difficulties of his age, indeed, there is something ruthless about his total dismissal of their validity, as in his comment in 'National Apostasy' (1848: 148) that the true Churchman is 'calmly, soberly, demonstrably SURE, that sooner or later, HIS WILL BE THE WINNING SIDE, and that the victory will be complete, universal, eternal'. There is clearly no room for dissent here. His advice, whether in prose or poetry, was simple: trust in the authority of the church and her earthly representatives, kings and priests; be humble; and have confidence that all will be well. In an 1833 sermon, he argues, clearly with contemporary biblical criticism in mind: 'Is there not something even *cruel*, in raising scruples and niceties, and unpleasant associations of various kinds, among those who as yet happily have never dreamed of criticizing the Bible?' ('Sunday Lessons', in Keble 1834: 11). Happiness lies in evading controversy, rather than defeating it. Keble's position on religious debate is again summed up in the sermon 'Hoping Against Hope' (1846): 'We may understand the heavenly voice as saying, "What if thou didst see clearly the theological grounds of this or that mysterious proposition, this or that article of the Creed? What wouldest thou do? Do the same now, and thou wilt be right"' (Keble 1848: 327). He takes this concept of trust from Butler's *Analogy*, which he cites here as the source of his argument that one should always take the 'safest way', the way of God. The path out of doubt lies in action, not in fruitless questioning.

This belief is embedded in most of the poems in *The Christian Year*, where doubt or unrest are introduced only to be immediately quelled in favour of submission.

'Fourth Sunday After Epiphany', for example, one of the most complex poems of the volume in terms of its metrical variation, begins with a description of a storm, representing the passions and emotional turmoil which 'heave the struggling heart' (L. 18) of the believer. But even as the storm is pictured we are left in no doubt as to who is in control:

> They know th' Almighty's love,
> Who, when the whirlwinds rock the topmost grove,
>   Stand in the shade, and hear
> The tumult with a deep exulting fear,
>   How, in their fiercest sway,
> Curb'd by some power unseen, they die away,
> Like a bold steed that owns his rider's arm,
> Proud to be check'd and sooth'd by that o'ermastering charm.   (ll. 9–16)

The introduction of 'love' in the opening sentence, which might seem an odd contrast with the threatening whirlwinds of the next line (surely more likely to show God's wrath than his love), gives a sense of safety, knowledge that 'they', those who trust in God, will not be harmed. The varying punctuation in lines 10–11 and 14–15 creates some irregularity, and the uneven line lengths, extending and contracting, might suggest an affinity with the 'rocking' or 'sway' of the storm. But the rhythms of the passage are relatively undisturbed, with the five central lines (10–14), neatly balanced: an iambic pentameter (12) is framed by two trimeters with a matching reversed first foot and strong initial stress, and by two pentameters with the same pattern (i.e. 'Hów, in their fiercest swáy | Cúrb'd by some pówer unséen, they díe awáy'). 'Sway' acts as a pun, in that it appears to indicate mastery, but in fact signals wavering, anticipating 'die away'. The implication in the final couplet is that it is not simply Nature which obeys God's 'o'ermastering charm' (both in the sense of charm as allure, charisma, and as a spell or enchantment), but the good Christian also, who is 'proud to be check'd' in the expression of stormy thoughts. This poem, which was apparently written with reference to Keble's disapproval of Byron's wild poetic career, reflects upon the role of the ideal poet as well as the perfect Christian: both might 'exult' in wildness, but only in the knowledge that it is securely regulated.

Keble's poems repeatedly enact this principle of bowing to God's will:

> O Lord my God, do Thou Thy holy will—
>   I will lie still—
> I will not stir, lest I forsake Thine arm
>
> ('Wednesday before Easter', 1–3)

This verse pattern is consciously reminiscent of George Herbert's poems of resignation, such as 'The Collar', but note that Keble stages his submission in the first two lines of the poem—not, as in Herbert's poem, in the last two—to ensure that there is no other possibility left open. The imagery here, of 'clinging to my Father's breast' (l. 5), is very common in *The Christian Year*, as the speaker or addressee is imagined as a child obedient to God and to the mother church. Keble's repeated use of such imagery makes the model he describes familiar and familial, rooting the principles of Christianity in the key Victorian ideology of the happy family home. Tennyson (1987: ii), of course, borrowed the imagery of the poet-supplicant as infant in *In Memoriam*, but without any such security of parental love:

> Behold, we know not anything;
> I can but trust that good shall fall
> At last—far off—at last, to all,
> And every winter change to spring.
>
> So runs my dream: but what am I?
> An infant crying in the night,
> An infant crying for the light,
> And with no language but a cry.   (LIV: 13–20)

The first stanza here recalls both Keble's general insistence on 'trust entire' ('First Sunday After Epiphany', 56) in the face of a lack of knowledge of God's purposes, and his particular use of winter and spring imagery as analogous to earthly and heavenly life, as in the close of 'The Circumcision': 'So life a winter's morn may prove | To a bright endless year' (67–8). Winter does eventually change to spring in *In Memoriam*, but Tennyson is far from confident about this here. He hesitates and questions, where Keble is sure, and his representation of himself as a crying child suggests fear, isolation, and the absence of sympathetic communication.

Although several of the poems in *The Christian Year* argue that the church must be roused, war waged on unbelief, and that priests, besides their homely duties, are engaged in 'pastoral warfare' ('Ordination', 44), the abiding vision is of serving God through quiet obedience in everyday life, centred on family, country, and community. Even in 'National Apostasy', Keble's most revolutionary statement, he writes:

After all, the surest way to uphold or restore our endangered Church, will be for each of her anxious children, in his own place and station, to resign himself more thoroughly to his God and Saviour in those duties, public and private, which are not immediately affected by the emergencies of the moment: the daily and hourly duties, I mean, of piety, purity, charity, justice.   (Keble 1848: 146)

This argument had, however, already been advanced in 'Morning', one of his most popular poems:

> We need not bid, for cloister'd cell,
> Our neighbour and our work farewell,
> Nor strive to wind ourselves too high
> For sinful man beneath the sky:
>
> The trivial round, the common task,
> Would furnish all we ought to ask;
> Room to deny ourselves; a road
> To bring us, daily, nearer God.   (ll. 49–56)

The measured pace of the iambic tetrameter and the confident couplets lend a ring of authority to the verse. Keble's focus on 'our neighbour and our work', as opposed to a retreat into religious solitude, situates the ideal Christian firmly in a Wordsworthian world of sympathy and community. This vision of the humble, hardworking life as the epitome of virtue runs through later Victorian fiction, in George Eliot's noble carpenter and forester Adam Bede, for instance, or in Charles Dickens's Little Dorrit and Arthur Clennam, who go down in the final page of the novel into 'a modest life of usefulness and happiness' even in the wilderness of London (Dickens 1987: 895).

The scene of *The Christian Year* is largely set in a pastoral landscape, where the simple sights and sounds of Nature assist the spiritual life: 'Homely scenes and simple views | Lowly thoughts may best infuse' ('First Sunday After Epiphany', 23–4). Every aspect of the English landscape will speak to the trained observer of God:

> See the soft green willow springing
>   Where the waters gently pass,
> Every way her free arms flinging
>   O'er the moist and reedy grass.
>
> Though the rudest hand assail her,
>   Patiently she droops awhile,
> But when showers and breezes hail her,
>   Wears again her willing smile.
> Thus I learn Contentment's power
> From the slighted willow's bower.   (ibid. 25–34)

The willow here should be interpreted as a figure for the believer, in the light of the text which heads the poem, 'They shall spring up among the grass, as willows by the water courses' (Isa. 44: 4). More broadly, the poem, which ends by celebrating 'modest ways | Trust entire, and ceaseless praise' (55–6), supports the Epistle for this Sunday: 'For I say... to every man that is among you, not to think of himself more highly than he ought to think, but to think soberly' (Rom. 12: 1). Keble (1840, 143) notes of patristic writing in Tract 89 that it reads nature as 'fraught with imaginative associations', a symbolic poetic language of faith. He argues that even analogies which might seem far-fetched, such as reading biblical references to trees by the water (as in this poem) as references to baptism and the cross, are justified by the poetic nature of biblical language. All aspects of nature can be read symbolically in relation to Christianity:

> Two worlds are ours: 'tis only Sin
>   Forbids us to descry
> The mystic heaven and earth within
>   Plain as the sea and sky.
>
>   ('Septuagesima Sunday', 41–4)

Again, while a close attention to nature is a religious move for Keble, it also pre-empts the natural realism of later Victorian literature. The English countryside and its symbolic associations play a crucial role in the novels of George Eliot and Thomas Hardy, for instance (though its resonances there are often considerably darker), in Hopkins's journals, or in Pre-Raphaelite paintings and poems such as Dante Gabriel Rossetti's 'The Honeysuckle' or 'The Woodspurge', where the detailed focus on nature under the impetus of strong emotion verges on the symbolic:

> Among these few, out of the sun,
> The woodspurge flowered, three cups in one.
>
> From perfect grief there need not be
> Wisdom or even memory:
> One thing then learnt remains to me,—
> The woodspurge has a cup of three.
>
> ('The Woodspurge', ll. 7–12, in
> Rossetti 1911: 205)

This short poem plays cleverly with the idea of symbolic readings. Rossetti is not unaware that the three in one of the woodspurge suggests the Trinity, but the poem hints at this only to render it meaningless. There are no lessons, applications, or analogies to be gained by the speaker, who is wholly absorbed in personal grief. Rossetti's simple language and rhyme scheme and the apparent natural analogy allude to Keble while rewriting his purpose.

Keble used his theories of symbolism and analogy to support the doctrine of 'Reserve', the theory that God's sacred truths are revealed gradually and indirectly, and only to those who have proved themselves worthy. Reserve was codified as a general Tractarian principle by Isaac Williams's Tracts 80 and 81, 'On Reserve in Communicating Religious Knowledge' (Williams 1938, 1940), but Williams himself linked the concept to his reading of Origen (one of the writers crucial in Keble's discussion of symbolic language) and to 'the conduct of the Kebles' (Williams 1892: 89). It was Keble, moreover, who advised Williams to publish his writings on the subject as part of the *Tracts for the Times*. Once again, then, Reserve is an idea which was already present, and emblematized by Keble himself, before it became primarily linked to High Anglicanism. Reserve was to prove a vital concept for poetry, in that it suggested that its function was not necessarily the direct expression or outpouring of emotion, but an expression veiled, indirect, and all the more powerful for being so.

The Christian Year demonstrates this by constantly, almost coyly, withdrawing from moments of dramatic action or revelation, and emphasizing the hidden, secret, or inexplicable nature of God's work. In 'All Saints Day', writing on the false pride of empires and cities, Keble asks,

> Think ye the spires that glow so bright
>   In front of yonder setting sun,
> Stand by their own unshaken might?
>   No—where th'upholding grace is won,
> We dare not ask, nor Heaven would tell,
> But sure from many a hidden dell,
> From many a rural nook unthought of there,
> Rises for that proud world the saints' prevailing prayer.   (ll. 41–8)

The decisive negative at the start of line 44 makes it appear that the poet is about to answer his rhetorical question, only for this to be denied in 'We dare not ask', as the poem retreats from the towers of the city, back into the pastoral nooks and dells of Keble's English countryside. 'Prevailing' is ambiguous, because it is unclear whether the saints' prayer is simply constant, or whether it 'prevails' in the sense of triumphing, actually upholding the splendour of the city. The reader (and poet) are not yet worthy to know the source of grace. 'Fourth Sunday in Lent' compares God's reserve to the natural modesty Keble saw as essential to Christian life:

> E'en human Love will shrink from sight
>   Here in the coarse rude earth:
> How then should rash intruding glance
> Break in upon *her* sacred trance
> Who boasts a heavenly birth?   (ll. 26–30)

The poet should shrink from revealing his emotions, mirroring his reticence in discussing God's secrets. Later poets play with this conceit. Christina Rossetti, as Emma Mason (2002) has recently discussed, frequently enacts the same move of hinting at an imminent revelation, then immediately retreating from it. Rossetti was deeply influenced by the High Anglican tradition, and many of her poems turn on the agonized suppression of emotional utterance, or on the attempt to reconcile the self to patience and humility in the light of God's apparent silence and concealment. The speaker of one of her religious sonnets commands:

> Lift up thine eyes to seek the invisible:
>   Stir up thy heart to choose the still unseen:
>   Strain up thy hope in glad perpetual green
> To scale the exceeding height where all saints dwell.
>
>   (Untitled ['Lift up thine eyes'], ll. 1–4, in
>   Rossetti 2001: 493)

These commands are based on a series of paradoxes, the invisible cannot be seen, an ever-exceeding height cannot be climbed. Revelation is always just out of reach. Yet the possible irony inherent in these riddling commands is counteracted in the final sestet:

> —But thou purblind and deafened, knowest thou
> Those glorious beauties unexperienced
>   By ear or eye or heart hitherto?—
> I know Whom I have trusted: wherefore now
>   All amiable, accessible tho' fenced,
>   Golden Jerusalem floats into view.   (ibid. ll. 9–14)

A mocking voice enters the poem here, questioning how the speaker can know that God's saints are in bliss in the absence of any sensuous, intellectual, or spiritual proof. The speaker's answer, 'I know Whom I have trusted', chimes with Keble's beliefs and provides an unassailable argument. Ultimately, although the heavenly city is 'fenced' from earthly knowledge, it is also 'accessible' to the faithful.

Ideas of reserve, analogy, the relation between man and nature, and the concept of the poet as priest, exalted but constantly subject to the will of something greater, infused Victorian religious poetry. The examples of later poetry given here, however, might suggest that many Victorian writers responded to *The Christian Year* by replacing Keble's optimism with pessimism, confidence with wariness and insecurity. While this is a generalization, it is not unsustainable. The growing challenges to Christianity as the century progressed meant that *The Christian Year*, with its near-absolute certainty of God's presence and admonitions to have faith and be patient, came to be read almost nostalgically. For Matthew Arnold, for example, Keble's godson, it was associated with his juvenilia and with the safety of the domestic circle (Kline 2004). His poems of the 1850s, in contrast, bitterly lament the lack of security, healthful feeling, and confident faith in modern life. George Eliot's Maggie Tulliver finds reassurance in *The Christian Year* as an ardent teenager seeking self-sacrifice; with the Bible and Thomas-à-Kempis, it is one of the three books which 'She read so eagerly and constantly... that they filled her mind with a stream of rhythmic memories' (Eliot 1981: 387). Like Arnold, however, Maggie partly grows out of this interest. Eliot's association of Keble's volume with *The Imitation of Christ* suggests that it already belongs to an older world. By the last decades of the century, the representative reader of *The Christian Year* is Catherine Leyburn from Mrs Humphry Ward's bestselling *Robert Elsmere*, whose rigid Anglicanism and ideals of devotion and submission leave her unable to cope with her husband Robert's radical reinterpretation of Christian faith. Ward, of course, was Arnold's niece, and her family had been deeply affected by the religious controversies of the period through her father's wavering between the Anglican and Roman Catholic communions. In her novel, Catherine's utter refusal to see any justification in Robert's questioning and testing of his faith, and her horror at his abandonment of the church, are very Kebleian: 'Catherine Leyburn knew of no supreme right but the right of God to the obedience of man' (Ward 1987: 103). While there is sympathy for her anguish in the text, her attitude is also perceived as damaging and fundamentally misplaced in the new world of the 1880s.

Keble's contribution to literature and theology, and the conservative ideals he espoused, came to seem increasingly outdated in the course of the nineteenth century. Yet his influence was also enabling. In retrospect, and in the light of a renewed critical interest in literature and religion, his writings begin to appear more quietly revolutionary than late Victorian writers (or Keble himself) could have anticipated. As Sheridan Gilley and Lawrence Starzyk have noted, he rewrote Romantic poetic theory for the Victorian period; and as recent critics have observed, his concentration on reserve, formality, and the cautious expression of strong emotion was a powerful tool in the hands of later poets, including significant numbers of women poets (Arseneau 2004; Francis 2004). Moreover, his poetry still raises the question of what it means to combine literature and theology successfully. Recalling Keble's contribution after his death, J. C. Shairp (1866: 238) wrote that 'Above all, he gave poetry to the Movement, and a poetical aspect'. By lending a 'poetical aspect' to one of the key developments in Anglicanism, and Victorian Christianity more broadly, Keble helped to highlight the role of imaginative literature in disseminating and founding religious principles. More than this, *The Christian Year*, intentionally or not, challenged any division between poetry, theology, and politics. It was a key example of how poetry could operate in realms other than, or as well as, the aesthetic. Coleridge (1870: 157) observes: 'I have heard of a clergyman in a rural parish in Worcestershire who was in the habit of reading, and explaining from the pulpit, in lieu of an afternoon sermon, the poem for the Sunday.' Keble's poems, themselves designed as glosses upon religious texts, become such texts in their own right and are themselves subject to analysis and interpretation. Very few other poems have been accorded such devoted reading. *The Christian Year* ensured that religious poetry would be taken seriously, demonstrated (in a difficult period for poetry publishing) that it could simultaneously be immensely popular, and encouraged poets to think in terms of affect. The theological principles of *The Christian Year* haunt much Victorian literature, and if those principles had not been embodied in literary form, it is unlikely that they would have become influential, familiar, and respected across so wide a spectrum.

WORKS CITED

ABRAMS, M. H. 1953. *The Mirror and the Lamp*. Oxford: Oxford University Press.

ARSENEAU, MARY. 2004. *Recovering Christina Rossetti: Female Community and Incarnational Poetics*. Basingstoke: Palgrave.

BLAIR, KIRSTIE. 2003. 'John Keble and the Rhythm of Faith'. *Essays in Criticism* 53/2: 129–50.

BRICE, ARTHUR MONTEFIORE. 1894. *Reginald Heber: Bishop of Calcutta*. London: S. W. Partridge.

COLERIDGE, JOHN TAYLOR. 1866. 'Death of the Author of *The Christian Year*'. *Guardian*, April 9: 6.

—— 1870. *Memoir of the Reverend John Keble*. 3rd edn. Oxford: James Parker.

CONDER, JOSIAH. 1825. 'Sacred Poetry'. *Eclectic Review* 42: 354–63.

CRUSE, AMY. 1935. *The Victorians and Their Books*. London: George Allen.

D'AMICO, DIANE. 1987. 'Christina Rossetti's *Christian Year*: Comfort for "the weary heart"'. *Victorian Newsletter* 72: 36–42.

DICKENS, CHARLES. 1987. *Little Dorrit*, ed. John Holloway. Harmondsworth: Penguin. First published 1857.

ELIOT, GEORGE. 1981. *The Mill on the Floss*, ed. A. S. Byatt. Harmondsworth: Penguin. First published 1860.

FRANCIS, EMMA. 2004. '"Her silence speaks": Keble's Female Heirs', in K. Blair (ed.), *John Keble in Context*. London: Anthem, 125–42.

HEBER, REGINALD. 1827. *Hymns, Written and Adapted to the Weekly Church Service of the Year*. London: John Murray.

JULIAN, JOHN. 1892. *Dictionary of Hymnology*. London: John Murray.

KEBLE, JOHN. 1828. *The Christian Year*. 3rd edn. Oxford: James Parker.

—— 1834. 'Sunday Lessons: The Principle of Selection'. *Tracts for the Times*, i. *1833–4*. London: J., G. and F. Rivington.

—— 1840. 'On the Mysticism Attributed to the Early Fathers of the Church'. *Tracts for the Times*, vol. VI (1838–40). London: J., G., and F. Rivington.

—— 1848. *Sermons, Academical and Occasional*. 2nd edn. Oxford: James Parker.

—— 1859. *On Eucharistical Adoration*. 2nd edn. Oxford: J. H. Parker.

—— 1877. *Occasional Papers and Reviews*, ed. E. B. Pusey. Oxford: James Parker.

—— 1886. *The Christian Year, with a Biographical Sketch of John Keble, Together with Some Remarks on the Influence of 'The Christian Year'*. Intro. Alexander Grant. London: John Hogg.

KEBLE, JOHN. 1912. *Keble's Lectures on Poetry, 1832–1841*, ed. E. K. Francis. Oxford: Clarendon.

—— 1914. *The Christian Year, Lyra Innocentium and Other Poems*. London: Oxford University Press.

KLINE, DANIEL. 2004. ' "For rigorous teachers seized my youth": Thomas Arnold, John Keble, and the Juvenilia of Matthew Arnold and Arthur Hugh Clough', in K. Blair (ed.), *John Keble in Context*. London: Anthem, 143–58.

MASON, EMMA. 2002. 'Christina Rossetti and the Doctrine of Reserve'. *Journal of Victorian Culture* 7: 196–219.

MONTGOMERY, JAMES. 1828. *The Christian Psalmist; or, Hymns, Sacred and Original*. 5th edn. Glasgow: William Collins.

MOZLEY, J. B. 1885. *Letters of the Reverend J. B. Mozley*, ed. A. Mozley. London: Rivingtons.

NEWMAN, J. H. 1872. 'John Keble', in *Essays, Critical and Historical*. 2 vols. London: Longmans, Green, 421–53. First published 1846.

—— 1979. *Letters and Diaries of John Henry Newman*, ed. Ian Ker and Thomas Gornall. 2nd edn. Oxford: Clarendon, ii.

—— 1994. *Apologia Pro Vita Sua*, ed. Ian Ker. Harmondsworth: Penguin. First published 1864.

NEWSOME, DAVID. 1993. *The Parting of Friends: The Wilberforces and Henry Manning*. 2nd edn. Grand Rapids: William B. Eerdman.

PEREIRO, JAMES. 2004. 'John Keble and the Concept of Ethos', in K. Blair (ed.), *John Keble in Context*. London: Anthem, 59–74.

PRICKETT, STEPHEN. 1976. *Romanticism and Religion: The Tradition of Coleridge and Wordsworth in the Victorian Church*. Cambridge: Cambridge University Press.

ROSSETTI, CHRISTINA. 2001. *The Complete Poems*, ed. Rebecca Crump. Harmondsworth: Penguin.

ROSSETTI, DANTE GABRIEL. 1911. *The Works of Dante Gabriel Rossetti*, ed. William Michael Rossetti. London: Ellis.

SCOTT, PATRICK. 1989. 'Rewriting the Book of Nature: Tennyson, Keble and *The Christian Year*'. *Victorians Institute Journal* 17: 141–55.

SHAIRP, J. C. 1866. *John Keble: An Essay on the Author of the 'Christian Year'*. Edinburgh: Edmonston & Douglas.

TENNYSON, ALFRED. 1987. *The Poems of Tennyson*, ed. Christopher Ricks. 2nd edn. 3 vols. Harlow: Longman.

TENNYSON, G. B. 1981. *Victorian Devotional Poetry: The Tractarian Mode*. Cambridge, Mass.: Harvard University Press.

WARD, MARY AUGUSTA [MRS HUMPHRY]. 1987. *Robert Elsmere*, ed. Rosemary Ashton. Oxford: Oxford University Press. First published 1888.

WILLIAMS, ISAAC. 1838. 'On Reserve in Communicating Religious Knowledge'. *Tracts for the Times 1836–1838*. London: J., G., & F. Rivington.

—— 1840. 'On Reserve in Communicating Religious Knowledge (Part 2)'. In *Tracts for the Times 1838–1840*. London: J., G., & F. Rivington.

—— 1892. *The Autobiography of Isaac Williams*, ed. George Prevost. London: Longmans.

YONGE, CHARLOTTE. 1871. *Musings over the 'Christian Year' and 'Lyra Innocentium'*. Oxford: James Parker.

FURTHER READING

BATTISCOMBE, GEORGINA. 1963. *John Keble: A Study in Limitations*. London: John Constable.

BLAIR, KIRSTIE (ed.) 2004. *John Keble in Context*. London: Anthem.

CHAPMAN, RAYMOND. 1970. *Faith and Revolt: Studies in the Literary Influence of the Oxford Movement*. London: Weidenfeld & Nicolson.

EDGECOMBE, RODNEY STENNING. 1996. *Two Poets of the Oxford Movement: John Keble and John Henry Newman*. London: Associated University Presses.

GILLEY, SHERIDAN. 1983. 'John Keble and the Victorian Churching of Romanticism', in J. R. Watson (ed.), *An Infinite Complexity: Essays in Romanticism*. Edinburgh: Edinburgh University Press, 226–39.

GOODWIN, GREGORY. 1986. 'Keble and Newman: Tractarian Aesthetics and the Romantic Tradition'. *Victorian Studies* 30: 475–94.

NOCKLES, PETER B. 1994. *The Oxford Movement in Context: Anglican High Churchmanship, 1760–1857*. Cambridge: Cambridge University Press.

STARZYK, LAWRENCE. 1973. '"That Promised Land": Poetry and Religion in the Early Victorian Period'. *Victorian Studies* 16: 269–90.

CHAPTER 37

JOHN HENRY NEWMAN

IAN KER

THE *Oxford Companion to English Literature* well illustrates the difficulty a theological writer such as Newman has in receiving proper treatment as a writer whose texts are also acknowledged to be of literary merit and influence. It is not that this standard literary reference work does not recognize his importance. Indeed, his entry is not much shorter than that on Carlyle or George Eliot, and about the same as that on Matthew Arnold. The problem is that, while the *Companion* knows that he is more than a minor literary figure, it concentrates unduly on those texts which are self-evidently 'literary' but which by themselves don't really justify the amount of space given to him. True, the *Apologia pro Vita Sua* is rightly described as 'a literary masterpiece' (Drabble 1985: 695). On the other hand, the inclusion of what must rate as one of Newman's least 'literary' works, *An Essay in Aid of a Grammar of Assent*, suggests considerable uncertainty about where to place the emphasis—indeed, the no less important theological work, *An Essay on the Development of Christian Doctrine*, which is ignored, has rather better literary credentials. *The Idea of a University* is mentioned, although without any acknowledgement of its status as one of the non-fictional prose masterpieces of Victorian literature. Inevitably, the verse, the *Lyra Apostolica* and *The Dream of Gerontius*, and even more the two novels, *Loss and Gain* and *Callista*, all minor works, occupy most of the rest of the entry.

The truth of the matter is that Newman was a minor poet and novelist, but one of the great writers of non-fictional prose, whose real literary achievement is to be compared with that of Victorian contemporaries such as Carlyle, Matthew Arnold (the critic), and Ruskin. The *Companion*, therefore, by shying away from the theological writings and concentrating on the overtly literary Newman, succeeds in almost totally missing the point. In particular, Newman was one of the greatest controversialists in English literature, whose satirical writings are also ignored by the *Companion*.

The only literary influence Newman himself ever acknowledged was that of the Roman orator Cicero, whose rhetoric and satire he paid tribute to. Even the *Apologia*, which unusually—with one exception—avoids controversy and polemic, is to a considerable extent the record of past controversies and abundantly documented with copious quotations from controversial and polemical writings. The exception is the final fifth chapter, which contains one of the two greatest extended rhetorical passages in Newman.

Ostensibly, Newman's target is Charles Kingsley who had provoked the controversy which led to the writing of the *Apologia*, but in reality this general defence of Catholicism is aimed as much at the two opposing wings of the Roman Catholic Church, the liberals and extreme papal Ultramontanes. Newman begins with a strong defence of the doctrine of infallibility as 'a power... for smiting hard and throwing back the immense energy of the aggressive, capricious, untrustworthy intellect', which he uncompromisingly welcomes as 'a supereminent, prodigious power sent upon earth to encounter and master a giant evil'. This unequivocal statement provokes the obvious objection that 'the restless intellect of our common humanity is utterly weighed down' by an infallible authority, 'so that, if this is to be the mode of bringing it into order, it is brought into order only to be destroyed'. The resolution of the contradiction lies in a third possibility, namely, that, far from being mutually contradictory, authority and reason depend upon each other precisely because, paradoxically, each is actually sustained by conflict with the other, for the 'energy of the human intellect... thrives and is joyous, with a tough elastic strength, under the terrible blows of the divinely-fashioned weapon and is never so much itself as when it has lately been overthrown'. Having stated the 'thesis' and 'antithesis', Newman surprises the reader with a 'synthesis' which is not a compromise between the two positions but rather an insistence on their interdependence: both need each other. The 'questionings' of theologians lead to doctrinal definitions by the infallible authority, the creeds themselves being the result of heresies. And then the theologians have to interpret and explain the definitions, a process which may lead to an intervention by authority, and so the interaction continues. As Newman explains in what is perhaps the most dazzling rhetorical passage in all his writings:

it is the vast Catholic body itself, and it only, which affords an arena for both combatants in that awful, never-dying duel. It is necessary for the very life of religion... that the warfare should be incessantly carried on. Every exercise of Infallibility is brought out into act by an intense and varied operation of the Reason, both as its ally and as its opponent, and provokes again, when it has done its work, a re-action of Reason against it; and, as in a civil polity, the State exists and endures by means of the rivalry and collision, the encroachments and defeats of its constituent parts, so in like manner Catholic Christendom is no simple exhibition of religious absolutism, but presents a continuous picture of Authority and Private Judgment alternately advancing and retreating as the ebb and flow of the tide;—it is a vast assemblage of human beings of wilful intellects and wild passions, brought together into one by the beauty and the Majesty of a Superhuman Power,—into what may be called a large reformatory or training-school, not as if into a hospital or into a prison, not in order to be sent to bed, not to be buried alive, but (if I may change my metaphor) brought together as if into some moral factory, for the melting, refining, and moulding, by an incessant, noisy process, of the raw material of human nature, so excellent, so dangerous, so capable of divine purpose.

In his theology of freedom and authority, then, Newman does not come down on one side or the other, nor does he attempt to take up a position in between. Instead, he upholds both in tension with each other, because he thinks the conflict is actually creative. G. K. Chesterton was to say the same sort of thing when he pointed out that you can only have a space if you have limits and boundaries. Newman's taut prose brilliantly conveys the clash of opposites, which in fact reflects the tensions in his own mind between a cautious conservatism on the one hand and a radical openness on the other. His characteristic method of argument, which underpins his rhetoric, is to keep in balance two diametrically opposed points of view, and then to achieve a resolution of the contradiction not by trying to find a middle way but by allowing the conflict to force a crucial shift of perspective that enables the dilemma to be seen in a new light and so to be resolved.

Having stated the case for authority as unequivocally as possible, he proceeds to emphasize the narrow limits of infallibility and its rare occurrence. He also stresses that the way authority is exercised may be wrong, but that does not affect its legitimacy. Again, history shows 'how the initial error of what afterwards became heresy was the urging forward some truth against the prohibition of authority at an unseasonable time'. And Newman is uncompromising in his insistence that, while such a reformer 'may seem to the world to be nothing else than a bold champion for the truth and a martyr to free opinion', in fact 'he is just one of those persons whom the competent authority ought to silence'. No doubt mindful of liberal Catholic criticism of himself for obedience to authority, he adds that, 'if the ruling power happens in its proceedings to evince any defect of prudence or consideration', then 'all those who take the part of that ruling authority will be considered as time-servers, or indifferent to the cause of uprightness and truth'. But the reader of Newman can never assume that a conclusion has been reached just because one 'aspect' of an 'idea', to use his own terminology, has been dealt with. There is always another aspect to be considered, which may open up a new perspective which may put the previous aspect in a new light. Indeed, the sentence just quoted does not end there, but with these words, directed not at the liberals but at their enemies, the Ultramontanes: 'while, on the other hand, the said authority may be accidentally supported by a violent ultra party, which exalts opinions into dogmas, and has it principally at heart to destroy every school of thought but its own'. And now Newman presses this aspect of the question, arguing that the proof that infallibility has not crushed intellectual freedom in the church is that it is 'individuals, and not the Holy See, that have taken the initiative, and given the lead to the Catholic mind, in theological inquiry'. 'Indeed,' he points out with studied irony, 'it is one of the reproaches against the Roman Church, that it has originated nothing, and has only served as a sort of...break in the development of doctrine.' But now, just in case the reader has been lulled into thinking that really Newman's heart lies with the liberals, he is quick to interject that 'it is an objection which I really embrace as a truth; for such I conceive to be the main purpose of its extraordinary gift'. However, he is unsparing in showing how history gives no support to the Ultramontane idealization of Rome as the oracle of truth. The greatest Western theologian belonged to the African Church, while Western theology was largely formed by the 'questionings' of such heterodox theologians as Tertullian and Origen. As for general councils, here history shows the crucial influence of individual theologians rather than the pope. Again Newman appeals to history to show how little authority has interfered with the freedom of theologians, but his appeal to the medieval church's practice of examining a controverted theological question at the local level with Rome as a last resort contains a veiled protest against the present practice of immediate involvement by Rome. He doesn't explicitly attack the authoritarianism of the Church of Pio Nono, but the rhetoric of reticence has its own eloquence as when he remarks that 'this mode of proceeding ... tends not only to the liberty, but to the courage, of the individual theologian', whereas, 'if he knew authority, which was supreme and final, was watching every word he said ... Then indeed he would be fighting, as the Persian soldiers, under the lash, and the freedom of the intellect might truly be said to be beaten out of him.' However, yet again the reader is surprised by the immediate reservation, that nevertheless 'when controversies run high', then 'an interposition may ... advisably take place; and again, questions may be of that urgent nature, that an appeal must, as a matter of duty, be made at once to the highest authority in the Church'. And then finally, there is one last shift of perspective as the insistent emphasis on the universality of the church that follows barely conceals an unfavourable allusion to the Italian monopoly of the Holy See (Svaglic 1967: 220, 224–6, 232–3, 237, 239, 240–1).

This last chapter of the *Apologia*, then, contains not only an important contribution to Newman's developing ecclesiology or theology of the church, but also some of the best prose he ever wrote. And, of course, one cannot separate the rhetoric from the thought: the sharply antithetical style simply reflects the method of argument whereby the contrasting aspects of a question are carefully balanced against each other to arrive at a synthesis, the scrupulous determination to do justice to the differing, even diametrically opposed points of view.

The other great extended passage, also an essay in itself, that I want to look at is the eighth Discourse in the first half of *The Idea of a University*. At the heart of the rhetoric of the Discourses is the tension between the unconditional insistence on the absolute value of knowledge in itself on the one hand, and on the other hand the equally firm conviction that knowledge is emphatically not the highest good. Thus, while on the one hand Newman will have no truck with those who wish to justify education solely on moral or religious grounds, on the other without any self-contradiction, he insists that it is better to have a simple religious faith than an educated intellect without religious belief. There is no question of any necessary incompatibility for Newman, but he recognizes the fact that religion and education, faith and reason, are not always found together. If, therefore, there has to be a choice between reason and faith, then Newman has no doubt as to his priority.

Thus, the various eulogies of the 'imperial intellect', which is the aim of education, are balanced against the eloquent expositions of the omniscience of God and the authority of the Catholic Church. Or there is the contrast in the final Discourse between the admission that a Christian literature is an impossibility, because it 'is a contradiction in terms to attempt a sinless literature of sinful man', and the insistence that nevertheless the study of literature must not be omitted from education because education is 'for this world' and 'it is not easy to learn to swim in troubled waters, never to have gone into them'. Conversely, the rapt evocation of the wonder of music in the fourth Discourse is promptly followed by a warning against its temptation 'rather to use Religion than to minister to it'. The ideal of a liberal education, then, is systematically qualified by reminders of its limitations. Thus the definition of a 'liberal' pursuit does not attempt to pretend that 'in point of worth and importance' there need be any comparison even with an 'illiberal' study: 'even what is supernatural need not be liberal, nor need a hero be a gentleman, for the plain reason that one idea is not another idea.' Newman warns against exaggerating the importance both of the university and of a liberal education. It is, he insists, 'as real a mistake to burden' liberal knowledge 'with virtue or religion as with the mechanical arts':

Its direct business is not to steel the soul against temptation or to console it in affliction, any more than to set the loom in motion, or to direct the steam carriage... it as little mends our hearts as it improves our temporal circumstances.... Quarry the granite rock with razors, or moor the vessel with a thread of silk; then you may hope with such keen and delicate instruments as human knowledge and human reason to contend against those giants, the passion and the pride of man.

An element of suspense hangs over the Discourses as the different aspects of the idea of a university come into focus and the perspective changes. Certainly, the most remarkable and dramatic shift of perspective occurs in the famous portrait of the 'gentleman' in the eighth Discourse. It is here that Newman concludes his exposition of intellectual culture with an eloquent depiction of its 'momentous' moral influences, 'all upon the type of Christianity... so much so, that a character more noble to look at, more beautiful, more winning, in the various relations of life and in personal duties, is hardly conceivable'. However, 'the work is as certainly not supernatural as it is certainly noble and beautiful', for there is a 'radical difference' between this 'mental refinement' and 'genuine religion'. And Newman proceeds to show how 'the tendency of the intellectual culture' is to become 'a false philosophy' and a 'spurious religion'. He takes as an example the Emperor Julian, 'in whom every Catholic sees the shadow of the future Antichrist', but who 'was all but the pattern-man of philosophical virtue'. Indeed, it is from the very 'shallowness of Philosophical Religion... that its disciples seem able to fulfil certain precepts of Christianity more readily and exactly than Christians themselves', so that 'the school of the world seems to send out living copies' of 'St. Paul's exemplar of the Christian in his external relations... with greater success than the Church'. Modesty is substituted for humility, and 'pride, under such training, instead of running to waste in the education of the mind, is turned to account'. A passage of marvellous irony follows, in which Newman admiringly extols the great and real social fruits of this new quality 'called self-respect', only to conclude with devastating effect: 'It breathes upon the face of the community, and the hollow sepulchre is forthwith beautiful to look upon.' Still, however, we are not allowed to forget that secular education can accomplish objects which seem to defeat religion, and we are reminded that it is a refined self-respect which 'is now quietly but energetically opposing itself to the unchristian practice of duelling . . . and certainly it seems likely to effect what Religion has aimed at abolishing in vain'.

The famous passage which follows, beginning with the well-known words, 'Hence it is that it is almost a definition of a gentleman to say he is one who never inflicts pain,' is so eloquent and presents such an attractive picture that many people have supposed that this in fact Newman's ideal. And indeed they are right in the sense that it is the ideal end of a liberal education—which

makes not the Christian, not the Catholic, but the gentleman. It is well to be a gentleman, it is well to have a cultivated intellect, a delicate taste, a candid, equitable, dispassionate mind, a noble and courteous bearing in the conduct of life; - these are the connatural qualities of a large knowledge; they are the objects of a University; I am advocating, I shall illustrate and insist upon them; but still, I repeat, they are no guarantee for sanctity or even for conscientiousness, they may attach to the man of the world, to the profligate, to the heartless . . .

The final terse sentence of this Discourse makes the point concretely and dramatically: 'Basil and Julian were fellow-students at the schools of Athens; and one became the Saint and Doctor of the Church, the other her scoffing and relentless foe.' It is a striking conclusion to one of the greatest passages of rhetoric in the English language. (Ker 1976: 371, 195, 197, 80, 101, 110–11, 164–5, 167, 174, 177–9, 110, 181.)

Newman was above all an 'occasional' writer, not because he needed a pretext or reason for writing, but because he was pre-eminently a controversialist. His brother Francis recorded after his death that he had learned his skills from Cicero and that he could have become an eminent barrister, since in his writings he was invariably arguing a brief, attacking or defending a thesis. In fact, Newman did very seriously consider a career at the Bar and one of his earliest writings was an essay on Cicero's oratory. It was controversy that stimulated Newman's literary powers, and the subject-matter was religion and theology. One aspect of Cicero that he specially emphasized was his use of satire, and this surely influenced Newman, who is not only one of the great controversialists but also one of the great satirists in the English language. This was recognized at the time by the leading literary critic R. H. Hutton, who wrote one of the best studies of Newman. Unfortunately, Hutton, followed by Wilfrid Ward, the author of the first serious biography, for some reason thought that the satirical Newman came into his own only after his conversion to Rome. It is true that the best satirical writings appeared in the years immediately after his leaving the Church of England, but we can date the first attempts at satire to 1833, the year the Oxford Movement began, when Newman attacked Thomas Arnold's published proposals for the reform of the Church of England, in which the liberal Arnold argued that religious inclusiveness was the only way of avoiding disestablishment. The sarcastic letters penned by Newman at the time are notable for the way he employs the kind of colloquial tone of voice that he would one day perfect in the public duel with Charles Kingsley that led to the writing of the *Apologia*. His central objection to Arnold's proposals is that, if comprehensiveness is the ideal and differences in belief unimportant, then why should not Roman Catholics and Jews, and even Muslims, belong to Arnold's inclusive national church? In other words, Arnold's argument is inconsistent since he certainly would want to draw the line. But to show that one's opponent is inconsistent is also to show that his position is absurd. And it is the theme of inconsistency which is at the heart of Newman's satirical writings. But the attack is nearly always on intellectual not moral inconsistency—characteristically, Newman thought that consistency was the mark of a saint. The exception proves the rule as when, writing as an Anglican on 'The Protestant Idea of Antichrist', he remarks with gleeful relish that the 'private life' of Thomas Newton, who was the 'main source' for the tradition, hardly inspired confidence: true, there was no doubting his 'kindness of heart and amiableness'—

but a man so idolatrous of comfort, so liquorish of preferment, whose most fervent aspiration apparently was that he might ride in a carriage and sleep on down, whose keenest sorrow was that he could not get a second appointment without relinquishing the first, who cast a regretful look back upon his dinner while he was at supper, and anticipated his morning chocolate in his evening muffins, who will say that this is the man, not merely to unchurch, but to smite, to ban, to wither the whole of Christendom for many centuries, and the greater part of it even in his own day...

But the anti-popery tradition is absurd anyway because of its manifest inconsistency in ordinary life:

how men, thinking that the Pope is the Beast of the Apocalypse, can endure the sight of any of his servants... or can sit with them in the same Council or Parliament, or can do business with them, buy and sell, trade and traffic, or can gaze upon and admire the architecture of churches built by Antichrist, or make much of his pictures,—or how they can read any book of his servants... all this is to us inexplicable.   (Newman 1871: 138–9, 148–9)

Again, writing as an Anglican, he satirizes the Protestant insistence on Scripture as the sole source of faith for its inherent inconsistency:

We [Protestants] uphold the pure unmutilated Scripture; the Bible, and the Bible only, is the religion of Protestants; the Bible and our own sense of the Bible. We claim a sort of parliamentary privilege to interpret laws in our own way, and not to suffer an appeal to any court beyond ourselves. We know, and we view it with consternation, that all Antiquity runs counter to our interpretation; and therefore, alas, the Church was corrupt from very early times indeed. But mind, we hold all this in a truly Catholic spirit, not in bigotry. We hold in others the right of private judgment, and confess that we, as others, are fallible men. We confess facts are against us; we do but claim the liberty of theorizing in spite of them. Far be it from us to say that we are certainly right; we only say that the whole early Church was certainly wrong. We do not impose our belief on any one; we only say that those who take the contrary side are Papists, firebrands, madmen, zealots, bigots, and an insult to the nineteenth century.   (Newman 1840: 420–1)

Newman seizes on Protestant hostility to those who abandon Protestantism as the proof that the principle of 'private judgment' is self-contradictory. Does it not prove that 'this great people is not such a conscientious supporter of the sacred right of Private Judgment as a good Protestant would desire'? He enjoys satirizing the glaring inconsistency in an exuberantly comic passage:

Is it not sheer wantonness and cruelty in Baptist, Independent, Irvingite, Wesleyan, Establishment-man, Jumper, and Mormonite, to delight in trampling on and crushing these manifestations of their own pure and precious charter, instead of dutifully and reverently exalting, as at Bethel, or at Dan, each instance of it, as it occurs, to the gaze of its professing votaries? If a staunch Protestant's daughter turns Roman, and betakes herself to a convent, why does he not exult in the occurrence? Why does he not give a public breakfast, or hold a meeting, or erect a memorial, or write a pamphlet in honour of her, and of the great undying principle she has so gloriously vindicated? Why is he in this base, disloyal style muttering about priests, and Jesuits, and the horrors of nunneries, in solution of the phenomenon, when he has the fair and ample form of Private Judgment rising before his eyes, and pleading with him...All this would lead us to suspect that the doctrine of private judgment, in its simplicity, purity, and integrity,—private judgment, all private judgment, and nothing but private judgment,—is held by very few persons indeed; and that the great mass of the population are either stark unbelievers in it, or deplorably dark about it; and that even the minority who are in a sense faithful to it, have glossed and corrupted the true sense of it by a miserably faulty reading, and hold, not the right of private judgment, but the private right of judgment; in other words, their own private right, and no one else's.   (Newman 1871: 340–1)

Newman was writing as a Tractarian trying to restore what he believed was the essentially Catholic character of the Church of England through the theory of the *via media* or middle way, between Protestantism on the one hand and Roman Catholicism on the other. But while Newman was very critical of what he saw as the corruptions and superstitions of the Roman Church, it is striking that he never attempted to satirize Roman Catholics—except in one passage (which he quotes in the *Apologia*) in an article of 1840 on the 'Catholicity of the Anglican Church', which he wrote in a desperate attempt to shore up the theory of the *via media* against an article that had deeply disturbed him, comparing the Anglo-Catholic position to the Donatist schism in north Africa at the time of Augustine. This solitary exception comes at the end of an attack on Roman Catholicism.

When we go into foreign countries, we see superstitions in the Roman Church which shock us; when we read history, we find its spirit of intrigue so rife, so widely spread, that 'Jesuitism' has become a by-word; when we look round us at home, we see it associated everywhere with the low democracy, pandering to the spirit of rebellion...We see it attempting to gain converts among us, by unreal representations of its doctrines...We see its agents smiling and nodding and ducking to attract attention, as gipsies make up to truant boys, holding out tales for the nursery, and pretty pictures, and gold gingerbread, and physic concealed in jam, and sugarplums for good children.

The word 'unreal' is worth noticing, indicating as it does that it is not the doctrines of Rome that are objected to by the author, but the way in which they are insinuated. And it explains the sentence that follows: 'Who can but feel shame when the religion of Ximenes, Borromeo, and Pascal is so overlaid?' (ibid. 71–2). Uniquely, then the Roman Catholic Church is made the object of satire, not for being herself but for not being her true self, for being inconsistent, unreal, and consequently ridiculous. In his Tractarian period Newman never doubted the consistency of the Roman Church, which could certainly be attacked and criticized but not satirized for the simple reason that a church so logically consistent, so objectionably consistent, so alarmingly consistent, could not be made the object of ridicule. This exceptional attempt at satirizing Rome is not, unsurprisingly, at all funny. In actual fact, Newman was to make the point explicitly as a Roman Catholic himself, when he quoted the saying, 'that ridicule is the test of truth,' commenting: 'Methodism is ridiculous, so is Puritanism; it is not so with the Catholic religion; it may be, and is, maligned and defamed; ridiculous it cannot be. It is too real ... to have aught to fear from the most brilliant efforts of the satirist or the wit' (Newman 1851: 393). He should have known; he was speaking from personal experience.

The one sustained work of satire from Newman's Anglican period, which is also his Anglican literary masterpiece, is the unpromisingly named *Tamworth Reading Room*, consisting of a series of letters published in *The Times* in February 1841, attacking a speech by Sir Robert Peel at the opening of a new library and reading-room at Tamworth, in which he suggested that education could substitute for religion as a basis of morality. How, Newman asked, could a knowledge of science have a morally uplifting effect? 'Can the process be analysed and drawn out, or does it act like a dose or a charm ...?' The truth is that such 'great teachers of morals' are engaged in 'the incessant search after stimulants and sedatives, by which unruly nature may ... be kept in order'. While the Tory Peel 'makes no pretence of subduing the giant nature, in which we were born, of smiting the loins of the domestic enemies of our peace, of overthrowing passion and fortifying reason', the Whig Lord Brougham at the founding of the secular London University

frankly offers us a philosophy of expedients: he shows us how to live by medicine. Digestive pills half an hour before dinner, and a posset at bedtime at the best; and at the worst, dram-drinking and opium,—the very remedy against broken hearts, or remorse of conscience, which is in request among the many, in gin-palaces not intellectual.

Newman demands, 'who was ever consoled in real trouble by the small beer of literature or science?' or when 'was a choleric temperament ever brought under by a scientific King Canute planting his professor's chair before the rising waves?' 'Such' he concludes, 'is this new art of living, offered to the labouring classes,—we will say, for instance, in a severe winter, snow on the ground, glass falling, bread rising, coal at 20d. the cwt., and no work'. There follows one of the great passages of satire in Newman:

That the mind is changed by a discovery, or saved by a diversion, and can thus be amused into immortality,—that grief, anger, cowardice, self-conceit, pride, or passion, can be subdued by an examination of shells or grasses, or inhaling of gases, or chipping of rocks, or calculating the longitude, is the veriest of pretences which sophist or mountebank ever professed to a gaping auditory. If virtue be a mastery over the mind, if its end be action, if its perfection be inward order, harmony, and peace, we must seek it in graver and holier places than in Libraries and Reading-rooms.

It is noteworthy that there is no attempt to satirize the arch-utilitarian Jeremy Bentham. And the reason is simple. There is nothing inconsistent in the idea that knowledge can replace religion as the basis for morality with the philosophy of Bentham, to whom the objection that 'To know is one thing, to do is another' is easily met by the answer that 'the knowledge which carries virtue along with it, is the knowledge how to take care of number one', since 'Useful Knowledge is that which tends to make us more useful to ourselves;—a most definite and intelligible account of the matter, and needing no explanation.' But unlike the 'lofty enthusiasm', the 'high aspiration, generous sentiment, and impassioned feeling in the tone of Lord Brougham and Sir Robert', Bentham 'had not a spark of poetry in him'. There is nothing inconsistent or unreal about that 'stern realist', whose 'system has nothing ideal about it' and who 'limits his realism to things which he can see, hear, taste, and handle'. What, on the other hand, could be more unreal than to think that knowledge ever 'healed a wounded heart' or 'changed a sinful one'? (Newman 1841: 285, 262–4, 266–70.)

In the *Apologia* Newman describes how he 'came to the conclusion that there was no medium, in true philosophy, between Atheism and Catholicity, and that a perfectly consistent mind … must embrace either the one or the other' (Svaglic 1967: 179–80). It is because he regarded both atheists and Roman Catholics as completely consistent that they are beyond the reach of his satire, for ridicule cannot touch the real. But it can touch Brougham, since 'Human nature wants recasting', but he is 'all for tinkering it'; as well as Peel, for, if we 'attempt to make man moral and religious by Libraries and Museums, let us in consistency take chemists for our cooks, and mineralogists for our masons' (Newman 1841: 277, 296).

Newman's first novel, *Loss and Gain*, which was also the first book he published as a Roman Catholic, opens his most creative period as a satirist. Running through the novel is a strong, often comic, sense of the real and the unreal. The issue for the hero Charles Reding becomes not so much which is the true religion, but which is the real religion. The doctrinal comprehensiveness of the Church of England is perceived not as a source of strength but as fatal to its reality, for two contradictory views cannot 'both be real'. In the face of broad or liberal Anglicanism, it is no longer a question of satirizing inconsistencies, but of satirizing inconsistency itself as an ideal. 'Our Church,' he said,

admitted of great liberty of thought within her pale. Even our greatest divines differed from each other in many respects; nay, Bishop Taylor differed from himself. It was a great principle in the English Church. Her true children agree to differ. In truth, there is that robust, masculine, noble independence in the English mind, which refuses to be tied down to artificial shapes, but is like, I will say, some great and beautiful production of nature—a tree, which is rich in foliage and fantastic in limb, no sickly denizen of the hothouse, or helpless dependent of the garden wall, but in careless magnificence sheds its fruits upon the free earth, for the bird of the air and the beast of the field, and all sorts of cattle, to eat thereof and rejoice.

There is another hilarious scene in a religious bookshop when the hero comes across an Anglo-Catholic friend who had once idealized celibacy, but who is now a clergyman engaged to be married. His bride cannot remember the name of the book she wanted: can it be 'The Catholic Parsonage'? or 'Modified celibacy'? No, it is 'Abbeys and Abbots'—'"I want to get some hints for improving the rectory windows when we get home…"' (Newman 1848: 34, 84–5, 351).

In a letter Newman insisted that his satire was directed against the same 'unreality and inconsistency of conduct' which he had laughed at as an Anglican (Dessain and Blehl, 1964: 399). But the doctrinal inconsistencies which he had come to see in Anglo-Catholicism and which are touched on in the course of the novel he would satirize at length in the first of his two major satirical works.

Lectures on certain *Difficulties Felt by Anglicans in submitting to the Catholic Church* were delivered in 1850. The contrast between the real and the unreal is central to the argument. Anglo-Catholics 'dream' that the Church of England is a branch of the Catholic Church, when in fact it is nothing more than a state Protestant church.

If, indeed, we dress it up in an ideal form, as if it were something real … as if it were in deed and not only in name a Church, then indeed we may feel interest in it, and reverence towards it, and affection for it, as men have fallen in love with pictures, or knights in romance do battle for high dames whom they have never seen. Thus it is that students of the Fathers, antiquaries, and poets, begin by assuming that the body to which they belong is that of which they read in times past, and then to proceed to decorate it with that majesty and beauty of which history tells, or which their genius creates.

Gentle irony gives way to a more brutal sarcasm as the real identity of the Church of England is revealed:

And, as in fairy tales, the magic castle vanishes when the spell is broken, and nothing is seen but the wild heath, the barren rock, and the forlorn sheep-walk, so is it with us as regards the Church of England, when we look in amazement on that we thought so unearthly, and find so commonplace or worthless.

As usual in Newman, the idea of consistency and inconsistency is closely involved in that of reality and unreality. Thus it is 'an intellectual absurdity'

That such as you, my brethren, should consider Christianity given from heaven once for all, should protest against private judgment, should profess to transmit what you have received, and yet from diligent study of the Fathers, from your thorough knowledge of St. Basil and St. Chrysostom, from living, as you say, in the atmosphere of Antiquity, that you should come forth into open day with your new edition of the Catholic faith, different from that held in any existing body of Christians anywhere … and then, withal, should be as positive about its truth in every part, as if the voice of mankind were with you instead of being against you.

It is no less absurd than arrogant to profess to 'have a mission to teach the National Church, which is to teach the British Empire, which is to teach the world'. Nor is it consistent to provide a defence for the Church 'which she has no dream of appropriating', to 'innovate on her professions of doctrine' and then 'bid us love her for your innovations', to 'cling to her for what she denounces', and 'almost anathematise us for taking a step which you would please her best by taking also'. The 'theories' on which the Oxford Movement was based 'claimed to represent the theological and the ecclesiastical teaching of the Fathers; and the Fathers, when interrogated, did but pronounce them to be the offspring of eclecticism, and the exponent of a State Church'. Anglo-Catholic theologians appealed to the authority of the Fathers:

There they found a haven of rest; thence they looked out upon the troubled surge of human opinion and upon the crazy vessels which were labouring, without chart or compass, upon it. Judge then of their dismay, when, according to the Arabian tale, on their striking their anchors into the supposed soil, lighting their fires on it, and fixing in it the poles of their tents, suddenly their island began to move, to heave, to splash, to frisk to and fro, to dive, and at last to swim away, spouting out inhospitable jets of water upon the credulous mariners who had made it their home.   (Newman 1850: 4–6, 157–8, 161, 386, 150)

The irony of *Difficulties Felt by Anglicans* is gently sympathetic; it is, after all, addressed to former associates and friends and directed against a form of religion in which Newman himself had once believed, and of which indeed he was the principal architect. Very different is the sarcasm of *Lectures on the Present Position of Catholics*, in which he confronts head-on the virulent anti-popery tradition, that had been inflamed by the restoration of the Catholic hierarchy. It contains the best of Newman's satirical writing, and he himself said he had 'ever considered it [his] best written book' (Dessain and Gornall 1974: 115). And yet it is a book which has not only been largely ignored by writers on Newman, but which can also claim to be one of the most underrated works in English.

As always, it is inconsistency that is Newman's target. Thus anti-popery, which objects to the Catholic belief in tradition, itself rests on 'tradition immemorial, unauthenticated tradition'. Indeed, because the 'anti-Catholic Tradition' is the most effective weapon at the disposal of the Established Church, its special task is 'to preserve it from rust and decay, to keep it bright and keen, and ready for action on any emergency or peril'. Or again, to change the image, the 'Establishment is the Keeper in ordinary of those national types and blocks from which Popery is ever to be printed off.' Since a few facts are useful for preserving the tradition, it is not surprising that 'preachers and declaimers' have 'now a weary while been longing, and panting, and praying for some good fat scandal, one, only just one ... to batten upon and revel in'. The prejudiced Protestant is the child of the tradition, 'and, like a man who has been for a long while in one position, he is cramped and disabled, and has a difficulty and pain ... in stretching his limbs, straightening them, and moving them freely'.

The book contains some of the most startling and vivid imagery—sometimes savage and Swiftian, sometimes grotesque and Dickensian—to be found anywhere in Newman's writings. He enjoys turning the images that have stained the Protestant imagination against Protestantism itself. Thus it is no benighted Catholic country but Protestant England, which, 'as far as religion is concerned, really must be called one large convent, or rather workhouse; the old pictures hang on the walls; the world-wide Church is chalked up on every side as a wivern or a griffin; no pure gleam of light finds its way in or from without; the thick atmosphere refracts and distorts such straggling rays as gain admittance'. Again, it is

familiar to an Englishman to wonder at and to pity the recluse and the devotee who surround themselves with a high enclosure, and shut out what is on the other side of it; but was there ever such an instance of self-sufficient, dense, and religious bigotry, as that which rises up and walls in the minds of our fellow-countrymen from all knowledge of one of the most remarkable phenomena which the world has seen?

In an

inquisitive age, when the Alps are crested, and seas fathomed, and mines ransacked, and sands sifted, and rocks cracked into specimens, and beasts caught and catalogued, as little is known by Englishmen of the religious sentiments, the religious usages, the religious motives, the religious ideas of two hundred millions of Christians poured to and fro, among them and around them, as if, I will not say, they were Tartars or Patagonians, but as if they inhabited the moon

And so the English Protestant who despises the enclosed monk or nun is shown to be just as 'enclosed', while, in spite of his vaunted knowledge of the world, he is wholly ignorant of the Catholics about whom he has so much to say and so confidently.

Analogies also reveal inconsistencies. The so-called 'omnipotence' of the Virgin Mary is no more to be taken literally than the 'Omnipotence of Parliament'. Just as the notice 'Ring the Bell' presupposes 'if you have business within', so indulgences presuppose but do not convey absolution. Protestants emphasize the value of freedom of thought, 'but towards us they do not dream of practising it'. The Protestant Reformers had used their 'private judgment' against the Church—but 'There was enough of private judgment in the world, they thought, when they had done with it themselves. So they forcibly shut-to the door which they had opened, and imposed on the populations they had reformed an artificial tradition of their own, instead of the liberty of inquiry and disputation.' Protestants vehemently reject the very notion of infallibility, but in practice regard as infallible their own objections to Catholicism. Protestants disapprove of images in Catholic churches, and yet they are quite happy to burn the pope in effigy—but 'How is it childish to honour an image, if it is not childish to dishonour it?' Toleration is the boast of Protestants, but they love to persecute Catholics. It is true that the Catholic Church does not recognize the absolute right to religious freedom that Protestantism does—but are Protestants to 'bring their own inconsistency as the excuse for their crime' of atrocities at least as bloody as any perpetrated by Catholics? Certainly the Protestant readiness to do so is hardly consistent with the view that Catholicism 'is so irrational that it will fall to pieces of itself'. Again, since honesty is one of the boasted virtues of Englishmen, it is paradoxical that it is by 'wholesale, retail systematic, unscrupulous lying . . . that the many rivulets are made to flow for the feeding the great Protestant Tradition' (Newman 1851: 43–5, 55, 74–5, 126, 139, 178, 180, 219, 275).

Finally, something very briefly should be said of Newman's novels, poetry, and letters. Apart from its satire, *Loss and Gain* as a novel of conversion does have one claim to originality: its introduction of a new kind of introspective self-questioning into English fiction. His other novel, *Callista*, is interesting as an imaginative attempt to recreate the world of the primitive church, in which an analogy between the situation of the early Christians facing persecution in the Roman Empire and that of Catholics in nineteenth-century England is clearly intended. But otherwise the book is more notable for theological than literary reasons.

Newman's long poem *The Dream of Gerontius* was, after Tennyson's *In Memoriam*, the best-known literary work on the subject of death and the afterlife in an age that was preoccupied with the subject. Today its fame derives from the oratorio which Edward Elgar completed in 1900. Theologically, it is especially interesting for its spiritual treatment of purgatory. But as a literary work, it has to be compared with Gerard Manley Hopkins's 'The Wreck of the Deutschland' as a specifically Catholic literary treatment of death. What above all distinguishes Newman's and Hopkins's poems from *In Memoriam* or other Victorian treatments of death is that for the two Catholic writers it is possible both to pray for the dead if they are in purgatory and to ask for their prayers if they are assumed to be in heaven. For Protestant writers, the dead person was no longer in contact or relationship with the living, apart from a continuing existence in the memory.

Newman's vast correspondence, unlike the letters of some other writers (such as George Eliot), not only has biographical importance but also adds appreciably to his literary standing. In that respect, it reminds us of the position his mentor Cicero's letters hold in his literary achievement. They enhance his position as one of the great writers of non-fiction prose, as well as constituting an immensely rich and varied contribution to the epistolary genre. There is a great variety of voice since Newman wrote in a highly personal way to each correspondent. The satirist who ridiculed the unreal in the sense of the inconsistent, the philosopher who contrasted 'real' with merely 'notional' knowledge, and the theologian who distrusted unreal theories that did not accord with historical facts, was also the letter-writer whose many voices are all attempts to do justice to the reality of each situation as it confronted him and as he tried to realize it for each correspondent.

WORKS CITED

DRABBLE, MARGARET (ed.) 1985. *The Oxford Companion to English Literature*, 5th edn. Oxford: Oxford University Press.

KER, IAN (ed.) 1976. *The Idea of a University*. Oxford: Clarendon.

NEWMAN, JOHN HENRY. 1840. London: Longmans, Green, and Co. Dates given are of first publication in book or pamphlet form, but all page references are to the relevant volume of the Longmans Green uniform edition of 36 volumes (1868–81).

—— 1841. *The Tamworth Reading Room*. London: Longmans, Green.

—— 1848. *Loss and Gain: The Story of a Convert*. London: Longmans, Green.

—— 1850. *Lectures on Certain Difficulties felt by Anglicans in submitting to the Catholic Church*. London: Longmans, Green.

—— 1851. *Lectures on the Present Position of Catholics in England*. London: Longmans, Green.

—— 1871. *Essays Critical and Historical*. London: Longmans, Green, ii.

—— 1964. *The Letters and Diaries of John Henry Newman*, ed. Charles Stephen Dessain and Vincent Ferrer Blehl, SJ. London: Nelson, xv.

—— 1974. *The Letters and Diaries of John Henry Newman*, ed. Charles Stephen Dessain and Thomas Gornall. Oxford: Clarendon, xxvii.

SVAGLIC, MARTIN J. (ed.) 1967. *Apologia pro Vita Sua*. Oxford: Clarendon.

FURTHER READING

HOLLOWAY, JOHN. 1953. *The Victorian Sage: Studies in Argument.* London: Macmillan.

HOUGHTON, WALTER E. 1945. *The Art of Newman's* Apologia. *New Haven: Yale University Press.*

KER, IAN. 1990. *The Achievement of John Henry Newman.* Notre Dame, Ind.: University of Notre Dame Press.

KER, IAN and HILL, ALAN G. 1990. *Newman After a Hundred Years.* Oxford: Clarendon.

PETERSON, LINDA H. 1986. *Victorian Autobiography.* New Haven: Yale University Press.

CHAPTER 38

....

MATTHEW
ARNOLD

....

LUKE FERRETTER

Modern poetry can only subsist by its contents: by becoming a complete magister vitae as the poetry of the ancients did: by including as theirs did, religion with the poetry, instead of existing as poetry only, and leaving religious wants to be supplied by the Christian religion.   (Arnold 1932: 124)

Arnold was not yet 30, and had only a single volume of poems to his name, when he wrote these words to Arthur Hugh Clough in 1851. He would not begin his works of literary criticism until the end of the decade, nor his biblical criticism until the 1870s. Nevertheless, the concern he expresses in this earlier letter with the close interrelationship of literature and religion is one that pervades not only his poetry, but all his literary criticism and theology. Arnold is not the first English literary critic of the Bible—he was acquainted early with Coleridge's *Confessions of an Inquiring Spirit*—but his literary criticism of the Bible was not surpassed in critical breadth or detail until the work of modern scholars such as Robert Alter and Frank Kermode. He was charged by T. S. Eliot, as by critics of his own day, with *reducing* religion to literature. John Campbell Shairp said of him in 1871, 'They who seek religion for culture-sake are aesthetic, not religious' (Dawson and Pforedsher 1979: 277). Eliot (1951: 436) wrote: 'The total effect of Arnold's philosophy is to set up Culture in the place of Religion, and to leave Religion to be laid waste by the anarchy of feeling.' This, however, is not the case. Although Arnold is convinced that popular religion is a thing of the past, outdated by the scientific spirit of the age, he is equally convinced that true religion will always meet the moral, emotional, and intellectual needs of the human race. It is through the process of literary criticism that he determines from the Bible in what this true religion consists. At the same time, his concept of religion determines for him the criteria of literary criticism. Throughout his work, as his letter to Clough suggests, Arnold does not think of literature except in terms of religion, nor of religion except in terms of literature.

By the 1860s, when Arnold turned in earnest to literary criticism, the Church of England had been forced for the first time to face the challenges of natural science and of German biblical criticism, both of which called into question the traditional basis of faith in the historical truth of the Bible. The geology of the first half of the century had cast doubt on the historical accuracy of the book of Genesis. In 1859, *The Origin of Species* argued that all the varieties of living things had evolved by a process of natural selection, calling into question the biblical doctrine of creation. Although the theory of evolution was well integrated into Christian thought only two or three decades later, Darwin's work cemented in the popular mind the conviction that 'science' contradicted 'religion'. Arnold's friend T. H. Huxley vigorously defended Darwinism against the theological prejudices of its opponents. In 1860, another publication shook the church, the *Essays and Reviews*, written by six clergymen and a layman. These authors set out to end the silence in the Church of England over questions of biblical criticism that had been disturbing educated Christians at least since George Eliot's translation of David Friedrich Strauss's *Life of Jesus* in 1846. In his contribution to the volume, Rowland Williams gave details of the results of German biblical criticism to date—the Pentateuch was a gradually compiled composition; Isaiah 40–66 was not written by the author of Chapters 1–39; the book of Daniel was written in the second century BC; and similar hypotheses, then entirely new to English theology—according to which it could not be maintained that every detail of the scriptural text was historically accurate. Benjamin Jowett, Regius Professor of Greek at Oxford, brought his learning in German liberal theology to bear on the question of scriptural interpretation. His first principle was this:

As the time has come when it is no longer possible to ignore the results of criticism, it is of importance that Christianity should be seen to be in harmony with them ... It would be a strange and almost incredible thing if the Gospel, which at first made war only on the vices of mankind, should now be opposed to one of the highest and rarest virtues—the love of truth.   (Shea and Whitla 2000: 502)

Like Coleridge before him, Jowett argued that the Bible must be interpreted like any other book, 'by the same rules of evidence and the same canons of criticism'. He was convinced that, once the Bible was read rightly in this way, Christianity, stripped of its layers of theological dogma, would again become acceptable to the minds of a scientific age.

The *Essays and Reviews* caused a public controversy. Clergymen of the Church of England had expressed in it views at variance with the church's articles of faith. Two of the book's authors—Rowland Williams and H. B. Wilson—were prosecuted for heresy, a move which kept the controversy in the public eye, and which backfired, since the judgement, although against the defendants, recognized that clergymen could hold an unexpectedly broad range of views on the historical accuracy of Scripture. The conviction was overturned on appeal. During the controversy, which was not settled until 1864, Bishop John William Colenso of Natal, who had read the *Essays and Reviews*, published the first two parts of *The Pentateuch and the Book of Joshua Critically Examined*. A former maths teacher at Harrow, Colenso argued that the numerical figures given in the Pentateuch showed that many of the events it describes could not actually be true. These arguments were easily dismissed, but the fact that a bishop of the Church of England was teaching that the Pentateuch was in part historically untrue was a scandal. Colenso was petitioned by all forty-one English bishops to resign and, when he refused, deposed by the Bishop of Cape Town. He appealed to the Privy Council, who held that his removal from office was illegal. After his return to South Africa as the lawful bishop of Natal, a second bishop was nevertheless consecrated, causing a schism in the diocese, as an expression of the church's view that the author of *The Pentateuch and the Book of Joshua Critically Examined* was not the rightful holder of the office.

Arnold's first extended treatment of the relationship between literature and religion was written in response to the first part of Colenso's book. In 'The Bishop and the Philosopher' (1862), he explains the relevance of the book to literary criticism: 'Literary criticism's most important function is to try books as to the influence which they are calculated to have upon the general culture of single nations or of the world at large ... Religious books come within the jurisdiction of literary criticism insofar as they affect general culture' (Arnold 1962: 41). A work of biblical studies, like a work of philosophy, history, or of any other science, is the proper object of the special criticism of the discipline to which it contributes. It is also, Arnold argues, the proper object of literary criticism, in so far as it also contributes to the culture of its age. Literary criticism, as Arnold conceives it, is the 'appointed guardian' of European culture, which constitutes 'the best that has been thought and said in the world' (ibid. 42; 1965: 233). If a work of biblical studies has an influence upon that culture, it becomes an object of literary criticism. Arnold divides religious books into two kinds—those which edify and those which inform. It is the latter which contribute to the development of culture, and with which literary criticism is concerned. Arnold's criticism of Colenso's book, 'which all England is now reading', is that it neither edifies nor informs. It is neither a successful religious work nor a successful literary work. Colenso had argued that his mathematical demonstrations, which most intelligent critics had ridiculed, proved that the Pentateuch is not a historically accurate report. By the standards of literary criticism, Arnold argues, his argument is a failure, since it fails to inform, or to develop the higher culture of Europe. Men of culture had known at least since Spinoza that there were contradictions in the Pentateuch, and German Biblical criticism had been pointing it out ever since. The question to which European culture seeks an answer is, 'What then?' (Arnold 1962: 49). How are we to understand the Bible, and to organize our religious lives after we have understood this criticism? Spinoza's superiority over Colenso is that he addresses these questions. Two hundred years before Colenso had even asked the questions, Spinoza had attempted to answer them. He calls on governments to establish national churches on the basis of the religion of the Bible rightly interpreted, rather than on the basis of the current metaphysical misinterpretations.

Spinoza's *Tractatus Theologico-Politicus* makes a contribution to the development of culture that the Bishop of Natal's book does not. Arnold (ibid. 76) writes of the latter, 'For literary criticism his book, as it at present stands, must remain a censurable production'.

In 'Dr Stanley's Lectures on the Jewish Church' (1862), Arnold responds to critics of his position on Colenso's book, using his friend A. P. Stanley's recently published lectures as a point of departure from which to develop these reflections on the literary value of religious studies. Stanley has understood a fundamental principle which Colenso has not, for Arnold—that religion is not primarily intellectual assent, but emotional attachment. He has understood that the Bible is a literary work. Arnold (ibid. 74) writes: 'There is truth of science and truth of religion: truth of science does not become truth of religion until it is made to harmonise with it. The fundamental truth of religion, for Arnold, is that human happiness consists in the practice of right conduct, motivated by emotional attachment. Any scientific proposition, if it is to make sense in the sphere of religious belief and practice, must be consistent with this fundamental truth. It is a difficult task to express scientific propositions in this way, and those who have been able to do so have been the great religious reformers of history. Luther was such a reformer, not because he criticized ideas like that of a mediatory priesthood, but because he showed how religion could continue after such a criticism. In the nineteenth century, the Protestant doctrines which grew out of this reformation are themselves subject to the critical ideas of the age, and a new reformation is necessary. In his religious works of the 1870s, Arnold addresses this task himself. In 1862, however, he sees religion in a kind of cultural hiatus, in which the old forms of its expression are no longer tenable but adequate new forms have yet to be articulated. In this period of transition, he argues, it is the literary qualities of the Bible which constitute the most adequate expression of the truths of religious experience: 'Who has not rejoiced to be able, between the old idea, tenable no longer, which once connected itself to certain religious ideas, and the new idea, which has not yet connected itself with them, to rest awhile in the healing virtue and beauty of the words themselves?' (ibid. 81). If we can no longer believe intellectually in the special intervention of Providence, for example, we can nevertheless commit ourselves emotionally to the words of Isaiah, 'In all their affliction, he was afflicted, and the angel of his presence saved them; and he bare them and carried them all the days of old' (Isa. 63: 9). Until we have been able adequately to integrate the insights of contemporary culture into religious life, until we have a newly formulated scientific theology, there is no better expression of the religious impulse than the poetry of the Bible. Although Arnold does not say as much, his concept of literary value in these essays in criticism of religious works is determined by his concept of religion. For a religious work to be judged favourably by literary criticism, to be judged to possess literary value, it must teach true religion—moral practice on the basis of emotional attachment—above all, and it must subordinate its propositions of religious science to this fundamental principle of true religion. The literary value of a religious book, that is, is commensurate with its religious value. This is the principle Arnold applies to the Bible as well as to the biblical studies of Colenso, Stanley, and Spinoza.

The next development of Arnold's understanding of the relationship between religion and culture occurs in *Culture and Anarchy* (1869). As described in the essays which comprise this book, culture has a close and complex relationship with religion, as the epigraph—*Estote vos ergo perfecti*, 'Be ye therefore perfect' (Matt. 5: 48)—indicates. If culture is the 'study of perfection' (Arnold 1965: 91), Arnold's epigraph reminds us that this is also a dominical definition of religion. In the first chapter of *Culture and Anarchy*, originally delivered as Arnold's last lecture as Professor of Poetry at Oxford, he argues that culture combines the 'scientific passion for pure knowledge' with the 'moral and social passion for doing good' (ibid.). Its object can be described in Bishop Wilson's words as, 'to make reason and the will of God prevail' (ibid.). Culture is concerned both with what constitutes reason and the will of God, and with making these the standards of individual and social life. Arnold's definition of the will of God is here, as always, rigorously non-supernatural. To know the will of God is 'to draw towards a knowledge of the universal order which seems to be intended and aimed at in the world, and which it is a man's happiness to go along with or his misery to go counter to' (ibid. 93). It is to obey the moral law, which constitutes human happiness. What is the relation of culture, conceived in this way as a study of perfection, to religion, whose greatest teacher enjoined his disciples to be perfect? In one sense, religion is superior to culture—it is 'the greatest and most important of the efforts by which the human race has manifested its impulse to perfect itself—religion, that voice of the deepest human experience' (ibid.), 'a yet more important manifestation of human nature than poetry' (ibid. 99). Religion also has the same goals as culture, namely to ascertain the nature of human perfection and to make this perfection prevail. It 'comes to a conclusion identical with that which culture . . . reaches' concerning the nature of human perfection: 'Religion says: *The kingdom of God is within you*; and culture, in like manner, places perfection in an *internal* condition, on the growth and predominance of our humanity proper' (ibid. 94). Jesus teaches that righteousness is not a matter of external observance but of the inner person; in the same way, culture is not a matter of social action but of the development of the self—of the harmonious development of the moral, emotional, and intellectual faculties. Again, for both culture and religion, this development is a continual and lifelong process. Finally, Arnold argues, because human beings are not only individuals but part of the human race, the perfection which is the goal of culture cannot consist only in individual self-development, but in the development of the whole race. 'The individual is required, under pain of being stunted and enfeebled in his own development if he disobeys, to carry others along with him in his march towards perfection' (ibid.). This requirement, too, culture shares with religion.

On the other hand, culture is superior to religion. In the first place, it can be more certain of the truth of its concept of reason and the will of God than religion, because it seeks 'the determination of this question through *all* the voices of human experience which have been heard upon it, of art, science, poetry, philosophy, history, as well as of religion, in order to give a greater fullness and certainty to its solution' (ibid. 93). Since culture consists in the study of all the productions of the human spirit, it has more comprehensive access to the totality of human reflection on reason and the will of God—including those that can be described as 'religious'. Nevertheless, according to Arnold, culture and religion come to the same conclusions. Culture's more effective superiority to religion consists in this, that whereas culture is a 'harmonious' development of all the powers or faculties of human nature, religion tends only to develop one of these powers, that of morality. Here Arnold makes clear that he is speaking of 'popular religion', the supernatural, historical, and dogmatic beliefs of Protestant orthodoxy, especially as these are held by the Nonconformist churches which exist for the sake of this orthodoxy. This is what he means when he says that 'culture goes beyond religion, as religion is generally conceived by us' (ibid. 94). The British middle classes, who constitute the social base of Nonconformity, have a powerfully developed sense of morality. What they lack is culture—the sense that a complete perfection, rather than moral perfection alone, is necessary not only to be truly happy, but also to be truly religious. They are under the impression that their churches teach all that is necessary for human perfection, but a mere glance at their way of life—which Arnold disparages as 'jealousy of the Establishment, disputes, tea-meetings, openings of chapels, sermons', a judgement that provoked some understandable objections from Nonconformist critics—shows that this is not the case. The religious institutions of Victorian Britain are failing as such—they have not made reason and the will of God prevail. What is necessary, therefore, is culture:

When our religious organisations—which I admit to express the most considerable effort after perfection that our race has yet made—land us in no better result than this, it is high time to examine carefully their idea of perfection, to see whether it does not leave out of account sides and forces of human nature which we might turn to great use; whether it would not be more operative if it were more complete.   (ibid. 104)

Arnold's begins his work of biblical criticism in *Culture and Anarchy*, as he argues that the Nonconformist churches, because of their single-minded pursuit of moral perfection, even misunderstand the religious teaching of the Bible, on which they base this pursuit. 'No man, who knows nothing else, knows even his Bible' (ibid. 184). As an example, Arnold cites the position of the Baptist leader C. H. Spurgeon in the debate on the disestablishment of the Irish church. In a letter published in *The Times*, Spurgeon derives his anti-establishment stance from the text, 'My kingdom is not of this world' (John 18: 36). This is not the meaning of the text, Arnold argues. It is Spurgeon's single-mindedness which has caused him to think that it is. Because he focuses all his concern on Protestant doctrine as such, he has misinterpreted the biblical text in the light of this concern. A more cultured reading, Arnold argues, the reading of a person who pursues intellectual and emotional as well as moral perfection, makes clear that, 'Jesus Christ's words mean that his religion is a force of inward persuasion acting on the soul, and not a force of outward constraint acting on the body' (ibid. 196). If the Nonconformist stance against church-establishment can be shown to follow from what Jesus meant, Arnold argues, then Spurgeon can be said to have interpreted the text correctly. This is not the case, though—especially with respect to worship, religious life is more effectively practised in the common tradition of an Established Church rather than in small and isolated congregations. Hence 'Mr. Spurgeon and the Nonconformists seem to have misapprehended the true meaning of Christ's words' (ibid. 198), since, if this is not expressed perfectly in the Church of England, it is nevertheless less inadequately expressed there than in Nonconformity.

This is the kind of claim Arnold pursues in *St. Paul and Protestantism* (1870), the first of the many biblical and religious studies which occupied him for the next seven years. In *St. Paul* (1869), Ernest Renan had argued that the influence of Paul's thought, along with the Protestant doctrine based upon it, was coming to an end. In Arnold's view, whilst the Protestant theologies which claimed to be based on the epistles of St Paul had indeed become unacceptable to the spirit of the age, this was not true of Paul's own thought. On the contrary, the influence of this thought, properly understood, was only just beginning. Protestant doctrines are a series of misinterpretations of Paul's letters, for Arnold, a series of acts of bad literary criticism. This can be demonstrated by a comparison of these doctrines with Paul's letters rightly interpreted, with what Arnold calls the 'true criticism of this great and misunderstood author' (Arnold 1968: 4). True criticism is, of course, cultured criticism. Although, because of his separation from us in time and place, we cannot be sure of knowing exactly what Paul meant, Arnold (ibid. 20) argues that we can understand his letters as closely as possible 'by reading him with the sort of critical tact which the study of the human mind and its history, and the acquaintance with many great writers, naturally gives for following the movement of any one single great writer's thought'. Culture, the 'pursuit of our total perfection by means of getting to know, on all the matters which most concern us, the best which has been thought and said in the world' (Arnold 1965: 233), allows us the most adequate understanding possible of the thought of an author such as St Paul. It takes a wide acquaintance with the history of the texts produced by the human spirit to understand the texts of the Bible. In *Literature and Dogma* (1873) and *God and the Bible* (1875), Arnold applies this principle to the whole Bible. Culture allows us to understand what kind of discourse the biblical texts constitute, the differences among its texts, and which of them are the more valuable. It implies both knowledge of the texts and the 'tact' to read them appropriately (Arnold 1968: 162).

One of the first principles of Arnold's biblical criticism is that the society in which he lives has become one which demands proof of a statement that claims to be true if it is to accept it as such. 'The scientific sense in man never asserted its claims so strongly', and statements like those of theology, which claim to be true, are met—especially by the working class, with which Arnold is increasingly concerned—by the demand for verification (ibid. 8). Now, the value of St Paul's thought, for Arnold, is that unlike Calvinist theology, it is verifiable. The first result of good literary criticism of Paul's letters is to make clear that the fundamental element in his thought is the 'desire for righteousness' (ibid. 23). 'I exercise myself, to have always a conscience void of offence toward God and toward men' (Acts 24: 16). In Hebrew thought, Arnold argues, God was first of all the source of goodness, the giver of the moral law. Access to God, for the Hebrews, meant access to the source of this law, and harmony with it. 'My soul breaketh for the longing that it hath unto thy judgements at all times' (Ps. 119: 20). St Paul's 'piercing practical religious sense' combined the Hebrew understanding of the goodness of God's law with a fervent desire to put it into practice. Paul's 'frequent, nay incessant' lists of moral habits to be pursued or avoided, Arnold argues, indicate, in their detail and their prominence, the depth of Paul's desire to understand and to practise righteousness. It is this love of righteousness, he even suggests, that accounts for Paul's conversion to Christianity, inasmuch as Jesus' teaching opened up new aspects of righteousness of which he had not learned in his Pharisaic training.

Now, the fact that Paul founds his religious teaching on the desire for righteousness, for Arnold, constitutes the 'scientific superiority' of this teaching to that of Calvinism, in which the practice of righteousness comes last in the order of ideas—as the Synod of Dort, for example, makes clear. For Arnold, the moral law is a fact of human nature, familiar to every human being from his or her own experience. Since St Paul bases his religious teaching on this moral law, he bases it on a scientifically verifiable fact: 'Things as they truly are, facts, are the object-matter of science; and the moral law in human nature, however this law may have originated, is in our actual experience among the greatest of facts' (ibid. 30). That there is a moral law, and that human happiness consists in obeying it, are verifiable facts, in Arnold's view. That moral experience consists in the conflict between what Paul calls the flesh and the spirit, between selfish desire and conscience, and that happiness follows from resisting the one and acting on the basis of the other, are also verifiable facts. Arnold cites a wide array of poets and philosophers, from Plato and Aristotle to Goethe and Wordsworth, who have also made these claims, as evidence that they constitute 'general experience' and a 'natural law' (ibid. 294–5). Arnold was acutely sensitive to the changing currents of the *Zeitgeist*—his religious work consists entirely in the reinterpretation of the Bible in the light of current scientific ideas. Nevertheless, like most of his contemporaries, he does not acknowledge the possibility that moral ideas are subject to the same process of historical change as those of science. As Vincent Buckley writes, in *Poetry and Morality* (1959): 'While he turns an adequately critical eye upon received religion, he does not turn an adequately critical eye upon received morality...Consequently, the sharply critical analysis of contemporary religion is possible to him only while he is passive, and even silent, in his criticism of the "best" contemporary moral thought and feeling' (Buckley 1959: 39). The moral teaching of the Bible cannot be verified 'as you verify that fire burns' (Arnold 1968: 370). Moral ideas are not facts of nature, not objects in themselves, but elements of a discourse, dialectically related to the progression of the *Zeitgeist* in just the same way as the theological ideas Arnold rejects as products of a bygone age. Although, in *Culture and Anarchy*, Arnold had argued that it was one of culture's functions to ascertain what constitutes reason and the will of God, in his biblical criticism he takes these to be universally accessible facts of human nature.

Arnold acknowledges that Paul needed Christ in order to obey the moral law: 'O wretched man that I am! Who shall deliver me from this body of death? I thank God through Jesus Christ our Lord' (Rom. 7: 24–5). But Paul does not speak of Christ in the pseudo-scientific terms of his Calvinist interpreters, Arnold argues; rather, he remains on the firm ground of verifiable experience. Jesus was to Paul above all the one who was without sin—whereas, in Calvinism, Jesus is without sin because he is divine, for Paul he is divine because he is without sin. The struggle Paul knew in his own experience against the flesh, against selfish desire, and which he was unable to overcome, Jesus had overcome. Jesus was a perfect example of the righteousness Paul so strongly desired, and through a process of emotional identification with this man who had fulfilled his desire, Paul found himself able to pursue righteousness as Jesus had: 'The struggling stream of duty, which had not volume enough to bear him on to his goal, was suddenly reinforced by the immense tidal wave of sympathy and emotion' (ibid. 43). This emotional identification with Jesus, Arnold argues, is what Paul meant by 'faith', or, more precisely, by 'faith that worketh through love' (Gal. 5: 6). Here again, he bases his teaching on verifiable experience, since 'it is evident to whoever can read the Bible with open eyes' that Jesus followed the moral law without being hindered by selfish desire (ibid. 42). Good literary criticism— whose aim is 'to see the object as in itself it really is' (Arnold 1962: 261)—shows that this is clearly taught in the Gospels.

In *Literature and Dogma* and *God and the Bible*, Arnold extends this project of cultured literary criticism to the whole Bible. The first thing that culture tells us about the Bible is that it is a literary work: 'To understand that the Bible is fluid, passing, literary, not rigid, fixed and scientific, is the first step towards a right understanding of the Bible' (Arnold 1968: 152). Arnold means that the language of the Bible, unlike that of theology, is not scientific language. It does not claim accurately to describe objects of its authors' knowledge. If theologians have proceeded upon the assumption that this is the case, it is because they have lacked the necessary culture to understand that it is not. The language of the Bible is poetic language, '*thrown out* at an object of consciousness not fully grasped, which inspired emotion' (ibid. 189). The biblical authors do not claim to know the object of which they speak—rather, they have experienced a force or power in their lives which has been of deep moral and emotional significance. The best way in which they have been able to speak of this force has been the 'language of figure and feeling', the language of poetry. This is true first, Arnold argues, of the word 'God'. All the excesses of systematic theology derive from a failure to understand that, in the Bible, 'God' is a literary term. Arnold (ibid. 170) writes: 'People use it as if it stood for a perfectly definite and ascertained idea, from which we might, without more ado, extract propositions and draw inferences, just as we should from any other definite and ascertained idea.' Theologians come to formulate definitions of God, such as that he is a 'Great Personal First Cause, who thinks and loves, the moral and intelligent Governor of the universe'. Arnold argues that such definitions of the term are not only bad science—since they cannot be verified—but that they are also not what the Bible means.

Religion, of which the Bible is the incomparable teacher in Western culture, for Arnold, has nothing to do with the pseudo-sciences of metaphysics or theology. The object of religion, Arnold (ibid. 173) argues, is *conduct*—the field of human action.

He considers that conduct—'eating, drinking, ease, pleasure, money, the intercourse of the sexes, the giving free swing to one's temper and instincts'—constitutes 'three-fourths' of human life. Religion is not merely morality, however, but 'morality touched by emotion' (ibid. 176). It is right conduct 'touched, strengthened and almost transformed' by emotional experience. It is precisely this emotionally suffused conduct to which the Bible refers with the word 'righteousness'. In *Ethical Studies* (1876), F. H. Bradley (1927: 315) criticized this definition of religion as a tautology. He argued that '*all* morality is, in one sense or another, "touched by emotion"', and that Arnold really means that religion is 'morality "touched" by *religious* emotion'. Arnold's definition has been defended by critics such as Basil Willey (1975: 251) and Ruth apRoberts (1983: 191). Bradley is right to point out, however, that moral action inspired by deep emotional attachment to that which enjoins such action—which is what Arnold means—is not a definition of anything other than itself. Morality plus emotion does not add up to religion. Rather, it is what Arnold has already taken as the scientifically acceptable core of the traditional religion—in his case, Thomas Arnold's already liberal version of the traditional religion—in which his generation was brought up.

A people as deeply engaged with righteousness as ancient Israel, Arnold (1968, 181) argues, could not fail to become aware of 'the very great part in righteousness which belongs, we may say, to *not ourselves*'. There is a large part of human conduct, he claims, that does not originate in human will or action. He calls this the 'not ourselves'. Now, that which is not ourselves is a vast area of human experience, and has inspired all kinds of religious forms. To the authors of the fundamental religious texts of the Old Testament, that aspect of it which impinged upon their consciousness above all was the '*not ourselves* by which we get the sense for *righteousness*, and whence we find the help to *do right*' (ibid. 182). The fundamental meaning of the word and the concept 'God' in the Old Testament, for Arnold, is 'the enduring power, not ourselves, which makes for righteousness' (ibid. 200). The biblical authors meant other things in addition by the word, but they did mean this, and they meant it consciously. This can be seen, Arnold argues, in the name with which they named the not themselves which impinged upon their consciousness. The meaning of the tetragrammaton, the Hebrew name of God, Arnold argues, is best rendered 'the Eternal'. Rowland Williams had commended this term in the *Essays and Reviews*, and Arnold knew that it was rendered thus in one of the French versions of the Bible. He had also heard children in the Jewish Free School he visited in his capacity as an inspector of schools use it in reciting the Ten Commandments (Arnold 1970: 59). By 'the Eternal', Arnold (1968: 183) claims, the Hebrew people did not mean 'the eternal cause', for example, nor that God's essence is his existence—they were not metaphysicians—rather, they meant 'the Eternal *righteous*, who loveth *righteousness*'.

Although Arnold's biblical criticism is on the whole learned, there is no warrant for this last claim. Most biblical critics agree that *ehyeh asher ehyeh*, 'I am who I am' (Exod. 3: 14) means something like 'I will be with you', a promise of God's saving presence to Israel. If the metaphysical concept of eternity is not present in the tetragrammaton, nor is the moral concept of righteousness. The most fundamental fault in Arnold's biblical criticism, however, lies in the double standard he applies to the concept of science. He rejects the propositions of dogmatic theology as unverifiable, replacing them with concepts which he claims are verifiable. God is 'the stream of tendency by which all things seek to fulfil the law of their being' (ibid. 10), and 'the enduring power, not ourselves, which makes for righteousness'. These statements about God do not refer to empirically verifiable facts, however, as Arnold claims, but are theological dogmas of precisely the same order as those which Arnold rejects. An early critic of *Literature and Dogma* rightly describes Arnold's own positions as 'generalisations of the nature of dogma. They are the intellectual forms in which the Divine seems true to him' (Dawson and Pfordresher 1979: 290). This is true. If it is an article of faith to claim that God is a person, it is no less an article of faith to claim that he is a stream of tendency or the eternal not ourselves which makes for righteousness. As James Livingston writes: 'There remains an ambiguity in Arnold's use of the terms "verification" and "scientific" that allows him to apply standards of verification to certain types of theological assertions which he does not appear in practice to apply to others' (Livingston 1986: 154). Arnold's concept of the power not ourselves that makes for righteousness is not the scientific core of the religion of the Bible, stripped of the unverifiable accretions of dogma, but simply another dogma. In *Culture and Anarchy*, Arnold speaks of his 'faith' in culture. We must add that Arnold's relation to the religion of morality touched by emotion is also one of faith.

The most basic religious insights of the Old Testament, for Arnold, are those concerning righteousness, and the happiness that follows from the pursuit of righteousness. 'Israel's original perception', he argues, is that 'Righteousness tendeth to life' (Prov. 11: 19). He dates this religious insight to the period of David and Solomon. As Israel suffers conquest, exile, and foreign rule, a series of accretions develop, such as the idea of the Messiah, who will bring in a new age of righteousness. These accretions Arnold calls *Aberglaube*, which he translates as 'extra-belief', or 'belief beyond what is certain and verifiable' (Arnold 1968: 212). The word's basic meaning is 'superstition'. When Jesus began to teach in Israel, the original intuition of the Hebrews that righteousness leads to life had become overlaid by centuries of anthropomorphic and eschatological *Aberglaube*. Jesus's teaching, Arnold argues, consisted in the 'restoration of the intuition' (Arnold 1968: 285). Jesus did not redefine the Old Testament's understanding of God—he meant by the term what it had always meant, 'the Eternal that loveth righteousness'. Rather, he redefines the idea of righteousness. To be precise, Arnold writes, 'He restored the intuition of God through transforming the idea of righteousness' (Arnold 1968: 286). He did this in three ways, Arnold argues, and these are what characterize Jesus as the most effectively inspiring religious teacher of all time. First, Jesus brought a *method* to the teaching of righteousness, the method of inwardness. Whereas religion had become a matter primarily of national and social conduct, Jesus taught that conduct was a matter of the inner person, of the will, of the emotions, and of thoughts. 'Those things which come forth from the heart, they defile the man' (Matt. 15: 18). This is Jesus's method, for Arnold—to attend not to external practices, but to inner life, and this is what he meant by *metanoia*, which is inadequately translated as 'repentance'—'a change of the inner man' (ibid. 289). Jesus not only showed his disciples in this way what righteousness was; he also showed them how to practice it. This is his *secret*, the secret of the 'peace' that his apostles preached along with repentance (Acts 10: 36). This secret can be summed up in St Paul's word *necrosis* (2 Cor. 4: 10)—'always bearing about in the body the dying of Jesus, that the life also of Jesus may be made manifest in our body', and in Jesus' teaching, 'Whosoever will save his life shall lose it: but whosoever will lose his life for my sake, the same shall save it' (Luke 9: 24). Jesus's method of inwardness quickly led his disciples to the realization that there were two lives within them, the life of impulse, passion, and desire, and the life of conscience and right conduct. Paul calls them 'the mind of the flesh' and 'the mind of the spirit' (Rom. 8: 6): 'One of them *life* properly so-called, full of light, endurance, felicity, in connexion with the higher and permanent self; and the other of them life improperly so-called, in connexion with the lower and transient self' (ibid. 292). Jesus taught that it is by dying to the lower form of life that a person can live the higher form of life. This is Jesus's secret, for Arnold, that happiness, peace, and joy follow from renouncing the desires of the 'ordinary self', in order to pursue the moral law of the 'best self'. All the great moral teachers have known this, he argues, but what distinguishes Jesus is his *temper*, which Arnold (ibid. 300) describes as one of 'mildness and sweetness'. To the texts we have already cited, if we are fully to understand the nature of Jesus's teaching, we must add a text such as 'Learn of me; for I am meek and lowly in heart: and ye shall find rest for your souls' (Matt. 11: 29). Mildness was the 'element' or the 'medium' in which Jesus thought and taught, for Arnold—both his method and his secret are suffused with this temper. Together, these produce the total impression of *epieikeia* (2 Cor. 10: 1), which Arnold translates as the 'sweet reasonableness' which characterizes the person and teaching of Jesus, and which makes him so much more attractive and effectively inspiring a religious teacher than any other poet or philosopher.

In his later literary essays, Arnold begins to attribute to poetry some of the functions of religion. In 'On the Study of Poetry' (1879), commissioned as an introduction to the literary figures in the anthology *The Hundred Greatest Men*, he reflects on the special value of poetry amongst the productions of the human spirit. It is superior to the plastic arts, since it is conceptual; it is superior to science, since its concepts are 'touched by beauty' and 'heightened by emotion'. It is more lasting than philosophy, and superior to religion, at least to the historical and supernatural beliefs upon which popular belief and scientific theology are based: 'The reign of religion as morality touched with emotion is indeed indestructible. But religion as men commonly conceive it—religion depending on the historicalness of certain supposed facts, on the authority of certain received traditions, on the validity of certain accredited dogmas—how much of this religion can be deemed unalterably secure?' (Arnold 1973: 63). Arnold has no doubt that the religion which he has argued is taught in the Bible, if it is properly understood, will continue to sustain the human spirit. Dogmatic Christian theology, however, will not withstand the scientific criticism of the age. It has staked its claim to be true upon the belief that the biblical texts report facts, but it is becoming increasingly clear that this is not the case. Poetry, on the other hand, is not so committed to facts—for poetry, Arnold (ibid. 63) writes, 'the idea is everything; the rest is its world of illusion, of divine illusion; it attaches its emotion to the idea, the idea *is* the fact'. Poetry is committed only to the truth of the way in which the poet expresses his perception of the world, which is not subject to verification or falsification by natural science. Arnold (ibid.) concludes: 'The strongest part of our religion today is its unconscious poetry. The future of poetry is immense, because in conscious poetry, where it is worthy of its high destinies, our race, as time goes on, will find an ever surer and surer stay.' By unconscious poetry, Arnold means the aesthetically valuable elements of liturgy, ritual, architecture, and devotional art, which are aspects of the religious practice of institutions such as the Anglican and Catholic churches. These aesthetic aspects of religious practice are what, in the face of the scientific critique of theological dogma, most fulfil the moral, emotional, and spiritual needs of contemporary men and women. Hence, it is conscious poetry—poetry written as such, and able therefore to achieve its full range of effects in this regard—which will, as popular religion begins to die out, increasingly fulfil these needs.

In 'On the Study of Poetry', written the following year as the introduction to *The English Poets*, edited by T. Humphry Ward, the husband of Arnold's niece, and reprinted as the first of the *Essays in Criticism, Second Series* (1888), Arnold continues this reflection on the function of poetry. Whilst the *Zeitgeist* had remained one in which religion was not radically criticized, the spiritual function of poetry had remained largely unacknowledged. Now this is no longer the case, it will become increasingly better understood: 'We should conceive of poetry as capable of higher uses, and called to higher destinies, than those which in general men have assigned to it hitherto. More and more mankind will discover that we have to turn to poetry to interpret life for us, to console us, to sustain us' (Arnold 1973: 161). The moral, emotional, and intellectual needs fulfilled by religion, for Arnold, will come to be met by poetry. Naturally, this will be true only of the best poetry. He defines poetry as 'a criticism of life under the conditions fixed by the laws of poetic truth and poetic beauty', and he argues that it is 'in proportion to the power of the criticism of life' in a given body of poetry that it will be able to assume the functions hitherto performed by religion of 'consolation' and 'stay' (ibid. 163). Aristotle had said in the *Poetics* that, compared to history, poetry was *philosophōteron kai spoudaioteron*, which Arnold renders as 'possessing a higher truth and a higher seriousness'. He argues that 'the substance and matter of the best poetry acquire their special character from possessing, in an eminent degree, truth and seriousness' (ibid. 171). The very best poetry combines these qualities of content with formal excellence in diction and movement. Chaucer does not have the 'high and excellent seriousness' that constitutes such poetry, for Arnold, although his criticism of life has 'truth of substance', nor does Burns. Homer, Dante, and Shakespeare, on the other hand, all have it. Arnold (ibid. 177) writes: 'It is this chiefly which gives to our spirits what they can rest upon; and with the increasing demands of our modern ages upon poetry, this virtue of giving us what we can rest upon will be more and more highly esteemed.'

As in his earlier critical essays, Arnold's concept of good poetry here is determined by his understanding of the Bible, the finest example of religious literature produced by the human spirit. Whilst poetry is destined to take over the functions of popular religion as the latter becomes increasingly untenable in the modern age, it does so in so far as it consists of the kind of discourse of which the Bible consists. Both poetry and the Bible, for Arnold, speak truly, although not scientifically—they speak truly about human life, three-fourths of which consists in conduct, in a form whose beauty allows us to commit ourselves emotionally to the practice of right conduct. If poetry will replace popular religion, for Arnold, this is only in so far as it consists of truly religious discourse. This is clear from Arnold's examples of the difference between morality and religion. He writes, 'Our religious examples are all here taken from the Bible, and from the Bible such examples can best be taken; but we might also find them from elsewhere' (Arnold 1968: 178). He then cites a speech from *Oedipus Rex*, and comments: 'That is from Sophocles, but it is as much religion as any of the things which we have quoted as religious. Like them, it is not the mere enjoining of conduct, but it is this enjoining touched, strengthened and almost transformed, by the addition of feeling' (ibid.). The difference between good poetry and truly religious discourse is ultimately one only of degree. Both inspire us to the true happiness of right conduct, on the basis of our emotional response to the beauty with which they express this truth. For Arnold, the Bible is the greatest poem ever written because of the supremely attractive figure of Jesus. Although Arnold does not put it in these words, we might suggest that, precisely in so far as Jesus was the greatest religious teacher in history, he was also the greatest poet.

Although some critics continue to defend the value of Arnold's thought for liberal theology, his biblical criticism is based on axioms no longer shared in the twentieth, let alone the twenty-first, century. Even by the end of the nineteenth century, the mid-Victorian crisis caused by the sense that science was in conflict with religion, and that the latter must be altered in the light of the former to remain acceptable to educated minds, had passed. Although Arnold's belief in the objective and verifiable existence of moral values continues to be shared by some, it was widely discredited by the second half of the twentieth century, in favour of more historical perspectives. After the horrors of the two World Wars, publicly shared values no longer seemed to constitute a certain basis for anything. Arnold's work has been more influential in literary studies than in theology. His concept of culture as an improvement of the self, analogous to religion, and which could take on the functions of religion in a secular society, continued to prevail in university English departments at least until the late 1960s. The very concept of 'literature' derives in part from Arnold's belief that poetry is a modern substitute for religion. Furthermore, he has continued to be influential in the interdisciplinary study of literature and theology. His argument that the Bible is a literary work, and must be read as such in order to be rightly understood, is still axiomatic in this field, even among those who continue to believe that it is also the Word of God. Arnold's belief that the moral and aesthetic truths of the Bible, rather than its supernatural claims, constitute the heart of its message to modern readers, is also widely shared. Although there are few card-carrying 'Arnoldian' critics writing in literature and theology today, the broad outlines of the discipline continue to be those sketched out by the work of one of its first great practitioners.

WORKS CITED

ApRoberts, Ruth. 1983. *Arnold and God*. Berkeley: University of California Press.

Arnold, Matthew. 1932. *The Letters of Matthew Arnold to Arthur Hugh Clough*, ed. Howard Foster Lowry. Oxford: Clarendon.

—— 1962. *The Complete Prose Works of Matthew Arnold*, iii. *Lectures and Essays in Criticism*, ed. R. H. Super. Ann Arbor: University of Michigan Press.

—— 1965. *The Complete Prose Works of Matthew Arnold*, v. *Culture and Anarchy*, ed. R. H. Super. Ann Arbor: University of Michigan Press.

—— 1968. *The Complete Prose Works of Matthew Arnold*, vi. *Dissent and Dogma*, ed. R. H. Super. Ann Arbor: University of Michigan Press.

—— 1970. *The Complete Prose Works of Matthew Arnold*, vii. *God and the Bible*, ed. R. H. Super. Ann Arbor: University of Michigan Press.

—— 1973. *The Complete Prose Works of Matthew Arnold*, ix. *English Literature and Irish Politics*, ed. R. H. Super. Ann Arbor: University of Michigan Press.

Bradley, F. H. 1927. *Ethical Studies*. 2nd edn. Oxford: Clarendon.

Buckley, Vincent. 1959. *Poetry and Morality: Studies on the Criticism of Matthew Arnold, T. S. Eliot and F. R. Leavis*. London: Chatto & Windus.

Dawson, Carl, and Pfordresher, John (eds.) 1979. *Matthew Arnold: Prose Writings. The Critical Heritage*. London: Routledge & Kegan Paul.

Eliot, T. S. 1951. *Selected Essays*. 3rd edn. London: Faber & Faber.

Livingston, James C. 1986. *Matthew Arnold and Christianity: His Religious Prose Writings*. Columbia: University of South Carolina Press.

Shea, Victor, and Whitla, William (eds.) 2000. *Essays and Reviews: The 1860 Text and Its Reading*. Charlottesville: University of Virginia Press.

Willey, Basil. 1975. 'Arnold and Religion', in Kenneth Allott (ed.), *Matthew Arnold*. London: G. Bell.

FURTHER READING

Allott, Kenneth (ed.) 1975. *Matthew Arnold*. London: G. Bell.

Chadwick, Owen. 1966–70. *The Victorian Church*. 2 vols. London: A & C Black.

DeLaura, David J. (ed.) 1973. *Matthew Arnold: A Collection of Critical Essays*. Englewood Cliffs, NJ: Prentice Hall.

Krook, Dorothea. 1959. *Three Traditions of Moral Thought*. Cambridge: Cambridge University Press.

MURRAY, NICOLAS. 1996. *A Life of Matthew Arnold*. London: Hodder & Stoughton.

REARDON, BERNARD M. G. 1971. *From Coleridge to Gore: A Century of Religious Thought in Britain*. London: Longman.

ROBBINS, WILLIAM. 1959. *The Ethical Idealism of Matthew Arnold*. London: Heinemann.

SCOTT, NATHAN A. JR. 1985. *The Poetics of Belief: Studies in Coleridge, Arnold, Pater, Santayana, Stevens, and Heidegger*. Chapel Hill: University of North Carolina Press.

SUPER, R. H. 1970. *The Time-Spirit of Matthew Arnold*. Ann Arbor: University of Michigan Press.

CHAPTER 39

C. S. LEWIS

CATH FILMER-DAVIES

OFTEN referred to as the greatest Anglican apologist of modern times, C. S. Lewis is also regarded as a 'popular' theologian. But although we might understand that his books, particularly his fiction, have been and to some lesser extent still are 'popular', there is nothing to suggest that his theology is at all popular in the sense of being embraced and welcomed by even his keenest readers. In many ways, it is at odds with some of the more liberal thought emanating from the Church of England in contemporary times.

There is also a distinction to be made between Lewis's overtly apologetic works—such as *Mere Christianity* (1952) and *The Problem of Pain* (1940), in which he was writing to order, as it were—trying to expound and defend orthodox beliefs, and his more personal theology, which is to be found in greater complexity (and to some greater perplexity) in his fiction. The distinction can be made because there is a different mode of self-disclosure at work in fiction; paradoxically, more of the person behind the fictional work can be, and is, revealed, because of the apparent security of the veil of the narrative which covers it. Fiction, in which the narrative and symbolism becomes pre-eminent for the reader, admits self-disclosure subversively, at a deeper layer of meaning than frank apologetics. This examination of the theology of C. S. Lewis then, while not disregarding the overtly apologetic works nor, indeed, belittling their importance, also takes serious account of the theology to be found at the heart of his fiction.

It is clear that, for many (such as Will Vaus (2004)), Lewis's theology seems to be primarily encapsulated in his theological digest *Mere Christianity*, but that work contains only a pale reflection of most of his theological thought. The reason is, of course, that in *Mere Christianity* Lewis was attempting to synchronize not his own theology but that of the mainstream Christian churches, and to do that in a way that would win acceptance from them all. He deliberately wanted to avoid anything that might cause contention or dissent, and although that little book has been of enormous value to its many readers, it hardly presents the complexity of thought that makes up the theological viewpoint of one of the twentieth century's most compelling lay theologians.

Of course, Lewis was an academic, an English literature don at Magdalen College, Oxford, but even his academic writings have a clarity and lucidity that makes them attractive to the general reader. His theological works have the same qualities, but are written from his own perspective as a layman. Thousands of readers have found in them a vocabulary and a tone which not only does not 'speak down' to them, but which is written, as it were, from in their midst, by one of their own. Lewis, of course, made no claim to theological qualification or to the specialist knowledge of the clergy or theologians. What he could—and did—claim was the universality of human experience which made his own experiences worth communicating to others, in the hope that they might speak also to the hearts of his readers.

Lewis's theology might be divided into three parts, each representing a stage in his own spiritual development. But whereas for some who make this journey past experiences are left behind, Lewis integrated them all into his final theological vision.

The three parts of Lewis's theological vision are; supernaturalism, the nature of good and evil, and the process of redemption. Each aspect of this vision emphasizes the key issue of his Christian faith: the surrender of the self to God.

SUPERNATURALISM

Although Lewis claimed to have lost his faith after the death of his mother, and to have remained an 'atheist' until his conversion to theism in 1930, the term he chose to describe his beliefs during that period is not entirely accurate. If Lewis's literary œuvre of the time is anything to go by, he was enchanted even then by the idea of the inconsolable longing for some reality that cannot be seen or experienced by humans, except in brief, tantalizing glimpses. This longing he called *Sehnsucht*, exploiting to the fullest the many ways in which the German word can be translated into English (homesickness, nostalgia, longing, desire).

Lewis at this stage might not have admitted that there was a God, but he certainly believed in some sort of transcendent Reality which he struggles to identify and to express in his early poetry. He was never, in any sense, a mere materialist; there was always 'Something Somewhere' which held his attention and claimed his adherence. Thus in an early poem, 'Song', he writes:

> Atoms dead could never thus
> Stir the human heart of us
> Unless the beauty that we see
> The veil of endless beauty be,

Filled full of spirits that have trod
Far hence beyond the heavenly sod
And seen the bright footprints of God.   (1919: 33)

At about the same time, in a letter to his friend Arthur Greaves, Lewis insisted, 'I believe in no God, least of all in one that would punish me ... but I do believe I have a spirit in me, a chip, shall we say, of universal spirit' (Letter to Arthur Greaves, 25 May 1918, Lewis 1979b: 221).

There was, in fact, a strong element of Platonism in Lewis's early thought which was hardly atheistic, although its supernaturalism was ill-defined and ranged from Romantic thought to some ideas which were consistent with his later Christianity. Robert Houston Smith (1981) believes that Lewis's religious thought was 'undergirded, enriched and occasionally overshadowed' by his devotion to 'a comprehensive religious philosophy ... a vibrant fabric that encompasses intellect, feelings, metaphysics, aesthetics and ethics' at the core of which is 'the conviction that everything in the universe is the manifestation of a single reality' (ibid. 1–2). Lewis was synthesizing elements of Platonism with Christianity long before his final commitment to the latter, and he continued to do so after his conversion.

He believed at this early stage also that nature was somehow warped or 'fallen'; the shells and bullets of the war leading him to surmise that 'Matter = Nature = Satan' (Letter to Greaves, 3 June 1918, 1979b: 213–14). The Christian Lewis wrote in 1961 that nature is a 'creature lower than ourselves. And a fallen creature—not an evil creature but a good creature corrupted, retaining many beauties but all tainted' (Letter to Dom Bede Griffiths, 10 December 1961; 1964a: 301). This notion of nature as a fallen creature appears in Lewis's final novel, *Till We Have Faces* (1956), and in other aspects of his fiction.

With Lewis's conversion to Christianity, these elements of his theological thought were retained. Platonism helped to confirm Lewis's commitment to sacramentalism. If *Sehnsucht* represented an unsatisfied desire for something more than the material world could offer, there was sense in the pursuit of a hidden reality. The notion of *Sehnsucht* bridged the chasm between Platonic and Christian supernaturalism. Lewis believed that the material world is merely the shadow which stimulates the desire for the real world. This concept is fundamental to an understanding of Lewis's beliefs.

The experience of *Sehnsucht* and the way it compels a synthesis between imagination and reason leads to the pursuit—and 'if faithfully followed, the discovery'—of truth (1981b: 205). Neither the imagination nor human reason can be natural, and Lewis uses the argument of the atheistic evolutionist and scientist J. B. S. Haldane to suit his own argument. Haldane (1940: 196) writes:

It seems to me immensely unlikely that mind is a mere by-product of matter. For if my mental processes are determined wholly by the motion of atoms in my brain, I have no reason to suppose that my beliefs are true. They may be sound chemically, but that does not make them sound logically. And hence I have no reason for supposing my brain to be composed of atoms.

Since the movement of atoms cannot, of itself, produce the faculty of reason, it follows, Lewis asserted, that reason is generated outside of nature. In other words, human reason is a supernatural faculty. Lewis observes that

Neither Will nor Reason is the product of Nature. Therefore either I am self-existent (a belief which no one can accept) or I am a colony of some Thought and Will that are self-existent. Such reason and goodness as we can attain must be derived from a self-existent Reason and goodness outside ourselves, in fact, a Supernatural.   ('Bulverism' (1941) in 1979a: 276)

Lewis believed that divine reason 'descends' as it were, into human minds, following the pattern that shows that higher entities can identify with, and include, lower. Lewis, always the rhetorician and polemicist, expressed the theory in this way:

solid bodies exemplify many truths of plane geometry, but plane geometry figures no truths of solid geometry: many inorganic propositions are true of organism, but no organic proposi-tions are true of minerals; Montaigne became kittenish with his kitten but she never talked philosophy to him. Everywhere the great enters the little—its power to do so is almost the test of its greatness.   (1947: 134–6)

The way in which the lower medium can make reference to the higher medium is symbolism; but symbolism cannot operate unless the higher medium is known and at least partly apprehended. But that term 'symbolism' does not always adequately describe this analogical process. In some instances—the use of writing to symbolize speech, for example—the term is applicable because the relationship between written sign and the spoken word is conventionally accepted. But in other causes, such as that of a painting, the representation of reality is a part of the reality it represents. Light in a painting is illumined by true light; the relationship between the two is much more than that between a conventional written sign and a sound. In the case of the picture, 'the thing signified is really in a certain mode present', Lewis observes. The relation-ship between the two is not so much symbolic as sacramental; it is not arbitrary but dependent upon an established connection and relationship between the represen-tation and the reality. This natural world not only represents supernatural reality; it is also part of it. It is logical therefore to deduce that there is an appropriate and parallel correspondence between human sensory perceptions and supernatural reality. Such a conclusion avoids Platonic asceticism while retaining the underlying concept of the Ideas and the Copies as a basis for sacramentalism. Furthermore, Lewis believed that in Christ the natural and the supernatural, the Copy and the Idea, the symbolized and the symbol, the archetype and the ectype, are all reconciled ('Transposition', 1980: 54–73). What is important in this context is the spiritual aspect of human beings. *Sehnsucht* arises from the spiritual aspect of humans; it is ultimately the longing of the human spirit for its own fulfilment and reconciliation with supernatural reality.

But the human spirit finds itself grappling with the desire for reconciliation on the one hand and an urge to rebel on the other. In traditional Christian theology, the human spirit must choose between God and the created but rebellious entity called 'the devil' or 'Satan'. In Lewis's writings, the struggle is depicted as being ultimately between God and the human being's own self, since the unsurrendered self slips gradually into corruption and becomes absorbed into the satanic. Only when the self is put to death, or surren-dered to God, does it become fully integrated and fully individual (1981a: 165; 1979b: 460–1; 1961b: 11). At the heart of Lewis's concepts of Good and Evil, then, lies the separation between spirit and nature, which has its origins in the fall. When humankind fell, its natural environment was also corrupted, which is the reason why nature cannot be worshipped. Humanity and nature are both in need of redemption. With the death and resurrection of Christ, the process by which humanity and, indeed, the natural order are reconciled to their creator was initiated. Its completion in individual lives depends upon individual choice between self and God.

Lewis's supernaturalism is best seen in his various works of fiction. It is distinguished by images by which he hoped to evoke the notion of *Sehnsucht* or longing as well as a sense of celebratory joy (for example, of music and dancing; Aslan is served, in the Narnian stories, by the god of merriment and wine, Bacchus). He was careful, however, to preserve a sense of awe in his depiction of the supernatural. Several times readers are warned, in *The Lion, the Witch and the Wardrobe*, that 'Aslan is not "safe"' (1950: 76). God is not a Santa Claus figure who will deliver gifts on demand; even the Father Christmas figure in *The Lion, the Witch and the Wardrobe* brings gifts—and useful, practical gifts at that, 'tools not toys' (ibid. 104) which can be employed in the battle against evil which is to come—not at the request of the recipients, but of his own selection.

THE NATURE OF GOOD AND EVIL

As a Christian, Lewis adopted orthodox views on sin and salvation, but the Platonic elements which so shape his supernaturalist beliefs also influence the way he conceives good and evil. He properly rejects, to begin with, the notion of dualism—the belief that two equal and opposite, absolute and divine powers exist in the universe. He rejects, as well, the idea that good and evil as a priori principles coexist in the nature of God. Only in the sense that God offers every created being the choice of whom to serve can Lewis be said to see evil as inherent in the nature of God. Humans tend to build for themselves false images of reality which become the focus of human desires and worship:

Only because God has laid up real goods for us to desire are we able to go wrong by snatching at them in greedy, misdirected ways. The truth is that evil is not a real thing at all, like God. It is simply good spoiled. That is why I say there can be good without evil, but no evil without good... Evil is a parasite. It is only there because good is there for it to spoil and confuse.   ('To Arthur Greaves', 12 September 1933, in Lewis 1979*b*, emphasis in original)

Lewis's supernaturalism, and his concept of 'good' are unapologetically hierarchical. In our prevailing climate of 'political correctness', Lewis's hierarchical views sit uneasily with the doctrine of equality and egalitarianism. But to Lewis, the notion of both symbol and sacrament point to a hierarchical order, not only in terms of the supernatural being 'higher' than the natural order but within both the supernatural and natural orders themselves. Thus Lewis follows without irony the Thomist doctrine of 'the Great Chain of Being'. His views on the marriage relationship and his political opinions also reflect the sacramentalism of hierarchy. Lewis admitted that the medieval model of hierarchical analogies 'delighted' him (1964b: 216) although he was quite aware of the error of applying it to the science of astronomy. Hierarchies are the foundation not only of the supernatural order but also of the natural order when it remains faithful to the supernatural paradigms existing for it. The hierarchical model has not dated, Lewis (1942a: 72) insists, because it belongs

to the ancient orthodox tradition of European ethics from Aristotle to Johnson himself... [According to this tradition] degrees of value are objectively present in the universe. Everything except God has some natural superior; everything except unformed matter has some natural inferior. The goodness, happiness, and dignity of every being consists in obeying its natural superior and ruling its natural inferior. When it fails in either part of this twofold task, we have disease or monstrosity in the scheme of things until the peccant being is either destroyed or corrected.

Lewis's 'doctrine of objective values' (the belief that some things are really true and others really false, about the kind of thing the universe is and the kind of thing human beings are (1943a: 29)) means that his view of the world is not 'democratic' ('democracy', to him, was a kind of necessary political and legal fiction). He makes this viewpoint quite clear:

I do not believe that God created an egalitarian world. I believe in the authority of parent over child, husband over wife, learned over simple, to have been as much a part of the original plan as the authority of man over beast... But since we have learned sin, we have found, as Lord Acton says, that 'all power corrupts and absolute power corrupts absolutely'. The only remedy has been to take away the powers and substitute a legal fiction of equality... Even the authority of man over beast has had to be interfered with because it is constantly abused.   ('Membership', 1980: 114)

And elsewhere (1961b: 19) he adds,

The claim to equality outside the strictly political field, is made only by those who feel themselves to be inferior. What it expresses is the itching, smarting, writhing awareness of an inferiority which the patient refuses to accept.
    And therefore resents...
Here is someone who speaks English rather more clearly and euphoniously than I—it must be a vile, upstage, lah-di-dah affectation. Here's a fellow who says he doesn't like hot dogs— thinks himself too good for them no doubt... If they were the right sort of chaps they'd be like me. They've no business to be different. It's undemocratic.

But demands for 'equality' are not the only manifestations of the self-worshipping, self-aggrandizing entity which contemporary psychology might call the ego and which Lewis called the *meum*. A demanding and tyrannical self can be seen in the mother of the 'patient' who is the focus of Screwtape's attention in *The Screwtape Letters* (1942b). She serves both as an example of how the human belly and palate produce querulousness, impatience, uncharitableness, and self-concern (ibid. 86), and also as an example of the 'all-I-want' state of mind, what Lewis calls 'the gluttony of delicacy', which focuses firmly on the self, regardless of the inconvenience and trouble it causes to others:

She is a positive terror to hostesses and servants. She is always turning from what has been offered her to say with a demure little sigh and a smile, 'Oh please, please ... *all* I want is a cup of tea, weak but not too weak, and the teeniest weeniest bit of really crisp toast'... Because what she wants is smaller and less costly than what has been set before her, she never recognises as gluttony her determination to get what she wants, however troublesome it may be to others.   (ibid. 86–7; emphasis in original)

The usurping god of the self, the *meum*, here demands offerings and oblations, appeasements if you like; the service and worship of others. The demand for worship is often disguised as pseudo-unselfishness, which, far from benefiting its recipients, actually confines them in the bondage of the warped and twisted, self-centred manifestations of that most basic and animal of human feelings which Lewis classifies as *storge* or 'affection' (in contrast with the three other kinds of love he identifies as *philia*, *eros*, and *agape*—friendship, sexual love, and (divine) unconditional love. He writes,

Affection is the most instinctive, in that sense the most animal, of the loves ... But ... the ravenous need to be needed will gratify itself either by keeping its objects needy or by inventing for them imaginary needs. It will do this all the more ruthlessly because it thinks (in one sense truly) that it is a Gift-love and therefore regards itself as unselfish.   (1963: 49–50)

A character which emphasizes Lewis's point here is Mrs Fidget in *The Four Loves*, who inflicts upon her family a regime of devotion which they do not want, including '[sitting] up to "welcome" you home if you were out late at night; two or three in the morning, it made no odds; you would always find the frail, pale weary face awaiting you, like a silent accusation. Which meant that you couldn't with any decency go out very often' (ibid. 61). Furthermore, this paragon who worked her fingers to the bone, imposed upon those around her an obligation to 'help' her, so that 'They did things for her to help her do things for them which they didn't want done' (ibid. 62). In other words, her miserable self-sacrificing created a bondage for her family from which they longed to escape.

Lewis makes plain, however, the fact that affection is a necessary part of human existence and 'is responsible for nine-tenths of whatever solid and durable happiness there is in our lives' (ibid. 66); but it does so only when affection is balanced by common sense and 'give-and-take decency', which means that it should be tempered with 'goodness ... patience, self-denial, humility, and the continual intervention of a far higher sort of love than Affection, in itself, can ever be' (ibid. 67). Mrs Fidget's activities were geared to one end only: to make her feel needed. Ceasing them would threaten her with the feeling of not being necessary to her family. Taken to their brutal extreme, her activities also allowed her to feel unappreciated, and to wallow in what Lewis calls 'the pleasures of resentment'; such pleasures, he adds, are available only to those who hate. In the way Mrs Fidget has invented needs for her family in order to serve her own needs, her own ego, there is indeed an element of hatred. The thing that makes such affection a manifestation of evil is the way in which it encourages those who indulge in it to demand 'appreciation' or worship. The self, and the 'love' in which it engages, becomes a god.

In the Preface to *The Screwtape Letters*, Lewis referred to the way in which human relationships can be warped and twisted into becoming embroiled in damaging and destructive behaviour:

Even in human life we have seen the passion to dominate, almost to digest, one's fellow; to make his whole intellectual and emotional life merely an extension of one's own—to hate one's hatreds and resent one's grievances and indulge one's egoism through him as well as through oneself. His own little store of passion must of course be suppressed to make room for ours.   (1961*b*: 10)

In Lewis's fiction, then, evil is shown in terms of self-enslavement, devouring and absorbing others in order to reinforce the burgeoning ego of the auto-idolater. Lewis argues always for submission and obedience to God as the only means by which a person can be truly individuated (that is, become what they have always been meant, in the Divine plan, to be). The process of salvation/redemption is that of surrender and submission; the 'self' must be put to death first and then rebirth and regeneration can take place. This belief is almost completely in accord with traditional fundamentalist thought, the praying of the sinner's prayer, and the 'acceptance of Jesus Christ as Lord'—although perhaps even that word 'acceptance' has overtones of the self about it, whereas Lewis's terms, 'surrender and sacrifice' do not.

If Lewis had a favourite scripture, he does not say so; but he certainly relies to a very great degree on the six-times iterated 'Whoever loses his life shall find it' (Matt. 10: 39; 16: 35; Mark 8: 35; Luke 9: 24; 17: 33; and John 12: 26), a theme exemplified in the death and resurrection of Christ himself. But self-surrender is certainly the major constituent of what is 'good' in Lewisian theology. The characters Devine and Weston in the Ransom Trilogy are paradigms for two kinds of evil: Devine for that of total self-indulgence, exploitation of the planet Malacandra's minerals for his own sake and for his own aggrandizement: 'For the most part his conversation ran on the things he could do when he got back to earth: ocean-going yachts, the most expensive women, and a big place on the Riviera figured largely in his plans' (1938: 34). He adds that he is not risking his life to obtain that wealth just 'for fun', yet 'fun'—self-indulgence and auto-idolatry—is exactly why he is taking those risks. Devine is less redeemable than his companion, who has devoted his life and energies to a cause outside himself. Weston, who serves a Life Force on the model of that posited by Schopenhauer and Shaw, is merely 'bent'; but Devine (whose adjectival name suggests self-worship) is, in the words of the angelic Oyarsa figure who rules the planet, 'broken, for he has... nothing but greed. He is now only a talking animal' (ibid. 157). Weston, nevertheless, still represents evil, for the Cause he serves has induced him to forsake all moral restraints and values and he will sacrifice any intelligent life which might impede the progress of his Cause. In the second book of the trilogy, *Perelandra* (1943*b*), Weston (named apparently for 'Western' secular values) becomes so inhuman and inhumane that he is reduced to the mere appearance of humanity: he is an 'un-man', a managed corpse (ibid. 139).

Devine's fate is depicted in the final book of the trilogy, *That Hideous Strength*; he begins as 'Lord Feverstone' who is 'a big man driving a big car to somewhere where they would find big stuff going on' (1945: 56). That somewhere is the ironically named NICE: the National Institute for Co-ordinated Experiments. (Someone in the British government has a bleak sense of humour: those initials are now used for a government agency, The National Institute for Clinical Excellence.) At the end of this novel, Feverstone—

whose name suggests the heat and sulphuric stones of hell—along with the NICE hierarchy—is consumed by a natural cataclysm in a wave of earth and a 'blinding violet flame' (ibid. 456). In other words, he meets his end by means of *fever* and *stones*.

Ransom, on the other hand, as his name suggests, is not only 'saved' spiritually and physically; he is also the means of the salvation of others. His job in *Perelandra* is to prevent the planet's innocent rulers from a fall such as that which befell their counterparts on earth, and his task in *That Hideous Strength* is to restore God-ordained order to the world and, in the relationship between Jane and Mark Studdock, to marriage. (Mark forsakes his ambition; Jane gives up her Ph.D. thesis, and is told to give up her dreams and to have children instead. Her barrenness is one of the causes of the outbreak of evil in the land.)

Throughout his fiction, Lewis depicts evil or unredeemed characters as self-centred and selfish and as engaging in spiritual (and emotional) *cannibalism*, an idea he found in David Lindsay's *Voyage to Arcturus* (Lewis 1965: 11). Such imagery pervades *The Screwtape Letters* which deals with the activities of demons, but in various forms, it is present in all Lewis's fiction. Among the spiritually cannibalistic are people who demand their rights: 'I only want my rights. I'm not asking for anyone's bleeding charity', says a ghost in *The Great Divorce* (1946) in which the narrator is guided through heaven, hell, and purgatory much as was Dante in his more famous *Commedia*. The ghost is told: 'Then do. At once. Ask for the Bleeding Charity' (ibid. 32). The vulgarism is transformed into a theological reality and becomes the self-sacrificing love of Christ which itself demands human surrender. In a compensation-crazy twenty-first century, Lewis's theology still has something to offer; and it also makes some harsh but accurate observations about contemporary relationships. The ghost called 'Robert's wife' seeks only to dominate and destroy her husband—and all for his 'good': 'Put me in charge of him', she demands, '... give him to me, do you hear? Don't consult *him*: just give him to me...How can I pay him out if you won't let me have him?' By contrast, in an echo of John Donne's Holy Sonnet X, the psalm of the redeemed in this otherworldly environment is, 'Overcome us, that, so overcome, we may be ourselves' (ibid. 95). In a Chestertonian paradox, Lewis believes that surrender to God will bring us to share in Christ's victory and death to the self to eternal life.

REDEMPTION

Lewis's views on redemption can be themselves divided into two parts: his Christology and his eschatology. Both can be seen most clearly in his fiction, although, as *Mere Christianity* makes clear, he had no doubt about the divinity of Christ or the trinitarian nature of God, as seen in his chapter 'The Three-personal God' (1981a: 160–5). And in the Narnian Chronicles, the Christ-figure Aslan lays down his life for Edmund, according to the 'Deeper Magic from Before the Dawn of Time' (1950: 160), which can be taken as referring to the will of the Father.

The essential difference between good and evil as expressed in the wills of human beings is the difference between Satan and Christ. Satan, symbolically represented in the book of Isaiah, states, 'I *will* ascend to heaven...I *will* set my throne on high... I *will* make myself like the Most High' (Isa. 14: 12, RSV; italics mine). Set against that is Christ's prayer in the Garden of Gethsemane, '*Not my will* but Thine...' (italics mine). That is the change in human perspective that Christianity should bring about in the lives of those who die to the self and accept Christ as Lord. That is the hub of Lewis's message of salvation. It is not a 'once saved, always saved' dogma, but rather, a continuous process of change and salvation, a testing in every event of human existence and every moment of human life. It is a tough, and not at all a 'popular' message, but that is what lies at the heart of Lewisian theology.

Nowhere, however, is that theology more explicit than in his final piece of fiction *Till We Have Faces: A Myth Retold* (1956). Not only are his views on supernaturalism, good and evil, and redemption portrayed here with searing insight, but also one more of his beliefs—that Jesus Christ embodies and actualizes all the truths in the myths and religions of the world. Lewis seems more comfortable when he places his theology in the context of myth, fairy tale, and even pagan religion, but he does so to emphasize the role of truth in myth and story in the way they prefigure and anticipate the redemptive work of Christ. He writes in his 1944 essay 'Myth Became Fact' that

As myth transcends thought, Incarnation transcends myth. The heart of Christianity is a myth which is also a fact. The old myth of the Dying God, without ceasing to be myth, comes down from the heaven of legend and imagination to the earth of history. It happens—at a particular date, in a particular place, followed by definable historical consequences...but it does not cease to be myth: that is the miracle.   (1979a: 66, 67).

Lewis emphasizes, of course, that God is more than a god, and Christ is more than Balder. In *Mere Christianity,* the tone at times suggests that Lewis's personal theology is being expressed with some vehemence:

I am trying here to prevent anyone saying the really foolish thing that people often say about [Christ]: 'I'm ready to accept Jesus as a great moral teacher, but I don't accept His claim to be God'. That is the one thing we must not say. A man who was merely a man and said the sort of things Jesus said would not be a great moral teacher. He would either be a lunatic—on a level with the man who says he is a poached egg—or else he would be the Devil of Hell. You must make your choice. Either this man was, and is, the Son of God: or else a madman or something worse. You can shut Him up for a fool, you can spit at Him and kill Him as a demon; or you can fall at His feet and call Him Lord and God. But let us not come with any patronising nonsense about His being a great human teacher. He has not left that open to us. He did not intend to.   (1981a: 52)

So Lewis is not by any means equating Christ's reality with his mythic precursors. But they were there, symbolically, just as figures in the Old Testament were there, symbolically, to represent Christ; figures such as Melchizedek, Moses, and Aaron for example. Similarly, Lewis uses his figure of Aslan in the Narnian Chronicles, and the figure of the god of the Grey Mountain in *Till We Have Faces,* as a sort of *pre-evangelium* to open the reader's eyes to the reality of the supernatural, and to present God's salvation through Christ in indirect ways through myth and story.

In the Narnian Chronicles, Aslan the Christ-figure is the son of the Emperor-over-the-sea, but Aslan is the true ruler of Narnia, and it is to Aslan that Narnians turn in times of trouble and from whom they ask help. Aslan, the lion, symbolically a king in the correspondences seen by Aquinas in the Great Chain of Being, and also the Lion of Judah, dies and is resurrected. Interestingly, the redemption is won for Edmund—just one person—which underscores the religious dogma that Christ would have been sacrificed had only one human needed redemption. And it is Aslan who is imitated by the Ape in *The Last Battle*, which prophesies two things: apostasy in the end times and also the domination of the 'Calormenes'—or perhaps, as some see them symbolically, those members of the Islamic faith who intend to impose their systems on others. This might well be distasteful to some, but to others it will seem merely insightful. On the other hand, of course, Lewis is careful to show, through his Calormene character Emeth (whose name means 'truth') that those who seek the truth, whatever their professed creed, will find it (1956*a*: 161–6).

The Narnian Chronicles also demonstrate Lewis's eschatology since the final volume of the series deals in fact with 'last things'. Apostasy, scepticism, outright lack of faith, impatience with a God who does not seem to act when action is most needed, a running after idols who pretend to be the Messiah, and finally enslavement to false systems, are all to be found in *The Last Battle*, as indeed they are foretold in various apocalyptic biblical passages. Lewis (1973: 109) warns that we are to be alert and watchful, for, in the words of John Donne, what if this present were to be the world's last night?

Lewis's eschatology was orthodox. Life on earth is not like watching a play that we know—such as, for instance, *King Lear*. We do not know the play, Lewis warns; we do not even know whether we are in Act I or Act V. 'The doctrine of the Second Coming teaches us that we do not and cannot know when the world drama will end,' Lewis says (ibid. 105). But just because the doctrine of the Second Coming is largely rejected by contemporary mythology, it is not to be rejected by believers (ibid. 106). Lewis is not advocating mass hysteria but merely the three propositions of the doctrine: (1) That Christ will certainly return; (2) that we cannot possibly find out when, and (3) that we must always be ready for him (ibid. 107). In the final Narnian Chronicle, *The Last Battle*, life goes on pretty much as it is going on in our mundane world. Religion is largely forgotten; people are annoyed and disbelieving because Aslan has not appeared for a long time; and other religions, in particular the religion of the Calormene god Tash, a giant man with a bird's head, are capturing the hearts and minds of the people. Indeed, some are even declaring that Aslan and Tash are the same, and the name 'Tashlan' is coined to describe this combined deity. Just so in contemporary times are people ready to believe that 'we all worship the same god' without any critical examination of exactly who and what gods they are likening to Yahweh and to Jesus Christ. Prophetically, Lewis has a ginger tomcat ask whether Aslan and Tash are really the same:

' "Assuredly," said the Calormene. "The enlightened Ape—Man, I mean—is in the right. *Aslan* means neither more nor less than *Tash*". "Especially, Aslan means *no more* than Tash?" suggested the cat. "No more at all," said the Calormene.' (1956a: 32) Yet the cat, and many others, find out that the two are most definitely not the same: they are opposite forces. The language is very strong indeed, as Aslan explains to Emeth why he has been saved:

'I and he are of such different kinds that no service which is vile can be done to me, and none which is not vile can be done to him ... if any man do a cruelty in my name, then though he says the name Aslan, it is Tash whom he serves and by Tash his deed is accepted.' (ibid. 165)

But of course the thing to be remembered is that in a work of fiction, 'any resemblances can be said to be coincidental'—between religions as well as between human beings. There is actually no really explicit or direct comparison between the Calormenes and the followers of Islam, though a link can undeniably be made. In any case, the real evil is not the religion but the willingness of Aslan's follower's to forsake him; and the real virtue is that some of the Calormenes seek the truth and do good. Lewis is careful to draw those distinctions as well. Those who, like the Ape, seek self-aggrandizement, lose their lives and their eternal souls; those who die to the self, even if foolishly, like Puzzle the Donkey, gain their lives and their eternal souls. The heavenly vision with which Lewis concludes this book is almost sublime in its understatement, but the joy it suggests is deeply moving. It is a reunion, not just among people who have known each other, but between each soul and Aslan/Christ. There is a real reward for those who lose their lives, because, as Lewis writes in his conclusion to *Mere Christianity*:

Submit to death, death of your ambitions and favourite wishes every day and death of your whole body in the end: submit with every fibre of your being, and you will find eternal life. Keep back nothing. Nothing that you have not given away will be really yours. Nothing in you that has not died will ever be raised from the dead. Look for yourself, and you will find in the long run only hatred, loneliness, despair, rage, ruin, and decay. But look for Christ and you will find Him, and with Him everything else thrown in. (1981a: 127)

The key to Lewis's theology, then, is this death to self, not in any Platonic ascetic sense, but rather in the sense of putting to death the egocentric will, the 'meum' that craves acknowledgement and worship. This very process is, for him, evidence of the redemptive grace at work in our lives since it occurs *after* the steps he followed in his own life—the recognition of the existence of the Supernatural, the acceptance of Theism, the acknowledgment of Jesus Christ as Saviour and Lord. His focus on dying to self does not shift from his earliest Christian writings to those of his final years.

Soon after his conversion, Lewis wrote in a poem which appears in his first apologetic work, *The Pilgrim's Regress* (1933):

> Because of endless pride,
> Reborn with endless error,
> Each hour I look aside
> Upon my secret mirror
> Trying all my postures there
> To make my image fair.

> Then and then only turning
> The stiff neck round, I grow
> A molten man all burning
> And look behind and know
> Who made the glass, whose light
> Makes dark, whose fair
> Makes foul, my shadowy form reflected there
> That Self-Love, brought to bed of Love may die and bear
> Her sweet son in despair.   (1981*b*: 184)

Lewis's postures and faces recorded here have their echo in the postures and faces of Orual in *Till We Have Faces*, whose good works might seem to make her 'fair' until she allows the 'Ungit-Self'—the self-worshipping *meum* as represented by the strange goddess worshipped in Orual's country of Glome—to die so that the god or goddess, the 'sweet son' or redeemed individual, might be born in the new self. Ungit symbolizes the fallen nature, all natural loves, desires and ambitions. As the Stoic philosopher, The Fox, explains: 'All . . . are born into the house of Ungit. And all must get free from her. Or say that Ungit in each must bear Ungit's son, and die in childbed' (1956*b*: 312). The pool by which Orual and her sister Psyche stand in their redeemed state represents both the water of death and the water of life, the water of rebirth.

As the novel makes clear, those who do not die to self are those enslaved to self and from there descend into outright evil. Those who do will find total fulfilment in Christ. This theological stance can be summarized in the words of the god to Orual, 'Die [to the self] before you die. There is no chance after.' This was Lewis's first Christian theological position: it was his final theological vision. Some might also say it was one of the twentieth century's finest.

Works Cited

HALDANE, J. B. S. 1940. *Possible Worlds*. London: Evergreen.

LEWIS, C. S. 1919. *Spirits in Bondage: A Cycle of Lyrics*. London: Heinemann.

—— 1938. *Out of the Silent Planet*. London: The Bodley Head.

—— 1940. *The Problem of Pain*. London: Bles.

—— 1942*a*. *A Preface to* Paradise Lost: *Being the Ballard Mathews Lectures Delivered at University College, North Wales, 1941*. Rev. and enlarged edn. London: Oxford University Press.

—— 1942*b*. *The Screwtape Letters: Letters from a Senior to a Junior Devil*. London: Bles.

—— 1943*a*. *The Abolition of Man or, Reflections on Education with Special Reference to the Teaching of English in the Upper Forms of Schools*. Glasgow: Fount.

—— 1943*b*. *Perelandra*. London: The Bodley Head.

—— 1945. *That Hideous Strength*. London: The Bodley Head.

—— 1946. *The Great Divorce: A Dream*. London: Bles.

—— 1947. *Miracles: A Preliminary Study*. London: Bles.

—— 1950. *The Lion, the Witch and the Wardrobe*. New York: Collier.

LEWIS, C. S. 1956a. *The Last Battle*. New York: Collier.

—— 1956b. *Till We Have Faces: A Myth Retold*. London: Bles.

—— 1961a. *The Screwtape Letters: Letters from a Senior to a Junior Devil*. London: Macmillan.

—— 1961b. *The Screwtape Letters and Screwtape Proposes a Toast* London: Bles.

—— 1963. *The Four Loves*. Glasgow: Fount. First published 1960.

—— 1964a. *Letters of C S Lewis Ed with memoir by WH Lewis*. London: Bles.

—— 1964b. *The Discarded Image: An Introduction to Medieval and Renaissance Literature*. Cambridge: Cambridge University Press.

—— 1965. *Screwtape Proposes a Toast and Other Pieces*. Glasgow: Collins/Fourt.

—— 1979a. *God in the Dock: Essays on Theology*, ed. Walter Hooper. Grand Rapids: Eerdmans.

—— 1979b. *They Stand Together: The Letters of C S Lewis to Arthur Greeves 1914–1979*, ed. Walter Hooper. London: Collins.

—— 1980. *The Weight of Glory and Other Addresses*, ed. Walter Hooper. New York: Macmillan. First published 1947.

—— 1981a. *Mere Christianity*. London: Fount. First published 1952.

—— 1981b. *The Pilgrim's Regress: An Allegorical Apology for Christianity, Reason and Romanticism*. Grand Rapids: Eerdmans. First published 1933.

SMITH, ROBERT HOUSTON. 1981. *Patches of Godlight: The Pattern of Thought of C. S. Lewis*. Athens, Ga.: University of Georgia Press.

VAUS, WILL. 2004. *Mere Theology*. New York: Intervarsity Press.

FURTHER READING

FILMER-DAVIES CATH. 1993. *The Fiction of C S Lewis: Mask and Mirror*. Basingstoke: Macmillan.

LEWIS, C. S. 1949. *Transposition and Other Addresses*. London: Bles.

—— 1951. *Prince Caspian*. New York: Collier.

—— 1952. *The Voyage of the Dawn Treader*. New York: Collier.

—— 1953. *The Silver Chair*. New York: Collier.

—— 1954. *The Horse and His Boy*. New York: Collier.

—— 1955. *The Magician's Nephew*. New York: Collier.

—— 1963. *Prayer: Letters to Malcolm*. Glasgow: Fount.

—— 1967. *Reflections on the Psalms*. Glasgow: Fount.

—— 1973. *The World's Last Night and Other Essays*. New York: Harcourt Brace Jovanovich.

LITURGY AS LITERATURE

BRIDGET NICHOLS

INTRODUCTION

Until relatively recently, a chapter on 'Liturgy as Literature' might have devoted most of its attention to the Anglican Book of Common Prayer, first issued in 1549, and familiar across the English-speaking world in the revised form published in 1662. Its distinction was that it contained vernacular texts of all the services that the newly reformed English Church offered, thus greatly expanding the limited provision for lay worshippers in such manuals as *The Lay Folks' Mass Book*. This collection, translated from French in the late thirteenth century, had the strategic aim of giving instructions on conduct and posture for those attending the mass, together with prayers to be recited by the laity during the elevation of the host.

There was a time when the whole of life could be described according to the Prayer Book. From baptism, through confirmation, marriage, the birth of children, sickness, and death, and in the daily and weekly rhythms of Morning and Evening Prayer and holy communion, existence was shaped by liturgy and the standard liturgical texts. Likewise, the secular calendar was aligned with the feasts of the church. As a character in George Eliot's *Middlemarch* puts it, summing up a sequence of unusual and suspicious events in the quiet and predictable life of an English midlands village in the early 1830s, '*I* don't want anybody to come and tell *me* as there's been more going on nor the Prayer-book's got a service for' (Eliot 1994: 676).

Even now, the Prayer Book continues to be held up in some quarters as the gold standard by which aesthetic judgements are made on modern liturgical texts. Yet in the current climate, it cannot be assumed that it is a possession common to whole populations. There are many reasons for this, including the use of modern language texts for worship in the greater number of Anglican (Episcopal) settings; the growth of other Christian denominations with their own liturgical traditions, as well as independent Christian churches which may not use formal liturgies at all; and the increasing secularization of Western society.

To add to the disintegration of certainties, there is also an internal division in much language about liturgy. Popular discussion often treats 'liturgy' and 'worship' as related but different entities. Liturgy is identified with text, worship with action; liturgy connotes intellectual activity, while worship suggests something affective and directly of the heart and spirit; liturgy means for many the study of the history and practice of worship through the deposit of written evidence, whereas worship indicates a living practice which is able to speak to the present. Worshippers within a single tradition may even define themselves by reference to one or other word. 'Liturgy' may thus be used pejoratively to signal ritualistic practice and elaborate ceremonial, while 'worship' may carry the positive suggestion of spontaneous expression and freedom from rules. This chapter refuses the distinction, and uses the two terms more or less interchangeably. Against this background, 'Liturgy as Literature' becomes a question rather than a statement. In its most elementary form, it asks how liturgy can be admitted to the category of literature, though as we shall see, the relationship is more subtle and more complex than this.

The question has been addressed, as one might expect, by scholars working in the interdisciplinary area of literature and theology or religion. David Jasper and Robert Detweiler, in *Religion and Literature: A Reader* (2000), preface their discussion of 'The Language and Literature of Worship' with a survey of the material they treat. It includes 'texts that have been employed in worship or acts of devotion, private or public. Beginning, again, with the Bible, [they] include literature from liturgy, drama, ritual, chant, devotion, prayer and sermon.' They acknowledge that 'a number of these texts would not normally be read as "literature" (for example, those from liturgies) but they contain poetry and prose of the highest order and have been enormously influential because of their ancient and public use' (Jasper and Detweiler 2000: 60). The Jewish-American liturgist, Lawrence Hoffman (2002: 743), defines liturgy as 'a literature . . . that exists not for private reading or meditation but for repeated public recitation'.

In very different ways, all of these voices acknowledge that liturgy has a claim to literariness, but that this claim rests on unusual grounds. For Jasper and Detweiler, the oddity is in thinking of the words used in worship as literature. Once that conceptual barrier has been removed, it is possible to identify a number of conventional literary genres. For Hoffman, the oddity is in the idea that liturgy could be anything other than public celebration, or that the liturgical text could have a literary life outside the activity of worship.

This chapter takes up the question again, broadening the scope from the kinds of liturgical texts which might be *read* as literature, to a consideration of how liturgical texts might *be* literary. While it accepts that some basic conditions should be kept in mind, for example the meeting of some of the aesthetic criteria applied to literary works, its interest is less in the uncertain business of identifying the attributes of liturgical texts that qualify them to rank as literature, than in the ways in which liturgy inhabits the English tradition. It is particularly interested in the way in which liturgical forms are influenced by other texts, and how, in turn, they exert their own influence.

Many starting points could have been chosen. I begin with what is surely the original and generative event in the relationship between liturgy and literature—the presence of the Bible in the liturgical text. This is both the background to everything that follows, and an important reminder that it is not always necessary to look outside the milieu of worship in order to discover the literary character of liturgy.

Although 1549 should be taken as the inauguration of a fully fledged collection of prayers and rites for public worship in English, a vigorous conversation between liturgy and literature had been developing through the Middle Ages. This convergence is explored as a preliminary to a consideration of the advent of an English Prayer Book. Subsequent sections concentrate on its rapid cultural embedding, and the expectation among secular writers that liturgical references would be recognized. This is an expectation that alters the closer we move towards the present, and as twentieth-century examples reveal, the assumption of familiarity becomes less confident.

Diminishing knowledge of the Prayer Book and waning confidence in its ability to speak to later generations stand, perhaps not entirely ironically, alongside the fact that it was in the twentieth century, particularly its second half, that the first significant opportunity for the composition of liturgical texts in English for four hundred years arose. By this stage, the poles had reversed, and it was liturgy's turn to seek at least some of its inspiration in literature. Successes and difficulties can be demonstrated, and all of them contribute to the introduction of a penultimate section on the writing of liturgical material in the contemporary setting.

A final reflection on a poem by the contemporary Scottish poet, Roddy Lumsden, draws attention to the conversation between liturgy and literature as a dynamic opportunity for making sense of ritual experience, often in unexpected ways. In a moment of illumination which seems to surprise the speaker as much as the reader, the meaning of a marriage 'a decade back' is rescued from assembled artefacts and understood as sacred transformation. Such convergences enact the creativity and the mystery of the bond between liturgy and literature.

LITURGY AND THE BIBLE

For the liturgy, the Bible is always the first textual encounter outside of itself. In a pre-literary way, it gives narrative shape to ritual action, particularly in the dominical sacraments of baptism and the eucharist. This transmutation of biblical sources into material for use in worship is strikingly illustrated in the eucharist, which takes its dramatic setting and its story from the accounts of the Last Supper in the Synoptic Gospels and from words quoted by Paul in the First Letter to the Corinthians

(Matt. 26; Mark 14; Luke 22; 1 Cor. 11). Although the exact nature of this meal continues to be a matter of scholarly debate, in its retelling it became a sequence of repeatable actions, centred on the words 'This is my body/ blood...Do this in remembrance of me', and recounting the breaking and giving of bread, and the giving of the cup. Catherine Pickstock, followed by others, has defined as 'non-identical repetition' the ceremony that is enacted according to the same pattern over and again, in Christian communities throughout the world, yet which is always a new event (Pickstock 1997: *passim*; Ford 1999: 152–7, 215).

Generations of worshipping communities have elaborated this practice, embedding the plain content of its core words in a surrounding texture of confession, praise, intercession, petition, and thanksgiving. Most of the inspiration for the developed structure is found in scriptural sources, from greetings modelled on those found in the Pauline Letters, to collects which might draw on the readings for the day, to interpolations such as the Sanctus ('Holy, Holy, Holy') in the Eucharistic Prayer itself, which uses words from Isaiah 6, and which records the shout of the angels who prostrate themselves before God in the prophet's vision of the glory of the Lord in the Temple.

The inclusion of readings from Scripture is mandatory in most acts of Christian worship, but transplanting Scripture into liturgy is never a neutral movement, for the liturgical action is a hermeneutical environment in which biblical literature is interpreted in the whole economy of the act of worship. Louis-Marie Chauvet (1992, 123) notes how material prescribed in a cycle of readings is often typologically arranged (i.e. to show the relationship between Old and New Testament texts), and thus 'produces...effects of meaning quite different from those which it has in the context of the Bible itself'. What he calls the 'hermeneutical reprocessing' of biblical material (e.g. in Bible translation) 'raises the question of the "liturgical Bible" in its relationship with the biblical canon'.

Amplifying the reading of the Bible in worship is its representation in canticles and prayers derived from biblical sources. Donald Gray's chapter on the Collects of the Book of Common Prayer (Ch. 33 above) gives an insight into this process. Since the eighteenth century, another important contribution to the biblical density of worship in England, and in the churches around the world which grew out of English missionary endeavour, has come from hymns, themselves a genre with both liturgical and literary affinities.

Vernacular hymns were not an immediate part of worship in Reformation England, and metrical psalms, notably those of Sternhold and Hopkins (1562) and Tate and Brady (1696), are probably the earliest form of congregational singing in English. The texts were never authorized for use in Church of England services, where the Psalmody was said, but sung psalms were permitted before and after the service.

It is not always easy to see how hymns differ from devotional poetry. J. R. Watson (1995: 74–5) distinguishes between a singable public utterance, and a personal and intense meditation, contrasting George Herbert and Henry Vaughan, who wrote personal compositions later used as hymns, with Charles Wesley, who wrote for congregational singing.

A survey such as this cannot hope to do justice to the English hymnographic tradition. I offer instead a very short example from one of Wesley's many hymns that shows the characteristics which might define a hymn as literary. It emerges from the operation of a daring theological imagination on an enormous range of internalized biblical and theological reference. In Watson's view, Wesley's advantage lay in knowing a single English version of the Bible, the King James, as his source text (ibid. 231). But Wesley does not simply quote Scripture: he translates it into a meditation capable of transcending finite experience and moving towards an eschatological vision. Here is the first verse of his morning hymn, 'Christ, whose glory fills the skies':

> Christ, whose glory fills the skies,
> Christ, the true, the only light,
> Sun of Righteousness, arise,
> triumph o'er the shades of night;
> Dayspring from on high be near;
> Daystar in my heart appear.

In the space of six lines, the hymn refers to the glory of Christ as described in the Epistle to the Hebrews (Heb. 1: 3); to Christ as the true light (John 1: 9); to the Old Testament image of the Messiah as the Sun of Righteousness (Mal. 4: 2); to the Lucan characterization of the Messiah, of whom John the Baptist is the forerunner, as the dayspring from on high (Luke 1: 78 KJV); and to the Second Epistle of Peter, with its acclamation of Christ as the Daystar (2 Pet. 1: 19). It is ideally suited to congregational singing because it is an immediate appeal to the presence of Christ with believers in the present moment. The claims it makes on Christ are easily appropriated by those who could not have put the thought into words in the same way. At the same time, the hymn's choice of biblical messianic imagery, clustered round the dominant theme of light, makes it an eschatological and almost apocalyptic picture of the Second Coming. The domestic and the awe-inspiring are fused here into a single utterance.

A hymn like this exemplifies the paradox that, despite the complexity of the biblical-hermeneutical environment of worship, meaningful devotional acts are possible with very little biblical knowledge. Popular devotion and folk religion can easily be undervalued or dismissed as the blind allegiance of ignorant people, yet as we begin to seek the origins of the exchange between liturgy and literature, their importance becomes visible.

Before an English Liturgy

The forms and rites of the church had been influencing the development of a vernacular literature, particularly poetry and drama, for a considerable time before the appearance of an English Prayer Book. Even the business of churchgoing—what today would be called the sociology of worship—caught the literary imagination.

Chaucer reflects on one kind of liturgical drama in his portrait of the Wife of Bath in the General Prologue to *The Canterbury Tales*. He dwells particularly on her refusal to allow anyone to precede her in the procession when the congregation moved forward to make their offerings of money at the celebration of the mass:

> In al the parisshe wif ne was ther noon
> That to the offrynge bifore hire sholde goon;
> And if ther dide, certeyn so wrooth was she,
> That she was oute of alle charitee.

> (Chaucer 1966: 21)

This frivolous vignette depicts a subplot, running concurrently with another dramatic event, the mass itself. Some medieval churchmen, Amalarius of Metz (*c*.750–850) prominent amongst them, interpreted its actions as the allegorical re-presentation of the events of Christ's death and resurrection. But the liturgical drama proper appears to spring from the *Quem quaeritis* dialogue in the medieval Easter liturgy, which animated the encounter between the women who went to anoint Jesus' body and the angels who met them at the empty tomb. Deriving its title from the initial words of the question, 'Whom do you seek?', it is first found in England in the tenth-century Winchester troper, where it seems to have been part of the Easter Vigil ceremonies rather than the eucharist of Easter morning. Much later, the dialogue would be rendered into English in the fifteenth-century Resurrection play in the Wakefield Cycle, now cut loose from its original ecclesiastical setting. By this time, the cast would have changed from clergy to lay people, perhaps members of a trade guild. O. B. Hardison (1965: 178–9) has called the *Quem quaeritis* 'the bridge whereby medieval culture made the transition from ritual to representational drama'. Put differently, it might mark the transition from a dramatic liturgy to a freestanding religious drama, and from this point the great cycles of plays developed, enacting the whole sweep of salvation history from the Creation to the Harrowing of Hell.

Poetry was another beneficiary of liturgical texts, often blending English and Latin. This can be seen particularly in the religious lyrics that appear more and more frequently from the fourteenth century onwards. Of these, the Scottish poet William Dunbar's Easter hymn, 'Done is a battell on the dragon blak', composed in the late fifteenth or early sixteenth century and celebrating the risen Christ's victory over the Devil, is a majestic example. Each stanza ends with the proclamation from the Easter liturgy, *Surrexit dominus de sepulchro* ('the Lord is risen from the tomb'), familiar even to those who did not understand Latin (Davies 1963: 253).

Perhaps there is no greater example of the coming together of a Latin liturgy and a developing English literature than William Langland's fourteenth-century dream-vision of Piers the Plowman. Langland's method assumes a total compatibility between the sacred and secular worlds. The poem is an allegory, and it is out of the experience of worship that the speaker learns of the identity of Christ, passing en route through encounters with the Seven Deadly Sins and with the principal Christian virtues of conscience and patience. Christ is found in the world, particu-larly in careful discernment of good and evil, and in the choosing of the good, but it is in the church that the victory of Christ is symbolically celebrated. The language of the church thus becomes the shape of life.

The poem takes place over the course of almost a year, culminating in Holy Week and Easter. Its eighteenth Passus, or book, chronicles each stage, using a method of ecclesiastical chronology based on texts set for the Offices of the days from Palm Sunday to Easter which would be entirely clear to a regular worshipper. The dreamer wakes *in ramis palmarum* (that is, on the morning of Palm Sunday, when this antiphon would have been used). The poem then progresses through the antiphons and psalms set for Holy Saturday, moving finally to Psalm 85, whose four virtues (Mercy, Truth, Peace, and Righteousness) become four maidens who 'danced until daybreak, when the bells of Easter morning rang out for the Resurrection' (Langland 1966: 217–30). This is an extraordinary feat of imagination, which brings the very texts of the liturgy to life.

Worship in the Vernacular—The Coming of an English Prayer Book

An English liturgy, encompassing public worship in all its dimensions, did not appear until 1549. The transition from worship conducted in Latin to an English rite is sometimes misrepresented as a sudden and shocking development. True, there was a decisive moment when the Latin books disappeared from churches in England, to be replaced by a single English book. But in reality, prayers in English had gradually been finding their way into popular use through the devotional books, or primers, used by educated members of the laity from the early part of the sixteenth century. Eamon Duffy (1992: 80) explains that, 'though the basic texts of the primers remained in Latin till after the break with Rome, the demand for vernacular material was evident in the evolution of early sixteenth-century primers, as more and more English material was added'. Ordinary people would certainly have begun to say the Lord's Prayer, the Hail Mary, and the Creed in English with the aid of their primers, in the same way that earlier generations had learned standard Latin devotions.

The 'little clergeon' so delightfully depicted by Chaucer in 'The Prioress's Tale' is an example of exactly this kind of rote-learning. It would certainly have been from a Latin 'prymer' that he was memorizing prayers when he heard other children memorizing and singing the beautiful antiphon of the Virgin, *Alma redemptoris mater*, and abandoned his own book to learn it:

> This litel child, his litel book lernynge,
> As he sat in the scole at his prymer,
> He *Alma Redemptoris* herde synge,
> As children lerned hir antiphoner.

> (Chaucer 1966: 161)

The method of ingestion, however, continued with the introduction of resources in English.

By the end of the 1530s, Archbishop Cranmer was experimenting with English forms of Morning and Evening Prayer. At the same time, primers were appearing for the first time in English. While much of the motive for these publications was the control of doctrine, they served a real purpose in enabling ordinary people, excluded from full participation in the services of the church by their lack of Latin, to say their prayers in English.

These early attempts were very rough in comparison with the texts that appeared in the First Prayer Book of Edward VI shortly afterwards (Cuming 1983: 56). Stylistically unrefined though they were, however, they laid the foundation on which the Book of Common Prayer would be built. They represent an initial exercise in writing liturgical English, a journey of discovery in which its users first began to exploit the rhythms and balances of their own language.

The Preface to the 1549 Prayer Book emphasizes the pragmatic aims of the new liturgy, and in a reaction against the extensive textual armoury required for all the services of the Latin liturgy, it commends plainness and simplicity over undue elaboration and the proliferation of books.

And moreover, whereas s. Paule would have such language spoken to the people in the church, as they might understande and have profite by hearyng the same: the service in this Church of England (these many yeares) hath been read in Latin to the people, whiche they understoode not, so that they have heard with theyr eares onely: & their hartes, spirite and minde, have not been edified thereby.…

[H]ere you have an order for praier… muche agreable to the mynde & purpose of the olde fathers, and a greate deale more profitable and commodious, then that whiche of late was used. It is more profitable, because here are left out many thynges, whereof some be untrue, some uncertein, some vain and supersticious: and is ordeyned nothyng to be read, but the very pure worde of God, the holy scriptures, or that whiche is evidently grounded upon the same: and that in suche a language & ordre, as is moste easy & plain for the understandyng, bothe of the readers and hearers. It is also more commodious, bothe for the shortnes thereof, & for the plaines of the ordre, & for that the rules be fewe & easy. Furthermore, by this ordre, the curates shal nede none other bookes for their publique service, but this boke & the Bible: by the meanes whereof, the people shall not be at so great charge for bookes, as in tyme past they have been.   (Brightman 1915: 34–6)

This finely crafted manifesto for universal access to the resources of worship, both linguistically and economically, must be treated with admiration and caution. On the one hand, it fostered the development of a mode of composition which, at its best, fused the art of translation with a fine sense of vernacular prayer. There are no illustrations more apt than some of the collects, which Donald Gray discusses in Ch. 33 above. On the other hand, there is always the danger of what David Jasper has called 'a powerful rhetoric of theological persuasion and coercion' (Jasper 1991: 385). It is present in the passage quoted above, and it is present in the doctrinal underpinnings of the Prayer Book's language of worship.

LITURGY IN LITERATURE

By the early seventeenth century, the Edwardine Prayer Book (only very slightly modified in 1559 under Elizabeth I) had been in use for fifty years, and was sufficiently familiar for allusions to be made to it in secular works. The swift rhetorical flourish which allusion is usually intended to achieve belies its serious foundations, for it depends on shared knowledge of material that is woven into the texture of the world in which it operates. Over a long period of time the contents of the Prayer Book were part of this weave, as the persistence of references confirms. A small number of examples will illustrate how secular and religious life were assumed to flow into one another.

Shakespeare's darkly comic portrayal of Malvolio in *Twelfth Night*, who is imprisoned as a madman and visited by the Fool in the disguise of Sir Topas the Curate, assumes that the audience recognizes in the scene a parody of the Order for the Visitation of the Sick. Adapted from a Latin predecessor, this service would have been familiar to the many who saw parish clergy at work. The Fool's salutation, 'Peace be in this prison', echoes the opening of the rite—'Peace be in this house'—and sets the tone for the cruelly amusing distortions that ensue.

Some forms were familiar because they were distinctive to services that occurred year after year. Writing a number of years later than Shakespeare, Andrew Marvell (1990: 24) could propose to his coy mistress that her refusal of his love might go on 'till the conversion of the Jews', confident that this would recall the second collect used on Good Friday. The prayer beseeches God to 'have mercy upon all Jews, Turks, Infidels and Heretics, and take from them all ignorance, hardness of heart, and contempt of thy word; and so fetch them home... to thy flock, that they may be saved among the remnant of the true Israelites' (Brightman 1915: 373). This conversion was not expected imminently. In fact, most readers would have known that a long time was envisaged, extending to the very end of time, when unlikely events might occur. By the poem's logic, a change of heart in this unwilling woman was a very unlikely event indeed.

Even the rubrics, or notes of guidance for the proper use of orders for public worship, were part of the common understanding. Henry Fielding's Parson Adams in *Joseph Andrews* (1742), refuses to marry Joseph Andrews and Fanny in the inn where they have unexpectedly found themselves, for there are formalities to be observed. The fictional eighteenth-century country clergyman 'would by no means consent to anything contrary to the Forms of the Church, that [Joseph] had no Licence, nor indeed would he advise him to obtain one. That the Church had described a Form, namely the Publication of Banns, with which all good Christians ought to comply...' (Fielding 1970: 144).

A century later, Dickens's account of the baptism of Paul Dombey in *Dombey and Son* (1847–8) makes a double demand. In order to understand the scene described, the reader must know something about baptism according to the Book of Common Prayer. It is especially important to know that those present are required to make responses. This explains the extraordinary behaviour of one of the christening party, the predatory spinster, Miss Tox, who hopes to marry the baby's recently widowed father. She 'kept her Prayer-book open at the Gunpowder Plot and occasionally read responses from that service' (Dickens 1970: 114–15). Here is the second part of the exercise, for the audience must grasp the comedy of this bizarre departure into the services of thanksgiving for King James I's escape from the conspiracy to blow up the Houses of Parliament in 1605, which were only removed from the Prayer Book in the 1870s. In her preoccupied state, Miss Tox's concentration has lapsed completely. None of this would have been lost on a Victorian readership.

Yet by this time, a measure of nostalgia is already entering some evocations of ordinary religious practice. Writing from a mid-Victorian vantage point, George Eliot (1980: 243) describes a village congregation in the late eighteenth century: 'None of the old people held books—why should they? Not one of them could read. But they knew a few "good words" by heart.' Easy familiarity with the Prayer Book was already on the wane, although time-honoured methods of instilling knowledge of its contents persisted. Thomas Hardy's Tess Durbeyfield likewise needs no book as she enters the valley of the Great Dairies to embark on a new life after the death of her baby son. The landscape around her causes a lift of the heart which demands a vocal response. 'She tried several ballads, but found them inadequate; till, recollecting the psalter that her eyes had so often wandered over of a Sunday morning before she had eaten of the tree of knowledge, she chanted: 'O ye Sun and moon . . . O ye Stars . . .' Tess had found herself automatically expressing her joy in the canticle in praise of creation known as the Benedicite, which is included in the Prayer Book Order for Morning Prayer (Hardy 2003: 103–4).

As liturgical texts become less and less part of everyday life, more attenuated ways of calling upon liturgical memory appear in literary contexts. Fragments of texts begin to appear in settings where there can be no certain expectation that they will be recognized as, for instance, in D. H. Lawrence's semi-autobiographical novel, *Kangaroo*. Lawrence (1971: 127) describes how the Australian Ben Cooley, nicknamed Kangaroo, 'sat there with a rapt look on his face: a pondering, eternal look, like the eternity of the lamb of God grown into a sheep.' This parody of the *Agnus Dei* in the eucharistic rite, and perhaps of New Testament references to Jesus as the Lamb of God (John 1: 29, 36; Rev. 12: 11, 22: 1) simultaneously recalls and deflates. It is too self-consciously mischievous to be blasphemous, and unlikely to cast a long shadow over the original words.

A much bleaker appropriation takes place when T. S. Eliot imports ecclesiastical language into a meditation on contemporary culture. Here are lines from 'East Coker', the second section of *Four Quartets*:

> The whole earth is our hospital
> Endowed by the ruined millionaire,
> Wherein if we do well, we shall
> Die of the absolute paternal care
> That will not leave us, but prevents us everywhere.
>
> (Eliot 1974: 202)

They echo the collect for the Seventeenth Sunday after Trinity:

Lord, we pray thee that thy grace may always prevent and follow us, and make us continually to be given to all good works; through Jesus Christ our Lord.

as well as one of the Prayer Book collects to be said after the offertory, when there is no communion:

Prevent us, O Lord, in all our doings, with thy most gracious favour, and further us with thy continual help, that in all our works, begun, continued, and ended in thee, we may glorify thy holy name, and finally by thy mercy obtain everlasting life.

Eliot's lines exploit the changed sense of 'prevent' as the BCP understood it (a benevolent and protective going before), to suggest a God whose own bankruptcy turns fatherly love into an inescapable, wearisome, and irritating presence. It is the kind of care that brings death by nothing more sinister than boredom.

Helen Gardner (1968: 61–2) wrote of Eliot's use of language with a Christian reference that, outside the circle of those accustomed to using such words in a similar setting, it might seem merely 'pious jargon'. She lamented the 'lack of contact between the traditional language of Christian worship and prayer and the most vigorous and lively writing in prose and poetry today', concluding that the age in which Eliot wrote was 'not an age in which a poet [could] use without self-consciousness the language of the Bible and the Prayer Book'.

Published in 1949, this assessment speaks of a discomfort that is perhaps necessarily provoked by a poem deeply concerned with the crisis of culture. To use Prayer Book language self-consciously is to acknowledge that it no longer seems effective, although there is no obvious alternative. Words change meaning and lose meaning, and living with that condition of loss is an intermediate and necessary stage. At least temporarily, this is a cry of dereliction.

It is significant that Eliot's writing has been an important point of reference for more recent writers of liturgy, but this is to anticipate a broader discussion of literature and its influence on the words crafted for use in worship.

LITERATURE IN LITURGY

So far we have considered literary references to liturgical utterances and activities. The opposite trend is less apparent as we consider the Book of Common Prayer, for two principal reasons. In the first place, the Prayer Book was being composed while the corpus of literature in English was very small. Opportunities for borrowing were therefore limited. In the second place, the Prayer Book services remained the sole form of worship for four hundred years. While secular literature flourished during this time, its influence did not impinge on a rigidly fixed language of worship.

An opportunity arose for English liturgists in the period of revision and experimentation that began in the 1960s and led to the publication of the *Alternative Service Book* in 1980. This project required the writing of a substantial body of new material, and the inclusion of literary specialists in the drafting committee's membership produced some distinguished prayers whose range of reference extended beyond what was classified as liturgy. (Interestingly, attempts to involve poets, among them W. H. Auden and Cecil Day-Lewis, were not nearly so successful.)

Some of these were treated with caution at the time and printed in an appendix of alternatives to the main text, among them two prayers written by David Frost. Each of them performs a variation on George Herbert's much-quoted 'Love III' (1941: 188), a poem automatically recalled by its opening line, 'Love bade me welcome; yet my soul drew back'. The first is an alternative form of confession:

> Father eternal, giver of light and grace,
> we have sinned against you and against our fellow men,
> in what we have thought,
> in what we have said and done,
> through ignorance, though weakness,
> through our own deliberate fault.
> We have wounded your love,
> and marred your image in us.
> We are sorry and ashamed,
> and repent of all our sins.
> For the sake of your Son Jesus Christ, who died for us,
> forgive us all that is past;
> and lead us out from darkness
> to walk as children of light.
>
> (Church of England 1980: 166)

Its opening words immediately liberate it from the conventional address, 'Almighty God, who...' The ensuing catalogue of failings culminates in the central lines (7–8) which echo Herbert's speaker, who hesitates to look on God (with whom Love must be identified) even though God has made his eyes. 'Truth, Lord; but I have marr'd them.' Love will have none of that, and insists on waiting on his sinful creature.

The second prayer is a Prayer of Humble Access, in which worshippers protest their unworthiness to receive communion, and implore God to have mercy on them. It is offered as an alternative to the familiar Prayer Book words, 'We do not presume to come to this thy table, merciful Lord':

> Most merciful Lord,
> your love compels us to come in.
> Our hands were unclean,
> our hearts were unprepared;
> we were not fit
> even to eat the crumbs from under your table.
> But you, Lord, are the God of our salvation,
> and share your bread with sinners.

> So cleanse and feed us
> with the precious body and blood of your Son,
> that he may live in us and we in him;
> and that we, with the whole company of Christ,
> may sit and eat in your kingdom.   (Ibid. 170)

There are echoes of the Prayer Book form, especially in the address to God, now amplified by 'most', and in the picture of sinners so unworthy that they cannot even claim the privilege of household pets that eat the crumbs under their owner's table— itself a Gospel image (Mark 7: 27–8). From Herbert, though, the prayer adopts a picture of an insistently loving God who, far from denying the sinner entrance to grace, refuses to be denied access to the sinner's own heart. 'Love took my hand', the speaker in Herbert's poem says. At its pivotal moment, the prayer changes from past tense to present tense, putting the despair of sin behind, and the practical business of healing and salvation in its place. The poem ends with Love insisting that the speaker sit down to be served at the table, summing up the determinative change in understanding of self in relation to God in six words: 'So I did *sit and eat.*' This image, framed in words drawn from the poem, becomes in the prayer the expression of hope that the saving promises of God will be celebrated at the banqueting table in heaven.

Both these prayers gain their vitality from an originality of vision, which interprets familiar elements in the tradition of worship through a new lens. As in the case of scripturally based hymns, it is not necessary to know Herbert to appreciate the forceful expressions of penitence and unworthiness as they are expressed here. To grasp the connection, however, is also to be reminded of the ongoing dialogue between the literary and the liturgical tradition. A reciprocal reading might thus explore the strong eucharistic resonances in the poem, perhaps extending to its hidden pun on the Latin *hostia*—victim; the loving *host* who welcomes the speaker, and the *host* which is the wafer used for holy communion.

In a perverse way, it is precisely when attention is drawn deliberately to sources that the dialogue ceases to be spontaneous in its effect and becomes forced. The third Eucharistic Prayer (Prayer C) in the Book of Common Prayer of the Episcopal Church of the United States of America celebrates the majestic achievements of God the Creator in its narrative of salvation, leading up to an acclamation in the 'Holy, Holy, Holy' of the Sanctus. Here, the praise of God's act of creation depends upon knowledge gained from space exploration and astronomy, and draws on the famous first picture of the earth taken from space—small, beautiful, green, and vulnerable:

God of all power, Ruler of the Universe, you are worthy of glory and praise. At your command all things came to be: the vast expanse of interstellar space, galaxies, suns, the planets in their courses, and this fragile earth, our island home.   (ECUSA 1979: 370)

Now read it against lines from Eliot's 'East Coker':

> O dark, dark, dark. They all go into the dark,
> The vacant interstellar spaces, the vacant into the vacant.
>
>   (Eliot 1974: 199)

and W. B. Yeats's poem 'The Dawn' from his 1919 collection, *The Wild Swans at Coole*:

> I would be ignorant as the dawn
> That has looked down
> On that old queen measuring a town
> With the pin of a brooch,
> Or on the withered men that saw
> From their pedantic Babylon
> *The careless planets in their courses...*
>
> (Yeats 1950: 164 emphases added)

Eliot's 'interstellar spaces' are neither comfortable nor immense gestures of divine power. They are empty and echoing, utterly negative, not displaying the mark of a creator or indeed of any form of cosmic order. Against claims that they are redeemed in liturgical use, it should be said that such redemption often tends to domestication and banality. In their own context they are dark, pending an eventual and better hope, but that does not relieve their contentless darkness. Yeats's planets, reunited with their adjective 'careless', have, in a different way, equally little to say about the kind of world order imagined in the prayer, and lend an air of frivolity at a solemn moment. This sense is heightened for anyone reminded by 'our island home' of W. S. Gilbert's 1870 operetta of the same title.

Quotation from the major 'canonical' poets of the twentieth century may have seemed safe in one sense, and a guarantee of respectability; it is profoundly unsafe from another point of view. Great care is needed in composing liturgical texts which quote widely from other forms of literature. At their best, such prayers are powerfully eloquent, and combine grace, economy, and renewed insight. Less successful examples end by distracting the worshipper with incommensurate cross-referencing, so that she combs her memory for the elusive phrase and forgets to concentrate on the activity of prayer. It is not surprising that many find this eucharistic prayer difficult to use.

Learning to Write Modern Liturgical Texts

These are transitional times for liturgical language, style, and structure. There are critical decisions to be made about the use of ordinary language and simple words, just as there are considerations governing more elaborate composition. English-language liturgy is in the interestingly provisional stage of not yet having criteria, agreed standards of excellence, or models of the best available writing, where a sixteenth-century style is no longer used. Liturgical committees in the mainstream Christian denominations concur on the use of inclusive language and simplified

syntax and punctuation, and the importance of concrete imagery, yet such agree-
ments do not lead to an assured mode for new composition.

A major challenge arises from the simultaneous perception that liturgical texts
should be written in a language and style that strive after grace as well as profundity,
but that they are also a pragmatic genre, and not produced with the intention that they
should become literature. We cannot therefore depreciate liturgy for not being literature. They are different categories, using many of the same media. David Jasper
suggests that '[t]he aesthetic argument is not as central to "liturgy" as it may be to
"literature", because liturgy is an exercise which demands a working language and
sometimes we need to be hardheaded and practical about it' (Jasper 1991: 385). The
theologian and Christian Socialist F. D. Maurice (1966: 4–5) put this even more strongly
in a sermon preached in a series on the Prayer Book in 1848. He told his congregation,
'I hope you will never hear from me any such phrases as our "excellent or incomparable" Liturgy.... I do not think we are to praise the liturgy, but to use it.... When we
do not want it for life, we may begin to talk of it as a beautiful composition: thanks be
to God it does not remind us of its own merits when it is bidding us draw nigh to Him'.

Maurice did not live in an age that was reassessing its liturgical needs to an extent
where new texts were being produced. He was able to concentrate exclusively on the
Prayer Book, and to warn properly against an aesthetic view that would obscure its
function as a means of enacting the commerce between human beings and God. For
contemporary worshippers in the major Christian denominations of the English-
speaking world, the situation is much more complex.

It would seem desirable to have some criteria for judging the merits of liturgical
texts, if only to guard against triviality on the one hand, and the dangerous delusion
that the effectiveness of acts of worship can be measured by aesthetic characteristics
on the other. Equally, it is difficult to lay down standards for acts of language which
draw simultaneous responses from faith, emotion, and intellect. Who can say
whether the sincerity of confession, or the assurance of divine forgiveness depends
on Prayer Book words? At the opposite extreme, who can argue that unless a
liturgical formula is fully intelligible, without any remainder of mystery, it achieves
nothing? Liturgy is not a linguistic product to be contemplated at leisure: it is
primarily a matter of words in action, freighted with the hope, joy, scepticism,
desperation of those who engage in worship.

To take an illustration, we might turn to David Frost's well-loved post-commu-
nion prayer:

Father of all, we give you thanks and praise, that when we were still far off you met us in your
Son and brought us home. Dying and living, he declared your love, gave us grace, and opened
the gate of glory. May we who share Christ's body live his risen life; we who drink his cup bring
life to others; we whom the Spirit lights give light to the world. Keep us firm in the hope you
have set before us, so we and all your children shall be free, and the whole earth live to praise
your name; though Christ our Lord.   (Church of England 1980: 144)

The Lucan account of the Prodigal Son (Luke 15: 11–31) provides the account of fatherly
love, forgiveness, and generosity which is used here to depict God's willingness to

approach his own fallible people in the person of Christ. The original story is imaginatively transformed, however, to gain breadth and freedom in the prayer. All God's lost children are thus found again in the living person and saving death of the perfect Son, and brought home to feast on his body and blood. Divine and human nature meet in a very real and active way in the person of the Son. The banquet held in the Prodigal Son's honour becomes entwined with the heavenly banquet of the Son of God, which is anticipated in every eucharistic celebration. This is a dense and rich piece of creation, achieved with a grace that avoids didacticism and self-consciousness, but none of this analysis fully defines the operation and powerful effect of the prayer, nor would such analysis be appropriate.

LITERATURE AS LITURGY/LITURGY AS LITERATURE

David Jasper (1991: 375) has spoken of liturgy as a participant in a more widespread 'crisis of language experienced within the postmodern condition'. Lawrence Hoffman (2002, 735) is more optimistic about the prospects open to liturgy in the contemporary climate, although perhaps with a measure of reserve. Liturgy, he suggests, inhabits 'a participational universe where meaning is negotiated at the horizon of meeting between the individual and the experienced world'.

It is at this point of negotiation that liturgy and literature can engage most fruitfully, literature providing what (borrowing and freely adapting from a recent Vatican Instruction on liturgical translation) I will call a 'sacral vernacular' for the exploration of ritual experience (Congregation for Divine Worship 2001: 22). Roddy Lumsden's poem, 'In the Wedding Museum', speaks this sacral vernacular with poise, humour, and disarming tenderness:

> This is why we're here and why we've swapped
> admission money for these crimson ticket stubs
> the guide has torn in two. The simple hall
> is kept at constant temperature; four walls
> of exhibition cases, glass and oak, are lined
> with printed cards. Let's take a look around.
> Two jars of morning air, lids sealed with lead.
> A linen sheet which graced the marriage bed.
> And here's a corkboard pinned with lists of guests,
> last-minute shopping lines, musicians' sets,
> the florist's chit. That bar-till roll is bull's-neck thick!
> This bucket's where I-can't-remember-who was sick.
> The marquee poles are here and champagne flutes
> are poking from each pocket of the bridegroom's suit.

> The sleeping bags of those who roughed it overnight.
> A burst guitar string, coiled like an ammonite.
> A wishbone which, for once, split half and half.
> A dozen albums filled with photographs.
> The bridegroom's tie, the best man's speech, the banns,
> some skewers from the barbecue, some cups and cans
> and candles. Here's a freeze-dried slice of wedding cake.
> And here's the dress itself, still crisp and vacuum-packed.
> This clod of earth's that very billionth part of Fife
> where man and woman changed to husband, wife,
> a decade back. And this is why we've come
> to visit this museum, ten years on,
> with these two children, blushing ear to ear,
> who're laughing, knowing this is why they're here.

(Lumsden 2000: 30)

The visit to the Wedding Museum may commence with the determination to retrieve the past, but it ends in an entirely new act of understanding. The poem's purposeful opening words and formal rhyming couplets strive against another process, in which secular experience is reimagined and finally even hallowed, to re-emerge as something other than what its participants had remembered.

The artefacts of the wedding day 'a decade back' have undergone no change, although they are now strangely unrelated in any system of meaning. Some of them have even entered a confusion of categories, so that the wedding dress in its vacuum packing offers the same edible possibilities as the freeze-dried cake. The best of modern technology has been applied to the task of arresting time, and the abrupt stops and emphatic caesurae that dictate the speed and movement of the poem reinforce this. We are forced to stop at each exhibit and recall its original tissue of associations. The poem demands that its audience at least entertain the possibility that experience could be objectified in this way—that it might even be recoverable from its symbolic remnants.

Yet this is precisely *not* why the couple are here. As they discover in meeting the fragment of a real place, what occurred was not a single event, but a sacramental transformation. This is an epiphany that stops the visitors in their tracks and halts the flow of the line in midstream: 'man and woman changed to husband, wife, | a decade back'. For a moment, it seems that time might stand still here for ever. But there is no leisure for rapt contemplation, even though the pause may invite this, for sacraments are local, incarnate, embedded, and rich in consequences. They command those who share them to return to the reality of daily existence.

The two blushing children, living evidence that the Prayer Book's orderly expectations of marriage have been met, signal their awareness of this at several levels. They are embarrassed in the most ordinary way by parents and sex and adult rites of passage. In quite another way, they are mysterious participants in the mythology of the creation of humanity out of the dust of the earth, made specific by location and time.

Herbert McCabe, a Dominican monk and theologian, spoke of the language of worship as an act of 'translinguification by which we find the language of the future in the signs of the present' (McCabe 1987: 178). Archbishop Michael Ramsey reflected in a different way on the mystery of the '"otherness" of the other world' which is invoked in prayer and worship. It is beyond the descriptive powers of language, 'yet Christians have loved to describe the other world.... So it is that some Christians, combining the imagery of another country with the sense of the present unseen fellowship with God, have written of the other world not as away from or 'after' this world, but as existing behind it or within it, hidden by the veil of our present ignorance' (Ramsey 1965: 28–9).

In the contemporary situation, where 'spirituality' has an integrity that may not include Christian claims, Lumsden achieves the 'translinguification' of past into present and future. His virtual tour through the Wedding Museum focuses the 'other world' through the time-bound contents of the display cases. This seems to me an icon of the way in which liturgy and literature should live with each other, for at best, they can teach each other's users 'why [they're] here'. The imagining of ourselves as capable of being transformed, whether through the encounter with the literary text, or by appropriating for ourselves what has been learned in worship from the hymnographers and writers of prayers who have guarded and regenerated the tradition of worship, is the beginning of a sacramental transformation.

WORKS CITED

BRIGHTMAN, F. E. 1915. *The English Rite*. London: Rivingtons, i and ii.

CHAUCER, GEOFFREY. 1966. 3rd repr. 1978. *Works*, ed. F. N. Robinson. 2nd edn. Oxford: Oxford University Press.

CHAUVET, LOUIS-MARIE. 1992. 'What Makes the Liturgy Biblical?—Texts'. *Studia Liturgica* 22: 121–33.

CHURCH OF ENGLAND (CENTRAL BOARD OF FINANCE). 1980. *The Alternative Service Book 1980*. London: Hodder & Stoughton.

CONGREGATION FOR DIVINE WORSHIP AND THE DISCIPLINE OF THE SACRAMENTS. 2001. *Liturgiam Authenticam: Vernacular Languages in the Books of the Roman Liturgy*. London: Catholic Truth Society.

CUMING, GEOFFREY. 1983. *The Godly Order*. London: SPCK/Alcuin Club.

DAVIES, R. T. 1963. *Medieval English Lyrics*. London: Faber.

DICKENS, CHARLES. [1848] 1970. *Dombey and Son*. Harmondsworth: Penguin.

DUFFY, EAMON. 1992. *The Stripping of the Altars: Traditional Religion in England 1400–1580*. New Haven: Yale University Press.

ELIOT, GEORGE. [1859] 1980. 6th repr. 1986. *Adam Bede*. London: Penguin.

—— [1871–2] 1994. *Middlemarch*. Ware, Herts.: Wordsworth Editions.

ELIOT, T. S. 1974. *Collected Poems 1909–1962*. London: Faber & Faber.

EPISCOPAL CHURCH OF THE UNITED STATES OF AMERICA (ECUSA). 1979. *The Book of Common Prayer*. New York: Church Hymnal Corporation.

FIELDING, HENRY. [1742] 1970. *Joseph Andrews and Shamela*. London: Oxford University Press.

FORD, DAVID. 1999. *Self and Salvation*. Cambridge: Cambridge University Press.

GARDNER, HELEN [1949] 1968. 6th repr. 1990. *The Art of T. S. Eliot*. London: Faber.

HARDISON, O. B. 1965. *Christian Rite and Christian Drama in the Middle Ages*. Baltimore: Johns Hopkins University Press.

HARDY, THOMAS. [1891] 1998; repr. 2003. *Tess of the D'Urbervilles*. London: Penguin.

HERBERT, GEORGE. 1941. 5th repr. *Works*, ed. F. E. Hutchinson. Oxford: Clarendon.

HOFFMAN, LAWRENCE. A. 2002. 'Jewish Liturgy and Jewish Scholarship: Method and Cosmology' in Martin Goodman (ed.), *The Oxford Handbook of Jewish Studies*. Oxford: Oxford University Press.

JASPER, DAVID. 1991. 'Between Literature and Liturgy: A Pragmatics of Worship'. *Anglican Theological Review* 73: 375–87.

—— and DETWEILER, ROBERT. 2000. *Religion and Literature: A Reader*. Louisville, Ky.: Westminster/John Knox.

LANGLAND, WILLIAM. [c.1370–90] 1966. *Piers the Plowman*, ed. John Burrow. Rev. edn. London: Penguin.

LAWRENCE, D. H. [1923]; repr. 1950; 5th repr. 1971. *Kangaroo*. Harmondsworth: Penguin.

LUMSDEN, RODDY. 2000. *The Book of Love*. Newcastle upon Tyne: Bloodaxe.

McCABE, HERBERT. 1987. *God Matters*. London: Mowbray.

MARVELL, ANDREW. 1990 *The Oxford Authors: Andrew Marvell*, ed. Frank Kermode and Keith Walker. Oxford: Oxford University Press.

MAURICE, F. D. [1849] 1966. *The Prayer Book*. 3rd edn. London: James Clarke.

PICKSTOCK, CATHERINE. 1997. *After Writing*. Oxford: Blackwell.

RAMSEY, A. M. 1965. *Sacred and Secular*. London: Longmans.

WATSON, J. R. 1995. *The English Hymn: A Critical and Historical Study*. Oxford: Clarendon.

YEATS, W. B. 1950. 13th repr. *Collected Poems*. 2nd edn. London: Macmillan.

FURTHER READING

BRADSHAW, PAUL. F. (ed.) 2002. *The New SCM Dictionary of Liturgy and Worship*. London: SCM.

BROOK, STELLA. 1965. *The Language of the Book of Common Prayer*. London: André Deutsch.

BROWN, FRANK BURCH. 1990. *Religious Aesthetics*. London: Macmillan.

BUCHANAN, COLIN. 1982. *What Did Cranmer Think He Was Doing?* 2nd edn. Bramcote, Notts: Grove.

DUFFY, EAMON. 2006. *Marking the Hours: English People and their Prayers, 1240–1570*. New Haven: Yale University Press.

FROST, DAVID. 1973. *The Language of Series 3*. Bramcote: Grove.

HOFFMAN, LAWRENCE. A. 1987. *Beyond the Text: A Holistic Approach to Liturgy*. Bloomington: Indiana University Press.

JASPER, DAVID, and JASPER, R. C. D. (eds.) 1990. *Language and the Worship of the Church*. London: Macmillan.

JEFFERY, PETER. 2005. *Translating Tradition: A Chant Historian Reads Liturgiam Authenticam*. Collegeville, Minn.: Liturgical Press.

NICHOLS, BRIDGET. 1996. *Liturgical Hermeneutics*. Frankfurt: Peter Lang.

TAYLOR, NORMAN. 1993. *For Services Rendered: An Anthology in Thanksgiving for the Book of Common Prayer*. Cambridge: Lutterworth.

PART SIX

THE GREAT THEMES

CHAPTER 41

EVIL AND THE GOD OF LOVE

ERIC ZIOLKOWSKI

Is he willing to prevent evil, but not able? Then is he impotent. Is he able, but not willing? then is he malevolent. Is he both able and willing? Whence then is evil?

Posed by the character Philo in David Hume's *Dialogues Concerning Natural Religion* (Part X), but routinely and misleadingly ascribed to Hume himself, these questions about God which find their source in Epicurus (quoted by Lactantius, *De ira Dei* 13) crystallize the traditional philosophical understanding of the problem of evil (cf. Feinberg 2000: 17–18). This problem, whether evoked by a case of natural evil, epitomized by the Lisbon earthquake of 1755 and the South Asian tsunami of 2004, or of moral evil, epitomized by the Shoah, poses a grave challenge to conventional theism and is deemed 'the guiding force of modern thought' (Neiman 2002: 2–3). Before examining the thematic relation between evil and the God of love in English literature, we should consider the theme's roots in the Bible, conceived not etymologically as *ta biblia ta hagia* (the holy books) but as a unified 'literary' document. It is in this sense that the Hebrew Bible or Tanakh furnished for Jack Miles his best-selling *God: A Biography* (1996: 354), and that the combined 'Old' and 'New' Testaments of the Christian Bible much earlier comprised for William Blake 'the Great Code of Art' ('The Laocoön', etching, *c.*1820).

Tanakhic Theodicy, the Agapic God, and Christian Theology

One reason the quandary of Hume's Philo seems irresolvable is that the Bible elicits as many questions as it answers about God and evil. Of the tanakhic texts that confront the problem of innocent suffering, Job comes first to mind, yet surpasses neither Ps. 44: 18–20 as a statement of the problem nor Prov. 16: 4 as a solution to it (Miles 1996: 304). Read in the canonical sequence of its 'books', regardless of historical-critical concerns, the Tanakh seems in no hurry to portray God as loving. Early in Genesis, he betrays a vindictive streak (e.g. his cursing and banishing of Adam and Eve) and a destructive inclination (e.g. through the Noahic deluge) that grimly complement his creator role. The same divine mean streak seems betrayed when two bears maul a mob of children who mocked a prophet of God (2 Kgs. 2: 23–5; see Ziolkowski 2001).

If this construal of God seems remote from his hackneyed reputation as God of love, it is because his loving image does not emerge until much further in the Tanakh, in the second portion of Isaiah, known as Deutero-Isaiah (Isa. 40–66). In Miles's view, from Genesis through Isaiah 39, God exhibits wrath, vengefulness, and remorse, but never love in a true sense (Miles 1996: 237; *pace* Exod. 34: 6b–7a; Num. 14: 18a). Meanwhile statements about God's having 'set his love upon' Israel, or that God 'loves' Israel (Deut. 7: 7a and 7: 8a; KJV, RSV) attest not to a tender emotion but to a strictly formal, covenantal love. God first evinces authentic lovingness in the Song of assurance to Israel that follows the four Servant Songs, which Christians read as auguring Christ. Here God, 'husband' of humiliated, exilic Israel, affirms that he will accept her back with compassion and 'everlasting love', having previously abandoned her 'in overflowing wrath' because of her pre-exilic infidelities (Isa. 54: 8). Whereas the noun for 'everlasting love' here is *hesed*, which connotes covenantal 'loyalty... rather than any more tender or personal feeling' (ibid. 243), this passage and others that follow (e.g. Isa. 62: 4–5) seem to reveal in God a new, genuine ardour, 'a pitying love or a loving pity' (ibid. 243, 245).

Not a little baffling is the tanakhic God's self-exonerating aside at Isa. 54: 15a: 'If anyone stirs up strife, it is not from me.' This does not square with his earlier boast that, in addition to forming light and creating darkness, 'I make weal and create woe [*ra'*]' (Isa. 45: 7a). Here, as in other passages that acknowledge God to be an author of *ra'* or *ra'ah* (Job 2: 10a; Amos 3: 6b), the noun in question denotes 'evil' (KJV, RSV, JPS). In quoting God's renewed promise to have compassion on Israel, Deutero-Isaiah adopts one of several possible opinions about the problem of evil. These are: (1) that the suffering of the innocent and the prospering of the wicked attest to an immoral world *ruled by a fiend*; (2) that the fact that the innocent sometimes prosper and the wicked sometimes suffer attests to an amoral and meaningless world *ruled by chance*; (3) that although the innocent sometimes suffer here and now, and although the wicked sometimes prosper, our temporal and spatial world is but a part of the real world, and at some later time or in some other place the innocent will be justly rewarded and the wicked justly punished, because the world as a whole is moral and *ruled by a just judge*; and (4) that the prosperity of the wicked need only indicate *a merciful world judge*, and that innocent human suffering, rather than simply being evil, meaningless, or compensated for in the future, may be meritorious, serving as a means by which the mysteriously just judge achieves universal justice (ibid. 247).

Although Deutero-Isaiah bypasses the first two options, neither of them is dissociable from the Bible. To be sure, modern thinkers such as Charles Hartshorne and Bertrand Russell will respectively aver that an immutable God could only be an impassive tyrant and 'inhuman monster' (Dodds 1986: 385 n. 388), or that if the world 'is the outcome of a deliberate purpose, the purpose must have been that of a fiend' (Russell 1957: 93). Yet Job's divinely condoned innocent suffering remains the tanakhic paradigm for the accentuation of God's 'fiend-susceptible side' (Miles 1996: 328) or what Neil Forsyth calls 'the darker aspect of God' that humans experience as 'evil', a perception that departs from the cosmological dualism manifest in the even more ancient but ever-resilient 'combat myth' in which God and his enemy are radically distinct (Forsyth 1987: 191).

Whereas the Tanakh nowhere sanctions the idea of a world governed by chance, modern literary expressions of that idea often reference the Bible. Pre-eminent examples include Thomas Hardy's poems 'Hap' (1866) and 'Before Life and After' (1909) and Samuel Beckett's tragicomic drama *Waiting for Godot* (*En attendant Godot*, 1952). As for Deutero-Isaiah, instead of dismissing God as fiendish (option 1) or the world as chance-governed (option 2), he presents God as just, usually by changing Israel's punishment to reward through an enlargement of the spatial or temporal context (option 3). He furthermore introduces the figure of a servant—Israel personified and, simultaneously, an actual person, perhaps the prophet himself—who, having suffered terrible affliction, will be rewarded after redeeming many (option 4; see Isa. 52: 13–53: 12; Miles 1996: 249). Deutero-Isaiah thus provides the Jews with a messianic vision and, later, the Christians with a prefiguration of Christ. He also helps to establish what will develop into the principal Western theodicy, up through the coining of that Greek compound noun in the 1690s by G. W. Leibniz to connote the human effort to demonstrate the justice (*dikē*) of God (*theos*). Finally, the prophet's new sense of God's *hesed* as 'a pitying love or a loving pity' anticipates the Pauline and Johannine formulations about God's *agapē* (Rom. 5: 8; 1 John 4: 8; cf. 4: 16; John 3: 16), an unconditional spiritual love of universal scope, distinct from physical, sexual love (*eros*).

The impact of this conception upon subsequent Christian theology cannot be overstated. Of the three *hypostases* or 'persons' of the Divine Trinity, the Son is assigned the attribute of love. For St Augustine (354–430), God's love is also manifest in human virtues (*De moribus ecclesiae catholicae* 1. 15. 25). St Thomas Aquinas's (*c*.1225–74) *Summa Theologica* (hereafter *ST*), agreeing with 1 John 4: 16 that 'God is love [*caritas*]' (*ST* I q. 20 a. 1 *sed contra*), elaborates that God loves all things (cf. Wis. 11: 24*a*), and the better things more than others (*ST* I q. 20 a. 2 arg. 1–I q. 20 a. 4 ad 5; cf. Augustine, *In Joannis evangelium tractatus* 110).

Paradoxically, it is in identifying God with love that Aquinas suggests its insepar-
ability from the notion of evil. God's love is evident to Aquinas through its being
the primary tendency of the will and of every appetitive faculty. Good and evil are the
proper objects of volitional and appetitive acts: the will and the appetite have
the good as their essential and special object, whereas evil is only their object
secondarily and indirectly. Therefore volitional and appetitive acts oriented towards
the good must precede those oriented towards evil, since 'what exists of itself, exists
prior to what exists of another [*quod est per se, prius est eo quod est per aliud*]' (*ST* I q.
20 a. 1 co). Evil, after all, is not a nature or being. Consistent with Augustine (e.g.
Enchiridion 12–14), the Pseudo-Dionysius (*c.*500; *Divina nomina* 4), and Boethius (d.
524; *De consolatione philosophiae* 3. 12–4. 4), Aquinas conceives of evil as existing not
of itself but only through a privation (*privatio*) of the good (*ST* I q. 48 a. 1 ad 1).

According to the anti-dualism of Christian theology from Augustine onwards,
good and evil are not equally potent in opposing one another. Nor does the relativity
of good and evil make them mutually dependent, so that, as a modern monist put it,
'Good is good only because there is evil, and God is God because there is a Devil'
(Carus 1900: 484). Instead, the entire world is good, as created by God (Gen. 1: 31); in
Augustine's words, 'all evil [*malum*] is either sin or punishment for sin' (*De Genesi ad
litteram imperfectus liber* 1. 3). That is, all moral evil originates in the fall of angelic
beings that rebelled against God, and of the first man and woman they tempted,
whereas all natural evils (earthquakes, storms, illness, etc.) are penalties for sin. (Of
the two major Christian explanations of evil, this Augustinian one has predominated;
the other, introduced by St Irenaeus [*c.*130–*c.*202], construes the fall as the starting-
point of human moral development [Hick 1966].) So even the devil is not, as the
Manichaeans imagined him, the autonomous, eternal power of darkness, the co-
equal foil of God's power of light. Rather, as the *satan* ('adversary') and one of God's
'sons' (Job 1: 6), this fallen angel is, as Luther sees him, the Lord's hangman, the agent
of divine wrath and punishment (Carus 1900: 342). Or he is, as Calvin sees him, a
degenerative creation of God, the author of all iniquity, and yet, as such, a servant of
divine justice (*Christianae religionis institutio* 1. 14. 16; 2. 4. 5).

EARLY PARADIGMS: ST PATRICK
AND *BEOWULF*

Although the mythologies of the pre-Christian peoples of the British Isles did not
lack in divinities associated with erotic love (e.g. the males Aengus and Maponos or
Mabon, and the females Branwen, Ailinn, Aidin, Aeval, and Creiddylad, the Welsh
type of Shakespeare's Cordelia), the idea of the agapic biblical God was introduced
only through the arrival of Christians in the first several centuries after the Roman

invasion (43 CE). It is uncertain, however, how much the attribute of love figured in this God's reputation among native Britons. From what is known about the later emergence of the Old English language, his agapic associations appear not to have been salient enough to warrant his being called, to the exclusion of all other divinities, 'the god of love.' According to the *Oxford English Dictionary* (2nd edn., s.v. 'god'), epithets 'chiefly referring to the department of nature or human activity or passion, over which a particular god was supposed to rule', are usually assigned to Graeco-Roman deities such as Mars or Ares (god of war), or Amor, Eros, or Cupid (god of love). Whereas one can only speculate how exposure to biblical thought and belief may have affected Celtic British conceptions of evil, the earliest use of the term *yfel* cited in the *OED* comes from the pen of the Venerable Bede (673–735). His vernacular song of death exalts the person who, before dying, considers 'What may be judged of his soul for good and evil [*yflæs*]' (trans. G. K. Anderson).

As lore about the early English saints and martyrs often concentrates upon their persecutions by malevolent pagans, it typically stresses God's vengefulness rather than his love. Thus, in an anecdote rehearsed by Bede, the decapitator of St Alban (third century) 'was not permitted to rejoice over the dead man, for his own eyes dropped onto the ground with the head of the blessed martyr' (*Historia ecclesiastica* 1. 7). The same harsh principle of divine retributive justice informs the warning issued two centuries later by St Patrick (c.390–c.460), the British-born apostle to Ireland, in his wrathful letter to the soldiers of the British prince and professed Christian, Coroticus, demanding that they be punished for slaying several Irish converts and enslaving others: 'Thus are all who do evil: they bring on death as their everlasting punishment [*mortem perennem poenam operantur*]' (par. 13). Patrick does mention divine love or *caritas*, but only to stress that any man who hands over Christians to Picts and Scots is 'far from God's love [*longe a caritate Dei*]' (par. 12). Revealingly, in his lyric hymn the *Lorica* ('Breast-Plate'), the closing litany of divine qualities through which he claims to 'arise' and be protected from adversities includes God's strength, might, wisdom, and so forth—but not God's love. In his *Confessio*, Patrick avows that it was Christ's love (*caritas*) that conveyed him to the Irish people (par. 13) and he persistently speaks of God as his personal protector against evil, 'injustices' (par. 33), and 'dangers' (par. 35). The report of Satan's nocturnal assault upon Patrick (par. 20) anticipates the literary vogue during the heroic age of the Germanic migrations, namely, a stern 'confrontation with evil—something to match the stature of a Beowulf. The lonely and superhuman struggles with demons... described in [Felix's] life of St Guthlac [*c.*673–714]... excited the admiration of a generation that looked for towering strength and personal prowess in its leaders' (Southern 1970: 217).

Regarding *Beowulf*, a landmark in the English literary portrayal of human conflict with evil, not all scholars accept J. R. R. Tolkien's famous thesis that the monstrous foes of the poem's titular hero *symbolize* evil (Tolkien 1936; see Tuso 1975: 116). The most significant Old English poem *Beowulf* was putatively composed as early as the eighth century, by which time England had been almost entirely Christianized. Notwithstanding the timeworn scholarly debates over whether *Beowulf* is a pagan or Christian poem, its coalescing of elements from both traditions is exemplified by

the monstrous persecutor of the Danes of Heorot. 'The figure of Grendel,' observes
Friedrich Klaeber, 'while originally an ordinary Scandinavian troll, and passing in the
poem as a sort of man-monster, is at the same time conceived of as an impersonation
of evil and darkness, even an incarnation of the Christian devil' (Tuso 1975: 104).
Grendel's epithets often recall Satan: 'creature of evil' (*wiht unhælo*; line 120; trans.
E. Talbot Donaldson hereafter), 'enemy of mankind' (*fēond man-cynnes*; line 164
[cf. 1276]), 'hell-spirit' (*helle-gāst*; line 1274; cf. 101, 788), 'God's enemy' (*Godes
andsaca*; line 1682; cf. 786), and so forth. His partial derivation from biblical mythology is further reflected by his descendence from the fratricidal, God-accursed Cain
(lines 102–8, 1263–7), a connection that introduces the Christian theme of divine
retributive justice: 'The Eternal Lord avenged the murder in which [Cain] slew Abel.
Cain had no pleasure in that feud, but He banished him far from mankind, the Ruler,
for that misdeed. From him sprang all bad breeds, trolls and elves and monsters—
likewise the giants who for a long time strove with God: He paid them their reward
for that' (lines 107–14).

Here, just as this allusion to trolls and elves constitutes residue from pre-Christian
myth, so is suggested the brutal, unquestioning approximation of a Christian
theodicy that Beowulf later blends with the pagan notion of 'fate' upon declaring
to the Danes his desire to fight Grendel:

The one whom death takes can trust the Lord's judgment [*Dryhtnes dōme*]. I think that if he
[Grendel] may accomplish it, unafraid he will feed on the fold of the Geats in the war-hall as
he has often done on the flower of men. You will not need to hide my head if death takes
me...he will bear away my bloody flesh meaning to savor it, he will eat ruthlessly.... Fate
always goes as it must [*Gǣð ā wyrd swā hīo scel*].   (lines 440–9, 455)

Framed as it is by the conflicting allusions to the Lord (*Dryhten*) and fate (*wyrd*),
this passage gives pause. Despite the poet's assertions elsewhere that God 'has always
ruled mankind' (*manna cynnes | weold wīde-ferhð*; lines 700–2; cf. 1057–8) and can
overrule a person's fate (line 1056), and despite attestations by King Hrothgar, the
poet, and Beowulf himself that the hero's victory over Grendel was achieved only
with God's assistance (lines 939, 1274–5, 1657–65) and that it was God that decided
Beowulf's victory over Grendel's malevolent mother (lines 1555–8)—despite all these
claims, and the repeated appellation *mihtig God* or '[al]mighty God' (lines 701, 1716,
1728), Beowulf's horrific fantasy of being vanquished and devoured by Grendel opens
up two different theological possibilities. One of these, captured above in the pagan
Anglo-Saxon notion that 'Fate always goes as it must,' is the belief that fate can
overrule God's will. This seems paradoxically supported by the poet's disclaimer
about Grendel's inability to drag away any Danes 'when the Ruler did not wish it' (*þā
metod nolde*; line 706), for the question naturally follows as to why God, if good, ever
did allow Grendel to assault or drag away human beings. On the occasion when
Beowulf could not keep Grendel in his grip, 'since the Lord did not wish it' (*þā metod
nolde*; line 966), one might wonder *why* God did not wish it. Such questions bear
upon the other theological possibility: might the Lord's judgement (*Dryhtnes dōme*)
in some instances seem cruelly unjust or at best indifferent?

Although readers sharing Klaeber's convictions about *Beowulf*'s 'Christian coloring' and about the poem's lack of 'a genuine pagan atmosphere' (Tuso 1975: 102, 103) might shrink from this last question, nowhere does the poem associate God with love. The closest approximation is the poet's comment that anyone will be well who, after death, seeks God and desires friendship or peace (*freoðo*) in God's embrace (line 188). Otherwise the conception of God as 'Ruler of Victories' (*sigora Waldend*; line 2875) is reminiscent of the Christian 'deity' the Roman emperor Constantine the Great had embraced some five centuries before, largely in the belief that this God had effected Constantine's military victory over Maxentius at the Mulvian Bridge (312 CE). Yet *Beowulf*'s God would have failed such a pragmatic theological test. While granting the poet's assurance that Grendel's 'heathen soul' (*hǣþene sāwle*; line 852) was claimed by Hell and submitted to 'the great judgment' (*miclan dōmes*; line 978), we are later left to wonder why the 'Ruler of Victories' allows Beowulf's battle with the wicked dragon to end in a fatal draw, with hero and beast lying dead beside each other (line 2910).

READING EVIL, EXPERIENCING LOVE

The culminating plea in the Lord's Prayer for deliverance from evil or the evil one (*ponēros*; Matt. 6:13) harks back to the psalmist's confidence in the Lord as protector from evil (*ra'*; Ps. 23: 4a) and shows evil in the Bible to be a concern far weightier and more urgent than a 'mere' literary theme. Hence, from the outset of the English identification with the church, the very act of reading—or listening, in the case of sermons, or viewing, in the case of sacred drama—could entail an existential anxiety over eschewing evil and embracing good in the quest of divine salvation. In his preface to his *Ecclesiastical History of the English People* (*Historia ecclesiastica gentis Anglorum*, completed 731) Bede asserts: 'For if history reports good things about good men, the attentive listener is stirred to imitate what is good; or if it recounts evil things about bad men, nonetheless the religious and pious listener or reader, shunning what is noxious and perverse, is incited more adroitly to pursue what he knows to be good and worthy of God.' By the late Middle Ages, the widely popular English Mystery Plays, often called Miracle Plays, had the similar purpose of inspiring conversions to God through the enactment of biblical episodes that emphasize the opposition between good and evil, obedience and disobedience, righteousness and sin. In a sermon against such dramas, a Wycliffian preacher rehearses their defenders' claims that the theatrical spectacle of the devil moving people to lechery and pride, and making people his servants, converts viewers to 'gode lyvynge' and turns them 'to the bileve, and not pervertith'. Seeing the passion of Christ and his saints performed, men and women have 'ben movyd to compassion and devocioun wepynge bitere teris'. And if some men are converted to God 'by ernestful doynge', and others, 'by gamen and play', it is also true that people must have recreation, and 'bettere it is, or lesse yvele, that thei han theyre recreacoun by pleyinge of myraclis than by pleyinge of other japis [japes]' (Pollard 1904: pp. xxii n.4–xxiii).

Several centuries later, in his 'Conclusion' to Part 1 of *The Pilgrim's Progress* (1678), John Bunyan adds a less optimistic theological twist to this concern over the reader's relation to good and evil. Although the Reformation had encouraged individuals to pursue salvation privately by reading and interpreting the Bible on their own, Bunyan warns of the eschatological hazardousness of the hermeneutic situation in which his religious allegory places readers: 'but take heed | Of mis-interpreting; for that, instead | Of doing good, will but thy self abuse. | By mis-interpreting evil insues [*sic*].' Such worrying over the ethical consequences of proper or improper interpretation will later dovetail with the debates among literary theorists of the Augustan Age over the relative merits of instruction and entertainment, edification and delight, didacticism and enjoyment. Moreover, despite the glaring difference between his Nonconformist affiliation and the Roman Catholicism of Alexander Pope, Bunyan's association of evil with misinterpretation does curiously call to mind a central argument of Pope's *Essay on Man* (1733–4), namely, that our perceptions of discord and chance in the world are but betrayals of our inability, on account of our human limitation, to recognize the perfect, divinely ordered harmony and direction of the whole cosmos: 'All Nature is but Art, unknown to thee; [...] All partial Evil, universal Good' (1. 289, 292). In analogizing the created world to a work of 'art' whose total perfection we lack the epistemological and hermeneutic capacity to fathom, Pope contributes to the tradition of so-called 'aesthetic' theodicy that finds its origins in Augustine (see Hick 1966: Ch. 4).

Although *The Pilgrim's Progress* makes rare allusions to God's love (as when 'Hopeful', paraphrasing Rev. 1: 5, tells Christian, 'He loved us, and washed us from our sins in his own blood'), the dominant emotion Bunyan's book is likely to foster in readers is terror at the thought of wrathful divine retribution for human evil (from the opening spectacle of Christian's flight from the City of Destruction to the closing glimpse of 'Ignorance' being sent straight to hell from the heavenly gates). In contrast, a separate, unparalleled branch of English literature had flourished in the fourteenth century that conveys its authors' sense of communing spiritually with the God of love. These mystics, most notably Richard Rolle (*c.*1300–49), Walter Hilton (d. 1396), Julian of Norwich (*c.*1342–1416), and the unknown author of *The Cloud of Unknowing*, focus upon 'nothing less than the way to God through love' (Windeatt 1994: 1).

Consistent with Jesus' claim to his disciples that the Father loved them because they loved the Son (John 16: 27), the mystics attest to the experience of being loved by God in reciprocity for their loving him (or her, in the case of Julian's seminal construal of God as 'modere'). This agapic relation typically climaxes in the 'marriage' of the soul with God. Believing 'that contemplacioun is a wunderful joye of Goddes love', Rolle avers that the person given to continual heavenly meditation is 'ravisshed in the swetnesse of Goddes love' (*Mendynge of Lyfe*, Ch. 12; Windeatt 1994: 19, 20). Likewise *The Cloud of Unknowing* characterizes God as 'a gelous lover' (Ch. 2; Windeatt 1994: 8), and the advertisement that prefaces the shorter of the two versions of Julian's *Shewings* promises 'many comfortabylle wordes and gretly styrrande to alle thaye that desyres to be Crystes looverse' (Windeatt 1994: 182). While Julian's revelations of divine love culminate with her analogizing the mutual love between God and the human soul to the love between a mother and child (see long version, sect. 63), no mystic elaborates more graphically the much commoner analogy to erotic love than Margery of Kempe (*c.*1373–*c.*1439), who recounts God's speaking to her about their need to 'ly togedir' in bed after their espousal: 'And therfor thu mayst boldly take me in the armys of thi sowle and kyssen my mowth, myn hed and my fete as swetly as thow wylt.... For I aske no mor of the but thin hert for to lovyn me that lovyth the' (*The Book of Margery Kempe*, Ch. 36; Windeatt 1994: 235).

Such divine rapture notwithstanding, the late-medieval English mystics hardly prove oblivious of mundane evil. *The Book of Margery Kempe* (Ch. 18) and *The Cloud of Unknowing* (Ch. 48) convey a wary cognizance that voices, visions, and other mystic delights can in some instances be wicked, demonic, and deceptive rather than good, divine, and authentic. Julian, equally aware of this distinction but fortunate enough to have a priest present to legitimate her own revelations (see *Shewings*, short version, sect. 2; long version, sect. 3), has a vision that affirms the Augustinian-Thomistic conception of the insubstantiality and non-essentiality of evil (long version, sect. 27). Although God leaves her then to puzzle over why he allows sin to exist, and later, over why heathens and disobedient Christians are excluded from his love and condemned forevermore to hell (long version, sect. 32), he does reveal to her how Christ's passion overcame and disempowers the devil. While the 'fende' remains as malevolently industrious as before the Incarnation, 'contynuelye he sees that alle chosene saules eschapes hym worschipfullye, and that es alle his sorowe', because 'he maye nevere do als ille as he wolde, for his might es alle lokene in Goddys hande' (short version, sect. 8; Windeatt 1994: 191; cf. long version, sect. 13).

This explication of how God delimits and thereby frustrates the devil's activities adumbrates the treatment of that subject in Milton's *Paradise Lost* (1667), the pivotal English literary effort to 'jusifie the wayes of God to men' (1. 26). Other adumbrations may be gleaned from several of the most important English poets before him.

THE CONCRETIZING OF EVIL AND THE DEVELOPMENT OF THEODICY IN PRE-MILTONIC POETS

The Augustinian notion that evil constitutes nothing *sui generis* suggests how important literary representations can be for endowing evil with an aura of concreteness and tangibility in forms of wicked personae, structures of malevolent actions, or the contours of evil images, symbols, or allegories. The insubstantiality of even the severest sorts of human malevolence is illustrated in Shakespeare's dramas, where the evil of such criminals as Aaron the Moor, Richard of Gloucester, Don John, and Iago 'is never really committed; it is only suffered. For the agents of evil are not moral; only their victims are. *Evil* is a word that describes the human and moral view of what they do' (Spivack 1958: 45). All these characters are derived at least in part from the personifica- tion of Vice (the devil's auxiliary), the constant and universal opponent of Virtue (God's auxiliary) in the allegorical conflict of the soul (psychomachia), the central theme of late medieval Morality Plays. As such, Shakespeare's villains violate human, social, and even cosmic nature, and 'merge into a single large affront to the unity and harmony of the world', with the result that their 'evil in its greatest magnitude expresses division and disorder' (ibid. 49). In causing a breakdown of social and cosmic order, their evil reciprocates the natural and moral evils that result from disjunctions in the universal order. As Ulysses observes in Shakespeare's *Troilus and Cressida*, 'But when the planets | In evil mixture to disorder wander, | What plagues and what portents, what mutiny!' The sea rages, the earth shakes, and the winds stir: 'frights, changes, horrors | Divert and crack, rend and deracinate | The unity and married calm of states | Quite from their fixure!' (I. iii. 94–6, 98–101).

In Shakespeare, the 'tragic dilation into religious significance of crimes which in our secular modern view have only a personal or social meaning' (Spivack 1958: 50) should not obscure the Bard's bridging of past theologizing with future seculariza- tion in one specific regard towards evil: his tendency to humanize and hence to modify the traditional notion of the devil, a term he frequently uses (cf. Carus 1900: 350–1). In *Othello*, for example, Iago compares himself to a devil (II. iii. 351–3) and is later perceived as such by Othello (v. ii. 287; cf. 301), who by then has called Desdemona a devil three times (IV. i. 240, 244) and been called one twice himself by Emilia (v. ii. 131, 133; cf. Spivack 1958: 52). Elsewhere, accordingly, Troilus psych- ologizes the idea of devilhood, construing it as a form of self-delusional human masochism: 'And sometimes we are devils to ourselves | When we will tempt the frailty of our powers' (*Troilus and Cressida* IV. iv. 95). Akin to this insight is the oft- quoted suggestion of Milton's Satan about the mind's ability to 'make a Heav'n of Hell, a Hell of Heav'n' (*Paradise Lost* 1. 255)—a suggestion which, though he himself later refutes it (4. 75), squares with modern sceptical understandings of heaven, hell, and the devil as mental fabrications.

An earlier, pre-Reformation image of the devil has him satirically garbed as the wandering yeoman encountered by the summoner in Geoffrey Chaucer's (*c*.1343–1400) 'Friar's Tale'. A far cry from *Beowulf*'s monstrous embodiments of evil, Chaucer's devil proves an eloquent interlocutor (an anticipation of Goethe's suave, cultured Mephis- topheles), and his explanation of why he must pursue the same vocation of bailiff that the summoner pursues lacks the ambiguity about the powers of God and fate that characterized the Old English poem. The devil acknowledges that he and his fellow 'feends' are 'Goddes instrumentz, | And meenes to doon his comandementz, | Whan that hym list, upon his creatures [. . .] Withouten hym we have no might, certayn' (*The Canterbury Tales* III [D] lines 1483–5, 1487). This acknowledgement, like Julian's insight a decade earlier that the devil's 'might es alle lokene in Goddys hande', conforms to

Augustinian theodicy and foreshadows the Miltonic disclosure that Satan in hell 'lay |
Chain'd on the burning Lake, nor ever thence | Had ris'n or heav'd his head, but that
the will | And high permission of all-ruling Heaven | Left him at large to his own dark
designs' (*Paradise Lost*, 1. 209–13; cf. Job 1: 12). Yet unlike Julian and Milton, Chaucer's
devil evokes this theodicy to affirm that his ultimate abduction of the summoner to
hell is divinely sanctioned.

References to Job are a thread joining Chaucer's pre- and Milton's post-Reformation portrayals of evil. In 'The Friar's Tale' the devil cites Job to exemplify how
sometimes, in causing woe in a person's life, devils are permitted by God 'Oonly the
body and nat the soule greve' (*The Canterbury Tales* III [D] line 1490), and in 'The
Clerk's Tale' Job is mentioned as an analogue to patient Grisilde, whose sadistic
husband betrays an awareness that the trials that he gratuitously imposes upon her to
test her steadfastness are nothing less than 'yvele' (IV [E] lines 932, 1052). In Milton's
Paradise Regained (1671) 'patient Job' likewise figures as a type of the tempted Son of
God in the wilderness, who extols him as 'the just man', divinely and universally
praised for having borne Satan's wrongs 'with Saintly patience' (3. 62, 93, 95).
A subsequent antithesis of Job is the disobedient Renaissance necromancer whose
legend inspires Christopher Marlowe's drama *The Tragical History of Doctor Faustus*
(1604; second version, 1616). Like the Job tale, the Faustus story hinges on an
agreement involving the devil. However, reflecting the oft-remarked trend of
human individualization fostered by the Reformation, the agreement this time is
not a bet made with Satan by God which frees Satan to test the faith of the unwitting
virtuous man (Job 1: 8–12), but rather a pact made wittingly and willingly with
Lucifer's demonic agent Mephistopheles by the blasphemous magus, granting the
magician's body and soul to the devil in exchange for twenty-four years of enjoying
the latter's service.

As disastrous as is his misassumption that his soul is his own possession to sign
away (*Doctor Faustus*, A-Text, 509; contrast Luke 12: 19–20), Faustus's most condem-
nable theological errors are his convincing himself that God does not love him, and
his vow to Lucifer 'never to look to heaven; | Never to name God, or to pray to him'
(A-Text 451, 728–79). These blasphemies allow Faustus' love of Beelzebub to become
'fixed' (453), betray his unforgivable 'Despair in God' (446), and ensure the futility of
his desperate plea just before the devils arrive in the end to drag him down to hell:

> See, see where Christ's blood streams in the firmament;
> One drop would save my soul, half a drop. Ah my Christ!
> Ah, rend not my heart for naming of my Christ—
> Yet will I call on him—oh, spare me Lucifer!
> Where is it now? 'Tis gone.
> And see where God stretcheth out his arm
> And bends his ireful brows.   (1484–90)

With its spectacle of the damned Faustus being denied even the 'half a drop' of
Christ's redemptive blood (see the paraphrasing of Rev. 1: 5 by Bunyan's 'Hopeful',
quoted earlier), this scene negates the affirmation a decade earlier by Edmund

Spenser's *The Faerie Queene* (1590–6) of the compassion that God out of gratuitous love shows even his basest, evilest creatures through angelic mediation:

> But ô th'exceeding grace
> Of highest God, that loues his creatures so,
> And all his workes with mercy doth embrace,
> That blessed Angels, he sends to and fro,
> To serue to wicked man, to serue his wicked foe.   (2. 8. 1)

BEYOND MILTON

In effect, *Paradise Lost* explores the reconcilability of Marlowe's vision of human fallenness and damnation effected through diabolic temptation and witnessed by God's 'ireful brows', and Spenser's vision of human salvation by God's grace alone (*sola gratia*) as Luther and Calvin conceptualized it. Given the devotion of an entire chapter to Milton in Part III of this *Handbook*, suffice it here to note that the imagining of evil and the God of love in post-Miltonic English literature has been largely, though certainly not exclusively, conditioned by *Paradise Lost*. Given Milton's possibly sympathetic portrayal of Satan, many have shared William Blake's opinion that Milton was 'of the Devils [*sic*] party without knowing it' ('The Marriage of Heaven and Hell' [1792–3], pl. 5). If, as Percy Bysshe Shelley stated in his essay 'On the Devil, and Devils' (1820), 'The Devil . . . owes everything to Milton' (quoted in Forsyth 1987: p. xiii), it would be not be an exaggeration to speak similarly about the debt owed to Milton by subsequent literary manifestations of theodicy.

This is especially true of the Romantics, most notably Wordsworth. For him, as for Blake, Milton embodied the paragon poet, and in *The Prelude* and *The Recluse* the Miltonic prognostication that human suffering will be justified in Christ's restoration of the lost Eden—a prognostication based upon the ancient doctrine of Adam's *felix culpa* (happy fault) or *felix peccatum* (happy sin), the 'fortunate fall'—is transposed into the view that 'paradise . . . can be achieved simply by a union of man's mind with nature' (Abrams 1973: 95). Concurrent with this transposition of theodicy to 'biodicy' is Wordsworth's adaptation of the 'theodicy of the landscape' that had evolved in a tradition extending from Chaucer's Dorigen in 'The Franklin's Tale' (see *The Canterbury Tales* V [F] 865–99), through Thomas Burnet's *Telluris theoria sacra* (1681–9, *The Sacred Theory of the Earth*), which posits that what is beautiful in nature constitutes 'the enduring expression of God's loving benevolence, while the vast and disordered in nature express his infinity, power, and wrath' (Abrams 1973: 101).

Reflecting this same tradition is Mary Shelley's *Frankenstein, or the Modern Prometheus* (1818), in which crucial encounters between Victor Frankenstein and the devilish monster he created from human corpses occur in such 'disordered', unsettling natural sites as the Alps and the Arctic. Shelley's novel, however, applies a new twist to the rationale the Miltonic Satan gave for his own malignity: 'If then his Providence | Out of our evil seek to bring forth good, | Our labour must be to pervert that end, | And out of good still to find means of evil' (*Paradise Lost* 1. 162–5). Although it is Frankenstein's rejection of his own creature that triggers the latter's murderous spree, neither the unloving creator nor his spurned monster imagines that any good can come from this evil, a word that recurs with telling frequency throughout the narrative. The monster actually reads *Paradise Lost* (among other classics), perceives his own partial affinities with both Adam and Satan, and later curses Frankenstein for having formed him without a companion to commiserate with his hideousness: 'God, in pity, made man beautiful and alluring, after his own image; but my form is a filthy type of yours. . . . Satan had his companions, fellow devils, to admire and encourage him, but I am solitary and abhorred' (1831 edn., Ch. 15).

A curious blending of Miltonic with Goethian-Faustian, German Romantic ideas about God, evil, and the devil occurs in Thomas Carlyle's satiric, rhapsodic prose-poetic novel *Sartor Resartus: The Life and Opinions of Herr Teufelsdröckh*, which was published serially in 1833–4, several years after *Frankenstein*'s third, revised edition (1831). Like the Genovese Frankenstein, who studied at the University of Ingolstadt, Carlyle's protagonist is a caricature of a Teutonic academic, a professor of transcendentalist philosophy at the fictive University of Weissnichtwo, Dr Diogenes Teufelsdröckh. He too is something of a modern Prometheus, with an 'electric Promethean glance' (Carlyle 1937: 134). However, with his surname meaning 'devil's dung', his outward appearance as 'some incarnate Mephistopheles' reflects his dualist conviction about the necessity of evil for the attainment of good: 'but for Evil there were no Good' (ibid. 126). This quasi-Irenaean idea—derived from Goethe's doctrine of character cultivation or *Bildung*, and passed on by Carlyle to the poet Robert Browning—supports Teufelsdröckh's sense that 'a Devil dwells in man, as well as a Divinity' (ibid. 239). Accordingly, like Frankenstein's monster, when depressed following a failed love affair, he identifies with Milton's fallen Satan. Having lapsed into a 'wholly irreligious' condition ('The Everlasting No'), plagued by 'Unbelief' that 'fixed, starless, Tartarean black', he paraphrases the arch-fiend, lamenting that 'ever. . . to be weak is the true misery' (ibid. 159, 162; cf. *Paradise Lost*, 2. 858, 1. 157). In wondering deistically whether 'there is no God, then; but at best an absentee God, sitting idle' (ibid. 159), he now envisions the universe as so spiritually sterile and mechanistic that he envies Goethe's anti-hero, for whom at least there was a devil to sign a pact with: 'Some comfort it would have been, could I, like a Faust, have fancied myself tempted and tormented of the Devil; for a Hell, as I imagine, without Life, though only diabolic Life, were more frightful: but in our age of Down-pulling and disbelief, the very Devil has been pulled down, you cannot so much as believe in a Devil' (ibid. 164).

Teufelsdröckh eventually escapes 'The Everlasting No', via 'The Centre of Indifference', into the condition of 'The Everlasting Yea', which he defines in scriptural language as loving God rather than pleasure (ibid. 192; cf. 2 Tim. 3: 4), but which he characterizes as a kind of newly evolved, non-creedal faith based on the belief that the suffering that life entails is surmountable through creative action and fulfilment of duty. From this vantage, Teufelsdröckh resolves that 'what is at present called Origin of Evil' is 'a vain interminable controversy', to which 'ever the Solution of the last era has become obsolete, and is found unserviceable' (ibid. 189).

As if to illustrate this last point, the armchair anthropologist James George Frazer decades later laid the groundwork for a very different construal of the human understanding of God and evil in his massive study of magic and religion among 'primitive' peoples, *The Golden Bough*. If Teufelsdröckh's contemplation of the universe as a hostile, purposeless, 'huge, dead, immeasurable Steam-engine' (ibid. 164) conveyed Carlyle's protest against the Industrial Revolution, Frazer's subversion of the distinction between 'savage' and 'civilized' expresses a late-Victorian discomfiture brought about in no small measure by increased exposure to the many foreign 'strange' peoples encompassed by the British Empire. Sensing 'the permanent existence of such a solid layer of savagery beneath the surface of society' (Frazer 1900: i. 74; 1911–15, i. 236; 1922: 64), Frazer acknowledges 'our debt to the savage': 'For when all is said and done our resemblances to the savage are still far more numerous than our differences from him' (Frazer 1890: i. 211; 1900: i. 449; 1911–15: iii. 422; 1922: 307). For Frazer, this rule applies no less to 'our' (i.e. modern, Western, Christian) conceptions of God and evil than to any other areas of our thought. The idea that our guilt and suffering are transferable to another being who will bear them for us—that is, the atonement doctrine—is, in Frazer's words, 'familiar to the savage mind' (Frazer 1922: 624). Likewise, he contends, there is an unbroken chain connecting the modern Christian conception of Godhead with 'savage' notions of a man-god, a human endowed with divine or supernatural powers, such as a magician or medicine man (ibid. 107).

As widely influential as *The Golden Bough* was upon twentieth-century English literary artists, no work seems more consonant with Frazer's blurring of the categories of 'civilized' and 'savage' than the Polish-born Joseph Conrad's story 'Heart of Darkness', which appeared in 1902, two years after the second, expanded edition of Frazer's work. *The Golden Bough*, that self-described 'voyage of discovery... [through] many strange foreign lands, with strange foreign peoples, and still stranger customs' (Frazer 1911–15: i. 43; 1922: 10), charts Frazer's sense of our 'mov[ing] on a thin crust which may at any moment be rent by the subterranean forces slumbering below' (Frazer 1900: i. 74; 1911–15: i. 236; 1922: 64). Likewise, the river journey of Conrad's Marlow into the interior of the Congo, the account of which is patterned partly after the underworld descent in Book 6 of Virgil's *Aeneid* (Feder 1955), forces him to confront 'the lurking death... the hidden evil... the profound darkness of its heart' (Conrad 1988: 35), and the illusoriness of the 'savage'/'civilized' distinction. Marlow's hunger and fatigue give him the sensation of 'getting savage', and the trip itself, with the glimpses it affords of the (to him) exotic, threatening, incomprehensible tribesmen on the banks, is 'like traveling back to the earliest beginnings of the world' (ibid. 25, 35). For his own part, Mr Kurtz, the mad, moribund, but charismatic chief of the ivory-trade Inner Station whom Marlow has journeyed to meet, holds the natives in awe like one of the savage 'man-gods' studied by Frazer. His dwelling encircled by heads on poles, Kurtz has—as Marlow reports—'presided at certain midnight dances ending with unspeakable rites, which...were offered up to him' (ibid. 50). Conrad's story is thus considered 'an attempt to describe evil, its theme being the lack of restraint that is its most obvious marker' (Mensch 2001: 26)—that is, the unrestraint of the European colonizing enterprise encapsulated in Kurtz. Even the Nigerian novelist Chinua Achebe, in branding *Heart of Darkness* racist, allows that Conrad 'saw and condemned the evil of imperial exploitation' in colonized Africa (Conrad 1988: 262).

Though the Frazerian literary concern with the underlying 'savagery' of society did not cease with Conrad, the focus sometimes shifted to children. Reminiscent of the puerile propensity to wickedness displayed in the biblical story of Elisha and the bears (a tale often invoked by English Calvinists in earlier centuries to warn children against succumbing to the rebellious promptings of their own sinful nature), a supremely pessimistic fictional exposé of the inherent barbarism ascribed to young boys is William Golding's novel *Lord of the Flies* (1954). Through the device of an aeroplane crash, which leaves a group of English schoolboys stranded on an ocean island, Golding's narrative portrays prepubescent savagery free of adult—or divine— interference, sharing a number of striking features with the Elisha tale mentioned above. The spectacle of a gang of children engaged in sociopathic, evil behaviour, outside adult or divine control, also occurs in Graham Greene's early short story 'The Destructors', which appeared the same year as *Lord of the Flies*; and Doris Lessing's futuristic novel *The Memoirs of A Survivor* (1974), which is often compared to Golding's novel (see Ziolkowski 2001: 163–4, 168–72). In all three works, although God is totally out of the picture, the naturalness with which children commit criminal or even savage acts is inexorably suggestive of original or 'inherited' sin.

The prospects of theodicy today are uncertain. On the one hand, Friedrich Nietzsche's declaration of God's 'death' in the nineteenth century has been succeeded by Emmanuel Levinas's pronouncement of 'the end of theodicy' in the wake of the Shoah (Larrimore 2001: 376–9). Yet this leaves unexplained the remarkably resilient, enduring popularity of the religious writings of C. S. Lewis, which often explore questions of theodicy: most notably, *The Problem of Pain* (1940), which seeks to reconcile the reality of suffering with the notion of a righteous and loving God by analogizing the life of souls to a game of chess defined by fixed laws, causal necessity, and other limitations; *The Screwtape Letters* (1942), a novel that records the letters of an elderly devil to his nephew apprentice, a demon assigned to ensure a young man's damnation; and the seven-volume Chronicles of Narnia (1950–6), which tell stories of Christian import about children of this world who pass into an imaginary, alternative world where struggles between good and evil are strongly pronounced. Of all his writings, however, none displays Miltonic theodicy more explicitly than *Perelandra*, the second novel of his fantasy Space Trilogy (1938–45). There, the protagonist Elwin Ransom—whose surname recalls the Pauline and Calvinist usage of that term to symbolize Christ's giving of himself in atonement for human sin (1 Tim. 2: 6; *Christianae religionis institutio* 3. 4. 30)—is miraculously transported to the planet Venus where he finds himself serving as God's agent to 'avert' what would amount to a second fall in the enactment of an Eden-like 'myth'. At the point when his demonically possessed antagonist, Weston (a scientist, like Frankenstein, by vocation), almost convinces Eve's Venusian counterpart that God *wants* her to be disobedient, Ransom suffers a moment of doubt in contemplating an ineluctable paradox of Christian theodicy: 'How if the enemy were right after all? *Felix peccatum Adae.* Even the Church would tell him that good came of disobedience in the end' (Ch. 9).

Though the atrocities of 11 September 2001 revitalized the terms 'evil' and 'evildoers' in the rhetoric of politicians and journalists, evil today is often construed as a cultural 'construct', and the *OED* finds the term to be 'little used' in modern colloquial English, 'such currency as it has being due to literary influence. In quite familiar speech the adj. is commonly superseded by *bad*; the n. is somewhat more frequent, but chiefly in the widest senses, the more specific senses being expressed by other words' (s.v. 'evil'). Nonetheless, regardless of what it is called, and of its inevitable permutations, evil undeniably persists in human affairs through abuses of free will and the denial of others' humanity, and thus is ensured a permanent place in the world of imaginative literature; indeed, images of malevolence become all the more prominent through their frequent extension to cinematic representation (see Cigman 2002). This is especially true of the detective story, that demonstrably film-friendly genre which, in the hands of its greatest masters (e.g. Arthur Conan Doyle and Dorothy L. Sayers), presents the sleuth's need to solve mysterious crimes as practically a moral imperative to exercise reason to the end of combating evil.

As for a sense of divine *agape* in our post-Nietzschean world, Ian McEwan's novel *Enduring Love* (1997) inauspiciously diagnoses one character's consumption by Godlike love as a form of psychopathology. The denizens of an increasingly secularized society will probably share the bafflement of Lewis's demonic Screwtape at 'This impossibility He [God] calls *love*', the seemingly contradictory ideal that 'The good of one self is to be the good of another': 'what becomes of my reiterated warning that He really loves the human vermin and really desires their freedom and continued existence?' (Lewis 2001: 94, 99).

WORKS CITED

ABRAMS, M. H. 1973. *Natural Supernaturalism: Tradition and Revolution in Romantic Literature.* New York: W. W. Norton.

CARLYLE, THOMAS. 1937. *Sartor Resartus: The Life and Opinions of Herr Teufelsdröckh*, ed. Charles Frederick Harrold. Indianapolis: Bobbs Merrill.

CARUS, PAUL. 1900. *The History of the Devil and the Idea of Evil.* Chicago: Open Court.

CIGMAN, GLORIA. 2002. *Exploring Evil: Through the Landscape of Literature.* Oxford: Peter Lang.

CONRAD, JOSEPH. 1988. *Heart of Darkness: An Authoritative Text, Backgrounds and Criticism*, ed. Robert Kimbrough. 3rd edn. New York: W. W. Norton.

DODDS, MICHAEL J. 1986. *The Unchanging God of Love: A Study of the Teaching of St. Thomas Aquinas on Divine Immutability in View of Certain Contemporary Criticism of this Doctrine.* Fribourg: Éditions Universitaires.

FEDER, LILLIAN. 1955. 'Marlow's Descent into Hell'. *Nineteenth-Century Fiction* 9: 280–92.

FEINBERG, JOHN S. 2000. *Many Faces of Evil: Theological Systems and the Problems of Evil.* Rev. and expanded edn. Wheaton, Ill.: Good News.

FORSYTH, NEIL. 1987. *The Old Enemy: Satan and the Combat Myth.* Princeton: Princeton University Press.

FRAZER, JAMES GEORGE. 1890. *The Golden Bough: A Study in Comparative Religion.* 2 vols. London: Macmillan.

—— 1900. *The Golden Bough: A Study in Magic and Religion.* Rev., enlarged, retitled. 3 vols. London: Macmillan.

—— 1911–15. 3rd edn. Rev. and enlarged. London: Macmillan.

—— 1922. Single-volume abridgment. London: Macmillan.

HICK, JOHN. 1966. *Evil and the God of Love.* New York: Harper & Row.

LARRIMORE, MARK (ed.). 2001. *The Problem of Evil: A Reader.* Oxford: Blackwell.

LEWIS. C. S. 2001. *The Screwtape Letters* with *Screwtape Proposes a Toast.* New edn. San Francisco: HarperCollins.

MENSCH, JAMES. 2001. 'Literature and Evil', in *Ethics and Literature,* ed. Dorothee Gelhard. Berlin: Galda & Wilch, 26–43.

MILES, JACK. 1996. *God: A Biography.* New York: Random House.

NEIMAN, SUSAN. 2002. *Evil in Modern Thought: An Alternative History of Philosophy.* Princeton: Princeton University Press.

POLLARD, ALFRED W. (ed.). 1904. *English Miracle Plays, Moralities and Interludes: Specimens of the Pre-Elizabethan Drama.* 4th edn., rev. Oxford: Clarendon.

RUSSELL, BERTRAND. 1957. *Why I am Not a Christian and Other Essays on Religion and Related Subjects.* New York: Simon & Schuster.

SOUTHERN, R. C. 1970. *Western Society and the Church in the Middle Ages.* Harmondsworth: Penguin.

SPIVACK, BERNARD. 1958. *Shakespeare and the Allegory of Evil: The History of a Metaphor in Relation to His Major Villains.* New York: Columbia University Press.

TOLKIEN, J. R. R. 1936. '*Beowulf:* The Monsters and the Critics'. *Proceedings of the British Academy* 22: 245–95.

TUSO, JOSEPH F. (ed.). 1975. *Beowulf: The Donaldson Translation, Background and Sources, Criticism.* Norton Critical Edition. New York: W. W. Norton.

WINDEATT, BARRY (ed.). 1994. *English Mystics of the Middle Ages.* Cambridge: Cambridge University Press.

ZIOLKOWSKI, ERIC. 2001. *Evil Children in Religion, Literature, and Art.* Houndsmill: Palgrave.

FURTHER READING

BRUNSDALE, MITZI. 1990. *Dorothy L. Sayers: Solving the Mystery of Wickedness.* New York: Berg.

COX, JOHN D. 2000. *The Devil and the Sacred in English Drama, 1350–1642.* Cambridge: Cambridge University Press.

DANIELSON, DENNIS RICHARD. 1982. *Milton's Good God: A Study in Literary Theodicy.* Cambridge: Cambridge University Press.

DENDLE, PETER. 2001. *Satan Unbound: The Devil in Old English Narrative Literature*. Toronto: University of Toronto Press.

Evil in English Literature. 2003. Proceedings from the 23rd All-Turkey English Literature Conference, 24–26 April 2002. Istanbul: Istanbul Universitesi.

FORSYTH, NEIL. 2003. *The Satanic Epic*. Princeton: Princeton University Press.

FREIBURG, RUDOLF, and GRUSS, SUZANNE (eds.). 2004. *'But vindicate the ways of God to man': Literature and Theodicy*. Tübingen: Stauffenburg.

GORDON, HAIM. 1997. *Fighting Evil: Unsung Heroes in the Novels of Graham Greene*. Westport, Conn.: Greenwood.

LAATO, ANTTI, and MOOR, JOHANNES CORNELIS DE 2003. *Theodicy in the Bible*. Leiden: Brill.

LANGER, LAWRENCE L. 1975. *The Holocaust and the Literary Imagination*. New Haven: Yale University Press.

MYERS, WILLIAM. 1991. *Evelyn Waugh and the Problem of Evil*. London: Faber & Faber.

PYRHÖNEN, HETA. 1999. *Mayhem and Murder: Narrative and Moral Problems in the Detective Story*. Toronto: University of Toronto Press.

SMITH, MOLLY. 1991. *The Darker World Within: Evil in the Tragedies of Shakespeare and his Successors*. Newark: University of Delaware Press.

SRIGLEY, MICHAEL. 1994. *The Mighty Maze: A Study of Pope's* An Essay on Man (*Acta Universitatis Upsaliensis. Studia Anglistica Upsaliensia*, 87). Uppsala: Uppsala University Press.

CHAPTER 42

DEATH AND THE AFTERLIFE

TINA PIPPIN

FOR WHOM THIS BELL TOLLS: THE PROXIMITY OF DEATH

IN 1623 as John Donne (1572–1631) lay sick he wrote meditations on his own and the overall human condition of sickness and death: 'Now this bell tolling softly for another, says to me, Thou must die. . . . Any man's death diminishes me because I am involved in mankind, and therefore never send to know for whom the bell tolls; it tolls for thee' (Meditation XVII, 1624, in Abrams 1968a: 917). Donne pointed to the certainty of sickness and death, the importance of faith, and the assurance of heaven for the believer. A little later a country doctor in England explored the metaphysics of death while writing a meditation on a funeral urn. Sir Thomas Browne (1605–82) commented, 'There is no antidote against the opium of time, which temporally considereth all things: our fathers find their graves in our short memories, and sadly tell us how we may be buried in our survivors. Gravestones tell truth scarce forty years' (*Hydriotaphia, Urn Burial*, ibid. 1249). Graves can be removed, monuments can fall, but each person wants to be remembered: 'God, who can only destroy our souls, and hath assured our resurrection, either of our bodies or names hath directly promised no duration. . . . But man is a noble animal, splendid in ashes, and pompous in the grave, solemnizing nativities and deaths with equal luster, nor omitting ceremonies of bravery in the infamy of his nature' (ibid. 1252). In the eighteenth century Jonathan Swift expressed the combination of finality and hope when musing on death: ' "His time was come; he ran his race; | We hope he's in a better place" ' (Swift, 'Verses on the Death of Dr. Swift', ibid. 1514). In the seventeenth century birth was fragile and death always near. Of course, how one was remembered depended on one's earthly life and works.

Death lyrics in poetic or prose form have a long history. These lyrics were popular in the Middle Ages in England, especially in the fifteenth century. Everyone will eventually die, and death treats all social classes equally. Since all humans sin, all are in need of repentance, and death lyrics brought an understanding to the mystery. The thinking or philosophizing over death in the West developed and evolved over time. Philippe Ariès observes that the first thousand years of Christian Europe presented a form of 'tamed death'. The person was usually forewarned of their near death, the death came at its appointed hour, and Christians and pagans died 'simply' (Ariès 1974: 2–12). Later more Christian exclusivism arose. From the end of the medieval era to the nineteenth century the central focus of individual death (and judgement) was the deathbed (ibid. 38). So for Ariès in the Middle Ages there are two stages in the development of thoughts about death: 'the familiar resignation to the collective destiny of the species . . . *Et morie-mur*, and we shall all die' and '*la mort de soi*, one's own death' (ibid. 55). The dying had one last chance to repent of any sins, face the 'final' judgement that would determine their afterlife with God or Satan, and accept the inevitable.

> When the turf is thy tower
> And the pit is thy bower,
> Thy flesh and thy white throat
> Worms shall consume.
> What helpeth thee then
> All the world to win?
>
> (XIII, 30 in Fowler: 78
> from Brown).

By the sixteenth century England was nearing its period as an imperial power in the world. It envisioned itself as a New Rome, an imperial power controlling earth, and also heaven and hell. New worlds came into sight, as well as new opportunities to push military advances and spread diseases to indigenous peoples. Death remained destiny, but of a different sort: whole peoples could be eradicated as a part of some grand imperialist plan.

The major shift in perceiving and representing death came in the eighteenth century with the change of focus from one's own death to the death of the other, '*la mort de toi* . . . whose loss and memory inspired in the nineteenth and twentieth centuries the new cult of tombs and cemeteries and the romantic, rhetorical treatment of death' (ibid. 56). The focus then shifted from the corpses to memorializing the dead through their tombs. The focus on the tomb and corpse brought the imaginative literature of the 'undead', vampires and other creatures who refuse in various ways to obey the laws of nature and God and go away permanently.

Percy Bysshe Shelley (1792–1822) explored the theme of death at age 18 in his political poem 'Queen Mab'. He wrote this elegy to Death:

> How wonderful is Death,
> Death and his brother Sleep!

> One, pale as yonder waning moon
> With lips of lurid blue;
> The other, rosy as the morn
> When throned on ocean's wave
> It blushes o'er the world:
> Yet both so passing wonderful!   (Keats and Shelley n.d.: 805)

Shelley gives an enthusiastic view of natural death, and then proceeds to critique institutional religion that supports murderous plots against atheists and heathen nations.

Perhaps the most famous English poem written about death, from this or any other period, comes from Thomas Gray (1716–71). His 'Elegy Written in a Country Churchyard' (1751) gives a view not only of a public graveyard but of the public nature of death in eighteenth-century England. Gray describes the gravesites as quite gently protected by nature, but death is still an everlasting state: 'Beneath those rugged elms, that yew tree's shade, | Where heaves the turf in many a moldering heap, | Each in his narrow cell forever laid. | The rude forefathers of the hamlet sleep' (Abrams 1968a: 1766–7). The ultimate truth for Gray is this: 'The boast of heraldry, the pomp of power, | And all that beauty, all that wealth e'er gave, | Awaits alike the inevitable hour. | The paths of glory lead but to the grave' (ibid. 1767).

For Gray the dead remain forever dead and are missed by the living. No communication comes from the dead; no ghosts haunt the living. The act of remembrance is of key importance: 'Far from the madding crowd's ignoble strife, | Their sober wishes never learned to stray' (ibid. 1768). Also part of memory is the hope of heaven. This poem is a meditation on a public space, a public monument to death, which in eighteenth-century England was generally connected to (or in) a church. The beauty of the countryside alludes to the beauty of the afterlife, although Gray makes no clear reference to the landscape of heaven. Here there is no battle between God and Satan, no souls crying out in the space in between Hell and Heaven, no grand Last Judgment and casting of souls to salvation or damnation. The demons do not lurk in this peaceful setting. Only the observer (poet and reader) and the dead bodies beneath the ground: 'Here rests his head upon the lap of Earth' (ibid. 1769). The dead are no longer productive, but the meditation on death certainly is.

The idea of the inevitability of death is, of course, a constant throughout English literature, but there is sometimes hope in remembrance and respect for the dead. One example of this connection with death and the dead is from Robert Southey (1774–1843). In his poem, 'My Days among the Dead Are Passed' (1823) he reflects: 'My thoughts are with the dead, with them | I live in long-past years [. . .] My hopes are with the dead, anon, | My place with them will be, | And I with them shall travel on | Through all futurity; | Yet leaving here a name, I trust, | That will not perish in the dust' (Abrams 1968b: 588). Leaving a legacy—of poetry and prose, of good works, a life well lived—will keep death from being an empty end of life.

A more negative examination of death occurs in the early to mid-twentieth century. D. H. Lawrence (1885–1930) expressed such productive meditation in his poem, 'The Ship of Death' (1929–30): 'Build then the ship of death, for you must take | the longest journey, to oblivion' (ibid. 1766). As with Donne and others who suffered personal illness and pain, Lawrence focuses on the finality of death while leaving room for a sliver of hope: 'And yet out of eternity a thread | separates itself on the blackness, | a horizontal thread | that fumes a little with pallor upon the dark [. . .] A flush of rose, and the whole thing starts again' (ibid. 1768). T. S. Eliot (1888–1965) also explores oblivion in his poem, 'The Waste Land' from 1921 in which, according to Abrams, 'death heralds no resurrection' (ibid. 1780). Eliot writes of a Jesus who suffers and dies but does not resurrect: 'He who was living is now dead | We who were living are now dying | With a little patience' (Eliot 1952: 47). The waste land is barren, dry, and desolate, reflecting modern urban life. Thus life in the desolate city becomes a sort of in-between state. This state of being in the middle, neither in heaven or hell, is the subject of many writers.

To Be or Not to Be, and All That's In Between

In some of the most famous lines ever spoken, the speaker addresses major human fears and desires:

> To be, or not to be—that is the question:
> Whether 'tis nobler in the mind to suffer
> The slings and arrows of outrageous fortune
> Or to take arms against a sea of troubles
> And by opposing end them. To die, to sleep—
> No more—and by a sleep to say we end
> The heartache, and the thousand natural shocks
> That flesh is heir to. 'Tis a consummation
> Devoutly to be wished. To die, to sleep—
> To sleep—perchance to dream: ay, there's the rub,
>
> .   .   .   .   .   .
>
> But that the dread of something after death,
> The undiscovered country, from whose bourn
> No traveller returns, puzzles the will,
> And makes us rather bear those ills we have
> Than fly to others that we know not of?   (III. i. 56–82)

Hamlet's soliloquy provides the setting for all other discussions of death and the afterlife in English literature. Shakespeare put the discussion on the stage and gave it tragic dimensions. In a world in which death was present in many forms (sudden death and lingering sickness unto death) heaven and hell took on special power. The pagan world of the spirits, along with the Apocalypse of John's souls under the altar crying for resurrection, forms the basis for afterlife belief. The borders of the afterlife and this world are often blurred—by guilt, sin, and desire. The saintly few went straight into heaven; those who committed mortal sins went into hell for all eternity. But what about those who were basically good throughout their lives but committed venial (or lesser) sins? An intermediate place of purification took hold of the medieval imagination, fuelled by Dante's fictional tour of hell. Heaven awaited these righteous-but-not-quite-righteous-enough souls, but first they must experience hell-like fires to be cleansed of their smaller sins. So purgatory emerged as a place of suffering, but a place that could be negotiated by those who prayed for the dead, or offered indulgences on their behalf, or by means of guardian angels who protected these souls against attacking demons. What began in the imagination of believers became a profitable doctrine in the Church.

When did the idea of purgatory emerge? The most definite answer comes from Jacques Le Goff, who places the beginning of the concept in 1170 CE through the appearance of the noun *Purgatorium* to designate a place and not only a state of mind (Greenblatt 2001: 265 n. 11). Most scholars disagree, finding the idea of an intermediate space in the early Church Fathers (e.g. Kabir 2001: 187). The Council of Lyons made purgatory an official doctrine in 1274 CE (Bynum and Freedman 2000: 296 n. 22).

In the English Middle Ages writings of trance-inspired visions of the afterlife were popular. Usually the visionary is sent to an interim place or purgatory to be cleansed before admittance into Paradise (heaven). In writings such as *The Voyage of St. Brendan* and *The Vision of Tundale* (c.1149 CE) and *St. Patrick's Purgatory* (c.1153 CE) the visionary sees hell, purgatory, and heaven (see Eleazar 1963: 377). *The Voyage of St. Brendan* is an Irish *imram*, what Alice Turner describes as 'a Christianized series of Sinbad-the-Sailor-like adventures' (used by C. S. Lewis in *The Voyage of the Dawn Tread* in the Narnia Chronicles—Turner 1993: 103, see n.). The most popular tale was *St. Patrick's Purgatory* which told the story of the Knight Owen. The hero searches for an earthly paradise while going through the requisite purification and punishment rites. Owen is the first person actually to travel to purgatory—and return to tell about it (see the discussion in Greenblatt 2001: 73–82). Greenblatt adds, '*Saint Patrick's Purgatory* may serve as a model for a type of literary experience: an expressive pattern of exploration, symbolic suffering, and psychic release that extends from Dante's *Purgatorio* to Seamus Heaney's *Station Island*' (ibid. 84).

Medieval literature on death and the afterlife is full of allegories, dreams, visions, ghosts, demons and angels, the Virgin, the fires of hell and purgatory, and the garden space of Paradise. One purpose of these bleak tales was 'to scare readers and listeners into right living so that they might immediately enter paradise' (Eleazar 1963: 385). There is a human need to imagine what we dread the most, and these stories brought a certain catharsis and thrill. They also staked out Roman Catholic claims in a world dealing with the impositions of paganism and the first stirrings of the Reformation.

Purgatory emerged in different forms, earthly and heavenly, allegorical and real, over the first millennium and a half of Christianity. Purgatory is a middle state, a physical place for the dead in between heaven and hell, and a state of the heart, for those who are not completely pure and sinless. In medieval Anglo-Saxon literature purgatory is, in one earlier form, an 'interim paradise' between death and judgement day (Kabir 2001: 1). This idea of an interim paradise was popular with Bede (673–735) and Aelfric (*c*.955–1010) and gained popularity in the Church. The interim paradise was an earthly paradise, a sort of heaven on earth, a reinvented Garden of Eden (Kabir 2001: 187–8). In his *Ecclesiastical History of the English People* (*c*.731 CE) Bede relates the otherworldly adventures of *Furseus* (633 CE) and of *Drythelm* (696 CE), the latter a man who dies and resurrects post-vision, in an interim purifying process (Eleazar 1963: 380). Heaven, hell, and interim paradise are described in these stories.

The dead scope out the afterlife; evidence of this is in the appearance of ghosts. In the later *The Gast of Gy* (*c*.1380 CE) a ghost of a dead man comes back to earth to haunt his widow's bedroom. A priest (armed with a consecrated host) and men (armed with weapons) arrive on the scene to interrogate and exorcize the Ghost. The Ghost then proceeds to tell them about purgatory (see Greenblatt 2001: Ch. 3). The prayers and intercessions of the living can benefit the dead by helping shorten what could be a long time in this place of suffering in the middle of the earth.

Ghosts are also present in Thomas More's (1478–1535) *The Supplication of Souls* (More 1990), a response to Simon Fish's Protestant book, *A Supplication for the Beggars*. Fish made a case against purgatory and the Church, and More replied in his extended book. In More's book the souls of the dead in purgatory cry loudly in order to be heard and not forgotten by the living. For those who do not believe in purgatory, hell is their destination. Not only do people have to fight Satan during their earthly lives, they also have to continue the contest as they suffer in purgatory. The dead in purgatory want to be remembered, and in return for supplication on their behalf they promise the living they will help them when they finally do arrive in heaven (Greenblatt 2001: 143–4). More fought the growing rationalism that poked holes in the belief in purgatory. He explores these ideas in his satirical book *Utopia* (More 2003), in which the traveller Raphael Hythlodaeus discovers the island of Utopia. More portrays Utopians as believing in eternal bliss after death. Death, but not sickness, is to be eased into joyfully. If anyone hesitates, it means they are hiding something bad they did in their life. About the dead in Utopia More writes, 'For they believe that the dead are present among us and hear the talk about themselves, though they are invisible through the dullness of human sight . . . that the dead come among the living observing their words and deeds' (Abrams 1968*a*: 417). For More death is something that demands remembrance: 'Now to my word: | It is "Adieu, adieu, remember me." | I have sworn't' (1. 5. 111. 13). He made a strong case for the complexities of the afterlife that mirrored his own support of the Roman Catholic Church as he served during the reign of Henry VIII and the growing reformation. More eventually lost his life in 1535 over his loyalty to Catholicism.

By the time of the Protestant Reformation the theology of purgatory became embroiled in the Protestant versus Catholic struggles of the time. Stephen Greenblatt (2001: 3) points out that purgatory was opposed as being 'not simply a fraud; it was a piece of poetry'. English poetry, from Old and Middle Anglo-Saxon literature through Shakespeare to the present, has this imaginary place embedded in stories of the afterlife. Suffering, which was the main point of the purging and purifying experiences of purgatory, lends itself well to human experience in any time. But Western Christianity explored the depths of suffering and the necessity for pain in this world and after. In this theology death only leads us into a next phase, a next step towards either heaven or hell. And in the Christian world that imagined purgatory, there remained the need to pray for the dead.

Purgatory gives the not-so-holy dead a second chance at redemption. Greenblatt (2001: 45) explains the transition using the example of John Donne writing from his sick bed: 'There are no ghosts, save the Holy Ghost, no suffrages, save preaching to the living. For the dying Donne there is an almost frantic hope of Heaven; there is an intense fear of Hell and a still more intense fear of putrefaction; but there is no Purgatory'. Donne often focused on death in his poems and sermons, working out the religious politics of his time through examining highly charged images such as purgatory. Donne (1973: 6) would rather refer to 'the manifold deaths of this world'. These deaths, and the final death, are in the hands of God: 'to this God our Lord belong'd these issues of death. . . . There we leave you, in that blessed dependency, to hang upon him, that hangs upon the cross' (ibid. 26). Believers have a path to resurrection and a future in God's kingdom because of Christ's sacrifice. The focus in Donne's last sermon is on God's suffering to open the path to heaven. Death and the afterlife can only really be imagined, left out of scientific verification. Purgatory falls away in the face of such hope of heaven.

Purgatory is a subset of heaven; all souls who arrive in purgatory are able to eventually make it to heaven. But the fire and other purification rites sound more like a mini-hell, even if angels sometimes protect the better of the souls. As D. P. Walker (1964: 59–60) describes the situation in the seventeenth century, the debate between Protestants and Catholics over death and the afterlife was centred on an acceptance or rejection of purgatory. Some Protestants got around the problem of absolutes— either eternal delight in heaven or eternal punishment in hell—by belief in an 'intermediate state' in which (according to Luther) the soul could still be saved in or after death. The issue concerned what to do with unbaptized babies (for Catholics) and the decent enough but not-quite-good-enough folks (for both Catholics and Protestants). And the main theological question was over theodicy: what was God's role in the judgement and post-judgement? Could God really instigate and dictate eternal torment? Was God that vengeful, vindictive, and cruel? The existence (and persistence) of hell necessitated an imaginative eschatology. The eternally tormented cried out for poetic justice. Yet in the midst of this theology of the afterlife arose a critique of purgatory, as the Church neatly fitted the doctrine into its economic benefits. In other words, critics of the doctrine of purgatory saw it as an integral part of the larger greed of the Church.

By Shakespeare's time the theological underpinnings of purgatory had been seriously undermined. Hamlet also does not think he is headed for purgatory. In his reading of Hamlet's narrative, Greenblatt follows the Ghost, making the Ghost a central character in his interpretation of the play. The Ghost is the spirit of Hamlet's father that is stuck in the middle state between heaven and hell. The Ghost announces,

> I am thy father's spirit,
> Doomed for a certain term to walk the night,
> And for the day confined to fast in fires
> Till the foul crimes done in my days of nature
> Are burnt and purged away
>
> (1. v. 9–13; see also 1. iv. 21–5; 11. ii. 575–6)

Greenblatt (2001: 233) points out that Hamlet is not drawn into the idea of purgatory here. Hamlet tries to maintain a Protestant theology that was put in place by the Church of England in the mid-1550s and later in Thomas Cranmer's *Book of Common Prayer* and the Thirty-Nine Articles. Article 22 states that purgatory and all things surrounding it (belief, prayers, and rituals) are 'rather repugnant to the word of God' (quoted ibid. 235). But the idea continues to exist that the Ghost comes from such a middle realm. Greenblatt speculates that the Ghost in Hamlet reflects Shakespeare's own Catholic father's spirit asking for assistance from purgatory. His father died in 1601, the same year Hamlet was written. Hamlet relates that death is 'the undiscovered country from whose bourn | No traveller returns' (iii. i. 81–2). Greenblatt (2001: 257) observes that purgatory is a space that lingers in the Protestant imagination, especially that of Shakespeare, even as he artfully dodged the Elizabethan censors. Purgatory takes to the theatre: 'the space of Purgatory becomes the space of the stage where old Hamlet's Ghost is doomed for a certain term to walk the night'. It is difficult to get rid of ghosts completely; the undead stalk the imagination, calling out from their unsettled place in the afterlife. Mary Wollstonecraft Shelley invented a living monster from the parts of dead people in her novel, *Frankenstein* (1818). Bram Stoker seized on this idea when he resurrected Vlad the Impaler in his *Dracula* novel (1897). Dracula as vampire represents the undead, the fear of being stuck in a sort of living hell in which one is neither fully alive nor fully dead, and heaven is unreachable. In the world of fantasy, as well as the real world, spirits can be demons in disguise, speaking falsehoods.

ETERNITY AND UTOPIA

Hell takes its cue from the *Apocalypse of Peter* and the *Apocalypse of Paul* in which elaborate tours of hell are related. The damned are confined for all eternity to a filthy pit of torture and fire. Angels and demons oversee the suffering: 'Ezrael, the angel of wrath, brings men and women with the half of their bodies burning and casts them into a place of darkness, the hell of men; and a spirit of wrath chastises them with all manner of chastisement and a worm that never sleeps consumes their entrails. These are the persecutors and betrayers of my righteous ones' (*Apoc. Peter* 9; Reddish 1990: 250). In these tours of hell each punishment fits the crime of the sinner. For example, 'those who harmed orphans and widows and the poor, and did not hope in the Lord' are placed naked in ice with their hands cut off (*Apoc. Paul* 39; Reddish 1990: 312–13). These apocalypses also briefly juxtapose a vision of heaven, or paradise in a third heaven in the *Apocalypse of Paul*. Dante built his space of damnation on these earlier visions, including many layers or levels to his underworld structure. The vision of hell as a place of eternal torment and fire has occupied and dominated the literary imagination.

Heaven, or paradise, and hell became allegories in some English literature, in particular during the seventeenth century. Throughout the last two thousand years these ideas of the afterlife had multiple meanings and variations. However, some dominant images and tellings stand out, from the *Apocalypse of John* through Dante to Milton. Milton built his visions on these images that spun from the biblical story of Eden in Gen. 2–3. Tours of either heaven or hell all had their beginning in the original earthly paradise.

Visions of a future paradise emerge from various contexts and theologies and take a variety of forms. Some are simple, spiritual unions with the divine. Others promote an elaborate world where desires, material and otherwise, are finally and fully completed. Other visions (such as Augustine's) remove all desire, especially sexual desire, from heaven. Heaven is sometimes a garden and sometimes a great city with streets of gold.

Images in the late medieval period often focused on heaven as an ideal garden. In his *Parliament of Fowls* (1380 CE) Geoffrey Chaucer (*c*.1340–1400 CE) envisioned as a dream an earthly, Eden-like garden paradise, a beautiful place with all kinds of trees and birds. 'A gardyn saw I ful of blosmy bowes | Upon a river, in a grene mede, | There as swetnesse everemore inow is | With floures white, blewe, yelwe, and rede, | And colde welle-stremes, nothing dede, | That swymmen ful of smale fishes lighte, | With fynnes rede and skales sylver bryghte' (lines 183–9; quoted in Fowler 1984: 151). He was imagining at once the Eden of Genesis, heaven, and sexual love (Fowler 1984: 151–2). The most ideal place in nature is the place of a glorified joining—of Adam and Eve— and of all lovers.

The fourteenth century was full of visions of the heavenly realm. The medieval English poem *Pearl* includes the vision of the New Jerusalem received from a young woman (the Pearl) who has died and relates the details of the city in a dream to her beloved who mourns her early death. One can enter the New Jerusalem only if one is totally spotless, free of sin. 'From outside, you may see that bright cloister, but you may not place a foot within it; you have no power to walk in the street unless you are clean without stain' (quoted in McGrath 2003: 27). Drawing on details from Revelation (Apocalypse of John) 21, the Pearl describes heaven as a splendid, jewel-filled place: 'As John the apostle saw it with his own eyes, I saw that city of great renown, Jerusalem, so new and royally adorned, as if it were light that had come down from Heaven' (ibid. 27). The focus on the beautiful vision of the heavenly city offers hope and comfort to the mourner as he grieves over Pearl's decaying body and fears his own future (ibid. 29).

These images of the medieval period continued to develop in English literature and religious culture. Wondering about what lay beyond this earthly life occupied the minds of many writers. Much thought of death and the afterlife was also common in the seventeenth century, a central century for the development of visions of the inevitable end of life and what comes after. One major theme in literary thinking on the afterlife, the New Jerusalem, continued to be part of this imagining. In one of the most enduring narratives, *Pilgrim's Progress*, John Bunyan (1626–88) contrasts the old and new Jerusalems. According to McGrath (ibid. 31): 'Yet Bunyan succeeded in establishing the journey from the "city of destruction" to the "heavenly city" as a framework for making sense of the ambiguities, sorrows, and pains of the Christian life'. The main pilgrim, Christian, sets out with others in search of the New Jerusalem. Angels called 'Shining Ones' tell them of the goal ahead: 'You are going now, said they, to the paradise of God, wherein you shall see the tree of life, and eat of the never-fading fruits thereof' (quoted ibid.). Bunyan's allegory of Christian suffering and final victory reinforced Puritan values and spirituality.

The imagery of heaven as an Edenic garden is a dominant motif in Christian thinking of the afterlife. John Milton (1608–74) drew on this idea of a paradise lost and regained, an Eden left and eventually returned to. In *Paradise Lost* Milton (2001) explores the Garden of Eden. Like Bunyan, Milton had suffered from and through the English Civil War (1641–52).

> By lik'ning spiritual to corporal forms,
> As may express them best, but what if Earth
> Be but the shadow of Heav'n, and things therein
> Each to other like, more than on earth is thought? (*PL* 5. 573–6)

In Paradise Lost earth begins as a mirror image of heaven. Both Eden and heaven reflect perfect worlds. No humans yet inhabit heaven, only God and the angels. On earth there is the beginning of human love (between Adam and Eve) in Eden. Adam and Eve have sexual intercourse and live very happily in marriage until driven out of paradise, thus fulfilling God's plan. Milton is imagining a sort of ideal love that is not tainted by adultery and other human lusts and sins. Milton had specific views of the afterlife: 'Since he upheld the mortalist position that the entire human being is nonexistent until the general Resurrection, the soul could not meet her beloved immediately after death' (McDannell and Lang 1988: 232). For Milton, any perfect society had the sex act as part of it, and this included heaven—even more so than on earth.

In Milton's world the architecture of heaven governs earthly space. According to McGrath (2003: 71), 'This fantastic and detailed elaboration of Eden struck a deep chord of sympathy with many of Milton's wealthier readers, who reorganized their estates to reflect the glories of this vision of Eden'. Death is kept at bay outside the decorative gates, just as it is outside the golden gates of heaven.

Milton's cosmology in *Paradise Lost* is thus that of heaven, earth, and hell. But the divisions are not so clear, as the mirroring of heaven and earthly Eden portray. Regina Schwartz (1988: 39) outlines this pattern from chaos to creation to fall to the ultimate re-creation of paradise: 'The Son had left the gates of heaven to encounter the Abyss at creation just as they leave the gates of Paradise to behold the world all before them. And God has promised to "raise another world," a new creation where man will find a place of rest, and perhaps in that paradise within, "the sea will be no more"'. Milton runs through biblical history from Genesis to Revelation, and even though Chaos lurks throughout, it is not allowed to triumph in the end.

Thus paradise is not only external, whether earthly or not. Northrop Frye (1965: 110–11) points out that there is another dimension for Milton: 'In *Paradise Lost*, of course, it is Paradise itself that is internalized, transformed from an outward place to an inner state of mind.... The heaven of *Paradise Lost*, with God the supreme sovereign and the angels in a state of unquestioning obedience to his will, can only be set up on earth inside the individual's mind.' Frye is noting the political context of Milton's time; when faced with corrupt monarchs it is necessary to seek freedom from within.

William Blake picked up on Milton's theme of heaven as the union of souls. His drawings have a certain aura of romantic love. In his illustration *The Last Judgement* (1806) Blake shows couples and their children being reunited on the trip upward to heaven (see discussion in McDannell and Lang 1988: 233–45). According to Blake, 'The Treasures of Heaven are not Negations of Passion, but Realities of Intellect, from which All the Passions Emanate Uncurbed in their Eternal Glory' (Blake 1966: 615). Heaven for Blake, as for Milton, becomes human-centred, and love and right relations carry on past this earthly life. 'Blake rejected both the notion that death is destructive and that life after death necessitates the discontinuity of earthly activities. Like Swedenborg, Blake assumed that whatever on earth contained true spiritual meaning continues after death' (McDannell and Lang 1988: 245).

Eden and its idyllic garden are the images invoked by many writers over the centuries. Examples include, Alexander Pope (1688–1744) in 'Windsor Forest' in which he uses political satire to subvert the British claims to Empire, Robert Browning's (1812–89) blank verse poem 'Sordello', and Percy Bysshe Shelley's 'Queen Mab: A Philosophical Poem'. The latter is a critique of religion with a secular spin on the future (McGrath 2003: 72–4). Shelley envisions:

> What now remains?—the memory
> Of senselessness and shame—
> What is immortal there?
> Nothing—it stands to tell
> A melancholy tale, to give
> An awful warning: soon
> Oblivion will steal silently
> The remnant of fame.
> Monarchs and conquerors there
> Proud o'er prostrate millions trod—
> The earthquakes of the human race;
> Like them, forgotten when the ruin
> That marks their shock is past.   (Shelley 1944: 811)

Still heaven holds magic for Shelley: 'As Heaven, low resting on the wave, it spread | Its floors of flashing light, | Its vast and azure dome, | Its fertile golden islands | Floating on a silver sea' (ibid. 810).

Shelley's contemporary Lord Byron (1788–1824) added a political touch to his view of heaven, for in his satirical poem, 'The Vision of Judgment' (1822), he has King George III ascend to heaven: 'All I saw farther, in the last confusion, | Was, that King George slipped into heaven for one; | And when the tumult dwindles to a calm, | I left him practicing the hundredth psalm' (Stanza 845; Abrams 1968b: 397). Byron rejoices in his exaggerated heaven, with St Peter, Satan, a host of political figures, and angels, of whom Byron explains, 'And true, we learn the angels all are Tories' (Stanza 205; ibid. 381). Even the king's enemies praise him.

But what is the key to entering heaven? In his 1526 translation of the Bible into English, William Tyndale first used the word 'atonement' for the reconciliation of humans with God (and to the New Eden). The King James Bible continues this association with its translation of Rom. 5: 11: 'We also joy in God through our Lord Jesus Christ, by whom we have now received the atonement' (quoted in McGrath 2003: 76). McGrath (ibid. 78) relates, 'Yet for writers such as Augustine or C. S. Lewis (1998–1963), the memory of Eden lingers, haunting humanity with its longing to regain entrance to this forbidden realm. Nature itself becomes a parable, charged with a divinely imbued potential to recreate the memory of Eden, and make us long to return to its now-deserted meadows.' The idea of a victorious, heroic Christ on the cross who rescues humanity from the devil and sin was central to much English theology.

Another popular idea was the 'harrowing of hell' in which the souls in hell are rescued by Christ's resurrection. One example of this theology comes from poet William Dunbar (1465–1520): 'Done is the battell on the dragon blak, | Our campioun Chryst confountet hes his force; The yetis of hell ar broking with a crak [. . .] Chryst with his blud our ransonis dois indoce' (quoted in Jasper 1989: 42). McGrath (2003: 92–4) points out that the idea of 'the harrowing of hell' developed in the Middle Ages (e.g. *Piers Plowman*) and continued in Lewis's *The Lion, the Witch, and the Wardrobe* in which the lion Aslan defeats the White Witch, resurrecting in the end to rescue the inhabitants of Narnia. McGrath further notes that throughout Lewis's writings is the theme of the 'longing for heaven'. Lewis had a romantic view and certainty of the paradise to come:

At present, we are on the outside of the world, the wrong side of the door . . . We cannot mingle with the splendours we see. But all the leaves of the New Testament are rustling with the rumour that it will not always be so. Some day, God willing, we shall get *in*.   (From the sermon, 'The Weight of Glory', quoted in McGrath 2003: 135)

Lewis's beliefs reflect the idea of heaven as a consolation for loved ones who have died, but also for one's own personal suffering. Heaven is a reward, the goal at the end of a life well lived.

George Herbert (1593–1633) introduces the idea of eternal rest in his poem 'The Pulley' (McGrath 2003: 120–1). There is the idea of a transcendent future place after death in which perfection dwells: ' "Let him be rich and weary, that at least, | If goodness lead him not, yet weariness | May toss him to my breast" ' (Abrams 1968a: 958). The true believers can dwell there too; therein lies great hope and comfort.

Other poets held out hope for a future, earthly utopia. For example, in the nineteenth century William Morris (1834–96), famous for his utopian novel, *News from Nowhere* (1891; Morris 2003), was influenced by Marxist renderings of work and socialism. In 'A Death Song' Morris mourns a friend beaten and killed by police in a socialist march they both participated in: 'We asked them for a life of toilsome earning—| They bade us bide their leisure for our bread; | We craved to speak to tell our woeful learning—| We come back speechless, bearing back our dead. | *Not one, not one nor thousand must they slay, | But one and all if they would dusk the day*' (Abrams 1968*b*: 1177; see n. 8). Morris's visions of the afterlife have an earthly anchor in his poem 'The Earthly Paradise: An Apology': 'Of Heaven and Hell I have no power to sing, | I cannot ease the burden of your fears, | Or make quick-coming death a little thing... So with this Earthly Paradise it is' (ibid. 1176). Morris hoped for a workers' utopia of more fulfilling work, better conditions, and much leisure time.

THE DREAD OF DEATH, AND LIFE

In Denys Arcand's film *Jesus of Montreal* (1989) an actor agrees to participate in a Montreal Passion Play if he is allowed to recite Hamlet's soliloquy. He fits the lines in perfectly in a scene in an underground tunnel beneath the Roman Catholic cathedral where the disciples await Jesus' return with halting hope. The lines fit fluidly, as if they are part of the Gospel's accounting of death and the afterlife. They provide a certain theological statement about human curiosity and wonderment at the end of life—imagining or experiencing the death of loved ones and of ourselves. 'But that the dread of something after death, | The undiscovered country, from whose bourn | No traveller returns, puzzles the will.' What we make of this mysterious future and otherworldly space determines how we proceed in this life. The dread is at once empowering and paralysing, for the visions produced by fear are endless and have endless possibilities.

In the Victorian period writers such as Alfred Lord Tennyson (1809–92) devote much space to exploring the concept of death, especially in attempting to understand the death of close friends and loved ones. In his lengthy elegy 'In Memoriam A.H.H.' (1833–50) he works through his grief over the sudden death of his friend Alfred Henry Hallam. In this poem Tennyson does not turn towards any positive assurance in a state of post-death happy-ever-after. Instead, he reveals the struggles to understand religion and science that emerged in the Victorian era. His grief process, from despair to tentative acceptance, flows through the poem, with doubt in the end winning out over faith in a transcendent certainty. Tennyson mourns, 'O Sorrow, cruel fellowship, | O Priestess in the vaults of Death, | O sweet and bitter in a breath, | What whispers from thy lying lip?' (Tennyson 2004: 3. 1–4). He also questions what one can gain from such grief; he does not see God but rather his own face: 'What profit lies in barren faith, | And vacant yearning, tho' with might | To scale the heaven's highest height, | Or dive below the wells of Death? [...] And on the depths of death there swims | The reflex of a human face' (ibid. 108: 5–8, 11–12). In the end though Tennyson returns to a more hopeful gaze on death and on God's role: 'That God, which ever lives and loves, | One God, one law, one element, | And one far-off divine event, | To which the whole creation moves' (ibid. Epilogue, 141–4).

In the twentieth century writers brought more existential angst. James Joyce (1882– 1941) brought a modernist sensibility to his agnostic thinking of death in writings such as 'The Dead' (1916), *Ulysses* (1922), and *Finnegans Wake* (1939). He wrote in the context of war, occupied France, and his own numerous eye surgeries. Many of these writers lived self-destructive, alcoholic lives. For example, Malcolm Lowry (1909–57) revisits Dante's *Inferno* in a novel based on his own experiences in Mexico, *Under the Volcano* (1947). The backdrop for the novel is war and the Mexican celebration of the Day of the Dead. The main character, a Consul in a small Mexican town, experiences a life of divorce, alcoholism, and death. His own death is the result of his self-destructive behaviour. The Consul meets his tragic end in a bar—he is shot by police. '"Christ," he remarked, puzzled, "this is a dingy way to die"' (Lowry 1947: 373). Through the setting and his character Lowry is telling the reader something about hell: it is something experienced in life. So too does poet Philip Larkin (1922–85) express the existential nature of death. In 'Poetry of Departure' he refers to death as 'This audacious, purifying, | Elemental move' (Larkin 1988: 85). In his poem 'Aubade' he muses, 'yet the dread | Of dying, and being dead, | Flashes afresh to hold and horrify.' Like the earlier English poets Larkin shares the anxiety over the proximity of death. But he does not dwell long on this reality and states boldly that 'Death is no different whined at than withstood' (ibid. 208–9).

Dylan Thomas (1914–53) offered his view of death in poems such as 'And Death Shall Have No Dominion', 'Here Lie the Beasts', 'Deaths and Entrances', 'After the Funeral', and 'Do Not Go Gentle.' Thomas's most famous lines, 'Do not go gentle into that good night... Rage, rage against the dying of the light' (Thomas 1971: 207–8), reveal his fascination with death and the unnamed and unknowable afterlife. In Thomas as in other twentieth-century poets who experienced either one or both World Wars on British land, death is something to be dreaded. This dread of death does not lead to imaginings of other places—of heaven, purgatory, or hell—but rather to a certain ranting at the existential death caused by oneself and/or others.

Another writer, Virginia Woolf (1882–1941), lived out that existential dread in creative ways in her novels. Her own experience of the death (from influenza and cancer) of family members, childhood sexual abuse, and mental illness (bipolar disorder) influenced her writing. For example, in her novel *Mrs. Dalloway* (1925; Woolf 1990) she explores the life of a shell-shocked hero-survivor of the First World War who commits suicide by throwing himself out a window. Mental illness eventually overtook Woolf and she succumbed to the desire for her own death.

W. H. Auden provides a glimmer of ambiguous hope in the midst of the chaos of the mid-twentieth century. In his poem, 'Hell', he declares, 'Hell is neither here nor there, | Hell is not anywhere, | Hell is hard to bear.' Auden plays with the idea that hell may or may not exist as a place, but he also plays with the idea that hell is an experience that allows for choices: 'It is so hard to dream posterity | Or haunt a ruined century | And so much easier to be' (Auden 1966: 171).

Novelist Graham Swift (1949–   ) took a postmodern turn in his multi-narrator novel *Last Orders*. In this story a group of friends travels to a pier on the coast to comply with a friend's last wish for the disposal of his ashes. The dead man's wife, who chooses instead to visit their mentally retarded daughter whom he never acknowledged, comments on death in the shadow of the Second World War: 'I thought the war might change things, put everything in its place.... I thought, he might be killed. Or I might. Or you might. A stray bomb on a home for the hopeless, no one need grieve, a mercy really. What a hard-nose. But what war did was to push things even further the way they'd gone' (Swift 1997: 239). War only adds to the already existing culture of death.

In English literature and theology the varieties of fictions on and of the End follow certain patterns and scattered genealogies, yet the connections to political and social realities of the times are always worthy of connection and comment. And so literature responds, in poetry, sermons, novels and plays, to humour death (or our dread of death).

All these writers mentioned here faced these limitations of understanding death and the afterlife. These writers wrote in the context of plague, of their own and others' sickness, of existential dilemmas, sudden death, or funerals. They spoke out of despair, joy, memory, politics, and hope. In the face of death they dreamed of afterlives, and carried us to other worlds, and to visions of our own world transformed.

WORKS CITED

ABRAMS, M. H. (ed.). 1968a. *The Norton Anthology of English Literature*. New York: W. W. Norton, i.

—— 1968b. *The Norton Anthology of English Literature*. New York: W. W. Norton, ii.

ARIÈS, PHILIPPE. 1974. *Western Attitudes toward Death: From the Middle Ages to the Present*, trans. Patricia M. Ranum. Baltimore: The Johns Hopkins University Press.

AUDEN, W. H. 1966. *Collected Shorter Poems: 1927–1957*. New York: Random House.

BLAKE, WILLIAM. 1966 [1972]. *Complete Writings*, ed. Geoffrey Keynes. Oxford: Oxford University Press.

BROWN, CARLETON. 1932. *English Lyrics of the XIIth Century*. Oxford: Clarendon.

BYNUM, CAROLINE WALKER, and FREEDMAN, PAUL (eds.). 2000. *Last Things: Death and the Apocalypse in the Middle Ages*. Philadelphia: University of Pennsylvania Press.

DONNE, JOHN. 1973. *Deaths Duel: A Sermon Delivered before King Charles I in the Beginning of Lent 1630/1*, ed. Geoffrey Keynes. Boston: David R. Godine.

ELEAZAR, Ed. 1963. 'Visions of the Afterlife', in Laura Cooner Lambdin and Robert Thomas Lambdin (eds.). *A Companion to Old and Middle English Literature*. Westport, Conn.: Greenwood, 376–97.

ELIOT, T. S. 1952. *The Complete Poems and Plays, 1909–1950*. New York: Harcourt Brace Jovanovich.

FRYE, NORTHROP. 1965. *The Return of Eden: Five Essays on Milton's Epics*. Toronto: University of Toronto Press.

GREENBLATT, STEPHEN. 2001. *Hamlet in Purgatory*. Princeton: Princeton University Press.

JASPER, DAVID. 1989. *The Study of Literature and Religion*. Philadelphia: Fortress.

JOYCE, JAMES. 1939. *Finnegans Wake*. New York: Viking.

—— 1992. *Ulysses*. New York: Random House. First Published 1922.

—— 1993. *The Dead*, ed. Daniel R. Schwarz. Boston: Bedford Books of St Martin's Press. First Published 1916.

KABIR, ANANYA JAHANARA. 2001. *Paradise, Death, and Doomsday in Anglo-Saxon Literature*. New York: Cambridge University Press.

KEATS, JOHN, and SHELLEY, PERCY BYSSHE. n.d. *Complete Poetical Works*. New York: The Modern Library.

LARKIN, PHILIP. 1988. *Collected Poems*, ed. Anthony Thwaite. New York: Farrar, Strauss, Giroux.

LOWRY, MALCOLM. 1947. *Under the Volcano*. New York: Reynal & Hitchcock.

MCDANNELL, COLLEEN, and LANG, BERNHARD. 1988. *Heaven: A History*. New Haven: Yale University Press.

MCGRATH, ALISTER E. 2003. *A Brief History of Heaven*. Oxford: Blackwell.

MILTON, JOHN. 2001. *Paradise Lost & Paradise Regained*. New York: Signet Classic.

MORE, ST THOMAS. *The Supplication of Souls*, in *The Complete Works of St. Thomas More*, eds. Frank Manley, Germain Marc'hadour and Richard Marius.

—— 1990. 2003. *Utopia*. New York: Penguin. Miller. New Haven: Yale University Press, vii.

MORRIS, WILLIAM. 2003. *News from Nowhere*. New York: Oxford University Press.

REDDISH, MITCHELL G. (ed.). 1990. *Apocalyptic Literature: A Reader*. Peabody, Mass.: Hendrickson.

SCHWARTZ, REGINA. 1988. *Remembering and Repeating: Biblical Creation in* Paradise Lost. New York: Cambridge University Press.

SHELLEY, PERCY BYSSHE. 1944. *The Complete Poems of Percy Bysshe Shelley*. New York: The Modern Library.

SWIFT, GRAHAM. 1997. *Last Orders*. New York: Vintage.

TENNYSON, LORD ALFRED. 2004. *In Memoriam*, ed. Reik Gray. 2nd edn. New York: W. W. Norton.

THOMAS, DYLAN. 1971. *The Poems of Dylan Thomas*, ed. Daniel Jones. New York: New Directions.

TURNER, ALICE K. 1993. *The History of Hell*. New York: Harcourt Brace.

WOOLF, VIRGINIA. 1990. *Mrs. Dalloway*. New York: Harvest.

FURTHER READING

ARIÈS, PHILIPPE. 1974. *Western Attitudes toward Death: From the Middle Ages to the Present*, trans. Patricia M. Ranum. Baltimore: The Johns Hopkins University Press.

FRYE, NORTHROP. 1965. *The Return of Eden: Five Essays on Milton's Epics*. Toronto: University of Toronto Press.

GORER, GEOFFREY. 1965. *Death, Grief, and Mourning in Contemporary Britain*. New York: Doubleday.

INNES, BRIAN. 1999. *Death and the Afterlife.* London: Brown Partworks.

JUPP, PETER C., and GITTINGS, CLARE (eds.). 2000. *Death in England: An Illustrated History.* New Brunswick, NJ: Rutgers University Press.

LE GOFF, JACQUES. 1984. *The Birth of Purgatory,* trans. Arthur Goldhammer. Chicago: University of Chicago Press.

SEGAL, ALAN F. 2004. *Life after Death: A History of the Afterlife in the Religions of the West.* New York: Doubleday.

CHAPTER 43

PASTORAL TRADITION IN RELIGIOUS POETRY

DAVID SCOTT

INTRODUCTION

THE common threads that run through this chapter are poetry, the ministry of the church, and under the general umbrella of that ministry, a pastoral consciousness. Poetry is but one type of literature. It is a way of writing about things in a particular tradition, form, and style that bears the poet's distinctive and authentic stamp upon it. The ministry of the church could seem to be quite a narrowing of the field, but here denotes that specificity in poetry which comes from those who have a relationship with God, are committed to the Christian church and who write poetry in English from that standpoint. The chapter also considers the church's ministry among people and not specifically with the poetry of hymnody, liturgy, or sermons. A pastoral consciousness refines that concept of ministry even more, and as a subject is related to the way in which the church engages with people at the level of pastoral care. This is poetry that emerges from the challenge of caring for people in their need; need which is physical and spiritual, and goes some way to being met by visiting, listening, comforting, counselling, and healing.

Several things influence these definitions. Occasionally, as in the cases of Chaucer and Wordsworth, we are not dealing with ministers of the church who write poetry out of their direct pastoral experience, but with lay commentators on that ministry.

Secondly, when we look at the history of the church in England, we see that for many centuries its clergy have been men. The voices of women have been eerily silent. However, the pastoral work of the church has often been the province of women, and with some, that has issued in poetry; for example, the contemporary poems of Kathy Galloway, a minister of the Church of Scotland, engage with the feelings and needs of women in her book *Talking to the Bones* (Galloway 1996).

The heart of the pastoral ministry has been significantly influenced in the Church of England by the parochial system. For about eight centuries, everyone residing in a geographical parish, whether they believed in God or not, had rights within the church and at least in theory could call on the church for help. Thus the church and its ministers have been seen as a focus of charitable giving and advice for the poor, and one of the institutions available to minister to those in need, practically and spiritually. Therefore the poetry that has arisen as a direct result of this unique relationship between priest and people obviously reflects the joys and pains of that relationship. It has been and is a unique dynamic and therefore to look at the pastoral tradition of religious poetry written in English is not a hole-in-the-corner project, but rather mines a major area of cultural and literary history.

This is poetry both of intense engagement, of reflective seclusion, and mutuality in the relationship of care. It records both the experience of the one in need, and also, before God, the one commissioned to meet that need. The roles of the one in need and the other ministering, easily get reversed. As T. S. Eliot put it, 'the wounded surgeon plies the steel' (Eliot 1969: 181) Those sent to serve may find themselves served.

THE BIBLICAL METAPHORS

Much of the poetic material in the pastoral tradition of English religious poetry has depended on images that have come to us in translation from the scriptural languages of Greek and Hebrew: Hebrew in the Old Testament and Greek in the New Testament. With the movement for translating the Scriptures into non-canonical languages by the heroic work of the fifteenth- and sixteenth-century Protestant scholars such as Tyndale, Wyclif, and Cranmer (see ch. 4, above, by Lynn Long) we begin to accumulate a body of images from the biblical sources in English poetry. For example, we find the image of God as the Shepherd in the Old Testament in Ezekiel and in the Psalms, and as the Good Shepherd in the New Testament in the Gospel of John.

The image of the Shepherd in Psalm 23 has affected the whole tenor of pastoral ministry within the church, with its multiple versions of putting God and the Shepherd together. This has created an image of what pastoral care, both within and beyond the church, is about. The Hebrew Scriptures are thick with daring images of God, but the need to put a face or form to something abstract for the pastoral work of the church has come to rest on this image of the Good Shepherd. Traditionally Psalm 23 was King David's psalm, but whoever wrote it, it was an act of inspiration to put the Hebrew words *Yahweh* and *roki* together, as simple and strong as pebbles in a pouch. God, the powerful other, the lawgiver and leader of the people, is to the poet also a shepherd, the one who comforts and protects and supplies the wants of those in need. Within the English literary tradition the psalm took its place in the Book of Common Prayer in the translation by Miles Coverdale (*c.*1539): 'The Lord is my shepherd: therefore can I lack nothing.'

In St John's Gospel the idea of the Lord as shepherd became what we could almost call a metaphysical poem: 'I am the good shepherd' (John 10: 11). In the Greek form this passage is not constructed as a poem, but as with so much of St John's Gospel, it is a piece of heightened prose, a meditation by the evangelist on the relation of Christ to the Father and to the disciples. The shepherd lays down his life for the sheep. So the image continues through from the Old Testament to the New, and becomes incarnated in Christ.

It is in the gospel records of Jesus' own shepherding of the disciples, and in the bringing into the fold those responding to his healing touch, that the model for pastoral concern, and consequently the poetry inspired by that model, has its roots. For example, the healing of the ruler of the synagogue's daughter (Mark 5: 35–43) has within it some touches and hints of the way that Jesus' mind is working, his priorities and sensitive insights that provide examples of what shepherding can be about in the human sphere. For example, the need for peace and quiet: 'And when he was come in, he saith unto them, Why make ye this ado, and weep? the damsel is not dead but sleepeth.' The authoritative command: 'And he took the damsel by the hand, and said unto her, Talitha cumi; which is being interpreted, Damsel, I say unto thee, arise' (KJV).

Another early and significant piece of writing from the first Prayer Book of Edward VI (1549) also points to the pastoral nature of the Christian ministry, and makes significant use of the 'shepherd' image. It is in the Ordinal, which is part of the bishop's charge to those intending to be ordained priest. In this passage the bishop about to ordain outlines the nature of the task, duties, and obligations of the priest:

We exhort you, in the name of our Lord Jesus Christ, to have in remembrance, into how high a dignity, and to how chargeable an office ye be called, that is to say, to be the messengers, the watchmen, the Pastors, and the stewards of the Lord to teach, to premonish, to feed, and to provide for the Lord's family: to seek for Christ's sheep that be dispersed abroad, and for his children which be in the midst of this naughty world, to be saved through Christ for ever. Have always therefore printed in your remembrance, how great a treasure is committed to your charge, for they be the sheep of Christ, which he brought with his death, and for whom he shed his blood.   (Church of England, n.d.: 286)

Within the Ordinal another important image is used, and that is of the church and its congregation being the body and spouse of Christ: 'The Church and congregation whom you must serve, is his spouse and his body. And if it shall chance the same church, or any member thereof, to take any hurt or hindrance, by reason of your negligence ye know the greatness of the fault, and also of the horrible punishment which will ensue' (ibid.). This adds another dimension to the pastoral nature of the clergy, and it is interesting to see how this has followed through into the poetry. The shepherd looks after the sheep, but in the end cannot be responsible for their waywardness. If, however, the church and congregation are seen as the very body and spouse of Christ, then the responsibility becomes that much more significant, closer, and more intimate, and the consequences of failure that much more disastrous. It is the pain of failure that can so haunt the pastoral task, and we shall see that being worked out in some of the poets writing in this tradition. With the increased sense of personal failure comes, in some theologies, an increase in the possibility of punishment and in others a greater depend-ence on the cross of Christ to shoulder the burdens and the responsibility. This too filters down into the variety of poetic traditions.

At the head of the canon of poets writing in Middle English, on the subject of the pastoral ministry of the Church, stands Chaucer (1340–1400). It is interesting to note that in the early nineteenth century William Wordsworth framed that canon in the *Duddon Sonnets* (1820), where he included Chaucer, Herbert, and Goldsmith.

Geoffrey Chaucer

Chaucer's Prologue to *The Canterbury Tales* (*c*.1387) contains a section on the Parson (The Persoun), ll. 477–528 in the Six Text Edition of the Chaucer Society (Skeat 1924: 32–4). The description of the Parson in the Prologue is of a 'holy and humble man of heart', in contrast to other religious figures such as the Summoner and the Pardoner. It could be that Chaucer consciously wrote to highlight the contrast, but the tone of praise sounds authentic, and is extraordinarily appealing in its uncomplicated goodness. It is the less important ecclesiastical figures who are on the pilgrimage in *The Canterbury Tales*, and Chaucer observes their degrees by the order in which he presents them in the General Prologue. The Parson follows the Prioress, the Monk, the Friar, and the Clerk. He is rich in good works, but humble in degree, and by his humility escapes the irony of Chaucer. On the contrary his unassuming and lowly status is a cause of wonder and praise.

Chaucer seemed to have great respect for the position of the parson, and had obviously met with a 'good man' to take for an example. He visited his parishioners:

> Wyd was his parisshe, and houses fer a-sonder,
> But he ne lafte nat, for reyn ne thonder,
> In siknes nor in mischef, to visyte
> The fereste in his parisshe, much and lyte
> Up-on his feet, and in his hand a staf.   (ll. 491–5)

The parson is an example to his people:

> This noble ensample to his sheep he yaf,
> That first he wroghte, and afterward he taughte;   (ll. 496–7)

Shame lies in the opposite, and here the text 'take keep' is not clear, but the implication seems to be that it is a pity if the sheep are clean and the priest is dirty:

> And shame it is if a priest take keep
> A dirty shepherd and a clene sheep.   (ll. 503–4)

Cleanness is a word with wide significance in the period and books were written on the subject, but basically it meant in the gospel words 'pure in heart' and therefore able to see God:

> Well oghte a preest ensample for to yive,
> By his clennesse, how that his sheep shold live.   (ll. 505–6)

It is, however, not only purity of heart that the Parson has to teach through example, but also the virtue of 'stability'. By staying in his post among his people, he gains respect and facilitates a more beneficial ministry:

> He sette nat his benefice to hyre,
> And leet his sheep encombred in the myre,
> And ran to London, un-to seynt Poules,
> To seken him a chaunteyre for soules,
> Or with a brotherheed to been witholde;
> But dwelt at hoome, and kept wel his folde,
> So that the wolf ne made it nat miscarie;
> He was a shepherde and no mercenarie.   (ll. 507–15)

Above all the parson was a follower of Christ, not with a 'spyced' (over-scrupulous) conscience, but in simplicity and faith, 'waiting after' and teaching Christ's love, which before teaching to others he had 'first to folwe … him-selve'.

GEORGE HERBERT

By the seventeenth century the picture is altogether more complex, particularly with regard to George Herbert (1593–1633). Herbert was late in coming to ordination, at the end of his short life. Having spent most of his time in the University of Cambridge as student and then public orator (1619–27), he wrote model poems for state occasions and entered into theological disputes with Presbyterians. With the death of James I, and the increasing influence of friends such as Bishop Lancelot Andrewes, his writing turned to more confessional themes, and his life to the service of God in the priesthood.

The task of the country clergy in 1630 when Herbert went to the parish of Bemerton, near Salisbury, was marked by a social divide between priest and people. His prose work 'A Priest to the Temple or, The Country Parson' set the parson up as an example to his flock in temperance, honesty, and in the disinterest with regard to worldly riches. He is 'a father to his flock', and 'when any of his cure is sick, or afflicted with loss of friend, or estate, or any ways distressed, fails not to afford his best comforts, and rather goes to them, than sends for the afflicted' (Herbert 1978: 249).

Herbert's poetry acknowledges the compassion of God. Yet, whereas in the prose work Herbert is speaking from above to below, in the poetry he writes very much as one under obedience to God himself and dependent on God's grace. It is much like the love of the Father for a child; perhaps the father Herbert never really had in his own life. The nature of the poem as poem, its intricacy with the play of images allows Herbert to express subtleties of feeling, which do not come across in the prose work. It is the poetry that takes us deeper into the heart and mind of the pastor, the one who under God is responsible for others. Yet this is sometimes at the expense of the detailed description of clerical life in 1630.

The poems only give us the briefest of glimpses into the daily life of his parishioners. The sweeping of a room is a rare physical or domestic image, and we hang onto it with such eagerness because it is so rare. Nor do we see into the houses of the poor, or find details of their clothes, or gardens, their illnesses, their ways of dying. We seem to have to wait for Wordsworth to take us into such interiors. What we do have are the struggles of the devout soul in the presence of Love itself. And as Herbert knew that territory in himself, we can imagine he also knew it in those he met and ministered to, served and counselled.

The poems are largely meditations on his inward state, the result of being honest with his own soul, in the manner of previous spiritual writers such as St Augustine, and more contemporary with Herbert, St Francis de Sales (1567–1622), whose 'Introduction to the Devout Life' was published in 1609. Such writers used their knowledge of their own inward journey to be of use to others. Herbert offered his poems to his friend Nicholas Ferrar with instructions to publish them only if he felt that they would be helpful to 'poor souls'.

It may be expecting too much of Herbert, of reading into the poems what is not there, but it is interesting to imagine how his practical experience of the ministry affected the poetry. Two brief insights will have to suffice. In the poem 'Redemption' Herbert is meditating on the incarnation of Christ, using the echoes of various New Testament events and parables. These could well have included the murder of the owner of the vineyard's son, the birth of Christ in poverty in a manger, and the fact that he lived and taught among sinners, to explain how Christ managed to redeem the world. It is the sense of Christ going down among the people that in a curiously discreet way gives us a sense of Herbert's own capacity for going among his people. The Christlike model could well have been his own.

More down to earth is the picture we get of Herbert at the end of a long Sunday. He had two churches to serve, Bemerton and Fuggleton. He also had some catechizing and some visiting, which brought him exhausted to his bed. In the poem 'Even-song' Herbert reflects how he has managed during Sunday:

> What have I brought thee home
> For this thy love? have I discharg'd the debt,
> Which this day's favour did beget?

> I ran, but all I brought, was fome.
>   Thy diet, care, and cost
> Do end in bubbles, balls of winde;
>   Of winde to thee whom I have crost,
> But balls of wild-fire to my troubled minde.
>
> (Herbert 1978: 64)

But God is kind, and says, 'It doth suffice | Henceforth repose; your work is done', and Herbert eventually finds solace in the 'ebony box', which is the night:

> Thus in thy ebony box
> Thou dost inclose us, till the day
> Put our amendment in our way,
> And give new wheels to our disorder'd clocks.   (ibid. 64)

In 'A Priest to the Temple' Herbert describes the activities of a parson's Sunday, and certainly it is a very full day, but there is none of this private sense of uselessness and anxiety which we find in the poems. After the services of the morning and catechizing in the afternoon, he writes, 'The rest of the day he spends either in reconciling neighbours that are at variance, or in visiting the sick, or in exhortations to some of his flock by themselves, whom his sermons cannot or do not reach.... As he opened the day with prayer, so he closeth it, humbly beseeching the Almighty to pardon and accept our poor services, and to improve them, that we may grow therein, and that our feet may be like hinds feet ever climbing up higher, and higher unto him' (ibid. 236).

The poetry seems to capture the true picture of the country clergy through the centuries, of feeling inadequate to the task. Herbert acknowledges the fact that God is love, and it is this love that gives true refreshment:

> My God thou art all love.
> Not one poor minute scapes thy breast,
> But brings a favour from above;
> And in this love, more then in bed, I rest.   (ibid. 64)

THE EIGHTEENTH CENTURY

In the eighteenth century and first half of the nineteenth century, George Crabbe (1754–1832), William Cowper (1731–1800), and John Clare (1793–1864) were all poets who had a descriptive eye for the clergy both in their social and religious roles. When he was 27, Crabbe took orders and became curate of Aldeburgh, having previously been apprenticed to a doctor, and practised medicine. In the poem 'The Parish Register', which he wrote in 1807, there is a section on marriage, in which he sees, with some foreboding, the couple coming towards him in church.

Next at our Altar stood our luckless pair
Brought by strong Passions and a Warrant there;
By long rent cloak, hung loosely, strove the Bride
From every eye, what all perceiv'd, to hide.
While the Boy-Bridegroom, shuffling at his pace,
Now hid awhile and then expos'd his face
As Shame alternately with Anger strove,
The Brain, confus'd with muddy Ale, to move;

(Crabbe 1998: 240)

Noted for his realism, 'Nature's sternest painter yet' as Byron described Crabbe, it is interesting to get that sense of a period in clerical pastoralia when the imperative to be 'nice' had not yet entered the profession. In 'The Parish Register III, Burials' there are some wonderful thumbnail sketches of various clerical types: Parson Peele, Dr Groundspear, and:

Then came *the Author-Rector*; his delight
Was all in Books; to read them or to write:
Women and Men, he strove alike to shun,
And hurried homeward, when his Tasks were done;
Courteous enough, but careless what he said
For points of learning he reserv'd his Head;
And when addressing either Poor or Rich
He knew no better than his cassock, which;   (ibid. 865–72)

However, he had no sense of his own dignity, and as a result did not turn 'from Gypsies, Vagabonds or Fools;'

It was his nature, but they thought it whim,
And so our Beaux and Beauties turn'd from him.   (ibid. 883–4)

As for other poets and poems in this period, the phenomenon of the evangelical movement gave rise both to satire and admiration. William Cowper coming under the influence of the Revd John Newton, the evangelical divine, with whom he collaborated on the *Olney Hymns* (1779), conveys a more serious side to the calling. In 'The Task, The Winter Morning Walk', Cowper points to the distinction between the preaching office of the clergy which may be very fine, but ultimately it is the deed which speaks of the inward being, the heart.

Do they themselves, who undertake for hire
The teacher's office, and dispense at large
Their weekly dole of edifying strains
Attend to their own music? Have they faith
In what with such solemnity of tone
And gesture they propound to our belief?
Nay—conduct hath the loudest tongue. The voice
Is but an instrument on which the priest
May play what tune he pleases. In the deed,
The unequivocal authentic deed,
We find sound argument, we read the heart,

(Cowper 1820: 170)

John Clare (1793–1864), more of an outsider to the church than Crabbe or Cowper, describes in his poem 'The Parish' (1824), how the parish lamented their departed vicar:

> Ah sure it was a mellancholly day
> That call's the good man from his charge away
> As the sad lecture oer his coffin preached
> They'd no more harvests now of hopes to reap
> Een children wept to see their mothers weep
> And pulled their gowns to ask and question when
> hed wake and come to give them pence agen.

(Clare 1985: 75)

Wordsworth, writing in the first half of the eighteenth century, lit on a character, Robert Walker (b. 1709) who provided for him the picture of a model pastor, and Wordsworth wrote about him both in *The River Duddon*, the notes to these poems, and in 'The Excursion'. Wordsworth styled him 'Wonderful' because of his shepherding of his parish flock for over more than sixty years, 'that lowly, great, good man'. Robert Walker was born in 1709 at Under-Crag in Seathwaite in the Duddon Valley, and 'being sickly it was deemed best to breed him a scholar'. After several years as a schoolmaster he added to that responsibility the curacy of Seathwaite 'in his native vale'. There he remained ministering until his death in 1805, the year that Wordsworth began writing the first of his Duddon Sonnets.

For Wordsworth, Walker was an example of fidelity to the pastoral task, honesty, integrity, and self-sufficiency. Walker sheared the sheep and carried the bales of fleeces across the hills for sale. He brought up his large family to be faithful to God, industrious, and scrupulously honest.

He sate up late, and rose early; when the family were at rest, he retired to a little room which he had built on the roof of his house. He had slated it, and fitted it up with shelves for his books, his stock of cloth, wearing apparel, and his utensils. There many a cold winter's night, without fire, while the roof was glazed with ice, did he remain reading or writing till the day dawned.   (Wordsworth 1964: 715)

In addition to these essentially human qualities, Walker also portrayed for Wordsworth a simple gospel life, bringing an example of peace and harmony to a troubled world, and perhaps to Wordsworth's own troubled soul. There is an element in the whole involvement with the memory of this pastor, of a yearning in Wordsworth for the monastic life of the church. The Church of England in the mid-nineteenth century was beginning to experiment with small religious communities, mainly for women. These communities came under close scrutiny and sometimes persecution from objectors. Wordsworth's poems laid a creative foundation for the flowering of the contemplative life in the church, and Walker's hidden ministry in the Duddon valley would have had, for Wordsworth, strong echoes of the Cistercian monks of the Middle Ages.

In *The River Duddon* sequence of poems, 'Seathwaite Chapel', in which the life of Walker is celebrated, follows a sonnet about the pagan history of the valley, its Roman forts and Druidical stone circles. So Wordsworth begins the sonnet heralding a new era: 'Sacred religion!' and continues:

> Mother of love! (that name best suits thee here)
> Mother of love! for this deep vale, protect
> Truth's holy lamp, pure source of bright effect
> Gifted to purge the vapoury atmosphere
> That seeks to stifle it:—as in those days
> When this low Pile a Gospel Teacher knew,
> Whose good works formed an endless retinue: (ibid. 300)

In a tightly knit valley community the Revd Walker's contact with his people was close. As the schoolmaster as well as the priest he taught his classes in the chancel of the church. He shared in the work of the community, visited them when they were in need, baptized, conducted the marriage services and the burials, and provided an example of a holy life.

In Book 5 of Wordsworth's poem 'The Excursion' the essence of the pastor's calling and vocation is powerfully described as a result of a request from a Recluse, one of the characters in the poem, for the pastor to share his insights more widely:

> There lies
> Around us a domain where you have long
> watched both the outward course and inner heart:
> Give us, for our abstractions, solid facts;
> For our disputes, plain pictures.   (ibid. 649)

The pastor is expected to know his people, both the living and the dead:

> as we stand on holy earth
> And have the dead around us, take from them
> Your instances . . .
> Epitomise the life; . . .
> So, by your records, may our doubts be solved;
> And so not searching higher, we may learn
> To prize the breath we share with human kind;
> And look upon the dust of man with awe.   (ibid. 649)

In his own statement, the pastor points interestingly away from himself to some members of his flock in whom he sees the virtues he would wish to see espoused in all:

> In powers of mind,
> In scale of culture, few among my flock
> Hold lower rank than this sequestered pair:
> But true humility descends from heaven
> Stoop from your height, ye proud, and copy these!
> Who in their noiseless dwelling-place, can hear
> The voice of wisdom whispering scripture texts
> For the mind's government, or temper's peace;
> And recommending for their mutual need,
> Forgiveness, patience, hope, and charity!   (ibid. 650)

JOHN KEBLE AND GERARD MANLEY HOPKINS

A renewed sense of seriousness and professionalism came back into the calling of the clergy with the growth of the Oxford Movement. That movement inculcated high standards in the sacramental life of the pastor, and many clergy went to work in the growing number of industrial areas in the country. John Keble (1792–1866), however, remained in the countryside in Hampshire after he left Oxford. Keble was a priest, a pastor, a poet, an Oxford don, a country clergyman, and the author of *The Christian Year* (1827), *Lyra Innocentium* (1846), and *Miscellaneous Verses* (1869).

The sick room has long been the preserve of the priest, administering the sacraments, reading Scripture, saying prayers, laying on hands of healing, bringing comfort, prompting penitence, waiting and sitting in silence. For poets too, notably for poet-priests it has been a place to ponder as in John Keble's 'Holy is the Sick Man's Room' from *Miscellaneous Verses*:

> Holy is the sick man's room.
> Temper'd air, and curtain'd gloom,
> Measured steps, and tones as mild
> As the breath of new-born child,
> Postures lowly, waitings still
> Looks subdued to duty's will,
> Reverent, thoughtful, grave and sweet:
> These to wait on Christ are meet.
> These may kneel where He lies low,
> In his members suffering woe.
> Nor in other discipline
> Train we hearts that to His shrine
> May unblamed draw near, and be
> With his favour'd two and three.
> Therefore in its silent gloom
> Holy is the sick man's room.
>
> (Keble 1869: 262)

The room is holy because in the presence of the sick, Christ enters in and makes it holy. 'In his members', that is among the Body of Christ, he suffers woe along with them. 'Train we hearts': we are encouraged to train our hearts to be ready for such occasions, so that we are a help in the sick room. There is a strong echo here of Jesus in the sick room of the ruler of the synagogue's daughter. That room and this that Keble writes about is a shrine, a place where holy things are kept. The sick are holy, because they are in need of God's healing.

Keble brings a particular character to the sick room. At first we are not clear what is happening in 'the curtain'd gloom', but it becomes clearer as our eyes get used to the dim light. Christ is present in the room where prayer is part of the waiting. We begin to understand and are assured and comforted by the presence of Christ. Friends gather round, with their 'postures lowly... reverent, thoughtful'.

If we put alongside that poem by Keble the poem 'Felix Randal' by Gerard Manley Hopkins, then we begin to see some significant differences. In Felix Randal we see a once strong farrier now sick and weakening. The general movement of Hopkins's poem is inspired by the transformation, physical and spiritual, of a man who in the days of his heroic vigour fettled the great grey drayhorse and now, having gone from strength to weakness physically, goes spiritually from weakness to strength 'being anointed and all'. But the priest is touched too, and is changed by the experience, 'spent' by it.

> This seeing the sick endears them to us, us too it endears.
> My tongue had taught thee comfort, touch had quenched thy tears,
> Thy tears that touched my heart
>
> (Hopkins 1992: 165)

Hopkins can only now sit and watch this man draw near to his death. All that can be done for him spiritually has been done. He reflects on the physical change that has come over this man, and how sickness makes a rough, impatient man tender. Hopkins finds himself becoming more sympathetic to him, as the farrier becomes a child again. 'How far from the forethought of', but now we think, are caused to think about the way God draws us back. Hopkins paints the character of the man so vividly, whereas Keble says nothing of the sick person, other than that in his sickness Christ is with him. The beat of the Keble poem is solemn, Victorian we might say; Hopkins, with his sprung rhythms, brings an element of thanksgiving, and the hope of heaven to it all, and releases poetry from its Victorian tread.

Together these two poems (the Hopkins so personally engaged, the Keble so self-effacing) exhibit something of the intrinsic restraints and the opportunities of holy orders. And both paradoxically are, for all their differences poems of self-giving. They are as they are because their authors were priests.

THE TWENTIETH CENTURY

Extraordinary circumstances create extraordinary characters, and from the First World War emerged the 'Woodbine Willie' phenomenon. Geoffrey Studdert Kennedy (1883–1929) (as he was sometimes called!) was a chaplain in the Great War, and earned his nickname by distributing cigarettes to soldiers. Born Irish, he perfected a colloquial verse which described the raw emotions of battle, comradeship, faith, and mud. Many of his poems are dialogues between himself and 'Tommies' with a cockney accent, and have in hindsight a rather weakening sentimentality about them. This has a lot to do with their persistent music-hall metre, but there is no faulting the involvement and courage that lies behind the poems.

In the poem 'His Mate' Studdert Kennedy is heard at his best. He is at the front line near Thiepval, burying the dead, while 'bullets rattle around me'. 'In one grave I laid two hundred | God! What sorrow and what rain!' It was duty and his calling to say swift prayers for them, 'common Christian prayer'.

> Then there spoke a dripping sergeant
> When the time was growing late.
> 'Would you please to bury this one,
> 'Cause 'e used to be my mate?'
>
> (Studdert Kennedy 1940: 41)

Details make up a strong picture here: a body 'with a red blotch on his hair':

> Though we turned him gently over
> yet I still can hear the thud,
> As the body fell far forward
> And then settled in the mud.   (ibid. 42)

The service takes place, this time with the whole service from 'I am the resurrection . . .' to the blessing. Almost at the end a 'sudden light shot soaring across the sky' which could have been a flare or an explosion or a mystical light, it is difficult to tell, but it is there long enough for the sergeant to be seen 'staring at a crimson clot of blood'. His own, his mate's, again, it is difficult to tell, but the message is clear:

> There are many kinds of sorrow
> In this world of Love and Hate
> But there is no sterner sorrow
> Than a soldier's for his mate.   (ibid.)

'Sterner sorrow' bears thinking about. 'Sterner' is a fine, strong, unexpected adjective, which gives the poem a point, a ballast, a seriousness. The priestly tasks are being done, but there is also something about the observation, the noticing that is priestly too, and the poetic and the priestly roles merge at this point. This could be one reason why poetry is such a useful medium for religious communication and understanding. Christ was the one who noticed. The eye and the heart of the Christ figure are allied to the mind and the ear of the poet.

Which brings us close, in time, to the poetry of R. S. Thomas (1913–2000), and back to that description of Chaucer's, 'wyd was his parisshe, and houses fer a-sonder'. Something of the lack of romanticism and sheer gritty refusal to be sweet hangs around the work of the finest religious poet of the twentieth century. A parish priest in Wales, the visits he made often took him on long walks, which gave him time to work on his theology, as in this poem, 'Ninetieth Birthday':

> You go up the long track
> That will take a car, but is best walked
> On slow foot, noting the lichen
> That writes history on the page
> Of the grey rock
>
> .   .   .   .

> As the road climbs
> You will pause for breath and the far sea's
> Signal will flash, till you turn again
> To the steep track, buttressed with cloud.
>
> (Thomas 1993: 107)

Fighting any hint of sentimentality, Thomas returns from his pastoral visits mainly with questions and a sense of bleakness. The 90-year-old of the poem lives in a time warp:

> You bring her greeting
> And praise for having lasted so long
> With time's knife shaving the bone.
> Yet no bridge joins her own
> World with yours, all you can do
> Is lean kindly across the abyss
> To hear words that were once wise.   (ibid. 107)

'Leaning kindly' is a interesting echo of 'Lead kindly', and shows the characteristic minimalism that Thomas is well known for. There is an element of modesty in it and shyness, of not allowing himself to feel successful in the world's terms, but taking from the human situation the minimum that is allowed by human nature under the eye of God.

Another purpose of visiting is to share the ironies and paradoxes of life. Thomas shares with the farmer the paradox of nature's beastliness and its beauties in this poem 'The Parish':

> Somewhere among
> Its green aisles you had watched like me
> The sharp tooth tearing its prey.
> While a bird sang from a tall tree.   (ibid. 101)

Watching, like Thomas in his favourite pursuit of observing birds, is something that figures largely in the pastoral mode. It is a 'keeping an eye on'; a fascination with the understanding that God is in the reality of things, far deeper than our brittle gloss on the matter, as in the poem 'Priest and Peasant':

> While I watch you and pray for you,
> And so increase my small store
> Of credit in the bank of God,
> Who sees you suffer and me pray
> And touches you with the sun's ray,
> That heals not, yet blinds my eyes
> And seals my lips as Job's were sealed
> Imperiously in the old days.   (ibid. 62)

The attitude of Thomas to his pastoral work that is conveyed in the poems is one of hard-won victories. The Welsh hill farmers and their families, the archetypal Cymdylan's on their tractors, are the antithesis of cosy; but there is also the sense of

Thomas viewing the parish in the light of eternity, aware of his individual limitations to change the world, and the people in it. He went at the pace of the land, and thought in millennia.

ENDGAME

Where this pastoral tradition might go in an age of little apparent belief, the slow disintegration of a church committed to a whole nation's well-being, and the strong and sometimes creative mix of faith traditions, is hard to predict. If the tradition itself was not touching some deeper chord than the narrowly confessional and institutional, then it would be good if it did die. However, there is something about the religious impulse at its best in literature which touches universal chords, such as compassion, sacrifice, empathy, and love in its religious manifestation. At its height this all-purpose word is known as *agape,* at its homeliest, the Do Good of Piers Plowman.

A nostalgic regret for the demise of the parson-poet which sends us scurrying to the second-hand bookshelves hunting for Andrew Young of Sussex, Danby of the North Riding, Baring Gould, Richard Jago, Charles Kingsley, Herrick, Crashaw, and Christopher Smart is perhaps inevitable. The gradual demise of the professional religious writers in residence, the clergy, and the crumbling of the parish system, must leave room for a poetry that charts the bereavement of a long tradition, but also continues to notice human vulnerability, and the proximity of that frailty, to glory. Yet the spiritual pastoral tradition will no doubt continue to recruit its poets: such as Rowan Williams's, noticing the 'dour council cleaner' and 'a thin mother with her child' battling with the rain and wind:

> Cartons and condoms and a few stray sheets
> of newspaper that the wind sticks
> across his face—

> The worn sub-Gothic infant, hanging awkwardly
> around, glued to a thin mother,
> Angelus Novus:

> Backing into the granite future, wings spread,
> head shaking at the recorded day,
> no, he says, refuse...

> (Williams 2001: 13)

The compassion is in the noticing, and in the empathy that the writer shares with the teenage mothers, in the struggle of bringing things to birth. The tradition will inevitably change as the institution changes and will be energized by insights into pastoral care gathered from many different circumstances. Engagement, compassion, realism, sacrifice, and truth are likely to remain the hallmarks of this poetic tradition, but poems will be gleaned from increasingly surprising sources. Away from the crust of English religious tradition, new notes will be struck, new chords tried out.

WORKS CITED

CHURCH OF ENGLAND. n.d. *The First Prayer Book of Edward VI*. London: Griffith, Farran.

CLARE, JOHN. 1986. *The Parish*. Hasmondsworth: Penguin Classics.

COWPER, WILLIAM. 1820. *Poems*. London: W. H. Reid.

CRABBE, GEORGE. 1988. *The Complete Poetical Works*. Oxford: Oxford University Press.

ELIOT, T. S. 1969. *The Complete Poems and Plays*. London: Faber & Faber.

GALLOWAY, KATHY. 1969. *Talking to the Bones*. London: SPCK.

HERBERT, GEORGE. 1978. *The Works of George Herbert*. London: SPCK.

HOPKINS, G. M. 1990. *The Poetical Works*. Oxford: Oxford University Press.

KEBLE, REVD. J. 1869. *Miscellaneous Poems*. Oxford: James Parker.

SKEAT, W. W. 1924. *Chaucer the Prologue to the Canterbury Tales*. Oxford: Oxford University Press.

STUDDERT KENNEDY, G. A. 1940. *The Rhymes of G. A. Studdert Kennedy*. Hodder & Stoughton.

THOMAS R. S. 1993. *Collected Poems. 1945–1990*. London: J. M. Dent.

WILLIAMS, R. 2001. *Remembering Jerusalem*. Oxford: Perpetua.

WORDSWORTH, W. 1964. *The Poetical Works of Wordsworth*, ed. Thomas Hutchinson Oxford: Oxford University Press. First published 1904.

FURTHER READING

COUNTRYMAN, L. WILLIAM. 1999. *The Poetic Imagination*. London: Darton Longman Todd.

LEVI, PETER. 1984. *The Penguin Book of English Verse*. Harmondsworth: Penguin.

MALCOLMSON, CHRISTINA. 2004. *George Herbert, A Literary Life*. London: Palgrave Macmillan.

THOMAS, R. S. 1997. *Autobiographies*. London: J. M. Dent.

CHAPTER 44

THE PASSION STORY IN LITERATURE

PAUL FIDDES

THE story of the passion of Jesus Christ, in its earliest forms, was already shaped by interpretation. Suffering and death on a cross, when set in the wider story of the life of Jesus, cried out for explanation. This was the story of a man who had announced the coming of the Kingdom of God and who had presumed to offer forgiveness, healing, and an acceptance of social outcasts on behalf of the God whom he called Father, and with whom he claimed an intimate acquaintance. It was a story that had ended in agonizing execution and an experience of forsakenness by friends, fellow countrymen, and—he himself felt—by his God.

So with different colourings, and from different perspectives, the early accounts of the passion of Jesus come with an interpretation. The very ways that the Apostle Paul and the four Evangelists tell the story, and the images and metaphors they employ, try to grapple with the mystery of 'atonement', the belief that through this death a union has been achieved between the Creator and a rebellious creation. Starting from formative images in the New Testament which were drawn from the temple, the battlefield, the slave-market, the law-court and family life, the thinkers and poets of the church made models or theories to explain how atonement worked: notable among these were ideas of sacrifice, victory, ransom, justification and persuasive love. But no theory of atonement was ever declared to be definitive by the church, so that hearers of the story were encouraged to find new meaning in their own responses. The story of the cross could always acquire meaning, and—when placed alongside stories of suffering elsewhere in human life—could enable meaning to be gained in new situations when it did not seem to be intrinsically present.

When the story of the passion is told in English poetry and prose we can thus identify versions of the great models and metaphors of atonement that were developed in Christian theology. We may also find these images combined in new and playful ways, producing an internal tension within the texts, creating an open space, and clearing the way for an endless expansion of meaning. This in turn can have an effect on the theology of the passion, breaking the borders of doctrine open for new exploration.

VICTORY AND SUFFERING LOVE

We can see such a creative opening-up of space in one of the earliest accounts of the passion in English literature, the eighth-century Anglo-Saxon poem usually titled *The Dream of the Rood*. The narrator describes a strange dream of a wonderful tree, which changes in appearance before his eyes, first ornamented with gold and jewels and then revealing the savage marks of conflict, covered in sweat and blood. The tree speaks, and tells us that it was cut down from the forest to bear 'the young warrior who is God Almighty'(þa geong Hæleð, þæt wæs God ælmihtig), and who is 'resolved to loose the bonds of humankind' (Dickins and Ross 1967: 25).

The dominant image is that of battle and victory, drawing upon a long tradition in the church which portrayed the passion as a defeat of all hostile powers. But this theme is held in tension with another, that of the suffering of Christ for human sins. There is a dramatic tension set up between the two, as nearly all the images of victory are ascribed to the figure of Christ, while nearly all the images of suffering are deflected onto the cross itself, which testifies to its pain like a sentient being. Thus the cross tells how the young warrior actively strips himself for the fight, hastens with resolute courage to climb the tree, and then rests limb-weary after the exhaustion of single combat as 'Lord of victories', watched over by his faithful followers. By contrast, the cross remembers how it was 'pierced with dark nails', drenched with blood, endured many grievous wrongs from wicked men, was 'wounded with weapon-points', stood weeping and was finally levelled to the ground. All the sympathy and pathos of the reader are directed towards the cross.

The juxtaposition between cross and the crucified one corresponds to the relation between the human nature of Christ (the cross) and the divine person of the Logos or Son of God (the warrior), reflecting the development of orthodox Christology in which the 'one person' of the Son of God could be said to suffer, but only in his humanity. Both the speaking cross and the narrator in his own voice refer to the divine Lord as suffering on the cross for the sins of humankind; it is Almighty God who 'tastes death', and the cross sees God 'violently stretched out'. But this is possible because the cross itself, standing for the human nature, accepts the injury inflicted:

> Feala ic on þam beorge   gebiden hæbbe
> wraðra wyrda.   Geseah ic weruda God
> þearle þenian
>
> .   .   .   .   .   .
>
>   Weop eal gesceaft,
>   cwiddon cyninges fyll.   Crist wæs on rode.

I have endured many cruel wrongs on that hill, where I saw the God of Hosts violently stretched out…All creation wept, lamenting the fall of the King; Christ was on the cross.   (ibid. 27–8)

What is striking about this poem is that it offers no explanation or theory as to *how* the victory and the suffering converge and can be attributed to the one Lord. There is a resonant space opened between these concepts, as dramatic as the space between the cross and the warrior. The impression given is that victory interprets the suffering, but we cannot quite see how. One way of bridging them in the patristic tradition (for example in Gregory of Nyssa's *Great Catechism*) was to regard the human suffering as a ransom offered to Satan, who otherwise had 'rights' over human beings because of the fall; Christ then triumphs victoriously over Satan who has taken the bait of his human nature, so that the deceiver is aptly deceived and human souls are released from hell. While there is a possible hint of this theme towards the end of the poem in the phrase 'he was victorious in his enterprise…when he came with the throng, the company of the spirits, into God's kingdom', the poet refrains from explicitly depicting a conquest over Satan. In this he differs markedly from the two Latin poems by Fortunatus on the victory of the cross, with which the text shows a familiarity.

The space opened up between the themes, as well as the non-specific nature of the triumph, draws readers in to make connections for themselves, as does the narrator himself who ends by reflecting in an elegiac way on his own life, in which he feels 'many yearnings' within himself, and in which he has known the sorrow of losing friends who 'live now in heaven, dwell in glory'.

In the period from the twelfth century onwards, the emphasis between suffering and victory moves very definitely in the opposite direction from the *Dream of the Rood*, towards extended and intense meditation on the suffering humanity of Jesus as a person. We can see, however, that tension and open space remains in place of any dogmatic theory. The medieval period was characterized by a revolution of feeling, by a new interest in the human figure of Jesus, and by an imaginative thinking about the human life of Jesus which found focus in his suffering and death. In the lyrics and in devotional prose such as that of Richard Rolle and Julian of Norwich the bleeding wounds of Jesus are a continual topic for devotion; first and foremost they are not wounds incidental to the battle (as in the *Dream of the Rood*), but an expression of divine love and pity which in turn awakens pity and love in the observer. The regal crown is replaced by the crown of thorns.

The passivity of Christ in his five wounds is supported by the activity of his words from the cross, which are extended into two liturgical forms which become part of the service for Good Friday: the lamentation or complaint and the reproaches. The first is based on the Lamentations of Jeremiah, centring upon 1: 12, 'Is it nothing to you, all you who pass by? Behold and see if there is any sorrow like my sorrow.' The second is based on Micah 6: 3: 'Oh my people, what have I done to you? In what have I wearied you? Answer me!'

Elaborations of the laments and reproaches in poetry and prose are designed to evoke a response of pity and love from the reader or hearer, who is being drawn into the scene of the passion; observers of the bloody drama become participants whose emotions have been engaged. The influence of Peter Abelard here is strong, who had called upon his readers to envisage the scene of the passion story and imagine themselves part of it, in order that divine love might prompt love in the human heart (Radice 1974: 151; Fairweather 1956: 284). This is far from what is sometimes called an exemplarist view of the passion, or merely copying the love of Jesus; there is confidence that the revelation of the love of God in the cross will actually *create* love in hard and sinful human hearts.

> Jesu Christ, my lemmon [lover] swete,
> That diyedst on the Rode Tree,
> With all my might I thee beseche,
> For thy woundes two and three,
> That also faste mot thy love
> Into mine herte fitched be
> As was the spere into thine herte,
> Whon thou soffredest deth for me.
>
> (Davies 1971: 117; cf. 98, 109, 120)

Just as today theologians lay stress on the transformative power of repentant love within the personality, the appeal of Christ, suffering in his human nature, was envisaged by poets and devotional writers as producing repentance and a radical change of life.

But alongside the suffering love of the crucified Christ, the scene of the passion continued to be interpreted as a victorious battle. The gap between the two themes is partly closed by now identifying Satan and Death as specific enemies. The 'ransom' theory which the *Dream of the Rood* was silent about takes a more visible place, with the affirmation that sinners have been 'bought' out of the power of Satan by the suffering and death of Christ.

> 'Moder, mercy, let me deye!
> For Adam out of helle beye,
> and his kun that is forlore.'
>
> (ibid. 87, cf. 111, 253)

However, this linking of suffering and victory is rarely put forward as a dogmatic synthesis. It is a moment of drama in the story of the passion rather than a dominant theory. Poets seem uneasy about the idea of the 'devil's rights' and satisfying the demands of Satan; they have perhaps taken note from Anselm that too much importance had been given to the claims of Satan and not enough to the claims of God on human life.

A second way of bridging the gap seized hold of the medieval imagination much more strongly. The tradition of Christus Victor was united with feelings of courtly love to portray Christ as the lover-knight who suffers and dies to win the love of his lady. By the end of the twelfth century the lover-knight had an established place in aristocratic life and literature, as is witnessed by the poem *The Owl and Nightingale* (Stanley 1972: 79–81). Christ the young warrior was to be recast in this form; the reproach of the divine lover was to become the plea of the divine lover-knight, with the human soul ('mansoul') as the hard-hearted lady whose love was to be won through conflict with her enemies or in jousting for her honour, as in the devotional manual, the *Ancrene Wisse* (Shepherd 1967: 21–2). The whole martial metaphor of the passion as found in the Christus Victor tradition can now be expanded into an allegory of love in which, for instance, the human nature of Christ is compared to the armour that the lover-knight wears. In a medieval lyric, the cross is like a horse which Christ rides: 'My palefrey is of tre' (Davies 1971: 116).

The allegorization of coat-armour as human nature takes a foremost place in William Langland's poem *Piers Ploughman*. The dreamer asks:

> 'Is þis ihesus þe iuster [jouster]' quod I   'þat iuwes [Jews] did to deth?
> Or is it Pieres þe plowman!   who paynted hym so rede?'

> (B. XIX. 6–11; Skeat 1869: 344)

In the process of the poem the figure of Piers Ploughman is less an individual than the state of being human. We are not surprised then, when Conscience replies that 'þise aren Pieres armes | Hise coloures & his cote-armure'. In contrast to the writers of meditative devotion, Langland uses an economy of detail in telling the story, the inflicting of the wounds being briefly portrayed ('nailed him with three nails naked on the cross'), but he does spend time in carrying through the jousting theme by describing the thrust of the spear into Christ's side by a 'knight', who is here presented as blind and so tricked into 'jousting' with the already dead Jesus when nobody else would dare to touch 'God's body'. Earlier writers had interpreted the cry 'I thirst' as a cry of love, longing for the human souls whom Christ desires. Langland keeps the cry back for a scene before the gates of hell, as the victorious Christ declares:

> For I, þat am lorde of lyf.   loue is my drynke,
> And for þat drynke today.   I deyde vpon erthe...

> (B. XVIII. 363–4; ibid. 339)

So Langland refers the cry to a thirst induced by fighting, evoking again the lover-knight. Christ assumes the arms of human nature, and fights on the cross, parched with love for human souls.

The ideas of ransom and the lover-knight do not just hint at the way that the theme of suffering love and victory might interact. They both offer an answer to the question with which Abelard was faced: that is, why does the display of God's love require a death? An answer, though not very satisfactory theologically, was given by the devil's rights. The alternative answer of Anselm of Canterbury, that the death of

Christ paid a debt and satisfied the honour of God (Davies and Evans 1998: 281–7), had no great impact on medieval poetry. But the theme of the lover-knight supplies an imaginative answer to the question: why is love shown by death? It is simply part of the story of the lover-knight that the knight dies in defence of his lady. This is what lover-knights *do*. As long as the picture held the imagination, it made perfect sense that the love of Christ demanded his death. We shall see that Langland offers another answer to this question, which finds new echoes in later ages when the theme of the lover-knight no longer compelled. For the moment, however, the themes of suffering and victory were held together by the strands of the devil's ransom and the lover-knight, though neither provides a tight theory that fills the space between them.

LAW AND MERCY

Anselm's challenge to move from a focus on the rights of the devil to the demands of the law of God was taken up by Reformation theology. Already we can see a preoccupation of Langland with a new tension, beyond that of suffering and victory. This is the dynamic of divine law and divine mercy. In Passus I of *Piers Ploughman*, Langland portrays the passion in the legal context of the demands of the law. The rich are advised that, although they have the power to summon the poor to court, they should show mercy just as God shows mercy to sinners who are arraigned because of their misdeeds. The divine Father 'looked on us with love and let his son die | meekly for our misdeeds to amend us all' (B. I. 165–6). There is no hint here of Anselm's theory that Christ has dealt with the demand of the divine law by paying God a debt of honour. The point is that love, exhibited in the death of Christ, 'modifies' the strict requirement of the law:

> Riȝt so is loue a ledere   and þe lawe shapeth,
> Vpon man for his mysdedes   þe merciment he taxeth.
>
> (B. I. 157–60; Skeat 1869: 18)

(In the same way love is a leader, and *shapes* the law; it asks for mercy upon man for his misdeeds.)

The mood of Langland here seems similar to the way that Isabella in Shakespeare's *Measure for Measure* urges the superiority of mercy to the law without having to be committed to any theoretical mechanism of satisfying the divine lawmaker. In reply to Angelo's statement that her brother is a 'forfeit of the law' and condemned to die, she replies:

> Why, all the souls that were, were forfeit once,
> And He that might the vantage best have took
> Found out the remedy...   (II. ii. 73)

Langland is impressed by the divine mercy which 'shapes' the law and wants to see this imitated in human social life. Moreover, he has an insight into the reason why the mercy and love of God needs to be exhibited in a death. When Peace appears as the emissary of love she explains that the purpose of the crucifixion is for God to experience the extremities of human sorrows and death: God becomes man 'to know what al wo is' (B. XVIII. 22), to know whether 'deth were soure or swete', and 'to se þe sorwe of deynge' ('to see the sorrow of dying') (C. XX. 217–24; Pearsall 1994: 328–9). Langland sets in parallel here the redemptive act of God and God's first-hand knowledge of 'what pain is'. In the light of Abelard and the medieval lyrics of love we might draw the conclusion that it is the experience of human suffering by God which is itself salvific, having the power to awaken love in the human heart. This is a far-reaching insight that has been echoed in modern theology of the atonement.

Langland—and Shakespeare too—thus leaves a gap between the divine law and the divine mercy, which is filled loosely by a 'shaping' or modification of law by love, impelled by the divine pity. The God who is love, says the figure of Repentance 'with þi self sone in owre *sute* deydest' (B. V. 495), thus bringing the two elements together in a pun. In Christ, God dies in the process of our 'law-suit', and as wearing the garments ('suit') of our humanity, knowing our sorrows: 'Ihesu cryst . . . In a pore mannes apparaille pursueth vs euere' ('Christ in a poor man's apparel pursues us always') (B. XI. 179–80). With the Reformation, however, the relation between the divine mercy and divine justice is made more rational, and the gap is closed more tightly. Calvin advanced a theory, often called penal substitution, according to which the law of God is satisfied or appeased by the fact that 'Christ made his soul a propitiatory victim for sin, on which the guilt and penalty being in a manner laid ceases to be imputed to us' (Beveridge 1949: i. 439).

In its severely Calvinistic form, this theory was alien to the passion poetry of John Donne and George Herbert. Just as medieval lyrics had called for their hearers to 'behold' and 'regard' the scene of the cross (injunctions taken from Lam. 1: 12), so Donne (leaning on the technique of Ignatian meditation) sees with the eye of the imagination the particular place where Christ was crucified. But as he situates himself in the scene, it is as a sinner who merits the wrath of God, showing himself to be an heir of the Protestant Reformation. In 'Good Friday, Riding Westward', for example, he is travelling away from the east and the site of the crucifixion, which positions him to receive correction on his back as Christ did:

> I turne my backe to thee, but to receive
> Corrections, till thy mercies bid thee leave.
> O thinke mee worth thine anger, punish mee,
> Burne off my rusts, and my deformity,
> Restore thine Image, so much, by thy grace,
> That thou may'st know mee, and I'll turne my face.
>
> (Gardner 1969: 31)

Despite emphasis on the wrath of God, however, there is some openness of meaning in the basic concept of penal suffering by which he interprets the passion. It is his delight in the elements of drama and wit—including paradox, double meaning, and unlikely juxtapositions of images—that leads him to find the notion of substitution attractive. The transfer of penalty expressed by 'Kings pardon, but he bore our punishment' ('Holy Sonnets' 7) belongs to the same range of antinomies as does 'Death, thou shalt die' ('Holy Sonnets' 6).

Donne in fact rarely commits himself to a metaphor itself, but to the emotion that it expresses, often in highly intellectual terms. The emotion is the sense of being a sinner before a God of righteous anger, called to exercise faith and moral choice. In this situation the story of the passion brings law and mercy together in a variety of ways which exceed any strict transaction between Christ and his Father. The Holy Sonnet ('Spit in my face yee Jewes, and pierce my side') which confesses that satisfaction cannot be offered for sin by the death of the sinner, and which admires the 'strange love' by which Christ bears our punishment, also continues Langland's theme that God has clothed himself in human flesh so that 'Hee might be weake enough to suffer woe'. In another Holy Sonnet Donne finds that Christ, the lamb slain from the beginning of the world, has made two wills, the first being the covenant of law and the second a covenant of 'all-healing grace'. There is no suggestion that the demands of the first are satisfied by the second, but rather, in the mood of Langland's 'shaping' of the law by love,

> Thy lawes abridgement, and thy last command
> Is all but love; Oh let that last Will stand!

> ('Holy Sonnets' 12; Gardner 1969: 12)

To see what a fully transactional account of transferred penalty would look like, we need only turn to John Milton, and *Paradise Lost*. Milton shows the loss, which was typical of the Commonwealth and Restoration period, of the tradition of meditating on the cross, so that the suffering love of Christ becomes less a means of inspiring the observer and more of a component in a transaction. Books 3 and 12 offer two long discussions of the theory of salvation, but hardly any picturing of the *events* of the passion. Law and mercy are related through a Calvinistic doctrine of transferred penalty, as in the scene in heaven where the covenant of grace (as mentioned in passing by Donne) is made between the Father and the Son. In high drama, God the Father calls for someone in the heavenly court to offer to be satisfaction for the demand of the law:

> Die [man], or justice must; unless for him
> Some other able, and as willing, pay
> The rigid satisfaction, death for death.
> Say, heav'nly Powers, where shall we find such love?
> Which of ye will be mortal to redeem
> Man's mortal crime, and just th'unjust to save?
> Dwells there in all heaven charity so dear?

> (3. 210–16; Bush 1967: 261–2)

The Son of God offers, 'On me let thine anger fall; | Account me man' (237–8). Instead of love 'abridging' or 'shaping' the law it now 'fulfills' the law, in the sense that only by suffering the penalty of death 'can high justice rest appaid' (12. 401).

Milton has recovered the insight of the Apostle Paul that the real powers which are hostile to human life are not Satan and legions of devils, but the 'existential' enemies of sin, law, and death (Rom. 7: 7–25). But God's dramatic appeal underlines the mechanical nature of a transaction: all that is needed is the death of a perfectly righteous person—apparently any death, anywhere—to pay off the debt owed to the law. What is lost here is the insight of Langland, following the logic of divine love in the medieval lyrics, that it is the suffering of God (albeit in human nature) that creates love in the human heart, and that this is what the passion is all about. Modern theologians have added that it is the awakening of repentant love which will in the end overcome the true enemies within human existence (Dillistone 1968: 367–86; Macquarrie 1977: 318–24; Fiddes 1989: 135–9).

SACRIFICE AND SACRAMENT

As in Donne's religious verse, the passion of Jesus is at the centre of George Herbert's poetry. In contemplating the scene of the crucifixion he is not, however, so concerned with the relation between law (with its companion, divine wrath) and mercy, as with another pair of concepts which set up a space into which the reader can be drawn. We might summarize these as sacrifice and sacrament, which find particular—though not exclusive—expression in the established analogy between blood and wine.

Herbert's gaze upon the cross returns constantly to its fluids, to the blood that flows from the wounds of Christ and the mingled blood and water that flows from the spear-thrust in his side. Sacrifice is understood not in a propitiatory way, but as the release of precious liquids from the victim, bringing refreshment, cleansing, and new life to the individual and the cosmos. This is in accord with Old Testament understanding of sacrifice as releasing a life-force which purifies and renews the tainted life of the community (Lev. 17: 11 'the life of the animal is in the blood'), and with established images in the church which already link the blood and water with the sacraments (eucharist and baptism) and with the 'water of life' which Jesus promises in the Fourth Gospel. Herbert stands firmly in the medieval tradition by declining to associate sacrifice, as had Calvin, with satisfaction.

Thus the penultimate verse of the poem headed 'The Sacrifice' links the fall of Adam, from whose side a rib was taken to craft Eve, with the spiritual nourishment provided by the Second Adam:

> Nay, after death their spite shall further go;
> For they will pierce my side, I full well know;
> That as sinne came, so Sacraments might flow.
>
> Was ever grief like mine?
> (Gardner 1967: 29)

The whole poem is a series of variations on the two traditional liturgical forms for Good Friday whose influence has already been mentioned: the complaints ('Was ever grief like mine?') and the reproaches ('What have I done to you?'). Within these established guidelines, Herbert intersperses a whole series of typological allusions and paradoxes. He constantly creates new resonances within established images, and not least with the image of blood. When he refers to the blood of Jesus as a 'cordiall', this evokes the traditional analogy of the cross with a wine-press: a phrase from Isa. 63: 2–3—'I have trodden the wine-press alone'—was believed to refer to the squeezing out of the life-giving blood of Jesus, like juice from grapes, and this reference is confirmed by the picture of the vineyard of Israel in the very next verse of Herbert's poem. But he then makes a new and unexpected connection with the crown of thorns: the vineyard according to Isa. 5 produces no grapes and becomes a place of thorns. Thus Christ, dying in the wine-press as the true vine, wears the thorns of Israel's guilt:

> Then on my head a crown of thorns I wear:
> For these are all the grapes Sion doth bear,
> Though I my vine planted and watred there.

In 'The Agonie' Herbert refers again to the picture from Isa. 63 of the man with blood-red garments who has trodden the wine-press:

> Who would know Sinne, let him repair
> Unto Mount Olivet; there shall he see
> A man so wrung with pains, that all his hair,
>   His skinne, his garments bloudie be.
> Sinne is that presse and vice, which forceth pain
> To hunt his cruell food through ev'ry vein.

In one of Herbert's transformative endings this is now explicitly related to the eucharist, by way of reference to the pierced side of Christ:

> Love is that liquor sweet and most divine,
> Which my God feels as bloud; but I, as wine.

Herbert makes the same connection in 'The Bunch of Grapes', while in a marvellous compression he also weaves in a reflection on the way that the cross deals with the demand of the law:

> Who of the Laws sowre juice sweet wine did make,
> Ev'n God himself being pressed for my sake.

The blood of Christ's wounds has 'paid the full price' ('Sunday') but this is never specified as satisfying a God of righteous anger. Christ's blood puts colour into the face of death ('Death') and into the cheeks of the church ('Church Rents'). It cleanses and heals wounds ('An Offering'), writes the story of the passion on the heart of the poet ('Good Friday') and fills the baptismal font in order to wash the human heart clean ('Love Unknown'). In this last image, while the blood of Christ is *compared* to the stream of water that came from the rock that Moses split, we are reminded that at the cross blood was also actually *mixed* with water from the spear-thrust, with the result that either blood or water can be associated with baptism.

It is the poet David Jones who in modern times has most echoed Herbert in drawing upon this association of sacrifice with life-giving fluids—blood, water, wine. In his long poem *The Anathemata*, he interweaves the story of the passion with the Welsh story of the knight Peredur (Percival in the Grail Legend), who embarks on a quest to revive the wasteland that his country has become, so that the waters are freed, streams flow again, marriages are consecrated, and the earth fructifies. So Jones offers a modern revival of the theme of Christ the lover-knight, 'riding the Axile Tree' (Jones 1972: 243), set against the background in his own time of suffering of soldiers in the First World War. By focusing on the theme of the 'freeing of the waters' he also offers another version of the cross as a 'fountain filled with blood' as a means of refreshment, healing, and cleansing. Through the death of Christ and its celebration in the eucharistic liturgy not only individual lives but a whole culture and society can be renewed, like pouring water onto parched ground. As the poet asks, echoing the traditional complaints and reproaches, 'what more should he do | that he hasn't done?' (ibid. 226).

The poem culminates in the consecration of the host on Good Friday ('here he takes the victim') and the cross is seen as the source for the sacraments which pour life into the whole universe. The deathly cry 'I thirst' ('sitio') is answered by the freeing of the waters, as the cross which is 'dry-stiped' becomes 'effluxed', moist with blood and water. This in turn recalls an earlier saying of a common seaman that Christ 'laboured long for us at the winepress' (ibid. 156), evoking once more the figure of the man in bloody garments from Isa. 63.

Compassion and the Self

In the space between sacrifice and sacrament there is room, especially in Herbert, for the divine grief, just as there was room for divine pity in Langland's juxtaposing of law and mercy. The cross absorbs all human grief, and all human tears flow into the sea of Christ's tears (Herbert's 'Affliction'). In William Blake we find a full flowering of the earlier tradition that the pity of Jesus for humanity lies at the centre of the passion. In the Lamb of God we see the man who truly lives by the divine image which is 'Mercy, Pity, Peace and Love', the human form divine. Moreover, this pity is brought into relation with the Pauline theme that 'The "I"—the self—is crucified with Christ' (Gal. 2: 20). For Blake, the passion of Jesus discloses the power of pity and forgiveness, which can enable the true and eternal Self in a human being to divest itself of the false self, or the state of Selfhood which is named Satan. Here is a revisioning of the story of the cross, where Jesus does indeed come into conflict with

Satan, but the Satan is nothing other than a 'spectrous' self, characterized by egocentricity, hypocrisy, and self-righteousness. It is this Satan, and not the true Jehovah, who demands reparation and satisfaction through blood ('The Ghost of Abel'; Keynes 1966: 780).

In his songs and prophetic books Blake is continually telling the story of the fall of humanity into division and resurrection again to wholeness. The self is divided, split into warring psychological elements, and the human being (symbolized as the Giant Albion, the eternal Man) must awaken from deadly sleep to recognize the situation and reclaim the true self. In his poem *Vala*, or the *Four Zoas*, Blake relates the fragmentation of the self, as the four life-forces (Zoas) fall into conflict with each other and rage against each other as the human person sleeps, unaware of the crisis situation. Urizen symbolizes the human faculty of reason, trying to control the world through imposing mechanistic laws of science and morality, limiting energy, desire, and forgiveness. Los symbolizes the human spirit of imagination, which should take the leading role in the human psyche, but after being usurped by reason he gives birth to 'the terrible boy' Orc, who is the inhibited spirit of desire. Reason and imagination are further split off from the faculty of Luvah, the emotions, and the dysfunctional quartet is completed by Tharmas, or instinctive life. The resurrection to unity can only come about through the integration of the life-forces, and the annihilation of the 'Spectre' which is the false self or the state of Satanhood. Since Reason has overthrown the imagination, Urizen is also closely associated with the Satan or Selfhood.

In Night 8 of *Vala*, Blake concerns himself primarily with the crucifixion. Urizen enters into an unholy alliance with Orc, who becomes the serpent coiled around the Tree of Mystery; that is, legalistic religion uses suppressed desire for its own ends. Jesus, the Lamb of God, appears 'infolded in Luvah's robes of blood', wearing the garments of human nature which are love. He has 'assumed the dark Satanic nature in the Virgin's womb', and has now come 'in the State called Satan . . . to put off Satan eternally'. He faces Satan, his shadow or state of Selfhood, who judges him in the Sanhedrin:

> Urizen call'd together the Synagogue of Satan in dire Sanhedrim
> To judge the Lamb of God to Death as a murderer & robber:
> As it is written, he was number'd among the transgressors.
>
>   .   .   .   .
>
>   The Lamb of God descended thro' the twelve portions of Luvah,
> bearing his sorrows & recieving [*sic*] all his cruel wounds.
>
> Thus was the Lamb of God condemn'd to Death.
> They nail'd him upon the tree of Mystery, weeping over him
> And then mocking & then worshipping, calling him Lord & King . . .
>
>   .   .   .   .
>
> . . . Jerusalem saw the Body dead upon the Cross. She fled away,
> Saying: 'Is this eternal Death? Where shall I hide fom Death?'
>
> (8. 272–4, 323–7, 331–2; Keynes 1966: 348–9)

The traditional battle between Christ and Satan at the cross can thus be understood as a conflict between imagination and rationalism, or the conflict of the eternal self (the human form divine) with the earthly selfhood. The one who bears the divine image divests himself of the satanic selfhood; in the words of a modern theologian 'One's own self is the last idol, and to give even oneself unreservedly is . . . to have vanquished the last demon' (Macquarrie 1977: 319).

Jesus overcomes Satan, not by Satan's own tools of force and restriction, but by exercising forgiveness in divine pity. The Daughters of Beulah praise Jesus as the one who awakes sleepers, because he is 'the pitying one' whose 'pity is from the foundation of the World' (*Vala* 8. 242). The cross brings about the last judgement, in which the Giant Albion awakes, error is recognized, Los regains the leading role in human consciousness, and human beings live on the products of both imagination and reason, symbolized in the making of eucharistic bread and wine. The man with blood-red robes (Isa. 63: 2) reappears when Jesus is clothed in the garments of Luvah, as does the winepress. Here, however, *all* human beings are to be trodden like grapes in the press, yielding up their selfhood, to make the wine of true humanity (*Vala* 9. 748–9, 770–1; Keynes 1966: 377).

A century later W. B. Yeats acknowledges his debt to Blake's use of symbols, but takes a quite different view on both the surrender of the self and the place of compassion in the death of Christ. He protests against the 'objectivity' of the cross and Christianity as a whole, and by this he does not mean simply a transactional view of the atonement such as penal substitution; he means any sense of submission to an external divine being who demands annihilation of the self in imitation of Christ. In this context, the idea of a suffering God is also dangerously objective; an ultimate divine suffering can insist on inhabiting and possessing the worshipper, driving out the human self. In Yeats's dance-play *Resurrection* there is a devastating speech on Christian submission by a Hebrew disciple who has been disillusioned by the fate of Jesus: 'Nobody before him had so pitied human misery . . . One had to sacrifice everything that the divine suffering might, as it were, descend into one's mind and soul, and make them pure. One had to give up all worldly knowledge, all ambition, do nothing of one's own will . . . God had to take complete possession' (Yeats 1952: 583, 585).

This kind of 'compassion', Yeats thinks, is effective with the 'objective' type of person whose suffering derives from external causes—such as poverty, sickness, and death—or from a sense of sin. Such people need an external saviour. This pity cannot reach the subjective type of person, the one who has an intellectual and psychological despair. Lazarus and Judas are examples of subjectives whom Christ encounters on the way to his cross in the dance-play *Calvary*, and whose despair lay beyond his sympathy. Lazarus, like the character in Oscar Wilde's parable 'The Doer of Good', has been frustrated in his desire to die and find peace, since—he complains—'alive I could never escape your love'. But he has been 'dragged to the light' like a rabbit pulled out of its hole (Yeats 1952: 452) This is the intrusive nature of objective religion; the solicitude of Christ will pursue him beyond the grave. Judas also wants his self to be free from Christ, and has betrayed him to gain this freedom, claiming that 'if a man betrays a God he is the stronger of the two' (ibid. 454).

The symbol for the subjective types is the bird—especially the heron, eagle, and hawk—and like these birds they seek to be alone, in desert, wilderness, and uninhabited places. The play begins with an image of a white heron brooding over a shallow stream, symbolizing the subjective person as a contemplative:

> Motionless under the moon-beam,
> Up to his feathers in the stream;
> Although fish leap, the white heron
> Shivers in a dumbfounded dream.   (ibid. 449)

The refrain of the play, 'God has not died for the white heron,' is echoed in the last line: 'God has not appeared to the birds.' Subjective types are immune from all externalities, even the sacrifice of an external saviour-God. They maintain their separate identity, discovering in meditation their own higher self, which is identical with the universal divine Self.

In portraying the passion Yeats gives us only one of the words from the cross: 'My Father, why hast Thou forsaken Me?' Christ suffers from the loneliness of an objective personality in the cross, while Judas and Lazarus as subjective types seek a self-sufficient loneliness. The word of forsakenness is followed immediately by the closing lyric: 'Lonely the sea-bird lies at her rest.' Yeats presents a tableau of the passion: Christ is on the cross, forsaken, the cross is held up by Judas, who cannot finally escape Christ, while the Roman soldiers dance around the cross in celebration of the God of Chance. Yeats surrounds the crucified man by those whom he cannot save with his love: the subjective types are beyond his kind of salvation, while the objective types present (the soldiers) are indifferent to his appeal.

Death and Suffering

In Blake and Yeats two aspects of the passion are held in tension: the divine pity expressed in the cross, and the putting to death of the human self. We can see the same tension in the novels of George Eliot, and especially in *Adam Bede*. But while in Blake the pity of the passion releases the true self from a false Selfhood, Yeats—echoing Nietzsche—warns that pity may overcome the self altogether.

The novelist Iris Murdoch is in agreement with Yeats that human beings cannot be dependent on an external, objective Saviour and his wounds. This is vividly portrayed in a vision of Christ that her character Ann Cavidge receives in *Nuns and Soldiers* (Murdoch 1991: 289–94). In response to her plea that she wants to be saved, 'to be made good', and 'to be washed whiter than snow', he gently insists that 'you must do it all yourself' and 'I am not a magician.' She cannot push away her responsibilities onto him, for he bids her (as he did Mary) 'Love me if you must my dear, but don't touch me.' She cannot cling to an easy Saviour, but must find the way of truth for herself through the tangles of her love, though Christ can be followed and even loved as one who took the path of truth himself. Christ has certainly suffered wounds on the cross and on the way to it, but they themselves cannot save; when she looks at his unscarred hands he says paradoxically, 'my wounds are imaginary'. That is, the suffering is 'not the point . . . though it has proved so interesting to you all!' Suffering has passed like a shadow; what *is* the point, what remains, is the challenge of facing death, which 'is one of my names'. Murdoch thus presents us with yet another tension in thinking about redemption—that between death and suffering.

Like Yeats, Murdoch urges us to serve an unreachable Good—Plato's unnameable Good—for no reward: being 'good for nothing' is a constant refrain in her novels. However, she is more aware than Yeats of the dangerous trap of the self, of building a world around the centre of one's self and being unable to notice objects and other persons as they truly are. Like Blake, she believes that we must engage in 'the long task of unselving' (Murdoch 1976: 174; 1970: 84). She thinks that we can be helped to break free of our self-enclosed shells by deliberately paying attention to the particularity of objects in the world. Stones appear often in her novels with this function, but works of art have a special place. An icon of the Trinity plays a central part in *The Time of the Angels* in this way, as does the engraved artwork on the bell in the novel of that name. 'Unselving' is also assisted by attention to the fact of death, and here we return to the visionary enounter of Christ with Ann Cavidge, bidding her to consider his death rather than his suffering. Murdoch thinks that confession and a seeking for salvation from God can mask the fact that we find our sins an interesting and absorbing subject. Suffering the torments of remorse about them can be a self-indulgence, which is simply another form of creating our own world around us. A sado-masochism of the cross can thus substitute suffering for the death which witnesses to the true death of the (self-centred) self. As Father Brendan expounds it (in *Henry and Cato*):

We live by redemptive death. Anyone can stand in for Christ . . . Death is the great destroyer of all images and all stories, and human beings will do anything rather than envisage it. Their last resource is to rely on suffering, to try to cheat death by suffering instead. And suffering we know breeds images, it breeds the most beautiful images of all.   (Murdoch 1976: 337)

Christ, however, did not cheat death by suffering instead. Christ was obedient to the Good unto a death whose horror he fully comprehended; as Nolan puts it in *The Unicorn*, 'true obedience is without illusion. A common soldier will die in silence, but Christ cried out' (Murdoch 1966: 66). This is being good for nothing, without reward—including a resurrection. So the mystical Christ can turn us to the Good, and in this sense only he is alive: 'if Christ saves, he lives' (Murdoch 1987: 490). The failed poet, Lucius, dies in making his best haiku, a miniature work of art celebrating death as 'the great teacher' (Murdoch 1976: 330). What matters about the passion of Christ is not a redemptive suffering, but the example of someone who faced death and saw it without illusion. Death is the great teacher because it teaches the death of the self.

Murdoch—together with George Eliot—has been a considerable influence on the novels of A. S. Byatt, and here too we find the tension between suffering and death. In her quartet of novels charting English cultural life from the early 1950s to 1970, beginning with *The Virgin in the Garden* and ending with *The Whistling Woman*, these themes gather especially round the character of Daniel Orton. As a young Anglican priest, he one day finds the body of his wife, Stephanie, electrocuted by a faulty refrigerator, and he relates this experience of death to the story of the passion of Christ in a way that becomes a leitmotif throughout the books. In the aftermath of his wife's death, Daniel tries to pray in church:

Christ had said that the Father cared for the fall of a sparrow, but though it was clear Christ had cared, it was not at all clear that the powers did ... The image of the hanging figure on the cross was a human cry for things to be otherwise, for human suffering to be at the centre, for man to be responsible for his own destiny and for the destroyed to come again ... (Byatt 1995: 423–4)

As with Murdoch, death is the great teacher. Daniel loves a Christ 'of devastating common sense' but does not address this Christ 'because he was dead' (Byatt 1994: 140). The shocking death of Stephanie makes us face the fact and the finality of death, as with the death of Cordelia in *King Lear*, Stephanie's favourite play. Byatt has more place for the suffering of the cross than does Murdoch, perhaps influenced by her other mentor, George Eliot. But the passion of Christ is not an example to be *imitated* by our own suffering; the crucified Christ, as the focus of human suffering, is a call to do something responsible about dealing with its causes.

Daniel remains uncertain about whether the suffering of Christ is also divine suffering, and so is less confident than Eliot's characters for whom 'man needs a suffering God', and who know that 'in all the anguish of the children of men infinite love is suffering too' (Eliot 1992: 371, 413). What he *is* sure about is that the image of a Father who causes his Son to die is totally unhelpful to those who suffer. When his rector prays, 'Dearly beloved Father who understands human mourning having given your own son for our sake', Daniel responds by hitting him (Byatt 1995: 425). As is underlined by the rejection of God as 'the avenger of blood' by Joshua Ramsden in *Whistling Woman* (Byatt 2002: 112–15), Byatt, like Blake, offers a protest against any reading of the passion story in which a divine Father directly inflicts suffering. While Joshua re-mythologizes the passion of Christ, setting it in a cosmic struggle between light and darkness, Daniel essentially humanizes the story, seeing it as a protest against all human suffering. Yet in *Babel Tower*, meditating on a recent victim of a capital punishment, Daniel concludes hesitantly that 'This is Christ, the divine man, a man tortured and executed ... and perhaps it is right after all to find God here' (Byatt 1997: 372–4).

Daniel's response is a fitting point on which to bring this account of the passion in English literature to an end. His hesitancy hints at a view of the passion which we have seen to have emerged constantly in the work of poets and novelists, that the suffering of God in the passion of Christ somehow has power to transform human minds and attitudes, to God and to fellow human beings. The echoes of this theme can be heard sounding, sometimes muted and sometimes more pronounced, in the space which is opened up by the tensions between the various images and concepts I have identified—between victory and suffering love, between law and mercy, between sacrifice and sacrament, between compassion and selfhood, and between death and suffering. Theologians need to live in these tensions as they develop doctrines from the story of the passion, and the work of creative writers can help theologians to see how the motifs and images by which they interpret the passion modify and correct each other. In particular, there is a need to listen to the problems about redemptive suffering which writers such as Yeats, Murdoch, and Byatt present. Their work suggests that belief in a divine suffering should enable those who identify with the cross to resist and overcome human suffering wherever it happens.

Works Cited

Beveridge, Henry (trans. and ed.) 1949. *Institutes of the Christian Religion by John Calvin*. 2 vols. London: James Clarke.

Bush, Douglas (ed.) 1967. *Milton. Poetical Works*. Oxford Standard Authors. London: Oxford University Press.

Byatt, A. S. 1994 (repr.). *The Virgin in the Garden*. London: Vintage.

—— 1995 (repr.). *Still Life*. London: Vintage.

—— 1997 (repr.). *Babel Tower*. London: Vintage.

—— 2002. *A Whistling Woman*. London: Chatto & Windus.

Davies, Brian, and Evans, G. R. (trans. and ed.) 1998. *Anselm of Canterbury. The Major Works*. Oxford World's Classics. Oxford: Oxford University Press.

Davies, R. T. (ed.) 1971. *Medieval English Lyrics: A Critical Anthology*. London: Faber & Faber.

Dickins, Bruce, and Ross, Alan S. C. (eds.) 1967, *The Dream of the Rood*. Methuen's Old English Library. London: Methuen Educational.

Dillistone, F. W. 1968. *The Christian Understanding of Atonement*. The Library of Constructive Theology. London: James Nisbet.

Eliot, George. 1992 (repr.). *Adam Bede*. Everyman's Library. London: David Campbell.

Fairweather, Eugene R. (trans. and ed.) 1956. *Abelard*: Commentary on the Epistle to the Romans, in *A Scholastic Miscellany: Anselm to Ockam*. The Library of Christian Classics. London: SCM, x.

Fiddes, Paul S. 1989. *Past Event and Present Salvation. The Christian Idea of Atonement*. London: Darton, Longman & Todd.

Gardner, Helen (ed.) 1967. *The Poems of George Herbert*. 2nd edn. The World's Classics. London: Oxford University Press.

—— (ed.) 1969. *John Donne. The Divine Poems*. Oxford: Clarendon.

Jones, David 1972 [1955]. *The Anathemata. Fragments of an Attempted Writing*. London: Faber & Faber.

Keynes, Geoffrey (ed.) 1966. *Blake. Complete Writings*. Oxford Standard Authors. London: Oxford University Press.

MacQuarrie, John. 1977. *Principles of Christian Theology*. Rev. edn. London: SCM.

MURDOCH, IRIS. 1966 (repr.). *The Unicorn*. Harmondsworth: Penguin.

—— 1970. *The Sovereignty of Good*. London: Routledge & Kegan Paul.

—— 1976. *Henry and Cato*. London: Chatto & Windus.

—— 1987. *The Book and the Brotherhood*. London: Chatto & Windus.

—— 1991 (repr.). *Nuns and Soldiers*. London: Chatto & Windus.

PEARSALL, DEREK (ed.) 1994. *William Langland. Piers Plowman*. The C-Text. Exeter Medieval English Texts and Studies. Exeter: University of Exeter Press.

RADICE, BETTY (trans. and ed.) 1974. *The Letters of Abelard and Heloise*. Harmondsworth: Penguin.

SHEPHERD, GEOFFREY (ed.) 1967. *Ancrene Wisse*. Parts Six and Seven. Nelson's Medieval and Renaissance Library. Edinburgh: Nelson.

SKEAT, WALTER W. (ed.) 1869. *The Vision of William Concerning Piers the Plowman by William Langland*. The Crowley Text; or Text B. The Early English Text Society os 38. London: Oxford University Press.

STANLEY, ERIC GERALD (ed.) 1972. *The Owl and the Nightingale*. Old & Middle English Texts. Manchester: Manchester University Press.

YEATS, W. B. 1952. *The Collected Plays*. 2nd edn. London: Macmillan.

FURTHER READING

BENNETT, J. A. W. 1982. *Poetry of the Passion. Studies in Twelve Centuries of English Verse*. Oxford: Clarendon.

DAVIS, STEPHEN T., KENDALL, DANIEL, and O'COLLINS, GERALD (eds.) 2004. *The Redemption. An Interdisciplinary Symposium on Christ as Redeemer*. Oxford: Oxford University Press.

DILLISTONE, F. W. 1968. *The Christian Understanding of Atonement*. Welwyn: Nisbet.

—— 1960. *The Novelist and the Passion Story*. London: Collins.

FIDDES, PAUL S. 1991. *Freedom and Limit. A Dialogue between Literature and Christian Doctrine*. Basingstoke: Macmillan.

—— 2000. *The Promised End. Eschatology in Theology and Literature*. Oxford: Blackwell.

GIFFIN, MICHAEL. 2002. *Jane Austen and Religion: Salvation and Society in Georgian England*. Basingstoke: Palgrave.

JASPER, DAVID. 1988. *The Study of Literature and Religion. An Introduction*. London: Macmillan.

KEEN, JILL AVERIL. 2002. *The Charters of Christ and Piers Plowman: Documenting Salvation*. Oxford: Peter Lang.

MURDOCH, BRIAN. 2000. *Adam's Grace: Fall and Redemption in Medieval Literature*. Woodbridge: Brewer.

SHERRY, PATRICK. 2003. *Images of Redemption*. London: T. & T. Clark/Continuum.

SYKES, STEPHEN W. (ed.) 1991. *Sacrifice and Redemption*. Durham Essays in Theology. Cambridge: Cambridge University Press.

WOOLF, ROSEMARY. 1968. *The English Religious Lyric in the Middle Ages*. Oxford: Clarendon.

CHAPTER 45

POSSIBILITIES OF REDEMPTION THROUGH THE NOVEL

DANIEL BOSCALJON

REDEMPTION is a powerful and uplifting theme that acknowledges the human potential to succeed after—or in spite of—having failed. Theological understandings of redemption focus on how humans can restore their relationships with God despite having fallen from grace into sin. Literature takes the same theme of brokenness and renewal and places it in the context of life on earth, thus including understandings of redemption that may stray from those theologically defined. In many ways, literature can be read as testing the boundaries of what can be redeemed, who can be redeemed, or what can be understood as an agent of redemption. Literature, not limited to theological assumptions of another world or an all-powerful creator, is able to explore how life on earth may be redeemed and how humans can mediate their own redemption. In this way, even 'secular' literatures can be seen as doing 'theological' work.

Although many pre-novelistic works of British literature utilize the theme of redemption—from *Gawaine and the Green Knight* to the plays of Shakespeare—I will limit my examination in this chapter to ways in which the theme of redemption is developed through the form of the novel. Instead of looking at books which seem to align readily to a more typical Christian theological notion of redemption (such as Charles Dickens's *A Christmas Carol*), I will look at books which rather unsettle or challenge previous understandings.

REDEMPTION AND SALVATION

Before showing the theological work done by secular novels, it is important to examine more specifically what the Christian understanding of redemption involves. Salvation and redemption are closely connected in many theological variations of Christianity, as salvation (generally understood as mediated by the crucifixion and resurrection of Jesus) is seen as both a necessary and sufficient part of redemption. *Comprehended* in this way, however, a difference between salvation and redemption can be articulated: knowing that one is saved is an event in the process of redemption. Understood as a process the times that precede salvation become as important as those that come after: in terms of redemption, sin is necessary for salvation to occur: instead of focusing on the elimination of suffering (past or future), the broader scope of redemption attempts to use the suffering as a meaningful element in the narrative.

Theological narratives of redemption therefore include the story of the individual's fall into sin, the acceptance of salvation and forgiveness of sins, and the reconciliation of the human with God. One example of this type of narrative is given in the parable of the Prodigal Son, attributed to Jesus in Luke's Gospel. The narrative includes a discussion of a 'fall', as the younger of two sons asks his father for his inheritance early, and then leaves home and squanders it. Destitute and abandoned by the 'friends' he has made, the prodigal son eventually sinks to the level of working with swine. Realizing that his father had been a kinder employer than his current master, the son moves towards home. He is seen by his father, who had kept watch for him since his departure, and who subsequently commands that a celebration commence. This particular narrative is interesting in that it is a story of redemption that omits any type of 'salvation' event, focusing instead on the constancy of the father's love and the changing relationship of father and son.

This parable does more than merely clarify the difference between salvation and redemption; it is also useful as a way of differentiating theological and literary notions of redemption. Even more than a discussion of the presence of sin, a theological understanding of redemption focuses on the action of the divine (or redeeming) agent in a single transitional event. In this case, the theologically significant element of the parable is the fact that the father stands watching for his erring son, whom he is willing to embrace and forgive. Although there is nothing that particularly comprises a 'salvation', the emphasis on the importance of an event (instead of the process as a whole) is how redemption is theologically understood—or at least that which generates the questions which theology seeks to answer. Literature, in contrast, looks at the process as being more significant than the event. By seeing suffering as more than a means to the end of salvation and by being able to explore agents of redemption other than a divine being, literature—which keeps the form of the theological construct while altering the content—is able to explore a variety of ways in which human suffering can be redeemed. The challenge taken up by those literatures that do not assume the existence of an all-loving being is to show how redemption, nonetheless, is a possibility.

The focus on the redemptive nature of the human journey through life instead of the unfailing love of God (in the parable, the prodigal son and not the father) leaves a question regarding the assurance of redemption. This chapter will paint, in broad strokes, three equally inevitable alternatives that allow redemption to be guaranteed despite the absence of a deity: suffering, death, and time. The separation of these as distinctive redemptive themes is not intended to be definitive: instead, it is meant to be used as a way of understanding how 'secular' literatures construct theological arguments, how novels with seemingly pessimistic tones nonetheless point to a hope of redemption, and how new literatures evolve to take the critique of earlier works into account. Redemption theologically understood, premised on the unfailing love of an eternal God, never changes. Literature, for which that foundation is not necessarily available, is much more versatile.

SEVENTEENTH AND EIGHTEENTH CENTURIES: REDEMPTION THROUGH SUFFERING

At the dawn of the English novel, fictions of the seventeenth and eighteenth centuries adhere more closely to biblical assumptions than many of the later fictions tend to do. Nonetheless, the creation of fictionalized accounts creates a space between text and truth, a space originally caused by the decision to focus on the narrativizable account of suffering as redemption instead of reiterations of the unchanging. The focus on the human instead of the divine as a source of redemption is the foundation upon which later authors of fiction are able to build.

The Pilgrim's Progress

John Bunyan's The Pilgrim's Progress (1678) is not only a narrative of redemption but also one of the most foundational and influential works of English literature (see also Ch. 34 by Robert Collmer). The narrative is presented within the context of the author's dream, a technique that allows Bunyan to interweave spiritual and physical dangers to Christian (the pilgrim) without differentiation. Christian's journey begins in the City of Destruction, where, reading, he learns of both his impending doom and the promise of an inheritance. He leaves after receiving a parchment roll from Evangelist, which instructs him to fly from the wrath to come and towards the Celestial City. The majority of the story details interactions between Christian and other characters, some of whom reveal truth, others of whom are deceptive. Although intended both as a description of saints in his time as well as a prescription for how to live a Christian life, Bunyan's decision to write an allegorical account of redemption presents many interesting consequences that he may not, perhaps, have intended.

Bunyan's choice to structure the story around the theme of redemption instead of salvation has the benefit of making for a longer (and perhaps more exciting) narrative, one which allows for Christian to be both saved and imperilled at various points along his journey. The fact that Bunyan's interest is more centred on redemption than salvation is first revealed by the distance between salvation (a minor event, when Christian's burden is removed) and redemption (the story's conclusion). Additionally Bunyan, focusing on the human efforts of Christian's journey, precisely *excludes* direct reference to divine agents. Perhaps the most striking example of this is the absence of love within the book—important if love indeed is the significant element in theological understandings of redemption. Not only does Christian seem to lack a sense of love for his family (rushing from them with little hesitation) or friends (also left behind), but love is silenced throughout the novel. While Christian's fellow pilgrims represent two-thirds of the Pauline trilogy (Faithful and Hopeful), no character is allowed to represent the greatest of these ('Loveful'). Charity, a type of love, is personified—indeed, it is she who reminds Christian of his family—but her interactions with Christian are brief. The bond that seems to unite the pilgrims is not love, but merely the shared goal of redemption.

While Bunyan is clear that Christian cannot *save* himself, the focus on the human figures (Christian, Faithful, Hopeful), combined with the absence of a clearly demarcated divine presence would seem to indicate that the possibility of redemption rests firmly on human shoulders. This is primarily seen through the efforts of Christian as he continues to progress towards his final goal, and is reinforced by the relationship of Faithful and Hopeful: Hopeful is inspired to make the journey towards redemption by the witness of Christian and Faithful, especially in Faithful's martyrdom. Lacking any mention of salvation, Hopeful's quest seems wholly focused on redemption.

The notion of anthropocentric redemption is maintained negatively as well: Christian's salvation seems secure, in so far as he never receives back the burden of sin that he had laid to rest at the cross. Christian's *redemption*, on the other hand, is continually in jeopardy. Threats to Christian's redemption are characterized as all that slows or hinders the pilgrims' progress: the Slough of Despond, the Valley of Humiliation, Vanity Fair, and the Castle of Giant Despair not only create tension within the narrative but also show the reader the type of obstacle able to be overcome. The gates to hell that appear throughout Christian's journey—portals of a purely spiritual persuasion—never truly threaten Christian in the same way but seem to exist as a reminder to the reader that there is a type of danger which exists outside redemption. By the end, however, in the absence of divine love, it seems as though Christian is redeemed through his suffering and through his exposure to danger, because of his confrontations with foes.

Redemption in Bunyan's world still adheres to Christian doctrine (specifically in a Puritan form) in its depiction of a fallen world populated by fallen characters whose natures make unlikely either salvation or redemption. Salvation remains a prerequisite for redemption, and those who pursue redemption without knowledge (Ignorance) are doomed to see their efforts fail. What is most important, however, is the way in which Bunyan alters theological notions of redemption. First, *The Pilgrim's Progress* sets a precedent for the novel in which humans and other non-divine agents can be both redeemed and redeemers. No longer is redemption in literature dependent on an almighty God; instead, humans can work to redeem others (as Hopeful was redeemed) or can pursue their own redemption (as did Christian). The redemption in all cases comes about through struggle and suffering. Second, *The Pilgrim's Progress* opens a literary understanding of redemption as a journey and not an event. If, in this case, redemption requires salvation, redemption is no longer reducible to a single (or even multiple) salvation event. Just as *The Pilgrim's Progress* is a transitional work between narrative and novel, so also does it serve as a bridge from religious to secular texts.

Clarissa

Samuel Richardson's monstrous tome *Clarissa* (1748–9), one of the longest novels ever written, expands on the parameters for redemption that Bunyan erected. *Clarissa*, like *The Pilgrim's Progress*, is not written in what came to be standard novel format but instead is composed as a series of letters. The story tracks Clarissa's stumble (through a lack of obedience), fall (as her virginity is taken), and redemption (through a resurrection of her body of letters in the form of the book that is being read). As opposed to Bunyan's dreamworld fantasy, *Clarissa* faithfully reproduces the reality of the letter-writers including the need for ink and paper. The perils of Clarissa's world are also, fittingly, more realistic than those faced by Christian. She is pressured to marry a man she detests, ends up trusting the wrong people (including Lovelace, whose lovelessness also contains an echo of Bunyan), and suffers both mentally and physically. While Clarissa is thought to be an angel by the book's end (although her faults are acknowledged by both her and her friends), her salvation (theologically understood) is only assumed, and is never presented within the text. The work centres on redemption, not salvation.

Clarissa is redeemed on three different levels. First, adhering to the traditional form of redemption as reconciliation, the final reunion with her friends is promised to occur in the afterlife. Second, acknowledging the need for her suffering to be made meaningful in the 'real' world, Richardson shows how the virtuous (Clarissa's friends) are rewarded with happy lives while the wicked (those who hinder her happiness) are punished by having shortened or unhappy lives. On a third level, because she identifies the hope of her redemption as resting in the assembly of the letters connected to her life and death, her redemption is re-created with every reading of the text. It is important to recognize that only the first of the three redemptions requires divine mediation, and that this redemption takes place outside the text. The redemption within the narrative is fully effected without the help of God: the gap between salvation and redemption is widened.

It is clear that the story of Clarissa comprises an inversion of the story of the Prodigal Son. The one who leaves is a disenfranchised daughter. The reconciliation of parent and child occurs only in the afterlife. Because Clarissa precedes her parents in death, it is her love and patience that will permit an eventual reconciliation. *Clarissa* opens options for how novels can utilize the theme of redemption for non-sacred ends: not bound to any level of content, authors can use the *form* of the redemption narrative to offer any type of argument or message. Through the inversion of the traditional narrative, Richardson is able to offer Clarissa redemption without salvation, a redemption that is humanely mediated on two distinct levels. He also goes further than Bunyan in separating salvation and redemption: not only is Clarissa's redemption permissible despite a lack of salvation, but in some ways her uniquely mediated redemption depends on her not being saved (in the earthly sense). The power of her story, the one that compels the reader to read, is the hope of seeing unjust suffering redeemed. It is important, finally, to notice that not all suffering is redemptive: as is exemplified by the punished state of her enemies, only unjust suffering can be triumphantly redeemed.

Nineteenth Century: Redemption Through Death

The literature of the nineteenth century ceases to romanticize the value of suffering. This is not to say that characters in novels no longer suffer—indeed, the protagonists of the nineteenth-century novels suffer at least as much (if not more) than their earlier counterparts. Although the characters suffer differently—and for different reasons—many nineteenth-century stories seem to point to the insufficiency of suffering alone to redeem the one who suffers. Perhaps this can be seen as a reluctance to accept suffering as a virtue or to be resigned to the afterlife to provide redemption.

The scepticism in these novels extends to a second realm of certainty: death. While death plays an important role in literature from Bunyan on, one can read the nineteenth century as testing death as that which can yield a redemption which suffering no longer seems to be able to offer. Both more certain and more final, the path towards death offers new possibilities for redemption that authors are able to examine.

Frankenstein

Mary Shelley's novel *Frankenstein* (1818) can be seen as setting the stage for the stakes of redemption which later authors will seek to problematize. The novel focuses on Frankenstein, a scientist who discovers how to reanimate flesh, and the creature whom he thus brings to life. Frankenstein, who had hoped that his experiments would bring redemption through abolishing death, finds that instead they bring only more death and more suffering. As is obvious, the novel details the dangers of pride and technology; also of importance is the way that it reconceptualizes the path to redemption. Although it follows works such as *The Pilgrim's Progress* and *Clarissa* in focusing on the journey of the protagonist, it pushes past them in two directions. First, more than assuming or ignoring the love of the Father as a partner in redemption, the 'father' in Frankenstein turns against the hideousness of his creation: the son's journey home will in no way be rewarded. Secondly, Shelley seems to cast doubt on the virtues of suffering: both Frankenstein and his creation tell of their sufferings and sorrows, but as each is the cause of the suffering of the other, neither finds his suffering to be either redeeming or redemptive.

The scope of this book's discussion, then, lies in the possibility of redemption in a world where neither the suffering of the son nor the love of the father necessarily brings about redemption. Both Frankenstein and the creature see themselves as unable to be redeemed due to their crimes against nature. Victor Frankenstein dies before seeing the creature's demise; the creature, in turn, finds no relief at his creator's death. The creature seeks death at the end—not for redemption—but merely to end the pain of loneliness and guilt. While both could have provided salvation to the other, both chose, instead, the route of destruction.

Despite having negated what were traditionally seen as the possibilities for redemption, the book opens up two new ways in which redemption may be enacted, types of redemption that continue to echo in literature for the rest of the century. One possibility for redemption—that pursued by Frankenstein—is in the telling of stories. While neither Frankenstein's life of suffering nor death are able to redeem him, he feels that if he is able to dissuade another human from a life of pride or science, that, perhaps, his life will not be wholly lost. This contains echoes of the story of the Prodigal Son, although, as should be expected, in a distorted manner: the father confesses his crimes to a son, far from home, in the hope that the son will learn and avoid similar mistakes of pride or faith in science. The second possibility for redemption is death: the creature, who, finding his desires for benevolence thwarted, becomes a killer and finally feels he can be redeemed only in ending his own life, acceding, in the end, to his creator's wish. Storytelling thus opens the possibility of redeeming others (as Hopeful was redeemed by the witness of Christian and Faithful), while death (more certain than a father's love) becomes a form of redemption which limits its scope to the one who dies.

Wuthering Heights

Emily Brontë's *Wuthering Heights* (1847) (see also Ch. 8, above, by David Klemm) makes a more drastic break from theologically grounded notions of redemption than either Bunyan or Richardson and continues in the direction that *Frankenstein* sets out. Brontë constructs a world that welcomes suffering and staves off redemption. Heathcliff, the adopted favourite of Mr Earnshaw, is intent on destroying his father's land and family after the older brother—Hindley—becomes jealous. The narrative follows the Earnshaws and the Lintons (the neighbouring family and estate) through three short-lived generations—almost everyone in the story dies at a relatively young age.

The narrative in *Wuthering Heights*, like that of *Frankenstein*, is doubly mediated—from Nelly Dean to Lockwood to reader. The difference between this book and the former lies in the effect of the story. While *Frankenstein*'s moral may have had an effect on the sea captain, who is presented as a younger version of Victor and actually 'tells' the story, Lockwood has little similarity to any of the characters involved in the main narrative. The story is told merely as a way to stave off boredom: Nelly Dean's role as observer of events hardly requires redemption, in any case. In this way, Brontë can be seen as eliminating the hope that Shelley had left open, that the telling of stories may be, in itself, redemptive. Instead, Brontë refocuses on the possibility of redemption in death, trying to reclaim the value of it by disregarding the assumption that death needs to redeem the one who dies.

This is not to say that Brontë completely undermines the foundation established by Shelley: the insistence on the insufficiency of suffering as a redemptive force is reiterated in *Wuthering Heights* in an even more powerful way. The characters in *Wuthering Heights* who interact with Heathcliff become infected with his taint, to the point that they, too, seem to be pushed beyond the possibility of redemption: Hindley is depraved, Catherine duplicitous, Linton doomed. Those who somehow escape him—Edgar or Joseph—are nonetheless repugnant (although fascinating). Not even Lockwood or Nelly Dean—the least troubled characters—come close to being as charming as Clarissa or as tragic as Frankenstein. Suffering abounds, but because Brontë creates a cast of relatively unsympathetic characters, the redemptive force of it is muted. In other words, Brontë offers a second, independent reason why suffering fails to redeem.

Nelly nonetheless wishes to engineer a redemption: as in *Clarissa* and *The Pilgrim's Progress*, redemption is made possible through the death of the main character—in this case, Heathcliff. Because the death involved is of one beyond redemption, the redemption of the others is merely made possible, not guaranteed. Lockwood is allowed to witness only that Cathy and Hareton—neither of whom are descended from Heathcliff (which makes the death of Linton Heathcliff, the son of Heathcliff, a welcome event)—are still kindly disposed toward one another, kissing between reading lessons. Whether or not they will continue the Earnshaw line, whether Hareton will end up taking after Heathcliff despite the lack of blood relation, whether, in the end, the book presents a comic or tragic view—all these questions remain unresolved. The future is left uncertain, further destabilized by the possibility that an undead, ghostly Heathcliff persists into the future.

Even though it presents a bleak account of human nature and does not provide for a guaranteed happy ending, *Wuthering Heights* nonetheless is a book that is important in the evolution of literature and redemption insofar as it reintroduces the element of love into the literary understanding of redemption. In the novel, the possibility of redemption lies in the love of Cathy and Hareton while Heathcliff, the unredeemed, neither loves nor is loved. The suffering in the book opens as Heathcliff disrupts the economy of love—taking from the father what Hindley thought ought to be his. Heathcliff continues such disruptions throughout the text, stealing Catherine's love from Edgar and Hareton's love from Hindley. This is the heart of Heathcliff's unredemptive nature, and why the possibility of redemption requires for him to die in order to allow love to exist once more.

Thus the effect of *Wuthering Heights*, like *Frankenstein*, is to unsettle views of redemption as certainties. Moving further than *Frankenstein*, Brontë also undermines the possibilities of storytelling or death to provide redemption (at least positively). Instead, Brontë troubles the binary established above, centring the possibility of redemption on love, but in an importantly negative sense. Redemption comes as a possibility with the death of the fiend, not with the certainty caused by the martyrdom of a saint or the unconditional love of a God. Brontë unsettles all previous anchors of redemption, exchanging certainties for possibilities.

Tess of the D'Urbervilles

Written towards the end of the nineteenth century, Thomas Hardy's novel *Tess of the D'Urbervilles: A Pure Woman* (1891) continues to look for redemption in a world in which both redemption and salvation are apparently absent. Placing the book in the context where the humans are the sport of the immortals (picking up on the theme of helplessness in the face of fate which *Frankenstein* also discusses), Hardy mocks the possibility of suffering being redemptive or able to provide any sort of meaning at all. In this world, sorrow begets sorrow and suffering begets suffering. As in *Wuthering Heights*, the hope of redemption is found in death—yet in a different way than that outlined by Brontë.

It is possible to look at Hardy as constructing a new argument on the foundations laid by Brontë, one that probes what it could mean to be unredeemed. Hardy does much to build the character of Tess in a way that parallels that of Heathcliff. Like Heathcliff, Tess destabilizes possible relationships by being inserted between characters, who, because of Tess, are denied fulfilling relationships. Like Heathcliff, Tess redeems others by dying, remaining unredeemed herself: death is a place where she can find fulfilment and wholeness—but her wholeness remains a hole, empty, ending as it begins. The dead in Hardy, unlike the ghosts of Brontë, sleep on unknowing. There is no afterlife hope of reconciliation. The removal of Tess—like that of

Heathcliff—allows another couple to move forward into the future together (in this case, Angel Clare with 'Liza-Lu, the spiritualized version of Tess).

Yet Tess marks an important addition to what is able to be included in a literary understanding of redemption: while she seems to conform to the form of Brontë's brute, the content of her character is radically different. This much, at least, is suggested by the subtitle which Hardy chose: 'A Pure Woman'. Both characters can be read as being non-redeemable, but Hardy unsettles the reader by expanding the possibilities for the unredeemed to include someone as gentle and loveable as Heathcliff is not. Tess's status as the unredeemed redeemer could be explained through two separate readings. First, Tess is written as a discontinuous character: there seems to be no core or central Tess who can be saved. In fact, much of Tess's agony lies in her inability to cling to any consistent sense of identity. A second reading could suggest that Tess is already a pure woman (by nature) and so, as such, requires no redemption. If it can be said that Brontë begins to blur the theological and literary understandings of redemption, Hardy can be said to bring the literary even closer to the theological by creating a pure central character who, punished unjustly throughout her life and into her death, mediates the redemption of others.

In addition to Tess as redeemer, Hardy's literary interrogation of the possibility for redemption can also be seen in the characters who are redeemed by Tess. Whereas Brontë's redeemed couple seemed a relatively obvious choice (the only central characters of marrying age left alive), Hardy constructs a world where the criterion for determining who is redeemed is much more nebulous. This, perhaps, is a more important move than that shown by Tess: rather than continuing to show that death fails to redeem those who die, or showing how a pure death can be as negatively redemptive as the death of the wicked, Hardy presents a world in which redemption operates randomly, rejecting any sort of causal structure upon which other narratives of redemption depended. Hardy constructs Angel Clare and Alec D'Urberville as doubles: both acknowledge the same man as a father (Angel biologically, Alec spiritually) from whom both end up turning away. Both are said to be husband to Tess, both are the chief causes of her misery and suffering, and both attempt to cover their crimes in the clothing of Christianity. The choice to redeem Angel (who refuses to consummate the marriage and abandons her) and not Alec (who rapes Tess and yet attempts to provide for her) seems either to speak to repentance as a random process, or one which favours those who by nature are spiritual (Angel, 'Liza-Lu) instead of earthly (Tess, Alec). Thus, while Hardy leaves open the possibility for death to be redeeming, the way that redemption is framed as either random or preordained (in either case left out of the individual's hands) simultaneously points to the need for individuals to mediate their own redemption (lest they be played as sport for immortals) and continues to erode the foundation on which this belief could be built.

Dracula

By undermining the security even of death (expanding on the doubts created by Brontë's ghosts) Bram Stoker's novel *Dracula* (1897) nonetheless rehabilitates death and storytelling as possibilities for mediating redemption. Accepting the worldview left by Hardy, that individual redemption is a futile endeavour, Stoker shifts the focus to the efforts of a group: while an individual's death may save neither the self nor another, the efforts of a group are shown to bear redemptive fruit. The novel, like *Tess*, includes fragmented personalities instead of a consistent core character, but by allowing the personalities to inhabit separate bodies, Stoker reinforces the redemptive possibility of the group in the face of individual annihilation.

Dracula fits nicely into the lineage of nineteenth-century novels discussed above, bearing a relation to the problems that surfaced in those novels individually. Stoker's answer to the question of how redemption is possible is thus an important one. The centre of the novel is an inhuman fiend, but worse than Frankenstein's monster, lacking the creature's original moral sensibilities. Like Heathcliff, Dracula is the father of a family whose death is required for redemption to occur. Both Mina and Lucy, like Tess and Clarissa, have their bodies violated against their will, a violation that produces suffering (which, in the case of Lucy, does not lead to redemption). The possibility of a fiend haunting in the shadows merges the threats of Frankenstein and Heathcliff in a more personal and sexualized way. But by making the unredeemable element of the text non-human, Stoker is able to disambiguate the notions of good and evil that troubled *Frankenstein*, *Wuthering Heights*, and *Tess*, ameliorating the process of redemption. This avoids the troubling notion that wickedness and evil are of human origin and shifts the focus once more on to how to redeem the suffering of the innocent.

Stoker, corresponding to the authors already mentioned, takes seriously the problems and questions raised concerning the possibility of attaining redemption but shows how a group can overcome the problems which an individual faces. Lucy and Jonathon suffer, but their suffering is not redeemed. Lucy dies, but while her flesh remains beautiful, she is nonetheless deadly. Far from redeeming the efforts of those who gave their blood to save her, she instead forces them to kill her again. Yet the form of the novel—resembling *Clarissa* in so far as it is a collection of fragments of other texts—serves to depersonalize the search for redemption. Instead of focusing on the apotheosis of the heroine (as Richardson did), the quest is the destruction of the titular character who (again unlike Clarissa) is denied a voice in the published fragments. The possibility of redemption is found only in the group as a whole, each member of the group possessing a unique characteristic or trait. The final efforts of the group are redeemed and embodied in the birth of Quincy Harker (this Quincy a memorial to the one who died in the final assault on Dracula). With Dracula's death, brought about by a joint effort, all of the living and the dead are redeemed. In telling Quincy Harker the story of what happened, the redemption will extend to future generations as well. By showing the success of group efforts, Stoker resurrects the possibilities for redemption raised in *Frankenstein* and denied in *Wuthering Heights*: storytelling and death.

In the end, because the space of the father has been filled with the face of the fiend, Dracula offers a picture of redemption much more palatable than those which preceded it, able on one hand to acknowledge the inability of individuals to confront the real terror of modern existence, while on the other asserting that redemption is nonetheless attainable as a mass in a way which depends only on the brave spirits of the human, not on the heart of an altruistic God. Nonetheless, even though the novel closes all the problems it opens (specific to the undead of Dracula), the need to be vigilant even over the dead to ensure death causes the reader to place faith exclusively in the bravery of a collective, instead of in death or anything lying beyond.

TWENTIETH CENTURY: REDEMPTION THROUGH TIME

By the middle of the twentieth century, death seemed to be as insecure a foundation for redemption as suffering. After the large-scale devastation and destruction that the World Wars and Holocaust wreaked upon the world, there was no need (or even option) to create narratives around such monsters as Dracula or Frankenstein. Something other than death or suffering, hopefully more certain, would need to be explored. Time, both impersonal and inevitable, became a third sphere that authors began to test as a foundation for redemption. The examination of time is not limited to science fiction. Instead, highlighting the element of time enables a return to the form of the individual's journey, important considering the dangers of masses and groups evidenced at the beginning of the century. Yet, although novels once again focus on the possibility for an individual to be redeemed, it should not be seen as a simple return to the redemptive efforts of the individual. By focusing on the redemptive qualities of time, experienced by all, the authors are able to circumvent the potential difficulty of dealing with fickle deities pointed out by Hardy.

A Clockwork Orange

Burgess's 1962 novel manages to show the need for redemption, its possibility to be mediated socially (as opposed to through individual or divine efforts), and the futility of all mediation in the face of time. The book is divided into thirds: the first part focuses on the extremely violent actions of the narrator, Alex, who conforms to the model of a prodigal son (with the addition of nastiness to the hedonism of Jesus's original character). The second part shows three different attempts at mediating Alex's redemption: religion, state, and science. Science—specifically a type of Pavlovian brainwashing that causes him to become nauseated when confronted with violence—allows Alex to rejoin society. The third part shows the ultimate failure of science truly to redeem Alex as he is left defenceless in a cruel world; the treatment is reversed and Alex is left alone.

The American version of the book—and the 1971 film by Stanley Kubrik—both end at this point. The British edition of the book includes one more chapter, where Alex meets another of his old gang, who now is married, and begins to realize that it may be time, at 18 years of age, to get married and have a son of his own. In reflection, he believes that the danger of youth is 'being like one of these malenky toys you viddy being sold in the streets...you wind it up grr grr grr and off it itties, like walking...But it itties in a straight line and bangs straight into things bang bang and it cannot help what it is doing' (Burgess 1986: 217). Burgess writes that the inclusion of the twenty-first chapter was not only intentional, but also meant to symbolize the completeness of the age of maturity (ibid. p. vi). There is no need for a father to redeem the son by love, there is no need for suffering, no need for death: time is all that is required for redemption to occur.

It is in this way that Burgess is able to show the problems with the collective or group solution to redemption, and come once again to the possibility of an individual's redemption, focusing on the possibility of being redeemed in this life, not the next. All that is required for redemption is growing up, maturing: the prodigal son will, by nature, return home of his own accord. If the father fails to welcome him, Burgess indicates that the son will simply be able to start a new family. Love becomes as unnecessary as suffering, society, or death as time alone is able to heal, restore, and redeem.

Time's Arrow

Martin Amis takes a different approach to the notion of time's redemptive power in his novel *Time's Arrow* (1991). The novel begins with the death and ends with the birth of the object-character (introduced as Tod T. Friendly), and the narrator (who both is and is not the character) is forced merely to watch as Friendly moves, in reverse, ever closer to his birth. The life is an interesting one: Friendly, a doctor, steals toys from children and beats prostitutes, who return to their pimps in order to be healed. Relationships 'begin' with a passionate argument, and 'end' with women walking away as if they had never met. In time, the mysteries of Friendly's life (why he becomes upset hearing about the Second World War, dislikes the 'other language' that he sometimes hears, or dislikes the smell of fire (especially fingernails in the fire)) are solved as the narrator sees Friendly redeem his history of cruelty to others: at Auschwitz, the object-character helps make people from the ashy weather with the help of Zyklon B. Eventually, Friendly, becoming ever smaller, returns to his mother's womb, innocent.

Life viewed from the narrator's perspective seems to need to be redeemed for the same reasons as Friendly would have viewed it. Death and suffering still exist, only the cause-and-effect relationship has been altered. However, even though bringing a roomful of people to life out of the sky's ashes (a return of the dream of Frankenstein) may redeem the object-character's history of violence to children and patients, the question of whether or not Tod T. Friendly's efforts as doctor and benefactor in his later years redeemed his past in the Nazi camps remains open. Does this type of temporal reversal merely place life in a different perspective, or is this a new (or the only?) path towards redemption? If Tod T. Friendly can be seen as a prodigal son, the re-entry into the womb shows the ultimate return home, having placed his future crimes safely in the past: is this the only guarantee of redemption?

The trick of time that Amis plays leads to an incredibly controlled and determined world: the narrator describes what happens without having any ability to interfere or intervene. The world is exclusively populated by clockwork oranges who behave as programmed. What the narrator sees is simultaneously absurd and placed outside the realm of morality, ethics, or religion. Suffering, death, religion, society—everything is obviated in the face of absolute certainty. Is this how we may be redeemed? And how greatly does this differ from the universal assurance of the love of a Heavenly Father?

Perhaps the key to understanding the role of redemption in the book rests not in the redeemed—the object-character—but on the narrator who continually watches over the character whom he simultaneously is and is not. The narrator is unable to be categorized as either redeemed or redeemer. While he identifies with the object-character at times, he is nevertheless simultaneously always distinct. In addition, his vigilance over Tod T. Friendly does not redeem him—again, this seems to be the role of time. Yet the role of vigilance is undoubtedly important, because the object-character is unaware of the reversal of time's arrow: it is through being observed and having the narrative related that redemption can occur.

Beyond suffering and beyond death, however, the possibility of being redeemed through experiencing a story persists even in Amis's world of reversals. The questions of whether or not I forgive the object-character his 'past', and whether or not I believe that I as a human can be redeemed are raised only because it is possible to experience a narrative, only because I can understand things as causally related. The promise of Amis's present is completely different from that which Burgess offers, simultaneously more optimistic and more pessimistic. The optimism is rooted in believing that there is the hope for redemption even for those who do not mature as they age: the pessimism comes from the impossibility of this form of redemption, from not knowing whether or not we will make the narrator's trip backwards as we die. The roles of vigilance and storytelling, reaffirmed in Amis's novel, point to a new way in which literature interprets the role of the Father. If the placement of observer within the self is as important to Amis's understanding of redemption as the reversal of time, then redemption may be within reach after all.

LITERATURE AS THE POSSIBILITY
OF REDEMPTION

As time progresses, suspicion over the possibility of anything 'certain' continues to grow. The theological view of redemption, resting in the ever-open arms of a Heavenly Father who remains vigilant for a lost son's reappearance seems, for some, a less than compelling view in a world that appears beyond the hope of redemption. The focus of the novel on the journey of the child may be dark and disturbing, or might challenge and undermine its own conclusions regarding by what means redemption is possible. However, as Bunyan surely realized, there is some comfort in the experience of a narrative. Every narrative, no matter how pessimistic its view of human nature, has at least the hope of redemption that Amis brings forth: that of reversibility.

Literature also broadens the scope of redemption beyond what some theologians would allow, questioning the possibility of different saviours and exploring redemptions that do not require salvation. Although these options often include a view of humanity at its most corrupt and fallen, it complements a theological perspective which some think fails to take the worst of human nature into account: while perhaps no person would be as evil and corrupt as Heathcliff or Dracula, the experimentation possible in literature working towards how narratives enable redemption is, at the very least, interesting. At most, literature is a necessary supplement to theological understandings of redemption, opening out ways in which we, as humans and as storytellers, can be redeemed.

WORKS CITED

AMIS, MARTIN. 1992. *Time's Arrow*. New York: Vintage.
BRONTË, EMILY. 1992. *Wuthering Heights*. Boston: Bedford Books of St Martin's Press.
BUNYAN, JOHN. 1987. *Pilgrim's Progress*. New York: Penguin.
BURGESS, ANTHONY. 1986. *A Clockwork Orange*. New York: Ballantine.
HARDY, THOMAS. 1998. *Tess of the D'Urbervilles*. Boston: Bedford Books of St Martin's Press.
RICHARDSON, SAMUEL. 1985. *Clarissa*. New York: Penguin.
SHELLEY, MARY. 1992. *Frankenstein*. New York: Penguin.
STOKER, BRAM. 2003. *Dracula*. New York: Penguin.

FURTHER READING

ADORNO, THEODOR W. 1997. *Aesthetic Theory*. Minneapolis: University of Minnesota Press.
FIEDLER, LESLIE A. 1967. *Love and Death in the American Novel*. London: Jonathan Cape.

SHERRY, PATRICK. 2003. *Images of Redemption: Art, Literature and Salvation*. London: Continuum.

STEWART, GARRETT. 1996. *Dear Reader: The Conscripted Reader in Nineteenth-Century British Fiction*. Baltimore: Johns Hopkins University Press.

CHAPTER 46

....

BODY AND WORD

....

ALISON JASPER

He is my helper and my enemy, my assistant and my opponent, a protector and a traitor.

(John Climacus)

INTRODUCTION:
THE WORD BECAME FLESH

....

In the twenty-first century scholars increasingly approach body and embodiment as a critical theme or discursive category and in this context it is clear that Christianity is not the first or only ideology to use, shape, and exploit the perceived pleasures, needs, and shortcomings of the body and embodiment to its own ends. Nevertheless Christianity appears to have been the source of some very powerful ideas about the body in European societies, at least since Constantine adopted it as the 'official' religion of the Roman Empire at the beginning of the fourth century.

There is today something of a common assumption that Christianity has always been implacably hostile in respect of the body or human embodiment. But theological sources reveal a story with a different and perhaps more predictable emphasis. The evidence suggests that the prevailing theological attitude to the body throughout this long period has been one, not so much of unrelieved negativity, as of equivocation. In words attributed to John Climacus, the seventh-century Syrian abbot of Mt. Sinai, for example, the body is viewed as both a helper *and* an enemy,

an assistant *and* an opponent, a protector *and* a traitor. And this Christian equivocation about sexual enjoyment, health and fitness, longevity, beauty, adornment,
physical cruelty, gender, sexuality, and the training of the body is clearly also reflected
in the work of writers of English poetry, drama, and literature to a significant degree
for well over a thousand years. Even in its earliest debates, in formulating the
extraordinary doctrines of incarnation and bodily resurrection, Christian leaders
and theologians have been strongly divided on the subject of body and embodiment,
moved by both extreme reverence and by an equally notable anxiety. They have
provided innumerable authors since that period with a palette of very strong colours
with which to enrich their own varied texts and narratives about embodied, human
existence, revealing a characteristic ambivalence about the value of human incarnation in the context of longings and hopes that often appear to transcend it.

In the Christian 'Old Testament', God's disembodied words (Gen. 1: 1) bring into
being all the features of the material world including embodied women and men, and
yet God himself remains excluded or 'protected'. God is the source, but the ineffa-
bility of his divinity is not risked by being brought any closer into contact with
materiality as it is linked—as a sort of contaminant—with human embodment. It
was then, hugely significant that Christianity should make the frankly sacrilegious
connection and claim, going further than the Hebrew invocation of divine creativity[1]
and order had ever done, that 'the Word became flesh' (John 1: 14). Thereafter,
human embodment can no longer be dismissed as mere materiality or creatureliness
since God was Jesus, in the vulnerability and extreme limitation of his historical,
human embodment just as much as he is Creator or indwelling yet immaterial
Spirit. Within the Christian dispensation, God's divine Word has not simply formed
and breathed life into material being from a safely disembodied position, screened off
from its risks, but, expressing the highest validation of that human embodment,
generated very flesh himself.

Yet it makes little sense to deny that in seventeen centuries, across the whole of
Europe into Asia Minor, and in the wake of massive colonial exploration and
expansion, Christianity's views of body and embodment have sometimes been less
than positive. Even though it is a state of existence created, sanctified and, more than
this, shared by God in divine incarnation, Christianity has also always assumed that
we need a bodily resurrection (1 Cor. 15: 12–19). Through their symbolic incorpor-
ation into the community of Christ's followers in baptism, Christians are invited to
escape from the finality of death, that otherwise defining bodily event, and to live and
flourish in the distinctive resurrection body (see 1 Cor. 15: 35–58). By describing the
Church as the sacramental body of Christ in the world, Christianity has clearly placed
a very high value on embodment as the defining form of God's involvement in
creation and in the ordering of human society (see 1 Cor. 12: 12–31; Rom. 12: 4–8). Yet

---

[1] The Johannine formulation of this fundamental Christian doctrine makes connections between the
creative word of God as it is described in Genesis and also personified in Hebrew and Greek Wisdom
literature as the female figure of Wisdom, with the Greek word λογος meaning word as the inward
thought or the principle of order and reason itself (Liddell and Scott, 1899).

even within that body of the Church, human life is, in fact, still subject to poverty, disease, ignorance, physical pain, the violence of desire, and particularly the finality of death. Even for the wealthy and fortunate, embodied existence is never entirely or consistently blissful. Even the wealthy and fortunate must die. To have appealed so widely and for so long, it is arguable that Christian theologians have always needed to acknowledge this darker side of embodiment and, crucially, to account for the persistence of death within the realm of material flesh[2] in God's paradisal creation.

The answer to which they typically resorted was, of course, that this blissful creation has been marred by human sinfulness and that this is what has brought suffering and death into an original paradise of unreflective innocence and what now maintains it there, even though their ultimate eradication may not, by virtue of Christ's own sacrificial death, be in doubt. Negativity about the body and embodiment finds its key expression in the term 'flesh' ($\sigma\alpha\rho\xi$) which appears in the Johannine formulation of 'The Word became flesh' (John 1: 14). 'Flesh' is the loaded term which refers to the body's supposedly intractable connection with wilful disobedience or unregulated desire, most powerfully configured in the narratives of creation as Christians inherit them from the Hebrew book of Genesis: when the bodily senses and appetites of the first man and woman were engaged in the service of their desire for forbidden knowledge (Gen. 3: 6), then disaster followed, including the 'disaster' of their fall into a knowledge of sexuality, of the difference between clothed and naked (Gen. 3: 11), and of the misery of sexual desire (Gen. 3: 16). This 'flesh' then is not the created body per se, but, at the end of Gen. 3, the equivocal embodiment of creatures expelled from the garden and from the presence of God into the realm characterized by knowledge, growth, and procreation, but also by thankless labour, patriarchal oppression, pain, and, most of all, death.

The use of the term 'flesh' does not then absolutely conflict with a principle of bodily goodness since God's original creation and intention for humankind's increase is good (Gen. 1: 26–31). But the link made between sin, embodiment with strong sexual overtones, and death within the Genesis narrative of creation and fall, and reproduced within Christian theology (for example, Rom. 5: 12–14; 1 Cor. 15: 12–19; Heb. 2: 14–18), makes 'flesh' sometimes seem synonymous with sinfulness, especially in its sexuality.[3] And the purity of body or embodiment is idealized beyond

[2] Christianity makes the demarcation between Word and flesh more extreme than either the creation story of Plato's *Timaeus*, for example, or the Genesis account, both of which presuppose that before anything took shape there was formless but nevertheless pre-existing materiality. In the Johannine account, 'Word' comes first, pre-exists any material, and calls being out of nothing.

[3] It is notable, of course, that although the Word became 'flesh', the picture of Jesus in the New Testament is entirely uninformative about his sexuality. There is no mention of marriage or of a wife. Some of the so-called 'apocryphal Gospels' unearthed in the 1940s at Nag Hammadi—established as mostly second-century documents strongly influenced by various forms of dualistic Gnosticism—give the figure of Mary Magdalene a larger role as one of the important followers of Jesus. In some cases—for example the *Gospel of Philip*—there is reference to Jesus kissing her. This has led to some fictional speculation at least that she might have been Jesus' wife or partner (see e.g. Roberts 1984). However, it is also possible that this intimacy is more symbolic than real, with Magdalene taking on, in some form, the personified role of Divine Sophia—God's creative Word in action—as represented in various traditions of Wisdom literature. See Pagels 1979.

realization except in eschatological and asexual terms. As a result, even if the body is not understood to be the root of the problem, it becomes necessarily subject to strict discipline and regulation in order to mitigate the consequences of body-bound, 'fleshly' thinking and motivations.

In consequence, men and women of the Christian era have been taught to be generally very circumspect or indeed downright suspicious around their bodies. They have been taught to distrust their feelings and bodily impulses as guides to wisdom and well-being because, in their connection to death, these too are thought to bear the traces of an ineradicable tendency to sinfulness. Augustine (354–430 CE), for example, saw sexual desire leading to genital sex as the mechanism whereby this tendency to sin, and thus death, is actually passed on from generation to generation. He didn't believe that this meant sex had to be avoided entirely. He even argued that sexual pleasure could be a 'pardonable indulgence' (*De Bono Coniugali* 2001: p. xviii) in marriage but he still makes it quite clear that the purpose of sanctified sexual intercourse—that is, within heterosexual marriage—should be the 'productive' business of procreation and that the best marriages were those in which there is as little sex as possible outside that definitive purpose. Sexuality is not, for Augustine, a good in itself. Even better than pleasurable intercourse leading to conception is bodily continence and holy virginity (*De Sancta Virginitate*: Augustine 2001: 7; see also Irigaray 2004). Sex is a problematic bodily activity with a godly purpose, framed in terms of the complementarity of women and men, but bearing a shameful stigma.

THE *ANCRENE WISSE* OR *GUIDE FOR ANCHORESSES* AND THE DELIGHTS OF DISCIPLINE

A relatively early example of the sort of literary equivocation about body and embodiment to which I am referring can be identified in the *Ancrene Wisse*[4] or *Guide for Anchoresses*—a manual read in both Middle English and Anglo Norman[5] from the early 13th Century and written by an unknown author for three well-born women who were about to dedicate their lives to God.[6] On the face of it, the *Guide for Anchoresses* (hereafter the *Guide*) reflects a deep distrust and anxiety about the

---

[4] I follow Bella Millett's usage of 'Wisse' rather than 'Riwle' as explained in Wada 2003. The edition referred to here, however, was translated from the Early Middle English, Corpus MS: *Ancrene Wisse*, by M. B. Salu and published in 1955 under the title *Ancrene Riwle*. I have therefore referred to this edition throughout as *Ancrene Riwle* or 'AR'.

[5] Anglo-Norman versions of this text remain in use into the fifteenth century. See Wogan-Browne 2001: 13.

[6] This was a largely solitary religious vocation in which the anchoress or anchorite typically spent the rest of their life in prayerful contemplation often installed in a single room or cell attached to a church. Sometimes, they could be approached for advice or counsel.

circumstances of embodied human existence that is transient and vulnerable to war, disease, and death and which, in terms of a Christian narrative, has already been corrupted by the actions of Eve 'our first mother' (*AR* 2001: 23) and needs firm control and regulation if it is not to lead us astray all over again. Already we seem to be steeped in the misogyny that associates women with a corrupted and corrupting materialism and leads both men and women away from engagement with their own embodiment as a source of positive physical or spiritual pleasure and energy. In the *Guide* the body's senses provide the aspiring anchoress with nothing but troublesome distraction and temptation. Just as Eve's eyes led her inexorably to taste the forbidden fruit, it is the sight of someone of the opposite sex that inflames both and leads them into mortal sin. Just as 'cackling Eve' let the devil know her weakness through her chattering tongue, like a hen whose noise draws the egg thief to her eggs (ibid. 29), so it is the tongue that leads the anchoress into pride in her own accomplishments (ibid. 28). Her ears let in gossip and backbiting which poison her repose and tempt her to indulgence of other sins. The advice is to shut out the outside world and distrust these bodily senses. Yet, interwoven with this manifest hostility and distrust, the joys of her spiritual path and its rewards are couched for the anchoress in consistently sensuous language that absolutely parallels the perils of her calling. There is no better way to describe the joys of heaven, it appears, than precisely in terms of what must, here and now, be censored or renounced:

But anchoresses, here enclosed, shall there have even more lightness and swiftness than others, if any can, and shall be as little shackled as they play in the wide pastures of heaven that the body shall be wherever the soul desires, in an instant... and anchoresses see God's hidden mysteries and decrees the more clearly who now, through the custody of their eyes and ear, give small attention to outward things. (ibid. 41)

And references abound in the *Guide* to the biblical Song of Songs, an ancient Hebrew poetic text featuring extremely sensuous language and erotic images. Both Jewish and Christian traditions witness to the Song of Songs as a metaphorical description of God's love for his people, or of Christ's love for the Church (Brenner 1993: 30). Yet, it is notable, in the work of St Bernard (1090–1153)—whose writing was clearly influential for the author of the *Guide*—that there is no absolute distinction between souls and bodies such that bodies and their material conditions can be safely disregarded or dismissed in the next life. Bernard sometimes refers to the body as 'miserable flesh' or 'foul and fetid flesh' ('*Sed unde hoc tibi, o misera caro, o foeda, o foetida unde tibi hoc?*'—Bernard of Clairvaux 1957–77: v. para. 2) but he also sees persons as souls together with bodies. For this reason, the resurrection of the body is essential and the soul is joyfully reunited with the body: 'Do not be surprised if the glorified body seems to give the spirit something, for it was a real help when man was sick and mortal... Truly the soul does not want to be perfected without that from whose good services it feels it has benefited in every way' (Bernard of Clairvaux 1974: sect. 11, paras. 30–3). Clearly whatever the limitations and troubles of the mortal life or the anxieties accorded by the body, resurrection *without* the body is not on the cards, and the sensual language of the *Guide* gains in nuance by this intertextual reference to Bernard's commentary. Certainly in the *Guide*, the anchoress is encouraged to envisage her relationship with God in the most flagrantly erotic terms. Our Lord's kiss is 'a sweetness and a delight of heart so immeasurably sweet that every worldly savour is bitter in comparison' (*AR* 2001: 44), and Jesus Christ chooses her for his beloved, her sweet voice and fair face being prized by him and him alone (ibid. 42–4). Of course, it is also clear in this text that 'the animal man who gives no thought to God' (ibid. 25) is body ruled by appetite and self-interest and must be controlled. This comparison with dark brutishness even implies a certain appreciation of its strength and vitality, but the very evident anxiety about control still confirms the idea that the author puts little confidence in human senses as the means to do the job. And yet it is the sensuous rather than the self-sacrificing nature of human love that provides the model for divine love, just as Bernard, once again making reference to the body's powerful appetites, describes resurrected embodied souls as 'drunk with love' (*Treatises* II Bernard of Clairvaux 1974: v). In any event, equivocation is seen in this example not as any kind of lukewarm antipathy to the body in general but as a powerful coincidence of sometimes quite passionately contradictory approaches to embodiment.

John Donne and the Delights of Bondage

The sixteenth and seventeenth centuries describe a period when Renaissance philosophy and art were beginning to allow a renewed and expanded engagement with classical Greek and Latin readings of the physical body in Western Europe. In the attention it devoted to the aesthetic values of the body,[7] for example, and even more explicitly, in its various well-developed senses of hierarchy,[8] these classical literary and philosophical intertexts have undoubtedly also contributed significantly to views of the body expressed in English literature. At this time, the body appears newly dressed as an object of scientific or medical enquiry and as a bearer of value, a revelation of divine beauty, goodness, and truth. Nevertheless, embodied existence is still characterized by unavoidable transience and vulnerability. This use of sensuality which pays homage to the powerful appeal of embodied, emotive, and sexual existence whilst also expressing fear of its potential to endanger a soul whose destiny, by God's grace, transcends the present moment, continues to be reflected for many centuries within the English language and not least in the writing of the metaphysical poets of the early seventeenth century, including John Donne.

---

[7] Artists and architects such as Leonardo Da Vinci (1452–1519) and Leon Battista Alberti (1404–72) referred to the work of the first-century BCE Roman architect and engineer, Marcus Vitruvius Pollio, whose architectural values, expressed in *De Architectura*, reflected a perceived connection between values in architecture and the idealized proportions of the human body.

[8] Writing about Plato's *Timaeus* as one of the foundational stories for Christian Europe, Rosemary Radford Ruether (1992: 24) comments, 'the just and ordered society corresponds to the hierarchy of the well-ordered self, with mind in control, the will under the lead of reason, and the appetites controlled by both'.

Of course Donne (1572–1631) is a man of his age, living in a climate of different spiritual and intellectual change and challenge from that of the *Guide for Anchoresses*. A contemporary of both Descartes and Hobbes, he is writing poetry in an age of intellectual and colonial exploration, in which printed books on an ever-widening field of experience and information are available to a university-educated man such as himself. He clearly has a personal history outside the clerical profession on which he does not scruple to draw. His youthful sexual adventures are immortalized in such poems as 'The Good Morrow' and 'The Flea', and the contrasts he later makes between this 'profane love' (Holy Sonnets vi; Gardner 1972: 99) and his love for God represent a disruption of traditional values and attitudes informed by taste and experience that go someway outside the purview of Christian theology or spirituality. Yet we also hear within Donne's poetry a very Christian theological concern for the communal 'body' of Christ's Church on earth within which the individual Christian must recognize his or her 'mutual duties' ('Good Lord, Deliver us!'; ibid. 95). This Christian voice challenges the smoothing out, depletion, or reduction incipient in views of the body determined by the energies of the emergent capitalist ideology of the age, for example, in so far as it reaffirms a view of body as a set of complex relationships determined as much by the Christian theological context of spiritual and communal values as by the freer play of material considerations. In the sensuality of language and the revealing imagery, especially of imprisonment—which reflects its framing in terms of both the Platonic view of embodiment (see Spelman 1999: 36) and Christian notions of atonement and redemption—Donne resists all attempts to dilute the fundamental irony and equivocation of Christian incarnation. In his poetry, the Christian is characterized as an anchorite, imprisoned in his own filth, or the unborn child, inhabiting prison/religious cells which are both body and womb ('The Progress of the Soul'; Gardner 1972: 100–1). Yet though eventually 'we must wake eternally when death shall be no more' (Holy Sonnets iii; ibid. 97), exulting in our liberation, the very thought that 'this earth | Is only for our prison framed' ('Good Lord, Deliver Us'; ibid. 95) is itself a prison from which Donne seeks deliverance. And what ultimately delivers Donne is God's own 'wellbelov'd imprisonment', which is to say 'Immensitie cloystered' in the dear womb of his mother (Holy Sonnets, 'La Corona'; Jasper and Prickett 1999: 209) and the mystery of God's own 'becoming body'.

WOLLSTONECRAFT AND THE BODY OF WOMEN AS A GILT CAGE

As English poets, writers and literary figures move into the eighteenth and nineteenth centuries is there still the same degree of 'drawing on' Christian understanding of body and embodiment as in earlier centuries? Attitudes are undoubtedly changing but a vocabulary of concepts, ideas, and ideological concerns from the past, albeit increasingly confused and at odds with each other, still remain current or at least significant. Mary Wollstonecraft (1759–97) lived at a time when respect for human rationality, viewed largely or completely apart from its divine Creator, vied with an equally powerful but very different Romantic sensibility that favoured emotion and feeling over reason and other traditional hegemonies or forms of power, including established religion. Against this combination of adversaries, evangelical Christianity in particular still sought to maintain its hold on an ever more slippery surface, sometimes by returning to the seeming certainties of a patriarchal Reformation faith in divine revelation through Scripture and the implicit social regulation of a fundamentally Calvinist economy. Yet over all, greater freedom from the authority of the church in political and social affairs gave scope and space for reviewing established categories, including the canons of Christian incarnational theology and, of course, its striking equivocations about body and embodiment.

Wollstonecraft appears to have had no quarrel with the idea of a providential God for most of her life, yet she did not hesitate to criticize attitudes which she believed to degrade women even when these coincided with conventional Christian opinion. It was undoubtedly her concern for the values of liberty and equality in the mode of Enlightenment rationality and revolutionary politics rather than a concern for, for example, the proper exercise of Christian responsibility or the better modelling of some notion of spiritual womanhood[9], that framed her concern for the issues of women's embodiment. In so far as she considered human beings subject to divine authority, she believed that men and women best cooperated with the Supreme Being by cultivating their reason as far as they could (Wollstonecraft 1992: 102). This made her more than a little critical of influential contemporary views of womanhood which drew, for example, on the biblical figure of Eve and had perhaps been given their most iconic expression in Milton's epic poem, *Paradise Lost* (1667—see e.g. Gilbert and Gubar 1984: 30–3; Daggers 2002: 4–6). Wollstonecraft suggested that Milton at least was demanding to have his cake and eat it too in the figure of Eve he created. He appeared to intimate, she suggested, that the ideal woman (Eve) conforms to what are sensually rooted (male) fantasies (Wollstonecraft 1992: 102) of soft and beautiful feminine embodiment—in which women behave as gently brutish, undemanding creatures, within an idyll of domestic orderliness and regulated reproduction—while at the same time expecting her to be the perfect companion and friend, intellectually and morally capable of sharing her husband's burdens and entering into all his practical and spiritual concerns. Wollstonecraft wants to persuade her readers that an education focused on maintaining in girls an undemanding softness is unlikely to yield much in the way of intellectual or spiritual companionship! She, of course, argues strongly that women and men *both* need to be educated to think and use their reason.

---

[9] An interesting comparison might be made here with the work of Wollstonecraft's contemporary, Hannah More. For example, More's novel, *Coelebs in Search of a Wife* (1809), while presenting a much more glowing account of Milton's Eve, also voices some disapprobation of Milton's tendency to sentimentalize her character in stereotypical terms (ibid. ii. 289).

Her evaluation of contemporary manners and education neither draws on nor is a critique of Christian theology in a direct sense. However, in so far as the stereotypical roles of men and women current at the time—which she largely deplores[10]—draw on Christian equivocation about body and women's bodies in particular, she could be said to be responding to it indirectly. Arguably what she is addressing is the sense in which Christian references to the sexualized body as a sign of human fleshliness or carnality in general have been subtly grafted onto a series of female stereotypes establishing, overall, a gendered view of bodily fragility, weakness, and moral inferiority and helping to provide a rationale for female objectification in terms of male desire. In general terms justifications provided for practices limiting or belittling to women at this period appear—as with Milton's Eve—to be controlling forms of idealization. A slightly later and similar idealization was the Victorian 'angel in the house'.[11] This conceptual trope within Victorian literature and thought traded in the reverential mystification of women yet undoubtedly also imprisoned them within the idealization of certain sorts of female body and behaviour, an alienating symbol for men as well as women in the vibrant variety of their actual lived experiences of human embodied relationships. Taking her stand on the principles of equality and liberty, Wollstonecraft, presaging later arguments within feminist theory, challenges the stereotyping, holding on to the argument that our views of womanhood are not so 'naturally' constituted but, to an important extent, formed by conventional practice that can be changed through education: 'Men and women must be educated, in a great degree by the opinions and manners of the society they live in' (Wollstonecraft 1992: 102).

Nevertheless with respect to the body in general Wollstonecraft clearly demonstrates a familiar equivocation echoing prevailing views on the subject. She adopts the hierarchical view of (male) Enlightenment thinkers—that sits quite comfortably at some points with traditional Christian teaching—that the body had to be transcended and that the power of reason was to be preferred to unregulated passion or untutored feeling. This is perhaps understandable since it was by pursuing a rational subjectivity that women of Wollstonecraft's class and period in history could most successfully provide themselves—by writing and publishing—with some culturally sanctioned and legitimated means of escape from a suffocating conformity to the cultural stereotypes described by Wollstonecraft (ibid. 103) as a distortion into 'useless members of society'. She wrote that the alternative view—that reason and rationality were not of primary significance for women—was a terribly dangerous illusion. And it is intriguing to note Wollstonecraft's (ibid. 103) brief but revealing reference, specifically regarding the bodies of women, to that familiar image of

---

[10] Wollstonecraft argues for example against the philosopher Jean-Jacques Rousseau's argument (1979 [1762]), that girls should be educated merely to please men in a physical and sexual sense (Wollstonecraft 1992: 107–8).

[11] For a description of this Victorian figure of desirable womanhood by the writer Virginia Woolf, see Pamela Sue Anderson, Ch. 48, below, 'Feminism and Patriarchy'. Anderson describes the modern philosopher Michèle Le Dœuff's view of the feminist as someone who never lets others do her thinking for her, a kind of subversive 'angel'.

imprisonment: 'Taught from infancy that beauty is woman's sceptre, the mind shapes itself to the body, and roaming round its gilt cage only seeks to adorn its prison'.

Wollstonecraft clearly accepts the hierarchical and hegemonic framework of body thinking that she had inherited—notable not least, of course, in her reference to the Platonic trope of embodiment as mind's imprisonment (ibid.) that has already figured in this chapter in reference to the poetry of John Donne. But unlike Donne, Wollstone-craft is not so much concerned with the notion of embodiment as individual human limitation but with the much more concrete political limitations imposed on women by existing patterns of education and conformity that were only exacerbated by a particular form of obsession with their bodies. She saw how easily women could become entrapped in a cage not essentially of their own making. At the same time, in response, rather than advocate that her readers turn their backs still further on the claims of body, she began, implicitly, to redefine some of those claims. She wanted her readers to liberate their daughters from existing controls that condemned them, as she believed, to poor appetites, weak health, and disappointing lives. As an educationalist, she was strongly convinced of a connection between vigour of body and keenness of intellect (ibid. 131). Emancipation was not just an intellectual category but included the body. In the end, it has to be said that she clearly could not fight all the presuppositions of a privileged masculinity, associated as it was with both the 'disciplining' of little girls to adopt their role as soft and delicate sexual bodies and the valorizing of a disem-bodied, 'masculine' reason. Even as it was, Wollstonecraft's essay was received with scorn and derision by the literary and political establishment of the time and she was branded by Horace Walpole as a 'hyena in petticoats' (ibid. 13)

Charlotte Brontë—Rattling the Doors of the Gilt Cage

Victorian Britain represents another period of considerable spiritual and intellectual upheaval in which the ascendancy of science and capitalism driven by the machinery of imperial and industrial expansion intensified the challenge to Christian theo-logical structures already stressed in a different sense by the counter-hegemonic and rebellious tendencies of intellectual, literary, and artistic Romanticism. Writing at this period of crisis and challenge, Charlotte Brontë's own Evangelical Christian upbringing and education in many ways brings into focus the complexity of the age in respect of questions about body and embodiment. Although Christianity may have been challenged, it, so to speak, still packed a punch for many people in this respect. Brontë was the child of an Anglican clergyman of Evangelical churchman-ship, who wished, according to her first biographer, Elizabeth Gaskell, 'to make his children hardy, and indifferent to the pleasures of eating and dress' (Gaskell 1857: part 1,

Ch. 3). In line with centuries of Christian theology, the connection of sin and mortality with bodily appetites and feelings still plays strongly into the lives of Brontë's family as, presumably, into many others like it. In *Jane Eyre* (1996 [1847]), we could perhaps say that Brontë tries out and tests a number of Christian Evangelical tenets relating to these 'lusts of the flesh', seeking the limits of their compatibility with what is acceptable to a still devoutly Christian author or her readers. While Mr Brocklehurst's thunderous condemnation of a little girl at Lowood school for having naturally curly red hair, for example, is clearly portrayed as excessive, unjust, and, moreover, humorously ineffectual,[12] Jane Eyre is a deeply serious character, far from indifferent to counsels against vanity and calls for sobriety. When Jane rejects St John Rivers' proposal of marriage, for example, it is not because she fails to appreciate the value—or the heroism—of sacrificing safety, domestic contentment, physical well-being and comfort, or life itself to a higher or more enduring cause. Though the figure of St John Rivers is judged hard and despotic by Jane (ibid. 452) when he tries to bully her into marrying him in the name of duty and principle, she finds it hard to detach herself entirely from a need for his approval or to disagree absolutely with him. Yet at the same time, given the limitations and sheer geographical, physical, and social marginality of her life, as a relatively poor clergy-man's daughter, Brontë's aspiration, whatever the obstacles, to robust, fulfilling, embodied presence in her world—expressed not least in her unceasing efforts to write and publish her work—speaks to her desire to be far removed from the almost comic Puritanism of a Mr Brocklehurst or the zealous evangelism of a St John Rivers. Brontë had every reason to be aware of the body's frailty and vulnerability to death and an understandable need for the comfort of her religion in its promise of resurrection (see Brontë 1996: p. xxxii). Only four of the six Brontë children, whose mother died painfully of stomach cancer in 1821 when Charlotte was 5, survived into adulthood. Two older sisters died at home at the ages of 10 and 11. She was only aged 39 herself when she died of tuberculosis, survived by none but her ageing father. Yet *Jane Eyre* at least ends on a complex and equivocal note: the final words of the novel reflect the conviction of Christian faith in the defeat of death and it is the rejected suitor described in thoroughly world-denying terms who receives an unmistakable apotheosis. Jane and St John's abortive relationship mirror Jane and Edward Rochester's contented marriage. This relationship, described in terms of budding woodbine covering a chestnut-tree that has been struck by lightning (ibid. 493), is resonant with Jane's earthy and earthly aspirations for physical intimacy and fruitful domesticity. Yet although Jane Eyre takes up her place in independence and contentment at Thornfield Hall, the book ends in expectations of a less worldly, 'fleshly' kind: 'Amen; even so come, Lord Jesus' (ibid. 502).

---

[12] When Mr Brocklehurst tells all the girls to turn their faces to the wall so that he can inspect and condemn the 'excrescences' of their hairstyles, Jane recalls, with an unmistakeable reference to Matt. 23: 25–6, '[l]eaning a little back on my bench, I could see the looks and grimaces with which they commented on this manoeuvre; it was a pity Mr Brocklehurst could not see them too; he would perhaps have felt that, whatever he might do with the outside of the cup and platter, the inside was further beyond his interference than he imagined' (Brontë 1996: 76).

D. H. Lawrence: Opening
the Closet Door?

D. H. Lawrence, writing in the early twentieth century, works in the shadow cast by the Great War (1914–18), with its terrible legacy of bodily maiming, death, and bereavement. However, Lawrence's writing shows little formal interest in the theology of the Christian Church as a means either to explain or offer consolation for this suffering. It rearranges the traditional association of death with the appetites of the body by linking desire—for touch, sex, and bodily exertion or a sensuous immersion in the non-human world of trees, weather, and water—with the real and proper life-giving energy of human lives. In opposition to traditional Christian theology, the body's instinctual life is a means of grace and not a hindrance to it. Yet a curiously familiar sense of equivocation remains. After their first sexual encounter, Mellors, in the notorious *Lady Chatterly's Lover*, which shocked the public with its explicit approach to sex when it was first published, admits to Connie that he is almost sorry (Lawrence 1994: 118). Sex with Connie is, for Mellors, some kind of acknowledgement of a return to life he should not and cannot resist: 'There's no keeping clear. And if you do keep clear you might almost as well die' (ibid.). Yet this also brings on him a 'new cycle of pain and doom' (ibid. 119). Death continues to feature as strongly as life in Lawrence's texts. There is, for example, constant reference to a deadness when there is refusal to acknowledge the claims of the body or the truth of embodied human natures. Like the Creator, walking in the garden in the cool of the evening (Gen. 3: 8–12), the narrative returns, again and again, to the ideal of truthful, unalloyed men or women who do not hide away or cover themselves in conventional manners, politics, or false feeling, deceiving themselves and others about their real desires. The poignant possibility remains of resisting the corruptions of the modern mechanized world obsessed with possessing, having, or knowing in small-minded or diminishing ways and 'acting in singleness' (Lawrence 1974: 36). And yet Lawrence's characters are 'fallen', 'subtly demoniacal' (ibid. 24), complex, and vulnerable. If Christian theology in its earliest days grappled with the problematics of embodiment—how to reconcile the goodness of material creation, including our human embodiment, with the suffering and pain of our actual embodied lives—these twentieth-century narratives are preoccupied with the same themes. It is as if the Christian mythic tale of creation remains a palimpsest on which Lawrence rewrites timeless preoccupations with the nature of embodied human subjectivity for a new age:

—Set the mind and the reason to cock it over the rest, and all they can do is to criticise and make a deadness. I say all they can do. It is vastly important. My God, the world needs criticising today—criticising to death. Therefore let's live the mental life and glory in our spite, and strip the rotten old show. But mind you, it's like this. While you live your life, you are in some way an organic whole with all life. But once you start the mental life, you pluck the apple. You've severed the connection between the apple and the tree: the organic connection.

And if you've got nothing in your life but the mental life, then you yourself are a plucked apple, you've fallen off the tree.   (Lawrence 1994: 37)

Yet Lawrence's readers are certainly urged to reassess their priorities by a powerful critique of existing cultural and religious dualities; the body is consistently presented as a route and means to human freedom and spiritual nourishment. Strength comes from acknowledging its claims and engaging wholeheartedly with its wisdom and sense whatever religious or social convention dictates. The human body has significance, moving beyond the superficiality of an ungrounded interest in sex, which invokes nostalgia for a past—an Edenic and idealized vision of human integration and bodily fulfilment:

Her tormented modern woman's brain still had no rest. Was it real?—And she knew, if she gave herself to the man, it was real. But if she kept herself for herself, it was nothing. She was old: millions of years old, she felt. And at last she could bear the burden of herself no more. She was to be had for the taking. To be had for the taking. (ibid. 117)

Of course, as the quotation illustrates, this Edenic vision is framed in terms of a frank and unapologetic heterosexuality. And it is not surprising that these narratives have drawn strong criticism from feminist critics. Kate Millet (1971: 316–17) in *Sexual Politics*, for example, claimed that Lawrence transformed masculine ascendancy into a mystical religion that celebrated the penis. Certainly embodied sexual relationships in *Lady Chatterly's Lover*, for example, are clothed in terms that would do full justice to the heterosexism of some modern Roman Catholic notions of gender complementarity (cf. Isherwood and Stuart 1998: 73–4). Connie is stripped for our inspection and readers may well flinch at the tone: 'She was not a little pilchard sort of fish, like a boy, with a boy's flat breasts and little buttocks. She was too feminine to be quite smart' (Lawrence 1994: 19). Yet at the same time this is not mere sexism. We are not told that Connie has no right or capacity to explore her own sexuality or that her body and pleasure is of less value or importance than her partner's. It is her initiative, her search, her discontent, and her escape that frame the novel. It is rather that the authorial voice—which we know to be male—seems entirely confident in asserting the nature of her concerns and desires as an embodied woman. Sometimes these narratives are extremely sensitive to the '*thousand* obstacles a woman has in front of her' (Lawrence 1974: 52) in a man's world, and Lawrence is certainly prepared to criticize specific faults and peccadilloes viewed as typically masculine just as much as those viewed as peculiar to the female (Lawrence 1994: 35). But the whole corpus of his work tends toward broad generalizations which re-emphasize stereotypical differences. For example, in an essay written in 1928, the same year as *Lady Chatterly's Lover* appeared, Lawrence characterizes a proper femininity—one that does not ape the masculine—as decidedly not of the mental life, characterized by a certain physical timidity and numbness that recognizes the male as boss. The essay describes the 'cocksure' modern woman as tragic (Lawrence 1969: 33) and strives to reassert the heroic vision of the male striking an attitude in defiance of 'challenge, danger and death on the clear air' (ibid.). Meanwhile, perhaps, the picture of what really strikes fear into the author's heart emerges, predictable in its expressive ambiguities about the body as alien, feminine, and in need of control: 'If women to-day are cocksure, men are hensure. Men are timid, tremulous, rather soft and submissive, easy in their ery henlike tremulousness. They only want to be spoken to gently' (ibid.).

In spite of all the invocations to men and women to be just themselves as individuals, there is here perhaps more about the attempt to move men and women around the texts like rather over-determined mythic symbols. In *Women in Love*, for example, Hermione Roddice is introduced to readers as a 'masculine' woman, too preoccupied with the intellect to the detriment of her womanly self: 'And all the while the pensive, tortured woman piled up her own defences of aesthetic knowledge, and culture, and world-visions, and disinterestedness. Yet she could never stop up the terrible gap of insufficiency' (Lawrence 1974: 18). Embodied heterosexuality seems an almost sacred principle within Lawrence's novels, but yet the familiar sense of equivocation finds expression in a constant anxiety or uncertainty about the connection between male and female characters that goes along with this principle (Lawrence 1994: 118—'Almost with bitterness he watched her go. She had connected him up again when he had wanted to be alone'). Characters may talk about love between men and women as if it could be some kind of absolute (Lawrence 1974: 63) yet, in Terry Eagleton's words, Lawrence seems to write as if he feels woman 'is forever trying to violate the man's proud singleness of being' (Eagleton 2005: 266). Eagleton (ibid. 271) goes so far as to say Lawrence hates women because they stand for 'the sensuous flesh which inhibits one's (male) drive to freedom and self-realization'. In this way we seem to fall back into ways of thinking that, without explicit reference, reflect something of the original connection between sin, sex, women, and death so particularly characteristic of patriarchal Christianity. At the very least, in its struggle to maintain both the connection and the separateness between the male and female, Lawrence's writing appears to be a preoccupation that has about it something of the intensity of the equivocation familiar from centuries of Christian reflection.

ALISON KENNEDY . . . BACK TO *ORIGINAL BLISS*

The novella *Original Bliss* by contemporary Scottish writer Alison Kennedy takes us back much more explicitly to the efforts of Christianity to control the body as dangerously 'fleshly', a troublesome, irrational necessity within God's unfathomable wisdom and providence that is the means both to the continuance of the race and of its sinfulness apart from God. In this work Kennedy is much more overtly preoccupied with the Christian subtext of our ongoing concern with body and embodiment, than was D. H. Lawrence, for example. The novella seeks to challenge the problematic implications of a least one important strain within Christian reflection on the body and embodiment by clearly linking domestic violence against women and the violence inherent in the production and procurement of pornography, to a reading of body theology that is identifiably Christian. Rejecting that interpretation of the Genesis narrative that sees it as an unproblematic demand for obedience, Kennedy's character, Helen Brindle, explicitly challenges obedience (Gen. 3: 11) in favour of sexual knowledge, implicitly accepting the authority of the body's desires— Mr Brocklehurst's 'lusts of the flesh'—as a better route to God than their denial. The original bliss of the title refers to Helen Brindle's relationship with God before her husband's violence and abuse destroy her comfort and confidence. Kennedy suggests that Helen's loss of faith is a symptom of this toxic relationship, but that her original bliss is also, in some sense, part of the problem. Her love of God who 'had given her everything, lifted her, rocked her, drawn off unease and left her beautiful' (Kennedy 1998: 162) is also equivocal in its implications. It is the best sense she has at the start of what bliss might be, but it has a dark side. She appears also to be trapped by a notion of God's love that demands unending, unconditional, agapaic self-sacrifice, all of which becomes hopelessly confused with her need to exercise an impossibly vigilant self-control in order to satisfy the arbitrary demands of her violently unpredictable and abusive husband. At the same time she is driven by a shockingly contradictory, and ultimately saving awareness of the erotic, linked to her authentic desire for a different embodied relationship that allows her self-expression and comfort. When she falls in love, Helen is drawn, irresistibly, to resist the path of least resistance that has confined her to lifeless conformity and physical oppression, in the rebirth of her own vitality, resistance, and will. It is against her view of the correctness of her actions, against the still present, if shadowy, oppressive sense of God's love/will for her, that she is drawn physically, sexually, and emotionally towards another man, and an adulterous affair with a pornography junkie. Helen's 'fall' into love is her return ticket to bliss, precisely in so far as she learns to reverse the Edenic patriarchal system of value or priority in such matters—putting her embodied desires before the need to control them through conventional obligations to God viewed as Loving.

Conclusion

I have used the term 'equivocation' to describe the sense in which Christian incarnational theology appears to have provided a resource or way of thinking about our embodied human condition. For British literary works produced across a period of over a thousand years, that is not wholly negative. Christian convictions about God's investment in the materiality of human existence bear witness to our perception of infinite human longings and seemingly endless possibilities as well as our fearful limitations. British artists and commentators during this period have not all accepted the authority of a Christian approach, and in the last two or three centuries many have aspired to challenge the more negative or limiting emphases of its teaching, including the exclusions implicit in its most patriarchal and colonial formulations. Arguably, the paradigm remains significant, however, continuing to provide both impetus and challenge to ongoing reflections on the nature of unavoidable human incarnation.

WORKS CITED

Ancrene Riwle, The (*AR*), 2001 [1955]. Trans. M. B. Salu. Exeter: Exeter University Press.

AUGUSTINE. 2001. *De Bono Coniugali; De Sancta Virginitate*, ed. and trans. P. G. Walsh. Oxford: Oxford University Press.

BERNARD OF CLAIRVAUX. 1957–77. *Sancti Bernardi Opera*, ed. J. Leclercq, H. M. Rochais, and C. H. Talbot. Rome: Editiones Cistercienses.

——— 1974. *The Works of Bernard of Clairvaux*, trans. Robert Walton. Washington, DC: Cistercian Publications.

BRENNER, ATHALYA. 1993. *A Feminist Companion to The Song of Songs*. Sheffield: Sheffield Academic Press.

BRONTË, CHARLOTTE 1996 [1847]. *Jane Eyre*, ed. Michael Mason. London: Penguin.

BYNUM, CAROLINE WALKER. 1995. *The Resurrection of the Body*. New York: Columbia University Press.

DAGGERS, JENNY. 2002. *The British Christian Women's Movement: A Rehabilitation of Eve*. Aldershot: Ashgate.

EAGLETON, TERRY. 2005. *The English Novel: An Introduction*. Oxford: Blackwell.

GARDNER, HELEN. 1972. *The Faber Book of Religious Verse*. London: Faber & Faber.

GASKELL, ELIZABETH. 1857. *The Life of Charlotte Brontë*. Online publication: <http://www.lang.nagoya-u.ac.jp/~matsuoka/EG-Charlotte-1.html>.

GILBERT, SANDRA M., and GUBAR, SUSAN. 1984. *The Madwoman in the Attic: The Woman Writer and the Nineteenth-Century Literary Imagination*. New Haven: Yale University Press.

IRIGARAY, LUCE. 2004. *Luce Irigaray: Key Writings*. London: Continuum.

ISHERWOOD, LISA, and STUART, ELIZABETH (eds.). 1998. *Introducing Body Theology*. Sheffield: Sheffield Academic Press.

JASPER, DAVID, and PRICKETT, STEPHEN (eds.). 1999. *The Bible and Literature: A Reader*. Oxford: Blackwell.

KENNEDY, A. L. 1998. *Original Bliss*. London: Vintage.

LAWRENCE, D. H. 1969 [1950]. *Selected Essays*, intro. Richard Aldington. Harmondsworth: Penguin.

——— 1974 [1921]. *Women in Love*. Harmondsworth: Penguin.

——— 1994 [1928]. *Lady Chatterley's Lover*, ed. Michael Squires. Harmondsworth: Penguin.

LIDDELL, H. G., and SCOTT, R. 1899. *Greek–English Lexicon*. Oxford: Clarendon.

MILLET, KATE 1971 [1969]. *Sexual Politics*. New York: Avon.

MORE, HANNAH. 1809. *Coelebs In Search of a Wife: Comprehending Observations on Domestic Habits and Manners, Religion and Morals*. 2 vols. London: T. Cadell & W. Davies.

PAGELS, ELAINE. 1990 [1979]. *The Gnostic Gospels*. Harmondsworth: Penguin.

ROBERTS, MICHÈLE. 1984. *The Wild Girl*. London: Routledge.

ROUSSEAU, JEAN-JACQUES. 1979 [1762]. *Émile: Or, On Education*, trans. Allan Bloom. New York: Basic Books.

Ruether, Rosemary Radford. 1992. *Gaia and God: An Ecofeminist Theology of Earth Healing*. London: SCM.

Spelman, Elizabeth V. 1999. 'Woman as Body: Ancient and Contemporary Views', in Janet Price and Margrit Shildrick (eds.), *Feminist Theory and the Body: A Reader*. Edinburgh: Edinburgh University Press.

Vitruvius 1960 [1914]. *The Ten Books on Architecture*, trans. Morris Hicky Morgan. New York: Dover.

Wada, Yoko (ed.). 2003. *A Companion to Ancrene Wisse*. Cambridge: D. S. Brewer.

Wogan-Browne, Jocelyn. 2001. *Saints' Lives and Women's Literary Culture: Virginity and its Authorizations*. Oxford: Oxford University Press.

Wollstonecraft, Mary. 1992 [1792]. *A Vindication of the Rights of Woman*, ed. Miriam Brody. Harmondsworth: Penguin.

Further Reading

Beauvoir, Simone de. 1972 [1949]. *The Second Sex*, ed. and trans. H. M. Parshley. Harmondsworth: Penguin.

Brown, Peter. 1988. *The Body and Society: Men, Women and Sexual Renunciation in Early Christianity*. New York: Columbia University Press.

Carrette, Jeremy R. 2000. *Foucault and Religion: Spiritual Corporality and Political Spirituality*. London: Routledge.

—— 2005. 'Intense Exchange: Sadomasochism, Theology and the Politics of Late Capitalism'. *Theology & Sexuality*, 11/2.

Coakley, Sarah (ed.). 1997. *Religion and the Body*. Cambridge: Cambridge University Press.

Conboy, Katie, Medina, Nadia and Stanbury, Sarah (eds.). 1997. *Writing on the Body: Female Embodiment and Feminist Theory*. New York: Columbia University Press.

Crary, Jonathan, Feher, Michel, Foster, Hal, and Winter, Sanford K. (eds.). 1989. *Fragments for the History of the Human Body*. 3 Parts. New York: Zone.

Eagleton, Terry. 2005. *The English Novel: An Introduction*. Oxford: Blackwell.

Foucault, Michel. 1978–86. *History of Sexuality*, trans. Robert Hurley. 3 vols. New York: Vintage.

Jasper, Alison (ed.). 2005. *Theology & Sexuality* 11/2. Special Issue: *Dangerous Sex*. London: Sage.

Melville, Pauline. 1990. *Shape-Shifter*. London: Bloomsbury.

....

CHAPTER 47

VISIONS OF
HEAVEN AND HELL

....

ELENA VOLKOVA

> ...in my flight
> Through utter and through middle darkness borne,
> With other notes than to the Orphean lyre
> I sung of Chaos and eternal Night;
> Taught by the heavenly Muse to venture down
> The dark descent, and up to re-ascend,
> Though hard and rare: Thee I revisit safe,
> And feel thy sovran vital lamp....
>
> (Milton, *Paradise Lost*)

THE DESCENT INTO HELL

....

There was only one Temple dedicated to Hades in Greece, and it only opened one day per year, perhaps because it represented the fact that people only descended into the realm of the dead once in their lives. Only priests were allowed to enter the temple on the Day of Hades. Mortals would be punished severely for penetrating the under-world, as Theseus found to his cost when he attempted to kidnap Persephone, the wife of Hades. However, the myths relate that there were certain men who did obtain permission to enter: Orpheus, the famed poet and musician, descended there in the hope of bringing back his wife Eurydice; Odysseus, hero of the Trojan War, breached the threshold of Hades while trying to find a way back home to his own land of Ithaca. But whereas the mellifluent Orpheus failed in his quest, the artful Odysseus reached his goal. Their contrasting outcomes may symbolize the fact that in the Greek religion there was no return to life, and that neither love nor art were able to conquer death: Odysseus succeeded only because he did not attempt resurrection. He only sought mystic knowledge that would enlighten him on his way home.

Thus in Greek mythology it is only the priest, the artist, and the hero—representing spirit, genius, and courage—who might approach or enter the world of the dead. The aim of their respective descents is to worship the god, to save people from death, and to return home.

In the Christian faith by contrast, God miraculously raises people from the dead and descends into hell after his own death on the cross. There he rescues the faithful and opens the door to heaven for them. This is the first thing Jesus Christ does after his crucifixion: he takes Adam and others out of the world of death and brings them to their heavenly home. The three mythological motifs surrounding the descent into the underworld remain however—worshipping God, saving the dead, and returning home: God the Son does the will of his Father, saves humanity from evil, and translates the faithful out of hell and into their heavenly home.

E. M. W. Tillyard in his book *Some Mythical Elements in English Literature* (1961) describes a window in King's College Chapel, dating from about 1530, which

> shows the first act of Christ after his death on the cross: that of leaving his body in the tomb, breaking Hell's gates, and haling out Adam, Eve and other patriarchs for transference to their new home in Paradise. This act was known as the harrowing or subduing of Hell. The King's chapel window, in point of treatment, is normally representative of the differing versions of this not entirely canonical series of acts; aesthetically it is one of the most eminent.   (ibid. 20).

Alister E. McGrath (2003: 92) mentions a fifteenth-century English alabaster panel, which depicts Christ as Harrower of Hell. The story of Christ's descent into hell derives from scattered passages of Scripture (analysed in detail in John Pearson's *An Exposition of the Creed*, 1659), but in fact cannot be attested by the Bible (though there are hints in 1 Peter) for it comes from the apocryphal *Gospel of Nicodemus*. Nevertheless the story was very popular in both the Byzantine and the Western artistic tradition and became part of the Apostles' Creed. Tillyard thinks that the reason for the story's popularity lies in the medieval desire to fulfil Scripture in its account of Adam's fall and to persuade 'the ears of illiterate' that it is the church as Body of Christ that can guarantee them salvation:

> As to establishing connections, the concrete rescue of Adam by Christ corresponded precisely with the perdition of Adam by Satan through the concrete act of eating the forbidden fruit. [...] If the doctrine of Redemption could be put in terms of Adam it would penetrate the simple man's mind more quickly and surely than through any other means. Looking at a mosaic or a fresco of Christ taking Adam by the hand, he could reflect: There I am; or there I could be, if I followed the commands of the Church.   (Tillyard 1961: 27–8)

Medieval writers often show first-hand knowledge of the *Gospel of Nicodemus*. All four mystery cycles (York, Chester, Wakefield, and Coventry), the fourteenth-century drama *The Harrowing of Hell*, as well as the poems *Northern Passion* and *Cursor Mundi*, include versions of the Harrowing of Hell as if it were canonical. Langland combines the myth with that of the Four Daughters of God (Pity, Truth, Justice, Peace).

In early Christian art Orpheus was identified with Christ; the image of the legendary artist was seen as analogy for 'the good shepherd', because of his descent into Hades to save his wife. In this respect, the Descent into Hell, or the Harrowing of Hell, is archetypal and may refer to the calling of any writer, and even to the religious understanding of literature in general: *every* artist *descends* into the 'hell' of human life, in the sense that he has to engage with the realm of sin and suffering, crime and punishment, darkness and despair to save people either from their blindness, negligence, despair, or desolation.

Literature tends to represent human life, the world in which we live and which we are called to transform, as a metaphor of hell. Any work of literature that deals with conflict, pain, suffering, grief, misery, and disaster (and which does not, at least indirectly?) bears an analogy to hell, where life lacks love, bliss, and harmony. Aristotle's definition of the perfect tragic plot as one in which we note a 'change in the hero's fortunes [...] from happiness to misery', or Northrop Frye's identification of *Paradise Lost* as an archetypal plot convention, may prove the point. This earthly 'hell' may be presented as a social environment (in George Orwell's *1984*, J. G. Ballard's *The Atrocity Exhibition*, William Golding's *Darkness Visible*, and many others, particularly in dystopia, war, and Holocaust literature), like a gloomy city ('Hell is a city much like London' in the words of Shelley's *Peter Bell*) or as a symbolic Waste Land inhabited by Hollow Men in T. S. Eliot's poetry. It also refers to an inward state: Satan cries 'Myself is Hell' in *Paradise Lost*, and he is echoed in T. S. Eliot's *The Cocktail Party*: 'What is Hell? Hell is oneself.'

Christ descends into hell led by his compassionate love towards those who suffer there. In the last quatrain of the York version of the *Harrowing of Hell* Adam says:

> To the, Lorde, be louyng
> > That us has wonne fro waa;
> > For solas will we syng,
> > Laus tibi cum gloria.

(To Thee, Lord, be praise, who has won us from woe; for solace we will sing, Praise to thee with glory.)

Langland explains that Christ went to Hell 'to learn what all woe is'; Blake, who identifies God with the Poetic Genius, echoes: 'Can I see another's woe, | And not be in sorrow too?' ('On Another's Sorrow'). It is then being in sorrow with the fallen world that makes the Poetic Genius descend into hell, reconsider, and recreate it. That is why, perhaps, the Poet is 'of the devil's own party', as Blake writes of Milton: hell is the realm *he* has to descend into and to deal with. Joyce Carol Oates (1976: 7) believes,

that the serious artist insists upon the sanctity of the world—even the despairing artist insists upon the power of *his* art somehow to transform what is given. It may be that his role, his function, is to articulate the very worst, to force up into conscience the most perverse and terrifying possibilities of the epoch, so that they can be dealt with and not simply feared; such artists are often denounced as vicious and disgusting when in fact they are—sometimes quite apart from their individual conception of themselves—in the service of their epoch, attempting to locate images, adequate to the unshaped, unconscious horrors they sense.

ANTINOMY OF FALLING/RISING

Thomas Green, in his *The Descent from Heaven: A Study in Epic Continuity* makes the story of the descent a major element of the epic and sees descending as an intrinsic part of the ascending process. Together they create a complex religious duality in the text. Green (1963: 390) develops this idea by analysing the *vertical imagery* in Milton's *Paradise Lost*: '*Paradise Lost* plays continually with the paradoxical duality of lowness—the lowness of humility and of moral degradation or despair—and with the duality of height—of spiritual eminence of exaltation and of pride. It plays also with the paradoxes of rising and falling, the abasement that exalts and the pride that abases'.

The falling–rising paradox, he continues, is a biblical commonplace, referring to the prophesies of Isa. 40: 4 ('Every valley shall be exalted, and every mountain and hill shall be made low'), and of Christ in Matt. 23: 12 ('Whosoever shall exalt himself shall be abased; and he that shall humble himself shall be exalted'), and to many other passages,[1] as well as in English poetry: Vaughan's 'The Morning Watch' ('O let me climb when I lye down'); Donne's *Devotions Upon Emergent Occasions* ('I am readier to fall to the earth, now I am up, than I was when I lay in bed . . . Even rising is the way to ruin!', 'Now I am up, I am ready to sink lower than before').

Northrop Frye, in his *Words With Power* (1990), regards the coherence of the Bible's narrative to lie in its 'U-Shaped plot'. It begins in the garden in paradise, is followed by the fall, and concludes with the final triumph of ascent to the Celestial City of the New Jerusalem. This plotline may be found on a biographical level in the many biblical stories of fall and rise, such as those of Joseph, Moses, Ruth, Job, David, Peter, and Paul, as well as framing a wide range of literary narratives.

Thus we can suggest that when a writer tries to 'articulate the very worst, to force up into conscience the most perverse and terrifying possibilities of the epoch' he does not necessarily experience the fall himself, but rather makes the imaginative descent in order to elevate his readers' minds.

---

[1] Ezek. 21: 26; 31: 10–18; 1 Peter 5: 5–6; Job 24: 24; Matt. 11–23; Luke 14: 11; 18: 14; Jas. 1: 9–10; Eph. 4: 9–10; Phil. 2: 5–10 (Green 1963: 388–9).

The Descent of Heaven to Earth

Where does the artist *descend* from? Barring the idea of a literal descent from life on a mountaintop (as in Nietzsche's *Zarathustra*), there must be some vertical dimension in his or her life, some height within that furnishes him or her with the perspective to see the distortion of human life. And from what is it distorted? On what step of Jacob's ladder, which unites heaven and earth, does this or that artist stand, if he or she sees humanity as 'crashing down all the steps of this Jacob's ladder that reached from paradise to a hell on earth'? (as Bernard Shaw writes in *Back to Methuselah*). What is his heaven like?

Robert Herrick sees it as some *whiter Island*:

> In this world (the *Isle of Dreames*)
> While we sit by sorrowes streams,
> Tears and terrors are our themes,
> > Reciting:
>
> .   .   .
>
> In that *whiter Island,* where
> Things are evermore sincere;
> Candor here, and lustre there
> > Delighting:
>
> > > (*The white Island: or*
> > > *place of the Blest*)

For most medieval writers (the authors of the Middle Irish *Vision of Adomnán* (Fis Adomnan), the Middle English *Pearl* and *Doomsday; Vision of the Monk of Eynsha,* and *The Vision of Tundale*) the ideal of perfection is that presented in the Bible, where heaven is a transcendent other world, an abode of God, angels, and saints, revealed in visions to Isaiah, Ezekiel, Daniel, and John.

Heaven may be used as a synonym for paradise, or the Garden of Eden. There are three types of paradise in the Bible: the first, the natural terrestrial one, is planted by God on earth for human habitation (Gen. 2: 8,10; 4: 16). It is not in heaven, but since it is the place where people can see God face to face and live in peace with him, it may be seen to partake of the Heavenly Kingdom. There is no spiritual difference between heaven and earth in the beginning: God creates both as parts of a new universe. The second appears only after Adam and Eve have been expelled from paradise. For a time, there is no Eden, but Christ's crucifixion opens the door to a celestial paradise. Finally, heaven is also represented mystically in the form of sacred or secular visions, in revelations or dreams. A personal 'dream' displays the author's meekness, and his or her lack of control over the dream. It is authorized by the One who gives it, and confirmed by those capable of interpreting.

The Revelation of St John the Divine is a major source of medieval literary visions. The author of the last book of the Bible sees a new heaven and a new earth united— God's eternal Kingdom is revealed to him as

the holy city, new Jerusalem, coming down from God out of heaven, prepared as a bride adorned for her husband. And I heard a great voice out of heaven saying, Behold the tabernacle of God is with men, and he will dwell with them, and they shall be his people, and God himself shall be with them, and be their God. And God shall wipe away all tears from their eyes; and there shall be no more death, neither sorrow, nor crying, neither shall there be any more pain: for the former things are passed away.   (Rev. 21: 2–4)

Biblical visions provide literature with the basic archetypes of heaven—those of the kingdom (up *there*), the garden (down *here*) and the city (descending from *there* to *here*). All of them also function as metonyms of God who dwells *there* in heaven, *here* in the earthly paradise, and descends twice—from heaven to earth, and from earth into hell.

The terrestrial and celestial paradises symbolically represent some kind of inner paradise—'the Kingdom of God is within you' (Luke 17: 21). Joseph Duncan's *Milton's Earthly Paradise: A Historical Study of Eden* analyses the tripartite interrelations between the natural, celestial and inner paradise in Milton:

Both the inner paradise of edenic innocence and the allegorical garden of virtues are lost, but the inner paradise of the regenerate may be gained and possessed in a fallen world. This paradise of inner grace, like the external, natural paradise, is created by God. Like the celestial paradise, it is foreshadowed and suggested by the loveliness of the natural paradise. In *Paradise Lost*, when Adam goes forth into the world, he possesses the paradise within, 'happier farr' than the external paradise he is leaving. [...] The inner paradise of innocence and the external paradise fuse to form a complex symbol of a spiritual state; and the inner life of Satan and the devils fuses with the external features of Hell to form a comparable symbol.   (Duncan 1972: 264, 266)

Milton's Satan tries to persuade himself that 'The mind is its own place, and in itself | Can make a Heaven of Hell, a Hell of Heaven' (1. 254–5) (the idiom is borrowed from Shakespeare's *A Midsummer Night's Dream*).

Another biblical source of heaven symbolism is Jesus's parables, where the Kingdom of Heaven is presented by symbolic things ('treasures in heaven' as opposed to 'treasures on earth', a 'pearl of great price', 'a grain of mustard seed', leaven) and people (a merchant seeking for pearls, a king who arranged a marriage for his son, a man who gives talents to his servants, ten virgins with lamps who go out to meet the bridegroom, a landowner who hired labourers for his vineyard). If the parable relates to man then he symbolizes either God himself (usually as king or master, who chooses the righteous for the kingdom), or the desire of the soul for heavenly riches. So they speak of the kingdom of heaven as both an objective domain of God and a state of one's mind.

Pearl, a fourteenth-century poem 'contains what is arguably the finest account of the New Jerusalem to have been written in the English language' (McGrath 2003: 25). It is a wonderful example of a dream vision, in which the biblical reference to a pearl—itself a symbol of the Heavenly Kingdom—is incorporated into the particular story of a jeweller who lost a most precious pearl. He speaks of it both as a jewel and as a human being, probably a 2-year-old daughter. The image is developed through the story: from a material thing—up to the heavenly Pearl Maiden, a guide to the celestial city that symbolizes Christ, his triumphant love, mercy, and grace. The dreamer is allowed to see the procession of Christ the Lamb and virgins, his brides in New Jerusalem, all of whom are crowned as queens of the kingdom. The Pearl Maiden may be understood to represent the jeweller's late daughter, or her soul, that reigns in heaven. *Pearl* actually offers an archetype of sorts for subsequent visions of heaven as it has many motifs that will be developed: that of paradise lost, since on a literal level the jeweller lost what he valued most on earth, but on a spiritual level he also lost his inner paradise (an aspect which will attain primary significance in Romanticism); it contains a reunion with the departed (which will be a leitmotif in the Victorian treatment of heaven); and it contains a pilgrimage story as an allegory of life (which will attain prominence in Chaucer and Bunyan).

In biblical and medieval visions heaven reveals itself to man as if a window were opened and symbols descended through it from God to earth, or as if God himself opened a door into the soul to reveal the essence of the Christian faith. Man, as the jeweller in *Pearl,* is given a lesson in perfection which he is supposed to learn in order to realize his own sins, repent, and change his life. This is very much the way heaven is opened to the biblical prophets: unexpectedly, as a gift sent by God from above (the *Apocalypse* is said to be 'The Revelation of Jesus Christ, which *God gave* [...] unto his servant John'). The King of Heaven speaks to his servants, or sends a messenger to his people for them to know what they should be or live like. Messengers and guides appear as angels in the Bible and in Milton; in the form of Virgil and Beatrice—in Dante; in the form of the Maiden—in *Pearl*; in the form of Solid People—in Lewis's *Great Divorce*, etc. A seer is a spectator in the heavenly theatre, who is supposed to enjoy the scene or the speech and draw a moral from them. Although *Pearl* is usually identified as an elegy, it may also derive from the sermon tradition, in so far as the Pearl Maiden preaches to the jeweller as a priest would amongst a community of believers, who seem to know the Scriptures but do not live accordingly.

Colleen McDannel and Bernard Lang in their *Heaven: A History* (1988) designate the medieval visions as theocentric and distinguish them from the anthropocentric ones which, they observe, begin with the focus on the human afterlife in the works of Swedenborg. A theocentric vision is an encounter with an otherwise invisible world, which *descends* to man in the moment it becomes visible, in the same way Christ descended to earth when he took on human flesh, or in the way it is revealed that the New Jerusalem will descend in the book of Revelation. In this sense visibility and verbalization, seen from a Christian perspective, are in themselves embodiments of the divine into images which may be associated with the incarnation of Jesus Christ.[2] Hence, the descent of heaven, or from heaven, is intrinsic to the religious nature of theocentric literature and art.

Incarnation for its part is theologically considered as the *kenosis* of Christ, 'emptying himself' of his divine prerogatives and subjecting himself to the laws of human birth and the lowliness of fallen human nature:

> O Thou who camest from above,
> the pure celestial fire to impart
> kindle a flame of sacred love
> upon the mean altar of my heart.
>
> (Charles Wesley, 1776)

---

[2] John of Damascus while defending icons against Iconoclasts in the eighth century, referred to incarnation: 'Of old God the incorporeal and uncircumscribed was not depicted at all. But now that God has appeared in the flesh and lived among humans, I make an image of the God who can be seen.'

Many hymns maintain the theocentric focus of beatific visions: this idea of the church is based on the image of the New Jerusalem, the city where heaven and earth (as church visible and invisible) are united and inhabited by the community of the righteous, who participate in the heavenly liturgy, singing praise to God together with the angels and the saints:

> That undisturbed Song of pure content,
> Ay sung before the saphire-colour'd throne
> To him that sits theron
> With Saintly shout, and solemn Jubily
>
> (Milton, *At A Solemn Music*)

While John Milton believed that such harmony was only possible in the prelapsarian world, he anticipated that it would soon be restored:

> O may we soon again renew that Song,
> And keep in tune with Heav'n, till God ere long
> To his celestial consort us unite,
> To live with him, and sing in endles morn of light.

The Imaginative Ascent to Heaven

We can note an increasing anthropocentric tendency in Renaissance literature, which introduces a new, active type of a visionary—an artist or narrator who creates an idea or picture of the transcendent by his own intellect and imagination. In Spenser's *An Hymne of Heavenly Love* and *An Hymne of Heavenly Beauty* the poet tries to lift his mind with the help of the divine love and beauty so as to reach heaven and enjoy the vision of it:

> Loue, lift me vp vpon thy golden wings,
> From this base world vnto thy heauens hight,
> Where I may see those admirable things,
> Which there thou workest by thy soueraine might,
> Farre aboue feeble reach of earthly sight
>
> (*An Hymne of Heavenly Love*)

Man is incapable of comprehending heaven; nor can his language verbalize it:

> I faine to tell the things that I behold,
> But feele my wits to faile, and tong to fold.
>
> (*An Hymne of Heavenly Beauty*)

Spenser gives a Neoplatonic picture of Heaven, where 'those *Idees* on hie, | Enraunged be, which Plato so admired, | And pure *Intelligences* from God inspired.' His heaven is hierarchal: Plato's ideas are part of the lowest level, 'where happy souls haue place', but higher and fairer are the heavens where a hierarchy of angels, *Powers, Potentates, Dominions, Cherubim,* and *Seraphim* preside (the ordering of these into three hierarchies in nine choirs Spenser borrows from the angelology of Dionysius the Pseudo-Areopagite (*c.* AD 500). Spenser's heaven is 'the eternal fountaine' of perfect love, beauty, truth, wisdom, bliss, grace, mercy, and might. But it is love and beauty that he glorifies first, which reign in human hearts as dim reflections of God.

The anthropocentric tendency is far stronger in Milton's poetry. *Lycidas* was composed on the occasion of the death of fellow Cambridge student Edward King, who drowned when his ship sank off the coast of Wales in August 1637. Milton employs his favourite falling–rising antinomy: 'So Lycidas sunk low, but mounted high'. Unlike the Pearl Poet, Milton does not need a divine sign to be certain that his *learned Friend* went up to heaven, and his emphasis remains upon the man. He does not rise to worship or serve God, and we are told that saints will 'entertain him' and 'wipe the tears for ever from his eyes'. In his poem *On Time*, Milton, developing the mythological image of the all-devouring Chronos, pronounces his certainty that all heavenly guided souls will dwell in heaven:

> Then long Eternity shall greet our bliss
> With an individual kiss;
>
> .   .   .   .   .
>
> Attir'd with Stars, we shall for ever sit,
> Triumphing over Death, and Chance, and thee O Time.

Having dominated in medieval and, to a lesser extent, Renaissance literature, there is a decided shift away from the biblical cosmology of earth in relation to heaven and hell for planetary mysticism in the metaphysical poets. In Crashaw's *Hymn to Sainte Teresa*, the moon, surrounded by maiden stars (supposedly representing St Mary and other virgins) has prepared room for St Teresa; the heavens, 'thy old friends', greet the saint 'and all in one weave a constellation | Of CROWNS, with which the King thy spouse, | shall build up thy triumphant browes'. Donne's *The Second Anniversary,* written on 'the religious death of Mistress Elizabeth Drury', abounds in planetary (esoteric?) imagery: the soul liberated by death from her 'living tomb' passes through many heavenly bodies: Hesper, Vesper, Mercury, Mars, the Sun, and finally reaches heaven. Astronomy and a new form of mysticism provide poetry with a new idea of the universe. As a result, the heaven of metaphysics gives a combination of biblical, classical, astrological images and scientific terms. To the bliss, love, holiness, worship, and other traditional associations of heaven Donne adds the knowledge which it implies and which can be obtained in its fullness only after death: 'In heaven thou straight know'st all, concerning it.'

The poetical rhythm and style tend to be lighter and more natural than in the Renaissance in spite of the metaphysical complexity of the message as, for example, in Herbert's poem 'Heaven', which is written in the form of a dialogue between the poet and echo about heaven:

> Then tell me what is that supreme delight?
> *Echo.*   *Light.*
> Light to the mind: what shall the will enjoy?
> *Echo.*   *Joy.*
> But are there cares and business with the pleasure?
> *Echo.*   *Leisure.*
> Light, joy and leisure; but shall they persevere?
> *Echo.*   *Ever.*

Each answer of the echo returns part of the last word in the question. The device is symbolic: it suggests that the essence of heaven is hidden in human language and may be derived from the similitude of words by means of rhyming, where the first rhyme-fellow (in the question of man) gives an earthly understanding of heaven, while the second one (that of the echo) reveals the mystery of heaven, which may be found either in the stem (the core of the word), as in *delight-light, enjoy-joy,* or through the consonance. Echo as a voice of heaven refers to the metaphysical understanding of rhyme as a device that reveals the hidden correspondence between things, which could help man comprehend the world as part of the spiritual universe, which wholeness and grandeur embraces all the divisions within it, where heaven and hell are parts of the global divine Providence, filled with the profound sense. The central symbol of echo also speaks of the growing anthropocentrism: heaven here is just a reflection of a Narcissus-like man.

This new metaphysical mode may be identified as microcosmic, for it is based on the idea of the human soul as a finite inner universe corresponding to the macrocosm of infinite existence. John Donne, in his *Second Anniversary,* writes that the heroine was 'to herself a State', 'a Church', and 'made this world in some proportion | A heaven'. Not only did she have a vast knowledge of heaven, she carried it within her soul and established it around her. Donne suggests that such souls, being a church unto themselves, can unite heaven and earth through their deeds and death:

> So by the soul doth death string heaven and earth;
> For when our soul enjoys this her third birth,
> (Creation gave her one, a second, grace),
> Heaven is as near, and present to her face,
> As colours are, and objects, in a room
> Where darkness was before, when tapers come.

In Traherne's 'Felicity', Dame Nature (playing the angelic role of messenger) reveals the infiniteness of the inner world to the poet: 'Dame Nature told me there was endless Space | Within my Soul, I spy'd its very face: | Sure it not for nought appears. | What is there which a Man may see | Beyond the Spheres?—FELICITY.'

Alister McGrath (2003: 116) in his *A Brief History of Heaven* observes that

taking delight in nature is [. . .] seen as nourishing our anticipation of beholding God face to face—of satisfying the desire that owes its origins to God, and can only be fulfilled by God. Paradoxically, nature generates a longing that it cannot itself satisfy, and thus leads us to find God and heaven. While this theme is developed by many theologians, perhaps its most systematic application is found in Romanticism and New England Transcendentalism. It is also a significant element in the writings of the metaphysical poets of the seventeenth century.

The most influential literary depiction of natural paradise may be found in Milton's epic. But the natural world is also praised as Edenic in the poetry of Thomas Traherne, William Cowper, William Blake, and, in the most sublime and detailed way, by William Wordsworth in *The Excursion* and *The Prelude* ('That paradise, the lost abode of man, | Was raised again: and to a happy few, | In its original beauty, here restored' (IX 717–19).) While amongst the metaphysical and Romantic poets 'the kiss of Eternity' (to paraphrase Milton) became more individual and more hylozoic in nature, the Protestant religious literature of the seventeenth century returned to the biblical images of heaven.

LIFE AS PILGRIMAGE: THE ROAD TO HEAVEN THROUGH HELL

The vision of heaven is often linked to the pilgrimage story as a way up to the Kingdom of God. Forrest Smith, in his *Secular and Sacred Visionaries in the Late Middle Ages,* observes that

imaginary journeys into the afterlife [...] flourished in the medieval imagination as an interpretation of the primary, essential spiritual pilgrimage of man. The otherworld journey had as its counterpart in the secular world a search for perfection in this life as the terrestrial City of God. The journey took on the weight of myth, and for the late Middle Ages it was a plastic, unifying myth of Christian experience. [...] Visions in whatever form stand uniquely as an intersection of the eternal and the temporal and the divine and the human.   (Smith 1986: 5, 7)

The most widely read English pilgrimage story was written by John Bunyan (1626–88). His *Pilgrim's Progress* presents scenes and characters that embody virtues and sins which may be understood to partake of heaven or hell. Christian and Evangelist (those who know and follow the Word of God), Goodwill, Interpreter (of the Bible), Patience, Discretion, Prudence, Piety, Charity, Hopeful, and Faithful certainly 'stand for the world to come'. With the help of them the pilgrim succeeds in the 'harrowing of hell', represented by the appearance of the characters Obstinate, Pliable, Worldly-Wiseman, Morality, Civility, Discontent, Shame, Ignorance, and other sinners, as well as by Apollyon, Beelzebub, and Legion, who are of infernal origin and construct a Vanity Fair on earth (according to a 'hell on earth' archetype) as a trap for the pilgrims to the Celestial City. All the characters are allegories of the proper and the improper, of true and false understandings of Christianity. Heaven in Bunyan has obvious allusions to the vision in Revelation: 'The city shone like the sun, the streets were paved with gold, and in the streets walked many people with crowns on their heads. They had palms in their hands, and carried golden harps with which to sing praises. Some had wings, and they spoke to one another saying, "Holy, holy, holy, is the Lord!"' Having approached paradise each pilgrim has to show a certificate to Enoch, Moses, and Elijah at the gate of the city to prove that he had passed all the way from the City of Destruction up to Heaven, which signifies the fullness of the spiritual battle one has fought. Bunyan's hero Christian is a warrior, who fights a spiritual war against sins and the enemies of God.

WAR IN HEAVEN

Milton also sees heaven through the lens of war. He places an unusual emphasis on the wrath of Jesus Christ, emphasizing his metaphoric status as the Lion of Judah rather than as the meek Lamb, particularly in the scene in which he drives a chariot against Satan's troops:

> So spake the Son, and into terrour changed
> His countenance too severe to be beheld,
> And full of wrath bent on his enemies.

Most critics believe that in the episode of the War in Heaven Milton sought to imitate the epic poetry of Homer, Virgil, Hesiod, Ariosto, Tasso, Spenser, and other poets. The Battle of the Angels abounds in epic allusions. But A. C. Dobbins in *Milton and the Book of Revelation: The Heavenly Cycle* (1975) has convincingly argued that the allusions and devices Milton used were not merely nods towards epic conventions: 'Milton's account of the War in Heaven is based upon a literal interpretation of Revelation 12: 7–9 and Revelation 6: 1–8' (ibid. 29).

J. R. Watson writes that sanctified by the authority of the Bible, the ideas of the Holy War and the spiritual inner war between good and evil may be found in the legends of medieval Christianity, in the Counter-Reformation ideology of the Jesuits, in Bunyan, Milton, John and Charles Wesley, and many other writers. In the seventeenth century 'the Great Rebellion, or the Civil War, produced a literature of conflict and of warfare applied to the spiritual state', while later we can even see 'the transition of the defensive mode to an offensive one in the fighting hymns of the 19th century' (Watson 1999: 13, 18, 22). Both Milton and Bunyan made their faith part of their politics. The ideological mentality of Bunyan, for example, seems not to know any Christian love for the enemy, or any compassion for those going to hell.

Milton's hell could be interpreted as a metaphor for a human society that has rebelled against God, gripped by fear and despair, which they try to dispel by different activities, such as sport, military training ('As at th' Olympian games or Pythian fields'), art ('Retreated in a silent valley, sing'), theology, philosophy ('Vain wisdom all, and false philosophy!'), travelling ('to discover wide | That dismal world').

THE THEODICY OF HEAVEN AND HELL

The seventeenth century is marked by a drastic reconsideration of the idea of hell. D. P. Walker in *The Decline of Hell* states that the doctrine of hell remained almost unchallenged for many centuries[3] because of the very strong scriptural authority until it began to lose its hold in the seventeenth century in the writings of the Cambridge Platonists Peter Sterry and Jeremiah White and in the visions of some Philadelphians—Jane Lead, the Petersens, and Richard Roach. 'An abominable aspect of the traditional doctrine of hell', Walker writes, 'was that the part of the happiness of the blessed consists in contemplating the torments of the damned. This sight gives them joy because it is a manifestation of God's justice and hatred of sin, but chiefly because it provides a contrast which heightens their awareness of their own bliss' (Walker 1963: 29). F. W. Farrar called this type of enjoyment 'an abominable fancy' and opposed the title of his own book *Eternal Hope* (1878) to the idea of eternal torments in hell.

Lindsey Hall in his *Swinburne's Hell and Hick's Universalism* suggests that there are various theological perspectives on hell: a strong view of hell ('which is the belief that God sends those who will not be saved to hell'); a weak view of hell ('God does not send people to hell, rather than they send themselves there'); the idea of annihilation and conditional immortality ('the unrighteous will cease to exist after death'); and universalism ('belief in universal salvation or apokatastasis') (Hall 2003: 10–17).

In the seventeenth century the traditional doctrine of eternal torments in hell raises a question of theodicy: can heaven coexist with hell? What kind of paradise might it be when the rest of humanity suffer in hell? Can the faith based on fear of punishment have any moral value? As Thomas Burnet ironically puts it:

> Consider a little, if you please, unmerciful Doctor, what a theatre of Providence this is: by far the greatest part of the human race burning in the flames for ever and ever. Oh what a spectacle on the stage, worthy of an audience of God and angels! And then to delight the ears, while this unhappy crowd fills heaven and earth with wailing and howling, you have a truly divine harmony.   (Walker 1963: 32)

The majority of the early Church Fathers assume hell literally to be a place of fiery torments, of darkness, weeping, and gnashing of teeth. Chaucer's Parson vividly depicts 'the horrible peynes of helle' giving a lot of references to patristic and medieval understanding of the subject. In James Joyce's *Portrait of the Artist as a Young Man* we can find a parody on the traditional naturalistic description of hell, inspired, as it seems, by the sermons and books of the infamous nineteenth-century Irish-English priest Fr. Furniss, whose surname speaks of his love of preaching eternal damnation to little children in terrible hair-raising details. Dan Kelly opens his

---

[3] It was as early as the third century when Origen developed the idea of the ultimate salvation for everyone and was condemned as heretic. Similar ideas were expressed by Gregory of Nyssa and Isaac of Nineveh, and later revived in the ninth century by Scotus Erigena.

sarcastic article 'Book Hell!' with a highly expressive quotation from Fr. Furniss's *The Sight of Hell*:

Perhaps at this moment, seven o'clock in the evening, a child is just going into Hell. To-morrow evening at seven o'clock, go and knock at the gates of Hell, and ask what the child is doing. The devils will go and look. Then they will come back again and say, the child is burning! Go in a week and ask what the child is doing; you will get the same answer—it is burning! Go in a year and ask; the same answer comes—it is burning! Go in a million of years and ask the same question; the answer is just the same—it is burning! So, if you go for ever and ever, you will always get the same answer—it is burning in the fire!   (Kelly 2002).

Steven Daedalus' priest Fr. Arnall preaches in Fr. Furniss's manner:

Imagine some foul and putrid corpse that has lain rotting and decomposing in the grave, a jelly-like mass of liquid corruption. Imagine such a corpse a prey to flames, devoured by the fire of burning brimstone and giving off dense choking fumes of nauseous loathsome decomposition. And then imagine this sickening stench, multiplied a millionfold and a millionfold again from the millions upon millions of fetid carcasses massed together in the reeking darkness, a huge and rotting human fungus. Imagine all this, and you will have some idea of the horror of the stench of Hell.

As Geoffrey Rowell shows in his *Hell and the Victorians* the doctrine of everlasting punishment was one of the central points of debate for the greater part of the nineteenth century. 'The Bible, after several decades of controversy and criticism, no longer occupied the position of unquestionable authority which it had once held, and even where men were still concerned to profess a biblical religion, there had been too much discussion of the texts concerning eternal punishment for them to be altogether unaware of the difficulties surrounding their interpretation' (Rowell 1974: 2).

MARRIED AND DIVORCED

William Blake in his *Marriage of Heaven and Hell* includes the doctrine of eternal torments among the list of the major Errors made by 'all Bibles and sacred codes'. Yet this is probably because Blake followed Swedenborg in naturalizing the supernatural, both heaven and hell, as imaginative projections. The narrator literally descends into 'hell': 'As I was walking among the fires of Hell delighted with the enjoyment of Genius, which to Angels look like torment and insanity, I collected some Proverbs; thinking as the sayings used in a nation mark its character, so the Proverbs of hell show the nature of Infernal wisdom better than any descriptions of buildings or garments.' Blake treats hell with the respect Christians traditionally pay to heaven and he looks for infernal wisdom instead of longing for the heavenly one. Blake's Hell is an ironic image of what the church has done to the idea of the human and the divine: both have been divided into two antagonistic counterparts (soul and body/heaven and hell) while man and world, both microcosm and macrocosm, are inseparable within them and driven by Energy, which is the source of the Poetic Genius.

The descent into hell (both as a place and a state of mind) is a very important Romantic motif, because the Romantics placed special emphasis on evil and its power over human hearts. The tradition started in the Gothic novel and was developed by S. T. Coleridge, P. B. Shelley, Lord Byron, E. A. Poe and other writers. The beatific imagery in Romantic poetry is often fused with infernal features: Byron's Cain *ascends* to the realm of Lucifer as a world of powerful knowledge; Coleridge's enchanting vision of Kubla Khan as an Edenic place is 'haunted | By a woman wailing for her demon-lover'; his Ancient Mariner suddenly descends from a happy state of mind ('Happily did we drop...', 'Hailed it in God's name') into the infernal realm of crime and punishment (a dead, cursed world with death-fires, witch's oils, drought, a lack of speech, the hatred of the dead but moving shipmates, the dead Albatross hanging around the Mariner's neck instead of the cross, the rotting sea, the lonely soul in agony), and finally through repentance and love restores inner joy and peace.

In his *Songs of Innocence and Songs of Experience*, Blake opposes the world of innocent paradise to that of conceptual evil which brings hell into human hearts and lives. But 'the fearful symmetry' (to use the title of Northrop Frye's book on Blake, adopted from Blake's *The Tyger*) of Blake's *Marriage* is so controversial that scholars tend to look for sources in other texts: mostly in Swedenborg's *Heaven and Hell*, in Boehme's *The Threefold Life of Man*, and Shakespeare (Nurmi 1957; Sabri-Tabrizi 1973). As for the 'harrowing of hell' motif, Blake establishes the priority of the active over the passive, includes the 'hell' of religious mistakes, and shows how people have made infernal things of heavenly ones. His active 'harrowing' of the traditional idea of hell is caused by his belief in the divine nature of the Poetic Genius: 'For Blake, Paradise was the human imagination, and he spent most of his time there. He not only believed in it firmly, but he acted on it unhesitatingly and consistently. His greatest achievement in his poetry and his design is "to carry us with him into such an imaginative world,"' states G. E. Bentley, who sees Blake as *The Stranger from Paradise* (Bentley 1999: 93–4).

Two of the famous Inklings circle, J. R. R. Tolkien and C. S. Lewis, challenged both of Blake's Romantic ideas—his marriage of heaven and hell and his cult of genius. Lewis separates what Blake had put together in *The Great Divorce*: in his tale, people arrive on the threshold of paradise but cannot enter it. Ultimately they reject heaven and return to hell because they have nothing of paradise within them: they are filled with self-centredness, ambition, and vanity, all of which are alien to the realm of God's love and self-sacrifice. Lewis's allegory may serve as an illustration of Cardinal Newman's idea that heaven 'would be Hell to an irreligious man', because in heaven every man must 'do God's pleasure' rather than 'choose and take his own pleasure' (Walker 1963: 125).

Tolkien's 'Leaf by Niggle' introduces the artist not as a saviour but as a 'little man', 'the sort of painter who can paint leaves better than trees', yet wants 'to paint a whole tree'. He is 'little' not because he is less talented than other artists, but in comparison to God as the true Artist of the Universe. The tree which Niggle fails to paint evidently refers to the world tree of mythology as a symbol of the universe. The artist has an ambition to be like God but can only echo the heavens in a Platonic way: it is only in heaven that he finally sees his own Tree completed, alive, 'its branches growing and bending in the wind that Niggle had so often felt or guessed, and had so often failed to catch. He gazed at the Tree, and slowly he lifted his arms and opened them wide: "It's a gift!" he said. He was referring to his art, and also to the result; but he was using the word quite literally.'

Tolkien allegorically presents the idea of synergy—the creative cooperation of God and man, which he designates as Creation and Sub-Creation. It is a process that requires all kinds of talents, which God furnishes to his people: Niggle (as an allegory of Art) and his neighbour Parish (an allegory of Life) together reach harmony in the paradise called Niggle's Parish. Both heaven in Tolkien's story and hell in Lewis's are nonetheless depicted in the quasi-Romantic terms of earthly life, where Edenic nature traditionally embodies heaven while Civilization (Town) represents the *infernal* world of darkness and death, the descent into which should paradoxically (as many things sound in Christianity) transfigure human souls. It should teach people the *heavenly* values of love and compassion, how to 'bear one another's burdens', which Charles Williams in his novel *Descent into Hell* (1937) calls the doctrine of Substituted Love.

Hell became one of the most significant metaphors of the twentieth century: after the development of psychoanalysis it is effectively presented as madness either of man or the world surrounding him (Hannah Greenberg's *I Never Promised You a Rose Garden,* Doris Lessing's *Briefing for a Descent into Hell,* Mark Vonnegut's *The Eden Express,* Ken Kesey's *One Flew Over the Cuckoo's Nest*).

We can conclude by saying that heaven and hell may be seen as two poles of the vertical dimension in literature. Originally based on the biblical story, they have been greatly reconsidered and developed as metaphors of the social and inner world: while the Descent into Hell may be seen as symbol of literature or of the writer called 'to make Heaven of Hell'.

However, both realms, heaven and hell, in spite of their diverse embodiment in literature, remain profound mysteries, the very inexpressibility of which inspires the poetic imagination:

> O world invisible, we view thee,
> O world intangible, we touch thee,
> O world unknowable, we know thee,
> Incomprehensible, we clutch thee!
>
> (F. Thompson, *The Kingdom of God*)

WORKS CITED

BENTLEY, G. E., Jr. 1999. *The Stranger from Paradise: William Blake in the Realm of the Beast. Religion and Literature: Through Each Other's Eyes.* Moscow: Rudomino.

DOBBINS, AUSTIN C. 1975. *Milton and the Book of Revelation.* Tuscaloosa: University of Alabama Press.

DUNCAN, JOSEPH E. 1972. *Milton's Earthly Paradise. A Historical Study of Eden.* Minneapolis: University of Minnesota Press.

FRYE, NORTHROP. 1990. *Words with Power.* Toronto: Viking.

GREEN, THOMAS. 1963. *The Descent from Heaven: A Study in Epic Continuity.* New Haven: Yale University Press.

HALL, LINDSEY. 2003. *Swinburne's Hell and Hick's Universalism.* Aldershot: Ashgate.

KELLY, D. 2002. 'Book Hell!' *Book Happy 7.*

McDANNEL, COLLEEN and LANG, BERNARD. 1988. *Heaven: A History.* New Haven: Yale University Press.

McGRATH, ALISTER E. 2003. *A Brief History of Heaven.* Oxford: Blackwell.

NURMI, MARTIN K. 1957. *Blake's 'Marriage of Heaven and Hell': A Critical Study.* Kent, Ohio: Kent State University Press.

OATES, JOYCE CAROL. 1976. *New Heaven, New Earth: The Visionary Experience in Literature.* London: Victor Gollancz.

ROWELL, GEOFFREY. 1974. *Hell and the Victorians.* Oxford: Clarendon.

SABRI-TABRIZI, G. B. 1973. *The 'Heaven' and 'Hell' of William Blake.* London: Lawrence & Wishart.

SMITH, FORREST S. 1986. *Secular and Sacred Visionaries in the Late Middle Ages.* New York: Garland.

TILLYARD, E. M. W. 1961. *Some Mythical Elements in English Literature.* London: Chatto & Windus.

WALKER, D. P. 1963. *The Decline of Hell.* London: Routledge & Kegan Paul.

WATSON, J. R. 1999. *Warfare and its Values / Religion and Literature: Through Each Other's Eyes.* Moscow: Rudomino.

FURTHER READING

ALMOND, PHILIP. C. 1994. *Heaven and Hell in Enlightenment England.* Cambridge: Cambridge University Press.

BECKER, E. J. 1899. *A Contribution to the Comparative Study of the Medieval Visions of Heaven and Hell, with Special References to the Middle-English Versions.* Baltimore: John Murphy.

IERSEL BAS VAN and SCHILLEBEECKS, E. (eds.) 1979. *Heaven.* New York: Seabury.

LUTTIKHUIZEN, G. P. (ed.). 1999. *Paradise Interpreted. Representations of Biblical Paradise in Judaism and Christianity.* Leiden: Brill.

RUSSEL, JEFFREY BURTON. 1997. *A History of Heaven: The Singing Silence.* Princeton: Princeton University Press.

TURNER, ALICE K. 1993. *The History of Hell.* New York: Harcourt Brace.

WHEELER, M. 1990. *Heaven, Hell, and the Victorians.* Cambridge: Cambridge University Press.

CHAPTER 48

FEMINISM AND PATRIARCHY

PAMELA SUE ANDERSON

A major obstacle inherent in patriarchy remains its barely perceptible reality for all of those women and men whose lives have been decisively ordered by the rule of the father. Toni Morrison, winner of the Nobel Prize in Literature, captures the imperceptible reality of racial domination with imagery of a fishbowl. Her readers are compelled to imagine the bowl as a transparent structure permitting the ordered life which it contains to exist in a larger world (Morrison 1993: 6–17). Her imagery reveals the ways in which apparently invisible structures of domination can suddenly become visible. With Morrison's cogent use of imagery in mind this chapter aims to recognize patriarchy by revealing both the transparent structure of male domination which has contained women's lives and the ways in which feminism has emerged with this revelation. The bare outlines of the former will be made evident here in a reading of English literature and theology; the latter will be seen as if the writer and reader were outside that ordered life, tackling 'the obstacle which does not speak its name' (cf. Le Dœuff 1991: 28).

THE REALITY OF PATRIARCHY AND THE EMERGENCE OF FEMINISM

Feminism and patriarchy form a conceptual pair. Together these two concepts can help men and women come to see what has been the significant reality of a woman's material and social relations with men, with other women, and with the impersonal agents of traditional institutions. As long as patriarchy in the most basic sense of father rule justifying the domination of women by men makes up the fundamental structure of societies in various explicit and implicit ways, feminism will have its *raison d'être*: to enable each woman to become aware of her own capacity to think for herself and to live in a situation of equality with men, women, and other institutional agents.

Yet patriarchy exists in different cultural forms (Butler 1990: 3–4, 35–38). Feminism also has its various forms, figures, and differences: contemporary feminists continue to disagree about their own self-definition (Anderson 1998: 67–70, 230–5; 2002: 103–20). Nevertheless, a common feature of every form of feminism is ultimately to remove the patriarchal structures which oppress women's lives, to eradicate the structures which devalue women's acting, thinking, feeling, and, especially here, their writing. At the very least, feminist authors in this context would agree that a woman deserves to have her reason, experience, authority, identity, and claims to truth given equal consideration to those of every man and every other woman.

In the history of English literature and theology, feminism and patriarchy are found, respectively, to enable or to inhibit women's reading and writing. In the useful terms of socialist feminism,[1] women's role, or their lack of a socially significant role, in the production of literature and theology is dialectically related to the material conditions of their lives (cf. Delphy 1984). From the seventeenth century at least women in the English-speaking world are known to have struggled against adverse material conditions in order to write poetry, plays, philosophical or theological essays, and correspondences of a literary nature. As will be discussed later, Virginia Woolf (1882–1941) offers a now classic description of the conditions necessary for a woman to write a literary piece of her own in *A Room of One's Own* (1929). Woolf claims that Aphra Behn (1640–89) is possibly the earliest English woman to prove 'that women could make money by writing' (Woolf 1993a: 59). Behn's contribution to the recognition of patriarchal oppression rests both in her personal struggle to be paid for written work and in her sexually explicit writings of poetry, drama, and especially of the fiction which possibly invented the novel: *Oroonoko, or the Royal Slave* (cf. Behn 1696).

Already in her own century Behn's writing is taken up by other women writers. Notably Catharine Cockburn (née Trotter, 1679–1749) writes a verse dramatization of Behn's 'Agnes de Castro' which is performed in 1695 at the theatre in Drury Lane. Highly significant in the present context is that Cockburn and her seventeenth-century predecessor Viscountess Anne Conway (née Finch, 1631–79) both also write philosophical essays on theological topics. From conversation and correspondence with the Cambridge Platonist Henry More (1614–87)[2] Conway develops her own

---

[1] For a fuller list of the different forms of feminism see n. 6.

[2] Henry More is a university tutor of Conway's brother and a friend of her husband, so someone through whom she has indirect access to debates in philosophical theology. As a seventeenth-century woman Conway is certainly not allowed a university education. For a woman of her time to develop her own ideas discursively is doubly difficult, since socially her role as daughter, sister, lover, or wife would prevent her direct access to learning, let alone the equality to think and write for herself. It is then highly

distinctive non-trinitarian and cogent philosophical arguments concerning God, Christ, and creation.[3] Her original account of metaphysical change and process, and in particular her argument that 'substance' incorporates body-mind-spirit, can still challenge Christian orthodoxy today and engage modern physicists in timely debates. Conway left a volume of her philosophical writings which More published for her posthumously in Holland; and it has been suggested that this work influenced the metaphysical ideas of the great German eighteenth-century philosopher Gottfried Leibniz (1631–79).[4] Equally, after her marriage to Reverend Patrick Cockburn, Catharine Cockburn writes well-argued theological essays on such matters as the resurrection (admittedly, defending the view of John Locke, 1632–1704) and on whether God ordains what is good and evil at will or according to the fitness to creation—about which she writes for and is read by certain clergymen of her day (cf. Cockburn, in Warnock 1996: 29–36). In addition, Mary Astell (1666–1731) should be recognized as another seventeenth-century woman writer who gains access and authority to writing seriously on theological ideas, in large part due to her dialogue with a Cambridge Platonist, John Norris (1657–1711). Her letters on both personal and philosophical matters reflect Astell's intellect as a woman, revealing both her self-education and the significant material conditions necessary for her writing (Astell and Norris 1695). Not unlike Conway, Astell writes on theological matters; and like Behn, she also creates poetry and drama.

The published essays by Conway, Cockburn, and Astell provide significant evidence of the feminism emerging as women and men begin to recognize the oppressive nature of English patriarchy. Moreover, it is extremely important that the writings and ideas of these women are taken seriously enough to be debated by prominent seventeenth- and eighteenth-century theologians and philosophers. None of Behn, Cockburn, Conway, or Astell explicitly articulates either a form of feminism or a definition of patriarchy. Yet Astell writes (for instance) in defence of women, especially on the miseries of marriage. In fact, she produces a searing critique of the powerlessness of women within the (patriarchal) marital institution (Astell 1730). Astell also proposes a 'Religious Retirement' where Anglican women could retreat to engage in religious observance, learning language, and other skills (Astell 1694). All these writings testify to the fact that a seventeenth-century woman in Britain could and did exhibit an awareness of male domination over women in social, theological, and literary institutions.

The content of the aforementioned women's writings and the material conditions in which the actual production of their works takes place support the claims of

significant that Conway has correspondence with and intellectual respect from More. See Le Dœuff 2002: 105–8; Warnock 1996: p. xxxvi; and Taliaferro and Teply 2004: 37–43.

[3] On the nature of the relationship between the master philosopher and the faithful student who follows (him), and its socially problematic nature for a woman's education in particular, see Le Dœuff 2002: 105, 117–20.

[4] For additional background on and excerpts from the writings of Conway and Cockburn, see Warnock 1996: pp. xxxv–xxxvii, 3–36. Also on Conway, see Taliaferro and Teply 2004: 37–43, 187–92.

socialist feminism. That is, change comes about when the concrete circumstances of women's lives are transformed by their socially significant involvement in producing new works, say, of a literary and theological nature. However, the feminist struggle against the domination of women by men continues to remain on the margins of eighteenth- and nineteenth-century societies. For example, the notable Hannah More (1745–1833), one of the English bluestockings, works to ameliorate women's education by writing political tracts and by setting up eleven village schools, with her sisters, after running possibly the most successful girl's school of the eighteenth century in Bristol.[5] Yet the inheritance of More's essays and novels, the seeds for future forms of feminisms, are more significant than any actual social changes to patriarchy in the late eighteenth and early nineteenth centuries.

Along with a historical account of feminism's gradual emergence in literature and theology under English patriarchy, it should be understood more broadly that every religious tradition serves as a primary space in which and by means of which gender hierarchy is culturally articulated, reinforced, and consolidated in institutional forms. In particular, women's exclusion from the production of significant literary and religious works globally re-enforces culturally specific gender hierarchies in the domination of women by privileging the ideas and images of men. Although English literature and (Christian) theology together make up only one great cultural and historical form in the production of sacred and aesthetic texts, they display an unvarying, global ambivalence on the subject of women. This ambivalence means that for every literary text that places well-domesticated womanhood on a religious pedestal, another text announces that, if uncontrolled, women are the root of all evil. There is plenty of evidence that this ambivalence concerning a woman in Western theological and literary texts continues across various cultures worldwide (for cross-cultural evidence see Filipczak 2004: 210–22).

In brief, the conceptual pair of feminism and patriarchy initially set out here supports a material analysis of women, men, and the impact of their theological and/or literary ideals on social reality. At the same time, it is important to acknowledge the existence of different forms of feminism, often existing side by side.[6] In concluding, a

---

[5] The English bluestockings is the name given to a group of educated, intellectual women who met for intellectual debates and flourished in London in the late eighteenth-century. The description derives from the stockings made from blue worsted rather than silk and goes back to the days when men in the Parliament of 1653 would not wear silk and instead wore those blue stockings. It seems that the derogatory nature of this label remains as imagery for those who would dress or act in an inappropriate manner, that is, like those who would not appreciate the significance of silk for ceremonial occasions. For a witty, insightful story about the emergence of 'the bluestockings' first in Parliament and then later as an epithet for women who met to discuss feminist issues, see Le Dœuff 2003: 1–4. Le Dœuff's story suggests that perhaps no one ever wore the warm worsted stockings; instead this imagery becomes a convenient way to refer to those who were thought capable of something highly inappropriate.

[6] Consider a rough account of the forms of feminism. Further on, it will become possible to picture the continuing rise and fall of these different forms of feminism as an ongoing movement with (as yet) unending waves. *Socialist feminism* assumes that the solidarity and interdependence of men as grounded on a material base enables men to dominate women. *Radical feminism* regards patriarchy as an all-pervasive and a-historical system. 'Radical' refers to the belief that patriarchy is deeply rooted, inherently hierarchical and aggressive, existing independently of social changes (for a fuller account of radical

critical comment will be given about a cross-current traversing the waves of feminism, that of *post-feminism*. Until then, bear in mind that the common goal of the various forms of feminism is the eradication of patriarchy. But this does not prevent feminism from accompanying patriarchy. Just the reverse is true. Feminism does and, arguably, should exist alongside patriarchy until ideally, the pair dissolves.

THE NECESSARY CONDITIONS FOR A WOMAN'S WRITING

The contemporary French feminist Michèle Le Dœuff offers English literary and cultural critics some intriguing detective work on the theological conceptions of woman and on the ideals of divine knowledge which have silenced women within the long tradition of English writers. Her standpoint as an outsider to this tradition sheds light on the narrowness of the vision of twentieth-century women authors in Britain, notably Virginia Woolf who is otherwise crucial in raising British consciousness on issues concerning patriarchy in literature and the material conditions necessary for women to be able to write. Le Dœuff's special interest in 'the philosophical imaginary' motivated her to dig into the collective history of literary and philosophical–theological ideas in order to work out how a woman came to produce her own ideas.[7] Crucial is Le Dœuff's documentation concerning the ways in which theological conceptions of woman have not only prohibited women's freedom and authority on matters of truth, reason, good, and evil, but have advocated a form of 'absolute altruism' whereby a woman becomes 'a nothingness in the eyes of the other' (Le Dœuff 1991: 280, also see, 108; and 2003: Ch. 1, 'Cast-offs').

feminism, see Rich 1995: 56–83; cf. Anderson 2002: 103–5). Yet the shifts from one economic or political structure to another, according to this radical conception, would not make any great difference to women's subjugation. *Difference feminism*, or at least one version of a form stressing sexual difference, identifies women's reproductive function as the primary site of female oppression; the biological family structure is, then, the ground of patriarchal constructions of women as a subordinate class. This use of class for female reproduction is essentially a refinement of a Marxist conception of class oppression (cf. Barrett 1979; and Barrett, in Woolf 1993a: pp. x–xvi). *Liberal feminism* is one of the earliest forms of feminism and continues to participate in various waves of feminism. It is identified by its political agenda to eradicate the social and legal inequalities suffered by women (cf. Wollstonecraft 1992; and Godwin 2001 esp. 43–4, 72–9). Finally, *postmodern feminism* has been taken up and expanded by those contemporary literary theorists who recognize patriarchy as an ideological structure permeating every aspect of life. Postmodern feminists tend to assume a post-structuralist conception of language as the ground of all meaning and value. According to this conception, language is structured by sets of binary terms. So, man/woman, rationality/irrationally, omnipotence/impotence, straight/curved, light/dark, etc. are not simply words, but paired terms with differential values. These binary terms give meaning to language-users; and, crucially, the second term is always given less value than the first. Postmodern theorists seek to confront the binary structure of literary texts. Feminist deconstructive strategies target the gendered binary constituting the various texts of patriarchal cultures.

7 For Le Dœuff's conception of 'the philosophical imaginary', see Le Dœuff 2002, esp. 'Preface: The Shameful Face of Philosophy', 1–20.

In so far as her identity is determined by patriarchal literary and theological traditions, a woman finds it virtually impossible to possess the authority which would be necessary to write with her own integrity of style, to have her own ideas, and have them read. Moreover, the conditions necessary for a woman to achieve authority, as a recognized 'author' of her own ideas, on particular theological matters would require the transformation of those moral ideals which portray woman as untrustworthy (cf. Wollstonecraft 1992; Le Dœuff 2003). Patriarchy is doubly embedded in the literary and theological imaginations, shaping the gendered nature of a woman's life, thought, and action. But a woman author is not simply a feminist because born female: a feminist will insist upon allowing no one else to think (or write) in her place.

Le Dœuff articulates with concrete stories and imagery the necessary conditions of a woman's literary creativity, even uncovering aspects making up a latent tradition of women thinkers.[8] These conditions constitute the sort of women's tradition Woolf sought: that is, women struggling for a feminist literary imagination. The perceptive reader recognizes a paradigmatic figure in Le Dœuff's feminist texts. An older and wiser figure than the Victorian 'Angel in the House',[9] or the medieval Christian 'helpmeet', emerges as if a dissenting angel who is no longer trapped in the house, or fishbowl! This figure enhanced by the philosophical imaginary encourages each individual woman to write, to create her own anecdotes of life with a feminist wit that enables hope for change in the collective historical experiences of women. The aim of this imaginary figure is to convey truth, in a post-Woolfian style, under new,

---

[8] Consider the existence of a European woman writer whose work is known to have been translated into the English vernacular in 1521. Christine de Pizan (1364–1430) overcomes the obstacle which prevents women from acquiring the necessary conditions to write, that is, the necessary education and material circumstances (place and time) to contribute to women's creativity. De Pizan not only had to have the (self)-education, but she had to refute *both* a tradition of Christian theology which conceived women as sinful like Eve (a view exaggerated at the time with a strongly misogynist reading of Paul's teachings in the New Testament on a woman's role in personal and social life) *and* a tradition of ancient philosophy, which conceived women as defective males (a view deriving from Aristotle's physics). These traditions which silenced women reflect views that were and are anti-feminist. In overcoming these de Pizan writes without living in complete submission to a man—whether husband, male confessor, or other patriarchal figure—and his God. Moreover, she does not claim a woman's ignorance, weakness, and frailty. Instead she cultivates certain intellectual virtues. Careful reading of de Pizan's text renders a startling possibility for this fourteenth-century lady: that (today) she be called a feminist—and that her feminism may have had an unacknowledged impact in the sixteenth century on women and men in the English-speaking world. Totally unaware of de Pizan, or any other woman writer as early as this, Woolf simply dismisses any possibility that a medieval or Renaissance woman could have had the education and material conditions which would have been necessary to write on her own (Woolf 1993a: 38–9). Despite Woolf's particular lack of imagination and knowledge of this historical period, feminism and patriarchy in English societies may have its earliest origins in reading a woman's writings from outside its cultural boundaries. Now, redressing any such acts of disinheritance, Le Dœuff digs into the texts of fifteenth-century Europe and retrieves this significant feminist inheritance for twenty-first century men and women. For her detective work on Christine de Pisan (which is the spelling used by Le Dœuff, but I have followed the spelling of the Penguin edition), see Le Dœuff 2003: pp. ix–x, 135–8. Le Dœuff describes de Pisan as her representative of a literary *epikleroi*, that is, a woman from whom later generations have inherited a certain knowledge and know-how (see ibid. 112–18).

[9] Virginia Woolf, 'Professions for Women' (Lecture for the National Society of Women's Service, 21 January 1931), in Woolf, 1993a: 357. For a description and discussion of Woolf's 'Angel in the House', see further below; cf. Le Dœuff 1991: 127–9; 2003: 77–8.

playful imagery and political passion, not unlike the expression of truth which render such feminist classics as *A Room of One's Own*.

The British feminist Michèle Barrett makes an explicit point about the continuing contemporary appeals to Woolf's highly significant text: 'A Room of One's Own, published in 1929, even now remains one of the clearest and most eloquent accounts that we have of women's writing' (Barrett, in Woolf 1993a: p. ix). Often in a literary critic's account of Woolf's novels, the 'feminist' nature of her creative writing is contested. But in contrast, the feminism of *A Room of One's Own* and *Three Guineas* (1938) is not so easily contested. In her 1929 text, Woolf argues that the writer is a product of her historical circumstances, and that material conditions have decisive significance for the very possibility of a woman writer. Rarely has an argument concerning feminism and patriarchy in English literature been presented more concisely and carefully. Without 'a room of one's own', that is, without the money, education, and social circumstances which would allow the right psychological elements for developing the creative process of the literary imagination, women will not be enabled to produce their own writings. This argument remains true at least for feminists who advocate female autonomy.

In addition, the later argument of *Three Guineas* has more significance today than it did when first published in 1938: at that time, the equation of masculinism and militarism was not so easily accepted. Woolf advocates giving three guineas, one to each of three separate funds with particular aims: the first guinea would go to a fund for rebuilding a woman's college; the second guinea to an agency for helping women find employment; and the third guinea would go to prevent war (i.e. the spread of fascism in 1930s Europe) by protecting intellectual and cultural freedoms. The heart of Woolf's argument is that these ostensibly separate funds point to an inseparable concern for women's financial independence; this would be gained through educa-tion and employment. So, at that time at least, women's education and employment were not only the essential preconditions for their independence but, according to Woolf's feminism, for the force against war. The connection of these preconditions to political debates (e.g. on war) may not have been (fully) understood in late-1930s Britain. Yet Woolf's argument is compatible with subsequent feminism in linking the private and public worlds: 'That fear, small, insignificant and private as it is, is connected with the other fear, the public fear, which is neither small nor insignificant, the fear which has led you to ask us to help you prevent war', that is, the tyranny of women's domestic servitude is one and the same as 'the tyrannies and servilities of the other' (Woolf 1993a: 270).

In these terms, present-day feminists will (generally) agree that Woolf had the capacity to anticipate the political concerns of future men and women. The crucial element in Woolf's argument is that a lack of an accessible tradition of women writers puts a brake on a woman's imagination and so constrains her own critical reflection on both private and public life. This argument continues to inspire and direct clearly vocal critics, editors, and theorists of English literature by and for women (see Barrett 1979; Brown-Grant, in Pizan 1999: p. xvi; Heilbrun 1989: 13, 15, 30; Le Dœuff 1991: 16; Moi 1988: 1–18; Rich 1995: p. xxv, 56 n.; Waugh 1989: 88–125). As the political question of war illustrates (in *Three Guineas*), in order to accomplish the common feminist goal of eradicating the tyrannies of patriarchy, female authors need to be allowed to create and develop their own imaginative tradition for the good of both women and men.

In this context, literature and theology together constitute a formidable force for good or evil in (re-)shaping women's lives. Feminism supports the struggles of women to write about human lived experiences, whether spiritual, personal, and/ or political. Feminists recognize the uniqueness of specific texts by women in the history of English literature, at least since the Middle Ages. Julian of Norwich (1342–after 1416) is said today to be the first woman writer in English who can be identified with certainty (see Spearing, in Julian of Norwich 1998 pp. vii–xx). Julian struggles over a number of years to write the 'Short Text' and 'Long Text' of her experience of divine revelations, or 'showings' of divine love (ibid. 1998). Her medieval culture would have strongly resisted her effort to write and especially to teach as a woman. This resistance would have been justified by appeals to Pauline writings in the New Testament (e.g. 1 Cor. 11: 3–10, 14: 33–5; also, 1 Tim. 2: 9–15). Moreover, any writing which discussed theological ideas in the vernacular (English) would have been suspect. Consequently, not only would Julian have worked for years on her texts in order to express her ideas well, but also would have taken care to keep her self-presentation modest. In Ch. 6 of the 'Short Text' of her visions Julian writes:

> I beg you all for God's sake and advise you all for your own advantage that you stop paying attention to the poor, worldly, sinful creature to whom this vision was shown, and eagerly, attentively, lovingly and humbly contemplate God, who in his gracious love and in his eternal goodness wanted the vision to be generally known to comfort us all. . . .
>
> But God forbid that you should say or assume that I am a teacher, for that is not what I mean, nor did I ever mean it; I am a woman, ignorant, weak and frail.   (ibid. 9–10)

Julian's text does not illustrate a woman's writing in a space free of patriarchy. As a woman in all humility she had to defer to the perfect goodness and authority of the patriarchal Christian God. Nevertheless, whatever can be said historically about Julian's theological strategy and literary force in claiming weakness, poverty, and sinfulness on her part, while acknowledging the strength, richness, and goodness on the part of God, she successfully acquires the time, space, and knowledge necessary for her writing *Revelations of Divine Love*. Moreover, in appealing to a God-given vocation this autobiographical writing appears at the beginning of a now long tradition of women writers who gain authority from a spiritual calling of service to others, from which these women would be otherwise prohibited. Later examples of similar spiritual appeals by women to a God-given authority are found in the writings and service of Margery Kempe (1373–1438), and, albeit in quite different cultural circumstances, in Margaret Cavendish (1623–73) and Florence Nightingale (1819–90).[10] None of these women writers who each consistently and unselfconsciously submits her ideas to

---

[10] On the inspirational role of the spiritual autobiographies of such women as Kempe and Nightingale, see Heilbrun 1989: 22–4, also see 118–19. In addition, for helpful background on the development of a feminist consciousness through creativity within, and resistance to, patriarchal traditions of literary and theological creativity, see the historical points on Margery Kempe, Margaret Cavendish, Florence Nightingale in Lerner 1993: 83–7, 173–4, 179 respectively.

structures of male authority can be identified as explicitly feminist. At most, it might be said that one by one each woman anticipates a still imperceptible feminism.

'I ask you to write more books...for your good and for the good of the world'[11]

Women writers continue to confront that barely perceptible reality which does not speak its name (cf. Le Dœuff 2002: 100–28; 1991: 28). To help detect this reality, Le Dœuff offers an account of 'feminist' knowledge:

the term feminist here in its most basic sense... [is] someone who knows that something is still not right in the relations between a woman and everybody else, in other words men, other women, the supposedly impersonal agents of institutions, and anyone else: some hitch that is strictly potential, of course, simply liable to manifest itself, but which you must learn to identify in everyday situations and conversations.   (Le Dœuff 1991: 28)

It is crucial to learn that as long as patriarchal structures condition a woman's life, her relations will not be right. This self-recognition is not simply a matter of women acknowledging a universal nature. Patriarchy is not, then, an a-temporal structure which all women at any time and in any place can identify as one and the same thing. For example, not all women have experienced the inner conflict(s) between the virtues of the Victorian angel and the desire for intellectual and social autonomy, especially as evident in the inner struggle to produce one's own ideas. Instead each woman must dig deep in her material and social relations to identify what is wrong in her everyday relations and communication.

Arguably, women in writing English literature and confronting socially and materially oppressive traditions have created their own ways to give feminist expression to their personal and political oppression. Although the present sketch cannot consider in detail the wide-ranging impact of the movement of feminism on patriarchal structures, it seeks nevertheless to make sense of the various ways in which feminism gradually emerges in relation to different understandings of patriarchy (cf. Gamble 2001: 293). Essentially, those women literary figures who have taken up the ultimate goal of feminism—i.e. the eradication of patriarchy—seek their own freedom to think, to write, and to gain authority in their lives and relationships. In strong sympathy with this emerging literary tradition the present detective work confirms and continues this

---

[11] These words from Virginia Woolf (1993a: 99). appear as an epigraph on the otherwise blank page before the 'Contents' in hooks 1999: 'when I ask you to write more books I am urging you to do what will be for your good and for the good of the world at large'.

process by picturing the movement of feminism as 'our collective historical experience' (Le Dœuff 1991: 242).

Following Woolf and Le Dœuff, feminists today can draw productively on the imagery in women's writings to make sense of this feminist movement. Woolf begins *The Waves* with the imagery of sun, sea, and sky: 'The sun had not yet risen. The sea was indistinguishable from the sky, except that the sea was slightly creased as if a cloth had wrinkles in it. Gradually as the sky whitened a dark line lay on the horizon dividing the sea from the sky and...' (Woolf 1992c: 3). And Le Dœuff carries on her use of imagery:

> The waves of hope rise and fall: 'The grey cloth becomes barred with thick strokes moving, one after another, beneath the surface, following each other, pursuing each other, perpetually. As they neared the shore each bar rose, heaped itself, broke and swept a thin veil of white water across the sand. The wave paused, and then drew out again, sighing.' These opening sentences from Virginia Woolf's *The Waves* might well contain the poetics of our collective historical experience. Successive waves of women have joyfully fought, convinced that once we had at last gained the right to, for example, a job, education, citizen's rights, or a sexuality freed from the chains of reproduction, something fundamental would have changed in the general female condition. A thin veil of white water across the sand: these gains have hardly even yet been gained... Inward migrations, exoduses, expansions, recessions, fresh waves: whether economic, cultural or political, the waves break more of us than they keep afloat. And even if they did keep us afloat, they would be deceiving us. There are enough ideological or political eddies in the Movement, enough inquiries going adrift, to make sure of that.   (Le Dœuff 1991: 242–4; cf. Woolf 1992c: 3).

In brief, a feminist literary tradition is shaped around the collective history of a movement, the ebb and flow of the imagery and political ideas of each woman writer. Shifts in the philosophical imaginary constantly move feminism either backwards or forwards. The imagery of the waves is a case in point. Woolf as a paradigmatic figure of and for a woman's writing speaks profoundly to her readers, even in this new century, about patriarchy and feminism. Feminist writers can profitably pick up and exploit her metaphorical and mystical language to express the rise and fall of hope in the feminist movement. The waves of feminism reflect a process within a wider political movement of women historically. This imagery gives expression to the complex patterns and shifts in the historical movement(s) of both the collective and the individual woman.

The moments of vision when Woolf seems at one with creation link women and fiction: the characters in her novels gain virtually mystical moments of insight, reflecting a writer's own efforts to transcend the real contingencies of familial and gendered relationships. Yet, despite the mystical nature of her explorations in *The Waves* and other novels, the author herself rails against Christianity in her letters to her sister Vanessa, as she does in her novels and political essays.[12] Obviously, her relationship to theology is not one of believer or academic theologian. What is most clear is that she blames the church for forbidding women's access to education (see Lee 1997: 226–7). Nevertheless, to understand her writings, the reader should detect

---

[12] Woolf 1975: i. 442; 1992b; Woolf 1993c: 205–7.

the patriarchal structures of Victorian Anglicanism haunting the self in the figure of Woolf's 'Angel in the House': 'It was she who bothered me and wasted my time and so tormented me that at last I killed her' (Woolf 1993a: 357). Woolf goes on to describe this Victorian angel:

She was intensely sympathetic. She was immensely charming. She was utterly unselfish. She excelled in the difficult arts of family life. She sacrificed herself daily... [she] preferred to sympathize always with the minds and wishes of others. Above all... she was pure. Her purity was supposed to be her chief beauty.... And when I came to write I encountered her with the very first words. The shadow of her wings fell on my page... she slipped behind me and whispered: 'My dear, you are a young woman. You are writing about a book that has been written by a man. Be sympathetic; be tender; flatter; deceive; use all the arts and wiles of our sex. Never let anybody guess that you have a mind of your own. Above all, be pure.' (ibid.)

This angel of Victorian patriarchy captures the female figure imagined, and then reinforced, by Christianity; that is, by what have been the Christian moral ideals in English literature and theology. Woolf's novels also exhibit a profound longing to (re)turn to a mother–daughter relationship, to reject the destructiveness of patriarchal relations as excavated in mothers, in daughters, in fathers and other men. Consider Clarissa Dalloway preparing for the dinner party in *Mrs Dalloway*, Mrs Ramsey and Lily Briscoe exploring mother–daughter (older–younger woman) roles in *To The Lighthouse*, the woman–man exploration of gender, androgyny, writing, and desire in *Orlando*, and Bernard seemingly transcending gender and life/death distinctions in *The Waves*. Upon reflection it becomes clear that each character and each event in Woolf's novels is shaped around a struggle to transcend the sexual or gendered roles of women and men who seek to understand not only the Victorian values of Woolf's own upbringing, but the Christian values which continue to determine the patriarchy of contemporary theology. Woolf's writings are pivotal in the present context both for her contribution to the philosophical imaginary and for her own significant, true (human) insights from which she draws most profoundly.

A paradigmatic figure for feminism and patriarchy may derive from Woolf, but the ideal is an even stronger, inspirational writer than Woolf herself. This paradigm will, ideally, inspire women (and men), through the collective characters and stories of a feminist imagination, to experience, reason, feel, seek truth, and imagine new relations between women and men, women and women, mothers and daughters, daughters and fathers, persons and nature, nature and knowledge which cannot be spoken. But this is not to make a (feminist) moral saint of any particular female writer.

Woolf herself provokes hotly contested and conflicting interpretations (cf. Moi 1988: 1–18). Some interpretations present Woolf exclusively as a modernist whose primary concern is to shape her writing according to a formal aesthetic. Ironically she has been criticized for failing to be 'shrill', 'strident', or 'angry' as a 'feminist' ought to be (Moi 1988: 1–8; Heilbrun 1989: 14–15; Waugh 1989: 88–125; Lee 1997: 476, 520–1). To be too eloquent and too controlled would be to fail to kill the Angel in the House. On such grounds, critics deny that Woolf's writings are consistent or genuinely feminist at all. Her general hostility to life might be criticized as madness; her hostility to Christianity might be called repressed anger; her preoccupation with her mother, her father, her familial relations verge on the narcissistic; her inner battle with hetero-sexual emotions/relations could smack of a general dishonesty in failing to confront her own sexuality. Ultimately, a woman's failure to recognize her own self-deception might render not only her art, but her politics self-destructive. Yet where else do we go, if not to an individual woman writer to create a feminist paradigm, to conceive the elements for hope that feminism and patriarchy will one day dissolve?

Despite the contestations of feminist critics, the figure of Woolf becomes a messenger of hope for those women who want to know what is necessary in order to reverse their silencing. Against the mutism of their own condition under patri-archy, feminism after Woolf advocates two grounds which will give a woman freedom for self-expression and literary creativity: (1) material conditions allowing independ-ence of thought and (2) social circumstances allowing time and place away from domestic labours.

Admittedly, creating a messenger of hope out of 'Virginia Woolf' in recognition of persisting forms of patriarchy and in an embrace of feminism will not satisfy (or, be acceptable to) her critics. Perhaps her critics are correct to see only weakness, madness, and repression in post-Woolfian literary imagery which, nonetheless, seems to break free from its origin in 1920s and 1930s Britain. A lack of explicitly directed anger about Woolf's own conditions as a writer has provided the grounds for critics to dismiss the possibility that her writings could direct other women. And yet the present contention is that Woolf's self-expression and literary creativity can become part of—along with the work of such women writers as those mentioned already—the source of imagery for a philosophical imaginary that will generate new visions for men and women.

Even if successfully imagined as a messenger of hope, Woolf's imperfections raise a more general question about precisely what guides expressions of feminism and patriarchy towards their own ultimate end. To answer this consider a slightly earlier attempt (on another continent) to confront the walls of patriarchy and imagine the literary struggle out of confinement. The late nineteenth-century American Char-lotte Perkins Gilman writes a small masterpiece, 'The Yellow Wallpaper' (1892), portraying a woman's deeply disturbing split-self awareness of confinement by her husband:

. . . for really I wasn't alone a bit! As soon as it was moonlight and that poor thing began to crawl and shake the pattern, I got up and ran to help her.

I pulled and she shook, I shook and she pulled, and before morning we had peeled off yards of that paper

. . . I kept on creeping just the same, but I looked at him over my shoulder.

'I've got out at last,' said I, 'in spite of you . . . And I've pulled off most of the paper, so you can't put me back!'

Now why should that man have fainted? But he did, and right across my path by the wall, so that I had to creep over him every time!   (Gilman 1981: 32, 36)

Gilman captures patriarchy in the imagery of walls, of crawling, shaking, creeping, seeking a way out of the constraining other, finding one's own inner world, however small it may be. Moving against one's oppressor enables the writer and the reader to build up a literary tradition that seeks to imagine and subvert the obstacle that does not speak otherwise.

In this manner, the patriarchal containment of a woman physically and mentally by both literature and theology reveals itself in the imagery at the heart of texts written by women who struggle to give expression to their social and material conditions. In turn, the authors of such texts and readers of such imagery generate messengers of hope—as inspirational figures—not only in fiction, but in social reality. Now, thinking back to the century before Gilman and Woolf, a late eighteenth- and early nineteenth-century mother–daughter pair of women authors comes to mind.

AESTHETIC EDUCATION AND THE MONSTROUS SUBLIME

Mary Wollstonecraft (Godwin) (1759–97) and Mary (Godwin) Shelley (1797–1851) enable a bridge across the eighteenth and nineteenth centuries. A political philosopher, if not a feminist in contemporary terms, Wollstonecraft argues persuasively against the prevailing opinion of woman's sexual character in her historical and cultural context. In particular, she responds to both Jean-Jacques Rousseau's account of the moral education of women in *Émile: or, On Education* (1762) and John Milton's portrayal of the first woman, Eve, in *Paradise Lost* (1667). Rousseau's political treatise and Milton's poetic text become the targets of Wollstonecraft's brilliant and energetic rebuttal of the prevailing literary and theological (in fact, political) opinion of a woman's moral nature. Wollstonecraft insists *contra* Rousseau that women were destined just as men were to acquire human virtues, if only given the freedom to have the moral education for these. Of course, this would go against the moral education necessary for women who were to stay at home and prevent the chaos which, it was thought (by Rousseau), would result from their presence in public life. Nevertheless, Wollstonecraft persists in asking, what if women were educated, and then, what if they were to confront Milton's theological reading of woman? While advocating the acquisition of human virtues by women Wollstonecraft exposes the way in which Milton turns the voice of Eve against herself:

Milton, I grant, was of a very different opinion [to me] . . .
  'To whom thus Eve with perfect beauty adorn'd.
  My author and disposer, what thou bid'st
  Unargued I obey; so God ordains;
  God is *thy law, thou mine*: to know no more'
These are exactly the arguments that I have used to children; but I have added, your reason is now gaining strength, and, till it arrives at some degree of maturity, you must look up to

me for advice—then you ought to *think* and only rely on God.   (Wollstonecraft 1992: 101; cf. Milton, *Paradise Lost*, 4 ll. 634–8; Wollstonecraft's italics)

The problem is that Eve's voice from Milton's magisterial poem resounds in the ears of the woman at the heart of the patriarchal tradition in English literature and theology. Eve's ignorance in submitting to (her) man is based upon an analogy to man's submissive obedience to his God. This patriarchal hierarchy is not easily dismantled. The implicit European Christian conception of a woman reinforces the hidden obstacle against a woman's own thinking. This obstacle is repeatedly identified in literature and reality, while the waves of feminism return to force themselves beyond that which obstructs women.[13]

At the end of the eighteenth and beginning of the nineteenth centuries, philosophical readings align beauty with certain feminine virtues and the sublime with masculine ones (cf. Burke 1990; Kant 1960). Although it may seem surprising that after Wollstonecraft's momentous text on the rights of woman (1792), the values attributed to the beautiful and the sublime rise up against women to cause a significant backlash on ideals of gender. Arguably Enlightenment moral and aesthetic education has a direct impact on conceptions of woman and man—to the detriment of the former. This is also the historical point at which the sublime becomes associated with the divine—often in place of the beautiful. But then another sudden change—twenty-one years after her mother's death as a result of her own birth— Mary Shelley subverts the theme of submissive female beauty and so undermines the powerful Enlightenment views of the sublime which had become a theological ideal par excellence. Before describing Shelley's subversive novel, consider the persuasive aesthetic-theological argument which shifts associations of the divine from the beautiful to the sublime.

The basic argument is initially that whatever God is, or creates, has to be perfect; and, in this case, if God is to fulfil the human desire for perfect fairness, fit, or countenance, God has to be the origin and end of perfect beauty. Or, turning this around, man's (*sic*) awareness of design in nature, including human nature, gives grounds for the existence of a perfect being who designed this order. Why, in this light, would late eighteenth-century conceptions of man and God gradually lead theologians from a concern for perfected beauty to a search for the sublime? Essentially the argument becomes, if divine perfection is greater than any human conception of perfect(ed) beauty and greater than any imitation of natural beauty, then this inexpressible perfection (i.e. maximal greatness) of the divine is best simply named 'the sublime'. It is, then, stressed that, unlike perfect beauty, the sublime is always ultimately inconceivable. What more can be said about the inconceivable sublime before the literary imagination reverts back, in the ebb and flow of Western European literary conceptions, to expressing experiences of beauty in nature?

In eighteenth-century Europe Rousseau's account of the different moral and aesthetic educations of men and women in *Émile* (1762) is given a critical response

---

[13] For an extremely witty and wise anecdote about an incredible contemporary ignorance of Mary Wollstonecraft, see Le Dœuff 2003: 108–10.

in Mary Wollstonecraft's *Vindication of the Rights of Woman* (1792). But Wollstone-craft's response is not taken up directly by her own contemporaries; it takes possibly another century before women championed her vindication.[14] Instead at the time Rousseau's assumptions concerning gender are appropriated by philosophers who take up Immanuel Kant's *Observations on the Feeling of the Beautiful and the Sublime* (1764). The latter raises heated gender debates (even today) about such statements as: 'The fair sex has just as much understanding as the male, but it is a *beautiful understanding* whereas ours should be a *deep understanding,* an expression that signifies identity with the sublime' (Kant 1960: 78).

A positive reading of Kant's claim acknowledges a certain level of equality in understanding between the male and female sexes. However, the gender differences between beautiful and deep understandings have negative implications when read alongside Kant's assertion that 'The virtue of a woman is a beautiful virtue. That of the male sex should be a noble virtue. Women will avoid the wicked not because it is un-right, but because it is ugly; and virtuous actions mean to them such as are morally beautiful. Nothing of duty, nothing of compulsion, nothing of obligation!' (Kant 1960: 81). At first glance women seem freed from the constraints of duty. But in Kantian terms this would imply excluding them from moral autonomy, since this autonomy would mean being free to act for the sake of duty alone. Moreover, additional gender connotations differentiate men from women by the former's ability to distance themselves from nature and move closer to the divine. This crucial gender difference shapes later associations of women with nature; and so women's beauty as a gift of nature becomes increasingly problematic as modern science and technology seek to dominate all nature as unruly and threatening rather than orderly and nurturing. What began, for some, as gender differences due to education becomes for many post-Enlightenment thinkers entrenched assumptions concerning fixed natural differences between women and men. Kant's gendering of beauty affects subsequent accounts of aesthetic education in profound ways. Even more worrying is that theological accounts of divine greatness as the sublime give further substantial ground to privilege men over women. From Kant to the twentieth-century French postmodernist Jean-François Lyotard, the problematic assumption persists that absolute beauty is unobtainable for women while men struggle to reorder the chaotic and corrupting forces of nature.

And yet hope emerges in a significant, ironic form which portrays a monstrous sublime. This upshot[15] of Kant's text implies a decisive lesson: once human desire and delight go beyond their proper limits human creations become monstrous.

---

[14] There are various arguments why this initial lack of positive response to her work and life might have been so (see Sanders 2001: 16–28). For further background to the reception of Wollstonecraft's (feminist) ideas after her death, see Pamela Clemit and Gina Luria Walker, 'Introduction', in Godwin 2001: 10–42.

[15] Crucial for a feminist writer's relationship to the history of literary and theological ideas are two sorts of readings of canonical texts: the first is the upshot of the text, which is the manner it has been understood by its (current) history; and the second is the possibility remaining in the text for the philosopher who is persuaded to return to it, to reread that text with fresh eyes; see Le Dœuff 1991: 168–70.

At the extreme the yearning connoisseur of beauty, despite a powerful recognition of unsurpassing beauty, fails tragically to be worthy of this perception. Without the mutual exchange between creator and creature, lover and beloved, monstrous forms of creativity manifest human unworthiness.[16] Instead of harmony, integrity, and splendour, the one-sided endeavour to create human beauty results in the monstrous sublime of death and destruction, 'where by its size it defeats the end that forms its concept' (Kant 1952: 100). In contrast to any ideal of the mutual exchange of human love in beauty the (monstrous) sublime undermines beauty: lifesaving potential is a creative yet fragile intimation of the divine. This monstrosity is powerfully represented in the Enlightenment myth of a new Prometheus in Mary Shelley's *Frankenstein* (1818).

Shelley's story about a man-made creature explores the tragedy and distortions of a scientific man who endeavours to replace divine with human creations, religion with science, and love with technology; the outcome is truly horrific. Shelley learns about a woman's rights and a revised moral ideal from a mother she never knew, and discovers for herself the productivity of the imagination. The brilliant young daughter captures, in her terrifying story of *Frankenstein,* the danger of displacing love. Hence she demonstrates with unforgettable imagery that the Romantic idea of human creativity cannot be sustained without the virtues of mutual love and justice; or, in the words of Frankenstein's monster: 'Cursed creator! Why did you form a monster so hideous that even you turned from me in disgust? God in pity made man beautiful and alluring, after his own image...but I am solitary and detested' (Shelley 1993: 105). Virtues—including beauty which accompanies justice as fair countenance—sustained by something transcendent of men and women (e.g. perfect order) would ensure that neither male nor female creativity results in the self-destructiveness of a chaotic and violent nature.

FEMINISM OR NOT

Angel or devil, submissive or strident, anti-feminist or thinking woman, each stark alternative repeats a pattern of patriarchal relations. 'A thin veil of white water across the sand...'—the imagery speaks volumes, if we treat the waves as representative of feminism's impact on patriarchy. Feminism has not yet had its last day. At the turn of this century the literary theorist Sarah Gamble assesses the feminist and post-feminist debates, and she concludes that

post-feminists are [not] wholly misguided in focusing attention upon what feminism has already gained for women. But it's also easy to be too optimistic and to take one's own

---

[16] This could be usefully put in contrast to Conway's account of the necessary interactions between the changing aspects of creation. See Conway 1982: 209–10.

privileged position as representative, which can lead to the conclusion that the time for feminism is past, and that those who still cling to activist principles are deluded and fanatical.   (Gamble 2001: 53)

Two points of caution: (1) it is crucial not to become too optimistic and ignore the deep ambivalences about women's identities which continue to undermine their authority as women and as writers of their own ideas; (2) it is essential that a woman is not afraid to affirm her uniqueness in seeking to write. She should, as Dorota Filipczak (2004: 210–22; cf. Jasper 2007) argues, aim at 'divining a self'. This divining means to locate oneself spiritually and socially in order to enable the autonomous female self to create a spiritual identity within her own political and religious context. Feminism and patriarchy struggle with both creative and destructive forms of language. The challenge is to explore that part of one's cognitive and imaginative capacities which constitutes the literary author as much as the theologian or philosopher of religion.

The paradigmatic figure which has gradually emerged in the previous pages is that of a dissenting angel. The post-Woolfian author seeks her own destiny, while appropriating Woolf's ultimate vision of light as it sets the sea ablaze. 'The surface of the sea slowly became transparent and lay rippling and sparkling until the dark stripes were almost rubbed out. Slowly the arm that held the Lamp raised it higher and then higher until a broad flame became visible; an arc of fire burnt on the rim of the horizon, and all around it the sea blazed gold' (Woolf 1992c: 3–4). Taking up the imagery from this novel, the reader imagines how years pass until another narrative interlude puts into play the sun, sea, sky, and waves. Here it is the end of another day:

The sun was sinking. The hard stone of the day was cracked and light poured through its splinters. Red and gold shot through the waves, in rapid running arrows, feathered with darkness. Erratically rays of light flashed and wandered like signals from sunken islands, or darts shot through laurel groves by shameless, laughing boys. But the waves, as they neared the shore, were robbed of light, and fell in one long concussion, like a wall falling, a wall of grey stone, unpierced by any chink of light.   (ibid. 173)

Thus, even when a feminist light is darkening, metaphor, imagery, narrative, and imagination seek to embody human knowledge. Creativity is one path to freedom, to free thinking, writing, and feeling. The creation of feminist knowledge(s) gives reality and substance to that part of the mind which exists to be developed. The creation of language and the creation of an inner world threaten to separate one from another, and yet this twofold nature of creativity remains essential for life itself. For the post-Woolfian feminist, mental states are themselves described, or spoken of, by external landscapes. The obstacle that does not speak its name is, nevertheless, shown in concrete practices and concrete exchanges. It is also tackled in the creation of characters, of narratives, of imagery by which glimpses of ineffable truths continue to rise and fall. Feminist creativity continues to produce messengers of hope for a world freed from oppressive material and social relations.

Works Cited

Anderson, Pamela Sue. 1998. *A Feminist Philosophy of Religion: the Rationality and Myths of Religious Belief*. Oxford: Blackwell.

—— 2002. 'Myth and Feminist Philosophy', *Thinking Through Myths: Philosophical Perspectives*, (ed.) Kevin Schilbrack, New York: Routledge.

Astell, Mary. 1694. *A Serious Proposal to the Ladies*. London: R. Wilkin.

—— 1730 [1700]. *Some Reflections on Marriage*. London: Wm. Parker.

—— and Norris, John. 1695. *Letters Concerning the Love of God, Between the Author of the Proposal to the Ladies and Mr John Norris*. London: John Norris.

Barrett, Michèle (ed.). 1979. 'Introduction', *Virginia Woolf: Women and Writing*. London: The Women's Press.

Behn, Aphra. 1696 [1688]. *Oroonoko, or the Royal Slave*, in *The Histories and Novels of the Late Ingenious Mrs. Behn*. London: S. Briscoe.

Burke, Edmund. 1990 [1757]. *A Philosophical Enquiry into the Origin of Our Ideas of the Sublime and Beautiful*, ed. Adam Phillips. Oxford: Oxford University Press.

Butler, Judith. 1990. *Gender Trouble: Feminism and the Subversion of Identity*. New York: Routledge.

Cockburn, Catharine. See Warnock 1996: pp. xxxvii, 29–36.

Conway, Anne. 1982 [1670]. *The Principles of the Most Ancient and Modern Philosophy*, ed. Peter Loptson. The Hague: Martin Mijhoff.

Delphy, Christine. 1984. *Close to Home: A Materialist Analysis of Women's Oppression*, trans. and ed. Diana Leonard. London: Hutchinson.

Filipczak, Dorota. 2004. 'Autonomy and Female Spirituality in A Polish Context: Divining A Self', in Pamela Sue Anderson and Beverley Clack (eds.), *Feminist Philosophy of Religion: Critical Readings*. London: Routledge, 211–22.

Gamble, Sarah (ed.). 2001. *The Routledge Companion to Feminism and Post-Feminism*. London: Routledge.

Gilman, Charlotte Perkins. 1981 [1892]. *The Yellow Wallpaper*. London: Virago.

Godwin, William. 2001 [1798]. *Memoirs of the Author of A Vindication of the Rights of Woman*, eds. Pamela Clemit and Gina Luria Walker. Ontario: Broadview.

Heilbrun, Carolyn G. 1989. *Writing A Woman's Life*. London: The Women's Press.

Hooks, bell. 1999. *Remembered Rapture: The Writer at Work*. London: The Women's Press.

Jasper, Alison. 2007. '"The Past is not a Husk . . . Yet Change Goes On": Liberating Feminist Theology for All Our Futures'. *Feminist Theology*, forthcoming.

Julian of Norwich. 1998 [1373; 1393]. *Revelations of Divine Love*, trans. Elizabeth Spearing. London: Penguin.

Kant, Immanuel. 1960 [1764]. *Observations on the Feeling of the Beautiful and the Sublime*, trans. John T. Goldthwait. Berkeley: University of California Press.

—— 1952 [1790]. *The Critique of Judgement*, trans. James Creed Meredith. Oxford: Clarendon.

Le Dœuff, Michèle. 2002 [1980]. *The Philosophical Imaginary*, trans. Colin Gordon. New York and London: Continuum.

—— 1991 [1989]. *Hipparchia's Choice: An Essay Concerning Women, Philosophy, Etc.*, trans. Trista Selous. Oxford: Blackwell: 2006, republished in a revised translation. New York: Columbia University Press.

—— 2003 [1998]. *The Sex of Knowing*, trans. Lorraine Code and Kathryn Hamer. London: Routledge.

Lee, Hermione. 1997. *Virginia Woolf*. London: Vintage.

LERNER, GERDA. 1993. *The Creation of Feminist Consciousness: From the Middle Ages to Eighteen-Seventy*. New York: Oxford University Press.

MILLETT, KATE. 1977 [1969]. *Sexual Politics*. London: Virago.

MOI, TORIL. 1988 [1985]. *Sexual/Textual Politics: Feminist Literary Theory*. London: Routledge.

MORRISON, TONI. 1993. *Playing in the Dark: Whiteness and the Literary Imagination*. New York: Vintage.

PIZAN, CHRISTINE DE. 1999 [1405]. *The Book of the City of Ladies*, trans. Rosalind Brown-Grant. Harmondsworth: Penguin 1521. *The Boke of the Cyte of Ladyes*. London: Henry Pepwell.

RICH, ADRIENNE. 1995 [1982]. *Of Woman Born: Motherhood as Experience and Institution*. New York: W. W. Norton.

SANDERS, VALERIE. 2001. 'First Wave Feminism', in Gamble 2001: 16–28.

SHELLEY, MARY. 1993 [1818]. *Frankenstein, or the Modern Prometheus*, ed. Marilyn Butler. Oxford: Oxford University Press.

TALIAFERRO, CHARLES, and TEPLY, ALISON (eds.). 2004. *Cambridge Platonist Spirituality*. Mahwah, NJ: Paulist Press, 37–43, 187–92.

WARNOCK, MARY (ed.). 1996. *Women Philosophers*. London: J. M. Dent.

WAUGH, PATRICIA. 1989. *Feminine Fictions: Revisiting the Postmodern*. London: Routledge.

WOLLSTONECRAFT, MARY. 1992 [1792]. *A Vindication of the Rights of Woman*, ed. Miriam Brody. Harmondsworth: Penguin.

WOOLF, VIRGINIA. 1975 [1888–1912]. *The Letters of Virginia Woolf*, ed. Nigel Nicolson and Joanne T. Trautmann. London: Hogarth.

—— 1992a [1925]. *Mrs Dalloway*. Harmondsworth: Penguin.

—— 1992b [1915]. *The Voyage Out*. Harmondsworth: Penguin.

—— 1992c [1938]. *The Waves*, ed. Gillian Beer. Oxford World's Classics. Oxford: Oxford University Press.

—— 1993a. [1929; 1938; 1931]. *A Room of One's Own; Three Guineas*; 'Professions for Women' (Appendix II), ed. with intro. and notes Michèle Barrett. Harmondsworth: Penguin.

—— 1993b [1928]. *Orlando*. Harmondsworth: Penguin.

—— 1993c [1927]. *To the Lighthouse*. Harmondsworth: Penguin.

FURTHER READING

BUCK, CLAIRE (ed.). 1992. *Bloomsbury Guide to Women's Literature*. London: Bloomsbury.

CLEMIT, PAMELA. 1993. *The Godwinian Novel: The Rational Fictions of Godwin, Bockden Brown, Mary Shelley*. Oxford: Oxford University Press.

KEMPE, MARGERY. 1985 [late 14th century]. *The Book of Margery Kempe*, trans. and ed. Barry Windeatt. London: Penguin Classics.

KENYON, OLGA (ed.). 1992. *800 Years of Women's Letters*. Stroud: Alan Sutton.

MITCHELL, JULIET. 1973 [1971]. *Woman's Estate*. New York: Vintage.

NIGHTINGALE, FLORENCE. 1979 [1852]. *Cassandra*. New York: The Feminist Press at CUNY.

WOLLSTONECRAFT, MARY. 1976 [1788]. *Mary, A Fiction*, with *The Wrongs of Woman*, ed. Gary Kelly. Oxford: Oxford University Press.

CHAPTER 49

....

SALVATION— PERSONAL AND POLITICAL

....

GEORGE NEWLANDS

A great deal of human striving may be understood as a search for salvation, intellectual, physical, and emotional. This search generates stories, which are recorded in texts both sacred and secular. It also generates actions, which are wrapped up with and often stimulate the stories. Religion, as part of human striving, searches for salvation through transcendence, and through the consequences for human life of divine action. In English literature the predominant religious tradition which has stimulated the articulation of notions of salvation has been Christianity. This chapter will therefore focus on Christian input into narratives of salvation.

Christian theology, arising from both worship and reflection on the biblical tradition, has seen salvation in both corporate and in individual terms, individual more in a 'Protestant' mode from Paul through Luther, corporate more in a Catholic mode from the Church Fathers to the Middle Ages. We see the travails of salvation personal, salvation religious, or salvation secular, explored in the writings of John Milton and John Bunyan, and in the fiction of Graham Greene, John Steinbeck, and John Updike. We see salvation political in William Blake's *Jerusalem*, in the work of George Orwell, and throughout the millenarian tradition.

In modern theology, salvation is most often seen as personal, both in conservative evangelical and in liberal theologies. More recently, however, there has also been an emphasis on salvation as political, in the liberation theologies, and as communal, in some post-liberal versions. Traditionally, salvation has been seen as salvation *for* and salvation *from*, in different dimensions. Salvation is *for* a great final goal and source of hope. Salvation is *from* some great evil. Salvation in Christianity is, above all, salvation through Christ. The large-scale modern systematic theologies of Karl Barth and Hans Urs von Balthasar can be read as dramas of salvation as incarnation and as atonement. A good overview of salvation which is sensitive to literary allusions and analogies may be found in F. W. Dillistone's old but still useful book *The Christian Understanding of Atonement* (1968).

Salvation is a hugely multifaceted theme. Salvation is from God, and as such it is understood as the goal to which all humanity has been directed from the beginning of the creation: to be saved is to become truly human. It can be conceived as rescue and restoration, as revelation and reconciliation, as representation and substitution, judgement and making righteous, incarnation and atonement, decontamination from the things of this world and attainment of a heavenly realm, something almost in the shape of a consumer durable and recognized as accompanied by prosperity, liberation, justice, and the establishment of specific forms, for example, of social and political orders. In the Christian tradition, salvation is through Christ alone: God comes into our world in the figure of Jesus Christ as a human being, in solidarity, in suffering, and in transfiguration.

In English literature the quest for salvation, broadly conceived, may be seen as a leitmotif of significant writing from Beowulf to Joyce. The classic sources are too many to list in detail, but a few would include the Grail legends and salvation through eucharist; Chaucer and the theme of pilgrimage to Canterbury; Shakespeare and in particular *The Tempest*, but also the tragedies; John Donne in the Holy Sonnets; George Herbert, especially in perhaps his best-known poem, 'Love bade me welcome'; John Milton in *Paradise Lost*; Samuel Taylor Coleridge in *The Rime of the Ancient Mariner*; Robert Browning in 'The Bishop Orders his Tomb'; or Oscar Wilde in *The Portrait of Dorian Gray*. More recently we might turn to C. S. Lewis, or the poets W. H. Auden, Edwin Morgan, or Geoffrey Hill.

Throughout this corpus of literature there is an ongoing interaction with theology. Lear's sufferings are a mirror of the dialectic between damnation and salvation, and the travail of human life on the edge. Donne's divine poems are, of course, saturated with theological reflection on salvation.

> Since Christ embrac'd the Crosse itself, dare I
> His image, th'image of his Crosse deny?
> Would I have profit by the sacrifice
> And dare the chosen Altar to despise?
>
> ('The Cross')

With Milton we are in a world of a tradition steeped in the consciousness of sin and the looming threat of hell.

> Of man's first disobedience, and the fruit
> Of that forbidden tree, whose mortal taste
> Brought death into the world, and all our woe,
> With loss of Eden...
>
> (*Paradise Lost*, Book 1. 1–4)

With Coleridge too we are riddled with guilt and maddened by consciousness of sin.

> The very deep did rot: O Christ!
> That ever this should be!
> Yea, slimy things did crawl with legs
> Upon the slimy sea.

> (*The Rime of the Ancient Mariner*)

With Browning we see the subversion of faith which still clings to the simulacra of salvation.

> And then how I shall lie through centuries
> And see God made and eaten all day long
> And feel the steady candle-flame
> Good strong thick stupefying incense-smoke.

> ('The Bishop Orders his Tomb.')

We may think of the influence of Coleridge on Cardinal Newman, of Kierkegaard on Auden, of the interface of faith and poetry in Gerard Manley Hopkins. If we extend literature in English to American literature, and colonial and post-colonial themes, then the field becomes even more diverse. Stories of paradise gained juxtapose with stories of paradise lost. Salvation is sometimes the healing of a desperate disease and sometimes a cosmic victory over evil.

If we extend literature in the direction of other media, the salvation theme becomes equally visible, in the films of the works of Tolkien or J. K. Rowling, or the passion narrative as seen through the eyes of Mel Gibson. Even the literature of the internet is flooded with salvation motifs, while much of the material from literature, such as the poems of George Herbert, centres on salvation. Some of the literature derives its strength from irony, as when Updike's unflinching gaze on our contemporary frailty is framed in his novel *In the Beauty of the Lilies* (1996).

Tragedy and salvation conflict at every level in the literary cosmos. Can there ever be a Christian tragedy, however, when the Gospel is of a sure and certain hope of resurrection? But this is more than simply a clichéd examination question. Lutheran and Catholic backgrounds often give a distinctive twist to literary explorations of the subject. Neither T. S. Eliot nor Auden would have written as they did without absorbing particular theological perspectives, for better or for worse, and without participating in particular sorts of Christian worship and practice. Indeed, it might be said that in a religion of incarnation there is always an imperative to a wider dialogue. Christian faith ever seeks to contribute to the search for common human values within the created order.

Salvation and damnation, literature and the liberal arts: these are enormous themes, and it is not easy to say anything worthwhile about them of a general nature. The more these themes are studied, the clearer it is that they are *infinitely heterogeneous*. Culture has infinite subdivisions, often with very different characteristics. But we should not give up hope entirely of making connections, for without connections there can be no common search for values, and we should try to avoid avenues in which all cats become grey in the night.

Salvation is a work of love. Where there is salvation there is love, and perhaps even where there is love there is salvation. Salvation is an idea, a vision, and an at least partly embodied reality. It encompasses forgiveness and reconciliation, and at the same time it cannot ignore evil and injustice. It is accomplished through agonizing conflict at many levels, intellectual, physical, political, spiritual. It relates to specific historical events in the past, to present reality, and to eschatological promise and expectation. It signals a specific quality of corporate concern for generosity and commitment in the present, and it remains provisional, open to future resolution. It points to life and to death, and to existential questions of meaning and value, for individuals and for communities.

A good example of theological dialogue with literature is given by the theologian Karl-Josef Kuschel in his book *The Poet as Mirror: Human Nature, God and Jesus in Twentieth-Century Literature* (1997). Kuschel is conscious of the contemporary isolation of theology. 'One does not need to read the most recent demographic surveys to know how remote religious language has become from the reality of life. In religious language, a particular order of the church and society has become frozen, and if it is transferred to changed social conditions, it must often seem comical or ridiculous' (Kuschel 1997: 8). He affirms George Steiner's claim that human beings can experience transcendence in the encounter with a great work of art, and notes that even Karl Barth could say that art could function as a parable of the reality of God. But, he continues, 'not every experience of mystery as a result of a work of art is itself an experience of God' (ibid. 18). Art contains only the possibility of truth, and can be subject to self-deception.

For the ultimate verification of human products as signals of the truth lies with God himself. . . . Works of art as places of the seeming true are symbolic illuminations of the mystery of human nature—that is my theological definition. For its part, Christian faith illuminates the human condition, the human mystery, in the light of the word of God, attested in holy scripture.   (ibid. 20–1).

In illustrating the theme of salvation in literature we can only dip into a tiny number of instances. Among the diverse group of theologians who constituted the Christian realists in the late 1930s and 1940s were two notable literary figures, T. S. Eliot and W. H. Auden.

Eliot was a friend of the Scots theologian John Baillie, and attended the Moot, that significant gathering of intellectual figures in England throughout the war years. Along with Karl Barth, William Temple, and others, he contributed an essay to the collection entitled *Revelation*, edited by Baillie and Martin (1936).

Baillie had left New York before Auden arrived in 1939. Auden was soon to become a close friend of Reinhold Niebuhr—a friendship eloquently testified to in their correspondence, which was published by Ursula Niebuhr in 1991. First it is important to see how much it matters to a literary figure *what sort of theology*, and what sort of churchmanship, he or she embraces.

Eliot's essay on revelation is the first in the *Revelation* collection. Eliot begins with the observation that 'it is because I am not a theologian that I have been asked to contribute'. He continues:

I am concerned with the general differences between those who maintain a doctrine of revelation and those who reject all revelation . . . I take for granted that Christian revelation is the only full revelation; and that the fullness of Christian revelation consists in the essential fact of the incarnation, in relation to which all Christian revelation is to be understood. The division between those who accept, and those who deny, Christian revelation I take to be the most profound division between human beings.

Here we see Eliot in his most conservative theological mode. Both Eliot and Auden were, of course, highly complex characters, and the complexities led to tensions which in their poetry and prose were often immensely creative. Both had a firmly realist sense of the difference between the sacred and the profane. Neither was partial to 'psychological mysticism', though both were deeply aware of the mystery of divine transcendence. Both were prisoners, at one level, of the theological and ecclesial perspectives they inherited, largely by serendipitous means, as we all acquire knowledge which we have not studied in professional courses. Both turned these accidents to their craft with profound effect, and produced literary work, at least on occasion, of the very highest order.

In his book *Christianity and Modern European Literature* (1997), Daniel Murphy has a fascinating chapter on Eliot entitled 'Darkness of God: T. S. Eliot's Quest for Faith.' Eliot moved from humanism to religion, as he himself explained in an essay 'Religion without Humanism' in 1931. He was especially fascinated by the *via negativa*, notably in the mysticism of St John of the Cross but also in Buddhism. These come together particularly, Murphy notes, in 'The Fire Sermon', in *The Waste Land*. While much of his early poetry had been openly critical of religion, *The Waste Land* explores the tension between belief and unbelief. Murphy quotes a letter of Eliot to Charles Williams: 'We are, I know not how, double in ourselves, so that what we believe we disbelieve, and we cannot rid ourselves of what we condemn.' The way of darkness is ultimately the way of light, as in the second of *The Four Quartets*, 'East Coker'. These religious themes are brought to a final resolution in 'Little Gidding'. In faith, and in life beyond death, the symbol of suffering and the symbol of God's love are one.

> And all shall be well and
> All manner of thing shall be well
> When the tongues of flame are in-folded
> Into the crowned knot of fire
> And the fire and the rose are one.
>
> (Eliot 1969: 198)

Perhaps in some ways mirroring the mood of foreboding of the 1930s in much of Europe, there is more of the cross than of the incarnation or even the resurrection in a great deal of Eliot's work. This gives it its power, but also a certain limitation. Together with Barth and Niebuhr, and also with Auden, Eliot drinks deep from the Augustinian tradition. To affirm the gospel as good news, as transformative within the created order, without either trivializing suffering or romanticizing the world, remains a difficult task. The German theologian Dietrich Bonhoeffer was to struggle towards this in his *Letters and Papers from Prison*. Auden was aware of the dilemma, but perhaps too steeped in the thought of Kierkegaard to be able to address it effectively.

I now turn to Auden, and again to his theological connections. Ursula Niebuhr wrote that:

Wystan Auden was a close and dear friend to Reinhold, me and our children. He was always kind, interested and generous; we, as did other friends of his, gave him a strong family setting....He and I had shared the same sort of English and Edwardian childhood. We both had doctor fathers: both of us had devout mothers...Anglican liturgy had also interested us both.   (Niebuhr 1991: 280)

She notes the influence of Kierkegaard on Auden, his use of the 'leap of faith' and also his sense of irony. She comments, 'We cherished this friend, his imagination, and what he saw and taught us about life, not only about the human situation but also about a certain vision of glory.'

Auden's correspondence reveals remarkable daily snapshots of the way he related religion to culture.

14 February 1946: Auden to Reinhold Niebuhr. 'Kierkegaard as usual put his finger on the sore spot when he said that the task of the preacher is to preach Christ the contemporary offense to Christians.'

30 May 1957: Auden to Ursula Niebuhr. 'Among other works have read Simone Weil's *La Pesanteur et la Grace*. Have you? Wildly exasperating, I think, but very important. An exposition of the *via negativa* carried to almost heretical lengths, i.e. for her it is not the Cross that is the stumbling block, but the Incarnation, or rather any of the references in the Gospel to Christ enjoying himself. However, it is more honest than any modern work I know about the characteristic experience of God in a sceptical schizophrenic age like ours.'   (ibid. 285, 290)

Norman Cary (1975) has noted that Auden, like Eliot, draws *a clear line between the sacred and the secular*, at least in theory. In *The Dyer's Hand*, Auden asserts that 'To a Christian, unfortunately, both art and science are secular activities, that is to say, small beer.' The artistic imagination is purely natural, and is liable to be moved by 'certain objects, beings, and events, to a feeling of sacred awe'. This smacks of pantheism. To the Christian, on the other hand, the truly sacred is not that which naturally arouses awe in the human imagination.

The Incarnation, the coming of Christ in the form of a Servant who cannot be recognized by the eye of flesh and blood, but only by the eye of faith, puts an end to all claims of the imagination to be the faculty which decides what is truly sacred and what is profane. A pagan God can appear on earth in disguise but, so long as he wears his disguise, no man is expected to recognize him nor can. But Christ appears looking just like any other man, yet claims that he is the Way, the Truth and the Life, and that no man can come to the father except through him. The contradiction between the profane appearance and the sacred assertion is impassible to the imagination.   (Auden 1963: 457)

There is an excellent discussion of Auden in the chapter entitled 'Credo ut Intelligam: W. H. Auden's Vision of Christian Co-inherence' in Murphy's book on modern European literature (Murphy 1997: 323–58). He comments: 'The writings of [Reinhold] Niebuhr, together with those of [Charles] Williams and Søren Kierkegaard, were largely responsible for shaping the Christian vision that dominated Auden's poetry from 1940 till his death in 1977.' Murphy mentions especially Niebuhr's works *An Interpretation of Christian Ethics* (1936), *Christianity and Power Politics* (1940), and *The Nature and Destiny of Man* (1941–3). From Kierkegaard, Auden derived a conception of the ethical as a fulfilment of the radical freedom of individual consciousness, and the act of moral decision as a leap from the aesthetic to the ethical. Auden sees truth as the product of a dialectical tension. 'The one infallible symptom of greatness is the gift of *double-focus*.' He also writes, 'We, being divided, remembering, evolving beings, composed of a number of selves, each with its false conception of self-interest, sin in most that we do' (quoted in Murphy 1997: 344).

Following Kierkegaard, Auden (1976: 675–6) stresses the inevitability of suffering, but also the resolution which ensues from it. Faith alone is what is required. Hope is founded on the cross and resurrection.

> Now, did he really break the seal
> And rise again? We dare not say;
> But conscious unbelievers feel
> Quite sure of Judgement Day.
> Meanwhile, a silence on the cross,
> As dead as we shall ever be,
> Speaks of some total gain or loss,
> And you and I are free
> To guess from his insulted face
> Just what Appearances he saves
> By suffering in a public place
> A death reserved for slaves.
>
> ('Friday's Child: In Memoriam
> Dietrich Bonhoeffer')

Auden's Kierkegaardian perspective provides an instructive foil to Eliot's confidence in Christendom, and indeed to the implicit correlation of religion and culture which we see in the theological tradition from Schleiermacher to Tillich.

In their entirely different ways the writers mentioned—and completely different examples could have been chosen—are doing what literature does best, that is, seeking to offer a critically realist account of human life as it actually is, and by showing their denial of these, highlighting values of love and justice. All are concerned with social issues and with the ultimate questions of human existence. By shedding light on darkness, or indeed by shedding darkness on light, each writer describes the contrasts between the actual and the desirable states of human community. A critical theology should be able to learn from these penetrating narratives of the human condition in seeking to make its own contribution towards understanding God's engagement with humanity, so that the jagged fragments of human need and divine reality are brought again into some sort of serious conjunction.

To allow these different commentaries on human dignity to engage with each other on their own terms, while facilitating a genuine mutuality in a common recognition of mutual need, is part of an intercultural theological venture which requires all the varieties of experience if it is to have any hope of success in construing salvation in a deeply fragmented world.

A poem is a poem and a novel is a novel, and neither are theological or sociological treatises. Yet the issues involved in the one instance may help in our understanding of the other, provided that we do not allow our judgement to be unduly skewed by any particular form of interpretation. Only God can provide the grand perspective in which all the connections are properly recorded. The theologian's task is the more modest one of seeking to trace some of the threads of comparison and contrast which may help to provide a human perspective on the issues and the ways in which we can move forward to a more humane society. Awareness that we are precisely *not* God may help us to avoid deifying partial aspects of this reality, as well as helping us to move towards God's preferred envelope of love, peace, and justice for our actions. Neither Christendom, nor exclusive whiteness nor blackness nor any other coercive stereotype will help us.

One of the basic questions raised by these examples from literature and theology is the relationship of God to history. A spiritualizing approach which removes God and the question of God from the often unpleasant realities of history is clearly useless, while an immersion in historical struggle which never shows any sense of transcendent presence within and through history is equally frustrating. Only a concept of God who can be reasonably believed to act in and through human history will engage the attention of serious seekers after common humanity and a God who is self-giving, self-affirming love.

In the Christian story, salvation comes through vulnerability, kenosis, unconditional generosity, and the avoidance of triumphalism. Yet its historical manifestation has, in practice, often exhibited the opposite characteristics, not least in relation to non-European peoples and non-Christian religions. Here are areas where the scope of the traditional imagination concerning salvation urgently needs to be widened through intercultural and cross-cultural dialogue, both religious and secular. We have to be aware of the limitations of a choice of examples far from our own domestic situation, which relieve us of the burden of pressing issues.

F. W. Dillistone's survey of atonement motifs, a major strand of salvation theology, includes essays on such central elements as eternal sacrifice, unique redemption, supreme tragedy, decisive judgement, all-embracing compassion, and all-inclusive forgiveness. But the scope of salvation is as broad as the scope of our imagination itself. Salvation has at the very least a historical dimension, a personal dimension, a political dimension, an anthropological dimension, a cosmological dimension, a spiritual dimension, an eschatological dimension; while loss of salvation, damnation, and alienation are the other side of the coin, and the stuff of tragedy.

It is worth underlining the huge literary power of the other side of salvation and the profound consequences of a world of lost innocence. The Glasgow poet Edwin Morgan brilliantly touches upon damnations, past and present. The 'silenced' are remembered only by chance: on Janet Horne, the last woman burned as a witch in Scotland in 1727 he comments (2002: 59)

> Dear God were you sleeping
> You were certainly not weeping
> She was not in your keeping.

On the contemporary face of the tradition of persecution he writes, in *The Trondheim Requiem* (ibid. 63–):

> We entered by the gate of fear
> We exited without hope, as smoke
> The chimneys pointed at the sky
> In silence, unaccusing, unaccused
>
> (The Yellow Triangle)
>
> Who shall chronicle our suffering?
> We have no lobby and no voice
> Where is our home, where is our country?
> Is that why our destroyers destroy?
>
> (The Brown Triangle)
>
> We were the lowest of the low.
> Further down you could not go
> Nature itself, they said, abhorred us.
> How should the Third Reich reward us?
>
> (The Pink Triangle)

Understanding of salvation closely mirrors the development of the understanding of the self as 'encultured'. It is hardly surprising, therefore, that salvation is a central underlying theme of much serious literature.

The search for salvation involves the search for transcendence. In this quest the European classical tradition of Christian theology, despite its tendency to attempt to colonize the mind of God, still has much to contribute. However fallibly, it has at least produced important constructive efforts to understand our conceptions of God, while still respecting the mystery. It has also contributed, in tandem with classical philosophy, to the search for universal ethical, political, and social values. For example, Steinbeck's novels of the Great Depression, especially *Of Mice and Men* (1937) and *The Grapes of Wrath* (1939) are driven by the search for a community's political and economic salvation.

To this tradition the recent emancipatory and liberation theologies continue to make important modifications. In highlighting the histories of alternative community they highlight the deficiencies of accounts which equally focused on Eurocentric community experience—in this entry we are speaking specifically of work produced in the United Kingdom.

Salvation is worked out in personal struggle, but also, as the tradition has shown us, in community. It is this community element which is a recurring emancipatory theme. This may bring out the ecclesial dimensions of Christian salvation theme—word and sacrament, participation and eucharist, worship and discipleship. Here too there are communities of damnation, where an irrational and wasteful dynamic tears communities apart, dragging individuals helplessly to destruction. The salvation theme is a theme of essential hope, but it is not an easy or unreflected hope.

Works Cited

AUDEN, W. H. 1951. *The Enchafed Flood*. London: Faber & Faber

—— 1963. *The Dyer's Hand*. New York: Random House.

—— 1976. *Collected Poems*, ed. E. Mendelson. London: Faber.

BONHOEFFER, DIETRICH. 1953. *Letters and Papers from Prison*, ed. Renate Bethge. London: SCM.

CARY, N. 1975. *Christian Criticism in the 20th Century*. New York: Kennikat.

DILLISTONE, F. W. 1968. *The Christian Understanding of Atonement*. London: James Nisbet.

ELIOT, T. S. 1936. 'Revelation', in *Revelation*, ed. J. Baillie and H. Martin. London: Faber & Faber.

—— 1969. *The Complete Poems and Plays*. London: Faber & Faber.

KUSCHEL, KARL-JOSEF. 1997. *The Poet as Mirror: Human Nature, God and Jesus in Twentieth Century Literature*, trans. John Bowden. London: SCM.

MORGAN, EDWIN. 2002. *Cathures*. Manchester, Carcanet.

MURPHY, D. 1997. *Christianity and Modern European Literature*. Dublin: Four Courts.

NIEBUHR, U. 1991. *Remembering Reinhold Niebuhr*. San Francisco: Harper.

Further Reading

NEWLANDS, G. 2004. *The Transformative Imagination*. Aldershot: Ashgate.

PATRICK SHERRY. 2003. *Images of Redemption: Art, Literature and Salvation*. London: Continuum.

PART SEVEN

AFTERWORD

CHAPTER 50

THE FUTURE OF ENGLISH LITERATURE AND THEOLOGY

ANDREW HASS

IF we try to give scope and shape to the future of literature and theology, we must remain as speculative and open-ended as any prognostications about art and ideas. New creations, we all know, resist predictability, since they depend upon uncontrollable forces—an inspiration, a catastrophic event, an instant discovery, the rare emergence of genius. One can only forecast from what one knows about the present, and even then guardedly. It is therefore not the specifics of future religious thought, nor the emergence of some new form of literature, that we would dare to anticipate. Rather, we can only hope to offer more general observations about where we might see literature and theology as a defined field heading in the near future, observations that arise from certain discernible features of our contemporary culture. The following discussion will lay out four such general features: post-secularity, globalization, culturality, and interdisciplinarity. None of these must stand alone; each will intersect with the other at some level. Collectively they all become determinate of the space that literature and theology, either as separate enterprises or as a joint entity, seem already to be filling. So what we intend to put forward here, at the end of a volume about the way literature and theology has emerged as a joint field of study within the Humanities, is not some programmatic approach to how scholarship in this field ought to be conducted, nor how artists interested in religion will necessarily ply their trade, nor how religions will make use of future literary productions, nor even how religion and art will once again seal their alliance. It is rather how several present phenomena or conditions will have some bearing on how we envision and practise a field that, in its very evolution, seems to be outstripping its own designations, 'literature' and 'theology'. To this end, we will take our four categories as markers of a wider state for which literature and religion, from Milton to Blake to Joyce, has always heralded, if not embodied: those moments of paradigmatic shift when we humans rethink our relationship to the divine.

POST-SECULARITY

As the end of the last millennium came to a close, there arose talk within certain philosophical circles of a 'return' to religion. Derrida stated in the mid-1990s: 'Today once again, today finally, today otherwise, the great question would still be religion and what some hastily call its "return"' (Derrida 1998: 39). It may seem odd that philosophy should speak of a return, as if religion had ever gone away. But we know that Western literature had been marking a slow retreat from religious expectation since the eighteenth century, so that by the *fin de siècle* of the following century, whether through Nietzsche or through Hardy, the death knell had been ringing for that form of Christianity which centrally informed our cultural value system and our underlying perception of reality. The twentieth century had been one of resignation to the inexorable forces of secularization, so that by the latter half, when the first noises of 'postmodernism' made their raucous entry, a thoroughly secularized West seemed a *fait accompli*. But with typical postmodern irony, religion began to creep back through the very ideas which seemed at first to seal its coffin. By the new millennium, the return seemed certain, with talk being generated well outside only philosophical circles, and, post-9/11, with society waking up to the consequences of religion's fervency. In the opening statement of his book *True Religion* (2003: p. vii), Graham Ward declares as the beginning of a 'manifesto': 'Religion is, once more, haunting the imagination of the West'. Whether or not linked with terrorism, it has begun again to inspire thinking in ways that, only a few decades previously, seemed all but unrecoverable.

Yet one thing we can say about this religious 'return' of late modernity: religion no longer stands in *opposition* to secularity, as if in some prolonged Cold War that began some two hundred years previously. This is not because of some détente, where both sides agree to ease the strain through compromise or good will. Nor is it that religion has regained its sure-footedness in the age of post-industrialization and the information age. It is rather that secularity has lost its position as an impenetrable positivist bastion against what it saw as the thinly protected myths of religion and spirituality. Secularism, as an *ism*,[1] has shown itself to be as vulnerable as it once claimed religion to be. Under the charge of a postmodern critique, secularism has proved as ideological as any religious doctrine or theology in its privileging of certain social and political realities over others, and in its dependence on categories of rationality grounded upon logocentrism, historicism, patriarchy, and stable notions of selfhood. Its claims to authority—scientific instrumentality on the one hand, individual freedom and autonomy on the other—have now been rendered questionable through various levels of sustained critique, and by bracketing out transcendence and divine possibility, it becomes nothing other than the inverse gesture of the deductive theology that begins with transcendence and divine possibility. Both positions assume stable a prioris that in their direct opposition might have once cancelled each other out, but now are equally implicated in those ideological indignities that the cultural critiques of such newer disciplines as gender studies and post-colonialism have been so eager to expose.

As one of the most far-reaching products of the Enlightenment, the antinomy of religion and irreligion has thus given way to a post-Enlightenment condition. Here, the adjective 'post-secular' has gained increasing use in reconsidering the various constituencies of the cultural domain: post-secular philosophy, post-secular reason, post-secular theology, post-secular social theory, post-secular art, and even, within the academy, post-secular studies (e.g. at London Metropolitan University). All these terms suggest that the young new millennium has not dispensed with religion or spirituality as something outmoded and unsustainable, but that religious or spiritual matters, whether in the form of lingering cultural vestiges or resurfaced interests, continue to influence and inform our fundamental thinking, actions, and creations.

One of the prominent effects of this post-secularity (as a state or condition, and not an ism) is that religion and art no longer bear an antagonism towards each other, as they once did within the religious/secular divide. Religion, having lost its supremacy as moral authority, can no longer expect literature to play the role of handmaiden to higher truths. Art, having lost its authority as the inviolable genius of culture, can no longer claim to be the new legislator of morality and reality. A new humility marks the post-secular age, whereby both sides understand that they are bound to one another. Theologically, we are no longer speaking about a readiness to acknowledge the importance of the language of art to describe the indescribable. Aesthetically, we are no longer speaking about a postmodern borrowing of religious relics from the past (images, symbols, concepts), to be used within an ironic mélange. Instead, we are speaking about a fundamental reconceiving of both sides, where religion, along with its theological discourse, admits it has always been party to poetics, and art, along with its aesthetic discourse, admits it has always been religiously invested. We have seen this mutuality arising out of certain discourses

---

[1] In distinction from Vattimo's understanding of 'secularization' in his notion of a 'theology of secularization', whereby the secularizing process in the history of the West in fact becomes the salvation of Christianity, in removing it from the natural religion of a peremptory God of violence, held in place throughout European history by metaphysics and onto-theology. See Vattimo 1999.

within Continental thinking about art, religion, and philosophy, whose language, particularly in its more recent phases, is already a language 'between'—between reason and imagination, between analysis and poetics, between direction and indirection, between critique and belief (see e.g. Blond 1998). But we see a further manifestation in recent post-secular art, which has intentionally situated itself between a this-worldliness and an other-worldliness. In this between-state, it sits poised with the affirmation that the material carries a dimension of the spiritual which the creative act, acting upon the material, allows us in some degree to penetrate. This is not a religious position as such, though it may work in traditional religious imagery and thought; but neither is it *not* religious, in that it willingly opens itself up to what traditional religions have always sought to give voice and expression to. It may not make a confessional plea for this, but it furnishes a space for its play.

The Scottish writer A. L. Kennedy has already been mentioned in this volume in relation to matters of the body (see Alison Jasper, 'Body and Word'). But we can also see in her stories this movement towards the post-secular, where the material and the spiritual find a renewed coexistence through the blended forces of bodily expression and religious yearning. In her novel *Paradise* (2004), for example, a Christlike sacrifice unfolds in fourteen chapters, each emulating a Station of the Cross. The protagonist, however, is not a hallowed figure, but rather a serious alcoholic, whose various stages of agony result from successive bouts of inebriation, sobriety, and blackout. Here the reemergence of the religious is not towards the abstract or metaphysical God who resides beyond the flesh and materiality of this world, but is through the uneasy marriage of the physical with the spiritual, as God once again is embodied in the weaknesses of the flesh, and the old abusive hierarchy of the body/soul dualism (the traditional patriarchal marriage) gives way to a new sanctification of love and identity founded on a mutual reliance.

GLOBALIZATION

Part of the breakdown of secularism has come from its inability to survive in other cultural contexts outside the West. And as most of the developed world now experiences present-day life on a global level, whether through media, the Internet, or travel, it has opened itself up to the influences of other views and cultural sensibilities. This outward shift has made a tremendous impact on how we understand both literature and religion. As we have pointed out many places before in this volume, the term 'English literature' has now become a deeply problematic term; but the notion of 'Western religion' also requires re-evaluation if it is to become something more than a mere historical marker.

For literature, globalization—'a process effecting worldwide linkages, joint action and the formation and maintenance of transnational institutions, made possible by recent advances in electronic communications and high-speed international travel' (Strenksi 2004: 631)—has made it increasingly difficult to define authors and their writing strictly on nationalist grounds. Post-colonial experience in particular has blurred the lines between national and cultural boundaries, and has brought both a theoretical ambiguity and a social ambivalence to the notion of the 'indigenous'. Even beyond strict post-colonial contexts, English authors may now find their cultural, aesthetic, or ideological inspiration from well outside anything we may have formally called 'English'. One might argue that, upon the dissolution of the British Empire, this shift was set up for us by Forster's *Passage to India* in 1924, and was continued mid-century with the likes of Malcolm Lowry and Graham Greene, both of whom understood the world as a shifting cultural and spiritual centre, which, as Greene constantly suggests, we ought not to consider as loss or retrogression but as an inexorable and even acceptable reality of modern life. We can see various literary responses to this shift in such works as James Fenton's collection of poetry *Out of Danger*, J. G. Ballard's novels of global dystopia, or Michael Ondaatje's rich stories of international passion, to name but a few.

For religion, globalization has created two divergent paths. In one direction, an expanding awareness of other traditions, together with that levelling spirit of acceptance which ideologically funds the liberal democracy standing behind and driving forward the globalizing movement, has promoted a willingness to embrace other modes of religious thinking and spiritual expression, leading to various forms of ecumenism, pluralism, and syncretism. In a second direction, increased exposure to foreign beliefs and practices has amplified the sense of the 'foreign' and the 'foreigner', to the point where any influences, accommodations, or indeed linkages with the 'other' are seen as an abiding threat, and conservation of one particular set of religious beliefs moves from a rigid apologetics to an ardent and at times militant fundamentalism. The divergence of these paths seems only to be widening, for as one becomes more hardline, the other becomes more reactive, in a strange dialectic of reciprocating response that allows neither to capitulate and neither to be overcome. (We saw this in the case of Salman Rushdie, where, despite the formal removal of the *fatwa* against him as the author of *Satanic Verses*, the division between Islamic fundamentalism and artistic freedom remains deep, keeping Rushdie a pariah in the circles of the one, while allowing him a certain hero's status in the circles of the other.) The re-emergence of literature and religion, or more widely of art and religion, as a mutual enterprise within the last half century or so has come about within and, one could argue, because of this religious and political bifurcation. But it has clearly done so within the context of this polarizing tendency: the democratizing nature of literature—the creative demands of producing and engaging with the text that dictate against hierarchical systems and binding authority—challenges the very conception of fundamentalism, in whatever form. The more militant religious fundamentalism becomes, then, the more literature and religion as a united front seem to arise as a counteracting force, as we saw in Margaret Atwood's seminal text *The Handmaid's Tale* (1985), or can see in the satirical levity of Mark Dunn's novel *Ella Minnow Pea* (2001).

Religious pluralism might be said to go even further in drawing literature to its side. There are a myriad of options to those who, in this post-secular and post-ecclesial society, now find themselves developing a new religious sensibility more by means of elective affinity or subjective choice than through inherited tradition. Available now are all traditions, approached not through priestly channels which grant religious access according to prescribed sanctification and ritual, nor through doctrine or dogma as they underwrite cultural expectations and mores, nor through familial allegiance that demands continuity of values, but through personalized exploration in which heterogeneity defines if not the end result then certainly the manner by which it is attained. Such exploration leads less to monolithic systems of belief or practice, and increasingly to a syncretism which remains unsystematic, undefined, or highly individualized and localized. Pagan becomes mixed with Christian, Western becomes mixed with Eastern, orthodoxy becomes mixed with unorthodoxy, canonical becomes mixed with non-canonical, all because the world now becomes a kind of marketplace of traditions and ideas from which to piece together a tailor-made spirituality. Within this kind of post-secularity, literature plays a significant role, since the idea of a sacred text gives way to a certain pan-textuality in which the world becomes a textual repository rife with spiritual possibilities, influences, and energies, and in which sacredness can be rewritten in various new manifestations not bound by priestly, credal, or cultic dictates. A novel indicative of this rewriting is Yann Martel's *Life of Pi*, in which the main character synthesizes three main religions, Christianity, Islam, and Hinduism, only to find this synthesis put to the test when he is stranded on a lifeboat with a Bengal Tiger. His personal account of his own story becomes a rewriting of faith, not simply for himself, but for the reader, who, against the primal backdrop of the open sea, must invest the story with more than just a willing suspension of disbelief—with the questions of truth and interpretation at the core of all faiths, and with the re-creative inspiration to see one through those questions, and to survive in the groundless plurality of our postmodern and post-postmodern worlds.

This globalizing effect will only increase as more people gain access to the means by which the world is made instantly available. The World Wide Web in particular has developed methods and attitudes fundamentally different from previous generations, and enhances the idea that the world is an intricacy of evolving networks whose centre or ground, if any exists, is indeterminable, and thus open to a continual resituating or reinventing. Reality becomes virtual, and textuality becomes de-authorized, so that truth and authority become pliable concepts, and belief turns on images and ideas free-floating in a cyberspace that takes 'democracy' to its most extreme incarnation. Here, any and all (i.e. of those who have access—still a key socio-economic factor) have unrestricted say in what constitutes, and what ought to constitute, the world we choose to live in. Within such cyber-democracy, literature and religion will continue to merge as a joint steering mechanism, particularly when the 'demos' encounter the obstacles of authoritarian and fundamentalist regimes by which 'religion' is dogmatically predetermined, and 'literature' is canonically enclosed or theocratically censored.

CULTURALITY

The question of culturality is closely linked with that of globalization. We have already suggested that in late modernity a reconception of roles has taken place, whereby religion and literature become mutually inclusive. But we need now to qualify this reconception further, because the issues go beyond simply a redefinition of two narrowly defined spheres of cultural experience. In the context of a widening globalization, and of a general tendency to perceive culture as an interlinked network of multifarious forces and influences, each acting upon the other in a sometimes hidden, sometimes explicit nexus of interpenetrations and symbolizations—what Mark C. Taylor (2001: 156—71), borrowing language from information theory and evolutionary biology, has compared to as a 'complex adaptive system'—the issues now embrace a broad spectrum of spheres, each one itself contributing to an evolving and shared totality in what we experience as 'culture'. Hence, when we try to think of literature and religion as a unified field, or as a confluence of forces, we must increasingly think of the many other forces that play into them, and help constitute them, so that our reconception necessarily involves taking culture as an organic whole, whose elements can no longer be seen in purely separate or autonomous terms. This is what is meant by the notion of *culturality*: 'spheres' of cultural experience, of which literature and religion are simply two possible manifestations, are no longer seen as individual components of an overall aggregate, but are part of an organicism, which is open and dynamic, yet ultimately inseparable, functioning as a co-evolving, co-adapting, co-determining system. 'Culture', we may say, is the accretion of a people's achievements, customs, and values as they are symbolized and given meaning within a given historical period; 'culturality' is the dynamic *interplay* between various realms of experience and between the conceptualizations of those experiences as they feed into one another across a wide range of social production and theoretical circumscription. Literature and religion will be increasingly understood and practised within such a culturality.

We might conceive of this culturality further if for the moment we turn to the language of cultural theory: religious production and literary production are bound up within a cultural logic that further draws them—amid other productions—inextricably together. As Frederic Jameson (1991: 5–6) has suggested, cultural logic denotes a 'systematic cultural norm and its reproduction' that are inseparable from the economic structures of late capitalism and that give 'an increasingly essential structural function and position to aesthetic innovation and experimentation'. This kind of logic works in a comprehensive manner, whereby all inputs into the system conform to an overriding 'determinant', which, for Jameson, is economically rooted in Marxian terms, but which is also purely self-reflexive, the logic governed by no other rationality than its own, and leading to no other *telos* or truth than what it internally offers itself as a groundless, endlessly reproduced desire, image, or virtuality (a *simulacrum*, as Baudrillard calls it). These are helpful distinctions, yet, as we will see further below, we have in some sense already moved beyond this kind of postmodern assessment of our situation. We can still speak of a cultural logic, and that logic no doubt is still economically determined, even within a globalized capitalism, but the self-reflexivity of postmodern experience, and of the theory that developed both to describe and to inform that experience—an astute insight of Jameson: that the theory itself is generated and held captive by the same forces it intends to critique—has now given way to an understanding or pursuit of something outside the logical apparatus. This is precisely where religion makes its return, as a proven discourse in carrying one beyond the self-contained structures of a pure immanence, a pure solipsism, or a purely secularized rationality and self-reflexivity. Yet *how* religion makes this return is still very much bound to a cultural question, or to a question of culturality—the processes of production that continue to determine cultural interplay—so that religion is no longer purely an imposing of transcendence upon immanence, or of otherness upon self, or, as Niebuhr (1951) would have it, of faith upon culture. Religion is not *pure* in any sense, either as pure transcendence, pure otherness, or pure faith. Religion is part of a cultural hermeneutic, where 'purity' itself is a concept alloyed with cultural forces and investment.

This investment increasingly manifests itself in artistic and literary terms. We get a glimpse of such manifestation in Graham Ward's book *True Religion* (2003). In attempting to give a 'genealogy of "religion"' through a cultural hermeneutics of the fourteenth to the twenty-first century, where '"True religion" is disseminated across social and historical processes...the poetics and politics of cultural determination, production and transformation', Ward (2003: 4) takes us to the literature of Shakespeare (*Romeo and Juliet*), John Donne, Daniel Defoe (*Robinson Crusoe*), Novalis, Herman Melville (*Moby Dick*), and Salman Rushdie (*Satanic Verses*), amongst other philosophers, cultural theorists and films. What Ward is trying to expose, in an argument here not bound to the Radical Orthodoxy programme he has otherwise been tied to, is not only that religion has returned in force within a postsecular culture, but that its return is caught up within a matrix of other cultural systems that link it, necessarily, to certain aspects of economy, politics, and art. To understand 'true' religion, we must understand and properly 'read' these other cultural systems or spheres, in which notions of truth are rendered, shaped, manipulated, sustained, postulated, and propagated. In speaking of Melville, for instance, Ward (ibid. 112–13) writes:

The changes to the understanding of 'religion' represented in *Moby Dick* find certain correlations in the political, the economic, the aesthetic, the metaphysical and the spiritual. The momentous growth in consumer culture that began in the nineteenth century paralleled the new Smithian economics of free trade and the avaricious drive for conquest, [and] are reflected back in the fears, fascinations and figurations of 'religion', the turns to cosmotheism, the Romantic metaphysics of the absolute spirit, the deity who dominates, and the aesthetics of the sublime.

To understand religion here is to understand literature, as much as it is to understand nineteenth-century economics, politics, philosophy, and aesthetics. 'True' religion is no more truer than the cultural realities of any given period, as they are appropriated by and experienced through the stories we tell of them. If then we are to continue to theologize—about religion in general, or within the specific religions any one of us may confess—we must incorporate our cultural practices and our creative expressions into our reflection and our understanding of the divine, which of course will profoundly change the nature of our theological discourse and the expectations we have of it. And such changes are well under way, in what we might consider as an emerging 'theography'.

In the writing of literature we already have examples of the way culturality integrates with theological concern as part of the 'mode' of fictionalizing. John Banville's earlier 'historical' novels (*Doctor Copernicus* (1976), *Kepler* (1981), and *The Newton Letter* (1982), which reinscribe history and historical characters in the face of science and its evolving view of reality) lead to the later novel *Shroud* (2003), in which Zoroastrianism, Nietzsche, Paul de Mann, Italian renaissance artists, the mythical Cassandra, Mary Magdalene, and Jesus are all wrapped up. The question of identity at the heart of the novel extends to the questionable, shifting, culture-bound 'identity' of religions and religious figures, such as the Shroud of Turin implies—a parchment on which (perhaps) God is rewritten. This question of religious history, and how it is 'storied', is also at the heart of Graham Swift's earlier *Waterland* (1983), where the question of God's revelation in history (or as history) figures powerfully through the narrator's wife Mary, who 'begets' a child from God in a rewriting of the virgin birth: she steals a baby from a supermarket because 'God told her to'. These kinds of novels—and there are plenty of examples, including those that rescript the sacred text itself, like Rushdie's *Satanic Verses* (1988) or Jim Crace's *Quarantine* (1997)—are not merely using religious or Christian imagery to freight their stories with vestiges of a once powerful and compelling past, earnestly or ironically. They are asking questions of the nature of religion itself, and rewriting religious understanding out of the cultural interchange between what has been, what is presently, and what can be in the future, an interchange which works across manifold and overlapping spheres of cultural interest and expression. Like a religious shroud, they are materializing new imprints of spiritual sensibility upon the multiform strands that make up our shared social and cultural fabric. And though this may appear to efface religion in its traditional form, it equally reinvests religion with, or as, a new form, even if yet a faint and indeterminate form. As such a theography increases—and all signs suggest that it will—this form will become more distinct, offering a new aesthetic as much as a new theological investiture.

An extension of this form can be seen in the growing state of post-colonial writing. Here, as with historiography and theography, political rewriting alters the fundamental perception of a given reality. But the politics involved here is a politics always informed by religion. Globalization, we have seen, obscures the distinction between foreign and domestic: what is produced domestically, and labelled domestic, is increasingly a product mixed with foreign parts, foreign labour, and foreign finances (including the products of art and literature). And post-colonial art certainly trades on this admixture. But post-colonial issues are far more than a product of pluralism. They arise as much, if not more, out of interplay between various levels of cultural determination that places some people in subjection to others. A theological hier-archy of the cosmos had governed the Western view of reality since at least the medieval scholastics, we know. As this hierarchy became married with expansionism, beginning with Columbus in the late fifteenth century and continuing until the twentieth century, global politics took with it the theological and religious ideology which gave it its justification. Post-colonial writing is an attempt to dissect the relationship between hierarchical assumptions in the air and socio-political realities on the ground. It might be argued that post-colonialism, as an ism, is more interested in the heights—that it is and will always remain theoretical in so far as it is expounded exclusively by academics and literati, and not by those struggling to live their lives between two differing yet amalgamated worlds (or more than two, as in the case of South Africa). No one marches in the streets in the name of post-colonialism. Yet it is precisely because post-colonial 'realities' are built upon presup-positions and assumptions—religious, political, economic, etc.—which, over time and under critique, are eventuated as a dilemma, that they do not yet find direct expression in praxis. Rather, one lives a dilemma, an 'anxiety', which if it is to be articulated, is articulated through forms which can expose and dismantle precon-ceptions of the most fundamental and far-reaching kind—religious preconceptions ultimately, those about how humankind is located within the cosmos or the universe, and what ought to inform the construction of our social formations, as much as the actions we take within them. Literature becomes a powerful medium for this articulation, because it is one of the few cultural instruments by which we can reconstruct and deconstruct interplay between cultural forces that are both indirect and direct, both abstract and concrete, both hidden and revealed.

It is for this reason that literature has been at the centre of post-colonialism's emergence from the beginning. Edward Said's *Orientalism* in 1978 certainly laid much of the ground for unmasking the hidden and deleterious forces at work behind the Western division of the globe into the 'Occident' and the 'Orient'. But in his later collection of essays, *The World, the Text, and the Critic* (1983), he puts forward the idea of the 'worldliness' of texts, that texts and textuality have always been deeply inculturated phenomena: 'It is not only that any text, if it is not immediately destroyed, is a network of often colliding forces but also that a text in its actually *being* a text is a being in the world'; 'texts have ways of existing that even in their most rarefied form are always enmeshed in circumstance, time, place, and society—in short, they are in the world, and hence worldly' (Said 1983: 33, 35). As a literary critic, he goes on to show, in writers that vary from Swift to Conrad to Joyce, just how 'worldly', how caught up in the mechanisms of cultural practice and ideology, texts are by virtue of being texts. And it is in this enmeshment that they are complicit in the privileging of one set of perspectives and priorities over another. 'Texts are a system of forces institutionalized by the reigning culture at some human cost to its various components' (ibid. 53). The human cost is what is central to Said's critique. And even if Said's own accounting of that cost will itself later come under critique from the likes of Homi Bhabha, it is incontrovertible that religion has contributed liberally to that sum.

It is highly doubtful that post-colonial issues and post-colonial writing will go away anytime soon, even though the geopolitical and social fallout of colonization may fade in the near future with some rapidity, and the term 'post-colonial' may give way to something that is more relevant to globalization. What do not seem to be fading are imperialisms. Thus as literature allows us not simply to expose but to redirect the interplay of cultural forces, both benign and coercive, we will continue to see the emergence of literature, cultural criticism, and religious reflection that makes visible, like metal filings around a magnet, the lines upon which those forces operate, and that pulls them, like a counteracting charge, in different directions.

INTERDISCIPLINARITY

Criticism, whether literary, cultural, political, or ideological, is not primarily, if at all, an exercise in debunking. As David Klemm's chapter on German criticism in this volume has indicated (see Ch. 8, above), it is a discipline of analysis, by which judgements upon a work are brought to a meta-level. As a discipline it functions in formalized settings, which themselves are caught up in culturality. The academy, the most formal of these settings, is a deeply cultural space, with productions and consumptions that have effect in the wider community. Criticism is worldly, said Said; theory is formed by a cultural logic, said Jameson; academic disciplines, we can add, are bound up in cultural interplay. The merging of literature and religion through the interrelation of cultural forces is reflective of a shift not merely in how these spheres are experienced, but indeed in how they are studied, categorized, and formalized as fields of enquiry. As experience merges, so too do the categories and formalizations, the criticisms and the critiques. Disciplines lose their strict identity, and begin to overlap, cross-fertilize, interpenetrate. In the short history of literature and theology/religion as a combined field of study, what we have seen is a categorical confusion about where the merger ought to be situated—in the departments of literature or religion? The tension between these two disciplines has never abated; in many ways, that tension has fuelled the enquiry. But as other disciplines and fields of study have become more and more implicated in the questions and the critiques, through post-secularity, globalization, and culturality, the tension has only gained strength. Having made the first move to combine the study of literature and theology, as charted in the introductory chapter of this volume, interdisciplinary floodgates have now swung wide open, so that the dyadic term 'literature and theology' is now almost a cipher into which one may pour any number of disciplinary labels.

In focusing on Edward Said above, we have already drawn attention to this interdisciplinarity within the academy. Said began his career as a literary critic of comparative literature. When the 1967 Arab–Israeli war broke out, politics became an inseparable part of his life's work. His politics was informed by literature and literary criticism, to be sure, but also by history, philology, sociology, anthropology, contemporary philosophy, political science, art, and even music. His writings reflect all these influences, indeed begin from all these points, so that by the end of his life, one was hard-pressed to isolate Said's discipline in singular terms, and the media began resorting to such general titles as 'public intellectual'. The development of postcolonial critique tells us that literature was too implicated in the world's social and political realities to remain within the self-contained confines of New Criticism, and that the role of the literary critic was radically changing ground. Said was no mere Renaissance man. Under the powers of Foucault's genealogies and post-structuralism's deconstruction, literature for Said transposed into *textuality*, the expanded grammar of cultural production and interpretation that carries one back into the material world through the critical parsing and syntactical analysis of its structures. And though he remained 'secular' in these textual pursuits, religion was a central and unavoidable construction in the grammar.

There are other interdisciplinarians for whom religion has been more than merely a component of a secular enterprise. One can think of such Europeans as Paul Ricœur and, more recently, Slavoj Žižek. The latter in particular has challenged our notions of what to understand as a text, bringing the visual arts, film, and popular culture into the mainstream of his wide religious, cultural, political, and philosophical discussions. In Britain, this textual expansion can be seen in David Jasper's *The Sacred Desert* (2004), subtitled simply 'Religion, Literature, Art, and Culture'. Here Jasper displays an intricate fusion of written works with music, paintings, video art, and cinema. Theology, spirituality, and mysticism weave with philosophy, social commentary, and personal diary. Poetry stands alongside novels, biographies, and travel literature. In expounding the space of the desert as the ultimate sacred space, his own written text becomes a manifestation of the space he is trying to elucidate: the desert narrative behind all literature, religion, art, philosophy, etc.—behind, that is, *all* disciplinary gestures, the quiet, shifting landscape 'that both kills and redeems and is absolutely indifferent and pure', a landscape that 'is never and always', a place that is both all text and no text whatsoever (ibid. 169). What such interdisciplinary studies will continue to provide, then, is a critical redefining of *what is text*, and in turn a critical redefining of the disciplines we use to pursue the question.

Perhaps the most significant manifestation of this critical interdisciplinarity today can be found in the extensive developments of feminism. There are of course many 'feminisms', each with their specific agenda. But if we can use the term 'feminism' in a general sense here as an extended form of a critical spirit, indeed a mode of critique, then what we have seen is a complete reorientation of how to approach any one discipline, and what makes up the content of that discipline. Feminist reappraisal has exposed coercive patriarchal structures, given voices to the marginalized, challenged the priorities of our value systems, and forced us to reconsider notions of self and identity. In this respect, it may be considered part of the legacy of 'critical theory'. But in all this it has done something yet more radical: it has caused us to shift how we conceive of reality and divinity. The issue of gender is not a war between two biological make-ups, two psychological and emotional constitutions. Ultimately, gender, as a social and cultural construct—this 'Theory' has taught us clearly—is a mode of existing in the world. Feminism, then, becomes a way of being, even, we could argue, for men. It is a way of being that takes into account, and lives out, an understanding of difference at the core of who we are. For all the philosophical and theoretical focus on difference at the end of the last century (not to mention *différance*), feminism appropriates difference existentially as a lived and embodied reality, not in a divisive manner, which sets differends against each other, but as a defining state of existing affirmingly within the manifold of the world, a heterophonous state that hears alterity not as clash but as a choral layering together of possibility. It works against systems of totality not because uniqueness and individuality are better, but because such systems have proved to be impoverished ways of describing and experiencing the possibility of the world (as much as any individualism has proved to be).

To this end, feminism is a metadiscipline in the highest order—though in the very opposite direction of a metaphysical order. Feminism rarely becomes its own department within the academy (though in America one can find departments of Women's Studies) because it is less an isolated field of study as it is a mode by which to approach all fields. Hence one can find a feminist appropriation of any field and discipline, from the Humanities to even the hard sciences (see e.g. Doell 1991: 121–39; and Fréchet 1991: 205–21). More importantly, it is changing our understanding of knowledge, and how we categorize and institutionalize knowledge. Not just previously marginalized knowledge that has arisen anew under the banners of gender, race, ethnicity, and sexuality, but *all* knowledge. Nor all knowledge as merely a product of ideation, but all knowledge as it is socially, culturally, and institutionally enmeshed. This change directly affects our disciplines. Granted, there is still a long way to go. But feminism is succeeding, despite resistance, in changing this interplay between engendering knowledge and formalizing knowledge, and bringing us to a fuller interdisciplinarity across all our enquiries, both within the academy and without.[2] More importantly, as a metadiscipline, it takes us beyond discipline as a purely intellectual sphere and activity, and forces us to the materiality, sociality, and culturality of our thinking and its differences. This is why literature has remained so central to feminist concern: it brings us out of our closets of abstraction, and shows us our material contingencies and the new possibilities that might thereby arise.

AFTERWARD

The question of discipline, and the critical discourse that emerges from disciplinary methodology, might suggest that literature and religion will remain a highly theoretical enterprise, one grounded in a certain critical or cultural theory. But the idea of

---

[2] For an excellent discussion of both the advances and obstacles of feminist critique within the academy, see Hartman and Messer-Davidow 1991.

'pure theory' (as someone such as Said might have envisioned it) has itself fallen prey to the same internal critique as that of 'pure religion'. We can see this critique in a recent turn in Britain towards a kind of thinking called 'after theory', as evidenced in the book titles of notable British literary critics Terry Eagleton and Valentine Cunningham: *After Theory* (2004) and *Reading After Theory* (2002) respectively.[3] Both these writers understand 'theory' here as the cultural theory that grew up particularly in the 1960s and 1970s, as put forward by many Western intellectuals either of the French (from Lacan to Derrida), German (Habermas), American (Jameson), or British (Raymond Williams) cast. It was such cultural theory that had direct influence on literary theory and criticism as it rode the wave of postmodernism through to the new millennium. Both writers suggest that this theory has had its heyday now, and that we are moving on to something else, something as yet undefined, but certainly 'after' (there is a deliberate avoidance of 'post-' here). Yet both also admit that such theory has made its mark indelibly upon our culture, and that there is no turning back to a moment before such theory, as if it was all a serious mistake. On the contrary, both go out of their way to show the immense importance and pervading influence such theory has had, and still has. But it no longer guides our most present concerns, they suggest, because its deficiencies are now too glaring, especially in the wake of 11 September 2001. How can it address the new global narrative of capitalism and its war on terror with a theory fundamentally loath to action, asks Eagleton? If reading comes after theory, as it always does, how do we carry on reading, as we must, asks Cunningham? Eagleton curiously recasts his Marxist allegiance within a Neo-Aristotelian and Christian persuasion, while Cunningham champions the primacy of the act, and tact, of reading as an engaged, tactile—not theorized or theorizing—activity. Both emphasize moral and ethical concerns as paramount and necessary, even if problematic. And Eagleton especially returns religion to its rightful place as a world-changing possibility, even if what it is changing is religious fundamentalism. Is this move 'after' theory, then, any more distinct than what we have been laying out above, somewhat theoretically, in relation to literature and religion?

We can say that the theory which Eagleton and Cunningham are suggesting is behind us now is a certain kind of theory that transposed itself into *literary criticism* within certain confines of academic practice. But it is precisely away from such literary criticism that, we suggest, 'literature and religion' moves, as it encounters the forces of post-secularity, globalization, culturality, and interdisciplinarity. Though one can argue these forces are themselves highly theoretical, they do not form a self-contained field, an orthodoxy until themselves, as Eagleton and Cunningham argue 'Theory' (or 'High Theory', as Cunningham calls it) had become. Here instead we are trying to lay out the *after* of a theory which, if it still contains theory, contains it in a far more integrated manner, a manner in which it is impossible to separate out 'theory' (in a decapitalized form) with the practice of reading and, indeed, living. What we are suggesting is that 'literature and religion', whether in

---

[3] And corroborated, for example, in French Studies by Colin Davis 2004.

Britain or elsewhere—or *for the very reason* it is both in Britain and elsewhere simultaneously, as a global phenomenon—is forcing us to rethink our perception of theory and criticism from the ground up, so that we are as much *after* theory in the sense of beyond one kind of Theory, and *after* theory in the sense of seeking out and pursuing a new kind altogether.

What will guide this pursuit, as it has already begun to do, is an increasing concern for ethics. If we consider 'High Theory' within a history of ideas, one could conceivably argue that it arose from the ashes of the Shoah: the ringing indictment of Adorno's famous line, that no poetry was possible after Auschwitz, impelled a body of thought which, in effect, allowed literature to remain 'impossible', while theoretical strategies played around it and 'extraneous' factors were brought in from the outside (though, as Theory would impress upon us, the 'extraneous' was always intraneous). And to this end Theory remained thoroughly political, in its attempts to keep literature, and eventually religion, from ever again reaching that 'most exquisite of art forms', the concentration camp. What else is postmodern art and theory than a refusal to let sovereign power back into its fold? If, as Agamben (1998: 188) suggests, there 'is no return from the camps to classical politics', then neither, said Theory, is there a return to the classic text. And if the camp remains, at least biopolitically, 'the hidden matrix...in which we are still living' (ibid. 166), we ought to understand Theory as leaving us with an indispensable legacy. But with 9/11, that matrix has been inexorably altered—that is to say, it is no longer hidden. If the camp represents the 'state of exception that has become the rule' (ibid. 168–9), then with the War on Terror, the exceptional terrorist attack, and in particular the suicide bomber, has been made into a rule which is all too evident. Suicide bombing is *the* biopolitical gesture of our times, now made explicitly public, with a deep theology at its root—a biotheology. As we face what it means to live in a world where a terrorist strike can be expected to happen at any time, and anywhere, the political energy that had fuelled Theory in the wake of Adorno is now transformed, not merely into a displacement of sovereign power through deconstructive means, but into an ethical demand for responsible action in the face of competing and polarizing ideologies.

Where the voice of poetry returns, or the voice of literature as such, is within this very matrix of now open and hostile religiosity, whether that of the suicide bombers or that of the religio-political forces set out in the name of freedom and democracy to uproot their insurgence and relieve History of its antagonisms. We are only now seeing art respond to this new world of terror. Of course the best art will not be programmatic, nor tendentious, but will create possibility out of what seems impossible or reality out of what seems unreal. And in this new world we will be forced to change our approach to the study of literature, and to the rereading of the classic text. As irresponsible action continues to pervade on all sides, not least in governmental response to individual terrorists—where the name 'Osama bin Laden' acts as the justification for full-scale wars—responsibility will need again to be sought in or informed by those texts we once deemed impossible not only to write but to read. 'Our sense of duty must often wait for some work which shall take the place of dilettantism and make us feel that the quality of our action is not a matter of indifference', writes the narrator in *Middlemarch* (Eliot 1965: 501). For us, the heady days of postmodern trifling are now behind us. But this does not mean we can return to the halcyon days of naive hermeneutics void of critical element, as if to read the text again in and of its own right. As the foregoing discussion has tried to show, there is no longer any such thing as 'in and of its own right'. On the contrary, one's 'own' is caught up in a matrix of conditions and forces, and thus the critical element has become all the more pressing, to the point where it can no longer afford the 'impossibility' of playful deferment and inaction. Criticism has reached a crisis, and finding its ability to respond in this crisis will be the great ethical necessity that drives it forward beyond itself, and back to the materially grounded text where the action has always taken place. As the statue of Hermione returns to life at the end of Shakespeare's *The Winter's Tale*, so we might hear anew literature say of its own flesh-and-blood possibility: 'her actions shall be holy as | You hear my spell is lawful' (v. iii. 104–5; Shakespeare 1969: 1367).

If 'literature and theology' began as an exploration of two fields implicated in each other's concerns, 'literature and theology' today stands as the place where textuality is implicated in our most intense cultural conditions. At this place we have moved beyond a matter simply for 'literature' or 'religion' alone, or in even concert. We are even forced beyond the 'now and in England' (see Elisabeth Jay, Ch. 1 above). If the earlier Eagleton was right, that the study of English literature in the nineteenth century arose as the result of 'the failure of religion' (see this volume, David Jasper, Ch. 2 above), then we might venture to say that the study of the text and textual hermeneutics in the twenty-first century will continue because of a particular resurgence of religion. But this resurgence is global, bound up with the interplay of all cultural forces, and germane to all disciplines seeking out how to position humanity amid the turbulence of its own violent times. If religion is back, it is back not as the totalizing foundation and confirmation of all reality. It is back as warring and wounded sovereignties without sure domains to rule. Literature can, and must, speak to this dilemma: the broken God without a home. In doing so, it may well supply that temporary shelter in which new ministration, if not dispensation, might be found.

Works Cited

Agamben, Giorgio. 1998. *Homo Sacer: Sovereign Power and Bare Life*, trans. Daniel Heller-Roazen. Stanford: Stanford University Press.

Atwood, Margaret. 1985. *The Handmaid's Tale*. Toronto: McClelland-Bantam.

Blond, Philip (ed.) 1998. *Post-secular Philosophy: Between Philosophy and Theology*. London: Routledge.

Crace, Jim. 1997. *Quarantine*. London: Penguin.

Davis, Colin. 2004. *After Poststructuralism: Reading, Stories and Theory*. London: Routledge.

DERRIDA, JACQUES. 1998. 'Faith and Knowledge: The Two Sources of "Religion" and the Limits of Reason Alone', in Jacques Derrida and Gianni Vattimo (eds.), *Religion*. Stanford: Stanford University Press.

DOELL, RUTH G. 1991. 'Whose Research Is This? Values and Biology', in Hartman and Messer-Davidow (1991).

ELIOT, GEORGE. 1965. *Middlemarch*, ed. W. J. Harvey. London: Penguin.

FORSTER, E. M. 1979 [1924]. *Passage to India*, ed. Oliver Stallybrass. Harmondsworth: Penguin.

FRÉCHET, DENISE. 1991. 'Towards a Post-Phallic Science', in Hartman and Messer-Davidow (1991).

HARTMAN, JOAN E., and ELLEN MESSER-DAVIDOW (eds.) 1991. *(En) Gendering Knowledge: Feminists in Academe*. Knoxville: University of Tennessee Press.

JAMESON, FREDERIC. 1991. *Postmodernism, or, The Cultural Logic of Late Capitalism*. Durham: Duke University Press.

JASPER, DAVID. 2004. *The Sacred Desert*. Oxford: Blackwell.

MARTEL, YANN. 2003. *Life of Pi*. Edinburgh: Canongate Books.

NIEBUHR, H. RICHARD. 1951. *Christ and Culture*. New York: Harper & Row.

RUSHDIE, SALMAN. 1988. *Satanic Verses*. New York: Picador.

SAID, EDWARD. 1983. *The World, the Text, and the Critic*. Cambridge, Mass.: Harvard University Press.

SHAKESPEARE, WILLIAM. 1969. *Complete Works of William Shakespeare*, ed. Alfred Harbage. New York: Viking.

STRENKSI, IVAN. 2004. 'The Religion in Globalization'. *Journal of the American Academy of Religion* 72/3: 631–52.

TAYLOR, MARK C. 2001. *The Moment of Complexity: Emerging Network Culture*. Chicago: University of Chicago.

VATTIMO, GIANNI. 1999. *Belief*, trans. Luca D'Isanto and David Webb. Stanford: Stanford University Press.

WARD, GRAHAM. 2003. *True Religion*. Oxford: Blackwell.

FURTHER READING

BANVILLE, JOHN. 2002. *Shroud*. London: Picador.

CUNNINGHAM, VALENTINE. 2002. *Reading After Theory*. Oxford: Blackwell.

DUNN, MARK. 2001. *Ella Minnow Pea*. London: Methuen.

EAGLETON, TERRY. 2004. *After Theory*. London: Penguin.

FENTON, JAMES. 1993. *Out of Danger: Poems*. London: Penguin.

HASS, ANDREW. 2003. *Poetics of Critique: The Interdisciplinarity of Textuality*. Aldershot: Ashgate.

JASPER, DAVID. 2004. *The Sacred Desert*. Oxford: Blackwell.

ROBINSON, MARILYNNE. 2005. *Gilead*. London: Virago.

SAID, EDWARD. 1978. *Orientalism*. London: Penguin Classics.

SWIFT, GRAHAM. 1983. *Waterland*. London: Picador.

WARD, GRAHAM. 2003. *True Religion*. Oxford: Blackwell.

INDEX OF CITATIONS

Index

Note: Page references in **bold** type indicate main discussion on prominent names and topics.

Index compiled by Meg Davies (Fellow of the Society of Indexers)